IMPORTANT

HERE IS YOUR REGISTRATION CODE TO ACCESS MCGRAW-HILL PREMIUM CONTENT AND MCGRAW-HILL ONLINE RESOURCES

For key premium online resources you need THIS CODE to gain access. Once the code is entered, you will be able to use the web resources for the length of your course.

Access is provided only if you have purchased a new book.

If the registration code is missing from this book, the registration screen on our website, and within your WebCT or Blackboard course will tell you how to obtain your new code. Your registration code can be used only once to establish access. It is not transferable.

To gain access to these online resources

1. **USE** your web browser to go to: **www.mhhe.com/hetherington6e**
2. **CLICK** on "First Time User"
3. **ENTER** the Registration Code printed on the tear-off bookmark on the right
4. After you have entered your registration code, click on "Register"
5. **FOLLOW** the instructions to setup your personal UserID and Password
6. **WRITE** your UserID and Password down for future reference. Keep it in a safe place.

If your course is using WebCT or Blackboard, you'll be able to use this code to access the McGraw-Hill content within your instructor's online course.
To gain access to the McGraw-Hill content in your instructor's WebCT or Blackboard course simply log into the course with the user ID and Password provided by your instructor. Enter the registration code exactly as it appears to the right when prompted by the system. You will only need to use this code the first time you click on McGraw-Hill content.

These instructions are specifically for student access. Instructors are not required to register via the above instructions.

The McGraw-Hill Companies

Mc Graw Hill | **Higher Education**

ISBN 0-07-313733-2 T/A HETHERINGTON: CHILD PSYCHOLOGY: A CONTEMPORARY VIEWPOINT, 6/E

Thank you, and welcome to your McGraw-Hill Online Resources.

MYC3-DQNU-W8JV-JQH8-46EY

REGISTRATION CODE
REGISTRATION CODE

The McGraw-Hill Companies

Mc Graw Hill | **Higher Education**

Child Psychology
A Contemporary Viewpoint

Child Psychology
A Contemporary Viewpoint

E. Mavis Hetherington
UNIVERSITY OF VIRGINIA

Ross D. Parke
UNIVERSITY OF CALIFORNIA, RIVERSIDE

Mary Gauvain
UNIVERSITY OF CALIFORNIA, RIVERSIDE

Virginia Otis Locke

SIXTH EDITION

McGraw
Hill

Boston   Burr Ridge, IL   Dubuque, IA   Madison, WI   New York   San Francisco   St. Louis
Bangkok   Bogotá   Caracas   Kuala Lumpur   Lisbon   London   Madrid   Mexico City
Milan   Montreal   New Delhi   Santiago   Seoul   Singapore   Sydney   Taipei   Toronto

Higher Education

CHILD PSYCHOLOGY: A CONTEMPORARY VIEWPOINT

Published by McGraw-Hill, a business unit of The McGraw-Hill Companies, Inc., 1221 Avenue of the Americas, New York, NY, 10020. Copyright © 2006, 2003, 1999, 1993, 1986, 1979, 1975 by The McGraw-Hill Companies, Inc. All rights reserved. No part of this publication may be reproduced or distributed in any form or by any means, or stored in a database or retrieval system, without the prior written consent of The McGraw-Hill Companies, Inc., including, but not limited to, in any network or other electronic storage or transmission, or broadcast for distance learning.

Some ancillaries, including electronic and print components, may not be available to customers outside the United States.

This book is printed on acid-free paper.

2 3 4 5 6 7 8 9 0 VNH/VNH 0 9 8 7 6

ISBN 13: 978-0-07-301231-5
ISBN 10: 0-07-301231-9

Editor in Chief: *Emily Barrosse*
Executive Editor: *Michael J. Sugarman*
Senior Developmental Editor: *Elsa Peterson*
Marketing Manager: *Melissa S. Caughlin*
Managing Editor: *Jean Dal Porto*
Project Manager: *Susan Trentacosti*
Art Director: *Jeanne Schreiber*
Lead Designer: *Gino Cieslik*
Text Designer: *Kiera Pohl*
Cover Designer: *Gino Cieslik*
Art Manager: *Robin Mouat*
Illustrator(s): *Judy and John Waller*
Manager, Photo Research: *Brian J. Pecko*
Cover Credit: *Margie Livingston Campbell (20th C. American).* Instrument Zoo II, *1997. Watercolor.* © M. L. Campbell/SuperStock.
Media Project Manager: *Alexander Rohrs*
Senior Media Producer: *Stephanie George*
Senior Production Supervisor: *Carol A. Bielski*
Permissions Editor: *Marty Granahan*
Composition: *10/12 Times Roman, by Techbooks/GTS LA*
Printing: *45 # Pub Matte, Von Hoffmann Corporation*

Credits: The credits section for this book begins on page C and is considered an extension of the copyright page.

Library of Congress Control Number: 2005925570

The Internet addresses listed in the text were accurate at the time of publication. The inclusion of a website does not indicate an endorsement by the authors of McGraw-Hill, and McGraw-Hill does not guarantee the accuracy of the information presented at these sites.

www.mhhe.com

To children everywhere

About the Authors

E. Mavis Hetherington

E. Mavis Hetherington is Emerita Professor of Psychology at the University of Virginia. Hetherington obtained her Ph.D. in Psychology at the University of California at Berkeley. She is a past President of Division 7, the Developmental Psychology Division of the American Psychological Association, the Society for Research in Adolescence, and the Society for Research in Child Development. Hetherington has been editor of *Child Development,* and associate editor of both *Developmental Psychology* and the *Journal of Abnormal Child Psychology.* Among her honors are Distinguished Scientist awards from the American Psychological Society, The National Council on Family Relations, the Society for Research in Child Development, and the American Psychological Association. Hetherington has authored and edited many books including *The Separate Social World of Siblings* (with David Reiss and Robert Plomin), *The Relationship Code* (with David Reiss, Jenae Neiderhiser, and Robert Plomin) and *For Better or Worse: Divorce Reconsidered* (with John Kelly). Her research interests are in the areas of childhood psychopathology, personality and social development, and stress and coping in families. Hetherington is well known for her work on the effects on children's development of divorce, one-parent families, and remarriage.

Ross D. Parke

Ross D. Parke is Distinguished Professor of Psychology and director of the Center for Family Studies at the University of California, Riverside. He is past President of the Society for Research in Child Development and of Division 7, the Developmental Psychology Division, of the American Psychological Association, and in 1995 he received the G. Stanley Hall Award from this APA division. Parke was elected a Fellow of the American Association for the Advancement of Science in 1997. He has served as editor of both the *Journal of Family Psychology* and *Developmental Psychology,* and as associate editor of *Child Development.* Parke is the author of *Fatherhood,* coauthor of *Throwaway Dads* (with Armin Brott), and co-editor of *Family-Peer Relationships: In Search of the Linkages* (with Gary Ladd), *Children in Time and Place* (with Glen Elder and John Modell), and *Exploring Family Relationships with Other Social Contexts* (with Sheppard Kellam). Parke's research has focused on early social relationships in infancy and childhood. He obtained his Ph.D. from the University of Waterloo, Ontario, Canada, and is well known for his early work on the effects of punishment, aggression, and child abuse, and for his work on the father's role in infancy and early childhood. Parke's current work focuses on the links between family and peer social systems, ethnic variations in families, and the effects of the new reproductive technologies on families.

Mary Gauvain

Mary Gauvain is a Professor of Psychology at the University of California, Riverside. She is a Fellow of the American Psychological Association and past Secretary/Treasurer of Division 7 (Developmental Psychology) of APA. She is also a member of the Society for Research in Child Development. She is currently an Associate Editor of the *Merrill-Palmer Quarterly* and on the Editorial Board of *Child Development.* She is the author of *The Social Context of Cognitive Development* and coauthor of *Readings on the Development of Children* (with Michael Cole). She is well known for her research on cognitive development, in particular her research on social and cultural contributions to the development of planning skills and spatial thinking. She obtained her M.A. degree in Sociology of Education from Stanford University and her Ph.D. in Psychology from the University of Utah. She has held postdoctoral positions in Developmental Psychology at the Graduate Center of the City University of New York and the Oregon Social Learning Center. Her current research focuses on the ecology of children's everyday lives and especially on how experiences in the family and cultural community provide opportunities for the development of cognitive skills.

Virginia Otis Locke

Virginia Otis Locke, clinician turned professional writer, is also a coauthor of *Introduction to Theories of Personality* (with Calvin Hall and Gardner Lindzey). Locke received her B.A. from Barnard College and earned an M.A. (and "A.B.D.") in the doctoral clinical psychology program at Duke University. She served as staff psychologist at St.Luke's–Roosevelt Medical Center in New York City and then, changing careers, became a freelance writer and editor, working on many books in the behavioral and social sciences. After several years, she joined the staff of Cornell Medical College/Columbia Presbyterian Medical Center as a writer and editor, and then, as a senior editor in Prentice Hall's College Division, she developed numerous textbooks in the behavioral sciences. Locke has also spent several years as an elementary school teaching assistant. Currently an independent writer again, she plans a new project that will be seriously related to psychology but not as serious as a textbook.

Brief Contents

Contents

8.
Cognitive Development: Piaget and Vygotsky   316

9.
Cognitive Development: The Information-Processing Approach 364

10.
Intelligence and Achievement 414

Preface

Child psychology is a field on the move, for the study of children's development continues to undergo rapid change. In recent years, theorists and researchers have taken giant steps in several areas. For example, they have offered the field new insights into the biological underpinnings of behavior. They have also revealed remarkable cognitive skills in infants, and they have explored the effects of new family arrangements on children's development.

In this sixth edition of *Child Psychology: A Contemporary Viewpoint* we continue to reflect the dynamic nature of the field of child psychology. Much of the new research we discuss highlights the central processes that account for developmental change within the different areas of child development. Designed primarily for use in child psychology or child development courses in either two- or four-year colleges, our book takes a topical approach to the course material. This allows us to help the student explore in depth such subjects as how the continuing interaction between genetic and environmental factors affects children's development, how children's learning of language helps them sharpen their cognitive skills, and how children's growing emotional skills help them in their relationships with peers and friends. Throughout the book we emphasize the interplay across the different areas of psychological growth—biological, emotional, cognitive, and social.

In this edition we have tried to ensure that our book continues to provide both students and instructors with a current and exciting overview of child development. Although we have made many revisions in this edition, our goal remains the same: to present the most important contemporary issues in child psychology in such a way that students not only will understand the material but will find it useful in their lives and in professional careers. We hope the academic community will find this new edition a valuable teaching tool as well as a comprehensive and current resource.

DISTINGUISHING CHARACTERISTICS OF THIS BOOK

Several characteristics continue to distinguish *Child Psychology: A Contemporary Viewpoint*. We offer balanced theoretical discussions, we explore both basic research and its practical applications, and, throughout the book, we integrate multicultural and cross-cultural research.

Balanced Theoretical Perspectives

Our topical approach lends itself to a sophisticated presentation of the theories that guide research in the many areas of child development. As the research continues to accumulate, however, the limitations of such theories become evident. For example, developmentalists have found that some of Piaget's classic studies are open to new and intriguing interpretations. Thus, rather than focus on a few grand theories that attempt to account for many aspects of development, we now recognize the value of more specific theories that guide research in particular topic areas, such as language, motor development, and emotional understanding. Thus, throughout this edition, to supplement the grand theories we explore newer approaches, such as dynamic systems theory, sociocultural perspectives, and evolutionary theory.

Child Psychology: A Contemporary Viewpoint strives both to be theoretically eclectic and to emphasize the multiply determined nature of development. In each discussion of a topic one or two causative factors predominate, but others are influential as well. For example, in our discussion of genetics and early development the predominant factors are biological, but learning principles and environmental factors play a role. When we discuss language and gender typing, we emphasize cognitive learning, information processing, and social interaction, but genetics takes the stage when we explore the biology of gender and the nativist view of language learning. Although cognitive theories such as the information processing and Piagetian approaches dominate our discussion of intellectual development, we also consider sociocultural processes as contributors to cognitive growth. Similarly, social and affective factors predominate in our coverage of family and peers, but we explore cognitive, behavioral, and biological issues as well. This approach underscores the contemporary recognition that child development evolves out of the interplay among biological, cognitive, social, and emotional factors.

PROCESS ORIENTATION   Our emphasis is on the *processes* of development, a hallmark of contemporary child psychology. Focusing on the processes that generate changes in the child's development enables students to learn what development comprises and what specific changes take place across time. By examining what changes and how, students come to understand why these changes occur. And in this way they gain insight into why two children with seemingly similar capabilities may develop very different ways of understanding and interacting with the world.

Some of our readers have been curious as to why some sections of our book cover adolescence more fully than others. This approach arises out of our process orientation. When the completion of a developmental process or a milestone in that process occurs in the teenage years, we follow the process from childhood through adolescence. Thus, for example, we discuss physical development through puberty, cognitive development into adolescence, and, as part of our exploration of changes in the nature of friendships across time, we follow beginning romantic relationships into adolescence. Because our book focuses, however, on the period of childhood, we do not cover adolescence for all developmental processes.

THEMES OF DEVELOPMENT   This edition of our book continues to characterize theoretical perspectives by focusing on several cross-cutting themes of development. We have trimmed the number of these themes to three: biological versus environmental influences, continuity versus discontinuity of development, and individual characteristics versus contextual and cultural influences. Throughout the book we illustrate these themes, and in our Epilogue we link the themes with broad principles that summarize our views about the research and theory-building needs of the field of child development.

Basic and Applied Research: A Reciprocal Relationship

In this book we present child psychology as a scientific discipline, illustrating the techniques used by psychologists in the field. It is important for students to become familiar with the methodological approaches that are unique to child psychology so that they can understand, interpret, and use the results of research intelligently. We present findings in sufficient detail to enable students not only to understand the steps in the research process but also to appreciate the complex nature of drawing valid conclusions about development.

Although some instructors prefer a basic research focus and others an applied approach, we emphasize the interactive nature of basic research and its applications.

Basic information about the processes of development can help us understand a wide range of real-life problems and, conversely, insights we gain from applying the results of scientific investigation can help improve research and sharpen our theoretical understanding. In Chapter 10, for example, we consider what the scientific community has learned about the fundamental processes of development from early educational intervention programs like Head Start. In Chapter 6 we discuss new research on homesickness that demonstrates the relevance of attachment theory for real-life problems. And, as we discuss in Chapters 1 and 14, basic research on imitation has helped us understand the effects of television on children's cognitive and social development. Throughout the book, teachers and students will find fascinating examples of the dynamic interplay between basic and applied research.

Sociocultural Diversity in Child Development

In this edition we have intensified our focus on the cultural, ethnic, and racial diversity of heterogeneous societies like the United States, as well as on differences among cultures around the world. Our expanded discussion of Vygotskian theory, with its strong emphasis on the role of culture, provides a framework for understanding how culture and development interact. We introduce the theme of cultural pluralism in Chapter 1 and have integrated it into every chapter; in each topical discussion we explore research with the many ethnic groups that make up U.S. culture as well as with people in nations around the world. In addition, our Perspectives on Diversity boxes highlight relevant cross-cultural and intra-cultural studies.

ORGANIZATION

Several organizational decisions and changes in this sixth edition distinguish our book from other texts in child development. To allow instructors greater flexibility, we have reduced the book by two chapters, so that it now comprises just 15. We have trimmed and combined Chapters 1 and 2 into a new introductory chapter that presents fundamental theoretical and methodological issues in heightened focus. This presentation enables students to move more rapidly into the content chapters. We have also deleted the chapter on schools, computers, and the media; we have distributed this material into other chapters, where we tie it more closely to related concepts and issues. For example, the topic of achievement is now part of Chapter 10, and the effects of the mass media on children are now discussed in Chapters 1, 13, and 14. By integrating our presentation of these issues into our discussions of specific developmental outcomes we are able to explore these matters in more meaningful ways.

SOME HIGHLIGHTS OF THE SIXTH EDITION

We have rewritten *Child Psychology: A Contemporary Viewpoint* to feature the most recent developments in theory and research. Every chapter includes new information, some of which we highlight below. Even more exciting is the addition of co-author Mary Gauvain to our team who joins us in this sixth edition. Gauvain, a renowned cognitive developmental psychologist, brings new depth to our treatments of cognition, information processing, and language learning. This added expertise balances Hetherington's and Parke's widely respected coverage of emotional and social development. In addition, Gauvain's expertise in sociocultural approaches and her research on cross-cultural and intra-cultural variations strengthen our coverage of the cultural aspects of development.

With Ginny Locke, former clinician turned professional writer, continuing to ensure the clarity, elegance, and effectiveness of our prose, our team not only maintains our authoritative voice but boasts increased breadth and depth. We believe this edition constitutes a major improvement, one that has made our text even better and more relevant to students' and instructors' concerns in this new century.

The following are some highlights of the new coverage in this sixth edition:

CHAPTER 1: CHILD DEVELOPMENT: THEMES, THEORIES, AND METHODS

- Theoretical, thematic, and methods discussions presented succinctly, moving students more quickly into specific-content chapters
- Clear, concise presentation of three major themes of development: biology versus environment, continuity of development versus discontinuity, individual characteristics versus contextual and cultural influences
- Emphasis on research methods that are unique and central to developmental inquiry
- Streamlined overview table of developmental themes and theoretical perspectives

CHAPTER 2: HEREDITY AND THE ENVIRONMENT

- Updated discussions of new reproductive technologies
- Updates on the Human Genome Project: Identification of protein-coding genes and progress in identifying genes that help account for specific diseases
- New notion that genes can shape the environment explored; three concepts of passive, evocative, and active genetic-environmental interaction discussed
- New research on temperament and later developmental problems for "difficult" babies

CHAPTER 3: PRENATAL DEVELOPMENT AND BIRTH

- New studies of the effects on the fetus of maternal stress, fear, and anxiety
- Updated U.S. and international data on infant mortality rates
- New information on low birthweight and its consequences for preterm infants' development
- New coverage of intervention programs for preterm babies
- Updated information on the incidence of AIDS in babies and on interventions for these infants

CHAPTER 4: INFANCY: SENSATION, PERCEPTION, AND LEARNING

- Updated material on the rapidly expanding areas of infant perception and memory
- New discussion of infant preparedness, including debates on early learning and biological preparedness; new research on early object knowledge
- Recent studies of haptic sensitivity in newborns

CHAPTER 5: THE CHILD'S GROWTH: BRAIN, BODY, MOTOR SKILLS, AND SEXUAL MATURATION

- New research on the association between brain development and musical study and performance
- New table of the latest brain assessment techniques, such as SPECT, fMRI, and TMS
- Updated material on the treatment of obesity and anorexia nervosa
- New section on sexual orientation and sexual identity

CHAPTER 6: EMOTIONAL DEVELOPMENT AND ATTACHMENT

- New section on the functionalist perspective's approach to emotional development
- New work on the recognition of emotions and the impact of abuse on a child's ability to recognize emotion
- New work on jealousy in young children; change over time in children's jealousy reactions
- New section on the role played by the family in children's emotional development
- Updated research on attachment relationships between fathers and their children
- New work on overcoming early problems and developing "secure" attachments in adulthood
- New research on increased aggression among children in child-care facilities

CHAPTER 7: LANGUAGE AND COMMUNICATION

- New research on challenges to the nativist view of language learning
- Expanded coverage of social contributions to language learning
- New research on whether to explain language by a unique cognitive processing system or a general learning system
- Expanded section on young children's queries—especially their "why" and "how" questions
- Additional coverage of metalinguistic awareness, including monitoring of speech

CHAPTER 8: COGNITIVE DEVELOPMENT: PIAGET AND VYGOTSKY

- Updates on research that examines the predictions of Piagetian theory, especially in the sensorimotor and preoperational stages
- New section on social cognition, including theory of mind and understanding of intentions
- Expanded and updated section on research stemming from Vygotsky's approach
- Updated section on cultural contributions to cognitive development, including the role of tools in intellectual development

CHAPTER 9: COGNITIVE DEVELOPMENT: THE INFORMATION-PROCESSING APPROACH

- New discussion of basic assumptions and models of information-processing theory
- Updated discussions of the enrichment and differentiation views of perceptual development
- New coverage of the connectionist models of information processing
- New section on cognitive tools, including symbolic and material supports for thinking
- Updated discussion of attention, including the role of attention in planning and recent research on memory, including organization and strategy development

CHAPTER 10: INTELLIGENCE

- Updated and expanded discussion of intelligence testing, including infant intelligence
- New discussion of how ethnicity and social class relate to IQ testing

- New material on changes in IQ over time, including the Flynn effect
- Updated section on achievement motivation, transferred from former chapter on schools

CHAPTER 11: THE FAMILY

- New section on co-parenting including such patterns as cohesive cooperation and gatekeeping
- New data on ethnic variations in child rearing
- Updates on incidence of pregnancy and STDs among teenagers
- New information on child abuse and neglect and the effects on children of sexual abuse
- New section on self-care and the latchkey child

CHAPTER 12: EXPANDING THE SOCIAL WORLD: PEERS AND FRIENDS

- New information on peer rejection and victimization
- New research on how close, same-gender friendships differ between boys and girls
- New section on romantic relationships among teenagers
- New data on whether parents or peers have more influence on children's behavior

CHAPTER 13: GENDER ROLES AND GENDER DIFFERENCES

- Integration of recent ideas on the evolutionary basis of gender differentiation
- New research showing that girls' slightly lesser ability to handle spatial reasoning is the basis for the erroneous belief that girls have poorer math skills
- Discussion of why girls continue to drop out of math courses
- New research on androgenized fetuses
- New section on siblings as shapers of gender identity
- New material on the effects on girls of a father's absence or unavailability

CHAPTER 14: MORALITY, ALTRUISM, AND AGGRESSION

- New section on the affective side of morality and the development of guilt in children
- New material on children's understanding of freedom of speech and of religion
- New findings with regard to the development of tolerance in children
- New material on relational aggression in girls

CHAPTER 15: DEVELOPMENTAL PSYCHOPATHOLOGY

- New data on the roles of peers and schools in children's substance abuse
- Updates on the symptoms and treatment of attention deficit-hyperactivity disorder
- Updates on suicide rates among various ethnic groups, especially Native American youth
- Update on the genetic roots of autism
- New boxed insert on the rate of mental health problems among affluent adolescents

SPECIAL FEATURES

In this edition we have expanded and refined our special features and now present nearly all illustrations in full color.

CHAPTER OUTLINES AND SUMMARIES Our chapter outlines facilitate students' survey of a chapter's contents and our comprehensive, bulleted summaries reiterate the chapter's main ideas.

STAGES OF PRENATAL DEVELOPMENT

The Zygote
The Embryo
The Fetus

Turning Points: An Overview of Prenatal Development

RISKS IN THE PRENATAL ENVIRONMENT

Environmental Dangers
Maternal Factors

Box 3.1 *Perspectives on Diversity: Prenatal Health Care and Infant Mortality*

BIRTH AND THE BEGINNINGS OF LIFE

Labor and Delivery
Prematurity and Low Birthweight

Box 3.2 *Child Psychology in Action: Of Babies and Bears and Postnatal Care*

VULNERABILITY AND RESILIENCE IN CHILDREN AT RISK

Box 3.3 *Risk and Resilience: What Factors Help Children Overcome Early Adversity?*

MAKING THE CONNECTIONS 3

SUMMARY

EXPLORE AND DISCUSS

3.

Prenatal Development and Birth

Anticipating the birth of a child can be one of the most joyous times in people's lives. Couples look forward to becoming parents and enjoy preparing for their baby's arrival. They may even try to influence the new family member by playing favorite music or reading to their unborn child!

Whether it's possible to influence a baby in such positive ways during pregnancy is not entirely certain, although as we will see, there is some evidence that babies learn in utero. Unfortunately, however, clear evidence indicates that the developing organism is vulnerable to a variety of negative influences. Some of these influences are genetic, as we saw in Chapter 2, and others are variations in the prenatal environment caused by factors and events affecting the mother as her pregnancy proceeds. An amazing number of adverse agents—including medications and diagnostic procedures; prescription, nonprescription, and other legal and illegal drugs; maternal age and *parity* (whether a woman has had a child before); illness, dietary deficiencies, and emotional distress; and environmental toxins—can contribute to deviations from the normal development of a child from its first weeks of gestation. In addition, events occurring during childbirth may threaten the viability or good health of an infant, and, as we might guess, the economic and social conditions in which a child is raised can affect its development from the very earliest days of its life outside the womb.

We begin this chapter by exploring the normal development of the human being from conception to delivery and then discuss the many factors that can threaten normal development throughout a pregnancy. We look at normal childbirth and at some of the complications of labor and delivery, including the problems of prematurity and low birthweight. We conclude the chapter with a review of the research that has explored the long-term effects of pregnancy and birth complications as well as the resilience some children show in the face of such difficulties. Throughout these discussions we will ask several questions: What are the most significant of these complicating factors? How does the timing of their appearance in the

---

SUMMARY

Stages of Prenatal Development

- Prenatal development is typically divided into three distinct periods (zygote, embryo, fetus). In reality, these periods represent continuous phases of development during which the organism, protected and sustained by the **amniotic sac**, the **placenta**, the **umbilical cord**, and, after the fifth month, the lanugo, undergoes a systematic series of sequential changes to become increasingly complex and differentiated.

- The period of the **zygote**, which lasts about two weeks, extends from fertilization to implantation, when the zygote becomes implanted in the wall of the uterus. The period of the **embryo** begins at that point and lasts until the end of the eighth week. During this period of rapid growth, most of the important organs and physiological systems develop, and the embryo is quite vulnerable to adverse environmental influences.

- The principles of **cephalocaudal development** and **proximal-distal development** govern the order in which various parts of the organism's body are formed and grow. According to the first principle,

physical growth begins in the area of the head and moves downward, toward the trunk and legs; according to the second, growth also proceeds from central areas, such as the internal organs, to more distant ones, such as the arms.

- The period of the **fetus** extends from the beginning of the third month until birth. Around the fourth and fifth months, the mother can feel the fetus move, and reflexes such as sucking appear. Nails appear, the skin grows more adultlike, and **lanugo** covers the body of the fetus. Although the major organ systems are well differentiated by this time, the central nervous system continues to develop at a rapid pace, reflexes develop, and regulatory processes and the respiratory system continue to mature. A danger at this time is **respiratory distress syndrome**, and if the child is born before the **age of viability**, or 22 to 26 weeks, it may not be developed enough to survive.

Risks in the Prenatal Environment

- During prenatal development, **teratogens**, agents that produce developmental abnormalities, may

BOX PROGRAM   Our boxed discussions highlight three important themes: the application of basic research to real problems of children's lives, the importance of understanding and supporting children's resilience in the face of risk, and the similarities and differences among children of many different cultures and ethnicities.

Box 4.1

Child Psychology in Action

PREVENTING SUDDEN INFANT DEATH SYNDROME (SIDS)

Each year in the United States about 10,000 babies die in their sleep from causes classified as **sudden infant death syndrome (SIDS)**, also known as *crib death*.

The prevention of SIDS requires identifying its most likely victims. So far we know that victims are more apt to be low-birthweight male babies who have a history of newborn respiratory problems, who were hospitalized longer than usual after birth, and who have abnormal heart-rate patterns and nighttime sleep disturbances (Mitchell et al., 1993; Rovee-Collier & Lipsitt, 1982; Sadeh, 1996). Their mothers are more likely to be anemic, to smoke or use narcotics, and to have received little prenatal care, although it should be stressed that most babies of women with this history are not affected. Usually, SIDS occurs during sleep in the wintertime, and it often follows a minor respiratory ailment, such as a cold. It is most common between the ages of 2 and 4 months and rarely occurs after 6 months (*American Academy of Pediatrics Report*, 2000).

The cause of SIDS is still a mystery. It is not due to accidental suffocation, to mucus or fluid in the lungs, or to choking on regurgitated food. Nor has there been any success in isolating a virus associated with SIDS, although this is still a possibility. Another possibility is that *apnea*, the spontaneous interruption of breathing that sometimes occurs during sleep, especially REM sleep, may be a factor in SIDS (Steinschneider, 1975). The brain stem, which controls breathing, may not be well enough developed in these infants to overcome brief cessations in breathing. Researchers are investigating whether babies who have unusually long apnea periods during sleep may be more prone to SIDS.

Parental smoking has also been suggested as a contributing factor to crib death (Frick, 1999). In addition, SIDS victims may have failed to develop adequate responses to nasal blockage and other threats to breathing (Lipsitt, 1990). Although newborns appear to have built-in defensive reactions to respiratory threats (e.g., when a cloth is placed over a baby's face, she will use her hands to try to remove it), between 2 and 4 months of age these reactions may change from reflexive behaviors to voluntary ones. Crib death is most common during this same age period. Perhaps failure to make a smooth transition from reflexive to voluntary defenses puts an infant at greater risk for SIDS.

Monitors that sound an alarm to alert parents when an infant's breathing is interrupted may be useful in preventing SIDS. Although the false alarms of these devices may place stress on the parents, the devices may help to save lives. It is also helpful for babies to sleep on their backs or sides, not on their stomachs; sleeping on the stomach may depress breathing (Willinger, Hoffman, & Hartford, 1994). Babies should not sleep on very soft mattresses or be surrounded by pillows that may obstruct breathing (*Am... Report*, 2000). Some resea... adopt the practices of ma... infant cosleeping is commo... and China where this practi... lower (McKenna & Mosko, ... some researchers to sugge... baby in breathing regulatio... However, this proposal is st... Phillips, 2000) and needs f...

Child Psychology in Action boxes pick up the thread of our research-application theme, focusing on how the results of basic research can be applied to the solution of problems in children's development. For example, in Chapter 2, the box on "The Human Genome Project" reports both the latest developments in describing the human genome and the implications of this work for the treatment of disease and disorders. In Chapter 9, the box "Should Young Children Testify in Court?" shows that although children's memory may be accurate, children are susceptible to such influences as the circumstances under which they acquired the original information and the characteristics of the person who later interviews them.

Box 6.2

Risk and Resilience

PEERS AS ATTACHMENT FIGURES

Anna Freud's classic account (Freud & Dann, 1951) of the behavior of six young German-Jewish orphans brought to England during World War II not only highlights the incredible resilience of these at-risk children, torn from their families and kept in concentration camps from age 1 through 4, but also illustrates the depth and intensity that peer attachments can have. When they were 4 years old, these children, most of whose parents had died in gas chambers, arrived at Bulldog Banks, a small English country home that had been transformed into a nursery for war children. Quickly, they formed intense, protective attachments to each other while they ignored or were actively hostile to their adult caretakers. Bulldog Banks was the first time any of them had experienced living in a small, intimate setting with adults who offered them kindness rather than cruelty.

In their early days at the nursery these six children were wild and uncontrollable. Within a few days they destroyed or damaged much of the furniture and all the toys given them. Most of the time they ignored the adults, but when they were angry, they would bite, spit, or swear at them, often calling them *bloder ochs* ("stupid fools").

The contrast between the children's hostile behavior toward their caretakers and their solicitous, considerate behavior toward one another was surprising. In one case, when a caretaker accidentally knocked over one of the children, two of the other children threw bricks at her and called her names. The children resisted being separated from each other even for special treats like pony rides. When one child was ill, the others wanted to remain with her. They showed little envy, jealousy, rivalry, or competition with each other. The sharing and helping behaviors of these children with one another was remarkable in children of this age.

Here are some typical incidents in the children's first seven months at Bulldog Banks (Freud & Dann, 1951, pp. 150–168):

- The children were eating cake, and John began to cry when he saw there was no cake left for a second helping. Ruth and Miriam, who had not yet finished their portions, gave him the remainder of

their cake and seemed happy just to pet him and comment on his eating the cake.

- In very cold weather one child lost his gloves, and another child loaned his gloves without complaining about his own discomfort.

Even in fearful situations, children were able to overcome their trepidation to help others in their group:

- A dog approached the children, who were terrified. Ruth, though badly frightened herself, walked bravely to Peter, who was screaming, and gave him her toy rabbit to comfort him. She comforted John by lending him her necklace.

- On the beach in Brighton, Ruth was throwing pebbles into the water. Peter, who was afraid of waves, did not dare to approach them. Suddenly, in spite of his fear, he rushed to Ruth, calling out: "Water coming, water coming," and dragged her back to safety.

When, finally, the children began to form positive relations with adults, they made them on the basis of group feelings. Their relationships with their caretakers had none of the demanding, possessive attitudes often shown by young children toward their own mothers. They simply began to include the adults in their group and to treat them, in some ways, as they treated each other. For those children in whom this phase of general attachment was eventually followed by a specific attachment to an individual caretaker, clinging and possessive behaviors did appear. But for all the children throughout their year's stay at Bulldog Banks, the intensity of such attachments to surrogate mothers was never as great as it would have been in normal mother-child relations, and the relationships were never as binding as those they maintained with their peers.

These children's circumstances were unusual, and we must therefore interpret this classic work with caution. At the same time, the children's behavior clearly demonstrates not only the intensity of attachments that can develop between young children but also the resilience that enabled these children to survive unimaginable horrors.

Risk and Resilience boxes explore the sometimes astounding resilience that children can display in the face of a wide variety of risks, including physical and mental disabilities, disease, poverty, deteriorated neighborhoods, and broken or dysfunctional families. These discussions focus not only on how we can support and encourage such resilience but how we can work to alleviate or eliminate the risk factors. For example, in Chapter 3, the box "What Factors Help Children Overcome Early Adversity?" focuses on Emmy Werner's classic and continuing work on risk and resilience on Hawaii's island of Kauai. In Chapter 7, the box "Children at Risk for Failure to Develop Language" discusses the System for Augmenting Language developed by Mary Ann Romski and Rose Sevcik, by which nonspeaking children with mild to severe mental retardation have been able, for the first time, to communicate with others by using a system of lexigrams and a computerized keyboard.

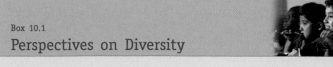

Box 10.1

Perspectives on Diversity

MAKING THE GRADE IN JAPAN, TAIWAN, AND THE UNITED STATES

The declining school achievement of U.S. children decried by the media has often been attributed to failures of the North American school system. Teachers and educators who, particularly in inner-city schools, have struggled to help children from varying backgrounds and life circumstances learn to read, write, do mathematics, and, most important, enjoy learning, have felt deeply wronged by these reports. Longitudinal studies by Harold Stevenson and his associates (Chen, Stevenson, Hayward, & Burgess, 1995; Stevenson, Chen, & Lee, 1993; Stevenson, Chen, & Uttal, 1990) have now provided evidence that in the earliest months of first grade, children in the United States already lag behind other children in academic achievement. Thus, although differences in academic performance may well reflect varying educational systems, that these differences appear when children have as yet had little exposure to formal education suggests more is involved than inadequate educational practices.

Over a 10-year period, Stevenson and colleagues administered tests of reading and mathematics ability to groups of first, fifth, and eleventh graders in classrooms in two U.S. metropolitan areas (Minneapolis, Minnesota, and Fairfax County, Virginia), in two East Asian cities (Beijing, China, and Taipei, Taiwan), and in Japan (Sendai). The U.S. students included four cultural groups—European, Chinese, African, and Latino Americans, although not all these groups were represented in every study. To the degree possible, the investigators retested the same students at different ages

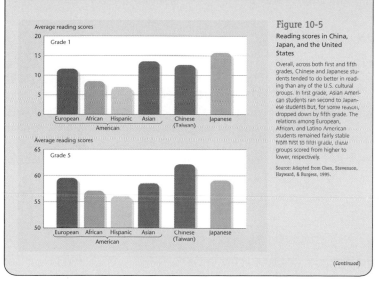

Figure 10-5

Reading scores in China, Japan, and the United States

Overall, across both first and fifth grades, Chinese and Japanese students tended to do better in reading than any of the U.S. cultural groups. In first grade, Asian American students ran second to Japanese students but, for some reason, dropped down by fifth grade. The relations among European, African, and Latino American students remained fairly stable from first to fifth grade; these groups scored from higher to lower, respectively.

Source: Adapted from Chen, Stevenson, Hayward, & Burgess, 1995.

(Continued)

Perspectives on Diversity boxes tie in with another of our major themes, examining research on the development of children's abilities, behaviors, and skills in different cultural communities throughout the world and among children of the many different cultural groups who make up the U.S. population. These boxes recognize the increasing importance of understanding and respect for all peoples, attitudes that need to be rooted in the world of the child. For example, in Chapter 1, the box "How Culture Can Affect Children's Cognitive Development" discusses how children's thinking is influenced by cultural experiences and practices, and that culture affects both what children think about and how they use their cognitive abilities to carry out intelligent actions. In Chapter 14, the box "Justice versus Interpersonal Obligations: India and the United States" demonstrates that Hindu Indians are much more likely to accord interpersonal considerations importance in making moral judgments than are Americans.

KEY TERMS AND MARGIN GLOS-SARY We have carefully reviewed key terms and have included some additional terms that we consider crucial to the student's learning of new material. These terms are set in boldface type and are repeated, with their definitions, on the same page in a margin glossary; the terms and their definitions also appear in the alphabetized Glossary at the back of the book. Terms that may be unfamiliar to students but that are not crucial to learning the material are shown in the text in italics.

problem-solving, and reasoning. From an information-processing perspective, each of these abilities plays an important role in how information is operated on. The organization of the information-processing system relies on the flow of information through it. Thus, the system is structured around what happens once information is selected for processing and enters the system, how information is retained in the system, and how information is used in thinking and problem solving.

Perception and Attention

A group of children exposed to the same sensory stimulation do not necessarily take in the same amounts and kinds of information. Each child's **perception** of the surrounding environment—that is, interpretation of information that comes in through the senses—may be the same, but his **attention** may be focused on different aspects of that environment. Attention involves the identification and selection of particular sensory input for closer inspection and more detailed processing. For example, one child in a classroom who is focusing on the teacher will hear and understand the lesson, but another child who is more interested in a whispered message from a neighbor may focus on that sound and regard the teacher's voice as background noise. How children's surroundings affect them depends on what aspects of the surroundings children attend to and what meaning these features have for them.

Perception and attention are tightly interwoven: Each depends on the other. To attend to something we must first perceive it, and to perceive something without attending to it is haphazard at best. The child's choice of what perceptions she will attend to, and in what manner, will determine how the environment's many sights, sounds, smells, touches, and sensations of movement affect her. And as both her perceptual capabilities and attentional strategies develop, they will continue to affect the information she acquires from any particular situation. As children develop, they combine attention with other cognitive processes: for example, they make use of planning, in the form of deliberate attempts to obtain knowledge from the environment that will make it possible for them to reach a goal.

perception The interpretation of sensations to make them meaningful.

attention The identification and selection of particular sensory input for closer inspection and more detailed processing.

"MAKING THE CONNECTIONS" GRAPHICS New to this edition are diagrams that enable the student to relate discussions in one chapter to topics explored in other chapters. These graphics underline the interrelatedness of issues across different domains of development.

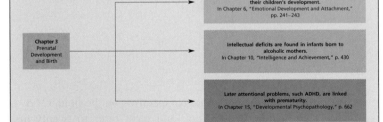

Making the Connections 3

There are many links between concepts and ideas presented in one area of development and concepts and ideas in other areas. Here are some of the connections between ideas in Chapter 3 and discussions in other chapters of this book.

Chapter 3 Prenatal Development and Birth

Fathers play a supportive role for both mothers and infants not just during childbirth but throughout their children's development. In Chapter 6, "Emotional Development and Attachment," pp. 241–243

Intellectual deficits are found in infants born to alcoholic mothers. In Chapter 10, "Intelligence and Achievement," p. 430

Later attentional problems, such ADHD, are linked with prematurity. In Chapter 15, "Developmental Psychopathology," p. 662

"EXPLORE AND DISCUSS" STUDY QUESTIONS Also new to this edition are study questions that appear at the end of each chapter. Our aim is to promote creative and critical thinking about the issues discussed in each chapter.

EXPLORE AND DISCUSS

1. How do changes in infants' thinking, as described by Piaget, contribute to the infant's increasing ability to interact with people and objects in the world?
2. Imagine you are an educational consultant and you have been asked to consult at a school where several second- and third-grade children are having difficulty understanding scientific concepts that involve the conservation of weight and volume. How would you explain this difficulty and what would

you advise the teachers to do to help these children?
3. If you were to design a new IQ test based on Vygotsky's idea of the zone of proximal development, what would it be like?
4. How could Vygotsky's ideas about culture and development be used to understand children's learning and development in a multicultural society such as ours?

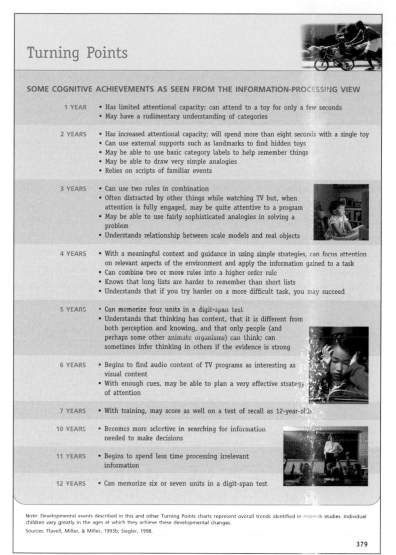

Turning Points

SOME COGNITIVE ACHIEVEMENTS AS SEEN FROM THE INFORMATION-PROCESSING VIEW

1 YEAR	• Has limited attentional capacity; can attend to a toy for only a few seconds • May have a rudimentary understanding of categories
2 YEARS	• Has increased attentional capacity; will spend more than eight seconds with a single toy • Can use external supports such as landmarks to find hidden toys • May be able to use basic category labels to help remember things • May be able to draw very simple analogies • Relies on scripts of familiar events
3 YEARS	• Can use two rules in combination • Often distracted by other things while watching TV but, when attention is fully engaged, may be quite attentive to a program • May be able to use fairly sophisticated analogies in solving a problem • Understands relationship between scale models and real objects
4 YEARS	• With a meaningful context and guidance in using simple strategies, can focus attention on relevant aspects of the environment and apply the information gained to a task • Can combine two or more rules into a higher order rule • Knows that long lists are harder to remember than short lists • Understands that if you try harder on a more difficult task, you may succeed
5 YEARS	• Can memorize four units in a digit-span test • Understands that thinking has content, that it is different from both perception and knowing, and that only people (and perhaps some other animate organisms) can think; can sometimes infer thinking in others if the evidence is strong
6 YEARS	• Begins to find audio content of TV programs as interesting as visual content • With enough cues, may be able to plan a very effective strategy of attention
7 YEARS	• With training, may score as well on a test of recall as 12-year-olds
10 YEARS	• Becomes more selective in searching for information needed to make decisions
11 YEARS	• Begins to spend less time processing irrelevant information
12 YEARS	• Can memorize six or seven units in a digit-span test

Note: Developmental events described in this and other Turning Points charts represent overall trends identified in research studies. Individual children vary greatly in the ages at which they achieve these developmental changes.

Sources: Flavell, Miller, & Miller, 1993b; Siegler, 1998.

379

"TURNING POINTS" CHARTS   These charts help students view children's evolving skills and abilities in terms of their chronology over the child's development. The charts, which record what is *typical* but do not take account of individual difference, appear in Chapters 4 through 9 and 12 through 14. We also highlight the chronologies of various specific evolving characteristics and skills in briefer tables throughout the book.

UPDATED RESEARCH   As our book title, *Child Psychology: A Contemporary Viewpoint,* promises, we provide the most up-to-date perspectives on the field. Of over 2,000 references, close to 900 are new to the book and most refer to twenty-first century work. Although nearly half are from the 1990s onward, we include research classics because they provide the frameworks for recent studies and help understand contemporary research.

ILLUSTRATION PROGRAM   We have expanded our program of illustrations and have revised many graphics and tables to achieve better clarity. Almost all of our photographs are now in full color and clear captions help students understand figures and photos and relate data to text discussions.

SUPPLEMENTS

A complete package of multimedia and ancillaries has been prepared for this book. The supplements listed here may accompany the sixth edition of *Child Psychology: A Contemporary Viewpoint.* Please contact your local McGraw-Hill representative for details concerning policies, prices, and availability, as some restrictions may apply.

For the Instructor

INSTRUCTOR'S MANUAL   Susan Perez, University of North Florida
This comprehensive resource is designed around a list of Learning Objectives which correspond with those in the Test Bank and the student Online Learning Center, forming a cohesive instructional package. In the Instructor's Manual you will find chapter outlines, lecture topics, class discussions, and demonstrations with handouts included. The manual also facilitates the integration of the textbook's boxed features (Child Psychology in Action, Risk and Resilience, and Perspectives on Diversity) into your lectures. Finally, each chapter includes a list of Supplementary Readings and a guide to multimedia resources.

TEST BANK   Jessica Dennis, California State University–Los Angeles; Kristie Morris, University of California–Riverside
Each Test Bank chapter includes the list of Learning Objectives, which correlate to those in the Instructor's Manual and the student Online Learning Center. The Test Bank provides more than 1,500 multiple choice, short answer, and essay questions. Additionally, each multiple-choice question includes the answer, the type of question (factual, conceptual, or applied), the learning objective it addresses, and the page in the main text where the corresponding material is presented.

DUAL PLATFORM COMPUTERIZED TEST BANK ON CD-ROM   The Computerized Test Bank is compatible for both Macintosh and Windows platforms. This CD-ROM provides fully functioning editing features that enable instructors to integrate their own questions, scramble items, and modify questions. Additional information regarding these features can be found in the accompanying CD-ROM documentation.

POWERPOINT SLIDES   Linda Ann Butzin, Owens Community College
The *Child Psychology* sixth edition PowerPoint presentations cover the key points of each chapter, serving as a springboard for your lectures. They can be used as is, or you may modify them to meet your specific needs.

INSTRUCTOR'S RESOURCE CD-ROM   For instructors' convenience, the Instructor's Manual, Test Bank, and PowerPoints are offered on a single CD-ROM.

ONLINE LEARNING CENTER: INSTRUCTOR CENTER   www.mhhe. com/hetherington6
This extensive Web site, designed specifically to accompany *Child Psychology,* sixth edition, offers an array of resources for both instructor and student. Among the features included on the Instructor's side of the Web site, which is password protected, are an online version of the Instructor's Manual, PowerPoint Slides, and links to professional resources. These resources and more can be found by logging onto the text site at www.mhhe.com/hetherington6. Contact your McGraw-Hill representative for your password.

   PowerWeb: This unique online reader, which is fully integrated into the Online Learning Center, provides readings, *New York Times* news feeds, and weekly updates with refereed Web links. You will be excited by this powerful tool for helping keep your lectures up to date and timely.

PAGEOUT   PageOut™ is the easiest way to create a Web site for your course. It requires no prior knowledge of HTML coding or graphic design, and is free with every McGraw-Hill textbook. Visit us at www.pageout.net to learn more about PageOut™.

MCGRAW-HILL'S VISUAL ASSET DATABASE (VAD) FOR LIFE-SPAN DEVELOPMENT   Jasna Jovanovic, University of Illinois at Urbana-Champaign

McGraw-Hill's Visual Asset Database is a password-protected online database of hundreds of multimedia resources for use in classroom presentations, including original video clips, audio clips, photographs, and illustrations—all designed to bring to life concepts in developmental psychology. In addition to offering ready-made multimedia presentations for every stage of the lifespan, the VAD search engine and unique "My Modules" program allows instructors to select from the database's resources to create customized presentations, or "modules." Instructors can save these customized presentations in specially marked "module" folders on the McGraw-Hill site, and then run presentations directly from VAD to the Internet-equipped classroom. Contact your McGraw-Hill representative for a password to this valuable resource.

MULTIMEDIA COURSEWARE FOR CHILD DEVELOPMENT   Charlotte J. Patterson, University of Virginia

This video-based, two CD-ROM set covers classic and contemporary experiments in child development. Respected researcher Charlotte J. Patterson selected the video and wrote modules that can be assigned to students. The modules also include suggestions for additional projects as well as a testing component. Multimedia Courseware can be packaged with the text at a discount.

As a full-service publisher of quality educational products, McGraw-Hill docs much more than just sell textbooks to your students. We create and publish an extensive array of print, video, and digital supplements to support instruction on your campus. Orders of new (versus used) textbooks help us to defray the cost of developing such supplements, which is substantial. We have a broad range of other supplements in psychology that you may wish to tap for your course. Ask your local McGraw-Hill representative about the availability of supplements that may help with your course design.

For the Student

LIFEMAP CD-ROM   Steven A. Schneider, Pima College

Packaged free with each new copy of the book, the LifeMap CD gives students an opportunity to expand and test their understanding of course material. In addition to a multiple-choice quiz with feedback for each chapter, the CD includes videos of children engaged in activities described in the text; interviews with children, teens, and parents; and comments from experts on various child development topics. Each video is accompanied by an overview, study questions, and Web links to encourage further exploration of the topic. The LifeMap CD also features an interactive timeline outlining the stages of human development from conception to adolescence.

ONLINE LEARNING CENTER WITH POWERWEB   Gail Edmunds

www.mhhe.com/hetherington6

This extensive Web site, designed specifically to accompany *Child Psychology,* sixth edition, offers an array of resources for both instructor and student. The student side of the Online Learning Center provides a variety of learning tools, including the Learning Objectives that match those in the Instructor's Manual and Test Bank; chapter outlines; quizzing including Key Terms flashcards, multiple-choice questions, true-false questions, and short answer/essay questions; and Web links for each chapter.

These resources and more can be found by logging on to the Online Learning Center at www.mhhe.com/hetherington6.

A PowerWeb passcard is bound into each new copy of the book—students should be sure to save it so that they can benefit from this unique online reader, which is fully integrated into the Online Learning Center. Here you will find readings, *New York Times* news feeds, and weekly updates with refereed Web links; tools for research, study, and assessment; and interactive exercises.

ACKNOWLEDGMENTS

We are grateful to the many contributors to the sixth edition of the *Handbook of Child Psychology* who kindly made prepublication copies of their chapters available to us. We know that readers of *Child Psychology: A Contemporary Viewpoint,* sixth edition, will benefit greatly from discussions throughout our book that draw on portions of this significant work.

We are fortunate that a number of people who teach the child development course have offered us their insights and suggestions for the manuscript of this book, and we offer them our gratitude: Belinda Blevins-Knabe, *University of Arkansas, Little Rock;* Lisa Chan, *California State University, Los Angeles;* W. Andrew Collins, *University of Minnesota;* K. Laurie Dickson, *Northern Arizona University;* Cynthia Erdley, *University of Maine, Orono;* Janet Frick, *University of Georgia;* Jody Ganiban, *George Washington University;* Barbara Hammonds, *Palomar Community College;* Kathleen Kleissler, *Kutztown University;* Ting Lei, *Borough of Manhattan Community College;* Kevin MacDonald, *California State University, Long Beach;* Alyssa McCabe, *University of Massachusetts, Lowell;* David Nelson, *Brigham Young University;* Claire Novosad, *Southern Connecticut State University;* Cathie Robertson, *Grossmont College;* Glenn Roisman, *University of Illinois at Urbana-Champaign;* Sharon Stein, *Ferrum College;* Margaret Szewczyk, *University of Illinois at Urbana-Champaign;* Lorraine Taylor, *University of North Carolina, Chapel Hill;* Jamie Walter, *Albion College;* and Bonnie Wright, *Gardner-Webb University.*

Our thanks to Graeme R. Hoste, Mary Gauvain's son, for his work in updating and organizing the references for this sixth edition of our book and for offering helpful ideas regarding illustrations and the presentation of graphic material in the text. We also want to thank Heather Guzman for her patient and professional assistance in preparing the manuscript.

Once again, this book has benefited from the expertise and dedication of the McGraw-Hill Higher Education staff. We thank Steve Rutter, Publisher, for his support of this project. Thanks also to Mike Sugarman, Executive Editor, for his support and enthusiasm for this new edition. Elsa Peterson, Senior Developmental Editor, has provided diligent oversight and has kept us on track during the book production process. Susan Trentacosti, Lead Project Manager, has supervised the production process smoothly. Brian Pecko, Manager, Photo Research, was very helpful in locating photos and illustrations that enhance the artistry of this new edition. Bea Sussman, copy editor, made an important contribution to the accuracy of the book. Robin Mouat, Art Manager, skilfully oversaw the preparation of graphs and other figures. Finally, Melissa Caughlin, Marketing Manager, brought great creativity to devising a plan for presenting our book to the talented McGraw-Hill sales force. To these people and to the many others on the McGraw-Hill team we express our gratitude.

E. Mavis Hetherington
Ross D. Parke
Mary Gauvain
Virginia Otis Locke

Child Psychology
A Contemporary Viewpoint

Pablo Picasso (1881–1973). *Claude with Horse,* 1949.

1.

Child Development: Themes, Theories, and Methods

Two-year-old Mariela has a pile of blocks in front of her of all shapes, sizes, and colors. She can put all her red blocks in one group and all the blue ones in another, regardless of their shape and size. At this age, Mariela does not sort all triangular blocks together if the triangular blocks are of differing colors. By the time she's 5, she'll be able to sort and re-sort a collection of objects that have several different sizes, shapes, and colors. For example, Mariela will be able to put all triangular blocks in one group regardless of their colors. And when she is 7 or so, she'll use this strategy of categorization in learning new information. For example, if her teacher gives her a list of words including *shirt, eyes, carrot, apple, nose, shoes, pants, cereal,* and *mouth* she will be able to learn the words more efficiently by classifying them into groups: items of clothing (*shirt, shoes, pants*), parts of the body (*eyes, nose, mouth*), and food (*carrot, apple, cereal*).

Justin, who is a year and a half, plays with his toys next to another child but doesn't talk to the other child or interact with him except, perhaps, to grab one of his companion's toys or scream if the other child has taken one of his. At this age, Justin has difficulty taking into account the other child's perspective. In contrast, when Justin is 6 or 7 he can and does engage in group play. He also understands that people have different points of view, although he believes that people act from their own self-interest. By the time he is in his midteens, Justin understands the need for positive human relationships, the desirability of being "good" rather than "bad," and the concepts of societal law and order.

What accounts for this gradual but steady evolution in the child's ability to perceive and describe complex relationships, to learn new things efficiently, and to relate to, interact with, and feel responsibility toward other people? The field of **child development**, a sub-area of the broader discipline of developmental psychology, seeks to answer these questions in two major ways. First, it endeavors to identify and describe *changes* in the child's cognitive, emotional, motor,

child development A field of study that seeks to account for the gradual evolution of the child's cognitive, social, and other capacities first by describing changes in the child's observed behaviors and then by uncovering the processes and strategies that underlie these changes.

and social capacities and behaviors from the moment of conception through the period of adolescence. Second, it attempts to uncover the *processes* that underlie these changes and that help to explain how and why they occur. In short, developmental psychologists are interested in what things change as children get older and how these changes come about. To understand the changes and processes that underlie child development, researchers devise theories, design empirical studies to test these theories, and suggest practical applications or social policies based on their research. This chapter introduces the study of child development by describing the main theories in the field and the methods scientists use to examine these theories.

Although today research in child development plays a significant role in the general field of psychology, this subdiscipline is a relatively young enterprise. It got its start barely a century ago, when the topic drew the attention of scholars from various regions of the world (Cairns, 1998). For instance, in Europe there were many pioneers, such as Charles Darwin, who conducted research on infants' early sensory and perceptual capacities and children's emotions, and Alfred Binet, who studied children's learning and how to assess children's intelligence. In Russia, Lev Vygotsky studied the influence of social and cultural experiences on human development. In the United States, G. Stanley Hall and James Mark Baldwin were early proponents of the value of studying developmental psychology and helped pave the way for the field in the United States. They were soon followed by John Dewey, who applied a developmental approach to education, and by Arnold Gesell, who charted the course and pattern of human growth.

Why is this field so young? Part of the reason is that our appreciation of childhood as a unique phase of life is a relatively modern phenomenon. As the French historian Philipe Aries documents in his classic work *Centuries of Childhood* (1962), for most of recorded history, little was written about children or childhood. By and large, people viewed children as miniature adults—a view particularly evident in the way adults treated children. For example, children were often laborers in factories and mines. In fact, it was not until the late nineteenth century that child labor laws were introduced to protect children from this kind of exploitation. By the end of the twentieth century, the scientific study of child development had a central role in psychological research, and its influence stretched into the arenas of social policy and legislation. During this relatively brief history, the field has gradually begun to embrace an increasing number of topics, often adding such new topics as a direct result of societal changes that affect child development in some particular way.

Proposing one of the first theories of children's emotional development, Charles Darwin (1809–1882) based much of his theorizing on his infant son's earliest emotional expressions. Although Darwin is more widely known for his theory of evolution, his work on children's emotional behavior continues to have considerable influence on the field of child development.

Such changes have included the establishment of compulsory schooling, the increased divorce rate, alterations in family size and composition, delayed parenting, and improvements in nutrition and health care. And recently, the large set of social changes captured under the term *globalization* has attracted the attention of developmental psychologists. For example, researchers have documented an increase in eating disorders among female adolescents who live in the South Pacific islands, where television didn't appear until late in the twentieth century. Globalization has brought these young girls the images of attractive and very thin role models, unknown in their own culture, and in an effort to keep up with the world, these teens have begun to endanger their health.

Better information about child development can help all members of society who care about the well-being of children, including parents, teachers, health professionals, and legislators (Lerner, Fischer, & Weinberg, 2000). Research findings can lead to helpful advice on a wide range of current issues, from creating and selecting effective day-care programs and handling children's temper tantrums to dealing with the effects on children of such things as child care and violence on television. Information on normal child development also helps those who work with and care for children with problems of physical and mental development. Such information may contribute to efforts to prevent and treat developmental difficulties.

To understand the study of child development, it is important to appreciate the central themes of development that underlie current theory and research, the main theoretical views that guide this research, and the methods that are used in it. Throughout our exploration of contemporary child psychology, we will ask how specific processes and experiences may account for different aspects of the child's development. We will also discuss how we can use what we learn to improve children's functioning and opportunities for development in important areas of their lives, especially relationships with family, friends, and peers; academic pursuits; and personal development.

THEMES OF DEVELOPMENT

As scientists have studied children's development, they have continued to confront and debate a number of significant themes. These themes address core issues in the study of psychological development, and theories of development typically account for each of these themes in some way. The primary themes, which we will discuss in more detail, pertain to the origins of behavior, the pattern of developmental change, and the forces that direct this pattern. In terms of the origins of behavior, psychologists are especially interested in whether development is the result of biological, or hereditary, influences, or whether it is primarily formed by environmental forces. Today scientists agree that both our biology and the social and physical environment that surrounds us affect development, although each may influence different aspects of development to different degrees and at different points during growth and change.

Questions about the pattern of developmental change concentrate mostly on whether change is discontinuous, or stagelike, with many qualitative shifts, or whether change is better described as a continuous and cumulative process in which developmental progress is clearly and directly tied to prior functioning. Finally, the third theme, which focuses on the forces that direct developmental change, is typically examined by considering whether a child's personal characteristics regulate his development or whether situational factors, such as other people or particular experiences or conditions within his family or his culture, play the more significant role in directing the course of development.

We will encounter all these themes repeatedly as we discuss the many aspects of development—biological, cognitive, linguistic, emotional, and social—throughout the text. We will also see that the different theories of child development we discuss in the next major section emphasize one or more themes to differing degrees.

Biological versus Environmental Influences

Most modern viewpoints recognize that both biological and environmental factors influence human development, but they disagree about the relative importance of each of these factors for different aspects of development. Biological extremists of the past believed that the course of development was largely predetermined by genetic and other biological factors; these genetic or biological processes led to the naturally unfolding course of growth called **maturation.** One early advocate of this view, Arnold Gesell, suggested, "All things considered, the inevitableness and surety of maturation are the most impressive characteristics of early development. It is the hereditary ballast which conserves and stabilizes the growth of each individual infant" (Gesell, 1928, p. 378). Opposing this view, other early theorists, such as the behaviorist John B. Watson, placed their emphasis strictly on the environment. Watson (1928) assumed that genetic

maturation A genetic or biologically determined process of growth that unfolds over a period of time.

factors place no restrictions on the ways that environmental events can shape the course of a child's development and claimed that by properly organizing the environment he could produce a Mozart, a Babe Ruth, or an Al Capone.

Today no one supports either of these extreme positions. Instead, modern developmentalists explore how biological and environmental factors, or nature and nurture, interact to produce developmental variations in different children. The interplay between biology and environment is evident in many ways. Research on child maltreatment, for example, finds that children with certain genetic characteristics are more likely to exhibit behavior problems than are children who do not have these characteristics (Plomin, DeFries, McClearn, & McGuffin, 2001). When children with these genetic dispositions live in abusive environments, they are more likely to be maltreated than other children. Thus, the *combination* of the child's genetic characteristics, the way he expresses these characteristics behaviorally, and the abusive environment itself puts a particular child at risk. The question then is not which factor is more important, but how the expression of the biological program that we inherit is shaped, modified, and directed by our particular set of environmental circumstances.

The interaction between biological propensities and the environment over the course of development is supported by the active nature of the human organism. Modern developmentalists hold that one critical biological predisposition crucial to psychological growth is that children are active agents who shape, control, and direct the course of their own development (Bell, 1968; Kuczynski, 2003). Children intentionally try to understand and explore the world about them. Moreover, socializing agents such as parents, peers, or teachers do not simply mold the child; instead, influence is a two-way process. That is, children also actively modify the actions of their parents and other people whom they encounter in their daily lives. Thus, the interaction between biology and environment is an active, dynamic process in which the developing organism is also a contributing force or agent in the process that propels development.

Continuity versus Discontinuity

Another major question that confronts developmental psychologists is how to describe the pattern of developmental change. Two basic patterns are debated. Some psychologists view development as additive, or quantitative; that is, they see it as a continuous process whereby each new event builds on earlier experiences, in an orderly way (Figure 1-1a). In this view, development is a smooth and gradual accumulation of abilities, without any abrupt shifts along the path. For many behaviors, this seems like an apt explanation. For example, as we learn a new skill—let's say how to swim—we usually observe gradual improvement, sometimes on a daily basis. Every day our stroke may get a little smoother or our pace a little swifter. However, sometimes we notice an abrupt change in our ability. Whereas yesterday we were swimming quite competently, today it seems as if some substantial improvement in our stroke has occurred—all our practice seems to have finally paid off. Compared with the earlier more incremental changes, our more recent changes seem more qualitative in nature, and our smoother swimming stroke now bears little resemblance to the choppy, halting strokes we used when we first began to swim. This latter type of change is of particular interest to developmental psychologists who view development as discontinuous. This view likens development to a series of discrete steps or stages in which behaviors get reorganized into a qualitatively new set of behaviors (Figure 1-1b).

Recently, some theorists (e.g., Siegler, 2000) have suggested that both continuity and discontinuity are needed to describe the complex pattern of human psychological development. Moreover, depending on how we study a process—especially how closely we study it—either continuous or more discontinuous changes may be more evident. For instance, if we look over a fairly long period of time, it is clear that there are

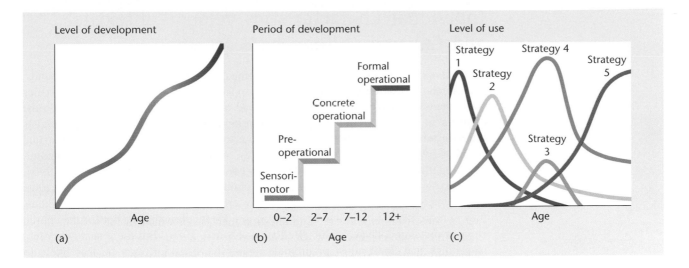

Figure 1-1   Continuity and discontinuity in the child's development

The continuous view (a) sees development as a gradual series of shifts in capacities, skills, and behavior with no abrupt changes. A discontinuous view (b) proposes abrupt, steplike changes that make each stage qualitatively different from the one that precedes it. Most contemporary developmentalists embrace a third view, which holds that development is fundamentally continuous but interspersed with transitions that may appear to be sudden or abrupt. For example, Siegler's "overlapping waves" model (c) suggests that children use a variety of strategies in thinking and learning at any given age. The use of each strategy ebbs and flows with increasing age and expertise, and only gradually do the most successful strategies predominate. As a result, from a long-range perspective, development appears generally continuous, but using a closer examination, we can observe specific qualitative changes.

Source: Part (c) from Siegler, Robert S.; Alibali, Martha W., *Children's Thinking*, 4th Edition, © 2005. Adapted and reprinted by permission of Pearson Education, Inc., Upper Saddle River, NJ.

marked, qualitative differences between the young infant's tentative motor abilities and the toddler's physical capabilities, or between the fourth grader's problem-solving abilities and the adolescent's competence at solving logical problems. Clearly, the quality of the skills a child possesses varies greatly in such comparisons. However, if we look more closely—let's say, as a child practices long division problems over a class exercise on this topic—we find that many developmental changes, such as a shift to a more efficient way of arranging the columns of numbers in the problems— are not abrupt but gradual. Thus, through close examination and analysis, we see a very different picture of development—one in which gradual change occurs as the child slowly learns to adopt the developmentally most advanced approach available at some given point in time (Figure 1-1c).

The theme of continuity and discontinuity as a way of describing the pattern of development is not as prominent as it once was. This is because most contemporary child researchers see development as basically continuous, but sometimes interspersed with periods of transition in which change may seem qualitative. These transitional periods are intriguing to psychologists who believe that the process of development is often revealed most clearly during such times of change. Other more recent research related to this theme aims to understand how behavioral continuities are sustained by an individual's experiences. This research sees the environment as a reciprocal force that either helps maintain behavioral continuity or disrupts this continuity. Although a disruption to behavioral continuity may sound problematic, it may not be so. What is important to consider is the behavior itself. For example, Rutter, Kreppner, and O'Connor (2001) have investigated how children who were reared early in life in deprived institutional settings changed in a positive direction after they were adopted into healthy families. Research on transitional periods and reciprocal continuity greatly expands our understanding of the pattern of development over time by considering the forces both inside and outside the child that contribute to continuity and change.

Individual Characteristics versus Contextual and Cultural Influences

Child development occurs in a variety of settings such as homes, schools, playgrounds, and streets. Do children's individual predispositions and personality characteristics cause them to behave similarly across a broad range of situations? How much do the contexts in which children live affect development? Developmental psychologists differ in terms of the importance they assign to individual factors versus contextual variables. Many resolve the controversy by adopting an interactionist viewpoint, stressing the dual role of individual and contextual factors (Magnusson, 1996a; Magnusson & Stattin, 1998). For example, children with aggressive personality traits may often seek out contexts in which they can display these characteristics; thus, they're more likely to join a gang or enroll in a karate class than to opt for the church choir or a stamp collector's club (Bullock & Merrill, 1980). But these same children, in settings that don't allow or promote aggressive behavior, may be less likely to behave aggressively and perhaps even be friendly and cooperative.

One way in which individual characteristics have been studied is by examining how different children respond when they are confronted with situational challenges to healthy development. As we grow and mature, we encounter a variety of risks that may alter our developmental trajectories for better or for worse. Such risks or challenges may change a child's course of development from a normal to a nonnormal course. Risk comes in many forms. Some risks are genetic or biological: for example, a serious illness, or living with a psychotic parent. Other risks are environmental, such as family income, education, divorce, or the death or remarriage of a parent. Individual children respond to such risks in very different ways. Many seem to suffer permanent developmental disruptions or delays. Others show "sleeper" effects; they seem to cope well initially, but exhibit problems later in development. Still others exhibit resilience under the most difficult of circumstances, and some, when they confront new risks later in life, seem better able to adapt to challenges than children who have experienced little or no risk (Cummings, Davies, & Campbell, 2000; Luthar, Cicchetti, & Becker, 2000). Studies of risk and resilience show clearly that development does not proceed along a single, common pathway.

Examination of the contribution that context makes to child development has led to increased interest in how culture relates to development. We know that children who grow up on a farm in China, in a kibbutz in Israel, in a village in Peru, or in a suburb in the United States have very different kinds of experiences. Developmental psychologists differ in how they incorporate the contribution of culture into their research. Whereas some researchers adopt a universal approach to development and assume that culture-free laws of development apply to all children in all cultures, others argue that the cultural settings in which children grow up play a major role in the pattern and pace of development. For example, in some cultures, children are encouraged to walk very early and are given opportunities to exercise their new motor skills. In other cultures, infants are carried or swaddled for long periods of time, which reduces their chance to walk until they are older. Today most developmentalists agree that examining child development across cultures can provide much insight. Such research provides information about variation in the range of human potential and expression that may emerge in different circumstances of growth (Rogoff, 2003). Moreover, cultures differ not only across national boundaries but within single countries. The United States, Australia, and Russia, for example, all contain a wide range of subcultural groups representing very diverse racial and ethnic traditions (Demo, Allen, & Fine, 2000).

The three themes we've been discussing—biological versus environmental origins, continuous versus discontinuous patterns of growth, and individual versus contextual and cultural influences on development—have inspired several different theories about child development. The main theories in the field do not always explicitly describe the position they take on each of these themes. More often, a theory embodies its position on these themes in a set of basic assumptions about what development is and how it proceeds. In the next section, as we discuss the main theoretical perspectives on child development, we will try to specify the various positions on these themes that are taken in each of the theories.

THEORETICAL PERSPECTIVES ON DEVELOPMENT

Theories about the way children grow and mature play a central part in a scientific approach to child development. To be a developmental theory, it is not sufficient that a theory focus on children or childhood per se. What is critical is that a theory describes psychological change or development over time (Miller, 2002).

Theories serve two main functions that are critical to the science. First, they help organize and integrate existing information into coherent, interesting, and plausible accounts of how children develop. Second, they generate testable hypotheses or predictions about children's behavior. In the field of child psychology, although there are several theories, no one theory currently dominates the field nor is any single theory comprehensive and able to account for all aspects of human development. As you will see, each theory is concerned with certain questions about development, and to answer these questions a theory focuses on particular aspects of development that are relevant to these questions. Different theories also favor particular methods or ways of studying development. At this point it is not useful to identify a theory as correct or incorrect. It is more helpful to evaluate the theories in relation to the questions they have tried to answer and how well they have met their goals.

In the following sections, we use five general perspectives—structural-organismic, learning, dynamic systems, contextual, and ethological and evolutionary views—to describe the main theories that influence the field of child development today. Although our grouping of these main theoretical approaches fits with the themes and ideas we emphasize in this book, we recognize that there are other ways to group them. We also aim to give you a sense of the breadth and diversity of different theoretical approaches to child development. Following our discussion of theory, we then turn to the methods psychologists use to study questions about child development that arise from these theories. We begin this section by discussing two theories that are among the earliest theoretical attempts to focus specifically on psychological development: Freud's psychodynamic theory and Piaget's theory of cognitive development.

Structural-Organismic Perspectives

Both Freud and Piaget developed their theories in the early twentieth century when scholars in a number of disciplines wanted to understand the workings of complex systems such as societies, kin systems, and the range of human languages. To tackle this issue, many of these scholars tried to describe the formal structure, or organization, of the system in which they were interested in the hope that this description could provide insight into how the system worked. This approach, called *structuralism,* was adopted by Freud and Piaget, both of whom were interested in psychological development. Although the theories that Freud and Piaget introduced focused on very different aspects of development—Freud was interested in emotional and personality growth, whereas Piaget was interested in intellectual development—both devised theories that incorporated their mutual interest in biology, especially evolutionary theory, which was

structural-organismic perspectives Theoretical approaches that describe psychological structures and processes that undergo qualitative or stagelike changes over the course of development.

psychodynamic theory In this view of development, which is derived from Freudian theory, development occurs in discrete stages and is determined largely by biologically based drives shaped by encounters with the environment and through the interaction of the personality's three components—the id, ego, and superego.

id In Freudian theory, the person's instinctual drives; the first component of the personality to evolve, the id operates on the basis of the *pleasure principle.*

ego In Freudian theory, the rational, controlling component of the personality, which tries to satisfy needs through appropriate, socially acceptable behaviors.

superego In Freudian theory, the personality component that is the repository of the child's internalization of parental or societal values, morals, and roles.

a prominent area of intellectual interest at the time. Thus, both Freud and Piaget used a **structural-organismic perspective** in their theories, in which psychological structures and processes within the child were seen as critical to development. More specifically, both held the perspective that the organism goes through an organized or structured set of stages or discontinuous changes over the course of psychological growth and that these stages are universal in that they are experienced by all members of the species. As you will see, despite these common features, these theories are markedly different from each other. In part this difference is due to the aspects of development each theory attempts to describe. They also differ in the influence they had on the formation of the field and how they influence contemporary theory and research in child development. First we discuss psychodynamic theory, which was introduced by Freud and came a bit earlier, and then we discuss Piaget's theory.

PSYCHODYNAMIC THEORY   In the early 1900s, Sigmund Freud, who was trained as a physician, began a revolution in thinking about human development by emphasizing how the experiences of early childhood shape the development of adult personality. This perspective, which is called **psychodynamic theory,** has had an enormous influence on psychological and psychiatric thinking for close to a century. However, many of Freud's specific concepts remain open to debate and controversy.

Freud's theory is very complex and covers many aspects of psychological functioning. Here we concentrate on the parts of this theory that have influenced developmental psychology. For Freud, the developing personality consists of three interrelated parts: the id, the ego, and the superego. The roles that each of these three components of personality play change across development as the infant, who is largely under the control of the **id,** or instinctual drives, gradually becomes more rational and reality bound. The id operates on the *pleasure principle,* which is oriented toward maximizing pleasure and satisfying needs immediately. As the infant develops, the **ego,** or the rational, controlling part of personality, emerges and attempts to gratify needs through appropriate, socially constructive behavior. The third component of personality, the **superego,** emerges when the child *internalizes*—that is, accepts and absorbs—parental or societal morals, values, and roles and develops a *conscience,* or the ability to apply moral values to her own acts.

To Freud, personality development—that is, changes in the organization and interaction of the id, ego, and superego—involves five discrete stages (see Table 1-1). In the first, *oral* stage, which extends through the first year of life, the infant is preoccupied with activities such as eating, sucking, and biting, and with objects, such as food, that can be put in the mouth. In the second to third year, the child enters the *anal* stage and learns to postpone personal gratification, such as the pleasure of expelling feces, as he is trained to use the toilet. Following the anal stage, the *phallic* stage begins, and children's sexual curiosity is aroused. Their preoccupation with their own sexual anatomy also alerts them to the differences in sexual anatomy between the genders. Freud saw this stage as critical to the formation of gender identity. According to Freud, sexual drives are temporarily submerged during the *latency* period, from about 6 years of age to puberty. During this period children avoid relationships with peers of the other gender and become intensely involved with peers of the same gender. In Freud's last stage, the *genital* period, sexual desires reemerge and are directed toward peers, a topic we return to in Chapter 12.

One of Freud's primary contributions to developmental psychology is his emphasis on how early experiences, especially in the first six years of life, influence later development. For him, the way in which the child negotiates each of the stages we've described—especially the oral, anal, and phallic stages—has a profound impact on her adult personality. For example, infants who have unsatisfied needs for oral stimulation may be more likely to smoke as adults. Or toddlers whose parents toilet trained them extremely early and in a very rigid manner may later be obsessively concerned

Table 1-1   Freud's and Erikson's developmental stages

Age Period	Stage of Development	
	Freudian	Eriksonian
0–1	**Oral.** Focus on eating and taking things into the mouth	**Infancy.** Task: To develop *basic trust* In oneself and others. Risk: *mistrust* of others and lack of self-confidence
1–3	**Anal.** Emphasis on toilet training; first experience with discipline and authority	**Early Childhood.** Task: To learn self-control and establish *autonomy*. Risk: *shame* and *doubt* about one's own capabilities
3–6	**Phallic.** Increase in sexual urges arouses curiosity and alerts children to gender differences; period is critical to formation of gender identity	**Play Age.** Task: To develop *initiative* in mastering environment. Risk: Feelings of *guilt* over aggressiveness and daring
6–12	**Latency.** Sexual urges repressed; emphasis on education and the beginnings of concern for others	**School Age.** Task: To develop *industry*. Risk: Feelings of *inferiority* over real or imagined failure to master tasks
12–20		**Adolescence.** Task: To achieve a sense of *identity*. Risk: *Role confusion* over who and what individual wants to be
20–30	**Genital.** Altruistic love joins selfish love; need for reproduction of species underlies adoption of adult responsibilities	**Young Adulthood.** Task: To achieve *intimacy* with others. Risk: Shaky identity may lead to avoidance of others and *isolation*
30–65		**Adulthood.** Task: To express oneself through *generativity*. Risk: Inability to create children, ideas, or products may lead to *stagnation*
65+		**Mature Age.** Task: To achieve a sense of *integrity*. Risk: Doubts and unfulfilled desires may lead to *despair*

with neatness and cleanliness. Although current developmental theory does not adopt Freud's exact views about what the important features of early experience are the idea that Freud introduced, namely, that events in infancy and childhood have a formative impact on later development, remains a central issue in the study of child development. Another contribution that Freud's thinking makes to contemporary developmental psychology is the preeminent role that emotional attachment early in life, especially to the mother, has in socioemotional development, as you will read in Chapter 6. Additionally, psychodynamic theories have been influential in certain areas of applied and clinical psychology, as we note in Chapter 15.

Freud also had followers who went on to devise their own theories of development, often containing concepts that stem from some of Freud's basic ideas. The most prominent of these theories was devised by Erik Erikson in his **psychosocial theory** of human development. In Erikson's theory, development is seen as proceeding through a series of organized stages. Erikson proposed eight specific developmental stages that unfold across the life span, and each stage is characterized by the personal and social tasks that the individual must accomplish as well as the risks the individual confronts if she fails to proceed through the stages successfully (see Table 1-1). Of these ideas, the most influential for current research in child development is Erikson's description of the stage of adolescence, in which the child focuses mainly on the search for a stable definition of the self—that is, for a self-identity. The danger

Erik Erikson (1902–1990) studied psychology in Vienna with Freud. His psychosocial theory continues to be influential today, especially for those who hold a life-span perspective on development.

psychosocial theory
Erikson's theory of development that sees children developing through a series of stages largely through accomplishing tasks that involve them in interaction with their social environment.

life-span perspective A view of development as a process that continues throughout the life cycle, from infancy through adulthood and old age.

Piagetian theory A theory of cognitive development that sees the child as actively seeking new information and uses two basic principles of biology and biological change: organization and adaptation.

A child psychologist at the Universities of Geneva and Lausanne, Switzerland, Jean Piaget (1896–1980) framed a theory of the child's cognitive development that has had great impact on developmentalists, educators, and others concerned with the course and determinants of children's development.

of not meeting this challenge successfully is role confusion, in which the individual cannot get a grip on who or what she wants to be. Problems in attaining identity in adolescence may lead to the avoidance of relations with others in adulthood.

Erikson's theory has also been influential in the study of development beyond childhood and adolescence. Erikson introduced concepts that pertain to adult development and fulfillment, including generativity and ego integrity. Some investigators in the field of developmental psychology have incorporated these ideas into a **life-span perspective,** which sees development as a process that continues throughout the life cycle, from infancy through adulthood to old age (Fagan & Hawkins, 2001; Snarey, 1993).

PIAGETIAN THEORY   The Swiss psychologist Jean Piaget introduced a structural-organismic theory to describe child development in a very different area of growth, intellectual development. Like Freud, Piaget was trained in the area of biology, and this training had enormous influence on his thinking about child development. The **Piagetian theory** of intellectual development uses two basic principles of biology and biological change: organization and adaptation. The principle of *organization* is seen in Piaget's tenet that the development of human intelligence is a biologically based process and, like the development of other aspects of the biological system, an organized process. Thus, the child's understanding of the world changes in an organized way over the course of development. Piaget used the principle of *adaptation* to describe the process by which intellectual change occurs. As a child grows, he interacts with the world, and these interactions promote an increasingly more complex way of understanding that is adapted to the world in which the child lives and functions. According to Piaget, two complementary cognitive processes play a major role in this adaptational process. Children use their current knowledge of how the world works as a framework for the absorption or *assimilation* of new experiences. And through the process of *accommodation,* children modify their existing knowledge in response to the new input from their environment. In Chapter 8 we discuss both processes in greater detail.

Piaget proposed that all children go through four stages of cognitive development, each characterized by qualitatively different ways of thinking, organizing knowledge, and solving problems. Whereas infants rely on their sensory and motor abilities to learn about the world, preschool children rely more on mental structures and symbols, especially language. In the school years, children begin to rely more on logic, and in adolescence children can reason about abstract ideas. For Piaget, young children are *egocentric* in their thinking—that is, they are more centered on their own perspectives than older children and less able to take the viewpoints or understand the feelings and perceptions of others. According to Piaget, cognitive development is a process in which the child shifts from a focus on the self, immediate sensory experiences, and simple problems to a more complex, multifaceted, and abstract understanding of the world.

The structural-organismic approach to child development that these two theories represent offers a type of wide-ranging description of development in which the structure of the developing system is the focus of the theory. We now turn to theoretical perspectives that emphasize learning; these approaches highlight process more than structure. Learning views, as we will see, consider change over the course of development to be more gradual and continuous than we found it to be in structural-organismic theories.

Learning Perspectives

The study of learning is one of the oldest subdisciplines of human psychology. In this section, we explore some of the learning theories that have been applied to developmental issues. We begin with the work of the behaviorists, consider the approaches of the cognitive social learning theorists next, and then explore the information-processing perspective on cognitive development.

BEHAVIORISM The behaviorist approach to development is exemplified in the work of John B. Watson, Ivan Pavlov, and B. F. Skinner. **Behaviorism** focuses, quite simply, on the learning of behaviors. This perspective holds that theories of psychology must be based on observations of actual behavior rather than on speculation about motives or other unobservable factors. This approach, when applied to psychological development, emphasizes the role of experience, and it is a gradual, continuous view. The same principles of learning shape development throughout childhood and, indeed, across the entire life span.

In the history of child psychology, the behaviorist view was influential. Watson used Pavlov's notion of **classical conditioning**—a type of learning in which two stimuli are repeatedly presented together until individuals learn to respond to the unfamiliar stimulus in the same way they respond to the familiar stimulus—to explain many aspects of children's behavior, especially emotions such as fear. For example, he conditioned an 11 month-old infant to fear furry animals by showing the baby, who was easily frightened by noises, a white rat and simultaneously making a loud noise. B. F. Skinner's notion of **operant conditioning,** a type of learning in which learning depends on the consequences of behavior, was also applied to children's behavior. Positive reinforcement of a particular behavior in the form of a friendly smile, specific praise, or a special treat was shown to increase the likelihood that a child would exhibit that behavior again. On the other hand, punishment in the form of a frown, criticism, or the withdrawal of privileges such as watching television can decrease the chance that a child will repeat that same behavior. Later researchers have shown the value of some of these ideas for understanding both how children's behaviors develop and how we can change such behaviors. For instance, Patterson and his colleagues (G. R. Patterson, 1982; G. R. Patterson & Capaldi, 1991) have shown how children's aggressive behavior is often increased rather than decreased by the attention that parents pay to such acts as hitting and teasing. Patterson has also shown that punishment of these kinds of acts by "time-out"—a brief period of isolation away from other family members—can help diminish aggressive behavior. Operant conditioning has been incorporated into many applied programs to help teachers and parents change children's behavior, including hyperactivity (restlessness, inattention, impulsivity) and aggression.

COGNITIVE SOCIAL LEARNING THEORY According to **cognitive social learning theory,** children learn not only through classical and operant conditioning but also by observing and imitating others (Bandura, 1989, 1997). In his classic studies, Bandura showed that children exposed to the aggressive behavior of another person were likely to imitate that behavior. For example, after a group of nursery school children watched an adult punch a large Bobo doll (an inflated rubber doll that pops back up after being pushed), the children were more likely to attack and play aggressively with the doll than were a group of children who had not seen the model. Neither the adult model nor the children had received any reinforcement, yet the children learned specific behaviors.

Further research on how the process of imitation aids learning has revealed the important contribution of cognition to observational learning. Children do not imitate the behaviors of others blindly or automatically; rather they select specific behaviors to imitate, and their imitation relies on how they process this information. Bandura has described four cognitive processes that govern how well a child will learn a new behavior by observing another person (Figure 1-2). First, the child must *attend* to a model's behavior. Second, the child must *retain* the observed behaviors in memory. Third, the child must have the capacity, physically and intellectually, to *reproduce* the observed behavior. Fourth, the child must be *motivated,* have a reason to reproduce the behavior.

behaviorism A learning perspective that holds that theories of psychology must be based on observations of behavior rather than on speculations about motives or unobservable factors.

classical conditioning A type of learning in which two stimuli are repeatedly presented together until individuals learn to respond to the unfamiliar stimulus in the same way they respond to the familiar stimulus.

operant conditioning A type of learning in which learning depends on the consequences of behavior; rewards increase the likelihood that a behavior will recur, whereas punishment decreases that likelihood.

cognitive social learning theory A learning theory that stresses the importance of observation and imitation in the acquisition of new behaviors, with learning mediated by cognitive processes.

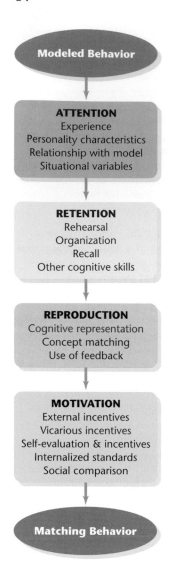

Figure 1-2

Bandura's model of observational learning

To produce a behavior that matches that of a model, a child goes through four sets of processes. Her ability to attend to the modeled behavior is influenced by factors in her own experience and in the situation; her skill in retaining what she has observed reflects a collection of cognitive skills; her reproduction of the behavior depends on other cognitive skills, including the use of feedback from others; and her motivation to produce the behavior is influenced by various incentives, her own standards, and her tendency to compare herself with others.

Source: Based on Bandura, 1989.

INFORMATION-PROCESSING APPROACHES   **Information-processing approaches** to development focus on the flow of information through the cognitive system, beginning with an input or stimulus and ending with an output or response, much like the way computers process information (Klahr & MacWhinney, 1998). In human information processing, output may be in the form of an action, a decision, an insight, a verbalization, or simply a memory that is stored for later use. Information-processing theorists are especially interested in the cognitive processes that a child uses to operate on knowledge and the gradual changes over the course of development in children's ability to use these processes. What cognitive processes does the child use? He attends to information, changes it into a mental or cognitive representation, stores it in memory, compares it with other memories, generates various responses, makes a decision about the most appropriate response, and, finally, takes some specific action. In some ways, these operations are analogous to the way computers deal with information; information in the form of symbols is entered into the system and this input undergoes a series of transformations—it is registered, organized, and stored, and finally it provides an answer, or output.

According to the information-processing perspective, the child, in order to understand or achieve meaning about some external event, engages in a series of cognitive processes or operations that change, transform, and manipulate information over time. This approach has been applied to a wide range of problems of cognitive development, including attention, memory, problem solving, and planning. In Chapter 9 we give particular attention to this approach. Information-processing theory is also proving valuable in studying how children develop an understanding of reading, mathematics, and science (Siegler, 2000; Siegler & Alibali, 2005). This approach has also provided a powerful analytic tool for understanding social behaviors, such as social problem solving and aggression (Kupersmidt & Dodge, 2004; Lemerise & Arsenio, 2000).

The classical, operant, and cognitive social learning approaches have been especially influential in the areas of social and emotional development. The information-processing approach has advanced understanding of cognitive development in individual problem-solving situations and in social transactions.

Dynamic Systems Perspectives

Another approach to child development concentrates on changes over time and considers these changes the result of the coordination of elements of a complex, integrated system. Dynamic systems theories are a diverse group that cover a wide range of topics in child development. In some theories, the focus is on the child herself and how the child, as a biological and psychological system, functions and grows in a physical world that both supports and challenges her development. For example, in learning to walk, infants must coordinate many physical abilities, including muscle strength, balance, and momentum, with the features of the physical world such as gravity and the properties of the walking surface. Only when the entire system of forces is coordinated and mastered does the child become successful at walking. In other system theories, the focus is on the child within the nexus of a social system, such as the family or school. For instance, many therapists who adopt a family systems approach contend that they cannot help a child unless the entire family is involved in the therapeutic process. Despite variation in the specifics of different system theories, all attempt to describe how child development arises from the system as a whole, not from any single factor. For example, a child who has muscle strength but lacks balance will not walk, or a child who needs to learn to cooperate more with others at home cannot succeed without the support of other members of his family.

For most system theories, what makes the system more than just a collection of parts is its dynamism; because its parts are in constant transaction, the processes in which they engage and the relationships they form and maintain become the primary focus of the system. In **dynamic systems theory,** individuals and their achievements can be understood and interpreted only within the framework of the interacting components of the dynamic system (Lewis, 2000). The term *dynamic* underscores the constant interaction and mutual influence of the elements of the system. (Table 1-2 summarizes some of the principles of the theory.)

Thus, the emphasis of dynamic systems theory is on process and transactions among elements of the system. The actions of a system and its members are constantly changing in response to ongoing interactions within the system. Systems theory has been applied to a variety of developmental issues, including motor development, perception, language, cognition, and social behavior (Sameroff, 1989; Smith & Thelen, 1993). We will encounter many different applications of systems theory throughout the book.

Contextual Perspectives

For a long time, developmentalists and other psychologists have realized that children as well as adults function not only in many different settings—such as the home, school, and workplace—but in broader contexts, such as communities and societies. In response to this view, some theorists have taken particular account of the effects

information-processing approaches Theories of development that focus on the flow of information through the child's cognitive system and particularly on the specific operations the child performs between input and output phases.

dynamic systems theory A theory that proposes that individuals develop and function within systems and that studies the relationships among individuals and systems and the properties by which these relationships operate.

Complexity
Each part of a system is unique but at the same time related to one or more of the system's other parts. For example, a family comprises individual members (mother, brother, niece), subsystems (a married couple; their daughter and her husband and children), and extended members (cousins, other more distant relatives, and sometimes even longtime family friends).

Wholeness and Organization
The whole system is organized and contains more than just the sum of its parts. For example, to understand a family system's functioning we must study not only the characteristics of individual family members and the relationships between them, but also the organization of all family relationships and the whole family as an interacting unit.

Identity and Stabilization
No matter how a system may change, the identity of the system remains intact. For example, the family unit continues even when new members join it and old members die. The system's tendency toward stability is maintained over time by the ongoing interactions among individual members and their relationships with one another. The continuing care parents give their children and the relations among group members help to maintain the family as a system.

Morphogenesis
This principle refers to changes in the system. A system must be able to grow and adapt to internal and external changes. Children go to school, leave home, and marry. Parents raise children, change jobs, and retire. Catastrophic change, such as divorce, may force a family system to reorganize itself, perhaps by adapting to a stepparent or to single parenthood. The family must also adapt to changes in social values and institutions such as economic cycles and social ills such as crime and discrimination.

Equifinality
This principle holds that most individuals reach essentially the same developmental milestones—even though, in the process, each one experiences varying combinations of genetic and environmental influences.

Table 1-2

Some principles of dynamic systems theory

Source: Based on Fogel, 1993; Holt, Fogel, & Wood, 1998; Lewis, 2000; Novak, 1996; Sameroff, 1989, 1994; Thelen, 1995.

of contextual factors, especially social and cultural surroundings, on the developing individual. Contextualists would be interested in a question such as, would an introverted or shy child born into a culture or a family that encourages social interaction be more talkative than an introverted child born into a culture or family that does not encourage social interaction? We consider three theoretical perspectives that illustrate contextual approaches to development: Vygotsky's sociocultural theory, Bronfenbrenner's ecological theory, and the life-span perspective, which emphasizes historical context.

VYGOTSKY'S SOCIOCULTURAL THEORY   The developmental approach referred to as sociocultural theory traces much of its roots to the writings of Lev S. Vygotsky, a Russian psychologist who worked in the early part of the twentieth century. A sociocultural approach to child development places particular emphasis on the impact of children's social and cultural worlds on their development. Despite his early death at the age of 37, Vygotsky has had a major impact on our thinking about development, in particular intellectual development, which was his primary area of research. Vygotksy's interest in the relation of social and cultural experience to psychological development makes sense when one considers that he grew up and worked in Russia during the 1917 Communist revolution, a period of tumultuous social change (Kozulin, 1990).

sociocultural theory A theory of development, proposed by Lev Vygotsky, that sees development as emerging from children's interactions with more skilled people and the institutions and tools provided by their culture.

The **sociocultural theory** of cognitive development, based on Vygotsky's views, proposes that the child's development is best understood as a product of social and cultural experience. Social interaction, in particular, is seen as a critical force in the development as the child and her more sophisticated partners—parents, teachers, and others—solve problems together and help the child as she learns. It is through the assistance provided by others in her social environment that the child gradually learns to function intellectually on her own, as an individual. According to Vygotsky, every child has a set of innate abilities, such as perceptual and memory skills. Input from the child's society, in the form of interactions with adults and peers who are more skilled than the child, molds these basic abilities into more complex, higher-order cognitive functions. Thus, the social world mediates individual cognitive development.

By emphasizing the socially mediated nature of cognitive processes, Vygotsky's approach offers new ways of assessing children's cognitive potential and of teaching

In the world's many cultures, children often begin at an early age to develop specialized skills. In Somalia, a son learns the care and management of camels from his father. In Kotzebue, Alaska, an Inupiat mother guides her daughter in mending fishnets.

Box 1.1

Perspectives on Diversity

HOW CULTURE CAN AFFECT CHILDREN'S COGNITIVE DEVELOPMENT

Sociocultural theories, such as that introduced by Vygotsky, place particular emphasis on the significance of culture in children's development. In his theory, Vygotsky put forward three important principles of cultural influence. First, cultures vary in the settings and practices they provide to facilitate children's cognitive development. Consider an example from Uzbekistan. Traditional Uzbekis, for the most part illiterate, responded to reasoning problems using concrete examples based on their experience. Alexander Luria (1971), an early collaborator of Vygotsky, showed that Uzbekis who learned to read and write, which are practices that are valued and promoted by many cultures, began to approach problems in different ways. For example, compared with traditional Uzbekis, they engaged in more abstract reasoning when they worked on problems such as logical syllogisms (Scribner, 1985).

Other researchers have come up with similar findings in other cultures of the world. For example, Saxe (1982) found that the Oksapmim people of Papua, New Guinea, relied on a rudimentary number system based on their own body parts to help them deal with the demands of daily life. However, as a result of formal education and changes in occupational and trading activities, the counting system is changing and becoming more similar to the procedures used in Western industrialized societies.

Vygotsky's second principle was that we must consider cultural contexts in assessing children's cognitive development. Cognitive tasks should be embedded in their appropriate cultural context; we may seriously underestimate children's development if we ignore the culturally specific nature of children's learning (Gauvain, 2001; Greenfield & Suzuki, 1998; Rogoff, 2003). A third principle is that children learn much about

their culture and the ways of thinking that are valued in their culture from more experienced cultural members, and the ways in which this information is conveyed may vary across cultures. Consider an example in which a student researcher was frustrated in attempting to learn a skill specific to a particular ethnic group by culturally determined teaching methods: The researcher undertook to study loom weaving with an experienced weaver of the Zinacanteco culture in Mexico. For two months the student observed while the weaver created her fabric; the weaver would often call the student's attention to a fine point of her technique, but she never allowed the student to lay a hand on the loom. Instead, she would say from time to time that inasmuch as the student had seen her do the weaving, she had learned it herself. Although the student kept silent, she did not agree; indeed, she wanted to shout, "Let me try it myself!" Understandably, perhaps, she was more than chagrined when, at last given the loom, her inevitable mistakes elicited the weaver's criticism that she hadn't watched and therefore hadn't learned (Greenfield & Childs, 1991). In the Zinacanteco culture, motoric quietude and a habit of responding rather than initiating have been valued qualities. A Zinacanteco student of weaving would have sat more quietly and attended more closely to the actions of the weaving master than did the U.S. student.

Theories that focus on cultural contributions to cognitive development are concerned with the ways in which both the processes and the content of human intelligence reflect the cultural context in which a person lives. By observing cognitive development in cultural context, developmental psychologists have a window into this important and fascinating aspect of human intellectual growth.

reading, mathematics, and writing (Brown & Campione, 1997; Gauvain, 2001; Rogoff, 2003). A vivid example of Vygotskian theory in action in the modern classroom is peer tutoring, in which an older child helps a younger pupil learn to read, write, add, subtract, and so on. Vygotsky has also increased our appreciation of the profound importance of cultural variation in development, as Box 1.1 illustrates. According to Vygotsky, the particular ways in which adults support and direct child development are influenced by culture, especially the values and practices that organize what and how adults and children think and work together on cognitive problems. Vygotsky was also interested in what he considered to be the psychological tools children use to understand their world. These tools, which are devised by cultures, take a variety of forms and include language, counting, mnemonic devices, algebraic symbols, art, literacy, and computers. As children develop, different tools help children to function more effectively in solving problems and understanding their cognitive world. Thus, tools of thinking, which are products of culture, become incorporated into the ways in which individuals think about and solve problems. We discuss this theory at greater length in Chapter 8.

ecological theory A theory of development that stresses the importance of understanding not only the relationships between organisms and various environmental systems, but the relations among such systems themselves.

BRONFENBRENNER'S ECOLOGICAL THEORY   Ecological theory
stresses the importance of understanding not only the relationships between the organism—such as the child—and various environmental systems—such as the family and the community—but the relationships among environmental systems themselves as well. The theory views children as active participants in creating their own environments and considers children's subjective experiences of their relationships and their surroundings just as important as the objective aspects of these phenomena.

Urie Bronfenbrenner (1979; Bronfenbrenner & Morris, 2006), a major advocate of ecological theory, provides a framework that describes the layers of environmental systems that impact child development. In his view, the child's world is organized "as a set of nested structures, each inside the next, like a set of Russian dolls" (1979, p. 22). As Figure 1-3 illustrates, these nested contextual influences range from the most immediate settings, such as the family or peer group, to more remote contexts

Figure 1-3

Bronfenbrenner's ecological model of development

Bronfenbrenner emphasizes the importance of the developing child's interactions with the people and institutions closest to her within the *microsystem* and *mesosystem,* as well as the effects on her life of a widening array of social and cultural institutions, attitudes, and beliefs within the *exosystem* and the *macrosystem.* The fact that all of these systems change over time is represented by the *chronosystem.*

Source: From *Child Development in a Social Context* (C. Kopp and J. Krakow, Eds.). Garbarino, J., "Sociocultural risk: Dangers to competence," p. 648. Copyright © 1982 Addison Wesley Publishing Company, Inc. Reprinted by permission of Pearson Education, Inc., Glenview, IL.

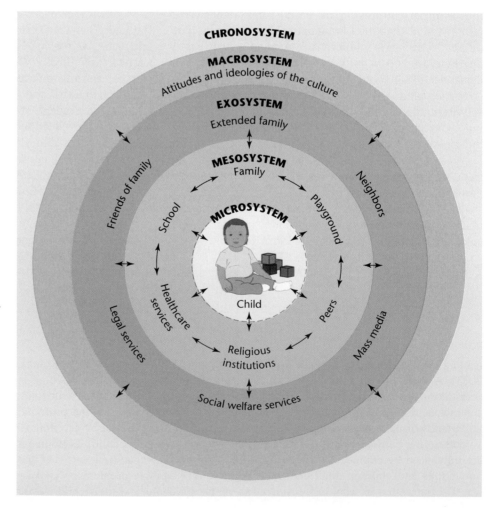

of the child's life, such as the society's systems of value and of the law. The **microsystem** is the setting in which the child lives and interacts with the people and institutions closest to her. Over time, the relative importance of these different interactions may change. For example, family may be most important in infancy, whereas peers and school become more important in middle childhood and adolescence. The **mesosystem** comprises the interrelations among the components of the microsystem. Thus, parents interact with teachers and the school system; both family members and peers may maintain relations with a religious institution; and so forth. The **exosystem** is composed of settings that impinge on a child's development but with which the child has largely indirect contact. For example, a parent's work may affect the child's life if it requires that the parent travel a great deal or work late into the night. The **macrosystem** represents the ideological and institutional patterns of a particular culture or subculture. Broad patterns of beliefs and ideology distinguish different cultures and countries, as well as different subcultures within a single country. Children who grow up in China experience a different social ideology than children who grow up in the United States.

Finally, these four systems—the micro-, meso-, exo-, and macrosystems—change over time. Bronfenbrenner's term for this time-based dimension is the **chronosystem.** Over time, both the child and his environment undergo change, and change can originate within the individual (e.g., puberty, severe illness, an accident) or in the external world (e.g., the birth of a sibling, entering school for the first time, parental divorce). Bronfenbrenner suggests that studying change over time is crucial to an understanding of the ecological context as a whole and its relation to child development. For Bronfenbrenner, development involves the interaction of a changing child with the changing ecological context in all of its complexity.

HISTORICAL CONTEXT AND PSYCHOLOGICAL DEVELOPMENT

The life-span perspective (recall our earlier discussion of Erik Erikson's views) incorporates the notion that historical factors may influence individuals' psychological development. This phenomenon is generally referred to as a *cohort effect*; the term *cohort* means a group of individuals who were born in the same year or during the same general historical period of time (e.g., the years of the Clinton administration). As such cohorts develop, they share the same historical experiences. Children who were born in 1980 were in late childhood when communism fell into disfavor in Europe and the Cold War ended (1985–1990). Children born in the United States in the 1950s were teenagers during the turbulent 1960s, and their adolescence was marked by considerable social upheaval.

A striking example of cohort effects is provided in Box 1.2, which describes the experiences of children and adults who lived through the Great Depression of the 1930s. As you can see, historical context is an important influence on the developing child, making development different for different cohorts of children. As this example illustrates, a life-span perspective has been particularly useful for understanding connections between child development and development into adulthood and the later years of life.

Ethological and Evolutionary Approaches

The final type of approach to studying development has come from the fields of ethology and evolutionary psychology. Since Charles Darwin introduced evolutionary theory, other scientists have sought to understand both the evolution of behavior and its adaptive, or survival, value to the species exhibiting it (Bjorklund & Pelligrini, 2002; Hinde, 1994). Central to this line of thought is the necessity to view and understand behavior in relation to the biology of the organism and the ecosystem in which the organism functions. For example, in studying social interactions among monkeys, one

---

microsystem In Bronfenbrenner's ecological theory, the context in which children live and interact with the people and institutions closest to them, such as parents, peers, and school.

mesosystem The interrelations among the components of the *microsystem.*

exosystem The collection of settings, such as a parent's daily work, that impinge on a child's development but in which the child does not play a direct role.

macrosystem The system that surrounds the *microsystem, mesosystem,* and *exosystem;* represents the values, ideologies, and laws of the society or culture.

chronosystem The time-based dimension that can alter the operation of all other systems in Bronfenbrenner's model, from *microsystem* through *macrosystem.*

Box 1.2
Risk and Resilience

CHILDREN OF THE GREAT DEPRESSION

What happens to children when economic disaster strikes? To find out, Elder & Shanahan (2006) studied children who, at the time of the Great Depression, were part of an ongoing longitudinal study in California of social and intellectual development. Some of the children were just entering school when the U.S. economy collapsed; others were teenagers. The fact that not all families suffered or lost their jobs enabled Elder to compare families who were severely deprived with those who remained relatively well off.

In the economically deprived families, dramatic changes in family roles and relationships affected children's development. The division of labor and power within the family shifted. As fathers' jobs disappeared and income dropped, mothers entered the labor market or took in boarders. As a result, the mother's power increased and the power, prestige, and emotional significance of the father decreased. The rates of divorce, separation, and desertion rose, especially among couples whose relationship was shaky even before the onset of bad economic times (Elder & Shanahan, 2006).

Roles changed for children, too. Girls were drafted into more household work, and the older boys took more outside jobs. Parent-child relationships changed in response to economic hardship; fathers especially became more punitive, less concerned about, and less supportive of their children. Boys tended to move away from the family, becoming more peer-oriented. They also frequently became ill-tempered and angry. Both boys and girls were moodier, more easily slighted, and less calm (Elder & Shanahan, 2006). Because younger children were more dependent on their parents and thus exposed to the altered situation at home for a longer period of time, the effects of the Depression were greater for children who were young when catastrophe struck.

Many of the effects on children were long lasting. When these children became adults, their values, work patterns, and marriages bore the marks of these earlier experiences. Men who were forced to enter the job market as teenagers because of economic hardship preferred secure but modest jobs over riskier but

These children, shown on their Missouri farm in 1940, were among the many whose families, whether on farms or in urban tenements and ghettos, were victims of the Great Depression. Although the stock market crash of 1929 triggered an economic collapse that hit its peak by 1933, the U.S. economy did not fully recover until the country began heightened defense spending in 1941, just before entering the Second World War.

higher-status positions. However, they were also less satisfied with their work and income.

In addition to vocational problems, men and women who had experienced adjustment problems in response to the Depression in the 1930s had marriages that were less successful. The marriages of men and women who had been ill-tempered children were less stable, and women with childhood difficulties often married men who were lacking in ambition and achievement (Caspi, Elder, & Bem, 1987; Elder & Shanahan, 2006). Finally, girls who were prone to temper outbursts as children became ill-tempered parents. Thus we see a three-generational impact of the Depression. Clearly, economic hardship left its imprint on the lives of many of these families. On the other hand, some families managed well in spite of economic hardship, particularly if family ties were strong before the onset of the Depression.

must consider species capabilities and needs as well as habitat, such as the kind of vegetation available to a band of monkeys for food and protection. Similarly, in attempting to understand human children's cognitive skills and behavior, it is important to understand clearly the child's biological nature and needs and the nature of the setting in which behavior takes place, such as a classroom, playground, or library.

ETHOLOGICAL THEORY   **Ethological theory** contends that behavior must be viewed and understood as occurring in a particular context and as having adaptive or survival value. The research this view has generated has captured the attention of child developmentalists, who observe many behaviors in human infants and children that are "species-specific" (unique to the human species) and that they believe may play an important role in ensuring that others meet children's basic needs. This hypothesis is supported by the finding that some behaviors are common to all human children regardless of the culture they are born into and in which they grow to maturity. Studies have found, for example, that emotional expressions of joy, sadness, disgust, and anger are similar across a wide range of modern cultures, including those of Brazil, Japan, and the United States, as well as of nonindustrialized cultures such as the Fore and Dori tribes of New Guinea (Ekman et al., 1987; La Freniere, 2000). One of the areas of developmental psychology that has been greatly influenced by ethology is the study of early relationships. In particular, John Bowlby's research on infant-mother attachment, discussed in Chapter 6, stems directly from the perspective offered by ethological theory.

Ethologists' basic method of study is the observation of children in their natural surroundings, and their goals are to develop detailed descriptions and classifications of behavior. Ethology has been very influential in increasing the popularity of observational approaches in modern developmental psychology. For developmental psychologists, ethological theory is useful for understanding that many behaviors seen across a range of cultures, such as smiling and crying, may have a biological basis and play an important role in ensuring that caregivers meet children's needs. For example, crying can be viewed as an "elicitor" of parental behavior; it serves to communicate that a child is distressed or hungry. It thus has clear survival value, for it ensures that parents give the young infant the kind of attention she needs for adequate development.

Although human ethologists view many elicitors, such as crying, as biologically based, they also assume that these types of behaviors are modified by environmentally based experiences. For example, children may learn to mask their emotions by smiling even when they are unhappy (La Freniere, 2000; McDowell, O'Neil, & Parke, 2000; Saarni, Campos, & Camras, 2006). Thus modern ethologists view children as open to learning and input from the environment; children are not solely captives of their biological roots. As we will see in Chapter 12, ethologists have also made important contributions to our understanding of how children's groups are organized. It turns out that monkeys and chickens are not the only ones to develop dominance hierarchies: Children, according to Hawley and Little (1999), develop specific organizational structures and "pecking orders" as well!

EVOLUTIONARY DEVELOPMENTAL PSYCHOLOGY   **Evolutionary psychology** has influenced the study of child development in a somewhat different way from that of ethology. Although ethologists and evolutionary psychologists share many of the same basic assumptions about the origins and social organization of behavior, evolutionary psychologists have had a major impact on the study of cognition and cognitive development. This perspective holds that the critical components of human evolutionary change are in the areas of brain changes and cognitive functioning (Cosmides & Tooby, 1987). This approach is influential in child development in that it directs attention to the types of capabilities and constraints of the cognitive system that enable

ethological theory A theory that holds that behavior must be viewed and understood as occurring in a particular context and as having adaptive or survival value.

evolutionary psychology An approach that holds that critical components of psychological functioning reflect evolutionary changes and are critical to the survival of the species.

humans to understand and act on the world in the ways that support their survival. In developmental terms, the main questions stemming from this view hover around when and how these cognitive capabilities emerge (Bjorklund & Pelligrini, 2002).

Although the focus in evolutionary perspectives is largely on cognitive processes and their development, these processes are seen as instrumental to human functioning more broadly (Bugental & Grusec, 2006). After all, one hallmark of evolution is the fact that human beings, who are capable of complex and creative reasoning, use this capability in all types of situations—from solving mathematical problems to figuring out how to escape from a dangerous or threatening force. Different contexts of development present humans with different problems to solve. For example, a child who lives on a remote island has many different types of experiences and problems to solve in his everyday activities compared with a child who lives in an urban, industrial center. Thus, one feature of human cognition, which is a product of evolution, is the adaptation of our intelligence to the types of problems that are important to solve in the environment we inhabit. Evolutionary developmental psychologists are interested in the process, especially in behaviors that children develop that are instrumental to survival.

Also of interest are the capabilities that human children develop that enable them to learn from their interactions with other people. For instance, Tomasello (1999) considers development of the ability to understand others' intentions to be a central feature of human cognitive development. Moreover, he argues that this ability appeared relatively late in human evolution and is a key distinguishing feature between humans and other primates. Through understanding that other people have mental states and intentions behind actions, children are able to learn meaningful, goal-directed behaviors by watching and interacting with others. Therefore, the behaviors children observe and learn are not just mindlessly imitated; they contain the meaning or intention of the human action. This capability guides children as they watch and interpret the actions of others and helps them adopt *and* adapt these actions to reach their own goals.

DEVELOPMENTAL THEMES AND THEORETICAL PERSPECTIVES: AN OVERVIEW

As we will stress throughout this book, the understanding of children's development can be approached from many perspectives and with a number of important themes in mind. Table 1-3 summarizes the theories we have discussed in relation to the themes of development. You can see from even these brief descriptions that these perspectives offer different accounts of development than do others. For example, Piaget's organismic theory is helpful in explaining children's cognitive development, whereas Bandura's cognitive social learning theory offers a perspective for explaining social development. Vygotskian theory is useful for understanding social and cultural contributions to children's thinking, whereas ethological approaches have been helpful in describing the development of early social relationships and of emotional expression and communication.

Many questions about child development benefit from the application of several different theoretical perspectives. Increasingly, we recognize that different aspects of development, such as language and emotional and social behavior, are interlinked. For example, children's learning takes place in social contexts with others—parents and peers—and the relationships children have with these individuals will affect what and how they learn from them. The ways that children perceive the environment may be influenced by the development of their motor skills because the visual information available to a crawling child is quite different from that which is available to a child who can walk. Similarly, language and cognitive development are better understood by recognizing their mutual interdependence. In short, every aspect of development is related to several others. This increasing acceptance of the interdependence of areas of

Table 1-3   Overview of developmental themes and theoretical perspectives

	THEMES		
Perspectives	Biology vs. Environment	Continuity vs. Discontinuity	Individual Characteristics vs. Contextual and Cultural Characteristics
Structural-Organismic Perspectives			
Freudian theory	Interaction between biology and environment	Discontinuity (stages of development)	High on individual traits
Erikson's theory	Interaction between biology and environment	Discontinuity (stages of development)	High on individual traits
Piagetian theory	Interaction between biology and environment	Discontinuity (stages of development)	Emphasis on individual characteristics
Learning Perspectives			
Behaviorism	Environment	Continuity (no stages)	High on situational influences
Cognitive social learning theory	Environment	Continuity (no stages)	High on situational influences
Information-processing approaches	Focus on environment but recognition of biology	Continuity (no stages)	High on situational influences although individual characteristics important
Dynamic Systems Perspectives			
	Interactions among all systems—biological, psychosocial, environmental	Continuity (no stages)	High on situational influences
Contextual Perspectives			
Vygotsky's sociocultural theory	Interaction between biology and environment	Discontinuous for some aspects of development	Situation and context are important
Bronfenbrenner's ecological theory	Focus on environment but recognition of biology	Continuity (no stages)	High on situational influences
Ethological and evolutionary approaches	Emphasis on biology, but environment plays role in eliciting and modifying behavior patterns	Varies among individual theories (e.g., depends upon theory's view of critical periods)	High on situational influences
Historical and life span perspectives	Focus on environment but recognition of biology	Continuity (no stages)	High on situational influences

development is leading to a greater acceptance of systems and contextual approaches to development. Ethological and evolutionary approaches add species-specific capabilities and needs to these views. Many contemporary developmental theories share at least some of the assumptions of these approaches. Most theorists tend to agree that it is often helpful to draw on several theories to help understand children's development; in combination, several theories can tell us a great deal more about the causes and course of children's development than any single one alone can. Now we turn to research methods, that is, how developmental psychologists test the ideas that stem from these various theories of child development. Although the theoretical perspectives we discussed are not wedded to particular methods, theories do tend to favor some methods over others. We will point out these theory-method links in our discussion.

Making the Connections 1.1

There are many links between concepts and ideas in one area of development and concepts and ideas in other areas. Here are some of the connections between ideas in Chapter 1's discussion of developmental themes and theories and discussions in other chapters of this book.

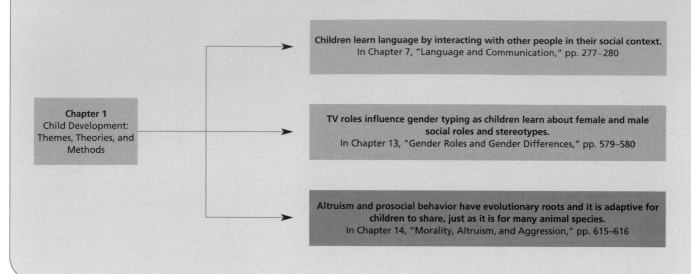

Chapter 1
Child Development: Themes, Theories, and Methods

Children learn language by interacting with other people in their social context.
In Chapter 7, "Language and Communication," pp. 277–280

TV roles influence gender typing as children learn about female and male social roles and stereotypes.
In Chapter 13, "Gender Roles and Gender Differences," pp. 579–580

Altruism and prosocial behavior have evolutionary roots and it is adaptive for children to share, just as it is for many animal species.
In Chapter 14, "Morality, Altruism, and Aggression," pp. 615–616

RESEARCH METHODS IN CHILD PSYCHOLOGY

A theory can provide us with insights, hunches, and ideas about human development, but to be useful, a theory must enable us to predict with some degree of accuracy such things as how children change as they grow older and why development unfolds as it does. In this section, we investigate some of the many strategies and methods used by psychologists who study child development. Like other scientists, child psychologists use the **scientific method** in their research; that is, they formulate hypotheses on the basis of a theory and use measurable and replicable techniques to collect, study, and analyze data in an effort to test the theory's usefulness. The main issues in a scientific approach to psychological development include selecting a sample, designing a study that taps development in some way, and ensuring that all ethical protections are in place.

Selecting a Sample

If you wanted to study the typical play activities of preschoolers, how would you go about collecting your data? How many children do you suppose there are at a given time in the United States? Rather a lot. Thus, you couldn't possibly study all of them, but you could select a **sample,** or a group of manageable size made up of individuals who, you hope, are representative of the entire population of preschoolers that you want to describe.

REPRESENTATIVENESS OF A SAMPLE   If we want our research conclusions to be applicable to the population our sample is designed to reflect, we must ensure the **representativeness** of that sample. That is, the persons we choose to study must possess nearly the same characteristics evidenced by the larger population in which we are interested and, depending on that population, we may need a very broad

scientific method The use of measurable and replicable techniques in framing hypotheses and collecting and analyzing data to test a theory's usefulness.

sample A group of individuals who are representative of a larger population.

representativeness The degree to which a sample actually possesses the characteristics of the larger population it represents.

24

sample in which, say, many social classes or ethnic backgrounds are represented. Consider the following example:

> A researcher wants to study the way children's vocabularies change over time. Living near a private nursery school in an affluent suburban community, she selects thirty 3-year-olds and thirty 5-year-olds from the school population and tests their vocabulary levels. Based on the performance of these children the investigator reports that she has a set of norms or guidelines for what may be expected of preschoolers' vocabulary knowledge. What's wrong with the researcher's conclusion?

The investigator has chosen her sample poorly, for, other things being equal, the parents of these children are likely to be well educated and to have verbal skills that surpass those of less educated parents. It's also possible that experiences at the school, where the ratio of teachers to students may be more favorable than in public schools, facilitate children's learning. Clearly, we can't generalize about the average vocabulary accomplishment of all children of ages 3 and 5 unless we sample a range of children from different backgrounds and in different instructional settings.

This example illustrates one of the major problems that a researcher faces in selecting a sample—namely, to try to recruit a group of people representative of the larger population about which the researcher wishes to hypothesize. Increasingly, investigators are finding it helpful to select several samples, each made up of people who vary in ethnicity, gender, and social class. By selecting multiple samples, they can be more certain that their conclusions about development do, in fact, apply to a broad range of people. Box 1.3 more closely examines the issue of representative sampling in a diverse population such as the United States.

LifeMap CD

Watch the video "Conducting Research on Adolescents" in Chapter 1 of your CD to hear a psychologist's insights on how research can have beneficial effects.

ANOTHER APPROACH: THE NATIONAL SURVEY   In an innovative approach to sampling called the **national survey,** researchers interested in a particular issue or issues select a very large, nationally representative group of people. For example, the National Longitudinal Survey of Youth (NLSY), begun in 1979 with a sample of young men and women who then ranged in age from 14 to 24, has interviewed its participants annually on such topics as experiences in the family, school, and work. The survey participants were drawn from 235 geographic areas across the United States. This broad sampling strategy has the advantage of allowing researchers to make general statements that may be applied to all Americans in the same age groups. It has a major disadvantage, however, in that national surveys are costly in terms of time and labor.

In recent years, the NLSY and other similar large-scale studies have begun to investigate such issues as the impact of day care, maternal employment, neighborhood quality, welfare reform, and divorce on children and families (Brooks-Gunn, Berlin, Leventhal, & Fuligni, 2000; Brooks-Gunn, Smith, Berlin, & Lee, 2001). Although these surveys' large samples allow them to reveal overarching patterns in people's

national survey A method of sampling in which a very large, nationally representative group of people are selected for a particular study.

Source: PEANUTS reprinted by permission of United Feature Syndicate, Inc.

Box 1.3

Perspectives on Diversity

MINORITY GROUPS IN CHILD DEVELOPMENT RESEARCH

In 1990 the non-European, non-white proportion of the U.S. population was 25 percent, and by 2020 it's expected to reach 30 percent (U.S. Department of Commerce, 1996). Today, about 50 percent of the U.S. population is either working-class or poor (Children's Defense Fund, 2001). Despite these statistics, most developmental research has virtually ignored non-European, non-middle-class children and families (Demo et al., 2000; Fisher, Jackson, & Villaruel, 1998). For example, as late as 1989, only 1.5 percent of articles in *Developmental Psychology* and other journals in the field pertained to African Americans. According to Graham (1992), despite the fact that the non-white U.S. population has been increasing steadily, this was a decrease from the proportion of articles (5.5%) published in the early 1970s!

Many minority people have moved from lower social classes into the middle class. Nevertheless, when researchers do include non-white, non-European individuals in their studies, they tend to sample only those of low socioeconomic status (Fisher et al., 1998). This practice may reinforce a stereotypic view of ethnic people as monolithic—that is, as a group of people who are *uniformly* poor and "different" from middle-class people—when in fact there are minority people in all social classes. In addition, research studies typically use materials and procedures developed from the perspective of the dominant culture and therefore often elicit responses from minority participants seen as deficient in some way (Fisher et al., 1998). As we will see in Chapter 10, this is particularly likely when using measures of cognitive functioning or intelligence.

This "deficit" orientation essentially rules out the possibility of exploring the skills and resources of people whose heritage and cultural patterns are different from the dominant North American patterns (Garcia Coll & Magnuson, 2000). It also prevents researchers from understanding the sociocultural bases for minorities' beliefs, attitudes, behaviors, and lifestyles from the points of view of minorities themselves and leads to the evaluation of research participants on the basis of the dominant group's perception of social reality.

Stimulated in part by such increasingly popular theoretical perspectives as Vygotsky's sociocultural theory, dynamic systems theory, and Bronfenbrenner's ecological theory, a new research paradigm emphasizing cross-cultural and multicultural comparisons is emerging (Fisher et al., 1998). This model proposes that to understand human growth and development, researchers must add cultural context as a parameter of equal importance to the biological, psychological, and social aspects of human life. Thus, to carry out useful research with ethnic minority participants, researchers need to understand the cultural values and practices of the groups they seek to study. New methods, such as ethnographic approaches that involve rich descriptions of the cultural practices of minority groups in their everyday environments, are becoming commonly used to improve our understanding of the unique characteristics and mores of different ethnic groups.

Cultural understanding needs to inform research instruments and methodology as well; questionnaires, interview protocols, and tests need to be adapted to the cultural characteristics of the group being studied. As Garcia Coll and Magnuson (2000) point out, the way a person interprets a task influences the way she or he performs it and, significantly, this interpretation is related not only to the specific features of the task but to the person's cultural experiences. If all children do not understand and interpret the goal of the task in the same way, can the tester legitimately compare the responses of different children? Equating tasks in terms of familiarity or cultural appropriateness is very difficult. However, it is reasonable to suppose that the more psychologists use culturally relevant materials and procedures and the harder they try to ensure that the child understands both the task and the examiner's interest in his or her responses, the more likely it is that the child will perform competently.

behavior and relationships among particular factors, these studies are less suited to answering specific questions about the processes that may account for different aspects of development. For this reason, a national survey is sometimes used in combination with a more intensive look at a smaller sample of people. Of the large national sample of children, for example, we might select a subsample of 100 or 200 and then study these children in some depth in order to achieve a better understanding of the processes that underlie changes over time in their thinking and behavior.

Methods of Gathering Data about Children

Once researchers have decided what group or groups they want to study, they must decide how they will study these youngsters. Essentially, there are three methods of gathering such data: We can ask children about themselves; we can ask people who are close to these children about them; or we can observe the children directly. Each approach has its advantages and limitations, and the researchers' choices depend on the kinds of questions they want to answer.

CHILDREN'S SELF-REPORTS   A **self-report** is information that a person provides about himself or herself, typically by answering a set of questions devised by a researcher. Soliciting such information from a child, as you may imagine, presents special problems. Compared with adults, children—especially younger ones— are apt to be less attentive, slower to respond, and to have more trouble understanding the questions that researchers ask. Despite these limitations on children's self-reports, some kinds of information are difficult to obtain in any other way (Cummings et al., 2000). As Zill (1986) notes, "The child is the best authority on his own feelings, even if he has some trouble verbalizing those feelings. And even in matters of fact—where adults have the advantage of a more fully developed sense of where, or when, and of how many—there are aspects of a child's daily life that his parents or teacher know little or nothing about" (pp. 23–24).

REPORTS BY FAMILY MEMBERS, TEACHERS, AND PEERS
A second way of collecting data on child development is to solicit information from people who know a child or children well. Most commonly, child development researchers seek this information from family members, teachers, and peers.

A strength of interviews with parents and other family members is that these reports are generally based on many observations made over time in a variety of situations. Another advantage of reports by family members is that even if parents and siblings are not totally accurate in their reporting, their perceptions, expectations, beliefs, and interpretations of events and behavior may be just as important as what we can only assume is objective reality (Bugental & Grusec, 2006; Collins & Repinski, 2001). For example, whether or not a child's parents explicitly insist on exceptionally good academic performance, a child's belief that her parents want her to do very well in school may greatly influence her behavior. There are some clear disadvantages in soliciting parental and other family reports about a child's growth and development. Human memory is not completely reliable. Also, because people are motivated to remember themselves in the best light possible, parents often remember themselves as more consistent, patient, and even-tempered with their children than more objective assessments might have revealed them to be.

Recently, in an effort to increase the accuracy of parents' reports about their children, investigators have devised a number of new interview strategies. For example, they may have parents report only very recent events so as to ensure more reliable memories, or they may phone parents every evening and ask which of a list of specific behaviors (such as crying or refusing to comply) their children have exhibited in the past 24 hours (Patterson, 1996; Patterson & Bank, 1989), or they may ask parents

self-report Information that people provide about themselves, either in a direct interview or in some written form, such as a questionnaire.

to keep a structured diary in which they record the child's behaviors at regular intervals (e.g., every hour: Hetherington, 1991a). Child development researchers have even asked parents to carry pagers, which experimenters then beep randomly, asking the parents to record their activities or feelings or those of their children (Larson & Richards, 1994). This approach allows for a random sampling not only of behaviors but of the situations in which these behaviors occur.

To learn about a child's behavior in school and other settings when parents aren't present, researchers can ask other people, such as teachers and peers. Investigators may ask teachers to rate children on a specific series of dimensions such as attentiveness, dependability, and sociability, in the classroom or on the playground. One technique researchers often use is to ask children, such as classmates, to rate how well a particular child's peers accept him. For example, investigators might ask all the youngsters in a classroom to rate each of their peers in terms of "how much I like to play with" him or her. The researchers then combine all the ratings to yield a picture of each child's social status in the classroom (Ladd, 2005; Rubin, Bukowski, & Parker, 1998).

Although children's self-reports, parental reports, and reports by others have their limitations, researchers have found that these reports offer them the best understanding of many issues. In addition, as we will see next, these kinds of reports are often used in conjunction with other data-gathering strategies.

DIRECT OBSERVATION   There is often no substitute for researchers' own **direct observation** of people, and students of child development may make such observations in naturalistic settings, such as participants' own homes, or in laboratories where they give children and sometimes parents a structured task to perform. Observational data are valuable resources in examining human behavior. However, such data are valid only to the extent that the presence of an observer or other demands of the situation do not distort the participants' behavior and responses.

These distorting factors are sometimes hard to avoid because children and parents often behave differently in different kinds of settings or when they know they are being

direct observation A method of observation in which researchers go into settings in the natural world or bring participants into the laboratory to observe behaviors of interest.

Research with very young children, like this 6-month-old infant, is becoming increasingly common as psychologists seek to expand our knowledge about early development. A video recording will permit closer study of this child's behavior after the observation session is over.

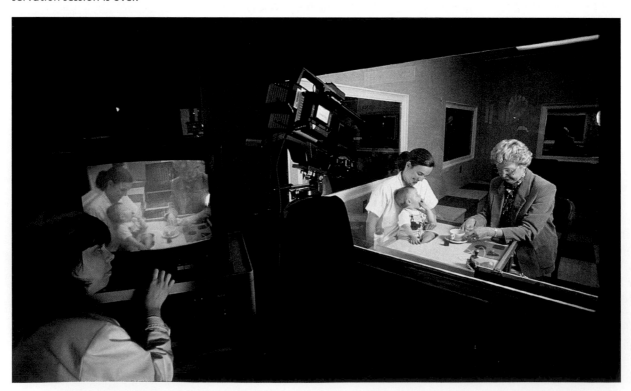

watched. Both adults and children tend to express less negative emotion and to exhibit more socially desirable behavior when observations are conducted in unfamiliar settings, such as a laboratory, compared with at home (Lamb, Suomi, & Stephenson, 1979). Even in home observations, customary behavior can be distorted by the presence of an outside observer. Parents, for instance, tend to inhibit negative behavior when they are being watched (Russell, Russell, & Midwinter, 1991). Attempts to minimize such distortions in studies in people's homes include the use of less obtrusive observational methods, such as video or tape recordings without the observer present, and by conducting many regular visits from an observer—for example, an observer being at a family's home each dinner hour over a period of several weeks (Feiring & Lewis, 1987). As surprising as it may seem, people can get used to such observational techniques; as observations proceed, one sees gradual increases in less socially accepted behaviors, such as quarreling, criticizing, and punishing (Boyum & Parke, 1995).

When researchers decide to observe children and their families directly, they must decide what kinds of behaviors to record (Bakeman & Gottman, 1997). If they're interested in a broad range of behaviors, they may use a **specimen record,** in which they record or videotape everything a subject does for a specified period of time. If they're interested in studying only a particular type of behavior, such as the way a child responds to her parents' directives, they may use a technique called **event sampling,** in which they record individuals' behavior, such as the child's response whenever the event of interest occurs. In the **time sampling** approach, the researcher records a set of predetermined behaviors that occur during a specific time period. Thus, if an investigator were going to observe a family for an hour, she might divide the hour into 120 thirty-second units, prepare a grid showing behaviors and time blocks, and then put a check beside each behavior that occurs in each block of time. This approach would yield the frequency of different kinds of behaviors during the hour. When a child development specialist is interested in a specific behavior, he may structure a situation to observe the behavior using a method called **structured observation.** Suppose a researcher is interested in the way mothers instruct their children about how to solve problems. The researcher may invite mothers and children to the laboratory to participate in a joint problem-solving session, perhaps one that involves putting together different types of puzzles, and observe how their interaction changes as the child attains skill and understanding of the task.

Observational methods remain central to the study of child development. The potential of these methods to provide insights into many aspects of child development is great. However, because of the limitations inherent in all these methods of gathering data, many investigators use several methods in the same study; for example, they combine observations with parent surveys or interviews. If the findings of a variety of methods converge, researchers can reasonably conclude that the findings are valid.

specimen record A technique by which researchers record everything a person does within a given period of time.

event sampling A technique by which investigators record participants' behavior only when an event of particular interest occurs.

time sampling A technique by which researchers record any of a set of predetermined behaviors that occur within a specified period of time.

structured observation A form of observation in which researchers structure a situation so that behaviors they wish to study are more likely to occur.

Research Design: Establishing Patterns and Causes

Selecting a sample and a method of gathering information enables us to describe some aspect of human development, but what will this information do for us? To make use of it, we need to design a study to determine how the various factors of development that we have described are related to and interact with each other, with the goal of identifying the reasons why development occurs as it does. In this section, we offer a brief discussion of the most common research designs—the correlational method, the experimental method, and the case study—that are used by psychologists to study the nature and process of child development. In describing these methods, we have chosen illustrations that pertain to a single topic: the effect on children's behavior of viewing violent television programs. Our aim is to show how different designs yield different approaches and answers to this question.

correlational method A research design that permits investigators to establish relations among variables as well as assess the strength of those relations.

THE CORRELATIONAL METHOD   Many questions in child development reflect an interest in whether some experiences of childhood are related to other experiences of childhood in a regular or systematic way. For example, many people are interested in whether educational television programs like "Sesame Street" are related to better performance when children enter school. To illustrate the **correlational method** of research, a design that enables researchers to establish that certain experiences or factors are related to each other and to assess the strength of the relations, let's examine a study that addressed this question. John Wright and Aletha Huston (1995) studied the TV-viewing behavior of preschool children in more than 250 families, all from low-income areas. The children were either 2 or 4 years old at the start of the study, and either 5 or 7 at its conclusion. The parents were asked to make detailed reports on how their preschoolers spent their time, including which TV shows they watched and for how long each day, and every year the children were given a variety of cognitive achievement tests, such as measures of mathematical skill and word knowledge. The researchers found that the more educational programs the children watched, the higher they scored on the tests (Figure 1-4).

Thus, these factors were positively correlated with each other in that scores for both measures increased. However, the more time children spent watching cartoons or adult programs, the lower they scored on these tests, which is a negative correlation; that is, as one score increased the other score decreased.

A correlation does not indicate causal relations between factors; it simply tells us that two factors are related to each other and indicates the strength or magnitude of that relation. The correlations found by Wright and Huston indicate that watching educational programs is related to children's cognitive performance, but they do not indicate that watching educational programs caused higher test scores. Any number of factors other than watching educational shows could have improved the children's test scores. For example, suppose that educational programs appeal most to children who have superior cognitive skills or who have parents who give them a great deal of encouragement and guidance in academic subjects.

If correlational research doesn't allow us to determine causation, why do we use it? For one thing, many questions are difficult to study in a controlled laboratory design. For example, the effect of viewing educational programs on cognitive development is cumulative, meaning it happens over a long period of viewing such programs. An experiment would be difficult to design that could control for such long-term exposure. Also, understanding causal processes is not the goal of all developmental research.

Figure 1-4

Watching "Sesame Street" makes scores rise

In one of the first studies of the effects of watching "Sesame Street," researchers found that on tests of identification of body parts; recognition of letters, numbers, and geometric forms; and classifying and sorting, preschoolers who frequently watched the show performed significantly better than those who watched rarely.

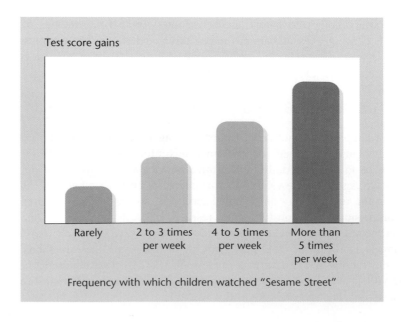

Many investigators are primarily interested in describing the patterns and paths of development as it naturally occurs, which the correlational method describes. Finally, ethical concerns associated with lab experiments may interfere with using this design in certain circumstances.

EXPERIMENTAL DESIGNS The primary way researchers investigate causal connections among factors is by experiment. An experiment can be carried out in a laboratory, the field, or in natural situations. In a **laboratory experiment,** researchers are able to control factors that may influence the variable they are interested in, and therefore their results allow them to draw conclusions about cause and effect. Researchers will hold constant, or equate, every possible influence except the one factor they have hypothesized to be the cause of the variable they want to study. They then create two groups of participants. One group, called the **experimental group,** is exposed to the proposed causative factor; the second group, the **control group,** does not receive or experience this factor. Researchers put people in these two groups by using **random assignment,** which will rule out the possibility that the people in each of the groups differ from one another in some systematic way that could distort the results of the experiment (more skilled people in the experimental group, for instance).

To understand how these various controls enable the laboratory experimenter to determine causality, let's look at a classic study of the relationship between watching violent television programs and aggressive behavior. Liebert and Baron (1972) randomly assigned 136 boys and girls ranging in age from 5 to 9 to either an experimental group or a control group. The children in both groups first saw two brief commercials selected for their humor and attention-getting value. Then half the children—those in the experimental group—saw three and a half minutes of a TV program about crime that contained a chase, two fistfights, two shootings, and a knifing. In contrast, the children in the control group watched a highly active but nonviolent sports sequence of the same time length. Finally, the children in both groups watched another 60 seconds of a tire commercial. The only difference in the material the two groups were exposed to was in the three-and-a-half-minute video they watched; one group saw violent episodes, the other no violence at all. This is the **independent variable,** or the factor the researchers deliberately manipulate. The researchers thus hypothesized that if the children in the experimental group later behaved differently from those in the control group, it would be reasonable to conclude that exposure to TV violence was the cause.

In the second phase of the study, the experimenters told each of the children that they were to play a game with another child in an adjoining room (whom they could not see and who, in fact, was purely imaginary). The researchers seated each child before a panel that had two buttons labeled "Hurt" and "Help" and told the child that the buttons were connected to a panel that the child in the other room sat before. This child was playing a game that required turning a handle, the experimenter explained, and if the child wanted to make it easier for her "partner" to turn the handle she could press the "Help" button; on the other hand, if the participant wanted to hinder the other child, pressing the "Hurt" button would turn the handle burning hot. Of course, this entire scenario was a deception, and nothing a child did hurt anyone else. (The issue of deception raises ethical questions that we discuss shortly.) The amount of aggressiveness the children display is the **dependent variable,** or the factor that researchers expect to change as a function of change in the independent variable. The researchers believed that by measuring how long and how often children depressed the "Hurt" button they could gauge how aggressively children in both the experimental and the control groups would behave toward another child. Liebert and Baron discovered that children who had seen the violent TV segment showed significantly more willingness to engage in interpersonal aggression than children who had watched the fast-paced but nonviolent sports program. This finding supported the researchers' hypothesis that exposure to TV violence can cause interpersonal aggression.

laboratory experiment A research design that allows investigators to determine cause and effect by controlling variables and treatments and assigning participants randomly to treatments.

experimental group In an experiment, the group that is exposed to the treatment, or the *independent variable.*

control group In an experiment, the group that is not exposed to the treatment, or the *independent variable.*

random assignment The technique by which researchers assign individuals randomly to either an *experimental* or *control group.*

independent variable The variable, or factor, that researchers deliberately manipulate in an experiment.

dependent variable The variable, or factor, that researchers expect to change as a function of change in the independent variable.

ecological validity The degree to which a research study accurately represents events or processes that occur in the natural world.

Although this study was carefully designed, like many laboratory experiments it has limitations that may prevent generalization from the experimental situation to the natural world. Ensuring a study's **ecological validity,** or its accurate representation of events and processes that occur in the natural environment, is often difficult. For example, Liebert and Baron edited their violent TV program to include more acts of violence in three and a half minutes than would normally occur in a randomly chosen TV segment of this length, even in a show that has a lot of violence. However, the exact duplication of natural circumstances is not the aim of all laboratory experiments. For example, as you will see in later chapters, experimenters usually gain important insights about people's perceptual capacities, such as how well they see and hear, through laboratory assessments. This is because, in the laboratory, researchers can precisely control the critical features of perceptual stimuli. For instance, they can increase the loudness of a sound by a single decibel to determine whether people can detect the change. For such questions, the laboratory is an ideal place for study. When we want to avoid artificiality and some of the other problems associated with laboratory experiments, we can sometimes conduct experiments in the field, which we discuss next.

field experiment An experiment in which researchers deliberately create a change in a real-world setting and then measure the outcome of their manipulation.

In a **field experiment,** investigators deliberately introduce changes in a person's normal environment and then measure the outcome of their manipulation. As an illustration, let's consider a field experiment that studied the impact of viewing TV violence on aggressive behavior in children that was conducted by Friedrich and Stein (1973). Preschoolers enrolled in a summer program were the participants in this study. During the first three weeks of the study, the researchers simply observed the children during their usual play sessions to achieve a baseline measure of the degree of aggressive behavior each child displayed under normal circumstances. Then, for the next four weeks, they showed the children, who were randomly assigned to one of three groups, a half-hour TV program each day. Some children always saw programs depicting interpersonal aggression, such as Batman and Superman cartoons; others saw programs with a message of caring and kindness toward others, such as "Mister Rogers' Neighborhood"; and others watched neutral shows, such as nature programs or circus movies.

Friedrich and Stein found that children who had been rated high in aggressive behavior before the TV watching started behaved even more aggressively after repeated exposure to aggressive cartoons, but not after exposure to the other two kinds of shows. For children who were rated low in aggression during the initial assessment period, watching interpersonal aggression seemed to have no effect; they were still less likely to behave aggressively. Children who watched neutral shows did not change either. The researchers concluded that exposure to TV violence can increase aggression in children, but only among children already likely to behave aggressively. These findings were especially interesting in that the researchers took care to minimize **observer bias,** that is, the tendency of observers who are knowledgeable about a research design or hypothesis to be influenced in their evaluations by that knowledge. The researchers who assessed the children's behavior after the viewings did not know which types of programs the different children had seen.

observer bias The tendency of observers to be influenced in their judgments by their knowledge of the hypotheses guiding the research.

One advantage of the field experiment over the laboratory experiment is that the results can be generalized more readily to real-life experiences. Friedrich and Stein did not edit the TV programs the children saw in any way, and these programs were among those that many of the children watched in their homes. Moreover, the children's aggressive behavior was measured in an everyday setting, not in a situation that allowed or encouraged them to behave aggressively. At the same time, the field experiment retains some important features of a laboratory experiment. Because the independent variable—the type of TV program—was still under the control of the researchers, and the participants were still randomly assigned to the various groups, Friedrich and Stein could be reasonably confident that they had demonstrated a causal connection—namely, that exposure to TV violence may encourage aggressive children to behave even more aggressively.

For ethical or practical reasons, researchers may not be able to introduce changes into the natural world. In these instances, they may elect to do a **natural experiment,** in which they measure the effects of events or changes that occur naturally in the real world. This approach is often called a *quasi-experiment,* because it is not a true experiment in that the research participants are not randomly assigned to experimental conditions. Instead, they select the children they study because the children are exposed to a set of conditions that are of interest to the researcher, such as enrollment in day care or a nutritional supplement program. One example of a natural experiment is a study that investigated the way the introduction of television into a community affected aggressive behavior among children (MacBeth, 1996). By monitoring the level of aggressiveness in children's play both before and after the debut of television in a small town in Canada, the investigator was able to show that aggressive behavior did in fact increase after TV arrived in town.

As our examples suggest, a great deal of research has been devoted to children's television viewing. Box 1.4 discusses this research and its impact on legislation.

natural experiment An experiment in which researchers measure the results of events that occur naturally in the real world.

THE CASE STUDY APPROACH Can we learn anything about development by studying a single child or perhaps a single group, such as a particular classroom? The study of individual persons or a group, called the **case study method,** does have a useful role in developmental research. The case study allows investigators to explore phenomena that they do not often encounter, such as an unusual talent, a rare developmental disorder, or a model classroom. It also facilitates more intensive investigation because the researcher's efforts are not spread across a large number of participants. In the 1800s, in one of the first recorded case studies, Charles Darwin (1872) kept a highly detailed diary of his infant son's emotional expressions, a record that became the basis for his theory of emotional development in infants and children. This early work also provided useful hunches, insights, and hypotheses that later investigators pursued in a more systematic fashion.

Sometimes a case study leads into a kind of experiment in which a psychologist or other researcher tries to bring about a change in a particular behavior, most often a behavior that is self-destructive or that involves aggressive behavior toward other people. For example, careful implementation and observation of a new treatment for child conduct problems may shed light on exactly how the treatment works for a particular child with certain behavioral patterns. The chief limitation of the single-case approach is the difficulty of generalizing from one individual to other people or situations.

case study method A form of research in which investigators study an individual person or group very intensely.

COMBINATION DESIGNS IN DEVELOPMENTAL RESEARCH
The several research strategies that we have discussed are the tools of research, and researchers can choose the best method among them for the questions they hope to answer. (Table 1-4 summarizes the differences among the research designs we've examined so far.) The choice of method depends on the question being asked and the ages of the children studied. Researchers may also combine these designs over a series of studies on the same topic. For example, a researcher may start off in an unexplored

Design	Control over Independent Variable	Control over Dependent Variable	Generalizability of Findings
Correlational method	Low	Low	Medium
Laboratory experiment	High	High	Low
Field experiment	Medium	Low	High
Natural experiment	Low	Low	High

Table 1-4

Research designs: Advantages and limitations

Box 1.4

Child Psychology in Action

HOW CAN WE MAKE BETTER USE OF RESEARCH ON CHILDREN AND TELEVISION?

The impact on children of the amazing growth of communications media within the twentieth century cannot be denied. From early radio, movies, and comic books to television and its electronic cousins—videotapes, video games, CD-ROMs, and the Internet—children have been bombarded with new information and experiences via the media. As we have seen in this chapter, some educational programs, such as "Sesame Street," have had a useful impact on young audiences. Many developmentalists have expressed the fear, however, that television may displace other, more valuable activities (Huston & Wright, 1998).

What has the wealth of research on children and television—much of it instigated by federal commissions and agencies—revealed? It has shown that some programs do help young children learn, but it has also made a strong case for the negative effects on children of watching programs filled with violence and sex as well as commercials that prey on the young child's limited understanding.

Although the U.S. Congress and the Federal Communications Commission have passed laws intended to influence commercial media, these laws have often failed to impose specific directives, such as banning certain content, mandating certain types of programs, or setting limits as to the period of time (e.g., early evening) or amount of time allotted to child-oriented programming. Moreover, the laws that have imposed such directives have often not been enforced. For example, although the Children's Television Act of 1990, drafted on the basis of research, required broadcasters to provide programs that would serve children's educational and informational needs, it had little initial impact not only because enforcement was minimal but also because some stations claimed an educational thrust for programs that few would call educational (e.g., "Teenage Mutant Ninja Turtles," and "Bugs and Tweety Show") (Kunkel & Canepa, 1994).

Attempts to legislate television programming run the risk of violating First Amendment rights to freedom of expression. Another barrier to the regulation of media content is economic in nature. The television industry is economically robust and maintains a powerful lobby in the nation's capital (Wartella, 1995). Still another barrier to regulation is the difficulty of reaching consensus as to just what kinds of material regulations should target. For example, the 1996 Telecommunications Act required television manufacturers to install in every set a special chip that would allow the consumer to block programs assigned particular ratings. However, agreement on such a system initially ran into several obstacles, including the problem of deciding on a rating for a particular program.

If television programming is unsuitable for children and essentially uncontrolled, what can parents and others do to protect their young charges beyond seeking stricter laws and government policies? According to Huston and Wright, such efforts may pale in the face of our need to recognize and act on our own enormous influence on children's use of television. "What, how, and how much television parents view has a direct impact on children not only because it provides a model, but because children are directly exposed to programs that parents are viewing" (Huston & Wright, 1998, p. 41). Setting an example as well as setting household limits are time-honored prescriptions.

A number of psychologists have recommended that parents and children coview suitable television programs; research has shown positive effects of this practice. If parents or others reinforce a program's content, helping young children identify and discuss characters and events and generally providing what psychologists call scaffolding (Chapter 8) for their understanding and interpretations, the children may benefit (St. Peters, 1993; Watkins, Calvert, Huston-Stein, & Wright, 1980). Research has also shown that parents can help children cope with fears aroused by specific television content (Wilson & Weiss, 1993). But so far, the evidence is that families don't engage often in such coviewing, at least not of programs that are child-oriented. Clearly, television viewing is a family affair, and families as well as networks and the government need to take responsibility for what children watch.

area by using a correlational approach to establish some possible relationships. Then she may use formal experimental approaches to achieve a clearer view of the causal links among the variables revealed by the correlational method. Finally, she may examine closely a single-case study, either of an individual or a group, to provide rich details about the process under study. In the field of child development, the use of multiple methods is becoming increasingly common.

Studying Change over Time

Recall that the main focus of research in child development is change over time. To study this topic, the field makes use of certain research techniques intended to measure the relation of age to some other variables through the progression of time. The main techniques used to study time are the cross-sectional, longitudinal, and sequential methods. These techniques for studying change are used in conjunction with the different data-collection methods and research designs chosen by an investigator. Thus, for example, a longitudinal study could use self-reports or observational data, and it could employ a correlational or an experimental research design.

THE CROSS-SECTIONAL METHOD   The most common strategy for investigating age-related differences in development is the **cross-sectional method,** in which researchers compare different individuals representing different age levels at approximately the same point in time. Imagine that you took a slice or cross section of layers of rock and were able to determine the age of the fossils found at the different layers. Cross-sectional research tries to accomplish this same goal. Essentially it compares different layers—specifically, age groups—of children on a topic, such as a behavior or cognitive performance, to determine how changes associated with age may unfold over the course of development. The cross-sectional method has both advantages and limitations.

cross-sectional method A research method in which researchers compare groups of individuals of different age levels at approximately the same point in time.

Consider the cross-sectional research done by Rheingold and Eckerman (1970) on the development of independent behaviors in young children. These researchers observed mothers and their children, with the children representing nine different ages between 12 and 60 months. There were six children (three boys and three girls) at each of the six-month intervals between 12 and 60 months of age; for example, there were six children who were 12 months old, six children who were 18 months old, and so on. The researchers used a seminaturalistic setting to observe the children's behaviors. They positioned the mothers and children at one end of a large lawn; the mothers sat in chairs, and the children were free to roam. Observers were stationed inconspicuously nearby and they recorded the paths of the children's excursions. A positive correlation between child age and distance traveled from mother was found. The average farthest distance from mothers for 1-year-olds was about 23 feet (6.9 meters); by 2 years of age children ventured about 50 feet (15.1 meters); 3-year-olds went 57 feet (17.3 meters); and 4-year-olds ventured 68 feet (20.6 meters).

Using the cross-sectional method, Rheingold and Eckerman were able to determine how independence differs across age levels by comparing the behaviors of groups of different children at different ages. However, this approach yields no information about the possible past determinants of the age-related changes observed because we can't know what these exact children were like at younger ages. We do not know if the child who is independent at 1 year is likely to be more independent at age 5 than a peer who exhibited little independence when he was 1 year old. Another research design, the longitudinal method, is better suited to tackling the issue of individual change over time.

THE LONGITUDINAL METHOD   One of the most ambitious projects in the study of child development is the Fels Longitudinal Study, which began in 1929 and continued until the 1970s to follow groups of children from birth to age 18. Parents enrolling their newborns in this study agreed to have the child weighed, measured, observed, and tested until he or she was old enough to graduate from high school. One lasting conclusion of this study, which could only be obtained by studying the same children over time, was that the stability of certain behaviors was affected by gender. Boys were more likely to show stable patterns of aggressive behavior from childhood to adulthood; girls were more likely to show stability in dependent-passive behavior (Kagan & Moss, 1962; see also Chapter 13).

longitudinal method A method in which investigators study the same people repeatedly at various times in the participants' lives.

This type of research uses the **longitudinal method,** in which researchers study the same individuals repeatedly at various points in their lives in order to assess patterns of stability and change over time. A longitudinal design allows researchers to follow the development of individuals and to explore possible causes of any observed pattern. It is a powerful method for evaluating the impact of earlier events on later behavior.

But the longitudinal method also has disadvantages. It takes years to collect longitudinal data, and researchers often want to obtain information more quickly. In addition, there is the problem of losing participants. Over time, people move, become ill, or simply lose interest, and the result is a shrinking sample that can affect the pattern of results. In addition, the theories and issues that generated the hypotheses and were used to direct data collection at the beginning of the study may not be of interest later on in the study. Another problem arises from what we call *practice effects,* or the effects of repeated testing. Since the same measures may be used in several successive years, participants' answers may be the result of their familiarity with the items or questions. In contrast, individuals who responded to these issues for the first time may give different answers.

A way to avoid some of these problems is to conduct a short-term longitudinal study. Here researchers track the same group of people but for a limited time period, usually a few months or a few years. Their focus is usually limited to a few key questions. For instance, Roger Brown and his colleagues (Brown, 1973) tracked the language development of three children, Adam, Eve, and Sarah, for a period of five years. Such research has the advantage of shortening the period of data collection and thereby avoiding dropouts in the sample.

A different kind of drawback to lengthy longitudinal studies is the problem of generalizing to generations other than the one being studied. As times change, people become exposed to different influences. Children today, for instance, grow up with many experiences virtually unknown to children growing up in their parents' or grandparents' generations: for example, computers, two parents working outside the home, day care, single mothers who have never married. Findings from a longitudinal study may lose relevance as times change and be descriptive of only a particular **age cohort,** that is, members of the same generation.

age cohort People born within the same generation.

THE SEQUENTIAL METHOD

A creative way around the problem of separating age-related changes from changes caused by the unique experiences of a particular age cohort is to use the **sequential method,** which combines features of both cross-sectional and longitudinal studies. In this method, researchers begin by selecting samples of children of different ages, as they would in cross-sectional research. Suppose, for example, that we wanted to study the change in the development of children's reading skills throughout childhood. We might begin by recruiting and testing three samples of children: 2-year-olds, 4-year-olds, and 6-year-olds. We would then test these same children again at periodic intervals, let's say every two years. Then at each of the two-year measuring points, we would add a new sample of 2-year-olds to the study, which would enable us to compare a larger number of age cohorts. Figure 1-5 displays the design of this study.

sequential method A research method that combines features of both the *cross-sectional* and the *longitudinal* methods.

There are several advantages of the sequential method. First, it allows us to examine age-related changes in children, because the longitudinal feature allows us to test the same children every two years. Second, the cross-sectional aspect of this approach allows us to examine the impact of the year of evaluation and testing or practice effects.

Third, in following each age cohort, it allows us to explore generational effects, or effects of the particular time period in which each group of children was born and raised. For example, perhaps the 6-year-olds originally recruited for this study entered kindergarten at a time when the mathematics curricula in the primary grades underwent much change. By comparing these and other age cohorts, we might be able to assess changes in children's mathematics abilities as instructional techniques changed. And finally, the design has a time-saving advantage. Six years after the start of the study, in 2006, we would have data on changes in mathematics ability that span a period of 10 years (look again at Figure 1-5). This is a four-year saving over a traditional longitudinal study.

When studying change over time, developmental researchers clearly have a choice of design and method (see Table 1-5 for a comparison of the pluses and minuses of all three strategies). In addition, research that stretches beyond national borders and considers cultural contributions provides a broader perspective on the nature and course of human development. Box 1.5 discusses some interesting examples of cross-cultural research.

From a practical point of view, it makes sense to select a research method that is well suited to the questions one is asking in a particular study. Nevertheless, as we said earlier, theoretical perspectives do tend to favor some methods over others. Generally speaking, this is because particular methods are in fact better suited to the kinds of questions posed by research that stems from a particular perspective. For example, Freud and other researchers in the psychodynamic tradition often use case studies because the latter provide the sort of personal detail they seek. Piaget focused on the systematic observation of children, typically in a laboratory and as the children attempted to solve particular problems. Into this observational approach he

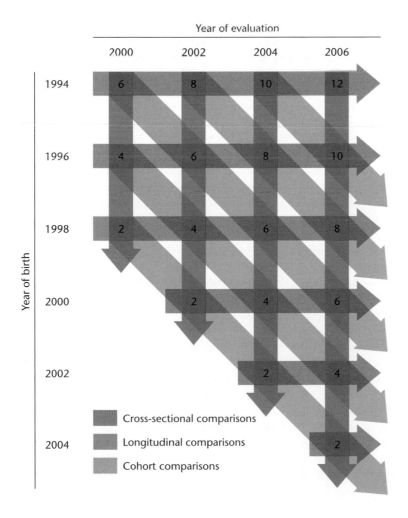

Figure 1-5

Design for a sequential study

This combination of the cross-sectional and longitudinal designs yields a third dimension of measurement that compares cohorts, or people of the same age, at different points in time. The numbers within the arrows are the ages of the groups of children to be studied. For example, in the year 2000 we would do a cross-sectional study of three groups of children, ages 2, 4, and 6. In 2002 we would add a new group of 2-year-olds and we would again measure the earlier groups of children, who would now be 4, 6, and 8. A number of different types of comparisons are possible from such a design. Can you describe some other comparisons that might be made?

Table 1-5 Comparative characteristics of methods of studying developmental change over time

	Cross-sectional	Longitudinal	Sequential
Time required	Short	Long	Moderate
Ability to control costs	High	Low	Moderate
Ability to maintain potential pool of participants	Excellent	Very problematic	Moderate to good
Continuity of staff	High	Medium to low	Moderate to high
Flexibility in adapting to new tests and measures	High	Low	Moderate
Likelihood of practice effects	Low	High	Medium
Ability to assess research issues:			
Normative development data at different ages	Excellent	Excellent	Excellent
Impact of early events on later behavior	Poor	Excellent	Good
Stability vs. instability of behavior	Poor	Excellent	Good
Developmental paths of individuals	Poor	Excellent	Good
Historical or cohort issues	Excellent	Poor	Good

often integrated a post-test interview in which he queried a child about the reasons for his or her behaviors during the problem-solving session because of his interest in describing the thinking that guides children's behavior at different stages of development.

Like Piaget, researchers who use a learning perspective have relied heavily on observational techniques, both in the field and the laboratory. Sometimes these investigators, particularly those who adopt an information-processing approach, use laboratory experiments in which much of the data they collect derives from observation. Observational analysis permits close inspection of behavioral changes to determine if any learning has occurred and has led to a reorganization of behavior relative to what was originally seen. Sociocultural theorists and ethologists also tend to rely on observational techniques, as do many researchers who work from a dynamic systems approach. These techniques may provide evidence of how interactions between a child and her social partner or the physical environment influence a change in behavior. Investigators who study large social systems, based either on a dynamic systems or an ecological perspective, and those who study long-range historical processes, such as life-span researchers, tend to use interview techniques, surveys, and objective demographic data such as health and longevity statistics. Such techniques capture broader social patterns and processes than are available in firsthand observations. Finally, those who use an evolutionary approach often rely on evidence obtained by paleoanthropologists or from comparative observations across species. This type of information may provide insight into species-level behaviors as well as patterns and differences across species or over very long periods of time.

If researchers from different theoretical perspectives rely on similar methods and perhaps even ask similar questions, where do the main differences between theoretical perspectives lie? The primary difference resides in the ways in which researchers of different theoretical persuasions interpret the data they collect. Two researchers working from different theoretical positions could observe the very same behaviors and interpret a child's behaviors quite differently. For instance, an observation of a child playing with an age-mate may provide the researcher who uses an information-processing perspective insight about the child's problem-solving skills. An ethologist may interpret the very same behaviors in relation to peer socialization and dominance hierarchies.

Box 1.5

Perspectives on Diversity

STUDYING DEVELOPMENT CROSS-CULTURALLY

Child developmentalists are becoming increasingly aware of the importance of defining the limitations of their findings and of determining whether the developmental insights gained by studies in one culture apply to children in other cultures. Is the timing of the onset of crawling and walking universal? Do children show the same emotions in all cultures?

We can often address fundamental development issues such as the relative roles of nature and nurture by comparing child development in different cultures. A finding that some aspect of development is similar in a wide variety of cultures may suggest that behavior patterns are universal. On the other hand, the discovery that a behavior differs markedly across cultures may suggest that environmental variables play a significant role in its development and expression (Gauvain, 2001; Turiel, 2001).

Consider the timing of motor development. Although we might expect the pattern of motor development to be universal, it is not. For example, in some African cultures, such as the Kipsigis people of Kenya or the people of Zambia, babies learn to crawl and walk at earlier ages than do infants in the United States (Harkness & Super, 1995). In these cultures parents teach their children to sit up, stand, and walk very soon after birth. In contrast, cultures such as the Ache who live in the rain forest of Paraguay discourage early motor development and keep children in close physical contact with their mothers. As a result, motor development is slowed down. If these patterns are not understood in relation to cultural practices, it would be all too easy to decide that children in some cultures develop motor skills more slowly or quickly than children in other cultures, when in fact the timetable of motor development in all cultures is tied to the cultural practices that provide support for the development of these skills.

In another interesting example of cross-cultural difference, the Nso children of Cameroon assume much more responsibility for the rearing of their siblings than do U.S. children (Nsamenang & Lamb, 1994). What implications may this behavior of Cameroon children have for the assumption of responsibility later in life? And consider patterns of play in Mexico. Whereas U.S. and Canadian adults serve as play partners for their children, in Mexican families sisters and brothers are more often play partners than are adults (Farver & Howes, 1993). These and other differences in socialization patterns may have profound effects on children's development, and these naturally occurring variations in cultural practices may provide important information about the impact of different childrearing conditions on later development.

Although cross-cultural research can be very informative, it is often difficult and expensive to conduct. Language differences and lack of familiarity with the underlying meanings of different customs and practices can often lead researchers to erroneous conclusions. Successful cross-cultural studies often benefit from the participation of cultural informants, usually local people who serve as translators and interpreters, who help researchers gain the trust of officials and other people with whom they need to collaborate and who often assist in interpreting research findings (Rogoff, 2003; Greenfield & Suzuki, 1998). As awareness of cultural contributions to development increases, cross-cultural research is becoming a more frequently used method in child psychology.

THE ETHICS OF RESEARCH WITH CHILDREN

In recent decades there has been a growing awareness of the ethical issues involved in doing research with children. Various government review boards and professional organizations, such as the American Psychological Association and the Society for Research in Child Development, have suggested guidelines for research in an effort to protect children from dangerous and harmful procedures (see Table 1-6).

In addition, all legitimate research projects involving children (and adults) are scrutinized and approved by review boards at the institutions where the research is

Table 1-6 A Bill of Child Participants' Rights in child development research

1. *The right to be fully informed.* Every child has the right to full and truthful information about the purposes of a study in which he or she is to participate and about the procedures to be used.

2. *The right to give informed and voluntary consent.* Every child has the right to agree, either orally or in writing, to participate in a research project. If a child is too young to understand the aims and procedures of the study and to make an informed decision, researchers must request the informed consent of the child's parents.

3. *The right not to be harmed in any way.* Every child has the right to know that he or she will not experience any physical or psychological harm or damage as a result of the research procedures.

4. *The right to withdraw voluntarily from research.* Every child has the right to withdraw at any time from continued participation in any research project.

5. *The right to be informed of the results of research.* Every child has the right to information about the results of the research project. If the child is too young to fully understand this information, it must be provided to the child's parents. It is understood that sometimes information is in the form of group measures or scores on a task rather than individual scores.

6. *The right to confidentiality.* Every child has the right to know that personal information gathered as part of the research project will remain private and confidential, and that it will not be shared with any other individuals or agencies.

7. *The right to full compensation.* Every child has the right to be fully compensated for her or his time and effort as a research participant, even if the child withdraws and does not complete her or his participation.

8. *The right to beneficial treatments.* Every child has the right to profit from any beneficial treatments provided to other participants in the research project. When experimental treatments are deemed beneficial—for example, participation in a program designed to enhance reading or math skills—participants in control groups who do not receive this treatment during the research study proper have the right to the same participation in the beneficial treatment after the project is completed.

Sources: American Psychological Association, 1992; Society for Research on Child Development Committee on Ethical Conduct in Child Development Research, 1993.

informed consent Agreement, based on a clear and full understanding of the purposes and procedures of a research study, to participate in that study.

carried out, including colleges and universities. This scrutiny ensures that researchers follow ethical guidelines.

All research with human subjects requires that researchers obtain **informed consent** from all participants before being included in a study. Informed consent is an agreement to participate in research based on a clear understanding of the purposes and procedures to be employed in the study. When participants are young children, parents or legal guardians must provide informed consent on their behalf as youngsters (under 7 or 8 years of age) may not have the cognitive capacity to fully understand the goals, risks, and benefits of the research (Institute of Medicine, 2004). Participants also have the right not to be harmed. This includes protection not only from physical harm, but also from psychological and emotional harm, such as feeling uncomfortable or embarrassed.

As easy as it is to list such rights of child participants in research, it is not always easy to determine the ethical course of action in a particular situation. Recall the experiment by Liebert and Baron (1972), discussed earlier, on the effects of viewing violent TV programs on children's later aggressive behavior toward other children in a "mock" game situation. Was it ethical to encourage the child participants in this study to choose to push the "Hurt" button and to let them believe that they were not only keeping another child from winning the game she was presumably playing but also causing her actual physical harm? Even though the scenario was a deception, and no child was actually harmed, how might the children have viewed themselves after they participated in the study? Might they have felt ashamed of themselves? Laboratory research involving deception is becoming less common. However, such questions remain important, and careful scrutiny of all ethical issues in research with children is critical.

Making the Connections 1.2

There are many links between concepts and ideas in one area of development and concepts and ideas in other areas. Here are some of the connections between ideas in Chapter 1's discussion of research methods in child development and discussions in other chapters of this book.

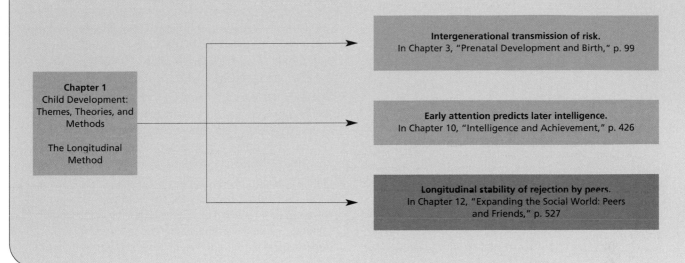

Developmental research is a tool for increasing our knowledge about children, and it is hoped that children at large, through this knowledge, will benefit. Recently some investigators and child advocates have called for more stringent criteria regulating the participation of children in psychological research. Others worry that too many additional restrictions will seriously impede the ability of psychologists to learn more about issues that may ultimately lead to benefits for children. The ethics of research in child psychology continue to comprise a topic of much debate.

SUMMARY

- **Child development** attempts to account for changes in children's abilities and behaviors as they develop by uncovering the processes that underlie these changes.
- Scientists also study children to develop practical information that can help those who care for children, such as parents, teachers, health professionals, and legislators.

Themes of Development

- Although in the past development was held by many to be the result of **maturation,** most modern developmentalists recognize the importance of both biological and environmental influences. Many psychologists are concerned with discovering the ways in which biological and environmental factors interact to produce developmental differences.

- Most contemporary developmentalists believe that children actively shape, control, and direct the course of their own development. A number of theorists view development as a continuous process, whereby change takes place smoothly and gradually over time, but others see development as a series of qualitatively different steps or stages. The more closely and more frequently we examine the child's development, the more gradual or continuous the process appears.

- Some developmentalists continue to debate the question of whether individual or contextual influences are more important in determining development.

Most developmentalists agree, however, that cultural contexts must be considered in any account of development.

Theoretical Perspectives on Development

- Theories serve two functions. First, they help organize and integrate existing knowledge into a coherent account of how children develop. Second, they foster research by providing testable predictions about behavior. Different theories take different positions on the issues or themes of development, and they also account for different aspects of development. In this sense they can be seen as complementary rather than as competing with each other.

- **Structural-organismic perspectives** focus on the organized components of the developing organism and how these change in a qualitative way over the course of human development. Two examples of structural-organismic theories are Freud's **psychodynamic theory,** in which the child is motivated by a set of basic biological drives that direct behavior, and Erikson's psychosocial theory. The concepts of **id, ego,** and **superego** are integral to Freud's notion of the development of personality, and Freud considered early experiences to be determining influences for later development. According to Freudian theory, later adult personality is a direct result of whether the child's drives were deprived or satisfied at each earlier stage.

- Erikson expanded Freud's theory to include social and cultural factors as influences on the child's development as well as to extend the theory into a **life-span perspective.** Erikson's **psychosocial theory** is organized around a series of fundamental personal and social tasks that the individual must accomplish at each stage.

- **Piagetian theory,** also a structural-organismic approach, focuses on intellectual development. In this theory the child is seen as actively seeking information and new experiences. Children adapt to their environment by assimilating new information or by accommodating their existing frameworks to new information. Development results from increasingly complex reorganizations of understanding as the child moves to more advanced levels of cognitive functioning.

- Learning perspectives emphasize how new behaviors are acquired and see development as a gradual and continuous process. The early learning theories, conceived within the traditional school of **behaviorism,** proposed that learning is regulated by environmental factors that modify behavior by either **classical** or **operant conditioning.**

- **Cognitive social learning theory** has extended the behavioral perspective to include imitation as another form of learning. According to this theory, children are selective about who and what behaviors they imitate.

- **Information-processing approaches** are derived from a learning perspective and focus on how children process information and use this knowledge to guide behavior. This approach has been applied to a wide range of problems in studies of cognitive development and social behavior.

- **Dynamic systems theories** view development from the system level in which individual behaviors are influenced by the other elements or members of the system. The continuing interactions among system members make development a highly dynamic process.

- Contextual perspectives focus on the contributions of social and cultural factors to psychological development. In his **sociocultural theory** of cognitive development, Vygotsky emphasized the interaction between the active child and her social environment. According to Vygotsky, the child grows and changes as a function of her own efforts and by the guidance of more skilled others.

- **Ecological theory** stresses the importance of understanding the relationship between the organism and various environmental systems, such as the family, school, community, and culture. Development involves the interplay between children and their changing relationships with these different ecological systems—the **microsystem, mesosystem, exosystem, macrosystem,** and **chronosystem.** The child's subjective experience of, or understanding of, the environment and the child's active role in modifying the environment are important aspects of this perspective.

- Historical approaches examine the contribution of cohort events to development. Psychologists who view development from a life-span perspective are particularly interested in the effects of historical events on human development.

- **Ethological theory** takes a biological-evolutionary approach to describing development. Ethologists, whose primary mode of study is direct observation of behavior in natural settings, study patterns of behaviors across human and infrahuman species and across human societies and cultures.

- **Evolutionary psychology** has influenced developmental research especially in areas related to cognitive development. The focus in this work is on how the cognitive capabilities and constraints of the organism may reflect survival needs and processes of human evolution.

Developmental Themes and Theoretical Perspectives: An Overview

- Some theoretical perspectives on child development are particularly useful in explaining certain aspects of children's growth and change, whereas other perspectives illuminate other aspects of development.

- Because every aspect of development is related to several others, it is often useful to apply several different theoretical perspectives to the analysis and study of a particular problem or issue. The interrelatedness of different domains of development makes a systems approach increasingly attractive.

Research Methods in Child Psychology

- Child psychologists use the **scientific method** in their research. They formulate hypotheses on the basis of theories, and they use measurable and replicable techniques to collect, study, and analyze data to test the usefulness of these theories.

- Selecting a **sample** is an important first step in doing research because it determines the extent to which the researcher's conclusions can be applied, or generalized, to people other than those who were studied. To ensure the **representativeness** of a sample, or the degree to which it accurately reflects some larger population, it must include individuals who represent the diversity of the larger population. Conducting a **national survey** is one way to ensure that a sample is representative of a broad range of people.

- Soliciting **self-reports** from children, usually by means of interviews, is one way to gather information about child development. Getting self-reports from children can be more difficult than getting them from adults, for children tend to be less attentive, slower to respond, and less likely to understand the questions put to them. Self-reports, however, are the only way to obtain information about such things as children's feelings and their unique perspectives on their lives.

- Another data-gathering method is to solicit information about a child from other people who know that child well, such as parents, siblings, teachers, and peers. Attempts to increase the accuracy of parents' reports about their children include focusing on specific current issues in the child's life and using structured procedures such as daily diaries or phone calls. Often, of course, there is no substitute for researchers' **direct observation** of children. Such observations can occur in natural settings, such as a child's home, or in a laboratory; in the latter case, a **structured observation** allows researchers to observe the child as

he performs some highly structured task. One limitation of direct observation is that, when children and parents know they are being watched, they act in more socially acceptable ways than they ordinarily would. To minimize such distortions, researchers try to observe unobtrusively for relatively long periods to enable subjects to adapt to the situation.

- When researchers use direct observations, they must decide what kinds of behaviors to record. They can record everything the participant does (a **specimen record**), record only particular events (**event sampling**), or identify which behaviors of a predetermined set occurred during a particular time period (**time sampling**). Because of the limitations of all data-gathering methods, researchers often use multiple measures of the same behaviors.

- The **correlational method** involves examining the relationship between two variables, such as children's aggressive behavior and the amount of aggression they watch on TV. If two factors are correlated, they are systematically related to each other, but a correlation does not tell us whether one factor causes the other.

- A **laboratory experiment** permits researchers to establish cause-and-effect relationships by assessing a specific behavior (such as aggression toward another person) in a controlled setting. A certain factor of interest (such as viewing TV violence) is introduced to an **experimental group** of participants, while a **control group** is exposed to some neutral factor. Researchers use **random assignment** to assign participants to either of these groups. The **dependent variable** is the behavior affected by the manipulation of the **independent variable.**

- Laboratory experiments cannot easily be generalized to real-world settings. A **field experiment,** in which a researcher deliberately produces a change in a real-life setting and measures the outcome there, has more **ecological validity.** However, researchers have to guard against **observer bias** when working in the field.

- Another way to increase the generalizability of findings is to conduct a **natural experiment.** In this case, the investigator measures the impact on children's behavior of some naturally occurring change. But because of lack of control over the independent variable and other factors that could affect behavior, it is often difficult to interpret the results of a natural experiment.

- The **case study method** takes an in-depth look at a single child or group (like a classroom), often (but not always) one with some uncommon feature that makes the child or group of special interest to developmentalists.

- The most common strategy for investigating developmental change over time is the **cross-sectional method,** in which researchers compare groups of children of different ages at a given point in time. This approach is economical in terms of both time and money, but it yields no information about change nor about the causes of any observed age-related differences in the child participants. The **longitudinal method** overcomes these two drawbacks of cross-sectional research because the researcher examines the same children at different points in their lives. But longitudinal research has its own disadvantages, including high cost, gradual loss of subjects, limited flexibility in using new insights or methods once the study has begun, and the question of the applicability of findings to other **age cohorts.**

- To overcome some of these limitations, researchers can use the **sequential method,** which combines features of both cross-sectional and longitudinal studies. This design enables researchers to compare not only groups of children of different ages at one point in time, and to track individual children over a period of years, but also to track age cohorts over a number of years.

- A major consideration when deciding on a research strategy is the effects the procedures will have on participants. Various government and institutional review boards, in addition to professional organizations, are involved in setting and maintaining guidelines for the proper treatment of human subjects in research. These guidelines include the right to **informed consent** before participating and the right not to be harmed. To determine if certain research procedures are ethical or not, the costs to participants must be carefully weighed against the potential benefits of increased knowledge about children's development.

EXPLORE AND DISCUSS

1. Do you think that all theories are equally useful for explaining all aspects of development? Or do you think that some theories are more helpful than others in explaining particular aspects of development, such as motor skills, social behavior, or cognitive development? If so, explain why.

2. Some theories, such as Freud's, are over 100 years old. Are old theories still relevant to contemporary children? Discuss the ways that you think some of the classic theories can be useful today.

3. What themes of development do you think are most important and why?

4. What research methods should you use if you want to determine what causes a particular behavior or event? Explain the difference between causation and correlation.

5. What are some of the limitations of longitudinal methods as a way of studying children? Do you think that these methods are worth the effort or not? Explain your answer.

6. Do you think the use of deception by Liebert and Baron in their study of the effects on children of viewing TV violence was ethical? Could it be justified on the grounds that we need to find a way to prevent aggression and violence among youth? What are some other ways researchers might evaluate the effect of TV violence on children?

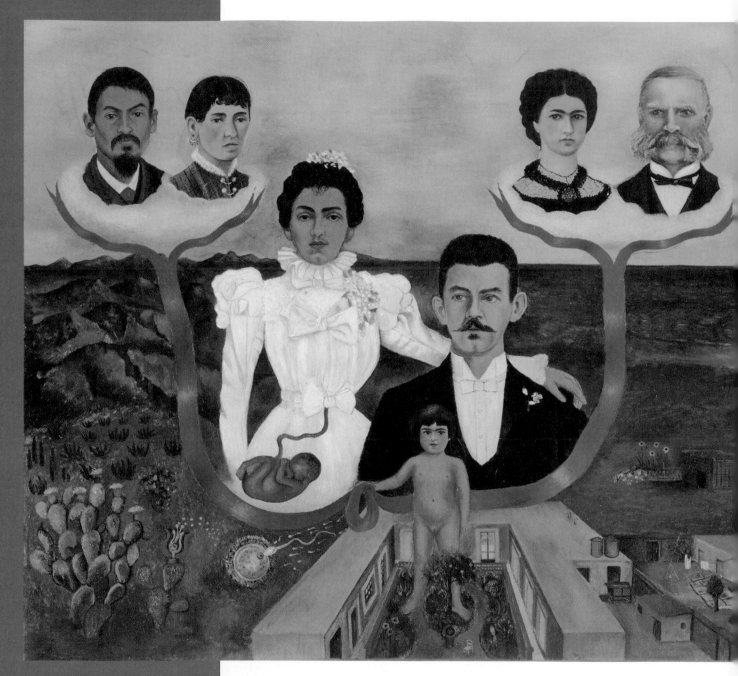

Frida Kahlo (1907–1954). *My Grandparents, My Parents, and I (Family Tree)*, 1936.
Museum of Modern Art, New York.

2.

Heredity and the Environment

One of the most striking things about newborns in a hospital nursery is their diversity. From the moment they're born, babies differ from one another not only in physical appearance but also in behavior. One baby may sleep most of the time; another may be quite alert, visually scanning the surroundings as if exploring them; a third baby may often be irritable and cry a lot. What contributes to these individual differences at such a young age? Before birth—according to some researchers, even before conception—transactions among a vast array of hereditary and environmental factors begin. Such transactions between genes and the environment make each newborn unique, and they continue to shape the individual's characteristics throughout his or her life span.

The concepts of genotype and phenotype provide a framework for exploring the interactions of genes and environment. A **genotype** is the particular set of genes that a person inherits from his or her parents and that determine such characteristics as height and eye color. With the exception of identical twins, no two people have exactly the same genotype. During the course of development, the genotype interacts with the environment in complex ways to produce the **phenotype,** which is the observable and measurable genetic expression of an individual's physical and behavioral characteristics. Psychologists study these kinds of characteristics—for example, motor abilities, intellectual skills, social behavior, emotionality, and personality traits—in an effort to increase our understanding of how genetic and environmental factors interact to produce each unique human being.

We begin this chapter by exploring what genes are and how they are transmitted from generation to generation. Next we examine how genes guide development, from determining a child's sex and many other of his or her characteristics to causing or predisposing children and adults to particular disorders. We go on to examine genetic testing and counseling for would-be parents who face the prospect of having a child with a troubling disorder, and we explore the growing field of genetic engineering. Then we consider heredity-environment

genotype The particular set of genes a person inherits from his or her parents.

phenotype The visible expression of the person's particular physical and behavioral characteristics; created by the interaction of a person's genotype, or genetic makeup, with the environment.

ovum The female germ cell, or egg.

sperm The male germ cell.

chromosomes Threadlike structures, located in the nucleus of a cell, that carry genetic information to help direct development.

meiosis The process by which a germ cell divides to produce new germ cells with only half the normal complement of chromosomes; thus male and female germ cells (sperm and ovum) each contain only 23 chromosomes so that when they unite, the new organism they form will have 46 chromosomes, half from each parent.

crossing over The process by which equivalent sections of homologous chromosomes switch places randomly, shuffling the genetic information each carries.

interactions: We discuss both the ways environmental factors influence the actual expression of an individual child's genetic makeup and, conversely, the way that genetic makeup can shape the environment. Finally, to further our understanding of how genes and the environment interact, we explore the relative contributions of these two forces to intellectual characteristics and functioning, to temperament and personality, and to the presence or absence in a child of mental and emotional distress.

THE PROCESS OF GENETIC TRANSMISSION

In the dark, warm, moist environment of a woman's *oviduct,* sperm and egg unite to create a new living organism with the potential to develop into a human being. This new organism, called a *zygote* (we discuss the zygote in detail in Chapter 3), owes its existence to this union of the male and female gametes, or reproductive cells, each of which carries genetic information. The egg, or **ovum,** the largest cell in the human body, is about 90,000 times as heavy as the sperm that penetrates it; nevertheless, it is still quite small, smaller even than the period at the end of this sentence. The **sperm,** the smallest cell in the body, packs its hereditary information in its head and uses the rest of its tiny body, composed of a long, whiplike tail, to propel itself through the woman's reproductive system in search of the ovum. One of the marvels of human development is that from these microscopic beginnings and over a period of just nine months, a 7- or 8-pound baby, 20 or so inches long, grows and becomes ready to enter the world.

Chromosomes and Genes

Chromosomes and genes are located inside a central cellular structure called a *nucleus.* At the moment of human conception, when sperm and egg unite, 23 chromosomes from each of these cells join together to create 23 chromosome *pairs,* or 46 chromosomes in all. The threadlike **chromosomes** carry genetic information that helps direct development. An individual's 46 chromosomes are said to come in 23 pairs because each chromosome contributed by the father's sperm is *homologous* (similar in shape and function) to one of the chromosomes contributed by the mother's egg. Copies of these original 23 homologous pairs of chromosomes are passed on to every cell in a person's body with one exception: the reproductive cells. Each reproductive cell contains only 23 single chromosomes instead of the usual 46 because during its development it undergoes a special form of cell division, called **meiosis,** in which its 23 chromosome pairs are halved (see Figure 2-1). The reason for this halving becomes clear when sperm and egg unite. Now 23 chromosomes from the sperm combine with 23 chromosomes from the egg to produce the correct number of 46 chromosomes for a new human being.

Both meiosis and sexual reproduction are crucial to the process of genetic transmission because each facilitates the production of a tremendous diversity of genetic combinations. During meiosis, when a male's or a female's set of chromosomes is halved to produce a germ cell—sperm or egg—that halving process mixes chromosomes that originated from the individual's father with chromosomes that originated from the individual's mother. Moreover, this mixing process is totally random. The only requirement is that one of each pair of homologous chromosomes end up in the new reproductive cell. This random assortment of homologous chromosomes makes possible the production of about 8 million different chromosome combinations in both a female's eggs and a male's sperm. Further genetic variability is added during meiosis by a process called **crossing over,** in which equivalent sections of homologous chromosomes randomly switch places (Figure 2-1), so that genetic information is shuffled even more. In view of all of these shuffling and sorting processes, it is no wonder the chances of any given man and woman producing two genetically identical children is one in many trillion (except, of course, when a single fertilized egg splits into identical twins).

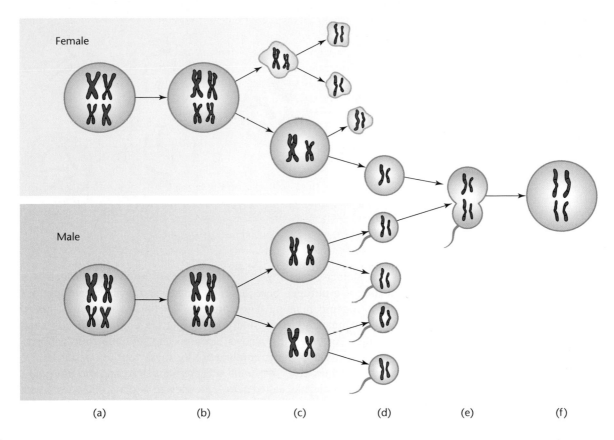

Female

Male

(a)   (b)   (c)   (d)   (e)   (f)

Figure 2-1   Meiosis: The reproductive cells divide to produce new germ cells with half the normal complement of chromosomes

As meiosis begins, all the chromosomes in the cell replicate themselves, as if they were about to undergo *mitosis,* or normal cell division (see Figure 3-2). In (a) we see the results of this replication (we show cells with only 4 chromosomes, or 2 pairs, rather than the full complement of 46 chromosomes, or 23 pairs). In (b) *crossing over* between chromosomes ensures the zygote's unique genetic inheritance. In (c), the male chromosome pairs separate to form 2 cells, each with 23 chromosomes. In the female, 2 cells are also formed, but one is nonfunctional and may or may not produce 2 more nonfunctional cells. In (d) the chromosomes separate once again, in the male forming 4 sperm cells and in the female a single ovum and a fourth nonfunctional cell. (The genetic material in the female's nonfunctional cells degenerates.) When a sperm cell fertilizes an ovum (e), a zygote is formed (f), with 23 chromosome pairs, or 46 in all.

In Chapter 3 we will follow the progress of the fertilized egg, or zygote, as it develops within the mother's body, becoming an embryo, then a fetus, and finally, at birth, a living human infant. Here we may ask, however, how the single cell created by the union of egg and sperm becomes a complex living being. By a process called **mitosis,** which occurs in both **autosomes** (chromosomes that contain matching pairs) and sex chromosomes (which we discuss on page 52), a cell duplicates its chromosomes and then divides into daughter cells that have the exact same number of chromosomes as their parent cell (see Figure 2-2). Thus the zygote divides and continues to divide, each time producing new cells that have the full complement of 46 chromosomes and gradually becoming a multicellular organism.

Genes, DNA, and Proteins

Scientists know that the binding element of a chromosome is a long, thin molecule of **deoxyribonucleic acid,** or **DNA.** This molecule, which stores genetic information and transmits it during reproduction, is made up of building blocks called nucleotides that are held together by two long, twisted parallel strands that resemble the two side

mitosis The process in which a body cell divides in two, first duplicating its chromosomes so that the new daughter cells produced each contain the usual 46 chromosomes.

autosomes The 22 paired non-sex chromosomes.

deoxyribonucleic acid (DNA) A ladderlike molecule that stores genetic information in cells and transmits it during reproduction.

Figure 2-2

Mitosis: The zygote divides and keeps dividing to produce a multicellular organism
In (a) we see a zygote with only 4 chromosomes rather than the 46 each cell normally contains. In (b), each chromosome splits in half (lengthwise) to produce a duplicate of itself. Next, in (c), the duplicates move away from each other as the cell begins to divide. Finally, in (d), the cell has divided in two, and each new cell has the same set of chromosomes as the other and as the original parent cell (a).

nucleotide A compound containing a nitrogen base, a simple sugar, and a phosphate group.

gene A portion of DNA located at a particular site on a chromosome and that codes for the production of certain kinds of proteins.

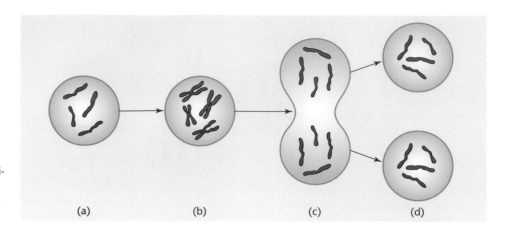

(a)   (b)   (c)   (d)

rails of a spiral staircase (see Figure 2-3). From each **nucleotide,** which is a compound consisting of a nitrogen base, a simple sugar, and a phosphate group, one of four different nitrogen-containing bases projects out toward the base opposite it to form one of the staircase's "risers." Only bases that are compatible with each other will bond together. As Figure 2-3 shows, adenine and thymine form a bond, as do cytosine and guanine, but no other combination of these four is possible in DNA.

How do chromosomes carry the units of hereditary information? Portions of the chromosome's DNA molecule, called **genes,** are located at particular sites on the chromosome, where they code for the production of certain kinds of proteins. The genetic code is "written" in the order in which the four bases occur in the gene, much as the

Figure 2-3

The structure of DNA
The two twisted strands of DNA form a kind of spiral structure that is composed of the complementary base pairs of nucleotides, adenosine-thymine or guanine-cytosine.

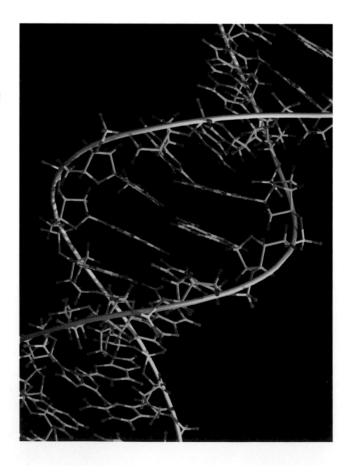

code for the meaning of a word is written in the order of its letters. Genes trigger the production of proteins only when a particular change in the environment signals them to activate. Now the gene, or DNA segment, splits down the middle so that its pairs of bases are no longer joined. According to the rules by which the four bases bond with each other, "free" nucleotides surrounding the gene connect to the exposed bases to form new pairs. The resulting copy of the gene then travels from the cell nucleus to the body of the cell, where protein synthesis takes place. The copy acts as a template for building protein molecules: Each sequence of three bases codes for one of the many amino acids (organic compounds) that combine to form different kinds of proteins.

When the protein molecule is assembled, it is ready to begin its work in the body. Each of the many different types of proteins serves a different function. Some proteins give cells their characteristic physical properties. For example, bone cells get their hardness, skin cells their elasticity, and nerve cells their capacity to conduct electrical impulses from the different kinds of proteins they possess. Other proteins do many other jobs within the body, such as triggering chemical reactions, carrying chemical messages, fighting foreign invaders, and regulating genes. It's the combined action of all the proteins in a human body that composes a living organism, each of whose specialized cells and organ systems has distinctive characteristics.

GENETIC INFLUENCES ON DEVELOPMENT

Scientists are learning more and more about how genes exert their influences on development. The central message they have gleaned is that, at least with respect to behavior, *genes never work in isolation, but always in combination with environmental influences* (Plomin et al., 2001; Turkheimer, 2000). A gene alone is useless. Its coded message cannot be "read" unless it is embedded in an environment that signals when and how it should respond. But because the topic of genetic-environmental interactions is so complex, in this and the next major section we'll focus on genetic influences apart from environmental ones. We'll return to the critical determining process of gene-environment interaction in the last two sections of the chapter.

The Transmission of Traits: A Basic Model

Two basic concepts are crucial to understanding genetic influences on development. First, at any given gene's position on two homologous chromosomes, there can be more than one form of that gene; these alternate forms are called the gene's **alleles.** One of these alleles comes from the person's mother, the other from the person's father. Second, if the alleles from both parents are the same, the person is said to be **homozygous** for that particular gene or for the trait associated with it. If the two alleles are different, the person is **heterozygous** for that particular characteristic. If *A* represents one allele and *a* another, the individual clearly can have one of three possible combinations: *AA, aa,* or *Aa (aA).*

When a person has one of the first two of these combinations (*AA* or *aa*), she or he is homozygous for the trait coded by the two identical alleles. Thus, for example, a person with two alleles for dark skin will have dark skin, and a person with two alleles for light skin will be light. When a person has a variant of the third combination, however, he or she is heterozygous for the trait for which each allele codes, and the result of this combination may vary. Sometimes the combination of two dissimilar alleles will produce an outcome intermediate between the traits for which each single allele codes. For instance, a light-skinned parent and a dark-skinned parent may produce a child of intermediate skin color. A second possibility is that both alleles will express their traits simultaneously; that is, the two traits will combine but will

allele An alternate form of a gene; typically, a gene has two alleles, one inherited from the individual's mother, and one from the father.

homozygous The state of an individual whose alleles for a particular trait from each parent are the same.

heterozygous The state of an individual whose alleles for a particular trait from each parent are different.

Table 2-1

Some common dominant and recessive traits

Dominant	Recessive
Curly hair	Straight hair
Normal amount of hair	Baldness
Dark hair	Light or blond hair
Blond or brunette hair	Red hair
Normal skin coloring	Albinism (lack of skin pigmentation)
Roman nose	Straight nose
Thick lips	Thin lips
Cheek dimples	No dimples
Double-jointedness	Normal joints
Normal color vision	Color "blindness" (red and green not distinguished)
Farsightedness	Nearsightedness (myopia)
Immunity to poison ivy	Susceptibility to poison ivy
Normal hearing	Congenital deafness
Normal blood clotting	Failure of blood to clot (hemophilia)
Normal protein metabolism	Phenylketonuria
Normal red blood cells	Sickle-cell anemia

codominance A genetic pattern in which heterozygous alleles express the variants of the trait for which they code simultaneously and with equal force.

dominant The more powerful of two alleles in a heterozygous combination.

recessive The weaker of two alleles in a heterozygous combination.

sex chromosomes In both males and females, the 23rd pair of chromosomes, which determine the individual's sex and are responsible for sex-related characteristics; in females, this pair normally comprises two X chromosomes, in males an X and a Y chromosome.

not blend. For example, the allele for blood type A in combination with the allele for blood type B produces the blood type AB, which has both kinds of antigens, A and B, on the surface of the red blood cells. This pattern is called **codominance** of the two alleles. A third possibility is that in a heterozygous combination, the characteristic associated with only one of the alleles may be expressed. The more powerful allele is said to be **dominant** over the weaker, **recessive** allele. An example is the dominant allele for curly hair combined with the recessive allele for straight hair; this combination produces a person whose hair is curly (Table 2-1). Fortunately, many deleterious alleles are recessive, which greatly reduces the incidence of genetic abnormalities in people. One of the reasons why many societies prohibit marriage between close blood relatives is that a harmful recessive allele possessed by one relative is more apt to be possessed by other relatives as well, thus increasing the chances that children of their intermarriage will be homozygous for the harmful trait.

Genes on the Sex Chromosomes: Exceptions to the Rule

The genes on the sex chromosomes provide an exception to the rule we've just discussed, for not all of these genes have two alleles. But before we examine this special situation, we must back up a bit in our story. As we said earlier, in every human being, 1 of the 23 pairs, or 2 of the 46 human chromosomes, are called **sex chromosomes;** these chromosomes have the important function of determining the individual's sex, and they differ in males and females (see Figure 2-4). A female has two large, homologous sex chromosomes, the XX chromosomes, one from her mother, the

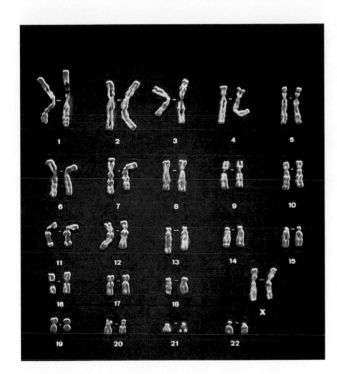

Figure 2-4

Normal chromosome arrangements
This *karyotype,* or photograph of chromosome pairs, shows the normal lineup of chromosomes in a female. The 22 pairs are similar in both sexes, but the 23rd pair differs. In the female, this pair has two X chromosomes, or an XX pattern, marked in the photo as "X." In the male, this pair has one X and one Y chromosome, or an XY pattern, discernible by the smaller size of the Y chromosome.

other from her father. A male, on the other hand, has one X chromosome from his mother and a smaller Y chromosome from his father; this pattern is referred to as XY. Because an X chromosome is about five times longer than a Y chromosome, it carries more genes. This means that some genes on a male's X chromosome will have no equivalent genes on his Y chromosome, and as a result, any recessive **X-linked genes** will automatically be expressed; the male's Y chromosome has no counteracting dominant genes. In females, X-linked recessive genes are expressed much less frequently because females, who have two X chromosomes, have a chance of inheriting a dominant and counteracting allele on the other X chromosome.

Hemophilia, a disorder in which the blood fails to clot, is an example of an X-linked recessive characteristic. Because the allele for hemophilia is recessive, a female who inherits it will have normally clotting blood as long as her second allele, inherited from her other parent, does not code for hemophilia. Only if she is homozygous for the recessive allele will her blood clotting be impaired. If a male is unfortunate enough to receive the hemophilia allele on his X chromosome, he is in greater danger of developing hemophilia. Like the female, he will develop the disorder if he receives another hemophilia allele on his Y chromosome; however, he will also develop hemophilia if he receives no counteracting gene on his Y chromosome. Only if the small collection of alleles on his Y chromosome happens to include one for normal blood clotting will he escape the disorder.

Many other X-linked recessive disorders are more common in men than in women, including diabetes, color blindness, certain forms of night blindness, atrophy of the optic nerve, one form of muscular dystrophy, and a disorder resulting in an inability to produce antibodies to fight certain bacterial infections. Males' higher rates of mortality as compared with those of females—whether through miscarriage before they're born, death in infancy, or early death in adulthood—are partly attributable to males' greater vulnerability to X-linked disorders. Even resistance to certain childhood diseases appears to be X-linked. Thus, although 120 males are conceived for every 100 females and 106 males are born for every 100 females, this numerical imbalance between the sexes is rapidly eliminated over the course of development.

X-linked genes Genes that are carried on the X chromosome and that, in males, may have no analogous genes on the Y chromosome.

hemophilia A disorder, caused by an X-linked recessive gene, in which the blood fails to clot; found more often in males than in females.

Interactions among Genes

So far we have presented a relatively simple genetic model in which a single allele or a single pair of alleles determines a particular characteristic. Although this model applies to certain human traits, many other characteristics are determined not by one pair of alleles, but by many pairs acting together. In fact, most characteristics of greatest interest to psychologists, such as intelligence, creativity, sociability, and style of emotional expression, are probably influenced by the interaction of multiple genes.

This interaction may help explain why some traits influenced by genes do not tend to run in families. Development of such traits usually depends on a certain configuration of many genes, and that particular configuration is not likely to be passed on from parent to child. A likely example is genius. Why are geniuses sometimes born to parents of quite ordinary intelligence, and why do geniuses go on to produce children who are not unusually talented? Such cases make sense if you consider genius a trait that emerges from a particular configuration of many genes, all interacting with each other (Lykken, McGue, Tellegen, & Bouchard, 1992; Turkheimer, 2000).

To further complicate the nature of genetic inheritance, we now know that a single pair of alleles may influence more than one trait. Moreover, they may do this not directly but indirectly, through their effects on the expression of still other genes. Genes that act in this manner are called **modifier genes.** One example is the modifier gene that affects the early development of *cataract,* a condition in which the lens of the eye becomes clouded, obscuring vision. Although the occurrence of early cataract is determined by a dominant gene, the nature of cataract formation is influenced by modifier genes. These kinds of genes determine, for example, whether the cloudiness forms along the periphery of the lens or at its center.

modifier genes Genes that exert their influence indirectly, by affecting the expression of still other genes.

Genetic Disorders

Genes can have both positive and negative effects on development. As we've seen, people can inherit harmful alleles of certain genes such as the ones that cause hemophilia or early cataract. It's also possible for a person to receive whole sets of genes that are not only harmful but fatal. In this section we will look at some of the genetic abnormalities that can interfere with normal development. Table 2-2 summarizes the chief characteristics of some of the disorders these abnormalities cause.

WHY HARMFUL ALLELES SURVIVE   A major reason why potentially harmful alleles survive is that they are not harmful in the heterozygous state; that is, when a person inherits both a normal allele and a recessive one. A good example is the allele that causes **phenylketonuria,** or **PKU.** PKU is caused by a recessive allele that fails to produce an enzyme necessary to metabolize the protein phenylalanine present in milk, the basic diet of infants. As long as a person also possesses a normal allele, the PKU allele has no ill effects. In fact, about 1 out of every 20 European Americans carries the recessive PKU allele and doesn't even know it. Problems arise only in infants unfortunate enough to be homozygous for the recessive gene. After birth, when these babies start ingesting milk, their bodies cannot break down phenylalanine. If these infants are not treated, toxic substances accumulate in their bodies, damaging the nervous system and causing mental retardation. Figure 2-5 shows that two heterozygous parents have a one in four chance of producing an infant who is homozygous for PKU. Most people who carry the PKU allele also have a normal allele, so they do not succumb to the disorder. Because these individuals survive and reproduce, however, the defective allele also survives from generation to generation, even though its effect may be seen only 25 percent of the time (when these individuals mate).

Some potentially harmful alleles may survive because they are actually beneficial in combination with a normal allele. An example of this kind of survival is provided

phenylketonuria (PKU) A disease caused by a recessive allele that fails to produce an enzyme necessary to metabolize the protein phenylalanine; if untreated immediately at birth, damages the nervous system and causes mental retardation.

Table 2-2 Some disorders that are caused by genetic defects

Disorder and Its Nature	U.S. Incidence	Cause	Method of Diagnosis	Current Methods of Treatment and Prevention
Hemophilia Blood disease characterized by poor clotting ability	1/10,000 (80–90% males)	Heredity: X-linked recessive trait	Blood tests	Hemophilia is treated at present by transfusions of clotting factors. New gene-splicing techniques may make it possible to provide these factors without running the risk of transmitting bloodborne infections through donated blood products.
Diabetes mellitus Body's inability to metabolize carbohydrates and maintain proper glucose levels	Type I - 1/200 Type II - 1/50	Heredity: multigene, exaggerated by environmental factors	Blood and urine tests	Sufferers can often control this disorder by special diet alone. In other cases oral medication and/or insulin injections are required to maintain the body's equilibrium.
Phenylketonuria (PKU) Inability to convert phenylalanine to tyrosine; untreated, leads to mental retardation	1/10,000	Heredity: recessive allele	Blood tests prenatally or at birth	Genetic counseling can indicate risk that a couple will have a PKU child. Modern genetic techniques can detect recessive alleles before such a child's birth, and immediately after birth a special diet can be instituted to prevent the disorder's toxic effects.
Sickle-cell anemia Blood disease characterized by malformation of red blood cells that are low in oxygen	1/600 African American infants affected; 1/13 African Americans are carriers	Heredity: two recessive alleles in combination	Blood tests	Blood transfusions have until recently been the only treatment. Drugs that turn on a normally dormant fetal hemoglobin gene may help prevent symptoms.
Down syndrome (trisomy 21) Physically and mentally retarded development; sometimes cardiovascular and respiratory abnormalities	1/1,000	Heredity: extra full or partial chromosome 21	Amniocentesis, alphafetoprotein assay, chorionic villi sampling, chromosome analysis	Special physical training; special education, including speech therapy. Surgical correction of problems with the heart and hearing are sometimes necessary.

(continues)

Table 2-2 *(concluded)*

Disorder and Its Nature	U.S. Incidence	Cause	Method of Diagnosis	Current Methods of Treatment and Prevention
Turner (XO) syndrome				
Underdeveloped secondary sex characteristics; infertility; short stature; social immaturity; webbed neck; cardiovascular and renal abnormalities	1/1,200–4,000 females	Chromosomal abnormality: only one X chromosome instead of two	Blood tests	Hormone therapy can promote development of secondary sex characteristics. Counseling; special education to lessen deficits in spatial understanding.
Triple X (XXX) syndrome				
Some physical abnormalities, including menstrual irregularities and premature menopause; some limitations on cognitive abilities	1/1,000 females	Chromosomal abnormality: extra X chromosome	Blood tests	Special education to improve cognitive skills.
Klinefelter's (XXY) syndrome				
Some female physical characteristics; sterility; mild to severe cognitive difficulties	1/1,000 males	Chromosomal abnormality: extra X chromosome	Blood tests	Testosterone treatments can enhance development of male secondary sex characteristics as well as sexual interest and assertiveness. Special education to improve cognitive skills.
XYY syndrome				
Unusual height; some cognitive impairment; attention deficit	1/1,000 males	Chromosomal abnormality: extra Y chromosome	Blood tests	Special education as needed.
Fragile X syndrome				
Physical abnormalities; mental retardation that deepens with time; psychological and social problems	1/2,000–4,000 males 1/5,000 females	Heredity: breaking of an X chromosome near its tip due to multiple repeats	Blood tests	No known treatment.

Sources: Lambert & Drack, 1996; Lin, Verp, & Sabbagha, 1993; Martini, 1995; Money, 1993; Nightingale & Meister, 1987; Postlethwait & Hopson, 1995.

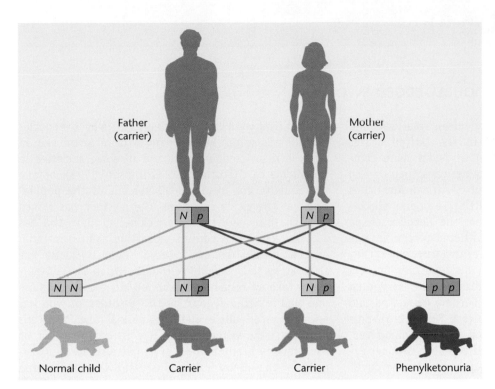

Father
(carrier)

Mother
(carrier)

Normal child   Carrier   Carrier   Phenylketonuria

Figure 2-5

Genetic transmission of phenylketonuria
When both parents carry the recessive allele for phenylketonuria, they have a one in four chance of producing a child with the disorder. If their dominant genes for normality (*N*) are passed to their offspring, the child will be normal. If the child receives one dominant and one recessive gene (*p*) it will be a "carrier"; that is, the child will not have the disorder, but it may pass the recessive allele to its own children. And of course if the child receives recessive genes from both parents, it will have phenylketonuria.

by a disease to which some African Americans as well as people in some African countries are subject: sickle-cell anemia. Box 2.1 describes this disorder and how its allele actually helps some people survive another life-threatening disease: malaria.

CHROMOSOME ABNORMALITIES   Developmental disorders can be caused not only by single genes or gene groups but also by defects in entire chromosomes. Almost 1 percent of all newborns have diagnosable chromosome abnormalities, and it has been estimated that 60 percent of early spontaneous abortions and 5 percent of later miscarriages are attributable to aberrations in chromosomes. Normally, such chromosome defects are not present in a child's parents, as are the defective alleles we've been discussing. Instead, they generally arise during the process of meiosis, when eggs or sperm are formed. In a great many instances, the aberration proves lethal, and the zygote produced by the union of sperm and egg spontaneously aborts. But sometimes, particularly when certain chromosomes are involved, a zygote is able to survive the abnormal condition, and a baby with a chromosome defect is born.

Down Syndrome   **Down syndrome** is characterized by physical and mental retardation and a distinctive physical appearance. People with this syndrome are typically of short stature and usually have almond-shaped eyes with a fold in the eyelid, as well as one or more other unusual physical characteristics. More troublesome is their heightened susceptibility to such illnesses as leukemia, heart disorders, and respiratory infections and their moderate to severe mental retardation. However, with advances in the treatment of these physical disorders (such as the use of antibiotics for pneumonia), the life spans of people with Down syndrome have greatly increased; currently about 70 percent of individuals with Down syndrome live into their sixties. Unfortunately, they are at greater risk for developing Alzheimer's disease in later life than the average person (Hayes & Batshaw, 1993).

Probably the most well-known chromosome disorder, Down syndrome is caused by a deviation in the set of chromosomes labeled number 21. Instead of a pair of these

Down syndrome A form of chromosome abnormality in which the person suffers disabling physical and mental development and is highly susceptible to such illnesses as leukemia, heart disorders, and respiratory infections.

Box 2.1
Perspectives on Diversity

SICKLE-CELL ANEMIA: A DOUBLE-EDGED SWORD

Sickle-cell anemia, a severe and often fatal disorder, affects about 60,000 people in the United States (Postlethwait & Hopson, 1995). It is far more common, however, among African Americans than among other Americans; about 8 percent of African Americans carry a recessive sickle-cell allele. The term **sickle-cell anemia** gets its name from the peculiar shape that the red blood cells of an afflicted person assume when they are low in oxygen (for instance, when they have just released oxygen to hard-working muscle cells). Rather than remaining disk-shaped, as normal red blood cells do, these cells become elongated and bent into the shape of a sickle (see Figure 2-6). This shape causes them to get stuck in small blood vessels, especially in the joints and the abdomen, resulting in severe pain, tissue damage, and possible death if critical vessels in the brain and lungs become blocked. Moreover, because these cells are abnormal, the spleen continually removes them from the blood, giving rise to chronic *anemia* (too few red blood cells). An allele on chromosome number 11 is the cause of sickle-cell anemia. When its companion allele is also recessive for this trait, the person develops the disorder. Among people who have one sickle-cell allele and one normal one, however, red blood cells rarely sickle except under conditions of low oxygen, such as in mountain climbing or under anesthesia, and, as a result, such people usually suffer no harmful effects from the defective allele.

Scientists were once puzzled as to why the sickle-cell allele is so prevalent among African Americans, in many African communities, and in some societies in the Middle East (Postlethwait & Hopson, 1995). Among the Baamba, for instance, 39 percent of the population has the sickle-cell gene. The mystery was solved with the discovery that the sickle-cell allele also has a positive effect: It confers protection against malaria, another deadly disease found in almost exactly the same areas as the sickle-cell allele. When malaria parasites take up residence in the red blood cells of someone who is heterozygous for this disorder, or who has one sickle-cell allele and one normal one, the cells become sickle-shaped when low in oxygen, just as such cells typically behave in people who are homozygous for the allele. But in this case, when the spleen removes the parasite-containing cells from the blood, it removes the malaria parasites as well. As a result, people with only one sickle-cell allele have built-in resistance to malaria—an enormous aid to survival.

Because the defective allele enables these people to fight off malaria, they tend to live longer than people who haven't a sickle-cell gene to protect them, and they reproduce more often; thus they pass the gene on to subsequent generations in increasing numbers. In this way, a potentially harmful gene not only survives but flourishes. Of course, for the person who is homozygous for sickle-cell anemia, or has two recessive genes for this disorder, the illness itself is so life-threatening

sickle-cell anemia A disorder, caused by a recessive gene, in which the red blood cells become distorted when low in oxygen, causing fatigue, shortness of breath, and severe pain and posing a threat to life from blockage of crucial blood vessels.

chromosomes, the person with Down syndrome has three chromosomes, which is why the disorder is also called *trisomy 21*. The extra 21st chromosome most often comes from the mother's egg, when her homologous pair of 21st chromosomes fails to separate during meiosis. Male sperm carry the extra chromosome in only about 5 percent of cases (Antonarakis & Down Syndrome Collaboration Group, 1991). And, for reasons that are not yet fully understood, this error occurs more often as women age (see Table 2-3). The father's age matters, too; the rates of Down syndrome births are higher for men over 50 (Hayes & Batshaw, 1993). Scientists have recently identified a gene that may play a role in the mental retardation associated with Down syndrome, but other genes likely play a role as well (Smith et al., 1997).

Infants with Down syndrome may develop fairly normally for their first six months, but unless they receive special therapy their rate of intellectual growth begins to decline after about a year. These children are generally slow to learn to speak and often have difficulty articulating words. They also have trouble attending to, discriminating, and interpreting complex or subtle information in their environments.

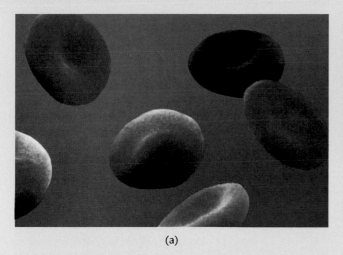

(a)

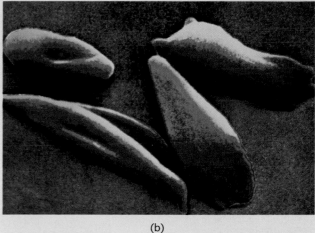

(b)

Figure 2-6 Red blood cell changes in sickle-cell anemia

Normal red blood cells are disk shaped (a), but in sickle-cell anemia these cells become sickled, or distorted, when they are low in oxygen (b). Among the symptoms of this disorder are pain in the joints and abdomen, chronic fatigue, and shortness of breath.

that the person's enhanced resistance to malaria is of little benefit to him or her.

Until recently, there was little hope for victims of sickle-cell anemia. The successful in utero treatment of a 4-month-old fetus for a condition called *severe combined immunodeficiency*, however, has made it possible now to think of treating sickle-cell anemia and other immune-deficiency and blood diseases before birth. In this groundbreaking surgery, physicians injected bone marrow cells from the fetus's father into its abdomen by means of a long needle inserted through the mother's abdomen, using ultrasound as a guide (Postlethwait & Hopson, 1995). Nearly a year and a half after his birth, the child was healthy and showed no sign of the rare genetic disease that had threatened his life outside the womb. Another promising treatment involves using a drug to turn on a gene for fetal hemoglobin that is normally dormant after birth. This fetal version of the gene is usually normal and reduces sickling (Atweh et al., 1999).

Maternal Age	Down Syndrome Detected at 9 to 11 Weeks by CVS	Down Syndrome Detected at 16 Weeks by Amniocentesis	Frequency of Down Syndrome among Births
20–24			1/1,400
25–29			1/1,100
30			1/900
35	1/250	1/250	1/385
40	1/80	1/70	1/100
45	1/25	1/25	1/40
Over 45	1/20	1/15	1/25

Table 2-3

Risk of Down syndrome infant, as detected by prenatal tests and at birth, by maternal age

Sources: Gardner & Sutherland, 1996; Hsu, 1998.

Children with Down syndrome can become active, achieving adults. Chris Burke, an actor and a Down person, starred in "Life Goes On," a TV evening sitcom, in which actress Patti Lupone played his mother.

Turner syndrome A form of chromosome abnormality found in females in which secondary sex characteristics develop only if female hormones are administered, and abnormal formation of internal reproductive organs causes permanent sterility.

Klinefelter's syndrome A form of chromosome abnormality in which a male inherits an extra X sex chromosome, resulting in the XXY pattern, many feminine physical characteristics, language deficits, and, sometimes, mental retardation.

These difficulties are reflected in problems of communication between children with Down syndrome and their caregivers; often parents are induced to talk more and to be more directive than the parents of normal children (Hodapp, 2002). Children with Down syndrome develop more competence when their caregivers provide them with stimulation and encourage them to be attentive to and involved in their environments. Although these efforts are more apt to enhance emotional, social, and motor development than cognitive development, training can help children with Down syndrome learn to read and write (Gibson & Harris, 1988; Hodapp, 2002). A number of children with Down syndrome become competent adults who hold jobs and live independently in group homes. A few people with Down syndrome have become actors and authors.

Sex-Chromosome Anomalies Abnormalities may also arise in the sex chromosomes, where they are rarely fatal to a developing organism but lead to various physical and physiological defects. For example, some females are born with only one X chromosome rather than the normal XX pattern. Usually this occurs because the father's sperm contained neither an X nor a Y chromosome. Girls with this XO pattern, called **Turner syndrome,** remain short, with stubby fingers, misshaped necks, and unusually shaped mouths and ears. They usually have normal intelligence, and they tend to be docile, pleasant, and not easily upset. As teenagers, they do not develop secondary sex characteristics, such as breasts and pubic hair, unless given female hormones. Because their internal reproductive organs do not develop normally, they remain sterile throughout their lives. Women with Turner syndrome tend to have problems in social relationships because they are immature and lacking in assertiveness (McCauley, Ito, & Kay, 1986). These problems are related in part to others' responses to these women's physical appearance. More important, women with Turner syndrome have difficulty discriminating and interpreting emotional cues and facial expressions in others, skills essential for appropriate social interactions (McCauley, Kay, Ito, & Treeler, 1987).

Another sex chromosome abnormality found in females is the XXX pattern, in which a girl inherits three X chromosomes instead of the normal two. These *triple-X* girls appear normal physically and have normal secondary sexual development, but their cognitive abilities are affected, especially their short-term memory and verbal skills (Robinson, Bender, & Linden, 1992; Rovet, Netley, Keenan, Bailey, & Stewart, 1996). When a male inherits an extra X chromosome, producing an XXY pattern known as **Klinefelter's syndrome,** he is sterile and has many female characteristics, such as breast development and a rounded, broad-hipped figure. Like the triple-X female, he tends to have verbal language deficits and reading problems and is sometimes retarded (Netley, 1986; Robinson, Bender, & Linden, 1992). Also likely to suffer some cognitive impairment is the male who inherits an extra Y chromosome, the XYY pattern once thought to be accompanied by excessive aggressiveness. Although XYY men are generally taller than normal men, they have not been shown to be any more aggressive or violent than others (Burns & Bottino, 1989).

Finally, some people carry an X chromosome that appears to be pinched or narrowed in some areas, causing it to be quite fragile. This **fragile X syndrome** is more frequent in males than females. It accounts for about 5 percent of retarded males whose IQ scores range between 30 and 55, although not all males with the syndrome are retarded (Hagerman & Cronister, 1996; Jacobs, 1991). In addition, people with fragile X syndrome often have physical abnormalities and psychological and social problems. Cleft palate, seizures, abnormal EEGs, and disorders of the eyes are some of the more common physical symptoms. Psychological and social problems include anxiety, hyperactivity, attention deficits, and abnormal communication patterns. Males may have deficits in social interaction, and females may be more likely to suffer from depression (Hagerman & Cronister, 1996).

In considering these chromosomal anomalies, it is important to remember that the environment influences the way genes are expressed. The severity of the symptoms that arise from hereditary disorders is often related to the degree to which the person has a supportive environment (Evans and Gray, 2000; Hodapp, 2002). We will return to the topic of how environmental conditions can lessen the effects of genetic abnormalities a little later in this chapter. It is also important to remember that with special therapeutic and educational methods, some manifestations of these abnormalities may be modified.

GENETIC COUNSELING AND GENETIC ENGINEERING

Advances in biology and genetics have opened new opportunities for shaping and controlling some aspects of development. For some time now, it has been possible to sample cells from a developing fetus to determine whether the fetus carries genes for any of the disorders we have discussed, as well as for many others. With this knowledge, gained through *genetic counseling,* parents may choose either to abort the birth of a child with abnormalities or to prepare for the arrival of such a child, who will need special care. For many people this is a very difficult choice. For example, ethical and religious beliefs prevent some couples from choosing abortion. In addition, because environmental factors can affect genetic predispositions, we cannot know for sure whether the anomalies we detect will inevitably result in serious problems. For example, although some XYY males engage in criminal activity, such men are relatively few; what would be the ethical implications, then, of a parental decision to abort a fetus with this chromosomal pattern?

More recent advances in the study of genes and their influence have made it possible to offer what we might call preventive genetic counseling. In this work, couples wanting to have a child can themselves be tested for various defective genes. If they find that they carry defective alleles, they may elect to adopt a child or to conceive a child through one of various *assisted reproductive techniques* in which a donor's egg or sperm may be substituted for one of their own germ cells. These techniques were originally developed to make parenting possible for couples who could not conceive and bear a child of their own. Box 2.2 describes some of the most common of these techniques.

Prenatal Diagnostic Techniques

It is possible that someday we will be able to replace defective genes in a fetus through gene therapy, thus preventing a genetically determined disorder before it happens. Already, physicians have been successful in injecting healthy bone marrow into a fetus to counteract an autoimmune disorder (Anderson, 1995). Before we discuss the exciting new work in this area, however, let us look at the major existing methods for testing the viability and health of a fetus.

fragile X syndrome A form of chromosomal abnormality, more common in males than in females, in which an area near the tip of the X chromosome is narrowed and made fragile due to a failure to condense during cell division. Symptoms include physical, cognitive, and social problems.

Box 2.2
Child Psychology in Action

THE NEW REPRODUCTIVE TECHNOLOGIES

The technique of *in vitro fertilization*—literally, fertilization "in glass" or in a glass dish—is most often used to make childbearing possible for a woman whose fallopian tubes are blocked. Physicians administer hormones to the woman to stimulate ovulation and then remove mature eggs from her ovary. They then place the eggs in a nourishing solution in a glass *petri* dish where they are mixed with the husband's sperm. If fertilization is successful, the zygote begins to divide, and when it is at the eight-cell stage, approximately two to four days later, it is inserted into the woman's uterus. For the pregnancy to be successful, the embryo must implant itself in the lining of the uterus. If the woman's uterus is not at the optimum stage to facilitate implantation, the embryo may be frozen and stored until the uterus reaches the proper stage.

In vitro fertilization was a remarkable breakthrough when Louise Joy Brown, the first baby conceived outside of her mother's body, was born in England in 1978. Since then, the techniques have become more common, with over 21,000 deliveries and 29,000 infants conceived via in vitro fertilization in the United States between 1996 and 2001 (American Society for Reproductive Medicine, 2002). The technique is used in a variety of situations. For example, when a husband has an insufficient supply of sperm or when the sperm are inadequate, physicians may use a male donor's sperm to fertilize the wife's egg. Or if the woman cannot produce an egg, the husband's sperm may be used to fertilize a female donor's egg, which is then implanted in the wife's uterus. The zygote produced by a husband's sperm and a wife's egg may be implanted in the uterus of a surrogate mother who carries the child to term. Using this technique, in 1991 a woman carried her own grandchild for her daughter, who had been born without a uterus. This feat of becoming a mother and a grandmother at the same time has since been repeated by other women. But the costs of in vitro fertilization are high whether the procedure involves using a woman's own eggs ($12,500 to $25,000) or donor eggs ($20,000 to $35,000). Insurance will often cover only part of the cost of the procedure, and sometimes it will not cover these costs at all (American Society for Reproductive Medicine, 2002).

Like many other medical breakthroughs, these new reproductive technologies have presented some ethical dilemmas (Murray, 1996; Schwartz, 2003; Shanley, 2001). How should prospective parents be screened?

amniocentesis A technique for sampling and assessing fetal cells for indications of abnormalities in the developing fetus; performed by inserting a needle through the abdominal wall and into the amniotic sac and withdrawing a small amount of the amniotic fluid.

chorionic villi sampling A technique for sampling and assessing cells withdrawn from the chorionic villi, projections from the chorion that surrounds the amniotic sac; cells are withdrawn either through a tube inserted into the uterus through the vagina or through a needle inserted through the abdominal wall.

COMMONLY USED TESTS The risk of disorder, as in an older expectant mother, may prompt parents to request the testing of a fetus. In **amniocentesis,** the most widely used technique for sampling fetal cells, a physician inserts a needle into the amniotic sac, or the fluid-filled membranous cover that surrounds and protects the fetus, and withdraws a little of the amniotic fluid. This fluid contains cells sloughed off from the fetus (such as skin cells), which pathologists can then analyze for their chromosomal and genetic makeup. The 16th week of pregnancy seems optimal for performing amniocentesis. By this time there are enough cells in the amniotic fluid to draw an adequate sample, yet the fetus is still small enough to avoid injury from the insertion of the needle. Nevertheless, this technique does carry a small risk of miscarriage; about one woman in 200 to 300 miscarries after this procedure.

Slightly more risky is **chorionic villi sampling,** which can be done as early as the 9th or 10th week of pregnancy. This procedure carries a slightly higher risk of miscarriage than amniocentesis and involves a slight risk of limb deformities as well. Physicians draw cells from the *chorionic villi*, fingerlike projections from the *chorion*, the outermost membrane that surrounds the amniotic sac. The villi help the zygote to embed itself in the uterine lining and then multiply to form the placenta. Although the villi are not part of the embryo itself, the chromosomes and genes in them are identical to the embryo's because they all arise from the same fertilized egg.

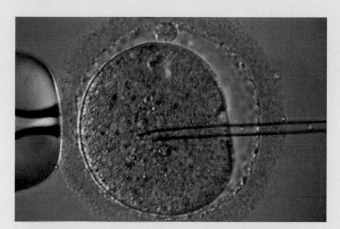

As part of an in vitro fertilization procedure, a technician inserts a human sperm cell into an egg in a petri dish.

have who has agreed to be a surrogate mother for another couple? With regard to surrogacy, there have been several celebrated cases in recent years in which the surrogate mother changed her mind about relinquishing custody. In one Massachusetts case—*Roscoe* (contracting parents) v. *Hoagland* (surrogate mother)— the court ruled in favor of the contracting parents, awarding them custody of the infant, even though the surrogate had decided to keep the baby (Blomeke, 1999).

Another major issue deals with the fate of frozen embryos. Can "extra" embryos be used for stem cell research? Embryos can be split and thereby cloned; should this technology be allowed? What would parents expect from identical twins born years apart? In the United States the stem cell research debate continues, although in some countries—for example, Great Britain—the use of nonfertilized embryos for medical research is permitted. In spite of these difficult questions, the hope, joy, and prospect of parenthood that the new reproductive techniques have given to many couples formerly unable to conceive or bear children seem to outweigh other considerations.

What criteria should be used in selecting sperm donors and in matching sperm to eggs? For example, should parents be offered sperm from a Nobel Prize winner? (A bank of such sperm was actually started some years ago.) What possibly unrealistic expectations might such parents have? What legal rights does a male donor have? What legal rights to the child does a woman

With a prenatal sample of cells in hand, it is possible to examine the fetus's chromosomes and genes for any signs of chromosome disorder. The critical abnormalities (such as missing or extra chromosomes) are clearly visible under a high-powered microscope. In addition, scientists have identified particular pieces of DNA, called *genetic markers,* that can serve as indicators of many disorders caused by one or more defective genes. For example, the gene for cystic fibrosis has been located on the midsection of chromosome 7, and a gene for familial Alzheimer's disease is found on the long arm of chromosome 21 (Lander, 1996). The latter discovery may in part account for the fact that Down individuals, as we've already noted, face a greater chance of developing Alzheimer's disease, for they have an extra chromosome 21. Without further research, however, we cannot be certain of this connection. Discovery of a birth defect, of course, raises the ethical issue of whether or not to abort the pregnancy— again a difficult personal decision for the couple.

One of the more personal hunts for a genetic marker was led by neuropsychologist Nancy Wexler, whose mother had died of **Huntington disease,** a fatal deterioration of the nervous system that begins in midadulthood, one that Wexler had a 50 percent chance of inheriting. Wexler charted patterns of Huntington disease in 5,000 Venezuelans who were all descendants of a woman who died of the disease more than 100 years ago. By using DNA samples from living relatives who had the disorder,

Huntington disease A genetically caused, fatal disorder of the nervous system that begins in midadulthood and is manifested chiefly in uncontrollable spasmodic movements of the body and limbs and eventual mental deterioration.

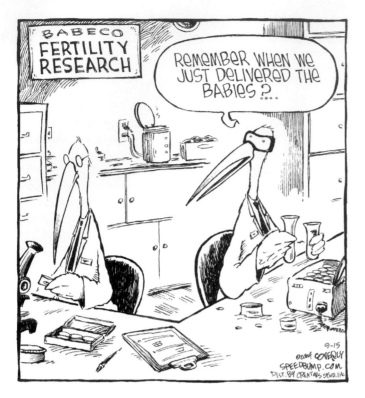

Source: SPEED BUMP. By permission of Dave Coverly and Creators Syndicate, Inc.

alphafetoprotein (AFP) assay A maternal blood test performed prenatally to detect such problems as Down syndrome, the presence of multiple embryos, and defects of the central nervous system.

ultrasound A technique that uses sound waves to visualize deep body structures; commonly used to reveal the size and structure of a developing fetus. Also called *ultrasonography.*

Wexler and geneticist James Gusella (Gusella et al., 1983) were able to identify a Huntington marker on chromosome 4. This discovery made it possible to develop a test for the Huntington gene.

Two other prenatal tests are now routinely done for most pregnancies, not just in cases of suspected risk based on family history. The **alphafetoprotein (AFP) assay** is a maternal blood test that can reveal the potential risk of certain fetal problems such as Down syndrome or defects of the central nervous system, as well as the presence of multiple embryos. If the test does uncover possible difficulties, parents in consultation with their physicians can undertake further tests. However, this is a conservative test with a high rate of *false positives*—that is, cases in which the test indicates that there may be a problem where none, in fact, exists. **Ultrasound,** or ultrasonography, a method of visualizing deep body structures, is now commonly used to detect gross physical abnormalities in a fetus. The technique, which scans the uterus by means of sound waves, produces a sonogram, or film, that shows the size and structure of the developing fetus and can determine the baby's sex. If parents want this information—some prefer to be surprised—they can stock up on blue or pink blankets with confidence. Ultrasound has other benefits as well. The opportunity to observe that the developing fetus is healthy and normal probably reduces parents' anxieties. Field, Sandberg, Quetal, Garcia, and Rosario (1985) found that women who had periodic ultrasound tests were less anxious as pregnancy progressed, had fewer birth complications, and delivered heavier, more alert, more responsive, and less irritable infants. Finally, unlike amniocentesis or chorionic villi sampling, neither the AFP nor ultrasound increases the risk of miscarriage.

ETHICAL AND POLICY ISSUES When prenatal testing reveals some major chromosomal or genetic abnormality in an unborn child, parents have the option of aborting the pregnancy. But this raises the ethical dilemma of deciding when an abnormality is severe enough to warrant an abortion. If a fetus has a lethal genetic disorder that will lead to a painful death in a few months or years, the choice is often easier than if the disorder is less devastating. What about a female fetus with Turner's syndrome, the XO chromosome pattern, or a male with the XXY pattern that gives rise to Klinefelter's syndrome? Although these children have both physical abnormalities and some cognitive impairments, they are capable of leading very productive lives. Confronting prospective parents with such difficult ethical choices is one result of developing the new technology to analyze chromosomes and genes (Murray, 1996). Even nongenetic testing, like ultrasound, is associated with some ethical problems. For example, in cultures where male children are preferred over females, this kind of prenatal assessment could lead to an increase in the rate of abortion for female fetuses (Murray, 1996; Shanley, 2001).

The new availability of genetic information also raises issues of ethics and policy in such areas as employment and personal insurance and among people who oppose abortion (Plomin & Rutter, 1998). For example, employers might decide to require in-depth genetic screening for potential employees and to reject individuals who have a gene that may someday put them at risk for cancer, heart trouble, or other diseases. Some writers have even suggested that industrial concerns might try to select employees for their lower likelihood of being affected by exposure to chemical toxins—and then fail to institute necessary procedures to protect employees. Equally disturbing is the possibility that insurance companies might decide to use information about the genetic risks people may have for certain diseases in order to exclude such individuals from insurance protection or to adjust rates for insurance coverage (Murray, 1996; Wadman, 1996). Finally, religious and social groups are concerned about the rising rate of abortion owing to the increased use of genetic screening. The prevalence of these potential abuses is unclear at this point, but the best way to develop guidelines for addressing such dilemmas may be to heighten public awareness of these issues (Bentley, 1996).

Gene Therapy

Scientists hope not only to locate the genes responsible for inherited disorders, but also to use gene therapy to ameliorate or even cure these problems. Gene therapy involves inserting normal alleles into patients' cells to compensate for defective alleles. The most effective current technique uses modified viruses (viruses from which harmful properties have been removed) to carry the new genes into the patient's cells. Scientists have adopted this strategy because viruses are by nature adapted to penetrate another organism's cells. Most often, target cells in the patient are first removed from the person's body, infused with the new gene by way of the virus, and then returned to the body. With federal approval, this procedure was first used in 1990 in treating a 4-year-old girl who had a deadly genetic disorder that shut down her immune system, leaving her defenseless against infections. Doctors inserted into some of the child's blood the gene needed to produce a critical enzyme that her immune system lacked. Ten years later, she continued to do well with some additional medication (Thompson, 2000). French scientists have also had some success with gene therapy for immune deficiencies (Fischer et al., 2000).

Not all the news about gene therapy has been good. Few effective treatments have been found despite more than 400 clinical trials. More ominously, patient deaths have been associated with some trials.

It may take some time before gene therapy is perfected, but much information has been gathered to assist scientists in their work. Box 2.3 describes the work of the Human Genome Project, whose aim was to map the identities and locations of all human genes in the hope of being able to prevent or treat more than 4,000 diseases to which our genes make one or another of us susceptible.

But again, as science enters this new age of genetic engineering, we confront significant ethical issues (Murray, 1996). As greater genetic manipulation becomes possible, how should we use it? And how, for the good of humankind, should we limit its use? It is one thing to replace a defective allele in a person who is seriously ill, and quite another to attempt to create a race of superhumans. Even more troublesome to many is our newfound ability to clone living creatures. Whether or not the U.S. Congress outlaws the cloning of human beings, scientists who are determined to accomplish this feat will undoubtedly find ways to achieve their goal. The potential benefits of many of our new technologies are great, but the dangers of using them unwisely may be even greater.

HEREDITY-ENVIRONMENT INTERACTIONS

In the past, many scientists took up opposing positions on what was familiarly referred to as the nature-nurture issue. Scholars who were more biologically oriented emphasized the role of heredity and maturational factors in human development, whereas those who were more environmentally oriented emphasized the role of learning and

Box 2.3

Child Psychology in Action

THE HUMAN GENOME PROJECT

The Human Genome Project (HGP) is an international cooperative scientific endeavor, funded by both private and public dollars, the aim of which is to locate all the genes of the human genome and then to sequence all human chromosomes (list the actual base pairs) accurately. The U.S. Congress authorized funding in 1988, and mapping and sequencing were completed in 2003 (International Human Genome Sequencing Consortium, 2004). Due to public and private lab cooperation and improved technology, the work was completed ahead of schedule. The final version of the human genome contains an estimated 20,000–25,000 human protein-coding genes, about 15,000 genes fewer than previously predicted (Venter et al., 2001).

Consider this description of the cataloging of the human genome:

> Some geneticists compare these segments (of genes) to books on a library shelf and for chromosomes 21 and Y, all the books now shelved are in the correct order. Researchers still can't decipher the locations or meanings of most phrases (genes) and letters (nucleotide sequences) within these volumes. At least, though, once an experimenter does discover which large segment contains a gene or base sequence of interest, he or she gets it straight off the "library shelf." (Postlethwait & Hopson, 1995, p. 281)

Work is also being done on animal genomes to increase our basic knowledge and to help provide more accurate models for the study and treatment of human diseases and conditions (U.S. Department of Energy, 2002; NIH, 2002). Work that compares the human genome sequences with animal genome sequences has given scientists some insights into the birth and death of genes in the human genome. Over 1,000 new genes arose in the human genome after our divergence from rodents some 75 million years ago. For example, there are two families of new genes in the human genome that encode sets of proteins that may be involved in the extended period of pregnancy unique to humans. Similarly, other genes have died or stopped functioning, such as those involved in olfactory or smell reception. This may account for humans having a poorer sense of smell than rodents.

The implications of the HGP are sweeping. Not only will it give us insight into the basic workings of the human body, but it will provide us with important insights into genetic diseases, such as sickle-cell anemia, Huntington disease, Turner syndrome, and Williams syndrome. These and several hundred other diseases are carried on single genes, but most illnesses, such as cancer or heart disease, are determined by interactions among multiple genes; figuring out the origins of most genetically caused illnesses will be a truly daunting task (Benson, 2004; Plomin, DeFries, Craig, & McGuffin, 2002).

experience. In the United States, where political and social philosophy stressed the importance of opportunity, education, and initiative, theories of biological determinism fell on rocky ground, and the environmentalist position of John B. Watson and the behaviorists flourished. In 1926, in the heat of the nature-nurture debate, Watson boasted:

> Give me a dozen healthy infants, well-formed, and my own specific world to bring them up in and I'll guarantee to take any one at random and train him to become any type of specialist I might select—a doctor, lawyer, artist, merchant-chief and, yes, even into beggar-man and thief, regardless of his talents, penchants, tendencies, abilities, vocations and race of his ancestors. (Watson, 1926, p. 10)

Contemporary psychologists, both in the United States and in other countries, see neither nature nor nurture as wholly responsible for the development of a human being. Instead, scholars focus today on how heredity and environment constantly interact to shape the developing person. Although they see genetic endowment as to some extent constraining what a person can become and do, most psychologists believe that social and environmental experiences exert a tremendous influence on the developing child.

A geneticist examines a computer display of a DNA sequencing pattern. These patterns are used to write the human genetic codes for protein production and for various structural and functional characteristics that are transmitted from generation to generation.

Despite the incredible scope of their assignment, researchers have made progress in identifying genes that may, in part, account for diseases such as Lou Gehrig's disease, some forms of Alzheimer's disease, epilepsy, and even cardiovascular disease and resistance to HIV (Lander, 1996). For example, Caspi and his colleagues (2003) have studied two genes identified through HGP that affect the breakdown and uptake of neurotransmitters in the brain. Interestingly, these pioneering researchers discovered that although these genes have effects on depression and antisocial behavior, these effects are seen only in people exposed to particular environmental stressors. Once again, we are reminded that genes do not act alone; their impact on human behavior depends on the particular environmental factors that also affect the individual.

As with genetic testing, there are ethical concerns about how doctors, employers, and insurance companies will use the data and about possible abuses of the new genetic information. For example, even if scientists determine that a person is genetically prone to develop a disease, he may never do so; as a result, caution in the use of this information is critical.

Not all are as wary as others. As James Watson, the Nobel Prize winner, argued, "When finally interpreted, the genetic message encoded within our DNA molecules will provide the ultimate answers to the chemical underpinnings of human existence" (Postlethwait & Hopson, 1995, p. 281).

Moreover, they see gene-environment interactions as highly complex. Not only do environments influence how genes are expressed, but genes can help to shape the environments to which people are exposed. We will explore both sides of this complex story.

How the Environment Influences the Expression of Genes

The concept of **range of reaction** helps explain how environments influence genes (Gottesman, 1963; Plomin, 1995). According to this concept, heredity does not rigidly fix behavior but instead establishes a range of possible developmental outcomes that may occur in response to different environments. As you might expect, individuals with different genetic makeups also have different ranges of reaction; their particular sets of genes set boundaries on their range of developmental possibilities. Of course, some traits such as eye color are determined by genes, but for the complex behaviors that concern child developmentalists, models that stress the interplay between genes

range of reaction The notion that the human being's genetic makeup establishes a range of possible developmental outcomes, within which environmental forces largely determine how the person actually develops.

Figure 2-7

Interaction between environment and genotype
Providing any child with an enriched, stimulating environment can substantially improve the child's performance on various measures of achievement. However, each child's genotype—in this hypothetical illustration the genotypes are represented by the labels "Child A," "Child B," and "Child C"—will determine the limits within which his or her performance may vary.

Source: Adapted from Gottesman, 1963.

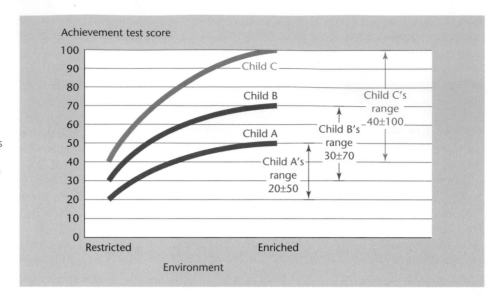

canalization The genetic restriction of a phenotype to a small number of developmental outcomes, permitting environmental influences to play only a small role in these outcomes.

and environment are more useful. And within those boundaries, the environment largely determines how the person will develop.

A good example of the interaction between range of reaction and the environment is provided by the hypothetical example that Figure 2-7 illustrates. Each of the three children represented by curves A, B, and C has a different range of possible scores on an achievement test. If all three children experience exactly the same level of environmental stimulation, child C will always outperform the other two. However, child B could achieve a substantially higher score than C if B experiences a more enriched environment than C does. (An enriched environment may have a high level of physical stimulation, such as a wide array of toys and books; social-emotional stimulation, such as the presence of highly responsive and attentive caregivers; or cognitive-linguistic stimulation, such as caregivers who talk and read a lot to a child.) Notice, too, that child C has the widest range of reaction: That is, the difference between child C's potential performance in either restricted or enriched environments is much greater than the analogous difference for child B and child A. Child A has both the lowest and the most limited range of reaction. This child not only scores below average (50) whether raised in a stimulating or unstimulating setting, but also shows less ability to respond to environmental enrichment.

When a reaction range is extremely narrow, even narrower than child A's, it is said to show strong **canalization** (Waddington, 1962, 1966). When a trait is highly canalized, development is restricted to just a few pathways, and more intense or more specific environmental pushes are required to deflect the course of development. For example, a baby's tendency to repetitively utter consonant-vowel combinations (called *babbling*) is strongly canalized, because babbling occurs even in babies who are born deaf and have never heard a human voice (Lenneberg, 1967). In contrast, intelligence is less highly canalized, for it can be modified by a variety of physical, social, and educational experiences.

Gilbert Gottlieb (1991, 1992; Gottlieb, Wahlsten, & Lickliter, 1998) has offered a modified view of gene-environment interaction, in which genes play a less determinative role in shaping development. According to Gottlieb's developmental systems view, "the concept of the genetic determination of traits is truly outmoded" (Gottlieb, 1991, p. 5). Instead, Gottlieb argues, individual development is organized into multiple levels—for example, genetic activity, neural activity (activity of the nervous system), behavior, and environment—all of which influence each other. As

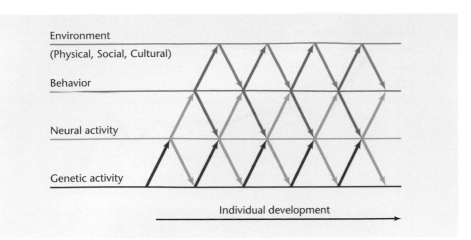

Environment
(Physical, Social, Cultural)

Behavior

Neural activity

Genetic activity

Individual development

Figure 2-8

Bidirectional influence in gene-environment interactions

In the developmental systems view, the influence each of the four levels of individual development wields is bidirectional; that is, each level influences both the one above and the one below it. Any level may also influence nonadjacent levels.

Source: Gottlieb, 1992.

Figure 2-8 shows, this influence is bidirectional; that is, it is directed both from bottom to top and from top to bottom. The figure offers a simplified explanation of how genes and environment mutually influence each other; for example, the prenatal environment could alter the expression of the genes, and the postnatal environment could, in part, determine whether a genetic predisposition found full expression in behavior. Thus, although each of the figure's levels generally influences the level directly above or below it, other interactions across nonadjacent levels are possible as well. In his work on mallard ducklings, Gottlieb found that ducklings' usual preference for the sounds of other ducks—a genetically governed preference—could be modified if the duckling were exposed before birth to sounds made by chickens. The duckling exposed to chicken sounds preferred these sounds over duck sounds.

The most important point of this systems view is the recognition that genes are part of an overall system and that their activity—that is, the expression of the characteristics they carry—is affected by events at other levels of the system, including the organism's environment. The message is clear: Both genes and environment are inextricably linked and always operate in a mutually dependent fashion in shaping development. It is impossible to treat genes and environment as truly separable, for both need to be considered together.

Another factor in gene-environment interaction is the stage of the child's development. Both developmental stage and the environment determine the likelihood that a genetically based trait or characteristic will be influenced by environmental forces. For example, as we discuss further in Chapter 3, if a fetus is exposed early in its development to the virus that causes German measles, the child is very likely to evidence some damage to its hearing. After the third month of pregnancy, however, fetal exposure to this virus generally does not affect the child's hearing. The window of opportunity for this particular environmental influence has largely closed because the fetus has reached a more mature stage of development.

Another example of the importance of critical periods can be seen in the treatment for PKU, the genetic disorder we discussed earlier. Babies today are routinely tested for PKU, and if they are found to be homozygous for the trait, they are placed on a special diet low in phenylalanine to prevent the buildup of toxins that results in mental retardation. In Figure 2-9 we see once again that in the interaction between genotype and environment there is a window of opportunity. The special PKU diet must begin immediately after birth, for delays of even a few months can have devastating effects on a child's intellectual development. On the other hand, if this diet is begun at once and continued until the nervous system is mature, a child with PKU can develop intellectual abilities close to normal. Whether a child must stay on this diet indefinitely

LifeMap CD

To learn more about the effects of a stimulating environment, watch the video "Nature and Nurture: The Study of Twins" in Chapter 2 of your CD.

Figure 2-9

Diet and intelligence in PKU children

Clearly, delaying the age at which a special diet is begun for the child born with phenylketonuria can have seriously negative effects on the child's intellectual functioning. If the diet is begun at birth, however, the child can eventually achieve an IQ score close to average (which would be 100; see Chapter 10).

Source: Adapted from Baumeister, 1967.

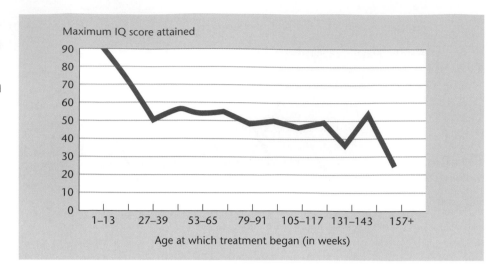

is a matter of controversy; at present, most experts recommend that women with PKU, at least, remain on it for life if they plan to bear children. If they don't do this, they may have to go back on the diet during pregnancy; if they fail to do this early enough, they may miscarry or the fetus may develop mental retardation (Verp, 1993). This example illustrates not only the importance of the timing of environmental influences but the complex way in which developmental outcomes—even those involving a genetically based predisposition—arise from the interaction between genes and environment.

How Genetic Makeup Helps to Shape the Environment

passive genetic-environmental interaction The interactive environment created by parents with particular genetic predispositions who encourage the expression of these tendencies in their children.

evocative genetic-environmental interaction The expression of the genes' influence on the environment through an individual's inherited tendencies to evoke certain environmental responses; for example, a child's smiling may elicit smiles from others.

active genetic-environmental interaction A kind of interaction in which people's genes encourage them to seek out experiences compatible with their inherited tendencies.

niche picking Seeking out or creating environments compatible with one's genetically based predispositions.

It is now widely accepted that gene expression is influenced by the environment. However, the idea that the environment can be shaped by genes is relatively new and is less commonly acknowledged. Scientists have proposed several ways in which people's genetic makeup can influence their environments (Plomin, 1995; Scarr, 1992, 1996; Reiss, Neiderhiser, Hetherington, & Plomin, 2000). In one of these pathways, known as the **passive genetic-environmental interaction,** parents with certain genetic predispositions may create a home environment that suits those predispositions and that may also suit and encourage the inherited predispositions of their children. Thus intelligent, well-educated parents may provide a home with books and stimulating conversation, enhancing their children's inherited tendencies to be bright and encouraging them to learn. In another pathway, known as the **evocative genetic-environmental interaction,** genes can influence the environment through people's inherited tendencies to evoke certain responses from others—that is, from their social environment. For instance, babies with an inborn tendency to smile often will probably elicit more positive stimulation from others than do very sober, unresponsive infants (La Freniere, 2000; Plomin, 1995). In this paradigm, the environment that has been altered by genetic expression has reciprocal effects on genetic makeup: The evoked stimulation reinforces the babies' smiling and ultimately, by a circular process, tends to magnify the babies' genetic predisposition (see Chapter 6).

Finally, genes can influence environment in a third way, namely through an **active genetic-environmental interaction.** People's genetic makeups may encourage them to actually seek out experiences compatible with their inherited tendencies (Scarr, 1996; Scarr & McCartney, 1983). In a process called **niche picking,** people search for, select, or build environments compatible with their predispositions. Thus, people genetically predisposed to be extraverted or gregarious actively seek the company of other people and become involved in a wide range of social activities. Or aggressive children are more likely to sign up for martial arts classes than a chess club (Bullock & Merrill, 1980). These experiences, in turn, enhance the expression of their genes for sociability. The importance of niche picking probably increases from childhood to adolescence and adulthood, as people gain more freedom to choose their activities and companions.

These influences of genes on environment underscore the difficulty of determining the relative contributions of heredity and environment to individual differences in development (Baumrind, 1993; Hoffman, 1991). If genes influence environmental experiences, which in turn influence genes, it is difficult to separate the factors involved in these complex feedback loops. Nevertheless, as we will see in the next section, researchers have attempted to calculate the relative influences of heredity and environment on individual differences in a large number of characteristics.

As children develop and have more freedom to choose companions and contexts, they may, in what is called niche-picking, select activities compatible with their genetic predispositions. They give expression to these predispositions by choosing endeavors that support them.

HEREDITY, ENVIRONMENT, AND INDIVIDUAL DIFFERENCES

An important issue that researchers contend with is the question of why people develop in such widely different ways. Why, for example, does one child achieve an IQ score of 105, whereas his sister has a score of 150? Why is one child so outgoing and sociable, another more introverted and shy? How can we explain why some children and adults are chronically aggressive, whereas others seek to cooperate and avoid confrontation? For years, psychologists interested in human personality have struggled with questions like these. The field of **human behavior genetics** arose in the 1960s when some scientists began to focus their attention particularly on the relative contributions that heredity and environment make to the array of individual differences observed in human behavior (Plomin et al., 1997, 2001).

Unlike biologists who study heredity, behavior geneticists can conduct their research without ever directly measuring chromosomes, DNA, or genes. Instead, using sophisticated statistical techniques, they calculate what are called **heritability factors,** or percentage estimates of the contribution that heredity makes to a particular ability or type of behavior. When discussing heritability factors, a caution is in order: These percentage contributions of heredity to individual differences should not be viewed as applicable to all groups of children or adults at all points in development. The relative contribution of heredity to an observed difference in human behavior depends on how wide a range of environmental influences the people studied have been exposed to. For example, when children experience virtually the same environment, we may assume that heredity plays the greater role in any individual differences in their behaviors. When environments are extremely different, however, things get more complex: Whereas environmental factors may exert greater influence on people's behavior, their very abundance may sometimes obscure the genetic influences at work.

British psychiatrist Sir Michael Rutter (1992) argues that people have many misconceptions about what the study of genetics contributes to our knowledge of human development (see Table 2-4). According to Rutter, the field of behavior genetics has

human behavior genetics The study of the relative influences of heredity and environment on the evolution of individual differences in traits and abilities.

heritability factor A statistical estimate of the contribution heredity makes to a particular trait or ability.

Table 2-4

Some misconceptions about the study of behavior genetics
Sources: Rutter, 1992; Shaffer, 1996.

- **Genes limit potential.** Wrong. Genetic factors do affect potential, but that potential is affected in turn by a child's environment. Change the environment, and the potential changes, too.

- **Strong genetic effects mean that environmental influences are not important.** Wrong. Although genetic effects account for individual variability, the environment may effect changes in the average expression of a characteristic. For example, the range of individual differences in IQ of children from disadvantaged families who are adopted into more advantaged families is more closely related to the IQ range of the children's biological parents. Nevertheless, these children show a general rise in IQ levels, demonstrating the effects of a stimulating environment.

- **Nature and nurture are separate.** Wrong. Both genes and environment are necessary for an individual to develop: "No genes, no organism; no environment, no organism" (Scarr & Weinberg, 1983).

- **Genetic influences diminish with age.** Wrong. The relation between genes and aging is highly complex. Some hereditary characteristics are most evident in early stages of development; some are more evident in later stages. For example, the age at which puberty occurs is largely under genetic control, whereas the contribution of genetic factors to individual differences in intelligence is more evident in older than in younger children.

- **Genes regulate only static characteristics.** Wrong. Genes affect developmental change as well. Deviations in the normally expected environment can upset the timetable for the child's physical and psychological development, producing gross delay. However, the time at which particular characteristics emerge and the sequence in which they appear are determined primarily by the child's genetic makeup.

as much to say about environmental influences on human beings as it has to say about genetic effects on humans. With the right research strategies, Rutter claims, it is possible not only to reveal the interaction between these two forces, but also to distinguish between them and to estimate the extent to which each contributes to any given trait or ability.

Methods of Studying Individual Differences

The method used most often to investigate the contributions of heredity and environment to individual differences is the study of family members whose degrees of biological relatedness are known. Studies of this type generally compare adopted children with their biological and adoptive parents, examine similarities and differences between fraternal and identical twins, or explore the effects of similar and different environments on twins and on ordinary siblings (Plomin et al., 2001; Rutter, Pickles, Murray, & Eaves, 2001).

ADOPTION AND TWIN STUDIES   In adoption studies, researchers usually compare characteristics of adopted children with those of both their adoptive and biological parents. Although the adoptive parents exert environmental influences on their adopted children, investigators can assume that there is no genetically determined similarity between these adoptive parents and their children. Adopted children, of course, have genes in common with their biological parents, but the latter exert no postnatal environmental influences on the children. (These kinds of studies include only adopted children who have no contact with their biological parents.) Based on these assumptions and conditions, researchers reason that any similarity of adopted children to their adoptive parents must be due to their social environment, whereas any similarity of the children to their biological parents must be the result of similar genetic makeup. Adoption studies also sometimes study the similarities and differences between biological siblings and adopted children who live in the same home. To cite one example, researchers have found that a biological parent's educational level is a better predictor of an adopted child's intelligence test scores than is similar information about the child's adoptive parents (Scarr & Weinberg, 1983). This suggests that genetic factors make an important contribution to intelligence.

In twin studies, researchers take a different approach to uncovering the contributions of heredity and environment to human differences. Often these studies involve comparing the similarities between identical and fraternal twins raised together in the same home. Identical, or **monozygotic,** twins are created when a single zygote splits in half and each half becomes a distinct embryo with exactly the same genes; both embryos come from one zygote (*mono* means "one"). In contrast, fraternal, or **dizygotic,** twins develop from two different eggs that have been fertilized by two different sperm, producing two different zygotes (*di* means "two").

Because they are conceived independently of each other, fraternal twins are no more similar genetically than any other pair of siblings; on average, they have half their genes in common. When comparing sets of identical and fraternal twins, researchers assume that each set has been raised in essentially the same type of environment. Thus, if identical twins show more resemblance on a particular trait than fraternal twins do, we can assume that the resemblance is strongly influenced by genes. We will see many examples in later chapters of the greater resemblance of identical twins as compared with fraternal twins on such characteristics as IQ, altruism, and aggression (see Chapters 10 and 14). On the other hand, if on a given trait the two kinds of twins resemble each other almost equally, we can assume that the resemblance is strongly influenced by the environment.

SHARED AND NONSHARED ENVIRONMENTS

Is it legitimate to make these assumptions? Some investigators have questioned the proposition that each member of a twin pair experiences the same environmental conditions. These investigators argue that identical twins, because of their identical genes and inherited predispositions, are treated more similarly by their parents, evoke more similar responses from people outside the family, and select more similar settings, companions, and activities than do fraternal twins (Baumrind, 1993; Scarr, 1996; Scarr & McCartney, 1983). Thus, these critics claim, identical twins have more **shared environments** than fraternal twins, and so any similarities in their traits must be attributed to both the environment and their genetic makeup (Plomin, 1995). Fraternal twins and siblings, they suggest, have more **nonshared environments,** or separate experiences and activities.

This viewpoint stresses that people are active creators of their own environments, not just passive recipients of environmental influences. In both deliberate and unintentional ways, people help to shape the many experiences they're exposed to. With this in mind, consider whether two siblings who live together in the same home encounter exactly the same family environment (Dunn & Plomin, 1991; Feinberg & Hetherington, 2001). In fact there are differences in people's experiences even within the same setting, differences based in part on who the people are as individuals. This perspective helps explain why adoptive siblings, and even biologically related ones, often show only a modest similarity on behavioral traits. Moreover, the initially modest similarity caused by a shared childhood home tends to decline with age, as personal niche picking exerts more and more influence on people's behavior (Reiss, et al., 2000; Towers, Spotts, & Reiss, 2003).

Children raised in the same family, then, have both shared and nonshared experiences. Shared conditions would include such factors as being poor or well off, living

monozygotic Characterizing *identical* twins, who have developed from a single fertilized egg.

dizygotic Characterizing *fraternal* twins, who have developed from two separate fertilized eggs.

shared environment A set of conditions or experiences shared by children raised in the same family; a parameter commonly examined in studies of individual differences.

nonshared environment A set of conditions or activities experienced by one child in a family but not shared with another child in the same family.

in a good or a bad neighborhood, and having parents who are employed or unemployed, in good health or physically or mentally ill (Reiss et al., 2000; Towers et al., 2003). Experiences not shared, in contrast, would include factors or events related to the individual characteristics of a particular child; for example, what specific activities that child engages in, or how he or she is treated because of age, gender, temperament, illness, or physical and cognitive abilities. Studies show that siblings, even twins, have many nonshared experiences that affect their development (Plomin, 1995; Plomin & Daniels, 1987). Even small differences in nonshared experiences may cause differences in how siblings develop. Furthermore, siblings' perceptions that their experiences—for example, the way their parents treat them—are different can affect their behavior whether or not these perceptions are accurate. In fact, some argue that nonshared influences are more important for understanding development than shared influences (Plomin et al., 2001). Increasingly, researchers are designing studies in which two siblings in the same family are examined rather than single siblings from different families in order to better evaluate the influence of nonshared versus shared environmental experiences (McGuire, 2001). Clearly, researchers in individual differences can no longer assume a homogeneous home environment for all siblings; be alert to this fact when you read the reports and conclusions of such studies.

Some Individual Differences and Their Contributors

In this section we have chosen to look at some of the findings of behavior genetic research in three important areas. We begin by examining the effects of heredity and environment on differences in intellectual abilities and we then explore differences in temperament and personality.

INTELLECTUAL CHARACTERISTICS   Interestingly, studies comparing the intelligence quotient, or IQ, scores of twins have been remarkably consistent in their findings (we discuss intelligence at length in Chapter 10). This research indicates that genes heavily influence similarities and differences in individual performance on intelligence tests. Generally, the closer the genetic links between two people, the more similar their IQ scores. As you can see from Table 2-5, which summarizes more than 100 family resemblance studies of twins, siblings, and other relatives,

Table 2-5

Resemblance in intelligence scores among family members*

Source: Adapted from Bouchard & McGue, 1981.

Relationship of Family Members	Correlation between IQ Scores
Identical twins reared together	.86
Identical twins reared apart	.79
Fraternal twins reared together	.60
Siblings reared together	.47
Parent and child	.40
Foster parent and child	.31
Siblings reared apart	.24
Cousins	.15

* Correlations are compiled from 111 different studies from all parts of the world. In general, the closer the genetic relationship of two people, the higher the correlation between their IQ scores.

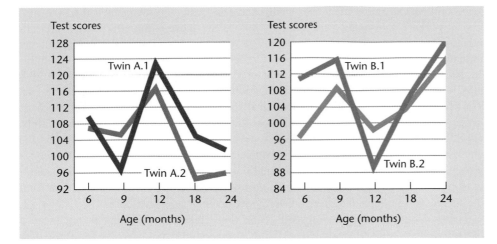

Figure 2-10

Twins' intelligence test scores over the first two years

The members of each of these two sets of identical twins paralleled each other closely in intelligence test scores as they developed over a period of about two years.

Source: Adapted from Wilson & Harpring, 1972.

identical twins reared in the same household are most similar in IQ scores (+.86 is a very high, positive correlation). The least similar in IQ scores are cousins, who have relatively few genes in common and are not raised in the same home (only +.15). As genetic similarity decreases, so does similarity in intelligence scores. Even identical twins raised apart have IQ scores that are more similar than are those of fraternal twins raised in the same home. Furthermore, although twin correlations of IQ decrease with age as the influence of a shared family environment diminishes, that decrease is greater for fraternal than for identical twins (McCartney, Harris, & Berniere, 1990).

Genes contribute not only to differences in general intellectual performance but also to differences in specific mental abilities as well, some more so than others. Differences in spatial and verbal abilities, for instance, are more influenced by genetic factors than are differences in memory and perceptual speed (Plomin, 1990). In a surprising finding, however, differences in creativity, that aspect of cognitive behavior that includes scientific and artistic innovation, show less genetic influence than differences in any other specific cognitive ability. It looks as if creative geniuses are largely made, not born!

Heredity affects not just differences in the level of mental development but also differences in the timing and rate of development. Just as children show spurts and plateaus in physical growth, they also show variations in the rate and timing of mental growth. Heredity apparently contributes substantially to these individual differences, as suggested by the fact that identical twins are more similar in this regard than fraternal twins (Wilson, 1983). For example, Figure 2-10 shows how the scores achieved by two sets of identical twins on infant intelligence tests rose and fell in much the same patterns over their first two years. Tests of infants typically show wide fluctuations over time; what is remarkable here is how similar the patterns of the fluctuations were for each pair of twins.

Adoption studies also reveal significant genetic contributions to individual differences in intellectual development (Plomin et al., 2001; Scarr & Weinberg, 1976). Even if children have been adopted in their first year of life, their intellectual performance at school age correlates more closely with their biological parents' intelligence ratings or scores than with those of their adoptive parents; moreover, the correlation with foster or adoptive parents declines with age (Scarr & Weinberg, 1983).

Bear in mind that the results of adoption studies do not mean adoptive parents fail to influence their adopted children's intellectual performance (Turkheimer, 1991, 2000). In one classic adoption study, adopted children were found to have IQ scores that averaged 20 or more IQ points higher than the IQ scores of their biological mothers (Skodak & Skeels, 1949). Because in this study the adoptive parents tended to be more highly educated and more socially and economically advantaged than the biological parents, this result was probably due to the more stimulating home environments that the adoptive parents provided. But note also that, despite this environmental influence on development, individual differences seemed still to be substantially influenced by genetic inheritance. The rank ordering of the children's IQ scores more closely resembled that of their biological mothers than that of their adoptive parents. The children whose biological mothers had the lowest IQ scores were likely to have lower IQ scores than the children whose biological mothers scored higher. Thus, although the absolute level of intellectual development was apparently boosted by the environmental influences provided by the adoptive parents, individual differences among the adopted children in intellectual performance—that is, their relative standings in this regard—appeared to stem more from their biological inheritance than from the increased intellectual stimulation provided in their adoptive homes.

Another qualification we must place on these research findings is that because the researchers studied primarily children adopted into middle-class families, they may have limited the expression of environmental influences. Among children adopted into families from a wider range of socioeconomic backgrounds, environment probably makes a greater contribution to individual differences in intellectual performance. For example, studies have shown that adopted children in economically disadvantaged homes have lower IQ scores and are more likely to drop out of school than those placed with more well-to-do families (Capron & Duyme, 1989; Duyme, 1988).

Thus, although twin studies and adoptive studies agree in showing that genetic factors make an important contribution to individual differences in IQ, environmental factors can also be important contributors to these differences, especially when there are wide disparities in the contexts in which individuals live. As you will see in Chapter 10, very poor or stressful environments can dramatically lower IQ scores, and cognitively stimulating environments or intervention programs can raise them.

TEMPERAMENT AND PERSONALITY   Even in infants' earliest days of life, we can see marked differences in what we call **temperament,** or the individual's typical mode of response to the environment, including such things as activity level, adaptability to new situations, and intensity of emotional expression. We use the term *temperament* to describe these kinds of individual differences in infants and children. In adolescence and adulthood these styles of responses to the world are often discussed as different aspects of *personality,* such as emotionality, activity, and sociability. (We revisit these issues in Chapter 6.)

Thomas and Chess (1986) have proposed a typology of temperament that has been widely accepted. This framework classifies infants as *difficult, easy,* or *slow-to-warm-up,* and each of these types is associated with a distinctive pattern of behavioral responses (Rothbart & Bates, 1998; Thomas & Chess, 1986). Difficult infants (about 10% of all babies) sleep and eat irregularly, become easily upset by new situations, and experience extremes of fussiness and crying. In contrast, easy babies (about 40%) are friendly, happy, and adaptable. Even in the same family, babies may exhibit both of these dramatically different temperaments:

> Nothing was easy with Chris. Mealtimes, bedtimes, toilet training were all hell. It would take me an hour and a half to get part of a bottle into him and he'd be hungry two hours later. I can't remember once in the first two years when he didn't go to bed crying. I'd try to rock him to sleep but as soon as I'd tiptoe over to put him in his crib his head would lurch up and he'd start bellowing again. He didn't like any kind of changes in his routine. New people and places upset him so it was hard to take him anywhere.
>
> John was my touchy feely baby. From the first day in the hospital he cuddled and seemed so contented to be held I could hardly bear to put him down. He didn't cry unless something was wrong—he was wet, or hungry, or tired. We took him everywhere because

temperament The individual's typical mode of response to the environment, including such things as activity level, emotional intensity, and attention span; used particularly to describe infants' and children's behavior.

Component	Description
Positive affect	Measured by a child's smiling, laughter, cooperativeness, and manageability
Irritable distress	Indexed by a child's irritability, fussiness, anger, frustration, and distress at limitations on her behavior
Fearful distress	Assessed by the length of time a child requires to adjust to a new situation, or his adaptability, and by the child's tendency to withdraw and show distress in new situations
Activity level	Indexed by the child's tendency to be more or less active
Attention span/persistence	Measured by a child's ability to concentrate, focus on a task, and continue to work at a problem
Rhythmicity	Assessed by the predictability or regularity of a child's behavior patterns

Table 2-6

Components of infant temperament
Source: Rothbart & Bates, 1998.

he seemed to enjoy new things. You could always sit him in a corner and he'd entertain himself. Sometimes I'd forget he was there until he'd start laughing or prattling. (Thomas & Chess, 1986)

The *slow-to-warm-up* child is low in activity level and tends to respond negatively to new stimuli at first but to adapt slowly to new objects or novel experiences after repeated contact with them. Essentially, these children fall somewhere between difficult and easy children; on first exposure to something strange they may look like difficult children, but they gradually show quiet interest, much like an easy child.

Rothbart and her colleagues (Putnam, Sanson, & Rothbart, 2002; Rothbart, 1981) have developed an alternative and increasingly popular measure of temperament known as the Infant Behavior Questionnaire. Compared with Thomas's and Chess's more global scheme, this newer approach describes more discrete aspects of temperament that can be more precisely measured. The six scales of this instrument are (1) positive affect, (2) irritable distress, (3) fearful distress, (4) activity level, (5) attention span/persistence, and (6) rhythmicity (Table 2-6). They have also developed a similar temperament measure for toddlers, young children, early adolescents, and adults (Goldsmith, Aksan, Essex, Smider, & Vandell, 2001; Putnam et al., 2002). Comparable scales across the span of development make this approach to temperament an influential one. Temperament, of course, is expressed in different ways as the individual grows older. For example, in infancy we may index persistence by the length of time a baby looks at an object, whereas in childhood we may measure this component by the length of time a child continues to work on a puzzle or problem.

Researchers have also compiled evidence for differences in newborn temperament among children of different ethnicities and races. For instance, Chinese American babies, in contrast to European American and Irish infants, have been described as generally calmer, easier to console, more able to quiet themselves after crying, and faster to adapt to external stimulation or changes (Freedman, 1974; Kagan, 1994; Kagan, Kearsley, & Zelazo, 1978). Similarly, Lewis, Ramsey, and Kawakami (1993) reported that Japanese infants between the ages of 2 and 6 months were less reactive than European American infants during well-baby examinations and that they were less likely to display intense distress at being inoculated.

A variety of cultural differences in the perception of infant temperament have been found for different East African societies. The Digo, for example, view the infant as active and able to learn within a few months after birth, whereas the Kikuyu view their infants as passive, keep them swaddled for the first year, and believe that real learning is not possible until the second year (DeVries & Sameroff, 1984). Parents provide different opportunities for learning depending on their assumptions about their infant's temperament. These findings underscore the ways in which cultural beliefs about the nature of infant temperament may, in part, shape the nature of the infant's early capacities. Even within cultures, temperamental differences may contribute to the type of caregiving that infants receive. Among the Masai of Kenya, under famine conditions, fussy, irritable infants are more likely to secure a greater share of available food than are calm, placid infants (DeVries, 1984). Cultural beliefs shape temperament, just as temperament shapes the ways in which caregivers behave (Kerr, 2001; Rothbart & Bates, 1998; Sameroff, 1994).

A higher rate of developmental problems appears in later life among children described by their mothers as difficult babies (Goldsmith et al., 2001; Halverson & Deal, 2001; Rothbart & Bates, 1998; Thomas & Chess, 1986). Two factors may contribute to this relationship: First, a less malleable child is likely to find it harder to adapt to environmental demands and so is more prone to stress and the toll it takes on emotional well-being. A second factor, which has been demonstrated in research studies, is that a child with a difficult temperament is more apt to elicit adverse reactions from other people and thus to suffer the psychological damage caused by social rejection. Children with difficult temperaments have been found to serve as targets for parental irritability, especially when the parents are under stress. Stressed mothers are especially likely to withdraw affection from temperamentally difficult boys and to show irritation with them (Hetherington, 1991b). If a mother is under multiple stresses and lacks a supportive family or friendship network, dealing with a difficult baby may disrupt the development of a harmonious mother-infant relationship and increase the likelihood that the child will exhibit developmental problems later (Crockenberg, 1981).

On the other hand, the finding that a difficult baby is not likely to suffer any long-term negative effects if its parents are calm and supportive (Hetherington, 1991b) suggests that the match between the child's temperament and the environment is important. This match between the child's temperament and the child-rearing environment is called **goodness of fit** by Thomas and Chess (1986). This model reminds us that the effects of temperamental predispositions will depend on how well parents and other agents of socialization are able to accept and adapt to each child's particular temperament. As we will see in our later discussion of moral development, fearful children have been found to develop greater self-control, or conscience, when their parents use gentle discipline; in contrast, however, parental strategies that focused on positive motivation were seen to promote more self-control in fearless children (Kochanska, 1997). As the goodness of fit model suggests, development progresses more smoothly when parents adjust their approach to suit the child's unique temperament.

How do heredity and environment affect temperament and personality? Scientists assumed for some time that both are at least in part genetically determined, although arguments have been made on both sides of the issue. Recent studies have suggested that prenatal environment and environmental factors at birth may make larger contributions than heredity to infant temperament (Riese, 1990). At the same time, genetic influences on temperament seem to become increasingly prominent throughout early childhood (Dunn & Plomin, 1991; Wachs & Kohnstamm, 2001). It may be that although some individual differences are partly genetic in origin, they are nevertheless susceptible to environmental influences, particularly interactions among family members (Grigorenko, 2002; Loehlin, Willerman, & Horn, 1988). Personality traits show some stability over time, which might suggest a genetic influence, but most

goodness of fit A measure of the degree to which a child's temperament is matched by her environment; the more effectively parents and other agents of socialization accept and adapt to the child's unique temperament, the better this "fit."

Making the Connections 2

There are many links between concepts and ideas in one area of development and concepts and ideas in other areas. Here are some of the connections between ideas in Chapter 2 and discussions in other chapters of this book.

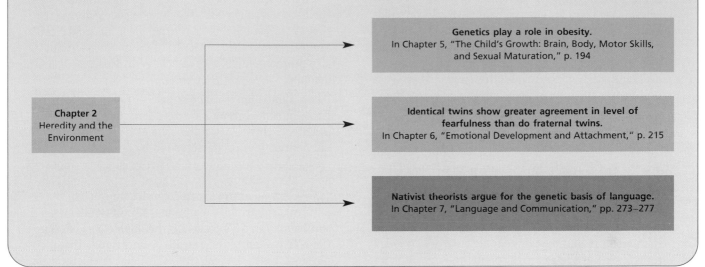

Chapter 2
Heredity and the Environment

Genetics play a role in obesity.
In Chapter 5, "The Child's Growth: Brain, Body, Motor Skills, and Sexual Maturation," p. 194

Identical twins show greater agreement in level of fearfulness than do fraternal twins.
In Chapter 6, "Emotional Development and Attachment," p. 215

Nativist theorists argue for the genetic basis of language.
In Chapter 7, "Language and Communication," pp. 273–277

psychologists today consider that both heredity and environmental factors contribute to personality in the same way that they do—as we've already noted   to other human characteristics.

Studies have shown that heredity contributes to individual differences in a number of temperament characteristics and personality traits, including some of the components identified by Rothbart and her colleagues: affect, or emotionality; fears and anxieties; activity level; attention span and persistence; and the tendencies to maintain high moral standards and to obey authority (Goldsmith, 1983; Kochanska, 1995). According to Plomin (1995), inheritance apparently contributes most to emotionality, activity level, and sociability. Temperament and personality show a declining link with genetic factors as people age, however, and differing life experiences seem more significant among older people (Plomin, McClearn, Pedersen, Nesselroade, & Bergeman, 1988).

SUMMARY

- During the course of development, the **genotype** interacts with the environment in complex ways to produce the **phenotype.** Scientists study the phenotypic expression of individual physical and behavioral characteristics in an effort to understand how genes and the environment interact to produce each unique human being.

The Process of Genetic Transmission

- Within each cell nucleus are threadlike structures called **chromosomes,** on which **genes** containing

the genetic code are located. Genetic variability is the result of (1) the huge number of chromosome combinations that are possible during the formation of sperm and egg cells; and (2) **crossing over,** which occurs during the kind of cell division called **meiosis** and involves the exchange of genes on homologous chromosomes. Sexual reproduction, or the union of **ovum** with **sperm,** also contributes to genetic variability, as 23 chromosomes from a woman unite with 23 chromosomes from a man to form the zygote. Through the process of **mitosis,** this new **autosome** divides and continues to divide, eventually producing a new, multicellular organism.

- Chromosomes are bound by molecules of **deoxyribonucleic acid (DNA),** which are made up of **nucleotides.** Genes, portions of the DNA molecule, are located at particular sites on the chromosome where they code for the production of certain kinds of protein. When a gene is activated, a copy of it travels from the cell nucleus to the body of the cell, where it serves as a template for building a protein molecule. Each of the many different kinds of proteins in the human body serves a different function. All of them, working together, are what make a living organism.

Genetic Influences on Development

- At any given gene's position on two homologous chromosomes, there can be more than one form, or **allele,** of that gene. If the two alleles are the same, the person is **homozygous** for that particular characteristic; if the alleles are different, the person is **heterozygous.** Heterozygous combinations may be expressed in three ways: (1) the person may have a trait intermediate between the traits that each of the two alleles codes for; (2) both alleles may express their traits simultaneously in an outcome called **codominance;** or (3) a **dominant** allele may overcome the other, **recessive** allele, resulting in the expression of the dominant allele's trait.

- The 23rd pair of human chromosomes are the **sex chromosomes,** differing in males and females. Females have two large homologous sex chromosomes, forming an XX pattern; males have one X and a smaller Y chromosome, an XY pattern. Because an X chromosome is about five times longer than a Y chromosome, it carries more genes. This means that, in males, some genes on the X chromosome have no equivalent genes on the Y chromosome; the person inherits only one each of these **X-linked genes.** If the inherited gene happens to be a harmful recessive allele, the associated genetic disorder will automatically be expressed. **Hemophilia,** a disease in which the blood fails to clot, is an example of an X-linked recessive trait.

- Many human characteristics are influenced by complex interactions among multiple genes acting together. This interaction of multiple genes may help explain why some traits influenced by genes do not tend to run in families. Their development depends on a configuration of many genes, and that whole configuration is not likely to be passed on from parent to child. Further adding to the complexity of genetic influences on development, a single pair of alleles may influence more than one trait, and if they are **modifier genes,** they may do so not directly but indirectly through the effects they have on how other genes are expressed.

- Harmful alleles survive generally because, as in **phenylketonuria (PKU),** they are not harmful in the heterozygous state. They may also survive, as they do in people who carry the allele for **sickle-cell anemia,** when they not only cause one disease but also protect people from another—in this case, from malaria.

- **Down syndrome** is one example of the many identifiable human chromosome disorders. It is caused by inheriting three 21st chromosomes instead of the normal two and is characterized by both physical and mental retardation and a distinctive physical appearance. Abnormalities can also arise in the sex chromosomes. Examples are **Turner syndrome** (an XO pattern), the triple-X syndrome, **Klinefelter's syndrome** (an XXY pattern), the double-Y syndrome (an XYY pattern), and **fragile X syndrome.** The physical, psychological, and emotional characteristics of people with these chromosome aberrations vary widely, depending upon the specific chromosome pattern and environmental factors involved.

Genetic Counseling and Genetic Engineering

- Advances in biology and genetics have opened new opportunities for diagnosing genetic disorders before birth. The two methods most commonly used to collect samples of fetal cells for genetic analysis are **amniocentesis** and **chorionic villi sampling.** Other diagnostic methods include the **alphafetoprotein assay** and **ultrasound.**

- Scientists hope eventually to locate the genes responsible for all inherited disorders. A breakthrough occurred when researchers identified the genetic marker for **Huntington disease,** making it possible to develop a test for the Huntington gene. With the aim of treating or curing genetic disorders, scientists are exploring gene therapy, which involves inserting normal alleles into a patient's cells to compensate for defective alleles. Theoretically, normal genes could even replace defective ones in sperm or egg cells, or they could be inserted into a newly created zygote.

Heredity-Environment Interactions

- The concept of the **range of reaction** helps shed light on how environments influence genes. According to this concept, heredity does not rigidly fix behavior but instead establishes a range of possible developmental outcomes that may occur in response to different environments. When a reaction range is extremely narrow, it is said to exhibit **canalization.** With a highly canalized trait, there are few pathways that development can take, and intense or more specific environmental pushes are required to deflect the course of development.

- Not only does environment influence genes, but genes also influence the environments to which people are exposed. In one way, called the **passive genetic-environmental interaction,** parents with certain genetic predispositions create a home environment that suits those predispositions and that may also suit and encourage the inherited predispositions of their children. In another way, known as **evocative genetic-environmental interaction,** people's inherited tendencies may evoke certain responses from others, as when a baby's inborn tendency to smile elicits positive stimulation from others. In a third way, called **active genetic-environmental interaction,** each person's genetic makeup may encourage him to seek out experiences compatible with his inherited tendencies. Also known as **niche picking,** in this form of interaction people who are, for example, naturally gregarious will look for opportunities to interact with other people in social activities.

Heredity, Environment, and Individual Differences

- An important question that researchers ask is why significant differences exist in individual development. **Human behavior genetics** seeks to answer this question by calculating **heritability factors**— percentage estimates of the contribution that genes make to some observed individual difference. Commonly, researchers study family members with known degrees of biological relatedness, such as **monozygotic** and **dizygotic** twins and adopted children, as well as the degree to which they inhabit **shared** or **nonshared environments.**

- Family resemblance studies consistently show that individual differences in IQ scores are substantially influenced by genetic factors. In addition, individual differences in certain more specific cognitive abilities, including spatial skills and verbal proficiency, are also influenced by genes, as are differences in the timing and rate of mental development. Nevertheless, an enriched environment can boost a child's level of intellectual development considerably.

- Heredity contributes to many individual differences in **temperament** and personality, especially differences in emotionality, activity level, and sociability. However, the contribution of heredity to differences in these traits appears to decline with age, as people's personalities become increasingly influenced by their life experiences.

- Whether early judgment of an infant as *difficult, easy,* or *slow-to-warm-up* has implications for a child's personality in later life may depend to a considerable degree on the **goodness of fit** between the child's temperament and the childrearing environment. A child's development can progress more smoothly and successfully when parents adjust their approach to suit their child's unique temperament.

EXPLORE AND DISCUSS

1. There is an ongoing debate about whether young people should be told if they are carriers of defective genes that may in the future lead them to have children with genetically caused disorders. Do you think children or even young adults should be given this information or not? Explain your position.
2. Two friends ask you about the heredity versus environment debate: One is a strong believer in the influence of the environment, and the other is committed to a belief in the importance of heredity. In light of our discussions in this chapter, what would you tell your friends to convince them that there are problems with both of these positions?
3. Many human characteristics have a genetic basis, and some of these characteristics can be modified by intervention. But should we modify a human characteristic just because we have the ability to do so? Do you think such interventions might lead to a societal view that some characteristics are more acceptable than others? Explain your answer.

House door panel with an X-Ray drawing of a pregnant woman. Collected in 1887 at Sieby Village, Geelvink Bay, Irian Jaya. Rijksmuseum voor Volkenkunde, Leiden, The Netherlands.

3.

Prenatal Development and Birth

Anticipating the birth of a child can be one of the most joyous times in people's lives. Couples look forward to becoming parents and enjoy preparing for their baby's arrival. They may even try to influence the new family member by playing favorite music or reading to their unborn child!

Whether it's possible to influence a baby in such positive ways during pregnancy is not entirely certain, although as we will see, there is some evidence that babies learn in utero. Unfortunately, however, clear evidence indicates that the developing organism is vulnerable to a variety of negative influences. Some of these influences are genetic, as we saw in Chapter 2, and others are variations in the prenatal environment caused by factors and events affecting the mother as her pregnancy proceeds. An amazing number of adverse agents—including medications and diagnostic procedures; prescription, nonprescription, and other legal and illegal drugs; maternal age and *parity* (whether a woman has had a child before); illness, dietary deficiencies, and emotional distress; and environmental toxins—can contribute to deviations from the normal development of a child from its first weeks of gestation. In addition, events occurring during childbirth may threaten the viability or good health of an infant, and, as we might guess, the economic and social conditions in which a child is raised can affect its development from the very earliest days of its life outside the womb.

We begin this chapter by exploring the normal development of the human being from conception to delivery and then discuss the many factors that can threaten normal development throughout a pregnancy. We look at normal childbirth and at some of the complications of labor and delivery, including the problems of prematurity and low birthweight. We conclude the chapter with a review of the research that has explored the long-term effects of pregnancy and birth complications as well as the resilience some children show in the face of such difficulties. Throughout these discussions we will ask several questions: What are the most significant of these complicating factors? How does the timing of their appearance in the *prenatal* environment modify their impact on the developing infant? Perhaps most important, how do *perinatal* factors (those occurring shortly before and/or after birth) affect the child's later development, and what *postnatal* events and conditions serve to sustain or modify the effects of prenatal and perinatal factors?

STAGES OF PRENATAL DEVELOPMENT

Conception usually takes place during a woman's ovulation or within a few days of it; the ovum, once released, lives only about three to five days. Prenatal development is understood, then, to encompass the 38 weeks, or approximately nine months, between conception and birth. Over these months the new organism changes in many ways. The kinds, numbers, positions, sizes, and shapes of cells, tissues, and bodily systems change, and these systems—for example, the central nervous system, which includes the brain and spinal cord—usually increase in size and complexity. On the other hand, some prenatal structures actually decrease in size or disappear. For example, at the end of the third week of pregnancy gill arches appear in the developing organism, but by the middle of the second month these remnants of an ancestral past have transformed into parts of the inner ear, the larynx, and the neck. The external tail that emerges between the second and fourth months also disappears.

The nine months of prenatal development are characterized in two ways. Traditionally, pregnancy has been described as occurring in three *trimesters,* or three periods of three months each, and we often speak of a particular event as occurring in one or another trimester. Increasingly, however, we talk about the three periods of (1) the zygote, (2) the embryo, and (3) the fetus. Although they are distinct in many ways, these periods should be thought of as comprising continuous phases of development, for from the moment the sperm penetrates the ovum, development involves a systematic series of sequential changes by which the organism becomes increasingly complex and differentiated. Figure 3-1 illustrates this series, from ovulation, when the ovum embarks on its journey to the uterus, to the end of the second trimester, when the fetus appears fully human.

The Zygote

zygote The developing organism from the time sperm and egg unite to about the second week of gestation; the period of the zygote comprises the implantation of the fertilized egg in the wall of the uterus.

The period of the zygote encompasses approximately the first two weeks of life, extending from the time a sperm fertilizes the ovum until that ovum, now a **zygote,** proceeds down the mother's fallopian tube into her uterus, where it implants in the wall of the uterus. When this occurs, about seven days after conception, the zygote is so tiny that probably 100 to 200 zygotes placed side by side would measure only an inch, and some 5 million would weigh only an ounce (Meredith, 1975). Gradually, tendrils from the zygote penetrate the blood vessels in the wall of the uterus, and the zygote forms the physiologically dependent relationship with the mother that will continue throughout the course of prenatal development.

The Embryo

embryo The developing organism between the second and eighth week of gestation; the embryonic period comprises the differentiation of the major physiological structures and systems.

The establishment of the zygote's secure relationship with the mother marks the beginning of the second prenatal period, the period of the embryo, a state of rapid growth that lasts from the beginning of the third week of gestation until the end of the eighth week. During this brief phase, in which the organism's most important physiological structures and systems differentiate, the **embryo** also becomes recognizable as a partially functioning tiny human being. From the time of fertilization until the end of this period the infant increases 2 million percent in size!

During this period, from the same, single fertilized egg, three crucial structures develop to protect and sustain the growing life within the mother's uterus: the amniotic sac, the placenta, and the umbilical cord. The **amniotic sac** contains the *amniotic fluid,* a watery liquid in which the developing embryo floats and which serves as a protective buffer against physical shocks and temperature changes. The tendrils that attach the embryo to the uterine wall increase in size and complexity to form a fleshy, disclike structure called the **placenta.** The embryo is joined to the placenta at the abdomen by the **umbilical cord,** a tube that contains the blood vessels that carry blood back and forth between the infant and placenta. (The umbilical cord attains a final length slightly greater than that of the growing organism, permitting it considerable mobility within the uterine environment.) However, semipermeable membranes within the placenta separate the bloodstreams of mother and child, allowing some substances to pass through, but not others. The placenta and umbilical cord thus transmit oxygen and nutrients to the infant and remove carbon dioxide and waste products from it, but they do not permit the direct exchange of blood. Early in gestation the nutrients in the mother's bloodstream exceed the needs of the embryo and are stored by the placenta for later use. Unfortunately, certain potentially destructive substances, such as drugs, hormones, viruses, and antibodies from the mother, do pass through the placenta to the embryo.

During the embryonic period, the inner mass of the new organism differentiates into three layers: the ectoderm, the mesoderm, and the endoderm. From the *ectoderm,* the hair, nails, parts of the teeth, the outer layer of the skin and skin glands, and the sensory cells and nervous system develop. The muscles, skeleton, circulatory and excretory systems, and inner skin layer evolve from the *mesoderm,* and from the *endoderm* come the gastrointestinal tract, trachea, bronchi, eustachian tubes, glands, and vital organs such as the lungs, pancreas, and liver. The especially rapid development and differentiation that occur at this time make the embryo more susceptible to environmental assault during this period than in any other—as a result, it is the period when most gross congenital anomalies occur. For example, about the fourth or fifth week of gestation the *neural folds* (formations that evolve ultimately into the central nervous system) begin to close. If something occurs to prevent the neural folds from closing completely, the child will have *spina bifida,* a disorder in which the spinal cord and the membranes that protect it may protrude from the spinal column (Corner, 1961, p. 14). Also at about the fourth week the organism's head begins to take shape, followed by the eyes, nose, and mouth. The blood vessel that will become the heart begins to pulsate. By the fifth week, buds that will form arms and legs begin to appear.

Note that fetal development is guided by two principles: cephalocaudal and proximal-distal development. By **cephalocaudal development** (the term *cephalocaudal* derives from the Latin words for "head" and "tail"), we mean a pattern of human physical growth that proceeds from the area of the head downward, to the trunk and legs. In **proximal-distal development** (again, from Latin words for "toward the center," "away from the center") growth occurs first in central areas, such as internal organs, and then outward to more distant areas, such as arms and legs. (We return to these principles when we discuss postnatal physical growth, in Chapter 5.)

By the end of the embryonic period, the growing organism's face and features are delineated, and fingers, toes, and external genitalia are present. Even at 6 weeks the embryo is recognizable as a human being, although a rather strangely proportioned one; the head is almost as large as the rest of the body. Primitive functioning of the heart and liver, as well as waves of the contractile movements of ingestion, have been reported late in this period.

Most *miscarriages,* or spontaneous abortions, occur during this period; for one reason or another the embryo becomes detached from the wall of the uterus and is expelled through the vaginal canal. The rate of spontaneous abortion has been estimated as high as one in four pregnancies, but many miscarriages remain undetected because they occur in the first few weeks of pregnancy. This high rate of natural abortion may be advantageous to the species, for the great majority of embryos aborted in this manner

amniotic sac A membrane that contains the developing organism and the amniotic fluid around it; sac and fluid protect the organism from physical shocks and temperature changes.

placenta A fleshy, disclike structure formed by cells from the lining of the uterus and from the *zygote* that, together with the *umbilical cord,* serves to protect and sustain the life of the growing organism.

umbilical cord A tube that contains blood vessels connecting the growing organism and its mother by way of the *placenta;* it carries oxygen and nutrients to the growing infant and removes carbon dioxide and waste products.

cephalocaudal development The pattern of human physical growth in which development begins in the area of the brain and proceeds downward, to the trunk and legs.

proximal-distal development The pattern of human physical growth wherein development starts in central areas, such as the internal organs, and proceeds to more distant areas, such as arms and legs.

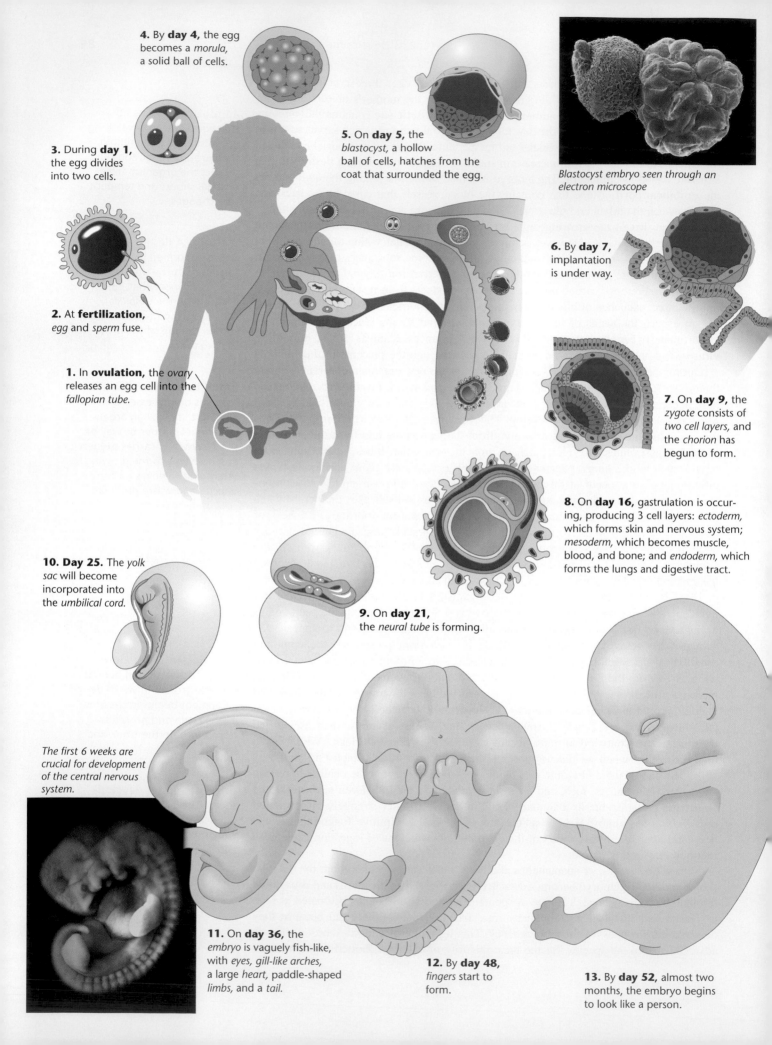

4. By **day 4,** the egg becomes a *morula,* a solid ball of cells.

3. During **day 1,** the egg divides into two cells.

5. On **day 5,** the *blastocyst,* a hollow ball of cells, hatches from the coat that surrounded the egg.

Blastocyst embryo seen through an electron microscope

2. At **fertilization,** *egg* and *sperm* fuse.

6. By **day 7,** implantation is under way.

1. In **ovulation,** the *ovary* releases an egg cell into the *fallopian tube.*

7. On **day 9,** the *zygote* consists of *two cell layers,* and the *chorion* has begun to form.

8. On **day 16,** gastrulation is occurring, producing 3 cell layers: *ectoderm,* which forms skin and nervous system; *mesoderm,* which becomes muscle, blood, and bone; and *endoderm,* which forms the lungs and digestive tract.

10. Day 25. The *yolk sac* will become incorporated into the *umbilical cord.*

9. On **day 21,** the *neural tube* is forming.

The first 6 weeks are crucial for development of the central nervous system.

11. On **day 36,** the *embryo* is vaguely fish-like, with *eyes, gill-like arches,* a large *heart,* paddle-shaped *limbs,* and a *tail.*

12. By **day 48,** *fingers* start to form.

13. By **day 52,** almost two months, the embryo begins to look like a person.

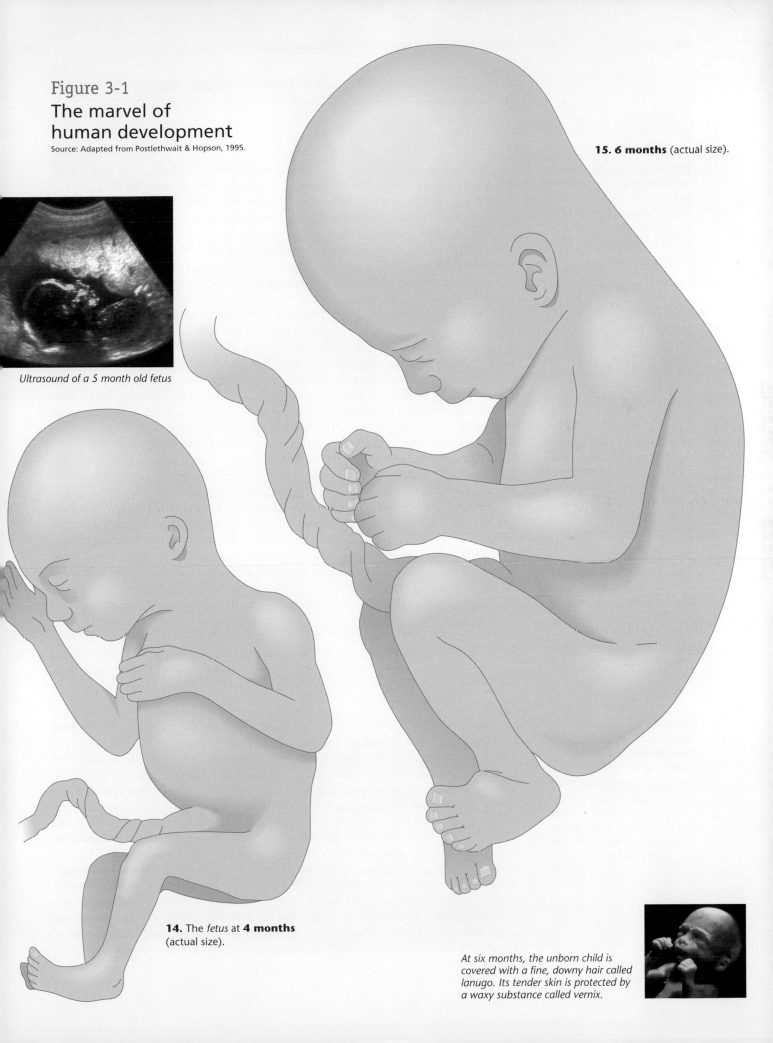

Figure 3-1
The marvel of human development
Source: Adapted from Postlethwait & Hopson, 1995.

Ultrasound of a 5 month old fetus

15. 6 months (actual size).

14. The *fetus* at **4 months** (actual size).

At six months, the unborn child is covered with a fine, downy hair called lanugo. Its tender skin is protected by a waxy substance called vernix.

have gross chromosomal and genetic disorders. Despite their relatively high rate, even early miscarriages can take an emotional toll on mothers and their partners.

The Fetus

fetus The developing organism from the third month of gestation through delivery; during the fetal period bodily structures and systems develop to completion.

During the third and final period of prenatal development, the **fetus**—the term for the developing organism from the beginning of the third month of gestation to delivery—experiences rapid muscular development. The development of the central nervous system also continues at a rapid pace during this period. The development of the brain itself is the major accomplishment of this period, although some parts of the nervous system (e.g., *glial cells,* which are discussed in Chapter 5) continue to develop for several years after birth. By the end of the third month the fetus will have all its body parts, including external genital organs. By the end of the fourth month, mothers usually report that they feel the fetus move. At around 5 months reflexes such as sucking, swallowing, and hiccuping usually appear. After the fifth month, the fetus develops nails and sweat glands, a coarser, more adultlike skin, and a soft hair, called **lanugo,** which covers the body. Most fetuses shed this hair in utero, but some continue to shed it after birth. By 6 months the eyes can open and close. If an infant is born prematurely at 6 months, the regulatory processes and nervous and respiratory systems are usually not mature enough for survival without intensive intervention. At this time the fetus cannot produce and maintain an adequate amount of *surfactant,* a liquid that allows the lungs to transmit oxygen from the air to the blood. Without surfactant, infants are often unable to breathe adequately, and they may develop **respiratory distress syndrome,** a condition of the newborn marked by labored breathing and a bluish discoloration of the skin or mucous membranes. This syndrome, which is often heralded by such symptoms as flaring nostrils and a gruntlike sound on expiration, can result in death.

lanugo A fine, soft hair that covers the fetus's body from about the fifth month of gestation on; may be shed before birth or after.

respiratory distress syndrome A condition of the newborn marked by labored breathing and a bluish discoloration of the skin or mucous membranes; can result in infant death.

age of viability The age of 22 to 26 weeks from conception, at which point the fetus's physical systems are advanced enough that it has a chance to survive if born prematurely.

The age of 22 to 26 weeks, sometimes referred to as the **age of viability,** is an important point in fetal development, because by this time the fetus's physical systems are sufficiently advanced that the child, if born prematurely, has a reasonable probability of surviving. With the exceptional resources available in modern intensive-care nurseries, infants as immature as 22 weeks can sometimes live. Notice in this chapter's Turning Points chart (pp. 90–91), however, that many systems are still developing; the respiratory system in particular continues to evolve into the ninth month of gestation. Not uncommonly, babies born before 28 weeks later display developmental deviations, especially if they encounter other adverse environmental conditions (Moore & Persaud, 1998).

RISKS IN THE PRENATAL ENVIRONMENT

teratogen An environmental agent, such as a drug, medication, dietary imbalance, or polluting substance, that may cause developmental deviations in a growing human organism; most threatening in the embryonic stage but capable of causing abnormalities in the fetal stage as well.

During the course of prenatal development, many agents may cause developmental deviations in the fetus. These agents are called **teratogens,** a term that derives from the Greek word *teras,* meaning "monster" or "marvel." Teratogens encompass a wide variety of agents, including prescription and nonprescription medications and drugs taken by the mother and environmental toxins, such as pollution. Although teratogens are essentially environmental factors, such factors as the mother's age, her diet, and her emotional state will affect the response of both mother and child to any given teratogenic agent. In this section, we will consider first the hazardous influences that abound in the environment at large, and then the risks that imperil the growing organism from within its maternal shelter.

In considering the effects of adverse prenatal and childbirth factors on development, we often tend to concentrate on the gross physical defects or mental impairments that sometimes result. However, an equally important issue is how these factors change the life experiences of the child and the responses of those around the child. How should a parent with a child at risk because of prematurity treat the baby?

How is the emotional bond that usually forms between parent and child affected by an infant's longer stay in the hospital because of prematurity, low birthweight, or other physical problems? Is the parent more anxious or more protective? Or may the parent sometimes reject the child? What happens to parent-child interaction if the infant is lethargic and unresponsive because of drugs administered during its delivery? Experiential factors such as these may ultimately be the most important in sustaining or minimizing the long-term effects of early adversity.

Before we begin to explore some of the possible threats to the health of the fetus or newborn, let us consider how teratogens exert their effects on prenatal development (Friedman & Polifka, 1996; Moore & Persaud, 1998; Vorhees & Mollnow, 1987).

1. *A teratogen exerts its effects largely during critical periods.* The effects of a teratogen vary with the embryo's developmental stage. As we've said (and as Figure 3-2 shows), during the embryonic stage the organism is most vulnerable

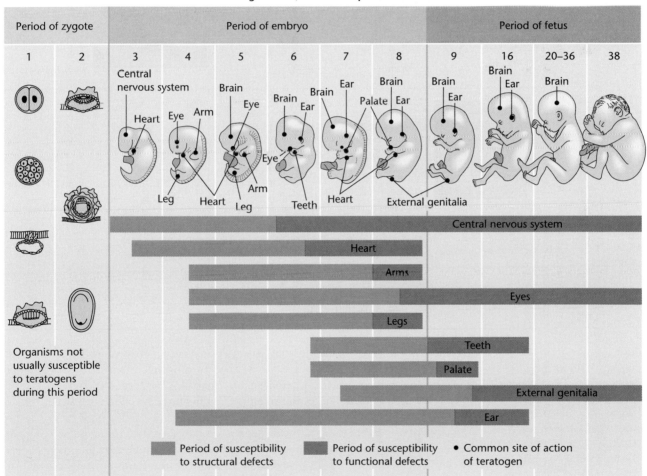

Figure 3-2 The child's prenatal susceptibility to teratogenic agents

Sensitivity of the growing embryo to teratogens is greatest in the first four to eight weeks of gestation, peaking about the fifth week. Normally, the zygote is not susceptible to specific teratogens, but if it does succumb to a teratogenic agent, its tiny mass is usually so defenseless that it dies. The defects that occur early in development, when critical organs are being formed, are generally structural; teratogenic agents that affect the fetus in later weeks are more likely to stunt growth or cause functional problems.

Source: Adapted from Moore, 1989.

Turning Points

AN OVERVIEW OF PRENATAL DEVELOPMENT

Month	Size & Weight	Nervous & Sensory Systems	Cardiovascular & Respiratory Systems	Musculoskeletal & Dermal Systems	Digestive & Urinary Systems	Endocrine & Reproductive Systems	Other Events
1 (Zygote)	0.2 in. .007 oz	Neural tube (B) Eyes, ears (B)	Heartbeat (B) Trachea & lungs (B)		Intestinal tract, liver, pancreas (B)		
2 (Embryo)	1.1 in. .09 oz	Nervous system organization, growth of cerebrum (B) Taste buds, olfactory system (B)	Heart structure, major blood vessels, lymph nodes (B) Blood formation in liver (B) Bronchial branching (B) Diaphragm (C)	Cartilage formation (B) Muscles that support central portion of body formed (C)	Intestinal subdivisions including salivary glands (B) Kidney formation (B)	Thyroid, pituitary, adrenal glands (B) Mammary glands (B)	
3	3.2 in. 1.6 oz	Basic spinal cord & brain structure (C)	Tonsils; blood formation in bone marrow (B)	Cartilage replaced with bone (B) Muscles that support appendages (e.g., legs, arms) formed (C) Skeleton visible in X rays by 14 weeks	Gallbladder, pancreas (C)	Genitalia (B) Differentiation of gonads into ovaries & testes	Fetus responds to stimulation Form is recognizably human Mother's abdomen visibly distended Mother can feel baby's movements
4	5.3 in. 5 oz	Rapid expansion of cerebrum (B) Eye & ear structure complete (C)	Blood formation in spleen (B) Lymphocytes migrate to lymphatic organs (B)	Lanugo & head hair form (B) Skin thin, wrinkled, translucent Sweat glands (C)		Genitalia distinct by 16 weeks	
5	8 in. 17 oz	Myelination of spinal cord (B)	Nostrils open (C)	Adultlike skin Eyelashes & eyebrows Nail production (B)	Intestinal subdivisions (C)		Fetus sucks, swallows, & hiccoughs Evidence of Babinski & grasping reflexes

First trimester (Months 1–3)

Second trimester (Months 4–5)

Fetus	6	11.2 in. 1 lb, 10 oz	CNS tract formation; layering of cerebral cortex (B)	Spleen, liver, & bone marrow (C); Formation of lung alveoli (B)	Perineal (sphincter) muscles (C)	Adrenal glands (C)	Survival outside womb relatively rare
Third trimester	7	14–15 in. 2 lb, 11 oz	Eyelids open; retina sensitive to light		Nail & hair formation (B)	Pituitary gland (C) Descent of testes into scrotum (B)	Survival outside womb not uncommon Rapid weight gain begins Sensitivity to sounds
	8	15–17 in. 4 lb, 6 oz	Taste receptors become functional	Pulmonary branching & alveolar formation (C)		Kidney structure (C)	
	9	19–21 in. 6 lb, 10 oz to 7 lb, 10 oz	CNS tract formation continues	Immune system becomes operative	Hair changes in consistency & distribution; Skeletal growth continues; Muscle mass & control increase	Descent of testes complete at or near time of delivery	
Postnatal development							Normal birth

Key: B = Begins to form   C = Completes formation
Sources: Based on Fischer & Lazarson, 1984; Martini, 1995; Moore & Persaud, 1998.

to assault; teratogens acting on newly differentiated cells may damage developing but yet unformed organ systems. Moreover, each organ system, developing at its own pace, has a different critical period (Little, 1992). For example, the most vulnerable period for the heart is between 20 and 40 days after conception (Friedman & Polifka, 1996). During the fetal stage, teratogen-induced abnormalities tend to occur only in locations or systems that are still maturing, such as the central nervous system and the genitalia.

2. *Each teratogen exerts certain specific effects.* Because individual teratogens influence specific developmental processes, they produce specific patterns of developmental deviations. For example, *rubella,* or German measles, in the mother affects mainly the fetus's heart, eyes, and brain. The drug thalidomide, which we discuss later, primarily causes malformations of the limbs.

3. *Either maternal or fetal genotypes may counteract a teratogen's effects.* Both maternal and fetal genotypes can affect the developing organism's response to teratogenic agents and may play an important role in determining whether offspring will display abnormalities. For example, not all pregnant women who have German measles produce defective infants. Infants who develop defects may do so because of their own genetic vulnerability or that of their mothers to a particular teratogen.

4. *The effects of one teratogen may intensify the effects of another.* The physiological status of the mother will influence the action of a teratogen. Factors such as nutrition and hormonal balance may modify the impact of a teratogen. For example, nutritional deficiencies, which may interfere with healthy prenatal development, may also intensify the adverse effects of drugs that the mother has ingested, such as cortisone.

5. *A particular teratogen may affect the fetus but have no discernible effect on the mother.* Levels of teratogenic agents that will produce malformations in the offspring may have no appreciable detrimental effects on the mother. Thus although the mother may take drugs, experience disease or irradiation, and maintain a deficient diet without visible ill effect, her child may exhibit gross abnormalities.

6. *A particular teratogen may produce a variety of deviations, whereas several different teratogens may produce the same deviation.* For example, if the mother contracts rubella early in her pregnancy, her child risks deafness. However, not only maternal rubella but also the mother's ingestion of drugs such as quinine or streptomycin may cause deafness in her infant.

7. *The longer a fetus is exposed to a particular teratogen, and the greater the intensity of the teratogen's effects, the more likely it is that the fetus will be seriously harmed.* This is the *dose-response* principle at work: In general, the higher the dose, the more severe will be the damage to the developing fetus.

Environmental Dangers

We know that illegal drugs, such as heroin, and other drugs in common use, such as alcohol and nicotine, are often quite harmful to human beings. Thus, it should come as no surprise that these substances can be extremely harmful—even life-threatening—to the growing organism, despite the protection afforded it by its mother's body. However, as we will see, mothers and the babies they carry for nine months may encounter many more and less well-known hazardous substances, any of which can do them—especially, the baby—considerable harm.

LEGAL AND ILLEGAL DRUGS Although most physicians and parents would probably agree that pregnant women should not take too many drugs, according to one estimate nearly 90 percent of women take some sort of drug during pregnancy (Cunningham, MacDonald, & Grant, 1993). In many of these cases, women may not yet realize that they are pregnant. Even so, a variety of over-the-counter (nonprescription) drugs, such as aspirin and diet pills, may have adverse effects on the fetus. For example, heavy use of aspirin has been associated with low birthweight, lower IQ, and poor motor control (Barr, Streissguth, Darby, & Sampson, 1990), although others have failed to confirm this link (Friedman & Polifka, 1996).

Many pregnant women may not be aware, however, that their choice of even nonalcoholic beverages is potentially harmful. Did you realize that too much caffeine can adversely affect a developing fetus? Recent studies found that women who drank three or more cups of coffee a day were at higher risk for miscarriage or for low-birthweight infants (Fernandes et al., 1998; Klebanoff, Levine, Der Simonian, Clemens, & Wilkins, 1999).

In this section we examine the effects on the fetus and infant of other legal drugs such as cigarettes and alcohol, as well as illegal drugs such as heroin and cocaine. In the next section we will consider the potential effects of drugs physicians often prescribe as well as the effects of some over-the-counter drugs. In Table 3-1 we provide you with an overview of this section as well as of the next two sections, on medical interventions and environmental toxins.

Nicotine and Alcohol   Despite the efforts of many groups in recent years to convince the public that nicotine and alcohol are just as dangerous and addictive as so-called hard drugs such as heroin and cocaine, people persist in using these substances. Researchers have found that both smoking and drinking are associated with disturbances in placental functioning and with changes in maternal physiology that lead to oxygen deprivation and thus to potential structural and functional changes in the fetus's brain (Chomitz et al., 2000). Nevertheless, it has been estimated that over 80 percent of pregnant women in the United States drink alcohol and over 30 percent smoke.

The rate of spontaneous abortions, prematurity, and low-birthweight babies is higher for mothers who smoke or drink than for those who do neither (Gilliland, Li, & Peters, 2001; Mills, 1999). In addition, *sudden infant death syndrome (SIDS),* in which infants under the age of 12 months stop breathing and die without apparent cause, is more common in the offspring of mothers who smoke, drink, or take narcotic drugs (Hunt, 2001). Women who are chronic smokers have premature infants almost twice as often as nonsmokers, and the more a particular woman smokes, the more likely she is to deliver prematurely. Babies born to smokers are also more susceptible to respiratory infections than are children of nonsmokers (Chavkin, 1995).

Recent studies have indicated that passive smoke—that is, smoke breathed in by nonsmokers—can also contribute to low birthweight among the babies of mothers who don't smoke (Friedman & Polifka, 1996). One study found that if fathers smoked during pregnancy, their babies were 3 ounces (88 grams) lighter at birth than babies of nonsmoking fathers (Martinez, Wright, & Taussig, 1994). In addition, British scientists have reported that men who smoke may transmit their own risk of cancer to their offspring. Studying 1,500 parents whose children died of cancer in the early 1950s, these researchers found that fathers who smoked a pack or more of cigarettes a day had a 42 percent increased risk of having a child with cancer (Sorahan, Lancashire, Hulten, Peck, & Stewart, 1997). Other studies have shown that passive smoke can cause delays in intellectual and behavioral development (Friedman & Polifka, 1996) and that babies exposed in utero to passive smoke are at increased risk for a variety of illnesses such as pneumonia, bronchitis, laryngitis, and otitis media (an inner ear infection) (Charlton, 1994). Clearly it is difficult for nonsmoking pregnant women to protect their unborn children from the dangers of nicotine when friends, coworkers, and even husbands smoke.

Table 3-1 The effect of drugs, medications, and environmental toxins on prenatal development

	Potential Negative Effects
Legal Drugs	
Nicotine	Prematurity, low birthweight, delayed intellectual and behavioral development, risk of pneumonia, bronchitis, laryngitis, inner ear infections; fathers' smoking may transmit risk of cancer to offspring
Alcohol	Fetal alcohol syndrome (physical defects, short stature, mental retardation, hyperactivity, stereotyped behaviors, congenital addiction leading to withdrawal syndrome); father's abuse of alcohol may cause genetic damage that leads to birth defects The combination of parental smoking and drinking may cause miscarriages, prematurity, low birthweight, and sudden infant death syndrome
Caffeine	Higher risk for miscarriage and low-birthweight infants
Illegal Drugs	
Heroin, morphine, methadone	In mother, difficulty conceiving; in infant, prematurity, low birthweight, addiction, withdrawal, death
Marijuana	In mother, difficulty conceiving; in infant, prematurity, low birthweight, high-pitched crying; no long-term effects
Cocaine	In mother, difficulty conceiving; in infant, prematurity, low birthweight; see text for further discussion
Lysergic acid diethylamide (LSD)	Chromosomal breakage
Medications/Treatments	
Diethylstilbestrol (DES)	In mother, miscarriage; in infant, prematurity, low birthweight; female child may develop cancer of the cervix; male child may have reproductive abnormalities and increased risk of testicular cancer
Thalidomide	Deformations of infant's face, limbs, fingers, and toes; malformations of heart and digestive and genitourinary tracts; malformations or absence of limbs
Quinine	Deafness in infant
Reserpine (tranquilizer)	Respiratory problems in infant
Tetracyclines	Defective skeletal growth in infant
Aspirin	Blood disorders in infant
Some anticonvulsant medications	Cleft lip and palate in infant; failure of blood coagulation
Anesthetics, local or general; epidural blocks	Short-term depression of infant's responsiveness, disruptions in feeding, behavioral disorganization, impaired attention, and motor abilities
Environmental Toxins	
Lead	Miscarriage, anemia, hemorrhage in mother
Methyl mercury	Cerebral palsy in infant
Radiation	In mother, miscarriage, stillbirth; in infant, microcephaly, stunted growth, leukemia, cancer, cataract

As early as 1800, abnormalities in children of alcoholic mothers were reported in England. Concerns were expressed that the high consumption of gin, euphemistically known as "mother's ruin," was leading to increased rates of dwarfism in women's offspring. Today, we know that **fetal alcohol syndrome** characterizes 6 percent of infants of alcoholic mothers (Day & Richardson, 1994). Even before birth the fetus's spontaneous movements may be suppressed, and young infants often display motor deficits (Streissguth, 1997). Infants with this disorder have a high incidence of facial, heart, and limb defects; they are 20 percent shorter than the average child of their age and are often mentally retarded (Streissguth, 1997). The mental retardation may be related to the loss of oxygen in the fetal brain when the fetus's breathing movements cease temporarily: It has been demonstrated that if in their last trimester women who are not heavy drinkers consume just 1 ounce of 80-proof vodka, the respiratory action of their fetuses may cease for more than half an hour (Fox et al., 1978). Indeed, the fetal damage from alcohol appears to be greatest in the last trimester. If women can cease drinking in this period, their babies tend to be longer, weigh more, and have a larger head circumference than those of women who continue heavy drinking (Streissguth, 1997).

Children with fetal alcohol syndrome may exhibit a wide range of abnormal behaviors: They may be excessively irritable, distractible, and hyperactive and may engage in behaviors such as repeatedly banging their heads or rhythmically rocking their bodies. They may also exhibit failure to become accustomed to repeated stimuli, and they may be slow or unable to learn to perform such actions as turning their heads or even sucking (Jacobson & Jacobson, 1996; Streissguth, 1997). Many babies born to alcoholic mothers go through withdrawal from the drug: They shake, vomit, are irritable, and generally exhibit symptoms akin to *delirium tremens,* the extreme withdrawal syndrome seen in adult alcoholics.

Although the worst cases of fetal alcohol syndrome are seen in babies born to clearly alcoholic mothers, even a pregnant woman's moderate social drinking— say, an ounce and a half of hard liquor or a glass of beer or wine per day—can cause abnormal behavior patterns in her baby (Abel, 1998; Mattson, Riley, Delis, & Jones, 1998). Furthermore, studies of older children indicate that many children whose mothers smoke or drink exhibit cognitive deficits, get lower IQ test scores, and have more problems with attention and academic achievement than other children (Connor, Sampson, Bookstein, Barr, & Streissguth, 2001; Streissguth, 1997). For example, studying more than 500 children, Streissguth and colleagues (Streissguth, Bookstein, Sampson, & Barr, 1995) found that prenatal alcohol consumption affected attention even in 14-year-olds. If it seems as if all the blame for prenatal damage to infants is placed on the mother, note that research has suggested that men who drink heavily may sustain genetic damage that leads to birth defects in their offspring (Cicero, 1994). Finally, smoking and drinking seem to interact negatively: Infants whose mothers use both alcohol and tobacco show more prenatal growth deficiencies than do infants whose mothers use only one of these substances (Little, 1975).

Heroin, Cocaine, and Other Drugs   Although drug use and abuse in the United States have waxed and waned in recent years, neither has entirely gone away, nor is either likely to do so soon. The prenatal effects of drugs such as heroin, morphine, methadone, cocaine, lysergic acid diethylamide (LSD), and marijuana are of increasing concern. Mothers who are addicted to heroin—a form of morphine—or to morphine itself or who use cocaine have offspring who are also addicted or who sustain toxic effects from these drugs. Babies addicted to one of these drugs go through withdrawal symptoms, some of which are similar to those we described in infants born to alcoholics: irritability, minimal ability to regulate their state of arousal, trembling, shrill crying, rapid respiration, and hyperactivity. Moreover, because these infants are often premature and of low birthweight, it is even more difficult for them to cope with

fetal alcohol syndrome A disorder exhibited by infants of alcoholic mothers and characterized by stunted growth, a number of physical and physiological abnormalities, and, often, mental retardation.

LifeMap CD

To learn more about fetal alcohol syndrome and its impact on the entire family, watch the video "Effect of Prenatal Exposure to Alcohol" in Chapter 3 of your CD.

the trauma of withdrawal symptoms (Lester, Boukydis, & Twomey, 2000). In general, the severity of the newborn's symptoms is related to the length, continuity, and intensity of the mother's addiction. If the mother stops taking drugs in the last trimester preceding birth, the infant is usually not affected appreciably (Lester et al., 2000). However, in some cases, symptoms can be severe enough to result in an infant's death in the first few days of its life (Lester et al., 2000; Phillips, Sharma, Premachandra, Vaughn, & Reyes-Lee, 1996).

At a time when an infant needs special attention and loving care, these infants' behavior may elicit the opposite kind of behavior from drug-using parents who have problems of their own. Although addicted babies' symptoms are likely to get the attention of a caregiver, these infants do not readily cuddle or cling to an adult. Moreover, when adults physically stimulate these infants or place them on their shoulders, they don't elicit the alertness that normal babies evidence. Clinging, alerting, and eye contact are the main behaviors by which infants initiate and sustain social interactions with their caregivers (Lester et al., 2000), and the lack of these behaviors in addicted newborns may disrupt parenting and have long-term adverse outcomes for parent-child relationships (Phillips et al., 1996).

As many as 200,000 American babies a year have mothers who used cocaine during pregnancy; in some inner-city areas, one in four births are to cocaine-addicted mothers (Chavkin, 1995). A specific set of cocaine-linked physical defects includes bone, genital, urinary tract, kidney, eye, and heart deformities; brain hemorrhages; and neuron damage. Lester and colleagues (2000) report that two common behavior patterns are found in the children of such mothers: One pattern is characterized by excitable, irritable behavior, and high-pitched prolonged crying; the other is depressed, unresponsive behavior with less crying of lower amplitude. The first pattern, which Lester suggests is associated with direct toxic effects of cocaine on the neurological system, is also accompanied by irregular, accelerated heartbeat, elevated blood pressure, and constriction in the upper airways. The second pattern is likely an indirect result of cocaine use and is related to low birthweight and stunted growth. Some children show a combination of both patterns, appearing lethargic and sleeping a great deal but then waking up screaming and resisting efforts to soothe them.

Finally, the effects of marijuana use on either fetal or infant development are unclear. Although investigators have observed reduced weight and size, as well as some short-term changes in behavior such as increased startle and sleep problems, we have no evidence of long-term adverse effects on infant development (Fried, Watkinson, & Gray, 1998; Lester et al., 2000). However, avoiding drugs during pregnancy is clearly the safest strategy for protecting the eventual health of the developing infant.

ENVIRONMENTAL TOXINS   Wide ranges of dangerous substances in the everyday environment are potentially harmful to children. Some of the most commonly encountered are radiation, lead, mercury, herbicides, pesticides, household cleaners, and even food additives and cosmetics. Although many environmental toxins have not been tested for their harmful effects on the growing organism, and much is still to be learned about prenatal neurotoxicity, we have known for years that radiation can harm the developing fetus; it is for this reason that pregnant women are advised to avoid X rays (H. Smith, 1992).

Lead is another well-documented problem for pregnant women, the developing fetus, and children. Women and babies may be exposed to lead, for example, by inadvertently inhaling automobile exhaust or by drinking water contaminated by industrial waste. Exposure to lead during pregnancy has been associated with a variety of problems in newborns, including prematurity and low birthweight, brain damage, and physical defects, as well as with long-term problems in cognitive and intellectual functioning (Dietrich, Berger, Succop, Hammond, & Bornschein, 1993). Lead-based paint, often found in older homes, also threatens babies and young children who eat peeling paint or simply breathe the dust from such paint. Ingestion of lead has been linked to poorer cognitive and academic abilities (Needleman, Leviton, & Bellinger, 1982; Voorhees & Mollnow, 1987).

Joseph and Sandra Jacobson (1996) have alerted us to the dangerous effects on pregnant women of another environmental hazard: polychlorinated biphenyls (PCBs), which were once used routinely in electrical transformers and capacitors. This use of these substances has been banned since the mid-1970s, when it was discovered that pregnant women who ate PCB-contaminated fish gave birth to infants with various deficits (Jacobson & Jacobson, 1996). These babies were smaller, less responsive, and less neurologically advanced than infants not exposed to PCBs. More recently, the Jacobsons and their colleagues have reported long-term effects of prenatal exposure to PCBs: Among these effects were lower IQ and poorer memory in 4-year-old children (Jacobson, Jacobson, Padgett, Brumitt, & Billings, 1992).

Even fathers' exposure to environmental toxins can have harmful effects on a developing fetus. Men who work in occupations that expose them to toxic substances such as radiation, anesthetic gases, mercury, or lead may develop chromosomal abnormalities that may affect their fertility or may increase the risk that their wives will miscarry or will bear infants with birth defects (Merewood, 2000). It would seem that any wife and husband planning to have a child should both monitor their exposure to environmental toxins. Some individual manufacturing companies have developed policies that protect pregnant women from job-related exposure to such toxins, and it looks as though these policies ought to include men as well.

MEDICAL INTERVENTIONS IN PREGNANCY AND CHILD-
BIRTH Because even many normal pregnancies are not without discomfort and symptoms that are distressing to the mother, physicians may prescribe drugs or diagnostic procedures to alleviate such problems. Medical X rays are now known to be harmful to the developing fetus and are avoided during pregnancy. Other procedures, such as ultrasound (which we discussed in Chapter 2), are now used instead to examine the fetus and to check for irregularities.

Some Therapeutic Disasters Between 1947 and 1964, the synthetic hormone **diethylstilbestrol (DES)** was often prescribed to help prevent pregnant women from miscarrying. Tragically, this drug turned out to be anything but therapeutic, for in the late 1960s scientists discovered its delayed effects. Many female offspring of the perhaps 2 million U.S. women who had taken DES during pregnancy developed vaginal abnormalities and cancer of the cervix in adolescence (Nevin, 1988). In addition, these young women also experienced a high rate of problems in pregnancy, including spontaneous abortion, premature deliveries, and babies with low birthweight (Linn et al., 1988). Moreover, it is now recognized that sons of women who ingested DES during pregnancy may have sustained damage to the reproductive tract, such as seminal fluid abnormalities (Giusti, Iwamoto, & Hatch, 1995; Wilcox et al., 1995).

Another therapeutic tragedy in the early 1960s made the public keenly aware of the often unknown and potentially devastating effects of drug use by pregnant women. **Thalidomide,** an antianxiety and antinausea drug, was prescribed by many physicians to relieve the symptoms of morning sickness. Increasingly, children were born with particularly unusual and often hideous abnormalities that included deformations of the eyes, nose, and ears; cleft palate; facial palsy; and fusing of fingers and toes, as well as dislocations of the hip joint and malformations of the heart and the digestive and genitourinary tracts. The most characteristic and most horrible deformity was something called *phocomelia,* in which limbs are missing and the feet and hands are attached directly to the torso in a way that to many resembled flippers (Moore & Persaud, 1998). Although there is some controversy on the point, the evidence suggests that thalidomide

diethylstilbestrol (DES) A synthetic hormone once prescribed for pregnant women to prevent miscarriage but discontinued when cancer and precancerous conditions were detected in their children.

thalidomide A drug once prescribed to relieve morning sickness in pregnant women but discontinued when found to cause serious fetal malformations. Current controversy surrounds its possible use in treating symptoms of such diseases as AIDS, cancer, and leprosy.

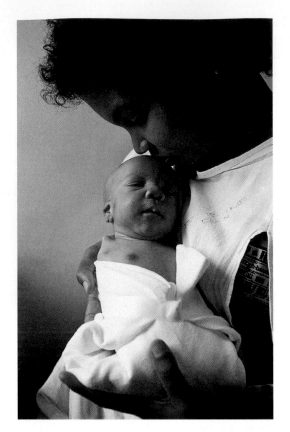

The tragedy of the thalidomide disaster is written on the face of this young Brazilian mother. Her love and her sadness are apparent as she kisses and cradles her newborn son in her arms.

babies who were reared in a normal home situation and who did not suffer from gross sensory deficits such as blindness or deafness were of normal intelligence (DeCarie, 1961).

The problems in establishing the consequences for offspring of maternal intake of a drug during pregnancy are illustrated clearly in the cases of both DES and thalidomide. The women themselves showed no adverse effects from these drugs, and in the case of thalidomide, only a small percentage of pregnant women produced children with deficits. In some animal studies the administration of this drug produced no adverse effects in offspring.

Diethylstilbestrol is still on the market today but is recommended now only for the alleviation of symptoms in advanced breast and prostate cancer. After being banned in 1962, thalidomide was made available in 1998 for the treatment of cancer and of other illnesses such as AIDS and leprosy.

Other drugs ingested by the mother may also affect the fetus. For example, if a pregnant woman with malaria is treated with quinine, her unborn child may be born deaf. In addition, it has recently been found that other drugs that are commonly administered to pregnant women for therapeutic reasons may have deleterious effects. Maternal ingestion of reserpine, a tranquilizer, may lead to respiratory problems in an infant. Some drugs used to combat maternal infections, such as the tetracyclines, may depress infant skeletal growth. There is some evidence that a pregnant woman's intake of certain anticonvulsant drugs may result in her baby's developing the condition of cleft lip and palate as well as failure of the blood to coagulate. Even the common aspirin, if taken in high doses by pregnant women, may produce blood disorders in offspring (Vorhees & Mollnow, 1987).

The effects of drugs are difficult to predict. Many drugs that have produced unfortunate effects were tested on animals and on nonpregnant adults and found to be harmless. However, we cannot generalize the findings from tests performed on animals and human adults to the situation of the rapidly developing fetus; teratogens may affect different species at different stages of development in diverse ways. The difficulties in predicting drug effects are also compounded by the wide individual differences among infants and mothers in vulnerability to drug effects. There is as yet little research on the long-term effects of maternal drug intake; clearly physicians must use great caution in prescribing drugs for women during pregnancy and labor.

Medications Used in Labor and Delivery In recent years, researchers have focused concern on the effects of local anesthetics, such as the spinal block, and general anesthetics when they are used to ease pain and to sedate women during labor. Babies of mothers who received large amounts of obstetrical medication during labor showed less responsiveness, less smiling, and more irritability for several days after birth, as well as depression, motoric disorganization, and disruptions in feeding responses (Brackbill, McManus, & Woodward, 1985). Genetic factors, the mother's general health, the length of labor, the size of the baby, and even the mother's attitude may modify the impact of obstetrical medications on the newborn (Lester, Als, & Brazelton, 1982). These medications, especially anesthetics, do cause impaired attention and motor abilities in the infant that are still evident at 1 month of age, but there are often no longer-term effects (Emory, Schlackman, & Fiano, 1996).

The use of general anesthesia, which renders the mother unconscious and which has the most deleterious effect on her infant, has declined greatly in recent years. Physicians generally use only modest amounts of drugs in labor and delivery (Hawkins, 1999). Regional anesthetics, either epidural or spinal, that numb the body from the waist down are the most common forms of pain relief used in labor and delivery. These types of medication, the least likely of all analgesics to reach the baby, are among the safest choices. However, even these "safe" painkillers may be associated with prolonged labor, though not increased risk of cesarean section (Zhang et al., 1999).

Maternal Factors

For the fetus, all teratogenic agents or their influences are mediated by the mother's body; however, some factors are directly related to characteristics of the mother herself. In this section we discuss how a mother's age, choice of diet, and emotional state may affect her unborn child. Then we will explore the diseases and disorders that may also have a negative impact on a developing fetus. As you read on you may find it useful to look at Table 3-2, which gives an overview of this material.

Table 3-2 Maternal characteristics, diseases, and disorders that can have a negative impact on prenatal development

	Potential Negative Effects
Characteristics of the Mother	
Age	Teenage mothers tend to live in risky environments, to neglect their health and diets, and to use drugs, thus raising their risk of delivering premature and low-birthweight babies; older mothers risk bearing a Down syndrome child as well as problems posed by illnesses that are more common as people age.
Diet	Malnourishment can lead to miscarriage, stillbirths, prematurity, low birthweight, physical and neural defects, smaller size in newborns, and sometimes cognitive difficulties.
Emotional state	Mothers who are stressed may have troubled pregnancies, miscarriages, long labor and delivery complications, and more need for childbirth anesthesia; their infants may be hyperactive and irritable and have feeding and sleep problems.
Diseases and Disorders	
Mumps	Infant may suffer malformation of some kind.
Rubella (German measles)	Infant may be born deaf or mentally retarded or have cardiac disorders or cataracts.
Rh factor incompatibility	If mother's and infant's blood types are incompatible (mother's negative, infant's positive), on subsequent pregnancies antibodies produced by mother's blood can kill the fetus.
Hypertension (high blood pressure)	Fetal abnormalities, miscarriage, fetal death.
Diabetes	Preeclampsia or eclampsia, associated with hypertension; possible stillbirth or death of newborn.
Gonorrhea	Infant may be infected in the birth canal.
Syphilis	Miscarriage; if infant survives it may be born blind, mentally retarded, or have other physical abnormalities.
Chlamydia	Miscarriage or stillbirth; surviving infant may acquire disease in birth process, or develop pneumonia or a form of conjunctivitis.
Genital herpes	Infected infant may be blind, mentally retarded, or have motor abnormalities or a wide range of neurological disorders. Half of surviving infants are seriously disabled.
Acquired immune deficiency syndrome (AIDS)	Infants infected often suffer neurological impairments, defects in mental and physical development, microcephaly (small head), and other physical abnormalities. More than half survive beyond 6 years of age, but most eventually die from this disorder.
Toxoplasmosis	Eye and brain damage in the developing baby.

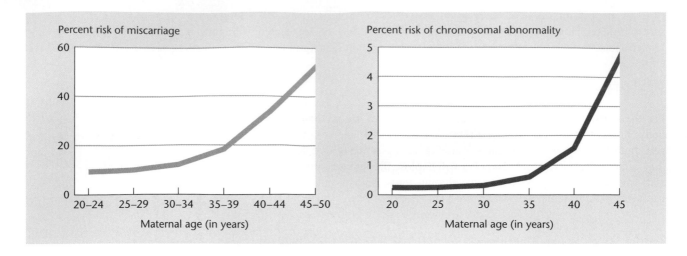

Figure 3-3   Maternal age and reproductive risk
As women age, the risks of miscarriage and of chromosomal abnormalities increase.
Source: From *Time*, April 15, 2002, p. 53. © 2002 Time Inc. reprinted by permission.

AGE AND PARITY   A woman's age and *parity*, or the number of children she has already borne, may interact in influencing the development of her fetus. Women who have their first child when they are under 15 or over 35 are likely to experience more problems during pregnancy and more complications during delivery than other women. Although this may be due to the immaturity of the reproductive system in teenagers or to deterioration in older mothers' reproductive systems, we know that in both groups these risks are also associated with the mother's health.

As we will see, there can be problems with early pregnancy, but waiting too long to become pregnant runs more risks, including difficulty in conceiving a child. Indeed, the chance of becoming pregnant declines steadily after age 27, and by age 40 it is less than 5 percent (among women who are trying to become pregnant). Similarly, as Figure 3-3 shows, the incidence of both miscarriage and chromosomal abnormality increase with the mother's age. Recall our discussion, in Chapter 2, of the older mother's risk of bearing a Down syndrome infant.

However, not just older mothers risk problems. Teenage mothers tend to encounter greater risks to their health and the health of their infants because they are often of low socioeconomic status and thus lack both good nutrition and prenatal care. Moreover, they tend to live in environments characterized by high rates of disease and environmental pollutants. One study of such young mothers, more than two-thirds from minority groups, showed that their children were at risk for delays in developing intellectual, language, and social skills (Sommer, Keogh, & Whitman, 1995). Another study of young mothers of similar backgrounds found that a mother's "cognitive readiness" for parenting—defined as knowledge of child development, parenting style preferences, and parenting attitudes—significantly affected her child's tendencies to develop anxiety and depression and to exhibit aggressive behavior (Whitman, Borkowski, Keogh, & Weld, 2001). Other studies have shown that because teenagers are more likely to have unhealthy personal habits, such as the use or abuse of drugs, they are more likely to have pregnancy complications like *toxemia* (a condition that results from the spread of bacterial products in the bloodstream) and to bear infants with lower birthweights (Smith, 1994). In addition, the failure of many teenagers to seek formal prenatal care contributes to the relatively high rate of infant mortality in the United States (see Box 3.1).

Box 3.1

Perspectives on Diversity

PRENATAL HEALTH CARE AND INFANT MORTALITY

It seems astonishing that more babies die at or soon after birth in the United States than in 21 countries worldwide (March of Dimes, 2001). After all, U.S. medicine and technology lead the world. Why, then, are our infant mortality rates so high? The answer is tied in large part to our less than adequate provision of prenatal health care to pregnant women (Children's Defense Fund, 2001).

In any 1 of 10 western European countries—Belgium, Denmark, England, France, Germany, Ireland, Netherlands, Norway, Spain, and Switzerland—pregnant women automatically receive prenatal and postnatal care at very little cost because it is subsidized by their governments; they also get from 9 to 40 weeks of paid maternity leave from work. (These services vary within the countries cited.)

Many pregnant women in the United States face a difficult situation. There are no uniform national standards to guarantee them either consistent high-quality maternity care or, of equal importance, financial coverage. Nationwide, at least 1.3 million U.S. women receive insufficient prenatal care each year, and many of these women are those who need this care most (Healy, 1995). The groups least likely to receive care are teens, the unmarried, the poor, the less educated, recent immigrants, and minorities (African Americans, Latinos, and American Indians). These women are at greatest risk of bearing babies with complications such as prematurity and low birthweight.

The data also reveal clear distinctions among racial-ethnic groups, with those at the lowest rung of the socioeconomic ladder receiving the least adequate care. For example, 85 percent of European American women receive first-trimester prenatal care compared with only 73 percent of African American and 74 percent of Latino American women (Children's Defense Fund, 2001). African American and Latino American women are also among the most seriously affected by poverty, unemployment or underemployment, lack of health insurance, and inadequate education.

According to Young and her colleagues (Young, McMahon, Bowman, & Thompson, 1989), other reasons why women do not seek prenatal care include motivational and multiple social problems. For example, in one study African American women in particular reported problems with scheduling and keeping appointments for prenatal care as a reason for delaying such care, whereas European Americans often noted that they didn't feel they needed prenatal care. Scheduling difficulties were more often cited by women under age 20 than by older women. Social problems most often cited were unemployment (presumably implying a lack of money), being a single parent (perhaps time and money), psychological stress, interpersonal conflicts with the baby's father, and family crises. Another reason may be women's fear and/or dislike of doctors (Kotelchuck, 1995).

Young and her associates also found that their participants often tended to deny the symptoms of pregnancy and to be reluctant to assume the role of an expectant mother. A majority of participants were single mothers with infants and toddlers, and many lacked social support. Research findings, however, seem to indicate that having social support may not guarantee that a woman will seek medical help and guidance during the prenatal period. In one study, researchers found that living with a husband or partner was more likely to impel a woman to seek prenatal care than having access to a supportive network (Casper & Hogan, 1990). Another group of researchers found that women who were enclosed within strong, mostly familial networks were less likely to seek prenatal care (St. Clair, Smeriglio, Alexander, & Celentano, 1989).

Within the United States the rates of infant (both fetal and neonatal) deaths have generally declined since 1960, but over the years the rates for African American infants have remained about twice those for European Americans. For example, in 1998, infant deaths among European Americans totaled 6 per 1,000 live births, but among African Americans there were 14.3 per 1,000 live births (Children's Defense Fund, 2001).

What can we do about this situation? The resistance in the United States to national health standards and/or a national health-care system has been monumental. As a result of this resistance and of the marked discrepancy between the wealthy and poor sectors of the population, a large group of poor mothers either have no access to prenatal care or do not take advantage of opportunities they do have. In view of the costs, both emotional and financial, of high infant mortality and high rates of premature and handicapped infants, it is important to make prenatal services widely available to women of all racial, ethnic, and socioeconomic groups.

When teenage mothers have adequate diets and prenatal care, they do not show higher rates of complications in birth or pregnancy than do mothers in their twenties (Moore & Brooks-Gunn, 2002; Smith, 1994). Among older mothers, emerging health risks—such as increases in hypertension, diabetes, and alcoholism—rather than age per se contribute to difficulties in pregnancy and birth. Despite the increased incidence of miscarriage, due in part to the greater likelihood of conceiving a child with chromosomal abnormalities, the vast majority of these women have normal pregnancies and healthy babies (Brockington, 1996).

CHOICE OF DIET   It is difficult to separate the effects of maternal malnourishment from those of a variety of other deleterious factors. The malnourished mother often exists in an environment characterized by poverty, poor education, inferior sanitation and shelter, and inadequate medical care. In the United States, malnutrition and high maternal and infant mortality are associated not only with negative socioeconomic factors but with ethnicity. African American and Latino families are often poorer than European and Asian American families, and African American and Latino women are more likely to be exposed to these harmful factors and to experience more of their destructive effects. The latter groups tend to begin childbearing earlier and to end it later, and to have poorer diets and poorer prenatal and delivery care. The environment of poverty to which the new mother returns with her baby sustains and compounds all of these effects.

Pregnant women are advised to gain about 25 to 35 pounds over the course of their pregnancies (Chomitz, Cheung, & Lieberman, 2000). Studies have shown that in the diets of pregnant women gross dietary deficiencies, especially of some vitamins, minerals, and proteins, are related to increased rates of miscarriage, stillbirth, and infant mortality. Moreover, such deficiencies are likely to lead to prematurity, physical and neural defects, and smaller size in neonates (Scholl, Heidiger, & Belsky, 1996; Shonkoff & Phillips, 2000; Sigman, 1995). Studies suggest that early malnutrition may interfere with the development of the nervous system. The specific form the damage takes depends, again, on the age at which the malnutrition occurs. For example, if the mother takes a supplement of folic acid daily she can lessen the likelihood that her fetus will sustain neural tube abnormalities, such as *spina bifida.* And if she takes folic acid in the last two months of her pregnancy she can also reduce her risk of having a premature birth (Scholl et al., 1996). Folic acid is found naturally in fruits and green vegetables, but many common foods such as bread, pasta, and rice also contain it. Thus it is easy to ensure that pregnant women receive adequate doses of this vitamin.

Impairment of a child's intellectual development due to prenatal malnutrition appears most marked when the mother's malnutrition has been severe and long lasting and when the effects of this dietary deprivation are sustained after childbirth by adverse nutritional, social, and economic factors (Sigman, 1995). Thus, a network of deleterious factors associated with prenatal malnutrition lead to continued ill effects on the child. Studies of short-term periods of famine attributable to such events as war suggest that no children sustain long-lasting intellectual deficits if previously well-nourished mothers go through a temporary period of malnourishment during pregnancy and if a child has a reasonably good diet and responsive caretakers following birth (Stein & Susser, 1976). On the other hand, studies of the impact of a drought in Kenya found that school-age children who suffered the worst malnutrition showed decreases in playground activity, social involvement, and classroom attentiveness (McDonald, Sigman, Espinosa, & Neumann, 1994).

Although it has been generally assumed that malnutrition has its greatest impact on social and motor development (Riciutti, 1993), a number of researchers have found that cognitive abilities are affected by poor nutrition as well (Lozoff, Jimenez, Hagan, Mollen, & Wolf, 2000; Sigman, 1995). Cognitive or academic difficulties may not only be the result of biological changes in the brain but may be linked as well with the sequelae of malnutrition—lowered energy, inattention, and lack of motivation and responsiveness. Nutrition supplement studies in Jamaica, Indonesia, and Colombia found that both motor and cognitive abilities improved when infants were given enriched diets (Grantham-McGregor, Powell, Walker, & Hines, 1991).

Finally, the effects on an infant of prenatal malnutrition may compound if tired, malnourished parents respond to their malnourished and irritable or nonresponsive infant with lack of support or rejection (Lozoff et al., 2000). For this reason, beside providing dietary supplements for malnourished families of low socioeconomic status, many successful intervention programs have focused on training economically deprived parents to interact with their children in a more sensitive, involved, and stimulating manner (Grantham-McGregor, Powell, Walker, & Chang, 1994; Ramey & Ramey, 1992).

EMOTIONAL STATE   The emotional state of the mother during pregnancy may affect her fetus and newborn (Brockington, 1996; DiPietro, 2004). Emotional characteristics may be transmitted genetically, and a pregnant woman's emotionality may induce metabolic or biochemical changes that affect the fetus. In fact, fetal stress hormones reflect those of the mother (DiPietro, 2004). Of course, a woman who is emotionally disturbed during pregnancy may also be emotionally unstable after childbirth and may bring inadequate caretaking skills to her important role as the main socializing influence on her baby. Studies have found that women who suffer sustained emotional distress tend to experience complications during both pregnancy and delivery. Some of these difficulties include nausea during pregnancy, premature delivery, spontaneous abortion, prolonged labor, delivery complications, and greater need for anesthesia during childbirth (Monk et al., 2000; Paarlberg, Vingerhoets, Passchier, Dekker, & van Giegn, 1995). Thus, in the findings of the studies we discuss next, genetic or prenatal factors or early infant learning and experiences could all have played a role.

Women who are anxious and under emotional stress during pregnancy tend to have infants who are physically more active in utero. After their birth, these infants tend to be hyperactive and irritable, to cry more, and to have feeding and sleep problems (Van Den Bergh, 1992), and they are less attentive at 8 months than other babies (Huizink, Robles de Medina, Mulder, Visser, & Buitleaer, 2002). And according to O'Conner and colleagues (2002), the effects on a baby of stress in the life of the woman who carries him aren't limited to the period of infancy. Women who experienced high levels of anxiety during pregnancy were twice as likely as nonstressed women to have children who, at the age of 7, exhibited behavioral difficulties, depression, and anxiety. In an even more dramatic demonstration, van Os and Selton (1998) tracked 100,000 men and women born in the Netherlands to mothers who were pregnant during the German invasion of the country in 1940. Compared with babies born in earlier or later years, the subjects in this study were more likely later on to develop schizophrenia.

Stresses during pregnancy can come from a wide array of problems, such as marital discord, disagreement about whether to continue the pregnancy, moving to a new locality, or illness and death in relatives. A woman's emotional distress during pregnancy may be temporary, or it may signal ongoing difficulties. Fear and distress during pregnancy may be part of a broader pattern of maladjustment, and this pattern of disturbance may be continued in the way these women handle their infants.

Interestingly, the effects of stress may be moderated by the support available to a pregnant woman (Brockington, 1996; DiMatteo & Kahn, 1997). When pregnant women were under severe life stresses, those with supportive relatives and friends had only a 33 percent rate of complications in pregnancy and childbirth compared with a 91 percent rate for women lacking social support (Nickolls, Cassel, & Kaplan, 1972). The effects on labor and delivery of the presence of a supportive companion are evident from a study of healthy Guatemalan women (Sosa, Kennell, Klaus, Robertson,

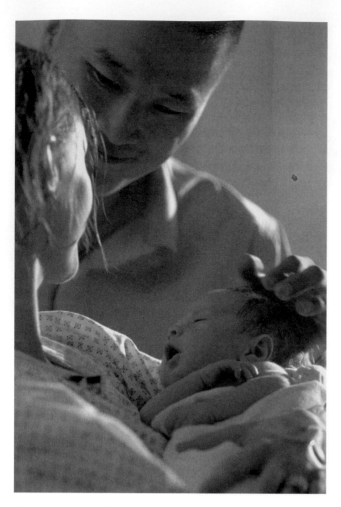

Sharing the joy of their baby's first hours of life is an experience many mothers and fathers treasure.

& Urrutia, 1980). Women in the experimental group were assigned a *doula,* a supportive female companion who talked to them, reassured them, rubbed their backs, and held their hands until delivery. The control group went through the normal hospital routine with no supportive person present. The mean length of labor was 19.3 hours for the control group and 8.7 hours for the women who had supportive companions. The latter also had fewer complications, such as the need for cesarean sections, and their infants were less likely to experience fetal distress. The presence of a trained, supportive companion has been found to have similar beneficial effects for women having babies in U.S. hospitals (Kennell, Klaus, McGrath, Robertson, & Hinckley, 1991).

In the United States in the mid-1970s, hospitals began allowing the husbands of pregnant women to be present, first during their wives' labor and then during delivery itself. Researchers have found that, in general, fathers' presence during labor and delivery has a beneficial effect on mothers, particularly in reducing their felt pain and their need for medication and in making their view of the birth experience more positive (Lindell, 1988; Parke, 1996, 2002).

On the other hand, the presence of the father alone may be less effective in reducing the need for cesarean deliveries than the presence of both the father and a support figure (Kennell & McGrath, 1993). Fathers' presence may be helpful, but dads may need more training and support if they are going to be as effective as more experienced support figures, such as doulas or nurses. At the same time, being present may benefit fathers themselves. For example, more fathers than mothers get to hold the baby while still in the delivery room, and many fathers have expressed high levels of emotional pleasure during this experience (Mosedale, 1991). Once the baby arrives healthy, the father's negative stress from the birthing ordeal may give way to relief, pride, and intense joy (Chandler & Field, 1997).

DISEASES AND DISORDERS   A wide range of maternal diseases and disorders can affect an infant's development either prenatally or during the birth process. Like the effects of other teratogenic agents, the effects of these disorders are often mediated by their appearance at a critical time. For example, if the pregnant woman contracts the viral disease *mumps* during her first trimester, her infant is much more likely to suffer some kind of malformation than if she were to contract the disease later in her pregnancy. Similarly, if a woman contracts *rubella* during the first month of her pregnancy, even if the attack is mild, her fetus risks cardiac disorders, cataract formation, deafness, and mental retardation (Cochi et al., 1989). If she contracts this illness in her third month or later, however, the likelihood that her infant will suffer disability declines substantially (Eberhart-Phillips, Frederick, & Baron, 1993).

Timing is also an issue in the potentially life-threatening condition of **Rh factor incompatibility,** in which an infant's blood is Rh positive (Rh+), whereas its mother's blood is Rh negative (Rh−). (Rh factors are antigens, or substances in the blood that can induce specific immune responses.) Because positive and negative blood types are incompatible, if by some chance fetal and maternal blood should commingle (as we've said, normally they do not), the mother's blood could produce antibodies that would attack the fetal blood cells, bringing about the death of the fetus. Because such

Rh factor incompatibility
A condition in which an infant's Rh-negative blood opposes its mother's Rh-positive blood and threatens fetuses in later births, when the mother's body has had time to produce antibodies that will attack fetal blood cells.

antibodies are scarce in a woman who is pregnant for the first time, Rh incompatibility is not an issue during a first birth. To prevent it from ever becoming an issue, Rh immune globulin can be administered to the mother after the birth of each child to prevent antibody formation and ensure the birth of other healthy children (Turner & Rubinson, 1993).

A number of other maternal conditions may increase rates of fetal abnormalities, miscarriage, and death. In the case of *hypertension,* also known as high blood pressure, the higher the mother's blood pressure, the greater the likelihood of prenatal complications. Women who suffer from *diabetes* face the possibility of delivering a stillborn child or a baby who will die shortly after birth. Diabetic women also have a greater chance of developing *preeclampsia* or, in its more serious form, *eclampsia* (also known as *toxemia of pregnancy*), which has such symptoms as very high blood pressure and excessive weight gain. Untreated, the condition can lead to death of the mother, the infant, or both. However, when diabetic mothers receive special care during their pregnancies, their babies have an excellent chance of being born healthy.

Other maternal disorders that can affect the infant adversely include several sexually transmitted diseases, usually contracted through sexual intercourse. These include gonorrhea, syphilis, chlamydia, pelvic inflammatory disease, herpes, and HIV/AIDS. AIDS can be transmitted also by infected blood or by infected needles used in blood transfusions or in illegal drug use. We may subdivide illnesses according to whether they're caused by bacterial, viral, or parasitic infections, such as **toxoplasmosis,** which is acquired by eating undercooked meat or by contact with feces, as in handling cat litter. Transmitted through the *placenta,* toxoplasmosis can cause eye and brain damage in a developing baby.

BACTERIAL INFECTIONS   **Gonorrhea,** which is spread for the most part by direct sexual contact with an infected person, can usually be treated with antibiotics. Left untreated, however, it can cause cardiovascular difficulties, arthritis, sterility, and, in women, *pelvic inflammatory disease,* which itself can cause an *ectopic,* or tubal, pregnancy. In an ectopic pregnancy, the zygote implants in the woman's fallopian tube rather than in her uterus, and the pregnancy must be terminated to save the mother's life (Turner & Rubinson, 1993). Although gonorrhea in the mother can be transmitted prenatally, most commonly an infant is infected as it passes through the birth canal. If not treated, the disease can cause blindness; for this reason, in most hospitals in the United States, a few drops of silver nitrate or penicillin are placed in the eyes of newborns to prevent infection.

Some chronic infections invade the developing embryo and remain active but do not exert their worst effects until later in development. For example, the deleterious effects on the fetus of maternal **syphilis** do not occur before 18 weeks of gestation, and therefore early treatment of a syphilitic mother may avert abnormalities in the child. If the mother is untreated, however, invasion of the fetus by bacteria from the mother may result in spontaneous abortion, blindness, mental retardation, or other physical abnormalities. Moreover, in some cases the negative effects of syphilis are not apparent even at birth but emerge gradually during the early years of development. In this case they are expressed in the form of deterioration in thought processes, judgment, and speech; a decline in motor and mental abilities; and, eventually, death. Although years ago syphilis was virtually a death sentence, today it can be cured if detected and treated early with antibiotics. Nevertheless, currently about one of every 2,000 newborns is infected with syphilis (National March of Dimes Foundation, 2001).

Although less well known, **chlamydia** is probably the most widespread bacterial infection among sexually transmitted diseases. Babies born to women with this infection often acquire it in the birth process and may develop pneumonia or a form of conjunctivitis. Mothers with chlamydia also risk spontaneous abortion and stillbirth. In addition, like gonorrhea, chlamydia can lead to pelvic inflammatory disease.

toxoplasmosis A parasitic disease acquired by eating undercooked meat or by contact with feces as in handling cat litter.

gonorrhea A sexually transmitted bacterial infection that, in a pregnant woman, can cause blindness in her infant; normally treatable with antibiotics.

syphilis A sexually transmitted bacterial disease that can usually be treated with antibiotics, but if untreated in the pregnant woman can cause miscarriage or blindness, mental retardation, or other physical abnormalities in her baby.

chlamydia Probably the most widespread bacterial sexually transmitted disease; can cause pneumonia or a form of conjunctivitis in a pregnant woman's baby.

genital herpes A common viral infection spread primarily through sexual contact; if contracted by an infant during birth, it can cause blindness, motor abnormalities, mental retardation, and a wide range of neurological disorders.

VIRAL INFECTIONS   One of the most common sexually transmitted diseases is **genital herpes,** which is spread primarily through intimate sexual contact. Of the approximately 4 million babies born in the United States each year, between 1,500 and 2,200 come into the world infected with herpes (National March of Dimes Foundation, 2001). If a herpes infection is detected in a pregnant woman before labor, a cesarean delivery will usually succeed in preventing the infant from coming into contact with the disease and thus protect it from contagion. The risk is especially great if the mother is having an active outbreak of herpes and the infant is exposed to the virus in the birth canal. Herpes can also be transmitted by exposure to the virus after birth, although this occurs less frequently. Because an infant does not have a fully developed immune system before 5 weeks of age, if it is infected with herpes, the disease can cause blindness, motor abnormalities, mental retardation, and a wide range of neurological disorders. Sixty percent of these babies will die; roughly 90 percent of the babies who survive are left with serious problems, including skin and mouth ulcers and eye and brain infections. Nearly half have major developmental disorders (Healy, 1995).

Of course, the viral infection that has caused the greatest alarm in recent years is the *human immunodeficiency virus (HIV)* infection and its expression in **acquired immune deficiency syndrome (AIDS).** At its first appearance in the United States in the early 1980s, AIDS was labeled a disease primarily of gay men. Gradually, however, it became apparent that the disease affected not only gay and bisexual men but their heterosexual partners, the offspring of these people, drug abusers who shared needles, and the recipients of blood transfusions when the blood came from infected persons.

acquired immune deficiency syndrome (AIDS) A viral disease that attacks the body's immune systems; transmitted to a fetus or newborn in the form of the *human immunodeficiency virus (HIV),* this disorder weakens the child's immune system and may ultimately cause its death.

Today, about 1 in 2,700 newborn infants is infected with HIV (March of Dimes, 2001). Most children are infected prenatally—through passage of the virus through the placenta during gestation or the birth process—or through the mother's milk. A few contract the disease through blood transfusions, usually for the treatment of hemophilia. About three-quarters of infected pregnant women are intravenous (IV) drug users or the sexual partners of IV drug users (Centers for Disease Control and Prevention, 2003; Institute of Medicine, 1999), and an infected pregnant woman has a 15 to 30 percent chance of transmitting the AIDS virus to her child. Recent advances in drug therapy, however, have reduced the likelihood of HIV transmission to newborns by two-thirds; one study found a reduction from 26 to 8 percent (Connor et al., 1994). As most children who develop AIDS are infected from birth, and because the disease progresses more rapidly in children, some 80 percent of U.S. children with AIDS are less than 5 years of age (Centers for Disease Control and Prevention, 2003). As Figure 3-4 shows, more than half of these children are African American and almost

Figure 3-4

U.S. children under age 5 with AIDS, 1996

Children in different ethnic and racial groups are at different levels of risk for AIDS. African American children are at highest risk for this disease, whereas Asian and American Indian children are the least likely to be infected.

Source: Based on data from Centers for Disease Control and Prevention, 1996.

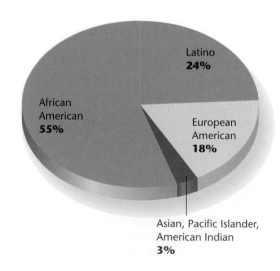

a quarter are Latino. European Americans make up 18 percent; the rest are Asian, Pacific Islander, or Native American (Centers for Disease Control and Prevention, 2003).

On average, AIDS is diagnosed at 4 years of age, and 54 percent of cases are diagnosed by the age of 7 (Hutton, 1996). These children often suffer neurological impairments, delays in mental and physical development, and such structural deformities as *microcephaly,* or an unusually small head, a square forehead, and widely spaced, slanted eyes. Of greater significance, of course, is the fact that AIDS is an autoimmune disease, or one in which the body's immunological forces are disabled and/or attack the body's healthy cells. Thus, these children are vulnerable to disease and infections of all sorts that cause their early deaths. Several recent studies indicate that, due to new and aggressive drug therapy, more than half of all HIV-infected infants are living beyond age 6; some even survive to adolescence (Hutton, 1996).

The parents of children with AIDS often have few resources; they are often drug users and both ill and poor. As a result they are frequently unable or unwilling to care for their HIV-infected children. Obtaining foster care for such children is very difficult, but infected children and their families are desperately in need of specialized care and support systems. Because at this time we have no cure for AIDS, many experts think that concentrating on preventive efforts, through education and programs aimed at modifying high-risk sexual behavior and drug abuse, is the only effective means of dealing with the problem (Tinsley, Lees, & Sumartojo, 2004). Both school-based and family-based prevention efforts are important in reaching the wide range of individuals who are likely AIDS sufferers, including school dropouts, runaways, and drug users (Kotchik, Shaffer, Miller, & Forehand, 2001; Tinsley et al., 2004). Clearly, we need more research on the prevention of high-risk behaviors in adolescents and young adults.

BIRTH AND THE BEGINNINGS OF LIFE

Birth is one of the most dramatic and significant events in the lives of parents and children. For parents, the last few weeks of pregnancy are typically characterized by joyous anticipation and, especially in first births, by apprehension about labor and childbirth, anxiety about whether the child will be normal, and concern about whether the mother will be permanently altered physically by pregnancy and delivery. Although both parents are exhausted by the process of birth, most are exhilarated, even awestruck, in seeing and holding their newborn for the first time. One new father said, "When I come up to see my wife . . . I go look at the kid and then I pick her up and put her down . . . I keep going back to the kid. It's like a magnet. That's what I can't get over, the fact that I feel like that" (Greenberg & Morris, 1974, p. 524).

Labor and Delivery

Birth is also a momentous physical and social transition for the infant. The baby moves from the warm, wet, dark environment of the amniotic sac to the cooler, dry, bright environment of an external world full of lights, objects, movements, touches, voices, and faces (Rank, 1929). Even before birth, the parents and child have established a relationship, and following birth the construction of this relationship becomes more intense and accelerated.

THE THREE STAGES OF CHILDBIRTH   Birth involves a series of changes in the mother that permit the child to move from the womb out into the external world. Figure 3-5 shows the way the fetus appears and is positioned in the uterus just before labor begins, as well as the three stages in the birth process.

The first stage of labor begins as the mother experiences regular uterine contractions that are usually spaced at 10- to 15-minute intervals; these contractions become

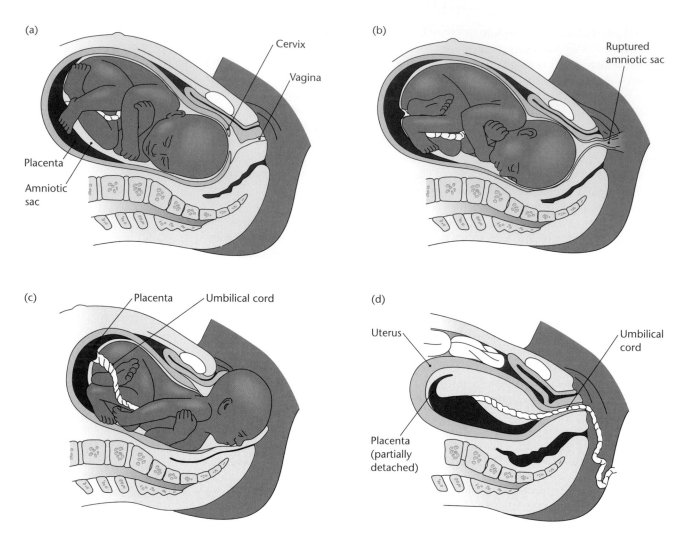

Figure 3-5   The stages of the birth process
With arms and legs folded and head pointed toward the birth canal, the fetus is ready to be born (a). In stage 1, the fetus moves toward the cervix as it gradually dilates (b). In stage 2, the fetus moves through the vaginal opening (c). In stage 3, the nourishing placenta detaches from the uterine wall preparatory to expulsion (d).
Source: Adapted from Vander, Sherman, & Luciano, 1994.

more intense and frequent as labor progresses. This first stage, which generally lasts between 8 and 14 hours for firstborn children and half that for later-born children, concludes when the cervix is dilated sufficiently to permit the infant's head to pass through it and into the vaginal canal.

In the second stage of labor, which usually lasts less than an hour, the infant descends through the birth canal and is delivered through the vaginal opening.

The third and final stage of birth takes only a few minutes, as the uterus expels the placenta.

NATURAL CHILDBIRTH: NOT SUCH A NEW IDEA Having a baby in the relatively isolated and unfamiliar setting of a hospital, separated from one's relatives and often from one's husband, was a practice that began in the nineteenth century as a response to a rise in health problems and in infant and maternal mortality associated with rapid urbanization and industrialization. Before that time, and still in many regions of the world, women gave birth in their homes, attended by relatives or a midwife.

Currently, 92 percent of U.S. women are still attended in childbirth by a physician (Centers for Disease Control and Prevention, 2000). However, pregnancy and birth are once again becoming a shared family experience, often occurring in the home or in homelike birthing centers. A common preparation for childbirth is the Lamaze method. The Lamaze childbirth technique uses breathing and muscle relaxation exercises to teach women how to manage the pain of labor and delivery. Many couples take classes during pregnancy to learn these techniques. Fathers are taught to help their partners with the relaxation procedures and to be a relaxation and breathing coach during the labor/delivery process.

The presence of a supportive partner, in combination with the Lamaze breathing techniques, does, in fact, lead to an easier labor and delivery. Mothers who are prepared for childbirth in this way experience shorter labors, require less medication, and are less stressed and more positive about the birth experience (Mackey, 1995; Wilcox, Kobayashi, & Murray, 1997). Midwife-assisted births (nearly 10%) have increased nearly 800 percent since the early 1970s (Carmichael, 2004; Wegman, 1994). Home deliveries by trained personnel or delivery in a birthing center are suitable for normal births; however, between 15 and 25 percent of women who begin labor in such settings are subsequently moved to a hospital because of birth complications (Olsen, 1997). Not all countries treat childbirth as a medical event. In Holland, for example, 35 percent of the babies are born at home and about 43 percent are delivered by midwives rather than physicians (Treffers, Eskes, Kleiverda, & Van Alten, 1990). Moreover, many of the new trends in home birthing go back to ancient times. The kneeling position, which some modern women prefer, was favored by native Hawaiian women up to the twentieth century, and the birthing stools that are gaining popularity in the United States are modeled after stools designed 4,000 years ago in Egypt (Carmichael, 2004). Most important, the rates of both infant mortality and postpartum depression are lower for home deliveries, partly because mothers who deliver at home are more likely to have had low-risk pregnancies. It would seem that for uncomplicated births, home delivery is an option, but in these birthings the risk of problems is higher than in medically assisted births.

CESAREAN DELIVERY The **cesarean delivery,** in which a baby is removed from the mother's uterus through an incision in her abdomen, is performed in a variety of situations. Labor may be unusually slow or prolonged, the baby may be in difficulty, there may be vaginal bleeding, or the baby's position may make a normal vaginal delivery impossible (e.g., the baby's feet may be in position to deliver first, or the baby may lie horizontally in the uterus). From the 1960s to the 1980s, the rate at which cesarean deliveries were performed increased from 5 to 23.5 percent of all births (Centers for Disease Control and Prevention, 1993). According to Localio and colleagues (1993), there are several reasons for this increase, including the convenience of physicians (they can schedule this procedure rather than be called to the hospital in the wee hours of the morning), convenience of patients, and an effort to minimize physician liability associated with the potential complications of vaginal delivery. Concerns have been raised that the rate of *cesarean section* (another term for this procedure) is unnecessarily high and that these procedures themselves may have unforeseen long-term adverse consequences. The rate at which cesareans are performed leveled out in the late 1980s and began dropping in the 1990s (Centers for Disease Control and Prevention, 2000).

Cesarean births place mothers at greater risk of infection and involve longer hospital stays. In addition, cesarean babies are exposed to more maternal medication

cesarean delivery The surgical delivery of a baby; the baby is removed from the mother's uterus through an incision made in her abdomen and uterus in a procedure also known as *cesarean section.*

during delivery; as a result, they have somewhat more trouble breathing and are less responsive and wakeful than other newborns (Emory et al., 1996). However, short-term studies of cesarean births suggest that this method of delivery has few effects on infants' cognitive or neurological development (Entwisle & Alexander, 1987). Although early mother-child interactions may be adversely affected, by the time the children are 1 year old, these relationships are positive (Reilly, Entwisle, & Doering, 1987). One advantage of cesarean births is that because mothers have a longer recovery period, during which it is often difficult for them to handle all the caretaking of their infants, fathers may become more involved than usual with their babies in the first few months (Parke, 1996).

BIRTH COMPLICATIONS Although labor and childbirth are normal processes in human development and, in the majority of cases, have no lasting adverse influences, they sometimes do affect an infant in negative ways. We've seen that sexually transmitted diseases can be passed to the infant as it moves through the birth canal. In addition, it has been found that more males than females are born with physical anomalies. This has been attributed in part to the role of the sex chromosomes (see Chapter 2) and in part to the larger size of, and hence greater pressure on, a male's head during birth. The majority of infants do not suffer serious impairment at birth, however. Fewer than 10 percent have any type of abnormality, and many of these difficulties disappear during subsequent development.

anoxia A lack of oxygen in brain cells.

Important birth factors related to developmental deviations and infant mortality are **anoxia** (lack of oxygen in the brain) and prematurity. Severe anoxia, which is usually associated with brain damage and sometimes death, is often found in infants of very low birthweight (Wegman, 1995). One of the methods frequently used to assess the condition of the newborn infant is the Apgar scoring system, named for its developer, anesthesiologist Dr. Virginia Apgar (Table 3-3). At 1 minute and 5 minutes after birth, the doctor or nurse measures the heart rate, respiratory effort, reflex irritability, muscle tone, and body color of the infant. Each of the five signs is given a score of 0, 1, or 2; the higher the score attained, the more favorable the baby's condition. A total score of 7 to 10 indicates that the newborn is in good condition, whereas a score of 4 or lower alerts medical staff to the need for immediate emergency procedures.

Table 3-3

Apgar evaluation of the newborn infant
Source: Adapted from Apgar (1953).

Sign	Score		
	0	1	2
Heart rate	Absent	Less than 100 beats per minute	100 to 140 beats per minute
Respiratory effort	No breathing for more than one minute	Slow and irregular	Good respiration with normal crying
Muscle tone	Limp and flaccid	Some flexion of the extremities	Good flexion, active motion
Reflex irritability	No response	Some motion	Vigorous response to stimulation
Color	Blue or pale body and extremities	Body pink with blue extremities	Pink all over

Description	Timing of Delivery	Average Weight at Delivery
Full Term	Average of 38 weeks from conception	7.7 lb (3,500 g)
Premature Preterm	Several weeks before due date	Less than 5.5 lb (2,500 g) but weight is often appropriate to time spent in utero
Small for date	Either at about due date or several weeks before	Less than 5.5 lb (2,500 g) and less weight than would be expected for time spent in utero; survival of babies who weigh less than 3.3 lb (about 1,500 g) is severely compromised

Table 3-4

Preterm and small-for-date babies

Prematurity and Low Birthweight

Premature babies are those born before they have completed the normal or full-term gestational period—remember, on average, 38 weeks from the mother's last menstrual period to delivery—and who are biologically immature in one or more ways. Premature infants are always of low birthweight; whereas on average the normal full-term baby weighs 7.7 pounds, "preemies" weigh less than 5.0 pounds. However, when a newborn's weight is appropriate for the amount of time he or she has spent in utero, the baby is considered **preterm** (see also Table 3-4). Preterm infants are generally born after 37 weeks or less. Because some writers have criticized the use of only gestational age and weight as indicators of prematurity, investigators are now considering such additional criteria as weight relative to stature of the parent, nutritional condition of the mother, and a variety of skeletal, neurological, and biochemical indexes (Goldberg & DeVitto, 2002).

Premature infants who weigh less than 5.5 pounds and whose weight is *less* than appropriate for their time in utero are called **small-for-date** babies. Note that a small-for-date baby may be born close to its due date (close to full term) but be of low birthweight. Although babies who weigh much less than 3 pounds have many odds against them, modern technology is increasingly successful in enabling very small babies to survive (Goldberg & DeVitto, 2002; McIntire, Bloom, Casey, & Leveno, 1999).

Most new parents look forward to holding, cuddling, and feeding their infants soon after birth and to leaving the hospital within two or three days with a healthy, vigorous baby. By 1996, as a result of health insurers' efforts to reduce medical costs, these two or three days had often shrunk to 24 hours for routine vaginal births. The wisdom of such "drive-through deliveries" was questioned by a number of authorities, largely because some problems, such as jaundice, may not be manifest until a baby is at home. One study found that babies who were sent home within 30 hours of birth were 28 percent more likely than babies kept in hospital longer to be readmitted within a week and 12 percent more likely to return within a month (Liu, Clemens, Shay, Davis, & Novack, 1997). Another study, however, found few negative effects of early discharge (Edmondson, Stoddard, & Owens, 1997). To be on the safe side, in 1997 the U.S. government passed the Newborns' and Mothers' Health Protection Act, which requires health plans to cover at least 48 hours of hospital care after a routine birth.

In the United States, African American mothers are twice as likely as European American women to have babies of low birthweight (less than 2,500 grams, or 5.5 pounds) and almost three times as likely to have babies of very low birthweight (less

preterm A term describing a premature baby who is born before its due date and whose weight, although less than that of a full-term infant, may be appropriate to its gestational age.

small for date A term describing a premature baby who may be born close to its due date but who weighs significantly less than would be appropriate to its gestational age.

than 1,500 grams, or 3.3 pounds). Among women of Latino origin, Mexican American women's chances of having such babies are about halfway between black and white women's chances (Goldberg & DeVitto, 2002). Several factors account for the higher risk of prematurity among minority women; among these are poor diet, inadequate prenatal care, and drug and/or alcohol use. But not all premature babies are born into one ethnic group or income level. In fact, premature and low-birthweight babies are more common in the cases of multiple births that often result from the new reproductive technologies—which are used more often by white or affluent women.

Being born premature sometimes results in developmental delays. As one mother observed:

> My preemie didn't do anything in normal sequence. I couldn't follow any of the books on typical child development. The doctors kept telling me he'd catch up. It took years, but eventually he did. (Tracy & Maroney, 1999, p. 214)

How typical is this mother's experience with her preterm baby's development? Extremely low birthweights are often associated with intellectual impairment, but in general, only children who weigh less than 3.5 pounds incur significant impairment in intellectual functioning (Goldberg & DeVitto, 2002; Rose & Feldman, 1996). Although most low-birthweight babies catch up in motor and intellectual development by the time they are 4 years old, about 15 percent of those who weigh less than 3.3 pounds (1,500 grams) and about 30 percent of those weighing less than 2 pounds at birth continue to show some kind of cognitive deficit (Goldberg & DeVitto, 2002).

Problems in academic achievement, hyperactivity, motor skills, and speech and hearing disorders occur more often in very-low-birthweight or premature babies than in maturely born infants (Anderson et al., 2003; Field, 1990; Goldberg & DeVitto, 2002). However, it is not clear whether these problems are the consequences of prematurity and low birthweight or the outcome of a number of related factors, such as delivery complications, temporary isolation, separation of parents and infant, neonatal anomalies other than prematurity, or the way parents respond to their infant's apparent frailty and small size (Field, 1990; Korner, 1989). We should also keep in mind that many extremely low-birthweight babies would not have survived 20 years ago, before the introduction of neonatal intensive care units with specialized treatment procedures, equipment, and highly trained staff. More very sick infants who require assistance are living, and it is when these high medical risks are compounded by adverse environmental circumstances that long-term developmental deviations may occur (Goldberg & DeVitto, 2002).

In the next two sections we discuss two aspects of these early experiences that have particularly concerned psychologists. First, in the early weeks of life the preterm infant in the isolette may be getting less sensory and social stimulation than the full-term baby receives. Second, early parent-child separation may interfere with the formation of affectionate bonds between parent and infant. We conclude this section with a look at the long-term effects of the complications of prematurity.

STIMULATION PROGRAMS FOR PREMATURE BABIES   Since the 1970s, researchers have experimented with administering extra stimulation to preterm and small-for-date babies and then comparing their development with matched infants who were not given special stimulation. Some experimenters have suggested that stimulation should approximate the conditions experienced in utero; thus, premature infants have been exposed to tape-recorded heartbeats as heard within the uterus (Barnard & Bee, 1983), to rocking hammocks (Neal, 1968), and to waterbed mattresses (Burns, Deddish, Burns, & Hatcher, 1983) that presumably simulate the rotation, movement, and rhythmic activity the fetus experienced within the amniotic sac. Other investigators have used stimulation characteristic of the experiences of full-term infants, such as mobiles, tape recordings of the mother's voice, manual rocking, talking and singing, and cuddling and stroking (Field, 2001a; Field, Hernandez-Reif,

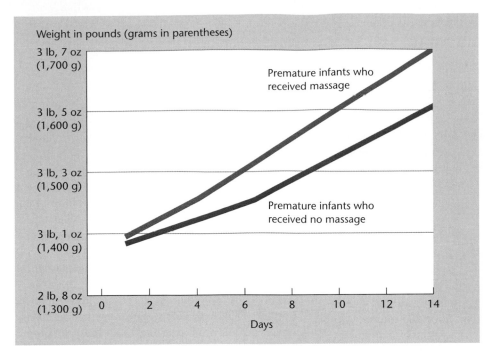

Figure 3-6

Everyone likes massage, including premature babies
A group of premature infants were given three 15-minute massages daily for 10 days, while another group received no massage. The infants given extra stimulation averaged 47% more weight gain per day, were awake and active more of the time, showed more mature behaviors on the Brazelton Neonatal Scale, and were in hospital for six days fewer than the other infants. Moreover, six to eight months later, the first group weighed more and performed better on the Bayley mental and motor scales than the second group.

Source: Reprinted by permission of the publisher from *Infancy* by Tiffany Field, p. 117, Cambridge, Mass.: Harvard University Press, Copyright © 1990 by the President and Fellows of Harvard College.

& Freedman, 2004; Goldberg & DeVitto, 2002). Both prenatal and postnatal-environment approaches have found that special stimulation can counteract some of the effects of the monotony experienced by infants in isolettes (see Box 3.2).

As Figure 3-6 shows, stimulated premature infants are more advanced in physical development (Field, 1990, 2001a, 2001b). They are also more advanced than unstimulated premature infants in neurological development as measured by infant reflexes, in sensorimotor and motor skills, in muscle tonus, in weight gain, and in exploratory behavior (Dieter, Field, Hernandez, Emory, & Redzepi, 2003; Goldberg & DeVitto, 2002). In addition, fewer incidents of *apnea* (temporary cessation of breathing, associated with later crib deaths) occur in stimulated infants (Korner, 1989). Stimulation clearly has at least a short-term salutary effect on the development of premature infants, although long-term gains are rarely found (Field, 2001a, 2001b; Korner, 1989).

Intervention programs facilitate not only the functioning of targeted systems but also of other systems that are about to develop. However, programs must be sensitive to individual differences (Als et al., 2003); not all premature babies benefit from additional stimulation (Goldberg & DeVitto, 2002). Children who are ill, who have intensive medical care routines that disrupt their sleep, or who are being weaned from breathing assistance or other physical support systems may not respond positively or may actually be distressed by added stimulation (Oehler, Eckerman, & Wilson, 1988). In attending to the needs of different children the question is not "whether stimulation for preterm infants is indicated but . . . stimulation for whom, what kind, how much, at what intervals, at what post-conceptual age, and for what purposes" (Korner, 1989, p. 12).

PREMATURE BABIES AND PARENTAL CONTACT It has been suggested that contact between the mother and her newborn in the first few hours of a child's life may facilitate the formation of emotional attachment (Klaus & Kennell, 1982). However, most research findings suggest that although early contact is potentially beneficial, it is not critical (Goldberg & DeVitto, 2002); many alternative routes can develop the parent-infant relationship. The most marked benefit of increased contact seems to be higher maternal self-confidence, which, particularly for the mother

Box 3.2

Child Psychology in Action

OF BABIES AND BEARS AND POSTNATAL CARE

Most babies go home from the hospital to brightly decorated rooms and cribs filled with soft, squishy animal companions. Now some premature infants in hospital isolettes are sleeping with such companions, too—a teddy bear from whose gentle "breathing" they may derive considerable benefit.

In most programs designed to stimulate premature infants, the stimulation is imposed on the infant whether she or he wants it or not. Evelyn Thoman (1987) designed a clever study to investigate whether premature infants can actively seek and regulate stimulation, rather than just being its passive recipients, and whether stimulation instigated by the infant will facilitate the infant's developmental progress.

Thoman placed a "breathing" teddy bear in the isolettes of one group of preemies, a nonbreathing teddy bear in the isolettes of another group, and gave a third group no teddy bears. She began her original study when the infants were 32 weeks old (counting from conception), 6 to 8 weeks younger than full-term (38 to 40 weeks) newborns. She continued her intervention for 3 weeks, until the babies were 35 weeks old.

The design of the breathing bear included a pneumatic pump that enabled it to "breathe" at a rate that could be individualized for each infant. Each bear's breathing rate was set at half of the infant's quiet-sleep respiration rate (Thoman, Hammond, Affleck, & DeSilva, 1995) on the theory that because premature babies have relatively fast respiration rates (about 60 breaths per minute in quiet sleep), such a rate might

be too fast for gentle stimulation. The breathing of the bear was expected to entrain the more irregular breathing of the premature baby without modifying his or her own endogenous rhythm, and researchers felt that the one-half rate, based as it was on that endogenous rhythm, would be successful in influencing each baby's irregular periods of breathing. Each infant controlled the amount of stimulation it received and the period of time the stimulation continued because it could either stay in contact with the bear or move away from it.

Thoman, in her original study, was interested, first, in the amount of time the infants spent in contact with the breathing and nonbreathing bears and, second, in whether contact with the breathing bear would indeed cause the child's respiration to become more regular. Thoman found that babies spent 63.4 percent of their time in contact with the breathing bear and 13.3 percent of their time with the nonbreathing bear. (Infants who had no bear spent 17.2 percent of their time in the area occupied by bears in the cribs of the two other groups of infants.)

Even these very young, premature babies were able to approach an available and attractive form of stimulation, and they clearly preferred the stimulation offered by the breathing bear to the passivity of the nonbreathing bear. Furthermore, the premature babies with the breathing bear showed more even respiration and more quiet sleep than did infants in the other two groups. Thoman speculates that this is

of a premature infant, enhances the sensitivity of her parenting (Klebanov, Brooks-Gunn, & McCormick, 2001).

Even in modern neonatal intensive care units that encourage parents to spend time with their premature infants, parents still have less early contact with these infants than with full-term babies. How does purposely increasing the amount of contact that mothers have with their premature infants affect mother-child relations? Recent work suggests that a particular form of mother-infant contact, namely skin-to-skin contact, seems to be beneficial in improving infant sleep patterns and cognitive development (Feldman & Eidelman, 2003; Tessier et al., 2003)

Some mothers report feelings of guilt, failure, and alienation from their infants and loss of self-esteem, and appear apprehensive about handling and caring for their fragile-appearing infants. When mothers of preemies are eventually able to take their babies home from the hospital, they tend to show less emotional involvement with

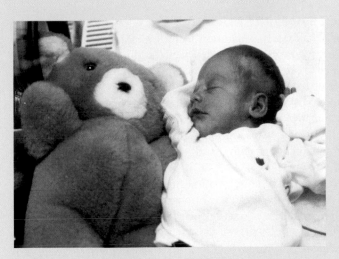

As this newborn snuggles up to a "breathing bear" it seems clear that the baby derives comfort from the bear's presence. This bear was designed by Evelyn Thoman for her studies of premature infants, who proved to benefit from the regulatory effects of the simulated breathing sounds.

and body movements; they replicated earlier findings and showed that the infants who spent more time with the breathing bear did indeed show a more regular respiratory pattern in quiet sleep. The breathing bear enabled more quiet sleep not only during the intervention but also several weeks after the intervention ended. They also showed that with practice the premature infants were successful in finding their breathing bears more quickly than the babies who had nonbreathing bears. Later, they added direct behavioral observation to the respiration recordings and found that the babies with breathing bears showed less waking and more quiet sleep, fewer startles in quiet sleep, and less crying. They were also more likely to smile than grimace during active sleep than babies with nonbreathing bears. The researchers conclude that the breathing bear serves to reinforce instrumental learning as premature babies seek and achieve contact with it. Finally, exposure to the breathing bear is good for mothers too: after six months mothers in the breathing bear group were less depressed and stressed than mothers in the non–breathing bear group (Novosad & Thoman, 2003).

An important area for future research will be the investigation of the neural and physiological correlates of affective expressions of preterm infants during both sleeping and waking, to improve not only our basic understanding of these behaviors but also the clinical care of our most vulnerable infants.

because the additional stimulation may have influenced the organization of brain processes associated with mature sleep patterns. Although physical and sensory maturity are normally associated with more advanced behavior, it may be that stimulating behavior and experiences also advance physical and sensory development.

Thoman and her colleagues (1995) introduced a pressure sensor under the baby to record respiration

them than do mothers of full-term babies (Goldberg & DeVitto, 2002). Especially if their infants have been in hospital for more than a month after birth (Corter & Minde, 1987). Preterm babies tend to make less secure emotional attachments to their mothers than do full-term infants (Mangelsdorf et al., 1996).

Some premature infants who fail to gain normal weight and height become battered or failure-to-thrive children (Bugental & Happaney, 2004). For example, there have been cases in which one twin had to be kept longer in hospital; when finally sent home, this child was abused or returned to the hospital as a failure-to-thrive child. This sort of situation might be attributed to early parent-child separation and lack of emotional bonding, but it might also result from adverse parental responses to characteristics of the low-birthweight child that make the infant unattractive. Premature babies' typical physical appearance, small size, high-pitched cry, feeding difficulties, and low responsivity may make them unappealing and also may increase parental frustration. More important than these factors, however, may be the fact that most premature infants are born to mothers who are poor, young, uneducated, and members of a minority group (Brooks-Gunn et al., 2000). It is likely that circumstances surrounding poverty, stress, and lack of support are at least as significant contributors to the abuse of a child as are birth-related difficulties.

LONG-TERM EFFECTS OF PREMATURITY   What are the long-term family effects of prematurity and early separation from the infant? Disruptions are more marked and enduring for economically deprived families than for middle-income families (Bradley et al., 1994; Klebanov et al., 2001). When such effects on parent-child attachment or on the child's cognitive development do endure, they seem to be attributable to a host of factors, in addition, of course, to the initial severity of the effects of prematurity: the child's responsiveness, the mother's competence, the family's environmental stresses, and the kind of support available to the parents from family members, nursing staff, and self-help groups (Gross, Spiker, & Haynes, 1997).

More often than it affects the parent-child relationship, the stress of raising a premature baby may have a negative impact on relations between the parents. Some research has reported a high incidence of marital discord in the first two years following a premature birth (Leiderman, 1983); on the other hand, if a couple view their coping strategies as complementary—if they can usefully share the task of caring for a child with special needs—the challenge may draw them closer (Affleck, Tennen, & Rowe, 1990). Recent intervention programs for low-birthweight children involving both parent training and child preschool classes have improved parenting and child outcomes (Klebanov et al., 2001). Clearly, to understand the effects of prematurity and early parent-child separation we must focus on the entire family system, an issue that we revisit in Chapter 11.

VULNERABILITY AND RESILIENCE IN CHILDREN AT RISK

In this chapter we have discussed a great number of events and conditions that can cause things to go wrong in pregnancy and childbirth. At this point you may be wondering if things ever go right! Indeed they do; most pregnancies proceed without major disruptions, and many couples find the period of waiting and preparing for the arrival of a child one of the happiest times of their lives.

Things do go wrong often enough, however, that scholars have attempted to understand and deal with the cases in which an infant's vulnerability to adverse perinatal influences either is compounded by subsequent conditions of its life or cannot be compensated for by more favorable factors in that life. Starting from the premise that there is a great variety in both the kinds of birth complications and the types of environmental conditions that can cause abnormalities in the child, a number of researchers have tried to uncover the reasons why some vulnerable children develop *resilience*, or the capacity to achieve competence and satisfaction in life despite initially challenging or threatening circumstances.

In trying to understand vulnerability and resilience, it is important to remember that both features of the environment and intrapersonal characteristics play roles in determining how successfully a child will develop. Researchers have proposed two sets of risk factors—biological and environmental. To capture the biological side, Pasamanick and Knoblock (1966) introduced the concept of the *continuum of reproductive casualty*. This notion suggested that the kinds of prenatal and perinatal biological factors that can affect the child negatively vary along a continuum of intensity that ranges from relatively minor perceptual, attentional, intellectual, motor, and behavioral disabilities to gross anomalies. On the environmental side, Sameroff and his colleagues (Sameroff & Chandler, 1975; Sameroff & Seifer, 1983) proposed a *continuum of caretaking casualty*: the environmental situation the infant enters also varies along a continuum of intensity, stretching from basically healthy (intact family, good caretaking, adequate financial support) to highly adverse (poverty, drug abuse, broken family, violence) (Sameroff & Chandler, 1975; Sameroff & Siefer, 1983). Although different groups of researchers have come up with varying specific factors, most agree that the seeds of resilience and the ability to overcome difficulties are sown in the interaction between risk factors and factors of protection or lack of protection (e.g., Luthar et al., 2000; Selman & Dray, 2005; Werner, 1995).

In an outstanding longitudinal study of the effects of birth complications on the development of the entire population of 698 children born in 1955 on the Hawaiian island of Kauai, Emmy Werner and her colleagues (Werner, 1995; Werner, Bierman, & French, 1971; Werner & Smith, 1977, 1982) set out not only to document these complications but also to assess their long-term consequences as well as the consequences over time of adverse early rearing conditions. (Note that among *all* children about 10 percent are born with some kind of handicap or anomaly.) As you can see from Box 3.3, these investigators learned along the way that the effects of adverse perinatal complications often lessen in intensity or disappear with age. This is in large part a function of the particular kind of caretaking environment in which children mature. Moreover, both children's vulnerability to high-risk conditions and their resiliency can change over time.

The Kauai study offered "a more hopeful perspective," according to Werner (1984), than does the general literature on children with problems, and it has been followed by other similarly designed studies that have tended to support its findings. Noting that there are great individual differences in the ways high-risk children respond to their environments, Werner (1993) points out that one of the first choices that must be made in planning intervention programs is to provide greater assistance to some children than others, and that means identifying the degrees of risk for children who have suffered prenatal and perinatal complications and who are born into some form of adversity:

> Intervention programs need to focus on children . . . who appear most vulnerable because they lack some of the essential personal resources and/or social bonds that buffer chronic adversity. Among [these] are the increasing numbers of preterm survivors of neonatal intensive care . . . children reared by isolated single parents with no roots in a community, and (pre-) adolescents with [behavioral] disorders who have poor reading skills. (p. 267)

More than one study has shown that a close and continuing relationship with another caring person is a highly significant factor in the development of resilience in a young person. Often the caring person is not a parent but a grandparent, an older sibling, a neighbor, a day-care provider, a teacher, a minister, a youth worker, or an elder mentor who can help tilt the balance from vulnerability to resiliency. Such a person can accept children's temperamental idiosyncrasies and allow them some experiences that challenge but do not overwhelm their coping abilities. A neighbor, a teacher, a mentor can guide a child in developing a sense of responsibility and caring and can reward him for helpfulness and cooperation; she or he can model for a child the conviction that life makes sense despite its adversities (Masten & Coatsworth, 1998). These ties, Werner (1995) argues, must be encouraged and strengthened, not weakened or displaced by legislative action and social programs.

Because most studies of risk and resiliency have focused on relatively urban, industrialized societies, future research, Werner (1993, 1995) proposes, should look at the many other physical and social settings in which children live. Child-care customs, gender-role socialization, and beliefs about children's needs vary greatly in the parts of the world where five out of every six children are born today: the countries of Asia, the Middle East, the continent of Africa, and South, Central, and Middle America.

Box 3.3
Risk and Resilience

WHAT FACTORS HELP CHILDREN OVERCOME EARLY ADVERSITY?

At the time that Emmy Werner and her colleagues (Werner et al., 1971; Werner & Smith, 1977, 1982) began their now-classic longitudinal study of all children born in 1955 on the Hawaiian island of Kauai, there was considerable literature on children born with serious defects or disorders and the course their lives could be expected to take. However, research on those factors that protect the individual and enable a small percentage of at-risk children to develop a remarkable degree of resilience was still in its infancy (Werner, 1995). Werner's study, which has followed most of its nearly 700 participants for more than 40 years, was one of the first to focus on such questions as: What is *right* with the children who develop this sort of resilience? and, How can we help other children to acquire this same near-invincibility in the face of severe adversity (Werner, 1995)?

When the participants in the Kauai Longitudinal Study were born, 47 percent suffered birth complications, and of these, a third were classified as specifically "at risk." In addition to experiencing moderate to severe birth complications, these children were born into poverty, their mothers had little formal education, and their family environments were characterized by discord, desertion, divorce, alcoholism, and/or mental illness. As we will see, despite these early stresses, fully a third of this at-risk group—10 percent of all participants—developed into confident, competent, and caring young adults.

All the children in this multicultural study—who were of Japanese, Filipino, and Hawaiian descent—were examined not only at birth but at 2, 10, and 18 years of age. At the first follow-up, 12 percent of 2-year-olds were rated deficient in social development, 16 percent were deficient in intellectual functioning, and 14 percent had health problems. The more severe the complications of birth and the more poorly the newborns had performed on various tests, the less adequate was their developmental level. Of particular interest was the relationship the researchers found between perinatal difficulties and environmental factors such as socioeconomic status. Infants who had severe perinatal complications and who were living in unstable families of relatively low socioeconomic status, with mothers of low intelligence, achieved lower IQ scores (lower by as much as 37 points) than infants living in the same kinds of conditions who had either no birth complications or only mild ones. By contrast, infants who had experienced severe birth complications but were living in stable family environments of high socioeconomic status, with mothers of high intelligence, obtained IQ scores that differed only slightly from the scores of infants in the same socioeconomic circumstances who had no birth complications. As toddlers, across all groups, the children who matured into resilient young adults were alert, autonomous, and more advanced in communication, self-help, and motor skills. They tended to seek out novel stimuli and had a positive social orientation.

By the age of 10, some two-thirds of the children classified "at risk" had developed serious learning or behavior problems (Werner, 1989). However, the effects of environmental variables had almost obliterated those of perinatal damage: No relationship was found between measures of birth complications and a child's IQ score at this age or later. Instead, the correlation between a child's intellectual performance and his or her parents' IQ scores and socioeconomic status increased as the child grew older; lower-class children showed marked deficits on cognitive measures. In short, the main effects of deviations caused by perinatal complications occurred early in a child's development; after that, development was increasingly influenced by environmental circumstances such as chronic poverty, family instability, and mental health problems.

When the children were 18, Werner and Smith (1982) tried to differentiate between children who had developed problems and a group of "resilient children" who were among the group that had been classified in infancy as "high risk" but who had not developed problems. The resilient children in families of low socioeconomic status seemed to share four personality characteristics: an active, resourceful approach toward solving life's problems; a tendency to perceive even their painful experiences constructively; the ability, from infancy on, to gain other people's positive attention; and a strong ability to use faith to maintain a positive vision of a meaningful life (Werner, 1984).

Thanks both to their own resilience and to environmental supports such as healthy child-rearing practices, fully a third of the at-risk children studied by Emmy Werner and her colleagues developed into self-confident, successful adults. These children had a positive and active approach to problem-solving, the ability to see some useful aspects of even painful experiences and to attract positive responses from other people, and a strong tendency to use faith in maintaining an optimistic vision of a fulfilling life.

Evidencing cognitive abilities such as effective reading skills by the fourth grade served as an additional protective factor (Werner, 1995). Finally, certain features of these children's social environment served as protective buffers: small family size, favorable parental attitudes, a continuous relationship with a caring adult (not necessarily the parent), low levels of family conflict, a smaller load of stressful life experiences, and the availability of counseling and remedial assistance. In addition, in middle childhood or adolescence, high-risk resilient children often assumed responsibility for the care of another person—a sibling, aging grandparent, or ill or incompetent parent. Both such "required helpfulness" and being cared for oneself were critical in buffering these high-risk children from adversity (Werner, 1984, 1995).

Although more high-risk girls than high-risk boys matured into resilient young adults, the periods of stress for each differed. In the first decade of life, boys appeared vulnerable to both biological and environmental stresses, but girls had more difficulty in the second decade of life. By the late elementary school years, boys were more able to cope with their earlier problems—the demands of school achievement and the control of aggression. Adolescent girls, however, confronted social pressures and sexual expectations that led to an increasing rate of mental health problems. The complexity of these interactions demonstrates the difficulty of separating the contributions of prenatal, perinatal, and experiential factors to long-term development.

On follow-up at age 30, three out of four participants had had some college education, almost all were fully employed, and the majority listed career or job success as their primary objective, followed by self-fulfillment. Of the women, 85 percent were married and working, and 75 percent had young children; only 40 percent of the men were married, and only 35 percent had children. Men seemed to have had more difficulty weathering the breakups of relationships than did women and to have become more reluctant to commit to new ones. Among the resilient adults who were parents, their primary goals for their children were the acquisition of personal competencies and skills. About three-quarters considered themselves happy and satisfied; a few had divorced, had experienced psychological problems requiring them to seek professional help, or had drug problems (Werner, 1995). But, again, investigators note that 10 times more of the participants in this study had problems related to the effects of poor environment than to the effects of perinatal stress. Indeed, birth complications, unless they involved serious damage to the central nervous system, were consistently related to impaired physical or psychological development only if they were combined with chronic poverty, parental psychopathology, or persistently poor rearing conditions (Luthar et al., 2000; Selman & Dray, 2005; Werner, 1991). Clearly, the environment plays a critical role in helping children overcome a poor beginning.

Making the Connections 3

There are many links between concepts and ideas presented in one area of development and concepts and ideas in other areas. Here are some of the connections between ideas in Chapter 3 and discussions in other chapters of this book.

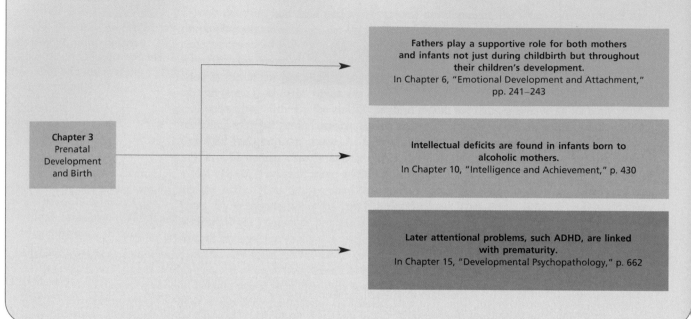

Chapter 3
Prenatal Development and Birth

Fathers play a supportive role for both mothers and infants not just during childbirth but throughout their children's development.
In Chapter 6, "Emotional Development and Attachment," pp. 241–243

Intellectual deficits are found in infants born to alcoholic mothers.
In Chapter 10, "Intelligence and Achievement," p. 430

Later attentional problems, such ADHD, are linked with prematurity.
In Chapter 15, "Developmental Psychopathology," p. 662

SUMMARY

Stages of Prenatal Development

- Prenatal development is typically divided into three distinct periods (zygote, embryo, fetus). In reality, these periods represent continuous phases of development during which the organism, protected and sustained by the **amniotic sac,** the **placenta,** the **umbilical cord,** and, after the fifth month, the lanugo, undergoes a systematic series of sequential changes to become increasingly complex and differentiated.

- The period of the **zygote,** which lasts about two weeks, extends from fertilization to implantation, when the zygote becomes implanted in the wall of the uterus. The period of the **embryo** begins at that point and lasts until the end of the eighth week. During this period of rapid growth, most of the important organs and physiological systems develop, and the embryo is quite vulnerable to adverse environmental influences.

- The principles of **cephalocaudal development** and **proximal-distal development** govern the order in which various parts of the organism's body are formed and grow. According to the first principle,

physical growth begins in the area of the head and moves downward, toward the trunk and legs; according to the second, growth also proceeds from central areas, such as the internal organs, to more distant ones, such as the arms.

- The period of the **fetus** extends from the beginning of the third month until birth. Around the fourth and fifth months, the mother can feel the fetus move, and reflexes such as sucking appear. Nails appear, the skin grows more adultlike, and **lanugo** covers the body of the fetus. Although the major organ systems are well differentiated by this time, the central nervous system continues to develop at a rapid pace, reflexes develop, and regulatory processes and the respiratory system continue to mature. A danger at this time is **respiratory distress syndrome,** and if the child is born before the **age of viability,** or 22 to 26 weeks, it may not be developed enough to survive.

Risks in the Prenatal Environment

- During prenatal development, **teratogens,** agents that produce developmental abnormalities, may affect the growing organism, resulting in physical and mental deviations. Seven general principles summarize the effects of teratogens on prenatal development, indicating that the type, timing, and duration of the teratogen, as well as the genotypes of the mother and child, play a role in the outcome.

- Mothers who smoke cigarettes or drink alcohol are more likely to bear premature or low-birthweight babies than women who do not smoke or drink. Even too much coffee can be harmful to the fetus. In addition, maternal drinking is related to **fetal alcohol syndrome,** which results in facial abnormalities, short stature, and mental retardation. Even modest amounts of alcohol and passive smoking have been related to negative effects in the offspring. Moreover, genetic effects of fathers' smoking and drinking may be passed to their offspring.

- In the case of illegal drugs such as cocaine or heroin, drug-addicted infants may exhibit symptoms that disrupt parenting and result in long-term adverse outcomes for both child and parent. Drug-using mothers may have particular problems dealing with such infants because of their own troubles.

- Drugs taken by the mother during pregnancy, whether legal or illegal, may have a negative impact on the developing fetus. Sometimes, as in the case of **thalidomide** and **diethylstilbestrol,** the effects of a prescription drug on the infant are not known until birth or much later.

- Some obstetrical medications used to ease pain and sedate women during labor and delivery may affect the newborn's behavior for several days after birth. However, there are often no longer-term effects of such drugs.

- Mothers who have their first child when they are over 35 or under 15 are likely to experience more problems during pregnancy and difficulties during delivery than women between these ages. In both groups, the risks are related to maternal health. Young adolescents are less likely to eat properly or to get prenatal care; older women are more likely to have hypertension, diabetes, alcoholism, and other problems related to age.

- Deficiencies in maternal diet are related to increased rates of prematurity, stillbirth, infant mortality, physical and neural defects, and small size. The specific form a defect takes is related to the age at which the malnutrition occurs and its severity and duration. Dietary supplements provided during pregnancy and after birth have been successful at reducing some of these effects, but the extent of the reversibility of such damage is not known. Continued ill effects seem to be related to the mother's history of dietary deprivation, the length and severity of the malnutrition, and continuing adverse nutritional, social, and economic factors following birth.

- Eating undercooked meat or coming in contact with feces, as in handling cat litter, can lead to the parasitic disease **toxoplasmosis,** which is transmitted through the placenta and can cause eye and brain damage in the growing baby.

- Maternal emotional disturbance has been related to complications during pregnancy and delivery and to hyperactivity and irritability in infants after birth. Discovering the causes underlying these relationships is difficult because women who are emotionally upset during pregnancy may be poorly adjusted in a variety of ways that affect their caretaking and their infant's adjustment after birth.

- A wide range of maternal diseases and disorders can affect prenatal development, including **Rh factor incompatibility;** high blood pressure; diabetes; rubella; and sexually transmitted diseases such as **gonorrhea, syphilis, chlamydia, genital herpes,** and **acquired immune deficiency syndrome,** or **AIDS.** The effects of maternal diseases are related to the stage of fetal development during which they are contracted and the length of time that they last.

Birth and the Beginnings of Life

- Birth involves a series of changes in the mother that permit the child to move from the womb to the outside world. These include uterine contractions during the first stage of labor that allow the cervix to become large enough for the child's head; the child's descent into the birth canal and emergence out of the canal during the second stage; and the expulsion of the placenta during the third stage. If problems arise before or during the delivery, a **cesarean delivery** may be performed by removing the baby through an incision in the mother's abdomen.

- Birth complications occur in only about 10 percent of deliveries. Some important birth factors related to developmental deviations and mortality are **anoxia,** or lack of oxygen in the brain; prematurity; and low birthweight. Premature babies may be **preterm** or **small for date.** Anoxia, early birth, and low birthweight have been associated with physical, neurological, cognitive, and emotional deficits. Most of these negative effects diminish with age, except in extreme cases. Stimulation programs have been successful with low-birthweight babies in combating the effects of isolation and the separation of infant from parents caused by keeping the infant in an isolette for the first weeks of life.

Vulnerability and Resilience in Children at Risk

- According to the concepts of the continuum of reproductive casualty and the continuum of caretaking casualty, both birth complications and the environmental situations into which a child is born may vary greatly along continua that stretch from the most favorable to the least favorable conditions for the child's well-being.
- Researchers who have studied the interaction of these continua have found that often more favorable early environmental conditions can compensate to some extent for adverse perinatal complications.

EXPLORE AND DISCUSS

1. How do you think our definition of "family" has changed as a result of the new reproductive technologies that allow families to have a child by means of a surrogate mother or through the use of donated sperm and/or eggs?

2. What advice would you give to a pregnant friend who drinks coffee and alcoholic beverages and smokes? Do you think that the government should prevent people from smoking or drinking during pregnancy? Explain your position.

3. Birth is a family affair, not just a mother's issue. How have the roles that fathers, other relatives, and even older siblings play in the birth process changed over the last several decades? How have hospital policies changed to accommodate new views of childbirth?

4. Medical science has permitted very small preterm infants to survive, but some of these children may face physical, social, and cognitive problems. Discuss the ethical issues involved in the medical practice of keeping increasingly smaller preterm infants alive.

Boris Kustodiev (1878–1927). *The Morning Bath. (The Wife and Son of the Artist.)* Russian State Museum, St. Petersburg, Russia.

4.

Infancy: Sensation, Perception, and Learning

Joseph's dad played folk songs to his 3-day-old son while rocking him in his cradle; Rebecca's mother started reading Shakespearean sonnets to her daughter when she was 1 month old; Jenny's grandmother bought Jenny picture books and a brightly colored mobile, but she waited to give them to Jenny's mother until she thought the child was "ready" for them—at 6 months of age!

Each of these adults had different ideas about a baby's sensory capabilities. Researchers today continue to learn more about the sensory and perceptual world of infants. They have found that babies can hear, see, and respond to interesting sights and sounds at a much earlier age than was once believed. The sensory world of a newborn is far from the "blooming, buzzing confusion" that psychologist William James once declared it. Newborns are able to organize information and to respond selectively to it even in the first few minutes after birth.

This chapter begins with a look at the newborn's earliest observed behaviors, including the baby's normal reflexes, the time spent in sleep or in wakefulness, and crying and ways of self-soothing; we also examine ways of assessing the newborn's health, maturity, and capacities. We then look at the growth and development of the infant's sensory and perceptual abilities—auditory, visual, taste, and touch. We conclude with a review of the different kinds of learning we discussed in Chapter 1 as evidenced by the infant and with a brief discussion of the baby's memory abilities.

THE NEWBORN

neonate A newborn baby.

Parents expecting one of those beautiful little creatures we see in television ads for baby products and in the print media are sometimes shocked at the appearance of their newborns, for at the moment of birth and for a little while afterward, most newborns, or **neonates,** are pretty homely little beings. Their noses, ears, and entire heads often bear the marks of the pressure exerted on them as they passed through the birth canal, and their skin is often red, wrinkled, and blotchy, partly as the result of floating for nine months in amniotic fluid. Their heads are oversized in proportion to their bodies (in fact, from childhood to adulthood the head goes from a quarter to an eighth of total body size), and their little legs appear weak, even useless. But despite these perhaps surprising characteristics—most of which disappear even before the newborn period of three to four weeks is over—most parents welcome their newborns with joy and love.

A New Baby's Reflexes

reflex A human's involuntary response to external stimulation.

Newborns are highly competent organisms. They have well-developed reflexes and sensory responses, and they are surprisingly well equipped to begin adapting to their new environments from the very first moments after birth. Moreover, their responses are not random and disorganized; rather, newborns show a capacity to respond in an organized, meaningful way early in life. Some of the first behaviors to appear are **reflexes,** or involuntary responses to external stimuli. Table 4-1 describes the newborn's major reflexes, some of which are permanent (e.g., withdrawal reflexes, such as the knee jerk), and others of which disappear during the first year of life. A number of these reflexes have obvious value in helping to ensure the newborn's survival. The rooting and sucking reflexes, for example, help the newborn to locate and obtain food, the eye blink helps to shield the eyes from excessively strong light, and the withdrawal reflex helps to protect the baby from painful and possibly harmful stimuli. The functions of other newborn reflexes are less obvious. Researchers speculate that some of them may have had survival benefits for the infants of our early ancestors.

Babies have lots of reflexes (many are described in Table 4-1) that serve as important indicators of physical well-being. The 6-week-old's Babinski reflex (a) tells the examiner that the child's lower spine is fully functional; the infant's palmar grasp (b) and rooting response (c) at 4 weeks of age both confirm the absence of depression.

(a)

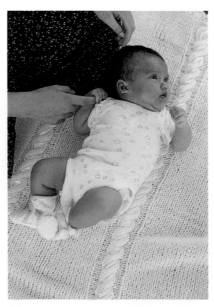

(b)

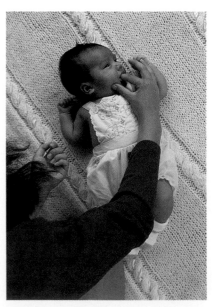

(c)

Table 4-1   The newborn's major reflexes

		Testing the Reflex		
Reflex	Method	Baby's Response	Significance of Response	Developmental Course of Reflex
Permanent				
Biceps reflex	Tap on the tendon of the biceps muscle	Baby displays short contraction of muscle	Absent in depressed babies or those with congenital muscular disease	Brisker in first few days
Eye blink	Flash bright light in baby's eyes	Baby blinks or closes eyes	Protects baby from strong stimuli	Relatively unchanging
Patellar tendon reflex ("knee jerk")	Tap on the tendon below the knee cap, or patella	Baby quickly extends or kicks leg	Weak or absent in depressed babies or those with muscular disease; exaggerated in hyperexcitable babies	More pronounced in first 2 days than later
Withdrawal reflex	Prick sole of baby's foot gently with a pin	Baby withdraws foot and pulls leg up, bending knee and hip	Absent when there is damage to the sciatic nerve, the largest nerve of the body	Constantly present during first 10 days; less intense later
Temporary				
Babinski reflex	Stroke bottom of foot from heel to toes	Baby's big toe curves up and other toes fan and curl	Absent in defects of the lower spine	Usually disappears near end of first year; replaced in normal adult by plantar flexion of big toe
Babkin or palmar reflex	With baby lying on his back, apply pressure to both of baby's palms	Baby opens mouth, closes eyes, and moves head to midline position	Inhibited in general depression of the central nervous system	Disappears at 3–4 months
Moro reflex	Suddenly allow baby's head to drop back a few inches; lower baby's overall position about 6 inches or make sudden, loud noise	Baby throws arms outward and extends legs; then brings both arms back toward center of body, clenching fists	Absent or consistently weak reflex indicates serious problem in central nervous system	Disappears at 6–7 months
Palmar grasp	Press a finger or cylindrical object against baby's palm	Baby grasps finger or object	Weak or absent in depressed babies	Initially strong; disappears by 3–4 months; replaced by voluntary grasp within a month or so
Plantar or toe grasp	Press on the ball of the baby's foot	Baby curls all toes, as if grasping	Absent in defects of the lower spinal cord	Disappears between 8 and 12 months
Rooting response	Stroke baby's cheek lightly	Baby turns head toward finger, opens its mouth, and tries to suck	Absent in depressed babies	Disappears at about 3–4 months and becomes voluntary
Stepping reflex	Support baby in upright position and move her forward, tilting her slightly to one side	Baby makes rhythmic stepping movements	Absent in depressed infants	Disappears at 3–4 months
Sucking response	Insert finger 1–1.5 inches into baby's mouth	Baby sucks finger rhythmically	Weak, slow, interrupted sucking found in apathetic babies; maternal medication during childbirth may depress sucking	Often less intensive and regular in first 3–4 days; disappears by 6 months

Abnormalities in a baby's reflexes during the first days or weeks after birth can be useful in identifying visual and hearing problems, and they can even help predict abnormal functions that don't appear until months or years later (Dubowitz & Dubowitz, 1981; Francis, Self, & Horowitz, 1987). Reflexes that are either weak, absent, or unusually strong can be a sign of brain damage. Moreover, some reflexes normally disappear; their failure to do so may be a sign of neurological problems. At birth, physicians often specifically test the newborn for certain reflexes to evaluate the soundness of the baby's central nervous system. As we saw in Chapter 3, infants exposed in utero to harmful agents, for example, cocaine, show a variety of neurological deficits that can be assessed by observing the infants' reflexive responses to specific kinds of stimulation (Phillips et al., 1996). Babies exposed to cocaine show abnormal patterns in the intensity of the sucking and rooting reflexes.

Infant States

Among the most fascinating aspects of the newborn's behavior are the changes that occur in the baby's state of arousal—that is, in its alternating states of sleep and wakefulness. Just as adults have recurring patterns of sleep and wakefulness, so do babies.

infant state A recurring pattern of arousal in the newborn, ranging from alert, vigorous, wakeful activity to quiet, regular sleep.

    The **infant state,** or the recurring pattern of arousal that ranges from alert, vigorous, wakeful activity to quiet, regular sleep, gives evidence of some important principles of human behavior (Table 4-2). First, human behavior is *organized* and *predictable*. Rather than occurring in a random, haphazard manner, infant states recur in a regular, periodic fashion as part of a larger cycle. Second, human beings are not passive, stirred into action only by outside stimulation. On the contrary, internal forces regulate much of our behavior and account for many changes in our activity levels (Schaffer, 1996). Psychologists who study infants know this all too well. Many have been frustrated when, after they have prepared an infant participant for an experiment, they find the infant has drifted off to sleep!

    This is not to say a baby's states can't be affected by outside forces; our later discussion of soothing techniques attests that they can be. Our point here is simply that internal forces play just as central a role in infant states as they do in adult states.

Table 4-2 Newborn infant states

State	Typical Duration	Characteristics
Regular sleep	8–9 hours	Infant's eyes are closed, and body is completely still. Respiration is slow and regular. Baby's face is relaxed, with no grimacing, and eyelids are still.
Irregular sleep	8–9 hours	Baby's eyes are closed, but baby engages in gentle limb movements and general stirring. Grimaces and other facial expressions are frequent.
Drowsiness	$\frac{1}{2}$–3 hours	Baby's eyes open and close intermittently and display recurrent rapid eye movements. Baby is relatively inactive. Respiration is regular, though faster than in regular sleep.
Alert inactivity	2–3 hours	Infant's eyes are open, have a bright and shining quality, and can pursue moving objects. Baby is relatively inactive; face is relaxed and does not grimace.
Waking activity	2–3 hours	Baby's eyes are open but not alert, and respiration is irregular. Baby frequently engages in diffuse motor activity involving the whole body.
Crying	1–3 hours	Baby makes crying vocalizations and engages in diffuse motor activity.

Sources: Wolff, 1966, 1987.

Evaluations of changes in fetal activity cycles and studies of infants born prematurely tell us that arousal patterns are formed well before birth (Sontag, 1944). In one study, even babies born two months prematurely exhibited regular changes in state that continued to develop and became more organized as the infants grew older (Holditch-Davis, 1990). As we discussed in Chapter 2, individual differences in state of arousal and the ability to regulate that state are important components of temperament.

In broadest terms there are two fundamental infant states—waking and sleeping. However, the waking state may be quiet, active, or distressed, as in fussing and crying, and the state of sleeping also includes variations. Here we will focus on sleeping and crying behavior.

SLEEP   The newborn, on average, sleeps about 70 percent of the time in a series of long and short naps that alternate regardless of whether it is night or day. By the time an infant is 4 weeks old, her periods of sleep are typically fewer but longer, and by the time she is 8 weeks old she is sleeping more during the night and less during the day (Ingersoll & Thoman, 1999). As Figure 4-1 shows, the infant also becomes less fussy as she gains better control over her states of arousal. By the end of the first year, most infants sleep through the night, much to the relief of their parents. This shift to a culturally accepted sleep-wake cycle illustrates how the infant's internal biorhythms become adapted to the demands of the external world (Ikonomov, Stoynev, & Shisheva, 1998).

Not all cultures organize sleep patterns in the same way that U.S. parents do (Harkness & Super, 1995; Morelli, Rogoff, Oppenheim, & Goldsmith, 1992). In the Kipsigis tribe of rural Kenya, infants are constantly with their mothers and regularly take naps throughout the day. In contrast to American babies, who gradually begin to sleep longer at night and less during the day, Kipsigis babies continue to take shorter and more frequent naps. Although these Kenyan babies eventually sleep through the night, they show this pattern much later than American babies (Super & Harkness, 1981).

Sleeping arrangements differ across cultures as well. In contrast to the U.S. custom of putting babies to sleep alone in their own rooms, many cultures encourage cosleeping arrangements, with parent(s) and infant in the same bed (Rogoff, 2003). Kipsigis babies sleep with their mothers, but when a new child is born, the older sibling sleeps

Figure 4-1   Infants' sleep patterns

At 2 weeks of age, infants tend to maintain about the same ratio of total sleep, active sleep, and fussy crying in the morning, afternoon, and at night, but by the time they're 8 weeks old they have begun to spend appreciably more time in quiet sleep during the nighttime hours.

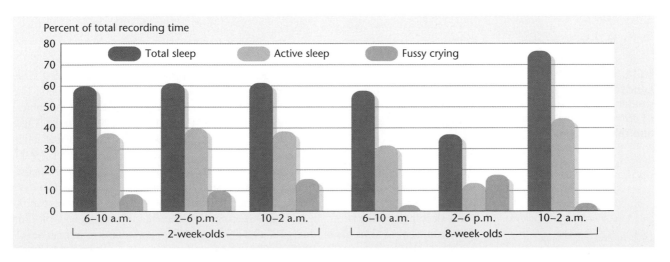

Source: Sostek & Anders, 1981.

Box 4.1
Child Psychology in Action

PREVENTING SUDDEN INFANT DEATH SYNDROME (SIDS)

Each year in the United States about 10,000 babies die in their sleep from causes classified as **sudden infant death syndrome (SIDS),** also known as *crib death.*

The prevention of SIDS requires identifying its most likely victims. So far we know that victims are more apt to be low-birthweight male babies who have a history of newborn respiratory problems, who were hospitalized longer than usual after birth, and who have abnormal heart-rate patterns and nighttime sleep disturbances (Mitchell et al., 1993; Rovee-Collier & Lipsitt, 1982; Sadeh, 1996). Their mothers are more likely to be anemic, to smoke or use narcotics, and to have received little prenatal care, although it should be stressed that most babies of women with this history are not affected. Usually, SIDS occurs during sleep in the wintertime, and it often follows a minor respiratory ailment, such as a cold. It is most common between the ages of 2 and 4 months and rarely occurs after 6 months (*American Academy of Pediatrics Report,* 2000).

The cause of SIDS is still a mystery. It is not due to accidental suffocation, to mucus or fluid in the lungs, or to choking on regurgitated food. Nor has there been any success in isolating a virus associated with SIDS, although this is still a possibility. Another possibility is that *apnea,* the spontaneous interruption of breathing that sometimes occurs during sleep, especially REM sleep, may be a factor in SIDS (Steinschneider, 1975). The brain stem, which controls breathing, may not be well enough developed in these infants to overcome brief cessations in breathing. Researchers are investigating whether babies who have unusually long apnea periods during sleep may be more prone to SIDS.

Parental smoking has also been suggested as a contributing factor to crib death (Frick, 1999). In addition, SIDS victims may have failed to develop adequate responses to nasal blockage and other threats to breathing (Lipsitt, 1990). Although newborns appear to have built-in defensive reactions to respiratory threats (e.g., when a cloth is placed over a baby's face, she will use her hands to try to remove it), between 2 and 4 months of age these reactions may change from reflexive behaviors to voluntary ones. Crib death is most common during this same age period. Perhaps failure to make a smooth transition from reflexive to voluntary defenses puts an infant at greater risk for SIDS.

Monitors that sound an alarm to alert parents when an infant's breathing is interrupted may be useful in preventing SIDS. Although the false alarms of these devices may place stress on the parents, the devices may help to save lives. It is also helpful for babies to sleep on their backs or sides, not on their stomachs; sleeping on the stomach may depress breathing (Willinger, Hoffman, & Hartford, 1994). Babies should not sleep on very soft mattresses or be surrounded by pillows that may obstruct breathing (*American Academy of Pediatrics Report,* 2000). Some researchers suggest that parents adopt the practices of many cultures where parent-infant cosleeping is common. In countries such as Japan and China where this practice is common, SIDS rates are lower (McKenna & Mosko, 1990). This pattern has led some researchers to suggest that cosleeping may aid the baby in breathing regulation (McKenna & Mosko, 1993). However, this proposal is still controversial (Shonkoff & Phillips, 2000) and needs further study.

---

sudden infant death syndrome (SIDS) The sudden, unexplained death of an infant while sleeping; also called *crib death.*

at the mother's back, indicating that breast-feeding and constant carrying are over for the older infant (Harkness & Super, 1995; Super & Harkness, 1981). Some mothers, like Mayan mothers in Guatemala, disapprove of the U.S. custom of separate beds for babies; indeed, they regard it as "tantamount to child neglect" (Morelli et al., 1992, p. 608). There are some exceptions in the United States, however. For instance, among Appalachian families, nearly 50 percent of children aged 2 to 4 cosleep with parents (Abbott, 1992). And recently middle-class U.S. families have shown more interest in cosleeping arrangements with infants, as evidenced by sales of bedside cribs for parents who want to have their infants nearby at night. Clearly, parents do not take lightly the matter of parent-child sleeping arrangements. In fact, the sleeping arrangements of parents and children "represent central ideas about family relationships and the proper course of human development" (Harkness & Super, 1995, p. 228). And as Box 4.1 suggests, cosleeping may also have specific health benefits for the developing infant (McKenna & Mosko, 1993).

By recording brain activity, investigators have distinguished different phases of sleep. The most important distinction is between **REM sleep** and *non-REM sleep*. REM, or rapid eye movement sleep, is often identified with dreaming because in adults it is during dreaming that the eyes, under closed eyelids, have been observed to dart around in rapid, jerky movements. (As yet we have no way of knowing if infants dream.) REM sleep is characterized also by fluctuating heart rate and blood pressure. Although we have yet to discover the full purpose of REM sleep, we do know that it has functional value: If just as they begin REM sleep people are repeatedly awakened and thus prevented from obtaining sleep of this type, they tend to be irritable and disorganized during their later waking hours.

In newborns, 50 percent of sleep is REM sleep, but as children age, REM sleep declines to about 20 percent (Berg & Berg, 1987; Ingersoll & Thoman, 1999). By the age of 18 and onward through adulthood, most people sleep about eight hours a day, and of that amount, only about an hour and a half to an hour and three-quarters is REM sleep. An **autostimulation theory** has been proposed to account for the high level of REM sleep in newborns. Researchers have suggested that the mechanism or process that causes REM sleep stimulates higher brain centers and that this in turn may stimulate early development of the central nervous system (Roffwarg, Muzio, & Dement, 1966). As the infant develops and becomes increasingly alert and capable of processing external stimulation, whether positive or negative in character, this type of built-in stimulation may become less necessary. If this theory is right, the speed with which infants reduce their percentage of REM sleep could depend on how much external stimulation they receive. Some researchers have found, for instance, that male newborns who have been circumcised and thus subjected to a high level of (negative) stimulation spend less time in REM sleep than uncircumcised infants, a finding consistent with the autostimulation theory (Emde, Harmon, Metcalf, Koenig, & Wagonfeld, 1971). High levels of positive stimulation seem to yield similar results. In one study, infants who were encouraged to stay awake and who were exposed to visual stimuli spent less time in REM sleep than infants in a control condition who were not provided these opportunities (Boismier, 1977).

REM sleep REM, or rapid eye movement, sleep is characterized by rapid, jerky movements of the eyes and, in adults, is often associated with dreaming.

autostimulation theory The theory that during REM sleep the infant's brain stimulates itself and that this in turn stimulates early development of the central nervous system.

CRYING At the other end of the continuum of infant states is crying. Crying is one of the infant's earliest means of communicating needs to caregivers, and three different patterns of crying, reflective of the infant's varying needs, have been identified (Schaffer, 1971, p. 61):

Pattern	Characteristics
Basic	Starts arrhythmically and at low intensity; gradually becomes louder and more rhythmic; sequence is cry-rest-inhale-rest. Linked to hunger, among other factors.
Angry	Same as basic pattern except that segments of crying, resting, and inhaling vary in length, and crying segments are longer. Causes include removing a pacifier or toy.
Pain	Sudden in onset, loud from the start, and made up of a long cry followed by a long silence that includes holding of the breath, and then by a series of short, gasping inhalations. Causes include discomfort from soiled diaper, a pinprick, or a stomachache.

Most mothers can distinguish among these different types of crying but only when listening to the cries of their own babies (Wiesenfeld, Malatesta, & DeLoache, 1981). In general, fathers are less skilled than mothers at distinguishing among types of cries, men are less skilled than women, and nonparents are less skilled than parents (Holden, 1988). These differences are probably related to varying amounts of experience with babies and differences in the amount of time spent caring for them.

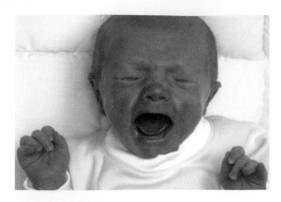

Newborns typically cry because of some form of physiological distress, such as hunger, the need for a diaper change, or digestive problems. By 3 or 4 months of age, a baby's crying—a clear form of communication—will often be related to psychological needs, such as his wish to be picked up and hugged or caressed or to be played with.

In the early months of life, crying is related to the infant's physiology; hunger, hiccups, or digestive problems may disturb him and lead to crying. By 3 or 4 months, however, crying is less associated with physiological distress and increasingly related to the baby's psychological needs. Similarly, by 3 to 4 months, most infants spend less of their days crying, their concerns are easier to interpret, and they are easier to soothe (Kopp, 1994; Shonkoff & Phillips, 2000).

Crying often works in eliciting a caregiver response. In one study, 77 percent of 2,461 episodes of crying studied were followed by some intervention on the mother's part (Moss, 1967). In a laboratory simulation study, both mothers and nonmothers responded to a crying baby doll by holding, talking to, and soothing the "baby" (Gustafson & Harris, 1990). This intervention becomes an opportunity for social interaction, so the parent is rewarded in two ways: The crying stops, and parent and child engage in a mutually enjoyable exchange (Lester, 1988).

For years, people have debated the wisdom of *always* responding promptly to a baby's cries. In the earlier part of this century, many people believed that rushing to soothe a crying infant would "spoil" the baby and encourage the infant to cry at the least little thing. Then, in the 1970s, research suggested that the opposite might be true: When mothers respond promptly to their crying infants, the frequency and duration of crying may actually *decrease* as the baby develops the expectation that the mother can be counted on to help (Bell & Ainsworth, 1972).

To test this latter hypothesis, Hubbard and van IJzendoorn (1991) observed infants in their homes over the first nine months of life. Crying declined greatly after the first three months, perhaps because the babies were adjusting to life in their new environments or because of changes in neurological organization (Nelson, 1999a). Individual differences in the duration of crying could not be explained by differences in how promptly mothers responded to their babies. However, the researchers did find that delays in the mother's responding seemed to cause a decrease in the number of crying bouts. This result makes sense if we differentiate between responding promptly to severe distress on the part of a baby and responding promptly to mild fussing over a minor matter (such as an uncomfortable body position), which through practice the baby might learn to cope with independently. Parents are generally able to distinguish between these levels of distress without difficulty. Delaying a response to this second kind of crying may help to make the baby more self-sufficient in dealing with minor irritations, and so the child fusses less often. The parent, however, must be a good judge of the causes of the baby's cries, for ignoring the cries of a severely distressed infant could have serious consequences.

Sensitivity to differences in cries and their meanings is as useful for physicians who treat the young as it is for parents. Crying patterns can be a helpful diagnostic tool that alerts pediatricians to possible abnormalities in early development (Worchel & Allen, 1997). For instance, infants with brain damage or with Down syndrome take longer to cry in response to a painful stimulus, require a more intense stimulus to elicit a cry, and produce a less sustained, more arrhythmic, and higher-pitched cry than normal infants (Lester, Corwin, & Golub, 1988). Sometimes, in a condition called colic, babies cry a great deal for no apparent reason. **Colic** (the word means pain) is a prolonged period of unexplained crying in infants that sometimes lasts several hours at a time. Infantile colic, which occurs in about 20 percent of infants, usually begins between 2 and 4 weeks of age, and its causes are not known (Lester, 2005). This loud, continual crying can be frustrating, even frightening, for parents. In most cases, it stops by the time the baby is 3 to 4 months of age. Although colic is usually harmless, in some cases it may indicate an illness, such as a hernia or an ear infection. And a high-pitched, urgent, "piercing" cry can help to differentiate babies with colic from those who simply cry a great deal or are ill (Lester, Boukydis, Garcia-Coll, Hole, & Peucker, 1992). The infant cry is not only an important communicative signal but also an early warning sign of developmental problems and illness.

colic A prolonged period of unexplained crying in an infant.

How to Soothe an Infant

As infants grow and mature they are less likely to cry or to engage in other behaviors that appear to signal distress. Because not all forms of distress go away, it seems that ways of dealing with distress are an increasingly important part of the baby's life. Thus, researchers have been interested in identifying techniques that may be effective in relieving an infant's agitation and distress.

INFANTS' ABILITIES TO SOOTHE THEMSELVES   To some extent, infants can relieve their own distress. One good way is by sucking, a highly organized response in which, even while still in utero, the baby routinely engages. After birth, sucking on things, including the baby's own thumb and hand, may soothe very young infants. Although it was long assumed that sucking was effective because of its association with feeding, researchers have found that, immediately after birth and before the baby's first oral feeding, simply sucking on a pacifier reduces a baby's distress (Field & Goldson, 1984; Kessen, Leutzendokff, & Stoutsenberger, 1967; Smith, Fillion, & Blass, 1990). It may be that sucking has a soothing effect because when the baby sucks, its overall body movements are lessened. Recent studies indicate, however, that sucking on certain specific substances more effectively calms infants than sucking on others. For example, sucking on substances with a sweet taste is more effective in calming young infants than sucking plain water (Smith & Blass, 1996). But the soothing techniques that work change as the infant develops. Some researchers have found that sucking on a sweet liquid appeared to be effective in calming a 2-week-old baby but was ineffective in soothing a 4-week-old unless accompanied by eye contact with an adult (Zeifman, Delaney, & Blass, 1996). By 4 weeks, the infant begins to rely on social contact with caregivers to soothe him and help regulate his states (Zeifman et al., 1996).

HOW PARENTS SOOTHE THEIR BABIES   Because infants pay more attention to events in their environment when they are in a calm but alert state, soothing babies and bringing them to a state in which they are neither too drowsy nor upset is one of the critical tasks of parenting. To find out how to achieve this optimal state was the goal of a classic study by Korner and Thoman (1970). These investigators assessed the effectiveness of six different techniques for bringing either a crying or a sleeping newborn into a state of calm alertness. Figure 4-2 shows that the most effective technique was holding the baby on one's shoulder. This position evoked bright-eyed

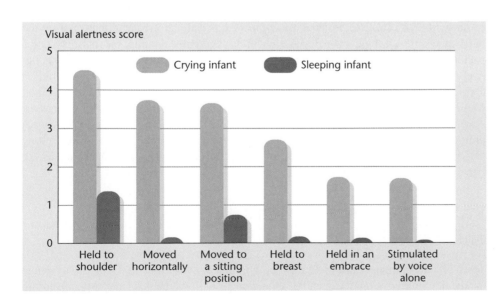

Figure 4-2

The effects of stimulation on an infant's visual alertness

In a classic study of how to bring an infant into a calm but alert state, holding the baby to one's shoulder was the most effective method.

Source: Korner & Thoman, 1970.

Perspectives on Diversity

HOW CULTURE AFFECTS SOOTHABILITY

Across cultures and nations there are wide differences in the ease with which babies in distress can be soothed (Shonkoff & Phillips, 2000; Rothbart & Bates, 1998). As we saw in our discussion of temperament in Chapter 2, some babies are easily calmed and others are really difficult to console (Moss, 1967).

Of particular interest are the many cross-cultural and subcultural differences in infant soothability. For example, studying infants in the United States, Freedman (1974) found that European American babies shifted more frequently between states of contentment and distress than Chinese American babies. The latter tended to calm themselves more readily when they were upset and were also more easily consoled by caretakers. Moreover, these differences persisted over the first few months of infancy and affected how the infants were treated. Kuchner (1980) found that Chinese American mothers allowed their infants to cry for longer periods before intervening but that Chinese American babies quieted quickly with minimal intervention (e.g., simply hearing their mothers' voices).

Soothability is also greater among babies in some other cultural groups, both within the United States and beyond its borders. Japanese babies, for example, and babies of the Zinacanteco Indian tribe of southern Mexico are more easily quieted than other infants

(Nugent, Lester, & Brazelton, 1989). Navajo babies in the American Southwest who, for about the first year of their lives, spend much of the day encased in a cradleboard are also easier to soothe than many other babies.

The *cradleboard,* which is used in other Native North American tribes and in other parts of the world as well, is made up of a wooden back, a hinged footboard, and a hoop that arches over and shields the baby's head and face. These components are held together by leather thongs, and the board itself is cushioned with bedding material and a blanket, the corners of which are tucked in tightly around the baby's body. A laced cover holds the baby and the bedding in place. Newborns and sleeping infants are swaddled from the neck down, but after about three months babies' arms may be left free (Chisholm, 1963).

Although the use of the cradleboard certainly limits a baby's motor actions, it confers another advantage that the bassinet, the crib, and the traditional Western carriage do not: It enables the baby to see what is going on around him from a more adultlike perspective (Chisholm, 1963). Because the cradleboard has a rigid back, it can be propped up against a wall or tree; the board is notched at the top so that it can be securely wedged in this upright position. (Of course,

---

visual scanning in 77.5 percent of the infants. Figure 4-2 also shows that the effect of a certain kind of stimulation depends heavily on the particular state the infant is in to begin with. For example, horizontal movement has a much greater effect on a crying baby than on a sleeping one. Because sucking can soothe infants, parents may use a pacifier with very young infants. This technique can comfort infants rapidly and effectively (Campos, 1989). A variety of other techniques are also effective in soothing a crying infant, including rocking, swaddling and massaging (Field, 2001a; Rock, Trainor, & Addison, 1999). In swaddling, one wraps the baby tightly in a blanket or cloth, thus keeping its arms and legs immobile (Byrne & Horowitz, 1981; Campos, 1989). Swaddling has been used successfully in many cultures; it is common, for example, among the Navajos and Hopis of the American Southwest (Chisholm, 1963; Valsiner, 1989). For discussion of cultural differences in babies' soothability, see Box 4.2.

Evaluating the Newborn's Health and Capabilities

Tests of reflexes (see Table 4-1) may be combined with other assessments to gauge the health, maturity, and capacities of a newborn (look back at the Apgar scoring

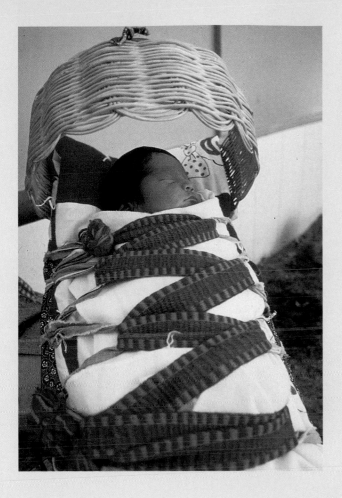

Tight swaddling provides a Havasupai infant with a feeling of comfort and security. Like many choices in child rearing, using the Native American cradleboard has clear tradeoffs. Although the cradleboard restricts a baby's movements (until the infant's arms are freed, at about 3 months), it also allows the baby to see and experience many things that an infant in a crib may miss, because the mother carries the cradleboard with her and can set it up against a firm backing.

when the child is sleeping, the cradleboard is laid flat.) Toys, beads, feathers, and other objects that interest the baby are often hung from the hoop, and when her arms are free she can reach and bat at these playthings.

Experts disagree on whether to attribute the Navajo infant's greater soothability to the relative motoric restriction of his first year; indeed, some authorities argue that the Navajo newborn is calmer at birth and that this relative quiescence is the reason for the use of the cradleboard (Chisholm, 1963). Some researchers suggest, however, that swaddling has a calming influence on the newborn (see, e.g., Tronick, Thomas, & Daltabuit, 1994). Perhaps simply having more to look at, as the cradleboard baby apparently does, encourages a calm, quiet, observational mode. Clearly, culture shapes the form and effectiveness of soothing techniques (Shonkoff & Phillips, 2000).

system displayed in Table 3-3). A variety of scales have been developed to standardize these assessments (Francis et al., 1987). One of the most widely used is the **Brazelton Neonatal Assessment Scale** (Brazelton, 1984; Brazelton & Nugent, 1995). As you can see from Table 4-3, this assessment instrument measures many of the capacities of the infant we discuss in this chapter: sensory and perceptual capacities (orientation to sights and sounds, habituation to sensory stimuli); motor development; infant states and the ability to regulate them; and signs that the brain is properly controlling involuntary responses (Brazelton, Nugent, & Lester, 1987).

The Brazelton scale has been used for a variety of purposes. Performance on the scale helps to identify infants at risk for developmental problems, and it can aid in diagnosing neurological impairment (Black, Schuler, & Nair, 1993; Eldredge & Salamy, 1988). The Brazelton scale is also useful in predicting later development. For instance, newborns who score high on it tend to score higher on later measures of cognitive, motor, or social development (Keefer, Dixon, Tronick, & Brazelton, 1991; Moss, Colombo, Mitchell, & Horowitz, 1988). Finally, the Brazelton scale has been used as an intervention technique, teaching parents about their newborn's capacities either by having them watch a health-care professional administer this test to their baby or by having them try the same tests with their baby themselves (Britt & Myers, 1994; Wendland-Carro, Piccinini, & Millar, 1999).

Brazelton Neonatal Assessment Scale A scale containing a battery of tests used to measure an infant's sensory and perceptual capabilities, motor development, range of states, and ability to regulate these states, as well as whether the brain and central nervous system are properly regulating involuntary responses.

Table 4-3   Brazelton Neonatal Behavioral Assessment Scale

Capacity for Habituation

Habituation, a form of learning in which repeated exposure to a particular stimulus leads to reduced response to that stimulus. The infant's ability to habituate is a measure of her capacity for attention to new things in her environment:

1. Light

2. Rattle

3. Bell

4. Pinprick

Orientation to Sights and Sounds

The baby's ability to focus on and track various stimuli is measured as an indication of his capacity to see, hear, and orient to things in his physical and social environment:

5. Visual focusing and following an inanimate object

6. Reacting to an inanimate auditory stimulus

7. Visual focusing and following a human face

8. Reacting to the sound of a human voice

9. Reacting to both the sight of a human face and the sound of the person's voice

Motor Development

These tests measure the infant's motor skills:

10. Baby's ability to pull to a sitting position

11. Defensive ability: Baby's ability to free himself of light cloth placed over eyes

12. Degree of alertness

13. General tonus

14. Motor maturity

15. Activity

State: Range in Degree of Arousal

Tests measure and record the variability and intensity of the infant's periods of arousal:

16. Peak excitement

17. Rapidity with which excitement builds

18. Irritability: Number of times the baby fusses and things appear to irritate her

19. Lability, or variability, of state: Frequency and intensity of changes in state

State: Regulation and Self-Regulation

These tests measure the infant's responsiveness to efforts to quiet or soothe her as well as her ability to quiet herself:

20. Cuddliness: A measure of the baby's willingness to be held and to conform to the examiner's body

21. Consolability with intervention: A measure of how long it takes an examiner to quiet a baby who is upset

22. Self-quieting: The baby's own efforts to soothe himself, as by thumb sucking

23. Whole hand to mouth

Autonomic Stability

Tests measure the infant's autonomic (uncontrolled) reactivity to various stimuli:

24. Tremors: Severe tremulousness may indicate problems in the central nervous system

25. Startles: The baby's tendency to react to sudden movement, loud sounds, and other strong stimuli with a startle response

26. Skin: Reactivity is assessed by measuring electrical activity on the surface of the skin

Source: Adapted from Brazelton et al., 1987.

Cross-cultural research on infant motor development has shown that a baby's behavior during the Brazelton assessment may predict later parent-infant interaction during feeding and play. Using the Brazelton scale, researchers identified superior motor performance by infants in the Gusii community of West Africa in comparison with American babies (Nugent, Lester, & Brazelton, 1991). This superior ability was found to be related to more vigorous handling by caregivers early in the child's life, including carrying the child on the mother's body in a sling, which has the effect of strengthening various muscles in the infant's body as she grips the mother (Keefer et al., 1991). The infants' motor abilities influence the way caregivers treat them, which, in turn, is influenced by cultural practices and behavioral routines. Together, these forces give infants opportunities to improve their motor control.

THE INFANT'S SENSORY AND PERCEPTUAL CAPACITIES

The sensory and perceptual world of infants is complex, especially when one considers the limited knowledge the infant has about the world in which he lives. Babies come to learn much about this world through their **sensations**—that is, what stimuli their sensory receptors detect—and their **perceptions**—their interpretations of the stimuli they detect (what they see and hear). Researchers have discovered that babies' sensory and perceptual capabilities are quite well organized even at birth, allowing infants to begin adapting immediately to their new environments.

sensation The detection of stimuli by the sensory receptors.

As this chapter's Turning Points chart (pp. 138–139) shows, the infant is especially well equipped to respond to his social environment, including human voices, faces, and smells. This suggests that a baby's sensory and perceptual systems may be biologically prepared to be sensitive to social stimuli. Such preparation is clearly adaptive, for a baby's responsiveness to other human beings increases caregivers' interest in the child and so enhances the child's well-being and survival. The infant's inborn sensitivity to social stimuli is one of the themes we will develop in this section of the chapter.

perception The interpretation of sensations to make them meaningful.

A second theme concerns the interdependence of the various sensory and perceptual systems—vision, hearing, taste, smell, and touch. To present the "facts" about these systems in an orderly way, we treat each one separately. In the real world, however, these systems develop together, and advances in one may trigger changes in another. Later in this section we will put the developmental pieces together and show how these systems influence each other, all working together to help the infant understand the world. Our discussion of the interplay of developing systems continues in Chapter 5, where we examine how changes in an infant's physical growth and motor capabilities, such as the emergence of crawling or walking, can have a profound effect on how a child perceives the world.

Unlocking the Secrets of Babies' Sensory Capabilities

Studying infants' sensations and perceptions is not easy. Without language skills, babies can't respond to direct questions as to whether one tone is louder than another or whether they see a difference between two colors. Very young babies even have trouble reaching or pointing toward something that interests them, and crawling in the direction of an interesting stimulus is far beyond their skills. Thus, many of the research methods we use to study sensation and perception in older children and adults

Turning Points

THE DEVELOPMENT OF SENSATION, PERCEPTION, AND EARLY LEARNING

EARLY WEEKS
- Baby can distinguish strong visual contrasts; hears sounds. Demonstrates size constancy and early forms of imitation.

1 MONTH
- Likes to look at faces; scans visually. Differentiates speech from other sounds. Has learned to tell difference between breast nipple, bottle nipple, thumb, and pacifier.

2 MONTHS
- Tracks objects visually from side to side. Likes to hear sounds with different intonations. Has learned that breast or bottle bring nourishment.

3 MONTHS
- Sees objects clearly, can sustain alertness, begins to localize sounds. Has recognition memory; remembers when cued.

4 MONTHS
- Looks more alert. Distinguishes colors, shapes, sizes. Can hear and respond to soft sounds; coordinates looking and listening. In immediate anticipation, at sight of bottle opens mouth.

5 MONTHS
- Attends to smaller objects; has better depth perception; recognizes a face even if it is upside down. Listens quietly to speech and shows signs of pleasure; takes more interest in sounds. Remembers pictures of faces.

6 MONTHS
- Recognizes familiar people easily; visual acuity approximates normal adult vision.

7 MONTHS
- Recognizes facial features and distinguishes male and female faces.

8 MONTHS
- Shows more interest in distant objects. Becomes quiet when others talk. Distinguishes between questions and declarative statements.

Note: Developmental events described in this and other Turning Points charts represent overall trends identified in research studies. Individual children vary greatly in the ages at which they achieve these developmental changes.

Sources: Haith & Benson, 1998; Kellman & Arterberry, 2006; Kopp, 1994; Saffran, Werker, & Werner, 2006.

are useless in studying infants. What's more, even if we determine that infants possess a certain sensory capability (e.g., distinguishing between the tastes of sweet and sour), how can we be sure they experience the same sensations as older children and adults? Sensations may mature or change with age.

In their efforts to solve these problems, psychologists have used research techniques that capitalize on whatever responses young babies are able to make. In particular, to probe an infant's sensory capabilities researchers have relied on information from the autonomic nervous system, which controls such functions as heart rate and breathing. For example, a change in a baby's respiration following a change in the pitch of a sound suggests that the infant heard the pitch change. A newborn's motor responses, although limited, can also give clues to sensory abilities. For instance, a slight turn of the head or kicking of the legs may be used to assess an early ability. Researchers have

9 MONTHS	• More visually aware of tiny objects; if given choice of picking up either large or small object will choose the smaller item. Begins to remember without cues. Uses knowledge to solve problems; aware of cause and effect; recognizes that his own actions may affect outcomes. "Uses" other people to make things happen.
10 MONTHS	• Begins to visually group similar objects. Discriminates an object within another: e.g., a cookie inside a jar. Investigates textures, designs, or parts of toys; repeats play sequences with different toys. Peers intently at pictures.
11 MONTHS	• Uses props as aids, e.g., uses chair to pull to standing position.
12 MONTHS	• Groups toys with like features, such as color or size. Checks own feet when walking. No longer discriminates speech sounds that are not in parents' language(s). Uses imitative learning. Deliberately introduces variations into play sequences. Memory is improved. 
15 MONTHS	• Makes groupings of objects that go together. Trial and error learning. More aware of functions of objects. Recognizes and uses more cause-and-effect relationships.
18 MONTHS	• Differentiates round puzzle pieces from square ones. Recall memory improved. Has primitive idea of what "should be": puts lids on jars; pays attention better; recognizes that others have possessions.
21 MONTHS	• Differentiates round, square, and triangular puzzle pieces and puts them in puzzle with help. Has some understanding of past, present, and future, some idea of categories.
24 MONTHS	• Tries to copy lines on paper. Elaborate play sequences show recognition of family members' specific roles. Begins to use strategy-like, or planned, behaviors.

also used the infant's well-developed sucking pattern as an index of the effect of sensory input. Infants' sucking patterns can change in intensity or duration in response to input from the environment. For instance, one technique used to study infants called the *violation-of-expectation* method introduces an unusual or impossible sight, such as an object floating in space or suspended without adequate support (Baillargeon, 1994). If the baby responds to this information with surprise, it suggests that he knows something about how objects normally work and that his expectation of this normal course of events has been violated. By noting changes while presenting a series of stimuli to an infant, researchers can determine that the baby has discriminated or detected a difference between stimuli or that she has expected certain patterns to occur.

Another commonly used technique of examining infants' abilities to distinguish visual stimuli is the **visual preference method,** which Robert Fantz (1963) pioneered.

visual preference method
A method of studying infants' abilities to distinguish one stimulus from another in which researchers measure and compare the amounts of time babies spend attending to different stimuli.

habituation A process of learning by which an individual reacts with less and less intensity to a repeatedly presented stimulus, eventually responding only faintly or not at all.

In this technique, the examiner presents an infant with two stimuli and measures the amount of time she spends looking at each. If the infant looks longer at one stimulus than at the other, we can assume that she can distinguish the two stimuli from each other. Looking longer at one stimulus may also indicate that the infant finds that stimulus more novel, more interesting, more complex, or more pleasurable than the other one, but such interpretations are speculative. We cannot know for sure why the infant looks longer at one stimulus than another.

In many of these methods of study, the ability to measure babies' responses as indicators of sensory capabilities depends on infants' tendency to **habituate** to a repeatedly presented stimulus—that is, to gradually lessen the intensity of their initial reaction until they respond only faintly or not at all. This index of learning is used in the Brazelton Neonatal Assessment Scale (see Table 4-3). To illustrate, imagine that if you were to shake a rattle near a baby's head, the child might display a *startle* response, thrashing his arms and legs and making general body movements. However, if you repeated the noise a second time, this response would diminish: The infant might give only a brief kick. And after a few more times, the infant would appear to ignore the sound completely and show no response at all. Now if you presented a different sound, such as a bell, the baby would once again show a reaction, until she habituated to the new noise. This reaction to the new sound tells you that the baby can distinguish between the rattle and the bell. Habituation can also be used to study the baby's ability to distinguish stimuli presented to the other senses—sights, smells, tastes, and tactile sensations. Therefore, habituation is widely used to explore infants' sensory and perceptual capabilities. In fact, this research technique was used to obtain much of the information that we discuss in the next few sections on the infant's senses of hearing, vision, smell, taste, and touch.

Hearing: Babies Are Good Listeners

Tests administered shortly after birth show that a newborn's hearing is extremely well developed (Saffran et al., 2006). This is not surprising when you consider that the development of the fetus's auditory system is completed well before birth (see Turning Points chart in Chapter 3). In one study researchers monitored changes in fetal body movements and heart rates and showed that even before birth, fetuses may hear complex sounds presented outside the mother's body (Kisilevsky & Muir, 1991). Such sounds are carried through the amniotic fluid to the fetus as a series of vibrations. Even more interesting is the evidence that infants may learn and remember what is read to them before they were born; as you can see in Box 4.3, fetuses can apparently learn to distinguish not only their mother's voices but the sounds and rhythms of the material their mothers are reading.

It's important to remember, however, that a newborn's hearing is not as well developed as an adult's. For a newborn, a sound must be louder—about 10 to 17 decibels louder—than the sound an adult can detect (Hecox & Deegan, 1985). (A *decibel* is a measure of sound pressure level, which we perceive as loudness.) Normal conversational speech is generally measured at about 60 decibels, the sound of a train at approximately 100 decibels, and a whisper at around 20 decibels. In addition, compared with adults, babies are less sensitive to low-pitched sounds; they are more likely to hear a sound that is high in pitch (Saffran et al., 2006). This may help explain why adults so often raise the pitch of their voices during *infant-directed speech,* also called *motherese* (Hoff, 2001). In speaking to babies, mothers and other adults and even older children (Shatz & Gelman, 1973) somehow know or quickly detect that a high-pitched voice is more likely to capture the child's attention. Over their first two years, however, babies rapidly improve in their ability to discriminate sounds of different pitch, until eventually they reach adult levels of discrimination (Saffran & Griepentrog, 2001).

Box 4.3

Child Psychology in Action

CAN INFANTS LEARN EVEN BEFORE THEY'RE BORN?

Speculating as to why newborn human babies perceive sound so well, Anthony DeCasper asked himself if perhaps they had already learned to listen in the womb. How could he test such a proposition? With a colleague, DeCasper designed a clever procedure in which babies could suck to control what they heard on a tape recorder: either their mother or a strange woman speaking to them (DeCasper & Fifer, 1980). As you will learn elsewhere in this chapter, newborns can learn to vary their sucking patterns. In this study, when infants sucked in a pattern of longer and shorter bursts, they activated their mother's voice on the tape recorder; a different sucking pattern activated the stranger's voice. The researchers found that infants sucked to hear their own mother's voice in preference to the voice of the stranger.

It could be argued, of course, that the infants heard their mother's voice from the time of birth and thus could have learned to prefer it in their first hours of life. To rule out this familiarity hypothesis, DeCasper and Spence (1986) designed another study in which 16 pregnant women were asked to read Dr. Seuss's famous children's book, *The Cat in the Hat,* to their fetuses twice a day for the last six and a half weeks of pregnancy. Some remarkable results occurred. After birth, when these women's infants could suck in one distinctive pattern to hear their mother's tape-recorded voice read *The Cat in the Hat,* or in another pattern to hear them read *The King, the Mice and the Cheese,* they sucked to hear *The Cat in the Hat!* Because in this test condition, the mothers read not just one of the poems but both of them, it seems pretty clear that what the babies preferred was not their mothers' voices per se, but their mothers' voices reading the poem to which the infants had been exposed prenatally.

Although these studies give us evidence that prenatal auditory experiences influence postnatal auditory preferences, we don't have a clear understanding of the exact mechanisms involved in prenatal learning. The sounds babies hear in utero, filtered through the mother's body and the amniotic fluid, must be different from the sounds of their mothers' voices as they hear them after birth. It may be that the component

Participants in experiments on fetal sensitivity to sound read *The Cat in the Hat* to their unborn babies. Whether such reading would give the baby a head start on learning language is still unknown, but the research showed that newborn babies prefer to hear not only their own mothers' voices, but also the specific pieces of poetry or prose their mothers read to them before they were born.

of maternal speech to which the fetus responds is *prosody*. Prosody includes the rhythm, intonation, and stress of speech and is carried by the sound frequencies that are the least altered in the prenatal environment. Because both of the books the mothers in DeCasper's and Spence's studies read to their babies are long poems but of very different meters, the infants may also have been expressing a preference for the familiar prosody.

The evidence is accumulating that newborns may exhibit a postnatal preference for a specific passage or melody experienced prenatally (DeCasper & Spence, 1986; DeCasper & Spence, 1991; Fifer & Moon, 1989). At the same time, despite the claims of marketers and other commercial enterprises, prenatal conditioning has its limits. It is unlikely to produce the supreme benefits claimed by those who want to sell stereo sets for babies, and it's not likely either to raise babies' IQs or radically modify their sociability. That said, there's no reason why expectant mothers shouldn't treat themselves and their unborn infants to their favorite music—a little Bach today, baby?

Babies are remarkably sensitive to other differences in the qualities of sounds; for example, they can express a preference for music as opposed to other sounds and for one type of music over another. Even newborns will alter their sucking patterns in one of the ways we've discussed if doing so allows them to hear music instead of general noise (Butterfield & Siperstein, 1972). By the time they are 2 months old, infants can distinguish among some types of musical sounds, such as those produced by bowing or by plucking the strings of a violin (Jusczyk, Rosner, Cutting, Foard, & Smith, 1977). By the age of 6 months, infants can even distinguish changes in melodies (Chang & Trehub, 1977; Trehub & Trainor, 1993; Schellenberg & Trehub, 1999). And infants who are 4 to 6 months old seem to prefer music composed of common chords to music composed of tone combinations not found in common chords (Kagan & Zentner, 1996; Schellenberg & Trehub, 1996). Kagan and Zentner (1996) suggest that "the human infant may possess a biological preparedness" to prefer certain types of music (p. 29). These early abilities have led some to speculate that listening to certain types of music may benefit development in some way. The most well-known example, referred to as the Mozart effect, suggests that listening to classical music can stimulate brain development and increase intelligence (D. Campbell, 2000). As intriguing as this idea sounds, research does not support the claim that listening to classical music or any kind of music, or even silence, increases intelligence (Hirsch-Pasek & Golinkoff, 2003).

Infants' attention to music, however, has been useful for learning about auditory abilities. Several researchers have found that 6-month-old infants are able to distinguish melodies whether they are based on Western musical scales or on Javanese (*plog*) scales, whereas adult participants did better with the Western scales (Lynch, Eilers, Oller, & Urbano, 1990). "This suggests that in early stages of development infants are equally adept at processing either scale type but that culture-specific experience enhances their ability to process one type of scale over the other" (Aslin et al., 1998, p. 177). As we will see in Chapter 7, research has revealed a similar shift in the infant's response to speech sounds. From initially responding to the speech sounds of many languages, within the first year infants come to respond only to those of the language the people around them speak.

Babies can also locate where a sound comes from and judge how far away it is, which is referred to as auditory localization. Even newborns will turn their heads toward the sound of a rattle, suggesting that they know what direction the sound came from (Clifton, 1992; Muir & Clifton, 1985; Muir & Field, 1979). The development of auditory localization has a unique course (Johnson, 1998). Babies are quite good at localizing sound in the first month of life, but between 2 and 3 months of age this ability seems to wane. Then, by 4 months of age babies can once again localize sounds well. This developmental pattern—which can be depicted graphically as a U-shaped curve because a period of high level performance is followed first by a performance drop and then by another high level performance—underlines an interesting point about auditory development. The better performances seen in the first and fourth months of life are controlled by different brain regions. At 1 month of age, this ability is controlled by subcortical brain systems in place at this time. However, over the first few months of life, the cortical regions of the brain develop and eventually take over some of the functions previously controlled subcortically. Thus, this U-shaped curve actually represents a shift in the way auditory localization is controlled by the brain.

By 6 to 12 months of age sound localization is augmented by even more complex auditory capabilities. Later in the first year babies get quite good at gauging a sound's distance, particularly when a sound is getting closer (Morrongiello, Hewitt, & Gotowiec, 1991). Because the ability to perceive approaching sounds can have survival value if the source of the sound is on a collision course with the listener, some researchers speculate that the auditory system may be programmed to facilitate this perception.

The human auditory system may also be programmed for special sensitivity to the sound of human voices (Aslin, 1987; Saffran et al., 2006). There seems to be something about a human voice that babies as young as 2 days old prefer to hear, particularly a voice that is high in pitch with exaggerated pitch contours (Fernald, 1992; Saffran et al., 2006). This preference for infant-directed speech, which is discussed at greater length in Chapter 7, plays an important role in language development and in the development of social relationships early in life. Mothers may be aware of these preferences, for when they are with an infant they speak in a high-pitched voice and sing in a high-pitched and melodic fashion. Perhaps this relates to the sensitivity to music that infants have, and it may account in part for the finding that lullabies are sung throughout the world to soothe infants. Babies ranging in age from 4 to 7 months prefer infant-directed playsongs and lullabies over non-infant-directed singing (Trainor, 1996).

Babies also learn to discriminate among voices very quickly; as we've seen, even newborns can distinguish their mothers' voices from those of other female voices. These abilities, which reflect the contributions of both innate factors and learning, facilitate the development of an emotional bond between parent and child by first channeling babies' attention to other human beings and then helping them single out important adults in their world. Even before babies can understand the words their parents say, the familiar tones and speech patterns lead to a pattern of interaction between infants and parents that facilitates these early social bonds. Thus, early auditory skills and preferences have functional significance for social development.

Finally, it is important to point out that despite the early and rapid developments in auditory abilities, hearing difficulties are rather hard to diagnose. In fact, deafness is often diagnosed as late as $2\frac{1}{2}$ to 3 years of age, which is a critical period for language acquisition. Because of the impact that hearing difficulties may have on other aspects of development, especially language acquisition, early and regular checks for hearing difficulties and ear infections, which can impair hearing considerably, are important.

visual acuity Sharpness of vision; the clarity with which fine details can be detected.

Only 3 months old, this little girl seems quite fascinated by the patterns in her mobile. She may be perceiving the patterns in their entirety, whereas earlier she could distinguish only parts of them. Thus, as vision develops, the same stimulus arouses different types of interest from the baby.

Vision: How Babies See Their Worlds

Some baby animals, such as kittens, cannot see at all for days after birth, but the eyes of a newborn human being are physiologically ready to begin responding to visual stimuli. Newborn humans can detect changes in brightness, distinguish movement in the visual field, and follow or track a moving object with their eyes (Field, 1990; Kellman & Banks, 1998). In this section we look at several important aspects of visual development.

THE CLARITY OF INFANTS' VISION **Visual acuity** is sharpness of vision, or the clarity with which a person can detect fine details. Since it is harder to see the details of a small object than a big one, acuity and viewing distance are related. If from 20 feet away you can read a letter of the alphabet that people with perfect vision can read from 40 feet, you have 20/40 vision, a relatively small deviation from the optimum of 20/20. The vision of infants under 1 month of age ranges from 20/200 to 20/800 (Courage & Adams, 1990; Dobson & Teller, 1978). This means that most objects not held close to a baby's face appear to her as quite blurry and indistinct. Visual acuity improves rapidly over the next few months, however, and seems to be within the

Figure 4-3

Visual discrimination in infants

At 1 week of age, infants can discriminate black stripes of this size from a gray field when they are a foot away from the target. This is only about one-thirtieth as fine a discrimination as an adult with normal vision can make, but by the time infants are 8 months old they see about one-fourth as well as adults, and they achieve adult levels by the time they're about 5 years old.

Source: Maurer & Maurer, 1988.

normal adult range by the time a child is between 6 months and a year old (Banks & Shannon, 1993; Kellman & Arterberry, 2006). One way visual acuity is assessed in infants is by testing how sensitive a baby is to visual details such as the width or density of a set of stripes in a pictorial image. Figure 4-3 displays the finest black stripes that most 1-week-old infants can discriminate from a gray field when the target is 1 foot away. Gradually babies develop the ability to detect more detailed patterns; thus, little by little they are able to detect stripes that are closer together (Kellman & Arterberry, 2006). To appreciate this ability to see details more clearly, examine Figure 4-4, which shows how well an infant can see a human face at 1 month and 1 year.

HOW BABIES SEE COLORS   Newborns have limited color vision. At 1 month, babies show little response to color, but 2-month-old babies can begin to see this feature of the environment. By 3 months of age infants can distinguish among most colors and can group colors into basic categories, such as reds, blues, and greens (Teller,

Figure 4-4

How well can infants see?

The photos represent a computer estimate of what a picture of a face looks like to a 1-month-old infant and 1-year-old infant. Infants at even 6 months can see quite well, and scientists presume that a child's vision continues to improve until it reaches the clarity of the normal adult's sight.

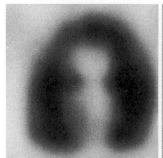 

1997; Teller & Bornstein, 1987). For instance, when presented with two shades of blue, a 3-month-old usually responds as if these colors were more similar than are one of these shades of blue and a shade of green.

Although such findings suggest that our ability to perceive color may be innate, there is some evidence that infants younger than 7 weeks can't make effective color discriminations (Banks & Shannon, 1993; Kellman & Arterberry, 2006). In fact, the structures and neural pathways important in color discrimination are quite immature during the first weeks of life, which may account in part for the limited ability to discriminate color in very young infants. Furthermore, testing color discrimination in very young children is difficult. For instance, researchers may fail to detect color discrimination in babies because methodological problems in testing young infants confound hue and brightness.

Some interesting recent research with infant monkeys indicates that early visual experience may be essential for normal color perception to develop (Sugita, 2004). In this study, the monkeys were raised, from 1 month of age, in a room in which the lighting was monochromatic and they could not see the normal spectrum of colors. When their color vision was tested at 1 year of age, their ability to distinguish colors was much poorer than that of normally reared monkeys. With training in color perception the monkeys reared in monochromatic illumination were able to develop some but not all of these abilities. Although these results pertain to monkeys and not humans, they suggest that early visual experience with color may be essential for normal color perception to develop.

HOW BABIES PERCEIVE PATTERNS   Psychologists have long debated whether the visual world of a young infant, like that of an adult, is organized into patterns or whether a baby sees merely unrelated lines, angles, and edges and only gradually learns through experience to perceive larger patterns. The nativist, or hereditary, position supports the first of these two viewpoints, arguing that pattern perception is innate. The empiricist, or environmental, position supports the second viewpoint and argues that experience is needed to piece the elements together into meaningful patterns. Most research findings suggest that both learning and experience are generally required to see patterns in an adult manner.

In one classic study, Salapatek and Kessen (1966) used an infrared camera to determine precisely where on a triangle newborns directed their eyes. They found that a newborn's gaze was not distributed over the whole triangle, as an adult's would be. The typical newborn centered attention on one of the triangle's angles, but sometimes also scanned part of an edge in a limited way. This suggests that although certain elements of a complex pattern attract a newborn's attention (angles, edges, boundaries), babies this young may not perceive whole forms. If they did, they would have scanned the entire triangle more completely. The scanning of forms improves quickly with age, however. By the age of 2 months, babies visually trace both the edges of a pattern and the internal areas (Aslin, 1987; Kellman & Arterberry, 2006; Salapatek, 1969). This suggests that they have made some advances in seeing the various parts of a pattern in a unified way.

By 3 months of age, babies are also almost as good as adults at picking unified patterns out of a moving form (Bertenthal, 1996; Bertenthal & Clifton, 1998; Booth, Pinto, & Bertenthal, 2002). For example, researchers use the technique of a point-light display to determine how infants interpret visual information from a moving form. If 10 or 12 points of light are attached to a walking person's head and major joints, and then an image of the person moving in a dark space is presented, adults quickly recognize this moving display as depicting a person. By testing babies 3 to 5 months of age with this same kind of stimulus, researchers have found that even infants this young can extract information about form from motion (Figure 4-5; Bertenthal, Proffitt, & Cutting, 1984). However, although infants 3 and 5 months old can extract a human figure's structure from information about its motion, they don't

LifeMap CD

To learn more about how infants perceive stimuli, explore "The Baby's Brain" interactive exercise in Chapter 4 of your CD.

Figure 4-5

Extracting information about form from movement

Three- to 5-month-old infants are able to detect a form from an upright walking person specified by an 11 point-light display (a). However, these same age infants do not appear to recognize the inverted light display of a walking person (b) or when 11 light points are presented in a scrambled arrangement (c). This pattern suggests that the infants apply different understanding or meaning to the perceptual displays and do not perceive these stimuli as just a collection of individual points of light.

Source: Bertenthal, Proffitt, & Kramer, 1987.

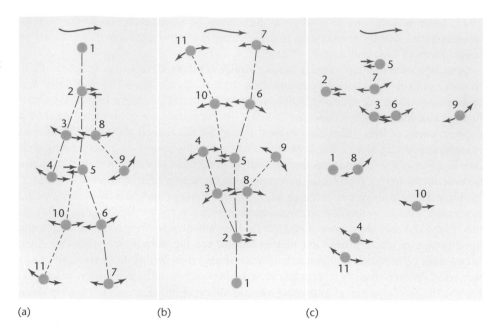

(a)   (b)   (c)

seem to recognize the form as a person until they are somewhat older—around 9 months of age (Bertenthal, Proffitt, & Kramer, 1987).

A PREFERENCE FOR FACES   The ability to perceive faces is a special kind of pattern perception that seems to develop along with the ability to see other kinds of forms. In the beginning, babies do not seem very good at seeing a face as a whole instead of a collection of parts. This conclusion is suggested by studies of the way young infants scan faces. As you can see in Figure 4-6, newborns approach a line drawing of a face the same way they deal with a triangle: They scan only small sections of the outermost contours of the face. Maurer and Salapatek (1976) found, however, that 2-month-olds quickly move their eyes to the internal features.

Other researchers, using adult participants' real faces, have documented these same developmental shifts in infants' scanning (Haith, Bergman, & Moore, 1977). These investigators highlighted a finding that can also be seen in Figure 4-6: Not only did

Figure 4-6

How infants scan the human face

A 1-month-old baby sticks pretty much to the outer perimeter of the face, although he shows some interest in the eyes. An infant who is 2 months old scans more broadly and focuses on the features of the face. She pays a lot of attention to the eyes and mouth, which suggests that some pattern detection may be occurring.

Source: Maurer & Salapatek, 1976.

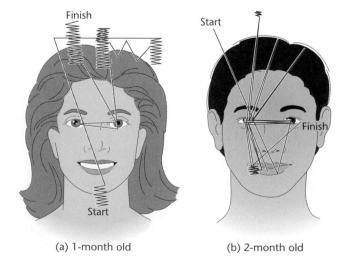

(a) 1-month old   (b) 2-month old

7-week-old infants spend less time on the contours of real faces, they looked at the eyes more than the younger infants did. But the fact that internal facial features, especially the eyes, strongly draw the attention of infants by 7 weeks of age does not mean that babies this young are seeing faces as unified wholes. Facial features may simply have an abundance of perceptual qualities, such as contour, contrast, and movement, that are intrinsically appealing to the infant. Even the discovery that newborns prefer their mothers' faces over the faces of strangers does not necessarily mean that newborns are seeing faces as adults do (Walton, Bower, & Bower, 1992). Instead, the newborn's recognition of and preference for the mother's face may simply reflect the baby's focus on one particular feature of her face. In fact, Pascalis and his colleagues (1995) found that 4-day-old newborns looked longer at their mothers' faces than at those of strangers only when the mother was not wearing a head scarf. This may suggest that the hairline and the outer contour of the face play an integral part in the newborn's face recognition.

How babies develop these impressive face-processing abilities is a subject of much debate. Some researchers believe that face processing is an innate human ability with an evolutionary basis and that little if any experience is needed to activate this type of processing. Others argue, however, that innate learning abilities not specific to faces enable infants to process all types of information presented by the environment, including faces. According to this view, over the first year of life infants use this general learning ability to process their many experiences with human faces. Gradually, this face-processing system learns to focus on the types of faces most important for infants to process—namely human faces—with importance determined by frequency of exposure (Turati, 2004). Evidence by Pascalis, de Haan, and Nelson (2002) supports this claim. They found that both 9-month-olds and adults could discriminate between pictures of human faces. However, neither these infants nor adults were skilled at distinguishing between monkey faces. In contrast, 6-month-olds are able to discriminate facial information for both human and monkey faces. Essentially, a narrowing, or specializing, in face processing occurs over the first year of life. This pattern is similar to the type of specialization that occurs in the development of speech perception (Werker & Vouloumanos, 2001), which we discuss in Chapter 7. The view that learning in infancy is regulated by a general rather than a specific set of processing systems brings these two similar learning patterns together and suggests that infants have the ability to learn information important to survival. If such information is repeatedly made available to infants in their experiences, they will learn to process it effectively.

Other research supports the notion that 7-week-old infants may still be too young to perceive faces as adults do (Nelson, 1987; Johnson, 1997). Before they're 2 months old, most babies cannot discriminate a "proper" schematic drawing of a face from a scrambled one (in which the features appear in the wrong locations; e.g., the nose where the mouth should be). By 3 months of age, however, they show a clear preference for drawings of faces with correctly positioned features. Instead of seeing a face as a mere collection of interesting parts, infants now perceive it as a unified whole (Mauer & Mauer, 1988; Olson & Sherman, 1983). Some research suggests that the pattern of information present in faces—for example, the great number of high-contrast areas seen in the upper portion of the face pattern—is preferred by newborns (Turati, Simion, Milani, & Umilta, 2002). This suggests that rather than being born with sensitivity to human faces per se, babies may be biased toward particular types of patterns that happen to coincide with the type of information presented in faces.

In one experiment, researchers showed $1\frac{1}{2}$- and 3-month-old infants the computer-generated stimuli displayed in Figure 4-7 (Dannemiller & Stephens, 1988). Although stimulus (a) looks much more facelike than stimulus (b), the two are identical except that the shading is reversed. At $1\frac{1}{2}$ months, babies showed no preference between

Figure 4-7

Evaluating infants' preferences for faces over other patterns

By the time they were 3 months old, infants looked longer at the face in (a) than its reverse (b). Finding that infants had no preference between patterns (c) and (d) established that it was the pattern of the face in (a) that they liked rather than its borders.

Source: Dannemiller & Stephens, 1988.

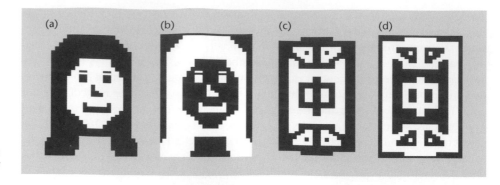

these two stimuli, but at 3 months they looked longer at (a), which is more easily seen as a face. Note that this was not simply because they had a preference for pictures with black borders and white interiors, for they showed no preference for stimulus (c) over stimulus (d). These findings suggest that by 3 months of age babies identify a face as a unique pattern. The shift from perceiving parts to perceiving whole patterns appears to occur at about the same time for both objects and faces. However, infants continue to look longer at, and show more brain activity in response to, faces as compared with objects (Johnson, 2000; Nelson, 1999a). Over the first year, infants also come to process facial information more quickly. A recent study of facial recognition found that, whereas 7-month-olds needed 14 trials to know a face well enough to recognize it reliably, 12-month-olds needed only about 9 trials (Rose, Jankowski, & Feldman, 2002). As we will see in Chapter 9, greater speed of processing is one consistent characteristic of cognitive change associated with age. Being able to extract information from stimuli quickly and reliably is a keystone of developing intellectual ability.

Beyond a general interest in faces, babies seem to prefer faces that are attractive. Judy Langlois and her colleagues (1987) showed groups of infants who were 2 to 3 months old and 6 to 8 months old color slides of women's faces. The researchers presented these slides in pairs: One of each pair had been rated attractive by adult judges; the other had been rated unattractive. Both the younger and the older babies looked longer at the "attractive" faces. In later research, Langlois and her colleagues (1990) supported their original findings, using both dolls that had been judged attractive or unattractive and adults who wore lifelike latex theatrical masks that had also been judged either attractive or unattractive. One-year-old children played more with the "attractive" doll and preferred to interact with the adults wearing the "attractive" mask, smiling at the adult, laughing, and withdrawing less often from him or her than from the person wearing the "unattractive" mask (see also Rubenstein, Kalakanis, & Langlois, 1999).

Why do infants prefer attractive faces? Some argue that such faces contain more of the features that the infant's visual system is organized to react to: Infants prefer high contrast, contours, curves, and vertical symmetry, and attractive faces may have more of these characteristics than unattractive faces. However, some research has shown that when attractiveness and symmetry are varied independently—for example, an attractive face that lacks symmetry or an unattractive yet symmetrical face is presented—babies, like adults, prefer attractiveness to symmetry (Samuels, Butterworth, Roberts, & Graupner, 1994). Thus, rather than symmetry explaining attractiveness, some suggest that there might be something about an attractive face that is interesting to babies. When faces identified as attractive have been examined more closely, what seems common across them is the averageness or prototypical aspects of these faces. It may be that their averageness is what makes attractive faces interesting to babies and adults alike (Slater, 2000). Attractive faces may simply be more average or facelike than unattractive faces. They are seen as better examples of faces because they contain many of the familiar features of other faces and are, therefore, more readily classified as a face. Or, alternatively, it may be that average faces are interesting because they are more difficult and time-consuming to process, especially to determine what makes such faces distinctive from other faces. We need a better understanding of why both infants and adults are interested in faces that judges have identified as attractive.

DEPTH PERCEPTION   Newborns' eyes do not work together in the way that the eyes of older children and adults do. The eyes of newborns move in the same direction only about half the time (Mauer & Mauer, 1988; Kellman & Banks, 1998), so young infants must rely on depth and distance cues available to each eye independently. Some of these cues involve motion. For example, as objects approach us they fill more of the visual field, and when we move our heads, the images of close objects move more than the images of distant objects. These kinds of changes associated with movement help babies judge depth. The ability to perceive depth improves with age, as eye coordination develops and more cues to depth and distance become available to the infant.

By 3 to 5 months of age babies can coordinate their two eyes and so can begin to see depth as adults do, using stereoscopic vision (Birch, 1993; Mohn & van Hof-van Duin, 1986). **Stereoscopic vision** is the sense of a third spatial dimension, depth, produced by the combination of the images perceived by both the left and the right eye, each of which reflects the stimulus from a slightly different angle. The brain's fusion of these two images creates the perception of depth. Proper use of the two eyes together at an early age is necessary for normal stereoscopic vision to develop. Babies born with crossed eyes (a condition called *convergent strabismus*) usually do not develop normal stereoscopic vision unless the eyes are surgically corrected before the age of 2 (Banks, Aslin, & Letson, 1975; Banks & Salapatek, 1983).

stereoscopic vision The sense of a third spatial dimension, that of depth, produced by the brain's fusion of the separate images contributed by each eye, each of which reflects the stimulus from a slightly different angle.

The ability to perceive depth has much practical value. For example, it helps keep us safe by preventing us from walking off cliffs and other high places. In fact, as this example suggests, depth perception is critical to survival. Thus, researchers have wondered if this knowledge is innate or built up from experience in some way. To investigate this issue, Gibson and Walk (1960) developed an apparatus called the **visual cliff** (see Figure 4-8). The visual cliff consists of an elevated glass platform with a pattern of some type directly beneath the glass on one side (the "shallow" side) and the same pattern several feet below the glass on the other (the "deep" side). Gibson and Walk found that babies 6 to 14 months old would not cross from the "shallow" to the "deep" side to get to their mothers even when the mother encouraged the child to do so. Thus, babies this age were fearful enough of heights to avoid them.

visual cliff An apparatus that tests an infant's depth perception by using patterned materials and an elevated, clear glass platform to make it appear that one side of the platform is several feet lower than the other.

This fear apparently does not exist in very young infants. When Campos and his associates (Campos, Langer, & Krowitz, 1970) placed $1\frac{1}{2}$-month-old babies first on the shallow side of a visual cliff and then on the deep side, the infants' heart rates *decreased,* which generally indicates interest rather than fear (fear is normally accompanied by an *increase* in heart rate). In contrast, when researchers placed older infants who could crawl on the deep side, these babies showed heart-rate accelerations, suggesting that they had learned to be afraid of heights (Campos, Bertenthal, & Kermonian, 1992; Campos, Hiatt, Ramsey, Henderson, & Svejda, 1978). Apparently, experience with locomotion is involved in the development of a fear of heights. Baby animals that are able to walk shortly after birth avoid the deep side of the visual cliff when they are only 1 day old. And when human infants who are unable to crawl are provided with 30 to 40 hours of experience in wheeled walkers, they begin to

Figure 4-8

Babies don't take chances
This baby is hesitant to venture beyond the safety of the visual cliff's "shallow" side, despite Mom's coaxing. Clearly, the child perceives the "deep" side as threatening.

show fear of high places (Bertenthal, Campos, & Kermonian, 1994; Campos, Svejda, Bertenthal, Benson, & Schmid, 1981). It is important to point out that in this research Campos and his colleagues were able to disentangle depth perception and fear of heights. Although these are related understandings of the world, they have different courses of development.

A final, interesting question about these findings asks: What is it about locomotion that triggers a fear of heights? Perhaps motion itself helps a baby to judge distances more accurately. Or perhaps moving about on one's own gives the baby an opportunity to fall and, as a result, he begins to recognize heights as potentially dangerous. When an infant falls or even nearly falls, the strong emotional reaction displayed by the caregiver may also prompt the baby to learn to fear heights (Campos et al., 1992; Lamb & Campos, 1982). Whatever the link, a fear of heights involves an interplay of biology and experience, along with the more basic ability to perceive depth.

SIZE AND SHAPE CONSTANCY   Regardless of how distant an object is, you can judge its size and shape. For example, even though a truck looks toylike from far away, you still perceive it as a normal-sized vehicle. This ability relies on **size constancy,** the tendency to perceive an object as constant in size regardless of changes in the distance from which you view it and regardless of the corollary changes in the size of the object's image on the retinas of your eyes (see Figure 4-9). Research with newborns suggests that this basic ability may be present from birth (Slater, Mattock, & Brown, 1990). However, demonstrating that a newborn displays this or any other ability does not mean that the ability is fully developed. As binocular vision develops, between 4 and 5 months, recognition of size constancy improves (Aslin, 1987; Kellman & Banks, 1998). Although great progress is achieved in the first 12 months, not until the child is 10 or 11 years old does this skill mature fully (Kellman & Banks, 1998).

Analogous to size constancy, **shape constancy** is the ability to perceive an object's shape as constant despite changes in its orientation and hence the angle from which one views it. The fact that even newborns are capable of shape constancy suggests that this ability may be present at birth, requiring minimal experience with the world (Slater & Morison, 1985).

size constancy The tendency to perceive an object as constant in size regardless of changes in its distance from the viewer and in the image it casts on the retinas of the eyes.

shape constancy The ability to perceive an object's shape as constant despite changes in its orientation and the angle from which one views it.

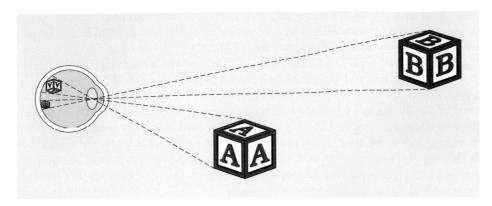

Figure 4-9

Size constancy
The two blocks pictured here are exactly the same size, and the viewer perceives them as the same size. However, because they are placed at different distances from the viewer, they cast retinal images of different sizes. Four-month-old infants will see the blocks as of different sizes, but by 6 months, babies have grasped the concept of size constancy and see the blocks as the same size.

Perhaps as researchers further improve their techniques for probing infants' visual capacities we will find evidence of even earlier competence in some other areas as well. Possibly, "perceptual constancies in general are an inherent function of the visual system," even though their range and accuracy may be improved by experience (Yonas, Arterberry, & Granrud, 1987, p. 7).

VISUAL EXPECTATIONS   Not only do babies begin to perceive colors, forms, depth, and perceptual constancies at an early age, but they also soon start to develop expectations about events in their visual worlds (Haith & Benson, 1998). To demonstrate this remarkable ability, Haith and his coworkers (Canfield & Haith, 1991; Haith, Hazen, & Goodman, 1988) presented pictures to babies in either a regular alternating sequence (left, right, left, right) or an unpredictable sequence (left, left, right, left, etc.). When the sequence was predictable, 3-month-olds began to anticipate the location of the next picture by looking to the side on which it was going to appear. And they developed this pattern of expectation in less than a minute! Younger infants did not show this ability to anticipate a picture's location based on a regular sequence. It may be that more cognitive or perhaps biological development is needed for this ability to emerge (Tamis-LeMonda & McClure, 1995).

Experience seems to contribute to the ability to perceive the trajectory or continuity of an object when part of the object or array of objects is obscured from view. Johnson and his colleagues (2003) showed 2- to 6-month-old infants a line or row of objects partly occluded by a screen; for example, a line of balls with several of the balls in the center of the image covered up by a screen. Two-month-olds showed little awareness of the continuity of the line of balls; 6-month-olds were aware of it, and 4-month-olds showed such awareness only when the occlusion period was of short duration (67 ms or milliseconds). It seems that the understanding of perceptual continuity emerges over the first six months of life. This type of understanding helps set the stage for more complex understanding of objects, discussed at greater length in Chapter 8.

This study, like others we have discussed, shows that the infant's overall level of visual ability is much greater than had been presumed only a few decades ago. It also indicates that even though the development of vision is greatly influenced by biology and its progress is rapid in the first year, visual experience plays a crucial role in this process (Johnson, 2001).

Smell, Taste, and Touch

Like vision and hearing, smell, taste, and touch are well developed at an early age. For instance, even newborns can discriminate among a variety of odors, and they show "appropriate" facial expressions in response to odors that adults rate as either pleasant or aversive. In one study, infants less than 12 hours old reacted to the odors of strawberry and banana with a look of satisfaction, whereas a whiff of fish or rotten eggs elicited a rejecting look (Steiner, 1979).

Young infants' well-developed sense of smell seems to provide another early guide to the people and things in their world. Macfarlane (1975) showed that 1-week-olds could distinguish the odor of their own mother's breast pad from the odor of the breast pad of another nursing woman, a stranger to the infants. When the two pads were positioned above the infant's head, the baby turned toward the mother's pad more frequently than toward the other. This preference was not evident in the first few days of life and seems to depend on babies learning to recognize the mother's special smell. Nor is it just the odor of a mother's breast secretions that is attractive; breast-fed babies come to learn and prefer the overall scent of their own mothers (Porter, Makin, Davis, & Christensen, 1992). Infants also prefer the odor of milk to the odor of amniotic fluid (Marlier, Schaal, & Soussignan, 1998).

Newborns also respond selectively to different tastes. In one study, 2-hour-old infants produced facial expressions in response to sweet, sour, bitter, and salty substances that are characteristic of the faces adults make when given these tastes (Rosenstein & Oster, 1988). Because these infants had not been fed anything but milk or formula, it appears that at least some taste preferences may be innate. However, it is important to stress that just because a taste preference is evident at birth, this does not rule out the possibility that *learning* occurred before birth and that the preference is not innate but learned. Research has shown that the human fetus can learn to like or avoid certain tastes (Hepper, 1992; Molina, Chotro, & Dominguez, 1995). Studying how learning about taste can occur in utero may be very important for understanding later development, such as how exposure to certain teratogens, like alcohol, might influence behavioral development postnatally (Lecanuet, Fifer, Krasnegor, & Smotherman, 1995). In addition to learning about taste preference that may occur before birth, research has also shown that such preference can develop in very early infancy. Mennella and Beauchamp (1996) found that infants exposed to vanilla-flavored milk were more accepting of the flavor of vanilla later on. Babies will accept garlic-flavored milk if exposed to garlic during breast-feeding. Animal studies indicate that the more varied the mother's diet, the more likely offspring are to consume novel foods after weaning (Mennella & Beauchamp, 1993). Perhaps one benefit of breast-feeding is that "it provides an opportunity for the infant to become familiar with the flavors of the foods of her or his mother, family and culture" (Mennella & Beauchamp, 1996, p. 19).

The sense of touch is activated long before birth (Field, 2001b); indeed, it may be one of the first senses to develop. As Klaus and colleagues (1995, p. 52) point out, "The skin is the largest sense organ of the body . . . , [and] babies are surrounded and caressed by warm fluid and tissues from the beginning of fetal life. . . . [Moreover,] the lips and hands have the most touch receptors; this may explain why newborns enjoy sucking their fingers." Babies are clearly responsive to different types of touch, from the positive quality of gentle stroking to the sometimes negative aspects of changes in temperature, texture, moisture, and pressure and the painful effects of drawing blood for testing.

Although it was once assumed that newborns were indifferent to pain, this is untrue. In fact, they are more sensitive to pain than older infants (Axia, Bonichini, & Benini, 1999). Evidence of the infant's sensitivity to painful procedures comes from studies of infant stress reactions; for example, male infants have shown higher levels of plasma cortisol (a stress marker) after a circumcision than before the surgery (Gunnar, Malone, Vance, & Fisch, 1985). Although it was once standard practice to perform circumcision and other invasive medical procedures on infants without using any pain-relieving drugs, advances in our understanding of the newborn's sensitivity to pain have changed these practices.

Not only do babies respond to touch—recall the positive impact that massage had on preterm babies (Field, 2001a)—but before the end of their first year they can learn to discriminate among objects using only their sense of touch (Streri & Pecheux, 1986). Researchers (Streri, Lhote, & Dutilleul, 2000) found that 2-day-old infants showed habituation to an object placed in their hands, suggesting that once tactile, or haptic, information is obtained, manual exploration of an object decreases. After the infants habituated to the first object, to rule out that this decrease was due simply to fatigue the researchers placed a new object in the baby's hands—and holding time increased. These observations suggest that neonates use touch to explore the environment and encode information, and that even very early in life infants have tactile sensitivity to object shape. Videotape analysis showed that the infants were not just grasping the objects rigidly; small movements of the baby's fingers were observed.

Intermodal Perception: How Infants Coordinate Sensory Information

Most of the time information comes into our senses through more than one sense modality. When do infants begin to coordinate information from different sensory sources into a single unified perception? For instance, when an infant sees a ball bounce or hears her father speak to her, does she perceive separate visual and auditory events? Or does she match the sight of the moving ball with the sound the ball makes as it hits the floor, and the sight of her father's mouth movements with his voice? **Intermodal perception** is the use of sensory information from more than one modality—in these examples, both vision and hearing—to identify a stimulus and make sense of it. It is also the identification of a stimulus that one has already identified by means of one sensory modality (e.g., vision) by means of a different modality (hearing).

Researchers have explored babies' ability to perceive intermodally by pairing two different sensory systems, such as vision and touch or vision and hearing. Exploring the first of these pairs, Meltzoff and Borton (1979) designed two different pacifiers, one smooth and one knobby (Figure 4-10) and gave 4-week-old infants a chance to suck one—or the other of them. Later, when the researchers let their small participants look at both pacifiers—but not suck on them—the infants looked longer at the pacifier that they had sucked on earlier than at the unfamiliar one. Pointing out that infants this age have had little opportunity to simultaneously touch and look at objects, the researchers concluded that human beings are able to recognize similar information obtained from different sense modalities without having to learn to coordinate this information (Meltzoff, 1981).

intermodal perception The use of sensory information from more than one modality to identify a stimulus and make sense of it; also, the identification of a stimulus already identified by means of one modality by the use of another modality.

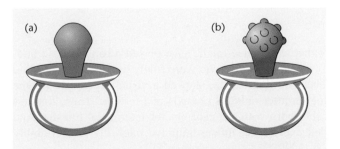

Figure 4-10

Testing a baby's intermodal perceptual abilities
Just by looking at these pacifiers, 4-week-old babies knew which one they had sucked earlier, no matter whether it was smooth (a) or knobby (b).

Source: From *Nature, 282* (1979), pp. 403–404. Meltzoff, A. N. and Borton, R. W., "Intermodal matching by human neonates." © 1979 Macmillan Journals Ltd. Reprinted with permission of Nature Publishing Group.

Figure 4-11

Combining vision and hearing to detect distance and direction
Babies can match an engine sound that is becoming louder with the toy train in (a), which is approaching the watching infant, and an engine sound that is growing fainter with the train shown in (b), which is moving away from the infant.

Source: Pickens, 1994.

(a)

(b)

To rule out the possibility that experience might have played a role in these findings, Kaye and Bower (1994) tested newborns who were solely breast-fed and had no experience with a pacifier. These newborns, too, showed a visual preference for the pacifier they had been sucking on after only 20 seconds of exposure. These findings suggest that infants are probably born with the capacity for intermodal transfer. And over the first year, with added experience, infants improve markedly in this ability (Mauer, Stagner, & Mondloch, 1999).

Studying when infants can coordinate vision and hearing, Elizabeth Spelke (1987) used two animated films and accompanying sound tracks of a kangaroo and a donkey, each bouncing at a different rate and producing sounds in keeping with its bouncing. Spelke then showed these two films, side by side, to 4-month-old babies as she played only one of the sound tracks from a speaker positioned between the two screens. The infants looked at the animal whose bouncing "matched" the sounds they were hearing. Because the infants had never seen or heard these animals, or their bouncing movements or sounds before, their reactions were clearly not the result of prior learning. Other studies have shown that babies this age can also "match" the sounds of particular words being spoken with the sight of a face whose lips are synchronized with those sounds, even though, as in the prior study, the visual stimulus is in one location (on a screen) and the auditory stimulus is in another (from a speaker positioned elsewhere) (Spelke & Cortelyou, 1981).

Intermodal matching can also help infants determine whether an object is approaching or retreating. Pickens (1994) showed 5-month-old infants films with sound tracks depicting a toy train either approaching the viewers or moving away from them (see Figure 4-11). Infants looked more at the approaching film when the decibel level of the sounds of the train increased and more at the retreating train when the sound of the train diminished. Infants did not show evidence of matching in other conditions in which the sound tracks were paired with videos depicting changes in the brightness of the train's image or showing the train moving horizontally with no change in its size. This experiment suggests that infants are able to integrate visual and sound information and can then use this information to help them judge distance.

The findings we've discussed in this section challenge the commonly held view that babies begin life experiencing unrelated sensations in each sensory system and only gradually learn to put the separate pieces together. Babies as young as 1 month can integrate vision and touch and babies as young as 4 months of age appear to experience a world of integrated visual and auditory sensations. An important path of future study is the discovery of the mechanisms that underlie infants' ability to perceive intermodally (Haith & Benson, 1998).

EARLY LEARNING AND MEMORY

Our discussions so far have concentrated on a particular kind of infant learning—that is, what babies know about the world's objects and their properties. Much of the research we've described has assumed that as babies develop and have experience interacting with people and things, they learn more about the world. How babies learn—in fact, how all humans learn—is a topic of long-standing interest to psychologists. As you will recall from Chapter 1, psychologists have been particularly interested in learning through imitation and learning through association, as in classical and operant conditioning. In this section we not only explore these kinds of learning in infants; we also consider what these and other kinds of learning abilities tell us about a baby's memory capabilities. As you will see, basic learning processes appear to be present very early in life. What changes over the course of development seems to be the nature of the information that babies are capable of learning and the speed and efficiency with which they learn.

Classical and Operant Conditioning

For years, psychologists have debated the issue of how early babies can learn through classical conditioning, and the controversy is not over (Rovee-Collier, 1987; Rovee-Collier & Shyi, 1992). For a refresher on the mechanisms of classical

Figure 4-12   How a baby may be conditioned to fear a doctor

At their first meeting (Stage 1), the baby may show no particular reaction to the doctor, but after the doctor gives the baby a painful injection that causes the baby to cry (Stage 2), the baby may expect the same pain at his next meeting with the doctor (Stage 3) and cry or act afraid even if he doesn't see a needle in her hand.

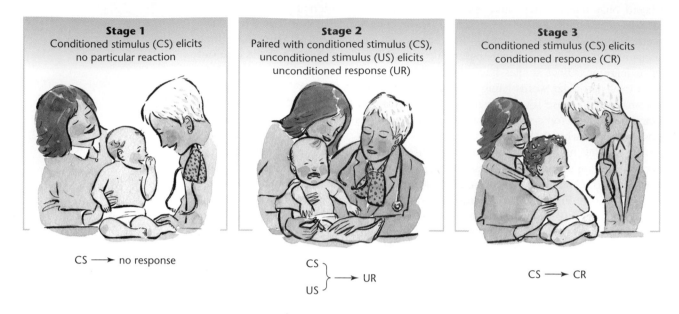

conditioning, look at Figure 4-12, in which we diagram the way a child might become conditioned to fear his doctor. On the one hand, there is some evidence that newborns can be conditioned in this way, especially in biologically meaningful contexts such as feeding. In one study, babies as young as 2 hours old learned to associate a stroke on the head with delivery of a sugar solution to their mouths, until eventually the stroke alone elicited puckering and sucking responses (Blass, Ganchrow, & Steiner, 1984). On the other hand, newborns have much more difficulty learning relationships that involve unpleasant stimuli, such as loud noises or things that are painful (Rovee-Collier, 1987). Perhaps because human infants have parents to protect them, it may be less critical at an early age to learn the stimuli associated with noxious events. However, there is also evidence that neurological mechanisms aiding the formation of negative associations develop later than neurological mechanisms facilitating positive associations (Rovee-Collier, 1987; Rovee-Collier & Shyi, 1992).

Operant conditioning, you will recall, involves learning to emit (or inhibit) some behavior because of the rewarding (or punishing) consequences it brings. Just as babies can be classically conditioned, they can also learn by operant conditioning (Gewirtz & Pelez-Nogueras, 1992). In the study we described in Box 4.3, DeCasper and Fifer (1980) used operant conditioning to induce sucking in newborns, with the mother's voice as a reward. The rate of sucking and the reward become associated with one another and are used to organize behavior. This research shows not only an early capacity for this kind of learning but also what seems to be a built-in propensity to enjoy contact with other human beings (which is why the sound of the mother's voice could serve as a reward). As in the case of classical conditioning, successful demonstrations of operant conditioning in newborns typically involve behaviors such as sucking or turning the head (related to the rooting reflex), behaviors that are components of feeding and thus of considerable importance to the baby's survival. Researchers take advantage of these early behaviors to investigate how infants learn specific behaviors.

Learning through Imitation

Acquiring behaviors through classical or operant conditioning (displaying a behavior, being rewarded, repeating the behavior, being reinforced again, etc.) is uneconomical in terms of time and energy because to be learned the behavior has to be experienced directly by the infant. Fortunately, infants are able to learn a great deal without any overt conditioning but simply by observing the behavior of other people. As you learned in Chapter 1, this is observational learning or learning through imitation.

Imitation begins early in life; it may even be possible in the first few days after birth. Meltzoff and Moore (1983), for example, found that babies between 7 and 72 hours old imitated adults who opened their mouths wide or stuck their tongues out—movements that are components of the sucking response. These findings are somewhat controversial. Many developmental theories, such as Piaget's, argue that imitation requires the capacity for symbolic representation, which is generally not achieved until the end of the second year of life (Chapters 1 and 8). Others argue that the infant who sticks his tongue out at the sight of an adult doing the same thing may not be truly imitating another's behavior (Anisfeld, 1991). There is evidence that the sight of any protruding object may cause newborns to stick out their tongues, not in imitation but because they see these objects as suckable.

Babies, however, are soon capable of genuine imitation. Nine-month-olds can imitate a series of modeled behaviors (such as pushing a set of buttons or shaking plastic eggs filled with pebbles). What's more, they can carry out these imitations not only immediately after seeing them but after an interval of 24 hours, with no opportunity to practice the behaviors in between (Meltzoff, 1988a; Meltzoff & Moore, 1994). At 14 months of age, infants can delay (or defer) imitation for one week (Meltzoff, 1988b). And between 14 and 18 months they can not only defer imitation, they can generalize it to new settings. For example, children this age who saw a peer model a new behavior at day care could imitate that behavior two days later in their own homes (Hanna & Meltzoff, 1993). By 2 years of age, children can reproduce behaviors later even when the materials they use to carry out the behaviors have changed (Herbert & Hayne, 2000).

This man and his little son are playing an age-old game that's fun for dad and instructive for baby. Imitation may be the sincerest form of flattery, but in newborns it's a basic way of learning!

What mechanisms underlie the ability of babies, especially young ones, to imitate behaviors that they see others perform? The answer is still unclear, but the process involves some form of intermodal matching (Meltzoff, 1990). For instance, newborns might form cognitive representations of the behavior they saw a model perform; they would then have to translate these initially visual perceptions into movements and actions that they themselves could perform. This interpretation suggests that babies may be ready for some form of representational thought at an earlier age than had been proposed, and that imitative learning relies on transforming these representations into action.

Memory in Babies

Even very young infants can remember what they see and hear over relatively long time spans. Two researchers found that newborns could remember a previously seen visual event over a 24-hour period (Werner & Siqueland, 1978). The babies in this study altered their sucking patterns when the color and pattern of a visual stimulus changed, even though they had not seen that stimulus for nearly a day. Other studies show that newborns can also remember speech sounds over a similar time period (Bauer, 2006; Swain, Zelazo, & Clifton, 1993; Ungerer, Brody, & Zelazo, 1978). In one study of mothers and their 14-day-old infants, the mothers repeated the words *tinder* and *beguile* to their babies 60 times a day for 13 days (780 exposures); as you may imagine, 2-week-olds rarely hear these particular words. At 14 and 28 hours after this marathon training ended, the researchers tested the babies' memory for the words. The infants showed not only that they remembered the words but that they recognized them better than their own names.

Older babies have even more impressive memory capabilities. In one study, 3-month-old infants first learned to make a mobile move by kicking one leg, to which the researcher had attached a long ribbon that was also attached to the mobile suspension bar (see Figure 4-13) (Rovee-Collier & Gerhardstein, 1997). Usually babies this age will forget the connection between a kick and a bobbing mobile after about eight days. However, with a brief reminder before the testing period, infants could remember the connection for as long as four weeks. The reminder, provided about 24 hours before the memory test, consisted simply of letting the babies see the mobile bobbing up and down for three minutes. During the reminder session, the babies' legs were not attached to the mobile, so they could not relearn the connection. The visual reminder was enough, however. Babies who had experienced the reminder kicked their legs more often in the testing session (when the ankle ribbon was again attached) than babies who had learned the leg-mobile connection but who had been given no reminder of it in the interim. Another cue that helps babies remember is the context or setting in which the original learning took place (Rovee-Collier, 1999). Babies were able to remember better when tested in the same setting in which they originally learned, such as the day-care center, rather than in a novel context, such as the laboratory (Hayne, McDonald, & Barr, 1997).

From the age of 3 months, babies' memory abilities improve even further. Consider a study in which infants who were about 10 months old saw pictures (e.g., a whale), touched objects (e.g., a clothespin), or heard sounds (e.g., a bell or a rattle). Upon returning to the laboratory when they were 3 years old—two years later—the children were more likely to touch the objects and recognize the sounds that they had been exposed to on their earlier visit than were children in a control group who had not had the earlier experience in the lab (Myers, Clifton, & Clarkson, 1987). This study suggests that children have some memory of events that happened to them before they could even walk or talk. Similar evidence comes from the research of Bauer (1996, 2002), who found that 13-month-old infants were able to

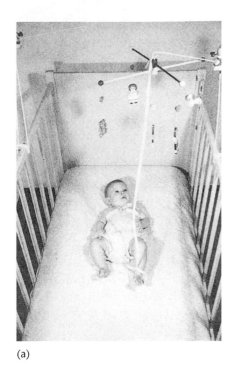

(a)

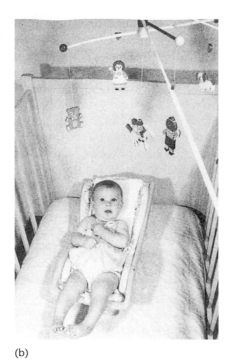

(b)

Figure 4-13

Memory lessons for babies

Rovee-Collier found that when she taught 3-month-old infants to make a mobile move by attaching the mobile to one of their legs with a ribbon (a) the babies forgot the association between kicking and moving the mobile after about a week. When this researcher gave these infants a "reminder" session, however, during which she removed the ribbon so that they could look at the mobile but couldn't make it move (b) and then reattached the ribbon (as in a), she found that most babies were able to remember the association for as long as four weeks

Source: Rovee-Collier, 1986.

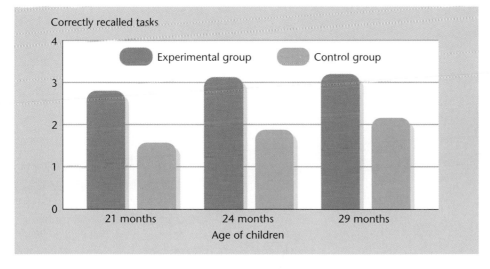

Figure 4-14

Young children have surprisingly good memories

Bauer and her colleagues tested young children ranging in age from 21 to 29 months on their memory for events in which they'd participated eight months earlier, such as setting up an inclined track and letting a car roll down the track, and found that the youngest group did very nearly as well as the oldest. All three groups recalled significantly more of the tasks than control groups who had had no experience with the tasks.

Source: Adapted from Bauer, 1996.

remember a simple sequence (e.g., putting teddy bear to bed) after an eight-month delay (Figure 4-14). In Chapter 9 we will revisit the topic of memory and examine in more detail the kinds of strategies that children develop to help them remember. Together these memory studies with infants and young children have led us to reevaluate the widely held belief that infants and children younger than 3 cannot recall the events of their lives. It appears that babies can recall much more of their early lives than we thought possible.

Making the Connections 4

There are many links between concepts and ideas in one area of development and concepts and ideas in other areas. Here are some of the connections between ideas in Chapter 4 and discussions in other chapters of this book.

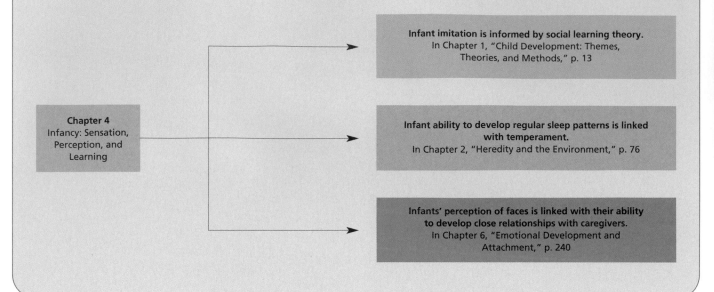

Chapter 4
Infancy: Sensation, Perception, and Learning

Infant imitation is informed by social learning theory.
In Chapter 1, "Child Development: Themes, Theories, and Methods," p. 13

Infant ability to develop regular sleep patterns is linked with temperament.
In Chapter 2, "Heredity and the Environment," p. 76

Infants' perception of faces is linked with their ability to develop close relationships with caregivers.
In Chapter 6, "Emotional Development and Attachment," p. 240

SUMMARY

- Babies can see, hear, and respond to interesting sights, sounds, and other sensory stimuli at a much earlier age than was originally believed.

The Newborn

- The newborn, or **neonate,** has a repertoire of **reflexes,** or involuntary responses to external stimuli. Many of these reflexes, some of which have obvious value in helping the newborn survive, disappear during the first year of life.

- Babies experience predictable changes in state, or recurring patterns of alertness and activity level, ranging from vigorous, wakeful activity to quiet, regular sleep. Two significant **infant states** are sleeping and crying.

- Between the ages of 2 and 4 months, babies may fall prey to **sudden infant death syndrome (SIDS).** Although the causes of SIDS are as yet unexplained, preventive measures for this fatal disorder include the cessation of parental smoking, preventing infants from sleeping on their stomachs, and parent and infant cosleeping.

- The **autostimulation theory** proposes that infants spend more than twice as much time as adults in **REM sleep** because such sleep stimulates higher brain centers that in turn promote development of the central nervous system.

- Crying, which is an effective means of early communication, follows distinct patterns that also change with development.

- Although there are wide differences among individuals, sexes, and races in soothability, certain caregiver techniques, such as holding the baby on the shoulder or swaddling it, are widely successful in helping to calm a distressed baby. Infants can also help to soothe themselves by sucking on a thumb or pacifier.

- Tests of reflexes may be combined with other assessments to gauge the health, maturity, and capacities of a newborn. The **Brazelton Neonatal Assessment Scale** is one widely used assessment tool.

The Infant's Sensory and Perceptual Capacities

- To study infants' **sensations** and **perceptions** investigators often make use of the infant's tendency to

habituate, or become used to, a given stimulus. Another technique is to use the **visual preference method,** in which researchers pinpoint a baby's preference for looking at one of two alternative stimuli. The violation-of-expectation method, in which investigators assess the infant's behavior following a surprise event, is also commonly used.

- At birth, babies are more sensitive to high-pitched than to low-pitched sounds, and for them to detect a sound it must be slightly louder than that for a normal adult. Overall, however, a newborn's hearing is very well developed. Newborns can distinguish among different kinds of sounds and tell what direction a sound comes from. They are also very responsive to human voices, which may be significant for later social and language development.

- Although visual capacities continue to develop throughout the first year of life, newborns are sensitive to brightness and can track moving objects. Initially they have poor **visual acuity** at distances beyond close range, although over the first three months acuity improves. Babies gradually begin to distinguish colors and improve in their ability to perceive patterns, including the patterning of human faces.

- The accurate perception of distance improves with age, as babies begin to coordinate their two eyes and use **stereoscopic vision.** Before babies can walk they can perceive depth, but experiments with the **visual cliff** demonstrate that with locomotion babies begin to show fear of heights. **Shape constancy** is something that even newborns seem to possess. **Size constancy** and visual expectations, however, appear to develop partly through experience.

- Newborns can discriminate among a variety of odors, and by 1 week of age they have learned to distinguish their mother's smells from those of other people. Newborns are also able to discriminate different tastes, and they display a preference for sweet over sour or bitter.

- The sense of touch is activated long before birth, and newborns are clearly responsive to both positive and negative types of touch; contrary to past beliefs, they are highly sensitive to pain. Infants also quickly learn to discriminate among objects based only on their sense of touch.

- From a very early age, using their capacity for **intermodal perception,** babies can integrate information from two different senses, such as the sounds that go with a certain sight.

Early Learning and Memory

- Newborns can be classically conditioned when a previously neutral stimulus is repeatedly paired with a pleasant stimulus. Eventually, the previously neutral stimulus alone comes to elicit the same reaction. *Classical conditioning* is more difficult in newborns when an aversive stimulus is involved.

- Newborns can also learn to emit a certain behavior when that behavior is repeatedly rewarded. Successful *operant conditioning* in newborns typically involves a behavior like sucking, which is of importance to the baby's survival. This suggests that young babies are best organized to learn conditioned responses that are functionally adaptive.

- Although newborns may be capable of some imitation, the basis of the ability to imitate others and the amount of such behavior the child displays change significantly with age.

- When given adequate retrieval cues for something they have learned, babies can remember information over substantial periods of time.

EXPLORE AND DISCUSS

1. What is the practical value of knowing about the young infant's sensory abilities? How might this information help in the early detection of problems and in the design of useful interventions to help children?

2. Based on your newly gained knowledge of infant's sensory and perceptual capacities, do you think that "the amazing newborn" is an appropriate description? Explain your answer.

3. How do you think that infants' visual and auditory abilities help them form relationships with their caregivers?

4. What would you tell a friend about the infant's ability to learn and remember new information?

Jacob Lawrence (1917–2000). *The Life of Harriet Tubman, #4: On a hot summer day about 1820, a group of slave children were tumbling in the sandy soil in the state of Maryland—and among them was one, Harriet Tubman. Dorchester County, Maryland.* 1940. Hampton University Museum.

5.

The Child's Growth: Brain, Body, Motor Skills, and Sexual Maturation

Tina's development was rapid from the start. She crawled and walked early, and by her first birthday she was forcing her parents to put their favorite vases on a high shelf, out of her reach. When she was 11 years old and in sixth grade she reached sexual maturity, well ahead of her classmates. Jason, in contrast, was a leisurely baby and took his time about everything. As a result the vases were safe in Jason's house until he was 14 months old. This pattern continued into childhood, and Jason was nearly 16 years old when he experienced his pubescent growth spurt.

The differences between these two children are not unusual; they illustrate two common findings. First, the rates at which children develop vary enormously among individual children, and second, rates also vary between the genders—at many points in childhood, girls develop more rapidly than boys. In this chapter, we examine the influence of biological and environmental factors on motor development and growth. First, we explore the development of the brain and the way genetic and environmental forces work together to determine brain growth and function. How is information transmitted within the brain? Do the two sides of the brain really control different functions? What happens if one side suffers damage? Next, we explore the motor and growth patterns that infants and children follow. What are the motor achievements of developing infants? What are the factors that speed up or slow down these emerging skills? Then we explore the ways in which children grow. How do biological and environmental factors modify growth patterns? Are children growing taller, and if so, why? What are the causes and consequences of being too thin or too fat? What role does nutrition play in growth? Can children who are deprived early of such things as proper nutrition "catch up" in growth? Finally, we explore the developmental milestone of puberty, its characteristics, and the factors that influence its course. How is the timing of puberty determined? What are the consequences of reaching sexual maturity earlier or later than other adolescents? Finally, we examine the development of gender identity and gender preference during adolescence.

BRAIN DEVELOPMENT IN INFANCY

In the prenatal period, as Figure 5-1 dramatically illustrates, the brain grows very rapidly, and it continues to grow at an amazing pace. Although at birth an infant's brain weighs only about 25 percent as much as a mature brain, by the time the baby is about 6 months old, its brain weighs half what an adult brain weighs, and the brain of the 2-year-old child weighs 75 percent as much as an adult brain (Figure 5-2; Shonkoff & Phillips, 2000).

The largest portion of the human brain consists of the two connected hemispheres that make up the **cerebrum,** a mass of tissue that embodies not only attributes particular to humans—such as speech and self-awareness—but also those that we human beings share with other vertebrate animals—such as sensory perception, motor abilities, and memory. The covering layer of the human cerebrum, the **cerebral cortex** (Figure 5-3), is highly convoluted and contains about 90 percent of the brain's cell bodies. Although we do not yet know how these cells control complicated traits, we do know that specific functions, such as seeing, hearing, moving, feeling emotion, thinking, and speaking, can be traced to specific regions of the cerebral cortex.

cerebrum The two connected hemispheres of the brain.

cerebral cortex The covering layer of the cerebrum that contains the cells that control specific functions such as seeing, hearing, moving, and thinking.

Figure 5-1

Fetal brain development

As the brain develops, the front part expands to form the cerebrum, the large, convoluted upper mass that in the adult dominates the upper and side portions of the brain. The cerebrum is covered by the cerebral cortex (see Figure 5-3), specific areas of which are devoted to particular functions such as motor, visual, and auditory activities. (The first five of the drawings in this figure have been enlarged to show details.)

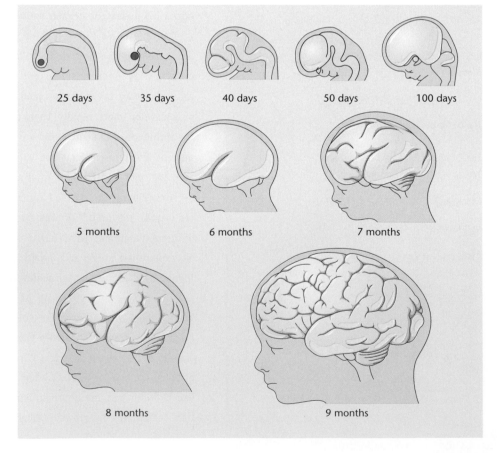

25 days   35 days   40 days   50 days   100 days

5 months   6 months   7 months

8 months   9 months

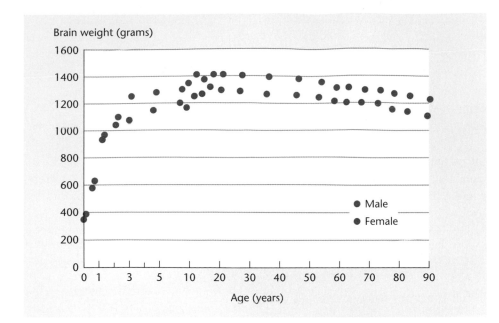

Figure 5-2

How brain weight increases with age

In this figure, the age scale for the early years has been expanded to show this period of rapid growth more clearly. As human beings mature, male brains tend to be heavier than female brains because of men's larger body size. Although scientists are discovering other differences between the brains of women and men, none of these differences have differential effects on either gender's intellectual abilities.

Source: Rosenzweig, Leiman, & Breedlove, 1996.

As we explore the development and functioning of the infant's brain, we examine the crucial importance of neurons and their interconnections, or synapses; the sequence in which brain functions mature; the topic of hemispheric specialization; and, related to this phenomenon, the brain's amazing ability to compensate for damage to one portion or even to an entire hemisphere. The Turning Points chart (pp. 166–167) in this chapter highlights some of the significant milestones in the development of the brain as well as important steps in the child's motor and physical growth; you may find it useful to refer to this chart as you read through this chapter.

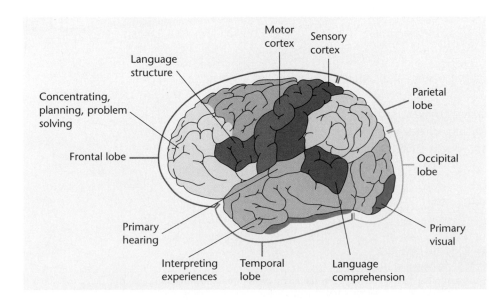

Figure 5-3

The brain's cortex

The cortex is divided into four *lobes*—frontal, temporal, occipital, and parietal—and specific areas within the lobes tend to specialize in particular functions. The left hemisphere, shown here, is generally associated with the processing of language, whereas the right hemisphere plays a greater role in visual and spatial processing. Because of the brain's plasticity, however, functions lost because of damage to one hemisphere, lobe, or area may be compensated for by another brain region.

Source: Postlethwait & Hopson, 1995.

Turning Points

GROWTH OF THE CHILD'S BRAIN, BODY, AND MOTOR SKILLS

AT BIRTH
- Infant's brain weighs one-quarter of adult brain weight; has 100 to 200 billion neurons and 2,500 synapses for every neuron. Baby generally assumes fetal position.

EARLY INFANCY
- Baby shows some evidence of hemispheric specialization. Most infants show right-hand dominance. When baby is held with feet touching flat surface, she makes stepping motions that resemble walking; this response disappears at about 2 months.

ABOUT 2 MONTHS
- Motor cortex of infant's brain begins to control voluntary movement. Baby lifts head and shoulders off mattress.

3 MONTHS
- Within first 3 months baby doubles his weight.

3–4 MONTHS
- Baby looks at and swipes at objects, retains toys put into her hand, but makes no contact with objects on a table. She holds head up for extended time, plays with her fingers, and kicks actively.

4 MONTHS
- Baby sustains head control and rolls from his tummy onto his back; sits with support.

4–5 MONTHS
- Baby contacts toys on table; grasps block precariously.

5 MONTHS
- Baby sits on adult's lap and grasps object; rolls from back to tummy, makes incipient crawling movements.

5–6 MONTHS
- There may be some indication of an inherited tendency to overweight.

6–7 MONTHS
- Baby bangs, shakes, and transfers toys from hand to hand; uses palmar grasp with a block; tries to grasp a raisin with whole hand.

7 MONTHS
- Baby sits alone.

Note: Developmental events described in this and other Turning Points charts represent overall trends identified in research studies. Individual children vary greatly in the ages at which they achieve these developmental changes. Milestones in sexual maturation are covered in Table 5-3.

Sources: Adolph & Bergen, 2006; Bertenthal & Clifton, 1998; Kopp, 1994; Shirley, 1931.

ABOUT 8 MONTHS	• Baby uses finger grasp with block, scissors grasp with raisin. Begins creeping; pulls up into unsteady stand but can't get back down; overall body control is better, with fewer unintended movements.
ABOUT 8 OR 9 MONTHS	• The brain's hippocampus, which aids in memory processes, becomes fully functional.
ABOUT 9 MONTHS	• Baby holds one block in each hand; approaches a raisin with index finger. Easily moves between sitting and lying; sitting is balanced and steady; stands holding furniture.
10 MONTHS	• Baby begins cruising (creeping); stands on toes while holding on but stands alone unsteadily; begins to use some implements, such as spoons.
11 MONTHS	• Baby is obsessed with learning to walk—walks when led; cruises till exhausted; feeds self with thumb and forefinger.
11–12 MONTHS	• Uses forefinger grasp of block and pincer grasp of raisin.
12–15 MONTHS	• Child's brain has about half again as many synapses as adult brain; synaptic pruning gradually reduces this number. Child stands alone and walks without assistance.
18 MONTHS	• Child runs and gallops.
2 YEARS	• In most children, right-handedness is fully established.
3 YEARS	• 90% of children show left hemisphere bias for language. Children can hop.
4 YEARS	• Children who will be obese later in life begin to gain weight at a faster rate than other children.
9 YEARS	• Boys catch up with girls in height, but then slow down again until about 14.
10 YEARS	• Some young girls succumb to anorexia or bulimia between 10 and the early 20s.
14 YEARS	• Girls' height gain slows down considerably while boys' gain takes off; boys' weight gain also shoots up.
16–17 YEARS	• Most young people have attained their full height.

Figure 5-4

A myelinated neuron

The neuron's axon terminates in synaptic knobs that, in synaptic connection with the dendrites of another neuron (see Figure 5-5) or with other types of cells, transmit messages through the nervous system. The myelin sheaths that encase much of the axon facilitate the transmission of signals rapidly and efficiently. Neurons are the longest cells in the human body, sometimes reaching more than 3 feet in length.

Source: From *Fundamentals of Anatomy & Physiology,* 3rd ed. by Frederic H. Martini, Fig. 12-7b, p. 389. Copyright © 1995 by Prentice Hall, Inc. Reprinted by permission of Pearson Education, Inc., Glenview, IL.

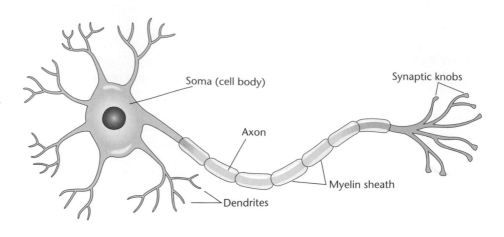

neuron A cell in the body's nervous system, consisting of a cell body, a long projection called an *axon,* and several shorter projections called *dendrites;* neurons send and receive neural impulses, or messages, throughout the brain and nervous system.

neuron proliferation The rapid formation of neurons in the developing organism's brain.

glial cell A nerve cell that supports and protects neurons and serves to encase them in *myelin sheaths.*

myelination The process by which glial cells encase neurons in sheaths of the fatty substance *myelin.*

neural migration The movement of neurons within the brain that ensures that all brain areas have a sufficient number of neural connections.

synapse A specialized site of intercellular communication where information is exchanged between nerve cells, usually by means of a chemical *neurotransmitter.*

synaptogenesis The forming of synapses.

Neurons and Synapses

Scientists believe that at birth or even earlier a baby's brain has most of its **neurons,** or nerve cells—100 to 200 billion of them (Nash, 1997), as many as there are stars in the Milky Way. In fact, recent estimates suggest that most neurons are present in the brain by the seventh month of gestation (Rakic, 1995). During the embryonic period, neurons multiply at a very rapid pace; according to Kolb and colleagues (2003), in a process called **neuron proliferation,** about 250,000 new neurons are born every minute!

Neurologists and others long assumed that the brain did not grow new neurons after birth, but recent studies (e.g., Gould, Reeves, Graziano, & Gross, 1999; Rosenzweig Leiman, & Breedlove, 1996) have suggested that the adult brain may have the capacity to regenerate nerve cells. Whether or not we grow new neurons, the brain increases in size as existing neurons grow and the connections between them proliferate. Brain growth also reflects the growth of **glial cells,** which surround and protect neurons, providing them with structural support, regulating their nutrient concentrations, and repairing neural tissue. Some glial cells are responsible for the important task of **myelination,** in which parts of neurons are covered with layers of a fatty, membranous wrapping called *myelin* (Figure 5-4). This insulation makes the neuron more efficient in transmitting information (Johnson, 1998). Most myelination occurs during the first two years of life but some continues into adulthood, a reminder that change in the brain is a lifelong process (Sampaio & Truwit, 2001).

Neurons are "always on the move" (Rosenzweig et al., 1996, p. 105) as they migrate to their final location. Guided by neurochemical processes, neurons move to a variety of places in the brain. This **neural migration** ensures that all parts of the brain are served by a sufficient number of neurons. The absence of an appropriate number of neurons in their proper locations may be associated with various forms of mental retardation and with disorders such as dyslexia or schizophrenia (Johnson, 1998; Kolb et al., 2003).

Perhaps as essential as neurons themselves are the connections that form between neurons, known as **synapses.** At these specialized junctions the extended *axon* of one neuron transmits a message to the projected *dendrites* of another neuron, usually by means of chemicals that cross the small spaces between the neurons (Figure 5-5). This activity is crucial to survival and learning, for as the brain's neurons receive input from the environment—before and after birth—they continue to create new synapses, allowing for increasingly complex communications. **Synaptogenesis,** or the forming of synapses, begins early in prenatal life, as soon as neurons begin to evolve. The brain forms synapses even more rapidly than it forms neurons; for example, at birth, in the brain's visual cortex alone there are 2,500 synapses for every neuron. And synapse formation goes on: In the visual cortex it reaches a peak when the child is about age 2, when there are about

Figure 5-5   Synaptic connection between two neurons

Across the small space between one neuron's synaptic knobs and another's dendrites or soma a chemical substance effects the transfer of information.

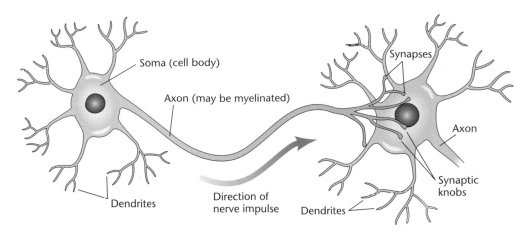

Source: From *Fundamentals of Anatomy & Physiology,* 3rd ed. by Frederic H. Martini, Fig. 12-7d, p. 389. Copyright © 1995 by Prentice Hall, Inc. Reprinted by permission of Pearson Education, Inc., Glenview, IL.

15,000 synapses for every neuron (Huttenlocher, 1994; Huttenlocher & Dabholkar, 1997). Even if there are fewer synapses per neuron in other parts of the cortex, this still would suggest trillions of synapses in the new young brain!

Are all these neurons and synapses necessary? Do they continue to function throughout life? The answer to both questions is no. The brain is programmed to create more nerve cells and more connections between these cells than are needed. This excess of neuronal function is designed to ensure that the developing child acquires the information and skills he needs for proper development. Across development, two processes reduce the number of neurons as well as of connecting fibers (Sowell et al., 2003). When new synapses are formed, some surrounding neurons die in what is called **neuronal death,** or *programmed cell death* (Kandel, Schwartz, & Jessell, 2000), apparently to provide more space for these crucial loci of information transmission. In **synaptic pruning,** the brain disposes of a neuron's axons and dendrites if that particular neuron is not often stimulated (see Figure 5-6). This again frees up

neuronal death The death of some neurons that surround newly formed synaptic connections among other neurons; also called *programmed cell death.*

synaptic pruning The brain's disposal of the axons and dendrites of a neuron that is not often stimulated.

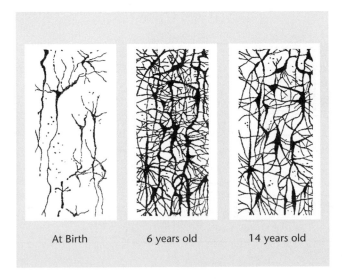

Figure 5-6

Developmental changes in neurons of the cerebral cortex

During childhood, the brain overproduces neural connections, establishes the usefulness of certain ones of these, and then "fine-tunes" the extra connections. Especially in the frontal cortex, overproduction of synapses may be essential for infants to develop certain intellectual abilities. According to some scientists, the connections that are used survive, and those that are not die.

Source: Reprinted by permission of the publisher from *The Postnatal Development of the Human Cerebral Cortex,* Vols. I–VIII by Jesse LeRoy Conel, Cambridge, Mass.: Harvard University Press, Copyright © 1939, 1975 by the President and Fellows of Harvard College.

space for new synaptic connections. The goals of both neuronal death and synaptic pruning are to increase the speed, efficiency, and complexity of transmissions between neurons and to allow room for new connections that develop as the child encounters new experiences (Huttenlocher, 1994; Kolb et al., 2003). Brain development is not simply an additive process but one that increases in efficiency and specialization. Loss in this case leads to a gain for the developing organism.

By adulthood, each of the brain's approximately 1 trillion neurons makes 100 to 1,000 connections with other neurons. That adds up to about 1 quadrillion synapses in the adult human brain (Huttenlocher & Dabholkar, 1997).

Sequential Development of the Brain

There is an orderly sequence to brain development during infancy. By autopsying the brains of infants and young children who die unexpectedly, Huttenlocher (1994) has traced the development of synapses in the brain and has found that the processes of forming and pruning synapses occur at different times for various parts of the brain. Most interesting is the link between the sequences of synaptic development and the onset in the developing infant of various motor, perceptual, and cognitive skills and abilities (Nelson, 1999a, b; Nelson, Thomas, & de Haan, 2005).

As the baby moves from mostly reflexive behavior in the early months of life to voluntary control over movements, the motor area of the brain develops most rapidly. When the infant is about 2 months old, motor reflexes such as rooting and the startle response (see Chapter 4) drop out, and the motor cortex begins to oversee voluntary movements such as reaching, crawling, and walking. Gradually the infant begins to master purposeful movements such as the effort to make contact with an object, which results at first in a kind of swiping motion.

As we have already noted, in the visual cortex the number of synapses per neuron is multiplied some six times within the first two years of life. But even within the first 4 to 12 months the number of connections rises to about 150 percent of those present in the adult brain. As a result of this proliferation, the baby's visual capacities are greatly enhanced; for example, she becomes more skilled at focusing on objects at different distances (Nelson, 1999a).

A similar sequence of synaptic and behavioral developments characterizes the evolution of the auditory cortex and other areas of the brain. The hippocampus, for example, which aids in memory processes, becomes fully functional at about 8 or 9 months. In the prefrontal cortex, which is involved in forethought and logic, synaptic density develops more slowly and does not reach its peak until after the first year (Nelson, 1999b; Nelson et al., 2005).

LifeMap CD

To learn more about how our brains develop from infancy to adulthood, view the "Brain Development" video in Chapter 5 of your CD.

Hemispheric Specialization

One of the most important organizing features of the brain is its left-right division into two halves or **brain hemispheres.** The left and right hemispheres, which are connected by a set of nerve fibers called the **corpus callosum,** are anatomically different and, in general, control different functions (Kandel et al., 2000; Stephen et al., 2003; Springer & Deutsch, 1993). Studies of people who have suffered damage to one side of the brain caused by head injuries or tumors give us important information about the functions in which each hemisphere normally specializes. At the same time, because a great deal of cross-wiring occurs between the hemispheres, the separation is by no means complete. Not only do both hemispheres play some role in most functions, but when one side of the brain suffers damage, the other half may take over some functions. Thus the brain has great plasticity and can adapt to adverse circumstances.

LEFT- AND RIGHT-BRAIN FUNCTIONS **Hemispheric specialization** begins early in life (Banish, 1998; Stephan et al., 2003; Turkewitz, 1991). Simple movement is controlled differentially, the left hemisphere of the motor cortex controlling the right side of the body, the right hemisphere controlling the body's left side. Researchers have demonstrated that in full-term and even preterm babies spoken syllables evoke electrical potentials that indicate that these infants' brains process speech syllables faster in the left hemisphere than in the right (Molfese & Molfese, 1980). But the brain's division of labor is more complex than this: **Lateralization** describes the further specialization of each side of the brain in specific perceptual and cognitive tasks. For example, the left hemisphere is associated with language processing, while the right hemisphere is involved in processing visual-spatial information.

The right hemisphere also processes nonspeech sounds like music, and the perception of faces (Nelson & Bosquet, 2000). When damage occurs to the right side of the brain, people may have difficulty attending to a task requiring visual-spatial perception, their drawing skills may deteriorate, they may have trouble following a map or recognizing friends, or they may become spatially disoriented (Carter, Freeman, & Stanton, 1995). The right hemisphere is also involved in processing emotional information, as shown by the fact that people with right-brain damage can have difficulty interpreting facial expressions (Dawson, 1994; Nelson & Bosquet, 2000; see also Chapter 6). At the same time, right-hemisphere damage can sometimes make people indifferent to or even cheerful about things that would normally upset them. Initially this suggested to some investigators (Springer & Deutsch, 1993) that the right side of the brain might have a special role in expressing negative emotions and inhibiting positive ones, the left side a special role in expressing positive emotions and inhibiting negative ones. This view has since been modified to suggest that the left hemisphere is activated in the expression of emotions associated with approaching the external environment, such as joy, interest, and anger, whereas the right region is activated in emotional expression that causes the person to turn away or withdraw from that environment, such as distress, disgust, and fear (see Figure 5-7, as well as Fox, 1991; Davidson, 1994).

The left hemisphere of the brain has traditionally been associated with language processing, and indeed it has been found that although people with left-hemisphere damage can recognize a familiar song and tell a stranger's face from an old friend's, they may have trouble understanding what is being said to them or speaking clearly (Springer & Deutsch, 1993). Interestingly, however, in persons who are deaf and use sign language to communicate—a language that involves motor movements of the hands—the right side of the brain takes over language functions. Neville and her colleagues (Neville et al., 1998; Neville & Bruer, 2001) studied deaf and hearing adults as they were engaged in language processing and found that electrical activity during this task was greater in the right hemisphere of deaf persons than it was in hearing adults' right brains. (See Chapter 7 for more discussion of language development.)

brain hemispheres The two halves of the brain's cerebrum, left and right.

corpus callosum The band of nerve fibers that connects the two hemispheres of the brain.

hemispheric specialization Differential functioning of the two cerebral hemispheres; the left controlling the right side of the body, the right controlling the body's left side.

lateralization The process by which each half of the brain becomes specialized for certain functions; for example, the control of speech and language by the left hemisphere and of visual-spatial processing by the right.

Figure 5-7   Emotions associated with left- and right-brain hemisphere activity
According to a recent theory, both hemispheres are involved in emotional expression, but the left focuses on feelings that trigger approach to the environment, the right on feelings that cause a person to turn away from the environment.

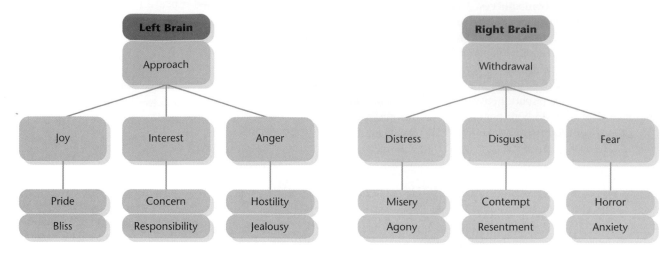

Source: Dawson, 1994.

As we will see, these and other findings have suggested that the brain may be even more capable of adapting to external change than we thought. If brain injury occurs in the early years of life, for example, infants and young children often recover their losses (Fox, Calkins, & Bell, 1994; Stiles, 2000). Young children enjoy this recovery advantage probably largely because the young brain is not fully developed, and hemispheric specialization is not yet complete. For instance, when the left hemisphere is damaged in early infancy, a child can still develop language ability close to normal (Bates & Roe, 2002). Even in adults, however, there is still a great deal of modifiability, and lost function can often be partially recovered through treatment. Even the old brain can be taught to relearn old tricks and acquire new ones (Black, Jones, Nelson, & Greenough, 1998).

As this teacher of the hearing impaired demonstrates "I love you" in American Sign Language to her eighth-grade student, it may be the right hemisphere of her brain that is particularly activated. As the text describes, there is evidence that in deaf and hearing-impaired people the right hemisphere takes over language functions.

CONSEQUENCES OF BRAIN LATERALIZATION Researchers have shown that the degree to which a newborn's brain is lateralized in processing speech sounds—that is, is prone to use one hemisphere rather than the other, is related to the child's language ability three years later (Molfese & Molfese, 1985). In infants who later exhibited better language skills, investigators found that the left hemisphere differentiated among speech sounds and the right hemisphere among nonspeech sounds. It has also been found, however, that a newborn's left-hemisphere dominance for processing language is not as extreme as that of an older child or an adult. Some 70 percent of infants show a left-hemisphere language bias, but 90 percent of 3-year-olds show this bias. In children who are 3 years of age and older, researchers find few developmental changes either in reliance on the left hemisphere for processing verbal information or in the superior ability of the right hemisphere to understand emotional cues (Bryden & Saxby, 1986; Johnson, 1998). Even these findings, however, may be challenged by studies such as one by Molfese, Morse, and Peters (1990), in which it appeared that the brain responses of 14-month-olds to speech and language materials and to matching these with concrete objects were multidimensional and involved a variety of differentiated processes, some of which were lateralized and some of which were not. Clearly, the assignment of brain function between the hemispheres is highly complex and requires continuing study.

One reason we need to know more about this issue is that theories about lateralization underlie current explanations of what is generally called **dyslexia,** or the difficulties some children (and adults) experience in learning to read (see Chapter 10). In fact, as many as 5 percent of U.S. children experience such problems. Typically, they have difficulty integrating visual and auditory information, for example, in matching written letters or words to the sounds of those letters and words. Some children confuse letters, for example, calling a "d" a "b"; others have difficulty breaking apart the letters and syllables of a word and, conceptualizing the word as a whole, have no clues with which to figure it out (Liberman, Shankweiler, Liberman, Fowler, & Fischer, 1976). Kraus and associates (1996) examined the responses of children with learning disabilities to different letter sounds by monitoring the electrical activity in their brains. Finding that the children showed no change in brain activity when, for example, the sound /ga/ replaced the sound /da/, these researchers concluded that there may indeed be a biological basis for dyslexia.

This and other similar disorders may have multiple origins, but one possible cause may be abnormal cerebral organization. Some researchers have suggested that poor readers do not show the normal lateralization pattern—that is, they process spatial information on both sides of the brain rather than primarily on the right and, thus, their left hemispheres may become overloaded, leading to deficits in such language skills as reading and understanding verbal information (Baringa, 1996; Witelson, 1983). This atypical cerebral organization, it is proposed, may be genetically determined or may be caused by environmental factors prenatally or after birth. Although a considerable body of evidence supports this hypothesis (e.g., Banish, 1998; Bryden, 1988), the view that reading difficulties are caused by faulty lateralization patterns is still controversial.

What about handedness? Like other functions, such as processing verbal information or understanding emotional cues, handedness is lateralized. About 90 percent of adults are right-handed, and a majority of young infants show right-hand dominance: They use the right hand more than the left for reaching, touching, and grasping (Dean & Anderson, 1997; Mauer & Mauer, 1988). Although young infants tend to shift between right and left hands, handedness is generally fully established by the age of 5 (Coren, 1992; Ozturk et al., 1999). Note, however, that some left-handed people are ambidextrous, able to use both hands for some tasks. This is consistent with the finding that such individuals' brains may be less clearly lateralized than the brains of right-handed people (Coren, 1992). The establishment of footedness is slower, and it appears to continue to develop until 4 or 5 years of age or even longer (Coren, 1992).

dyslexia A term for the difficulties some people experience in reading or in learning to read.

The Brain's Plasticity: Experience and Brain Development

As we have seen, the brain continues to develop so rapidly after birth that we cannot hold genes alone responsible for the multitude of neural connections formed. Stimulation from the environment clearly plays a crucial role in brain development, strengthening the synapses and modifying brain chemistry to improve the brain's overall efficiency. The human brain's **plasticity,** or the responsiveness of its neural structures and functions to input from the environment, is one of its most remarkable features.

Two types of experiences influencing brain development have been distinguished: experience-expectant and experience-dependent processes (Greenough & Black, 1999). **Experience-expectant processes** are universal, experienced by all human beings across evolution. Such experiences as touch, patterned visual input, sound such as that of voice and language, affectionate expression from caregivers, and nutrition are all expected in normal environments. These are critical for normal brain development and trigger processes such as synaptic development and pruning, which we have already described. Identifying these processes underscores the important role that the stimulation provided by a normal environment plays in brain development. As we have stated in Chapter 1, genes are important, but they need input from the external environment to promote normal development of all systems, including the brain. In fact, when there is interference with normal stimulation, such as occurs in the case of congenital cataract, the visual system is deprived of "experience-expectant" stimulation and fails to develop properly, resulting in blindness. In a series of classic experiments, Riesen (1947) showed that when chimpanzees were raised in the dark for the first year and a half of life, their retinas (the light-sensitive areas at the back of eye) failed to develop properly. In this case the animals were deprived of the experience-expectant stimulation they needed for proper brain development.

Experience-dependent processes describe the kinds of environmental stimulation that are unique to each individual. These processes involve experiences we encounter in our particular family, community, and culture. Children in Mozambique will encounter different language, customs, and activities than will children in North America. While a child in Mozambique may learn to hunt, fish, and make pottery, a child in our culture will be exposed to video games, computers, and supermarkets—clearly vastly different experiences. Our brains respond to these different types of environments by developing synaptic connections that encode these unique experiences. While the child in Mozambique may develop aspects of the motor cortex that correspond to the skills associated with hunting and fishing, the American child develops other parts of the brain that reflect the fine motor and eye-hand coordination needed for success at video games or for searching the Internet.

Evidence from both animal and human studies supports the predictions of these two postulated types of experience. Animal research shows that the size, structure, and even the biochemistry of the brain can be modified by experience. In a series of pioneering studies, Rosenzweig and his colleagues (Benloucif, Bennett, & Rosenzweig, 1995; Rosenzweig, 2003) placed young rats from the same litters in two very different environments. The enriched environment consisted of large, brightly lit, communal cages with wheels, ladders, platforms, and other toys that were changed daily to ensure that the rats had a steady stream of new learning experiences. In addition, every day the investigators gave the "enriched" rats an opportunity to explore a large obstacle course or maze. In contrast, the researchers placed the remainder of the rats in an "impoverished" environment, in which each was alone in a totally bare, isolated cage located in a quiet, dimly lit room. When the researchers compared the brains of the young rats after the rats had spent nearly three months in their respective worlds, they discovered several important differences that apparently resulted from the different

plasticity The capacity of the brain, particularly in its developmental stages, to respond and adapt to input from the external environment.

experience-expectant processes Brain processes that are universal, experienced by all human beings across evolution.

experience-dependent processes Brain processes that are unique to the individual and responsive to particular cultural, community, and family experiences.

environments. (In case you wonder about the relevance of the rat's brain to the human's, the basic neural structures of the two brains are very similar.)

For one thing, the weight of the rats' brains was affected, especially the weight of the cerebral cortex, which controls higher-order processes. An enriched rat's cortex weighed about 4 percent more than the cortex of an impoverished rat, and some regions of the cortex were affected more than others. The occipital region, which controls vision, made the greatest gain in weight (6%), whereas the area responsible for touch showed the least gain (only 2%).

Early experience can also affect the biochemistry of the brain and the structure of its neurons. An enriched environment tends to increase the complexity of neurons as measured by the number of dendrites they develop (Black et al., 1998; Jones & Greenough, 1996), and this proliferation of neural branches may help account for the increase in brain size associated with environmental enrichment. More dendrites per neuron means more synapses formed with other neurons, which in turn means that more information can be sent via these synaptic connections. At the same time, the activity of key chemicals in the brain, especially in the cerebral cortex, increases significantly as a result of an enriched rearing environment.

And it may not be just the young who can benefit from enriched experiences. Studies have shown that changes in brain weight, structure, and biochemistry are not restricted to the immature brain. Adult rats exposed to impoverished or enriched environments after being reared in normal laboratory conditions show changes like those we see in young rats (Black & Greenough, 1998). Still, the effects of differential experience may be greater during the earlier periods of life.

Recent research suggests that variations in environmental stimulation can affect the human infant's developing brain as well. As we will explore in detail in Chapter 7, studies of infant language acquisition illustrate the brain's plasticity. Although infants respond to the sounds of all languages at first, over the first year of life they become more selective, responding increasingly to sounds they hear in their own language (Kuhl et al., 1997). Kuhl and her colleagues suggest that infants' brains develop "auditory maps," or templates, designed to respond to certain auditory features and not others. These maps then guide infants in recognizing the language they are exposed to in their early environment. It is as if different sets of neuronal connections become programmed to respond to particular aspects of speech.

Recent studies have suggested that establishing certain kinds of neural connections can facilitate others. Sarnthein and colleagues (1997), for example, have proposed that the natural harmonies of music may help the brain develop a wiring diagram that can promote the kind of spatial-temporal reasoning that is central to success in math or the game of chess. After six months of weekly piano lessons, 3- and 4-year-olds improved markedly in this kind of reasoning as demonstrated by their ability to look at a disassembled picture of an elephant and to tell the researcher how to put the pieces together. In contrast, children in other groups who received either stimulation such as singing lessons and training with a computer keyboard and mouse or no stimulation showed little improvement. The research suggests that neural circuitry in the brain may be changed by music training, but there is no direct evidence of this, nor is it clear that these young pianists will be either better musicians or better math students in later years. However, recent work (Munte, Altenmuller, & Jancke, 2002) suggests that specialized brain development is associated with heavy involvement in particular activities, such as music; cellists, for example, have been shown to have expanded development of motor cortex that is associated with the type of hand-eye coordination needed to be a successful cello player. The brain is indeed highly plastic and thus responsive to the kinds of unique environments we create for ourselves through our choices of activities.

Just as stimulation can enhance the development of the brain, so can lack of stimulation or exposure to traumatic events damage the brain or cause it to malfunction. Recent studies suggest that in abused children both the cortex and the *limbic system*—centers in the brain that are involved with emotions and infant-parent attachment—are 20 to

LifeMap CD

To explore more detail on neurons and neurotransmitters, watch the "Neurons: How They Work" video in Chapter 5 of your CD.

30 percent smaller than in other children and that these areas have fewer synapses (Perry, 1997). Investigators have also found that infants raised in high-stress environments, such as a violent, crime-ridden neighborhood, may develop higher levels of cortisol, a natural steroid that increases the activity of the part of the brain involved in vigilance and the control of arousal. Hypothesizing that these children might be more likely to develop hyperactivity and impulsive behavior, Gunnar and her colleagues (Gunnar, 1994; Nachmias, Gunnar, Mangelsdorf, Parritz, & Buss, 1996) found that higher cortisol levels were indeed associated with lower inhibitory control. Newer techniques such as *positron-emission tomography,* or PET, and other techniques for studying brain function and activity (see Table 5-1), have permitted neuroscientists to

Table 5-1 Techniques for studying human brain function and structure

Technique	What it Shows	Advantages (+) and Disadvantages (−)
EEG (electroencephalograph): Multiple electrodes are pasted to the outside of the head.	Lines that chart the summated electrical fields resulting from the activity of billions of neurons	+ Detects very rapid changes in electrical activity, allowing analysis of stages of cognitive processing − Provides poor spatial resolution of the source of electrical activity. EEG is sometimes combined with magnetoencephalography (MEG), which localizes electrical activity by measuring magnetic fields associated with it.
PET (positron-emission tomography) and SPECT (single-photon emission computed tomography): Positrons and photons are emissions from radioactive substances.	An image of the amount and localization of any molecule that can be injected in radioactive form, such as neurotransmitters, drugs, or tracers for blood flow or glucose use (images indicate specific changes in neuronal activity)	+ Allows functional and biochemical studies + Provides visual image corresponding to anatomy − Requires exposure to low levels of radioactivity − Provides spatial resolution better than that of EEG but poorer than that of MRI − Cannot follow rapid changes (faster than 30 seconds)
MRI (magnetic resonance imaging): Exposes the brain to a magnetic field and measures radiofrequency waves.	Traditional MRI provides high-resolution image of brain anatomy. Functional MRI (fMRI) provides images of changes in blood flow (which indicate specific changes in neural activity). A new variant, diffusion tensor imaging (DTI), shows water flow in neural fibers, thus revealing the "wiring diagram" of neural connections in the brain.	+ Requires no exposure to radioactivity + Provides high spatial resolution of anatomical details (under 1 mm) + Provides high temporal resolution (slower than $\frac{1}{10}$ second)
TMS (transcranial magnetic stimulation): Temporarily disrupts electrical activity of a small region of brain by exposing it to an intense magnetic field.	Normal function of a particular brain region can be studied by observing changes after TMS is applied to a specific location.	+ Shows which brain regions are necessary for given tasks − Long-term safety not well established

Source: Bernstein & Nash, 2005.

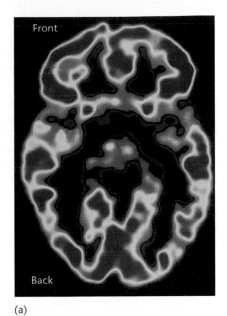 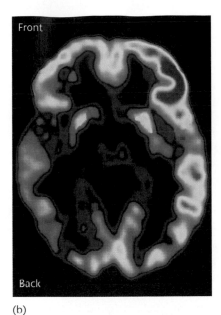

(a)   (b)

Figure 5-8

How early deprivation can affect brain activity
In the brain of a normal child (a), positron-emission tomography (PET) reveals many regions of high activity (red), whereas in the brain of an institutionalized Romanian orphan who suffered extreme deprivation from birth (b) there are many fewer such regions and more areas of less activity. The degrees of brain activity, from highest to lowest, follow the color sequence red, yellow, green, blue, and black.

Source: Begley, 1997.

track changes in infant brains over development as well as to detect the effects of trauma on the developing brain. PET scans use radioactive tracers to image and analyze such things as the flow of blood through the body's organs and metabolic activity in specific portions of an organ. As Figure 5-8 shows, early deprivation characterized by an unstimulating and unresponsive environment—a Romanian orphanage—can have a profound impact on the developing brain.

MOTOR DEVELOPMENT

What course does the infant's motor development follow? In this section we look first at the way an infant reaches and grasps and at how early she acquires these skills. One of babies' early achievements is the ability to reach, grasp, and pick up objects. These skills are important because they provide another way, in addition to seeing and hearing, that infants can explore and learn about their new world. "Once infants can reach and grasp objects, they no longer have to wait for the world to come to them; their hands now bring objects close enough for exploration" (Bertenthal & Clifton, 1998, p. 38). We also explore infants' first efforts to reach things beyond their immediate grasp—their attempts to crawl to an interesting object and, ultimately, to walk to it. As you will see, cultural practices and other environmental conditions can affect the timing of the emergence of effective locomotion (Bradley, Corwyn, Burchinal, McAdoo, & Garcia-Coll, 2001).

Reaching and Grasping

"Manual control ranks as one of the human infant's greatest achievements in the first two years of life" (Bertenthal & Clifton, 1998, p. 58), and the first step the baby takes toward this control is to reach for objects in his view. As we saw in Chapter 4, even newborns display a grasping reflex and a rudimentary form of reaching—called "prereaching"—that involves uncoordinated "swipes" at objects that babies notice. Around 2 months of age these primitive forms of reaching and grasping decline (Hofsten & Rönnqvist, 1993). At 3 months, infants initiate a new and more complex and efficient pattern, namely, *directed reaching* (Thelen et al., 1993; Spencer

& Thelen, 2000). By the time they are about 5 months old, normal infants in average environments generally succeed not only in reaching in a directed way for an object but in successfully grasping it. By this age, they can even touch objects that glow in the dark and move (Robin, Berthier, & Clifton, 1996) and can grasp lighted objects that become invisible (McCarty & Ashmead, 1999)—amazing feats for 5-month-olds.

Why does reaching develop so slowly? To be a skilled "reacher," the child needs to develop many components including muscles, postural control, control over the movement of her arms, hands, and legs, and a variety of perceptual and motor abilities. Only when all parts of the system are ready to work together can the infant become competent in reaching and grasping objects (Adolph, 2005; Thelen, 2001; Thelen & Smith, 2005). This "putting the pieces" together view of how reaching develops is consistent with the dynamic systems view of development that we reviewed in Chapter 1. In experiments with institutionalized infants whose normal environments were severely restricted, White (1967) showed that enriching infants' visual world could advance their abilities to attend to objects and to reach for them. Hanging colorful toys over the babies' cribs, providing them with multicolored sheets and bumper pads, and ensuring that the infants were handled more often by caretakers, the researchers found that the experimental babies exhibited visually directed reaching by the time they were a little over 3 months old and about 40 percent faster than control subjects. At the same time, these infants ignored the new conditions for the first five weeks of the experiment and cried more than the other babies during that time. This could suggest that maturation, too, played a role. Maybe if we want to accelerate a child's development, we need to provide her with new experiences paced just ahead of her emerging capacities, but not so far ahead that she can't incorporate these experiences into her repertoire of behavior. Yet another factor may have played a role in White's studies: The lack of sensitive caregiving in the institutional environment may have discouraged the infants from exploring—a reminder that contextual and biological factors interact in affecting development.

Using a finger grasp to pull a puzzle piece out of its place with one hand and with the other to hold a second piece in waiting shows some advanced skill on the part of this 7-month-old baby. On average, infants are 8 months old before they can use this type of grasp.

Maturation alone cannot account for the emergence of the skills of reaching and grasping. Although Halverson (1931) proposed an orderly developmental sequence based essentially on maturation of the brain and influenced little if at all by environmental factors, recent research indicates that this view was incorrect. Although a strong developmental progression occurs in the frequency and skill with which infants employ various grips (Bertenthal & Clifton, 1998; Siddiqui, 1995), and neurological development undoubtedly sets some limits on infants' abilities to contact and grasp objects, task parameters in the form of object size and shape affect grasping skill at every age (Newell, Scully, McDonald, & Baillargeon, 1989).

One way to illustrate the role that the environment—in this case, the task confronting the infant—plays in the emergence of grasping is to consider how the size and shape of an object alters the infant's grasping behavior. By varying the proportions of the objects they present to 4- and 8-month-old babies, investigators have found that an infant's grasping is actually quite complex. For example, infants vary their grips according to the size and shape of an object as well as the size of their own hands relative to the object's size (Newell et al., 1989). Infants use a grip involving the thumb and index finger (or the thumb, index finger, and middle finger) for small objects, but for large objects they use either all the fingers of one hand or all of both hands. Moreover, these patterns are consistent over time: Both younger and older infants show sensitivity to the size and shape of an object relative to the size of their hands. There is an age difference, however, in the way younger and older babies decide how to grasp an object (Newell et al., 1989). Four-month-olds rely more on touch to determine grip configuration, whereas 8-month-olds use vision as a guide; the latter technique is more efficient, of course, because it allows the child to preshape his hand as he reaches for an object (Newell et al., 1989).

Over the first year of life, the infant's progress in controlling his hands is remarkable. Infants not only become skilled reachers and graspers (Siddiqui, 1995) but begin to explore using objects such as spoons as tools (Connolly & Dalgleish, 1989). Moreover, they learn to use gestures in social communication: At about 1 year of age they are able to follow a parent's pointing finger to the target object rather than focus on the finger alone (Butterworth & Grover, 1990), and only a month later they can point themselves to attract other people's attention (Franco & Butterworth, 1996). By age 2, they can build and knock over towers of blocks, and by age 3 they can copy vertical lines on a page.

Locomotion

According to Thelen and Smith (1994, 2006), the development of locomotion consists of three clear phases or transitions. The first of these has long puzzled researchers: When you hold a baby upright and let his feet touch a flat surface, tilting his body slightly from side to side, the baby responds by reflexively moving his legs in a rhythmic stepping motion that resembles walking. But this stepping reflex disappears by the time the infant is about 2 months old. Not until the second half of the baby's first year does the second transition see the reappearance of stepping movements. In the third and final transition, infants who are about 1 year old begin to walk without support.

Psychologists have offered various accounts of how independent walking develops. Some maturational theorists believe it depends on the development of the motor cortex (McGraw, 1940). Others view it as a response to cognitive plans or representations that themselves are partly the product of the experience of watching other people walk (Zelazo, 1983). Still others suggest that a motor "program" in the spinal cord

Taking your first steps must be an emotional experience; the joy and excitement on the faces of both the 11-month-old baby and the child's 7-year-old sister are contagious. Perhaps these positive emotions are also contributing to the baby's slightly advanced ability; on average, children walk alone at about 12 months.

guides locomotor development (Forssberg, 1985). None of these explanations, how-ever, have been very successful in accounting for the mysterious disappearance and reappearance of stepping.

A more useful approach may be the dynamic systems view proposed by Thelen (Thelen, 1995; Thelen & Smith, 2006), which holds that walking skills are determined by the interplay of a variety of factors: emotional, perceptual, attentional, motivational, postural, and anatomical. According to Thelen, just as in the case of reaching, all these components must be "ready," and the developmental context (in this case, the weight of the baby's body in proportion to the strength of her legs) must be right before she can walk. On this view, the newborn's stepping response disappears for a 10-month interval before true walking emerges because anatomical factors conspire against the infant as she develops throughout the first year—that is, the baby's size and weight become too much of a load on the emerging motor system, masking the child's step-ping capability (Thelen, 1995).

If this explanation is right, infants between the ages of 2 months and 12 months should be able to step as long as they're given the stability and postural support necessary to stretch each leg forward and back while in an upright position. Thelen (1995; Thelen & Smith, 2006) tried to provide such support for walking by holding 7-month-old infants on a motorized treadmill. Immediately, they performed alternating stepping move-ments that were remarkably similar to more mature walking. Thelen and her colleagues found that 7-month-olds could even adjust their walking speed when the treadmill moved at different rates for each leg (Thelen, Ulrich, & Niles, 1987).

In another study based on a dynamic systems approach, Clark and Phillips (1993) investigated the way infants less than a year old learned to coordinate not only their two legs but the two main parts of each leg—the thigh and the shank—and then com-pared the infants' efforts to walk with adult walking. Weekly, these investigators filmed infants who were able to stand, to observe how walking emerged. They found that stability replaced instability as the infants began to achieve systemic coordination of each leg; that is, the angles at which both thigh and shank moved, the timing of their movements, and the interrelationships of thigh and shank began to resemble adult leg motion. These researchers did not intervene in their young participants' efforts at walking. However, the fact that two of the infants achieved stability in coordinating their leg movements after only three months of walking supports the idea that loco-motor development may be more advanced in the middle of the first year than was thought. Perhaps infants just need the right conditions, whether specific interventions or simple attention, to be able to "strut their stuff"!

Upright walking is only the beginning, of course, and by the time the average child is 7, she acquires the more complex skills of running, galloping, and hopping (Cratty, 1999; Robertson & Halverson, 1988). Running, which appears not long after walk-ing, is well established by the time the child is a year and a half old (Forrester, Phillips, & Clark, 1993), and galloping emerges at about the same time (Whitall & Clark, 1994). Hopping, which requires balance and strength, emerges a little later. In one study, only one child among twenty 2-year-olds could hop, but all 3-year-olds were able to hop (Halverson & Williams, 1985). As with walking, a dynamic systems approach provides the best explanation of this developmental progression: These skills depend on improvements in balance and coordination and on the opportunity for prac-tice (Adolph & Berger, 2006; Bertenthal & Clifton, 1998; Diedrich & Warren, 1995).

How Locomotion May Affect Other Aspects of Development

One important result of locomotor development is the growing degree of indepen-dence it provides. Babies who can crawl or walk can explore their environments more fully and initiate more contact with other people. This newfound independence, in turn, changes the way others respond to the child. No longer can parents place the baby on a blanket in the middle of the floor, expecting that he will be there when they turn around. The baby can now move at will throughout his home, leaving what seems to the pursuing parents like a trail of mayhem—torn magazines, overturned coffee cups, the luscious cherries that filled a favorite bowl squashed and mixed with pottery shards on the living room carpet. Not surprisingly, parents are likely to interrupt the infant's activities by relocating the child, distracting him, prohibiting actions with the ubiquitous "No, no!" or making objects or entire areas inaccessible (Green, Gustafson, & West, 1980). Clearly, not only do parents influence their children; children influence the attitudes and actions of their parents as well.

The onset of locomotion also affects the way babies understand their perceptual world (Adolph & Berger, 2006; Adolph, Vereijken, & Denny, 1998; Schmuckler & Tsang-Tong, 2000). Babies begin to develop a fear of heights only after they begin crawling (Campos & Bertenthal, 1989; Bertenthal et al., 1994), perhaps partly because at this stage they are better able to solve spatial problems. In one study, researchers compared precrawling infants, belly-crawling infants, and babies who crawled proficiently on hands and knees for their ability to solve a hidden-toy problem. All the babies watched while a toy was hidden in one of two containers. Then the researchers rotated each infant 180 degrees and left him or her to find the toy. Good crawlers were more likely to solve the problem than noncrawlers or belly crawlers, which suggests that locomotion helps infants deal better with changes in spatial orientation. Motor development and perception should be viewed as interdependent parts of a child's "action system," or his system of orienting and moving in his environment.

Another illustration of the link between perception and action is provided by a study of the impact of self-produced locomotion on infants' use of visual perceptual information to control their posture (Bertenthal & Bai, 1989). The investigators either moved the room in which their infant participants were situated or moved the walls of the room in such a way that the infants had to make postural adjustments to stay upright. Interestingly, only infants who either were at the crawling stage or had experienced self-produced locomotion in a walker were able to use the perceptual feedback from the distortions of the moving room to adjust their posture by moving their feet and shifting their weight. Prelocomotor infants of the same age were unable to use this critical visual feedback to help maintain their posture. Again, self-produced locomotion appears to induce shifts in other developing systems—in this case the visual perception system (Bertenthal & Clifton, 1998; Campos & Bertenthal, 1989). In children at risk because of some developmental disability, however, the action system may be in jeopardy; see Box 5.1.

Thus, as we see so often in development, changes in one domain have important implications for changes in another. Research has also suggested that early walking may be related both to a greater amount of positive interaction and to more "testing of the wills" between mother and child (Biringen, Emde, Campos, & Appelbaum, 1995); the latter refers to mothers' efforts to stop a particular act by her child. What might be the reason for these correlations? The researchers speculate that either the early walkers may have been strongly predisposed toward walking and at the same time have had more difficult child-parent relationships or that these young hikers may have been trying to achieve independence *because* they confronted such difficult and challenging relationships. Gender turned out to be a variable in this research as well, for the researchers found that mothers tended to perceive their male infants more positively but also, interestingly, to have more confrontations with them. Perhaps future studies will shed some light on the reasons for—and the stability of—this finding.

The Role of Experience and Culture

Although overall limits to motor development may well be set by physical maturation, within those limits the timing of the onset of various skills may be affected by

Box 5.1

Risk and Resilience

BLIND INFANTS STRUGGLE TO "SEE"

Being unable to see puts an infant at risk for many difficulties. As Figure 5-9 shows, blindness retards motor development considerably, especially the baby's first efforts to raise his body with his arms and his attempts to stand up by holding on to furniture, to walk alone, and to reach for objects (Adelson & Fraiberg, 1974). This limited mobility can have serious consequences: "It lessens [the blind infant's] ability to explore independently, to discover by himself the objective rules that govern things and events in the external world" (Fraiberg, 1977, p. 270). As we will see, studying the motor development of blind infants not only helps researchers devise ways to help these at-risk children but gives us more information about the interdependence among various sensory and motor systems.

No matter how resilient a blind infant may be, he or she clearly needs help in learning about and functioning in the physical and social environment. On the assumption that blind infants need assistance in learning to associate sound with the information they get from touch, Fraiberg (1977) developed a program that maximizes babies' opportunities to make sound a guide for touch. Parents of blind infants were encouraged to talk to their babies both as they were physically approaching them and during routine activities such as feeding and dressing. Fraiberg's program also called for parents to provide their infants with toys that make sounds and to make sure that these toys were within their infants' easy reach so as to encourage both coordinated two-hand activity and the exploration of objects that make sounds. With the help of these interventions, infants learn to use a combination of sound and touch as a way of identifying people and things. And it does make a difference. In comparison to blind children who do not receive such extra stimulation, stimulated blind babies are less delayed in standing and walking, even though they are still behind sighted infants in motor development.

Technology is also playing a role in building blind infants' motor capabilities. In the 1980s, experimenters in Scotland suggested that an electronic device that produces echoes from nearby objects might help blind babies to "see." The blind infant might learn to use this feedback to judge her distance from an object and even perhaps to assess the object's size and texture. Bower (1979, 1989) had blind infants wear an echo-producing device for several months and found that by using the echo feedback, the babies could judge their distance from objects and even sometimes an object's size and texture. The infants' reaching ability was improved, and they were able to do things more typical of sighted infants.

Because much research in this area has focused on devices that must be carried and manipulated by the user, the so-called electronic travel aids (ETAs) that have been developed are designed for blind adults. Adults have found ETAs, which use laser or sound-wave technologies, to be particularly useful in enabling them to avoid contact with other pedestrians and to detect the presence of nearby objects (Blasch, Long, & Griffin-Shirley, 1989). Two of the newer sensor devices, which provide information to the user in synthesized speech, require that places frequented by the public, such as hotels and public buildings, install special transmitters whose signals can be picked up by the device (Bentzen & Mitchell, 1995). Thus, for example, a transmitter in a hotel lobby might, when activated by a scanning sensor, inform the person that "Elevators are

societal and other factors (Bradley et al., 2001). Studying children in a number of European cities, researchers found fairly wide variations in the age at which walking begins: Parisian children, for example, walk earlier than their peers in London or Stockholm (Hindley, Filliozat, Klackenberg, Nicolet-Neister, & Sand, 1966). These differences suggest that the onset of walking may be influenced by cultural factors of some sort, perhaps including differences in nutrition and experience as well as differences in biological makeup.

Two related factors that may stimulate children's early motor development are physically handling infants and giving them exercise in various motor skills. As you can see

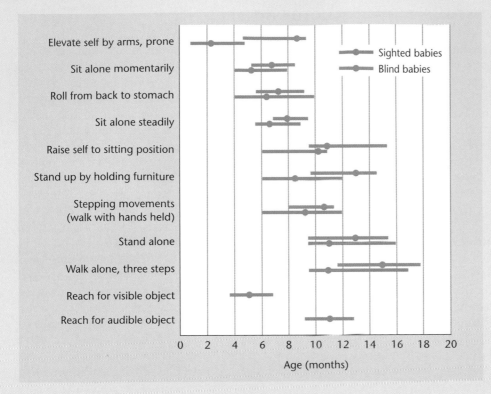

Figure 5-9

Motor development in blind and sighted babies

Clearly, being sighted helps an infant to develop motorically, but in some movements, such as rolling over and sitting up, blind babies are not very far behind sighted infants. The squares and circles indicate the average ages at which particular activities emerge in blind and sighted babies; the extent of each line indicates the age range within which babies may begin specific activities.

Sources: Adelson & Fraiberg, 1974; Bower, 1979.

to your right." For the preverbal child perhaps scaled-down versions of ETAs might be developed, but it's not beyond imagining that for the child who has acquired good language skills the newer "talking sign" devices might be adapted to home and school use.

One interesting possibility under investigation is a device composed of a camera and a computer contained in eyeglass frames and hooked up to a receiver implanted within the brain that may allow a blind person to "see" actual letters in the form of *phosphenes,* or the colored displays that we all see with our eyes shut (Stone, 1990). Among the drawbacks to this approach is that, at least for now, the device can display only one letter at a time, making "reading" for the blind person a very tedious process and, it would seem, hardly preferable to auditory input. There are no miracles in the offing, but if research continues, and if blind youngsters and adults can maintain their resilience as they try newly available techniques, perhaps the difficulties they confront may be lessened in time.

from Box 5.2, although such practices vary among cultures, mothers in developing societies tend to encourage their children's motor development. According to Hopkins (1991), less-advanced societies may place more pressure on parents to promote children's physical development simply to ensure their survival. It's possible that families in such societies put special value on physical strength because their local economies are characterized by more jobs that call for motor skills. But as Box 5.2 suggests, other factors such as climate and religious and spiritual beliefs also influence infant-rearing styles.

Research in the United States has shown that practice in motor behavior can hasten walking and other skills. Figure 5-10 shows the results of an early study of the role of

Perspectives on Diversity

HOW INFANT-REARING CUSTOMS CAN ALTER MOTOR PATTERNS

Cross-cultural studies have provided us with some insights into how specific ways of caring for newborns and infants can alter motor patterns. In general, it seems that when parents or other caretakers give babies special physical attention, including manipulation, massage, exercise, and specific practice of skills, the infants are likely to achieve certain motor milestones somewhat earlier than children not given such care and opportunities. As the text suggests, whether such advanced skills are useful to children may depend on the nature of the society in which they live.

In Zambia, a mother carries her new baby with her everywhere in a sling on her back. When the child is able to sit, the mother leaves her sitting alone for considerable periods of time, giving her plenty of opportunity to practice motor skills. Zambian babies, like many African and West Indian infants, show early development of motor skills (Goldberg, 1966; Hopkins & Westra, 1988). A little north of Zambia, in Kenya, Gusii infants are conditioned from birth to vigorous movement; Keefer and her colleagues have observed mothers and other adults handle newborns "with much more vigor than is tolerated with American infants" (Keefer et al., 1991, p. 49). Apparently, such things as being careful not to let a baby's head drop are unknown among the Gusii, who commonly toss their infants into the air after a bath not only to shake off excess water but to help the baby to get over her fright at such treatment! According to these researchers, Gusii children are healthy, robust, and responsive, and, when older, they are among the hardest-working children in the world. They are loved and well cared for, and as adults they maintain strong attachments to their mothers.

Studying mothers and babies in Jamaica, British West Indies, and comparing them with English mothers and children, Hopkins and Westra (1990) found that Jamaican mothers expect their infants to sit and walk alone two or three months earlier than English mothers expect their babies to achieve these skills. Moreover, soon after their babies are born, Jamaican mothers practice what is called "formal handling," in which they regularly massage their infants and stretch their arms and legs. Among Jamaican immigrants in England, mothers also use formal handling, and Hopkins (1991) found that, once again, children who were handled tended to be more motorically advanced than those who were not. When native Jamaican infants are 2 or 3 months old their mothers begin to give them practice in stepping. Jamaican mothers don't encourage crawling, which they think dangerous and apelike, and instead encourage sitting and then walking, skills they consider crucial to becoming a successful adult (Hopkins & Westra, 1990).

Among the Zinacantecos of Mexico, newborns are carried most of the time, tightly swaddled, and even have their faces covered for the first three months of life. One reason for this practice is climatic: These Mayan peoples live in the highlands of the state of Chiapas, where the extreme cold could endanger newborns' lives (Greenfield & Childs, 1991). But there may be other cultural and even economic reasons. For

specific practice in fostering the onset of walking and other motor skills. Zelazo and colleagues (1972) asked mothers of newborns to give their infants practice in the stepping reflex a few minutes a day. Not only did these 2- to 8-week-old babies make more walking responses, but they walked independently at an earlier age than a control group of babies who were given no practice. Even infants who engaged in passive exercise like that provided by the Jamaican mothers discussed in Box 5.2 walked later than the "practiced" infants or than infants who received no exercise at all. In a later study these investigators found that practice in sitting yielded similar results: Babies who were given practice in sitting for three minutes a day were able to sit upright longer than infants in a no-practice control group (Zelazo, Zelazo, Cohen, & Zelazo, 1988). More recently, Adolph, Vereijken, and Shrout (2003) showed that everyday experience plays a major role in both the onset of walking and in improvements in walking ability. Not surprisingly, infants with more

example, Zinacantecos believe that the art of hand-weaving, which not only is traditional in their culture but has become an income-producing activity, must be practiced with calm, quiet, and close attention. Green-field and Childs (1991) suggest that the early restraint of motor activity may promote the ability to master this kind of endeavor. These researchers, like Brazelton (1972), found that Zinacanteco infants had less-advanced motor skills than babies in the United States but also that the Mexican babies were more alert, observing their surroundings attentively for longer periods than the U.S. infants and not crying or flailing about, "demanding that someone react to them" (Greenfield & Childs, 1991, p. 147).

Swaddling seems to have another purpose for the people who live in fishing towns near Udupi in Karnataka State in southwestern India. Studying families in the coastal lowland village of Malpi, Landers (1989) concluded that swaddling may enable the child to habituate to, and shut out, disturbing sounds, movements, or other threatening phenomena. In Malpi babies, however, swaddling and being carried daily did not seem to interfere with motor activity, probably in large part because both mothers and grandmothers typically handled newborns with abrupt and vigorous movements and gave them daily baths that included strong massage. Although mothers did not encourage their infants to explore and master their worlds independently, the fact that in their first three months these babies grew 50 percent more than an American sample and performed better on the Bayley Scales of Infant Development suggests the involvement of some other influence. In fact, the Hindu view of the child

as a gift of God who should be protected, indulged, and showered with affection may be at work here. Indian mothers cuddle and cater to their babies, responding immediately to the least sign of distress and feeding them on demand, at the breast, sometimes until they are 2 or 3 years old. According to Landers (1989), this immediate response may encourage infants to interact vigorously with their environment, confident that they will succeed in eliciting feedback.

Finally, situational variables that parents cannot control may affect children's motor development. Consider the situation of families living, in the 1990s, in then-contemporary apartment buildings in Beijing. The rooms in some of these relatively low-income apartments were small and cramped, and floors were rarely carpeted. Campos et al. (2000) found that parents tended to put their infants on soft featherbeds and pillows to prevent them from hurting themselves on hard floors. Furthermore, their babies' crawling was restricted by the lack of room to roam. The researchers observe that because of the soft cushioning some infants failed to develop adequate upper girdle and abdominal strength as well as strength in other muscle groups that are critical to crawling behavior. As a result, crawling itself was delayed in these infants. As wealth increases in China's cities, the investigators suggest, families are likely to be able to afford more spacious and carpeted living quarters than they could a decade ago. In this event Campos and colleagues' findings will provide a good example of cohort effects: Infant development in future generations may be facilitated by changes in environmental variables made possible by an improved and strengthening economy.

walking experience were the most skilled walkers. More surprising is the amount of practice infants do. Diary records indicate that walking infants practice keeping balance in upright stance and locomotion for more than six hours a day. According to Adolph and colleagues (2003), "They [the infants the experimenters observed] average between 500 and 1,500 walking steps per hour so that by the end of each day, they may have taken 9,000 walking steps and traveled the length of 29 football fields!" (p. 494)

But practice apparently does not make perfect. For one thing, the effects of practice are highly specific. Practice in stepping does not affect sitting, and practice in sitting upright does not affect stepping. And the effect of practice on the emergence of motor skills is not enormous; no stepping-trained baby has walked at 3 or 4 months of age (Zelazo et al., 1988). Thus, at least in developed societies, attempting to speed up a child's motor development by giving her specific practice does not actually accelerate

Figure 5-10

Can practice really make perfect?
Newborns who engaged in active exercise of the walking reflex showed a clear increase in this response over babies who took part in passive exercise or no exercise at all. The practiced babies also walked earlier than the other children in this experiment.

Source: Adapted from Zelazo, Zelazo, & Kolb, 1972.

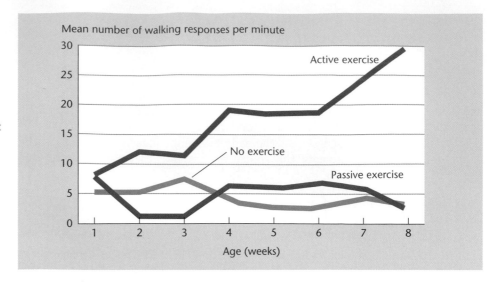

development. Only longitudinal studies could tell us whether such practice might have any long-term effect on a child's general physical and psychological well-being.

PHYSICAL GROWTH

One of the most actively investigated areas of child development, physical growth, as we noted in Chapter 3, is guided by two classic principles: First, the human infant is characterized by *cephalocaudal development*—that is, growth in infancy occurs from the head downward. Thus the brain and neck develop earlier than the legs and trunk. Second, growth also follows a *proximal-distal pattern*. In other words, development occurs from the center outward; for example, the internal organs develop earlier than the arms and hands.

Height and weight are the two principal measures of overall growth, and both dimensions are of great interest and concern to many, particularly people in the United States. Although no one has ever shown that tall people are brighter, more creative, or superior in any nonphysical way to shorter people, life insurance statistics have demonstrated a positive correlation between height and professional accomplishment! In addition, according to Krogman (1972), during the Great Depression of the 1930s, shorter men were first to be laid off of their jobs, and in U.S. presidential elections, victory has gone to the taller candidate 15 times. (For the record, Abraham Lincoln, at 6 feet, 5 inches, was America's tallest president, and Lyndon Johnson, at 6 feet, 3 inches, ran a close second.) According to one estimate (Bilger, 2004), over a three-year period, the average six-foot business executive earns $166,000 more than a 5-foot peer; that's an average of eight hundred dollars more per week per year! Although taller isn't necessarily better, for some reason Americans tend to think it is, and continue to hope that their children will not be too short.

The regular appearance of books describing innovative diets and frequent openings of new Weight Watchers clubs testify to the concern of adult Americans about weight and weight gain. Infant Americans, however, are encouraged to gain weight; parents and other relatives and friends greet each new pound with delight. According to Lipsitt and Werner (1981), babies grow faster within their first half year of life than ever again. They nearly double their weight in the first three months and triple their weight by the end of the first year. From then on, infants' growth rate slows down, but babies still increase their weight by five or six times by 3 years of age. It is just as well that the rate of weight gain slows in adulthood or we would all be obese!

In this section we discuss the various factors that influence the infant's and child's growth in both height and weight, beginning with possible genetic factors and turning next to such environmental factors as nutrition, hygiene and sanitation, and poverty. We then look at the interesting evidence that people—at least in more developed countries—have been growing taller. Our final discussion in this section focuses on the growing problems of obesity and eating disturbance in the United States as well as on methods of preventing and treating these disorders.

Do Genes Affect Height and Weight?

Although both height and weight can be influenced by environmental factors, research suggests that genetic factors strongly influence these physical characteristics (Tanner, 1990). Data from the Colorado Adoption Project, a longitudinal study that compares several hundred adoptive and biological parents, and adopted and natural children, indicate that genetic factors may determine as much as two-thirds of the variance in these characteristics (Cardon, 1994). Using a measure called the body mass index (BMI), a measure of body fat, this study has found that the tendency to be overweight or obese is strongly influenced by genetic factors, although this pattern does not stabilize until a child is somewhere between ages $5\frac{1}{2}$ and $6\frac{1}{2}$. Although people often try to predict a child's future height and weight from his birthweight, this is a risky venture. Body mass may not stabilize for a few years, and factors such as a mother's small size may mask a baby's potential for growth. For example, a fetus may grow more slowly during the last few weeks to make childbirth easier for the woman with a small frame. (Some small women do produce future linebackers, however!) On the other hand, we can predict how tall a child will be in adulthood if we know the child's gender, his or her height at the age of 9, and his or her mother's and father's heights (Roche, 1979). Presumably this is because environmental factors, which we discuss shortly, have had their maximal influence by that time.

Gender has a clear effect on height and weight, as you can see from Figure 5-11. Girls tend to be a bit taller than boys from the age of 2 until about the age of 9, when boys catch up. At about $10\frac{1}{2}$ girls experience a growth spurt, shooting well up above boys of their own age. At about 14, however, girls' height seems nearly to plateau, whereas boys continue to grow taller until they are about 18. The pattern for weight

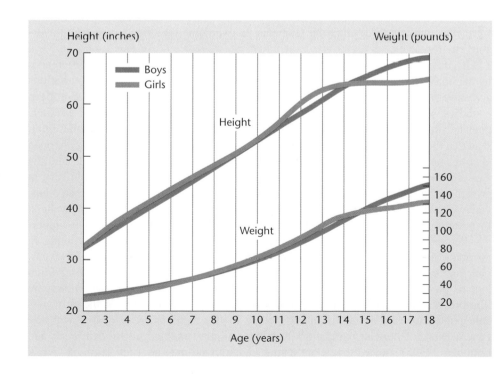

Figure 5-11

Male and female growth in height and weight
As they approach puberty, girls tend to gain height and, to a lesser degree, weight, faster than boys, but by the age of 14 or 15, boys surpass girls on both dimensions.

Source: National Center for Health Statistics, 1976.

Being taller than their dance partners is a common experience for girls between the ages of about 11 and 14, for boys their ages are typically 2 to 3 inches shorter than they are. These preteens don't seem to mind, though.

is not greatly dissimilar, although girls tend to weigh less than boys in the early years and then to exceed them in weight until about 14, when their weight gain slows down while boys' gain continues to accelerate (Tanner, 1990).

It's important to note that there are also wide individual differences in maturation rates. Because these differences become particularly obvious at adolescence, it is often assumed that they begin in adolescence. In fact, however, these differences are present at all ages, so that early maturers are always ahead of late-maturing peers. Tanner (1978, 1990), an early pioneer in the study of physical growth, coined the term *tempo of growth* to describe this variability in the timing of changes in infants' and children's growth. As Tanner observed, growth is like a musical score: "Some children play out their growth andante, others allegro, a few lentissimo. It seems that heredity plays a large part in setting the metronome, but we do not know the physiological mechanism" (Tanner, 1978, p. 78).

The Influence of Environmental Factors

Growth is determined not only by genetic factors but also by such environmental influences as nutrition, physical and psychological disorders, and climate (Tanner, 1990). When environmental conditions are favorable, individual growth curves tend to be very similar, but in the presence of one or more unfavorable conditions, such as inadequate nutrition, growth rates are often seriously depressed (Pollitt, 1994). Bradley and colleagues (1994) found that among a group of children living in poverty, those few (only about 10%) whose care was more responsive, accepting, stimulating, and organized and who lived in safer, less crowded homes were functioning in the normal range for growth and other important parameters such as cognitive and social skills. Those children with fewer than three of these protective aspects of caretaking were very unlikely to develop the resilience to overcome the effects of their unfavorable environments.

Of considerable interest are the variations in growth rates attributed to differences in nationality, ethnicity, and socioeconomic class. There are fairly wide variations across regional areas; for example, peoples in northwestern and western European countries, such as Scandinavia, are taller than southern Europeans, such as the Mediterranean cultures. Within the continent of Africa and among the countries of Central America there are also substantial variations in height and weight; for example, African Nicotics become 7 feet tall, whereas the Pygmies of Zaire, Rwanda, Burundi, and the western coastal areas are on average only about 4 feet tall. Moreover, people vary in growth within the same country; for example, in Brazil and India people in urban areas, where nutrition and the standard of living is higher, tend to be taller than rural dwellers. In addition, researchers have revealed that in the United States, children in upper-middle-class families are both taller and heavier than children of families living in poverty (Martorell, 1984). Among a number of Latino American groups—for example, Puerto Ricans and Mexicans—as many as 39 percent of families with children live in poverty (Baca Zinn & Wells, 2000). This may account for the finding by Martorell and his colleagues (1994) that, aside from gender, poverty was the only variable related to shorter stature among people in these groups as compared with the general North American population. Reporting similar findings in Sweden, Peck and Lundberg (1995) showed that short stature in adulthood may be a reflection of several adverse childhood conditions, including poverty—which subsumed poor nutrition and substandard housing—and psychological stress within the family.

NUTRITION   Good nutrition is critical for proper development throughout development, from infancy to adolescence. In this section we examine the role of nutrition in normal growth as well as under adverse circumstances such as famine, which may make good nutrition impossible. We also explore effects on normal development of both overeating and eating too little.

Bottle- versus Breast-Feeding   We begin in infancy, where one of the first challenges parents face is the choice to feed their new baby breast milk or bottled formula. Although over the last century ideas about the relative virtues of each fluctuated—in some decades, experts promoted the bottle, and in other periods breast-feeding was the rage—we know today that breast-feeding is clearly preferable for babies' healthy development (Blum, 2000).

What are the advantages of this approach to infant nutrition? As Table 5-2 outlines, a host of benefits for both infants and their mothers are associated with the

Table 5-2   Advantages of breast-feeding for infants and mothers

Infants	
Short-Term Benefits of Breast-Feeding	**Long-Term Benefits of Breast-Feeding**
Breast milk contains nutritionally balanced ingredients, including proteins, cholesterol, and lactose that together support development of the brain and nervous system	Breast-fed children have slightly higher IQs than bottle-fed children.
Supports appropriate weight gain	Breast-fed children demonstrate better reading comprehension.
Strengthens infant's immune system and reduces risk of diarrhea and infectious diseases	Breast-fed children are less likely to have childhood cancer, allergies, or diabetes.
Promotes more efficient absorption of iron, lessening likelihood of iron deficiencies	Breast-fed children have denser bones in preadolescence.
Reduces likelihood of SIDS	
Lessens likelihood of allergies	
Builds denser bones	
Makes shift to solid food easier	
Mothers	
Breast-Feeding	
Builds closeness to her baby	
Promotes faster weight loss after baby's birth	
Delays ovulation (but is not a reliable form of birth control)	
Is convenient	

Sources: Blum, 2000; Dewey, 2001; Fredrickson, 1993; Hoppu, Kalliomoki, Laiho, & Isolauri, 2001; Harwood & Fergusson, 1998; Jones, Riley, & Dwyer, 2000; Lifshitz, Finch, & Lifshitz, 1991; Newman, 1995.

choice to breast-feed. These include protection against infectious disease, better development of the brain and nervous system, and a reduction in the likelihood of SIDS (see also Chapter 4). For mothers, this method of feeding is more convenient (no refrigeration or warming is required). It helps women lose the weight gained during pregnancy and delays ovulation. And it promotes closeness between mother and baby. Breast-feeding is particularly important for mother and child in developing countries. Relative to the income of most families in these countries, formula is expensive; because of this women often dilute formula, thus extending the supply but endangering the health of their babies. The lack of clean water often leads to infected formula and increased rates of illness. According to UNICEF (United Nations Children's Fund), bottle-fed babies in developing countries are fourteen times more likely than breast-fed babies to die from diarrhea and four times more likely to succumb to respiratory ailments.

> If all babies were fed only breast milk for the first six months of life, the lives of an estimated 1.5 million infants would be saved every year, and the health and development of millions of others would be greatly improved. (UNICEF, 2004)

Many mothers in poor countries choose bottle-feeding and formula because they think it is best for their babies, but too often with disastrous results.

Who breast-feeds in Western countries? In the United States, about 60 percent of mothers breast-feed for several months, but after the baby reaches 6 months of age and begins eating some solid foods, this percentage drops sharply. Women over 25 who are of higher socioeconomic status and better educated are more likely to breast-feed. But even among this group, returning to employment outside the home reduces breast-feeding. Some mothers specifically choose, from the beginning, not to breast-feed, and others are forced to make this decision by the presence of medical conditions, such as AIDS or tuberculosis, or because they are being treated for illness with medications. In spite of concerns that infants will suffer if not breast-fed, babies who receive appropriate formula-based bottle nutrition develop normally, especially in Western countries where bottle-feeding is safe. But breast-feeding is still preferable and, as we have suggested, may give the infant some advantages.

Nutrition and Physical Growth   Research in a number of countries has revealed that nutrition plays a controlling role in physical growth. Wartime restrictions on food consumption on the home front in order to provide adequate nutrition for fighting forces have proved a useful barometer of the changes caused by reduced nutrition. In Europe, for example, during World Wars I and II, a general retardation in growth reflected the reductions in nutritional intake caused by wartime restrictions. In contrast, during the period between these two major wars, from 1920 to 1940, there was a general increase in growth (Tanner, 1990). Interestingly, this increase was seen more in weight than in height and in boys more than in girls. Wartime research also revealed that nutritional factors can affect the age at which children enter puberty; during World War II, girls in occupied France did not achieve menarche (the onset of menstruation) on average until they were 16 years old, which is approximately three years later than the prewar norm (Howe & Schiller, 1952). Probably stress associated with wartime contributed to these outcomes as well.

Studies of people during times of peace have also highlighted the role of nutrition in growth. In a study in Bogota, Colombia, Super and his colleagues (Super, Herrera, & Mora, 1990) demonstrated that the provision of food supplements for entire families from midpregnancy until a child was 3 years old effectively prevented severe growth retardation in children at risk for malnutrition. Moreover, the children who received the food supplements remained taller and heavier than control children at 6 years of age, three years after the intervention ceased. Equally impressive are the results of a study by Ahmed and colleagues (1993) in rural Bangladesh which found that changing traditional unhygienic practices by means of educational and supportive interventions improved children's health, their growth rates, and their nutrition. By developing safer methods of food preparation and waste disposal and thus lessening the possibility of food contamination, local people were able to reduce the incidence of diarrhea, which interferes with the absorption of needed minerals and vitamins and depletes the body of these essential substances.

Finally, a survey study of research on the effects of poverty on child development in both the United States and other nations highlighted the importance of providing nutritional supplements and controlling disease among disadvantaged children (Pollitt, 1994). **Iron-deficiency anemia,** a condition in which insufficient iron in the diet causes listlessness and may retard children's physical and intellectual development, is common among poor minority children and children in low-income countries. Supplemental feeding can improve these children's rate of growth and cognitive performance (Pollitt, 1994; Watkins & Pollitt, 1997). For example, a group of studies in Colombia, Guatemala, Jamaica, Taiwan, Indonesia, and the Harlem area in New York City showed that among children at risk, supplemental feeding enhanced both motor and mental development during the first two years of life. Researchers found that higher scores on the Bayley Scales of Infant Development (discussed in Chapter 10) and other scales documented improved motor performance during the children's first year.

iron-deficiency anemia A disorder in which inadequate amounts of iron in the diet cause listlessness and may retard a child's physical and intellectual development.

CATCH-UP GROWTH   In the face of the overwhelming need of millions of children living in poverty around the world, we need to ask not only what we can do to prevent malnutrition and inadequate growth but what, if anything, we can do to help those who are older catch up to their more fortunate peers. As we saw in Chapter 3, humans have a strong tendency to regain a normal course of development after an early setback, such as those prenatal deficiencies may cause. A similar corrective principle, referred to as **catch-up growth,** operates after birth: Children who have suffered early environmental injury or deprivation are eventually able to catch up to normal physical growth. Tanner (1970) noted that children's growth trajectories are governed both by genetics and by the energy they absorb from the natural environment: "Deflect the child from its growth trajectory by acute malnutrition or illness, and a restoring force develops so that as soon as the missing food is supplied or the illness terminated the child catches up toward its original curve" (p. 125).

catch-up growth The tendency for human beings to regain a normal course of physical growth after injury or deprivation.

The degree of catch-up growth a child can achieve will depend on a variety of factors, including the duration, severity, and timing of the original deprivation and the nature of the subsequent treatment or therapy. In a study of the effects of intervention following severe malnutrition, Graham (1966) found that malnourished infants who had a 5 percent deficit in height were able to catch up, but those with a 15 percent deficit remained significantly shorter, benefiting only somewhat from nutritional supplements. And catch-up growth following severe malnutrition may be limited to only some aspects of growth. In a 20-year longitudinal study of severely starved children, a program of nutritional intervention failed to enable full development in head circumference (and presumably brain development) and produced only some catch-up in height (Stoch et al., 1982). This impact of malnutrition on brain development may, in part, account for the intellectual and attentional deficits malnourished children show (Sigman, 1995; Shonkoff & Phillips, 2000).

Timing is also critical in determining the degree of catch-up growth. For example, pathology and undernutrition early in life can have serious consequences, and children starved in utero through some sort of placental imperfection usually show only partial catch-up (Pollitt, Gorman, & Metallinos-Katsaras, 1992; Tanner, 1990). In general, the earlier and more prolonged the malnutrition, the more difficult it is for interventions to be fully effective in achieving normal growth. A supportive, stimulating, and safe family environment may play a role in catch-up growth as well (Bradley et al., 2001; Valenzuela, 1997).

Figure 5-12

Height gains across the centuries and millennia
By 1997, the average American had gained 2.5 to 3 inches in height since the early eighteenth century, and expectations are that both men and women will double this gain by 2050. By that time we'll have become a foot and a half taller than our prehistoric ancestors!

Source: Richard Steckel, Ohio State University, 1997.

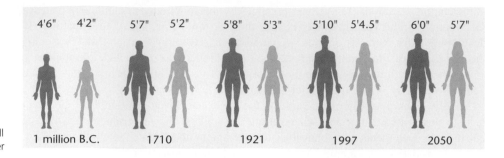

| 4'6" | 4'2" | 5'7" | 5'2" | 5'8" | 5'3" | 5'10" | 5'4.5" | 6'0" | 5'7" |

| 1 million B.C. | 1710 | 1921 | 1997 | 2050 |

secular trend A shift in the normative pattern of a characteristic, such as height, that occurs over a historical time period, such as a decade or century.

People Are Growing Taller

According to British scientists who have measured bones exhumed from gravesites, between the eleventh and fourteenth centuries the average Englishman was about 5 feet, 6 inches tall, whereas today the average adult British male is 5 feet, 9 inches tall. This kind of change is often called a **secular trend**—a shift that occurs in the normative pattern of a particular characteristic, such as height or weight, over some historical time period, such as a decade or a century (Figure 5-12). Should we keep updating our norms of height on the basis of this sort of gain—about a half inch every hundred years? Yes, probably, but note also that the same increases in height may not occur at every level of society. For example, if we look at the U.S. population from the point of view of socioeconomic status, we find that—at least in the country's current social, nutritional, and medical environment—most people in the upper 75 percent have probably reached their maximum growth potential (Hamill, Drizd, Johnson, Reed, & Roche, 1976). People in other segments of society do continue to make gains, and in some other countries change is following yet other patterns. In the Netherlands, for instance, people are continuing to gain in height and weight regardless of socioeconomic level; the average Dutch male is now 6 feet, 1 inch and Dutch women now average 5 feet, 8 inches in height (Bilger, 2004). In Japan, England, and Norway increase in stature has apparently come to a halt (Roche, 1979; Tanner, 1990).

Americans are not only growing taller but, as a consequence of their added height, Americans' feet are growing longer too, gaining about a third of an inch in each generation! The average college student's grandfather probably wore a size 7 shoe, whereas today the average American male wears between size 9 and 10. And not only are Americans and their feet increasing in size; Americans are achieving these growth increases at earlier ages than in the past. A hundred years ago, people didn't attain adult height until the early or midtwenties, but today many 16- or 17-year-olds are often as tall as, or taller than, their parents.

There are several possible reasons for these historical trends toward greater height and weight. First, health and nutrition have been improved in many countries of the world. Growth-retarding illnesses have come under control, particularly those that strike in the first five years of life, such as *marasmus* (caused by insufficient protein and calories) or *kwashiorkor* (caused by insufficient protein). Children with marasmus are frail, wrinkled, and cease to grow. Children with kwashiorkor are familiar from news reports: These are the children with bloated stomachs, skin lesions, and thinning hair. In many areas nutritional intake has been improved in terms of both quantity of food consumed and balance among the essential food groups (Tanner, 1990). Medical care and personal health practices have also improved; as we have seen, even in impoverished areas such as rural Bangladesh, efforts have been under way to introduce good hygiene and sanitary practices. Second, socioeconomic conditions have generally improved; child labor is less common, and living conditions such as housing and sanitation have improved. Third, the influence of genetic factors has

Happiness floods the faces of this Saudi Arabian couple as they pose with their son after his graduation ceremonies at a Texas college. Towering over his parents, the graduate demonstrates that the newer generation of young people are indeed taller than their parents.

been affected by such things as intermarriage among people of different racial and ethnic backgrounds, which produces increases in height and weight in the offspring of such unions.

Because these trends are largely environmentally determined, if we should experience major changes in the environment brought about, for example, by spectacular medical discoveries, natural disasters like famine, or an increase or decrease in environmental pollution levels, the average height of the population could shift again. Clearly, depending on what direction such changes might take, people could keep growing taller or could lose stature.

Are We Growing Heavier? Obesity and Eating Disorders

Both children and adults in the United States are growing heavier. **Obesity,** the condition in which a person's weight is 30 percent or more over average weight for his or her height and frame, has been on the rise since the early 1960s (Raynor & Epstein, 2001; and see Figure 5-13). This rise has occurred despite the fact that U.S. children are born into a society that reveres youthful, healthy good looks. Although Americans' preference for tall, slender people over short, overweight people may seem narcissistic, the emphasis on losing weight and keeping fit is based partly on realistic concerns about physical health and the avoidance of illness. Unfortunately, the desire to be attractive and physically fit leads many to a near obsession with weight-reduction clubs, magazines about weight and diet, and fad diets, and it is young girls who are most likely to suffer from this preoccupation with weight. In a recent study of 5- to 8-year-old Australian children, nearly 60 percent of the girls wanted a thinner figure, whereas 35 percent of the boys wanted to be thinner. Girls hoped to be thinner as teenagers as well (Lowes & Tiggerman, 2003). Indeed, by midadolescence perhaps 70 to 80 percent of American girls have been on at least one diet (Attie & Brooks-Gunn, 1989; Cowley, 2001). Why? Perhaps because their models have been getting thinner; participants in the Miss America Pageant weigh much less than they did 20 years earlier (Silverstein, Petersen, & Perdue, 1986). In this section we look at this continuing American struggle to be thin and consider the problems of obesity and of eating disorders such as anorexia and bulimia.

obesity A condition in which a person's weight is 30 percent or more in excess of the average weight for his or her height and frame.

Figure 5-13

Overweight (obese) children and adolescents, 1963–2000
Over close to 40 years, obesity (being 30 percent or more over average weight) roughly tripled among both teens and preteens.

Source: National Center for Health Statistics, 2002.

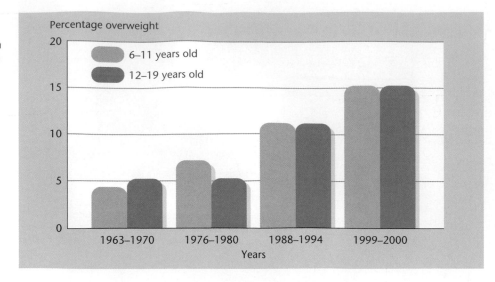

WHY DO CHILDREN GAIN TOO MUCH WEIGHT? In North America, nearly 25 percent of children are obese (Cowley, 2001). And although preadolescents and adolescents have the highest rates of obesity, about 5 to 10 percent of preschoolers are obese (Raynor & Epstein, 2001). One study found that among adults this trend toward obesity was most evident in people of Latino and Native American background, whereas in younger groups, prepubescent African American girls were heaviest. Wolf and colleagues (1993) found that among a sample of elementary and high school girls, about half of whom were between the ages of 11 and 14, African Americans tended to be the heaviest; Asian Americans were the least likely to be overweight. Preschool-aged African American children show less tendency toward overweight; this may be partly because African American women tend to bear children at relatively young ages and thus to have smaller babies and to give their children a slower start at weight gain (Kumanyika, 1993).

Genetic factors seem to play a crucial role in obesity. For example, in a longitudinal study Cardon (1994) found considerable stability in body mass index (a measure of a person's weight in relation to her height; abbreviated as BMI). Although environmental factors contributed to weight gains at certain ages, overall stability in BMI was explained by genetic mediation. Adoptive and twin studies have also shown a primary genetic effect. Stunkard and colleagues (Stunkard et al., 1986b), for instance, found a strong relationship between the weight of adopted children and their biological parents' weights but no relationship between adoptees and their adoptive parents' weights. Similarly, identical twins are twice as likely to resemble each other in weight as are fraternal twins (Stunkard, Foch, & Hrubeck, 1986a). And twins reared apart who did not share a common environment have still shown marked similarity in weight (Bouchard, 1994).

Other evidence of the role of inheritance comes from studies of early infant behavior. Milstein (1980) found that newborn infants with two overweight parents were more responsive to the contrast between a sweet-tasting solution and plain water than were infants of normal-weight parents. This indication of a preference predicted the children's weight at 3 years of age, suggesting that the preference for sweet tastes early in life may increase the risk for obesity. It seems fairly likely that babies' sucking patterns are genetically determined, and, interestingly enough, these patterns can help predict later weight (Agras, 1988). Later work (Jeffrey, 2001) has confirmed that overweight infants tend to become obese children and adolescents and that they continue to be obese even into adulthood.

All this sounds as though genetic factors dominate the issue of obesity, but wait: Education and income also play a role. For example, the better educated you are and the more money you earn, the less likely you are to be overweight! Although this may sound spurious, in fact some research with different groups in the United States suggests that socioeconomic factors may be at work. For instance, Kumanyika (1993) reports that among a sample of adults, the scale of overweight ran roughly as follows: Most overweight were the Pima Indians (Gladwell, 1998), followed by Hawaiian Americans, African Americans, Mexican Americans, Puerto Ricans, and Cubans; European Americans were the least overweight. Chances are that among these groups the European Americans had the highest incomes. One factor in their comparative slenderness may have been their ability to pay for such luxuries as health club memberships and foods with fat-reduced content.

There is also evidence that modeling by others strongly affects children's eating behaviors; although we might assume that the fact that obese parents tend to have obese children reflects inheritance, Ray and Klesges (1993) have found that children are very likely to imitate adults' food choices and eating behavior. In addition, they have observed that the parents of children who are obese not only encourage them to eat more than their nonobese siblings (explaining that they're bigger, so they need more food!) but also offer such eating prompts nearly two and a half times as often as parents of normal-weight children do. As Box 5.3 shows, teaching children how to recognize when they are hungry and to stop eating when they feel full may help prevent obesity. Rewarding children for eating everything on their plates, however, may teach them to rely on external instead of internal cues in deciding whether to eat, a practice that for some children may lead to eating whenever food is in sight. It is important to distinguish between reaching the point of being overweight, on the one hand, and becoming and remaining obese for some time, on the other. As we will see in the next section, once overweight is well established a person may have difficulty shedding the extra pounds.

Obese children and adolescents often suffer from a variety of physical problems, including hypertension and diabetes. They may also run the risk of having high cholesterol levels, which can predispose one to high blood pressure and other cardiovascular problems. But according to recent research, a positive relation between body fat and cholesterol levels may appear only in boys (Labarthe, 1997; Pinhas & Zeitler, 2000). Overweight children suffer psychologically as well, for they have more body-image disturbances than their nonobese peers, and the latter often discriminate against them (Bierman, 2004). Peers tease them more, exclude them from groups, and choose them last for athletic activities. For their part, because they fear other children will ridicule their bodies, chubby children often seek excuses to avoid gym class and thus get less exercise than they should. Overweight adolescents date less and are less likely to be admitted to prestigious colleges than their thinner classmates. Clearly, the costs of being obese can be very high.

TREATING OVERWEIGHT CHILDREN   Although obesity has been on the rise among children (Tinsley, 2003), there has also been an unfortunate lack of enthusiasm for treating this disorder—and it *is* a disorder—among physicians and other health personnel (Grilo, 2001). Why should health professionals be reluctant to deal with obesity? Most likely, it's because attempts to alter this condition have so often met with failure and high rates of recidivism. Treatment failures, however, may not reflect solely the strong genetic influences that we've discussed. They may also highlight the fact that we haven't found the right ways to encourage the healthy eating and physical activity habits that can help both children and adults improve their physical and mental health, their physical appearance, and their feeling of well-being.

Two principal ideas are central for controlling children's weight. First, it is important to involve the family—parents and perhaps siblings as well—in any treatment

Box 5.3
Child Psychology in Action

LEARNING NOT TO "CLEAN YOUR PLATE"

Parents play a major role in teaching children about eating. They help children learn what to eat, when to eat it, and how much to eat (Rozin, 1996). Unfortunately, parents may also teach children to rely more on external cues—such as feedback from them or the mere presence of food—than on cues that come from their own bodies that tell them when they're hungry and when they're not. When a child says, "I'm full" and the parent says, "No, finish what's on your plate," the parent is giving a clear message that it's the external cue that's important.

Birch and colleagues (Birch & Fisher, 1995; Birch, McPhee, Shoba, Steinberg, & Krehbeil, 1987) showed that children can learn to rely on either internal or external feedback, depending on adult responses to their eating behavior. Twenty-two preschoolers attended a series of special snack sessions over a six-week period. In one group the adult researchers helped the children focus on their sensations of hunger and fullness and stressed how these internal reminders tell us when to eat and when to stop eating. The children felt their stomachs and discussed how eating changes our feelings of hunger. In a second group, external cues were the focus. A bell rang to signal "snack time," and children were rewarded with such things as stickers for cleaning their plates.

Then the groups were combined and everyone was given a yogurt snack to eat, after which they were given a chance to eat another snack of cookies and granola bars. Children in the first group, who had been taught to rely on their internal signals, consumed less of the second snack, but children who had learned to depend on external cues such as rewards and adult urging ate just as many cookies and granola bars as they had yogurt no matter how full they were. It seems that the social context can influence which kinds of cues children learn to rely on in choosing to eat or stop eating.

This work helps us to understand why children are getting fatter. As you know, portion sizes are increasing, and "supersizing" is common in fast-food establishments. It wouldn't matter if children regulated their food intake so they stopped when they were full, but by the age of 5, children will eat more when portions are larger (Rolls, Engell, & Birch, 2000, and see Figure 5-14). Younger children (3-year-olds) seem to know better, for portion size does not alter their consumption.

Reviewing research on children's eating behavior, Ray and Klesges (1993) find that children can be encouraged to eat more healthily in a number of ways. According to these authors, allowing children to have more control over their food choices and the amounts they consume may help children learn more about how foods help us balance energy. In addition, involving children more in food-related activities such as helping to shop for and prepare foods may give them more awareness of the importance of good nutrition.

program. Second, increasing a child's physical expenditure of energy in innovative ways seems to help in the effort to achieve ideal weight for height (Tinsley, 2003; NICHD Child Care Network, 2003).

Stunkard (1958), a pioneer researcher in the field of obesity, once remarked that few obese people stay in treatment and of those who do, most don't lose weight, and of those who do lose weight, most regain it. However, as Rodin (1981) has reminded us, this seeming inability to learn to control one's weight is not simply a lack of discipline:

> Obesity is unusual because being fat is one of the factors that may keep one fat. . . . Many an overweight person . . . complains, "But I eat so little." Despite the disbelieving and reproachful looks of . . . lean friends, the perverse fact is that it often does take fewer calories to keep people fat than it did to get them fat in the first place. . . . Obesity itself changes the fat cells and body chemistry and alters levels of energy expenditure. Each of these factors operates to maintain obesity once it has developed. (p. 361)

We do not yet know enough about the mechanics of the genetic predisposition to fatness, the ways in which such a predisposition may be compounded by body chemistry, or the ways in which environmental change can affect obesity. But perhaps

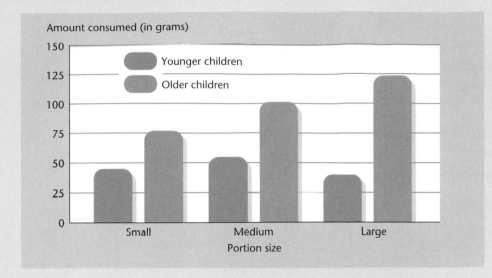

Figure 5-14

Do we get smarter with age—or not?

Researchers served two groups of children one of three different-size portions of macaroni and cheese at lunch. The $3\frac{1}{2}$-year-old children were not affected by the portion sizes, but among the 5-year-olds, the bigger their portion the more they ate.

Source: Rolls, Engell, & Birch, 2000.

Perhaps the most difficult pill for parents to swallow is the suggestion that they need to model good eating behavior for their children. According to Ray and Klesges, "the major finding to emerge in the research on the influence of adult behavior on the eating behavior of children is that children are more likely to eat a food when they see an adult eating it" (1993, p. 59). In addition, children apparently tend to develop the same food preferences as those of their parents. If parents eat a balanced diet that includes the major food groups, their children are likely to follow suit, but if parents eat large amounts of foods with saturated fatty acid content, children may eat similar amounts of such foods and may eat more of them than peers who eat healthier diets. Perhaps parents should look at this apparent restriction on their behavior as an opportunity rather than a restraint. The need to teach their children healthy eating habits might be just the nudge they need to watch their own diets and keep in shape!

an increasing awareness of the complexities of this disorder will encourage a more enthusiastic approach on the part of health professionals.

Behavioral approaches to treatment that recognize the important role that environmental cues can play in regulating eating behavior look promising (Tinsley, 2003). Parents often encourage their children's overeating not only by tying eating to external cues but by their own eating behavior. Researchers such as Epstein (Epstein, Valoski, Wing, & McCurley, 1994; Epstein et al., 1995; Epstein, Saelens, Myers, & Vito, 1997) and Nader (1993) are finding that working with entire families in attempting to reverse these processes may be successful. Other researchers (e.g., Israel, 1988) have also found that such interventions as reducing the likelihood of stressful interactions with family members at mealtime can help curb overeating.

Epstein and his colleagues (Epstein et al., 1994) found that by encouraging parents to serve as models of good eating and physical exercise, over the 10-year period of their study, 34 percent of their child participants succeeded in losing 20 percent or more of their overweight poundage; at the close of the study, 30 percent were no longer obese. As always, to "take it off and keep it off" requires not only watching your food choices, but burning off those calories as well.

Figure 5-15   Reducing sedentary activities helps reduce weight

Children who spent less time watching TV and playing computer games lost the most weight. Neither a specific exercise regimen nor the combination of exercise and reduction of sedentary activities worked as well!

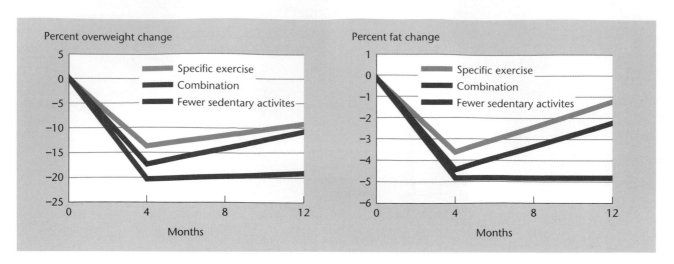

Source: Epstein et al., 1995.

A study by Epstein and colleagues suggests that choice may be very important in getting children to lose weight (Epstein et al., 1995). These researchers gave children two options: They could spend less time in sedentary behaviors, such as watching TV and playing computer games, or they could increase their physical activity—for example, riding an exercise bike or exercising to an aerobics tape. As you can see from Figure 5-15, decreasing sedentary activity was clearly more effective in producing weight loss than were either specific exercise or a combination of the two options. Based on significant improvements in fitness among the children who reduced their sedentary activities, the investigators speculate that these children may have substituted other, higher-energy-expenditure activities of their own choice. Parents had been instructed to make easily available such things as skates and bicycles.

Relatively few studies have been done, however, of the independent effects of exercise on children's weight (Gutin & Manos, 1993; Tinsley, 2003), and the topic remains controversial. For example, Sallis and colleagues (Sallis et al., 1993), found a nonsignificant decrease in levels of body fat in a group of fourth-grade children who participated in special physical education activities over a period of two years. Reviewing much of the literature, Gutin and Manos (1993) make an interesting suggestion: "Because children need to ingest sufficient energy and nutrients to assure healthy growth, energy restriction is not the method of choice for prevention of obesity. Shifting from a high fat to a high carbohydrate diet, however, may increase the TEF [the thermic effect of food, i.e., its productive channeling into energy-consuming activity] and [thus] have a subtle long-term preventive effect" (p. 123). These authors suggest that if children are made aware of the importance of a balanced diet, they may be more motivated to maintain their food intake at a constant level when they start an exercise program, and as a result the increased physical activity may gradually reduce fatness.

EATING DISORDERS IN ADOLESCENCE   Just as obesity can cause both physical and psychological problems, so being underweight can bring on distressing and even life-threatening conditions. The two most common eating disorders

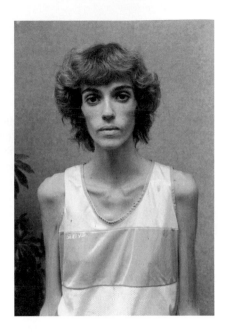 

The treatment of anorexia can be remarkably successful. From this girl's shocking appearance at diagnosis, one might not have believed that she could exude the health and happiness her posttreatment image shows.

in the United States, anorexia and bulimia, afflict far more women than men and generally strike between the age of 10 and the early twenties. Although there is some indication (Tinsley, 2003) that eating difficulties tend to decline in frequency in the transition to adulthood (and after college), a number of women continue to be dissatisfied with their bodies and to indulge in repetitive dieting. Men, on the other hand, who are less affected in adolescence and early adulthood, may begin to gain weight after beginning college and for the first time become concerned with dieting and body image.

People with **anorexia nervosa** have an unaccountable dread of being fat and diet constantly to avoid that state. They see themselves as obese even if they are quite slender and although they may be preoccupied with food and may even hoard it, they eat less and less. Young women in particular (relatively few young men are anorexic) may lose up to 25 percent of their body weight (some lose even more) and may become so weak that they must be hospitalized to redress fluid and electrolyte imbalances. Without continuing intervention, these skeletal creatures, who often have been attractive, bright, and achieving young women, may die from starvation or suicide (Neumarker, 1997; Tinsley, 2003).

Bulimia nervosa is an eating disorder in which the person—again, typically a young woman in adolescence or early adulthood—goes through recurrent periods of seemingly uncontrollable binge eating followed by either vomiting or the use of laxatives to compensate for the bingeing and to prevent weight gain. Sometimes this disorder is seen in young women pursuing activities such as gymnastics or ballet that stress slimness (Sherwood et al., 2002). Bulimics, like anorexics, risk fluid and electrolyte abnormalities, and the loss of stomach acid through vomiting and the frequent induction of diarrhea can cause other metabolic problems (American Psychiatric Association, 2000).

Most cases of bulimia emerge during the late teens and early twenties, whereas anorexia may begin at a variety of points throughout adolescence, especially at puberty (Attie & Brooks-Gunn, 1989). Bulimia is thought to affect between 1 and 3 percent of adolescent and young women (American Psychiatric Association, 2000), anorexia probably less than 1 percent. Both disorders are more prevalent in industrialized societies such as the United States, Canada, Australia, Japan, New Zealand, South Africa, and European countries.

anorexia nervosa An eating disorder in which the person, usually a young woman, is preoccupied with avoiding obesity and often diets to the point of starvation.

bulimia nervosa An eating disorder in which people, usually young women, alternate periods of binge eating with vomiting and other means of compensating for the weight gained.

Despite some outward similarities, the two disorders are quite different. Unlike anorexics, young women with bulimia rarely diet to the point of starvation and death; anorexics, however, do sometimes engage in bingeing and purging. In contrast to anorexic young women, who tend to be of normal weight before the illness takes holds of them and to be socially withdrawn, bulimics are sometimes obese before the onset of illness and are typically extraverted and have voracious appetites. Women with both disorders may exhibit depressive symptoms, but whereas bulimics often have poor self-image and low self-esteem, anorexics have a tendency toward *obsessive-compulsiveness* (the tendency to have recurrent obsessions or compulsions to do particular things that take up time and energy and that may cause marked psychological distress), perfectionism, and a strong need to control their environments (Fairburn, Cooper, Doll, & Welch, 1999; Levenkron, 2000). It may be that controlling their food intake is, for some anorexics, the only control they feel able to exert over their lives.

Most anorexics and bulimics are of European American descent and relatively high socioeconomic status (Benokraitis, 1996). They often have family histories of eating disorders and/or of substance abuse (alcohol, marijuana, uppers, downers). Anorexic girls often come from families that are high-achieving and protective and may describe their mothers as dominating, intrusive, and overbearing and their fathers as "emotional absentees" (Carson & Butcher, 1992). It is important to remember, however, that family members' behavior often affects other members, and some of these characteristics may represent responses to the behavior of the anorexic girl. According to Fisher and Brone (1991), the families of bulimic adolescents are often chaotic, conflict-ridden, and stressed, and family members have difficulty communicating their feelings.

Treating anorexia may require initial hospitalization and physical intervention. Although in-hospital behavioral modification techniques have succeeded in normalizing anorexics' eating behavior and in achieving weight gain, the effects of this type of therapy seem to be short-lived (Mehler & Crews, 2001). Longer-term psychotherapy that includes the family has had some success (Miller & Pumariega, 2001). However, according to one estimate, fewer than half of adolescents with this disorder make a complete recovery (Zerbe, 1993), and 5 to 10 percent die either from starvation or by overt suicide (American Psychiatric Association, 2000). Treating bulimia is generally more successful than helping adolescents with anorexia. A variety of approaches, including individual and family psychotherapy, support groups, nutrition education, and, in cases where depression is evident, antidepressive medications, have been successful in treating bulimia (Mitchell et al., 2001; Tinsley, 2003). Unfortunately, many adolescents never seek treatment for this disorder.

SEXUAL MATURATION

puberty The onset of sexual maturity.

Whereas physical growth, except for one of two growth spurts, is more or less gradual, sexual maturation arrives with rather a flourish. Suddenly, a girl begins to menstruate, a boy has his first ejaculation, and both know or come to know that they are no longer children but young adults, capable both of fully expressing their sexuality and of reproducing their species. **Puberty,** or the onset of sexual maturity, has long been held as a time of stress for the adolescent, when the intensity of new drives and the social pressures for new behaviors and new responsibilities may cause conflict and confusion. We begin this section by considering the actual changes that occur with puberty, and then explore the question of whether young people, just as they seem to be growing taller, are generally experiencing puberty earlier and earlier. We discuss whether maturing earlier or later than one's peers has a significant effect on a young person. Finally, we examine the issue of sexual identity, including the development of same-sex preferences.

The Onset of Sexual Maturity

Puberty is marked by the sudden bodily growth and changes that take place when the hypothalamus, at the base of the brain, stimulates the **pituitary gland** (see Figure 5-16) to secrete certain hormones. **Hormones** are powerful and highly specialized chemical substances produced by the cells of certain body organs and that have a regulatory effect on the activities of certain other organs. In this case, the pituitary gland's hormones cause the *adrenal cortex* (the outer layer of an adrenal gland) and the *gonads* (in males, the testes, and in females, the ovaries) to initiate a growth spurt. As Table 5-3 shows, in girls this spurt begins with breast development, and in both sexes the appearance of pubic hair is an early sign of puberty. These characteristics, along with voice change in boys, are considered *secondary sex characteristics,* which are not directly involved in sexual reproduction. *Primary sex characteristics,* which are involved in the reproductive process and which evolve a few years after the first secondary characteristics appear, include, in males, **spermarche,** or the capability of the testes and associated internal organs to produce sperm-containing ejaculate. In females, primary sex characteristics include the changes in the reproductive organs that culminate with **menarche,** or the beginning of *ovulation.* Each month an egg, released from an ovary, begins its journey through the fallopian tubes to the uterus; there, if the egg is not fertilized, it is expelled in the menstrual flow.

In both female and male adolescents, the rising concentrations of hormones stimulate the development of both primary and secondary sex characteristics. In females, **estrogens** are crucial to the maturation of the reproductive system, including the ovaries, fallopian tubes, and uterus, and to the onset of ovulation and menstruation. **Progesterone** helps regulate the menstrual cycle and readies the uterus for the reception and nurturing of a fertilized egg. In males, **testosterone,** the most important of several *androgens,* is essential to the maturation of the penis, testes, and other organs of the reproductive system and to the production of sperm. Male sexual motivation is influenced by testosterone; female sexual motivation is less dependent on hormonal secretions.

As you can see from Table 5-3, even the attainment of puberty's secondary sex characteristics is gradual, with menarche and spermarche occurring two to three years after the beginning of the maturation process. Nevertheless, it is because these two

pituitary gland A so-called master gland, located at the base of the brain, that triggers the secretion of hormones by all other hormone-secreting, or endocrine, glands.

hormones Powerful and highly specialized chemical substances produced by the cells of certain body organs and that have a regulatory effect on the activity of certain other organs.

spermarche In males, the first ejaculation of semen-containing ejaculate.

menarche In females, the beginning of the menstrual cycle.

estrogens Hormones that, in the female, are responsible for sexual maturation.

progesterone A hormone that, in females, helps regulate the menstrual cycle and prepares the uterus to receive and nurture a fertilized egg.

testosterone A hormone that, in the male, is responsible for the development of primary and secondary sex characteristics and is essential for the production of sperm.

Corpus callosum

Parietal lobe

Frontal lobe

Pituitary gland

Temporal lobe

Spinal cord

Occipital lobe

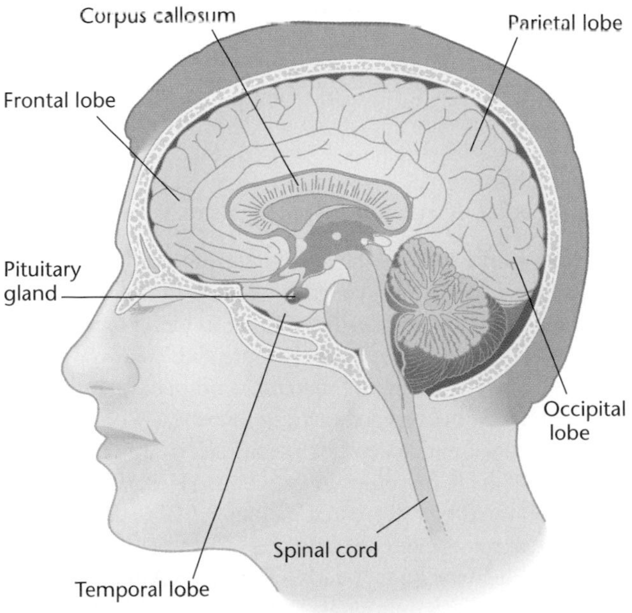

Figure 5-16

The pituitary gland

Cutting through the cerebrum, we can see the location of the pituitary gland, which controls the secretion of important human hormones including those that stimulate cell growth and replication.

Source: Adapted from Postlethwait & Hopson, 1995.

Table 5-3 Sexual maturation: A timetable

Average Age of Onset	Girls	Boys
10	Breasts (breast buds) begin to develop	
11	Pubic hair appears; it is sparse and slightly pigmented	**Testes and scrotum begin to grow**
12		Pubic hair, lightly pigmented, begins to appear
12 to 13	Underarm hair begins to appear	
13	Breasts continue to enlarge; areola and nipple project above contour of breast	**Spermarche: first ejaculation of semen**
13 to 14	**Menarche: beginning of menstruation**	
14	Pubic hair becomes denser, but area covered is smaller than in adult woman	Underarm and facial hair begin to appear
15	Breasts and pubic hair coverage are fully mature	**Penis, testes are fully developed** Pubic hair coverage is complete Mustache and beard hair begin to grow

Note: Primary sex characteristics are in boldface type.

Sources: Petersen & Taylor, 1980; Tanner, 1978; Turner & Rubinson, 1993.

later events signal such a marked change in the person, not only physically and physiologically but psychologically, that they are considered a major turning point. For some women, menarche is the "true" or real onset of puberty (Brooks-Gunn & Ruble, 1984); few accounts of this aspect of maturation are more eloquent or more poignant than the following diary entry written by Anne Frank, not long before she perished at the hands of the Nazis:

> Yesterday I read an article about blushing [that] . . . might have been addressed to me personally. Although I don't blush very easily, the other things in it certainly fit me. [The author] writes that . . . a girl in the years of puberty becomes quiet within and begins to think about the wonders that are happening to her body. . . .
>
> I think what is happening to me is so wonderful, and not only what can be seen on my body, but all that is taking place inside. . . .
>
> Each time I have a period—and that has only been three times—I have the feeling that in spite of all the pain, unpleasantness, and nastiness, I have a sweet secret, and that is why, although it is nothing but a nuisance to me in a way, I always long for the time that I shall feel that secret within me again. (Frank, 1967, cited by Katchadorian, 1977)

In industrialized countries, at least, young women have been reaching puberty at earlier ages than before. In the United States, for example, young women in the late 1960s tended to experience menarche nearly two years earlier (at 12.5 years) than their mothers had (at 14.4 years) (Herman-Giddens et al., 1997). As Figure 5-17 shows, in the countries of Finland, Norway, and Sweden, the age of menarche dropped about three and a half years in a little over a century. Some researchers (e.g., Roche, 1979; Wyshak & Frisch, 1982) have suggested that this trend to earlier menarche is slowing down among middle-class girls in the United States, but other investigators (Herman-Giddens et al., 1997; NHLBI Growth and Health Study Research Group, 1992) suggest that among certain groups, for instance African American girls, the onset of menarche is now even earlier—at age 8 or 9. The heavier body builds of African American girls may account for the earlier timing of puberty (Kimm et al., 2002). The reduction in age

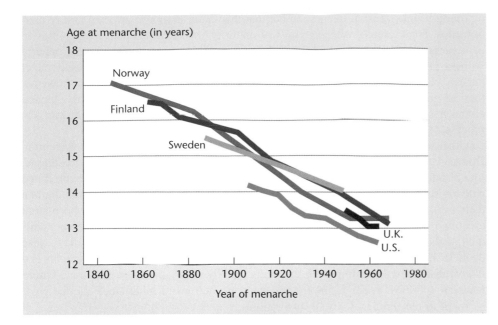

Figure 5-17

Decline in the age of menarche

In the Scandinavian countries represented here, the age of first menstruation declined considerably over a little more than a century and a half. Although the data for the United Kingdom and the United States do not cover the same time period, their trend suggests that the rate of change in menarche in all these countries is similar.

Source: Roche, 1979.

at menarche has not been uniform around the world. Little change has occurred among Eskimo groups or in some groups in India (Roche, 1979). In Denmark, change has ceased (Helm & Grolund, 1998). In certain underdeveloped countries, such as some parts of New Guinea, the median age of menarche is very late—17.5 to 18.4 years (Malcolm, 1970). Is sexual maturation synonymous with sexual attraction? Researchers McClintock and Herdt (1996) say no, arguing that sexual attraction appears first at about the age of 10, four years after the adrenal androgen dehydrocpiandrosterone (DHEA) has begun to rise conspicuously (this androgen is said to be a precursor of both testosterone and estradiol, sex hormones in men and women). These researchers found that significant numbers of the heterosexual and homosexual young people they studied reported first feelings of sexual attraction at about the age of 10, and they argue for an adjustment in our understanding of puberty so as to accommodate the view of sexuality as a continuous process that begins well before the traditional time of puberty.

What Determines the Timing of Puberty?

Inheritance seems to play some role in the timing of menarche; girls whose mothers matured early tend to mature early themselves. But environmental factors also have something to say about when this important event occurs. For example, the choice of a profession can to some degree alter the timing of menarche: Gymnasts, figure skaters, and ballet dancers who practice intensively, perform regularly, and diet to keep fit may delay the onset of menstruation by as much as one year (Brooks-Gunn & Warren, 1985). In fact, of the dancers studied by Brooks-Gunn (1988) only 30 percent were described as either early or "on time," in contrast to 80 percent of a comparison group of girls who were not dancers. And even after girls reach menarche, they may not stay on a regular schedule if they train hard and keep their weight low; for example, runners and gymnasts sometimes stop menstruating, or become *amenorrheic*. Such girls can literally turn their menstrual cycles on and off by stopping and restarting their training regimen (Brooks-Gunn & Warren, 1985).

Parent-child relationships can also alter the timing of sexual maturation (Brooks-Gunn & Moore, 2002). In a longitudinal study, Steinberg (1987) found not only that systematic changes in family systems around the time of puberty affected the timing of young people's sexual maturation but that this maturation also affected family relationships. For example, whereas physical maturity was accompanied by decreases in adolescent-parent closeness and increases in the child's desire for autonomy, puberty seemed also to increase conflicts between youth and parent. So far, it seems as if puberty causes a distancing between child and parent. Steinberg also found, however, that the greater the distance between the generations, the earlier young people tended to reach sexual maturity, whereas the closer parent and child were, the slower the process of maturation seemed to be.

Other researchers, (Brooks-Gunn & Moore, 2002; Ellis, McFadyen-Ketchum, Dodge, Pettit, & Bates, 1999; Moffitt, Caspi, Belsky, and Silva, 1992), for example, found that family conflict and father absence from the family scene were correlated with earlier menarche in girls. A genetic inheritance model might equally well explain their results with respect to father absence. Statistics show that women who mature early and have children early are likely to divorce, which leaves these women's children without fathers. Because the female children's genetic inheritance may cause them to mature early, the finding of high correlation between early menarche and father absence would simply be an artifact of the more complex situation. Future research will have to determine the relative contributions of inheritance and the environment to the timing of sexual maturation.

The Effects of Early and Late Maturation

Does normal individual variation in the rate of maturation make a difference? It depends on your gender. For boys, there are clear advantages in maturing early but some drawbacks as well. Early maturation creates problems for girls, but intervening factors such as parental support and the nature of a girl's peer group can modify the effects of more rapid sexual maturity. Moreover, both boys and girls may be strongly affected by challenging environmental transitions, such as changing schools, that often occur concurrently with biological changes (Wigfield, Eccles, & Schiefele, 2006).

Pioneering in this area of research, Jones and Bayley (1950) tracked the development of 16 early-maturing and 16 late-maturing public school boys over a six-year period. The late-maturing boys were rated lower in physical attractiveness, masculinity, and grooming than their faster-developing peers. The late maturers were also rated as more childish, more eager, and less relaxed, and as generally engaging in more attention-seeking behaviors. Peers regarded the late maturers as restless, bossy, talkative, attention seeking, and less likely to have older friends.

Later maturers and their parents have lower aspirations and expectations for educational achievement. On the basis of a national study of 493 boys, Duke et al. (1982) found that late maturers were less likely to want to complete college and that the parents of these boys did not expect them to graduate from college. Teachers, too, rated later maturers as lower in academic achievement than average or early maturers. And the late maturers scored lower on IQ and achievement tests. Perhaps parents and teachers provide more opportunities for early maturers and expect more from them because of their more adultlike physical appearance. However, boys who became late maturers had lower IQ scores as early as 8 years of age, and so their later physical appearance may have had nothing to do with parents' and teachers' actions during these boys' adolescence. This study raises a couple of possibilities: either that there are subtle biological differences between early and late maturers that, even before puberty, may elicit differential treatment from others, or that there are intrinsic genetic differences that affect not only rate of physical growth but intellectual capacity as well.

But for boys there is a downside to reaching maturity early: Early-maturing boys are more likely to engage in delinquent behavior, to express more hostility, and to experience more stress than their late-maturing peers. Owing to their obvious physical maturity, they are often accepted by, and associate with, older males—often leading them to more risk-taking and more problems (Ge, Conger, & Elder, 2001; Ge, Brody, Conger, Simons, & Murray, 2002).

Girls may not find early maturation advantageous. To begin with, early maturers may not be as prepared for the changes in their bodies and body functions because their development typically occurs before schools offer health classes. And, unfortunately, mothers apparently discuss these changes less often with early-maturing daughters (Brooks-Gunn, 1988). Early-maturing girls tend to have a poorer body image than on-time or late maturers, in part because the weight gains accompanying the onset of maturation violate the cultural ideal of thinness for girls (Halpern, Udry, Campbell, & Suchindrau, 1999; Graber, Petersen, & Brooks-Gunn, 1996). As you can see from Figure 5-18, the trends for positive body image for girls and boys are almost diametrically opposed: Early-maturing boys have a far more positive body image than late-maturing boys; early-maturing girls tend to have negative body images, whereas late-maturing girls have positive self-images. Notice, however, that like boys who mature late, the latest-maturing girls tend to have some problems with body image. Early-maturing girls have been found to have more adjustment or behavioral problems (Brooks-Gunn & Moore, 2002; Dick, Rose, Viken, & Kaprio, 2000). Lacković-Grgin, Dekovic, and Opačić (1994) found that late-maturing girls were more likely to have good self-esteem but that healthy relations with the mother were a more important determining factor. Thus early maturers who were close to their mothers often had as good, if not better, self-esteem than late maturers whose relations with their mothers were poor. On the other hand, researchers have also found that early maturers have more difficulty inhibiting impulses and exhibit more depressive affect (Ge, Conger, & Elder, 1996; Wichstrom, 1999).

Longitudinal studies in Sweden (Magnusson, 1988, 1996; Stattin & Magnusson, 1990; Stice, Presnell, & Bearman, 2000) have reported that early-maturing girls have a smaller network of close friends and are more likely to engage in "adult behaviors" (such as smoking, drinking, and sexual intercourse) at a younger age than late maturers. Apparently this is because earlier maturers tend to associate with older peers who are closer to them in terms of physical status and appearance. Although many people believe that early sexual maturity leads to early sexual behavior and to unwed teen pregnancy and childbearing, as we will see in Chapter 11, the reasons for adolescent pregnancy and parenting are far more complex than this.

Although early maturation seems to entail some risks for girls, experts (Brooks-Gunn, & Moore, 2002) suggest caution in interpreting research results to date. First, not all early maturers will have a poor body image or will date, smoke, or drink earlier. Second, individuals also differ on whether they perceive early maturation as "on

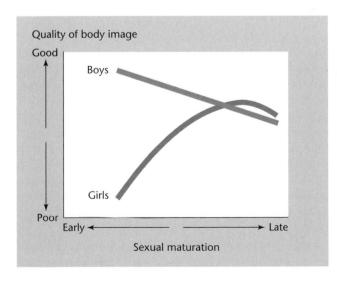

Figure 5-18

Body image in adolescent girls and boys

For boys, the relation between body image and timing of puberty is a straight line: the sooner the better. Girls tend to have more positive body images the later they mature, but if maturity comes exceedingly late, their body images may suffer.

Source: Tobin-Richards, Boxer, & Petersen, 1984.

time" (normal) or "off-time" (deviant), depending on such things as the attitudes, beliefs, and behaviors of their particular reference groups. "In the final analysis, a girl's adjustment to the changes of puberty will probably depend more on the kinds of support, encouragement, and guidance she receives from parents, and the values and expectations of her own particular peer group, than it will on whether maturation is early, average, or late" (Conger & Petersen, 1984, p. 121).

The impact of the transition to sexual maturity cannot be fully appreciated in isolation from other changes in young people's lives. Some adolescents attend junior high school after sixth grade, whereas others stay in elementary school through eighth grade and then go on to high school. Many have found that youth moving through the former type of system experience more adjustment difficulties (Wigfield et al., 2006; Rudolph et al., 2001). In addition, some adolescents date early and others delay this step. Simmons, Blyth, and their colleagues (Simmons & Blyth 1987) found that girls who entered puberty early and at the same time changed schools and started to date had lower self-esteem than other girls. Girls who moved their residences or experienced a major family disruption (divorce, death, remarriage) suffered even more loss in self-esteem and grades, and their participation in extracurricular activities decreased (Simmons, Burgeson, Carlton-Ford, & Blyth, 1987). Attending a coed school also increases problems for early-maturing girls (Caspi, Lyman, Moffitt, & Silva, 1993; Ge et al., 1996).

The challenges of coping with multiple and simultaneous life changes are not limited to girls. Boys who experienced sexual maturity accompanied by a variety of other changes, such as change of school, moving to a new neighborhood, or engaging in early dating, had poorer grades and participated less in extracurricular activities than boys who experienced fewer life transitions (Simmons et al., 1987). These findings underscore that the impact of the timing of puberty can best be understood in the context of other transitions and illustrate the ability of the environmental context to help or hinder children's abilities to cope with biological change.

Sexual Orientation and Identity

Most adolescents develop a heterosexual orientation, but a small percentage of children and adolescents realize that they prefer members of their own sex as sexual partners. According to recent estimates (Rotherman-Borus & Langabeer, 2001), between 3 and 6 percent of adolescents identify themselves as gay, lesbian, or bisexual. These are only estimates, for awareness of one's sexual orientation and of one's attraction to same-sex partners comes at different times to different individuals. For some, this occurs in early or middle childhood, but others reach adulthood before recognizing their same-sex preferences. What are the origins of same-sex preferences? Both biological and environmental causes have been proposed.

BIOLOGICAL CAUSES   Some genetic evidence supports the notion that identical twins are more likely to show similar sexual orientations than are fraternal twins (Barley, Pillard, Neale, & Agyei, 1993). Other studies (Hamer, Hu, Magnuson, Hu, & Pattatucci, 1993) suggest that variations in DNA may make it more likely that some boys will develop homosexual preferences. Still other research has implicated the level of prenatal hormones as a possible predisposing factor. For example, women exposed to a synthetic estrogen (diethylstilbestrol, or DES) during the prenatal period were more likely to be lesbian or bisexual than women who were not exposed to DES (Meyer-Bahlburg et al., 1995). However, not all women who were exposed developed lesbian or bisexual orientation, which suggests that environmental factors also play a role in the development of sexual orientation.

ENVIRONMENTAL CAUSES   Family experiences doubtless play a role in this process. Some researchers have argued that distant or hostile relationships with parents of the same gender may lead children to reject behavior typically associated with their same-gender parents (McConaghy & Silove, 1992; Bailey, Bobrow, Wolfe, & Mikach, 1995). Indeed, gay men have recalled distant relationships with their fathers, while lesbian women have reported poorer ties with their mothers. It has also been suggested that the gender of one's siblings may contribute to gay or lesbian identity. In one study, boys who are born later in the family and who have a larger-than-usual number of older brothers were more likely to develop homosexual orientations (Blanchard, Zucker, Bradley, & Hume, 1995). At the same time, there is little support for the view that gay and lesbian parents will produce gay and lesbian children. In fact, children of gay and lesbian parenting partners are just as likely to be heterosexual in their sexual orientation (Patterson, 2002). In short, none of these theories has received extensive support, and viewpoints that emphasize multiple pathways to gay/lesbian identity and that involve both environmental and biological factors are likely to be the most fruitful in helping us understand this matter.

DEVELOPMENT OF GENDER IDENTITY AND SEXUAL PREFERENCE

Although we will explore the issue of gender roles in detail in Chapter 13, we introduce here the issue of gender identity and sexual preference. By *gender identity* we mean the perception of oneself as either masculine or feminine; by *sexual preference* we mean one's choice of a same- or opposite-gender person as a sexual partner.

The recognition that one prefers a member of the same sex as a sexual partner is often a gradual process that is marked by a series of milestones. Many gay or lesbian adults report recalling that as children they had feelings that differed from those of their peers (Bailey & Zucker, 1995). One team of researchers has shown that some children as early as fourth grade express doubts about their heterosexuality (Egan & Perry, 2002; Carver, Egan & Perry, 2004). These children responded more negatively to such questions as "Some girls (boys) definitely think they'll get married one day" or "Some girls (boys) definitely think that they will be a mother (father) one day." Compared with children more confident in their heterosexuality, children who questioned their sexual identity reported more impaired self concepts. They expressed less interest in activities stereotypically linked to their own gender, such as babysitting for girls and building model planes and cars for boys. In addition, they were more likely to feel different from others of their gender and to express dissatisfaction with their own gender assignment.

Interestingly, the patterns were similar for both boys and girls. Across-time analyses suggested that sexual questioning leads to impaired self-concepts rather than the other way around. There is great variability in when sexual questioning begins: The work cited and other studies (e.g., Savin-Williams & Diamond, 2000) suggest that it may start in early and middle childhood, but it may not begin until considerably later. This is especially true for women; a significant minority shift toward a lesbian orientation after being heterosexual or even after motherhood (D'Augelli & Patterson, 2001; Rotherman-Borus & Langabeer, 2001). Although the studies of sexual questioning by children suggest that the process of achieving a sexual identity and orientation starts early, this does not mean that all children who have questions about their sexual orientation will necessarily grow up to be gay or lesbian. At the same time, both prospective and retrospective studies suggest that gay and lesbian adults often report that such sexual questioning is part of their childhood history (Bailey & Zucker, 1995). In addition, cross-typed behavior (e.g., boys playing with dolls) is often found in the childhood of gay men.

According to Savin-Williams (1998) the next step in the journey toward full acceptance of minority sexual identity is "test and exploration." During this phase, the youth becomes ambivalent about same-sex preferences and begins tentatively to explore these feelings. Next, during the identity acceptance phase, young people begin to accept their orientation and preferences for individuals of the same sex. They may share their sexual preferences with family and friends and may act on those preferences. Adolescent boys begin to label themselves as gay by age 13 and to engage in sex with other boys by age 15. Boys and girls, however, follow slightly different developmental pathways. Boys act first and label later, while girls do the opposite. Boys have sexual encounters with other males and only later label themselves as gay, whereas girls' identify themselves as lesbians and later engage in sexual encounters with other females (Savin-Williams & Diamond, 2000).

Identity integration is the final milestone in this identity process. At this juncture, gay, lesbian, and bisexual individuals accept their orientation and acknowledge their identity to others in their family, school, and community. About 55 percent of college students of either sex disclosed their sexual identity to their parents; a decade ago only 45 percent disclosed such information (Savin-Williams & Ream, 2003). And young people are disclosing themselves earlier than in the past—at 17 instead of in the mid-twenties, as they did a decade ago (D'Augelli, 2004). Parental gender may determine their choice of confessor: Youth of both genders are more likely to tell their mothers than their fathers (a reflection of the greater closeness of the mother-child bond). And adolescents use more direct face-to-face disclosure methods with mom than with dad. Researchers have found that children tended to disclose to fathers indirectly—that is, through someone else to whom they had spoken (Savin-Williams & Ream, 2003). Mothers (48%) are more accepting of their son's gay sexual orientation than are fathers (35%) (D'Augelli, 2004). Similarly, mothers are more accepting of their daughters' "coming out" as lesbian than are fathers (D'Augelli, Hersberger, & Pilkington, 1998). There is considerable prejudice in many parts of society toward nonheterosexuals, and many (20 to 40%) experience discrimination, rejection, and outright verbal and sometimes even physical hostility (D'Augelli, 1998, 2004). Even family members and friends may react negatively to the disclosure of minority sexual orientation.

In a recent study (Savin-Williams & Ream, 2003), when a child disclosed his gay or her lesbian self-identification, nearly 50 percent of parents reacted slightly negatively, expressed denial, or were intolerant or rejecting. However, after these initial reactions, the majority of parent-child relationships either maintained their quality or improved it, especially mother-child dyads. Friendships suffer too; many report a loss of friends as a result of "coming out" (D'Augelli, 2004), but the presence of friends who share the same sexual orientation helps disclosing youth adjust (Savin-Williams, 1998, 2001). Moreover, ethnicity and religion are important predictors of acceptance. Some ethnic minorities—especially Asian Americans and Latino Americans—are less tolerant than are European Americans of nonheterosexual orientations (Dube, Savin-Williams, & Diamond, 2001). Similarly, some members of conservative religious groups are less likely to be accepting of sexual-minority youth (D'Augelli, 2004).

For some youth, negative consequences follow disclosure. Suicide attempts are more common among gay and lesbian youth than among heterosexuals (D'Augelli, 2004), and youth who are victims of verbal or physical assaults are more likely to have mental health problems. On occasion, gay teenagers have actually been killed by others owing simply to their sexual preferences. The widely publicized October 1998 murder of Matthew Shepard, in Laramie, Wyoming, led to protests in Washington, D.C., the nation's capitol, by those who sought to raise awareness of the potential consequences of antihomosexual beliefs and behavior.

self-acceptance A general sense of one's personal worth combined with a positive view of one's sexual orientation.

Young people who achieve **self-acceptance**—a general sense of personal worth combined with a positive view of their sexual orientation—and who have the support of their families are less likely to suffer mental health problems when they encounter discrimination by others (Hershberger & D'Augelli, 1995). But these supports may be powerless in the face of violence. Although the media and various educational programs are making the general public more aware of the problems of gay, lesbian, and bisexual youth, these individuals still face discrimination, struggles, and outright challenges to their efforts to gain acceptance in society.

Making the Connections 5

There are many links between concepts and ideas in one area of development and concepts and ideas in other areas. Here are some of the connections between ideas in Chapter 5 and discussions in other Chapters of this book.

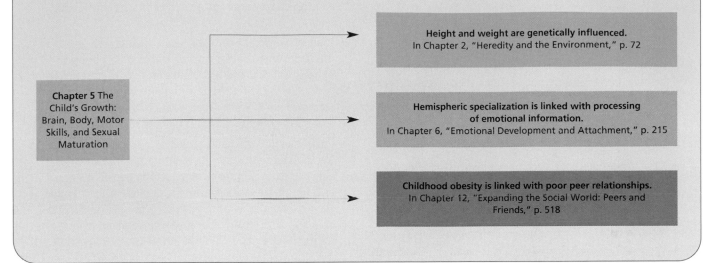

Chapter 5 The Child's Growth: Brain, Body, Motor Skills, and Sexual Maturation

Height and weight are genetically influenced.
In Chapter 2, "Heredity and the Environment," p. 72

Hemispheric specialization is linked with processing of emotional information.
In Chapter 6, "Emotional Development and Attachment," p. 215

Childhood obesity is linked with poor peer relationships.
In Chapter 12, "Expanding the Social World: Peers and Friends," p. 518

SUMMARY

Brain Development in Infancy

- The largest portion of the human brain, the **cerebrum**, is covered by a highly convoluted layer called the **cerebral cortex**. The cortex is divided into a number of regions whose cells control specific functions such as seeing, hearing, feeling, moving, and thinking. In the developing organism, **neuron proliferation** rapidly increases the number of the brain's nerve cells, or **neurons**. Although most of the brain's neurons are present at birth, many subsequent changes take place in their sizes, the numbers of connections, or **synapses**, among them, and the production of the surrounding, supportive **glial cells**. These changes, such as **myelination**, increase the speed, efficiency, and complexity of transmissions between neurons.

- **Neural migration** distributes neurons throughout brain regions. The abundance of synapses, formed by **synaptogenesis**, and of neurons is trimmed over time through **neuronal death** and **synaptic pruning**.

- The human brain is organized in two halves: the two **brain hemispheres** are connected by the **corpus callosum**. The right hemisphere controls the left side of the body and is involved in the processing of visual-spatial information, face recognition, and interpreting emotional expressions. The left hemisphere controls the right side of the body and is important for understanding and using language. Both **hemispheric specialization** and **lateralization** are evident early in infancy and are well developed by age 3.

- **Dyslexia**, or difficulty in learning to read, may reflect abnormal lateralization patterns, such as the processing of spatial information on both sides of the brain rather than primarily in the right hemisphere, the normal arrangement.

- The environment plays a critical role in brain development. In rats, enriched environments that permit a great deal of activity and exploration are related to increases in brain size, in the number of connections among neurons, and in the activities of key brain chemicals. Apparently, the brain has great **plasticity**, which allows it to compensate for defects or damage in one area or even one hemisphere.

- The development of the child's brain is influenced by two types of experience. **Experience-expectant processes** are universal, shared by all human beings across evolution, such as the touch of another person or the sound of voice and speech.

Experience-dependent processes are those that a person encounters in his own particular family or culture; for example, a child in Mozambique may learn to fish, whereas a U.S. child will learn to surf the Internet. These different activities promote the development of different parts of the brain.

Motor Development

- Research suggests that infants grasp objects in a variety of different ways, depending on the object. Research based on dynamic systems theory has shown that patterns of specific reaching and grasping behavior reflect both coordination tendencies in an infant's general, nonreaching arm movements and environmental influences such as task requirements.

- The development of walking follows a U-shaped course, beginning with a stepping reflex at birth that disappears after a few months, followed by the emergence of independent, voluntary walking a number of months later, usually around the first birthday.

- A dynamic systems approach to explain this pattern suggests that the development of walking depends on the combined readiness of a variety of factors, and when the baby's weight becomes too much of a load on the emerging motor system, stepping ability may be temporarily masked. Cross-cultural studies indicate that environmental influences, such as repeated practice of a skill, may either enhance or slow a complex motor skill such as independent walking.

- The relations between locomotion, other aspects of development such as perception, social interaction, and problem solving, and environmental forces are complex. In general, the greater a child's motor skills, the more his general development is enhanced; at the same time, negative factors such as conflicted child-parent relations may sometimes promote developmental skills such as walking.

Physical Growth

- Infants' and children's growth is guided by the two basic principles of cephalocaudal development and proximal-distal development, discussed in Chapter 3. Growth proceeds at different rates during different stages of development and is fastest during the first six months of life.

- Adult height is difficult to predict from a baby's size, which tends to be more closely related to the size of the mother. Successful predictions can be made in later childhood based on the child's height, gender, and parents' heights.

- Most authorities are agreed today that breast-feeding provides infants with better support for healthy growth than bottle-feeding. Breast-feeding ensures healthy development of the brain and nervous system; it strengthens the infant's immune system and protects against infectious diseases; and it helps build denser bones. Bottle-feeding is especially risky in developing countries, where the cost of formula is so high that women often dilute it with water that may not be clean.

- Inadequate nutrition may result in severely depressed growth rates. During World Wars I and II, height, weight, and age of puberty were affected by lack of adequate nutrition. Other environmental factors that may affect growth rates include illness, disease, and climate.

- Environmental influences such as nutrition and housing interact with other factors to produce a considerable variation in growth rates among people of different nationalities, ethnicities, and socioeconomic classes. The effects of poverty may be seen in such disorders as **iron-deficiency anemia,** common among minority children and children in low-income countries.

- Following environmental injury or deprivation, a strong corrective principle appears to operate in the case of physical growth. The degree of **catch-up growth** will depend on the duration, severity, and timing of the deprivation, in addition to the nature of the subsequent treatment or therapy. In general, the earlier and more prolonged the malnutrition, the more difficult it is to regain a normal level of growth.

- **Secular trends** in many countries show that people have become taller over time. Although in the United States people in the most advantaged groups may have reached their maximum potential in height gain, people in other segments of society continue to grow taller; both genetic and environmental factors influence this tendency.

- Although the problem of **obesity** may begin in infancy and childhood, only about one-quarter of obese infants will remain obese 20 years later. The two critical periods for the development of obesity are during infancy and at about 4 years of age. Recent research indicates that genetic factors may play a role in determining later obesity; however, parents' strategies for getting their children to eat may contribute as well.

- In addition to physical problems, such as hypertension and diabetes, obese children and adolescents may experience body-image disturbances and may suffer discrimination by peers and adults. Effective diet programs for children focus on changing the eating patterns and exercise behaviors of both the child and other family members.

- Eating disorders include **anorexia nervosa,** which may occur early in adolescence and results from reduced intake of calories, and **bulimia nervosa,** which typically occurs in later adolescence and is characterized by food binges and purging through vomiting.

Sexual Maturation

- **Puberty,** the onset of sexual maturity, is triggered when the **pituitary gland** stimulates other endocrine glands to secrete **hormones,** including **estrogens** and **progesterone** in females and **testosterone** in males, that initiate a growth spurt. This milestone in growth is marked by changes such as the start of breast development and **menarche** in girls, and the enlargement of the testes and **spermarche** in boys. Girls tend to reach menarche earlier in the more advanced countries, but there is still considerable variation in the onset of menstruation throughout the world.

- Inheritance is a strong factor in the timing of menarche, although environmental conditions such as conflict within the family and the absence of the father may also exert an influence on when a young girl reaches menarche.

- The timing of physical maturation can affect the child's social and emotional adjustment. Research indicates that the effects for late-maturing boys and early-maturing girls are largely negative. In general, the impact of the timing of puberty is best understood in the context of other transitions, such as school transitions and family disruptions, which may help or hinder the child's ability to cope with biological changes.

- There are wide individual differences in rates of maturation. However, in general, girls mature earlier than boys; on average, major changes occur two years earlier for girls. Although early maturation is usually seen as advantageous for boys, girls sometimes find early maturation stressful, developing poor body images and engaging in so-called adult behaviors such as drinking and smoking at an early age.

Sexual Orientation and Identity

- Most adolescents develop a heterosexual orientation, but a small minority identify themselves as gay, lesbian, or bisexual. Genetic and hormonal factors, as well as family influences, may contribute to the development of same sex preferences.

- Awareness of gender preferences may begin in early childhood or be delayed until adolescence. The identity process involves several steps from initial questioning one's sexual identity to a final phase of identity integration.

- Disclosure is often accompanied by initial negative reactions from family and friends but varies by ethnicity and religious beliefs. Family support can help buffer nonheterosexual adolescents from the negative effects of discrimination.

EXPLORE AND DISCUSS

1. The development of the brain can be modified by environmental factors that range from useful stimulation to the extreme deprivation often suffered by children reared in orphanages. What implications does this plasticity of the brain have for the heredity-environment debate?

2. Motor development is influenced by a variety of factors. What role may culture play in the timing of children's walking? Discuss the proposition that some cultures are more skilled in certain motor areas than others.

3. Children and adolescents are becoming increasingly obese. What factors do you think account for this alarming trend?

4. Why do you think that young people are reaching sexual maturity at earlier ages than in the past?

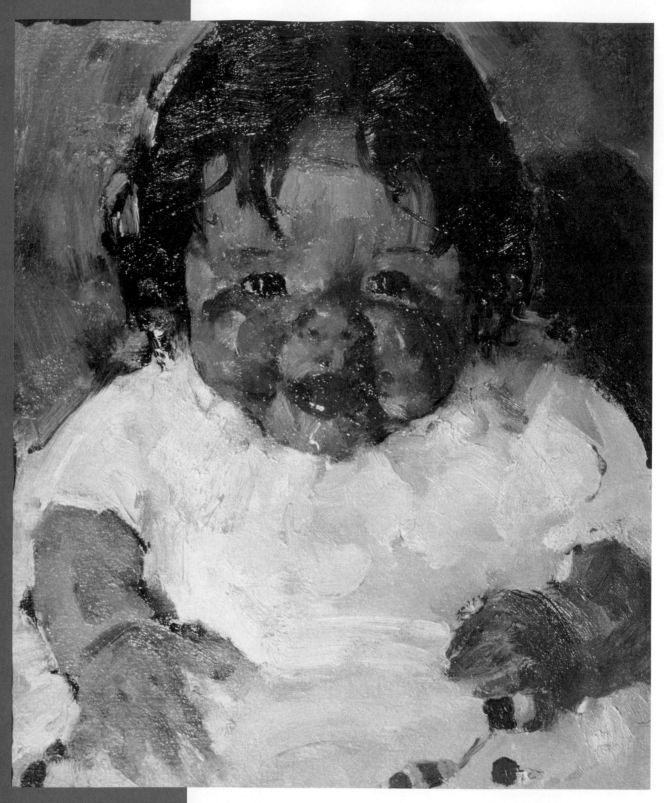

Martha Walter (1875–1976). *California Indian Child,* c. 1920. David David Gallery, Philadelphia.

6.

Emotional Development and Attachment

Children display a wide range of emotions, even from the time they are infants. Babies communicate their feelings, needs, and desires to others through the expression of emotion. The smiling infant tells others that something is pleasurable to him, and his frown communicates displeasure. Babies also influence the behavior of other people by their expression of emotions. When a baby smiles, for instance, caregivers are almost sure to approach her, pick her up, talk to her, caress her; when a stranger approaches, on the other hand, her screams are apt to stop the stranger from picking her up. The older child may use smiling as a sign of welcome and express anger as a way of deterring a potential aggressor. In addition to using their own emotions to communicate with and regulate their worlds, children learn to read the emotional signs that other people display. Both processes—the production and the recognition of emotion—are essential to useful interactions with other people, and they enable babies to begin to exert some control over their social world.

We begin this chapter by examining why emotions are important and a variety of theories that help explain emotional development. Next we explore children's earliest expressions of emotion and their beginning efforts to recognize emotions in other people. We then look at three of the earliest emotional expressions—smiling, laughter, and fear—in some detail. Then we look at the development of some of the complex emotions such as pride, shame, guilt, and jealousy. Next we discuss how children learn to regulate their emotions and how the family contributes to the socialization of different aspects of emotional development. Concluding our discussion of emotion, we explore how children think about emotions as they learn to match emotions to situations and begin to develop an awareness of their ability to experience more than one emotion at a time. We then turn to the study of attachment, first reviewing several theories of how attachment relationships form and then tracing the evolution of these relationships between infants and parents, siblings, and others.

In the last section of the chapter we explore the nature and quality of attachment relationships, considering such issues as the role of parenting styles in these relationships and the effects of attachment quality on the child's cognitive and social development as well as on her sense of self. We conclude by examining the important question of the effects of child care and multiple caregivers on the children of working parents.

EARLY EMOTIONAL DEVELOPMENT

emotions Subjective reactions to the environment that are usually experienced cognitively as either pleasant or unpleasant, generally accompanied by physiological arousal, and often expressed in some visible form of behavior.

What are **emotions?** Emotions, such as joy, anger, and fear, have several important aspects: They are subjective reactions to the environment; they are usually experienced cognitively as either pleasant or unpleasant; they generally are accompanied by some form of physiological arousal; and they can be communicated to others by some behavior. Thus, for example, Becky, the family's newest member, may react to the taste of a different formula with disgust, experiencing it as unpleasant, and if we were to measure her heart rate we might find it had accelerated. Moreover, because Becky has not yet learned to hide her emotions, as adults sometimes do, she would doubtless let her family know in no uncertain terms of her displeasure. Watching her wrinkle up her face, spit up, and cry, Becky's parents could be pretty certain of the source of her unhappiness.

Why Are Emotions Important?

Emotions have a wide variety of functions in the lives of children. First, as we just noted, emotions are means of letting others know how we feel. Second, our success in communicating our emotions and in learning to interpret other people's emotions is linked with our social success. Being able to express and interpret emotions is just as important as being able to solve a cognitive problem. Just as we have intellectual or cognitive intelligence, we develop emotional intelligence as well. As Daniel Goleman, in his popular book *Emotional Intelligence* (1995), has documented, being able to navigate successfully in the world of your own and other people's emotions is a critical ingredient of social and occupational success.

Emotions are linked to children's mental and physical health as well. As we explore in greater detail in the chapter on psychopathology, children who become excessively sad and despondent may develop other problems such as poor concentration and withdrawal from social interaction with others. In extreme cases, such children's self-worth may deteriorate seriously. Physical health suffers too when emotional development goes wrong. Children reared in environments in which they are emotionally and socially deprived, such as orphanages, often develop later problems with the management of stress and anxiety. The fact that these children have more difficulty modulating their reactions to stress is revealed by heightened levels of *cortisol* (a biological marker of stress response) that, in turn, may lead to problems of physical health (Gunnar, 2000; Rutter, 2002). Even children reared in ostensibly normal homes may suffer impaired physical health when they are exposed to emotional hostility between their parents (Gottman, Katz, & Hooven, 1996). Clearly, emotions have a wide range of effects on children's development.

Perspectives on Emotional Development

A child's emotional development is influenced by many factors: her genetic inheritance, the conditions of the environment into which she is born, her interactions with family members and, later, with peers—these and other factors all play important roles in determining her emotional makeup. In this section we examine four theoretical perspectives on emotional development: the genetic-maturational, learning, cognitive, and functionalist perspectives. Each of these four perspectives may be useful in explaining certain aspects of the child's development at certain stages of her life. And, as you will see, all views overlap to some degree.

THE GENETIC-MATURATIONAL PERSPECTIVE   According to the genetic-maturational view, emotions are best seen as products of biological factors. Individual differences in temperament play a central role in how intensely children react to emotionally arousing situations and in how well they are able to regulate their reactions. And right- and left-brain hemispheres control joy and fear expressions, respectively (see Chapter 2). Twin studies and cross-cultural research support the biological underpinnings for the development of emotions. Identical twins show greater similarity than fraternal twins in both the earliest times of their first smiles and the amount of smiling in which each engages (Plomin et al., 1997). Studies of smiling in premature infants support the role of genetic-maturational factors in the onset of smiling. The normal *conceptual age* (age since conception) of a newborn human is 40 weeks, and most full-term babies begin to smile about 6 weeks after they are born, or at a conceptual age of 46 weeks. Premature infants who are born at 34 weeks often do not smile until 12 weeks after birth, which for them is also 46 weeks since conception (Dittrichova, 1969). A certain amount of physical maturation and social stimulation must occur before a baby is ready to start smiling. The interplay between genetics and the environment accounts for the timing of smiling. A genetic-maturational basis for negative emotions, such as fear, is supported by both twin and cross-cultural studies. Again, identical twins are more similar than fraternal twins in their fear reactions to strangers and in their general degree of inhibitedness (Plomin et al., 1997; Robinson, Kagan, Reznick, & Corley, 1992).

THE LEARNING PERSPECTIVE   The learning perspective is particularly useful in explaining individual differences in emotional expression. In general, different emotional expressions have different onsets, frequencies, and intensities in different children. The frequency with which children smile and laugh seems to vary with the nature of the environment in which they are raised (Denham, 1998). Parents can help their children learn to manage and understand their emotions by rewarding only certain emotional displays. Or they can interfere by being punitive and by dismissing their children's emotional expressions and experiences (Gottman et al., 1996). Common sense suggests that parents who respond with enthusiasm to their smiling infant will tend to encourage him to smile more. This has in fact been verified in studies showing that when adults, particularly familiar caregivers, respond to a baby's smile with positive stimulation, the child's rate of smiling increases (Rovee-Collier, 1987).

Learning experiences can also elicit and reinforce fear responses. Recall our example, in Chapter 4, of how a child may become classically conditioned to fear the doctor who gave him a painful shot on his first visit. Children may learn other fears through operant conditioning when one of their own behaviors, such as climbing up on a high ladder, is followed by a punishing consequence, such as a painful fall. And they can learn still other fears simply by observing others. For example, a child may watch her mother react fearfully to a bee or to a large dog and later imitate her mother's reaction (Bandura, 1989). In all these cases, the child's particular set of fears depends on what she has learned.

THE COGNITIVE PERSPECTIVE   The cognitive view focuses on the infant's growing ability to acquire knowledge about the world. This general perspective, which we will discuss at greater length in Chapters 8 and 9, proposes that infants acquire mental representations, or *schemata,* of objects in their world and develop increasing ability to assimilate new stimuli as instances of these representations

(Denham, 1998; Sroufe, 1996). Recall from our introduction to Piaget's theory in Chapter 1 that assimilation is the process by which we incorporate new events into our existing knowledge base. For instance, if the smiling face of a stranger appears before a baby about 2 months old, the child typically will stare soberly at the person for a few moments and then break into a smile (Zelazo, 1972). It is as if the baby suddenly recognizes the face for what it is, "matching" it to a scheme for "face" stored in memory. This recognition gives the child pleasure, hence the smile. According to Sroufe (1996), the baby engages in a tension-relaxation cycle: Confronting a novel event causes a buildup of tension; the infant responds with cognitive effort to master the meaning of the event; when the infant is successful, her tension is released and she smiles.

THE FUNCTIONALIST PERSPECTIVE   The functionalist perspective is a contemporary approach to emotional development (Saarni, Campos, & Camras, 2006). According to this theory, emotions serve to help us achieve our goals and adapt to our environment, and it emphasizes the role of emotions in establishing and maintaining social relationships as well as the role that social cues play in regulating our emotional perceptions and expressions. This approach incorporates many features of the learning and cognitive perspectives in a unified view of emotional development.

How does this perspective approach emotional development? It assumes that the purpose of emotion is to help us achieve our goals. We all have goals that we try to reach—for example, to make a new friend, or to stay out of danger. And goals arouse emotions: joy and hope arise as we anticipate forming a new friendship; fear may engulf us in a scary situation. In both cases, the emotions aroused help us reach our goals. The emotion of fear may lead us to flee the dangerous situation, enabling us to achieve the goal of self-preservation.

The functional approach also recognizes the social nature of emotions. We use information provided by others' emotional signals to guide our own behavior. For instance, the way someone you view as a potential friend reacts emotionally to your social overture will be a critical determinant of how you feel. If she responds positively and smiles, you'll be happy and carry on, but if she frowns you'll probably not be pleased and will try to make friends with someone else. So, you evaluate the situation and use the feedback from others as a guide. Finally, memories of the past serve as a guide in shaping how the child will respond emotionally to a situation. Children who have routinely been rebuffed by potential friends will be more wary, whereas children who have been socially successful will be more confident in this situation. In both cases, emotions regulate children's behavior and enhance their adaptation to their environment.

No one theoretical perspective alone is likely to integrate all aspects of emotional development. Instead, different theories are useful in answering different questions. Emotional responses are shaped by a complex interplay between biological factors and the many forces of the environment that the child experiences. As we look at different aspects of emotional development, we will consider how each of the four perspectives we have examined helps us understand issues of emotional development.

How Infants and Children Express Their Emotions

Most parents pay a great deal of attention to their newborn infants' behaviors and activities, and witnessing displays, such as smiling, frowning, and laughing many times over, they are inclined to agree that infants display a wide range of emotions at a very early age. In one study, 99 percent of mothers said that their 1-month-olds clearly displayed interest; 95 percent of mothers observed joy; 85 percent, anger; 74 percent, surprise; 58 percent, fear; and 34 percent, sadness (Johnson, Emde,

Pannabecker, Stenberg, & Davis, 1982). These women based their judgments not only on their babies' behavior (facial expressions, vocalizations, body movements) but on the nature of the situations in which those behaviors occurred. For example, a mother who watched her baby staring intently at the mobile above her crib was likely to label the infant's emotion "interest," whereas she might call the emotion expressed by a gurgling, smiling baby "joy." As you continue through this chapter, you may find it useful to refer to the Turning Points chart (pp. 218–219), which offers a brief chronology of the milestones of emotional development in a typical child.

As we consider emotions, we will find it useful to distinguish between primary and secondary emotions. Primary emotions—such as fear, joy, disgust, surprise, sadness, and interest—emerge early in life and do not require introspection or self-reflection. Another set of emotions, the secondary, or self-conscious, emotions—such as pride, shame, guilt, jealousy, and embarrassment—emerge later in development and depend on our sense of self and our awareness of other individuals' reactions to our actions (Lewis, 1998; Saarni, 1999). We consider primary emotions first; later in the chapter we explore secondary emotions.

But is the human infant really capable of such a broad array of emotions that are recognizable in terms of adult expression and behavior? We have to be careful here, for it's not clear that young infants' emotional expressions are the same as what seem to be analogous adult expressions or even that infants are expressing the same sets of feelings. For example, what looks like anger in a baby may actually represent a generalized state of distress (Camras, Malatesta, & Izard, 1991). Carroll Izard, a pioneer in the study of infant emotion, holds that newborns do express specific emotions (Izard, 1994; Izard, Fantauzzo, Castle, Haynes, & Slomine, 1995). According to Izard, the first expressions to appear are *startle, disgust* (as in response to bitter tastes), *distress* (in response to pain), and a *rudimentary* or *reflex smile* that seems unrelated to external events. (The *true social smile,* a reaction to specific external stimuli, such as voices or faces, appears in most babies between about 4 and 6 weeks of age.) However, Izard proposes, not until babies are about $2\frac{1}{2}$ or 3 months old do they begin reliably to display facial expressions of anger, interest, surprise, and sadness (Izard et al., 1995). For example, although few 1-month-olds show anger expressions when their arms are gently restrained, by the time infants are 4 to 7 months old some 56 percent show clear expressions of anger at this restriction (Stenberg & Campos, 1989). These kinds of early emotions are probably influenced at the outset by genetic-maturational factors. Over time, learning, cognitive, and functional perspectives come into play. Moreover, Izard and his colleagues (1995) have found considerable stability of emotional expression between $2\frac{1}{2}$ and 9 months of age. That is, both the basic morphology, or form, of these expressions and their rate of occurrence were stable across the 7-month period. Interest, joy, sadness, and anger dominate the infant's repertoire during this period. Fear expressions enter the infant's emotional repertoire around 7 months (Camras et al., 1991), and shyness comes slightly later, between 6 and 8 months of age. Not until the second or third year do we see more sophisticated emotions, such as pride, guilt, or contempt, which involve evaluating the self or others according to specific behavioral standards.

Are you wondering how researchers can distinguish among infants' expressions of all these emotions? The answer is by means of coding systems that pay careful attention to changes in a baby's facial expressions and bodily movements. These systems assign finely differentiated scores to different parts of the face (e.g., lips, eyelids, forehead) and to specific infant movement patterns. Researchers then use these scores to judge whether an infant has displayed a particular emotion (e.g., Izard et al., 1995).

Not unlike adults, infants usually display emotions in response to particular external events (Sroufe, 1996). For example, researchers have evoked anger in 7-month-olds by offering them a teething biscuit and then withdrawing it just before it reaches the baby's mouth (Stenberg, Campos, & Emde, 1983). Two-month-olds respond

Turning Points

THE EVOLUTION OF EMOTIONAL EXPRESSION AND THE SENSE OF SELF

EARLY WEEKS	Shows distress by crying
1 MONTH	Generalized distress; may be irritable by late afternoon
2 MONTHS	Shows pleasure; mildly aroused by sight of toy; social smile
3 MONTHS	Excitement and boredom appear; smiles broadly and often; cries when bored; may show wariness and frustration
4 MONTHS	Laughs, especially at certain sounds; crying lessens; gurgles with pleasure; shows beginnings of anger
5 MONTHS	Usually gleeful and pleased but sometimes frustrated; shows primitive resistant behaviors; turns head from disliked food; smiles at own image in mirror; some babies may begin to show wariness of strangers
6 MONTHS	Matches emotions to others, e.g., smiles and laughs when mother does; fear and anger may appear now or later
7 MONTHS	Fear and anger; defiance; affection; shyness
8 MONTHS	More individuality in emotional expression; touches and explores body parts
9 MONTHS	Shows negative emotions when restrained; frowns when annoyed; actively seeks others' comfort when tired; nighttime crying may reappear; recognizes self in mirror; most babies display real fear of strangers
10 MONTHS	Intense positive and negative emotions; occasionally testy; uses reflection in mirror—e.g., seeing toy in mirror, may move toward toy
11 MONTHS	Greater variability in emotions; individual temperament is more evident; learning to associate names of body parts; may insist on feeding self
12 MONTHS	Becomes distressed when others are distressed; cries when something is not to liking; may show signs of jealousy; laughs often at own cleverness; struts/preens when walking; loves to look at self in mirror; wants to show mastery, and plays on own

Note: Developmental events described in this and other Turning Points charts represent overall trends identified in research studies. Individual children vary greatly in the ages at which they achieve these developmental changes.

Sources: Kopp, 1994; Saarni, Campos, & Camras, 2006; Sroufe, 1996.

15 MONTHS	More mood swings; is more caring to age-mates; annoyed by dirty hands; strongly prefers certain clothing; may fret or cry often but usually briefly
18 MONTHS	Can be restless and stubborn; may sometimes have tantrums; sometimes shy; shows shame; uses adjectives to refer to self; uses objects like a blanket or a favorite stuffed animal to soothe self

21 MONTHS	Makes some efforts to control negative emotions; can be finicky and exacting; makes more efforts to control situations; begins to understand parents' values; refers appropriately to self as *good* or *bad*
24 MONTHS	Can be contrary but also appropriately contrite; responds to others' moods; very intense; may be overwhelmed by changes; can be upset by dreams; refers to self by name; identifies self by gender; talks about self by using *I* and a verb, such as *hurt* or *need;* keen to experience world on own terms; begins to understand emotional display rules
30 MONTHS	Begins to show shame, embarrassment
36 MONTHS	Shows pride, guilt

48 TO 60 MONTHS	Shows increased understanding and use of emotional display rules
72 MONTHS	Begins to understand how two or more emotions can occur simultaneously

with a distress expression to being inoculated by a physician, whereas 6-month-old babies respond to the same stimulus with an expression of anger (Izard, Hembree, & Huebner, 1987). It seems that babies respond to emotional provocations in predictable ways at specific ages (Denham, 1998).

Do emotional experiences change across development? It is commonly thought that adolescents are moodier than younger children are. To test this assumption, Larson and his colleagues (Larson, Monetia, Richards, & Wilson, 2002) used an Experience Sampling Method (ESM) in which they used an electronic pager to beep preadolescents and adolescents in fifth through twelfth grades at random times during the day for two one-week periods. When beeped, the adolescents were to rate their emotional states (happy-unhappy, cheerful-irritable, friendly-angry) at that moment. Emotional states became less positive across early adolescence, but this downward change in average emotions ceased in grade 10. Not only are there general shifts in the pattern of positive and negative emotions across the age period, but the variability or fluctuations in emotional experience changes too. Specifically, girls were more variable in their emotional ratings during the high school years than boys. What accounts for the differences in daily emotions? Stressful life events (e.g., residence change, job loss in the family, divorce, death) were associated with more negative emotional states in both early and late adolescence. And emotions are linked with adjustment as well. Both younger and older adolescents who reported more positive daily emotions were less depressed and had fewer behavior problems and higher levels of self-esteem than those who reported fewer such feelings.

Are there gender differences in emotional expressiveness? Indeed there are (Brody, 2002), and they may surprise you. In one study, 6-month-old boys displayed both more positive (e.g., joy) and more negative (e.g., anger) expressions of emotion than girls (Weinberg, 1992). Others have found that boys cried more in response to frustration and took longer to recover when upset than girls (Fabes, Eisenberg, Nyman, & Michealieu, 1991). How can we reconcile these findings with the widely accepted and highly differentiated behaviors considered proper for men and women in U.S. society—lack of emotional expression in men (except, perhaps, for the expression of anger) and often intense emotional expression in women? According to Brody (2002), this apparent contradiction represents a "developmental shift" caused by different ways of socializing girls and boys with respect to the expression of emotions. To begin with, Brody suggests, parents may encourage more emotional expression in their infant daughters because their daughters' expressions are less intense and thus perhaps harder for parents to recognize. Brody also proposes that because girls tend to be more verbal at an earlier age than boys, parents may be likely to talk with a girl about emotions, heightening the possibility that the child will consider feelings important topics for expression and discussion (Dunn & Hughes, 2001). Finally, because parents tend to socialize children in accordance with the prevailing notions of what is socially acceptable, they may encourage emotionality in girls and try to suppress it in boys. Do you agree with Brody that these parental behaviors may in some cases produce a "self-fulfilling prophecy" (1996, p. 141)? These observations underscore the importance of the interplay between the child's actual characteristics and current cultural expectations. Thus, not only are the learning and functionalist perspectives on emotional development important, but we see again the value of an ecological viewpoint.

RECOGNIZING EMOTIONS IN OTHERS

Another challenge for the developing child is to learn how to recognize the emotions others express. According to Malatesta (1982), in the three months between the ages of 3 and 6, babies are exposed to others' facial expressions some 32,000 times! Learning to interpret these expressions of emotion is a formidable task for an infant.

But during this peak period for face-to-face interaction with parents or other caretakers, facial expressions are an effective way for parents to communicate their feelings and wishes to a child who cannot yet understand speech.

In mother-infant face-to-face interactions, babies tend to recognize positive emotions far more frequently than negative ones (Izard et al., 1995). More specifically, babies may develop the ability to recognize joy earlier than they can recognize anger. In one study, infants between 4 and 6 months of age looked longer at a face showing an expression of joy than at one showing anger (La Barbera, Izard, Vietze, & Parisi, 1976). And, consistent with the functionalist perspective, recognizing joy before anger has functional value for a baby:

> Recognition of joy can provide rewarding and self-enhancing experiences for the infant. Such recognition can also strengthen the mother-infant bond and facilitate mutually rewarding experiences, particularly if the joy recognition leads to joy expression. . . . [In contrast], anger recognition is not adaptive in the first half year of life. It seems reasonable that the threat of an anger expression would call for coping responses that are beyond the capacity of the 6-month-old. (La Barbera et al., 1976, p. 537)

The joy-anger recognition sequence is also consistent with the course of the infant's own emotional displays. As we will see, smiling and laughter emerge before fear.

The nature of early experience alters children's ability to recognize emotions, as the learning perspective on emotional development would predict. For example, $3\frac{1}{2}$-month-old infants recognize their mothers' emotional expressions earlier than they recognize such expressions in either fathers or strangers. Moreover, when mothers spent more time interacting directly with their babies, their infants were more successful at recognizing their mothers' emotional expressions (Montague & Walker-Andrews, 2002). However, both the quality and the quantity of interactions between parents and infants make a difference in children's ability to recognize emotions. Abused children who experience high levels of threat and hostility are able to identify anger expressions more easily than nonabused children are, but they are less capable of detecting expressions of sadness (Pollak & Sinha, 2002). The early family environment clearly plays a role in shaping children's abilities to recognize emotions.

It is probably harder for babies to learn to recognize expressions of emotions in others than it is for them to learn to express emotions accurately themselves. Citing the fact that around the world people use similar facial expressions of emotion, some researchers believe that producing these expressions is at least in part genetically determined (Ekman, 1994; Izard, 1994). If this were so, it would help to explain also why both babies and children are more accurate at producing emotional expressions than at interpreting them (Denham, 1998; Field, 1990). Nevertheless, by the time they are 2 or 3, children show production and recognition skills that are positively correlated: Toddlers who send clear emotional signals also tend to be good at identifying emotions (Magai & McFadden, 1995). Both these abilities continue to improve with age, probably contributing to the older child's ability to participate more often and more successfully in peer group activities as well as to his more sustained and sophisticated social interactions (Denham, 1998).

THE BEGINNINGS OF SPECIFIC EMOTIONS

With this general overview of early emotional development as a guide, let's turn to some specific examples: the development of smiling, of laughter, and of fear. All three of these show that emotions serve important functions in organizing the ways in which babies interact with others in their social worlds.

Smiling and Laughter: The First Expressions of Pleasure

reflex smile A smile seen in the newborn that is usually spontaneous and appears to depend on some internal stimulus rather than on something external such as another person's behavior.

At age 6 months, Liah smiled widely whenever her mother reached down to pick her up; by 12 months, Liah was laughing and giggling every time she and her dad played peek-a-boo. What events elicit the smiling and laughter, and what is the developmental course of joy and pleasure? As we have already noted, if you watch closely, you can see smiles even in newborn infants. These **reflex smiles** (Wolff, 1987) are usually spontaneous and appear to depend on the infant's internal state, but the exact nature of the internal stimulus is as yet unknown. Whether or not researchers can shed light on the origin of the baby's reflex smiles, these smiles serve a good purpose. Most caregivers interpret these smiles as signs of pleasure, and this gives the caregivers pleasure and encourages them to cuddle and talk to the baby. In this sense, these smiles may have adaptive value for the baby, ensuring critical caregiver attention and stimulation. Overall, early as well as later smiling helps keep caregivers nearby and thus becomes a means of communication and aid to survival (Saarni, 1999).

Between 3 and 8 weeks of age, infants begin to smile in response not only to internal events but to a wide range of external elicitors, including social stimuli such as faces, voices, light touches, and gentle bouncing (Sroufe, 1996). Infants are particularly interested in people and faces, and a high-pitched human voice or a combination of voice and face are reliable smile elicitors for babies between 2 and 6 months old. When 3-month-old infants were shown a human face and puppets whose faces varied in their resemblance to a human face, the infants smiled almost exclusively at the human face (Ellsworth, Muir, & Hains, 1993). Babies aren't such gullible little creatures; they know the "real thing" when they see it!

As infants grow older, they tend to smile at different aspects of the human face (Saarni et al., 2006). As we saw in Chapter 4 (see Figure 4-6), when 4-week-old babies look at human faces they tend to focus on the eyes, but by the time they're 8 or 9 weeks old they examine the mouth as well. Smiling behavior follows a similar pattern: At first babies smile at the eyes, then the mouth, and finally the entire face and the facial expression. By the time they are about 3 months old, babies also start to smile more selectively at familiar faces (Camras et al., 1991), a fact that lends some support to the notion that smiling has begun to signal pleasure and not just arousal. For example, 3-month-olds show greater increases in smiling when their smiles are reinforced by reciprocal smiles and vocalizations from their mothers than when they are reinforced by equally responsive women who are strangers (Wahler, 1967); these findings are consistent with the learning and functionalist perspectives. A baby's pleasure at watching a familiar face is revealed in other ways as well. For instance, one study found that 10-month-olds generally reserved a special kind of smile for their mothers, rarely offering it to strangers (Fox & Davidson, 1988). These special smiles (called *Duchenne smiles* after Guillaume Duchenne, the French physician who noticed this pattern more than 100 years ago) are likely to involve not just an upturned mouth but wrinkles around the eyes as well, making the whole face seem to light up with pleasure (Ekman, Davidson, & Friesen, 1990). Apparently babies display genuine smiles more in interacting with caregivers than when smiling alone (Messinger, Fogel, & Dickson, 2001).

Of course, not all babies smile with equal frequency at their caregivers: There are individual differences in the amount of smiling a baby does. Some of these differences have to do with the social responsiveness of the baby's environment. For example, as Figure 6-1 shows, Israeli infants reared in a family environment smiled more often by the second half year than infants raised in either a kibbutz (a communal living arrangement—see "Styles of Caregiving") or an institution, where the level of social stimulation is presumably lower (Gewirtz, 1967). Gender also seems to affect

LifeMap CD

For an evolutionary perspective on how humans display emotions, view the "Language of the Face" video in Chapter 6 of your CD.

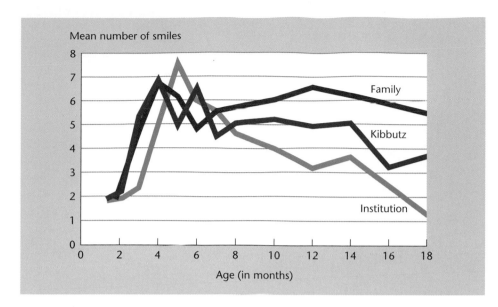

Figure 6-1

Smiling and the environment

Although initially Israeli infants raised either by their families, in a kibbutz, or in an institution smiled at about the same rate, by the time they were 8 or 9 months old they had begun to display different rates of smiling that continued to diverge. Kibbutz children smiled more than those who were institutionalized, but children raised at home smiled most of all.

Source: Adapted from Gewirtz, 1967.

babies' smiling: In the newborn period, at least, girls generally show more spontaneous smiles than boys do (Korner, 1974). Nor are gender differences in smiling restricted to infants—teenage girls smile more than teenage boys (La France, Hecht, & Levy Paluck, 2003). This higher rate of smiling has led some observers to suggest that girls may be genetically better prepared for social interaction than boys, because their greater tendency to smile more often draws others to them (Saarni, 1999). This view supports the genetic-maturational perspective. On the other hand, as we saw earlier in our discussion of Brody's (2000) work on gender differences in emotional expression, parents generally elicit and expect more emotions from girls than boys, which suggests that both genetic and environmental factors need to be considered. And there are national and ethnic gender differences in smiling (La France et al., 2003). Compared with their peers in Great Britain, children and adults in the United States and Canada show larger sex differences in smiling. Perhaps Europeans have less stereotyped views of gender differences and treat boys and girls more similarly than do North Americans. And European American males and females differ more in their smiling rates than do African Americans, among whom males and females show smaller differences in their smiling behavior. This ethnicity difference is consistent with the finding that African American parents treat boys and girls more similarly than European American parents do (see Chapter 13).

Infant smiling clearly becomes more discriminating as children develop. However, overall it also increases as a form of social behavior. It plays a central role in the infant's greeting behavior and occurs more frequently when the infant is with other people than when he is alone (Fogel, 1993; La Freniere, 2000; Sroufe, 1996).

Laughing, at which infants become quite skilled by the time they're 4 months old (Sroufe, 1996), is if anything even more useful in maintaining the baby's well-being (Nwokah, Hsu, Dobrowolska, & Fogel, 1994). If smiling gradually becomes a sign of pleasure, laughter leaves us with little doubt of a baby's positive emotion, and it plays a very important role in caregiver-infant interaction.

What sorts of events elicit laughter across the first year of life? Sroufe and Wunsch (1972), using mothers as their experimental assistants, examined the amount of laughter elicited in babies between 4 and 12 months of age by a wide array of visual, tactile, auditory, and social-behavioral stimuli—for example, a human mask or a disappearing object; bouncing the child on an adult's knee or blowing on the baby's hair; making lip-popping, whispering, or whinnying sounds; and playing peek-a-boo, covering the baby's face, or sticking out the tongue.

Figure 6-2

What makes children laugh?
Between the ages of 4 months and a year, children were most consistently likely to laugh at visual and social stimuli, such as a disappearing object or playing peek-a-boo.

Source: From Sroufe & Wunsch, 1972.

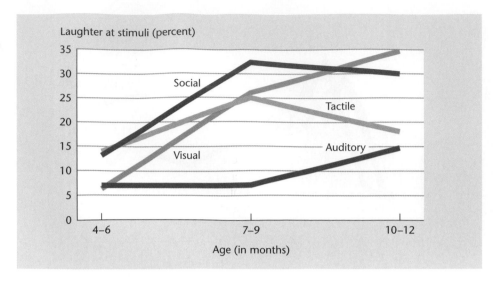

As Figure 6-2 shows, up to about 7 months of age babies are increasingly likely to laugh at visual, tactile, and social events, but their reactions to auditory stimulation remain stable. Note, however, that the nature of the stimuli that elicit laughter changes as the child develops. From 7 months on, both social and tactile stimuli begin to be less effective, but response to visual stimuli continues to increase. Toward the end of the first year, babies respond more to social games, visual displays, and other activities in which they can participate, such as covering and uncovering the mother's face with a cloth or playing tug-of-war with a blanket. By the end of the first year and throughout the second year, infants increasingly smile and laugh in response to activities that they create themselves (Sroufe, 1996), such as practicing their motor accomplishments by pulling themselves to a standing position or laughing after making a jack-in-the-box pop up. As children grow older, laughing increases and becomes more of a social event (Saarni, 1999). In one study of 3- to 5-year-olds, nearly 95 percent of laughter occurred in the presence of other children and adults (Bainum, Lounsbury, & Pollio, 1984). Acting silly was most often the elicitor of laughter among the nursery school set.

Fear: One of the First Negative Emotions

Timothy, at the age of 8 months, is exploring some toys in his playpen. He looks up and sees a strange woman standing near, watching him. Timothy turns back to his toys briefly, then again solemnly looks at the stranger, whimpers, turns away, and begins to cry. In the continuing search for regularities in early development, few phenomena have captured as much time, effort, and interest as this type of exchange between an infant and a stranger. Apparently, at the same time that babies are beginning to display signs of positive emotion in smiles and laughter, they are also learning to be fearful of some events and people, especially unfamiliar ones (La Freniere, 2000).

FEAR OF STRANGERS   The negative emotional response called *fear of strangers* evolves more slowly than the positive emotional expressions we've just discussed. Sroufe (1996) distinguishes two phases in the emergence of fear. At about 3 months of age, Sroufe maintains, infants show *wariness,* in which they respond with distress to an event that includes both familiar and unfamiliar aspects and which they therefore cannot comprehend and assimilate. This argument is consistent with the cognitive perspective on emotional development. By the time they are 7 to 9 months old, babies show true *fear*, which is an immediate negative reaction to an event that has specific meaning for them, such as seeing the face of a total stranger (e.g., "I don't know what this is, and I don't like it").

Even at 4 months of age, babies smile less at unfamiliar adults than they do at their mothers, showing early signs that they recognize familiar people. But they are not yet distressed by the presence of a stranger. In fact, they show great interest in novel people as well as novel objects. Often they look longer at a stranger than at a familiar person, and if the mother is present, they will frequently look back and forth between her face and the stranger's, as if comparing them. Then, at about 5 months of age, this earlier reaction of gaze and interest starts to be replaced largely by giving a stranger a sober stare. At 6 months, although babies still are most likely to react to strangers with a sober expression, they're also likely to display distress. A distress reaction then gradually increases in frequency over the next half year, and by 7 to 9 months, the earlier wary reactions give way to clear expressions of fear. Figure 6-3 summarizes this progression from interest and exploration to fear over the first year of life (Emde, Gaensbauer, & Harmon, 1976).

Fear of strangers, or **stranger distress,** has become enshrined in the psychological literature as a developmental milestone and at one time was thought to be both inevitable and universal. Researchers now know that it is neither (La Freniere, 2000). Stranger distress emerges at about 7 to 9 months of age in several cultures, including the Hopi Indians (Dennis, 1940) and in Uganda (Ainsworth, 1963). However, in other cultures, such as the Efe (Africa), that emphasize shared caregiving among relatives babies show little stranger fear (Tronick, Morelli, & Ivey, 1992). Whether a baby is fearful of a stranger depends on a host of variables, including who the stranger is, how he or she behaves, the setting in which the person is encountered, and the child's age (Mangelsdorf, Watkins, & Lehn, 1991). Moreover, babies are not all alike in their reactions to strangers. For some, greeting and smiling may be a frequent reaction,

Somewhere around the age of 7 to 9 months children begin to experience fear, especially in response to unfamiliar people or events. This child clearly doesn't want the little Dalmatian puppy anywhere near her.

stranger distress A fear of strangers that typically emerges in infants around the age of 9 months.

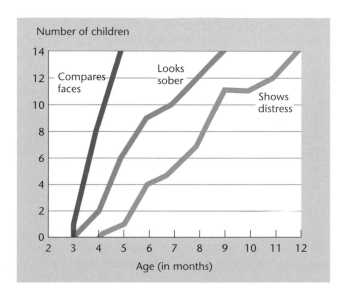

Figure 6-3

The onset of stranger distress

At 8 months of age, half of the children studied were showing distress at the appearance of strangers, and within a month or two this distress reaction was clearly dominant.

Source: Adapted from Emde, Gaensbauer, & Harmon, 1976.

and fear is not typical (Rheingold & Eckerman, 1973). Let's look at some of the factors that affect infants' reactions to strangers: individual infants' tendencies to fearfulness, the context, and characteristics of the strangers themselves.

INDIVIDUAL DIFFERENCES IN FEARFULNESS   There are wide individual differences among infants and young children in their reactions to strangers and other potentially fear-arousing people and events. As we saw in Chapter 2, infants and children differ widely in temperament. For instance, Kagan (1998) has identified a subset of children whom he calls "behaviorally inhibited." These children tend to be shy, fearful, and introverted, often avoiding even their peers, and they are more anxious and upset by mildly stressful situations than are other children (Kagan, 1998). Behaviorally inhibited youngsters tend to show atypical physiological reactions—such as rapid heart rates—in stressful situations, and their fearful responses and shyness tend to endure across time, from toddlerhood on into the early school years. According to Kagan, inhibitedness may be a stable characteristic of some children. However, warm, supportive parents can reduce fearfulness and lessen the likelihood that their children will continue to be abnormally shy and fearful (Gunnar, 1998; Kagan, 1998).

Other evidence that individual makeup contributes to a child's fearfulness comes from the finding that there is considerable consistency in the way a particular baby reacts to a variety of strangers, regardless of differences in the strangers' personal characteristics (Smith & Sloboda, 1986). Babies who are more sociable show less wariness in encounters with strangers than less sociable infants (Bohlin & Hagekull, 1993). These individual differences can be viewed as temperamental variations which is consistent with the genetic-maturational perspective on emotional development.

Finally, individual differences in positive and negative emotionality are related to children's adjustment (Lengua, 2002). For example, 10-year-olds who exhibited high levels of negative emotionality (fearfulness and irritability) were more likely to have adjustment difficulties. They tended to be depressed and to have conduct problems. Children who were judged emotionally positive (rated high on smiling and laughing) had high self-esteem and social competence, indicating better adjustment.

THE INFLUENCE OF CONTEXT   Consistent with the functionalist perspective on emotional development, contextual factors help determine the way an infant will react to a stranger. One such factor is the setting in which the encounter occurs. Ten-month-olds show little fear of the strangers they meet in their own homes, but nearly 50 percent of youngsters of this age group are fearful when encountering a stranger in the unfamiliar setting of a researcher's lab (Sroufe, Waters, & Matas, 1974). Similarly, babies who sit on their mothers' laps while a stranger approaches rarely show any fear—but when they're not in physical contact with their caregiver, they may show fear when a stranger approaches (Bohlin & Hagekull, 1993; Morgan & Ricciuti, 1969). Apparently, it is not just the presence of an unfamiliar person but the degree of security the baby feels in the surrounding context that determines her reaction.

Another situational factor in a baby's response to a stranger is the extent to which the mother's face, voice, and body signal either comfort and serenity or apprehension and alarm. When a baby sees his mother reacting positively to a stranger, he tends to follow suit and responds much more positively, smiling more, approaching the stranger, and offering his toys (Feinman & Lewis, 1983). Conversely, when the mother adopts a worried look in the presence of a stranger, her baby is apt to cry more and smile less (Boccia & Campos, 1989; Mumme, Fernald & Herrera, 1996). These studies illustrate **social referencing** in infants—that is, the process of "reading" emotional cues in other people to help determine how to act in an uncertain situation (Saarni, 1999). Much of this work has been stimulated by the functionalist perspective on emotional development. This social referencing undergoes clear changes over time

social referencing The process of "reading" emotional cues in others to help determine how to act in an uncertain situation.

(Walden, 1991). As infants develop they are more likely to look at the mother's face than at other parts of her body. Babies between 14 and 22 months old were clearly more aware that their mother's face was the best source of information than were babies 6 to 9 months old (Walden, 1991). Infants grow also in their tendency to check with their mothers before they act. Younger infants often act first and look later, a strategy that could lead to trouble in a dangerous situation. The fact that even infants learn to use others' emotional expressions as a guide to their own actions underscores the importance of emotion for regulating social behavior (Saarni et al., 2006).

A third contextual factor is the degree to which the situation allows the infant some control over the extent and pace of the interaction (Mangelsdorf et al., 1991). When a baby can have an impact on how a stranger acts, he tends to be less apprehensive. In one study, when 1-year-old infants could control the noise and movement of a toy monkey (a strange event) that clapped cymbals together (Gunnar, 1980), they were less fearful than when they had no control over the toy's actions. Predictability of the noises was another factor that lowered distress in this situation. Even putting the clapping on a regular, fixed schedule (such as a cycle of four seconds on and four seconds off) was enough to cause infants to be less fearful (Gunnar, Leighton, & Peleaux, 1984).

CHARACTERISTICS OF THE STRANGER   Babies' emotional reactions to strangers are also affected by a stranger's personal characteristics. In one study, for instance, researchers showed babies between 7 and 19 months of age a strange man, a strange woman, a strange 4-year-old girl, the baby's mother, and the mirror reflection of the baby's own self (Lewis & Brooks, 1974). All the people (and the baby's own mirror image) presented to the babies were positioned at four different distances from them: 15 feet, 8 feet, 3 feet, and actually touching the baby. Two principal findings of this study, shown in Figure 6-4, were that the babies' reactions were conditioned both by the characteristics of the stranger—the 4-year-old child was

Figure 6-4   Proximity and age of a stranger affect babies' reactions

In this study of stranger distress, the gender of a stranger had no effect, but his or her age did. The infants did not perceive the 4-year-old stranger as threatening but reacted very negatively to both adults. Distance from the infants had relatively little effect on the way they perceived the young stranger, but the closer the adult strangers got, the more intensely the babies showed their distress. In comparison, the infants reacted quite positively both to their own reflections and to their mothers, and this tendency increased with proximity.

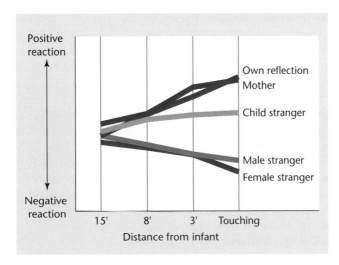

Source: Adapted from Lewis & Brooks, 1974.

Perhaps if Mom hadn't backed away to take a picture, this 1-year-old wouldn't have felt so threatened by Santa Claus.

apparently less threatening than the adults—and the closeness of the stranger to them—the closer the adult stranger got, the more negative the child's reaction.

To find out whether it was the size of the stranger or something about the stranger's facial configuration that caused infants to show more apprehensiveness toward adult strangers, Brooks and Lewis showed infants three more strangers: an adult, an adult midget, and a child (1976). The fact that the babies reacted significantly more negatively to the adult midget than to the child suggests that largeness is not the trait that triggers their apprehension. Probably, something about an adult's face seems less benign than a child's. Unfortunately, a "baby-faced" adult was not available to test this hypothesis!

A stranger's behavior also affects the degree of stranger distress an infant displays (Mumme et al., 1996; Ross & Goldman, 1977). When confronted by an active, friendly stranger who talks, gestures, smiles, imitates the baby, and offers toys, most 12-month-olds show little fear. In fact, they tend to be highly social and enjoy playing games with the stranger. In contrast, a passive stranger, who looks soberly at the infant, does not elicit this positive reaction. Apprehension, it seems, is elicited as much by behavior that seems threatening as by the simple sight of a stranger's face.

SEPARATION PROTEST   Some kinds of fear do appear to be universal and are present in all cultures. A common fear in childhood is associated with being separated from one's mother or other familiar caregivers. This fear, called **separation protest,** tends to peak in Western infants at about 15 months and, as Figure 6-5 shows, displays a remarkably similar timetable in such diverse cultures as those of Guatemala and the Kalahari Desert region in Botswana. As we will see later in the chapter, separation protest also occurs in infants in child care when working parents drop them off at a child-care center. Although *separation anxiety,* as this fear is also called, generally becomes less and less common in childhood, it sometimes reappears in other forms: Box 6.1 describes a recent study of homesickness among children at camp and suggests some useful ways of coping with this kind of distress.

separation protest An infant's distress reaction to being separated from his or her mother, which typically peaks at about 15 months of age.

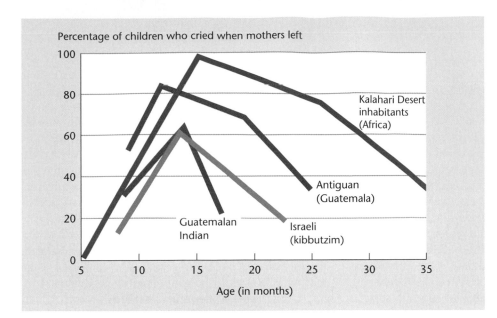

Percentage of children who cried when mothers left

Figure 6-5

Separation protest

Although children of four different cultures varied considerably in the intensity of their protest at their mothers' departures, they all tended to reach a peak of distress at about the same age, between 13 and 15 months.

Source: Reprinted by permission of the publisher from *Infancy: Its Place in Human Development* by Jerome Kagan, Richard B. Kearsley, and Philip R. Zelazo, p. 107, Cambridge, Mass.: Harvard University Press, Copyright © 1978 by the President and Fellows of Harvard College.

Complex Emotions: Pride, Shame, Guilt, and Jealousy

The appropriate display of more complex emotions, such as pride, shame, guilt, or jealousy, requires the ability to differentiate and integrate the roles of multiple factors in a situation, including the role of personal responsibility. Often called secondary, or "self-conscious," emotions because they rely on the development of self-awareness, these emotions begin to emerge toward the middle of the second year. For example, children may show embarrassment by blushing and turning away and they may express envy or jealousy by pouting when other children receive more desirable toys (Lewis, 1995). When a child is pleased with her accomplishments, she shows pride, but when she perceives that someone finds her wanting or deficient—perhaps she has failed an easy task—she shows evidence of shame. The feeling of guilt, which requires the development of a sense of personal responsibility and the internalization of moral standards, emerges a bit later than pride and shame (Tangney, 1998).

This boy is clearly proud and happy at winning a yellow ribbon in the Special Olympics.

PRIDE AND SHAME   Crucial to distinguishing between children's experiences of pride or shame is their emerging sense of the differences between "easy" and "difficult" and between "success" and "failure" (Lewis, 1992). Lewis and his colleagues (Lewis, 1992; Lewis, Alessandri, & Sullivan, 1992) found that by the time they were 3 years old, children were more likely to express pride if they succeeded at difficult tasks than at easy ones. They also expressed more shame if they failed an easy task but expressed little if any shame if they failed a difficult task. Solving a problem that was not particularly difficult elicited joy in these youngsters, but succeeding on a difficult task produced pride; failing a difficult task caused sadness, but failing an easy task aroused shame; see Figure 6-7 (Lewis et al., 1992).

Box 6.1
Child Psychology in Action

COPING WITH HOMESICKNESS

Homesickness, which is common in the middle and later childhood years, usually arises when children are away from home for periods of more than a day. Summer camps, boarding schools, college, foster homes, and hospitals are among the sites in which researchers have studied homesickness in children (Thurber & Weisz, 1997). *Homesickness,* a longing to be with one's family or regular caretakers, may be expressed in depressive or anxious behavior; in acting out, as in aggressive behavior; or in complaints about physiological problems, such as headache, stomachache, and other pains of an ill-defined nature.

How do children cope with homesickness? According to Thurber and Weisz (1997), a child's beliefs about his ability to exert control over a situation strongly determine his choice of coping mechanism. If a child who is sent to live with relatives because of economic distress at home believes he can change his situation, he may exert *primary control* by running away from his aunt's house and returning to his own home. Often, however, a child is unable to change his situation or finds that attempts to do so are unsuccessful and lead only to feelings of helplessness and depression. In this event, a child may instead elect *secondary control,* changing himself or his behavior to adapt to the unwanted situation. Thus, a child placed in a boarding school many miles from home might write letters home every day to feel in touch with his family, or he might join specific activities in which he had participated at home. A third way of dealing with homesickness is to *relinquish control,* or to give up trying to change things and seek solace in expressing sadness through a means such as crying or withdrawing from others.

Because some stressors are controllable and others are not, coping is often a mix of primary and secondary measures, the child trying first one and then another. The choice of coping measure depends on specific constraints of the situation, such as camp rules, as well as on individual characteristics, such as age, perceived ability to control events, and cognitive sophistication.

To study homesickness, Thurber and Weisz (1997) chose two summer camps, one for girls and one for boys, and found that overall, both boys and girls tended to use secondary control methods to cope with homesickness, most often doing something that was fun in order to forget their negative feelings. Among these youngsters, who ranged in age between 8 and 16 but who were on average $12\frac{1}{2}$, the most homesick were those most likely to relinquish control, making little effort to cope with their unhappiness. On the other hand, the least homesick were those who appeared to know how to use different combinations of both primary and secondary methods to cope with their

Children's understanding of pride also depends on their ability to entertain multiple emotions—such as pleasure at doing a task well and happiness that others appreciate the accomplishment (Saarni, 1999)—and on their sense of personal agency, or effort. To evaluate this understanding, Thompson (1989) told stories to 7-, 10-, and 18-year-olds involving accomplishments that individuals achieved either by their own efforts or by luck and then asked them questions about the stories. The 7-year-olds used the term *proud* in discussing good outcomes regardless of whether the actors in the stories had succeeded through their own efforts. More discriminating, the 10- and 18-year-olds realized that "feeling proud" can occur only when the good outcomes that occur are the result of a person's own effort, not of luck or chance.

GUILT   Only gradually do children develop an appreciation of the central role of personal responsibility in their behavior and thus an understanding of guilt. According to Graham, Doubleday, and Guarino (1984), this understanding emerges in

Figure 6-6 Coping with homesickness

When they were homesick at camp, both girls (G) and boys (B) preferred to talk with someone about it rather than act out in the hope of being sent home. However, this trend was much stronger in girls than in boys.

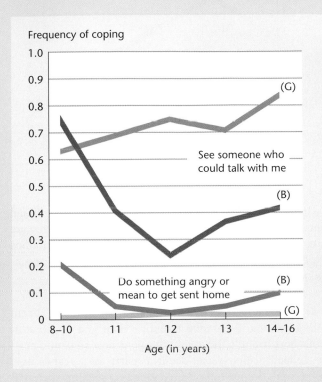

Frequency of coping

See someone who could talk with me

Do something angry or mean to get sent home

Age (in years)

Source: Adapted from Thurber & Weisz, 1997.

unpleasant feelings; this group was also the least likely to relinquish control.

Girls were more likely to call upon specific coping devices than were boys. However, there was also a significant gender difference in respect to the use of the primary control device of seeking out "someone who could talk with me and help me feel better, like a leader or one of my friends." Although 8- to 10-year-old boys and girls differed little on this parameter, from 11 on, girls were far more likely than boys to use this social-support approach to solving the problem of homesickness (Figure 6-6). As we've suggested earlier in the book, and will discuss at greater length in Chapter 13, girls seem to be more socially oriented from early on.

Thurber and Weisz (1997) conclude that useful intervention in homesickness involves helping children to understand that being homesick isn't just an unhappy emotion but an emotional reaction to circumstances, some of which they can control and some of which they can't. It's important to help children to distinguish these components of the problem and to help them develop specific coping methods at both the primary and secondary levels. Then one can show children how to apply each type for maximum benefit and help them understand why relinquishing control is not effective.

middle childhood. Asking 6- and 9-year-old children to describe situations in which they had felt guilty, these researchers found that only the older children had a clear understanding of this emotion and its relation to personal responsibility. For example, even when they had had little control over the outcome of a situation, 6-year-olds often described themselves as feeling guilty: "I felt guilty when my brother and I had boxing gloves on and I hit him too hard . . . sometimes I don't know my own strength." In contrast, 9-year-olds recognized that to feel guilty, it is critical to be responsible for the outcome of a situation: "I felt guilty when I didn't turn in my homework because I was too lazy to do it." Other studies (Saarni, 1999) have reached similar conclusions—namely, that young children focus on simple outcomes, whereas older children, who focus on the role of personal responsibility, understand that unless they themselves caused the outcome they need not feel guilty. Of course, guilt plays an important role in moral development, especially in terms of regulating behavior or as a response to rule violation (see Chapter 14).

Figure 6-7

Pride, shame, and task difficulty
The more difficult the task, the less shame children felt if they failed at it and the more pride they felt when they succeeded.

Source: Lewis et al., 1992.

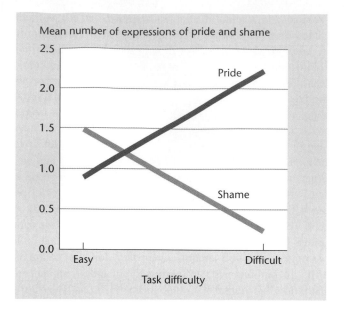

Although we often explore the development of human capacities such as emotional expression and cognitive competence separately, remember that these capacities are mutually dependent. For example, it's clear that the development of specific emotions is closely entwined with such cognitive advances as the ability to understand causality and, hence, personal responsibility.

JEALOUSY Jealousy is a common emotion that we all experience. From early childhood, when a sibling gets more parental attention than you do, to adolescence, when you resent your best friend's flirtation with your new romantic partner, you experience jealousy. Indeed, jealousy can occur as early as 1 year of age. In one study, children showed signs of jealousy (e.g., sadness, seeking maternal attention, anger) when mothers directed their attention away from their child toward an infant-size doll, a newborn infant, or a peer (Case, Hayword, Lewis, & Hurst, 1988; Hart, Field, DelValle, & Letourneau, 1998). Jealousy is a social emotion; it occurs among three people who have established important social relationships. Generally speaking, two people who have been friends for many years don't experience jealousy in interacting with a new acquaintance.

Recently, Volling, McElwain, & Miller (2002) explored jealousy among younger (12 months old) and older (2 to 6 years old) children. When mothers or fathers played with one child and encouraged her or his sibling to play alone, both younger and older children expressed jealousy of the sibling who received parental attention. Not surprisingly, the way that children express their jealousy changes across development. Volling and colleagues found that, in response to a jealousy-provoking scenario, younger children displayed distress, whereas older siblings showed sadness and anger. And jealousy reactions are costly: Children who react with jealousy may be less able to focus on their play activities than children who show less jealousy. As in the case of other complex emotions, such as pride and shame, cognitive understanding of emotions helps modify children's jealous reactions. Especially in older siblings, a more sophisticated understanding of emotions may be associated with less jealousy and less disturbed behavior.

Finally, the experience and expression of jealousy depend on the nature of the relationship in which this unpleasant emotion arises. When children have a secure and trusting relationship with their mothers and fathers, jealousy between siblings is less prevalent. Moreover, when parents are in a positive marriage, children are less likely to show jealous reactions with their siblings. Close relationships between child and parent and between the parents themselves serve as a protective factor in buffering children from jealousy reactions.

LEARNING TO REGULATE EMOTIONS

Learning how to regulate the expression of their emotions is a major challenge for infants and children. In this section, we trace the developmental changes in emotional regulation and the role of the family in this developmental progression. Often they get their first clue from something they began learning even before they were born: They found that putting their thumbs in their mouths helps soothe them. From this unintentional act of control, infants move to the more deliberate regulation of their emotions. For example, when they encounter a frightening event they may turn away, place their hands over their faces, or distract themselves by some form of play (Bridges & Grolnick, 1995). Children's methods of emotional control continue to change as they grow older. Mangelsdorf, Shapiro, and Marzolf (1995) found that 6-month-olds who confronted a stranger typically looked away or became fussy, whereas 18-month-olds more likely used self-soothing and self-distraction to cope with uncertain or arousing situations.

The Emergence of Emotional Display Rules

As infants become toddlers and head toward the preschool years, parents and others start to require them to exert even more control over their emotional expression. Under this pressure, gradually "the intense and unregulated expressions of infancy give way to expressions that are more modulated" (Malatesta, Culver, Tesman, & Shepard, 1989). Several things illustrate this greater self-control over emotions: Emotional expressions become less frequent, less distinct, less intense and exaggerated, and less variable and more conventionalized (La Freniere, 2000; Saarni, 1999). For example, a hungry baby may cry in uncontrollable frustration, whereas an older child whose mealtime is delayed will merely pout and complain. And emotional regulation abilities are important predictions of later adjustment. Children in preschool who were better at regulating their anger showed less externalizing behavior when they entered school—those who were able to distract themselves by shifting attention away from the frustrating situation were less aggressive and disruptive in kindergarten (Gilliom, Shaw, Beck, Schonberg, & Lukon, 2002).

At the same time, children begin to learn **emotional display rules** that dictate what emotions to show under what circumstances. This often means learning to separate the visible expression of an emotion from its inner experience. Conforming to various social norms, children 8 to 10 years old learn to smile even when they feel unhappy, to feign distress that is not really felt, or to mask amusement when they know they shouldn't laugh (Garner & Power, 1996; Saarni et al., 2006). But children as young as 2 may show an understanding of display rules for emotions (Lewis & Michaelson, 1985). In their earliest attempts to follow these rules, children typically mirror others' behavior by simply exaggerating or minimizing their emotional displays. Moreover, children acquire knowledge about display rules before they are proficient regulators of their own emotional displays (Saarni, 1999).

emotional display rules Rules that dictate which emotions one may appropriately display in particular situations.

Culture plays an important role in how children appraise situations, communicate emotions, and act on their feelings. Studying three cultural groups—Brahman and Tamang societies in rural Nepal and a rural town in the United States—Cole, Bruschi, and Tamang (2002) compared the reactions of children to difficult emotionally arousing situations. They interviewed second, fourth, and fifth graders about how they would react to a difficult interpersonal situation, such as someone's spilling a drink on their homework or accusing them falsely of stealing. How would they feel? Would they want others to know their feelings? Why or why not? And what would they do in the situation? As expected, culture clearly influences children's emotional responses. Among the Tamang, a Buddhist group who endorse interpersonal harmony, children were more likely than the other two groups to respond to difficult situations with shame. In contrast, children of the Brahman society, which teaches self-control in social interactions and the careful control of emotions, did not reveal anger or shame in response to their emotionally upsetting problem. Different again were the American children, who were more likely to endorse the display of anger—an emotion consistent with the American value of self-assertion. U.S. children were more problem-focused and action-oriented than the children in the two Nepali groups, who were more accepting of difficult situations and less likely to seek to alter the situation. Clearly, cultural and religious customs and values shape the ways that children react to emotionally upsetting events. Learning to follow cultural display rules seems to be an important developmental accomplishment. It seems that competence in implementing these rules is linked with better social relationships with peers (McDowell, O'Neil, & Parke, 2000; Parke, McDowell, Kim, & Leidy, 2005).

The Family's Role

Families play a major role in children's emotional development. Suzanne Denham (1998), a leading emotions researcher, has outlined three ways in which families influence children's emotions (Figure 6-8). First, family members' own patterns of emotional expressiveness serve as models for the child's emotional expressiveness. Second, parents' and siblings' specific reactions to children's emotions encourage or discourage certain patterns of emotional expressiveness. Third, parents often act as

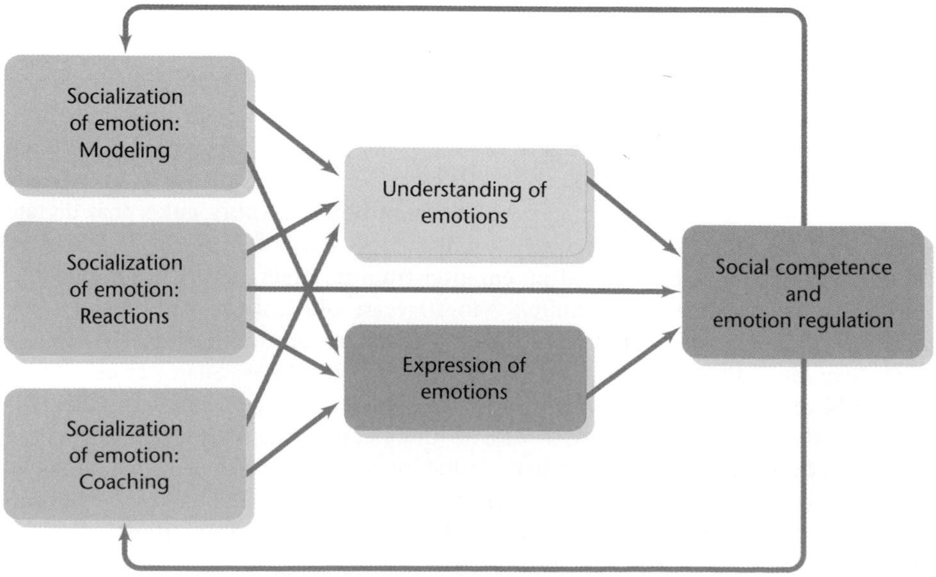

Figure 6-8

A model of emotional socialization

Parental socialization practices lead to changes in understanding and expression of emotions—which, in turn, lead to changes in children's social competence and in their abilities to regulate their emotions.

Source: Denham, 1998.

emotional coaches by talking about emotions and explaining and exploring children's understanding of their own and other people's emotional responses.

Just as children learn to share toys, to say their ABC's, and sometimes to hit people by watching others, they learn a great deal about how and when to express emotions by watching members of their family:

> Claire learned about anger and sadness. She witnessed an argument between her mother and father. The mother began to cry out of frustration and sadness over the long-standing, unresolved conflict. Claire watched with eyes wide. Then she got tearful herself. (Denham, 1998, p. 106)

Families vary in their emotional expressiveness. Some are subdued and restrained in their emotional reactions; others are more demonstrative and engage in more intense and frequent emotional displays. Many studies have shown similarities between parents and their children in both level of emotional expressiveness and types of emotions typically displayed (Eisenberg et al., 2001; Halberstadt, Crisp, & Eaton, 1999). Children who grow up in a positive emotional home with lots of happiness and joy are more likely to exhibit positive emotions (Halberstadt et al., 1999). However, children who are reared in a negative family environment characterized by hostility and conflict are more likely to display negative emotions, such as anger and sadness (Halberstadt et al., 1999). To take an extreme example, children who have been abused by parents, particularly girls, are more likely to display shame and less likely to show pride than their nonabused peers; according to Alessandri and Lewis (1996), this reflects the intense and frequent negative feedback these girls receive from their parents. Children can learn both by watching how parents react emotionally to them, as well as by observing how parents and other family members react emotionally to each other. Watching mom and dad argue or siblings squabble or a mother smile at a baby sister are all ways of learning about the world of emotions.

Or sometimes parents' reactions contribute to children's emotional repertoire by helping them cope more effectively with their emotions and by improving their understanding of what emotions may appropriately be displayed:

> Stacey's mother bought a new wading pool and had high hope for the fun the family could have. Whether told to wait, get in or get out of the pool, Stacey cried and wouldn't be consoled. Nothing could please her. Finally she had a mini-tantrum, lying down on the floor, knocking over a chair, and kicking out at things. Her mother told her she couldn't act like that . . . she let Stacey cry a while and then consoled her, hugging her and discussing what had happened. Then everyone went back to the pool and had a good time! Stacey learned that some intensities and means of expression are not acceptable and that talking about rather than venting feelings can have a positive outcome. (Denham, 1998, p. 107)

And there is evidence that parental reactions are, indeed, important contributions to children's emotional development. Children whose parents help them with their emotions are better able to manage emotional upset on their own and are also more accepted by their peers (Gottman et al., 1996). When parents are punitive or dismissive of their children's emotions, the children are hampered in regulating their own emotions (Eisenberg, Fabes, & Murphy, 1996; McDowell & Parke, 2000; Parke et al., 2005). Dismissive parents may belittle the child's emotion (e.g., "There's no reason for you to be [sad][angry] . . . ") or show little interest in how the child is feeling (e.g., "Don't worry about it—go watch TV"). Punitive parents may scold or punish their child for expressing emotions, especially negative ones such as anger or sadness. Dismissive or punitive parents "fail to use emotional moments as a chance to get closer to the child or to help the child learn lessons in emotional competence" (Goleman, 1995, p. 191).

Some parents actively deal with the world of emotions by coaching their children and by discussing emotions with them. Anikka learned about emotions while looking at a picture book with her mother. In the story they read, a new puppy tried to run away into the path of a school bus:

Mother: They were frightened . . . [They] grabbed the dog and brought it to safety. See the worried looks?

Anikka: They look so scared.

Anikka learned some new vocabulary for the emotion of fear, new cues for fear, and a new reason to be fearful—when the safety of a loved one is endangered (Denham, 1998, p. 107).

Parents who are good emotional coaches value emotional expression, are aware of their own emotions, and are willing to help their children with theirs. Help often takes the form of talking about feelings, for children whose parents discuss emotions are better at taking the perspective or viewpoint of others and at understanding their own and others' emotions. For example Hughes and Dunn (1998) found that 3-year-old children's conversations with their mothers and siblings about feeling states were closely related to the same children's ability, at the age of 6, to understand other people's emotions. Children from families in which there was more discussion of feelings were better able to recognize others' emotions than children raised in families in which feelings were less often discussed. In general, the better a child understands emotions, the more skilled he is at such social behaviors as problem solving and conflict resolution and the more likely he is to be accepted by peers (Denham, 1998; Garner, 1996; Parke & O'Neil, 2000).

It is important to remember that not only parents but peers and siblings as well function as socializers of emotion. When children display anger, their peers often respond with anger or rejection (Denham, 1998; Fabes, Eisenberg, Smith, & Murphy, 1996). Similarly, siblings often shape children's emotional reactions by their positive or negative responses or by alerting a parent to their siblings' angry emotional outbursts (Dunn, 1988). Interactions with siblings also contribute to a child's development of emotional understanding. Pretend play with siblings or friends, often characterized by conflict and other intense emotional experiences, is associated with increased understanding of other people's feelings and beliefs (Dunn & Hughes, 2001).

Finally, as we have often noted, socialization is a two-way process, and parent, peer, and sibling reactions are shaped by the characteristics and behavior of the children who are the objects of their endeavors. Recall from our discussion of temperament (Chapter 2) how children differ in the intensity of their reactions to events and how easily and quickly they calm themselves. These temperamental differences probably play an important role in the socialization of emotion. Children of difficult temperaments, for example, may require more direct intervention, such as coaching, than children with easy temperaments. Clearly, children play important roles in their own emotional socialization.

HOW CHILDREN THINK ABOUT EMOTIONS

Not only do children act on their emotions, they learn to think about those emotions as well. If we understand how children think about feelings, we are in a better position to understand why they act emotionally.

A child is invited to a birthday party; another child's favorite pet dies; a third child hears a loud, unexpected bang. When do children become able to think and talk about the varying emotional reactions likely to accompany these different kinds of events? When do they begin to understand the coexistence of multiple emotions? When can they empathize with another person, predicting how that person will feel in a given situation? We will try to answer these questions in this section.

Matching Emotions to Situations: Emotional Scripts

Over time, children undergo shifts in the ways they express emotions. They develop a more complete understanding of the meanings of emotion terms and of the situations that evoke different kinds of feelings. According to Saarni (1999), this understanding can be seen as a collection of **emotional scripts,** or complex schemes that enable the child to identify the type of emotional reaction likely to accompany a particular kind of event.

From a young age, children create a number of such emotional scripts. In a classic study, Borke (1971) told 3- and 4-year-old children simple stories about such things as getting lost in the woods or having a fight or going to a party and asked the children to tell her the emotions they thought the characters in the different stories would be likely to feel. The children easily identified situations that would lead to happiness, and they were reasonably good at identifying stories that were linked with sadness or anger. Later Levine (1995) showed that 3- and 4-year-old children could also describe situations that evoked other emotions, such as excitement, surprise, and fear. Clearly, young children know which emotions go with which situations.

Children's emotional scripts gain in complexity as they mature. For example, 5-year-olds generally understand only those situations that lead to emotions with a recognizable facial display (e.g., anger, displayed in frowning) or that lead to a particular kind of behavior (e.g., sadness, displayed in crying or moping about). By the time they are 7, however, children can describe situations that elicit more complicated emotions with no obvious facial or behavioral expressions, such as pride, jealousy, worry, and guilt. And by the time they reach 10 or 14, children can describe situations that elicit relief and disappointment (Harris, Olthof, Meerum Terwogt, & Hardman, 1987). A similar developmental sequence is found in a variety of cultures, including Great Britain, the United States, the Netherlands, and Nepal (Harris, 1989, 1995).

emotional script A complex scheme that enables a child to identify the emotional reaction likely to accompany a particular sort of event.

Multiple Emotions, Multiple Causes

Another aspect of emotional understanding that develops only gradually is the awareness that one can have more than one feeling at a time and that one can even experience two or more conflicting feelings at the same time. Although toddlers and even young infants show signs of experiencing conflicting feelings, children's ability to understand and express their knowledge of emotions emerges slowly and lags well behind their capacity to experience ambivalent emotions (Wintre & Vallance, 1994). According to Harter (Harter, 2006; Harter & Buddin, 1987), children show a clear developmental sequence in their ability to understand multiple and conflicting feelings. From their study of children between the ages of 4 and 12, Harter and Buddin (1987) derived the five stages of emotional understanding shown in Table 6-1. As you can see, it is not until the fourth stage, at about the age of 10, that children acquire the ability to conceive of opposite feelings existing simultaneously.

As they develop, children learn to consider more and more aspects of an emotion-related situation, such as the desires, goals, and intentions of the people involved. Children realize that people's emotional expressions are produced by inner states and that these expressions are not responsive solely to the characteristics of the situation. For example, young children often get angry when someone thwarts, wrongs, or frustrates them, regardless of whether the wrongful act was intentional—but children 7 years old and up, like adults, tend to reserve their anger for situations in which they think a person intended to upset them (Levine, 1995). We return to this issue of inferring others' internal mental states in our discussion of theory of mind in Chapter 9.

Table 6-1

Children's understanding of multiple and conflicting emotions

Sources: Based on Harter, 2006; Harter & Buddin, 1987.

Approximate Ages	Children's Capabilities
4 to 6	Conceive of only one emotion at a time: "You can't have two feelings at the same time."
6 to 8	Begin to conceive of two emotions of the same type occurring simultaneously: "I was happy and proud that I hit a home run"; "I was upset and mad when my sister messed up my things."
8 to 9	Describe two distinct emotions in response to different situations at the same time: "I was bored because there was nothing to do and mad because my mom punished me."
10	Describe two opposing feelings where the events are different or different aspects of the same situation: "I was sitting in school worrying about the next soccer game but happy that I got an A in math"; "I was mad at my brother for hitting me but glad my dad let me hit him back."
11 to 12	Understand that the same event can cause opposing feelings: "I was happy that I got a present but disappointed that it wasn't what I wanted."

THE DEVELOPMENT OF ATTACHMENT

attachment A strong emotional bond that forms between infant and caregiver in the second half of the child's first year.

Closely related to emotional development is the development of **attachment,** a strong emotional bond that forms in the second half of the first year between an infant and one or more of the child's regular caregivers. Visible signs of attachment are the warm greetings the child gives her parents when they approach, smiling broadly, stretching out her arms, and her active efforts to make contact when picked up, touching her parent's face and snuggling close. Attachment can also be seen in a child's efforts to stay near his parents in an unfamiliar situation, crawling or running to them, and holding on to a leg. Attachment can also be seen in the distress that older babies show when their parents leave them temporarily; its negative counterpart is expressed in the separation protest that we discussed earlier.

The emergence of attachment is one of the developmental milestones in the first year of life. It is of great interest to researchers not only because it is so intense and dramatic but because it is thought to enhance the parents' effectiveness in the later socialization of their children. Children who have developed an attachment to their parents presumably want to maintain their parents' affection and approval and so are motivated to adopt the standards of behavior the parents set for them.

Attachment is such an important and widely studied topic that we devote the rest of this chapter to it. We begin this section with several theories of why attachment develops, including psychoanalytic, learning, and ethological theories. We next look at the way attachment evolves over the first two years of life and then consider the special characteristics of attachment to fathers and to peers. In the last section of the chapter we discuss variations in the quality of attachment and in the consequences of such variations.

Theories of Attachment

A variety of theories have been offered to explain the development of attachment, including psychoanalytic, learning, and ethological theories. Each position makes different assumptions about the variables that are important for the development of attachment and about the processes underlying the development of an attachment relationship.

PSYCHOANALYTIC THEORY According to Freud's classic **psychoanalytic theory of attachment,** which we introduced in Chapter 1, babies become attached to their caregivers because the caregivers are associated with gratification of the infant's innate drive to obtain pleasure through sucking and other forms of oral stimulation. On this line of thinking, a woman who breast-feeds her baby is particularly important to her child's oral gratification. The baby becomes attached first to the mother's breast and ultimately to the mother herself. Although this argument from traditional psychoanalytic theory has fallen out of favor today, the stress it places on a person's inner needs and feelings and its focus on mother-infant interaction remain important influences in the study of infant attachment.

psychoanalytic theory of attachment Freud's theory that babies become attached first to the mother's breast and then to the mother herself as a source of oral gratification.

LEARNING THEORY Like psychoanalytic theory, the **learning theory of attachment** has traditionally associated the formation of mother-infant attachment with the mother's reduction of the baby's primary drive of hunger. Because the mother provides the infant with food, a *primary reinforcer,* she herself becomes a **secondary reinforcer.** Presumably, this ability to satisfy the baby's hunger forms the basis for infant attachment to the mother or any other caregiver linked to feeding.

learning theory of attachment The theory that infants become attached to their mothers because a mother provides food, or primary reinforcement, and thus becomes a secondary reinforcer.

Many studies, however, have challenged the view that feeding is critical for the development of attachment. In what is probably the most famous of these, Harry Harlow separated infant monkeys from their real mothers and raised them in the company of two surrogate mothers. One "mother" was made of stiff wire and had a feeding bottle attached to it; the other was made of soft terrycloth but lacked a bottle (Harlow & Zimmerman, 1959). Especially in moments of stress, the baby monkeys preferred to cling to the cloth "mother," even though she dispensed no food. Attachment to this surrogate mother clearly didn't require the reduction of hunger.

secondary reinforcer A person or other stimulus that acquires reinforcing properties by virtue of repeated association with a primary reinforcer.

Research on humans tells a similar story. Schaffer and Emerson (1964) found that babies formed attachments to their fathers and other frequently seen adults who played little or no role in the child's feeding. They found that babies whose mothers were relatively unresponsive and distant, except for routine physical care, but whose fathers were attentive and stimulating tended to form paternal attachments, even though they actually spent more time with their mothers.

The central point of the learning theory explanation is that attachment is not automatic; it develops over time as a result of satisfying interactions with responsive adults. Some learning theorists suggest that the visual, auditory, and tactile stimulation that adults provide in the course of their daily interactions with an infant are the basis for the development of attachment (Gewirtz, 1969). According to this view, babies are initially attracted to their regular caregivers because they are the most important and reliable sources of this type of stimulation. As interactions with these caregivers continue over weeks and months, infants learn to depend on and to value these special adults in their lives, becoming attached to them.

COGNITIVE DEVELOPMENTAL THEORY According to the **cognitive developmental view of attachment,** before specific attachments can occur, the infant not only must be able to differentiate between her mother and a stranger but also must be aware that people still exist even when she cannot see them. That is, she must have developed what Piaget terms *object permanence,* or the knowledge that objects, including people, have a continuous existence apart from her own interaction with them. As we will see in Chapter 8, there is some evidence that children as young as $3\frac{1}{2}$ months have an awareness of object permanence, although Piaget believed that this awareness did not begin to evolve until 7 to 8 months of age.

cognitive developmental view of attachment The view that to form attachments infants must differentiate between mother and stranger and understand that people exist independent of the infant's interaction with them.

Advances in the infant's cognitive development can also account, in part, for the gradual shift in the ways attachment is expressed. Physical proximity to attachment figures becomes less important as children grow older. Children are now increasingly able to maintain psychological contact with a parent through words, smiles, and looks.

In addition, because they are also better able to understand that parental absences are sometimes necessary and usually temporary, they are less upset by separations. Parents can reduce their children's distress over separations further by explaining the reasons for their departures. In one study, for instance, 2-year-olds handled separation from their mothers much better when the mothers gave them clear information ("I'm going out now for just a minute, but I'll be right back") than when the mother left without a word (Weinraub & Lewis, 1977).

ETHOLOGICAL THEORY   Another approach that has emphasized the reciprocal nature of the attachment process is John Bowlby's **ethological theory of attachment** (1958, 1969, 1973). Both evolutionary theory and observational studies of animals helped shape this theory, and an important early demonstration of the value of the ethological approach was provided by Lorenz's (1952) classic studies of imprinting in ducklings. By the process of **imprinting,** newborn birds and the young of other infrahuman animals can develop an attachment to the first object they see during a brief, critical period after their birth. In Lorenz's case, the young ducklings he studied became attached to Lorenz himself! Bowlby suggested that attachment has its roots in a set of instinctual infant responses that are important for the protection and survival of the species. The infant responses of crying, smiling, sucking, clinging, and following (visually at first and later motorically) both elicit the parental care and protection that the baby needs and promote contact between the child and the parents. Just as the infant is biologically prepared to respond to the sights, sounds, and nurturance provided by the parents, so the parents are biologically prepared to respond to the baby's eliciting behaviors. As a result of these biologically programmed responses, both parent and infant develop a mutual attachment.

The value of Bowlby's position lies in its emphasis on the active role in the formation of attachment played by the infant's early social signaling systems, such as smiling and crying. Another attractive feature is the theory's stress on the development of mutual attachment, whereby both partners, not just one, become bonded to one another (Cassidy, 1999; Thompson, 2006). From this perspective, attachment is a relationship, not simply a behavior of either the infant or the parent (Sroufe, 2002). More controversial is Bowlby's suggestion that these early behaviors are biologically programmed. As we have seen, for example, there is considerable evidence that smiling has social as well as biological origins.

How Attachment Evolves

Attachment does not develop suddenly and unheralded but rather emerges in a series of steps, moving from a baby's general preference for human beings over inanimate objects to a child's real partnership with its parents. Schaffer (1996) proposes four phases in the development of attachment; these are outlined in Table 6-2. In the first phase, which lasts only a month or two, the baby's social responses are relatively indiscriminate. In the second phase, the baby gradually learns to distinguish familiar from unfamiliar people. As you learned in Chapter 4, even very young infants can distinguish their mothers' faces, voices, and even smells from those of other women. However, although a baby under 6 months of age can make these discriminations between his mother and other caretakers and prefers familiar caregivers to strangers, he does not yet protest when familiar caregivers depart; he is not yet truly attached to these people. In the third phase, which begins when the baby is about 7 months old, specific attachments develop. Now the infant actively seeks contact with certain regular caregivers, such as the mother, greeting them happily and often crying when those people temporarily depart. The baby does not show these behaviors to just anyone—only to *specific* attachment figures. When the child passes the 2-year mark and enters toddlerhood (from about 2 to 5), the attachment relationship moves into the final phase—the so-called goal-corrected partnership

---

ethological theory of attachment Bowlby's theory that attachment derives from the biological preparation of both infant and parents to respond to each other's behaviors in such a way that parents provide the infant with care and protection.

imprinting The process by which birds and other infrahuman animals develop a preference for the person or object to which they are first exposed during a brief, critical period after birth.

Table 6-2 Phases in the development of attachment

Name	Age Range (months)	Principal Features
1. Preattachment	0–2	Indiscriminate social responsiveness
2. Attachment-in-the-making	2–7	Recognition of familiar people
3. Clear-cut attachment	7–24	Separation protest; wariness of strangers; intentional communication
4. Goal-corrected partnership	24 on	Relationships more two-sided: children understand parents' needs

Source: Schaffer, 1996.

(Bowlby, 1969). At this point, owing to advances in cognitive development, children become aware of other people's feelings, goals, and plans and begin to consider these things in formulating their own actions. As Colin (1996) noted, "the child becomes a partner in planning how the dyad will handle separations" (p. 72).

Attachment to Fathers and Others

Infants develop attachments not only to their mothers but to their fathers and to a variety of other persons with whom they regularly interact. When children are a little older, for example, they often develop attachments to siblings or other peers. Moreover, according to anthropologists (Harkness & Super, 1995), mothers are exclusive caregivers in only about 3 percent of human societies. In as many as 40 percent of societies, mothers are not even the major caregivers. And, as we will see later, the quality of attachment relationships can vary greatly (Thompson, 2006).

FATHERS Today's American fathers often take a much more active role with their infants than fathers in past generations; just like mothers, fathers develop mutual attachments with their babies (Parke, 2002). Fathers who have the opportunity to interact with their infants in the first few days after the infants are born tend to hold, touch, talk to, and kiss them just as much as mothers do (Parke, 1996; Parke & O'Leary, 1976). And later in their first year of life, the children of these dads showed patterns of attachment to their fathers quite similar to their attachment to their mothers.

In one study, older babies showed similar patterns of attachment to their mothers and fathers in a situation in which a friendly but unfamiliar visitor observed the children in their homes with both parents present (Lamb, 2004). In this nonstressful situation, the babies showed no preference for either parent in their attachment behavior. They were just as likely to touch, approach, and be near their fathers as their mothers. In other, stressful situations, however, babies generally look to their mothers for security and comfort if she is available (Belsky & Cassidy, 1994). This is probably because the mother has most often served this role in the past.

But although babies can be strongly attached to their fathers, American fathers are usually less involved than mothers in an infant's routine care; this is true also of grandfathers as compared with grandmothers (Smith & Drew, 2002). Significantly, American fathers participate more in caregiving when the mother is supportive of the father's involvement and views him as a competent caregiver (Beitel & Parke, 1998). Father involvement in infant care also increases when the mother is less available for such reasons as recovery from a cesarean section delivery (Pederson, Zaslow, Cain, & Anderson, 1980) or employment outside the home (Coltrane, 1996).

In some cultures, particularly hunter-gatherer societies where the search for food and other necessities requires the efforts of both men and women, fathers may be more likely to share in child care. According to Hewlett and colleagues (1998), fathers among the Aka, who live in the southern part of the Central African Republic and the northern reaches of the Domestic Republic of Congo, provide more direct care to their babies than fathers in any other known society. Among the Efe, however, another forager society, in Congo, child care is considered a woman's responsibility, and although Efe fathers spend a great deal of time with their infants, a relatively small percentage of that time goes into direct child care (Morelli & Tronick, 1992). Among the Agta, in Cagayan, Philippines, a hunter-gatherer society in which women and men share labor and subsistence activities almost equally, mothers remain the primary caregivers (Griffin & Griffin, 1992).

In many cultures, fathers have a special role in the infant's development—that of playmate. The quality of a father's play with a baby generally differs from a mother's: Fathers engage in more unusual and physically arousing games (especially with their sons), whereas mothers tend to stimulate their babies verbally and to play quieter games such as peek-a-boo (Parke, 1996, 2002). Even when fathers have assumed the role of their babies' primary caregiver, they tend to display this physically arousing style of interaction (Field, 1978; Hwang, 1986). Although American fathers, as well as fathers in other countries such as Australia, Great Britain, and Israel, spend four to five times more time playing with their infants than caring for them, apparently not all fathers engage in rough-and-tumble play with their children (Lamb, 1987; Roopnarine, 1992). Fathers in India, Central Africa, and Sweden are apparently less likely to engage in this style of play (Hewlett, et al., 1998; Roopnarine, 1992). Even U.S. fathers who enter parenthood at a later age (over 35) tend to be less physical in their play than younger men (Neville & Parke, 1997).

Mothers and fathers continue to show these different styles of play as their children grow older, well into the early childhood years (MacDonald & Parke, 1986). We don't yet know whether these mother-father differences in play mode are the result of biology or experience, but whatever their cause, infants tend to react more positively to a father's style of play than to a mother's (Parke, 2002). When given a choice of play partners, 18-month-olds in one study reliably chose their fathers more often than their mothers (Clarke-Stewart, 1978), but perhaps this preference for dads may be less pronounced in contemporary families in which both parents are working and away from their children during the day. Probably children like playing with their fathers because they make more exciting and unpredictable playmates.

OTHER OBJECTS OF ATTACHMENT

Although infants' most significant attachment relationships are usually with fathers and mothers, as Table 6-3 shows, a variety of other individuals are important in the infant's social world, including peers, siblings, and relatives such as grandparents, aunts, and uncles (Berlin & Cassidy, 1999; Smith & Drew 2002). Peers can become important attachment figures, even for very young children. For example, one investigator found that in a preschool where some children were transferring to new schools, both those who were leaving and those who were staying behind experienced a variety of

Young American fathers are particularly likely to engage in rough-and-tumble play with their young sons.

Attachment Target	Percentage of Infants Attached	
	Initially	At 18 Months
Mother	95	81
Father	30	75
Grandparent	11	45
Relative other than sibling	8	44
Sibling	2	24
Other child	3	14

Table 6-3

The breadth of children's attachments

Source: Schaffer, 1996.

reactions, including increased fussiness, heightened activity level, negative affect, illness, and changes in eating and sleeping patterns (Field, 1986). These reactions were viewed as separation stress associated with the loss of familiar peers. For an even more dramatic illustration of the ability of young children to form close attachment relationships with one another, see Box 6.2. Further, as children reach adolescence, they develop attachment relationships with friends and with romantic partners (Furman, Simon, Shaffer, & Bouchey, 2002). For a discussion of romantic attachments, see Chapter 12.

THE NATURE AND QUALITY OF ATTACHMENT

Like most aspects of human development, the formation of early attachments is not uniform from one child to another or from one relationship to the next. Many children form what appear to be highly secure attachments. The important adults in their lives seem to serve as a source of nurturance and affection that gives these youngsters confidence to explore the world and become more independent. For other children, however, attachments seem much less secure and dependable. Researchers describe such variations as differences in the *quality* of attachments.

Before we examine some of the specific factors that may affect the nature and quality of individual child-parent attachments, such as parenting styles and infant temperament, let us consider a classic body of work that has provided a means of characterizing attachment relationships of different qualities. Mary Ainsworth's studies, based on her concept of the *secure base* and using the so-called Strange Situation, have been replicated many times and in many parts of the world.

Methods of Assessing Attachment Relationships

Proposing that infants organize their attachment behavior around a particular adult so that they seem to be using the adult as a **secure base** for exploration or a safe haven in the event of distress, Ainsworth made valuable observations of infants' attachment and exploratory behavior at about 1 year of age (Ainsworth, 1973; Waters, Vaughn, Posada, & Kondo-Ikemura, 1995). The striking differences in the infants' behaviors

secure base According to Ainsworth, a caregiver to whom an infant has formed an attachment and whom the child uses as a base from which to explore and as a safe haven in times of stress.

Box 6.2
Risk and Resilience

PEERS AS ATTACHMENT FIGURES

Anna Freud's classic account (Freud & Dann, 1951) of the behavior of six young German-Jewish orphans brought to England during World War II not only highlights the incredible resilience of these at-risk children, torn from their families and kept in concentration camps from age 1 through 4, but also illustrates the depth and intensity that peer attachments can have. When they were 4 years old, these children, most of whose parents had died in gas chambers, arrived at Bulldog Banks, a small English country home that had been transformed into a nursery for war children. Quickly, they formed intense, protective attachments to each other while they ignored or were actively hostile to their adult caretakers. Bulldog Banks was the first time any of them had experienced living in a small, intimate setting with adults who offered them kindness rather than cruelty.

In their early days at the nursery these six children were wild and uncontrollable. Within a few days they destroyed or damaged much of the furniture and all the toys given them. Most of the time they ignored the adults, but when they were angry, they would bite, spit, or swear at them, often calling them *bloder ochs* ("stupid fools").

The contrast between the children's hostile behavior toward their caretakers and their solicitous, considerate behavior toward one another was surprising. In one case, when a caretaker accidentally knocked over one of the children, two of the other children threw bricks at her and called her names. The children resisted being separated from each other even for special treats like pony rides. When one child was ill, the others wanted to remain with her. They showed little envy, jealousy, rivalry, or competition with each other. The sharing and helping behaviors of these children with one another was remarkable in children of this age.

Here are some typical incidents in the children's first seven months at Bulldog Banks (Freud & Dann, 1951, pp. 150–168):

- The children were eating cake, and John began to cry when he saw there was no cake left for a second helping. Ruth and Miriam, who had not yet finished their portions, gave him the remainder of their cake and seemed happy just to pet him and comment on his eating the cake.
- In very cold weather one child lost his gloves, and another child loaned his gloves without complaining about his own discomfort.

Even in fearful situations, children were able to overcome their trepidation to help others in their group:

- A dog approached the children, who were terrified. Ruth, though badly frightened herself, walked bravely to Peter, who was screaming, and gave him her toy rabbit to comfort him. She comforted John by lending him her necklace.
- On the beach in Brighton, Ruth was throwing pebbles into the water. Peter, who was afraid of waves, did not dare to approach them. Suddenly, in spite of his fear, he rushed to Ruth, calling out: "Water coming, water coming," and dragged her back to safety.

When, finally, the children began to form positive relations with adults, they made them on the basis of group feelings. Their relationships with their caretakers had none of the demanding, possessive attitudes often shown by young children toward their own mothers. They simply began to include the adults in their group and to treat them, in some ways, as they treated each other. For those children in whom this phase of general attachment was eventually followed by a specific attachment to an individual caretaker, clinging and possessive behaviors did appear. But for all the children throughout their year's stay at Bulldog Banks, the intensity of such attachments to surrogate mothers was never as great as it would have been in normal mother-child relations, and the relationships were never as binding as those they maintained with their peers.

These children's circumstances were unusual, and we must therefore interpret this classic work with caution. At the same time, the children's behavior clearly demonstrates not only the intensity of attachments that can develop between young children but also the resilience that enabled these children to survive unimaginable horrors.

in what is known as the **Strange Situation,** a carefully worked-out scenario in which a mother twice leaves her baby alone or with a stranger and returns twice to be reunited with her child (see Table 6-4), enabled Ainsworth to assess the infant-mother relationships and to classify them according to their nature and quality. This procedure is typically used with infants at 8 or 9 months of age. Subsequent research both expanded on Ainsworth's work and added a longitudinal feature, comparing children's behavior at the ages of 1 and 6. (Main & Cassidy, 1988; Solomon & George, 1999).

As we examine Ainsworth's classification system, you may find it useful to look at Table 6-5, which summarizes four categories of attachment relationship: secure, insecure-avoidant, insecure-resistant, and insecure-disorganized attachment. As we note here, the importance of these classifications lies in their value in predicting differences in infants' and children's later emotional, social, and cognitive development. Of the white, middle-class children studied, Ainsworth classified some 60 to 65 percent as displaying **secure attachment** to their mothers, because they readily sought contact with her after the stress of her departure in an unfamiliar setting and were quickly comforted by her, even if initially quite upset. These babies also felt secure enough to explore a novel environment when the mother was present. They did not whine and cling to her, but actively investigated their surroundings, as if the mother's

Strange Situation A testing scenario in which mother and child are separated and reunited several times; enables investigators to assess the nature and quality of a mother-infant attachment relationship.

secure attachment A kind of attachment displayed by babies who are secure enough to explore novel environments, who are minimally disturbed by brief separations from their mothers, and who are quickly comforted by their mothers when they return.

Table 6-4

The Strange Situation scenario

Episode Number	Persons Present	Duration	Brief Description of Actions
1	Mother, baby, and observer	30 seconds	Observer introduces mother and baby to experimental room, then leaves. (Room contains many appealing toys scattered about.)
2	Mother and baby	3 minutes	Mother is nonparticipant while baby explores; if necessary, play is stimulated after 2 minutes.
3	Stranger, mother, and baby	3 minutes	Stranger enters. First minute: stranger silent. Second minute: stranger converses with mother. Third minute: stranger approaches baby. After 3 minutes mother leaves unobtrusively.
4	Stranger and baby	3 minutes or less	First separation episode. Stranger's behavior is geared to that of baby.
5	Mother and baby	3 minutes or more	First reunion episode. Mother greets and/or comforts baby, then tries to settle the baby again in play. Mother then leaves, saying "bye-bye."
6	Baby alone	3 minutes or less	Second separation episode.
7	Stranger and baby	3 minutes or less	Continuation of second separation. Stranger enters and gears behavior to that of baby.
8	Mother and baby	3 minutes	Second reunion episode. Mother enters, greets baby, then picks baby up. Meanwhile stranger leaves unobtrusively.

Table 6-5   Children's attachment behavior in the Strange Situation: A typology

1 Year Old	6 Years Old
Secure Attachment	
On reunion after brief separation from parents, children seek physical contact, proximity, interaction; often try to maintain physical contact. Readily soothed by parents and return to exploration and play.	On reunion, children initiate conversation and pleasant interaction with parents or are highly responsive to parents' overtures. May subtly move close to or into physical contact with parents, usually with rationale such as seeking a toy. Remain calm throughout.
Insecure-Avoidant Attachment	
Children actively avoid and ignore parents on reunion, looking away and remaining occupied with toys. May move away from parents and ignore their efforts to communicate.	Children minimize and restrict opportunities for interaction with parents on reunion, looking and speaking only as necessary and remaining occupied with toys or activities. May subtly move away with rationale such as retrieving a toy.
Insecure-Resistant Attachment	
Although infants seem to want closeness and contact, their parents are not able effectively to alleviate their distress after brief separation. Child may show subtle or overt signs of anger, seeking proximity and then resisting it.	In movements, posture, and tones of voice, children seem to try to exaggerate both intimacy and dependency on parents. They may seek closeness but appear uncomfortable (e.g., lying in parent's lap but wriggling and squirming). These children sometimes show subtle signs of hostility.
Insecure-Disorganized Attachment	
Children show signs of disorganization (e.g., crying for parents at door and then running quickly away when door opens; approaching parent with head down) or disorientation (e.g., seeming to "freeze" for a few seconds).	Children seem almost to adopt parental role with parents, trying to control and direct parents' behavior either by embarrassing or humiliating parents or by showing extreme enthusiasm for reunion or overly solicitous behavior toward parents.

Sources: Adapted from Ainsworth, Blehar, Waters, & Wall, 1978; Main & Cassidy, 1988; Main & Hesse, 1990; Solomon & George, 1999.

insecure-avoidant attachment A type of attachment shown by babies who seem not to be bothered by their mothers' brief absences but specifically avoid them on their return, sometimes becoming visibly upset.

insecure-resistant attachment A kind of attachment shown by babies who tend to become very upset at the departure of their mothers and who exhibit inconsistent behavior on their return, sometimes seeking contact, sometimes pushing their mothers away.

presence gave them confidence. In familiar situations, such as the home, these children are minimally disturbed by minor separations from the mother, although they greet her happily when she returns.

Ainsworth classified the remaining children she studied as insecure in one of several ways. Exhibiting **insecure-avoidant attachment** were children who typically showed little distress over the mother's absence in the Strange Situation, at least on her first departure. However, these children actively avoided their mothers on their return: They turned away from mothers, increased their distance from them, and paid them no attention. After the mother's second departure, during which time many of these babies became visibly upset, they again avoided her on her return. Later researchers have found that this first insecure pattern typically characterizes about 20 percent of American samples.

A second type of insecure relationship is called **insecure-resistant attachment.** Researchers have found that infants who display this type of attachment (and who make up about 10 to 15 percent of American samples) often become extremely upset when the mother leaves them but are oddly ambivalent toward her when she returns. Intermittently they seek contact with her and then angrily push her away.

The third type of insecure relationship, identified by later researchers, is called **insecure-disorganized attachment** (Solomon & George, 1999). When babies who display this kind of behavior are reunited with their mothers in the Strange Situation scenario, they seem disorganized and disoriented. They look dazed, they freeze in the middle of their movements, or they engage in repetitive behaviors, such as rocking. These children also seem apprehensive and fearful of their attachment figures and are unable to cope in a consistent and organized way with distress in the presence of their caregivers. Note that all these attachment classifications reflect the quality of the relationship between the child and the parent, not traits of either the child or the parent. Interestingly, as Table 6-5 shows, similar child-parent relationship patterns can be observed in these children and parents when the children are 6 years old (Main & Cassidy, 1988).

New methods for assessing attachment have been developed in recent years. Relying on the judgments of caregivers who are familiar with the child's behavior, the **Attachment Q Sort (AQS)** (Solomon & George, 1999; Waters, 1995) calls for the mother or other caregiver to sort a set of cards containing phrases that describe the child's behavior (e.g., "rarely asks for help," "keeps track of mother's location while playing around the house," "quickly greets mother with a big smile when she enters the room") into sets ranging from those that are most descriptive of the child to those that are least descriptive. The method, which is useful for children between the ages of 1 and 5, was designed to facilitate making ratings, in naturalistic settings, of a broad variety of attachment-related behaviors (e.g., secure-base behavior, attachment-exploration balance, and affective responsiveness). As we will see later, other investigators (Main & Cassidy, 1988; Solomon & George, 1999) have developed later-age assessments of attachment that closely resemble the Strange Situation and permit across-time comparisons between children in infancy and at later ages.

Finally, other innovative procedures for assessing attachment have been developed that do not rely on mother-child separations. The California Attachment Procedure (CAP) focuses on how mothers manage children's fear and upset in response to stressful events such as loud noises or a scary robot instead of maternal separations (Clarke-Stewart, Goosens, & Allhusen, 2002). This approach has been used with children at 18 months and more accurately classifies the attachment of children who are accustomed to routine separations from their parents such those involved in child care, a topic we address later in the chapter.

A question that continues to interest researchers is whether Ainsworth's model is equally useful in different cultures both within the United States and in other countries. As Box 6.3 discusses, the model does seem to have considerable applicability, although there are wide differences in the ways children of different cultures organize their secure-base behavior.

The Parents' Role in the Quality of Attachment

We have said that attachment is a *relationship,* developing out of the interaction between infant and parent. Both parents and infants contribute to the nature of the attachment relationship, and we begin, in this section, by considering the parents' input. We will explore ways that parents influence other aspects of development in Chapter 11. We look at the baby's contribution to the relationship in the section that follows.

STYLES OF CAREGIVING   Ainsworth was the first to describe how parents' styles of interacting with their infants are linked with the kinds of attachment relationships that infants and parents develop. Mothers of securely attached infants,

insecure-disorganized attachment A type of attachment shown by babies who seem disorganized and disoriented when reunited with their mothers after a brief separation.

Attachment Q Sort (AQS) An assessment method in which a caregiver or observer judges the quality of a child's attachment based on the child's behavior in naturalistic situations, often including brief separations from parents.

Box 6.3

Perspectives on Diversity

ATTACHMENT TYPES IN DIFFERENT CULTURES

Can Ainsworth's Strange Situation be used in cultures other than that of the United States to assess the character of children's relationships with their parents? For example, do *secure, avoidant,* and *resistant* mean the same things in Ganda that they mean in the United States? If mothers and fathers in Norway encourage their young children to develop independence earlier than U.S. parents, how may this affect the interpretation of "avoidant" behavior on a child's reunion with parental figures? A number of researchers have addressed these and other questions relating to the universality of Ainsworth's concepts. They have found that although overall the attachment categories seem to have considerable applicability across cultural groups, important variations do occur in the way infants of different racial-ethnic groups give expression to secure and insecure attachment relationships.

Another important question is the origin of particular attachment behaviors and relationships. According to Thompson (2006), parental solicitude is affected not only by personality factors and personal belief systems but also by such things as the availability of environmental resources and a parent's degree of freedom to care for a child rather than be stressed or exhausted by the effort to obtain the necessities for survival. On this view, all three major types of attachment can be seen as adaptive responses by infants to parental investment patterns. Thus, in assessing attachment behaviors among parents and children in the resource-poor environments found not only in developing countries but also in areas within more developed nations, it is important to consider the many factors that may contribute to attachment behavior.

Secure Attachment Relationships

When babies are accustomed to almost constant contact with their mothers, they may react differently to reunion in the Strange Situation, either not seeking contact or failing to be comforted by it, and because behavior at reunion is the primary basis for determining attachment classifications, understanding cultural variations in caretaking is crucial. Secure attachments may be present even when infants' behavior in the Strange Situation at first seems to indicate otherwise.

For example, the Ganda infants Ainsworth studied showed more distress in response to brief separations from their mothers than U.S. babies, but on investigation it was revealed that separations of only a brief period of time are infrequent in this African society. Ganda mothers leave their babies for hours at a time while they work in their gardens, and other relatives look after the children in their absence (Colin, 1996). Thus, when they left their babies in the experimental situation, the infants expected a long absence and reacted accordingly.

In the United States, most 1-year-olds are encouraged to engage in activities by themselves—to play with toys, exercise motor skills, and even to nap alone. Few U.S. parents bring their babies into their own beds, but in many parts of the world it is common for infants to sleep with their parents. For example, babies in Japan usually sleep in the same bed with their mothers, and parents don't hesitate to take a child into their bed when the youngster cries or asks to be fed (Colin, 1996; van IJzendoorn & Sagi, 1999). Infants in Japan show much stronger reactions to the departure of the mother than U.S. babies do.

Distinctive reactions to the Strange Situation are also found among ethnic groups within the United States. For example, European American mothers tend to stress active, exploratory behavior, personal development, and self-control in their infants, whereas Puerto Rican mothers are more likely to stress close contact, quietness, responsiveness, and respectfulness in their infants (Harwood, Miller, & Irizarry, 1995). As a result, European American babies may appear to be avoidant in comparison with Puerto Rican infants.

Avoidant Attachment Relationships

In Germany and Sweden, evidence of avoidant relationships is seen more often than in the United States, reflecting the fact that parents in these countries tend to stress early independence somewhat more than American parents do (Colin, 1996). And according to Schaffer (1996), infants in Great Britain are also more likely to evidence avoidant relationships than U.S. babies,

though not as likely as German infants. These tendencies appear even among babies showing secure attachment. For example, secure infants in the Netherlands use their mothers as a secure base while interacting across a distance, whereas in the United States secure-base behavior involves close physical contact both initially and on reunion (Colin, 1996; van IJzendoorn & Sagi, 1999).

In contrast, avoidant reactions are uncommon among Japanese babies, partly because children in Japan are socialized to maintain harmonious personal relationships; ignoring or turning away from someone would be considered rude (Colin, 1996). Moreover, in one Japanese study, most mothers rushed to pick up their infants on reunion, before the babies could give any sign that they wanted contact. Presumably these mothers hurried to alleviate the distress they assumed their babies were experiencing.

Resistant Attachment Relationships

Japanese and Israeli babies seem more likely than American infants to show resistant behavior in both phases of the Strange Situation. In the case of the Japanese infants, this may well be because they are in close contact with their mothers from the time they are born, including, as we've noted, sharing their parents' beds (Rothbaum, Weisz, Pott, Miyake, & Morelli, 2000). For these infants the stress of separation seems much greater than it is for Western babies.

Babies living on Israeli kibbutzim probably show resistant attachment behavior in the Strange Situation for different reasons. Although an infant Israeli "kibbutznik" is usually raised by a hired caretaker (in Hebrew, a *metapelet*), this person is not always highly motivated to engage in infant care and, typically having responsibility for three children, may be unable to respond sensitively to each of them in optimal fashion (Aviezer, Sagi, Joels, & Ziv, 1999; Sagi et al., 1995). The child customarily spends only a few hours with her parents, at supper time, and unless she sleeps at home, she may be watched at night by a person who must monitor all the babies in the nursery building. As a result, "even secure attachments might be expected often to be tinged with resistance and/or preoccupation

with the caregiver, who may often have been unavailable" (Colin, 1996, p. 155).

Can We Rely on the Strange Situation in Cross-Cultural Contexts?

In view of the foregoing findings, we may ask whether the Strange Situation is truly applicable to assessing attachment relationships in babies of other cultures. Given the cultural practices we've described that either neutralize the effects of separation or make it excessively threatening, it can be argued that this measurement device needs revision or replacement.

Does the fact that children from Germany and Sweden who may be well adjusted in terms of their upbringing nevertheless appear to have avoidant—and thus, by definition, insecure—attachment relationships undermine the usefulness of the assessment in those cultures? And perhaps the test situation is just too stressful for Japanese and Israeli babies? Several researchers have argued that as long as the experimenter shortens separation episodes for babies who are highly distressed by the scenario, the procedure probably produces valid classifications across cultures. Or possibly new approaches that we discussed in the text, such as the California Attachment Procedure (CAP), will be useful in cross-cultural studies, since it avoids stressful separation episodes (Clarke-Stewart, et al., 2002).

The newer Attachment Q Sort (AQS) that we discuss in the text allows for more input by infants' caretakers into the assessment process, but even this device may be culture-bound. Although Posada and colleagues (1995) found considerable overall cross-cultural consistency in their study of mothers' Q sorts in China, Colombia, Germany, Israel, Japan, Norway, and the United States, they report that sociocultural similarity both within and across cultural groups was modest, and that there is considerable diversity in the ways that children behave in separation situations. The issue of multicultural applicability of attachment assessment measures may remain unresolved until researchers undertake multiple naturalistic observations of infant-caregiver dyads in many cultures and social contexts (van IJzendoorn & Sagi, 1999).

sensitive care Consistent and responsive caregiving that begins by allowing an infant to play a role in determining when feeding will begin and end and at what pace it will proceed.

for instance, usually permit their babies to play an active role in determining the onset, pacing, and end of feeding early in life. This behavior in and of itself doesn't promote a secure attachment, but it identifies a mother as generally responsive to her baby's needs. The mother of a securely attached infant is also consistently available to her baby; she does not sometimes ignore her baby when he or she signals a genuine need for her (Belsky, 1999; Braungart-Rieker, Garwood, Powers, & Wang, 2001). This style of parenting, called **sensitive care,** is widely associated with the formation of secure attachments. Moreover, this link between sensitive parenting and attachment security is not exclusive to the U.S. and European samples; studies of Australian mothers and infants have found this link, as has research in some South American countries, such as Brazil (Harrison & Ungerer, 2002; Posada et al., 2002).

Maternal sensitivity is very important in fostering a baby's secure attachment, but *insightfulness* on the mother's part can contribute greatly to the bonding process. An insightful mother appreciates her infant's perspectives, motives, and feelings, makes accurate and empathic interpretations of her baby's signals, and adjusts her responses to suit the baby's needs. Insightfulness prevents a mother from focusing too much attention on her child's behavior and gives her the flexibility to consider his particular motives and intentions rather than follow some preset notion of infants' needs and wants. To assess insightfulness, researchers (Koren-Karie, Oppenheim, Dolev, Sher, & Etzion-Carasso, 2002) showed mothers videotapes of their interactions with their 12- to 17-month-old babies (playing with the baby, diapering her, being distracted during interaction) and asked mothers: "What do you think went through your child's head; what did she/he think, feel?" Mothers who were more insightful, recognizing and appreciating their child's mental life, were rated as more sensitive mothers and their infants were rated more securely attached. Both insightfulness and sensitivity were independent predictors of attachment security, suggesting that insightfulness is a further correlate of secure attachment. Even babies have a rich mental life, and the extent to which a parent appreciates this and tries to understand it is a predictor of the quality of the infant-mother attachment relationship.

A number of parenting styles are associated with insecure attachments. Cassidy and Berlin (1994), for example, have found that mothers of babies with an insecure-avoidant type of attachment tend to be *unavailable* and *rejecting*. These mothers are generally unresponsive to their infants' signals, rarely have close bodily contact with them, and often interact with them in an angry, irritable way. And the parents of infants with insecure-resistant attachments exhibit an *inconsistently available* parenting style (Belsky, 1999). Mothers who display this style respond to their babies' needs at times, but at other times they do not, and in general they offer little affection and are awkward in their interactions with their infants.

approach/avoidance behavior A pattern of interaction in which the infant or child shows an inconsistent pattern of approaching and retreating from a person or an object.

The most deficient forms of parenting are found among parents whose attachment with their infants is of the insecure-disorganized type; these parents often neglect their babies or abuse them physically. The **approach/avoidance behavior**—the tendency to show an alternating pattern of approaching a person or object and retreating or escaping from it—that infants with this type of attachment display when reunited with their caregivers in the Strange Situation may actually be an adaptive response; these babies do not know what to expect, given the abuse they have already suffered (Solomon & George, 1999). Carlson, Cicchetti, Barnett, and Braunwald (1989) found that mistreated infants were significantly more likely to develop insecure-disorganized attachments (82%) than were children who were not mistreated (19%). Another factor often associated with this pattern of attachment is maternal depression. Babies of depressed mothers show not only approach/avoidance behavior but sadness upon reunion. Observations of such mothers with their 6-month-old babies have revealed little mutual eye contact and minimal mutual responsiveness; instead, mother and baby each tend to avert their gaze (Field, 1990; Greenberg, 1999). The presence of a nondepressed caregiver such as a father can, in part, mitigate the negative effects of maternal depression on infant's development (Hossain et al., 1994). Studies of the Dogan, who live in Mali, West Africa, suggest that frightening or frightened maternal behavior is linked with disorganized attachment patterns—a finding similar to those reported in the United States and the Netherlands (Lyons-Ruth & Jacobvitz, 1999; True, Pisani, & Oumar, 2001). In this situation, as in the case of abuse, the parent is seen as a source of both comfort and fear, which leads to the infant's disorganized behavior.

The beginnings of these different parenting styles and the different kinds of attachment they encourage can be seen even in the earliest months of life. Mothers who offer sensitive care tend continuously to adjust their behavior to their baby's, so that the two are engaged in a kind of synchronous, smooth-flowing dance, which has been described as interactive synchrony (Van Egeren, Barratt, & Roach, 2001). This term, **interactive synchrony,** describes parent-child interaction patterns in which the parent shifts his or her behavior in response to the infant's signals so that the infant and parent continue to be engaged in the interaction. Some of the parent-infant pairs that fail to achieve early interactive synchrony also fail to develop a secure attachment in the baby's second half year of life. Maternal unresponsiveness to infant signals can play an important role in the emergence of an insecure attachment, just as a mother's sensitivity to her baby's needs can help promote secure attachment. This was shown in a longitudinal study in which infants and their mothers were observed in their homes at 1, 3, and 9 months of age in order to assess the mother's general responsiveness to the child (Belsky, 1999; Isabella, 1993). At 12 months, the quality of the mother-infant attachment was assessed in the Strange Situation. Securely attached babies had more synchronous patterns of interaction with the mother (even at 1 and 3 months of age) than did insecurely attached babies. The mother-infant interactions of the insecurely attached children were more one-sided, unresponsive, or intrusive. Mothers of insecure-avoidant infants, for instance, were verbally intrusive. They continued to talk to the baby even when the child signaled a lack of readiness to tolerate more verbal stimulation. Mothers of insecure-resistant infants were generally unresponsive as well as underinvolved.

Attachment processes do not cease in infancy, but continue to be important in later phases of development such as adolescence. Just as infants gain comfort from using mother as a secure base, adolescents continue to find value in the quality of the attachment relationship with their mothers. When the mother was supportive and attuned to the adolescent's needs and self-perceptions and when the mother and adolescent were able to maintain their relationship through disagreements, the adolescents' attachment relationship with their mother was more secure (Allen et al., 2003). Being able not to idealize but instead to accept a realistic portrayal of one's mother was another correlate of adolescent attachment security. Just as a secure base allows the infant to begin to explore her physical world, a secure base as expressed by a positive and supportive mother-adolescent relationship allows the adolescent to explore independence in ideas and behaviors. The forms of attachment relationships shift across development, but the fundamental dynamics remain the same.

What can we learn about attachment from infant-parent interactions in other cultures? An interesting comparison can be drawn between U.S. parenting styles and those of Israeli parents, some of whom live with their families in a kibbutz, or communal village, where they generally rear their infant children in group-care arrangements. In all kibbutzim (plural of kibbutz), babies stay in the infant-care center during the day, and in some they stay in the center even at night, but in others they spend the night with their families. Sagi and his colleagues (Sagi, van IJzendoorn, Aviezer, Donnell, & Mayseless, 1994), using the kind of natural experimental design we discussed in Chapter 1, examined the effects of these contrasting child-rearing arrangements on attachment relationships. Some of their results are summarized in Table 6-6, which shows that infants who slept at home with their families were more likely to

interactive synchrony A term that characterizes mother-infant interactions in which the mother constantly adjusts her behavior to that of her baby, responding to and respecting the baby's signals as to when she is ready for and wants engagement and interaction.

Table 6-6

Attachment in children raised in an Israeli kibbutz

Source: Adapted from Sagi, van IJzendoorn, Aviezer, Donnell, & Mayseless, 1994.

Attachment Type	Children Who Spent the Night		
	In the Care Center	At Home	All Children
Secure	6 (26%)	15 (60%)	21 (44%)
Insecure-avoidant	0	0	0
Insecure-resistant	7 (30%)	2 (8%)	9 (19%)
Insecure-disorganized	10 (44%)	8 (32%)	18 (37%)

develop secure attachments than babies who spent the night in the infant center. As you can see, among the children who spent the night at home, the secure and insecure-resistant attachment groups represented proportions similar to those of the American groups that we've already mentioned. Note that no infants were classified as having insecure-avoidant attachments. Babies reared in kibbutzim rarely exhibit such attachments, for kibbutzim caregivers seldom exhibit rejecting behavior or pressure children to act independently (van IJzendoorn & Sagi, 1999). The differences observed between the sleep-at-home and sleep-at-the-kibbutz babies were not related to any other factors, for the researchers equated their young participants on such things as temperament, early life events, mother-infant interaction in play, quality of day-care environment, and maternal characteristics such as job satisfaction and anxiety about separation from children. The researchers suggest, therefore, that it may have been the mothers' greater opportunity to respond sensitively to their babies' needs during the evening and nighttime hours that increased the mothers' overall sensitivity to their infants (Colin, 1996).

Even more convincing evidence of the impact of maternal sensitivity on the attachment relationship comes from an experimental study in the United States by Anisfeld, Casper, Nozyce, and Cunningham (1990). Lower-income inner-city mothers of newborns were divided into two groups: An experimental group received soft baby carriers, and a control group was given rigid carriers of the "car seat" type. The researchers predicted that the soft infant carriers would increase physical contact between infants and mothers and facilitate the development of maternal responsiveness; in fact, the mothers given the soft carriers were indeed more responsive to their infants' vocalizations at $3\frac{1}{2}$ months. Moreover, attachment measured at 13 months was affected as well: 83 percent of the babies in the experimental group were securely attached to their mothers, whereas only 39 percent of the control group babies were securely attached to their mothers.

Of course, relationships between parents and infants do not develop in a vacuum. They are affected by and affect other relationships among family members, as well as relationships outside the home. For example, there is a link between marital adjustment and infant-parent attachment: Secure attachment is more likely when marital adjustment is good (e.g., Belsky, 1999; Thompson, 2006). Although the birth of a child is generally associated with a decline in marital satisfaction (Cowan & Cowan, 2000), mothers whose infants become securely attached usually report less dissatisfaction with their marriages than mothers whose children are insecurely attached (Belsky, 1999). As you will see when we discuss the family in Chapter 11, marital and parent-child relationships are often closely connected.

IS THERE INTERGENERATIONAL CONTINUITY IN ATTACHMENT?   The kind of care that parents received when they were infants is another influence on the quality of attachment that develops between them and their own children (Bretherton & Munholland, 1999). From our mothers and fathers, we all acquire what Bowlby (1973) calls **internal working models** of the self and parents. According to Bowlby, these models are mental representations about oneself, one's own parents, and the styles of interaction one experienced as a child. Working models are often referred to also as *attachment representations*. Note that it is not the actual experience of the parent when she was an infant that forms this model but rather how she reconstructs or interprets these early experiences. Because of these internal working models, people tend to re-create their own childhood relationships when they themselves become mothers or fathers.

To investigate this notion of intergenerational continuity, Main, Kaplan, and Cassidy (1985) interviewed 40 middle-class mothers about recollections of their own relationships with their mothers during infancy and childhood. Supporting Bowlby's theory, the mothers' memory patterns did relate to the quality of their current attachment relationships with their own infants. As Table 6-7 shows, Main classified the women into three groups: autonomous, dismissing, and preoccupied. The *autonomous* group, who had developed secure attachment relationships with their infants, revealed in their interviews that although they valued close relationships with their parents and others, they were at the same time objective. They tended not to idealize their own parents but had a clear understanding of their relationships with them and were able to describe both their positive and negative aspects even if the relationship was strong enough to overcome any weaknesses. The *dismissing* group, who had avoidant attachment relationships with their babies, had a different set of memories; they dismissed and devalued attachment and frequently claimed that they couldn't recall incidents from their childhoods. On the other hand, the recollections they did report were often of idealized parents: "I had the world's greatest mom!" The third, *preoccupied* group was made up of the parents of resistant infants. Preoccupied with earlier family attachments, these mothers recalled many conflict-ridden incidents from childhood but couldn't organize them into coherent patterns.

Intergenerational continuity is not always straightforward, for some children and adults are able to overcome early adversity and insecure attachments and eventually develop satisfying interpersonal relationships with their spouses, partners, and offspring. Several cross-sectional studies have supported the existence of this resilient group of individuals, now called "earned secure" people (Paley, Cox, Burchinal, & Payne, 1999). Roisman and colleagues (2002), who used data from a 23-year longitudinal study, showed that individuals can indeed overcome early problems and develop "secure" attachment relationships. Even though these young adults had negative childhood experiences, those who overcame their past and developed secure internal working models of attachment relationships had high-quality romantic relationships in their

internal working model
According to Bowlby, a person's mental representation of himself as a child, his parents, and the nature of his interaction with his parents, as he reconstructs and interprets that interaction; also referred to as an *attachment representation*.

 LifeMap CD

To learn more about why researchers study attachment and some of the results they have found, view the "Attachment Theory" video in Chapter 6 of your CD.

Table 6-7

Relationships between mothers' and children's attachment status

Sources: Main, Kaplan, & Cassidy, 1985; Schaffer, 1996; Hesse, 1999.

Attachment Category		
Mother	**Child**	**Mother-Child Relationship**
Autonomous	Secure	Mother's mind not taken up with unresolved concerns about her own experience; mother thus able to be sensitive to child's communications
Dismissing	Insecure-avoidant	Mother reluctant to acknowledge her own attachment needs and thus insensitive and unresponsive to child's needs
Preoccupied	Insecure-resistant	Mother confused about her attachment history and thus inconsistent in her interactions with her child

early twenties. The romantic ties of these "earned secure" young adults were comparable to those of individuals who were continuously secure and of higher quality than those of individuals with insecure attachments.

Studies with fathers have yielded similar results (Crowell & Treboux, 1995; van IJzendoorn, 1995). For example, in a longitudinal study, German researchers found that fathers' recollections of their own relationships with their parents during childhood were indeed linked to their relationships with their own children (Grossman & Fremmer-Bombik, 1994).

Perhaps the most convincing evidence of intergenerational continuity comes from Fonagy, Steele, and Steele (1991), who interviewed pregnant women about their attachment histories and then measured infant-mother attachment when these women's babies were 1 year of age. This research design enabled the investigators to rule out the possibility that a parent's current experience with her baby was shaping her memories of her own childhood. Once again, these researchers found strong support for the relations between parental recollections of childhood family relationships and the attachment relationship between the women and their children.

The Effect of Infant Temperament

As you learned in Chapters 2 and 4, some babies are more difficult to interact with and care for than others. Might this affect the quality of attachments that these infants develop? Although attachment is a process of mutual influence, researchers have paid less attention to the infant's contribution than to the parental one. Some, however, have found a link between certain temperament characteristics in infants and the kinds of relationships they develop with their parents. For instance, irritable newborns or those with difficulties orienting to people and to objects may be more apt to develop insecure attachments (Spangler & Grossman, 1993; Susman-Stillman, Kalkoske, Egeland, & Waldman, 1996). Perhaps these early difficulties reflect underlying problems in adaptive mechanisms that continue to influence a child's behavior and interactions with others as he matures. We must be cautious in drawing such conclusions, however, because many other researchers have failed to find clear links between early infant temperament and later infant-parent attachment (Vaughn & Bost, 1999).

If infant temperament does have some influence on the development of attachment, that influence is probably mediated by many other factors. A "difficult" infant isn't necessarily destined to have a poor relationship with her parents. Parents who have a difficult or irritable baby can usually cope successfully if they receive help and support from other family members and friends. When adequate social support is available to the mother, an irritable baby is no more likely to become insecurely attached than a nonirritable one (Crockenberg, 1981; Van den Boom, 1994). If a mother is socially isolated

(a)

(b)

Some babies are fussy and difficult no matter how lovingly parents care for them (a), and others are easygoing, right from the start (b).

or has poor relationships with other adults, however, she is more likely to have problems fostering secure attachment in a difficult infant (Levitt, Weber, & Clark, 1986). Thus, the effect of temperament on attachment cannot be separated from the influence of the total social context in which the baby is developing (Sroufe, 1996; Vaughn & Bost, 1999).

Stability in the Quality of Attachment

There is substantial stability in the quality of attachment from one period of time to another. As you saw earlier in the chapter, among infants tested with their mothers in the Strange Situation, the same attachment patterns were detected both at 12 months and at 6 years of age (Solomon & George, 1999). Although attachment behavior in these children at different points in time didn't correlate perfectly—for example, 100 percent of the children rated securely attached at 12 months were rated similarly at 6 years of age, but only 66 percent of the children rated insecure-disorganized at 12 months were rated similarly at 6 years of age—the overall findings support the notion that attachment behavior is highly stable. Lending cross-cultural support to this idea is a German study that found that first-year attachment classifications predicted 78 percent of sixth-year classifications (Wartner, Grossman, Fremmer-Bombik, & Suess, 1994). Moreover, Waters and colleagues (2000) found that 72 percent of their sample classified as secure versus insecure in infancy were similarly rated 20 years later—an impressive level of stability of attachment across the life span. Even in adulthood attachment representations tend to be relatively stable: 78 percent of couples received similar Adult Attachment Interview classifications before marriage and 18 months later (Crowell, Treboux, & Waters, 2002).

But general stability in the quality of parent-child relationships doesn't mean that change is impossible (Waters et al., 2000). In both the American and German studies, substantial minorities of children with insecure attachments as infants did manage to develop better relationships with their parents by school age. This is particularly likely when a child's parents begin to experience less stress in their lives (fewer financial worries, for instance, or less marital tension) and so are able to become more available to their child and to interact in ways more responsive to the child's needs (Thompson, Lamb, & Estes, 1982). Alternatively, secure infant-parent attachment relationships can become insecure if the life circumstances of the family deteriorate due to job loss, divorce, illness, or abuse. More infants (44%) who later experienced negative life events changed attachment classifications from infancy to adulthood than children (22%) in families with no significant negative events (Waters et al., 2000).

Professional intervention can help improve a troubled parent-child relationship (Bakermans-Kranenburg, van IJzendoorn, & Juffer, 2003). In a Dutch study, mothers who were taught to be more sensitive to their infants developed better attachment relationships with them than did the mothers of a control group of infants (van den Boom, 1994). Whereas 68 percent of the experimental group were classified as securely attached at 12 months of age, only 28 percent of the control group was securely attached. Another 58 percent were insecure-avoidant and 16 percent were insecure-resistant. Clearly, attachment relationships continue to develop and are responsive to changes in the behavior of both parent and child (Thompson, 2006; Waters et al., 2000).

The Consequences of Attachment Quality

Does the quality of an infant-parent attachment have serious implications for the child's development? As you will see, early interactions with attachment figures do indeed seem to shape children's continuing development, particularly their development of cognitive and social skills and a sense of self (Thompson, 2006).

COGNITIVE DEVELOPMENT   An early secure attachment appears to be related to more complex exploratory behavior at 2 years of age (Main, 1973). Moreover, as the child continues to develop, this intellectual curiosity is reflected in an intensified interest and enjoyment in solving problems. This positive approach to problem solving is seldom seen in toddlers who were insecurely attached as infants. Matas, Arend, & Sroufe (1978) found that securely attached 2-year-olds were more enthusiastic, persistent, cooperative, and effective in solving problems than their insecurely attached peers. The former group showed less frustration, less negative affect, less crying and whining, and less aggression toward their mothers. In addition, the securely attached toddlers engaged in more symbolic or pretend play—for example, transforming a block of wood into an imaginary car or a stick into a witch's broom. Nor are the effects of attachment status on cognitive outcomes restricted to infants and toddlers. High-quality parent-child relationships and higher early maternal sensitive responsiveness were linked with better cognitive development at age 7. In turn, attachment disorganization was linked with poorer cognitive outcomes (Stams, Juffer, & van IJzendoorn, 2002). In this case the relations were not due to shared genetic factors, since the children were all adopted at an early age. In a longitudinal study in Reykjavik, Iceland, Jacobsen and Hofmann (1997) found that children who at age 7 were securely attached were likely to be more attentive and participative in the classroom at the ages of 9, 12, and 15. They maintained higher grades than children judged avoidant, ambivalent, or disorganized in their attachment.

It's not only mothers' and fathers' relationships with their child that are important to her or his cognitive development but the child's relations with other significant caregivers as well. A cross-national study in the Netherlands and Israel examined families of working parents who employed a third primary caregiver for child care (van IJzendoorn & Sagi, 1999; van IJzendoorn, Sagi, & Lambermon, 1992). The quality of the whole attachment network (mother, father, others) in infancy predicted the children's intelligence scores when they were 5 years old; the greater the attachment security, the higher the test score.

These studies underscore the link between the quality of the parent-child relationship and cognitive development—but they do even more: They also point out that the success of adult experts in facilitating children's learning, as proposed by Vygotsky, may, at least in part, depend on the quality of the attachment relationship. (We introduced Vygotsky's theory in Chapter 1 and will revisit this theory in more detail in Chapter 8.)

SOCIAL DEVELOPMENT   Many studies support the idea that the quality of the caregiver-infant relationship is important for later social development (Thompson, 2006). A recent longitudinal study in which children were traced from infancy to age 19 illustrates the importance of the early attachment for later social behavior (Carlson, Sroufe, & Egeland, 2004). Securely and insecurely attached youngsters developed very different social and emotional patterns. At 4 to 5 years of age, teachers rated securely attached children as showing more positive emotions and as having greater empathy for others and more ability to initiate, respond to, and sustain interactions with other people. Securely attached children also whined less, were less aggressive, and displayed fewer negative reactions when other children approached them. Not surprisingly, their teachers rated them more socially competent and socially skilled and as having more friends than other children, and their classmates considered them more popular than others.

At 8 and 12 years of age, the securely attached continued to be rated as more socially competent, more peer-oriented, and less dependent on adults. Moreover, they were more likely to develop close friendships than their less securely attached peers. Attachment history also predicted friendship choices: Children with secure attachment histories were more likely to form friendships with other securely attached peers. At age 19, the socioemotional functioning of those adolescents with a history of secure attachment was rated higher as well. In comparison with peers who had a history of insecure attachment, these young adults were more likely to have close family relationships, long-term friendships, sustained romantic involvement, higher self-confidence, and greater determination regarding personal goals. Others have found similar links between the quality of early attachment and later school-age peer competence and friendship patterns (Contreras, Kerns, Weimer, Gentzler, & Tomich, 2000; Schneider, Atkinson, & Tardif, 2001). The long-term consequences of attachment security are evident not just in biologically related families but also in families of adopted children. Infants who were adopted before 6 months of age and who developed high-quality infant-mother relationships and secure attachments were better adjusted socially at age 7 (Stams et al., 2002). This work underscores the importance for later adjustment of good early caregiving and suggests that the effect is not simply due to a shared genetic history.

Just as Bowlby argued, the links between attachment and social outcomes are forged by children's internal working models. In their longitudinal study, Carlson and colleagues (2004) assessed children's cognitive working models of relationships at various times throughout childhood and adolescence. For example, in the preschool years, these researchers evaluated children's relationship expectations, attitudes, and feelings. Securely attached children's relationship models were characterized by expectations of empathy between play partners, a high expectation of sharing during play, and constructive approaches to conflict resolution (e.g., taking turns, seeking adult acceptance, getting another toy). During adolescence (age 12) securely attached children construed their friendships as close, emotionally connected, and skilled in conflict resolution. These investigators showed that cognitive working models and social behavior mutually influence each other across time. In other words, cognitive representations in the preschool period predict social behavior in middle childhood; in turn, the representations in middle childhood predict social behavior at 12 years of age, and these cognitive models predict social outcomes at 19 years of age. Moreover, across time, social behavior at one point predicts later cognitive representations. For example, social behavior in middle childhood influences a child's cognitive working models in early adolescence. Figure 6-9 depicts this pattern of across-time influence between cognitive and behavioral levels. Other studies find similar links between working models and social behavior (Cassidy, Kirsh, Scolton, & Parke, 1996). Together, these studies illustrate the interplay among attachment, cognitive understanding, and children's social outcomes.

Emotions play a role in accounting for the links between attachment and social competence, too. For example, attachment to his mother affects the way a child processes emotional information and understands and regulates his emotions. Securely attached children tend to remember positive events more accurately than negative events, whereas insecurely attached children do the opposite (Belsky, Spritz, & Crnic, 1996). And securely attached preschoolers are better at understanding emotions than insecurely attached children (Laible & Thompson, 1998). Finally, Conteras et al., (2000) found that securely attached children are better at regulating their emotions, which in turn accounted for their superior social relationships with peers.

In trying to understand children's social behavior, it is also important to consider both infant-mother and infant-father attachment relationships (Berlin & Cassidy, 1999; Lamb, 2004). Even very young children may develop different relationships with each parent. In a study of 1-year-old infants, Main and Weston (1981) classified babies according to whether they were securely attached to both parents, to their mothers but not their fathers, to their fathers but not their mothers, or to neither parent. To determine whether the infants' relationships with their mothers and fathers affected their social responsiveness to other people, Main and Weston then observed the infants' reactions to a friendly clown. The infants who were securely attached to both parents were more responsive to the clown than those who were securely attached to only one

Figure 6-9   A model of across-time influence of social behavior and cognitive working models on children's adjustment

This model illustrates the ways that cognitive working models, or representations of relationships, influence each other across development. Together, earlier social behaviors and relationship representations influence social functioning in adolescence. Rectangles contain the specific measures used at each time point.

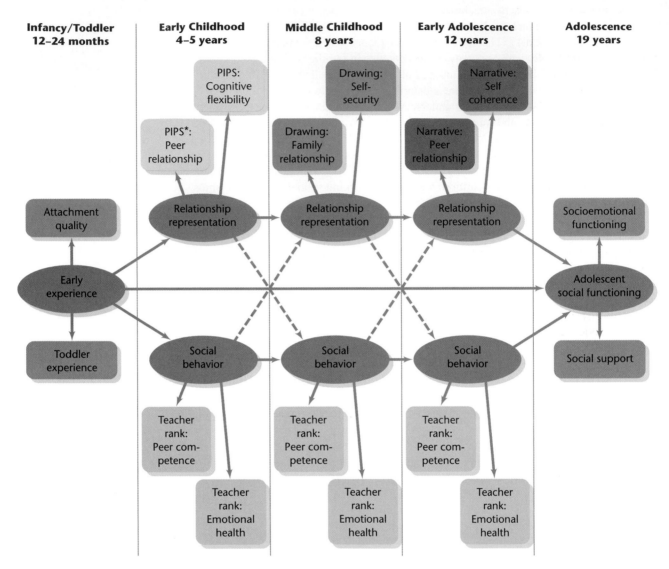

*PIPS: Preschool Interpersonal Problem Solving Assessment Interview.

Source: Carlson et al., 2004.

parent and insecurely attached to the other, and the babies who were insecurely attached to both parents were the least responsive of all. These results suggest that a less-than-optimal relationship with one parent is offset by a better relationship with the other parent—and that therefore it is not enough to study just mothers or fathers alone. Viewing the parents as part of a family system is the best way to understand their role in child development (Parke & Buriel, 2006).

In summary, a healthy attachment to parents facilitates exploration, curiosity, and mastery of the social and physical environment. Early healthy attachment also increases the child's trust in other social relationships and permits the later development of mature affectional relationships with peers. Longitudinal studies aimed at defining the links between early parent-infant interaction and later relationships in adolescence and adulthood suggest the long-term stability of the cognitive and social effects of early attachment. Clearly, developmental history leaves its mark (Thompson, 2006).

THE SENSE OF SELF   The *sense of self*, or the awareness of the self as differentiated from other people, is crucial to the child's development (Harter, 1998, 2005). As this awareness evolves, it becomes increasingly complicated, incorporating notions such as self-concept, self-esteem, self-confidence, and self-respect, all of which comprise cognitive and social as well as emotional factors.

When do children begin to recognize themselves as different from other people? How does the complex network of feelings and cognitions associated with a person's sense of personal identity evolve? Babies as young as 18 weeks of age happily gaze at their reflections in a mirror, but not until they are well past 1 year old do they realize that they are looking at a reflection of themselves. A classic method of examining self-identity in the child has been to allow the child to look into a mirror for a bit and then to put a spot of rouge on the child's nose and return her to the mirror (Brooks-Gunn & Lewis, 1984; Lewis, 1991). We assume that if the child recognizes that the mirror reflection is of herself, she will be likely to touch her nose. Children under 1 year of age seem to believe that the reflection is another child and sometimes touch it or try to look behind the mirror for the other child, but they don't try to touch their noses (Brooks-Gunn & Lewis, 1984). Sometime during the second year of life children begin to recognize their own images, and by the time they are 2 almost all children give evidence of self-recognition, giggling, showing embarrassment, or acting silly at the sight of their rouged noses (Figure 6-10). On average, children are 20 months old before they fairly consistently locate or touch the rouge on their noses. Later, they learn to use self-referent terms such as *I* and *me* and to distinguish themselves by age and gender. Table 6-8 presents the stages in the development of self-awareness in the first two years of life.

Is it possible that the sense of self develops in human children even earlier than 20 months? Some researchers have suggested that infants as young as 3 months may

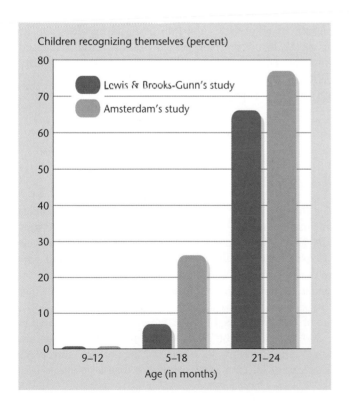

Figure 6-10

What's that on my nose?

When experimenters dabbed rouge on children's noses, in two separate studies the children showed similar behavior. Those less than a year old didn't recognize themselves in the mirror, but by the time they were 2, most children realized that mirror images of children with rouge on their noses were images of themselves.

Sources: Schaffer, 1996; Lewis & Brooks-Gunn, 1979.

Table 6-8

The early stages of self-awareness

Source: Schaffer, 1996.

Age in Months	Behavioral Indications
0–3	Infant shows interest in social objects but does not distinguish between self and other.
3–8	Child's first signs of self-recognition, based on *contingency clues* (fact that mirror image moves in tandem with child's movements), are tentative and unreliable.
8–12	Notion of self permanence emerges. Child reliably recognizes self based on contingency clues, begins to use *feature clues* (child's own physical features as seen in video or photograph).
12–24	Basic self categories, such as age and gender, are consolidated. Child reliably recognizes self based on feature clues.

have some sense of self-awareness (e.g., Schaffer, 1996), and others have even suggested that a sense of self develops prenatally, citing the behavior of some infrahuman creatures that make clear distinctions between themselves and others (Angier, 1997). Still others (e.g., Porges, 1995), however, point out that a considerable difference exists between survival-adapted tendencies to look out for oneself and a real consciousness of that choice or of one's relationship to others.

However these complicated questions may be answered, we do have some evidence that the quality of the child-parent attachment relationship affects the child's developing self-concept. Moreover, the value that one places on the self varies with the quality of attachment (Thompson, 2006). In one study, Cassidy (1988) assessed the attachment relationships of 6-year-olds and the children's self-concepts. Children who were securely attached viewed themselves in a positive way, although they were able to acknowledge their less-than-perfect qualities. In contrast, insecure-avoidant children tended to present themselves as perfect, and insecure-ambivalent children showed no clear pattern of responses. A group of children classified as insecure-controlling (similar to the insecure-disorganized classification discussed earlier) had negative self-concepts. These results strongly suggest that the quality of early attachment is related to the degree to which children view themselves positively and realistically; both of these capacities are important aspects of social adjustment.

Multiple Caregivers and Attachment: The Effects of Child Care

The 1999 U.S. Census revealed that more than two-thirds of American children under the age of 6 had both mothers and fathers who worked outside the home, and 10 million children *under the age of 6* were being cared for by someone other than their parents (U.S. Bureau of the Census, 1999). Although many children of working parents are cared for entirely by their parents, siblings, and other relatives, between 60 and 80 percent of children under 5 spend many hours a week in some form of day care—that is, care provided by one or more nonfamily members in the child's own home, in the caregiver's home, or in an organized child-care facility (see Figure 6-11) (Clarke-Stewart & Allhusen, 2005). It should be stressed that both parents often are forced to work in order to maintain the economic well-being of the family—thus placing an infant or child in outside care is often a necessity rather than a choice.

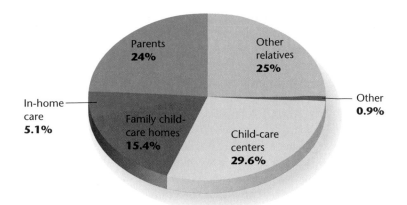

Figure 6-11

Who is caring for our preschoolers?
Nearly half of all preschoolers whose mothers worked outside the home were cared for by their parents or other relatives. An almost 50 percent increase over the number of children cared for by relatives in 1993, this reveals families' inability to meet the costs of commercial child care.

Sources: Children's Defense Fund, 1998; U.S. Bureau of the Census, 1999; Clarke-Stewart & Allhusen, 2002.

According to John Bowlby, having not only parents but a number of other caregivers share in caring for an infant may impair the quality of infant attachment. This proposition has been central to the controversy surrounding the advantages and disadvantages of child care for the infant's and young child's social development. There is no evidence that being in child care actually prevents the formation of an attachment between infants and their parents. Children who spend time in child care form close relationships with their mothers and fathers, just as children raised at home do (Clarke-Stewart & Allhusen, 2002, 2005; Lamb & Ahnert, 2006). As we saw earlier, children do show separation protest in response to being left by their parents even when they are clearly attached to their parents.

However, some evidence suggests that the *amount of time* children spend in day care does affect the nature of child-parent relationships (NICHD Early Child Care Research Network, 1997). In an extensive study of 1,300 families in 14 different locations in the United States, researchers found that the more time their children spent in day care, the less sensitive mothers were toward their infants at 6 months of age, at 15 months, and at 3 years of age. The study also found that children in day care were less affectionate toward their mothers at 2 and 3 years of age. These associations, however, were relatively weak. Recent evidence from Israel is consistent with the argument that not only the amount of time in child care, but also child-care quality, are important to consider in understanding the links between child care and attachment. In a large-scale study of over 750 12-month-old infants, Sagi and his colleagues (2002) found that infants in **center care**—an arrangement in which children are cared for in a "school-like" environment by professional caregivers—were more likely to be insecurely attached than infants cared for by mothers, other relatives, paid caregivers, or **family child care**—an arrangement in which an individual cares for three or four children in her home. Center care in Israel is of poor quality and has a high infant-caregiver ratio (i.e., each caregiver must look after a considerable number of infants), characteristics that account for the increased level of attachment insecurity among center-care infants.

Some earlier studies have suggested that infants who are in day care because their mothers are employed full time—especially babies who begin full-time day care before they're 1 year old—are more likely to be classified as insecurely attached than infants of nonemployed or part-time working mothers (Barglow, Vaughn, & Molitor, 1987; Belsky & Cassidy, 1994; Belsky & Rovine, 1988). Again, however, the correlations were not strong. Moreover, in a review of day-care studies, Clarke-Stewart (1989) found that although on average 36 percent of the infants of full-time working mothers became insecurely attached, 29 percent of the infants of nonemployed or part-time working mothers also developed insecure attachments.

center care A child-care context in which children are cared for in a "school-like" environment by professional caregivers.

family child care A child-care arrangement in which an individual cares for three or four children in her home.

How might we explain why roughly a third of the babies of working mothers, regardless of whether they are in day care or are cared for at home, develop insecure attachments? It is of course possible that day-care babies are somewhat more apt to develop an insecure attachment because their mothers are less available to them or because they interpret her absence as rejection (Barglow et al., 1987; Belsky & Rovine, 1988). However, other explanations are also possible (Clarke-Stewart & Allusen, 2005; Lamb & Ahnert, 2006). For instance, mothers who dislike caring for a baby (and who thus tend to be less sensitive caregivers) may be more inclined than other mothers to take full-time jobs. Or possibly the stress associated with handling both a baby and work interferes with a working mother's ability to promote secure attachment. These alternative explanations suggest that day care itself may not exert an influence on attachment but rather that something associated with a parent's use of day-care facilities, such as holding a full-time job, may reduce parental effectiveness at being a consistently sensitive and responsive caregiver. As Clarke-Stewart (1989) puts it, it may not be that "40 hours of day care is hard on infants but that 40 hours of work is hard on mothers" (p. 270).

Thus, even with the latest findings on day care, it seems unlikely that day care alone is responsible for a lesser degree of security in these relationships (Clarke-Stewart & Allhusen, 2002). What's more, good day-care providers can sometimes compensate for less than optimal care from parents by giving children an opportunity to form secure attachments outside the home (Howes, 1999). Research shows that children with an insecure attachment to their mothers, but a secure attachment to a day-care provider, tend to be more socially competent than insecurely attached children who have not formed such a strong compensatory relationship outside the family. Interestingly, this positive effect of day care is not restricted to American children; similar findings have been recorded in the Netherlands and in Israel (van IJzendoorn & Sagi, 1999).

Stability of staff may be an important determinant of the relationship quality that emerges between care providers and children in day care. Barnas and Cummings (1994) found that 21-month-old toddlers more frequently sought out caregivers who had been on staff for longer periods of time and who were rarely absent and could thus be relied upon to be there for them. When the children were distressed, these familiar figures were able to soothe them more effectively than were caregivers whose employment records were unstable. Clearly, minimizing staff turnover is important to provide a stable, predictable environment for child care (Lamb & Ahnert, 2006). In addition, a training program aimed at improving the quality of care provided by family day-care providers can have real impact on the attachment relationships developed between children and nonparental caregivers (Galinsky, Howes, & Kontos, 1995).

The higher the level of training of staff members, the more likely children are to develop secure attachment relationships with their caregivers (Clarke-Stewart & Allhusen, 2005). There are other important benefits of training as well. For example, children in high-quality programs are less likely to engage in delinquent and other antisocial behavior as they grow up, and they are less likely to need special education later on or to be retained in a grade. Kindergarten teachers have estimated that one in three children enters the classroom unprepared to meet its challenges (Lamb & Ahnert, 2006), and inadequate day care for preschoolers may be among the factors responsible for this finding. Another difficulty is that good day care is far more accessible to the affluent than to low-income families (Figure 6-12). This problem may worsen as a result of the 1996 federal welfare law that replaced Aid to Families with Dependent Children (AFDC) with a new program called Temporary Assistance for Needy Families (TANF). The newer program requires parents of all but the very youngest children to work and thus will increase the demand for day-care facilities (Children's Defense Fund, 1997). Some states have taken action to fund additional assistance for children. Partnerships among the state, the business community, and parents like those provided for by Florida's Child Care Partnership Act and the Early

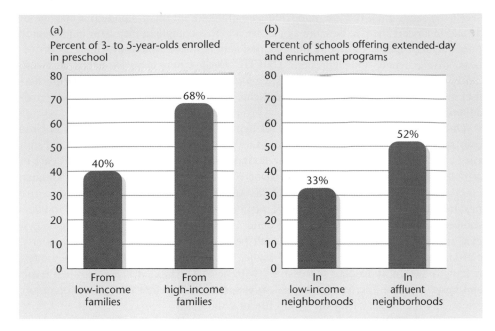

(a)
Percent of 3- to 5-year-olds enrolled in preschool

(b)
Percent of schools offering extended-day and enrichment programs

Figure 6-12

Are child care and enrichment programs only for the affluent?

Children from high-income families are not only more likely to be enrolled in preschool (a), but they are also more likely to have access to enrichment and before- and after-school programs (b).

Source: Children's Defense Fund yearbook, 1997, 2004.

Childhood Initiative undertaken in Pennsylvania look promising. Other states, however, have elected less farsighted programs—for example, licensing child-care providers who lack even a high school diploma or a GED (Children's Defense Fund, 1997).

Good-quality child care tends to enhance children's language abilities and cognitive skills, and infants with child-care experience adapt more quickly and explore more in an unfamiliar setting (Belsky, Steinberg, & Walker, 1983; Clarke-Stewart, 1993). These children play more with peers and are more socially competent, and they exhibit more self-confidence and are less fearful of unfamiliar adults (NICHD Early Child Care Research Network, 2001), especially when they have a secure infant-care provider relationship (Howes, 1999).

These infants and toddlers may learn important social and cognitive skills in this multicultural day-care facility. Especially in small centers with favorable staff-child ratios, age-appropriate activities, and responsive caregiving, day care can be a positive and enriching experience for young children.

At the same time, it's true that child-care children are often reported, at the age of $4\frac{1}{2}$ and in kindergarten, to be more aggressive and less compliant than their home-reared peers. As the amount of time in nonmaternal care increased, there was more assertiveness, disobedience, and aggression (NICHD Early Child Care Research Network, 2002, 2003). However, these rates of aggression and noncompliance are within normal ranges and do not indicate that child-care children are, in any sense, socially maladjusted (Lamb & Ahnert, 2006).

One reason for the increased levels of aggression is that extended periods in child care may be stressful for some children. In a recent study, researchers measured salivary cortisol (levels of cortisol provide an index of stress) in children at child care or at home in the morning and late afternoon (Watamura, Dongella, Alwin, & Gunnar, 2003). At child care, 35 percent of infants and 71 percent of toddlers showed a rise in cortisol across the day; at home, 71 percent of infants and 64 percent of toddlers showed decreases. Children who were better adapted to the child-care context, as evidenced by their greater involvement with peers, exhibited lower cortisol. Similarly, children at child care, who were rated higher in social fearfulness—which may interfere with the ability to play successfully with peers—exhibited higher cortisol levels and larger increases across the day. Clearly, some children fare better and cope more effectively than others with the group life of child care.

Of course, child-care quality is an important factor (Lamb & Ahnert, 2006). Optimal social development, as measured by better relationships with teachers and peers, is more often observed in high-quality day-care centers, where there are lower staff-to-child ratios, more interaction between staff and children, better caregiver training, more space, and better equipment than in poor-quality centers (Clarke-Stewart & Allhusen, 2002). Moreover, the effects of day-care quality continue even after children reach school age. In one study, high-quality preschool day care was related to less child hostility and better orientation to tasks in kindergarten. Poor-quality day care, however, coupled with early entry into day care (before the age of 1), was related to a higher level of destructiveness and less consideration for others (Howes, 1999). In another study, even four years after being enrolled in high-quality day care, children were rated friendlier, more inclined toward positive emotions, more competent, and better at resolving conflicts (Vandell, Henderson, & Wilson, 1988). There is no question that day-care quality is associated with children's later social and emotional development, but the long-term effects are greater for children from disadvantaged homes (Clarke-Stewart & Allhusen, 2005).

Making the Connections 6

There are many links between concepts and ideas in one area of development and concepts and ideas in other areas. Here are some of the connections between ideas in Chapter 6 and discussions in other chapters of this book.

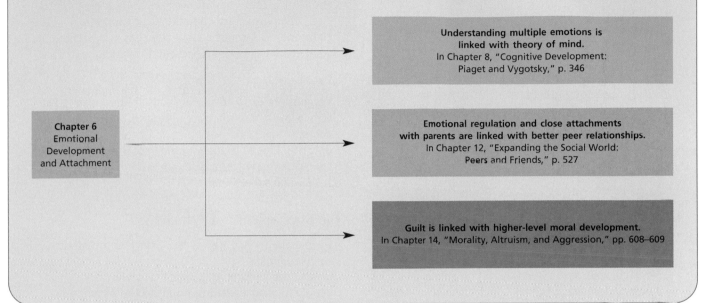

Chapter 6
Emotional Development and Attachment

Understanding multiple emotions is linked with theory of mind.
In Chapter 8, "Cognitive Development: Piaget and Vygotsky," p. 346

Emotional regulation and close attachments with parents are linked with better peer relationships.
In Chapter 12, "Expanding the Social World: Peers and Friends," p. 527

Guilt is linked with higher-level moral development.
In Chapter 14, "Morality, Altruism, and Aggression," pp. 608–609

SUMMARY

- Through emotional expression infants not only communicate their feelings, needs, and wishes to others but even regulate other people's behavior.

Early Emotional Development

- Babies begin expressing their **emotions** quite early in life. Startle, disgust, and distress are among the first true emotions to appear. Next to emerge is the social smile, in which true pleasure is expressed, and this is followed soon thereafter by delight, anger, joy, and surprise. Fear arrives a bit later, and still later come complex emotions such as pride and guilt. In general, emotions become more differentiated from one another over time and are more tied to specific situations.

- In infancy, boys are more emotionally expressive than girls, but in a developmental shift caused perhaps by the socialization efforts of parents and other caregivers, girls soon begin to express more emotions and boys to restrict emotional expression.

Recognizing Emotions in Others

- Another challenge that infants confront within the first half year of life is that of learning to recognize emotional expressions in others. Babies' typically easier recognition of positive emotions than of negative ones has functional value, for it strengthens the bond with mothers and other caretakers. In general, children are more proficient at producing than at recognizing emotions, but the two abilities are positively related: Children who are skilled at one are typically skilled at the other.

The Beginnings of Specific Emotions

- Smiling in infants follows a general developmental pattern, beginning with the newborn's **reflex smile,** which depends on the child's internal state. Next, at 4 to 6 weeks of age, come smiles elicited by external events, including social stimuli such as faces and voices. By 12 weeks, infants begin to smile selectively at familiar faces and voices, and their smiles differ depending on the situation. By 4 months, infants begin to laugh, and the number and kinds of events that elicit laughter change with their development. Both laughter and smiling may play a critical role in maintaining the proximity of the caregiver to the baby.

- Although not all infants develop **stranger distress** in their second half-year, when they do, the fear emerges gradually. Many factors determine how an infant will react to a particular stranger. Babies tend to be less fearful in a familiar setting and when they feel as if they have some control over the situation. **Social referencing** helps them interpret emotional cues in other people so as to know how to behave in a new situation. They also are less fearful of unfamiliar children than of unfamiliar adults, and they are less likely to be afraid of friendly, outgoing strangers.

- Various explanations for the development of smiling, laughter, and fear of strangers have been offered, including genetic-maturational, learning, and cognitive perspectives. Each of these perspectives may be useful some of the time, depending on the child's developmental level and the type of emotional reaction being considered. In some cases the appearance of a phenomenon across a range of cultures lends some support to a particular view; for example, the common experience of **separation protest** may suggest the contribution of inherited factors.

Learning to Regulate Emotions

- A major challenge for infants is to learn how to regulate their own emotions, to modify or control them when desirable. Gradually emotional expressions become less frequent and less intense. By the preschool years, children begin to follow **emotional display rules,** which dictate what emotions to show under what circumstances.

- Culture affects these rules, and the display of such emotions as anger and shame may be sanctioned in one culture but disapproved of in another.

- Family members, both parents and siblings, influence the child's developing patterns of emotional expression. Parents serve as models for emotional display, and by reacting to a child's emotional expressions both parents and siblings can encourage or discourage such displays. Children whose parents serve as coaches, helping them to understand and manage their emotions, are better able to handle emotional upset on their own and in addition are better accepted by their peers. Belittling or dismissing a child's emotions or punishing her for her expressions may prevent her not only from learning how to manage her own feelings but from understanding other people's emotions.

How Children Think about Emotions

- As children mature they develop an understanding of the meanings of emotion terms and of the situations that trigger particular feelings; each **emotional script** within this collection helps the child identify the feeling that typically accompanies a given situation. They also learn that they can experience more than one emotion at a time and that two or more such emotions may conflict, and they begin to consider the desires of others in predicting the emotions that others will experience in particular contexts. Learning to differentiate and integrate multiple factors in a situation helps children to understand more complex emotions like pride, guilt, and shame, as do both the ability to understand causal sequences and specific experience in discussing feelings with caretakers and others.

The Development of Attachment

- During the second half of the first year, infants begin to discriminate between familiar and unfamiliar caregivers, and to form **attachments** to the important people in their lives. According to the **psychoanalytic** view, the basis for the mother-infant attachment is oral gratification. The **learning** view stresses the role the mother plays as a **secondary reinforcer.** The **ethological** view stresses the role of instinctual infant responses that elicit the parent's care and protection. Analogous to infant-parent bonding is the process of **imprinting,** which among birds and other infrahuman animals can forge bonds between newborns and anything they see just after their birth. According to the **cognitive developmental view,** the infant must be able to differentiate his mother from a stranger and must be aware that his mother continues to exist even when he cannot see her.

- Attachment emerges over the first 6 to 8 months in a consistent series of steps. The first step, which seems to be innate in newborns, is a preference for other humans over inanimate objects. The second step, which begins soon after birth, is learning to discriminate familiar people from unfamiliar ones. Finally, in the third step, babies develop attachments to specific people. These attachments are revealed in the infants' loud protests when attachment figures depart and their joyous greetings for caregivers when reunited with them.

- Infants develop attachment relationships not only with their mothers but with their fathers, siblings, peers, and others. In many cultures fathers have the special role of playmate in the development of their babies; fathers' play with infants tends to be physical, whereas mothers' play is quieter and more verbal.

The Nature and Quality of Attachment

- The quality of an infant's attachment can be assessed in a scenario called the **Strange Situation,** in which the child's interactions with the mother are observed under mildly stressful conditions. This scenario evolved out of the notion that infants use the adult to whom they've become attached as a **secure base.** Typically, some 60 to 65 percent of infants are classified by this method as **securely attached** to their mothers, whereas the rest fall into three categories of insecure attachment: **avoidant, resistant,** or **disorganized.** Attachment classifications generally remain stable over time unless major changes occur in the lives of family members.

- The **Attachment Q Sort (AQS),** a newer method of assessing attachment, makes it possible to rate a broad range of attachment-related behaviors in a naturalistic setting.

- The quality of an infant's attachment to parents is determined by early parent-child interactions. Parents who display **sensitive care,** responding to their infant's needs and giving the baby a sense of control over the environment, seem to have more securely attached infants. **Interactive synchrony** requires that the mother constantly adjust her behavior to her baby's, engaging him when he is ready and backing off when he is not.

- Parents' **internal working models** of their own experience with their parents are likely to influence their attachment relationships with their babies. Both mothers and fathers who have been classified as autonomous, dismissing, and preoccupied have been shown to be more likely to have secure, avoidant, or resistant infants.

- A baby's temperament may play a role in the quality of the infant-parent attachment, but this occurs probably only in combination with other factors, such as the caregiver's behavior. Early attachments shape a child's later attitudes and behaviors. Children who were securely attached as infants are more likely than others to see themselves positively, to have high self-esteem, to be intellectually curious and eager to explore, and to have good relationships with peers and others.

- The quality of attachment is relatively stable across time, but changes in the environment may act to improve or lessen that quality, and professional intervention can help improve a troubled attachment relationship. Early secure attachment appears to be related to cognitive advancement and to the development of social skills. In addition, the more secure a child's attachment relationship, the more likely she is to develop a positive self-concept.

- Although there is no evidence that having multiple caregivers or spending time in a child-care center prevents the formation of a secure child-parent attachment relationship, some studies have indicated that the amount of time spent in such care is negatively correlated with the sensitivity mothers express toward their children and the affection children show to their mothers. Other studies have indicated that infants of working mothers are slightly more likely to be classified insecurely attached than those of non-working mothers, but the percentage difference is not large. It has been suggested that, rather than the mother's absence, it is the stress of working and also raising a child that interferes with the development of a strong attachment relationship.

- Quality and stability of child-care center staff are important ingredients in the security experienced by children in the care of these part-time caretakers. When quality of care is good, children may benefit both cognitively and socially. The quality of **family child care** is less certain, depending as it does on the one individual who cares for three or four children in such an arrangement.

EXPLORE AND DISCUSS

1. Our focus in this chapter has been on emotion. What role do you think families play in children's emotional development?

2. How does culture alter children's emotional development? Do you think that children show the same emotions in all cultures? Explain your answer.

3. How important to the development of attachment are specific caregiver functions, such as feeding, diapering, and bathing? Do you think other kinds of activities, such as play, are important as well? Or, because mothers are still the primary caregivers, will infants not develop attachments to other people, such as fathers, siblings, or grandparents?

4. Do you think that spending time in a day-care center puts a child at risk for later problems of development, such as, for example, difficulty in forming close personal relationships with other people? If you were counseling new parents, what guidelines would you offer them with regard to choosing a suitable day-care center for their baby?

Jacob Lawrence (1917–2000). *Library II*, 1960. Private Collection, New York.

7.

Language and Communication

Christa and her mother are talking about a recent event, a Halloween party that Christa, who is 19 months old, attended (from Engel, 1995):

Mother: (while looking at a doll clown) You looked like this. Remember the other day we dressed you up like this? Huh? Where'd you go? You went to a party? You went to a Halloween party. Remember? I put pom-poms on your dress?

Christa: Pom-pom.

Mother: Pom-poms. And d'you remember what you got at the party?

Christa: Pom-pom.

Mother: You got pom-poms, yeah. We fixed your pom-poms up when we came home. And what else did you get? A balloon?

Christa: Balloon.

Mother: And the pumpkin.

Christa: Pumpkin, pumpkin, pumpkin.

Mother: (pointing to a pumpkin on the table) There he is.

Christa: Pumpkin.

In this discussion, the mother contributes a large part of the conversation. She introduces the topic, connects it to a shared event, and reminds her child of her experiences. The child participates in several ways. She repeats words the mother uses that are interesting and important to her. She also answers questions, although she is greatly reliant on mother's help in doing so. By participating in this exchange, Christa is learning much about language and how to use it, such as turn taking, the question-answer format, and several new words. She is also learning about the kinds of ideas and events people find interesting to talk about, as well as how to use language to refer to a mental event, in this case a memory of a party.

Early conversations can also involve functional goals. For example, here 20-month-old Megan and her mother are playing with toys and other objects (from Budwig, 2002):

Megan: I want that one. (lifting the childproof container with the nut inside)

Mother: Oh you want that one, okay.

Megan: (tries to open container, fails) *My* open that!

Mother: What?

Megan: *My* open that, mommy. (handing container to mother)

Mother: Wanna open that?

Megan: Yeah.

Mother: (opens container)

Here the child wants to achieve a goal, but she is unable to do so. She uses language to make her desire known to someone who may be able to help her, her mother, and she and her mother have several exchanges to clarify exactly what it is that Megan wants. Here the child is learning something very important about language and how to use it: how to convey your own goal to someone else and then enlist your partner's aid in reaching that goal.

In both of these exchanges, what children learn about language occurs in the act of using language itself. This is a common way in which young children learn about and practice early language skills. Sometimes conversations between young children and older children or adults focus explicitly on helping children learn language, especially conventional forms of speech in a community. Here is an exchange, observed by Watson-Gegeo and Gegeo (1986), between a 15-year-old Kwara'ae girl in the Solomon Islands and her 27-month-old brother, Fita.

Sister: Then when you're full you just speak like this, "I don't want any more now."

Fita: What?

Sister: "I don't want to eat any more now."

Fita: I don't want?

Sister: Then you just speak as I said, like this, "I don't want any more now."

Fita: I don't want.

Sister: "I'm full now."

Fita: Full now.

Sister: "I'm—I'm full, I don't want to eat any more now."

Fita: Don't want to eat any more now.

Notice how the sister repeats the phrasing and encourages her brother as he repeats after her. Such exchanges provide guidance as children learn language and, as this conversation illustrates, children learn how to communicate information that is important for everyday functioning in socially appropriate ways. These three examples illustrate some of the many remarkable aspects of language learning in childhood. One of the child's most impressive developmental achievements is the mastery of language. Language is one of the most complex systems of rules a person ever learns, yet children in a wide range of different environments learn to understand and use their native languages quite rapidly. Their ability to do this suggests that human infants are prepared in some way to acquire language skills. However, biological preparation is insufficient in that the language abilities the child develops must fit with the community in which he or she lives. Thus, a crucial part of language learning is the social support provided by others as children learn to speak and use language to accomplish their own goals. In other words, one feature of our biological preparedness to learn languages is our ability to learn language in the context of social interaction.

What is **language?** It is a system of communication in which words and their written symbols are combined in rule-governed ways that enable speakers to produce an infinite number of messages. Language serves a wide range of purposes for the developing child: It helps him interact with others, communicate information, and express his feelings, wishes, and views. Children can use language to influence other people's behavior, to explore and learn about their environment, and to escape from reality by using their imaginations (Halliday, 1975). Language helps children to organize their perceptions and thinking, control their actions, and even to modify their emotions.

An important part of children's language learning is the development of **communicative competence,** which is the ability to convey thoughts, feelings, and intentions in a meaningful and culturally patterned way (Haslett, 1997; Hymes, 1972; Schaffer, 1974; Tomasello, 2006). Communication is by definition a two-way process; we send messages to others and receive messages from them. Thus, using **productive language,** we produce communications, and using **receptive language,** we receive communications from others.

We start this chapter with an overview of the primary components of language; next we explore the dominant theories of how language develops in the infant and young child. Then we discuss the structure of language including words, sentences, and grammar. After this discussion, we examine how children begin to understand and use language to communicate. Finally, we consider language development for children who learn two languages at once.

THE COMPONENTS OF LANGUAGE: PHONOLOGY, SEMANTICS, GRAMMAR, AND PRAGMATICS

Children learn about the sounds, meaning, structure, and use of language simultaneously. However, for purposes of study, scholars divide language into four main areas: phonology, semantics, grammar, and pragmatics.

Phonology, the system of sounds that a particular language uses, includes not only the language's basic units of sound, or **phonemes,** but rules about how we put phonemes together to form words and rules about the proper intonation patterns for phrases and sentences. Phonemes are considered *basic* units of sound because they are the smallest sound units that affect meaning; changing a phoneme changes the meaning of a word. For example, by changing the initial phoneme in the word *bat,* we can make the very different word *cat.* By changing the middle phoneme, we can make yet another word, *bit.* A very important feature of phonologic rules is that they are *generative;* that is, they are applicable beyond the cases on which they are based. A native English speaker, for instance, knows that *kib* is not a word in English, but it is nonetheless a possible sound pattern in the language's system. In contrast, *bnik* is not possible in English.

The study of word meanings and word combinations is called **semantics.** Comprehension of language requires not only a knowledge of specific words and their definitions but also an understanding of how we use words and how we combine them in phrases, clauses, and sentences. Thus, as children mature intellectually throughout their school years, their semantic knowledge continues to grow. Even adults continue to expand their vocabularies to encompass new knowledge. For example, a first-year psychology student must learn a whole new vocabulary of psychological terms.

Grammar describes the structure of a language and consists of two major parts: morphology and syntax. The subfield of grammar studies called **morphology** concentrates on the smallest units of meaning in a language, such as prefixes, suffixes, and root words. These units are called **morphemes.** Rules for altering root words to produce such things as plurals, past tenses, and inflections are part of a language's morphological system. **Syntax** is the aspect of grammar that specifies how words are

---

language A communication system in which words and their written symbols combine in rule-governed ways and enable speakers to produce an infinite number of messages.

communicative competence The ability to convey thoughts, feelings, and intentions in a meaningful and culturally patterned way.

productive language The production of speech.

receptive language Understanding the speech of others.

phonology The system of sounds that a language uses.

phoneme The basic unit of a language's phonetic system; phonemes are the smallest sound units that affect meaning.

semantics The study of word meanings and word combinations, as in phrases, clauses, and sentences.

grammar The structure of a language; consists of *morphology* and *syntax.*

morphology The study of morphemes, language's smallest units of meaning.

morpheme A language's smallest unit of meaning, such as a prefix, a suffix, or a root word.

syntax The part of grammar that prescribes how words may combine into phrases, clauses, and sentences.

Siblings are often good teachers for younger children, encouraging them to look at and manipulate interesting objects and giving names to shapes, colors, and noises that toys make.

pragmatics A set of rules that specify appropriate language for particular social contexts.

combined into sentences. For example, each language has syntactic rules for expressing grammatical relations such as negation, interrogation, possession, and juxtaposition of subject and object. The rules of syntax allow us to vary word order so that we are not limited to one way of saying what we mean providing what we say is still syntactically correct. For example, we can say "After class I went to the library and listened to some music," but the syntactically incorrect sentence, "I listened to some music after class and I went to the library," is ambiguous and unclear.

The fourth component of language, **pragmatics,** consists of rules for the use of language in particular contexts (Bates, 1999). Thus, pragmatics directly concerns effective and appropriate communication. For example, a child learns to speak differently to her younger brother than to her parents, simplifying language for her brother just as her parents initially simplified their language for her. She also learns that certain forms of language are more appropriate in some situations. For example, a child may have a better chance of getting what she wants if she asks a schoolmate, "May I have one of your crayons?" instead of demanding, "Gimme a crayon!" Researchers in pragmatics study these and other issues, such as how children learn to take turns speaking, to remain silent while others speak, and to speak differently in such different settings as the classroom and the playground.

THEORIES OF LANGUAGE DEVELOPMENT

As in many other subfields of child psychology, those who study language development debate how much heredity contributes to the evolution of language and how much children's experiences contribute to the emergence of their ability to communicate by means of language. Most theorists today maintain a middle ground, recognizing the roles that both genetic and environmental factors play in language development. To gain a full understanding of this interactionist approach, we first explore the environmental, or learning, view and then the biological, or nativist, view.

The Learning View: Claims and Limitations

Traditional learning explanations of language development use the principle of *reinforcement* to account for this process. For instance, the learning theorist B. F. Skinner (1957) posited that parents or other caretakers selectively reinforce the child's babbling sounds that are most like adult speech. By giving attention to these particular sounds and showing approval when their baby utters them, parents encourage the child to repeat them. When the child repeats the sounds, the parents or caregivers approve again, and the child, in turn, vocalizes these particular sounds more often. Thus, according to Skinner, by giving their greatest approval to the infant's closest approximations to adult speech sounds, parents shape their child's verbal behavior into what increasingly resembles adult speech.

Other learning theorists (Bandura, 1989; Bullock, 1983) propose that the child learns primarily through *imitation* or observational learning. According to this view, the child picks up words, phrases, and sentences directly by imitating what she hears. Then, through reinforcement and *generalization,* or applying what she has learned to new situations, the child learns when it is appropriate to use particular words and phrases. Learning theory accounts, however, have not fared well as a sole explanation of language acquisition for several reasons. First, the number of necessary specific connections—that is, linkages between a baby's vocalization and a parent's reinforcing response—to even begin to explain language is so enormous that a child could not acquire all of them in even a lifetime, not to mention a few short years. Second, naturalistic studies of parent-child interaction fail to support the learning theory account. For example, mothers are just as likely to reward their children for truthful but grammatically incorrect statements as they are to reinforce the children for grammatically correct utterances (Brown & Hanlon, 1970). Parents are concerned to teach their children acceptable behavior as well as correct language. It is difficult to see, then, how reinforcement alone might account for how the child learns grammar (Brown, 1973; Pinker, 1994).

A third argument against a learning explanation is that we cannot predict the vast majority of language utterances from specific utterances by others. For example, utterances that are closely tied to environmental cues, such as "Hello," "Watch out!" or "You're welcome," are relatively rare. For most sets of circumstances, language entails more creative responses than can be accounted for by a learning view. Fourth, learning theory accounts have not explained the regular sequence in which language develops. Children in our culture, and other cultures, seem to learn the same types of grammatical rules in the same order. For example, they learn active constructions before passive constructions: They learn to say, "Taisha and Neville prepared the posters for the class presentation" before they learn to say "The posters for the class presentation were prepared by Taisha and Neville." Finally, the learning explanation basically portrays the child as playing a rather passive role in language development although, as evidence we discuss later attests, the child plays an active and creative role in discovering and applying general rules of language.

For all these reasons, strict learning-theory accounts of language acquisition are not considered viable. An alternative explanation—the nativist view—suggests that language acquisition unfolds as a result of the unique biological properties of the human organism.

The Nativist View: Claims and Limitations

Linguist Noam Chomsky (1968), the most influential advocate of the nativist position, proposed that children are born with an innate mental structure that guides their acquisition of language and, in particular, grammar. Chomsky termed this structure a **language acquisition device (LAD).**

Nativists assert that certain *universal features* common to all languages are innate. For example, sentences in all languages contain a subject, verb, and object. The nativist approach sees language as an abstract system of rules that cannot be acquired by traditional learning principles. Rather, nativists argue that the normal human child is biologically predisposed to acquire human language. Following from this assumption, nativists contend that because language ability is an inherited species-specific characteristic, all languages of the species must display universal features—that is, they must share certain basic characteristics. By examining features such as the sounds used in speaking, the way words are organized in sentences, and how meaning is determined in various languages, investigators have concluded that a set of common principles does underlie all human languages (Slobin, 1985, 1992). For instance, speakers of all languages create a vast number of spoken words by combining a relatively small set of particular sounds. Each of the world's languages uses only a limited sample of all the possible vocal sounds humans can make. Finally, all languages have grammars, and nativists claim these grammars share certain formal properties as well (e.g., the subject-predicate relationship).

Also, in support of their position, nativists point out that in many different cultures, normal children acquire language relatively quickly and learn it well (Maratsos, 1989; Meisel, 1995; Pinker, 1994). Even in situations in which children receive fragmented

language acquisition device (LAD) Chomsky's proposed mental structure in the human nervous system that incorporates an innate concept of language.

Box 7.1

Perspectives on Diversity

CAN CHILDREN CREATE NEW LANGUAGES?

The most striking evidence that children may possess an innate program or template for grammar comes from the work of Derek Bickerton (1983, 1990), who has studied creole languages around the globe. The **creole language** often arises in a context in which people who speak different languages for some reason end up together in a single culture. We see this, for instance, in Hawaii, the southeast coast of North America, New Orleans, the Carribbean, the Guyanas, Africa, islands in the Indian Ocean, Indonesia, and the Philippines, where peoples from countries of Asia, Africa, Europe, and the Americas came together and formed polyglot societies. Although the adults in these situations crafted a common language that could be used to communicate, this language, called *pidgin*, lacked grammatical structure. However, the children in these cultures, regardless of their parents' native languages, used a language derived from pidgin, called *creole*, which had a single structure and linguistic system. Moreover, the creole languages persisted into succeeding generations in similar form. How could the children of these different racial and ethnic groups have evolved languages that resemble each other if they did not possess some sort of inner template of a universal grammar?

In these multicultural societies, many of which were made up of people imported, sometimes against their will, to labor on colonial plantations, communication began with workers' development of a pidgin language, a simplified linguistic system created out of two languages that suddenly come into contact with each other. As Table 7-1 shows, pidgin lacks grammatical complexity: Its sentences are often no more than

Table 7-1 Some utterances in Hawaiian pidgin English

Pidgin:	*Ifu laik meiki, mo beta make time, mani no kaen hapai.*
Direct translation:	If like make, more better make time, money no can carry.
Meaning:	"If you want to build (a temple), you should do it just before you die—you can't take it with you!"
Pidgin:	*Aena tu macha churen, samawl churen, haus mani pei.*
Direct translation:	And too much children, small children, house money pay.
Meaning:	"And I had many children, small children, and I had to pay the rent."

Source: From Bickerton, 1990.

strings of nouns, verbs, and adjectives. For this reason and because pidgin is highly individualistic, varying from speaker to speaker, its usefulness is limited. Such limitations may be what led the children of pidgin speakers to develop the more complex type of communication represented by creole languages.

The language children in polyglot societies develop is much richer in grammatical structure than pidgin (Bickerton, 1983). And interestingly, creole languages that develop in different places throughout the world are

---

creole language A language spoken by children of pidgin-language speakers that, in contrast with pidgin, is highly developed and rule governed.

critical period A specific period in children's development when they are sensitive to a particular environmental stimulus that does not have the same effect on them when encountered before or after this period.

and incomplete environmental input, children can learn language. Thus, nativists argue that the child must be preset to acquire language. As Box 7.1 suggests, some of the most striking evidence for the possibility of an innate predisposition for language comes from the study of children who learn language even with restricted input.

Another source of support for the nativist view is evidence that human beings learn language far more easily and quickly during a certain critical period of biological development. A **critical period** is a time during which a child is sensitive to a particular environmental stimulus that does not have the same effect on him when he encounters it before or after this period. The critical period for language stretches from infancy to puberty. Before puberty, a child may achieve the fluency of a native speaker in any language without special training, but after puberty, it is extremely difficult to

very similar in their structure, no matter what the contributing languages! Even more remarkably, the speech of first-generation creole-speaking children does not differ from that of later generations of speakers, which suggests that the acquisition of this new language happens very rapidly. Together, the uniformity of language across speakers and geographic locales and the speed of language acquisition argue against any simple explanation that children who learn creole are simply borrowing from the contact languages in a haphazard fashion.

What are the implications of these observations for theories of language acquisition? According to Bickerton (1983),

> The evidence from creole languages suggests that first-language acquisition is mediated by an innate device . . . the device provides the child with a single and fairly specific grammatical model. It was only in pidgin-speaking communities, where there was no grammatical model that could compete with the child's innate grammar, that the innate grammatical model was not eventually suppressed. The innate grammar was then clothed in whatever vocabulary was locally available and gave rise to the creole languages heard today. (p. 121)

In 1977, Nicaragua opened its first school for deaf people. Before school opened, the lack of an organized school system prevented the deaf from much interaction. In the new school, children and adults were taught to lip-read and to speak Spanish. This approach yielded little success, but the students were also able to freely engage in gestural communication. Slowly a rudimentary sign language emerged among the students. As new children of various ages entered the school, they learned this language from their peers. Senghas and Coppola (2001) investigated the complexity of this gestural language in relation to how long children were at the school and at what age they entered. If the complex grammar of language was found only among the children, then they could conclude that the knowledge stemmed from innate abilities available to the child until he or she reaches the critical period. If the most complex components of the language were found only in adults learning the new sign language, they could conclude that higher cognitive levels are needed to grasp the hardest parts of language. The investigators found that the most complex patterns of speech originated in children under the age of 10, and that adults were unable to make use of these structures in either comprehension or production. Thus, children were able to create and learn gestures that conveyed complex linguistic structures, whereas adults who were past the critical period were unable to do so. This conclusion provides powerful support for the theory that humans are designed to learn language at an early age.

The case is certainly not closed. Some critics like Tomasello (1995) have argued that adult influences may play a role in the emergence of creole. And others argue that creole languages reveal the common uses of language across cultures rather than simply reflect properties of the human mind (Jourdan, 1991). Finally, as Hoff (2001) points out, the fact that creole languages developed a long time ago makes it difficult to know exactly what processes underlie them. At this point, it seems that the interactionist view (see pp. 277–281), which suggests that both biological factors and environmental influences provide the best account of language acquisition, may offer a viable alternative explanation for the creole languages.

learn a first language (see Figure 7-1). Dramatic examples come from several famous case studies. In the winter of 1800, a 12-year-old boy was discovered living on his own in the woods near Aveyron, France. The boy had no language, and in spite of efforts by Jean Itard at the National Institute for Deaf-Mutes in Paris, the boy was able to learn only a few words. No one knows why. Perhaps the boy was impaired at birth, or perhaps language can only be acquired before puberty (Lane, 1976). In another, modern case, 13-year-old "Genie" was discovered to have been kept locked in a room by her mentally ill father from the time she was 18 months of age (Curtiss, 1989; Rymer, 1993). Although Genie was more successful in learning to communicate than the wild boy in France, she never acquired normal language. These cases strongly suggest a critical period for language acquisition (Hoff, 2001). Further

Figure 7-1

It helps to learn a new language early in life
On a test of English grammar, native speakers of Chinese and Korean who had immigrated to the United States before they were 7 years old scored as well as native speakers of English. The older immigrants were when they arrived in America, the less well they did on the test.

Source: Newport, 1990; redrawn from Johnson & Newport, 1989.

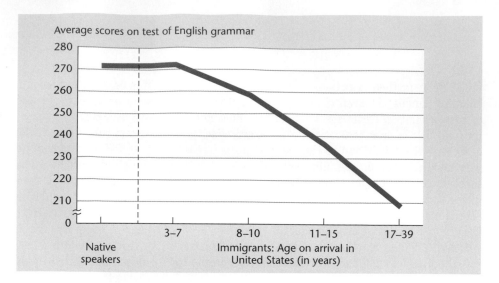

support for this claim is found among young children whose speech is disrupted by brain injury and who often recover their language capacity rapidly and completely. If the brain damage occurs after puberty, however, the prognosis for the recovery of language is poorer. Nevertheless, the fact that there is considerable variation, even among adults, suggests that despite the existence of a critical period, other contributions are also important (Goodglass, 1993).

Often people have cited the ability of animals to learn language as evidence against the nativist viewpoint, but the conclusions are mixed. Although learning theorists contend that language can be aquired by other intelligent animals given appropriate training, and nativists dispute this point, determining whether animals other than humans learn language depends on the definition of language a scientist uses as well as on the assumptions about what goes on in the human mind when people use language.

If one is to define language as a use of symbols as referents, then the average sheepdog is able to learn a language when it learns dozens of whistles for various actions. However, generally when evaluating animal language, linguists consider certain features as defining language, including the understanding of order and other syntactical cues ("Bob hit Jim" as opposed to "Jim hit Bob"), and the creation of novelty based on syntax (putting together two known words to create a novel meaning). Using these guidelines, there does seem to be some evidence of language in many species, ranging from the African grey parrot (Pepperberg, 2000) to dolphins (Herman & Uyeyama, 1999) and various primate species, most notably the bonobos, exemplified by Kanzi (Savage-Rumbaugh & Shanker, 1998). Other researchers, such as Kako (1999), argue that their language abilities place these animals at about the level of a 2-year-old human. Thus, they are still lacking crucial aspects of language learning such as the use of prepositions, demonstratives, and conjunctions. Although some of the most cognitively advanced species of animals seem to acquire some aspects of language, at least in specially designed environments, as of yet no animal has come close to acquiring the numerous complex linguistic subtleties that children as young as 3 acquire in the average home. Finally, if one assumes that using human language effectively entails understanding the mind and its properties, then the likely candidates for language acquisition are narrowed considerably. Whether such abilities exist in nonhuman primates, such as chimpanzees, is difficult to answer (Povinelli, Bering, & Giambrone, 2000; Tomasello, 1999).

Like the learning view, the nativist explanation of language development has its limitations. First, few theorists agree about the exact nature of the types of grammatical rules that children learn. In fact, several theorists have offered alternative explanations of the early grammar acquisition process that differ from Chomsky's original formulation (Maratsos, 1989, 1998; Pinker, 1994; Slobin, 1985). Second, language learning is a gradual process and is not completed as early as nativist accounts would predict. As we will see later in the chapter, specific aspects of grammar continue to develop in the elementary school years and even beyond.

Third, this perspective makes it very difficult to account for the many languages human beings speak throughout the world. Despite the nativist claim that languages possess universal features, it is difficult to envision features that produce such different grammatical structures, including the many varying forms of syntax and the way a universal feature leads to the enormous variety of sound combinations in the world's languages. Fourth, the nativist view gives the social context of language little recognition. We now know from research that takes an interactionist approach to language development that social influences play a much larger role in language development than is proposed in a nativist view. Additionally, the theoretical assertion that language milestones are acquired in a universal stage sequence is not supported by empirical research stemming from an interactionist approach (Nelson, 1998). The communicative context of language development, especially adult-child communication, plays a significant role in the pacing of this developmental process.

It seems likely that human beings are biologically prepared *in some way* for learning language. However, it seems quite unlikely that biological principles alone can account for all aspects of language development.

The Interactionist View

Most modern theorists of language development take the interactionist view, recognizing that language is learned in the context of spoken language but assuming as well that humans are in some way biologically prepared for learning to speak. Interactionists are concerned with the interplay between biological and environmental factors in the acquisition of language. The child's own active role in her development of normal speech complements the role played by socializing agents like parents (Gallaway & Richards, 1994; Morgan, 1990). Even in the examples we used to open this chapter, in which the adult or older child contributed a substantial part of the communication, the young children played active roles in conversations. In addition, language acquisition is not separate from other aspects of development (Bloom & Tinker, 2001). Rather, language development occurs in a rich behavioral and developmental context in which children try to accomplish meaningful goals and engage in relationships with others. Language development supports the expression and accomplishment of these important human acts. Although biology is considered an important contributor, the interactionist approach does not make assumptions about what this innate contribution is like. Interactionist theorists today are trying to discover just what this biological contribution is, a pursuit that Bates and Goodman (1999) refer to as determining the "nature of nurture" (p. 33).

In the interactionist view, normal language develops as a result of a delicate balance between parent and child understanding—when parents speak to children in a way that recognizes how much the children already know and understand, they increase enormously their children's chance of comprehending a novel message (Bloom, 1998; Ninio & Snow, 1996; Tomasello, 2006). You will recall from Chapter 1 that Vygotsky proposed this sort of help from older and more experienced people as necessary to children's learning. We will explore Vygotsky's concepts in greater depth in Chapter 8 (Gauvain, 2001a; Rogoff, 1990, 1998; Vygotsky, 1934).

FACILITATING CHILDREN'S LANGUAGE DEVELOPMENT
An advocate of the social interaction view, Jerome Bruner has proposed that the environment provides the language-learning child with a **language acquisition support system,** or **LASS** (Bruner, 1983; Snow, 1989). In contrast to nativists like Chomsky,

language acquisition support system (LASS) According to Bruner, a collection of strategies and tactics that environmental influences—initially, a child's parents or primary caretakers—provide the language-learning child.

Many games parents play with their young children help them learn words as well as pragmatic features of language such as turn taking and the meaning of pauses.

Bruner emphasizes the parents' or primary caretakers' role as facilitators of language acquisition. What does Bruner suggest the LASS consists of? During children's earliest years, parents support their development of language and their comprehension with several strategies. For example, parents often introduce objects to a child to provide a basis for their mutual play and speak about objects and events that are present and easily visible to the child. They monitor their child's apparent goals or intentions closely, often commenting on them. In general they try to modulate, correct, or elaborate their child's behavior rather than specifically redirect it. Although parents don't usually conceive of these tactics as deliberate teaching techniques but see them rather as natural efforts to carry on conversation with their children, they are very specifically facilitating their children's learning.

We turn now to a series of techniques that adults use to facilitate language acquisition in young children. These techniques include playing nonverbal games, using simplified speech, and elaborating on and rewording children's own utterances to help them sharpen their communicative skills.

Playing Nonverbal Games   Parents make some of their first efforts to "converse" with their children in early nonlinguistic games like peek-a-boo or patty-cake. Children learn some structural features of spoken language, such as turn taking, from these games. And because these kinds of games involve regular, repetitive, and thus predictable behaviors, they may also lay a foundation for the systematic rules of language. At first, young babies aren't capable of either initiating or responding in these playful "conversations," to say nothing of taking turns. Parents help them learn these social skills by carrying more than their share of early dialogues and by waiting for pauses in the infant's vocal or motor behavior and then inserting an appropriate response. This supportive activity of parents may contribute not only to later give-and-take in conversation but also to social turn taking in play and other more complex games (Garvey, 1990).

infant-directed, or child-directed, speech A simplified style of speech parents use with young children, in which sentences are short, simple, and often repetitive and the speaker enunciates especially clearly, slowly, and in a higher-pitched voice, often ending with a rising intonation. Also called *motherese*.

Using Simplified Speech   Another part of LASS is parents' habit of modifying their speech when they talk to infants and children. Typically, they use a simplified style, called **infant-directed,** or **child-directed, speech** (also called *motherese*), in which they speak in short, simple sentences that refer to concrete objects and events and that often repeat important words and phrases. In this style of speech, parents also talk more slowly and in higher-pitched voices, enunciate more clearly, and often end sentences with a rising intonation (Fernald, 1992; Fernald & Morikawa, 1993). The simplified grammar and syntax may help children learn the relationships between words and objects and may also give them some understanding of the rules of segmentation—that is, how speech is divided into words, phrases, and sentences. The acoustic variations can help highlight important words. For example, in reading to 14-month-olds, mothers consistently positioned a word that identified a picture ("that's a *shirt*" or "that's a *boy*") at the end of a phrase and spoke in exaggerated pitch, thus capturing their infants' attention (Fernald & Kuhl, 1987; Fernald & Mazzie, 1991).

Research has shown that newborns and 4-week-olds prefer to listen to infant-directed speech than to adult-directed talk (Cooper & Aslin, 1990) and that babies are equally responsive to this style of communication whether it is used by men or women (Pegg, Werker, & McLeod, 1992). And infants show a preference for infant-directed speech even when speech is in a nonnative language. For example, even when English-learning infants listened to Cantonese, they still appeared to prefer infant-directed speech (Werker, Pegg, & McLeod, 1994).

Exaggerating speech, placing important words at the ends of sentences, and raising pitch and intonation not only help adults gain infants' attention; simplified speech also tends to elicit signs of positive emotions, such as smiles, and may increase the chances that the child will understand the message (Pegg et al., 1992; Werker & McLeod, 1989). But does the use of a simplified code actually facilitate children's language learning? In fact, simplified speech may not always be helpful. In one study, children who had progressed beyond the one-word stage were more likely to respond appropriately to an adult form of a command ("Throw me the ball") than to a simplified form ("Throw ball"). As we have seen in other areas of development, a level of complexity that is slightly ahead of children may be the most effective in eliciting their attention and may maximize their learning (Hoff-Ginsberg & Shatz, 1982; Sokolov, 1993). When infants or children show signs that they are not comprehending, adults often revert to simpler speech (Bohannon & Warren-Leubecker, 1988). In general, parents adjust their speech to a child's level of linguistic sophistication, using a wider and wider range of words and parts of speech as children mature (Hoff, 2001; Shatz, 1983).

Other Influence Techniques Parents facilitate early communication in several other important ways. Consider the following exchanges between a mother and her child:

Child: Daddy juice.

Adult: Daddy drinks juice.

Child: Give Mama.

Adult: Give it to Mama.

In the technique of **expansion** illustrated here, the adult imitates and expands or adds to the child's statement. Expanding on children's statements facilitates language development, including vocabulary (Weizman & Snow, 2001). Moreover, following up on the child's interests and attention is more supportive of learning than switching the child's attention to another topic (Dunham, Dunham, & Curwin, 1993; Tomasello & Farrar, 1986). Brown (1973) has estimated that among middle-class families, about 30 percent of the time parents' speech to their children is composed of such expansions, but that lower-class parents use this technique much less often. Parents are especially likely to use this expansion strategy after a child has made a grammatical error (Bohannon & Stanowicz, 1988).

Although expansion sometimes helps a child's learning, a combination of expansion and recast is more effective. In a **recast,** the adult listener renders the child's incomplete sentence in a more complex grammatical form. For example, when the child says, "Kitty eat," the adult may recast the sentence as a question: "What is the kitty eating?" Or a child's "My ball" might become "Here is your ball." Through recasting, children's adult partners are, in effect, both correcting children's utterances and guiding them toward more appropriate grammatical usage. Moreover, some researchers have shown that children whose parents have recast their utterances appear to develop linguistically at a faster rate, using questions and complex verb forms at an earlier age than is common (Nelson, 1989; Nelson, Carskadden, & Bonvillian, 1973; Nelson, Welsh, Camarata, Butkovsky, & Camarata, 1995). As we do not know how often parents use recasts, we cannot yet say how powerful a role recasting plays in normal language acquisition.

expansion A technique adults use in speaking to young children in which they imitate and expand or add to a child's statement.

recast A technique adults use in speaking to young children in which they render a child's incomplete sentence in a more complex grammatical form.

We do know, however, that children often imitate their parents' expansions and recasts, especially when they are incorrect. When children's speech is correct, they are unlikely to imitate the adult's speech (Bohannon & Stanowicz, 1988). Perhaps children are more aware of their mistakes than we realize! Of particular interest is that children's imitations of their parents' expansions are often grammatically more advanced than their free speech, illustrated in this example from Slobin (1968):

Child: Pick-mato.

Adult: Picking tomatoes up?

Child: Pick 'mato up.

IS SOCIAL INTERACTION CRUCIAL TO LANGUAGE DEVELOPMENT?

Some theorists hold that although social interaction is necessary to language acquisition, the specific devices of expansion and recasting, together with children's imitation, may not be necessary. First, no universal pattern of social linguistic support characterizes all parents within or across cultural groups (Hoff, 2001). In fact, there are impressive individual differences among the linguistic environments that parents within a given cultural group provide their children (Hart & Risley, 1999; Shatz, 1983). In addition, not all cultures use the devices typical of the American middle class (Minami & McCabe, 1995; Peters, 1983). For example, among the Kaluli of New Guinea and in American Samoa, people speak to the very youngest children as if they were adults (Ochs, 1988; Schieffelin & Ochs, 1987), despite the fact that they believe young children are incapable of communicating intentionally. Evidently there are forms of interaction that we do not yet entirely understand but that nevertheless ensure that children around the world (including American Samoans) develop language at the same general pace.

How can we determine whether parental corrective feedback plays a role in the child's development of language? To determine whether this feedback—called **negative evidence** by language scholars because it shows the child what is *not* correct in her utterances—is a critical and necessary force in language learning, Pinker (1994) has proposed four criteria for evaluating this contribution—specifically negative evidence must be *present, useful, used,* and *necessary.* How do these criteria fare in the face of research? To begin with, negative evidence may not always be present or, perhaps, may rarely be present. Although most language scholars, especially learning theorists and interactionists, agree that parents correct their children's grammar on occasion, some nativists disagree and, as research has shown, in some societies parents apparently do not offer such correction (Bohannon & Stanowicz, 1988; Morgan, Bonamo, & Travis, 1995).

Second, to be useful, negative evidence needs to be provided in a form children can process. Nativists have offered two specific reasons why children may not be able to use corrective feedback. First, such feedback occurs only a portion of the time. Second, the evidence of children's use of feedback is indirect, for parents expand or recast rather than tell a child specifically what he said is wrong (Pinker, 1989, 1994).

Third, can we show that children actually use this type of feedback to improve their learning of grammar? In a study by Farrar (1992), children were more likely to imitate a recast such as "The dog is running," corrected from "The dog running"—a form of negative evidence—than they were to imitate other forms of feedback like topic continuations, such as "Would you like some water?" in response to "I'm hot." Although this study suggests that negative evidence does indeed appear to be particularly helpful in grammar acquisition, others disagree and argue that negative evidence offers no special advantage for learning grammar (Morgan et al., 1995; Morgan & Demuth, 1996).

Finally, if negative evidence were necessary, we would have to show either that all children receive it or that children who do not receive it do not learn language

negative evidence According to Pinker, corrective feedback that parents may give to young language-learning children.

adequately. As we have said, no universal pattern of language input characterizes all parents within a given cultural group, and some children who receive no corrective feedback do learn their language.

The final word on the role of parental influence in language acquisition is not yet in. Those who advocate the interactionist view hold that although the child is probably biologically prepared for learning language, there is also strong support for the role of environmental input in the child's development of language. For instance, recent longitudinal research exploring the relation between maternal responsiveness and the achievement by children of language milestones indicates that a mother's responsiveness to her child's activity at 9 and 13 months of age predicts language development (Tamis-LeMonda, Bornstein, & Baumwell, 2001). Maternal responsiveness was defined as any meaningful, positive change in the mother's behavior within 5 seconds of a child's action—for example, if the child picked up a cup and the mother said, "That's a cup." Other research demonstrates that 18-month-old infants are more adept at learning words in social referential contexts in which an experimenter produced a novel word as part of the interaction than in a situation in which the experimenter and child interacted but the novel word came from another source, such as a recording device (Campbell & Namy, 2003). These studies suggest that social contributions play an important facilitative role in language acquisition.

THE ANTECEDENTS OF LANGUAGE DEVELOPMENT

Communication skill is not achieved solely by learning words. If we restricted our focus to verbal communication only, we could easily underestimate how early in life communication begins. To fully understand the development of human communication, we must consider the many sounds babies make as well as the many looks, movements, and gestures by which they convey meaning before they can begin to talk. These prelinguistic achievements are important precursors of actual language use (Adamson, 1995).

Preverbal Communication

Some of infants' earliest communications take place during interactions with their first caregivers (Fogel, 1993; Uzgiris, 1989). Parent and infant often engage in a kind of dialogue of sounds, movements, smiles, and other facial expressions. Smiles, in particular, seem important in helping infants learn how to coordinate vocalizations and to translate expressions into effective communication (Yale, Messinger, Cogo-Lewis, & Delgado, 2003). Although these early transactions may seem at first glance to be "conversations," a closer look suggests that they be described as "pseudo-conversations" or "pseudo-dialogues," because the adult alone is responsible for maintaining their flow (Schaffer, 1977). Babies have limited control over the nature and timing of their responses, so adults insert their behavior into the infants' cycles of responsiveness and unresponsiveness. For instance, a baby gurgles and her mother replies by speaking to the infant. She first waits for the child's response, but if none is forthcoming, she may prompt the baby by changing her expression, speaking again, or gently touching the child. Such interactions

Gestures such as pointing and touching can help children connect a physical object with the word a parent or other adult is pronouncing.

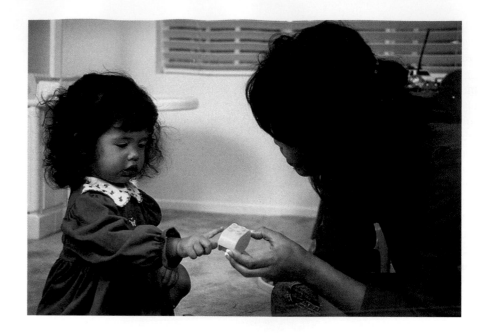

help the infant become a communicative partner by the end of her first year (Golinkoff, 1983; Schaffer, 1977, 1996).

Gestures and expressions play an important role in this process (Goldin-Meadow, 2006). Between 3 and 12 months of age, infants improve greatly in their ability to use gestures to communicate (Fogel, 1993). By at least the time when babies are 3 or 4 months old, adults offer and show things to them, and 6-month-old infants respond with smiles, gestures, movements, and sounds. When babies are about 6 months old, they begin to use a pointing gesture to guide others' attention to particular objects. Surprisingly, it's not until children are a year old that they can follow the point of another person. These steps in pointing signify milestones in language development. Through pointing, both in directing and in following, children can receive labels for objects that interest them and learn a great deal about the world around them (Golinkoff & Hirsh-Pasek, 1999). When a preverbal infant uses a gesture to call an object to someone's attention, her action is called a **protodeclarative** because it functions like a declarative statement (Bates, 1976). Babies can also use gestures to get another person to do something for them—for example, a child may point to a teddy bear on a high shelf to get someone to give it to her. Older preverbal children use this **protoimperative** form of communication very effectively, often checking to make sure that the listener is looking in the right direction and is able to respond to this form as an imperative or command (Bates, 1976, 1987; Bates, Thal, Whitsell, Fenson, & Oakes, 1989). When two communicative partners attend to the same visual information, this behavior is referred to as *joint visual attention* (Adamson & Bakeman, 1991). Some children develop their own unique gestures—such as waving their hands, jumping up and down, or nodding their heads—to attract adult attention to themselves or to an object of interest.

As children learn language, they often combine words and gestures for more effective communication (Adamson, 1995). A child may point to an object and then comment verbally to emphasize the meaning of the words. However, children's ability to use and understand gestures may develop independently of verbal language. It's only in the third year of life that children begin to recognize that gestures and language can be part of the same message and that if they are, they require an integrated response (Bates, 1987; Shatz, 1983). Across time, children reduce their use of gestures as they rely increasingly on their verbal skills to communicate their needs and wishes (Adamson, 1995; Bates, 1987).

protodeclarative A gesture that an infant uses to make some sort of statement about an object.

protoimperative A gesture that either an infant or a young child may use to get someone to do something she or he wants.

Early Language Comprehension

The foundations for receptive language skills emerge early. Well before they are able to speak themselves, babies can attend selectively to certain features of others' speech. In fact, newborns prefer listening to speech or to vocal music than to instrumental music or other rhythmic sounds (Butterfield & Siperstein, 1972). As we saw in Chapter 4, infants quickly become skilled listeners. Even a 2-day-old infant can distinguish his mother's voice from the voice of an unfamiliar woman. Moreover, like adults, infants respond with different parts of their brains to speech and nonspeech sounds. Electrical activity, for example, increases in the left half of the infant's brain in response to speech, whereas the right side responds to music (Molfese, 1973; Molfese & Betz, 1988; Neville, 1991).

CATEGORICAL SPEECH PERCEPTION The finding that infants perceive some consonants categorically is one of the most remarkable discoveries of recent decades (Aslin et al., 1998; Werker & Polka, 1993). Infants hear "one range of acoustic signals all as /p/ and a different range of acoustic signals as /b/ but no acoustic signal is perceived as something in between a /p/ and a /b/" (Hoff, 2001, p. 113). This phenomenon is known as **categorical speech perception,** or the *phoneme boundary effect.* In a classic study of discriminatory ability, one group of 5-month-old babies listened to 60 repetitions of the sound *bah,* followed by 10 repetitions of *gah;* a second group listened to 60 repetitions of *gah,* followed by 10 *bah* repetitions; and a third group heard only 70 repetitions of *bah* (Moffitt, 1971). The babies in the first two groups showed a marked heart-rate response when the experimenters suddenly presented the new consonant sound, *gah* or *bah,* respectively, which is evidence that the infants perceived the change. Babies in the third group showed no change in heart rate, suggesting that this sort of change as seen in the babies of the first two groups was not simply a reaction to the continuation of sounds. This ability to discriminate speech sounds is evident from as early as 1 month of age and holds true for a variety of other consonants, such as *m, n,* and *d* (Aslin, 1987; Aslin et al., 1998; Miller & Eimas, 1994). Infants' discrimination abilities rapidly improve; by the time they are 2 months old, infants can tell the difference between /a/ and /i/. Even more remarkable, 2- to 3-month-old infants can recognize the same vowel even when it is spoken by different people at different pitches (Marean, Werner, & Kuhl, 1992).

> **categorical speech perception** The tendency to perceive as the same a range of sounds belonging to the same phonemic group.

Findings like the foregoing add fuel to the nativist fire, for they seem to suggest that infants are indeed born with some innate mechanism for perceiving oral language. However, although evidence suggests that infants have an innate tendency to find the boundaries in sound patterns, as we saw in Chapter 4, the tendency to organize and group incoming information into patterns is not unique to processing the sounds of speech. Moreover, speech is more easily separable into perceptual categories than are other sound stimuli (Aslin, 1987; Aslin et al., 1998). In addition, Kuhl and Miller's (1975) finding that chinchillas show categorical speech perception and can discriminate between /b/ and /p/ casts further doubt on the notions that this ability is uniquely human and that humans are uniquely prepared for language acquisition! Instead of being a specifically linguistic property of auditory perception, categorical speech perception is thus seen as a property of the mammal's aural system that language simply utilizes (Kuhl et al., 1997; Miller & Eimas, 1994). In fact, language may have evolved "to take advantage of this pre-existing property of mammalian audition" (Hoff, 2001, p. 116).

BEYOND CATEGORICAL PERCEPTION Categorical speech perception is not the only skill babies exhibit that may help them learn language. In Chapter 4, we discussed a study by DeCasper suggesting that infants may learn some features of language prenatally; recent evidence suggests that infants can identify key properties of their native language's rhythmic organization either prenatally or during the first few days of life (Aslin et al., 1998). For example, 4-day-old French babies increased their sucking rate when listening to French speech as opposed to Russian (Mehler et al., 1988). Another study (Mehler, Dupoux, Nazzi, & Dehaene-Lambertz, 1996) suggests that infants respond to the rhythmic properties of speech: French babies were unable to distinguish changes in Japanese speech based on the rhythmic unit around which Japanese utterances are organized, but they could distinguish changes involving the elementary rhythmic unit of French.

Whatever innate abilities infants have for perceiving speech sounds, these abilities constantly interact with experience over the language-learning period. Research suggests that as babies develop, they lose their ability to distinguish the sounds of languages to which they haven't been exposed (Werker, 1989). For example, one study found that infants of English-speaking parents could distinguish between sounds that are unique to Swedish only until the age of 6 months (Kuhl, Williams, Lacerda, Stevens, & Lindblom, 1992). Similar findings occur for other languages as well. Jusczyk, Friederici, Wessels, Svenkerud, and Jusczyk (1993) found that by the time American infants were 9 months old, they "tuned out" Dutch words, and Dutch infants were similarly unresponsive to English words. Findings like this underscore the likely dual role of innate and experiential factors in the early recognition of speech sounds.

Although babies become highly skilled at discriminating the speech sounds of their native language at an early age, it takes time for them to learn to focus on important sound distinctions in everyday speech. As we've seen, 1-month-old infants can detect the differences between the consonant sounds of *bah* and *gah*. However, in one study of children up to 18 months of age, children had more difficulty with these same kinds of distinctions when the sounds were embedded in words and sentences. Also, it is critical to word learning that infants come to understand that phoneme sounds are equivalent across different speakers (deVilliers & deVilliers, 1979). Marean, Werner, and Kuhl (1992) found that infants as young as 2 and 3 months of age were able to recognize the consistency of a speech sound, for example /i/, even when pronounced by different speakers.

Although infants demonstrate many specialized language abilities, including the ability to discriminate among a variety of phonemes, learning a language requires learning which of the many discriminable differences in speech sounds actually signal differences in meanings. Indeed, this task "requires considerable exposure to language and is not complete even at the end of the second year" (deVilliers & deVilliers, 1979, p. 19). Children must develop skills that go beyond discriminating pure sounds—skills such as attending to and categorizing phonemic differences in the flow of communication.

Recent evidence suggests that infants can segment fluent speech and recognize words in ongoing speech better and much earlier than we had thought possible—by the end of their first year (Aslin et al., 1998), and perhaps even as early as $6\frac{1}{2}$ to 7 months of age (Thiessen & Saffran, 2003). Moreover, research suggests that infants have the capacity to make the kinds of distinctions that indicate word boundaries in the flow of speech (Hohne & Jusczyk, 1994; Morgan, 1994; Morgan & Saffran, 1995; Saffran, Aslin, & Newport, 1996). Infants use a variety of cues such as strong syllables (e.g., *tar* in *guitar*), stressed monosyllables (e.g., *cup, dog,* or *bike*), a strong syllable followed by a weak one (e.g., *fowler, turban*), or rhythmic properties to help define the boundaries of words, including pitch and pauses (Jusczyk et al., 1993; Jusczyk, Houston, & Newsome, 1999; Morgan, 1994; Thiessen & Saffran, 2003).

According to other research (Saffran et al., 1996), 8-month-old infants can detect new words in unfamiliar artificial language even when they have no idea what the words mean. Researchers had infants listen to two minutes of nonsense syllables mixed with "words" from an artificial language, which the researchers devised to eliminate the possibility that the infants were picking out words based on what they had already learned at home. Using a habituation paradigm, the researchers noted that

$\dfrac{1}{2r}$

$\Sigma 1$

$\displaystyle\sum\sum \Big/ 2 \quad \dfrac{\Sigma\,\Sigma}{8\,1}$

$9!$

$\dfrac{1}{1}$

when the tape was played a second time, the babies did not pay attention to the words—an indication that they had already learned them. This suggests that in the second half of the first year, babies are capable of detecting words in ongoing speech (Aslin, Woodward, LaMendola, & Bever, 1996). Fortunately, infants have the ability to detect words in sentences, because this is how most words are introduced to the young language learner. When researchers Woodward and Aslin (1990) asked mothers to teach new words to their 12-month-olds, the mothers presented their infants with most of the words in sentences. They presented only 20 percent of the words as words alone.

Babbling and Other Early Sounds

It is not just receptive language abilities that develop rapidly in infancy. Babies are actively producing sounds—even though not language—from birth onward. Anyone who has been awakened in the wee hours of the morning by the sound of a baby happily "talking" to herself knows that infants are neither quiet nor passive in the process of early language learning. They make a great many sounds, as if "gearing up" for their ultimate production of speech.

The production of sounds in the first year of life follows an orderly four-stage sequence summarized in Table 7-2. Crying, which begins at birth, is an important way of indicating distress and serves as a rudimentary means of communication. **Cooing,** the production of vowel-like sounds, starts at the end of the first month. Cooing, so named because it often consists of *oo* sounds that resemble the sounds pigeons make, often occurs during social exchanges between infant and caregiver. **Babbling,** or producing strings of consonant-vowel combinations, begins in the middle of the first year. Finally, at the close of the first year, **patterned speech** appears. In this pseudospeech, the child utters strings of "words" made up of phonemes in his native language and that sound very much like real speech—even in intonation—but are not. These various stages overlap, and even patterned speech and true speech may occur together as the child's first meaningful words begin to appear.

Not only does the early production of sounds follow an orderly sequence, but the kinds of sounds made at each of the first three stages are quite similar across different language communities. For instance, young Chinese, American, and Ethiopian babies all babble similar consonant-vowel combinations, even though they are exposed to different phonemes in their native languages (Thevenin, Eilers, Oller, & LaVoie, 1985). Even the early babbling of deaf babies sounds similar to the babbling of babies who can hear (Lennenberg, Rebelsky, & Nichols, 1965). Deaf infants born to deaf parents who sign (rather than speak) babble with their hands and fingers at the same age as hearing children babble vocally; moreover, their movements show similar structure in terms of syllabic and phonetic patterning (Bloom, 1998; Petitto, Holowka, Sergio, & Ostry, 2001). These similarities between manual and vocal babbling suggest

cooing A very young infant's production of vowel-like sounds.

babbling An infant's production of strings of consonant-vowel combinations.

patterned speech A form of pseudospeech in which the child utters strings of phonemes that sound very much like real speech but are not.

Table 7-2

Stages of sound production in the infant's first year

Stage	Begins	Description
Crying	At birth	Signals of distress
Cooing	At about 1 month	Oo sounds that occur during social exchanges with caregiver
Babbling	Middle of first year	Strings of consonant-vowel combinations
Patterned speech	Close of first year	Strings of pseudowords, made up of phonemes in native language, that sound like words

"a unitary language capacity that underlies human signed and spoken language acquisition" (Petitto & Marenette, 1991, p. 1495). Overall, these findings suggest that the pattern of development of early sounds that infants make is a function of maturational changes in vocal structures and in the parts of the brain that control producing sound.

In the middle of the second half-year, however, cultural differences in the prespeech sounds that babies make begin to emerge. For instance, babies exposed to one of two different native languages, Arabic or French, which contrast significantly in voice quality and pitch, may begin to show differences in their babbling at around 8 months of age (Ingram, 1989). Japanese and French words contain more nasal sounds than Swedish and English words, and in the latter part of the first year, French and Japanese babies' babbling contains more nasal sounds than that of their Swedish and English counterparts (De Boysson-Bardies et al., 1992). It is as if the babies are now starting to "tune in" to the language they hear spoken around them. This view is supported by the fact that older deaf infants fail to develop the more complex forms of babbling that start to resemble real speech, as hearing infants do (Oller & Eilers, 1988). It seems that exposure to speech is required for the development of these later, more advanced forms of babbling. Interestingly, the amount of time exposed to language, not just the baby's physical maturation, appears to be an important factor. Babies who are born prematurely, and who are therefore exposed to language earlier (in terms of their gestational age) than full-term babies are, begin complex babbling sooner than full-term infants (Eilers et al., 1993).

Thus, although historically linguists have argued that there is no relationship between babies' early vocalizations and their later speech (Jakobson, 1968), this more recent evidence challenges this view. The babblings of infants over their first year resemble the child's first meaningful words in a variety of ways (Carroll, Snowling, Hulme, & Stevenson, 2003; Elbers & Ton, 1985; Oller, Wieman, Doyle, & Ross, 1976). As one language expert has noted: "Late babbling contains sounds very much like those that are used in early attempts to pronounce words. . . . Babbling is indeed relevant to the child's developing linguistic skills" (Sachs, 1985, p. 49). Evidently, a child's early vocalizations are not only orderly in their development but also related to later speech. In terms of the foundations for both receptive and productive language skills, the human infant is very well prepared for learning to talk.

SEMANTIC DEVELOPMENT: THE POWER OF WORDS

naming explosion The rapid increase in vocabulary that the child typically shows at about the age of 1½.

Despite children's early skills in both receptive and productive language, research suggests that children's understanding of language far exceeds their capacity to express themselves clearly (see Figure 7-2). These findings may help to explain the fact that children don't develop their vocabularies in a strictly linear fashion. Like other aspects of development, vocabulary acquisition proceeds in bursts. The **naming explosion,** a term coined by Bloom (Bloom, Lifter, & Broughton, 1985), is the rapid increase in vocabulary that most children begin to show at the age of about 1½, when typically they can comprehend between 50 and 100 words. Children usually utter their first words between 10 and 15 months (Fenson et al., 1994). In one well-documented case, a 16-month-old learned 44 words in a single week!

By the age of 2, the average child knows approximately 900 root words, and by 6, when he is in either kindergarten or first grade, he knows 8,000! Whether this increase occurs in spurts or more gradually is currently under study. Some recent research suggests that although some children—about 20 percent—display a true spurt or explosion in vocabulary, most children add words gradually (Ganger & Brent, 2004). Whatever the answer here, clearly, the remarkable growth of vocabulary over the first five years of life is a dramatic example of the human capacity for language

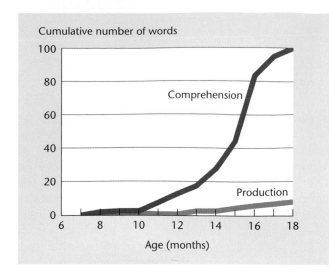

Figure 7-2

Receptive and productive language in infants
Children's comprehension outpaces their production of words. On average, children understood nearly 100 words by the time they were 18 months old but could produce only 8 to 10.

Source: Huttenlocher, 1974.

and communication. How do children learn words? Imagine that you have taken a job in a foreign country, and your first task is to learn the language. A native of the country points to a dog lying on a rug and says, *"Xitf."* How do you know whether *xitf* refers to the dog, the dog's twitching ear, the dog's fur, the fact that the dog is sleeping on the rug, the fact that the dog is the speaker's pet, or indeed, the rug itself? Clearly, the acquisition of object names is no simple matter. Let's look a bit more closely at this issue.

How Children Acquire Words

There are many different views of how children create a linguistic link between the mind and the world, a mental word-to-world map (Waxman & Lidz, 2006). Some theorists argue that children simply form an association, others contend that the social aspect of this process is important, and still others take the middle ground. According to Smith (2000), word learning is based on associations, combined with attention to perceptual similarity. Through experience, children realize that words label categories based primarily on similarity of overall object shape. If a child sees many tables that are often given the label *table,* over time he will realize that most things with a flat top and four legs get the label of *table.*

Another view is that children use mainly social cues from adults to learn what a word labels (Bloom, 2000; Tomasello, 1998). Many findings show that simply hearing a label in the presence of an object is not enough for an infant to learn that the word is a symbol for the object. For example, simply seeing a novel toy on a table and hearing an automated voice saying *glorp* will not cause the child to attach the label *glorp* to the object. Children depend on social cues such as pointing and the speaker's eye gaze.

Still other theorists claim multiple cues are available to infants for word learning, but how much they depend on each type of cue changes with age (Hollich et al., 2000). In this viewpoint, younger children do rely on perceptual similarity to realize when a word is the correct label for an object, but as they get older they become more dependent on social and linguistic cues. There is evidence that 16-month-olds will not accept a common label for two objects that are extremely different looking, but 20-month-old infants are willing to trust the speaker and give two perceptually distinct objects the same label (Nazzi & Gopnik, 2001).

Although the task of word learning may seem difficult, infants seem to come into the task with some constraints or principles that aid them. (See Box 7.2 for a

Box 7.2

Perspectives on Diversity

CHILDREN AT RISK FOR FAILURE TO DEVELOP LANGUAGE

Youth with moderate or severe mental retardation often need extensive and ongoing support in more than one major life activity; one of the most important is communication. Youth with moderate and severe retardation range from those who do learn to speak, although slowly and often with limited success, to those who are unable to develop spoken communicative skills at all, even with considerable speech and language instruction.

Using one of the methods developed by investigators of nonhuman primate communication, Mary Ann Romski and Rose Sevcik (1996) have shown that such youth who have never developed oral speech can learn to communicate intelligibly with adults and peers. In an approach based on Vygotskian concepts, each of 13 young boys with moderate to severe retardation worked with a partner (a teacher or a parent) who demonstrated and encouraged the child in using a computerized device that enabled him to select a particular symbol or lexigram, referred to as the System for Augmenting Language (SAL), on a keyboard to produce a single word or phrase (Figure 7-3). When the child presses a given key, the computer produces a synthesized voicing of the word or phrase and also prints it on a screen. The literature on children with severe retardation had claimed that such children could learn only with continuous prompting. Romski and Sevcik found, however, that a majority of their participants, 12 years old on average, who used the SAL device rapidly learned to associate symbols with words and phrases. By the end of the two years, most of the participants could both comprehend and produce a majority of the vocabulary words presented to them in instruction sessions. More than half of the participants even demonstrated the skill of fast-mapping, immediately associating a new name with a new object/symbol.

Romski and Sevcik chose to use arbitrary visual-graphic symbols rather than representational pictures in this work in part because they wanted to study "the process of learning to communicate symbolically" (p. 61). They introduced only a small number of symbols at a time to participants, beginning with a set of 12 symbols relevant to mealtime—symbols for specific foods, drinks, and utensils. The next group of words introduced related to leisure time activities—for example, *ball, game, magazine, television*—and the third group were social-regulative words and phrases such as *hello, excuse me, I want,* and *thank you*. A final group consisted of words tailored to individual participants' needs—for example, they added the word *work* to the lexicon of a participant who had a part-time job.

By the end of the two-year period, all participants had acquired 53 single words or two-word phrases in the first two categories, 16 words or phrases in the third group, and additional words or phrases in the final category. Moreover, many used their lexicons to engage in communication with people in the community without the use of the computer and synthesized speech. Thus, the participants' speech production had to stand on its own. For instance, one youth, classified as severely retarded, went to a mall music store and requested assistance of a clerk by asking "HELP TAPE" and then showing the clerk a photograph of the tape he wanted. With tape in hand the youth then said "THANK YOU" (Romski & Sevcik, 1996, p. 145).

According to Romski and Sevcik, some parents have been reluctant to offer SAL training to their children because they fear it will impede the children's efforts to learn to speak. Very few data in fact are available on the outcome of the early use of intervention with speech-output communication devices. Clearly, there is room for a great deal more research in this area. Among other things, we need to know what early predictors, such as specific behaviors or difficulties, may differentiate children who will not develop speech from those who will. We also need to determine whether early intervention with SAL could not only help children who are at risk for failure to develop language to communicate but perhaps help provide the cognitive stimulation and trigger the motivation that

Figure 7-3 Communicating with a computer and lexigrams

(a) Lexigrams like these, each made up of some combination of the nine elements shown, appear on the upper keypad of the computerized device (b). When a child presses the key for, say, *hot dog*, the words are sounded in synthetic speech and are also printed on the display screen of the computer.

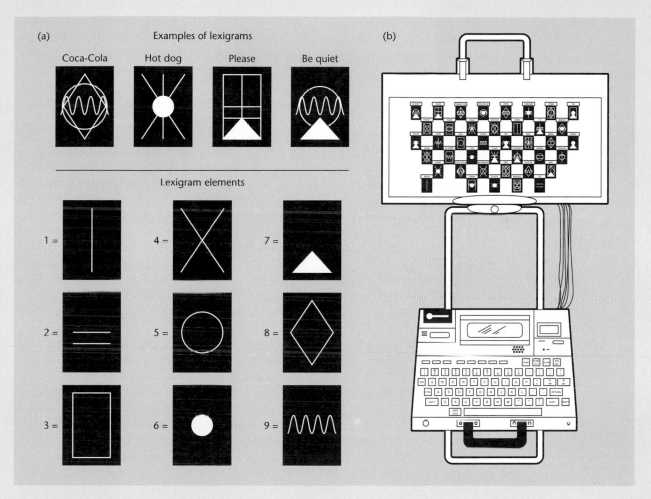

Source: Adapted from Romski & Sevcik, 1996.

might facilitate their learning of oral speech. Whatever its ultimate usefulness, SAL training has revealed the presence of cognitive capacities in children with mental retardation who, by traditional measures, had been considered only minimally functional. The work suggests that such young people can learn language under the right conditions and can apply it in social interaction.

discussion of how even children with mental retardation can learn to use words.) Markman (1989) was the first to introduce the idea of word learning principles. For example, the *whole object constraint* involves the assumption that a new word refers to the entire object and not to one of its parts or properties. Children as young as 18 months appear to make use of this constraint. For example, when 2-year-old Jamal visits the zoo and hears the word *anteater* for the first time, he assumes that anteater refers to the animal, not its nose, body, or behavior.

After Markman introduced the concept of constraints, many researchers began to notice other constraints that children seem to follow in word learning (Markman & Hutchinson, 1994; Merriman & Bowman, 1989). As a result, Hollich and colleagues (2000a) have compiled a set of six principles "deemed necessary and sufficient to account for how children get word learning 'off the ground'" within the framework of their Emergentist Coalition Model (ECM). These principles are less strict than the more nativist view Markman proposed because the principles themselves undergo change with development and because the use of these principles depends on a combination of both inborn biases and word-learning experience.

These six principles begin with the basic necessity to understand language. For example, the first thing a child must understand is the principle of *reference,* or the idea that words stand for objects, actions, and events. Later in development children come to understand more complex principles such as the *Novel Name-Nameless Category (N3C).* Similar to Markman's (1990) *mutual exclusivity bias,* N3C states that upon hearing a novel label, infants assume it labels a novel object over a familiar one. In a representative experiment, Golinkoff, Hirsh-Pasek, Bailey, and Wenger (1992) placed four objects in front of a 28-month-old. Three of the objects were familiar (a ball, a shoe, and keys) and one was unfamiliar (a tea strainer). The experimenter asked for the *glorp.* Consistent with N3C, children selected the unnamed object as the referent for *glorp.* In a control condition in which no label was used, but children were asked to retrieve an object, children selected the unnamed object only at a chance level.

The ECM principles are a good answer for many who criticized Markman's theory as being too nativist. Unlike Markman's theory, the ECM places a strong emphasis on the necessity for social interaction in word learning. According to Nelson (1998), to acquire a full understanding of the course of semantic development, we must look more closely at the social communicative context in which word learning occurs. Some researchers have found, for example, that parents clearly influence vocabulary growth. In one example, the amount of time parents spent reading to their 2-year-olds was significantly related to the children's language skills when they were 4 years old (Crain-Thoreson & Dale, 1992). Another study found that the more parents talked to their children, the larger the children's vocabularies became (Huttenlocher, Haight, Bryk, Seltzer, & Lyons, 1991). And some recent research on word learning suggests that the assumption a child makes about shared or common knowledge is an important factor in her learning a new word. Diesendruck and Markson (2001) demonstrated that what a 3-year-old knows about the knowledge and intentions of another, what the researchers call *pragmatic reasoning,* is used to decide which piece of information in a situation, such as a word or a fact, is new. In this study, the child plays with two novel objects, such as the top part of a turkey baster and an odd-shaped soap dish. The experimenter calls one of the objects by a novel name, such as *zev,* and does not label the other object. He tells the child that the objects belong to a puppet named Percy, who is away. While the child is playing with the objects, Percy returns and asks the child to give him the *jop.* Although Percy was not present when the first object was labeled for the child, children were more likely to select the object that had not been previously labeled by the experimenter, apparently assuming that Percy, who owned the toys, knew that name and would have used it if that was the toy he wanted. It seems that discourse and pragmatic understanding provide clues that children use to learn words (Nelson, 1996).

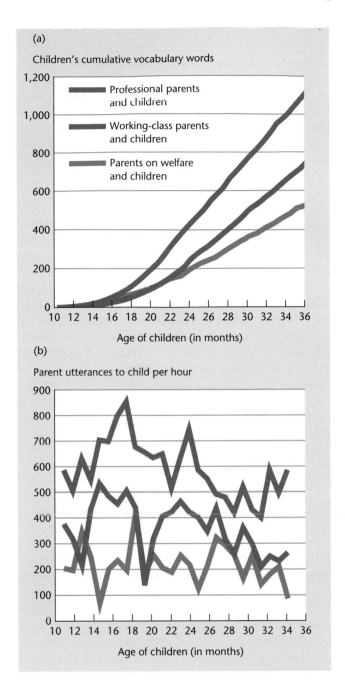

(a)

Children's cumulative vocabulary words

- Professional parents and children
- Working-class parents and children
- Parents on welfare and children

Age of children (in months)

(b)

Parent utterances to child per hour

Age of children (in months)

Figure 7-4

Social class and vocabulary development

Note: Key in (a) applies also to (b). (a) Over a period of a little more than two years, children from working-class families (middle to lower socioeconomic status) built vocabularies about two-thirds as large as those acquired by children from professional families; children from families who were on welfare acquired vocabularies only half as large as those of the children from higher-class families. (b) The frequencies with which parents in each of the three groups talked to their children correlated quite well with children's vocabulary size. Parents in professional families, whose children had the largest vocabularies, talked to their children the most. Parents in working-class families, whose children had the next largest vocabularies, talked less often. And parents in welfare families, whose children had the smallest vocabularies, talked even less.

Source: Hart & Risley, 1995.

Some of the strongest support for the social environmental approach comes from studies of vocabulary development in children of differing socioeconomic classes. Hart and Risley (1999) studied the language environments of 42 children, ranging in age from 10 months to 3 years, by observing them in their homes. These investigators found that social class, language environment, and children's vocabulary were all highly correlated: The higher the social class, the richer the language environment, and the greater the growth in the child's vocabulary (see Figure 7-4). A large study conducted by Weizman and Snow (2001) extended these results by investigating the home language environments of children in low-income families at age 5 and the vocabulary performance of these same children in kindergarten and second grade. Two important findings emerged. First, the researchers found substantial variation in these children's homes in language experience; not all low-income mothers communicate with their children in the same way. Some mothers produced a much richer language experience for children than others did. Second, children's language experience at home at age 5 was positively related to their later vocabulary performance in school.

Whether language is supported at home or outside the home, social stimulation is important to its development. Three-year-old children who attend day-care centers with stimulating language environments, in which there is much conversation between children and their teachers and caregivers, have more words for letters, colors, and shapes—the kinds of words that help prepare them for school—than children who attend programs with fewer conversational opportunities (NICHD Early Child Care Research Network, 2000).

More recently, the idea that language learning is a special and uniquely human aspect of development has been challenged by researchers who advance the view that language learning, including word acquisition, results from more general learning processes (Bloom, 2000). Basic cognitive abilities, such as perceiving, attending, and remembering, are seen as sufficient to explain how effectively and quickly children learn many things, including new words (Samuelson & Smith, 2000). Evidence used to support this claim includes that obtained by Markson and Bloom (1997) and Diesendruck and Markson (2001), who found that 3- to 4-year-old children acquire novel words, such as the name of a new object, and novel facts (like who gave the object to the child), in the same fashion. This evidence suggests a point we discussed earlier, namely that similar processing abilities are used to ascertain what information in a situation is new, be it a word or a fact, and that these abilities underlie all types of learning, including words (Bloom, 2000). In short, two cognitive mechanisms are not needed to explain word learning and learning of other information—one cognitive process or learning system suffices. The notion that there is an evolutionary basis for language learning among humans does not rule out such a general learning system. Indeed, a more general and powerful learning system may be best suited to the large and varied set of problems humans need to understand and master to survive (Nelson, 1996; Tomasello, 1999).

What Kinds of Words Do Children Learn First?

Analyzing the kinds of words children acquire, and the ways in which they use them, can give us important information about children's cognitive development and the degree of sophistication with which they form concepts. Studying the first 50 words learned by a group of 18 young children, Nelson (1973), in a classic study of early word acquisition, classified these words into six categories. Mothers kept diaries of each new word their children produced until the children produced 50 words. On average, children reached the 50-word level by the time they were $1\frac{1}{2}$, but there was a great deal of individual difference. Some infants learned their first 50 words by 15 months, whereas others took 24 months. As Figure 7-5 illustrates, about 65 percent of the 50 words were naming or object words, whereas words denoting action made up only about 14 percent. Schwartz and Leonard (1984) found about the same proportion of action words, and other research has determined that nouns are learned more easily than verbs (Childers & Tomasello, 2002).

One explanation for why children may learn object words first is that the concepts that object words encode are simpler than those that action words encode (Gentner, 1982; Huttenlocher & Smiley, 1987). To learn object words, children must match objects with their appropriate linguistic referents (Gentner, 1982), but to learn action words, or verbs, children must also form an understanding of the connections between objects and actions (Huttenlocher & Lui, 1979). However, several researchers have pointed out that the object words children learn first generally represent objects they can act on and thereby produce a change or movement. For example, the words *shoes, socks,* and *toys,* all of which children manipulate, are more common than words for things that they cannot move or

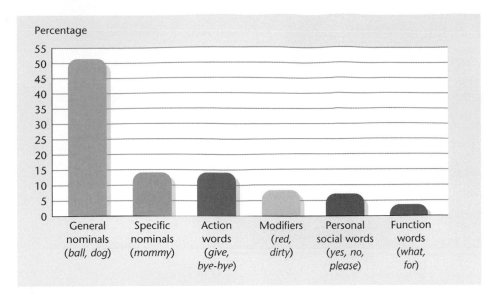

Figure 7-5

Words that children use first
According to the classic work illustrated here, naming or object
words make up almost two-thirds
of the vocabularies of children
between 1 and 2 years old.

Source: Based on data from Nelson, 1973.

change in some way, such as *table, stove,* or *tree* (Clark, 1983). Huttenlocher, Smiley, and Charney (1987) found that children are better at learning action words for things they can actually do themselves. For example, a 2-year-old is more likely to learn the word *walk* than *skip* because she is physically able to perform the action of walking.

Some researchers (e.g., Bloom, 1993, 1998) have challenged the assumption that object names predominate in early vocabularies. Studying children who ranged in age from 9 months to 2 years, Bloom found that object words represented only a third of the words the children learned. And Gentner (1982), whose study encompassed the first 100 words learned by her child participants, found that some children's vocabularies included as many as 30 percent action terms. Similarly, Tardif (1996) found that 21-month-old children learning Mandarin Chinese used equal numbers of verbs and nouns in their speech. In part, this is because in some Asian languages verbs play a more prominent role in speech and often occur in a prominent place at the end of a sentence (Hoff, 2001). The fact that Japanese mothers spend less time labeling objects than American mothers may also account for the less pronounced bias toward noun production among Japanese children (Fernald & Morikawa, 1993).

It is important to note that the principles and constraints discussed in object learning must also apply to verb learning. With this in mind, Merriman, Evey-Burkey, Marazita, and Jarvis (1996) investigated children's use of the *mutual exclusivity* bias in verb learning. Two-year-olds watched a TV screen that on one side had an actor doing an action that the children had a word for, like clapping, while on the other side a different actor did something that the children had no word for, like rolling his arms in circles. Overall, both the actions were equally interesting to the infants, but when the children were asked to "Look at the person glorping," they were more likely to look at the novel action. This is similar to Golinkoff and colleagues' (1992) finding in which children assumed a novel label applied to a novel object.

Errors in Early Word Use

Characteristic errors in children's early word use can help illuminate the learning process. Two such errors are overextension and underextension. In **overextension**, children use a single word to cover many different things. For example, everyone has heard a young child use the word *doggie* for horses, cows, giraffes, and all sorts of four-legged animals. Extensions such as these, which are based on perceptual

overextension The use, by a young child, of a single word to cover many different things.

Table 7-3

Some examples of children's overextensions

Source: From *Language Development*, 2nd edition by Hoff. © 2001. Reprinted with permission of Wadsworth, a division of Thomson Learning: www.thomsonrights.com. Fax 800-730-2215.

Word	Referents
Ball	Ball, balloon, marble, apple, egg, wool pom-pom, spherical water tank
Cat	Cat, cat's usual location on top of TV even when absent
Moon	Moon, half-moon-shaped lemon slice, circular chrome dial on dishwasher, ball of spinach, wall hanging with pink and purple circles, half a Cheerio
Snow	Snow, white tail of a spring horse, white flannel bed pad, white puddle of milk on floor
Baby	Own reflection in mirror, framed photograph of self, framed photographs of others

similarity, are common. Another example is using the word *ball* for round objects such as cakes, pancakes, oranges, the sun, and the moon. Overextension is common; about a third of young children's words are overextended at one time or another (Nelson, 1977). (See Table 7-3 for examples of children's overextensions.)

Rescorla (1980) investigated how and when children between 1 year and 18 months overextend words. The findings reveal that overextensions are both less common and more predictable than was previously assumed. By observing children from 12 to 18 months, she found that one-third of the children's words were overextensions. However, only a few different overextensions made up this share of their speech. She also discovered that overextensions usually show one of three themes or characteristics. First, overextensions can be categorical, meaning children will use one word within a category for another closely related word—for example, they will use the name of one color for another. Second, the words are used for something perceptually similar, as when a child calls all four-legged animals *doggie*. Finally, overextensions can reflect a relationship. For example, a child might use the word *doll* for an empty crib where the doll should be. As children's vocabularies develop and increase, they use fewer overextended words (Bloom, 1993; deVilliers & deVilliers, 1992; Rescorla, 1980). In **underextension,** a less common type of error, children use a single word in a highly restricted and individualistic way. For example, a child may use the word *car* only when she sees her father's yellow Chevy and may call all other automobiles, including her mother's green Ford, *trucks* (Bloom, 1993, 1998). The use of underextensions suggests that a child's understanding of a word is too restrictive or limited to a small set of meanings.

In speaking with their young children, parents may not initially give every variant of a class of objects its correct name and may thus trigger some word errors. Mervis and Mervis (1982) found that mothers tended to use single nouns to label certain toys and objects; for example, they called both lions and leopards *kitty cats*. Although this may help the child at first, enabling him to pick out a stuffed animal rather than a truck from an array of toys on a shelf, it may lead to overextending categories.

Another explanation for overextension is that they are not really errors in the usual sense of the term. As a child's vocabulary is limited, she may try to find a linguistic form that fits with an element of experience (Bloom, 1993, 1998). As Bloom notes, "It seems entirely reasonable for the child to use an available word to represent different but related objects—it is almost as if the child were reasoning, 'I know about dogs; that thing is not a dog. I don't know what to call it, but it is like a dog.'" (1976, p. 23). For the child, applying words in different contexts is a type of hypothesis testing, a process that continues throughout childhood but is particularly evident in the first three years, when the child begins to relate word

underextension The use, by a young child, of a single word in a restricted and individualistic way.

Table 7-4

Speech samples 10 months
apart
Source: Adapted from Brown & Bellugi,
1964; McNeill, 1970.

Child at 28 Months

"What dat?"

"Where birdie go?"

"Have screw . . ."

"Get broom . . ."

Child at 38 Months

"Who put dust on my hair?"

"You got some beads?"

"I broke my racing car."

"It's got a flat tire . . . when it's got flat tire it's need to go . . . to the station."

forms with objects (Kuczaj, 1982). Gradually, as the child's discriminations and vocabulary improve and her conceptual categories become more stable, her accuracy in word use increases.

THE ACQUISITION OF GRAMMAR: FROM WORDS TO SENTENCES

In their early years, children achieve an incredible amount of learning about language, and the rapidity with which children learn the complexities of language continues to fascinate developmentalists. As Table 7-4 shows, in a period of just 10 months a child may go from barely intelligible speech to clear communication.

In this section we examine a great deal of this leap in clarity and sophistication of communication. You may find it helpful to refer to the Turning Points chart on pages 296–297 to keep track of the sequence of development encompassed. We begin with the child's use of single-word utterances and then consider the evolution of two-word sentences, the emergence of modifications such as plurals and possessives, the development of questions and of negating sentences, and the beginning of learning how to understand the meanings of others' utterances.

Can One Word Express a Complete Thought?

Are first words simply words? Or are they early attempts to express complete thoughts? When a young child points to a toy airplane on a high shelf and says "Down," or when he takes a spoon from his mother and says "Me," is there more to his utterance than meets the ear? In the first case, parents may assume that the child is requesting that the toy be taken down off the shelf; in the second example, they might guess that the child is saying, "I want to do it myself."

Dale (1976) has noted: "First words seem to be more than single words. They appear to be attempts to express complex ideas—ideas that would be expressed in sentences by an adult" (p. 13). The term **holophrase** has been given to such single words that appear to represent a complete thought. Whether or not children are really expressing in these single-word utterances thoughts that could be expressed in sentences—thoughts that include subjects, objects, and actions—remains an unanswered question.

holophrase A single word that appears to represent a complete thought.

Turning Points

LANGUAGE MILESTONES FROM INFANCY TO MIDDLE CHILDHOOD

BIRTH	Cries
	Perceives others' speech
	Prefers human voices
1–6 MONTHS	Decreases crying
	Makes soft sounds
	Coos, laughs, gurgles
	Imitates short string of vowel sounds; alternates making sounds with another person
	Makes consonant sounds; "says" consonants increasingly often
	Responds to prosodic features of speech (e.g., inflection and pitch)
	Intonations move toward speech patterns heard most often
	Recognizes own name
6–12 MONTHS	Babbles strings of consonant-vowel combinations
	May babble more in familiar than unfamiliar settings
	Sounds resemble speech
	Shows increasing preference for own language over unfamiliar language
	Produces sound for familiar toy or object; experiments with sounds
	Babbling develops a sentence-like quality
	May "say" a word—*bah* for *bottle, mah* for *mother*
	May say *no* but doesn't always mean *no*
	May say two or three words; uses same word for category, such as *wah* for both *water* and *milk*
	Intentional communication begins

Note: Developmental events described in this and other Turning Points charts represent overall trends identified in research studies. Individual children vary greatly in the ages at which they achieve these developmental changes.

Sources: Hoff, 2001; Kopp, 1994; Tomasello, 2006; Waxman & Lidz, 2006.

Two-Word Sentences

telegraphic speech Two-word utterances that include only the words essential to convey the speaker's intent.

Somewhere between $1\frac{1}{2}$ and 2 years of age, the child begins to put two words together in what is often called **telegraphic speech.** Like telegrams, these two-word utterances include only the crucial words needed to convey the speaker's intent. Thus, although children generally use nouns, verbs, and adjectives, they are likely to omit other parts of speech such as articles and prepositions. The child's speech is novel and creative

12–18 MONTHS	Forms one-word sentences at first Tries hard to make self understood Makes symbolic gestures Imitates words; may repeatedly use a new word May use a few two-word sentences May use adjective to refer to self (*good boy*) Understands naming processes
18–24 MONTHS	Begins naming explosion; average child goes from 50 to 900 words in about six months Uses two-word sentences Rapidly expands understanding
24–36 MONTHS	Decreases gesturing Gives up babbling Increases use of plurals, past tense, definite and indefinite articles, some prepositions Uses three-word combinations Shows excellent comprehension Gradually increases use of sentences to communicate
36–48 MONTHS	Uses *yes/no* questions, *why* questions, negatives, and imperatives Embeds one sentence within another (using clauses) Uses overregularizations Vocabulary increases by about 1,000 words Coordinates simple sentences and uses prepositions
48–60 MONTHS	Uses pragmatic rules of communication in increasingly sophisticated way Uses humor and metaphor
5 YEARS AND BEYOND	Uses more complex syntax Further expands vocabulary (to about 14,000 words) Develops metalinguistic awareness

and is not merely a copy of adult language. Table 7-5 shows some two-word sentences used by young children speaking either English or one of several other languages (Slobin, 1985). Notice how these two-word phrases resemble one another in terms of the relationships between the words, or the basic structure or grammar of language, no matter how different the languages in which they were spoken. This similarity in relations extends to the sign language many deaf people use. As Box 7.3 shows, in acquiring American Sign Language (ASL), deaf children start out with many of the same word combinations that hearing children produce as they acquire oral language.

Table 7-5   Two-word sentences in several languages

Function of Utterance	Language					
	English	**German**	**Russian**	**Finnish**	**Luo**	**Samoan**
Locate, name	*there book*	*buch der* [book there]	*Tosya tam* [Tosya there]	*tuossa Rina* [there Rina]	*en saa* [it clock]	*Keith lea* [Keith there]
Demand, desire	*more milk*	*mehr milch* [more milk]	*yeshchë moloko* [more milk]	*anna Rina* [give Rina]	*miya tamtam* [give-me candy]	*mai pepe* [give doll]
Negate	*no wet*	*nicht blasen* [not blow]	*vody net* [water no]	*ei susi* [not wolf]	*beda onge* [my-slasher absent]	*le' ai* [not eat]
Describe event or situation	*Bambi go*	*puppe kommt* [doll comes]	*mam prua* [mama walk]	*Seppo putoo* [Seppo fall]	*odhi skul* [he-went school]	*pá u pepe* [fall doll]
Indicate possession	*my shoe*	*mein ball* [my ball]	*mami chashka* [mama's cup]	*täti auto* [aunt car]	*kom baba* [chair father]	*lole a' u* [candy my]
Modify, qualify (attributive)	*pretty dress*	*milch heiss* [milk hot]	*mama khoroshaya* [mama good]	*rikki auto* [broken car]	*piypiy kech* [pepper hot]	*fa'ali'i pepe* [headstrong baby]
Question	*where ball*	*wo ball* [where ball]	*gde papa* [where papa]	*missä pallo* [where ball]		*fea Punafu* [where Punafu]

Notes: Luo is spoken in Kenya. The order of the two words in each "sentence" is generally fixed in all languages but Finnish, in which children are free to use both orders for some types of utterances.

Source: From Slobin, Dan I., *Psycholinguistics,* 2nd ed., © 1979, Adapted by permission of Pearson Education, Inc., Upper Saddle River, NJ.

Why are the early utterances of children similar in terms of the meaning of what they talk about? Language can be viewed as a way of expressing what one knows or understands about the world. As children's capacity for understanding events in the world around them continues to grow, and because children around the world tend to have encounters with similar kinds of basic situations in life, their learning of language is tied to their cognitive development. Such fundmental experiences include the distinction between self and other; the concept of causality; and an understanding of objects. Thus, wherever they live, in whatever society, children beginning to speak express similar relationships and events, such as agent-action relations, possessives, and person and object identity. The development of cognitive capacity and the development of language are undoubtedly closely related (Carey, 1994; Clark, 1983).

Learning the Rules

One of the most interesting aspects of early grammar acquisition is the way children learn how to modify the meanings of the words they use, an accomplishment that also illustrates the close ties between semantic and grammar development. Roger Brown (1973), in his classic longitudinal study of Adam, Eve, and Sarah, followed these three children from 2 to 4 years of age, and noted, among many other things, that they acquired certain morphemes in a regular order. For example, during this period, the children began to use qualifiers that indicate plurality or a possessive relationship. Table 7-6 lists the 14 morphemes that Brown studied in the order in which his young participants acquired them. Although Adam, Eve, and Sarah each acquired these morphemes at a different rate of speed, the order in which each child acquired them was the same.

Form	Meaning	Example
1. Present progressive: -ing	Ongoing process	He is sit*ting* down.
2. Preposition: in	Containment	The mouse is *in* the box.
3. Preposition: on	Support	The book is *on* the table.
4. Plural: -s	Number	The dog*s* ran away.
5. Past irregular: e.g., went	Earlier in time relative to time of speaking	The boy *went* home.
6. Possessive: -'s	Possession	The girl*'s* dog is big.
7. Uncontractible copula be: e.g., are, was	Number; earlier in time	*Are* they boys or girls? *Was* that a dog?
8. Articles: the, a	Definite/indefinite	He has *a* book.
9. Past regular: -ed	Earlier in time	He jump*ed* the stream.
10. Third person regular: -s	Number; earlier in time	She run*s* fast.
11. Third person irregular: e.g., has, does	Number; earlier in time	*Does* the dog bark?
12. Uncontractible auxiliary be: e.g., is, were	Number; earlier in time; ongoing process	*Were* they at home? *Is* he running?
13. Contractible copula be: e.g., -'s, -'re	Number; earlier in time	That*'s* a spaniel.
14. Contractible auxiliary be: e.g., -'s, -'re	Number; earlier in time; ongoing process	They*'re* running very slowly.

Table 7-6

English-speaking children's first 14 morphemes

Source: Based on Brown, 1973.

Notice that the order in which these morphemes are acquired is sensible: Simpler morphemes are acquired earlier than more complex ones. For example, plural forms, like *-s*, are learned before the copula (meaning a linking word) *be*. Similarly, Golinkoff, Hirsh-Pasek, and Schweisguth (2001) found that children began to understand morphemes, for example they learn that *-ing* is a morpheme generally used with actions much earlier than they can produce the same morphemes. In Chapters 8 and 9, we will see that this same general principle of progressing from the simple to the more complex characterizes children's cognitive development as well.

Slobin (1985) suggests that children go through four phases in their application of grammatical rules like the use of plurals. In phase 1, they try but fail. In phase 2, they succeed in memorizing some of the irregular verbs, such as *broke* and *went,* but do not yet acquire a grammatical rule. This kind of learning, of course, is quite inefficient. Imagine how time-consuming it would be if children had to learn separate, specific rules for each new word that they encountered. They might learn, for example, that two dogs is expressed as *dogs,* but they'd have to learn in a separate lesson how to pluralize other words such as *cat* or *house.* In Slobin's third phase, children learn general grammatical rules that can be used with new as well as familiar words. Only in the fourth phase, however, do children—at 7 or 8—finally approach adult usage, recognizing when to apply these rules. A crucial achievement of this last phase is learning when *not* to apply a rule.

Adult language is full of irregularities and other exceptions to the rules. When children are first learning a language, they ignore these irregularities and rigidly apply the rules they learn. In **overregularization** of rules, children apply a rule for forming regularities in cases where the adult form is irregular and does not follow the rule. For instance, a young child may start out using the words *went* and *came* correctly but, after learning that *-ed* forms the past tense for many verbs, he may begin to use this ending for all verbs, producing *goed* and *comed* (Slobin, 1985). Similarly, a child

overregularization The application of a principle of regular change to a word that changes irregularly.

Child Psychology in Action

LANGUAGE LEARNING IN THE DEAF

Deaf children learning American Sign Language (ASL) produce word combinations very similar to those produced by hearing children around the world (Goldin-Meadow, 2006; Lederberg, Prezbindowski, & Spencer, 2000; Meier & Newport, 1990). Compare the examples in Table 7-7 with those in Table 7-5: In both the deaf child's phrases and those uttered by hearing children, we see locating and naming, indication of possession, making a demand, and describing or modifying. (For the ASL signs for some of the words in Table 7-7, see Figure 7-6.) Among deaf children, the length of utterances increases steadily, just as it does among hearing children, and like hearing children, those who use sign language tend to overextend words (Bellugi, van Hoek, Lillo-Martin, & O'Grady, 1993; Petitto, 1993). Nor are young signing children always accurate, as with the early words of their speaking peers. For example, intending to point to their mouths in signing (which might indicate "speech" or "speaking"), children may miss and point to their chins (which could mean "preference" or "favorite").

Although the steps that children follow in learning language, whether gestural or spoken, are similar, recent evidence suggests that deaf children may learn sign language faster and earlier than hearing children learn spoken language. In a longitudinal study of 13 infants being reared by deaf parents, Bonvillian and his colleagues (Bonvillian, Orlansky, Novack, & Folven, 1983) found that these children

Table 7-7 Some two-word combinations in a deaf child's signing

Sign	Meaning
Daddy work	"Daddy is at work."
Barry train	"That's Barry's [her brother's] train."
Bed shoes?	(Asking where her slippers are)
Daddy shoe	(Attempting to persuade her father to take off his shoes and play in the sand)

Source: Meier & Newport, 1990.

learned signs several months earlier than hearing children learned words. Most hearing children do not utter their first recognizable word before the end of the first year. The signing infants produced their first recognizable sign by the time they were 9 months old. By the age of 17 months, these children began to combine two or more signs; again they were two to three months ahead of hearing children. However, the advantage doesn't appear to last. After 2 years of age, the differences between signers and speakers disappear (Bonvillian, Orlansky, & Folven, 1990). What might account for the early discrepancy? The most plausible explanation is that the motor centers of

often uses the word *feet* until she learns the regular plural ending; then she may switch to *foots* or sometimes *feets*. Occasionally, after learning that some plurals are formed by adding -*es* (e.g., *boxes*), a child will come up with *footses* for a time.

Children also sometimes create regularized singular words from an irregular plural. For example, a child the authors knew overregularized a verb form, asking "I'm magic, amn't I?" Overregularization is found not only in the United States but in other countries, where children applied the rules they learned broadly to form novel "regularized" words and phrases that did not occur in adult speech (Slobin, 1982).

Despite great interest in overregularization among researchers, questions remain about why and how often children overregularize language in their speech. Additionally, it has been shown that some children are more likely than others to overregularize (Maratos, 1993), which suggests that children's interest in or skill at the rules of language may vary individually. Finally, some researchers suggest that it is not language development per se that explains overregularization. Rather, memory development may contribute to this behavior because learning all the complexities and rules of

(a)

Father, Dad
With the palm of the right hand facing left and fingers up, tap the thumb on the center of the forehead.

(b)

Work, employment
With both hands in form of fist, tap the heel of the right hand on the back of the left hand, twice.

(c)

Train, railroad
Using the index and middle fingers of both hands, move the right two fingers back and forth several times on top of the left two fingers.

(d)

Shoes
With both hands in the form of fist, hit the thumb sides of both hands together several times.

Figure 7-6

Some signs in American Sign Language

In early two-word communications like those listed in Table 7-7, a deaf child might combine the signs in (a) and (b).

Source: Adapted from Costello, 1983.

the brain develop more rapidly than do the speech centers. When the latter catch up with the former, language learning may proceed at a similar pace in both deaf and hearing children:

> In spite of these early differences in rate of language acquisition, the really important aspects of language and the really important abilities the child brings to the problem of learning are independent of the modality in which the linguistic system operates. Language is a central process, not a peripheral one. The abilities that children have are so general and so powerful that deaf children proceed through the same milestones of development as do hearing children. (Dale, 1976, p. 59)

In fact, because learning signs is a bit easier than learning to say words, largely due to factors related to brain development and the requirements of coordination that each of these communication systems entails, even hearing babies have been found to use signs earlier than speech to communicate (Acredolo & Goodyn, 1998). In recent years, teaching hearing children signs and gestures so they can communicate with their parents before children are skilled with spoken language has become an increasingly popular way for parents and young children to interact.

language places great demands on memory. Because young children are developing memory skills at the same time they are developing language, these processes may influence each other, and behaviors such as overregularization may be a result (Marcus, 1995).

Approaching Formal Grammar

In the third year of life comes "a grammatical flowering" (deVilliers & deVilliers, 1992, p. 378). Simple sentences start to become subtle and more complex as children show early signs of understanding the rules of adult grammar (Valian, 1986). Among children's many achievements is the beginning use of auxiliary and modal verbs (deVilliers & deVilliers, 1992). *Mode,* or "mood," is the capacity of verbs to convey factual statements, expressions of possibility (e.g., the subjunctive), or imperatives. One of the auxiliary verbs children begin to use at this stage is the verb *to be,* which appears in many English sentence structures and thus opens up the possibility of many new forms of expression. Children begin to use tenses other than the present: "I kicked it." And they begin to use pronouns and articles and even begin to create complex sentences: "The teddy and doll are gonna play" (deVilliers & deVilliers, 1992, p. 379). Let us take a closer look at two of these grammatical milestones: questions and negatives.

QUESTIONS   To express a question, young children may first use an assertion such as "sit chair" or "you like dis?" simply raising their voices at the end to indicate that they are asking a question (deVilliers & deVilliers, 1979). In the latter part of the third year children begin to ask "wh" questions—those that start with the words *what, when, who, why,* and *which*—as well as questions that begin with *how.*

Between ages 2 and 3, children's "wh" constructions may fail to include the auxiliary verb, and they can be heard to say things such as "Where you going?" A little later they include the auxiliary without inverting it—for example, "Where you are going?" Finally, they incorporate all the rules for producing a "wh" question—for example, "Where are you going?"

An important feature of "wh" questions is that they enable children to exercise their curiosity. "Why" and "how" questions in particular facilitate their learning of new things. Callanan and Oakes (1992) asked parents of 3-, 4-, and 5-year-old children to keep diaries over a two-week period of their children's "why" and "how" questions. They found, as every parent knows, that the frequency of these questions increases over these years. They also found that at all ages these questions tended to be complex—that is, children rarely asked about the world just by stating "why" or "how." Rather, these questions usually included referents, ideas, and observations—for example, "Why is the sky blue?" or "How does the telephone know which house to call?" Children are active purveyors of knowledge of the world, and they use their emerging skill at questioning as an important tool for obtaining this knowledge. Again, we see that language and cognitive development are closely tied, each serving the other and together promoting the child's overall progress.

NEGATIVES   Some of the earliest evidence of children's expression of negation comes in nonverbal form, for example, by shaking their heads. The simplest verbal

Animated conversations like this one are a sign of the "grammatical flowering" that generally characterizes the third year of life.

forms involve the word *no* either alone or affixed to the beginning of a phrase—for example, a child may say "No doggie" to mean the dog is not here. As children develop, they learn to form different kinds of negatives. Expanding on Bloom's (1970) argument that three distinct types of negation appear in a particular developmental order, Tager-Flusberg (1985) proposed the following categories of negatives in the order of their appearance in young children's speech:

Type of Negation	*Explanation*	*Example*
1. Nonexistence	Remark as to the absence of something	"No cake" or "all gone cookie"
2. Rejection	Opposition to something	"No wash hair"
3. Denial	Denial that a statement made or implied by someone else is true	"That not Daddy"

Language researchers have found that these same types of negations appear in the same order in Japanese as in English (Bloom, 1991; Clancy, 1985). As children's language skills develop, more complex forms of negation appear that include auxilary verbs and are similar to forms used by adults—for example "I didn't do it" or "He isn't my friend" or "She shouldn't eat that."

The development of these two types of speech—questions and negatives—is only a sample of a wide range of grammatical accomplishments during the preschool years. By 3 years of age, children begin to use sentences so complex that they "drive non-linguists to their descriptive grammar books" (deVilliers & deVilliers, 1992, p. 379). Again, progress is gradual but orderly. At first children tack on relative clauses—for example, "See the ball that I got." It's only later that they interrupt a main clause with a subordinate clause: "The owl who eats the candy runs fast" (Slobin, 1985; Maratsos, 1998). And they ask and answer complex questions: "Where did you say you put my doll?" (deVilliers & deVilliers, 1992, p. 379).

Although most fundamental forms of grammar are acquired by $4\frac{1}{2}$ to 5 years, the process of grammar acquisition is not over during the preschool years. Specific aspects of syntax continue to develop through the school years, as children experience exceptions and try to understand them (Maratsos, 1998).

How Children Make Sense of What They Hear

Children need not only to speak grammatically correct sentences but to understand the meaning of sentences they hear or read. Although we have been discussing language production, it is important to remember that productive and receptive language are closely linked. Several researchers have shown that children are apparently able to use syntactic and semantic cues to help them understand sentences at a very early age, sentences that are more complex than those they can produce. Syntax provides clues about the meanings not only of nouns (or object words) but of verbs (or action words) as well. For example, some types of verbs appear in some sentences and not others (Hoff, 2001). Verbs such as *hit* and *hug* refer to an action that one person does to another, and therefore such verbs usually appear in sentences in which the verb is preceded by a noun, the doer of the action, and followed by a different noun, the recipient of the action (e.g., *Joe hugged Molly*). Other verbs, such as those that refer to an action with no recipient, such as *laugh* or *slip,* appear in sentences in which there is just one noun, the doer (e.g., *Paul laughed*). According to Gleitman and her colleagues (Fisher, Hall, Rakowitz, & Gleitman, 1994; Gleitman, 1990), children use a kind of "syntactic bootstrapping" to figure out word meaning. According to this theory, once children learn how to parse utterances into syntactic units, they use this knowledge to distinguish the meanings of verbs they may not yet understand. In other words, they use what they already know about syntax to support or "bootstrap" their learning and use of new syntactical forms.

According to Goodman (1989), even $1\frac{1}{2}$- to $3\frac{1}{2}$-year-old children use semantic and syntactic cues to identify spoken words. In a sentence completion task, Goodman presented children with spoken sentences and asked them to fill in a final missing noun. For example, to the utterance "Mommy feeds the _____," children responded "baby." In a word identification task, children listened to complete sentences and pointed to pictures to identify the final word in each sentence. In one condition of this task, the word called for by the sentence meaning was among those pictured, but the word actually spoken was represented by another picture. For example, children listened to the sentence "Ann drives the duck" and then looked at pictures of a duck, a truck, a dog, and a book. Although the word spoken was *duck,* children chose the truck. When the children heard the sentence "The man sees the duck," however, they chose the duck picture.

Does the ability to use semantic and syntactic information improve with age? Entwisle and Frasure (1974) demonstrated that this is very probably so. Using a "noisy telephone" technique, in which background noise was used to make auditory material difficult to hear, these researchers asked groups of children 6, 7, 8, and 9 years old to listen to three sentences. The children were then asked to repeat the sentences as accurately as possible. Because the noise blocked out parts of the sentence, the children had to rely on their knowledge of how sentences are generally formed to fill in the missing words. Here are the sentences:

Bears steal honey from the hive.

Trains steal elephants around the house.

From shoot highways the passengers mothers.

In the *meaningful* first sentence, both semantics and syntax are correct. The *anomalous* second sentence is syntactically correct, although it makes no sense. In the *scrambled* last sentence, both syntax and semantics are jumbled, making this presumably the most difficult sentence for children to reproduce. As you can see from Figure 7-7, the older the child, the more he or she was able to benefit from the available syntactic and semantic clues. At all ages, the more such clues the children had, the better they did; all age groups experienced similar difficulties with the sentence in which these clues were totally absent.

Figure 7-7

Learning to use semantic and syntactic clues

The more syntactic and semantic clues offered by sentences heard against background noise, the more successful children were at repeating the sentences. All children had difficulty with the *scrambled* sentence that lacked any clues, but when clues were present, as in the *meaningful* and *anomalous* sentences, older children made better use of them than younger children.

Source: Entwisle & Frasure, 1974.

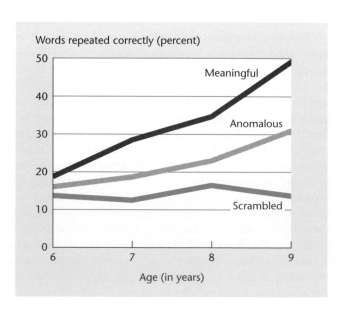

Children's comprehension of many complex constructions remains poorly understood. We still don't know when or how children are able to understand "John was thought by Mary to have been scratched by Sam" or "Whom do you think Mary could ask Sam to talk to about that?" (Maratsos, 1983). Clearly children continue to develop in both their production and understanding of complex syntax well beyond the early school years; a comparison of children's speech at the first- and eighth-grade levels testifies to these developments in production. Moreover, listening to a third-grade English lesson and a college seminar on Shakespearean sonnets clearly indicates that both comprehension and usage continue to develop for many years.

LEARNING THE SOCIAL AND CREATIVE USES OF LANGUAGE

Language, by its very nature, is a social phenomenon; it enables the child to communicate with other people. What becomes very important as children develop, therefore, is the decision as to what words and phrases to use in differing social situations. The rules for this usage, which we have already identified, are known collectively as *pragmatics*. Speakers have a variety of pragmatic forms, such as getting people to do things for them and thanking people for their help, and they need to know how to express these forms appropriately, depending on the situation and the other people involved. This focus on the social situation is seen even in the child's early one- and two-word expressions. When verbal expressions clearly refer to situations or sequences of events rather than to just one object or action, we call these expressions **speech acts.**

Communication becomes **discourse,** or socially based conversation, when children's speech is appropriate to both audience and situation and when children have become able to listen and respond to another's speech. The latter achievement includes the important ability to recognize one's own lack of understanding and to request additional information.

Children not only learn the social uses of language, they also develop the ability to use creative or figurative language at quite young ages. Even preschool children can understand creative devices such as metaphors, and this capacity builds gradually over childhood. In this section we begin by looking at some of the rules of pragmatics and then turn to the ways children learn first to communicate and then to be good listeners. The final part of the section examines the evolution of figurative language.

speech acts One- or two-word utterances that clearly refer to situations or to sequences of events.

discourse Socially based conversation.

The Rules of Pragmatics

Even when a child has mastered meaning and syntax, she is not yet fully equipped to be an effective communicator. She must learn another set of rules, namely, how to use language appropriate to a given situation. To be an effective speaker requires a complicated set of skills. First, the child must engage the attention of her listeners so they know that she wants to address them and that they should listen. Second, effective speakers have to be sensitive to listeners' feedback. If children don't know when others fail to understand them, or don't know how to change their messages to make themselves clear, they are not going to be very successful communicators. Third, speakers must adjust their speech to the characteristics of their listeners, such as age and cultural and social background. For example, the fifth-grade child must learn that in addressing his classmates he can use words and concepts that he can't use when he makes a presentation to kindergartners. Being a good communicator requires that you adapt your message to consider "who the listener is, what the listener already knows, and what the listener needs to know" (Glucksberg, Krauss, & Higgins, 1975, p. 329).

A fourth rule requires that children learn to adjust their speech to suit the situation. Children and adults learn to talk differently on a playground or street than they do in a church or a classroom. A fifth guideline points out that communication is a two-way process. To participate in a conversation, one must be not only an effective speaker but a skilled listener; learning to listen is just as important as learning to speak. A sixth rule underlines the importance of understanding one's own communicative skills—that is, children must learn to evaluate both their own messages and the messages they receive from others for clarity and usefulness. They must also learn to correct their own messages when necessary and to let another speaker know when they do not understand the speaker's communication, often specifying the information they need from the speaker (Glucksberg et al., 1975).

How early do children acquire these various communication skills? How do these skills develop? How do children use these skills to shift across different types of communicative situations? We explore these questions next.

LifeMap CD

To explore a special and controversial aspect of children's speech, view the video "Children's Eyewitness Testimony" in Chapter 7 of your CD.

Learning to Adjust Speech to Audience

By 2 years of age, children are remarkably adept both at engaging the attention of a listener and at responding to listener feedback. Videotaping ten 2-year-olds in their day-to-day interactions in a nursery school, Wellman and Lempers (1977) recorded 300 referential communicative interactions in which the communicator's intent was to point out, show, or display a particular object or referent to another child. The results were striking in their demonstration of these children's competence as speakers. The toddlers addressed their listeners when both were either interacting or playing together (82%) or when the listeners were at least not involved with someone else (88%). The children also directed communications to others when they could see each other (97%), when they were physically close to each other (91%), and, to a lesser extent, when the listeners were looking directly at them (41%). Similarly, the children made sure that when they spoke, they were close to the thing they were talking about (92%) and that the listener was also close to the thing referred to (84%), to make it more likely that the listener would understand the message.

In light of these precautions, it is not surprising that these young speakers were very effective in engaging their listeners. In fact, 79 percent of messages met with an adequate response from listeners. Moreover, speakers showed an awareness that certain situations were particularly difficult and adjusted their communications accordingly. They communicated more in difficult situations—for example, when there was an obstacle between the listener and the thing referred to. Finally, these children were responsive to feedback from their listeners. For example, more than half the time, when the speakers received no response, they repeated their messages in some form, but they repeated messages only 3 percent of the time when they received an adequate response. In sum, these 2-year-olds were surprisingly sophisticated speakers.

Children as young as 2 years of age learn to adjust their speech when talking with other children of different ages. In several studies (Dunn, 1988; Dunn & Kendrick, 1982), 2- and 3-year-olds used more repetitions and more attention-eliciting words (*hey, hello,* and *look*) when talking to their baby brothers and sisters than they did when addressing their mothers. Researchers (Gelman & Shatz, 1977; Shatz, 1983, 1994) have also found that children make the same kinds of adjustments when they speak to people outside the family. Contrast the following statements directed at an adult and a child (Shatz & Gelman, 1973):

[Four-year-old to unfamiliar adult]: You're supposed to put one of these persons in, see? Then, one goes with the other little girl. And then the little boy. He's the little boy and he drives. And then they back up. And then the little girl has marbles. . . .

[Four-year-old to unfamiliar, younger child]: Watch, Perry. Watch this. He backing in here. Now he drives up. Look, Perry, look here. Those are marbles, Perry. Put the men in here. Now I'll do it.

Despite the sophisticated level at which children can communicate, children's communicative competence does face some limitations. Preschoolers, for example, are more effective in a one-to-one conversation; they do less well when they must compete for their turn with adults and other children. Before they are $4\frac{1}{2}$, according to Ervin-Tripp (1979), children interrupt and are interrupted more often when in a group of other speakers than when talking to another child alone. Children don't track the conversations of two or more people easily, and they have trouble gauging when to enter the conversation and judging when it is their turn. Children are more competent when speaking about single familiar objects that are present in their immediate environment than when speaking about absent objects (absent in time or space) or their own feelings, motivations, thoughts, or relationships (Dunn, 1988; Shatz, 1983, 1994).

How do children acquire the ability to converse on an increasingly sophisticated level? Learning the social aspects of language is similar to learning other forms of social behavior. Children learn through direct instruction from parents and teachers, and they learn by observing other important people in their lives (Bandura, 1989; Dunn, 1988). They also learn by listening to people talk about conversations—who said what to whom and how this or that person responded (Miller & Sperry, 1987).

Learning to listen carefully to another's message is an important achievement, and adults can help children learn to attend to objects and events in the environment.

Much of what children learn from parents about the culturally appropriate use of language involves the acquisition of social conventions and moral rules. For example, one of the child's first lessons in formal communication involves learning how to use polite, socially accepted words and phrases, such as *hello, goodbye, please,* and *thank you* (Grief & Gleason, 1980); these simple social routines are common to all cultures (Schieffelin & Ochs, 1987). Children must also learn when, where, and to whom it is appropriate to express negative feelings and thoughts, such as anger (Miller & Sperry, 1987).

Learning to Listen Critically

To learn from a communication, you must be able to recognize when a message sent to you is not clear. Young children are often unaware that they do not understand a message. In one experiment, Markman (1977) gave first and third graders instructions to a game that left out critical information essential to playing the game. The third graders noticed the inadequacy of the instructions more readily than the younger children; indeed, the latter were generally unaware that information was missing and had to be urged to try to play the game before realizing that they didn't know enough to do so.

However, if the task is simple, even 3-year-olds can recognize an ambiguous message when they hear one and can act in appropriate ways to resolve the communication gap. In one study (Revelle, Wellman, & Karabenick, 1985), an adult made a variety of requests of 3- and 4-year-olds during a play session. Sometimes the requests were ambiguous—for example, the investigator might ask for a cup without specifying which of four different cups she or he wanted. In other cases, a request was impossible—"Bring me the refrigerator" (the only refrigerator available was a real and very large one). Even the 3-year-olds showed clearly that they recognized when a request was problematic, and preschoolers knew how to remedy the communication problem by requesting more information. For example, when asked to bring the refrigerator, more than one 3-year-old asked, "How? It's too heavy." Revelle and associates suggest that the essential skills in monitoring communication are realizing that problems can arise, recognizing problems when they do occur, and knowing how to fix them. Three- and 4-year-olds seem to possess all of these fundamental monitoring skills; as we'll see later, all are important in the development of metalinguistic awareness.

Children can be taught to be more effective listeners, but there may be a minimal age at which children can learn to listen critically. Two studies have shown that when 6- to 10-year-old children were encouraged to ask a speaker questions to clarify his or her communication, they performed more effectively than children who were not given this lesson in listening (Cosgrove & Patterson, 1977; Patterson & Kister, 1981). Because 4-year-olds did not benefit from this instruction, it suggests that this type of listening strategy may be a moderately advanced communication skill.

The Use of Figurative Language

Figurative expressions such as "the pillowy clouds" and "he croaked like a frog" convey powerful images. These expressions communicate something about a concept by comparing it with a similar concept from a different category. When do children begin to produce and comprehend metaphor and other forms of figurative speech?

According to Winner, McCarthy, Kleinman, and Gardner (1979), an 18-month-old child called a toy car a snake while twisting it up his mother's arm, and a 26-month-old exclaimed "Corn, corn!'" while pointing to a yellow plastic baseball bat. Utterances such as these are known as "child metaphors" because, although they are not strictly metaphors, they violate the conventions of naming (they refer to things by a name different from their literal names) or compare two objects that belong to different categories.

Children's comprehension and use of metaphor begins early and develops gradually to encompass a wider and wider range of figurative linguistic input (Gentner & Stuart, 1983; Vosniadou, 1987; Winner, 1988). To understand increasingly complex metaphors, children need to broaden their general knowledge and to hone their linguistic skills (Vosniadou, 1987). Without adequate knowledge, even adults would find it difficult to compare things from widely different frames of reference. In addition, metaphoric expressions can take a variety of linguistic forms, some of which may be easier to understand than others. For example, similes, which are based on nonliteral similarity, make explicit comparisons, using the words *as* or *like* (our second example at the beginning of this section). This makes them easier for children to understand than metaphors, in which the comparison is implied (as in our first example) (Vosniadou, 1987).

Very young children can comprehend figurative speech if metaphors are simple and occur in the appropriate context (Winner, 1988). Although the beginnings of metaphor comprehension emerge during the preschool years, understanding is not complete until the late childhood years. Children's ability to produce and comprehend metaphoric language depends critically on what they already know. However, presenting children with metaphors and encouraging them to think in figurative ways may help to advance and enrich their conceptual development. One kindergarten class, after listening to the teacher read Christina Rossetti's poem "The Clouds," came up with an amazing number of ideas as to why the poet likened clouds to sheep and the sky to a blue hill—including that clouds are "curly."

Metaphoric competence is based on children's ability to see similarities among objects and events in the world around them, an ability that also plays a fundamental role in categorization. Both categorization and the use of metaphor allow children to use their existing knowledge to understand new things. Metaphors in particular reflect the transfer of knowledge from well-known to less familiar domains and, as such, may serve as important mechanisms in acquiring new knowledge (Vosniadou, 1987).

METALINGUISTIC AWARENESS: KNOWING ABOUT LANGUAGE

One of the crowning achievements in language development, and one of the latest to develop, is the ability not merely to know language in the sense of being able to speak and understand it but to know *about* language. That is, children become aware that they know language and can think and talk about language itself.

Do children understand that words are made up of discrete sounds? Can children tell you what a word is? When can children describe the differences between grammatically correct and incorrect sentences? Do children monitor their own speech and make corrections when needed? **Metalinguistic awareness,** the understanding that language is a rule-bound system of communicating, includes the ability to talk about the various properties and uses of language as well as to monitor language as it is used (Whitehurst & Lonigan, 1998). This understanding and ability emerges well after children are proficient producers of sounds and sentences (Bullinger & Chatillon, 1983). Before they are 5 years old, children have trouble recognizing that words are groups of sounds, and they are baffled if you ask them to tell you the first sound in their names. Nor are words any easier to talk about. Before the age of 8, children confuse words with the objects that they describe. Words are *cats, toys,* and *cars,* but children have trouble articulating the concept that words are elements of language and independent of the objects or events they refer to (Ferreira & Morrison, 1994). Not until children are about 10 years old do they define words as "meaning something" (Berthoud-Papandropoulou, 1978). The ability to adjust speech to the listener's needs develops gradually over childhood and reflects this increased understanding of the social world and of language itself.

To test children's understanding of grammar, we can ask children to judge between grammatical and ungrammatical sentences and acceptable and unacceptable syntax. In one investigation, deVilliers and deVilliers (1972), using the clever technique of asking children to teach a puppet to talk correctly, tested children's ability not only to judge but to correct word order in sentences describing specific actions. Sometimes the puppet spoke in correct word order; for example, "Eat the cake." At other times the puppet reversed word order: "Dog the pat;" and at still other times the puppet used correct syntax but described actions that were impossible: "Drink the chair." The children both told the puppet whether the sentence was right or wrong and then helped the puppet rephrase it the "right way."

The researchers found a clear relationship between the children's level of language development and their metalinguistic awareness; as their ability to produce and comprehend sentences increased, their awareness increased as evidenced by their ability

metalinguistic awareness
The understanding that language is a rule-bound system of communicating.

phonological awareness
The understanding of the sounds of a language and of the properties, such as the number of sounds in a word, related to these sounds.

to correct the puppet's "wrong" utterances (deVilliers & deVilliers, 1992). According to Dale (1976), the process of becoming aware of language continues throughout development, and "in its highest form, it becomes the basis of aesthetic pleasure in poetry and prose" (p. 128).

Phonological awareness is one specific aspect of metalinguistic awareness directly related to the appreciation of the aesthetics of language. This understanding includes knowledge of the sounds of language and of properties related to these sounds, such as how many sounds are in a word. Rhyming is a particularly interesting instance of phonological awareness because of the delight children seem to take in discovering that words can rhyme and in learning how to make this happen. Children as young as 2 years of age have been observed making rhymes. Learning and passing on oral rhymes are common in the preschool and early school years. Here is a rhyme that was common among children in England in the early 1900s (Opie & Opie, 1959):

> Mrs. White had a fright
> In the middle of the night
> She saw a ghost eating toast
> Half-way up the lamp post

The fact that a rhyme, like this one, may make little sense does not seem to bother children; it even seems to make it more appealing. Children's interest in and use of rhymes reflects phonological awareness and can help create social connections and enjoyment for children. Phonological awareness also has significance for learning to read. Research has shown that children's phonological awareness before they enter school is positively related to success in reading both in the early grades and later (Goswami, & Bryant, 1990).

BILINGUALISM AND LANGUAGE DEVELOPMENT

bilingualism The acquisition of two languages at the same time.

The distribution of ethnic groups in the United States is changing rapidly. By about 2005, in some parts of the United States a majority of children will not speak English as their first language. What are the implications of **bilingualism,** in which children learn two languages simultaneously, for the language acquisition process? Although many experts have expressed concern that the task of learning two languages interferes with children's language learning more generally, this may not be the case. Although children who learn two languages may learn both languages more slowly than some of their peers learn one language, the performance gap disappears as children develop. Most evidence (Bialystok, 1997; de Houwer, 1995; Hakuta, 1986) suggests that children who are 5 or older when they learn to speak two languages have smaller comprehension vocabularies than monolingual children. In contrast, studies of children between 8 months and $2\frac{1}{2}$ years old found that bilingual and monolingual children had comprehension vocabularies of about the same size (Pearson, Fernandez, & Oller, 1993). Although a bilingual child may have in each of her languages a vocabulary that's smaller than a monolingual child's vocabulary, her total production vocabulary—her vocabularies in both languages combined—may be equal in size to the monolingual child's production vocabulary (Pearson et al., 1993).

Research (Hirsch & Kim, 1997) has suggested that when children learn two languages simultaneously, from infancy, the languages share the same brain region (called *Broca's area*) that is responsible for the execution of speech as well as for some grammatical aspects of language. However, when children learn a second

Despite research that suggests that children are capable of learning two languages equally well at the same time, bilingual education remains a highly controversial issue among both educators and parents.

language later in childhood or adulthood, this brain region is divided, with a distinct area reserved for the second language. If these findings are valid, we might speculate that they underlie the apparent greater ease of learning a second language early in childhood. Perhaps future studies will shed more light on this issue.

One important determinant of how well children master each of two languages is how often they are exposed to each one. Very few children, for example, are exposed to equal inputs of Spanish and English. As researchers recently found in Miami, a city that is home to a large Cuban population, children who received less than 25 percent of their language input in Spanish were unlikely to become competent Spanish speakers (Pearson, Fernandez, Lewedeg, & Oller, 1997). As in the case of many other kinds of lessons, exposure is an important determinant of how well children will learn.

Learning a second language often has specific benefits. Studies have shown that children who learn two languages are more cognitively advanced, have better concept formation, are more flexible in their thinking, and have better attentional control (Bialystok, 1999; Diaz, 1983, 1985; Goncz & Kodzopeljic, 1991; Rosenblum & Pinker, 1983). Not only do language and cognitive development benefit from bilingualism, but children's social behavior may improve as well. Lambert (1987) studied English-speaking children who participated in a French language immersion program in Quebec, Canada. In comparison to control pupils, the "immersion" students had less stereotyped attitudes toward French Canadian peers. Moreover, the immersion experience resulted in more mature and productive "social perspectives." For example, they offered more sophisticated solutions to solving cultural differences between French and English Canadians. In sum, learning two languages may not be as problematic as some thought but rather an advantage and an opportunity. Evidence of the benefits of bilingualism must be interpreted with caution, however. Children who are successful at multiple languages may be a select group (Diaz, 1983). We do not know how many children try to learn several languages and fall short of becoming bilingual. In other words, we don't know whether the samples used to date in explorations of the benefits of bilingualism are fully representative.

Making the Connections 7

There are many links between concepts and ideas in one area of development and concepts and ideas in other areas. Here are some of the connections between ideas in Chapter 7 and discussions in other chapters of this book.

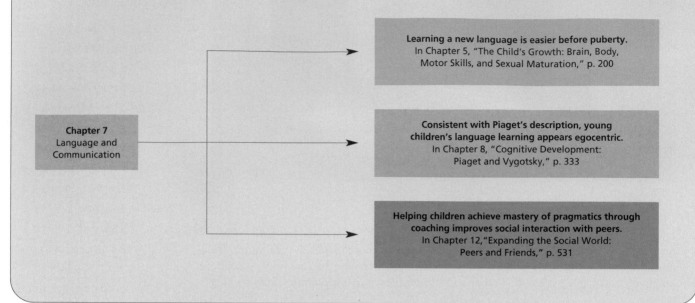

Chapter 7
Language and
Communication

Learning a new language is easier before puberty.
In Chapter 5, "The Child's Growth: Brain, Body, Motor Skills, and Sexual Maturation," p. 200

Consistent with Piaget's description, young children's language learning appears egocentric.
In Chapter 8, "Cognitive Development: Piaget and Vygotsky," p. 333

Helping children achieve mastery of pragmatics through coaching improves social interaction with peers.
In Chapter 12, "Expanding the Social World: Peers and Friends," p. 531

SUMMARY

- **Language** serves a variety of purposes for the developing child. It facilitates interpersonal communication, helps organize thinking, and aids in learning. The development of **communicative competence** is an important part of children's language learning.

- Communication requires us to use both **productive language,** transmitting messages to others, and **receptive language,** in which we receive and understand messages others send us.

The Components of Language: Phonology, Semantics, Grammar, and Pragmatics

- We can divide the study of language into four areas. **Phonology** describes a language's systems of sounds, or the way basic sound units, called **phonemes,** are connected to form words. **Semantics** is the study of the meaning of words and sentences.

- **Grammar,** which describes the structure of a language, includes **syntax** and **morphology; morphemes** are a language's smallest units of meaning. **Pragmatics** consists of rules for the use of appropriate language in particular social settings.

Theories of Language Development

- The traditional learning view explains language development by the principle of reinforcement. Other learning theorists argue the child learns language primarily through imitation. Although learning principles seem to be important in modifying language usage, they do not explain how children might acquire the enormous number of reinforcement linkages required to communicate effectively. Neither do they account for the regular sequence of language development, children's creative utterances, or the fact that children learn to speak grammatically even when parents fail to reinforce grammar.

- According to Noam Chomsky's nativist approach to language development, children have an innate **language acquisition device (LAD)** that enables them to learn language early and quickly. Support for this position comes from the finding of certain universal features in all languages, such as the use of a relatively small set of sounds and the combination of words into what in English are called *sentences,* as well as from evidence that there may be a **critical**

period for learning language. Critics point out that there is little agreement about the exact nature of the early grammatical rules that children learn and argue that language is not acquired as rapidly as nativists once thought. They also point out that the wealth of variant grammatical and syntactic rules around the world argues against any sort of universality and that the nativist view ignores the social context in which language develops.

- Most modern theorists take an interactionist view, recognizing that children are biologically prepared for language but require extensive experience with expressed language for adequate development. According to this view, children play an active role in acquiring language by formulating, testing, and evaluating hypotheses about their languages' rules.

- In proposing a **language acquisition support system (LASS),** Jerome Bruner emphasizes the critical roles parents and other early caregivers play in the child's language development. American middle-class mothers in particular support a child's beginning language by using **infant-directed,** or **child-directed, speech,** or simplified language with their children, by playing nonverbal games with them, by using the technique of **expansion** to expand or add to children's statements, and by **recasting** children's incomplete sentences in grammatical form. Many cultures do not use such specific techniques, nor do they demonstrate that **negative evidence** is a critical force in language learning.

The Antecedents of Language Development

- Infants acquire early training in the give-and-take of conversation through "pseudodialogues" with their parents, and by the time they are 1 year old, they are highly skilled at nonverbal communication. Using **protodeclaratives** and **protoimperatives,** young children can make statements about things and get other people to do things for them.

- Infants' capacity for receptive language begins as early as the first month of life, as demonstrated in their **categorical speech perception,** the ability to discriminate among consonant sounds as well as their ability to recognize some vowel sounds by the age of 2 months.

- As children are exposed to their native languages, their abilities to distinguish and categorize phonemes are refined and specialized for the sounds of their own languages.

- Precursors to productive language include **cooing, babbling,** and **patterned speech.** Babbling occurs in many cultures, and the babbling of deaf babies is very similar to that of hearing infants.

Semantic Development: The Power of Words

- Children's acquisition of vocabulary proceeds in bursts, the first of these occurring at about a year and a half in the **naming explosion.** Other aids to rapid learning of new words include a number of constraints that allow children to make judgments about a new word, such as knowing that it refers only to an object or that it is different from other words they already know.

- Children may learn object or naming words first, although some research has suggested that such words make up only a third of early vocabularies. A common error is that of **overextension,** in which a child uses a single word to mean many different things. In **underextension,** a child may restrict a word to only one representative of a category.

The Acquisition of Grammar: From Words to Sentences

- The one-word utterances that children begin to produce from about 1 year on are known as **holophrases** to indicate that these words often appear to represent a complete thought.

- Somewhere between $1\frac{1}{2}$ and 2, children begin to use **telegraphic speech,** which generally includes only nouns, verbs, and adjectives. In **overregularization,** children apply rules for regular formations in all cases, including those where formations are properly irregular.

- At about the age of 3, children begin to form more complex sentences, showing signs of understanding some of the rules of adult grammar, including "wh" and *how* questions and how to form negatives.

- The process of acquiring grammar continues throughout the school years. Using a kind of "syntactic bootstrapping," children as young as $1\frac{1}{2}$ or 2 years old use semantic and syntactic cues to help them understand sentences.

Learning the Social and Creative Uses of Language

- Because language is a social phenomenon, children must learn to raise their level of communication beyond **speech acts** to true **discourse,** which includes a complicated set of skills such as engaging the listener, sensitivity to listeners' feedback, adjusting speech to characteristics of listeners and to particular situations, being a good listener, and how to let others know that their messages are unclear.

- Even preschoolers are remarkably sophisticated speakers, but because they have difficulty tracking multiple speakers and judging when it is their turn to speak, they are more effective on a one-to-one basis than in a group. Children improve their conversational sophistication through direct instruction and by observing and listening to others speak.

- Perhaps as early as at $1\frac{1}{2}$, children can understand and produce some forms of figurative speech, although some early efforts, known as child metaphors, are not true metaphorical expressions. Presenting children with metaphors, and encouraging their skills at categorization, may facilitate their learning to use existing knowledge in understanding new things.

Metalinguistic Awareness: Knowing about Language

- When children achieve **metalinguistic awareness** at about the age of 10, they can both understand that language is a system of rules for communication and discuss the properties and uses of language. Although they can use many rules at an earlier age, they have difficulty separating words from the objects or events they represent and grasping the concept that words are elements of language.

- **Phonological awareness** appears earlier. Even preschool children have some understanding of the sounds of language and of how to use these sounds in different ways, for example, in creating rhymes.

Bilingualism and Language Development

- The evidence indicates that **bilingualism,** in which children learn two languages simultaneously, does not place children at a disadvantage in terms of language proficiency. In fact, learning two languages may have benefits, such as advanced cognitive skills, more flexibility of thought, and greater acceptance of peers from other cultural backgrounds.

EXPLORE AND DISCUSS

1. How do you think language development affects a child's social and emotional development?
2. Why is it important for a child's language development that she or he talk to adults as well as to other children?
3. Preschool children ask lots of *why* questions, sometimes even exhausting parents by the sheer number of their queries. If a child asked you a why question, such as "Why don't doggies cry?" or "Why are circles round?" how would you answer?
4. Is there an upper limit on the number of languages a child can learn to speak fluently? If so, what do you think this limit is, and why is there a limit?

Chinese painting, Northern Song dynasty, 1127–1279. *Children playing in an autumn garden,* 13th century CE. National Palace Museum, Taipei.

8.

Cognitive Development: Piaget and Vygotsky

How do we make sense of the world and all the people and objects in it? As adults, we take what we know about the world for granted. For example, when was the last time you wondered if an object continues to exist even when you can't see it? Or when you questioned that an object that is unsupported or released from a height would fall downward and not float up in the air? Or when you stopped to think about when and how you came to understand the symbols and gestures that people use to communicate with one another? **Cognition** is the term used to describe the mental activity through which human beings acquire, remember, and learn to use knowledge. Cognition is complex and includes many processes, such as perception, attention, learning, memory, and reasoning. It is such a broad concept that most of the topics covered in this book have some relation to cognitive development. After all, human beings are thinking creatures and much of our behavior reflects this fact. Research on cognitive development focuses specifically on how and when intellectual abilities and knowledge of the world first emerge in childhood and then change as a person grows older.

In this chapter and its companion, Chapter 9, we discuss several different approaches to the study of cognitive development. In this chapter, we describe two of these approaches. First, we explore Jean Piaget's theory of cognitive development, which emphasizes developmental changes in the organization or structure of children's thinking processes. Then we consider Lev Vygotsky's sociocultural theory of cognitive development, which suggests that a child's interactions with the social world produce advances in thinking and understanding. In Chapter 9 we will explore the information-processing approach to cognitive development. This view concentrates on how people use their cognitive abilities to process information and carry out intelligent action. Developmental psychologists who adopt this approach focus on age-related changes in cognitive abilities.

PIAGET'S THEORY OF COGNITIVE DEVELOPMENT

cognition The mental activity through which human beings acquire and process knowledge.

One of the most important and influential theories of cognitive development is that of the Swiss scientist Jean Piaget (Beilin, 1992). Part of Piaget's great influence on the field stems from the fact that his theory raised many interesting questions about intellectual development (Piaget, 1926, 1929, 1950, 1985). As a result, this theory has stimulated many other researchers' ideas about cognitive development. Piaget's theory is also a controversial view in that many developmentalists have challenged both his methods and his conclusions. First, we describe Piaget's theory, and then we turn to the main criticisms of this approach.

Piaget was precocious: He began his own scientific research at a considerably younger age than most other people do. His primary interest was biology and, at the age of 10, he published his first scholarly article on a rare albino sparrow. As a result of both this publication and his subsequent writings on mollusks, Piaget was offered the position of curator of the mollusk collection at the Geneva Museum of Natural History—a position he declined, as he was still a schoolboy at the time! As Piaget continued his studies, his interest in biology continued. However, he also became interested in philosophy, especially the study of knowledge, or *epistemology*. As a young man, Piaget pursued these interests by studying in Paris with Alfred Binet, who was working on the development of the first intelligence test (discussed in Chapter 10). As he helped Binet develop standardized IQ tests for children, Piaget made two important observations. First, he noticed that children of the same ages tended to make the same mistakes and to get the same answers wrong. Second, he noticed that the errors of children of a particular age differed in systematic ways from those of older or younger children. Piaget's theory of cognitive development began to take shape as he thought about these errors; in particular, he thought they revealed distinct age-related ways of thinking and understanding the world. Thus, for Piaget, children's incorrect responses on tests were more enlightening than their correct responses, and he used these errors as a basis for understanding changes in how children think.

Jean Piaget spent his career studying the development of children's thinking. Working in his native Switzerland, Piaget based much of his theory on direct observations and interviews with children.

To study children's thinking, Piaget primarily used two methods: interviews and observations. In his interviews, he would present children with a problem to solve or a question to answer and then ask them to explain their thinking. In his observational research, which he used mainly with very young children, he would present a problem and then watch how the children behaved as they tried to solve it. Some psychologists criticize Piaget for these methods and prefer controlled experiments that allow for tests of specific hypotheses. In the latter part of his career, Piaget did try to test some of his hypotheses with more controlled experiments.

Piaget began his research on cognitive development in the 1920s, but it was not until the early 1960s that Piaget's impact on developmental psychology began to be felt in the United States. In 1963 John Flavell published *The Developmental Psychology of Jean Piaget,* the first comprehensive summary and analysis of Piaget's work to appear in English. Developmental psychology was ready for these ideas. At this time, child psychology was largely a descriptive field that lacked a theoretical focus. Psychologists had done little research on cognitive development, and although some had studied intelligence—primarily how to describe and measure it—few had attempted to explain the development of cognitive function and abilities. Moreover, the prevailing theoretical view in American psychology at the time was behaviorism, which gave little importance to the mind as a significant component of child development.

Piaget's theory, which proposed that over development the child acquires qualitatively new ways of thinking and understanding the world, was innovative and intriguing. For developmental psychologists, this theory was an attractive alternative to behaviorism, for it was a genuine developmental theory derived from direct observations of how children's abilities and limitations change as they grow from infancy to adolescence.

PIAGET'S MAIN TENET: THE CHILD ACTIVELY SEEKS KNOWLEDGE

Piaget argued that children play an active role in acquiring knowledge—that is, rather than passively waiting for information from their environments to present itself, children actively seek out information. In addition, when children encounter new information, they actively try to fit it in with the knowledge they already possess. In other words, children construct the understanding they obtain from these encounters. Thus, this theory is referred to as a **constructivist view.**

Children develop a great deal of information about the world. Piaget was particularly interested in a specific type of information: that which pertains to the logical properties of, and relations among, objects and physical features of the world. It's important to emphasize this interest of Piaget's because it may seem difficult to reconcile his constructivist approach, which stresses how children actively construct understanding, with his view of mental changes as universal—that is, characteristic of all human beings regardless of where they live. The reason these two ideas can exist side by side in Piaget's theory is that he held that the ability to understand the logical properties of the world is a capability of the mind. Piaget considered understanding these logical properties to be essential to human functioning. Furthermore, he thought that this type of understanding is available to the human mind because, over the course of evolution, the mind developed this capability in response to the properties of the world itself.

Piaget set out to discover precisely how children at different points in their development think about the world and how systematic changes in their thinking and their understanding of the world come about. Although he was careful to point out that children vary in their achievement of different cognitive advances, he provided approximate ages at which these achievements occur. The Turning Points chart covers many topics discussed in this chapter (pp. 320–321) and includes a summary of Piaget's descriptions of the milestones of cognitive development.

constructivist view The idea that children actively create their understanding of the world as they encounter new information and have new experiences.

Cognitive Organization

Piaget believed that, over the course of development, children's knowledge of the world gets organized into increasingly more complex cognitive structures. A *cognitive structure* is not a physical entity in the brain but an organized group of interrelated memories, ideas, and strategies that the child uses in trying to understand a situation. Piaget built much of his theory around the notion of the **schema** (plural, **schemata**), a cognitive structure that is much like a concept that forms the basis for understanding and interacting with the environment. In short, a schema is an organized unit of knowledge.

schema (plural, *schemata*) An organized unit of knowledge that the child uses to try to understand a situation; a schema forms the basis for organizing actions to respond to the environment.

Turning Points

THE CHILD'S COGNITIVE DEVELOPMENT FROM INFANCY THROUGH LATE CHILDHOOD

1 MONTH The child becomes more efficient in the use of reflexes and can invite stimulation that allows this use; begins to adapt reflexive behaviors to different environmental conditions (e.g., sucks differently when nurses, drinks from a bottle, and has thumb or pacifier in mouth); shows recognition memory and can learn basic associations

2 MONTHS Can anticipate: stops crying at sight of mother's breast or the bottle; expects and shows interest in animate behavior from humans; exhibits organized and selective looking; is interested in faces

3 MONTHS Reacts to newness with body stiffening; quiets at sight of interesting toy; shows longer looking time at specific objects, investigative type of attention; has more voluntary control of looking; makes eye contact; social looking time increases; shows mutual gaze; face-to-face play becomes common

4 MONTHS Repeats body actions that are pleasurable and satisfying; can reach out and gently probe objects; evidences anticipation (e.g., opens mouth at sight of bottle); may be capable of simple grouping or categorization; reacts differently to some usual and unusual physical events

5 MONTHS Visually follows an object as it moves out of direct line of vision; remembers pictures of faces; looking time increases; increasingly focuses attention on objects as well as people

6 MONTHS Learns behaviors of familiar people; reacts to changes in familiar events

7 MONTHS Explores objects by manipulation; drops objects from heights; may understand the notion of physical support; is more attentive when playing

8 MONTHS Likes to make things happen and combines learned behaviors in this effort (e.g., shaking, banging, and dangling toys); displays basic problem-solving abilities; attends to play; often mouths toys as a way of exploring

9 MONTHS Begins to remember without cues; uses knowledge to solve problems; seems aware of some cause-and-effect relations; recognizes that own actions may affect outcomes; gets other people to make things happen; able to look at more distant objects or images; exerts increased control over own actions; begins to show goal-oriented attention; can alternate attention between a person and an object

10 MONTHS Explores inside and outside surfaces of toys; repeats play sequences with different toys; investigates textures, designs, or parts of toys; may be able to reason about hidden objects; looks intently at pictures

11 MONTHS Uses tools to accomplish goals (e.g., uses a chair to stand up); is more easily entertained; begins to put knowledge of containment to use (e.g., tries to stack cups)

Sources: Flavell, 1963; Gauvain, 2001a; Kopp, 1994; Siegler & Alibali, 2005.

1 YEAR	Actively plans to achieve a goal; examines objects comprehensively; uses imitative learning; deliberately introduces variations into play sequences; recognizes self in mirror; shows increased ability to look at complex visual stimuli; frequently looks at partner's face; starts to follow the glances and points of others
15 MONTHS	Continues to use systematic trial-and-error learning; is more aware of the functions of objects; may use dolls in play; recognizes and uses more cause-and-effect relationships; shows clear evidence of social referencing
18 MONTHS	Likes to experiment with the properties of objects; has better recall memory; has basic idea of "what should be" (e.g., puts lids on jars); recognizes that others have possessions; can use language to direct attention
21 MONTHS	To some degree, understands past, present, and future; uses scripts to organize activities into episodes; has some understanding of the idea of categories (e.g., colors)
2 YEARS	Can think symbolically and use language to direct attention and regulate behavior; can remember behaviors and reproduce an action long after observing it; can plan how to solve a problem mentally rather than use trial and error; begins to understand conservation; engages in fantasy play; recognizes that family members have specific roles; shows creative problem solving
3 YEARS	May be able to see the perspectives of others; may grasp conservation of number
4 YEARS	Begins to realize that others have different perspectives from own; may be able to understand part-whole relations; has memory span of about four items
5 YEARS	Has improved language and problem-solving skills; can use certain mental operations to solve problems but uses them intuitively, without a clear understanding of how and why they work
7 YEARS	Has achieved conservation of number, mass, liquid, length; begins to describe self in more abstract terms
8–10 YEARS	Can anticipate and consider the thoughts of others; achieves conservation of weight and area
11–12 YEARS	Achieves conservation of volume; begins to think deductively; can sort things in complicated combinations of attributes
12 AND BEYOND	Thinking becomes more flexible and capable of abstraction; can apply logic to ideas and problems that violate reality; can entertain many possible solutions of a problem

organization Combining simple mental structures into more complex systems.

Organization is, for Piaget, the ability to combine simple mental structures into more complex systems. Our earliest schemata, when we are newborns, are in the form of innate reflexes and related patterns of physical action that help us interact with the world. Through these interactions, we build or construct knowledge. For example, newborns will suck reflexively on anything that touches their lips. This organized sucking behavior, or schema, occurs in response to a wide range of stimuli and therefore functions as a way of relating to the environment and of beginning to learn about it. Over time and with experience at sucking, this schema changes, as the newborn sucks differently on different objects and uses this schema for different purposes, such as eating and exploring objects. Newborns possess many other basic reflexes or schemata, such as grasping, kicking, and looking, all of which help the infant engage with and learn about the world.

operations Schemata based on internal mental activities.

As children grow older and gain experience, they shift gradually from using schemata based on overt physical activities to those based on internal mental activities. Piaget called these mental schemata **operations.** The earliest operations are formed when younger babies internalize their physically based schemata, including strategies, plans, and "rules" for solving problems, so that they become parts of organized mental structures. Thus, an action-based grasping schema can become part of a complex plan for possessing a desirable object.

Over time and experience, schemata get combined to form more complex behaviors. For example, a looking-grasping-sucking schema helps babies obtain desired objects and explore them orally. When a substantial number of changes in schemata occur, Piaget hypothesized that children change from one organized way of understanding to an entirely new way of approaching the world. He described these large-scale organizational changes as stages and suggested that, over the life course, there are four stages of cognitive development. These stages are described in detail in the next major section of the chapter.

Cognitive Adaptation

adaptation Adjusting one's thinking to fit with environmental demands.

Piaget proposed that children continually modify their schemata in relation to their own experiences, and referred to this process as **adaptation.** Adaptation of a schema is a bit like a two-way street. It always involves determining how new information fits with existing knowledge as well as how existing knowledge may need to change to incorporate new information. Thus, Piaget described adaptation as composed of two processes, called assimilation and accommodation, which interact to modify children's schemata. To understand a new experience, children at first try **assimilation**—that is, they try to apply what they already know, their existing schemata, to the new experience. For example, as babies are confronted with new objects, they try to assimilate those objects to their looking-grasping-sucking schema. In most cases they are successful, and object after object gets seen, grasped, and placed in the mouth.

assimilation Applying an existing schema to a new experience.

However, sometimes babies encounter an object that is hard to assimilate. For example, a large inflated beach ball is very difficult to grasp and suck. Now the infant must modify her strategy for exploring objects (her looking-grasping-sucking schema) and adopt a new approach. Using the method of **accommodation,** she may hold the ball in her arms instead of her hands and lick it with her tongue instead of sucking on it. In this way, she has modified an existing schema to fit the characteristics of the new situation. At times, more extreme accommodation is called for, when children must give up old schemata entirely and find a different way of relating to a new situation. For example, no matter how hard they try, babies cannot catch hold of a stream of running water, nor grasp and draw a beam of light to their mouths. These new experiences demand new ways for exploring and understanding the world, and so babies' organized patterns of thought and behavior expand. Over time, assimilation

accommodation Modifying an existing schema to fit a new experience.

and accommodation work together to organize children's knowledge and behavior into increasingly complex structures.

In Piaget's theory, cognitive development is based on modifications to schemata that result from innate predispositions of the human child to actively seek knowledge, to organize this knowledge, and to adapt it to their needs. In these concepts of cognitive development, Piaget's early interest in biology, especially evolutionary theory, is evident.

THE STAGES OF COGNITIVE DEVELOPMENT

Piaget viewed intellectual growth in terms of progressive changes in children's cognitive structures. Small changes in understanding and interacting with the world eventually manifest themselves in large-scale changes referred to as **stages of development.** Each stage is qualitatively different from the one that precedes it. Because stages are built through experience, children do not reach these stages at exactly the same ages. However, all children pass through the stages in the same order, and no stage can be skipped. This is because the attainments of earlier stages are the building blocks of the later stages and thus are essential for these later developments to emerge. Piaget saw intellectual development as occurring in four main stages: the sensorimotor stage, the preoperational stage, the stage of concrete operations, and the stage of formal operations (see Table 8-1). Notice the terms "preoperational" and "operations" in the three later stages. Piaget felt that infants in the sensorimotor stage did not possess mental structures, or operations. But after infancy, when children have symbolic ways of representing the world in their minds, cognitive development involves changes or modifications to mental structures or operations. According to Piaget, as children pass through these four stages, they change from infants who are

stages of development
Comprehensive, qualitative changes over time in the way a child thinks.

Table 8-1 Piaget's stages of cognitive development

Stage	Age Range (years)	Major Characteristics and Achievements
Sensorimotor	0–2	Child's thought is confined to action schemes and sensory experiences. He differentiates self from objects and other people; seeks stimulation and prolongs interesting sights and experiences; develops object concept, including object permanence; achieves basic understanding of causality, time, and space; grasps means-end relationships; begins to imitate behaviors previously experienced; engages in imaginative play; and, late in the stage, shows the beginnings of symbolic thought.
Preoperational	2–7	Child begins to use symbols to represent objects and experiences and to use language symbolically; shows intuitive problem solving. Her thinking is semilogical, characterized by irreversibility, centration, egocentrism, and animism. She begins to think in terms of classes, see relationships, and grasp concept of conservation of numbers.
Concrete operations	7–12	Child is capable of logical reasoning, but this ability is limited to physically real and present objects; he grasps concepts of the conservation of mass, length, weight, and volume; his thinking is now characterized by reversibility, decentration, and the ability to take the role of another; he can organize objects into hierarchical classes (classification) and place objects into ordered series (seriation).
Formal operations	12 on	Child acquires flexibility in thinking as well as the capacities for abstract thinking and mental hypothesis testing; she can consider possible alternatives in complex reasoning and problem solving.

incapable of mental operations and are totally dependent on concrete sensory and motor activities to know the world into emerging young adults capable of great flexibility of thought and abstract reasoning.

The Sensorimotor Stage

sensorimotor stage Piaget's first stage of cognitive development, during which children change from basic reflexive behavior to the beginnings of symbolic thought and goal-directed behaviors.

Dramatic achievements in children's intellectual development occur during the **sensorimotor stage,** which spans approximately the first two years of life. By interacting with their environment in active ways, children build on their basic reflexes and, from these origins, formulate a way of understanding and interacting with the world. By the end of infancy, around 2 years of age, children begin to form mental representations of objects and events and to use this information in developing new behaviors and strategies for attaining goals and solving problems. The increasingly efficient use of mental or symbolic processes leads directly into the second major stage of development, the preoperational stage.

Before we discuss the preoperational stage, it is important to describe the six substages of the sensorimotor stage. Each of these substages is marked by a notable increase in the complexity of the child's cognitive activity. One of the child's major cognitive achievements that occurs during the sensorimotor stage is the development of the object concept. Although understanding and using objects is fundamental to human activity, we are not born with knowledge of objects. Rather, this knowledge must be constructed by the child over the course of his or her encounters with objects. According to Piaget, young infants do not have a conception of **object permanence.** For the very young child, when mother goes out of the room or when a favorite toy drops over the edge of the crib, it is not only "out of sight" but "out of existence" (Flavell, 1985). According to Piaget, gradually and in a predictable sequence over the sensorimotor stage, infants learn that objects exist when they are not in direct contact with them (Table 8-2). By

object permanence The notion that entities external to the child, such as objects and people, continue to exist independent of the child's seeing or interacting with them.

Table 8-2   Acquiring the object concept and an understanding of object permanence

Substage	Age (months)	Child's Behavior
1 Basic reflex activity	0–1	Focuses only on objects directly in front of him
2 Primary circular reactions	1–4	Begins to operate on objects with action schemes; initially this occurs accidentally and then becomes less accidental; looks a long time at place where an object disappeared but does not search visually or manually for the object
3 Secondary circular reactions	4–8	Can operate on objects and repeats actions toward objects; can visually anticipate where an object may be; searches for partially concealed objects
4 Coordination of secondary circular reactions	8–12	Will search for completely hidden objects but has tendency to repeat old actions by searching where objects were previously hidden (A-not-B error)
5 Tertiary circular reactions	12–18	Lots of trial-and-error experimentation with objects and how they move; searches for objects that have been concealed while she was watching but has difficulty if an object is displaced more than once
6 Inventing new means by mental combination	18–24	Object concept is fully developed; child searches and finds objects easily, even if the object has been hidden and displaced several times in a row before he is allowed to search

observing his own three children and the ways in which they engaged with objects at different times between birth and 2 years of age, Piaget was able to describe the development of the object concept in considerable detail. We discuss Piaget's thinking in respect to the object concept in the next several paragraphs, as we describe the six substages of the sensorimotor stage.

Substage 1: Basic Reflex Activity (0 to 1 Month)

In the substage of **basic reflex activity,** infants become more proficient in the use of their innate reflexes, such as grasping and sucking. Piaget saw the infant as an active organism, and, it is true that babies exercise, or practice, these reflexes as much as possible. They grasp and suck on a variety of objects as a way of providing stimulation for themselves. Much of their initial exploration of objects occurs through involuntary reflexive behaviors. However, over the first month of life, many of these involuntary behaviors are replaced by behaviors that are similar in form but are controlled voluntarily by the developing cortical system. For example, over the first month or so of life, the grasping reflex that is present in newborns, and that occurs if someone places an object in an infant's palm, gradually subsides. In its place, the infant begins to use her hands voluntarily to grab onto objects that come within reach. In terms of the object concept, from birth to 1 month, infants look only at objects that are directly in front of them.

Substage 2: Primary Circular Reactions (1 to 4 Months)

This substage is called **primary circular reactions** because during this time, infants produce repetitive behaviors that are focused on the infant's own body. In particular, babies repeat and modify actions they find pleasurable or satisfying. Often they have initiated these actions by chance. For example, a baby may accidentally bring a finger close to her mouth and start sucking on it. Finding this behavior pleasurable, the infant attempts to reproduce the exact behavior that produced the interesting event—in this case, by seeking the finger to suck on it again. If the sucking schema continues to produce satisfying behavior, the baby will tend to repeat it over and over again. Piaget chose the term *reaction* for this sort of behavior because the child is responding to an initiating event. He called these earliest reactions *primary* because they involve basic motor responses of the child's own body, and he termed them *circular* because they occur repeatedly. In terms of the object concept, infants display no comprehension that objects have an existence of their own. When a toy vanishes, they don't look for it. In fact, if the toy drops from a child's hand, he will stare at his hand rather than follow the falling object's path to the floor. Thus, when a young infant is not perceiving an object, he behaves as though it does not exist.

Substage 3: Secondary Circular Reactions (4 to 8 Months)

Not until the infant enters the substage of **secondary circular reactions,** at about 4 months of age, does he becomes interested in making things happen outside his own body. Secondary circular reactions involve repetitive behaviors focused on external objects, hence the term *secondary*. During this substage, the child's reactions are still circular—that is, he repeatedly engages in behaviors that please him. For example, the infant may shake a rattle, hear an interesting sound, shake the rattle again, hear the sound once more, and so on, over and over. Notice also that the baby now is capable of combining schemata, such as grasping and shaking, to produce relatively more complex behavior patterns.

It is tempting to say that at this substage the infant's behavior has become intentional—that is, that the child mentally forms the goal of shaking the rattle to hear the pleasant sound. However, Piaget did not attribute such intentions to the child until the fourth substage of

basic reflex activity An infant's exercise of, and growing proficiency in, the use of innate reflexes.

primary circular reactions Behaviors focused on the infant's own body that the infant repeats and modifies because they are pleasurable and satisfying.

secondary circular reactions Behaviors focused on objects outside the infant's own body that the infant repeatedly engages in because they are pleasurable and satisfying.

This 7-month-old child seems quite absorbed in shaking his rattle. Using its different parts, he may get the rattle to make more than just one intriguing sound; this illustrates the substage of secondary circular reactions.

the sensorimotor stage. At this third substage, he viewed the child's shaking of the rattle as caused by the fact that the rattle was in the child's hand. If the rattle were out of the baby's grasp, Piaget said the baby would not find the rattle and shake it.

In this substage, the infant begins to show some awareness of the permanence of objects. A child is more likely to search visually for an object if its loss is associated with interruption of her own movements than if another person has hidden it. In addition, a child will now anticipate the path of a moving object, looking at a location where it can be expected to appear. She will search for a partially visible object, but not a covered one, and even if she watches as an object is covered, she will not attempt to retrieve it. For example, if an adult hides a desired toy under a blanket, the infant will not search for the toy, even though she saw it being hidden.

Substage 4: Coordination of Secondary Circular Reactions (8 to 12 Months)

coordination of secondary circular reactions An infant's combination of different schemata to achieve a specific goal.

In the substage called **coordination of secondary circular reactions,** the child develops more sophisticated combinations of behaviors directed toward objects that reflect intentionality. At this point in development, Piaget held, the child is able to plan deliberately to attain a goal. Furthermore, schemata can be combined to reach these goals. For example, the child can now combine a hitting schema with her reaching and grasping schemata in order to move one toy out of the way so she can reach another. Thus, this substage marks the beginning of problem-solving behavior. Notice how the hitting schema is now used not only in a new situation but as an intermediate step in an effort to achieve a specific goal—that is, as part of a more elaborate set of intentional behaviors or a plan.

During this substage, the child's concept of object permanence continues to evolve. The child now begins to search for completely concealed objects, which gives evidence of her growing realization of object permanence. However, although the child will search successfully for an object hidden in one location, if the object is moved or displaced to another location as the child watches, the child will continue to search in the first hiding place. This type of displacement error is referred to as the A-not-B error because the child continues to search in the first hiding place, identified as A, even after, in the child's presence, the object is put in a second spot, identified as B.

Substage 5: Tertiary Circular Reactions (12 to 18 Months)

tertiary circular reactions Behaviors in which infants experiment with the properties of external objects and try to learn how objects respond to various actions.

In the substage of **tertiary circular reactions,** children begin to experiment with external objects. It is called tertiary because, now, actions not previously associated with objects are used on objects, and this helps the child understand more about how objects and actions on objects work. Children use trial-and-error methods to learn more about the properties of objects and to solve problems. Unlike the earlier substages in which the child repeated *exact* behaviors, infants are now capable of producing *similar* but not exact behaviors. Piaget referred to infants who had acquired this capability, which allows for novel exploration, as "little scientists." For example, children at this age often experiment by deliberately dropping objects to see what happens to them. They will vary the way they drop an object, the position and distance of the drop, the place from which they drop it, or the characteristics of the surface on which it lands. In this way they may learn, for instance, that whereas a rubber ball bounces *off* the floor, a cup of applesauce spreads all *over* the floor.

In this substage, the infant is finally able to recognize the permanence of an object hidden from view. The child will now track an object visually and search for it where it disappeared. But despite this new awareness, Piaget suggests, children in this stage still have difficulty conceiving of more than one displacement of an object. While playing a hiding game with his own son, Laurent, Piaget hid his watch repeatedly behind one of two cushions, and Laurent consistently searched for the watch under the correct cushion. However, as Laurent watched, Piaget then placed the watch in a box, put the box behind a cushion, and then surreptitiously removed the watch from the box, leaving the watch alone behind the cushion. He then handed the box to

This 11-month-old is a little ahead of schedule, for she's already beginning to experiment with dropping things to see what happens to them, illustrating the substage of tertiary circular reactions. From this height, her toy probably did nothing too startling, but it may have moved in interesting ways.

Laurent, who opened it and found it empty. Laurent did not search for the watch behind the cushion. Apparently, the concept of object permanence held for him only when he could observe every displacement of the watch. Although the child is no longer puzzled by the type of hiding problem described in the A-not-B error of substage 4, understanding this type of hiding, called *invisible displacement,* is not within the child's capability.

Substage 6: Inventing New Means by Mental Combination (18 to 24 Months)

It is not until the sixth and last substage of **inventing new means by mental combination** that children begin to think symbolically and engage in internal, or mental, problem solving. Actions on objects can now be considered mentally, and this ability enables the child to use objects in more deliberate and complex ways. **Symbolic thought,** or the use of mental images and concepts to represent people, objects, and events in the world emerges in this final substage. The child can now invent ways to attain a goal by *mentally* combining schemata; he is no longer limited to physically exploring, manipulating, and acting on objects. Symbolic capabilities are evident in the child's emerging ability to use language; in the representation of objects in drawings; in fantasy play; and in **deferred imitation,** in which the child mimics an action some time after observing it.

Finally, at this last substage, children fully acquire the concept of object permanence. They are able to make inferences about the positions of unseen objects even when the objects have been hidden or displaced several times.

CRITICISMS OF PIAGET'S VIEW OF THE DEVELOPMENT OF THE OBJECT CONCEPT

The development of object permanence has great importance in Piaget's theory. However, his claims regarding the acquisition of this concept have not gone unchallenged. One common criticism is that in all the tasks Piaget used to study the development of object permanence, he measured only the child's manual search behavior. Many investigators have argued that because of developmental limitations, such as poor hand-eye coordination, some children who have

inventing new means by mental combination Children begin to combine schemata mentally and rely less on physical trial and error.

symbolic thought The use of mental images and concepts to represent people, objects, and events.

deferred imitation Mimicry of an action some time after having observed it; requires that the child have some sort of mental representation of the action.

acquired the concept of object permanence may be unable to reveal it in manual search activities.

To study this possibility, Renée Baillargeon (1986, 1993) designed a task that allowed her to measure the amount of time infants look at a situation involving objects, which she referred to as an event, to try to reveal information about infant's understanding of objects before they are capable of manually searching for an object. Baillargeon presented 6- and 8-month-old infants with what seemed to be an impossible event: One solid object appeared to move through the space occupied by another solid object. The infant sat in front of a large stage on the left side of which was a long inclined ramp (see Figure 8-1a). At the bottom of the ramp, directly in front of the infant, was a small screen that could be raised and lowered. After the screen had been lowered, a small car rolled down the ramp along a track, disappearing behind the screen and reappearing at the other side of the screen. This event was repeated until the infant became habituated to it—that is, until he stopped looking at the display.

Next the infant saw one of two test events (Figures 8-1b and 8-1c). Both of these events were identical to the habituation event except that when the screen was raised, the infant saw a box placed behind it and then hidden by the lowered screen. The two test events were differentiated by the precise placement of the box. In the possible event (Figure 8-1b), the box was placed behind the track, and therefore out of the car's path. In the impossible event (Figure 8-1c), the box was placed on top of the track, directly in the car's path. This time when the car disappeared behind the screen and reappeared at the far side of the screen, it appeared to have rolled right through the box! (During the impossible event, the box was actually removed through a door in the back of the stage.)

What did Baillargeon find? Infants looked longer at the impossible event than at the possible event. And in later studies using the same basic experimental procedure,

Figure 8-1   Testing infants' grasp of object permanence

As 6- to 8-month-old babies watched, a car rolled down a ramp, disappeared behind a screen and reappeared at the other side (a). After infants saw a box placed *behind* the ramp, the car again rolled down the ramp, disappearing and reappearing once again (b; a possible event). After infants saw the box placed *on* the ramp, where it would obstruct the car's passage, the car once again rolled down the ramp, disappearing and reappearing as before (c; an impossible event). Babies looked longer at the event in (c) than at the event in (b).

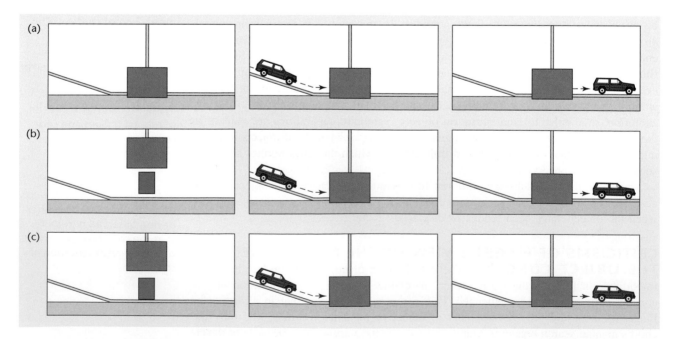

Source: Adapted from Baillargeon, 1986.

Baillargeon and her colleagues (see Baillargeon & Wang, 2002) found that even infants as young as $3\frac{1}{2}$ months of age could demonstrate an awareness of object permanence under these conditions. These findings, which run counter to Piaget's claims, have led to further research indicating that infants know a great deal more than Piaget imagined. However, although these findings challenge Piaget's views about the timing of the development of the object concept, debate continues as to whether they challenge his fundamental assumptions about this development, such as its origins in basic reflexes, the sequence with which this understanding unfolds, and the increasing complexity in object knowledge over the sensorimotor stage.

NEW RESEARCH DIRECTIONS AND EXPLANATIONS OF KNOWLEDGE IN INFANCY

Object permanence may not be the only principle of the physical world that children understand earlier than Piaget thought. There may be some other understandings about the world so fundamental to cognitive development that these too appear very early in life. Developmental psychologists refer to these types of understanding as **core knowledge systems** (Spelke, 2000). Such knowledge systems include ways of reasoning about ecologically important objects and events. Specific examples include some understanding of physical laws, such as those which pertain to the solidity of objects and the continuity of objects behind partial visual obstructions. Knowledge about what can happen to objects, or *event knowledge,* may also exist very early in life (Baillargeon & Wang, 2002). For example, the understanding that some objects can be put inside other objects, called a *containment event,* and that some objects can be hidden behind other objects, called an *occlusion event,* may be present in very young children. Another core knowledge system that has been proposed is understanding of the approximate numbers of items in a group, called *numerosity.* Early evidence of these types of understanding have led some developmental psychologists to call infants "naive physicists" (Wellman & Gelman, 1992), in that babies appear to demonstrate a surprisingly rich understanding of the world around them.

Research on early event knowledge has relied primarily on the *violation-of-expectation* method described in Chapter 4. For example, Hespos and Baillargeon (2001) studied the behavior of $4\frac{1}{2}$-month-old infants when they were shown two types of events, one possible and one impossible, regarding the occlusion and the containment of objects (Figure 8-2). In this experiment, the infants watched as an object, a tall cylinder, was either lowered behind a screen (the occlusion condition) or lowered inside a container (the containment condition). The investigators studied two types of events, the possible or expected event and the impossible or unexpected event. In the expected events, the objects used to occlude or contain the cylinder were as tall as the cylinder and therefore physically able to hide the cylinder from view. In the unexpected events, the objects used to occlude or contain the cylinder were shorter than the cylinder; in fact they were only half as tall as the cylinder. In the unexpected events, the cylinder was, nonetheless, hidden entirely from view in the two hiding conditions (a trap door was used to make this impossible event work). What did the infants do? They looked longer at the unexpected than at the expected events when they were in the occlusion condition but not in the containment condition. In another study that included older infants but used the same experimental design, $7\frac{1}{2}$-month-old infants, but not $5\frac{1}{2}$- or $6\frac{1}{2}$-month-old infants, looked longer at both the unexpected occlusion and containment events (Baillargeon, 2002). These findings suggest that this type of event knowledge develops very early, though it appears gradually over the first year of life.

Young infants' understanding of numerosity has also led to some surprising results. For example, Xu and Spelke (2000) showed 6-month-old infants a visual light display on a screen that contained arrays of dots. Over the initial trials, the positions and sizes

According to the Piagetian view of object permanence, this 10-month-old child is pretty much on track, searching for an object that was completely concealed. Renée Baillargeon has demonstrated, however, that even $3\frac{1}{2}$-month-old infants may be aware that objects exist whether or not they're visible.

core knowledge systems Ways of reasoning about ecologically important objects and events, such as the solidity and continuity of objects.

Figure 8-2

Exploring infants' knowledge of events

Drawings representing the unexpected test events for the occlusion condition (a) and the containment condition (b). Babies as young as $4\frac{1}{2}$ months looked longer at the unexpected test event in the occlusion condition, but it was not until babies were $7\frac{1}{2}$ months old that they looked longer at the unexpected test event in the containment condition.

Sources: Adapted from Baillargeon & Wang, 2002; Hespos & Baillargeon, 2001.

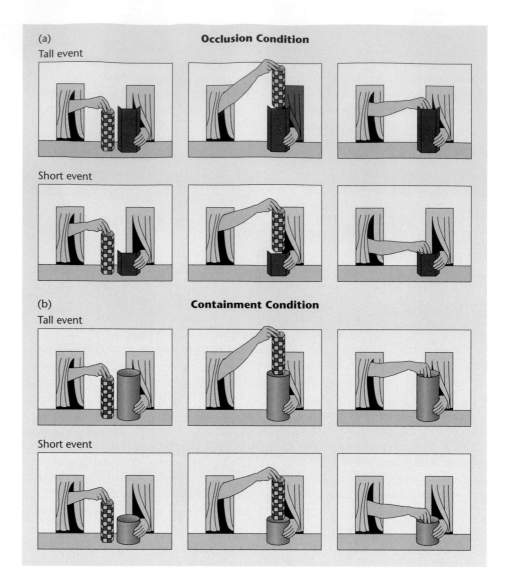

of the dots changed but the number of the dots remained the same. There were two learning conditions: Half of the infants saw 8 dots and half of the infants saw 16 dots. After the infants became habituated to the displays—that is, they had a decrease in their looking time—they were then shown a set of displays that alternated arrays with 8 dots and 16 dots. These were called the *test trials*. During the test trials, infants looked longer at the arrays that included the novel number of dots for their learning condition. That is, infants who were shown 8 dots in the learning trials looked longer at the 16 dot arrays in the test trials, and infants who were shown the 16 dots in the learning trials looked longer at the 8 dot arrays. The researchers interpret these results as evidence that the infants have a basic understanding of numerosity.

Together, these studies suggest that infants know more about the world than Piaget proposed. They also indicate that such early achievements develop over time. As Flavell and colleagues (Flavell, Miller, & Miller, 1993b, p. 62) point out, it is clear that "very young infants do not know all there is to know"! They achieve some skills at about 3 or 4 months of age and others when they're 6 or 7 months old. In addition, infants may learn general principles quite early but be unable for some time to grasp the subtleties of applying these principles. This argument proposes that infants are born with highly constrained learning mechanisms that guide the development of their reasoning about the physical world (Gelman & Williams, 1998). By "highly

Figure 8-3

Finding objects that have moved into a hidden space
When a ball rolled down a ramp and into one of the spaces behind the screen with the small doors, children had to open the door behind which they thought they'd find the ball. The movable barrier that protruded above the screen, and that stopped the ball's rolling, gave them a clue as to which door led to the ball.

Source: Berthier et al., 2000.

constrained" we mean that infants are, in a sense, constrained by the way they are biologically prepared to learn certain kinds of information or principles about the world. This theoretical position does not necessarily imply that the baby's understanding is innate but rather that infants' biological organization predisposes them to learn some critical features of their environment quite rapidly.

Currently, there is substantial interest among developmental psychologists in the general proposition that not all knowledge is the same and that some knowledge may be more fundamental and foundational to learning both early on and throughout life. In fact, this general claim is consistent with some of Piaget's main arguments. However, a number of researchers have criticized the studies that examine early understanding in infancy on several fronts. Some have argued that longer looking time indicates that the infant can discriminate between two events but it does not tell us why the infant looks longer at some information than at others. In other words, the reason behind the infant's longer looking remains unclear (Haith & Benson, 1998). Other psychologists have argued that perceptual processes rather than conceptual processes explain an infant's longer looking at an impossible event or changes in the number of objects in a display (Bogartz, Shinskey, & Schilling, 2000; Cashon, & Cohen, 2000; Rivera, Wakeley, & Langer, 1999).

Finally, other psychologists have discovered what appears to be a paradox in early conceptual development—namely that the knowledge identified in infants on tasks such as those just described is not clearly evident in children between 2 and 3 years of age (Keen, 2003). For instance, in one study toddlers were asked to find a ball after it rolled down a ramp and stopped behind a screen (Berthier, DeBlois, Poirier, Novak, & Clifton, 2000), as depicted in Figure 8-3. The ball could be stopped at any one of several locations behind the screen by a movable barrier that protruded above the screen, and therefore served as a cue as to where the ball had stopped. To find the ball, the child opened one of the small doors that were in the screen. Children under 3 years of age were unsuccessful at finding the ball. Moreover, adaptations to the apparatus, such as making the small doors transparent, did not help 2-year-olds perform any better on this task (Butler, Berthier, & Clifton, 2002). However, with this additional information, $2\frac{1}{2}$-year-olds performed better than they had with the opaque doors.

How can the differences between the infant performance described in the research above, and the toddlers' performance in these studies be explained? Keen (2003) suggests that these differences may be due to differences in the task demands and the thinking that these different types of tasks require of the children. In addition, Keen points out that in order to solve some of these problems, children need not only to have knowledge of the solidity or continuity of objects, but they also need to know how to solve problems related to objects, such as searching for objects when they are displaced. Searching for objects requires that the child understand how objects move and be able to create a plan that coordinates her own actions with her predictions about how the object will move. In other words, exactly what young children understand about objects at different ages, how this understanding develops, and when and how children are able to use objects to carry out their own goal-directed actions are questions for future research. As these criticisms suggest, this new direction of research has introduced a lively and provocative debate to the study of infant cognition.

Researchers are uncertain about exactly how infants attain knowledge of the physical world and about what mechanisms equip the infant to demonstrate the remarkable feats we've discussed. Clearly, we need to revise our views of what infants know and how early they know it. It is also clear that the account of infant cognition outlined in Piaget's six sensorimotor substages cannot explain many of the recent findings of early infant capabilities. Moreover, Piaget's use of motor activity as a gauge of the infant's understanding of physical concepts seems to have led him to underestimate the infant's cognitive abilities (Flavell et al., 1993b). Recent discoveries notwithstanding, although Piaget did not capture the entirety of the young infant's cognitive capacities, there is no question that he was a pioneer in providing the first description of the sequence of how the infant achieves and modifies cognitive understanding. Moreover, the little cross-cultural research that has been done on the sensorimotor stage supports Piaget's general framework. Longitudinal research conducted with Baoulé children between 6 and 30 months of age in Côte d'Ivoire revealed the same six substages Piaget described (Dasen, Inhelder, Lavallée, & Retschitzki, 1978).

The Preoperational Stage

The major characteristic of the **preoperational stage** is the child's development of the **symbolic function,** or the ability to use symbols, such as words, images, and gestures, to represent objects and events mentally. One of the preoperational child's major accomplishments is the acquisition of language. Language broadens the child's problem-solving abilities greatly and enables the child to learn from the verbalizations of other people. This ability to represent experience symbolically changes over the two substages of this stage, called the preconceptual and intuitive substages.

The Preconceptual Substage (2 to 4 Years)   In this substage, the emergence of symbolic capabilities is evident in children's rapid development of language, their great interest in imaginative play, and their increasing use of deferred imitation. Other important characteristics of children's thinking during the **preconceptual substage** are animistic thinking and egocentricity. The child who demonstrates **animistic thinking** tends to attribute life to inanimate objects. For example, the child may believe that plants feel pain when he picks their flowers or that the wind talks to his friends, the trees. In the following exchange between Piaget and a preconceptual child, the sun appears quite lifelike indeed:

Piaget: Does the sun move?

Child: Yes, when one walks it follows. When one turns around it turns around too. Doesn't it ever follow you too?

Piaget: Why does it move?

Child: Because when one walks, it goes too.

Piaget: Why does it go?

Child: To hear what we say.

Piaget: Is it alive?

Child: Of course, otherwise it wouldn't follow us, it couldn't shine. (Piaget, 1960, p. 215)

---

preoperational stage In this stage, the ability to use symbols facilitates the learning of language; this stage is also marked by semilogical reasoning, egocentricity—in which the child sees the world from her own point of view—and intuitive behavior, in which the child can solve problems using mental operations but cannot explain how she did so.

symbolic function The ability to use symbols, such as images, words, and gestures, to represent objects and events in the world.

preconceptual substage The first substage of Piaget's preoperational period, during which the child's thought is characterized by the emergence of *symbolic function,* the rapid development of language, animistic thinking, and egocentricity.

animistic thinking The attribution of life to inanimate objects.

Figure 8-4   Understanding different perspectives: Piaget's three-mountain test

We show Piaget's classic test, which used a tabletop model to represent three mountains. As the text discusses, contemporary researchers have found that young children can understand the perspectives of others, represented by dolls or imaginary people, better under a number of conditions: when the mountains look more realistic; when the children are allowed to rotate small models of the mountains; and when the reason for taking another's perspective is made more meaningful or sensible to children.

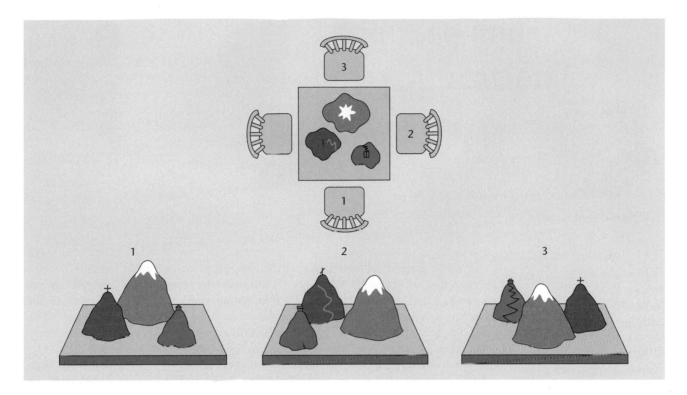

Just as Piaget's claims about the limitations on children's knowledge of object permanence have been questioned, so too has his hypothesis regarding animistic thought. For example, Bullock (1985) and others have pointed out that the objects Piaget used to test the limits of children's animistic thought, such as the sun, the moon, and the wind, are often open to magical interpretations. In contrast to Piaget's observations, Massey and Gelman (1988) found that when they used simple and familiar objects, children as young as 4 were quite good at deciding whether animate objects, such as mammals, or inanimate objects, such as statues, could move on their own.

Piaget's discussion with the preconceptual child about the sun reveals another characteristic of preconceptual thought: **egocentrism.** Children tend to view the world from their own perspective and to have difficulty seeing things from another person's point of view. For instance, notice in the foregoing dialogue that the sun follows the child, imitates the child's movements, and listens to the child.

To test the child's ability to see things from another person's perspective, Piaget designed what is known as the three-mountains test (see Figure 8-4). Models of three mountains of varying sizes are placed on a square table, and chairs are placed at all four sides of the table. The child is seated in one chair, and the experimenter places a doll in each of the other three chairs, one at a time, and each time asks the child to describe what the doll sees from the three different positions. The child may select one of a set of drawings or use cardboard cutouts of the mountains to construct the doll's views. Piaget found that preoperational children could not consistently identify the doll's view from each of the three locations. In fact, on this task Piaget found that children were not successful until later in the stage of concrete operations, when they were 9 or 10 years old.

egocentrism The tendency to view the world from one's own perspective and to have difficulty seeing things from another's viewpoint.

Figure 8-5   Another way to study children's perspective-taking abilities

In this model, Hughes devised four small rooms (A, B, C, and D) from among which a boy doll could choose a hiding place where the policeman doll, from various positions around the model, could not find him. Most children between 3½ and 5 years of age were able to provide correct answers to questions about this scenario.

Source: Donaldson, 1978.

Piaget's three-mountains task, and his interpretations of when children develop perspective taking skills, have been challenged by many researchers on several grounds. First, in his original test he used simple models of mountains that lacked salient characteristics by which one could differentiate one view from the next. Second, the task of reconstructing the display, or even of choosing the appropriate drawings, may be beyond the ability of a young child. And, third, choosing the correct perspective may simply not be an activity that makes sense to young children. Making two simple changes in Piaget's design, Borke (1975) obtained very different results: (1) The investigator placed familiar things, such as snowcaps, trees, or houses, on the sides of the mountains to make them more distinctive and (2) he asked children to rotate a small model of the display to present the appropriate view rather than reconstruct the display or choose from drawings. Children as young as 3 were then able to identify the correct perspective from each of the three different positions (also see Newcombe & Huttenlocher, 1992). Hughes (1975, cited in Donaldson, 1978) tackled another aspect of this task, changing the design by making the task more understandable to the children. Rather than having three mountains, he sat the children at a table on which there were two "walls" that intersected in a cross. Thus, there were four areas or corners of the table, each set off from each other by these walls (see Figure 8-5). Hughes then introduced two dolls, a boy doll and a policeman doll, and asked the child a series of questions about where the boy doll could hide so that the policeman could not find him. Children performed quite differently on this task than on Piaget's three-mountains task. Most of the children between 3½ and 5 years of age were able to provide correct answers to the questions. In fact, the 10 youngest children, whose average age was 3¾ years, had a success rate of 88 percent. These results suggest that when the task is made more accessible and comprehensible to children, they are able to perform much better than Piaget originally claimed.

intuitive substage The second substage of the preoperational stage during which the child begins to solve problems by using mental operations but cannot explain how she arrives at the solutions.

The Intuitive Substage (4 to 7 Years)   Piaget called the second substage of the preoperational stage "intuitive" because, although the child can employ certain mental operations, such as ways of classifying, quantifying, or relating objects, she does not seem to be aware of the underlying principles used in performing these operations. In other words, the child in the **intuitive substage** can solve problems with these operations but cannot explain why she solved them in a particular way. The preoperational child also has difficulty understanding part-whole relations, as illustrated in class-inclusion problems, such as the following: A child is given 7 toy dogs and 3 toy cats, a total of 10 animals. If the child is asked whether there are more dogs or more cats, he can answer correctly that there are more dogs. However, if the child is then asked if there are more dogs than there are animals, the child responds that there are more dogs. Piaget proposed that the child is responding incorrectly because he is unable to focus simultaneously on a part of the set of animals (the subset of dogs) and on the whole set of animals.

Developmentalists have criticized Piaget's research on part-whole relations, suggesting that the way he posed his questions confused young children. When Smith (1979) used simpler questions that still addressed children's ability to use part-whole relations, such as "A pug is a kind of dog, but it's not a shepherd. Is a pug an animal?" she found that children as young as 4 displayed knowledge of the part-whole relation between dogs and animals by correctly answering that a pug is an animal. Further research has shown that using collective terms such as *family* to describe a whole set (e.g., "Who would have more pets, someone who owned the baby dogs or someone who owned the whole family?") highlighted the part-whole relations between the objects and improved the performance of preschool children (Markman, 1973).

PREOPERATIONAL THOUGHT: SOME LIMITATIONS   The main limitation in preoperational thinking is that the child is semi-logical. We see one of the most vivid examples of semilogical thinking when preoperational children perform conservation tasks. To understand **conservation** the child must recognize that even when an object's appearance is altered in some way, the object's basic attributes or properties remain the same. For example, we present the child with two identical glasses, each of which contains the same amount of liquid. The liquid in these glasses is then poured into two other glasses of different sizes, such that one glass is tall and thin and the other glass is short and wide. The result of the pouring is that although the liquid remains the same quantity—nothing has spilled or been taken away—the water levels in the tall and short glasses are now different.

Two basic attributes of a physical object, in this case the liquid, are at issue here. One attribute pertains to the identity of the object, which is a qualitative property. To probe a child's understanding of identity in this example, we can ask her: Is the water in the different-shape glasses the same water that was in the two original glasses of the same shape? Preoperational children have no difficulty with this question and, therefore, understand *object identity,* a qualitative attribute of objects. The second attribute of a physical object that can be assessed is the quantity of the object—in this case, whether the amount of the liquid before and after the pouring is the same. Preoperational children have great difficulty with object quantity questions and respond that the amounts of liquid in each of the two different-shape glasses, though previously the same, are now different. Thus, these children can conserve the identity or quality but not the amount or quantity of objects—they are semilogical.

This semilogical pattern of reasoning among preoperational children has been demonstrated on a wide range of conservation tasks, such as those involving liquid, mass, volume, and area (see Figure 8-6). What

conservation The understanding that altering an object's or a substance's appearance does not change its basic attributes or properties.

This child's decision as to whether the two glasses hold equal amounts of colored water will reveal whether he's attained an understanding of the conservation of liquid.

Figure 8-6   Some Piagetian tests of conservation
These tests are discussed at further length in the text.

1. Number

Experimenter shows child two rows of plastic chips. Child agrees there are the same number of chips in each row.

Experimenter increases length of one row by adding space between chips (or by squeezing other row) and asks child whether each row still has the same number of chips.

2. Mass, or substance

Experimenter presents child with two identical balls of clay or plasticene. Child agrees that each has the same amount of clay.

Experimenter rolls one ball into breadstick or sausage form and asks child whether the two objects still have the same amount of clay.

3. Length

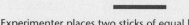

Experimenter places two sticks of equal length before child, who agrees they are of the same length.

Experimenter moves one of the sticks to the right and asks child whether sticks are still of the same length.

4. Liquids

Experimenter fills two glasses of the same size and shape to the same level with water. Child agrees each glass has the same amount of water.

Experimenter pours the water in one of the glasses into a taller, thinner glass and asks child if each glass with water in it now contains the same amount of water.

5. Area

Experimenter shows child two sheets of cardboard, on each of which square blocks are placed in identical positions. Child agrees that each sheet has the same amount of open (uncovered) area.

Experimenter then scatters the blocks about one of the cardboard sheets and asks child whether the two sheets now have the same amount of open area.

6. Weight

 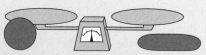

Experimenter places two balls of clay of the same size on a scale and asks the child if they weigh the same.

Experimenter then reshapes one ball and, before replacing it on the scale, asks the child if the two pieces of clay still weigh the same or if one weighs more.

7. Volume

Experimenter drops each of two balls of clay of the same size into two glasses of water; the child has already agreed that the glasses have the same amount of water.

Experimenter removes one piece of clay, reshapes it, and, before putting it back into the glass, asks the child if the water level will be higher or lower than or the same as the water level in the other glass.

Source: Based on Lefrancois, 1973.

processes of reasoning may lead the child to make this error in judgment? She has witnessed the experimenter pouring the same quantity of water from one container to another, or she has seen the investigator simply changing the shape of an object, such as forming clay into a ball or a sausage. Piaget proposed that preoperational children's semilogical reasoning is explained by three characteristics: the inability to grasp the notion of reversibility, the tendency to focus on the end state of an action or a task rather than the means to this end state, and centration, which is closely related to egocentrism.

The child's inability to understand **reversibility** means that the child cannot mentally reverse or undo an action. For example, preoperational children presented with the liquid-conservation task that we have outlined do not reason that if the water in the tall, thin glass is poured back into the short, wide glass it will reach the same height it had before. This *inability to reverse a series of mental steps* manifests itself in many other responses of the child between 2 and 6 years old. For example, an investigator asks a 4-year-old boy,

"Have you a brother?"

The child replies, "Yes."

"What's his name?"

"Jim."

"Does Jim have a brother?"

"No." (Phillips, 1969, p. 61)

The preoperational thinker also tends to have an **ends over means focus**—that is, the child focuses on the end states rather than the means by which the end states were obtained. In particular, he tends to overlook the process or transformation by which the change occurs. Again, in the liquid-conservation task, the preoperational child ignores both the experimenter's action of pouring the water from one glass to the other and the rising water level in the glass. Instead, the child focuses on the end state of the process—that is, the high water level in the tall container that now appears different from the water level in the short container.

Finally, **centration** in thinking leads preoperational children to center their attention, or focus, on only one dimension of an object or situation. In our test example, children base their reasons for why they think the amount of water in the containers is no longer equal on either the height of the water or the width of the glass. This tendency to attend to only one attribute of what one observes and to ignore multiple aspects of the problem prevents the child from grasping the notion of conservation, which involves several changes simultaneously.

Experimenters have studied children's understanding of conservation using many substances (see Figure 8-6). According to Piaget, it is the *order* in which children acquire these concepts that is important, and this order is what remains the same among all children. So regardless of the age at which a child understands the conservation of weight, she will always achieve an understanding of the conservation of area and volume later on. Cross-cultural studies have found considerable variation in the age at which children acquire the concept of conservation fully, and variation in the ages at which they acquire this concept with respect to various substances (Mishra, 1997; Rogoff, 2003). In Western societies, in general, children achieve conservation of liquids, mass, and length sometime between the ages of 6 and 7; they can conserve number a little earlier, by about age 6. Grasping the notions of the conservation of weight, area, and volume takes somewhat longer, emerging, respectively, at about age 9, between 9 and 10, and after age 11. Cultural variation in the onset of these particular conservation abilities has been found, and such varied findings have been linked to the values these particular abilities have in different communities (Dasen, 1975; Gardiner & Kosmitzki, 2005). For example, children who live in communities in Mexico in which pottery making by adults is important develop conservation of mass earlier than

reversibility The understanding that the steps of a procedure or operation can be reversed and that the original state of the object or event can be obtained.

ends over means focus Consideration of only the end state of a problem in evaluating an event; failure to consider the means by which that end state was obtained.

centration Focusing one's attention on only one dimension or characteristic of an object or situation.

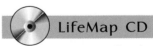

LifeMap CD

To see some Piagetian conservation experiments in action, watch the video "Development of Concept of Conservation" in Chapter 8 of your CD.

children who do not live in such communities (Price-Williams, Gordon, & Ramirez, 1969). Although only moderate differences in the acquisition of specific conservation abilities have been found (Newman et al., 1983; Rogoff, 1990), such differences raise interesting questions about the connection between cultural values and practices and the development of cognitive skills (Goodnow, Miller, & Kessel, 1995).

HORIZONTAL DÉCALAGE: VARIATION WITHIN A STAGE

horizontal décalage The term Piaget used to describe unevenness in children's thinking within a particular stage; for example, in developing an understanding of conservation children conserve different objects or substances at different ages.

Given that Piaget argued that his stages were organized or structured ways by which children understand the world, does the fact that children do not acquire the ability to conserve all types of substances at the same age present problems for this theory? In other words, if children develop the logical abilities to perform one type of conservation task, shouldn't they, from the perspective of a stage theory, be able to perform all such tasks? Piaget recognized this inconsistency in the appearance of conservation abilities and called this phenomenon **horizontal décalage** (the French word *décalage* can be translated as "time lag"). Piaget proposed that this unevenness in children's cognitive achievements at given ages reflects the differing degrees of abstraction required to understand the conservation of particular objects or substances. For example, he suggested that conserving mass requires the fewest abstract operations, whereas conserving volume requires the most; as a result, conservation of mass is acquired earlier. Although the notion of horizontal décalage is interesting, it does not explain the deeper question of how this gradual type of change can be reconciled with Piaget's stage approach.

By looking at the child's specific conservation skills more closely, many other studies (e.g., Gelman, 1990; Halford, 1990; Sugarman, 1987) have found that Piaget underestimated the young child's ability to conserve. For instance, Rochel Gelman (1972) explored Piaget's claim that children do not conserve number until they are 6 years old. Piaget had shown children two rows of objects, each row containing the same number of objects spaced at equal intervals. After the children responded that both rows contained the same number of objects, Piaget changed the appearance of one row by increasing (or decreasing) the space between the objects; he again asked the children if the two rows had the same number. Preoperational children replied that the transformed row contained more (or fewer) objects than the other.

Gelman designed a simpler conservation task called "the magic mice paradigm," and tested children younger than 6. In one study she showed a 3-year-old child two plates; one contained three toy mice, the other contained two. Then Gelman covered both plates and asked the child to pick one plate and identify it as either the "winner" or the "loser"; she did not mention number. Across a number of trials the plate with the three mice was consistently identified as the "winner," and the experimenter gave children a prize every time they correctly identified the winner. Once the child had come to recognize the three-mouse plate as the winner, the experimenter surreptitiously altered the winning plate by either decreasing the number of mice on the plate to two, or changed the spacing of the mice to match the two-mouse plate (i.e., the three mice were pushed closer together). Gelman found that when the mice had merely been pushed closer together on a plate, children as young as 3 years of age could still correctly identify it as the "winning" plate, suggesting they had conserved the number of the mice over a superficial transformation. Gelman's results directly contradicted the prediction made by Piaget that the children would not conserve number simply because the objects, the mice in this case, were pushed closer together. It appears that children can conserve number at a far younger age than Piaget had hypothesized.

These findings, along with many others, suggest that if we present children with simpler or more accessible versions of conservation tasks or teach them to attend to all the relevant aspects of the stimuli being presented, they can often demonstrate their understanding of conservation. This lesson has been made particularly clear in cross-cultural research. In the study in Mexico of the children of potters, mentioned previously, those children who initially performed poorly on conservation tasks that were conducted with materials unfamiliar to them went on to perform quite well on a test of conservation of mass when they were dealing with familiar materials, such as the clay and other substances used in making pottery (Price-Williams et al., 1969).

To test the notion that failure to conserve may occur because the child attends to some irrelevant aspect of the stimulus, such as shape, length, or height, Jerome Bruner (1966) presented preoperational children with a modification of Piaget's liquid-conservation task. As the experimenters poured the water from the short glass to the tall glass, they placed a screen in front of the tall glass; thus, although the children could see them pouring water from the short glass, they could not see the changing water level in the tall glass. When the distracting changes in the height and width of the water column were not visible to the children, most were able to conserve, recognizing that the same amount of liquid must be in the container.

In sum, the evidence suggests that Piaget was probably right about the timing of the acquisition of conservation for some tasks. However, if a task is simplified or made more comprehensible, children can conserve at earlier ages than Piaget suspected.

The Stage of Concrete Operations

Piaget described dramatic changes in the characteristics of children's thinking during the **concrete operations stage,** which extends from about the age of 7 to the age of 11 or 12. At this time, children become more flexible in their thinking, owing to an increased understanding of reversibility and a greater ability to attend to more than one dimension of a problem at a time. Logic and objectivity increase, and children begin to think deductively. They are able to conserve quantity and to classify or group things in a logical way. However, their thinking at this point is tied to concrete reality—that is, they can often solve problems only if the objects necessary for problem solution are physically present. For example, suppose we present a child with three children of varying heights in differently composed pairs. In pair 1, the child sees that Melissa is taller than Zoe, and in pair 2 she sees that Zoe is taller than Fabiana. Without seeing Melissa and Fabiana together, the child can reason that Melissa is taller than both Zoe and Fabiana. If, however, instead of presenting the three girls physically, we present the problem to our participant verbally, as "Melissa is taller than Zoe and Zoe is taller than Fabiana; who is the tallest of the three?" the concrete operational child will have difficulty solving the problem based on verbal information alone.

Children also make marked advances in the ability to classify objects during the concrete operations stage. The preoperational child gradually acquires the ability to classify on a consistent basis, by characteristics such as size, shape, or color. In contrast, the concrete operational child can sort objects according to more complicated combinations of their attributes. For example, the child can sort a group of flowers into a major class and a subclass: yellow roses, yellow tulips, yellow daisies, red roses, red tulips, and red daisies. Concrete operational children become able to understand such multiple classifications even when they must make subtle distinctions on the relevant dimensions, such as differentiating between shades of yellow or different types of daisies. Moreover, they are able to ignore irrelevant features such as number or size of petals (Fischer & Roberts, 1986).

Again, developmentalists have questioned whether the solution of such problems is based on the underlying changes in mental operations that Piaget proposed. Some investigators have suggested that in tests of inference, such as judging the relative length of several sticks based only on a verbal statement, what poses difficulty for the concrete operational child is not the lack of physical stimuli but the lack of memory capacity. If children could be trained to remember the rather complicated components of this problem, these researchers propose, perhaps they could solve it even without

concrete operations stage
Stage in which the child is able to reason logically about materials that are physically present.

the physical presence of the sticks. Bryant and Trabasso (1971) did exactly this and demonstrated that when procedures ensure that children can remember the information about the problem they are given, concrete operational children can make logical inferences without having to have the physical materials present.

Although Piaget held that the ability to classify develops during the preoperational and concrete operational periods, we now have evidence that even infants can place objects into categories based on perceptual similarities. Researchers have shown that babies as young as 3 to 4 months old can form categories of animals that include dogs and cats but exclude birds, or categories that include cats and lions while excluding dogs (Eimas, 1994; Eimas, Quinn, & Cowen, 1994; Haith & Benson, 1998; Quinn, Cummins, Kase, Martin, & Weissman, 1996). Infants as young as 3 months of age have been found to categorize animals and vehicles based on perceptual similarities, and also based on different types of motion—for example, motion of a dog versus motion of a car (Arterberry & Bornstein, 2001). Apparently children can classify objects at a much earlier age and in a more sophisticated fashion than Piaget believed possible.

Finally, we should note that researchers who have undertaken cross-cultural studies of Piagetian concepts, especially understanding associated with concrete operations, have generally demonstrated the importance of culture in determining what concepts will be learned and when. Box 8.1, pp. 342–343, not only illuminates this notion but points out that intelligence itself may be defined differently in different societies.

The Stage of Formal Operations

formal operations stage
Stage in which the child becomes capable of abstract thinking, complex reasoning, and hypothesis testing.

In the concrete operations stage, the child begins to build the foundation of logical thinking. How do thought processes in the **formal operations stage,** which begins at age 11 or 12, differ from those typical of the concrete operations stage? Perhaps the most significant changes are those in flexibility of thought, in the use of mental hypothesis testing, in the ability to entertain many possible alternatives for the solution of problems, and in the ability to think about thinking (Kuhn & Franklin, 2006).

One particularly interesting change in thinking that appears in adolescence is the ability to think of and contrast both real and ideal states of the world. Adolescents can think about abstract problems that are not based in reality. That is, they realize that logical rules can be applied to ideas even if these ideas violate reality. For example, consider the problem, "If all blue people live in red houses, are all people who live in red houses blue?" The concrete operational child would have difficulty getting beyond the fact that there is no such thing as blue people. In contrast, the child in the formal operations stage can move beyond the unrealistic content to focus on applying logical solutions to the question posed. Children in this stage are also able to review several possible alternatives or hypotheses in a problem-solving situation. They can consider different ways of arranging the world, they can think about and discuss philosophical issues such as truth and justice, and they can imagine alternative lifestyles and universes—hence, this is the stage when science fiction becomes of interest.

An example from a task used by Inhelder and Piaget (1958) illustrates the differences between children in the two stages. In this task, participants are presented with an assortment of objects and a container of water and asked to use these materials to find an explanation for why some objects float and others do not. What the children are actually being asked is to derive Archimedes' law of floating bodies, which states that an object will float if its weight per unit (or density) is less than that of water. Thus, if two objects are of equal weight, the larger object is more likely to float than the smaller object. Concrete operational children may focus on weight or size as a reason why things float or sink—for instance, they may say that the heavier or bigger objects are more likely to sink. They may even arrive at a double classification that involves the categories large and heavy, large and light, small and heavy, or small and light. However, they are still unable to consider alternatives not directly observable in the physical world. For example, they cannot predict that a large and heavy piece of wood will float even though it is bigger and heavier than a small lead weight.

In contrast, in the formal operations stage, the child can free herself from the obvious cues of weight and size and conceptualize a variety of possible alternatives to arrive at the concept of density. Piaget describes the comments of a child who has just entered the period of formal operations grappling with this kind of problem: "It sinks because it is small, it isn't stretched enough. You would have to have something larger to stay at the surface, something of the same weight and which would have a greater extension" (Inhelder and Piaget, 1958, p. 38).

Developmentalists continue to debate Piaget's notions about cognitive development in this last stage and to search for the best ways to describe the child's thinking at this time (Keating, 1990; Kuhn & Franklin, 2006; Overton & Byrnes, 1991). Actually, not all adolescents or, for that matter, all adults, in all societies reach the stage of formal operations and achieve the flexibility in problem solving that Piaget associated with this period (Kuhn & Franklin, 2006). Unlike concrete operational thought, which seems to be acquired to some degree in all societies, the attainment of formal operations is strongly influenced by culture (Moshman, 1998; Rogoff, 2003; Shweder et al., 1998). In groups that do not emphasize symbolic skills or in which educational experiences are limited, the stage of formal operations may occur late in development or may even be absent (Moshman, 1998). Even in Western communities in which symbolic skills and educational attainment are highly valued and available, adolescents and adults are more likely to achieve the capacity for logical abstract reasoning within their particular areas of interest or expertise than in other domains. For instance, abstract thinking has been documented in traditional cultures in tasks of much importance to the group, such as court cases (Jahoda, 1980), land disputes (Hutchins, 1980), and navigating on the open seas (Gladwin, 1971). In addition, scientific training in such subjects as physics, chemistry, and the philosophy of logic has been found to be associated with greater ability to use formal operations. Thus, formal operational thinking is strongly tied to social and cultural experiences.

Piagetian Concepts and Social Cognition

Although Piaget was interested in the individual's cognitive development and paid little attention to the child's evolving social awareness and behavior, a number of his important conceptions bear on social cognition and have stimulated research in this area. His concept of object permanence, for example, has relevance for the development of self-recognition—conceiving of the self as an entity distinct from the environment and from others—and the development of attachment, or a continuing and emotionally meaningful connection to another person. Piaget's views on egocentrism and on developmental changes in egocentric thought also have implications for the development of social cognition. Recently, researchers have investigated the development of children's understanding of mental processes and of the mind itself, referred to as *theory of mind* (Harris, 2006). Because understanding of the self and others has tremendous consequences for children's social functioning, we discuss it here.

THE SELF AS DISTINCT FROM OTHERS A central process in the development of social cognition is differentiation of the self from the nonself; that is, of the self from the environment—including other human beings, nonhuman beings, and objects in that environment (Harter, 2006). This differentiation process has its roots in early infancy: Even young babies seem to expect certain responses from people. For example, if you face a 2-month-old child without moving or speaking, the infant will become distressed (Tronick, 1989). Babies also learn to expect and use

Box 8.1

Perspectives on Diversity

CULTURE AND THE DEVELOPMENT OF COGNITIVE SKILLS

According to many theorists (e.g., Cole, 2006; Rogoff, 2003; Shweder et al., 1998), cognitive competence is culturally relative. Therefore, an individual's cognitive skills must be assessed in the context of the culture in which she develops. Moreover, if we define intelligence as adaptation to the environment, as did Piaget, it is not surprising that paths of cognitive development will diverge in cultures with different environments, expectations, and needs. Competence in any particular cognitive skill and the timing of when certain cognitive abilities are emphasized in a child's development are directly linked to culture. Thus we cannot take the measure of any specific task—such as object permanence or conservation—as indicative of a child's (or adult's) level of cognitive advancement, for some cultures emphasize the need to learn certain kinds of concepts while others stress other kinds. Even when cultures emphasize similar concepts, the timing of this emphasis—in terms of when opportunities are provided for children that support the development of these skills—may vary.

Pierre Dasen (1984) has examined the evidence for these claims. Comparing the performance of children of two very different cultures on tasks measuring their understanding of the conservation of liquids and of horizontality (the latter requires the child to understand that when a vessel containing a liquid is tilted at various angles the surface plane of the water will always be horizontal), Dasen found interesting differences. Whereas 90 percent of Inuit children, of Cape Dorset (in Canada's Northwest Territories), understood horizontality by the age of 8 (100% by age 12), only 60 percent grasped the conservation of liquids even by the age of 15 (see Figure 8-7a). In contrast, only 50 percent of Baoulé children, of Côte d'Ivoire, got the idea of horizontality by age 15, but 100 percent had an understanding of the conservation of liquids by the age of 10 (Figure 8-7b). Commenting on these results, Dasen suggests that people value and develop "those skills and concepts that are useful in the daily activities required" in their ecocultural settings. The Inuit, who are nomadic hunter-gatherers, value spatial skills and as a result acquire ideas like horizontality quite quickly, but they have less interest in quantitative comparisons. The Baoulé, on the other hand, are an agricultural people who, because they produce food, store it, and exchange it in the markets, assign considerable value to quantitative concepts, especially those concepts involved in measurement.

In further exploration of this notion that cognitive skills or intelligence vary among cultures, Dasen asked Baoulé adults (who were illiterate) to list the skills that they most valued in their children. The resulting compilation reflected a balance of social skills, on the one hand, and cognitive or more technological skills, on the other. In their view, the most important attribute of the intelligent child was the readiness to carry out tasks in the service of the family and the community. This included initiative, or performing a task without being asked, as well as competence, honesty, and responsibility. The second most often mentioned quality embodied respect for elders, politeness, and obedience. Many qualities that rank highly in U.S. concepts of intelligence, such as fast learning, observational skills, attention, memory, literacy, school intelligence, and manual dexterity were also included in the list, but even these abilities were seen as valuable only when they were put into the service of the social group.

In addition to differences in the acquisition of specific concepts and skills, cultures may vary in their overall approach to acquiring knowledge and understanding. For instance, Tharp (1994) explored differences between Native American and European American children with respect to the cognitive dimension of holistic versus analytic thinking. In holistic thought, the parts or units of something—such as a family or a group of people or ways of understanding or using a set of objects—get their meaning from the larger system to which they belong, that is, from their relation to the overall pattern. Analytic thinking emphasizes how the whole can be broken into units or parts, and these parts can be examined separately to reach some understanding of the whole. According to Tharp, Native Americans are more likely to think holistically, whereas European Americans think more analytically. Moreover, opportunities for children to develop cognitive skills in these respective communities reflect these different approaches to thinking. For example, when Yukon elders prepared a 16-week plan for teaching children how to make moccasins of caribou skin, they began with preparations for the hunt; moccasins did not appear until the 15th week. To their way of thinking, "it is not possible to understand the moccasin outside the

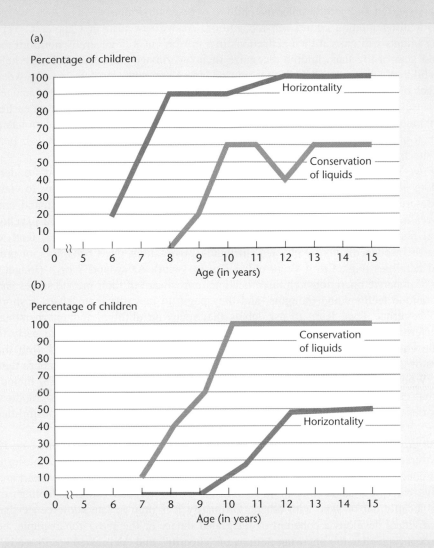

Figure 8-7

Conservation among Inuit and Baoulé children

Achievement of the concepts of horizontality and the conservation of liquids between the ages of 6 and 15 among (a) Inuit children of the Canadian Northwest Territories and (b) Baoulé children of Côte d'Ivoire.

Source: From *International Journal of Psychology, 19* (1984). Dasen, P. R., "The cross-cultural study of intelligence: Piaget and the Baoulé," p. 410. International Union of Psychological Science. Reprinted by permission of Psychology Press. http://www.psypress.co.uk/journals.asp.

context of the leather, which is not understandable outside the spiritual relationship of the caribou to the land" (Tharp, 1994, p. 90). If European Americans had prepared this plan, Tharp suggests, they would probably have given the children the pattern and the tools to cut the leather in the first 15 minutes.

The holistic thinker needs to understand the entire *context* of the thing he is attempting to understand, and this may mean understanding several levels of context. In the preceding example, the moccasin must be seen in the context of the leather of which it is to be made, the leather must be seen in the context of the caribou from which it comes, and the caribou must be seen in the context of the land it inhabits and with which it interacts. This approach leads to an emphasis on observational learning and, often, superior visual and spatial skills are a result. It may also lead, however, to difficulties for children raised in one culture when they must attend school and prepare to work and function socially in a culture in which a different cognitive style is dominant.

As these studies suggest, culture alters not only the *rate* at which children learn but the *ways* in which they learn as well. At the very least, the dominant culture needs to understand the cultural-historical background of the children it seeks to educate, so that no child is considered unintelligent or unteachable because of her cognitive style.

responses from other people to guide their own behavior, as in the process of social referencing. As we saw in Chapter 6, when a young child encounters an unfamiliar person, he may look to his mother to see how she responds to the stranger. If she appears relaxed and comfortable, the child may respond similarly.

With differentiation comes self-recognition. As we saw also in Chapter 6, very young infants will gaze at their reflections in a mirror, but it is generally not until the second year of life that children recognize their own images in a mirror. Piaget held that children achieve a full understanding of object permanence some time between the ages of $1\frac{1}{2}$ and 2 years, about the same time that they first see their mirror images as themselves. The fact that developmentalists have now found evidence of an earlier understanding of object permanence does not necessarily alter the relationship between object permanence and self-recognition; it may be that the former is a prerequisite for the latter.

As we will see in the next section, developmental changes in the child's understanding of herself seem to parallel developments in the way the child begins to view and describe others. The child's view of herself becomes more differentiated and involves more descriptions of values, motives, intentions, and other internal psychological phenomena as she grows older. Preschool children (5 or younger) tend to define themselves mainly by physical attributes, possessions, overt behaviors, or preferred activities (e.g., I'm 4 years old; I like to swim). At around 7 or 8 (Piaget's stage of concrete operations) children become more aware of their private selves and their unique feelings and thoughts, and they begin to describe themselves in more complex terms. They learn to use labels that focus on abilities and interpersonal characteristics, such as *smart, dumb, nice,* and *mean* (Harter, 2006). From early to middle childhood, children's self-constructs become increasingly aligned with the values of their cultural community, such as in terms of the roles and preferences they have. Whereas European American children tend to report autobiographical memories that emphasize their own roles, preferences, and feelings, the autobiographical memories of Chinese children tend to emphasize social roles and responsibilities (Wang, 2004).

The growing ability to think in the abstract allows the adolescent (from 11 or 12 on) to create a more integrated view of the self. For example, a young adolescent might conceive of himself as intelligent by combining the qualities of being smart and creative but at the same time think of himself as an "airhead," linking feelings of being socially out of sync with others. Ordinarily it is only in late adolescence that the individual develops a coherent or integrated theory of the self—for example, he may reconceptualize the opposing notions of "cheerful" and "depressed" as "moody," thus resolving apparent contradictions in his sense of self (Harter, 2006).

ROLE TAKING: UNDERSTANDING OTHERS' PERSPECTIVES

With development, children become less egocentric and more able to understand the thoughts and perspectives of others. And instead of viewing others in terms of observable attributes and traits, children come to appreciate people's more abstract and psychological characteristics such as emotions, motives, and intentions (Yuill & Pearson, 1998). The biggest increase in such psychological description of others occurs in middle childhood, around the age of 8. But it is not until adolescence or early adulthood that people become aware of the full complexity of human thoughts, feelings, and intentions or grasp the idea that behavioral characteristics may vary with situations or internal states (Flavell & Miller, 1998; Harter, 2006). For example, here is how a 16-year-old boy described his brother:

> My kid brother . . . loves to be with people. . . . Most of the time he's good-natured and a lot of fun . . . but when we play soccer . . . he can't keep up with teenagers [and] he gets mad when he loses the ball. . . . Later I've found him crying in his room . . . he gets so frustrated he can't help it. It's tough being the youngest.

Table 8-3

Role taking: Developing the ability to take different perspectives

Source: Adapted from Selman & Jacquette, 1978.

Stage 0 Egocentric Perspective

The child does not distinguish his own perspective from that of others nor recognize that another person may interpret experiences differently.

Stage 1 Differentiated Perspective

The child realizes that she and others may have either the same or a different perspective. Although she is concerned with the uniqueness of each person's cognitions, she can't judge accurately what the other person's perspective may be.

Stage 2 Reciprocal Perspective

Because the child can see himself from another's perspective and knows the other person can do the same thing, he can anticipate and consider another's thoughts and feelings.

Stage 3 Mutual Perspectives

Now the child can view her own perspective, a peer's perspective, and their shared, or mutual perspective, from the viewpoint of a third person. For example, she can think of how a parent, teacher, or other peer might view both her and her friend's perspectives as well as their mutual perspective.

Stage 4 Societal or In-Depth Perspectives

Children (and adults) can see networks of perspectives, such as the societal, Republican, or African American point of view. People understand that these varying perspectives not only exist in awareness but involve deeper, perhaps unconscious representations, such as feelings and values.

Some developmentalists argue that the shift away from an egocentric orientation underlies improved communication skills as well as the development of moral standards and empathic understanding of and concern for others (Eisenberg, Fabes, & Spinrad, 2006; Harter, 2006). The development of these abilities is basic to the child's socialization, and we will return to this topic in greater detail later, in Chapter 14. Here it will be useful to consider the role of perspective taking proposed by Selman and his colleagues (Selman, 1980; Selman & Byrne, 1974; Selman & Jacquette, 1978), in which this decentering process goes through five distinct stages (see Table 8-3). These stages begin with the child's egocentric behavior and then proceed into more complex social understanding and social consideration in children's reasoning ability. As children move through these stages, they learn not only to differentiate between their own perspectives and those of others but to understand others' views and the relations between these views and their own.

Although there are normative patterns in the development of perspective taking, some people develop greater abilities at social role taking or, as Figure 8-8 indicates, attain these abilities earlier than others. What kinds of factors contribute, or are related to, individual differences in role-taking abilities? Performance on standard intelligence tests shows a modest relation to social role-taking ability (Shantz, 1983), and, as we discuss in Chapter 14, some studies have found positive relations between prosocial behavior, such as helping and sharing, and role-taking skills. For example, Eisenberg and her colleagues (Eisenberg, 1992; Eisenberg, et. al, 2006) found that laboratory measures of role taking correlated with how often children engaged in altruistic behaviors—such as offers of help and responsible suggestions to other children—on the playground and in the classroom.

THEORY OF MIND There has been much interest recently among researchers in when and how children come to understand the mind and how it works. This area

Figure 8-8   Role taking at different ages

Between the ages of 4 and 6, children shift from an egocentric perspective to a more differentiated one. From here on, progress in appreciating others' views is less dramatic but steady.

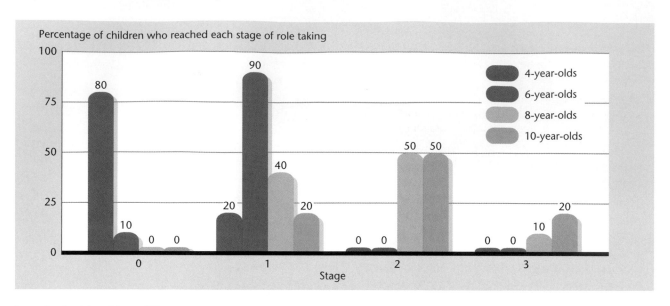

Source: Based on Selman & Byrne, 1974.

theory of mind Understanding of the mind and how it works.

of study, known as **theory of mind,** covers topics ranging from the development of the ability to distinguish appearance from reality to children's understanding of dreams, beliefs, intentions, desires, and deception (Harris, 2006). Researchers are also interested in when and how children come to think of the self and other people as psychological beings.

Much of the research on this topic has concentrated on children's performance on tasks that ask them to understand the thinking of other people. One common task, called a *false-belief task* (Wimmer & Perner, 1983), involves telling a child a story and then asking him what a character in the story thinks. For example, an investigator might tell a child a story in which a young boy named Maxi puts his candy in a cupboard in the kitchen and goes into another room to play. When Maxi is off playing, his mother moves his candy from the cupboard to a drawer. After a while, Maxi returns and wants his candy. At this point, the researcher would ask the child where Maxi will look for his candy. Older preschoolers, 4- to 5-year-old children, typically say that Maxi will search in the cupboard, indicating that they assume that Maxi will look where he believes the candy is, not where they themselves know the candy to be. In other words, they attribute a belief, or mental state, to Maxi and use this belief as a basis for their response. To answer in this way, the child needs to hold two understandings or representations of the situation in his mind simultaneously: what the child himself knows to be true and what Maxi believes to be true.

Three-year-old children respond quite differently. Unlike the older children, the 3-year-olds focus on the real situation, not on Maxi's mental state, and say that Maxi will look for the candy in the drawer where his mother put it. In other words, the child has a belief about where the candy is that is incorrect or false. These results suggest that our understanding of mental states, and the role these states play in guiding behavior, develops over the years of early childhood. This basic pattern of results has been replicated in a wide range of studies (Wellman, Cross, & Watson, 2001). However, the findings may not be as robust as they once seemed to be, and some researchers have contested both the results and their interpretation (Mitchell, 1997). Some investigators have also pointed out that there may be a difference between the development of a theory of mind in relation to fictional information, as in dreams and pretend play, and the development of an understanding of kinds or states of knowledge, such as false beliefs (Lillard, 1993). At present, it appears that this complex intellectual capability originates early in life, it exists in almost all people—the main exception being children with autism—and it does not seem to exist in other primates (Lillard, 1998; Povinelli & Giambrone, 2001; Sigman & Capps, 1997). It seems that human beings have a special ability to identify with other human beings as mental agents with needs, desires, and intentions that guide their behavior. The potential for interacting with, and learning from, others that this capability makes possible is profound (Harris, 2006; Tomasello, 1999).

Most research on children's theory of mind has been conducted with children in Western, middle-class communities in which discussions about the mind, its uses, and what people think are common. Children in Western middle-class communities are not only privy to conversations about the mind from an early age, but parents encourage them to participate in these conversations. Parents often ask children what they are thinking about, what other people believe, and about all kinds of mentalistic constructs such as dreams and imaginary friends. In addition to parents, siblings may also play a role in this developmental process. Perner, Ruffman, and Leekam (1994) showed that young children who have more siblings with whom they interact perform better on false-belief tasks. However, the ages of the siblings matter. Children with nontwin siblings performed better on theory of mind tasks than children who were twins and had no other siblings (Cassidy, Fineberg, Brown, & Perkins, 2005).

Are changes in children's understanding of mind universal—that is, do these changes appear in all cultures? Avis and Harris (1991) conducted a study of children's reasoning about people's beliefs and desires in the Baka community, hunter-gatherers who live in central Africa. These researchers found that by 5 years of age, most of the children they studied were able to predict correctly what an adult would find in a container that they had left for a moment and that, while they were gone, had been emptied. These results are consistent with other findings that show successful performance by preschool-age children in non-Western communities on theory of mind tasks (Vinden, 1996). This does not mean that social and cultural experiences do not contribute in important ways to this development—they do, and variation both within and across cultures in the development of theory of mind have been shown (Lillard, 1998). However, what is clear from this research is that during childhood an important set of capabilities known as theory of mind develops and that human social experiences around the world support this process.

EVALUATION OF PIAGET'S THEORY

Despite the importance of Piaget's theory for our understanding of children's thinking at different points in the child's development, his theory has come under criticism from many developmentalists. Some of these criticisms were mentioned earlier in relation to the particular stage of development to which they apply. Now we consider the strengths of Piaget's theory more generally and offer an overall assessment.

Strengths of the Theory

As we noted in Chapter 1, theories are useful for two reasons: They integrate and give meaning to a wide array of information, and they lead to new research by stimulating hypotheses and providing direction into new areas of exploration. Piaget's theory achieved both of these goals. With his stage model and his underlying concepts such as schemata, cognitive organization, and adaptation, Piaget integrated a broad spectrum of issues regarding concepts of the physical world—such as conservation, classification, and number—into a single, coherent theory. In addition, Piaget's theory has stimulated an enormous amount of research. According to Miller (2002), the most important ideas that Piaget introduced to the field are the following:

Children actively seek and construct knowledge

Development follows an invariant sequence

Errors are informative and may provide important clues about developmental patterns in children's thinking

Cognitive development, particularly in the first two years, does not depend on language; the child's perceptual-motor systems provide important routes to knowledge

Piaget's astute observations produced some surprises that still intrigue—and in some cases perplex—developmental psychologists. Why do infants behave as if objects disappear when they go out of sight? Why do preschoolers not conserve the quantities of substances when their shapes or appearances are altered? Why is it that school-age children can think logically about problems, even difficult problems, but when these problems are abstract (concrete materials are not available), they cannot use their skills at logical thought?

Did Piaget Judge the Child's Abilities Accurately?

A great deal of current work has suggested that infants and children may know a lot more than Piaget thought. In other words, Piaget may have underestimated the timing or onset of children's cognitive abilities. Our earlier discussion of infants' remarkable cognitive achievements, such as grasping object permanence at $3\frac{1}{2}$ months and understanding causality at an early age (Baillargeon, 1993), together with recent findings in infant perceptual ability (discussed in Chapter 4), suggest that the infant may possess greater cognitive skills than Piaget discerned (Flavell, 1985; Sugarman, 1987). Piaget also appears to have underestimated the abilities of older children. Many children in the preoperational and concrete operational periods seem to be more cognitively advanced than Piaget's stage theory of development would suggest (Gelman & Baillargeon, 1983; Halford, 1990). For example, 3- to 5-year-olds have shown a rudimentary ability to understand conservation. In a study in which preschoolers watched sugar dissolve in a cup of water, they believed that the water would taste sweet—even though they could not see the sugar—and that it would weigh more as a result of the added sugar (Au, Sidle, & Rollins, 1993). Other studies show that children as young as 4 or 5 years old can take others' perspectives (Newcombe & Huttenlocher, 2003). However, it remains an open question whether showing cognitive abilities at an earlier age than Piaget proposed represents a major challenge to his theory. After all, Piaget was less concerned with the age of onset of the abilities he studied than with their order of appearance.

Does Cognitive Development Proceed in Stages?

According to Piaget's view, children's cognitive development undergoes qualitative shifts from one stage to another, and these stages are presumed to follow each other in an invariant order. Moreover, the child cannot proceed to the next stage until she has mastered the ways of thinking characteristic of the current one.

Recent evidence (Siegler & Alibali, 2005) suggests that cognitive development may not occur in the stagelike steps that Piaget proposed. However, whether change seems more discontinuous or continuous may be a result of the way in which change is studied, especially with respect to the length of time between measurement points. For example, if we evaluate a child's abilities at 6-month intervals or even years apart, changes in these abilities may seem abrupt and discontinuous. However, if we look closely at the changes that occur within a shorter period of time, an hour or a day or even across several weeks—let's say as a child tries to solve a particular problem—we may find that the child's progress appears more gradual and continuous. In addition, the sequence of intellectual growth that Piaget proposes, especially within stages, may not be as unvarying as he suggests. The results of cross-cultural studies indicate that growth may be modified by cultural and experiential factors (Dasen, 1984; Rogoff, 1990). Moreover, in spite of Piaget's pessimism about the child's ability to proceed more quickly through instruction, the evidence is now clear that active intervention, such as training in problem-solving strategies, can accelerate development (Field, 1987; Gelman & Baillargeon, 1983; Siegler & Alibali, 2005).

Piaget also paid little attention to the social context of cognitive development, and therefore contributions of culture and social experience are not part of his theory. He also did not consider children's emotional states and emotional development and the ways that these may relate to cognitive development. Except in his theory of children's moral development (Chapter 14), Piaget generally ignored the contributions of social phenomena and emotions to cognitive development. However, his ideas have relevance to intervention in both education and counseling. Using Piaget's basic framework, one could design an educational or counseling approach for a child to fit the child's current level of understanding. In fact, there is a long history of connections between Piaget's theory and educational practice. Piaget admired the ideas of Maria Montessori, especially her views on the close relation between thought and action (Lillard, 2005). He drew on these ideas in his theory and even conducted many of his observations of young children's thinking at a modified Montessori school in Switzerland. In addition, approaches to child counseling may be informed by Piaget's ideas. Consider how Piaget's theory could be helpful in counseling a young child who is struggling with his parents' divorce or a parent's death. Would a preoperational child be likely to interpret such situations egocentrically and perhaps blame himself for his parents' divorce? Or would a preoperational child, because of limited understanding of the distinction between what is real and what is not, be prone to wishful thinking, perhaps believing that if he just wished hard enough his deceased parent would come back to life? Although Piaget did not deal directly with such issues, clearly an understanding of the capabilities and limitations associated with the different stages of thinking that he described could help guide an educator or therapist as he works with children in need.

Overall Assessment

Despite new findings and their resulting criticisms, Piaget's theory has had an enormous impact on the study of the child's development of cognitive skills. In fact, his theory was a major force in introducing cognition into developmental research in the latter half of the twentieth century (Beilin, 1992). Although his theorizing and methods were sometimes flawed, Piaget asked and answered important questions in innovative ways, and his ideas have stimulated a vast amount of research and theorizing among other behavioral scientists. If one test of the worth of a theory is its ability to generate interesting ideas for further study, Piaget's theory, without question, passes this test with "flying colors."

VYGOTSKY'S SOCIOCULTURAL THEORY OF COGNITIVE DEVELOPMENT

The developmental theory put forth by the Russian psychologist Lev S. Vygotsky focuses specifically on an area of concern that Piagetian theory did not address: the important influence of children's social and cultural worlds on their cognitive development (Vygotsky, 1978a). Despite his early death at the age of 37, Vygotsky's ideas have had a major impact, especially in recent years, on research in cognitive development. Vygotsky's interest in the impact of social and cultural experience on psychological development is understandable when one considers that he grew up and worked in the early twentieth century, a time of tumultuous social change in his native land (Kozulin, 1990). When Vygotsky was young, Czar Nicholas ruled Russia. At this time, the social divisions within the society were clearly marked, and these divisions had enormous effects on the lives of the Russian people. Jews were treated particularly badly, and Vygotsky was Jewish. In 1917, the year Vygotsky graduated from Moscow University, the Russian Revolution began and the entire society was in upheaval. After the revolution, as Vygotsky launched his career as a psychologist and developed his theory, civil war and famine ravaged the country and the entire social structure of the nation changed dramatically. Although some aspects of Vygotsky's life improved, others did not and because he had fallen into political disfavor in Stalinist Russia, at the time of his death his work was banned. As a result, information about his theory was delayed in reaching beyond Russian borders, and it wasn't until the late 1970s that Western psychologists began to explore his views (Wertsch & Tulviste, 1992).

Vygotsky's view of cognitive development is called a sociocultural approach because it proposes that cognitive development is, in good part, the result of children's interaction with more experienced members of their cultural community—parents, teachers, older children, and others. The child and her partners solve problems together, and through the assistance that her partners provide, the child has the opportunity to participate in intelligent actions beyond her current individual capabilities. Through these experiences, she gradually learns to function on her own in a more advanced intellectual way. As you can see, this approach is in marked contrast to Piaget's, for whom the individual was the unit of study. Although Vygotsky held that each child is born with a set of innate capabilities, such as attention, perception, and memory, he believed that input from the child's social and cultural worlds, in the form of interactions with more expert adults and peers, directs these basic capabilities toward more complex, higher-order cognitive functions. Consistent with this view, Vygotsky held that language has a particularly important role in the child's intellectual development.

Vygotsky had an abiding concern with the processes involved in development; he did not simply observe the end point or products of development. Vygotsky accounted for changes or shifts over the course of development by the types of mediation that children rely upon to understand their world. Across development, the emergence of different types of **mediators,** or psychological tools and signs—such as language, counting, mnemonic devices, algebraic symbols, art, and writing—permit the child to function more effectively in solving problems and understanding his cognitive world. In addition to focusing on mediators as critical to cognitive development, Vygotsky also emphasized that mediators represent the social and cultural context of development. As a result of mediation, children's thinking becomes increasingly aligned over the course of development with the social and cultural context in which growth occurs.

We begin by discussing Vygotsky's notion of mental functions. Here we will see how mediators enable the child to move to new levels of psychological processing. We then examine Vygotsky's concept of the *zone of proximal development,* a concept

mediators Psychological tools and signs—such as language, counting, mnemonic devices, algebraic symbols, art, and writing—that facilitate and direct thinking processes.

that expands on his idea that children learn through social interaction and that has given rise to such concepts as scaffolding and guided participation. We next explore the influence of culture on children's cognitive development. Finally, we examine the effects of culture on children's learning and use of language.

Elementary and Higher Mental Functions

In Vygotsky's theory, an important transition in children's cognitive development occurs between elementary and higher mental functions. **Elementary mental functions** are biological in basis and emerge spontaneously in children's interaction with the world. These and other "natural" forms of mental functioning, which include basic attention, perception, and involuntary memory, are transformed by the child's interaction with his society and culture into what Vygotsky referred to as higher mental functions. **Higher mental functions,** such as voluntary attention, intentional remembering, and logical and abstract thinking, represent a new level of psychological processing for the child. These functions entail the coordination of several cognitive processes and the use of mediators, such as language and other symbol systems, which children learn to use as they interact with their environment.

Vygotsky's discussion of memory illustrates the difference between these two types of mental functions. Vygotsky proposes that the elementary form of memory is constructed of images and impressions of events. This type of memory is very close to perception; it is unintentional and its content is directly influenced by the environment. The more complex or higher form of memory involves the use of signs to mediate memory functions—for instance, the child may write something down to help her remember it. Later on, she may read this note to remind herself or pass this information on to others. In this example, the child uses literacy as a tool to elaborate on or extend the natural functioning of memory. Mediational systems, like language and other tools that aid intelligent action, such as literacy, are products of culture (Cole, 2006). They are devised by a group and transmitted across generations. Higher mental functions combine basic mental processes with cultural products or tools. Moreover, children learn how to use these tools through the assistance of people in their culture who are more experienced than the child in their use. In other words, higher mental functions have sociocultural origins. The child's culture provides him with a writing system and other mediators that enable him to develop higher-level cognitive skills, and the members of his culture guide his understanding and use of these tools over the course of development. Thus, in Vygotsky's approach, the usual boundaries between individual cognitive development and the social world are broken down.

elementary mental functions Psychological functions with which the child is endowed by nature, including attention, perception, and involuntary memory, that emerge spontaneously during children's interaction with the world.

higher mental functions Psychological functions, such as voluntary attention, complex memory processes, and problem solving, that entail the coordination of several cognitive processes and the use of *mediators*.

The Zone of Proximal Development

Because of his interest in the social origins of intellectual functioning, Vygotsky was less concerned with children's individual intellectual abilities at a particular point in time than he was with the child's potential for intellectual growth through social experience (Cole, 1985; Wertsch, 1985; Wertsch & Tulviste, 1992). To assess this potential and to understand how intellectual development occurs, Vygotsky proposed the notion of the **zone of proximal development (ZPD),** defining this zone as the difference between a child's "actual developmental level as determined by independent problem solving" and his "potential development as determined through problem solving under adult guidance or in collaboration with more capable peers" (Vygotsky, 1978a, p. 86). The child's zone of proximal development is not static. The zone or region of sensitivity to learning is defined initially by the child's existing knowledge or competence in an area of intellectual growth. With proper support for learning, the child's level of competence in this area changes, and the child's zone of proximal

zone of proximal development (ZPD) The region of sensitivity for learning characterized by the difference between the developmental level of which a child is capable when working alone and the level she is capable of reaching with the aid of a more skilled partner.

Box 8.2

Child Psychology in Action

ADULT PARTNERING GUIDES CHILDREN IN EFFICIENT PLANNING

Do children solve a planning problem more efficiently when given guidance by a more skilled partner? According to Vygotsky, children should do better under these conditions. To find out, Radziszewska and Rogoff (1988) asked 9-year-olds to plan an errand in collaboration with either another 9-year-old or a parent as a partner.

Partners were given a map of an imaginary town (see Figure 8-9) and two lists of errands and were asked to plan a trip to obtain materials for a school play (e.g., to buy uniforms from the theatrical supplies store, paint brushes from the paint shop, and so on). Partners were asked to plan an efficient route to save gas, which required that the participants decide from which stores to purchase the needed supplies and then develop a plan that incorporated all these stores in sequence, without backtracking or other unnecessary travel.

Adult-child dyads were better planners than peer-child dyads. The adult-child dyads planned longer sequences of moves (average of 4.9 stores per move) than the peer-child dyads (average of 1.3 stores per move). Nearly half of the adult-child dyads planned the whole route at the onset, whereas none of the peer-child dyads showed this kind of careful

planning. Children learned other helpful strategies when they worked with an adult, such as exploring the map of the town before making any moves and marking stores that they wished or did not wish to shop at with different colors. Of great importance was the children's active involvement in the planning decisions, which the adults often verbalized to help the children's understanding. In contrast, peer partners often dominated the decision-making process, ignored their coworkers, and communicated very little.

Not only did children profit more from participation with an adult, but they were able to transfer their learning to later planning tasks that they executed by themselves. In an independent planning test, children who had worked in adult-child dyads in the first test produced more efficient routes (20% shorter) than children who had been in peer-child dyads.

As Vygotsky would have predicted, "children appear to benefit from participation in problem-solving with the guidance of partners who are skilled in accomplishing the task at hand" (Rogoff, 1990, p. 169).

development changes accordingly. The concept of the zone of proximal development is twofold. First, it represents an alternative approach to the assessment of intelligence—examining children's intellectual potential under optimal conditions—that is, conditions that are tailored to the child's specific learning needs and that build on the child's present capabilities. Second, the zone of proximal development represents a way of understanding how children's intellectual development may occur through social interaction with more skilled partners. As such, it builds bridges between the mind of the individual child and the minds of others.

Developmental researchers have illustrated the value of this approach in studies of children's learning by showing that children's attention, memory, problem-solving skills, and ability at planning future actions can indeed be improved when adults or peers who are more skilled provide children with specific help and guidance (Brown & Campione, 1997; Gauvain, 2001a; Rogoff, 1990, 1998). According to Vygotsky, working within a child's zone of proximal development—that is, with the assistance of an adult or more experienced peer—allows the child to participate in her environment in more complex and competent ways. In other words, in social interaction

Figure 8-9 How adult guidance can help children plan efficiently

This map of an imaginary town shows the efficient route an adult-child pair planned for acquiring all the materials they would need to prepare for and stage a school play.

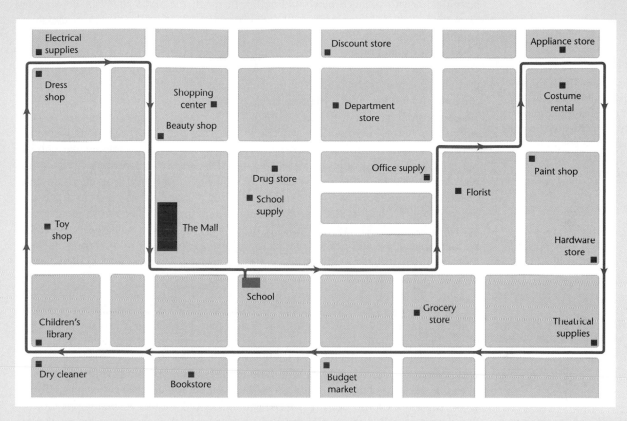

Source: Radziszewska & Rogoff, 1988.

targeted toward the child's zone of proximal development, a child has the opportunity to engage in more advanced cognitive activities than she could undertake on her own. This is because more experienced partners are able to break down an activity into components to make it more understandable and accessible to the learner. More experienced partners also help the learner by modeling new strategies for solving the problem and by encouraging and supporting the child's involvement in the more complex components. Finally, the more experienced partner may take on or assume some of the more difficult task components so that the learner can concentrate on other aspects. For example, an adult may keep track of how many items have been retrieved in a task that involves planning and carrying out errands in a model grocery store, thereby allowing the child to concentrate on the best way to get the remaining items on the grocery list (Gauvain, 1992).

Because adults are more experienced than peers with many of the skills entailed in informal instructional situations, such as turn taking and creating an overall plan for the activity, some evidence indicates that adult assistance is superior to that given by peers. In the study described in Box 8.2, the children who were guided in a planning problem by adults demonstrated more competent planning. In particular, they devised more efficient plans than the children whose partners were same-age peers. This is not to say that peer interaction cannot benefit children's cognitive development; it can. But it appears that children learn different things from social interaction with an adult partner and a partner who is a peer (Gauvain, 2001a). Whereas adults provide children with more overt and explicit opportunities to learn about a task, peers can help children learn how to coordinate a task with others, to negotiate and share activities, and to practice newfound skills. In short, the skills that can be obtained from both adult-child and peer-child cognitive interactions are important to social and cognitive development.

Vygotsky's theory has had considerable impact in the fields of psychology and education in recent years. **Scaffolding,** a form of instruction inspired by Vygotskian thinking, is a process by which the teacher adjusts the amount and type of support he offers to fit with the child's learning needs over the course of an interaction. In a classic demonstration, Wood, Bruner, and Ross (1976) taught 3- and 5-year-olds to build a pyramid out of interlocking wooden blocks through both verbal and physical scaffolding. This scaffolding involved modeling the steps, encouraging the child to put the blocks in the right slots, and helping the child by segmenting the task into more easily understood steps. By careful monitoring of the child's progress, the tutor was able to constantly adjust the task to make it manageable for the child and provide assistance when needed. In scaffolding, which has been demonstrated in a variety of tasks (Gauvain, 2001a; Rogoff, 1990, 1998), the teacher or more experienced partner gradually reduces the amount of support he provides as the child becomes more skilled, so that eventually the child can execute the task in a skilled fashion independent of the partner's help.

One example of the application of these ideas to the classroom comes from the research of Annemarie Palinscar and Ann Brown (1984), who introduced an instructional technique called **reciprocal instruction** that is based on Vygotsky's notion of the zone of proximal development. This tutoring approach enhances children's reading comprehension by having the learner work in close and supportive collaboration with more experienced partners who help children develop skills critical to comprehension, such as explication and elaboration. Ann Brown and her colleagues (Brown, 1994; Brown & Campione, 1997) have also introduced another related application for the classroom called the **community of learners** model of classroom instruction. In this approach, adults and children work together in shared activities, peers learn from each other, and the teacher serves as an expert guide who facilitates the process by which children learn from both the teacher and each other. Rogoff and her colleagues (Rogoff, 1998; see also Rogoff, Goodman Turkanis, & Bartlett, 2001) see the community of learners model as similar to traditional apprenticeship learning in trades and skilled activities, in which learning involves both relationships between teacher and apprentice and interactions among apprentices themselves. It is important to stress that the teacher in the community of learners approach plays two roles—one as a scaffolding agent for the students and the other as a participant in the learning process. The students, who vary in knowledge and ability, also actively help each other learn through their interchanges.

Another somewhat different approach to children's learning in informal instructional situations is **guided participation.** This perspective, introduced by Rogoff (1990), emphasizes the ways in which children learn as they begin to understand and are guided by the values and practices of others in their cultural community (Rogoff, 2003). This approach highlights the fact that adults regularly support learning in the context of everyday activities by directing children's attention to, and involvement in, these activities. Sometimes these activities are child focused, such as in play or an organized game, but oftentimes they are adult activities in which the primary purpose is not to instruct children but to carry out the activity itself. In these situations, adults often support children's involvement in specific but meaningful ways. For example,

scaffolding An instructional process in which the more knowledgeable partner adjusts the amount and type of support he offers to the child to fit with the child's learning needs over the course of the interaction.

reciprocal instruction A tutoring approach based on the ideas of the *zone of proximal development* and *scaffolding*.

community of learners An approach to classroom learning in which adults and children work together in shared activities, peers learn from each other, and the teacher serves as a guide.

guided participation Learning that occurs as children participate in activities of their community and are guided in their participation by the actions of more experienced partners in the setting.

as a mother tries to make a cake her child may ask if he can help. The mother may agree and then structure the task in a way that gives the child some real responsibility in the activity, such as stirring the ingredients that the mother has assembled. The mother then carefully supervises the child and provides assistance when needed. In this example, the child is involved as a meaningful participant whose actions are guided by the adult. Over time, if the child remains interested in and continues to be involved in making cakes with his mother, the child's involvement and the mother's activity will both change as the child's competence increases. Thus, according to Rogoff, cognitive change occurs as children participate in intelligent actions alongside more experienced partners. Furthermore, over the course of participation, as a child's roles and responsibilities in joint action change, the child's understanding of the activity also changes. In this view, the child is not merely a passive learner who follows the instructions or prompts of the more experienced partner. Rather, the child is a full and active participant who co-constructs, with the partner, new ways of understanding and learning about an activity. For Rogoff (2003), guided participation is one of the most prevalent and critical forms of learning that children experience throughout the world, though the distinct forms and emphasis it takes varies across cultural communities.

The Role of Culture

An important feature of Vygotsky's approach is his emphasis on the significance of society and culture in accounts of cognitive development (Cole, 2006; Gauvain, 2001b; Rogoff, 1990, 1998; Wertsch & Kanner, 1992). Vygotsky proposed two important principles of cultural influence in cognitive development. First, cultures provide institutions and social settings that facilitate cognitive development. Formal institutions, such as schools and businesses or other forms of employment, can significantly alter the ways in which people think. In these settings, teachers, employers, and others emphasize and promote particular approaches to solving problems, including the use of certain tools that aid problem solving. In every culture, both symbolic tools, such as language and mathematics, and material tools, such as pencil, paper, and computers, are products of that culture that support intelligent action. In fact, once certain cultural tools become incorporated into intelligent action, it is difficult to imagine how the activity would occur without such tools. Think for a moment about how you would remember your class material without the cultural tool of literacy, which mediates your learning in instrumental ways. Literacy helps you organize and record your thoughts for later reference and study. Less formal social institutions and social settings also influence cognitive development. For example, in cultures in which verbal explanation is highly valued, cultural practices related to this value, such as oral narratives and storytelling, assume much importance and are part of children's everyday experience and cognitive development in that community (Heath, 1998).

Although there has often been a tendency to consider industrialized and technological societies as more intellectually skilled than nonindustrial societies, sometimes a particular cognitive approach characteristic of a more traditional culture is more precise and useful than one common in industrialized nations. For example, the way children learn to organize and encode spatial information varies according to linguistic and cultural conventions (Levinson, 1997). Speakers of Guugu Yimithirr, an indigenous community in Australia, describe directions and location in absolute rather than relative terms. For example, they will guide a stranger by saying, "turn to the west" rather than "turn to the left." Contrary to what Western people might have thought, these people are more accurate in making certain spatial judgments than Europeans are because of the way they organize their understanding of spatial topology and the way this understanding is encoded in language.

Vygotsky's second principle of cultural influence states that in any attempt to assess children's cognitive development we must consider cultural contexts—if we ignore the culturally specific nature of children's learning, he claimed, we run the risk of seriously underestimating children's development (Greenfield & Cocking, 1995; Greenfield & Suzuki, 1998; Rogoff, 2003). Indeed, many cross-cultural studies have documented that children learn highly sophisticated and complex cognitive skills important in their culture (Cole, 2006; Rogoff, 2003). These skills are conveyed to children largely through social experiences, especially social interactions with more experienced cultural members (Gauvain, 2005). More experienced cultural members play significant roles in this process of cognitive socialization because they function as the most immediate representatives in children's lives of culturally organized ways of thinking and acting. Researchers have studied several social processes that promote children's learning of culturally valued skills, such as observational learning (Morelli, Rogoff, & Angellio, 2003), the social regulation of attention in infancy (Bornstein, Tal, & Tamis-LaMonda, 1991; Martini & Kirkpatrick, 1981), deliberate efforts to transfer knowledge from more to less experienced partners (Serpell & Hatano, 1997), social coordination during joint cognitive activity (Rogoff, 1998), and cognitive socialization through conversation and joint narratives (Mullen & Yi, 1995). Taken together, this research suggests that social opportunities for children's learning appear in many forms and that culture determines the frequency and manner with which these processes occur.

Vygotsky's theory not only leads us to an appreciation of different cultures and their values but actually connects cultural values and practices directly to cognitive development. Mathematics provides an interesting example of this kind of link. Children in Western societies often acquire and use rudimentary counting systems before they begin attending school (Saxe, Guberman, & Gearhart, 1987; Wilkinson, 1984), but it is generally in the early elementary grades, from kindergarten and on up, that children master the principles underlying counting and acquire more complex numerical concepts. In societies in developing areas of the world, however, children often acquire the ability to solve mathematical problems without the benefit of a formal education. How do they do this? From a Vygotskian perspective, how does the surrounding culture support such children's learning?

Geoffrey Saxe (1988, 1991) has studied the acquisition of mathematical concepts in children with little or no education, focusing particularly on young street vendors (10 to 12 years old) in Brazil. These children make their living by selling candy and fruit to the people riding on buses or walking through the downtown areas of Brazil's major cities. Saxe found that this occupational pursuit had several interesting effects on the children's mathematical abilities. Because of the severe inflation Brazil's economy was experiencing at the time of Saxe's study, these children often dealt successfully with large numerical values while conducting their daily business. When the researcher asked the children to identify and compare multidigit numbers based on bills and coins, they performed quite well. On the other hand, when they were asked to read multidigit numerical values in written form, even values that were smaller than those in the monetary problems, the children performed quite poorly. Perhaps because these young vendors often dealt with numbers in the thousands in their daily sales, they found Saxe's small-number comparisons more difficult than comparisons based on large numbers. Or it may be that they could not deal with numbers out of the context of their selling activities.

The findings of several other researchers who have studied the Brazilian street vendors are discussed in Box 8.3. As this box shows, the children's daily interaction with addition and subtraction, as well as their lack of formal schooling, has led them to develop ways of performing mathematical functions that work for them in their daily activities but that affect their ability to deal with mathematical concepts in an academic setting. If, as Vygotsky insisted, we take culture into account in evaluating such children's cognitive skills, we must recognize the sophistication of their competence,

Box 8.3

Risk and Resilience

STREET MATH AND SCHOOL MATH IN BRAZIL

Most human beings use mathematics and numerical reasoning every day of their lives. People calculate the costs of items in the supermarket, divide a pizza equally among friends, balance their checkbooks, and estimate how far it is to the market and other destinations. In most cases, people learn the necessary skills to accomplish these mental acts in grade school, but not all children or adults have the opportunity to acquire a formal education. How do those without that opportunity perform such daily tasks or manage to conduct a complex and demanding business with some degree of success? Can children learn to function effectively on mathematics tasks, even if they lack the opportunity to learn mathematics in a formal school setting? As the study we discuss here illustrates, even without formal training and in the face of hardship and risk, children demonstrate an amazing ability to develop the cognitive skills needed for their everyday functioning.

Carraher, Schliemann, and Carraher (1988) studied young vendors on the streets of Brazilian cities. These children, who are usually between 9 and 15 years of age, sell all kinds of goods, including coconuts, oranges, and other fruits, as well as candy and sweets, to pedestrians and riders of public transportation. Carraher, Schliemann, and Carraher (1988) were interested in the ability of these children to solve common mathematical problems. After all, they reasoned, success at their trade relied on mathematical skill. Oftentimes items would be sold in bulk, such as three oranges for 10 cruzados (the monetary unit in Brazil), but a customer may only want two oranges, and the seller would need to figure out a fair price or risk losing the customer (Saxe, 1991). Also, inflation is rampant in Brazil, and the prices of one day may be different from the prices yesterday. As a result, there is no fixed pricing scheme for the children to memorize. To study these children's skill at mathematical calculations, the experimenters presented five young vendors, who ranged in age from 9 to 15 years old, with either a common commercial transaction between a vendor and a customer—one similar to the transactions the children were accustomed to handling daily—or an exercise in computation framed as it would be presented in a school setting.

The young vendors revealed striking differences in their abilities to perform the two different types of task. When they were tested using the familiar commercial transaction, the children were correct 98 percent of the time, but when the same mathematical problems were presented in the form of an academic exercise, the percentage of correct answers dropped to 37. One notable difference in the children's response to the two tasks lay in method: The young vendors solved the commercial problem mentally but resorted to pencil and paper to solve the school-like problem. Most striking, however, were the differences in mathematical strategies that the children used in the two situations. The following protocol from one of the children illustrates these differences (Nunes & Bryant, 1996):

Commercial Transaction Problem

Customer: I'll take two coconuts. (Each coconut costs 40 cruzados, and the customer pays with a 500-cruzado bill.) What do I get back?

Child Vendor (before reaching for the customer's change): Eighty, ninety, one hundred, four hundred and twenty.

School-Type Problem

Test Question: What is 420 plus 80?

Child's Response: The child writes 42 on one line and 8 underneath and obtains 130 as the result. She apparently proceeds as follows: She adds the 8 and the 2, carries the 1, and then adds 1 + 4 + 8, obtaining 13. With the 0 already in the sum, she gets 130. Note that the child is confusing multiplication and addition rules.

The child has approached the same problem (420 + 80) in two distinctly different ways. In the street she uses an "add-on" strategy efficiently to arrive at the correct answer, whereas in the academic setting she applies strategies learned in school incorrectly. As Vygotsky would have predicted, this study underscores the importance of context for understanding cognitive development. It also illustrates how mediators—in this case, mathematical symbols and strategies—are integrated with thinking. Finally, it underlines the resilience of children at risk and their ability to survive and learn even complex cognitive skills despite the lack of opportunity for formal schooling.

which certainly exceeds what we might have expected. Together, these studies of young street vendors underscore the importance of considering the cultural context in our evaluations of children's cognitive development.

The Role of Language

Language plays a central role in Vygotsky's sociocultural approach to cognitive development. The acquisition and use of language is a primary component of children's developing intellectual abilities in a social context because language provides children with access to the ideas and understandings of other people. It also enables children to convey their own ideas and thoughts to others. Moreover, language, which is a cultural product, functions as the primary symbolic cultural tool that mediates individual mental functioning. In other words, once children learn to use language, it gradually becomes incorporated into their thought processes and, as a result, language both facilitates and constrains thinking.

egocentric speech According to Vygotsky, a form of self-directed dialogue by which the child instructs herself in solving problems and formulating plans; as the child matures, this becomes internalized as *inner speech.*

inner speech Internalized *egocentric speech* that guides intellectual functioning.

EGOCENTRIC SPEECH AS A COGNITIVE AID According to Jerome Bruner, Vygotsky was "forever intrigued with the inventive powers that language bestowed on mind—in ordinary speech, in the novels of Tolstoy and the plays of Chekhov . . . [and] in the play of children" (Bruner, 1987, p. 2). For Vygotsky, thought and speech are independent in early development. However, around the second year of life they begin to join together when children begin to use words to label objects. Within a year, speech assumes two forms: social, or communicative, speech and **egocentric speech** (also called "private speech"). Vygotsky's view of egocentric speech differs markedly from Piaget's concept. For Vygotsky, egocentric speech is a form of self-directed dialogue by which the child instructs herself in solving problems or formulating plans. Thus, egocentric speech becomes a tool for intellectual growth and allows the child to become a more effective and skilled learner. For example, in his efforts to solve a dinosaur puzzle, a child might say, "First I'll put the tail piece here, then the claw goes over here and the head right there." By age 7 or 8, this form of speech becomes internalized in the thought process and becomes **inner speech,** a form of internal monologue that guides intelligent functioning. This view is quite different from Piaget's conceptualization of egocentric speech.

For Piaget, egocentric speech merely reflects a mental limitation of the preoperational stage in which the child's self-focused way of thinking leads children to explain natural phenomena in reference to the self—for example, by claiming that the moon follows the child home at night. The egocentric child, in Piaget's view, makes no effort to adapt his point of view in a way that makes it understandable to others. Moreover, unlike Vygotsky, who considered egocentric speech as one step in the path of the development of internalized knowledge, Piaget thought that egocentric speech served no useful cognitive function. Finally, Piaget suggested that egocentric speech diminishes at the end of the preoperational period, as the child's perspective-taking abilities improve, whereas Vygotsky thought that this kind of speech becomes internalized as thought.

Who is right? Most of the evidence favors Vygotsky's version. For example, children use more private or self-speech when encountering a difficult cognitive task; as a result, their performance improves, suggesting that children use this form of speech as a cognitive aid (Berk, 1992). In addition, in a longitudinal study of the developmental sequence of this kind of speech, Bivens and Berk (1990) found that egocentric speech does in fact move from external (audible, self-directed speech) to internal (silent, self-directed speech) between 7 and 10 years of age, supporting Vygotsky's view. Thus, language seems to serve as an aid for regulating cognition as well as a tool for communicating.

USING THE ZONE OF PROXIMAL DEVELOPMENT IN TEACHING LANGUAGE Vygotsky's notion of the zone of proximal development (ZPD) has had considerable impact in the field of elementary education and has formed the basis for the theory of instruction adopted by a well-known educational experiment, the Kamehameha Early Education Program, or KEEP, in Hawaii (Tharp & Gallimore, 1988). In this program, Native Hawaiian children receive language instruction as well as instruction in other subjects, such as reading, all based on the ZPD concept. This program is learner-centered (Bransford, Brown, & Cocking, 1999) in that it was designed to incorporate the knowledge, skills, values, and beliefs that learners bring to the classroom and their lessons. The KEEP program was particularly concerned with how the practices that Hawaiian children experienced at home could be incorporated into the classroom. For example, the Native Hawaiian tradition of storytelling was used to develop the classroom practice of "talk-story," an approach to literacy instruction in which the teacher and the children jointly produce narratives about the focus of the day's lessons (Au & Jordan, 1981). This approach emphasizes social participation, along with story creation and comprehension, and its use has been related to improvements in the standardized reading scores of Native Hawaiian children.

The KEEP teacher's instructional repertoire includes the techniques of modeling, questioning, and feedback, all of which are part of the method of scaffolding and central to the reciprocal instruction approach devised by Palinscar and Brown (1984). For example, in the following exchange a teacher uses repetition, rewording, and expansion as she questions the child and seeks to clarify his statement (Tharp & Gallimore, 1988, pp. 143):

Child: Probably, probably have snow on the . . . stuff and . . . thing, thing was heavy and thing fall.

Teacher: Oh, you mean there might be so much snow and ice on the plane that it couldn't fly?

In the next example, the teacher questions a child, offers cognitive structuring (explaining, providing meaning), and gives the child feedback (Tharp & Gallimore, 1988, pp. 143–144):

Teacher: What do we put in our mouth underneath our tongue?

Child: A temperature . . .

Teacher: No, that's what we find out. Your temperature goes up. That means your body gets hot.

Many KEEP classroom lessons are planned and carried out in such a way that they "teach language without making the children conscious that they are learning language" (Tharp & Gallimore, 1988, p. 139). Through the provision of models and feedback as in the foregoing examples, children in the KEEP program are enabled to use new language forms and features. Tharp and Gallimore (1988) argue that minority or other "nonstandard dialect speakers" can benefit greatly from opportunities to converse throughout goal-oriented activities with a responsive yet uncritical teacher who speaks standard English. As Tharp and Gallimore point out, however, this kind of teaching is not common in U.S. schools.

EVALUATION OF VYGOTSKY'S THEORY

Vygotsky's approach, which emphasizes the culturally organized and socially mediated nature of cognitive processes, offers a perspective from which to view cognitive development within the contexts in which this development actually occurs. As such, it overcomes some of the limitations of Piaget's intensive focus on cognitive development as an individual or solitary endeavor.

Strengths of the Theory

Vygotsky's theory has helped to make developmental psychologists more aware of the importance of the immediate social contexts of learning and cognition. In particular, through the notion of the zone of proximal development and the related concepts of scaffolding and guided participation, this approach has pointed to new ways of assessing children's cognitive potential and of teaching reading, mathematics, and writing. Reciprocal instruction, the community of learners model, and the KEEP project are excellent examples of the application of these principles to educational settings. Moreover, Vygotsky's approach has increased our appreciation of the profound importance of culture in cognitive development. This approach is particularly useful in a multiethnic society, like the United States, in that it provides a theoretical base for examining the ways that children of different cultural and ethnic traditions approach cognitive tasks. Vygotsky's theory also provides a way of conceptualizing the role played by tools of thinking in cognitive development. This theory addresses how tools such as literacy and numerical systems, which are products of culture, get passed on across generations and become incorporated into the ways children learn to think and solve problems as they grow.

Does Vygotsky's Theory Describe Developmental Change?

microgenetic change
Changes associated with learning that occur over the time of a specific learning experience or episode.

Although Vygotsky's theory has recently inspired a great deal of research activity, the theory has several limitations, largely pertaining to its explanation of development. Although the approach emphasizes change over time in a specific learning experience, referred to as **microgenetic change,** and the role of long-term historical influences on intellectual development embodied in cultural practices and tools, this approach is not very specific in relation to age-related, or *ontogenetic,* change. Vygotsky did not provide a detailed description, as Piaget did, of how children's thinking changes with age (Miller, 2002). Furthermore, like Piaget's theory, this approach does not describe how changes in physical, social, and emotional capabilities contribute to changes in children's cognitive abilities. Nor is it clear how cultural contexts are designed to support and promote the latter. Although decisions about the contexts in which cognitive development occurs, and which are made available to children at different points of growth, are critical to this theoretical view, Vygotsky did not attend to the coordination of social and cultural opportunities and maturational changes in great detail.

Overall Assessment

In a sense, Vygotsky left developmental psychology a unique framework for thinking about cognitive development rather than a fully specified theory. The task of filling in the details of this theoretical position remains a challenge for the future. However, for now, most developmentalists agree that this approach holds great promise as a way of thinking about cognitive development in social and cultural contexts.

Making the Connections 8

There are many links between concepts and ideas in one area of development and concepts and ideas in other areas. Here are some of the connections between ideas in Chapter 8 and discussions in other chapters of this book.

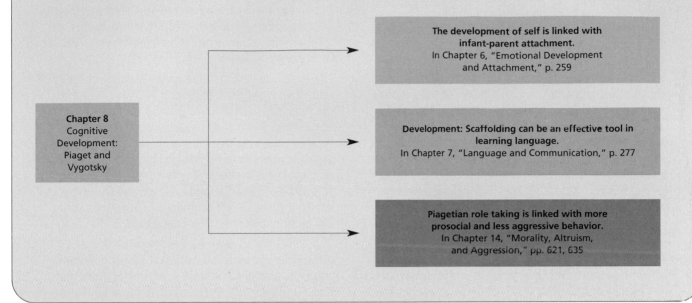

Chapter 8
Cognitive Development: Piaget and Vygotsky

The development of self is linked with infant-parent attachment.
In Chapter 6, "Emotional Development and Attachment," p. 259

Development: Scaffolding can be an effective tool in learning language.
In Chapter 7, "Language and Communication," p. 277

Piagetian role taking is linked with more prosocial and less aggressive behavior.
In Chapter 14, "Morality, Altruism, and Aggression," pp. 621, 635

SUMMARY

- **Cognition** is the mental activity and behavior that allows us to understand the world. It includes the functions of learning, perception, memory, and thinking, and it is influenced by biological, environmental, experiential, social, and motivational factors. A variety of theories have been proposed to explain the pattern of cognitive development seen in children.

Piaget's Theory of Cognitive Development

- Piaget's theory concentrates on the cognitive capabilities of children of different ages. Piaget based his theory on observations of his own and other children as they answered questions during structured and unstructured interviews.

Piaget's Main Tenet: The Child Actively Seeks Knowledge

- According to Piaget, children actively seek out information and adapt it to the knowledge and conceptions of the world that they already have. In this **constructivist view,** children construct their understanding of reality from their own experiences. Children organize

their knowledge into increasingly complex cognitive structures called **schemata.**

- Children possess many different schemata, and these change as the children develop. In the newborn, the schemata take the form of innate reflexes and reaction patterns, such as sucking. As the child grows and gains experience, the schemata shift from motor activities to mental activities called **operations.** These operations become increasingly complex with age.

- Piaget suggested that schemata are modified according to the principles of **organization** and **adaptation.** Organization is the predisposition to combine simple physical or psychological structures into more complex systems. Adaptation involves the two complementary processes of **assimilation,** or fitting new experiences into current cognitive schemata, and **accommodation,** or adjusting current schemata to fit the new experiences.

The Stages of Cognitive Development

- Piaget divided intellectual development into four stages that reflect changes in children's cognitive structures. The attainments of earlier stages are essential to reach later periods of development. All children go through the stages in the same order, although not necessarily at the same ages.

- During the first two years of life, called the **sensori-motor stage,** a child makes the transition from relying on reflexes to using internal representations of external events. Piaget divided this period into six substages, during which the child physically explores the environment, developing such abilities as **symbolic thought** and **deferred imitation.** Throughout these substages, which include **basic reflex activity, primary circular reactions, secondary circular reactions, coordination of secondary circular reactions, tertiary circular reactions,** and **inventing new means by mental combination,** children gradually come to understand the world including **object permanence.** Critics of Piaget have suggested that children may acquire object permanence, as well as other ideas about the properties of objects and such principles of the physical world as causality, earlier than Piaget thought.

- Recently, researchers interested in early knowledge systems have begun to study the understanding by very young infants of the physical world, including physical laws such as containment and numerosity. Much of this research considers this type of understanding basic to human functioning and refers to it as **core knowledge.** Debate continues as to whether core knowledge systems are innate or learned early in life, as well as how to interpret the evidence from very young infants that explores these ideas.

- The major developmental milestone during the **preoperational stage** is the development of the **symbolic function,** or the ability to use symbols such as words, images, and gestures to represent objects and events. This can be seen in the rapid development of language, in imaginative play, and in an increase in **deferred imitation.** Piaget divided this stage into the **preconceptual substage** and the **intuitive substage.**

- During the preconceptual substage, children's thinking is limited by **animistic thinking,** the tendency to attribute lifelike characteristics to inanimate objects, and by **egocentrism,** a tendency to view things from one's own perspective and to have difficulty seeing things from another person's perspective. A shift away from egocentrism may be related to the development of role-taking abilities.

- During the intuitive substage, children are able to use certain mental operations, but they do not seem to be aware of the principles used because they cannot explain them. Limitations in their thinking are still found in problems involving part-whole relations, classification, and conservation.

- The most important acquisition of the preoperational stage is an elementary understanding of the notion of **conservation.** Typically, the child learns to conserve number at the end of this stage but cannot yet conserve other physical properties such as mass and volume. The concept of **horizontal décalage** explains this unevenness of children's cognitive achievements. In recent years, however, critics have suggested that children may achieve notions of conservation earlier than Piaget believed.

- Piaget proposed that three characteristics of preoperational thought limit children's thinking. The first is the child's inability to understand **reversibility,** or the notion that logical operations can be changed back to their original state and that this change demonstrates the logical steps that were involved in an operation. The second is the tendency to maintain an **ends over means focus,** looking at the end state itself rather than at the process of transformation. The third characteristic is **centration,** or focusing on only one dimension of a problem.

- During the **concrete operational stage,** children acquire the ability to perform most of the tasks that they were unable to master in the preceding stage, including conservation of various substances, classification, and part-whole relations.

- Children in the **formal operations stage** can use flexible and abstract reasoning, test mental hypotheses, and consider multiple possibilities for the solution to a problem. Not all children or adults attain this stage. The nature of a problem, and the opportunity to attend formal schooling that emphasizes this type of thinking, are related to the use of formal operations.

- Although Piaget did not emphasize how the child learns to distinguish self from others, his concepts of egocentrism and object permanence have clear implications for this process and the beginnings of social cognition. Recent research on children's **theory of mind** is uncovering when and how children come to understand the properties of the mind, including that the mind guides the child's own behavior and the behavior of others.

Evaluation of Piaget's Theory

- Piaget's theory integrates and illuminates a broad spectrum of issues pertaining to children's understanding and use of knowledge, and it has stimulated an enormous amount of research. Among the most significant of Piaget's many ideas are that children actively construct their knowledge of the world, that the errors they make provide important clues about their thinking, and that cognitive development can be discerned in perceptual-motor behavior as well as in language skills.

- Current evidence indicates that infants and children grasp many concepts, such as object permanence, causality, conservation, and the perspectives of another, considerably earlier than Piaget thought. Research also suggests that the sequence of development may not be invariant as Piaget believed, that it may be modified by cultural experiences, and that development may not occur in the distinct and qualitatively different stages Piaget proposed.

- Piaget's ideas have been very influential in the field of cognitive development. Despite flaws in his theorizing and methods, Piaget asked and proposed answers to important questions in an innovative way, stimulating the work of other investigators.

Vygotsky's Sociocultural Theory of Cognitive Development

- Vygotsky's theory emphasizes the critical role played by the social world in facilitating the child's development. According to his theory, children generally internalize thought processes that first occur through interaction with others in the social environment. Qualitative transitions between **elementary mental functions** and **higher mental functions** occur because of shifts in the use of **mediators** such as language and other symbols. The acquisition and use of language plays a primary role in children's developing intellectual abilities.

- Vygotsky's interest in the child's potential for intellectual growth led him to develop the concept of the **zone of proximal development.** In recent years, this concept has led to the study of **scaffolding,** an instructional process in which the teacher adjusts the amount and type of support offered to the child to suit the child's abilities, withdrawing support as the child becomes more skilled. The concepts of **reciprocal instruction,** a **community of learners**, and **guided participation** also stem from these ideas. In reciprocal instruction and the community of learners models, individuals—whose learning abilities vary—support children's learning through social interaction.

- Guided participation emphasizes how cognitive development proceeds throughout the world as children actively participate, and are guided by more experienced people, in activities valued in their cultural community.

- Two principles of cultural influence inform Vygotsky's theory. First, cultures vary widely in the kinds of institutions, settings, and tools they offer to facilitate children's development. Second, in assessing children's cognitive development, we may seriously underestimate children's cognitive development unless we consider these variations and cultural contexts.

- Language plays an important role in Vygotskian theory. As children begin to use social speech, **egocentric speech,** and **inner speech,** they learn to communicate and to form thoughts and regulate intellectual functions.

Evaluation of Vygotsky's Theory

- Vygotsky drew attention to the importance of the social and cultural context in which learning and the evolution of cognitive skills take place and to the influence of peers and adults on the child's development. He pointed out that the particularities of a given culture determine the nature and manner of functioning of social interactions and of the societal institutions that influence how children think and learn. Interest in the effect of social and cultural variation on the child's development has created a research focus that is especially useful in multiethnic societies such as the United States.

- Vygotsky's approach mainly offers a general outline that addresses unique and important questions about the nature and course of cognitive development. The theory's focus is on **microgenetic change,** for it examines change over a learning episode rather than change associated with age (ontogenetic change). Vygotsky's ideas, especially in their emphasis on the social and cultural aspects of learning and cognition, challenge future researchers to explore the role of context in greater depth.

EXPLORE AND DISCUSS

1. How do changes in infants' thinking, as described by Piaget, contribute to the infant's increasing ability to interact with people and objects in the world?

2. Imagine you are an educational consultant and you have been asked to consult at a school where several second- and third-grade children are having difficulty understanding scientific concepts that involve the conservation of weight and volume. How would you explain this difficulty and what would

you advise the teachers to do to help these children?

3. If you were to design a new IQ test based on Vygotsky's idea of the zone of proximal development, what would it be like?

4. How could Vygotsky's ideas about culture and development be used to understand children's learning and development in a multicultural society such as ours?

Christian Pierre (b. 1962). *Modern Madonna,* 1996. Private Collection.

9.

Cognitive Development: The Information-Processing Approach

Every day of their lives children encounter cognitive challenges, such as getting dressed and ready for the day, remembering to do things like taking their homework to school, and solving problems like figuring out a math assignment or why their best friend is mad at them. This chapter focuses on the cognitive skills that children use to address these types of daily challenges as well as the way these skills change across childhood. We focus on approaches to cognitive development that are derived from an information-processing view of cognition (Klahr & MacWhinney, 1998). Although this view of cognitive development shares many of the concerns that drove Piaget and Vygotsky as they devised their theories, research based on an information-processing view takes quite a different approach to the study of the human mind. Moreover, there is no single information-processing theory of cognitive development. Information processing is, rather, a general approach to how questions about cognitive development are formulated and studied. In essence, all theories based on an information-processing view consider human beings as possessing an array of cognitive processes that help them to understand and make use of information they get from their experiences in the world.

The information-processing perspective originated in the study of adult, or mature, cognition and has been adapted in several different ways to the study of earlier cognitive development. One such approach considers the different processes or steps that the mind goes through as information flows through it. This approach is called a *multistore model* because it describes different ways in which information is processed so that the mind can operate on it. Another more recent adaptation sees the mind as composed of networks of information. Called a *connectionist view,* this approach describes cognitive processing as making connections among the various components of the neural network. The connectionist view relies extensively on computer modeling as a way of examining how knowledge may be organized and interrelated in a networked mental system. Another adaptation involves combining many of Piaget's ideas but focusing on cognitive processing rather than on stages of development. As we will see, this view, referred to as a *neo-Piagetian approach,* proposes that the stage-related structural changes that Piaget described are brought about by changes in the ways children process information.

After describing the multistore, connectionist, and neo-Piagetian approaches, we explore several basic cognitive abilities and discuss how these abilities change with development. We begin by describing changes in perception and attention that support the child's growing ability to perceive and select from the wealth of sensory input confronting her. Next, we consider memory and the child's developing competence in storing and retrieving information. We then discuss children's increasing ability to solve various kinds of problems, such as those involving logical and numerical reasoning, with particular attention to the role that the construction and use of strategies play in this endeavor. Finally, we look at children's knowledge of their own mental capabilities, referred to as *metacognition.*

As you study this chapter, keep in mind that the many different theories and approaches to cognitive development discussed in Chapters 8 and 9 are not necessarily in contention with one another. In many cases, the theories address different aspects of both cognitive development and the cognitive system. To date, no comprehensive theory of cognitive development—one that explains all of mental functioning and its development—has emerged. Although such a theory stands as one goal of the field at large, researchers realize that the human cognitive system is extremely complex and adaptive. It may be that no single theory will ever be able to explain this entire process. Thus, understanding each different theory and approach to cognitive development in its own right—and considering how well it explains the aspect of cognitive development it sets out to explain—is, at present, the best way to understand what is known about children's thinking and the way it develops.

INFORMATION-PROCESSING THEORY

information-processing approaches Theories of development that focus on the flow of information through the child's cognitive system and particularly on the specific operations the child performs between input and output phases.

Information-processing approaches to the study of cognition uses the computer as an analog for describing how the human mind works. Information-processing theorists propose that, like the computer, the human mind is an organized system that processes information through the application of a series of logical rules or steps. Information from the environment, or input, initially enters the cognitive system through the processes of perception and attention. This information is then encoded into some symbolic form so that it can be examined mentally. Then it is either expelled because it is no longer needed or saved so that at some later point it can be retrieved and used for thinking or solving problems. Like the computer, the mind is seen as limited in both the amount and nature of information it can process. Finally, just as the computer can be made into a better information processor by changes in its hardware (e.g., circuit boards and microchips) and its software (programming), so are human thinkers able to become more sophisticated in the use of the mind through changes in their brains and sensory systems (hardware) and in the rules and strategies (software) that they learn over the course of development. Psychologists who study cognitive development from this perspective are particularly interested in changes in the flexibility of the system and in the kinds of things that constrain or limit the way children process information. Like the computer and its operation, the human brain and its functioning is highly complex in terms of both what it can and what it cannot do.

A primary quality of the human cognition system is its flexibility. Human beings can adapt and adjust to many different task circumstances and requirements and can set and alter their goals in a given situation as needed. However, the human cognitive system has two primary limitations: It is limited in the amount of information that it can process at any one time, and its speed of processing is limited. You have probably noticed that computers can process information faster than the human mind. Does this mean that the human mind is deficient in some way? No, but the computer and the mind are indeed different in some fundamental ways. The rapid-fire speed of the computer reflects its singular, goal-directed nature: In solving a problem, it considers the information that a person has programmed it to consider. When the human mind undertakes to solve a problem, however, it has the freedom to consider as broad a range of issues and implications as it wishes and as a result it takes longer to do the job. Thus, in evaluating information-processing approaches to cognitive development it is important to remember that the human mind comprises a truly unique kind of information-processing system.

Before we discuss some of the principal ways in which the information-processing perspective informs various approaches to cognitive development, we need first to consider the four basic assumptions that are shared by all psychologists who study cognitive development within the general information-processing framework. Then we will turn to a description of some of the more specific approaches that are couched within this framework.

Basic Assumptions of the Information-Processing Approach

According to Siegler and Alibali (2005), the information-processing approach is characterized by several main assumptions. First, information processing theorists hold that *thinking is information processing*. In other words, mental activity, or thinking, involves taking information into the mind and operating on it in ways that make the information more understandable and usable. In terms of cognitive development, this assumption directs attention to questions about how the processes that underlie human cognition, such as perceiving, encoding, representing and storing information, change as children get older and have more experience with the world.

A second basic assumption of an information-processing perspective that has direct bearing on cognitive developmental research is its emphasis on the *mechanisms of change*. With development, children become better able to attend to and represent information in their minds; this process, known as encoding, helps them solve problems more effectively. Children also become better at devising new ways or strategies for managing and manipulating information to solve problems. Because cognitive skills that are highly valued and practiced become routine or automatized, the child's cognitive system is increasingly freed up to work on other problems or on new aspects of a problem. Finally, children learn to apply or generalize their cognitive skills to new problem situations. These four key mechanisms, encoding, strategy construction, automatization, and generalization, which are discussed in more detail later in the chapter, work together to bring about change in children's cognitive skills.

Information-processing theory also assumes that cognitive development is a *self-modifying process*. In other words, the child uses the knowledge and strategies she has acquired from earlier problem solutions to modify her responses to a new situation or problem. In this way, she builds newer and more sophisticated responses from her own prior knowledge base. Thus, children play an active role in their own cognitive development.

Another assumption of an information-processing approach is that *careful task analysis* is crucial. According to this view, not only the child's own level of development but the task or problem situation itself influences the child's cognitive performance. Therefore, through careful task analysis, the researcher can understand what the person needs to solve the problem. This information, coupled with accurate observation of the way the child actually performs the task, can reveal much about how children of different ages understand, approach, and solve problems. Careful task analysis often involves *error analysis,* or attending to the errors children make. This involves examining incorrect answers for evidence of less sophisticated, albeit systematic, strategies that children apply to problems. Such analysis often relies on a method called **microgenetic analysis,** which involves very detailed examination of how a child solves a problem over a single learning episode or over several episodes that occur close in time (Crowley & Siegler, 1993; Siegler, 1994; Siegler & Stern, 1998). This method is rather like watching action in slow motion as the investigator observes in great detail the way a child arrives at a problem solution. One important observation that has emerged from microgenetic analysis is that as children learn they often have available several problem-solving strategies that compete with each other (Siegler, 1996). However, gradually the most effective strategy comes to dominate the child's problem-solving repertoire.

Taken together, these four assumptions offer a perspective on cognitive development that emphasizes the different ways that children, over the course of development, understand and operate on information they obtain from the world. The next section discusses several of the approaches or models that are derived from an information-processing perspective and that guide research on cognitive development today.

Information-Processing Models

Several types of models are used to describe cognition from an information-processing perspective. In this section, we discuss three models that have been influential in the adaptation of an information-processing perspective to the study of cognitive development. These are the multistore model, the connectionist models, and the neo-Piagetian model. Each of these models attempts to characterize important aspects of the way that the mind operates as it processes information.

THE MULTISTORE MODEL   The basic organization of information in the human cognitive system is described in a model introduced by Atkinson and Shiffrin (1968) and referred to as the **multistore model** of human information-processing (Figure 9-1). This model describes how information enters and flows through the mental system as it is processed. As an initial step, we acquire information from the environment through our senses. This sensory information enters the system through the **sensory register.** Although the information in the sensory register is stored in its original form—that is, images are stored visually, sounds aurally, and so forth—this storage is very brief. Sperling (1960) showed that the sensory register can store visual sensory information for only one second! In addition, this storage capacity changes little over development: Research has shown, for example, that 5-year-olds and adults have the same time limitations on their ability to store sensory information (Morrison, Holmes, & Haith, 1974).

In the next step of processing, information that enters the sensory register is transformed, or encoded, into a mental representation of some sort that is then placed in the storage area referred to as **short-term, or working, memory.** Short-term memory can best be thought of as the "work space" of the mind (Bjorklund, 2005). Short-term memory is limited in the number of meaningful units or chunks of information that it can hold at any one time, as well as in how long it can hold this information without any active effort to retain it. Without a specific effort, such as rehearsal, we generally lose information from short-term memory within 15 to 30 seconds. Although this temporal limitation is a feature of short-term memory that we might often try to get around, its functional significance is that our conscious processing can respond to a rather continuous flow of incoming information. The ability to use active retention strategies, such as rehearsal, can make a huge difference in how long information can be held in short-term memory. And, because the ability to use strategies like rehearsal improves with age, older children have more proficient short-term memory than

microgenetic analysis A very detailed examination of how a child solves a problem over a single learning episode or over several episodes that occur close in time.

multistore model A model of information processing that depicts information as moving through a series of organized processing units—*sensory register, short-term memory,* and *long-term memory.*

sensory register The mental processing unit that takes information from the environment and stores it in original form for brief periods of time.

short-term, or working, memory The mental processing unit in which information may be stored temporarily; the "work space" of the mind, where a decision must be made to discard information, work on it at present, or transfer it to permanent storage in *long-term memory.*

Figure 9-1   A multistore model of information processing

A model of information processing that describes the flow of information through various stores of the cognitive system.

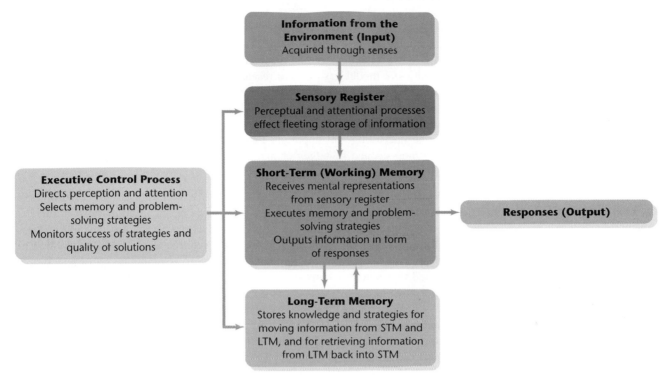

Note: The Executive Control Process is discussed on page 373.

Source: Based on Atkinson & Shiffrin, 1968.

younger children. For example, the faster a child can rehearse a piece of information—let's say, a new word—the shorter the time that will elapse between repetitions of the word during rehearsal and, therefore, more information can be retained (Hitch & Towse, 1995). Figure 9-2 shows how older children's more rapid rehearsal enables them to remember more words.

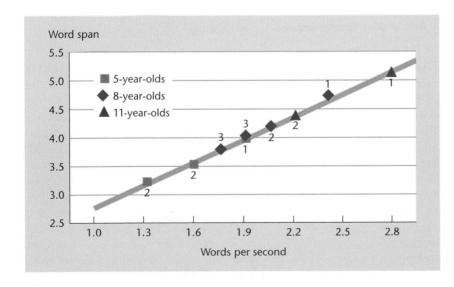

Figure 9-2

Memory skills improve with age

Experimenters asked children in three age groups to memorize a list of words. The older the child, the faster she could pronounce the words in rehearsing them and the more words she could retain in working memory. (Numbers by data points indicate number of syllables in word.) For example, 11-year-olds could pronounce 2.8 single-syllable words per second and could remember about 5 single-syllable words, whereas 5-year-olds could pronounce 1.9 single-syllable words per second and could remember about 4 single-syllable words.

Source: From Siegler, Robert S.; Alibali, Martha W., *Children's Thinking*, 4th Edition, © 2005. Adapted and reprinted by permission of Pearson Education, Inc., Upper Saddle River, NJ.

long-term memory The mental processing unit in which information may be stored permanently and from which it may later be retrieved.

Long-term memory is the term used to describe the mental processing unit in which knowledge is retained over a long period of time. Long-term memory contains information about objects, events, rules, types of problems and ways to solve them, and general knowledge about the world, such as vocabulary and what flowers smell like. In addition, long-term memory stores the strategies for building new knowledge, such as ways of encoding, representing, and retaining information. Information transferred from short- to long-term memory can be retained for an indefinite period of time.

The multistore model has directed research in cognitive development in a number of ways. In particular, this research has examined changes in short-term memory and the way these changes influence the development of long-term memory or the knowledge base. Developmental research based on this model is described here, along with many of the interesting and important findings that this research has revealed about cognitive processes and how they change over childhood.

connectionist models Information-processing approaches that are based on the biological idea of neural networks and that often use computer simulation; these models emphasize human cognition's different layers and networks of cognitive processing.

CONNECTIONIST MODELS   An alternative conceptualization of how information is processed in the cognitive system is offered by the **connectionist models** of human information processing. Connectionist models represent a biologically oriented approach to information processing and are often referred to as neural networks. The approach stresses that information in the brain exists in an elaborate set of neural connections and that much of thinking involves the simultaneous processing of information spread in various ways throughout the network, or *parallel distributed processing.*

From a cognitive developmental perspective, psychologists who adopt a connectivist approach are interested in how connections are organized, how they change over the course of development, and how different connections are activated as a child thinks and solves problems (Elman et al., 1998). Learning and development are seen as the result of changes in the strength and pattern of an individual's neural connections. Researchers have attempted to simulate cognitive development in various areas of mental functioning using connectionist ideas, including language learning, object knowledge, and conceptual development (MacWhinney, 1996; Munakata, McClelland, Johnson, & Siegler, 1997; Plunkett, Karmiloff-Smith, Bates, Elman, & Johnson, 1997). Connectionist models, though still relatively new, have much potential for capturing the complexity of human thinking and learning. The contributions that developmental psychologists can make to this approach are important in that a full understanding of neural networks will require a description of how these networks change with development. A major limitation to date in this approach is the heavy reliance on computer models. Critical tests of how these models map onto human thinking at different points in development are still needed (Miller, 2002).

neo-Piagetian theories Theories of cognitive development that reinterpret Piaget's concepts from an information-processing perspective.

executive control structure According to Case, a mental blueprint or plan for solving a class of problems.

NEO-PIAGETIAN   INFORMATION-PROCESSING   MODELS
Neo-Piagetian theories attempt to integrate Piaget's thought with that of an information-processing perspective. According to Robbie Case (1992, 1998), the proponent of one of these theories, the stagelike development of children's abilities described by Piaget is based both on improvements in memory capacity and executive control. Like Piaget, Case divides development into four stages (Table 9-1). Each of these stages is characterized by increasingly sophisticated executive control structures, which organize thinking. An **executive control structure** is a "mental blueprint or plan for solving a class of problems." An executive control structure has three components (Case, 1984): a representation or description of the problem situation; a representation of the objective or goal of the problem; and a representation of the appropriate strategy or procedure for attaining the goal. Table 9-1 provides examples of how developmental changes in the executive control system lead to different ways of processing information about the world. Case and his colleagues have applied this theory to a variety of different tasks and domains, including scientific reasoning, music

Table 9-1 Case's stages of cognitive development

	Examples of Mental Representations and Operations
Sensorimotor Control Structures (Birth to 1½ Years) Infants' mental representations are linked to their physical movement. Their executive control structures are combinations of physical objects and motor actions.	A child sees a frightening face (sensory) and runs out of the room (motor).
Relational Control Structures (1½ to 5 Years) Children's representations include knowledge of relationships among objects, people, and events. They also include internal representations on which they can act. Children's executive control structures now include cause-and-effect statements and explicit goal structures.	The child produces a mental image of the frightening face (representation) he saw the day before and draws a picture of it (action on representation).
Dimensional Control Structures (5 to 11 Years) Children begin to use logical processes to understand the physical world, as in comparing two dimensions such as distance, number, and weight. They can represent complex stimuli mentally and can act on these representations with simple transformations.	A child may realize that two friends don't like each other (complex representation) and may tell them that they could all have more fun if they were all friends (simple transformation).
Abstract Control Structures (11 to 18½ Years) Building on the dimensional control structures of the preceding stage, children begin to use abstract systems of thought that allow them to perform higher-order reasoning tasks and more complex transformations of information.	The child may realize that such direct attempts to create friendships rarely succeed (abstract representation) and thus may not tell his friends what he proposes but instead plan activities they will all engage in with the hope that greater familiarity and contact will produce the desired relationships (complex transformation).

Sources: Case, 1985; Siegler, 1998.

sight reading, solving spatial problems, conceptual development, reasoning about social problems, and mathematics (see Case, 1998, for a review of this research). Many of the instructional techniques based on these ideas show promise for fostering children's understanding.

Cognitive Processes: What Are They? How Do They Contribute to Development?

As children grow and develop, they become more skilled and efficient in using **cognitive processes,** which are the ways that the human mental system operates on information. Thus, the information-processing perspective is focused on gradual and quantitative changes in mental functioning. Although information-processing theorists have proposed many different cognitive processes that change gradually with development, we focus on four primary ones: encoding and representation, the construction of strategies, automatization, and generalization. These four processes are critical to the development of the information-processing system over the course of childhood, and most information-processing models attempt to describe each of these processes. Finally, we discuss the role that executive control processes play in organizing and monitoring cognitive functioning.

cognitive processes Ways that the human mental system operates on information.

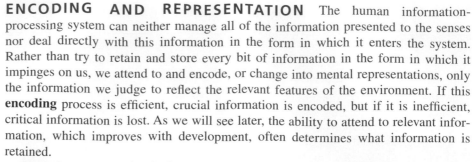

encoding The transformation of information from the environment into a mental representation.

mental representation Information stored in some form (e.g., verbal, pictorial, procedural) in the cognitive system after the person has encountered it in the environment.

strategies Conscious cognitive or behavioral activities used to enhance mental performance.

Using objects of different shapes, colors, and sizes (sometimes called *manipulatives*) can help children in the early grades learn to count, do simple arithmetic problems, and sort objects into categories.

ENCODING AND REPRESENTATION The human information-processing system can neither manage all of the information presented to the senses nor deal directly with this information in the form in which it enters the system. Rather than try to retain and store every bit of information in the form in which it impinges on us, we attend to and encode, or change into mental representations, only the information we judge to reflect the relevant features of the environment. If this **encoding** process is efficient, crucial information is encoded, but if it is inefficient, critical information is lost. As we will see later, the ability to attend to relevant information, which improves with development, often determines what information is retained.

Mental representation is the term used to describe information that is stored mentally in some form (e.g, verbal, pictorial, procedural) after a person has encountered the information in the environment. A mental representation depends on the child's understanding that one thing (e.g., a word such as *chair*) can stand for or "represent" something else (e.g., an actual chair). Some developmentalists have proposed that change in the type and complexity of mental representations underlies much of cognitive development (Bjorklund, 2005). And researchers disagree as to when in development a child can form mental representations; as to whether any representations are innate; and as to whether changes in representations are more qualitative or quantitative.

Encoding and representation are important in information processing and cognitive development. The efficiency with which information is encoded affects the type of processing one can apply to the information, and the complexity of the representation determines how elaborate and detailed the developing connections are.

STRATEGIES The use of strategies is one of the most important processes proposed by the information-processing approach. **Strategies** are conscious cognitive or behavioral activities used to enhance mental performance. Strategies can be applied at all levels of the information-processing system. For example, there are strategies for optimal storage and retrieval of information and for logical problem solving. An example of strategy use appears in children's counting. When we present younger children with an addition problem such as "3 + 14," they will attempt to solve it by using the *count-all* strategy, counting from 1 up to the first term of the problem (i.e., 3) and then continuing to count the number of the second term (i.e., 14 more) until they arrive at the answer of 17. Older children, in contrast, will use a more efficient strategy known as the *min rule.* Using this strategy to solve the problem just described, a child will begin counting from the larger of the two addends (14) and continue upward, adding the amount of the smaller number, thus counting "14, 15, 16, 17" to arrive at the answer and thereby does the minimum amount of counting necessary for solving the problem (Groen & Parkman, 1972).

The main purpose of a strategy is to decrease the load on the child's information-processing system by increasing the efficiency of the system as a whole and thus freeing up space for the various other tasks necessary for solving the problem. Another way to increase the efficiency of the information-processing system is to automatize certain aspects of the solution process.

AUTOMATIZATION   **Automatization** involves making behaviors that once were conscious and controlled into unconscious and automatic ones. A good example of automatization is an adult's learning to drive a car with a stick shift. At first, every shifting of the gears is slow and strained, the driver concentrating on each aspect of shifting in order to do it right. With practice, however, the driver can shift gears quickly and efficiently, unaware of the individual steps involved and often unaware of shifting altogether. In the same way, the child who has developed a memorization strategy for calculating simple addition or multiplication problems comes in time to use this strategy without thinking about it (Siegler & Alibali, 2005). For example, a child who has memorized the mathematical formula that $2 + 2 = 4$ can use this stored knowledge in giving a quick answer to the question "What is 2×2?". In contrast, a child who hasn't memorized the formula may have to stop, think, and perhaps count on his fingers ($[1 + 1] + [1 + 1]$) to figure out the answer.

automatization The process of transforming conscious, controlled behaviors into unconscious and automatic ones.

GENERALIZATION   Initially, the strategies that children develop to solve a given problem tend to be quite specific to the task at hand. Through the process of **generalization,** children apply a strategy learned while solving a problem in one situation to a similar problem in a new situation. Generalization does not happen overnight, though, and children may need to gain familiarity with the use of a rule, using it many times over, before they can successfully generalize it to new situations. Suppose, for example, that the child who used the min rule in the earlier addition problem had arrived at this solution in school. Coming home after school he finds that his mother has bought some jelly beans, and he decides to count the jelly beans so that he and his brother will have the same number of candies. Even though he applied the min rule successfully at school, now that he is presented with a set of concrete objects—a different situation—he may revert to the less sophisticated and more time-consuming strategy of counting all the items. However, with time and experience using the min strategy, more general use of it across problem situations occurs.

generalization The application of a strategy learned while solving a problem in one situation to a similar problem in a new situation.

The Role of the Executive Control Process

All the processes we've discussed are designed to help children increase their efficiency in processing information; crucial to the efficient use of these skills are knowing when to use them and monitoring their use to make sure they are effective. For this reason, an **executive control process** is postulated in the information-processing perspective in order to reflect the active role of the person in regulating cognitive processing. The executive control process guides the child in the selection and adaptation of strategies to particular problems and monitors the success of the problem-solving approach that a child uses. Toward the end of this chapter, we discuss metacognition, which relies on the executive control process.

executive control process A cognitive process that serves to control, guide, and monitor the success of a problem-solving approach a child uses.

Through the executive process, the child directs her intake of information (perception and attention). She can choose what problem she will work on, decide how much effort she will make toward its solution, select the strategies she will apply in this effort, avoid distractions and interruptions that hamper her efforts, and evaluate the quality of her solution. Between the ages of 3 and 12, brain systems that develop—in particular, changes in the prefrontal cortex—are central to the development of the executive control process. Over these years, the child's executive process shows dramatic development. Whereas the preschooler often seems dominated by a task and may apply a single ineffective strategy to a variety of tasks until she is overwhelmed by frustration, the 12-year-old is able to master a wide range of intellectual tasks, orchestrating her strategies to find the best solution to the problem at hand.

Figure 9-3

Knowledge and children's memory
In this test of the hypothesis that amount of knowledge in a particular domain plays a greater role in memory than simple memory capacity, young chess players recalled more chess-piece positions than non-chess-playing adults could (a), and they needed fewer trials than the adults to reach perfect recall (b).

Source: Chi, 1978.

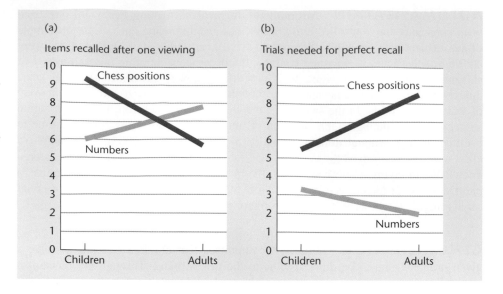

LifeMap CD

To learn more about how information-processing abilities develop, watch the "Mnemonic Strategies in Memory" video in Chapter 9 of your CD.

Effects of Knowledge on the Information-Processing System

One critical feature of information processing that we have yet to discuss is the role of knowledge itself (Keil, 2006). A child's familiarity with the domain or type of problem he is trying to solve plays a major role in his abilities to process information and solve problems (Wellman & Gelman, 1998). Research has shown that when children are given problems in an area in which they know a great deal, they will equal, and even surpass, the performance of less knowledgeable adults (Bedard & Chi, 1992; Chi, 1978).

To study this topic, Michelene Chi (1978) tested both children and adults on their ability to recall either a set of numbers or specific chess-piece positions. The children were experienced chess players, but the adults had only a basic understanding of the game. Chi found that although the third graders and eighth graders could not remember as many numbers as the adults on an immediate recall test, and needed more viewings to reach perfect recall, they far surpassed the adults in remembering chess-piece positions, both immediately and with repeated viewings (Figure 9-3). Chi concluded that the children's knowledge of chess played an important role in their memory performance and that the adult's superiority in recalling numbers may have reflected their generally greater familiarity with number systems.

These results suggest that domain expertise can enhance cognitive processing in children in a familiar domain, but that this expertise does not influence performance in other domains. These results also challenge stagelike views of cognitive development, which emphasize a coherence to the children's ways of thinking within a particular stage. It appears that when children have expertise in a domain, they function at a more advanced level in this domain than they do when they are thinking about problems outside that domain.

DEVELOPMENTAL CHANGES IN SOME SIGNIFICANT COGNITIVE ABILITIES

In this section, we consider what has been learned about the development of some important cognitive abilities when they have been studied using an information-processing approach. These abilities include perception, attention, planning, memory, problem-solving, and reasoning. From an information-processing perspective, each of these abilities plays an important role in how information is operated on. The organization of the information-processing system relies on the flow of information through it. Thus, the system is structured around what happens once information is selected for processing and enters the system, how information is retained in the system, and how information is used in thinking and problem solving.

Perception and Attention

A group of children exposed to the same sensory stimulation do not necessarily take in the same amounts and kinds of information. Each child's **perception** of the surrounding environment—that is, interpretation of information that comes in through the senses—may be the same, but his **attention** may be focused on different aspects of that environment. Attention involves the identification and selection of particular sensory input for closer inspection and more detailed processing. For example, one child in a classroom who is focusing on the teacher will hear and understand the lesson, but another child who is more interested in a whispered message from a neighbor may focus on that sound and regard the teacher's voice as background noise. How children's surroundings affect them depends on what aspects of the surroundings children attend to and what meaning these features have for them.

Perception and attention are tightly interwoven: Each depends on the other. To attend to something we must first perceive it, and to perceive something without attending to it is haphazard at best. The child's choice of what perceptions she will attend to, and in what manner, will determine how the environment's many sights, sounds, smells, touches, and sensations of movement affect her. And as both her perceptual capabilities and attentional strategies develop, they will continue to affect the information she acquires from any particular situation. As children develop, they combine attention with other cognitive processes: for example, they make use of planning, in the form of deliberate attempts to obtain knowledge from the environment that will make it possible for them to reach a goal.

HOW PERCEPTION DEVELOPS The two main theoretical perspectives on perceptual development revolve around a basic but unresolved controversy: Do we construct the meaning of a new object by *enriching* our perception of the object with stored knowledge, or do we become more efficient at detecting and *differentiating* an object's features, which are already endowed with suffcent information to support human perception? Piaget advocated the enrichment view, which emphasizes how the organism makes sense of perceptual experience and is consistent with a constructionist perspective. In contrast, the developmental psychologist Eleanor Gibson advanced a differentiation view that emphasizes how perceptual skills are coordinated with environmental input that is, in itself, informative.

The **enrichment view** of perceptual development proposes that each time a child perceives an object he learns a little more about that object as he integrates new information with old. For example, the first time a child sees a cat, he may view it as little more than another fuzzy, four-footed animal. The next time he sees the cat, he may elaborate his cat schema to include "purrs and likes milk." Yet another time he may try to pick the cat up but find it too heavy. Cats then become fuzzy, four-footed animals that purr, drink milk, and are heavy. According to this view, the information received from the environment is, by its nature, limited in what it conveys to a person. Thus, it must be modified and enriched by the mind, specifically information from existing schemata. Over development, as children add new information to an object's schema they also reorganize and elaborate the schema so that it becomes fuller and more detailed. This type of developmental change was described in our discussion of Piaget's theory in Chapter 8.

perception The interpretation of sensations to make them meaningful.

attention The identification and selection of particular sensory input for closer inspection and more detailed processing.

enrichment view The notion that the child acquires additional information about an object from each repeated experience with it, further modifying and enriching these data with information from existing schemata.

differentiation view The notion that the child learns to identify and discriminate among the important features of objects and relationships from the rich source of information sensory input provides.

In contrast, Eleanor Gibson's (1969; Gibson & Pick, 2000) **differentiation view** proposes that sensory input is in itself a rich source of information and not in need of enrichment. Instead, the child's task is to learn to identify and discriminate among the important features of objects from the vast flow of sensory information with which he comes in contact. Gradually, the child learns to attend to the relevant attributes of objects and to make increasingly finer discriminations among objects and events. Gibson terms the relevant attributes of objects or events *invariants,* by which she means that these characteristics do not vary or change under different conditions even though they may appear to change. For example, a gray cat may appear nearly black in dim light (e.g., indoors, by a small table lamp) but nearly white in bright light (e.g., outdoors on a sunny day). But the cat's black collar will always appear darker than its fur, regardless of the light. The relationship between the brightness of the cat and of its collar does not change; an object's brightness relative to other objects in its surroundings is a perceptual invariant.

According to Gibson's view, it is the invariant properties of objects and events to which the perceptual system attends and which uniquely describe information in the environment (Gibson & Pick, 2000). Thus, perceptual development entails learning to attend to the relevant invariants of objects and events and using this information to find differences among similar stimuli. For example, as we saw in Chapter 4, newborns tend to notice the edges and angles of faces but not the internal features such as the nose or mouth. As babies develop, however, they begin to notice and distinguish more features, such as color, texture, and the central parts of an object. Moreover, children learn to ignore an object's irrelevant features and to focus on the important ones.

Gibson was especially interested in the interplay between perception and action. The action-relevant features of objects are called *affordances* because they tell us what actions an object affords or allows us to perform—for example, a ball affords throwing, a chair affords sitting (Gibson, 2000). Gradually, children learn to recognize the action properties or potentials of objects, or affordances, and to use this information to guide their goal-directed behaviors. For example, Berger and Adolph (2003) found that 16-month-old infants in a laboratory play area who crossed a bridge that did not have handrails were more cautious than were infants who crossed a bridge that had handrails. Figure 9-4 illustrates this task. Children in this study perceived that the presence of a handrail affords a different type of locomotion, and they adjusted their walking accordingly.

Figure 9-4   Crossing a bridge with and without a handrail

By 16 months of age, infants will walk differently over a bridge, depending on whether a handrail is present (a) or not (b). According to Gibson's view of perceptual development, the infants perceive the handrail to afford a different type of locomotion or movement and they use this affordance when it is available to aid their walking. By the way, the infants were quite safe during this experiment. An experimenter was nearby to ensure their safety and the area beneath the bridge was lined with padding.

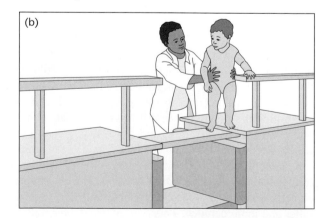

Source: Berger & Adolph, 2003.

Gibson's theory has had a major impact on research on early perception—however, some of the assertions in the enrichment view, especially those pertaining to the development of concepts about objects and events, remain important in early cognitive development. Even young babies seem not only to detect features but also to impose meaning on their perceptual world. In short, some of the ideas behind both the enrichment view, especially the active construction of meaning, and the differentiation view, primarily regarding the detection and selection of information in the environment, appear to play a role in perceptual development.

ATTENTION: CHOOSING WHAT IS PERCEIVED   When a topic is interesting, attention seems simple and effortless. In fact, however, attention is a very complex process, affected by the perceiver's sophistication and by both the type of information and the way it's presented. Children have difficulty controlling their attention when they are young. As they develop, they face the formidable tasks of learning to attend to what is relevant in a situation and of learning systematic strategies for planning how to solve a problem.

Control of Attention   Very young children can sustain their attention for only short periods. However, this ability increases steadily over development (Ruff & Rothbart, 1996). Even over the first year of life, there are a number of changes in the focus and duration of attentional behaviors. Between 2 and 3 months of age, the focus of the infant's attention shifts from the external contours of objects toward their internal features. From 3 to 9 months of age, infants show increasing control over their attention, and by 9 months of age infants can use attention to solve rudimentary problems such as getting toys from behind barriers (Willatts, 1990). Ruff and Rothbart (1996) see this type of behavior as indicative of the beginning of a higher form of attention, one that coordinates information that is physically present, such as a barrier, with information available in some form of mental representation or memory, in this case a hidden toy. Over the first few years of life, the duration of attention increases and distractibility decreases. Ruff and Capozzoli (2003) found that 10-month-olds were far more distractible than 26- and 42-month-olds when playing with toys appropriate for their ages. The youngest group responded more frequently to distracters, which in this case were images and sounds from a video player, and they also looked at these

Attention is important in learning to read. Children respond best to material that's appropriate to their age level, and at about 3 they begin making marked gains in their ability to focus their attention.

Figure 9-5

Attention in the face of distracters
In the third year of life, children are already showing some skill at being able to focus their attention when distracting information is present.

Source: From Ruff & Rothbart, 1996.

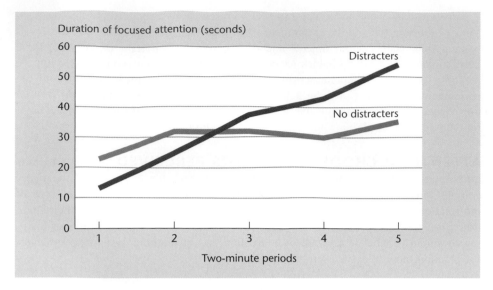

distracters longer than the older children. Interestingly, some of the 42-month-old children increased their attentional focus in the presence of the distracters. This pattern suggests that children as young as 42 months of age may be less distractible when an activity fully engages their attention. The observation is consistent with research with preschool and school-age children, which shows that distraction can sometimes facilitate children's performance. For example, Turnure (1970) found that preschoolers did better on a learning task when they listened to sounds that had nothing to do with the task, such as typing or a recording of a children's song (see Figure 9-5). Other research (Higgins & Turnure, 1984; Humphrey, 1982) suggests that older, school-age children perform better on learning tasks when there are visual or auditory distracters present than when they are not present. Together, these results suggest that even preschoolers are learning to hone their attention to relevant information, that with increasing age children are less easily distracted, and that older children are more able than younger children to narrow the focus of their attention in the presence of distracters to carry out the task at hand. The Turning Points chart (p. 379) notes these and other advances in children's cognitive skills.

With development, children are more likely to attend to material appropriate to their intellectual level than to other types of information (Anderson, Lorch, Field, & Sanders, 1981). Even young children are quite sensitive to the importance of information being presented; when questioned about a program they had viewed, 4- and 6-year-old children were more likely to recall important facts from the program than unimportant facts (Lorch, Bellack, & Augsbach, 1987). Finally, the manner of presentation is important—for example, researchers have found that children younger than 6 are more interested in the visual than in the audio content of programs (Hayes, Chemelski, & Bernbaum, 1981). Thus, when watching "Sesame Street," they are more likely to be interested in Big Bird's funny appearance, big feet, awkward movements, and wry facial expressions than in what he is saying.

Learning to Attend to What's Relevant   If the child is to learn, she must acquire the strategy of **selective attention,** in which she focuses on the relevant aspects of a task and ignores the irrelevant features. Shifts in selective attention are evident as early as 2 to 3 months of age. Whereas neonates may look longer at an object just because it is larger or brighter than another object, by 2 to 3 months of age infants begin to select what to look at based more on the form or pattern of the information available (Ruff & Rothbart, 1996). As children get older, the ability to attend selectively increases and enhances children's ability to learn.

selective attention A strategy in which one focuses on some features of the environment and ignores others.

Turning Points

SOME COGNITIVE ACHIEVEMENTS AS SEEN FROM THE INFORMATION-PROCESSING VIEW

1 YEAR
- Has limited attentional capacity; can attend to a toy for only a few seconds
- May have a rudimentary understanding of categories

2 YEARS
- Has increased attentional capacity; will spend more than eight seconds with a single toy
- Can use external supports such as landmarks to find hidden toys
- May be able to use basic category labels to help remember things
- May be able to draw very simple analogies
- Relies on scripts of familiar events

3 YEARS
- Can use two rules in combination
- Often distracted by other things while watching TV but, when attention is fully engaged, may be quite attentive to a program
- May be able to use fairly sophisticated analogies in solving a problem
- Understands relationship between scale models and real objects

4 YEARS
- With a meaningful context and guidance in using simple strategies, can focus attention on relevant aspects of the environment and apply the information gained to a task
- Can combine two or more rules into a higher-order rule
- Knows that long lists are harder to remember than short lists
- Understands that if you try harder on a more difficult task, you may succeed

5 YEARS
- Can memorize four units in a digit-span test
- Understands that thinking has content, that it is different from both perception and knowing, and that only people (and perhaps some other animate organisms) can think; can sometimes infer thinking in others if the evidence is strong

6 YEARS
- Begins to find audio content of TV programs as interesting as visual content
- With enough cues, may be able to plan a very effective strategy of attention

7 YEARS
- With training, may score as well on a test of recall as 12-year-olds

10 YEARS
- Becomes more selective in searching for information needed to make decisions

11 YEARS
- Begins to spend less time processing irrelevant information

12 YEARS
- Can memorize six or seven units in a digit-span test

Note: Developmental events described in this and other Turning Points charts represent overall trends identified in research studies. Individual children vary greatly in the ages at which they achieve these developmental changes.

Sources: Flavell, Miller, & Miller, 1993b; Siegler, 1998.

Figure 9-6   Paying attention to what's important

All the children in this study initially looked inside every box, finding pictures of animals in those with cages on their doors and pictures of household items in the boxes that displayed houses. When researchers asked 3-year-olds to recall where particular animals were, they opened house as well as cage doors, but 8-year-olds ignored the irrelevant house boxes and checked only the cage ones.

Source: Miller & Seier, 1994.

Research by Miller and her colleagues (Miller & Seier, 1994; Miller & Weiss, 1981) has shown that in the school years, children improve markedly in their ability to focus their attention on relevant information. These researchers presented 7-, 10-, and 13-year-old children with a learning task in which they asked the children to remember the location of a number of toy animals, each of which was hidden behind a different cover. As the experimenters lifted each cover to show the children each target animal, the children also saw a household item, such as a frying pan or an iron. The children's task was to remember the target object (the toy animal) while rejecting the irrelevant object (the household item). Not surprisingly, the older children were much better than the younger ones at recalling the target objects.

In another study, investigators (Miller & Seier, 1994) gave children a study period in which they could open up any of the boxes in which objects had been placed to help them remember the location of the target objects (again, animals). There were pictures of cages on the doors to the boxes containing animals and pictures of houses on the doors to the boxes holding household objects (Figure 9-6). Older children (8-year-olds) focused on the first set of boxes and ignored the second set. However, the youngest children (3-year-olds) looked equally at both kinds of boxes during the study period. Modifying attentional strategies paid off: The older children remembered more than the younger children. In short, older children use more selective search strategies, whereas younger children use more exhaustive methods.

To investigate how children's attentional and information-search strategies change over time and how these strategies affect both children's acquisition of information for making decisions and the quality of those decisions, Davidson (1996) presented second- and fifth-grade children with four elaborate visual displays. Each display (called an "information board") provided information on six varieties of an item (the four items were bicycles, books, computer games, and kites) and on six dimensions of the items (e.g., color or special features). It also contained a brief "Decision Story" that outlined the problem and the need for a decision (Table 9-2). The experimenter told the children to point to the dimension on which they wanted information and to say when they thought they had enough information to make a decision. For the story

Table 9-2 Illustration of an information board and its corresponding story

Bicycle	Amount of Color on Bicycle	Size of Bicycle	Number of Speeds
Bicycle A	Lots of color	Just right	Some speeds
Bicycle B	Lots of color	Too small	Some speeds
Bicycle C	Some color	Too big	Lots of speeds
Bicycle D	Little color	Just right	No speeds
Bicycle E	Little color	Too big	Some speeds
Bicycle F	Some color	Just right	No speeds

Bicycle	Amount of Rust on Bicycle	Special Features	Number of Your Friends Who Have Bicycle
Bicycle A	No rust	Lots: Horn & light	Some friends
Bicycle B	Some rust	No features	Some friends
Bicycle C	Lots of rust	Lots: Horn & light	No friends
Bicycle D	No rust	Some features	Lots of friends
Bicycle E	Some rust	Lots: Horn & light	Lots of friends
Bicycle F	Lots of rust	No features	No friends

Decision Story
Sarah likes to ride her bicycle, but it is getting old and rusty. Sarah wants to buy a new bicycle with lots of special features like a horn and a light. Sarah's parents took Sarah to the bicycle shop so she could pick out a new bike. The bicycle shop was filled with many beautiful bikes. Sarah knew that she wanted a bike with some speeds and with lots of color. Sarah is having a hard time deciding on a bicycle. Can you find a bicycle that she would like?

Source: Davidson, 1996.

illustrated in Table 9-2, the most effective search strategy would be to focus on the dimensions of color and speed, ignoring the rest; narrowing the search to bicycle A or B, Sarah would choose A because it also has lots of special features and is the right size.

Davidson found that the younger children (on average, 8 years old) tended to use exhaustive searches, whereas the older children (11 years old) used more selective search strategies. However, when the experimenter highlighted some of the decision dimensions by placing cards displaying one of the dimensions directly above the appropriate column on the board, both second graders and fifth graders became more selective and thus more efficient in their searching. Such assistance by the experimenter improved the performance of the young children beyond what they could do on their own, as predicted by Vygotsky's (1978a) notion of the zone of proximal development, discussed in Chapter 8. But even with such assistance, the younger children still did not reach the level of performance of the older children, suggesting that some maturational contribution is also an important part of this development.

As Figure 9-7 shows, the processing of relevant information increases steadily throughout the elementary and high school years. Processing of irrelevant information,

Figure 9-7

Children's changing attention to relevant and irrelevant information
Children steadily increase their attention to relevant information, but their concern with irrelevant information weakens and drops off quickly after junior high.

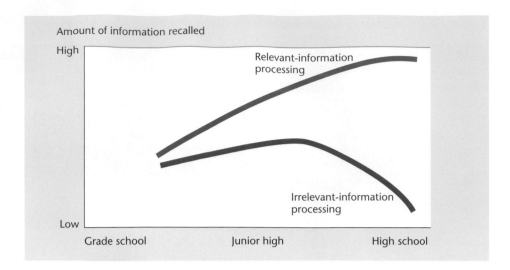

however, increases slightly until the age of 11 or 12 and then decreases rapidly. This view of children's developing attentional focus fits well with the predictions of the information-processing view of development—that is, that increasing efficiency in the child's cognitive processing helps fuel cognitive development.

Attention and Planning   One of the reasons older children are more adept at deploying attention is that they are able to develop a plan of action to guide their attention as they solve problems. As children get older, the types of problems they try to solve get more complex. With development, the ability to attend selectively combines with **planning,** which is the deliberate organization of a sequence of actions oriented toward achieving a goal, and enables the child to orchestrate his problem-solving behaviors by anticipating actions in advance.

The coordination of attention and planning is illustrated in a classic study by Elaine Vurpillot (1968) that used the drawings of houses presented in Figure 9-8. Suppose

planning The deliberate organization of a sequence of actions oriented toward achieving a goal.

Figure 9-8   A test of children's ability to gather and filter information
How quickly can you perform a task given to young children—to determine which pairs of houses, either pair (a) or pair (b), are identical?

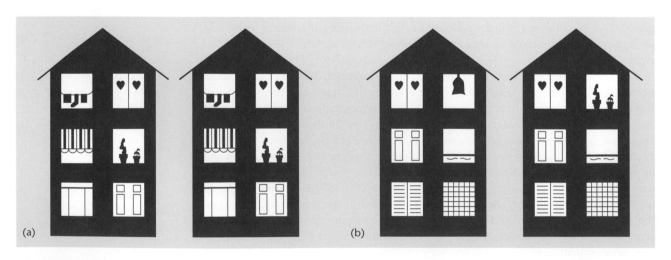

Source: Vurpillot, 1968.

that you were asked to determine whether each pair of houses was identical. How might you approach this problem? Probably, you would compare the six pairs of corresponding windows in each pair of houses until you found a pair in which the objects displayed did not match. If all the pairs matched, you would conclude that the houses were identical. When Vurpillot administered this task to children, she found that younger children were far less likely than older children to apply a systematic plan to extract the necessary information. Filming the children's eye movements as they made their comparisons, she found that younger children tended to look at the windows randomly and even made judgments without ever looking at the windows that were different.

Should we conclude from this research that the young child is unable to plan an efficient use of her attention? In studies in which researchers put a task into a meaningful context, even young children are able to integrate their attention into a problem-solving plan effectively. For example, Miller and Aloise-Young (1995) gave preschool children (ages 3 to 4) a task that required them to open doors to reveal two arrays of pictures and then to determine if the arrays were the same or different. When the task was embedded in an engaging story context, the children were able to attend to the appropriate contextual information and plan their solution more effectively. However, even in meaningful contexts, preschoolers can run into difficulty regulating their attention while they plan because they are less able to inhibit or suspend action during an ongoing activity, which is critical to planning (Kochanska, Murray, & Harlan, 2000).

Planning is often done in social situations and, therefore, it becomes a joint cognitive activity. As we saw in Chapter 8, Vygotskian theory reminds us that social and cognitive development are closely linked. In everyday life, parents, older siblings, or other more competent partners such as relatives, friends, and teachers are often available to guide young children in planning more efficiently. Using a model grocery store, Gauvain and Rogoff (1989) compared the planning behavior of 5- and 9-year-olds working with a peer, an adult, or alone. The older children were better at organizing their attentional resources and planning ahead, and children who planned in advance of action devised more efficient routes. Children were more likely to use attentional strategies and plan efficiently when they worked with a peer or adult partner, especially when the partners shared task responsibility. Sharing responsibility for carrying out a task helps children understand the task from the perspective of another person. Learning about the thinking of another appears to enhance the child's own understanding of the problem.

Memory

Memory is one of the most extensively studied topics in cognitive development. An interest in human memory and how it develops is not surprising if one considers what memory is. Everything you know you remember in some way. In fact, if you do not remember something, it is reasonable to say that you do not know it. Thus, the terms *memory* and *knowledge* are interchangeable. Acts of memory range from rapid-fire, basic processes, such as word and face recognition, to the recall of complex knowledge systems and events, such as the rules of chess and how a family coped with the Great Depression. The development of memory is a major accomplishment in children's development.

Because of the broad scope of information included in the term memory, it is not surprising that memory is a multifaceted process and that there are several different types of memory (Schneider & Bjorkland, 1998). Some types of memory are more influenced by experiential factors than are others. As we have discussed, short-term, or working, memory is the conscious areas of memory. Long-term memory is where knowledge that we retain for long periods of time is stored. Long-term memory's vast

semantic memory All the world knowledge and facts a person possesses.

episodic memory Memory for specific events, often autobiographical in nature.

memory span The amount of information one can hold in short-term memory.

If this child is dialing a telephone number from memory, she is probably demonstrating a greater memory span than is common among children her age.

array of information, which includes all the world knowledge and facts a person possesses, is called **semantic memory.** Included in semantic memory is memory for specific events, or **episodic memory** (Bauer, 2006). Much of the latter is autobiographical in nature, for it includes memories of important events or experiences that have happened to an individual. Later we discuss the development of autobiographical memory, which has been the topic of much recent research.

The act of remembering can be either intentional or unintentional. Much of everyday experience involves unintentional forms of remembering. It is rarely necessary to exert intentional effort to recall such things as language (e.g., vocabulary), behavioral routines (e.g., how to get ready for school in the morning), and personal experiences (e.g., what happened yesterday). In contrast, intentional memory, also called *explicit memory,* requires overt effort during storage and retrieval. Much of the research on the development of memory focuses on the strategies children use to remember information intentionally. Strategies such as rehearsal, organization, and elaboration are some of the techniques that, over time, children use increasingly to help them store and recall information.

The three areas of memory that gain strength and efficiency with time are (1) basic capacities, or the amount of information that can be held in short-term memory and how efficiently and quickly this information can be processed; (2) strategies or techniques that enhance the transfer of information from short-term to long-term memory; and (3) world knowledge, the larger context of information into which the child can fit new information. We will discuss each of these aspects in turn. Following our discussion of memory, we turn to the related cognitive process of problem solving. In practice it is not easy to separate the cognitive functions of memory and problem solving. Think about it. If you couldn't hold things in memory or retrieve them efficiently, you would find it impossible to solve any kind of problem. However, because it is important to understand memory ability and problem solving on their own before considering how they may work together, we discuss memory in this section and problem solving in the next.

BASIC CAPACITIES   We discuss three basic and interrelated capacities of the memory system and how these develop: the amount of information that can be held in short-term, or working, memory, referred to as memory span, the efficiency of memory processing, and the speed of this processing. Research on these basic capacities raises interesting questions about how they develop and contribute to the functioning of the memory system more generally. Recent research has shown that these basic capacities, in particular processing efficiency and processing speed, are intricately related to each other and have a clear impact on the effectiveness of working memory (Demetriou, Christou, Spanoudis, & Platsidou, 2002).

Memory Span   Suppose you are asked to repeat a sequence of numbers. Let's say the sequence begins with three digits, and then progressively more numbers are added. Eventually, you will be unable to repeat all the numbers correctly, for the sequence will have exceeded your **memory span** for this kind of information. The amount of information that a person can keep in mind—that is, in working memory—at any one time is limited. For example, memory for a series of numbers (digit span) is about eight units for college students, six or seven units for 12-year-olds, and four units for 5-year-olds (Brener, 1940; Starr, 1923). There are several explanations for this age-related change. Some argue that it represents a change in actual capacity—that is, the actual amount of information than can be held in short-term memory increases with development (Pascual-Leone, 1980, 1989). Others argue that there is no solid evidence for a capacity change as children develop (e.g., Dempster, 1985), and they point to evidence that shows that young children, as compared with adults, can remember more items from lists of items that interest them, such as toys. Such findings demonstrate that interest or motivation plays a role in memory span, and capacity changes may not be necessary to explain changes associated with age (Lindberg, 1980).

Another explanation for older children's and adults' greater memory span is that they use one or more strategies that help them organize such information in a way that facilitates remembering it (Chi, 1976). In particular, the older person may "chunk" the information into smaller, more easily remembered groups of numbers (Miller, 1956). Thus, whereas the young child may not be able to remember the sequence 1 4 9 2 1 7 7 6 1 8 1 2 because it is too long, the adult can recall the sequence because she "chunks" the numbers into meaningful groups: 1492, 1776, 1812. Notice that world knowledge, which increases with age, enables this ability to chunk.

Processing Efficiency   The first time a child uses a memory strategy, such as chunking, it takes up a fair amount of space in working memory. However, with practice, the use of such strategies becomes more automatic and, as a result, space in working memory becomes available to work on other problems or strategies. Case (1996) proposes that one of the important developmental changes in basic memory capacities is that the memory system simply gets more efficient. Case divides *executive processing space* into two distinct components: operating space and short-term storage space. *Operating space* is the amount of space necessary for a particular cognitive operation to take place (e.g., identifying a word). *Short-term storage space* refers to the amount of mental space devoted to short-term memory storage. Case proposes that, with development, children become more efficient in their execution of operations; consequently, they need less operating space to perform an operation. As Figure 9-9 shows, this decrease in the amount of operating space frees up more short-term storage space. With increased storage space, children can now attempt to solve complex problems that may contain a great deal of information to be remembered.

Case (1985) attributes the child's increasing efficiency to two factors: streamlining of executive control structures (e.g., as the result of strategies, such as chunking and automatization) and biological maturation, such as changes in the myelination of nerves. Recall from Chapter 5 that as the child grows, the process of myelination coats the axons of neurons in such a way as to increase the efficiency of neuronal firing and, presumably, the efficiency of brain function. Although Case's position on the role of biological maturation in cognitive development has yet to be fully tested (Siegler & Alibali, 2005), his emphasis on the role of increasing efficiency in the use of memory is well supported.

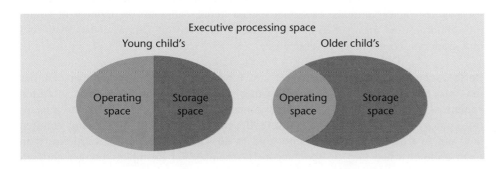

Executive processing space
Young child's   Older child's

Operating space   Storage space   Operating space   Storage space

Figure 9-9

The use of executive processing space

According to Case, as children learn to process information more quickly and efficiently, their diminishing need for operating space frees up more space for storing information.

Source: Adapted from Case, 1985.

Processing Speed   Processing speed, which is often assessed by reaction time, is the time it takes an individual to carry out a given mental act, such as recognizing a stimulus or reading a word. Processing speed is intricately linked with processing efficiency; the more efficient a process, the quicker it is. Kail (1991, 2000) has demonstrated that speed of processing increases linearly with age from childhood to early adulthood. Moreover, he has suggested that age-related increases in the speed of information processing are responsible for much of the improvement that occurs in children's cognitive abilities as they develop.

Developmental changes in processing speed are similar for tasks that are very different from one another, such as reading comprehension, mental addition, retrieving names from memory, and visual search (Kail, 1995). According to Kail, the fact that we see developmental changes in processing speeds in many different tasks with widely varying task components and requirements suggests that change in processing speed is a fundamental aspect of cognitive development. Because the pattern of development is similar across different types of tasks, Kail (1991, 2000) contends that a common mechanism underlies speed of processing across different tasks. We also know that processing speed is not simply due to practice. With development, children increase the speed with which they accomplish tasks that they encounter regularly and those that they rarely encounter (and therefore have little opportunity to practice) (Kail, 1995; Miller & Vernon, 1997). Finally, Kail and Park (1994) found the same relation between processing speed and age in Korean children and American children, which suggests that this may be a universal developmental process. All these findings suggest that increases in processing speed exert a significant influence on children's age-related improvements in task performance.

MEMORY STRATEGIES   Memory strategies are deliberate, planful procedures that help people carry out memory-related tasks. Because what can be held in short-term, or working, memory is limited, if we want to remember something that exceeds these limitations it is critical to use some specific technique or strategy. Additionally, the importance of being able to store and retrieve information efficiently from long-term memory also relies on strategies. People use a wide range of strategies to increase the likelihood that they will remember needed information at a later time. Some of these strategies involve external supports such as taking notes in lectures or writing down appointments on calendars. Other memory supports are purely mental (e.g., repeating a person's name to yourself several times so you can remember to ask a friend about her later). Adults commonly use the memory strategies of rehearsal, organization, and elaboration, and developmentalists have studied these three strategies to determine when and how they emerge in childhood and what role they may play in enhancing children's memory.

Although researchers often study these strategies separately, it would be a serious mistake to assume that children have only one strategy available to them at any one time (Schneider & Bjorkland, 1998; Siegler, 1996). Children's use of multiple strategies was demonstrated in a study by Coyle and Bjorkland (1997) in which they presented second-, third-, and fourth-grade children with sets of words (e.g., *house, pencil, carrot, bean, dog, book, cat, potato*) that could be organized into categories such as vegetables, animals, or school-related items. Although the number of strategies children used to organize the words increased over age (Figure 9-10), even second graders used a variety of strategies.

Rehearsal   One of the simplest strategies for recall is to repeat a number of times the information to be remembered, either mentally or out loud. This is called **rehearsal.** Research has shown that the spontaneous use of verbal rehearsal as a memory strategy increases with age (Flavell, Beach, & Chinsky, 1966). Young children tend not to rehearse unless explicitly told to do so, and they are less efficient than older children when they do spontaneously rehearse. For example, younger children

rehearsal A memory strategy in which one repeats a number of times the information one wants to remember, either mentally or orally.

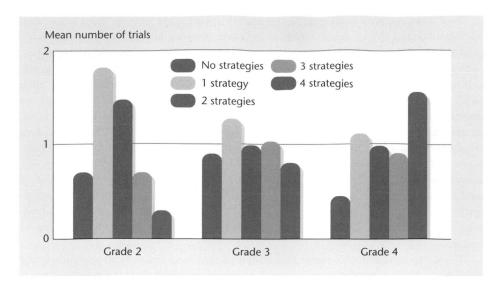

Mean number of trials

No strategies   3 strategies
1 strategy   4 strategies
2 strategies

Grade 2   Grade 3   Grade 4

Figure 9-10

More strategies, more memory

In a memory task, the oldest children used more strategies and recalled more words. Quite a few of the youngest children used multiple strategies, but their recall was less accurate.

Source: Coyle & Bjorklund, 1997.

will repeat the items to be remembered only once or twice when more repetitions are needed, and they are less likely to repeat earlier items (Naus, 1982). However, even young children can employ and benefit from rehearsal strategies if instructed to use them (Keeney, Cannizzo, & Flavell, 1967).

In a classic study, John Flavell and his colleagues (Flavell et al., 1966) showed a series of pictures to a group of children ranging from kindergartners to fifth graders and asked them to recall the sequence in which an experimenter pointed to a subset of the pictures. Watching the children's lip movements for a sign that they were rehearsing by naming the pictures to themselves, the researchers found that the children who used spontaneous verbal rehearsal had better memory for the pictures and that the use of such rehearsal increased dramatically with age. Whereas only about 10 percent of kindergarten children rehearsed the names of the objects in the pictures, more than 60 percent of second graders and over 85 percent of fifth graders did so. Later research by Ornstein, Naus, and Liberty (1975) modified this finding somewhat by showing that it was not the frequency of rehearsal that predicted performance differences in younger and older children. Rather, the style of rehearsal differs in younger and older children, and this explains the performance differences associated with age. Younger children are more likely to rehearse each item one at a time as it is presented to them. Older children are more likely to rehearse each item in a group with previously rehearsed items. It seems that the use of a more cumulative rehearsal strategy that includes several items at a time is more effective in aiding memory of items in a list. Although younger children can be trained to use a cumulative rehearsal strategy (Cox, Ornstein, Naus, Maxfield, & Zimler, 1989), older children are more likely to use this strategy spontaneously.

Organization   When we store information, we often organize it in a way that makes it more meaningful and thus easier to remember. How does the process of actively altering and rebuilding information change as children get older? An answer to this question is found in research on the use of the memory strategy known as **organization,** or the process of imposing an organization on the information to be remembered by means of categories and hierarchical relationships.

organization A memory strategy that involves putting together in some organized form the information to be remembered; usually entails categorization and hierarchical relations.

Competing in a spelling bee usually requires a child to spend a lot of time rehearsing specific words and their spellings. And winning a prize can be a powerful motivator for using such cognitive strategies!

Over time, children make increasing use of organization to help them remember. The spontaneous use of organization to facilitate memory appears late in elementary school (Hasselhorn, 1992). By grade 4, most children use organizational strategies, such as categorizing and sorting, on a wide range of tasks and they use these strategies effectively (Bjorklund, 2005). For example, as children mature they are more likely to use categories and verbal labels to help them remember. Suppose that we present a series of cards containing pictures of a *sweater, hat, apple, orange, jeans, sandwich, gloves, coat, milk,* and *dress* to children of different ages. Older children would be more likely than younger ones to form the cards into two groups of similar objects: *apple, orange, sandwich,* and *milk* as food items and *sweater, hat, jeans, gloves, coat,* and *dress* as items of clothing (Schneider & Bjorklund, 1998). In addition, children who use this strategy are better able to recall the items in a subsequent test (Best, 1993; Best & Ornstein, 1986) and more likely to argue for the advantages of this organizational strategy when asked to teach a younger child how to remember.

Are we to assume that young children are incapable of learning to use categorization? No, indeed. Children as young as 2 or 3 years old have been found to use basic category labels to help them learn and remember (Waxman, Shipley, & Shepperson, 1991). Also, recall from Chapter 8 that assistance from more skilled people such as parents and teachers may enhance a child's cognitive performance. Researchers have been able to teach children as young as 7 to use organizational strategies like categorization. For example, Ackerman (1996) prompted 7- and 12-year-olds to categorize a set of words (e.g., *horse, pig, cow*) by asking them "Are all of these animals?" Older children generally recalled more than younger ones, but, with training, 7-year-olds did as well as their older peers.

Another way to help children use an organizing strategy in remembering is to give them a contextual cue. For example, we may give children a set of words to remember (e.g., *horse, pig, goat*) and a place (e.g., *farm*) where they might see these animals. Children who are provided with such a context or place cue do better at recall than children who are not provided with this information. Context reminders are particularly useful when a task is hard—for example, if you've only one word to remember, say *pig,* it's very helpful to have a context cue, like *farm.* Recall from Chapter 4 that even infants can recall better when contextual cues are available.

Finally, children's motivation can also influence strategy use. Guttentag (1995) presented third graders with pictures of common objects to be recalled (25 pictures in five categories), and used these measures to explore the effects of intrinsic motivation, success-dependent rewards, and active participation on children's willingness to invest time in an organizing strategy. Active participation (being allowed to place the pictures themselves) led all children to use the organizational strategy and thereby facilitated their recall. Reward for achievement appeared to affect strategy use only in highly motivated children, and these children generally did better at the task than children whose motivation was low.

elaboration A memory strategy in which one adds to information to make it more meaningful and thus easier to remember.

Elaboration   Using the strategy of **elaboration,** we add to the information we want to remember in order to make it more meaningful and thus easier to place in long-term memory. This is a useful strategy because, although it might seem to add to the information burden, we are much more likely to remember something that is meaningful to us (Kee, 1994; Schneider & Bjorklund, 1998). The *Peanuts* cartoon in Figure 9-11 shows how Charlie Brown elaborates the numbers of his locker combination with major league players' numbers to provide a meaningful context for three seemingly random numbers. As with other strategies we discuss, as children get older they are more likely to use elaboration spontaneously and effectively.

Elaboration involves the association of items to be remembered with other information, which can be in verbal or visual form. An example of elaboration that used both of these forms can be seen in a study that involved training fifth- and sixth-grade

Figure 9-11

Charlie Brown's elaboration
strategy

Source: PEANUTS reprinted by permission
of United Feature Syndicate, Inc.

children to use a "keyword" strategy. In this research, Michael Pressley and colleagues (O'Sullivan & Pressley, 1984; Pressley, Cariglia-Bull, Deane, & Schneider, 1987) were able to improve the children's memory performance greatly. These researchers first prepared a list of 15 real cities in the United States, choosing only cities whose names sounded in part like a concrete object the children would know (e.g., the name Lock Haven contains the word *lock*). They then showed the children the list of city names, which included the major product of each city. Instructing the children in the keyword method, they told the children to notice the object that appeared in the city's name and to construct an image that linked the object and the city's major product. As an example, they pointed out that Lock Haven's major product is paper and showed the children a picture of a lock attached to a newspaper. Children who learned this keyword strategy recalled many more city-product pairs than children who had not received the keyword training.

Why Do Young Children Not Use Strategies?   Why do young children fail to use strategies to help them remember? By and large, older children use more strategies to help them remember than younger children do. There are three explanations as to why young children fail to use strategies that older children and adults find so useful. First, children may possess a **mediational deficiency:** This suggests that they simply can't make use of strategies for incorporating information into long-term storage. The fact that children can be taught to use such strategies, however, makes this proposal seem unlikely.

A second explanation proposes that young children have a **production deficiency:** This suggests that although they may know certain strategies for remembering, they are unable to generate and use these strategies spontaneously. One implication of the production deficiency explanation is that younger children who do not produce strategies to aid memory are not doing anything while they are trying to remember something. Although the strategies that young children use may not be the same strategies that older children and adults use, and although they are not always effective, they

mediational deficiency
Inability to use strategies to store information in long-term memory.

production deficiency
Inability to generate and use known memory strategies spontaneously.

are nonetheless strategic acts by the child. For example, DeLoache and Brown (1983) observed children as young as 18 months of age as they tried to remember the hiding place of a toy in their own home after a brief waiting period. While some of the strategies children used aided memory, such as staring or pointing at the hiding location during the entire waiting period, others were less effective, such as repeating the name of the toy over and over with little or no attention to the hiding place. Other research has shown that preschoolers can use a variety of strategies when solving problems and that their use of these strategies becomes more efficient with practice. Thus, even young children can produce memory strategies spontaneously, but the complexity and effectiveness of their strategies are limited in comparison to the strategies of older children.

utilization deficiency Inability to use a known memory strategy or to benefit from the use of such a memory strategy.

Finally, some researchers have suggested a third explanation, namely, that children have a **utilization deficiency** (Bjorklund, Miller, Coyle, & Slawinski, 1997; Miller, 1990; Miller & Seier, 1994). When they are in the early phases of strategy acquisition—for example, when learning how to rehearse—children may produce an appropriate strategy spontaneously but be unable to profit from using it. To illustrate, in one study, 9- and 10-year-old children were trained in the use of organizational memory strategies for remembering items in a list, such as sorting items into categories and devising categories that are easier to remember (Bjorklund, Schneider, Cassel, & Ashley, 1994). Later, when the children were tested on their memory for the items, the children showed that they had retained the strategies they had been taught in the training session. However, despite the use of these strategies, their memory for the items decreased. In other words, they used the strategies but the strategies did not appear to facilitate their memory of the items.

Children's ability to benefit from memory strategies may reflect a trade-off between the costs and benefits of using the strategy (Miller, Seier, Probert, & Aloise, 1991). When a strategy is new and, therefore, a less practiced skill—as is often the case for younger children—using the strategy may consume much mental effort. Therefore, children may opt sometimes not to use it or to use it only haphazardly. As children become more adept at strategy use, the costs decrease while the benefits increase. Although such findings suggest that such a utilization deficiency appears to exist, there remains some controversy on this point (Waters, 2000). In addition, when such deficiencies occur they are short lived. With practice, children quickly learn to use a new strategy to aid memory (Coyle & Bjorklund, 1997).

KNOWLEDGE OF THE WORLD   As our discussion of elaboration illustrates, what individuals have learned from past experiences—what they know about the world in general—influences what they understand about a present event and what they will recall about it later. We saw an example of the effects of **world knowledge** on children's memory in our discussion of Michelene Chi's work with child chess experts and adult novices. Chi and others have further documented the differing cognitive performances of novices and experts, suggesting the important role that the knowledge base plays in memory (Bedard & Chi, 1992; Chase & Simon, 1973; Chi, 1978; Chi & Koeske, 1983).

world knowledge What a child has learned from experience and knows about the world in general.

Children obtain knowledge of the world in many ways: through direct experience, through processes of formal and informal instruction, and via information they glean from their society and family. This knowledge also influences their memory abilities. Research based on Vygotsky's sociocultural view of development has focused on society's role in children's use of memory strategies and their overall memory performance (Gauvain, 2001a). Unfortunately, a great deal of cross-cultural research investigating children's memory processes has applied experimental techniques commonly used in Western society to non-Western populations. As a result, children in non-Western communities, who are less familiar with these techniques and types of questions, often perform poorly on them (Cole, 1996; Rogoff, 2003). However, when memory tasks are presented in culturally familiar contexts, children in non-Western cultures perform as well as, or better than, children tested in the United States.

Meaningfulness and Goals Rogoff and Waddell (1982) presented 9-year-old Mayan children in Guatemala and 9-year-old U.S. children with a memory reconstruction task. The children watched as 20 familiar objects were placed into a panorama model of a town that contained familiar landmarks (each model was appropriate to the culture of the group being tested). These objects were placed in their appropriate locations; for example, boats on lakes and furniture in houses. The objects were then removed from the display, and after a short delay, the children were asked to re-create the display they had seen prepared. Rogoff and Waddell found that the Mayan children performed slightly better than the North American children.

What led to the Mayan children's advantage? Rogoff (2003) speculates that the performance of the American children was hampered by the fact that about a third tried to use the strategy of rehearsal. However, this strategy, which is often taught in U.S. schools, is best suited to memorizing unrelated lists of objects; it may be only minimally effective in this spatial reconstruction task. In contrast to the U.S. children, the Mayan children appeared to rely on visual memory—they used the spatial relationships of the objects to organize their memories, which seems to have enhanced their performance.

In another study designed to explore the role not only of meaningful or familiar context but also of the goal of the activity in children's memory ability, Rogoff and colleagues (Mistry, Rogoff, & Herman, 2001; Rogoff & Mistry, 1990) enlisted the help of the parents of a group of 4-year-olds. In the Lab condition, in which a meaningful context and goal were not mentioned during the task, parents presented their children with 10 pictures of lunch-related items such as cheese, bread, juice, and a napkin. After repeating the names of all 10 items, they asked the children to go to the experimenter at the other side of the room and tell her all the items they remembered. In the Lunch condition, parents told children at the outset that they were making a sack lunch and needed all the ingredients from the "grocer" (played by the experimenter). The parent showed the child the pictures of the 10 items, and the child then went to the "grocer" and asked for the items. On average, children in the Lab condition remembered only 2.7 items, whereas children in the Lunch condition remembered 5.3 items. It seems that a meaningful context and a clear goal for the activity are important to children's remembering.

These findings echo Vygotsky's (1978a) view that memory in everyday life occurs in the course of meaningful, goal-directed activities. In other words, to remember something in and of itself is rarely our goal. Instead, we usually remember something so that we can do something else. For example, we remember the directions to the store so that we can go shopping, or we remember the items on a list so that we can assemble them for an event, like a meal or a party or packing a suitcase. Oftentimes when memory is tested in laboratory situations, remembering is the goal of the activity. Therefore, people who have more experience with activities in which memory functions as a goal in and of itself, which is frequent in school settings, do better on such tasks than people who have less experience with school. Furthermore, when a laboratory task is designed to resemble a more everyday type of memory activity—one in which remembering is embedded within a meaningful, goal-directed situation—the difference in memory performance between individuals who have much versus little experience with school is reduced or eliminated.

Despite the likelihood that a meaningful activity will improve memory performance, there are some situations in which a meaningful, goal-directed activity may not elicit optimal remembering in children. Consider the question of children's reliability as witnesses, an issue that has begun to concern society as children have increasingly been asked to testify in court. Often the cases in which children serve as witnesses involve domestic conflict or, worse, domestic and/or child abuse that is sometimes of

Box 9.1
Child Psychology in Action

SHOULD YOUNG CHILDREN TESTIFY IN COURT?

How accurate are children when asked to give testimony in a court of law? Research has indicated that suggestions by others, especially adults, may strongly influence a young child's reporting of past events. Several investigators have explored this issue by having children listen to brief stories and then following up the presentation by introducing inaccurate information (e.g., Ceci, Ross, & Toglia, 1987; Doris, 1991; Ornstein, Larus, & Clubb, 1992). In general, these researchers have concluded that young children are more often affected by inaccurate information than older children are.

Ceci and his colleagues (Bruck & Ceci, 1999; Ceci & Bruck, 1998; Ceci, Leichtman, & White, 1998) undertook an extensive series of studies to explore these effects of suggestion on children's memory. In one study, the experimenters engaged preschool children in a game similar to "Simon Says." A month later an interviewer talked with each child about the activity. In one condition of the experiment, the interviewer was accurately informed about what happened during the activity, and in the other, the interviewer was given false information. When the interviewer was accurately informed, the children's recall was 93 percent accurate. However, when she was misinformed, 34 percent of children 3 to 4 years old and 18 percent of children 5 to 6 years old corroborated false statements about what had happened during the experiment itself. The experimenters concluded that the younger the child, the more likely she was to be influenced by false information.

On the premise that children testifying in sexual abuse cases are often exposed to statements such as "X is bad," or "X did bad things," these investigators designed another study to test the effects of such information on children's memories of an event (Leichtman & Ceci, 1995). In the first condition of this study, a stranger named "Sam Stone" spent two minutes with 3- to 6-year-old children at their day-care center. On four later occasions, an interviewer asked the children about Sam's visit, trying to elicit as much detail as possible but taking care not to ask questions that would suggest answers. On a fifth occasion, a new interviewer elicited the same information and then asked specifically about two events that had not occurred during Sam's visit. Only 10 percent of the youngest children confirmed that these events had occurred, and of these, 5 percent said they had not actually seen or heard these events. Only 2.5 percent insisted on confirming the events when challenged.

In this study's second condition, starting a month before Sam's visit, the experimenters told children specific stories about how clumsy Sam was. After Sam had visited with the children, during which time he showed none of the behaviors that had been described, the children were again interviewed four times. This time, however, on each occasion, the interviewer stated a

a sexual nature. Although these situations are highly meaningful to children, as Box 9.1 suggests, other factors such as the influence of inaccurate suggestions by others and repeated questions may undermine the contribution that meaningfulness can make to memory performance (Eisen, Goodman, & Quas, 2002).

Knowledge of the Self: Autobiographical Memory   Here is how Ben, a 5-year-old boy, explained to his teacher how his $2\frac{1}{2}$-year-old brother Graeme sustained a bloody, but ultimately minor, cut to the head.

Teacher: What did you do over the holidays?

Ben: There was an accident.

Teacher: Oh, what happened?

Ben: My brother jumped on the bed and cut his head on the table. And then, after he cut his head, then the paramedics came and two fire trucks and an ambulance.

number of untruths about Sam, such as that he ripped a book during his visit and marked a teddy bear up with a crayon. On a fifth occasion, a new interviewer asked the children for a free narrative about Sam's visit. Among the youngest children, 72 percent reported seeing Sam perform one or more of the misdeeds they'd been told about after the fact. When the interviewer asked if they had actually seen Sam do these things, the percentage dropped to 44. Even when challenged, however, 21 percent maintained that they had seen these events.

Regardless of whether children's testimony is accurate or has been altered by suggestions from others, a jury's perception of a child witness is usually not favorable. Both laypeople and legal scholars believe that children make poor witnesses (Yarmey & Jones, 1983), considering them inferior to adults in recall memory. In one study, mock jurors believed that children under 11 could not provide accurate testimony (Leippe & Romanczyk, 1989). Paradoxically, these same adults believed that children make more *honest* witnesses than adults!

As yet we have an uncertain picture of the child's ability to give an accurate account of past events (Saywitz & Lyons, 2002). As in the case of many other cognitive functions, a variety of factors affect recall. For example, an interviewer who is intimidating and forceful may well affect children's accuracy, but a kind and supportive interviewer may elicit accurate information from a child (Goodman, Bottoms, Schwartz-Kenney, & Rudy, 1991). In addition, research has found that when a child has been an active participant in a situation, rather than a spectator, she is less likely to be susceptible to others' misleading suggestions (Lindberg, Jones, McComas-Collard, & Thomas, 2001; Rudy & Goodman, 1991). The type of question asked, and whether and how it is repeated, may also affect children's responses (Lyons, 2002).

Current research has moved beyond description to focus on the mechanisms that may account for children's ability to recall events accurately. Some cognitive mechanisms include strength of memory, semantic knowledge, knowledge of scripts, and linguistic comprehension. For instance, Ricci and Beal (1998) showed that children who were more accurate in their original memory of an event were less likely to answer inaccurately when a question was repeated. Also playing a role are socioemotional factors, such as avoiding punishment or embarrassment, keeping promises made to others, eschewing personal gain if it involves being deceitful, and personality characteristics. As we have repeatedly noted, cognitive and social factors operate together in accounting for the kinds of effects we have discussed here. Finally, this work reminds us that the lines between basic and applied research are often blurred. Although the research reviewed tells us about children's testimony, it also informs us about children's cognitive and social development.

Teacher: Oh, how awful! Then what happened?

Ben: Mommy went with him to the hospital in the ambulance. I stayed home with Nana.

In this example, an adult, the child's teacher, elicited details that brought out more information about the event from the child's memory. She also defined an emotional context and steered the child along as he recounted the story. The child used the occasion to describe the aspects of the event that were important and understandable to him. He used the **narrative form,** an account of an event that is temporally sequenced and conveys meaning (Bruner, 1990). In his narrative, he described the event, as well as information about himself, his family, and his own experience during the event. Even though what Ben said is brief, he makes it clear that this was an emotionally arousing experience for him. Even a short narrative may have deep meaning or value for a child (Engel, 1995). This value is enhanced because memories such as this one are personal in an interesting way. They define an individual's own history. However,

narrative form A temporally sequenced account that conveys meaning about an event.

because there are often social contributions to these memories as children discuss them with others, this history is also shaped by other people who inform the child about what aspects of his memory are interesting or important to remember. Since the event in this example garnered interest and attention from an adult, it may increase the likelihood of Ben's retelling the story and, therefore, rehearsing it, which will help him remember the event. Even the interpretations of others regarding an event may become part of the memory if the retelling triggers a certain response. For instance, if a child describes an experience that adults find amusing, the event may then be remembered not only in terms of the actions and the sequences of these actions, but also in terms of its effect on others.

autobiographical memory
A collection of memories of things that have happened to a person at a specific time or place.

A person's memories about things that happened to her at a specific time or place are part of the person's **autobiographical memory** (Bauer, 2006). Autobiographical memory emerges in the early years of life, when a child is about $2\frac{1}{2}$ years old, and it develops substantially over the preschool years (Nelson, 1993). Autobiographical memories are linked in both process and content to children's social experiences. Researchers estimate that during family interaction, discussion of past events occurs as often as five to seven times an hour (Fivush, Haden, & Reese, 1996). Parents talk directly to children about the past. In addition, in the presence of their children, parents talk to each other about the past. Early in the child's life, shared memories are mostly one-sided, with the parent taking on much of the responsibility for reminiscing. But by the age of 3, children's contributions to shared remembering increase. Also, around this time memories begin to endure rather well. Children as young as 3 years of age can remember specific event information over a fairly long time period (Fivush & Hamond, 1989).

Shared conversations about the past also help children have better memory for the event (Haden, Ornstein, Eckerman, & Didow, 2001; Hamond & Fivush, 1991). The fact that these conversations typically tie these memories to something of personal significance helps children acquire knowledge about themselves, other people, and the world in which they live (Engel & Li, 2004). Furthermore, this type of personal storytelling or shared reminiscence is not unique to particular families or cultures. This practice is culturally widespread (Miller & Moore, 1989). Some research indicates that the early conversations parents and children have about past events also serve to communicate cultural values to children. Wang (2004) asked preschool and early school-age children from China and the United States to recount four autobiographical events, and then she asked the children a series of questions about these events. She found that the memories of the American children included lots of personal details that emphasized the child's own experiences and feelings. In contrast, the Chinese children recalled memories that concentrated on social aspects of their lives, such as social interactions and daily routines. These patterns are consistent with different emphases on autonomy and social connections and with the parenting styles in these two cultural communities, which have been studied by Ruth Chao and are discussed in Chapter 12.

During social interaction, children learn much about what to remember, how to formulate their memories, and how to retain them in a retrievable form (Fivush, 1988; McCabe & Petterson, 1991). Hudson (1990) conducted a study with a group of 10 mothers and children when the children were between 24 and 30 months of age. She found that early in the observational period, the children had limited ability to talk about past events. They were mainly dependent on their mothers to cue these memories. However, once their memories were activated, and they had more experience with these types of conversations, the children became active participants. Moreover, their contributions did not simply repeat what their mothers had said but sometimes included new information about the event. Thus, in the second year of life, children are beginning to recollect their own past experiences, and these recollections often occur in the course of conversations that are heavily scaffolded by adults and organized around a narrative structure.

Such shared memory experiences carry much import in young children's lives. They contribute to the development of the self, and thereby help create what Nelson (1996) calls the historical self. They also contribute to the cultural self in that shared memories influence both the content and the process of remembering along the very lines valued by the community in which development occurs. Finally, they give children the opportunity to rehearse these memories and, in so doing, to learn some very important things about the memory itself and the whole process of remembering.

Problem Solving and Reasoning

Every day people try to achieve many and varied goals. Some of these are modest, such as having a good breakfast. Some are grand, such as completing a long project at school or work. In order to reach these goals, people organize their actions in ways that are directed toward meeting their goals. Identifying an action goal and delineating steps or means to reach this goal is called **problem solving.** Problem solving is a central feature of human intelligence. In fact, some psychologists equate problem solving with thinking. An important feature of problem solving is overcoming obstacles that interfere with reaching the goal. Thus, problem solving usually involves a goal and one or more obstacles that need to be overcome to reach this goal.

During children's development, their problem-solving abilities become more sophisticated; the strategies they possess become better developed and they acquire new strategies. To illustrate the impact these changes have on children's problem-solving abilities, we examine development in four areas of problem solving: solving problems by using rules that guide thinking; solving problems by analogy, or using information from one problem to solve another; using cognitive tools, such as the structure of routine behaviors or forms of representation; and using deductive reasoning.

problem solving The identification of a goal and of steps to reach that goal.

RULE-BASED PROBLEM SOLVING   Robert Siegler (1983, 1991) has studied the role that the learning and application of rules play in children's problem solving. In his research, using Piaget's balance-scale problem, in which children must predict which way a balance with different weights placed at different distances from the fulcrum will tilt, Siegler (1978) concluded that even preschoolers can systematically apply rule-based strategies to solve problems. As you can see from Figure 9-12, what makes this a difficult problem is the necessity to consider two dimensions: both the number of weights on each side of the balance's fulcrum and the distance from the fulcrum at which each set of weights lies. Siegler proposed that children's strategies for solving the problem include rules at four levels of sophistication:

Rule I: The side with more weights is heavier.

Rule II: If weights on both sides are equal, the side whose weights are farther from the fulcrum is heavier.

Rule III: If one side has more weights but the other's weights are farther from the fulcrum, you have to guess at the answer.

Rule IV: Weights $\times$ distance from fulcrum equals *torque;* the side with greater torque is the heavier.

Siegler found that 3-year-olds appeared not to use rules at all; about half of 4-year-olds used Rule I, and all 5-year-olds used Rule I. Among 9-year-olds, about half used Rule II and half used Rule III, and 13- and 17-year-olds almost always used Rule III. Interestingly, although Rule IV embodies the reasoning Piaget attributed to the child in the period of formal operations, only a minority even of college students used it!

Figure 9-12   Balance-scale problems and strategies for solving them

Using Robert Siegler's Rule IV will get you the correct answers on all these problems. Interestingly, your next best chance to get as many correct answers as possible is to use Rule II. Why? Answers to all problems appear below the figure, upside down.

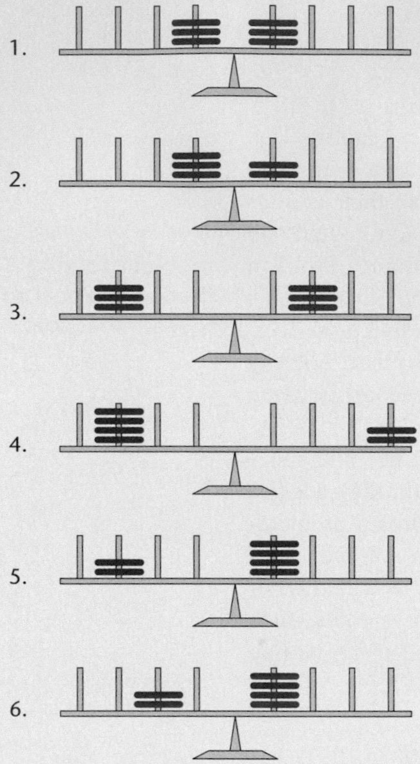

	Percent of Correct Answers Expected When Each Rule Is Used			
	Rule I	Rule II	Rule III	Rule IV
1.	100	100	100	100
2.	100	100	100	100
3.	0 (Will say balance)	100	100	100
4.	100	100	33 (Chance responding)	100
5.	0 (Will say right down)	0 (Will say right down)	33 (Chance responding)	100
6.	0 (Will say right down)	0 (Will say right down)	33 (Chance responding)	100

Problems 1 and 6: balance; problems 2–5: left down.

Source: From Siegler, Robert S.; Alibali, Martha W., *Children's Thinking*, 4th Edition, © 2005. Adapted and reprinted by permission of Pearson Eduction, Inc., Upper Saddle River, NJ.

When Siegler analyzed the task carefully to try to discover why young children couldn't solve many of the balance-scale problems, he hypothesized that perhaps limited memory and/or lack of knowledge were at fault. When he allowed children to continue viewing the original balance arrangement (low memory demand) and gave them direct, detailed, and repeated instructions (knowledge), those as young as 5 were often able to solve the problems.

Recently Siegler (1996) and Siegler and Chen (2002) have extended this view by pointing out that not only do children have rule-based reasoning, but they also have a variety of strategies for solving problems at any given time. To solve a problem, children choose from the strategies they have available. What is important developmentally is the kinds of strategy choices available at a particular point in time, how children decide which strategy or strategies to use, and the effectiveness and success with which children use these strategies during problem solving. Siegler (1996, 2000) calls this process an adaptive strategy choice approach to problem solving because, with development, the child makes strategy choices that are an increasingly better fit, or adapted to, the task at hand.

Piaget believed that children had to reach the stage of formal operations before they could solve complex problems such as measuring and calculating relative weights. Later researchers, among them Robert Siegler, have found that if younger children have enough information they may be able to solve such problems.

SOLVING PROBLEMS BY ANALOGY Suppose you are trying to learn how to use a personal computer and are having difficulty understanding the maze of directories, subdirectories, and files that are involved in using a computer. In this situation, drawing an analogy between the workings of the computer and that of an office filing system may be helpful. Directories on the computer are the same as filing cabinets, subdirectories are drawers in the filing cabinets, and files are the documents inserted in the drawers.

The use of *analogy*—or the inference that if two or more objects or situations resemble each other in some respects, they are likely to resemble each other in yet other respects—is a powerful problem-solving strategy (Brown, 1989). The inference drawn between the *source analog,* or the familiar situation, and the *target analog,* or the unfamiliar situation, may help an individual deal with a novel situation as well as provide the basis for learning a more general category that encompasses both the familiar and the novel (Gentner & Holyoak, 1997). Despite the power of this cognitive mechanism, both children and adults often find it difficult either to think of or to make use of analogies (Gick & Holyoak, 1980). One reason may be that psychological testing has often focused on the classic A:B as C:? type of analogies (e.g., "foot is to leg as arm is to what?") in which the important relations that need to be evaluated in the analogy may be unclear.

However, when simpler relations are used, even 1-year-old infants were able to use the perceptual similarity between objects as a basis for solving a problem (Chen, Sanchez, & Campbell, 1997). However, recognizing perceptual similarity is a simple type of analogical reasoning. Recognizing the relations of objects across two pairs of objects is more difficult, though even young children are able to demonstrate such reasoning. In a study with preschoolers, pictures represented the A, B, and C terms of the analogy, for example, chocolate (A):melted chocolate (B) as snowman (C):? (Goswami & Brown, 1990). The investigator would then show children five picture choices, one of which was of a melted snowman, and children would be asked to choose the picture that best represented the answer (D). Three-year-olds were correct 52 percent of the time on these types of problems, 4-year-olds were correct 89 percent of the time, and 5-year-olds were correct 99 percent of the time.

Of course, the question remains as to how analogical reasoning based on perceptual similarity and relational similarity fit together. In one study, 4-year-olds did better on a relational analogy task when there was also perceptual similarity across the objects (Holyoak, Junn, & Billman, 1984). Other researchers have noted that both children and adults are more likely to draw analogies if there is surface similarity between the situations (e.g., names of characters in a story) in the two problems

(Goswami, 1995). For instance, children found it easier to reenact a story about a jealous friend with new characters if the new hero looked something like the original one (Gentner & Toupin, 1986).

Interestingly, in a study of children's ability to solve a problem by drawing an analogy between the problem and one in a story they had been told, it appeared that the children's difficulties stemmed not from inability to reason in this way but, apparently, from failure to recall the details of the story. Brown, Kane, and Echols (1986) asked 3- to 5-year-old children to "help the Easter Bunny move the Easter eggs across the river" and into a basket on the "opposite bank" by using several materials provided by the experimenter: a flat piece of paper, a cardboard tube, a walking cane, tape, scissors, string, and a few other objects. Earlier, the experimenters had told the children a story in which a genie was faced with the problem of moving jewels from one bottle to another. The genie had solved the problem by rolling his magic carpet into a tube and sliding the jewels from the mouth of one bottle to the other through this tube.

The children found it quite difficult to help the Easter Bunny with his problem, however. Very few of the 3-year-olds were able to solve the problem, and even some of the 5-year-olds failed to figure out that they could use the cardboard tube to move the eggs across the river. However, when the experimenter gave the children a hint to help them recall the genie story, their rates of problem solution increased dramatically. This suggests that it was not inability to reason by analogy that kept them from solving the problem but rather inability to recall the details of the analogy-containing story. Researchers who have replicated this study have found that pointing out to children the goals of the story's protagonist aids in analogical transfer (Chen & Daehler, 1989), as does giving children multiple examples of the problem solution (Crisafi & Brown, 1986).

Analogical reasoning may play an important role in knowledge acquisition in that it helps the child broaden and deepen his understanding of the relations between objects and across similar types of objects. These expanded connections make possible more information-processing abilities and more complex understanding (DeLoache, Miller, & Pierrsoutsakos, 1998).

COGNITIVE TOOLS If we had to figure out, entirely on our own, what to do in every situation that is repeated day after day (e.g., bathing, dressing, and eating meals) and to find our way to school, work, and other familiar places, we would have little time or energy to devote to new events and activities. Children quickly become competent in many such routine situations. By providing guides or structures telling us how to proceed, routines aid thinking. In addition, children also learn to use other features of their environment, both material and symbolic features, to help them solve problems. Psychologists refer to these types of external aids as cognitive tools because they function in the same way that a tool like a hammer does when you try to build something. A tool is an extension of your action. It enables you to carry out an activity that you could not carry out in the same way or at all without the use of the tool. Sociocultural psychologists are particularly interested in the understanding and use of tools to aid cognition because such tools are products of a culture that mediate cognitive activity and that are passed on to children socially through the efforts of other members of the culture (Vygotsky, 1978a).

To illustrate the important role that these tools play in intellectual development, we concentrate on three particular tools: scripts, cognitive maps, and symbolic representations. These three cognitive tools are quite different from each other in terms of what cognitive activities they support. Scripts are relevant to behavioral routines and everyday practices. Cognitive maps are relevent to our understanding and use of large-scale space. And symbolic representations, such as models, allow us to envision features of the world in ways that help us plan actions and see relations that would otherwise be difficult to understand. Together, these three types of cognitive tools show how important such tools are to cognitive functioning and how much of what we do every day depends on the understanding and use of such tools. Other tools that have been of interest to those who study cognition include literacy (Olson, 1994), written and pictorial plans for action (Goody, 1977), and computers (Norman, 1993).

Scripts   A 2-year-old not only participates in many activities during the day, but she seems also to have a good understanding of her "role" in these situations. If you doubt this, just try to deprive a child of the piece of candy she usually gets in the grocery store checkout line. How do children structure information from past experiences to achieve an understanding of the present situation and develop a plan for appropriate behavior? One way that people deal with everyday situations is by forming scripts for many routine activities. **Scripts** provide basic outlines of what one can expect in a particular situation and what one should do in that situation (Nelson, 1993; Schank & Abelson, 1977).

This child's script of how to get ready in the morning will help him remember all the different things he has to do at this time of day and the order in which he should do them.

script   A mental representation of an event or situation of daily life, including the order in which things are expected to happen and how one should behave in that event or situation.

Children as young as 20 months know about and rely on the sequences of activities in familiar events such as bedtime, mealtimes, or parties (Bauer & Thal, 1990). And 3- to 4-year-old children can remember a large number of events in the correct order (Fivush, Kuebli, & Clubb, 1992). Even infants and toddlers learn to organize their representations of events along scriptlike lines. Bauer and her colleagues (Bauer, 2002; Bauer & Dow, 1994; Bauer & Mandler, 1992) have shown that by the end of the first year, infants use temporally ordered rules in their recall of a sequence of events. For example, these researchers presented infants with a familiar sequence, such as giving a teddy bear a bath *(put teddy in the tub, "wash" teddy with a sponge, "dry" teddy with the towel)*. Not only were infants able to reproduce the familiar sequence with a high degree of accuracy, but they were able to do this with novel events as well *(make a rocking horse move with a magnet)*. Studies by Bauer and associates suggest that the central aspect of the script—that is, the ability to represent events in temporal order—is learned very early in life (Bauer, Wenner, Dropik, & Wewerka, 2000).

One way researchers have demonstrated early understanding of scripts is to observe what a child does when a routine event is changed in some way and violates the expectations of the script. Even young children find such changes very confusing and disconcerting. In fact, young children are more rigid in their applications of scripts than older children and adults (Wimmer, 1980). For example, when asked to recall stories, young children will eliminate inconsistent elements of a story to preserve the expected sequence of events or to add events that they were expecting to happen but that did not (Fivush et al., 1996; Myles-Worsley, Cromer, & Dodd, 1986). Moreover, if you present 20-month-olds with an incorrect sequence (e.g., *dry, wash, put teddy bear in tub*), they sometimes correct the order to the real-life script (*wash* before *dry*). When the order of a well-understood script is violated, toddlers often say, "That's so silly."

Scripts help children remember over a long period. In one instance, kindergarten children visited a museum, a special event for youngsters. Not only did the children develop and remember a general museum script when questioned six weeks and even one year later, but they were able to remember details of their personal museum visit at these times as well (Fivush, Hudson, & Nelson, 1984). Children can distinguish the general from the personal script, and, it seems likely, the general script helps them remember personal experiences better by providing a way to organize specific memories. For example, children who visited Disneyworld when they were 3 to 4 years of age remembered both general elements of what a special event like a trip to an amusement park is like—such as we all woke up early and got ready to go—and many specific details of their visit—such as the particular rides they went on—when they were interviewed 18 months later (Hamond & Fivush, 1991).

The development of scripts may reflect some basic properties of the human memory system. According to Nelson (1996), the memory system may be designed to emphasize details of recurrent events, like routine behaviors. Such information would facilitate actions by providing people with behavioral expectations for both the self and others; these expectations, in turn, would support social interaction. In addition, such information might free up space in the information-processing system so that an individual could pay attention to new or unexpected information that might come up within the course of a routine.

Cognitive Maps   Just as children need to be able to negotiate their way through the routine events of the day, so too they must find their way through the spatial environment. Spatial cognition—that is, the processing of visual information and spatial relations—is critical to human functioning (Newcombe & Huttenlocher, 2003). Many cognitive tools have been devised to support spatial thinking, including maps, directions, and, most recently, global positioning systems, or GPS. Children learn to use material tools to aid their understanding and use of spatial information, and this capacity changes a great deal throughout childhood. For example, young children often interpret symbolic representations, such as the symbols used on maps, quite literally: They may assume that the outline of an airplane on a map means that there's a real airplane, rather than an airport, at that location (Downs & Liben, 1986). As children grow, they become better able to use this kind of information accurately to negotiate new surroundings (Liben, 1999; Uttal, 2000). Moreover, parents and other more experienced cultural members play important roles in helping children learn to use maps and other tools; this input then influences how children learn to think about and use space (Gauvain, 1993).

In addition to material tools for describing space, humans develop the ability to organize and retain in memory information that can be used to guide behavior in space, such as finding locations and traveling to a destination. Even very young children manage to maneuver their way through familiar places, avoiding obstacles and barriers in their paths (Heth & Cornell, 1980). They do this with the aid of **cognitive maps** (Tolman, 1948), which are mental representations of the spatial relations within a physical or geographic place—for example, a room, a playground, or a town.

As children mature, they become more skillful at constructing mental and physical maps of places they know (home, school, and neighborhood) and routes they have traveled. According to Siegel and his colleagues (Anooshian & Siegel, 1985; Siegel & White, 1975), children develop the abilities required to form cognitive maps of the spatial environment in three steps (see Table 9-3). In the first step, they learn to recognize specific landmarks, acquiring *landmark knowledge,* and in the second step, they put several landmarks together to form what is called *route knowledge.* In the final step, children acquire the ability to combine routes learned earlier

cognitive map A mental representation of the spatial layout of a physical or geographic place.

Table 9-3

Developing an understanding of space and mapping

Source: Siegel & White, 1975.

Step 1	Using landmark knowledge	Children use landmarks, such as the yellow house or the red fire hydrant, to help orient themselves in space.
Step 2	Using route knowledge	Children can integrate several landmarks (e.g., yellow house, red hydrant, and blue mailbox) into a sequence that forms a route through space that leads unfailingly to the baseball field or the nearby store.
Step 3	Developing mental maps	Children can create an overall mental or cognitive map of a familiar area that incorporates landmarks and routes learned earlier.

into an understanding of the spatial relations, thereby taking possession of cognitive or *mental maps* of entire areas.

Landmark or place learning emerges early in life. On simple tasks, 3-year-old children can evaluate the accuracy of location information using landmarks, and can then use this information to improve their search for an object (Newcombe, Huttenlocher, Drummey, & Wiley, 1998). Over childhood, children get better at identifying and using landmarks, and such changes are aided by children's everyday experiences exploring space. Cornell and colleagues (2001) observed children between 6 and 12 years of age as they traveled through and used natural environments around their homes where they were allowed to travel on their own, referred to as their *home range.* In this research, experimenters observed the patterns of visual scanning that children used during a walk in their home ranges. The distance and the duration of these walks were also recorded. Researchers undertook this study because of a request from the police in Edmonton (in Canada's province of Alberta). In the hope of obtaining information that would help them in searching for a lost or missing child, the police wanted to know how children of different ages travel around their neighborhoods when they are on their own (see Figure 9-13). When children get lost, their ability to find their way home may depend on the visual scanning they do while they walk, how far they travel, and how long they are willing to walk.

Cornell and his colleagues (2001) found that the distance and length of time a child would travel on his own increased significantly from 6 to 12 years of age. As children get older, they are more likely to try new routes and to travel beyond the limits of where their parents expect them to travel. Older children scan the environment more than younger children as they travel and they pay more attention to landmarks. In fact, 8-year-olds are quite knowledgeable about the landmarks in their home range, but this

Figure 9-13

The home range

This overview map shows the child's home (H) and his intended destination (ID). The "crow's flight" is the distance identified by the solid line to the ID and the actual path the child took to the ID is identified by the dashed line. Notice that because the child cannot walk through barriers in the environment, the child's path of travel is longer than the crow's flight distance. If a child was reported as lost or missing, this information would be used by police to create a search plan for the child.

Source: Cornell, Hadley, Sterling, Chan, & Boechler, 2001.

information is not as well integrated with way-finding information as it is for 12-year-olds. For example, 12-year-olds, but not 8-year-olds, will attend to the location of landmarks in relation to intersections and other choice points on their routes.

For children throughout the world, from early to middle childhood, the home range (Munroe, Munroe, & Brasher, 1985) expands considerably, and children often travel outside the areas their parents expect them to visit. Thus, the development of spatial skills that may facilitate children's way-finding is critical to children's ability to explore their environments safely and to adults' capacity to help their children when needed.

Symbolic Representation   According to Judy DeLoache (1995, 2000), being able to use symbolic tools, such as scale models and pictures, is a great aid in solving real-world problems. In her research on how children use models as representations of actual objects, DeLoache (1987) showed children who were 31 and 39 months old a furnished, normal-size living room and a miniature model of the same room, complete with furniture. She also showed them a normal-size doll and a miniature version of the doll. She hid the tiny doll in the model room while the children watched and then asked the children to find the larger version of the doll in the life-size living room, explaining that it was hidden in the same place in that room as the miniature doll was hidden in the model room. Figure 9-14 shows these steps in another, similar study in which DeLoache used toy dogs instead of toy dolls.

The older children had no problem finding the doll, but the younger children could not do so, although by retrieving the miniature doll from the model room, they showed that they remembered where it had been hidden. DeLoache proposed that the problem for the younger children was their inability to form a *dual representation*. That is, they couldn't conceive of the model room both as an object in its own right and as a representation of the larger, real room. To test this hypothesis, DeLoache and her colleagues (DeLoache, Miller, & Rosengren, 1997) presented two groups of children with different accounts of the hidden doll problem. Both groups saw the full-size room and the doll hidden in this room. The researchers then presented the model room to the first group and hid the miniature doll. To the second group, however, they explained that "a shrinking machine" had shrunk the full-size room and then the researchers revealed the small, model room. The $2\frac{1}{2}$-year-old children in this study had

Figure 9-14   A room is a room but is it the same room?

In a classic series of experiments, Judy DeLoache has tested the ability of young children to conceive of a model room not only as a representation of a full-size room but as an object in itself. Here, DeLoache hides a small toy dog in a scale-model room while a 3-year-old child watches (a). The child retrieves a normal-size toy dog from the analogous place in the full-size room (b). The child retrieves the small toy dog from its hiding place in the scale-model room (c).

(a) Hiding toy in model   (b) Finding toy dog in room   (c) Finding toy in model

Source: Courtesy of Judy S. DeLoache, University of Illinois at Urbana-Champaign.

no difficulty finding the miniature doll in the "shrunken" room. DeLoache and her colleagues suggest that the shrunken room version of the task was easier for the children because it did not require them to understand that the small room stood for or represented the large room symbolically. Thus, the children in the second group did not need to understand the *relation* between two objects—the large and small rooms, as children in the first group did. Instead, children in the second group had only to recognize the room in its new, "shrunken" form.

For DeLoache and colleagues (DeLoache et al., 1997; DeLoache & Smith, 1999), the notion that very young children may not be capable of dual representation has several practical implications. It may be that teaching basic mathematic concepts by using blocks of different sizes to represent different numerical quantities may present difficulty for very young children. Similarly, using anatomically correct dolls when interviewing young children about possible sexual abuse may not be as effective as psychologists have thought.

DEDUCTIVE REASONING In our discussion of Piaget's cognitive development theory, we noticed that Piaget placed great emphasis on children's ability to perform tasks based on logical reasoning, as evidenced in their understanding of such concepts as conservation and class inclusion. All these skills rely on children's ability to use logic, especially in the form of **deductive reasoning.** Although we have seen that in a number of cases children's cognitive abilities are far greater than Piaget believed, children do often find tasks based on deductive reasoning quite difficult.

deductive reasoning Logical thinking that involves reaching a necessary and valid conclusion based on a set of premises.

Transitive Reasoning One of Piaget's classic reasoning tasks involves **transitive inference,** or the mental arrangement of things along a quantitative dimension. Recall from Chapter 8 that children younger than 6 or 7 could not deduce that Melissa was taller than Fabiana when given the information "Melissa is taller than Zoe and Zoe is taller than Fabiana." Piaget attributed this failure to an inability to use the logic of transitive inference. An alternative hypothesis, proposed by Halford (1990), is that children do understand transitive inference but use an incorrect strategy to solve this kind of problem. For instance, one strategy young children use is to assume that the most recently mentioned object is also the largest; in this case, the strategy leads them to an incorrect inference. Another strategy is to assume automatically that one of the given objects is longer than the others, regardless of what the experimenter actually said (Brainerd & Reyna, 1990). Both these strategies reduce the child's memory load but often lead to erroneous conclusions. Children often fail to encode, retrieve, and use information correctly and effectively in transitive inference tasks (Rabinowitz, Grant, Howe, & Walsh, 1994).

transitive inference The mental arrangement of things along a quantitative dimension.

Propositional Logic and Hierarchical Categorization Two other forms of deductive reasoning that have been studied by developmental psychologists are propositional logic and hierarchical categorization. In **propositional reasoning,** the logic of a statement is evaluated based on the information in the statement alone. Oftentimes, cognitive psychologists study propositional reasoning by having people evaluate a set of statements called a *syllogism* that, in order to be solved, requires a deduction based on the premises available in the statements. For example, the Russian psychologist Alexander Luria (1976) tested the propositional reasoning of adults who had varying experiences with schooling and literacy by using the following syllogism:

propositional reasoning Logical thinking that involves evaluating a statement based on the information in the statement alone.

In the Far North, where there is snow, all bears are white.

Novaya Zemlya is in the Far North and there is always snow there.

What color are the bears there?

Piaget considered logical syllogisms such as this quite difficult and claimed that to solve them required formal operational thinking. However, simpler versions of logical syllogisms were presented to 4- and 5-year-old children by Hawkins and her colleagues (1984). Here's an example of these syllogisms:

Pogs wear blue boots.

Tom is a pog.

Does Tom wear blue boots?

The children in this study performed very well on these types of syllogisms—for example, by stating that Tom wears blue boots because he is a pog, which suggests that some of the basic skills needed for deductive reasoning of the type that is tapped in logical syllogisms may start to appear in the late preschool years.

hierarchical categorization
The organization of concepts into levels of abstraction that range from the specific to the general.

Hierarchical categorization, or *class inclusion* pertains to the organization of concepts into levels of abstraction that range from the specific (e.g., *dog*) to the general (e.g., *animal*). It is one thing to know that there are dogs and there are collies; a much more sophisticated appreciation of categorization is required to understand that a collie is a kind of dog, such that all collies are dogs but not all dogs are collies. Although some studies have suggested that children do not view such class-inclusion problems in the same way as adults and older children, some evidence suggests that even very young children are capable of forming categories based on hierarchical relationships (Haith & Benson, 1998; Mandler, 1998; Trabasso et al., 1978).

Mandler and Bauer (1988) studied 12-, 15-, and 20-month-old infants' knowledge of categories using a method called *sequential touching,* which takes advantage of young children's tendency to touch and manipulate objects within their grasp. These experimenters recorded the order in which an infant reached for objects that were placed, as a group, within the child's reach. Ensuring that the infants viewed objects from both specific levels (*dogs* and *cars*) and general levels (*animals* and *vehicles*), they presented a child with, say, two dogs and a horse, or two cars and a truck, and found that children touched sequentially objects that belonged to the same hierarchical category (e.g., all the dogs). This pattern of sequential touch was strongest at the specific level and present to a lesser extent at more general levels. Thus, it appears that even infants have some knowledge of class-inclusion relationships and, further, that they are able to use this information to form categories for familiar objects (Mandler, 1998; Quinn & Eimas, 1998).

Beyond infancy, research shows that children also use category information to determine whether one object shares a quality they've been told another object possesses (Gelman & O'Reilly, 1988). Children will also extend common behavioral characteristics based on category membership (Gelman & Markman, 1987). When told that a particular black and white cat can see in the dark, 3- and 4-year-old children said that a brown cat can see in the dark but that a skunk cannot. Language development, especially names or labels for objects, contributes substantially to concept development and the ability of children to use concepts to categorize objects hierarchically. Markman and Hutchinson (1984) gave 2- to 3-year-old children a set of three objects and asked the children to sort the objects "where they belong," sometimes labeling objects and sometimes giving them no labels. When the experimenters did not label an object, for example, a police car, the children put it with either a same physical category object (another car) or a same thematic category object (a police officer), apparently at random. When the experimenters did apply labels to objects, they used nonsense words rather than an object's real name. For example, they referred to the police car as a *daz.* Given this label, most of the children placed the police car with another car, apparently seeing both as having the same category membership. Other researchers have replicated this effect (e.g., Mandler, 1998), and some have reported similar findings using Japanese words instead of nonsense syllables (Waxman & Gelman, 1986).

In summary, children's ability to form hierarchical categories is evident from a very young age. This ability, together with other deductive reasoning skills, contributes in significant ways to how children think and solve problems.

NUMERICAL REASONING   The ability to think about and use numbers is an important developmental achievement that has significant implications for children's success at school (Ginsburg, Klein, & Starkey, 1998). Children begin to master some critical principles of counting at an astonishingly early age. Rochel Gelman has studied extensively what preschool children do and do not understand about number systems. Her findings, including her work with 3-year-olds on number conservation (Chapter 8), led Gelman to propose five basic principles of counting that lead to children's competence with numbers (Gelman & Gallistel, 1978):

1. The one-one principle: Each object should be counted once and only once.
2. The stable-order principle: Always assign the numbers in the same order.
3. The cardinal principle: A single number can be used to describe the total of a set.
4. The abstraction principle: The other principles apply to any set of objects.
5. The order-irrelevance principle: The order in which objects are counted is irrelevant.

A simple example will show these principles in action. Suppose we show a child 10 pennies, placed in a row, and ask her to count them. Pointing to each one, she proceeds to count them aloud, "1, 2, 3, 5, a, b, c, 10, 15, 12." When she finishes, we ask her to count them again, starting from the other end. Again she counts all 10 of the pennies, counting each one once and only once. "How many pennies are there?" we ask. "Twelve" is her sure reply. We then ask her to count 10 marbles. She repeats: "1, 2, 3, 5, a, b, c, 10, 15, 12." Again, we ask, "How many?" "Twelve."

Can we say that this child understands numbering and counting? Based on the principles just outlined, the answer is yes. Despite her use of an unconventional number sequence, she does seem to understand the critical principles of counting. She assigned only one number to each of the objects and always assigned the numbers in the same order, showing that she understood the one-one and stable-order principles. She had no problem switching the order in which she counted the objects, nor did she mind counting both pennies and marbles, demonstrating her command of the order-irrelevance and abstraction principles. Finally, when asked how many objects there were, she replied "Twelve," showing that she understood the cardinal principle.

Children may be competent in some or all of these principles at different points in their development. For example, a 3-year-old may grasp the one-one principle and the cardinal principle. However, he may be able to apply the stable-order principle only to sets with five or fewer members because his numbering becomes unstable after five (e.g., he counts 1, 2, 3, 4, 5, 10, 18, 7 on one occasion and 1, 2, 3, 4, 5, 7, 18, 10 on another). Such a child would be able to solve Gelman's mouse task (Chapter 8) but would fail on more complex number conservation tasks. Through such a careful analysis of the component skills involved, Gelman has provided a detailed and accurate description of young children's numerical reasoning abilities (Gelman, 1978, 1979, 1980).

In addition to learning to count, many other abilities are important to numerical reasoning. These abilities include the conservation of number, first described by Piaget (1965) and discussed in Chapter 8. This is the understanding that the amount of a set remains the same despite superficial transformations. For example, understanding that moving a line of eight checkers closer together on a table does not change the number of checkers in the line. Some research has shown that counting ability and conservation of number are related to one another. Saxe (1979) distinguished children, who ranged in age from 4 to 6 years, by their counting and number conservation abilities. Some children who had good counting skills were unable to conserve; however, all the children who could conserve numbers also had good counting skills. These results demonstrate that counting ability is a necessary but not sufficient condition for the type of reasoning entailed in number conservation.

Researchers have studied when children develop skills in other areas of numerical and mathematical reasoning, including enumeration, number facts, arithmetic, word

Box 9.2

Perspectives on Diversity

IT'S EASIER TO COUNT IN CHINESE THAN IN ENGLISH!

Chinese-speaking children may have an advantage over English-speaking children when it comes to counting. According to Miller and colleagues (Miller, Smith, Zhu, & Zhang, 1995), the Chinese language offers a more consistent "base-10" naming system than the system used in English. This may make it easier for young children to learn to count.

As Miller and associates point out, the base-10 Arabic system of numbering (1, 2, 3 . . . 10, 11, 12 . . . , etc.) is now used throughout the world, but *names* for numbers in different languages reflect older and sometimes more complex number systems. These researchers divided the number-naming systems of both (Mandarin) Chinese and English into four segments of interest: 1 to 10; 11 to 19, 20 to 99, and 100 and above. In the first segment, Chinese and English do not differ in difficulty of learning, they propose, for both languages require children to master an unordered sequence of names. There's no way to predict, for example, that *jiu* follows *ba* or that *nine* follows *eight*. In the second segment, however, Chinese follows a consistent base-10 rule (e.g., in Mandarin Chinese, the number 11 is called literally "ten-one"), whereas the English system is inconsistent and mixed: The names *eleven* and *twelve* seem to bear no relation to *one* and *two*, and the names for 13 through 19 both place unit values before the tens values and modify the names of both (*thir-teen, fif-teen*).

Between 20 and 99, both languages follow a base-10 approach in naming, except that Chinese uses unmodified unit and tens names (e.g., "two-ten-four," for 24) whereas English modifies the first unit name—but not the second—and the tens names (e.g., *twenty-four*).

Finally, above 100, the naming systems in both languages are fairly consistent in using the base-10 format, with only a few exceptions.

Based on an early study in which they found some differences in mathematical skills favoring Chinese over U.S. children entering school for the first time, Miller and colleagues formulated several hypotheses. If these differences in fact reflected a more easily comprehended number naming system, then (1) Chinese children should show substantial skills advantages after all children begin to learn to count above 10, (2) U.S. children should have more trouble with counting in the teens than Chinese children, and (3) differences should generally be related to the system of number names and not involve other aspects of counting. Engaging 99 Chinese children and 98 U.S. children—all between 3 and 6 years old—in a series of tasks that involved counting, these investigators confirmed their predictions. As you can see from Figure 9-15, there were no substantial differences between the two groups in counting up to 10, but as children began to count in the teens, a significant difference between Chinese and U.S. children emerged. This differential ability was evident until both groups began to count in the 100s, where they again performed similarly. Chinese children were somewhat more successful in counting actual displays of between 14 and 17 objects, but they did not differ from U.S. children in ability to solve simple mathematical problems or to count arrays of 10 or fewer objects. Although this finding might seem to violate the researchers' third prediction, it is consistent with the notion that U.S. children will have the greatest difficulty with number naming in the teens.

---

problems, and number relations (Ginsburg et al., 1998). In recent years, evidence has accumulated that Asian children display greater mathematical skills than American children do (Geary, Fan, & Bow-Thomas, 1992; Stevenson & Lee, 1990). Box 9.2 suggests that, as seen in Chinese and U.S. children, this difference may begin to emerge very early in life and may reflect verbal as well as quantitative abilities.

METACOGNITION

As cognitive beings, we don't just remember things, solve problems, and form concepts—we have an awareness of the strengths and limitations of our cognitive processing and of the way we control or regulate it to achieve such mental feats. In

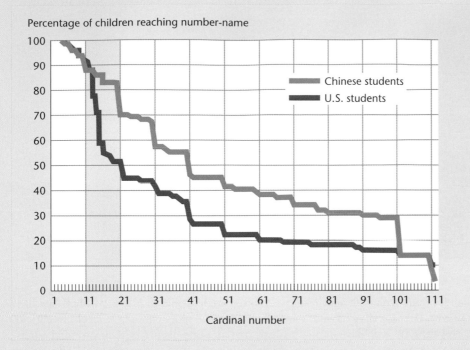

Percentage of children reaching number-name

Chinese students
U.S. students

Cardinal number

Figure 9-15

Counting in Chinese and English

The colored band at the left of the graph highlights the teens (11–19) when Chinese and U.S. children begin to diverge in counting skills, possibly owing to the non-base-10 structure of English names for these numbers.

Source: Miller et al., 1995.

Given that neither the Chinese nor the English language is likely to change its number-naming system, how can we help American children acquire counting skills more efficiently and effectively? According to Miller and colleagues, obstacles that the English system presents can interfere with such math operations as arithmetic carrying and borrowing. Other studies have suggested not only that Chinese children display more sophisticated addition strategies when they first enter school but also that counting strategies for certain kinds of problems predict adult performance on those problems. Although these researchers suggest that it may be important both to familiarize U.S. children with Arabic numerals at an earlier age and to emphasize use of the digits over the use of number words, they also point out that this approach might interfere with other methods used to teach American children the tens-structured addition method. Perhaps the answer lies in both parents and teachers—in the Vygotskian style—encouraging children more to learn math skills.

other words, we know about knowing (Flavell, Green, & Flavell, 1995b). These two components of **metacognition**—knowledge about knowing and control of cognitive functioning—are interrelated and act on each other (Brown, 1975). The child's understanding of her cognitive abilities and processes, of the abilities of others, and of the task situation will influence the strategies she uses in overseeing and monitoring her learning. In turn, her abilities and her experience in planning, monitoring, checking, and modifying cognitive strategies will contribute to her knowledge about cognition and to her success or failure on intellectual tasks. Metacognitive skills have significant implications for children's success in the classroom (Bransford et al., 1999).

There are a number of developmental changes in metacognition. The child's own awareness of how much he knows and is able to remember in any particular instance

metacognition The individual's knowledge about knowing and his control of cognitive activities.

Table 9-4

Limitations on young children's metacognition

Source: Flavell, Green, & Flavell, 1995b.

Young Children

- Underestimate the amount of thinking they and others do.
- Don't understand the concept of a "stream of consciousness."
- Fail to appreciate that someone sitting quietly and not obviously "doing" something might be engaging in mental activity.
- Don't understand that activities such as looking, listening, or reading involve thinking. When someone is engaged in such an activity, preschoolers do not automatically understand that the person's mind is active. Similarly, they don't recognize that *they* have been thinking when engaging in these kinds of activities.
- Cannot infer what another person might be thinking about, even when they realize the person is thinking.
- Fail to understand that when you focus attention on one thing, you are often not able to think about other things.
- Have difficulty saying, when asked, whether they were thinking or what they were thinking about, even when their responses are prompted and facilitated.
- Tend to understand thinking in terms of its products rather than in terms of the process of thinking itself.

changes quite a bit with age. Younger children are less able to assess whether they have studied material well enough to remember it than are older children (Flavell, Friedricks, & Hoyt, 1970), who have a more realistic and accurate picture of their own and others' memory abilities than do younger children (Flavell, 1985; Flavell et al., 1970; Yussen & Berman, 1981). Further, older children are also more likely to appreciate that one's memory ability varies from occasion to occasion and that memory ability may vary among individuals in any age group. An older child recognizes, for example, that he doesn't learn well when tired or anxious. Although young children recognize that older children are better at remembering (Wellman, 1978), unlike older children, they fail to attribute this difference to study strategies (Kreutzer, Leonard, & Flavell, 1975).

In this section, we examine two other important areas of research on metacognition: children's knowledge of tasks and how to go about them, and their knowledge of specific strategies for learning and remembering. The development of a theory of mind, discussed in Chapter 8, is also directly related to metacognition. The limitations in young children's understanding of the mind that are related to the types of metacognitive abilities discussed here are listed in Table 9-4.

Knowledge about the Task

The ability to monitor one's comprehension is critical for a wide range of problem-solving and communication tasks. Do I understand the directions to get to the party tomorrow? Do I understand the instructions for this week's science project? To be an effective processor of information, the child has to be sensitive to her present state of knowledge so that she can seek out the information she needs to further her understanding.

One way that children get information about their present state of understanding is by monitoring their task performance. This provides children with feedback about how they are doing so far on the task and what may still need to be done to finish it. Markman (1977, 1979) assessed children's ability to monitor their comprehension of task instructions. In one study, Markman (1977) gave first, second, and third graders inadequate instructions for playing a card game. The experimenter dealt each child four cards, which had letters on them, and explained the game:

We each put our cards in a pile. We both turn over the top card in our pile. We look at cards to see who has the special card. Then we turn over the next card in our pile to see who has the special card this time. In the end, the person with the most cards wins the game. How would you like to try to play this game with these instructions?

The experimenter made no mention either of what the "special card" might be or of how one acquired more cards. The first graders were far less likely to realize the inadequacy of the instructions than the second and third graders, who asked for more instructions before attempting to play the game. One-quarter of the first graders never asked a question, and most recognized that a problem existed only when they were asked to repeat the instructions or when they began to flounder in playing the game. It was because these children had failed to execute the instructions mentally that they did not notice the problem.

Do children realize that some things are harder to learn than others? Apparently, yes. Even 4-year-olds know that a long list of objects is harder to remember than a very short list and that success on the harder task is more likely if one makes a greater effort (Wellman, 1978; Wellman, Collins, & Glieberman, 1981). Many kindergartners and first graders know that it would be easier to relearn information (e.g., a list of birds) that one had forgotten than to learn it for the first time. Further, even young children realize that it is easier to recognize items than recall them (Speer & Flavell, 1979). Of course, younger children are not aware of some aspects of memory—for example, only older children appreciate that it is easier to retell a story in their own words than to repeat it verbatim (Kurtz & Borkowski, 1987).

Knowledge about Strategies

Children know a great deal more about using strategies to help in memorizing and solving problems than we might think. They seem particularly sensitive to the value of external aids to memory—for example, leaving your books where you will see them in the morning and writing notes to yourself. According to Lovett and Pillow (1995), even children who were not yet literate suggested the latter ploy! Children are also aware of the value of associations in memory (e.g., remembering your mother's age by adding 30 to your own) and develop an understanding of the use of "mental searches" for information (Wellman, 1977). As children grow older, their understanding of what strategy is appropriate increases (O'Sullivan, 1996), and sometimes they reveal a rather sophisticated understanding of memory strategies. When asked how she would remember a phone number, a third grader responded:

"Say the number is 633-8854. Then what I'd do is—say that my number is 633, so I won't have to remember that, really. And then I would think, now I've got to remember 88. Now I'm 8 years old, so I can remember, say, my age two times. Then I say how old my brother is, and how old he was last year. And that's how I'd usually remember that phone number."
"Is that how you would most often remember a phone number?" the experimenter asked.
"Well, usually I write it down." (Kreutzer et al., 1975, p. 11)

How can we define the relationship between metacognition and performance on cognitive tasks? Unfortunately, this relationship is not straightforward (Miller & Weiss, 1981). Some situations, for example, are more likely to engage the child's metacognitive activity than others. Carr and Jessup (1995) found that first graders to third graders who understood which strategy they were using employed some strategies more correctly when solving math problems. If children understand that a strategy like rehearsal is useful, do they actually use it in situations in which it would help them remember things? The answer is, not always. But it is important to remember that even adults don't always apply strategies they know to be effective in situations where they would be useful. It is unrealistic to expect children always to act at an optimal level of cognitive functioning when adults do not always do so.

Making the Connections 9

There are many links between concepts and ideas in one area of development and concepts and ideas in other areas. Here are some of the connections between ideas in Chapter 9 and discussions in other chapters of this book.

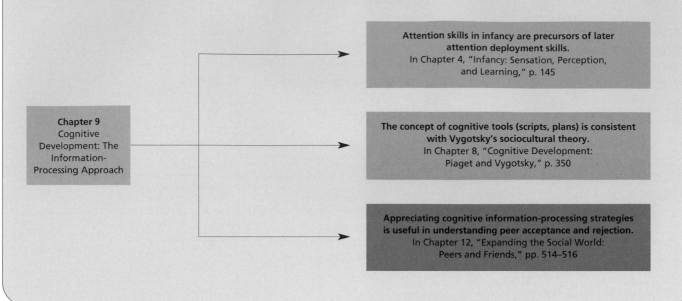

Chapter 9
Cognitive Development: The Information-Processing Approach

Attention skills in infancy are precursors of later attention deployment skills.
In Chapter 4, "Infancy: Sensation, Perception, and Learning," p. 145

The concept of cognitive tools (scripts, plans) is consistent with Vygotsky's sociocultural theory.
In Chapter 8, "Cognitive Development: Piaget and Vygotsky," p. 350

Appreciating cognitive information-processing strategies is useful in understanding peer acceptance and rejection.
In Chapter 12, "Expanding the Social World: Peers and Friends," pp. 514–516

SUMMARY

Information-Processing Theory

- The **information-processing approach** views the human mind as a system that processes information according to a set of logical rules and limitations similar to those with which a computer is programmed. Research using this perspective tries to describe and explain changes in the processes and strategies that lead to greater cognitive competence as children develop.

- Several basic assumptions of information-processing approaches are present to some degree in all these views. These assumptions are that thinking is information processing, mechanisms of change are important to describe, the cognitive system is self-modifying, and careful task analysis will aid researchers in examining the information-processing system. One type of task analysis used in this perspective is **microgenetic analysis,** which examines how children solve problems in close detail.

- The **multistore model** of information processing proposes that information enters the system through the **sensory register** and is encoded and stored in either **short-term memory** or **long-term memory. Connectionist models** propose that memory is based on the interconnections of information in neural networks in the brain. **Neo-Piagetian theories** attempt to apply information-processing ideas to explain Piaget's stage-related changes.

- The basic structures of the information-processing system do not change with development; instead, development occurs through changes in the speed and efficiency of the processes one applies to the information. Four important processes considered to be important in development are **encoding** and **mental representation, strategies, automatization,** and **generalization.** Some theorists also posit an **executive control process** that monitors, selects, and organizes the various **cognitive processes** applied to the information. In addition, knowledge plays a critical role in children's abilities to encode and represent information.

Developmental Changes in Some Significant Cognitive Abilities

- Although every child may perceive the same things in a particular environment, each child's attention

Memory

- Start reading to the kids at about 1 years old (almost 1)
  - Pop up books
- Read to the kids before they ~~get~~ go to bed ~~and to~~ because it builds an emotional connection. (also when they are "wake ~~up~~ because that when it will sink in)
- They will model the parents since they read.

Serial Position Curve

% of Recall

Primary

Recency

SH M

word Position

← 10 yrs old kids are similar because they start to rehearse

- Adults will remember 7 words in their short term memory.
- Atkins Shiffrin

$$SS \rightarrow SHM \rightarrow LTM$$

5-9 words

mediation vs. Production Deficiency
- Serial position curve

- short term memory capacity of a kid is smaller, its like 4. They don't rehearse
- mnemonic : chunking up words to make it easier to remember
- Flavell
  - kids have a production efficiency.

may be concentrated on different aspects of that environment.

- Two main perspectives describe how experience affects perceptual learning. The **enrichment view** proposes that children add information to existing schemata over repeated contacts with an object, elaborating or enriching a schema until they can distinguish among different objects. The **differentiation view** emphasizes that children gradually learn to attend to, identify, and make increasingly finer discriminations among objects and events.

- As children mature they can control and focus their attention for longer periods. In addition, older children are better than younger children at modifying their attention to fit task requirements. Older children also implement more systematic plans to focus their attention when gathering needed information, especially when planning a course of action, although younger children can make use of attention-focusing strategies when these are provided to them.

- Our **memory span,** or the amount of information we can hold in short-term memory, improves between infancy and adulthood. Some researchers suggest that this is due to the development of increased capacity based on changes in the brain. Others suggest that the difference is due to greater efficiency in the cognitive system.

- The spontaneous use of verbal **rehearsal** as a memory strategy clearly increases with age. Although even young children can use rehearsal as a strategy if instructed to do so, they typically fail to generalize the strategy to new tasks. Another strategy that improves with age is **organization** in which children use categorization and hierarchical relationships to process and store information. As with rehearsal, young children can successfully learn to use this strategy if instructed or reminded to do so.

- **Elaboration**—a strategy that involves adding to information to make it more meaningful and thus easier to remember—appears to aid children's retention. The fact that elaboration improves recall, despite the accompanying increase in informational load, underlines the importance of meaning in memory.

- Research suggests that the failure by young children to use strategies may result, not so much from a **mediation deficiency,** but from **production** and **utilization deficiencies,** which may in turn spring from an interaction between the costs and benefits of using a particular strategy. As children become more adept at strategy use, costs decrease and benefits increase.

- **World knowledge,** or what a person has learned about the world from past experiences, influences what the person will understand and remember about a present event. Evidence for the role of world knowledge comes from studies indicating that experts remember more than novices, and that when memory tasks are presented in culturally familiar contexts, children in Western and non-Western cultures perform equally well.

- One important application of developmental research on memory is in children's eyewitness testimony. Recent studies suggest that children may not be reliable witnesses because they are susceptible to suggestions by others. However, children are more resistant to misleading questions when an interviewer is supportive and when they have been actively involved in the recalled event.

- **Problem solving** involves a high level of information processing because it mobilizes perception, attention, and memory to reach a solution. Over development children use different and more complex rules to guide their problem solving on logical tasks. Although analogy is a powerful tool in problem solving, young children and even adults often have difficulty recognizing and using analogies. **Deductive reasoning** develops later in childhood, though simple versions of such tasks have shown some early evidence of both **propositional reasoning** and **hierarchical categorization.** Cognitive tools aid thinking, and examples of such tools are scripts, cognitive maps, and symbolic representations.

- **Scripts** of routine activities provide children with basic outlines of how events occur in many familiar situations so that their behaviors in those situations become almost automatic. Children as young as 3 know about and use scripts to guide their actions.

- Children also use **cognitive maps** and physical maps to negotiate their way through their surroundings. Very young children develop the ability to understand symbolic representations, such as models and pictures, that represent objects or places and the real objects and places in the real world.

- Children's competence with numbers is based on five basic principles of counting that develop during the preschool years. Counting skills may to some degree reflect the number-naming system of a child's native language.

Metacognition

- **Metacognition** refers to the individual's knowledge and control of cognitive activities. Metacognitive knowledge, which develops over childhood, includes the child's knowledge about the self, his theory of mind, and his knowledge about the task and about specific strategies.

- Although young children understand the importance of some task parameters for memory, even first graders are not good at monitoring their comprehension of information about a task. Young children are aware of the importance of memory strategies, and they are particularly sensitive to the use of external memory cues. However, older children have a more accurate and realistic view of their own memory abilities, and they are able to separate their own beliefs and desires from reality.

EXPLORE AND DISCUSS

1. When we reach $2\frac{1}{2}$ to 3 years of age and begin to use language rather effectively, we talk to other people quite a bit as we try to remember the events we have experienced. Do you think our early memories are actually memories of our own experiences and our reactions to them or are they more like a social redefinition of these experiences? Explain your answer.

2. Given what you have read in this chapter about changes in thinking and problem-solving abilities in childhood, do you think it is a coincidence that formal schooling begins at around 6 to 7 years of age? Why or why not?

3. Research by DeLoache and her colleagues on changes in how children understand models has interesting implications for how young children understand many of the toys they play with. Think about some of children's favorite toys—for example, farm sets and model trains. What do you think very young children think about these types of toys and how does their understanding of the toy change as they get older?

4. Child testimony is a very important and complex issue. What do you think might be the best way to interview a preschooler who is the only witness to a crime? Would you use a different interview approach if the child was 7 to 8 years of age? Why or why not?

Anonymous. *Wolfgang Amadeus Mozart as a child at the pianoforte*, 18th century. Mozart House, Salzburg, Austria.

10.

Intelligence and Achievement

What do you think intelligence is? Psychologists studying this question asked a wide variety of people—including some of their colleagues—what behaviors they think are characteristic of intelligence (Sternberg, Conway, Ketron, & Bernstein, 1981). Interestingly, these interviews revealed a consensus. People generally agreed that three behaviors are central to intelligence: problem-solving ability, verbal ability, and social competence. But this agreement among laypeople and psychologists is not a scientific definition. For that, we must specify how to measure intelligence and how to use such measurement in predicting behavior, particularly in areas where intelligence is thought to play a critical role such as academic performance. In addition to knowing how to measure intelligence, we also need to identify the factors that affect intelligence and its development, and to discover how these factors may be modified so as to improve intelligent behavior.

In this third chapter on cognitive functioning, we take a slightly different approach to the topic. In Chapters 8 and 9 we were concerned with cognition and cognitive processes in general, and we were more interested in similarities among people than in their differences. In this chapter, however, we want to know how individuals use their cognitive skills. We want to know how individual intelligence is measured and why people appear to differ in intelligence and in their achievements in cognitive activities. Thus we will discuss such questions as: Are differences in intelligence caused by genetic factors, environmental influences, or both? And, are these apparent differences permanent, or can they be changed? We then consider the matter of achievement, examining various factors that affect children's performance on intelligence tests and in the schoolroom, and we explore the interaction among social class and ethnicity as they impinge on intelligence. Then, after considering the results of some interventions to improve cognitive functioning, we look at intellectual giftedness and mental retardation, and conclude with some ideas about creativity in young children.

THEORIES OF INTELLIGENCE

In attempting to formulate useful theories of intelligence, scientists have focused on three primary issues: whether intelligence is unitary or multifaceted; whether it is determined by genetic or environmental factors; and whether it predicts academic success and success outside of school. The first of these questions, which was hotly debated in the early years of the twentieth century, asked whether intelligence is a single characteristic of an individual that cuts across all behaviors or whether intelligence has many components and an individual can be intelligent in some but not all of these components. Today, it is generally accepted that intelligence is multifaceted and that both genetic and environmental influences contribute to a person's intelligence. The argument is far from over, however, for now investigators concentrate on such issues as whether heredity is more influential than the environment or the other way around and the degree to which the genetic factors in intelligence may be altered by environmental conditions.

The third question asks how important intelligence, as measured by IQ tests, is in predicting children's and adults' success in school and real-life situations. Is it useful in predicting academic success, job stability, and good health and adjustment? Throughout the chapter we will find some answers to these and other issues, but we'll also raise more questions. Let's look now at several ways of understanding the elusive concept of intelligence.

The Factor Analytic Approach

To many people, it may seem obvious that intelligence has many components. We all know we are better—or smarter—at some things than at others. Can we then assume that each of us has more of certain kinds of intelligence than of others?

In the belief that intelligence is unitary, or a single ability, early investigators asserted that a general factor of ability permeates or connects all a person's multiple abilities. Researchers have tested this theory by performing **factor analysis,** a statistical procedure that can be used to determine which of several factors, or scores, are closely related to one another without overlapping each other's contribution. An early factor analyst, Charles Spearman (1927), proposed that intelligence is composed of a **general factor (g)** and a number of **specific factors (s).** Spearman regarded g as general mental energy, or ability, which was involved in all cognitive tasks, and he saw s factors as factors unique to particular tasks. A person with a high g would be expected to do generally well on all tasks. Variations in her performance on different tasks could be attributed to her possession of varying amounts of s factors.

Interest in g and the notion of a unitary concept of intelligence was challenged decades ago by Lewis Thurstone (1938), who proposed that seven primary skills comprise intelligence: verbal meaning, perceptual speed, reasoning, number, rote memory, word fluency, and spatial visualization. More recently, Carroll (1993, 1997) and other researchers (Johnson, Bouchard, Kruegar, McGue, & Gottesman, 2004) have confirmed the existence of a general factor of cognitive ability. It seems that people who do well on one kind of cognitive test (e.g., reading comprehension) are indeed likely to do well on other such tests (e.g., listening comprehension or folding paper into specific shapes, as in Japanese *origami*). However, intelligence researchers also recognize that individuals vary in their competence across different domains. For example, Carroll (1993, 1997) proposes a hierarchically organized model involving both a general, g, factor and more narrowly defined abilities, such as vocabulary knowledge in one's native language, basic mathematics skills, or the ability to discriminate musical pitch. According to this model, children vary both in overall level of intellectual power and in how proficient they are in specific aspects of cognitive functioning. This "middle ground" position nicely characterizes the current view of modern approaches to the study of intelligence.

factor analysis A statistical procedure used to determine which of a number of factors, or scores, are both closely related to each other and relatively independent of other groups of factors, or scores.

general factor (g) General mental energy, or ability, involved in all cognitive tasks.

specific factors (s) Factors unique to particular cognitive tasks.

The Information-Processing Approach: Sternberg's Triarchic Theory

The interest of information-processing researchers in the processes involved in intellectual activity has led to a new approach to intelligence and intelligence testing. Information-processing specialists believe that to understand intelligence, we must supplement traditional IQ tests with procedures that assess the components of information processing, such as the memory and problem-solving abilities people use in performing intellectual tasks (Sternberg, 1985).

Sternberg's (1985, 2001) **triarchic theory of intelligence** is an important example of this approach. As this theory's name implies, it proposes three major components of intelligent behavior: information-processing skills, experience with a given task or situation, and ability to tailor one's behavior to the demands of a context. These three components work together in organizing and guiding intelligent behavior. *Information-processing skills,* discussed in Chapter 9, are required to encode, combine, and compare varying kinds of information. *Experience,* the second component of Sternberg's model, considers how much exposure and practice an individual has had with a particular intellectual task and how readily an individual can automatize information over repeated experiences with a task. For example, if one child has never studied long division and another child has studied it for several years, we should make different judgments about these children's relative intelligence based on their performance on a long-division test (Sternberg, Wagner, & Okagaki, 1993).

Context, Sternberg's third component, recognizes that intelligence cannot be separated from the situation in which it is exercised. Because people must function effectively in many different situations, they must be able both to adapt to the requirements of a situation and to select and shape other situations to meet their own needs (Sternberg, 1985). Thus, one dimension on which the intelligence of a particular behavior can be measured is its suitability and effectiveness in a particular context (Ceci, 1996; Sternberg & Wagner, 1994). For example, consider how the young Brazilian street vendors we discussed in Chapter 8 were able to adapt their functioning to the requirements of the situations in which they used these skills.

In an extension of his triarchic theory, Sternberg has developed a theory of **successful intelligence,** which he defines as "one's purposive ability to adapt to, shape and select environments so as to accomplish one's goals and those of one's society and culture" (Sternberg, 2001, p. 350). Successful intelligence requires three abilities: analytical, creative, and practical. *Analytical abilities* include those taught and tested in most schools and colleges, such as reasoning about the best answer to a test question. *Creative abilities* are involved in devising new ways of addressing issues and concerns. *Practical abilities* are used in people's everyday worlds of work, family life, and social and professional interactions. Much practical knowledge is tacit in that it is not explicitly formulated and it is rarely taught directly to children; it is learned by observing others. Nonetheless, this kind of **tacit knowledge** is shared by many people and guides behavior. Sometimes tacit knowledge is referred to as common sense (Sternberg & Wagner, 1993). Table 10-1 displays an example of a test item that Sternberg and his colleagues use to measure tacit knowledge, or the ability to make practical choices, in college study behavior. Sternberg (2001) found that tacit knowledge of this sort, though not associated with IQ score, predicted the salaries and job performance of adult workers.

Applications of Sternberg's triarchic theory to school curricula have shown much success in helping children learn class material (Sternberg, Torff, & Grigorenko, 1999). Moreover, children who were instructed with curricula based on the triarchic theory reported enjoying the material more than children taught the same information in a more traditional fashion. This research suggests that this approach to intelligence when applied in the class setting may benefit children's learning as well as enhance their motivation to learn.

triarchic theory of intelligence A theory that proposes three major components of intelligent behavior: information-processing skills, experience with a particular situation, and ability to adapt to the demands of a context.

successful intelligence Ability to fit into, mold, and choose environments that best fulfill one's own needs and desires as well as the demands of one's society and culture. Includes analytical, creative, and practical abilities.

tacit knowledge Implicit knowledge that is shared by many people and that guides behavior.

Table 10-1

Tacit knowledge: A sample test question

Source: Adapted from Sternberg & Wagner, 1993.

College Student Life

You are enrolled in a large introductory lecture course. Requirements consist of three exams and a final. Please indicate how characteristic (on a scale of 1 to 5, from least to most characteristic) it would be of your behavior to spend time doing each of the following if your goal were to receive an A in the course:

_____ Attend class regularly.

_____ Attend optional weekly review sections with the teaching fellow.

_____ Read assigned text chapters thoroughly.

_____ Take comprehensive class notes.

_____ Speak with the professor after class and during office hours.

Gardner's Theory of Multiple Intelligences

theory of multiple intelligences Gardner's multifactorial theory that proposes eight distinct types of intelligence.

Howard Gardner (1983, 1998) has proposed a **theory of multiple intelligences.** Initially, he suggested that human beings possess seven kinds of intelligence—linguistic, logical-mathematical, spatial, musical, bodily-kinesthetic, intrapersonal, and interpersonal (see Table 10-2). Then, in 1999, Gardner added an eighth form of intelligence, which he called naturalist intelligence. At this time, he noted that the number of types of intelligences may be even greater than eight and he suggested a

Table 10-2   Gardner's theory of multiple intelligences

Type of Intelligence/Description	Examples
Linguistic: Sensitivity to word meanings; mastery of syntax; appreciation of the ways language can be used	Poet, teacher
Logical-mathematical: Understanding of objects, symbols, the actions that can be performed on them, and the interrelations among these actions; ability to operate in the abstract and to identify problems and seek explanations	Mathematician, scientist
Spatial: Accurate perception of visual world; ability to transform perceptions and mentally re-create visual experience; sensitivity to tension, balance, and composition; ability to detect similar patterns	Artist, engineer, chess player
Musical: Sensitivity to musical tones and phrases; ability to combine tones and phrases into larger rhythms and structures; awareness of music's emotional aspects	Musician, composer
Bodily-kinesthetic: Skilled and graceful use of one's body for expressive or goal-directed purposes; ability to handle objects skillfully	Dancer, athlete, actor
Intrapersonal: Access to one's own feeling life; ability to draw on one's emotions to guide and understand behavior	Novelist, psychotherapist, actor
Interpersonal: Ability to notice and distinguish among others' moods, temperaments, motives, and intentions; ability to act on this knowledge	Political or religious leader, parent, teacher, psychotherapist
Naturalist: Insight into the natural world; ability to identify different life forms and species and the relationships between them	Biologist, naturalist

Sources: Gardner, 1983, 1999; Torff & Gardner, 1999.

(a)

(b)

possible ninth form, which he called spirituality or existential intelligence. Three of the types of intelligence in his initial list, linguistic, logical-mathematical, and spatial, are similar to the kinds of abilities assessed in traditional intelligence tests. The remaining types have been much less widely studied, yet, according to Gardner, they are equally important to human functioning. For example, interpersonal intelligence may be of crucial importance to a parent, a nurse, or a teacher; bodily-kinesthetic intelligence may greatly facilitate the performance of a dancer or an athlete and even a sports medicine professional.

Each type of intelligence, Gardner proposes, is considered a unique form of intelligence with its own developmental path guided by its own forms of perception, learning, and memory. For example, linguistic intelligence emphasizes verbal and memory abilities and generally develops over years of educational experience, whereas bodily-kinesthetic intelligence, which emphasizes understanding of body mechanics and its coordination with perceptual abilities, may manifest itself quite early in life. In addition, Gardner suggests, a single individual can display different combinations of these intelligences, and different cultures or periods of history may emphasize or value some of these forms of intelligence more than others. In this way, Gardner's view of intelligence corresponds with the ideas presented in the domain-specific views of intelligence discussed by evolutionary psychologists (recall our discussion of evolutionary psychology in Chapter 1).

Gardner's theory has its critics, however. Some investigators have pointed out that Gardner's intelligences may not all be separate entities—that is, some may be closely tied to others, whereas others may be distinct (e.g., Carroll, 1993; Weinberg, 1989). Also, few efforts have been made to rigorously evaluate Gardner's theory using standard assessment techniques, or to develop tests based directly on the theory (Benbow & Lubinski, 1996; Sternberg & Wagner, 1994).

These caveats aside, Gardner's theory has been used to improve public education. Most notably, Gardner's work with Harvard University's Project Zero has resulted in more individualized and varied instruction through use of different curricula aligned with his multiple intelligences. And Gardner, Sternberg, and their colleagues collaborated on the Practical Intelligence for Schools, or PIFS, program, designed to teach the tacit knowledge needed to succeed in school. Evaluations of these programs have

Building a model out of tinker toys, as this U.S. child is doing (a), illustrates Howard Gardner's spatial intelligence. Playing an indigenous flute, like this Quechan child from Peru (b), illustrates Gardner's musical intelligence.

shown them to have had positive effects on student motivation, achievement, and behavior (Gardner, 1999; Sternberg, 2001).

THE TRADITIONAL APPROACH: TESTING INTELLIGENCE

Although developmentalists and other psychologists have become increasingly interested in the *processes* that contribute to intellectual functioning, the study and testing of intelligence has traditionally focused on its *products*—that is, on the specific knowledge and skills displayed on intelligence tests. On the basis of such tests, researchers have developed the **intelligence quotient (IQ),** an index of the way a person performs on a standardized intelligence test relative to the way others her age perform. Although the term IQ is widely used, it is often misconstrued; some people think IQ is innate and does not change. But research has shown that IQ *can* change over the life span, for it can be modified by experience.

In discussing intelligence and intelligence testing, it is important to remember that we can only *infer* intellectual capacity from the results of an IQ test. Although we assume that capacity and performance are related, we can measure only performance. We cannot measure capacity directly. Moreover, there is always some discrepancy between capacity and performance owing to the particular circumstances of a performance, such as the precise construction of a test or the test taker's emotional state during the test.

Why do we need to measure intelligence? There are three primary purposes in intelligence testing: predicting academic performance, predicting performance on the job, and assessing general adjustment and health. The earliest intelligence tests were designed to meet the first of these goals, and most existing intelligence tests, such as the Binet and Wechsler scales, predict academic achievement quite well. Predicting how well a person will succeed at a job is the second goal of intelligence testing, and according to Gottfredson (1997), such measures are the most powerful predictors of overall work performance. A third use of intelligence testing is in assessing people's general adjustment and health. The Binet and Wechsler tests that we discuss in this section can detect signs of neurological problems, mental retardation, and emotional distress in children as well as adults. The Bayley scales and other infant tests are useful in assessing developmental progress in infants as well as neurological disorders or mental retardation.

Unfortunately, traditional tests do not make predictions as accurately for some groups in our society as for others. Many critics, for example, have pointed out that these tests often require knowledge that children with fewer advantages than others may not have. As a result, traditional tests may unfairly classify some people as less intelligent than they actually are. Indeed, there have been times when, on the sole basis of IQ-test performance, entire cultural groups have been identified as less intelligent than other groups who have had greater educational opportunities. As a result, researchers have, for some years, been attempting to develop what are known as **culture-fair tests**—that is, tests that attempt to exclude or minimize the kind of experientially or culturally biased content in IQ tests that could prejudice test takers' responses. The Raven Progressive Matrices Test, which requires people to identify, distinguish, and match patterns of varying complexity, and the Kaufman test we discuss shortly are such tests.

We begin this section with a brief discussion of infant intelligence tests and then examine the two sets of traditional tests that are most widely used for testing IQ beyond the years of infancy—the Stanford-Binet tests and the Wechsler scales. Next we examine the relatively new Kaufman assessment measure, which attempts to measure the processes by which people acquire information and solve problems. We then turn to the methodology of test construction, including the ways in which psychologists develop norms for test scoring and the kinds of procedures they adopt to ensure the validity and reliability of their tests. We conclude the section by considering the stability of intelligence as well as what factors may effect changes in intelligence over time.

intelligence quotient (IQ) An index of the way a person performs on a standardized intelligence test relative to the way others her age perform.

culture-fair test A test that attempts to minimize cultural biases in content that might influence the test taker's responses.

Measuring Infant Intelligence

The **Bayley Scales of Infant Development,** or BSID (Bayley, 1969, 1993), are probably the best known and most widely used of all infant development tests. Because these tests were designed to be used with the very young, they include many nonverbal test items chosen for their ability to measure specific developmental milestones. The Bayley scales are used with infants and children between 1 month and $3\frac{1}{2}$ years of age, and they are generally used to assess children suspected to be at risk for abnormal development. For example, the Bayley *mental* scale includes such things as looking for a hidden object and naming pictures, whereas the *motor* scale includes such items as grasping ability and jumping skills. In a third part of the test, the examiner observes the child's behavior, making notes about such things as sociability and displays of fear. Although these scales are useful in identifying infants at risk for unhealthy development, the Bayley scales and other older tests of infant intelligence are poor predictors of later cognitive levels. This may be because they rely primarily on sensorimotor measures, whereas child and adult tests involve verbal and other later-emerging skills.

Newer tests, such as the Fagan test, measure information-processing skills in order to address the need for early prediction of educational risk and the avoidance of cultural bias. The **Fagan Test of Infant Intelligence** was built on the notion that infants display their intelligence in their capable use of such processes as encoding the attributes of objects, seeing similarities and differences between objects, forming mental representations, and retrieving those representations (Fagan, 1992). You'll recall that in Chapter 4 we discussed habituation and the infant's tendency to pay attention to what is novel in his environment. Based on this notion of early attention to novelty, the Fagan test estimates an infant's intelligence by measuring the amount of time the infant spends looking at a new object compared with the time he spends looking at a familiar object (Fagan et al., 1991). Using a set of 20 photographs of human faces, arranged in pairs, the examiner begins by showing a baby one photograph of the first pair for 20 seconds. Then the examiner pairs that photograph with its mate, showing the baby the two photos together for 5 seconds, and then again for another 5 seconds, this time reversing the two photos left to right (to avoid any tendency for the infant to "choose" one side). The score the infant receives is made up of the total time he spends looking at the novel photograph throughout a presentation of all 10 pairs. In research on whether infants from different cultures would be equally adept at this task, Fagan and his colleagues found that there were practially no differences between the average scores obtained by nearly 200 infants representing European Americans, African Americans, Bahrainians, and Ugandans. Although this test predicts later cognitive development better than older tests, the correlations with later development remain weak to moderate (Sternberg, Grigorenko, & Bundy, 2001; Tasbihsazan, Nettelbeck, & Kirby, 2003). However, as we've said, infant tests are useful for diagnostic screening to determine a child's need for early intervention services.

The Stanford-Binet Test

Widely used by psychologists both in schools and in health settings, the **Stanford-Binet Test** is the modern version of a test devised in the early 1900s by Binet and Simon at the request of the Paris school system. At that time, because of new compulsory education laws, the city's schools were overcrowded, and school administrators wanted to identify children who were unable to learn in traditional classroom settings and who would benefit from special education.

Binet and Simon, who believed that intelligence was malleable and that children's academic performance could be improved with special programs, took an innovative approach to the construction of their test (Binet, 1909/1973; Siegler, 1992). Critical of earlier psychologists, who had tried to assess intelligence by measuring simple sensory or motor responses, Binet and Simon asserted that to differentiate among individuals,

Bayley Scales of Infant Development A set of nonverbal tests that measure specific developmental milestones and are generally used with children thought to be at risk for abnormal development.

Fagan Test of Infant Intelligence A test of how infants process information, including encoding attributes of objects and seeing similarities and differences across objects; designed to be culture-fair.

Stanford-Binet Test The modern version of the first major intelligence test; emphasizes verbal and mathematical skills.

one had to sample higher mental functions such as comprehension, reasoning, and judgment. They developed an array of intellectual tasks involving such things as the ability to attend to an environmental cue and the ability to recognize logical absurdities. They also included tests of skills taught in school, such as recalling details of a story read aloud, naming the days of the week, and counting coins. In addition, they built into their test age-related changes in children's learning—that is, they recognized that as children grow they become able to solve increasingly complex problems (Siegler, 1992).

In refining their tests, Binet and Simon selected items to reflect children's competence at different age levels. Binet introduced the concept of **mental age,** which is an index of a child's actual performance level as contrasted with his true age. Thus, if a 6-year-old child gets as many items correct as the average 7-year-old, the 6-year-old's mental age is 7; she performs as well as a child 7 years old. The mental age concept was later captured in the intelligence quotient, for which the German psychologist William Stern devised the following formula:

$$IQ = MA/CA \times 100$$

where IQ equals mental age (MA) divided by chronological age (CA), multiplied by 100. Thus, if a child's mental age equaled her chronological age, she would be performing like an average child of her true age, and her IQ would be 100. If her performance were superior to other children her age, her IQ would be above 100. If it were inferior, her IQ would be less than 100.

Today's Stanford-Binet test, a revision of the Binet-Simon measure, has been designed to include items that tap other than language and math skills and to reflect intelligent performance. The extent to which academic experience influences such performance, however, is not entirely clear.

The Wechsler Scales

The **Wechsler Intelligence Scales,** developed by David Wechsler (1952, 1958), include the Wechsler Preschool and Primary Scale of Intelligence (WPPSI), the Wechsler Intelligence Scale for Children (WISC), and the Wechsler Adult Intelligence Scale (WAIS). Although these tests show the influence of Binet's tests, Wechsler designed them specifically to yield separate verbal and performance IQ scores as well as a combined, full-scale IQ score. The most recent update of the WISC, which is the fourth version (Wechsler, 2003), was designed to better represent current research and thinking in cognitive development, especially in areas related to how children process information. As you'll recall from Chapter 9, these areas include memory, strategy use, and processing speed. The descriptions of the WISC subtests from this recent version shown in Table 10-3 highlight the fact that performance items are somewhat less likely to be influenced by formal education or cultural factors. As a result, a child who has a specific learning problem, such as a difficulty with language, may do quite well on these items, even if he performs poorly on the verbal subtests. Children who come from homes that lack some of the advantages other children enjoy may also be more successful on these performance tests.

Rather than use mental age as a basis for estimating intelligence, Wechsler created the **deviation IQ,** which is a number that reflects the higher, lower, or similar position of the test taker's score in relation to the score obtained by the average child of the same age. How is this different from the concept of mental age? The deviation IQ scoring system, which like the Binet IQ takes 100 as an average score, is based on extensive testing of people of different ages in many parts of the United States and on the statistical computation of mean scores for each age group. In computing these average scores, psychologists use a statistic called the *standard deviation* to identify the extent to which non-average scores deviate from the norm. As a result, an individual's score may be at the mean, or it may be one or more standard deviations above or below the mean.

---

mental age An index of a child's actual performance on an intelligence test as compared with his true age.

Wechsler Intelligence Scales Three intelligence tests for preschool children, school-age children, and adults that yield separate scores for verbal and performance IQ as well as a combined IQ score.

deviation IQ An IQ score that indicates the extent to which a person's performance on a test deviates from agemates' average performance.

Table 10-3   The Wechsler Intelligence Scale for Children, Fourth Edition (WISC-IV)

Subtests	Descriptions and Some Examples	Skills Thought to Tap
Similarities	The child is asked to tell how paired words are alike (e.g., *How are a cup and a glass alike?*).	Concept formation; categorization
Vocabulary	The child is asked to define each word in a list of words of increasing difficulty.	Concept formation; long-term memory; vocabulary
Comprehension	A series of questions ask the child to explain why certain actions or practices are desirable (e.g., *What should you do if you lose a friend's toy?*).	Factual knowledge; long-term memory; intellectual interest
Information	For each item, the child answers questions that address a broad range of general knowledge topics (e.g., *How many days are there in a week?*).	Factual knowledge; long-term memory; intellectual interest
Word reasoning*	The child is given successive clues and asked to identify the common concept being described in a series of clues (e.g., *"This is squishy and full of holes"* or *"You use it to wash things with"*).	Verbal abstraction and comprehension; analogic and general reasoning ability; integration and synthesis of different types of information; domain knowledge; generation of alternative concepts
Block design	The child is shown an actual model of a red-and-white design or a picture of it and is asked to re-create the design, using blocks whose sides are either red, white, or half red and half white.	Visual-motor coordination; concept formation; pattern recognition; spatial ability
Picture concepts*	The child is presented with 2 or 3 rows of pictures of familiar objects and must choose one from each row to form a group with a common characteristic (e.g., *things to eat* or *things to play with*).	Fluid reasoning; abstract categorical ability
Matrix reasoning*	The child looks at an incomplete matrix, a grid of 4 equal-size squares in which all but 3 of the squares are filled with designs. The child must look then at a separate display of 5 possible designs and choose the one that will complete the matrix.	Visual information processing; abstract reasoning skills
Picture completion	The child is asked to look at a series of pictures and, for each one, to point out what is missing from the picture (e.g., *a car with a missing wheel; a rabbit with a missing ear*).	Visual organization; perceptual reasoning; concentration
Digit span	The examiner says several sequences of digits, each longer than the preceding one, and the child is asked to repeat them either in the order in which the examiner said them or in reverse order (e.g., *2-7-4; 3-1-9-6; 8-4-2-7-5*).	Mental alertness and attention; cognitive flexibility; short-term memory
Letter-number sequencing*	The examiner reads to the child a sequence of letters and numbers and asks the child to recall the numbers (in ascending order) and the letters (in alphabetical order).	Working memory—sequencing, mental manipulation, attention, short-term auditory memory, visual-spatial imaging, processing speed
Arithmetic	The child is asked to solve, without physical aids such as pencil and paper, arithmetic problems that the examiner presents orally. The test is timed.	Working memory; mathematical skills
Cancellation*	The child is shown an array of pictures of objects and asked to find and mark every picture of a certain class of objects as fast as possible (the test is timed) (e.g., *in an array of pictures of miscellaneous things such as flowers, furniture items, animals, cleaning implements, the child might be asked to find and mark all the pictures of animals*).	Visual selective attention; processing speed

* Subtests marked with an asterisk are new to the WISC in its fourth edition.

Source: Items similar to those in the *Wechsler Intelligence Scale for Children, Fourth Edition.* Copyright © 2003 by Harcourt Assessment, Inc. Reproduced with permission. All rights reserved. *"Wechsler Intelligence Scale for Children"* and *"WISC"* are trademarks of Harcourt Assessment, Inc. registered in the United States of America and/or other jurisdictions.

The Kaufman Assessment Battery for Children

Kaufman Assessment Battery for Children (K-ABC) An intelligence test designed to measure several types of information-processing skills as well as achievement in some academic subjects.

The first test to focus largely on processing skills is the **Kaufman Assessment Battery for Children (K-ABC)** (Kaufman & Kaufman, 1983). The test measures several types of information-processing skills grouped into two categories: *sequential processing* (solving problems in a step-by-step fashion) and *simultaneous processing* (examining and integrating a wide variety of materials in the solution of a problem). The test also assesses achievement in academic subjects, such as vocabulary and arithmetic, and efforts have been made to design the test items (many nonverbal) to be culture-fair. In fact, the designers of this test used a wide and representative sample of many American cultural and socioeconomic groups in establishing norms for the test.

An interesting innovation is that if a child fails early items on a subscale, the examiner teaches the child how to complete these items before the child does the rest of the subtest. According to the designers of the test, this ensures that no child who is capable of learning an unfamiliar task receives a failing score on it. The Kaufman test has been criticized for offering only a limited range of items that tap information-processing functions, such as short-term memory, and should focus more on problem solving (Conoley, 1990; Sternberg, 1985). Nevertheless, the Kaufman test is a creative approach to the measurement of intelligence that applies insights from the information-processing approach to intelligence testing.

Constructing Measures of Intelligence

psychometrician A psychologist who specializes in the construction and use of tests designed to measure various psychological constructs such as intelligence and various personality characteristics.

Devising an intelligence test depends first and foremost on the theory of intelligence held by the test constructor, or **psychometrician.** For example, if the theory emphasizes the products of intelligence, the test will include many subtests that ask for specific information. A test based on the information-processing approaches will include items designed to tap processing functions and speed and the strategies by which a person attempts to solve a problem. Certain goals and principles, however, are shared by all constructors of intelligence tests, and it is to these issues that we now turn. We look first at how norms for a test are established and at how the test is standardized; then we consider the important issues of determining a test's validity and reliability.

DEVELOPMENT OF NORMS AND STANDARDS A person's performance on an intelligence test is always described by his position relative to the performance on the same test of others in a specified group; the person is thus considered either average, above average, or below average in relation to other group members. **Test norms** are the values that describe the typical test performance of a specific group of people.

test norms Values, or sets of values, that describe the typical test performance of a specific group of people.

Age is a particularly critical factor when setting norms for children's test performance. Although children generally improve their test performance as they grow older, their score relative to the scores of other children of their age continues to be the significant factor in evaluating their intellectual development.

Psychometricians do not agree on whether comparison groups in intelligence testing should be equated on such factors as level of education, socioeconomic class, or gender. Nevertheless, in evaluating test performance we should always consider how closely the attributes and experiences of the person being tested approximate those of the group that was used to establish the test norms. For example, it would be inappropriate to use the same set of norms in evaluating the performance of children raised in an isolated Papua New Guinea tribe without access to formal schooling as we use to evaluate the performance of middle-class, European American children. And as we will discuss later, norms for the latter group may not be appropriate even for the children of minority groups within North America.

Because the conditions under which a given test is administered may influence performance and can vary widely, it is extremely important that we subject a test to **standardization,** in which test constructors attempt to ensure that on every testing occasion the procedures that examiners follow, the instructions they give to examinees, and test scoring are identical, or as nearly so as possible.

ASCERTAINING VALIDITY AND RELIABILITY
For any test to provide useful information about an individual, it must be valid—that is, it must measure what it claims it measures. It must also be reliable—that is, an individual's scores must be consistent over different times of measurement.

In establishing the **validity** of an intelligence test, psychometricians most often correlate performance on the test with some other measure, called a criterion, that is believed to reflect the capacity being tested. The most frequently used criteria are achievement test scores, grades in school, teachers' ratings of cognitive ability, and performance on other intelligence tests. Intelligence tests are much more successful in predicting school performance than in predicting things like creativity or social skills. Even within school performance, intelligence test scores are more closely related to mathematical problem solving and reading comprehension than to ability in drama, art, or music.

Reliability—the extent to which a test yields consistent results over time or successive administrations—is also critical for evaluating the utility of an intelligence test. To be useful, a test's scores must not fluctuate unpredictably from one administration to another. This is because a chief goal of these tests is to *predict* the individual's performance *beyond a single administration of the test*. Although reliability captures how much a test is useful across administrations, a related but broader issue is that of the stability of intelligence, to which we turn next.

standardization The process by which test constructors ensure that testing procedures, instructions, and scoring are identical, or as nearly so as possible, on every testing occasion.

validity The extent to which a test actually measures what it claims to measure.

reliability The degree to which a test yields consistent results over time or successive administrations.

Stability of Measured Intelligence

Is intelligence an absolute quality that remains stable, or fixed, over time, or can it change as a function of experience? To answer this question we need to understand many things about intelligence, intelligence testing, and the limitations of intelligence measures. Tests like the Binet and Wechsler scales, which focus on the products of intelligence and measure current performance, have generally demonstrated that IQ scores are not stable over time but fluctuate. As investigators have begun to use newer tests that focus on the processes of intelligent functioning, however, the evidence for stability has been mounting.

In this section, we review longitudinal studies in which children have been tested repeatedly over long periods to examine the question of the stability of intellectual functioning over time. We will also address a second, related question: Are the average intelligence levels within a population stable across time?

As we will see, the evidence to date suggests that there is both stability and change in intellectual functioning over time. This finding highlights a third question: Can intelligence be changed by purposeful effort? Throughout the rest of the chapter, we explore the many ramifications of this important issue.

PREDICTIVE VALUE OF INFANT TESTING
Most of our information on the consistency of performance on intelligence tests derives from longitudinal studies in which children—in some cases as young as 1 month old—have been repeatedly tested over time. Some of these studies are the Berkeley Guidance Study, the Berkeley Growth Study, and the Fels Longitudinal Study, in which individuals were followed for periods of time ranging from 20 to 50 years. These and other early studies have found no significant relation between intelligence test scores recorded in infancy and those attained later in childhood or even adulthood (Figure 10-1; see also Honzik, 1983; Lewis, 1983; McCall, Hogarty, & Hurlburt, 1972). However, as these early studies

Figure 10-1

Predicting IQ scores

The height of each curve represents the degree to which children's early intelligence test scores correlated with their Stanford-Binet IQ scores when they were 8 years old. The longer the time lapse between earlier and later testing, the less predictive value the earlier score held. Notice that in the Berkeley Growth and Stockholm studies, the earliest scores were actually negatively correlated with later ones.

Source: Honzik, 1976, 1983.

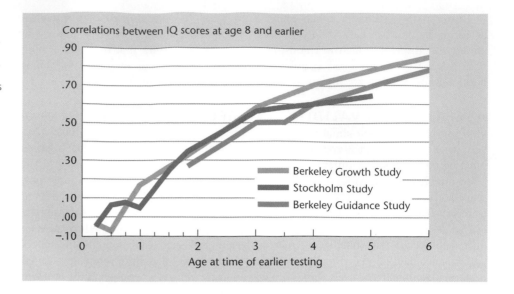

recovery The ability to recognize a new stimulus as novel and to direct attention to it in preference to a familiar stimulus.

tended to compare infants' sensorimotor skills with later problem-solving and verbal skills, it may be that these two kinds of abilities have little relation to one another.

More recent research using newer and different infant tests has found higher correlations with later cognitive measures (e.g., Fagan, 1992; Rose & Feldman, 1995). These studies have largely focused on information-processing abilities, such as some of the attentional processes that we described in Chapter 4, particularly habituation and recovery. Investigators have focused on the infant's ability to habituate—recall that this means to discontinue attending to a stimulus after several presentations—interpreting this behavior as the ability to familiarize oneself quickly with new material. In addition, studying the process called **recovery,** researchers have measured infants' ability to recognize a totally new stimulus as novel and to direct their attention to it in preference to a stimulus with which they're already familiar.

What kinds of correlations are found between measures of infant attentional processes and later IQ scores? Fagan and his colleagues found significant but moderate correlations between infants' visual preferences and attention at 7 months of age and their intellectual functioning at 3 and 5 years (Fagan et al., 1991). Bornstein and Sigman (1986) also found moderately strong relations between such attentional measures in young infants and the scores these children achieved on traditional intelligence tests at ages 3 to 6. Other researchers have found that infant preference for novelty was a better predictor of later intelligence scores, sometimes even into adulthood, than were standard infant intelligence measures such as the Bayley test (DiLalla et al., 1990; Rose, Feldman, Wallach, & McCarton, 1989). However, not all studies show such positive relations (Tasbihsazan et al., 2003).

Although we may be tempted to conclude that early individual differences in habituation and response to novelty reflect genetic predispositions, it's important to recognize that a child's environment has the opportunity to affect her attentional processing probably from birth. In fact, one study indicated that attentional processing in 5-month-olds was related to the infants' mothers' responsivity (Bornstein & Tamis, 1986). Moreover, differences in attentional processing in infants may reflect variation stemming from factors other than intellectual abilities, such as temperament (Karass & Braungart-Rieker, 2004). Thus, parental behaviors and the child's own emotionally related characteristics may well have a significant impact on infant intelligence.

CHANGES IN CHILDREN'S IQ OVER TIME The fact that correlations between infant testing and later measures of intelligence, though often significant, are moderate suggests that there is room for change as a child develops (Bornstein & Sigman, 1986). However, most research indicates that from the middle years of childhood onward, intelligence tests are fairly reliable predictors of later performance on such tests. For example, Honzik, MacFarlane, and Allen (1948) found a correlation of .70 between children's IQs at ages 8 and 18. Nonetheless, there is also evidence of considerable variability in children's IQs. Many of the children tested in the Fels study, mentioned earlier, shifted considerably upward in IQ scores between the ages of $2\frac{1}{2}$ and 17 (McCall, Appelbaum, & Hogarty, 1973): One of every three children scored higher by some 30 points, and one in seven shifted upward more than 40 points. On rare occasions, individuals have improved their IQ performance as much as 74 points. Investigators have also observed that high-IQ children are likely to show greater amounts of change than low-IQ children.

Some of the variability demonstrated in IQ scores reflects the fact that different children develop cognitively at different rates of speed, just as they experience physical growth in spurts and at different ages (Garlick, 2003). These variations in cognitive development affect the reliability of IQ scores. Interestingly, studies suggest that changes in IQ are most likely to occur at the ages of 6 and 10. According to some researchers, this change at age 6 may have been predicted by Piaget and his followers, as discussed in Chapter 8. Piaget described a shift in children of about that age to higher levels of reasoning and conceptual ability. Reasons for the shift at the age of 10 are less clear.

Experiential factors may also contribute to changes in IQ. Stressful life events, such as parental divorce or death or a geographical move or change in schools, can cause at least temporary disruptions in cognitive performance. Indeed, children who show the most dramatic changes in IQ over time have often experienced major changes in their life circumstances, such as foster home placement or a serious illness (Honzik, 1983).

In addition to examining the stability of individual IQ scores over time, some researchers have studied the stability of the average IQ for a group over time. Examining studies of different populations in the United States and other developed countries done between 1932 and 1978, Flynn (1984, 1998) found that the average IQ score in these nations increased by about 15 points during this time; this trend is known as the **Flynn effect.** Gains were observed in measures tapping problem-solving ability, but not in measures involving learned material. The explanations for these gains in the group average are still being debated; they range from improved nutrition, changes in testing formats and procedures, and exposure to technology and media.

Flynn effect Increase in the average IQ score in the populations of the United States and other developed countries since the early 1900s, a phenomenon identified by J. R. Flynn.

WHY DO PEOPLE DIFFER IN MEASURED INTELLIGENCE?

Closely related to the question of the stability of intelligence is one of the most controversial issues in the study of human intellectual functioning: how individual differences in intelligence develop. The modern controversy on this issue was touched off over 30 years ago when psychologist Arthur Jensen (1969) claimed that as much as 80 percent of differences in IQ among people were attributable to genetic, or inherited factors, and only a small proportion of differences to social-environmental factors. What was so shocking about Jensen's 1969 paper was his charge that the differences he recorded between IQ scores attained by African Americans and European Americans were attributable to inheritance, and that they demonstrated that blacks were inherently less intelligent than whites. In effect, Jensen was consigning an entire group to a lower level of functioning and asserting that these differences were immutable. Although some researchers have supported Jensen's view, many more researchers have opposed it, in general asserting that social and environmental factors have as much influence on intelligence as inherited factors (Neisser et al., 1995).

In this section, we review some of the research on the side of heredity and then examine the evidence for the role of social and environmental factors in intelligence. Because the issue of the effects of ethnic and social-class differences on intelligence is so important we have reserved much of our discussion of this topic for the major section entitled "Ethnicity, Social Class, and Intellectual Performance."

How Much of Intelligence Is Inherited?

As we saw in our Chapter 2 discussions of the relative roles of heredity and environment in the development of many human characteristics, there is considerable support for the importance of heredity in intelligence. Most estimates of the heritability of intelligence—that is, the proportion of the variability in intelligence attributable to genetic factors—have supported a figure of about 40 to 50 percent for middle-class European Americans (McGue & Bouchard, 1987; Plomin, 1990a; Plomin & Petrill, 1997). This suggests that the remaining 50 to 60 percent of the variability is a function of environmental factors, both social (family, peers, school) and nonsocial (dietary and disease factors, toxins, pollutants). Many psychologists disagree with this more or less 50-50 proposition, however. Some, like Stephen Ceci (1996), hold that the estimates of the heritability of intelligence are too high; others, like Jensen, insist that they are too low. In 1994 a book by Richard Herrnstein and Charles Murray, which argued that intelligence is in part genetically based, rekindled many of these arguments about the origins of intelligence. Since its publication, a number of other investigators have endeavored both to state the "mainstream" view of the issues surrounding this area of study and to encourage researchers in the field to become more sensitive to and concerned with the practical implications of their work (Gottfredson, 1997; Neisser et al., 1995). For instance, Gottfredson (2004) discusses how different conceptions of the contributions of inheritance and environment to IQ influence the way classrooms and curricula are structured and suggests how policies and actions in schools related to these views can affect children's opportunities for social mobility through education.

Although present knowledge suggests that some aspects of intelligence may stabilize during childhood and change little from then on, this does not mean that people are born with immutable levels of intelligence. As we will see later in this chapter, a considerable body of research has shown that environmental manipulations are indeed capable of creating changes in measured intelligence.

associative learning
According to Jensen, lower-level learning tapped in tests of such things as short-term memorization and recall, attention, rote learning, and simple associative skills. Also called *level I* learning.

cognitive learning According to Jensen, higher-level learning tapped in tests of such things as abstract thinking, symbolic processing, and the use of language in problem solving. Also called *level II* learning.

VIEWS THAT EMPHASIZE HERITABILITY OF IQ The measures of intelligence used in studies to support arguments for high levels of heritability in IQ are often based on traditional views of intellectual functioning. For instance, Jensen (1969, 1993), who has been the most outspoken proponent of the heritability, or genetic, position, proposes two types of learning, both inherited but each distinct from the other. **Associative learning** (*level I* learning) involves short-term memory, rote learning, attention, and simple associative skills. For example, we might ask a child to look at a group of familiar objects and then later to recall these objects or to memorize a list of numbers and then to recall them. **Cognitive learning** (*level II* learning) involves abstract thinking, symbolic processes, conceptual learning, and the use of language in problem solving. An example of cognitive learning is the ability to answer questions like the following:

What should be the next number in the following series? 2, 3, 5, 8, 12, 17, . . .

How are an apple and a banana alike?

Most intelligence tests measure mostly cognitive learning abilities. Some, however, include a subtest or two of associative learning ability. According to Jensen, only cognitive learning predicts school achievement. Further, Jensen suggests that associative learning is equally distributed across all people but that level II learning is more concentrated in middle-class and European American groups than in working-class or African American groups. And, some scholars claim, because people tend to marry within their own social and ethnic groups, the differences between cognitive learning across populations, as measured in IQ tests, will tend to increase over time (Herrnstein, 1971; Herrnstein & Murray, 1994).

These conclusions have been called into question by studies comparing the IQs of people with differing numbers of genetic markers for African ancestry. Such studies have found no association between the number of markers of African ancestry and IQ (Nisbett, 1998). In addition, Williams and Ceci (1997b) have shown that the IQ gap between racial groups has been decreasing, rather than increasing, in recent years.

CULTURE AND INHERITANCE   In evaluating the findings of studies of intelligence, it is important to distinguish between estimates of heritability based on individuals within a particular group and estimates used to make comparisons across groups. When we estimate heritability based on people within a group, our estimates are going to be higher because these people, by definition, share some characteristics that may be both inherited and environmental. What's more, environmental conditions will influence the extent to which an inherited ability can be expressed. Let's take as an example a person's height, a physical characteristic of human beings that, when children have good nutrition and are immunized against serious diseases, is essentially the result of inheritance (Kagan, 1969). Because the majority of North Americans are well nourished, the genes associated with height express themselves fairly directly in the actual height of an American child. However, all inherited characteristics interact with environmental forces to some degree, and so does height. In cultures where extremely adverse health and/or nutritional factors overwhelm the genetic contributions to physical stature, this contribution is lessened relative to more advantageous situations. Most starving children, if they live to adulthood, remain small of stature, regardless of the typical height of the ethnic-racial groups to which they belong.

Thus, because heritability may contribute to height differentially in two different cultures depending on the environmental conditions—specifically, the nutrition and health-related factors of each culture—it would be incorrect to apply the same heritability estimates or indexes to both groups. In similar fashion, many argue, it is inappropriate to use estimates of the heritability of intelligence obtained from one group in interpreting findings based on the study of another group unless it can be demonstrated that the critical contributions from the environment to support the development of IQ are present across these groups. Thus, heritability measures for middle-class European American families with reasonably similar backgrounds and life circumstances may be quite different from such measures for minority or working-class groups whose circumstances may differ dramatically from the middle-class groups. In short, genes depend on the environment for their expression (Moore, 2001). Poor nutrition, disease, and stress due to myriad factors—for example, economic deprivation, overcrowded living quarters, homelessness, lack of sleep, neglect, abuse—may overwhelm and thus minimize the genetic contribution to intelligence and intellectual performance (Garcia Coll, 1990; Huston, McLloyd, & Garcia Coll, 1994). As a result, the heritability estimates calculated for middle-class European American families simply do not apply to individuals from other, less advantaged groups in the United States or throughout the world.

THE MALLEABILITY OF INHERITED CHARACTERISTICS
Finding evidence for genetic influence on intelligence in a population does not suggest that differences among individuals are unchangeable (Plomin & Petrill, 1997). Let us consider some other kinds of developmental differences, such as blindness and deafness, that we know in some cases are influenced by genetic factors. The fact that these conditions may be genetically induced hasn't interfered with the ability of special education programs to help affected children. And as we noted earlier in this chapter, probably the most persuasive evidence that the black-white IQ difference has a strong environmental component is that this very difference has been declining over the last several decades (Brody, 1992; Neisser et al., 1995). Scores on tests of achievement in mathematics and reading show similar trends (Williams & Ceci, 1997b). From the early 1970s to the late 1980s, the gap between the scores of black students and those of white students narrowed by between a third and a half. Some recent research has shown that when characteristics of the home environment are taken into account, the gap narrows still further (Brooks-Gunn, Klabanov, Smith, Duncan, & Lee, 2003).

Environmental Factors

Even strong advocates for the genetic basis of human intelligence understand that children are brought up in circumstances that range from the most favorable to the most destructive. Furthermore, most scholars recognize that the quality, amount, and patterning of stimulation offered to children in these varying conditions strongly affect their cognitive and intellectual development. In this section we consider some of the factors that can affect the child's intellectual abilities before or during its birth; in addition, we explore the important influences of the family, the school and peer culture, and the community.

PREGNANCY AND BIRTH   As we pointed out in Chapter 3, such factors as poor maternal nutrition can have highly influential and lasting effects on a child. Moreover, an extensive body of research details the negative effects on intellectual development of such things as maternal disease, such as AIDS, or a mother's alcoholism or addiction to other drugs. In addition, events attending the process of birth, such as oxygen deprivation, can have destructive effects on a child's mental functioning. Deficits or defects traced to such factors are considered **congenital,** meaning that they occur during gestation or at birth. Rather than genetic in origin, they are either transmitted directly from the mother to the fetus or result from events during the birth process.

congenital Characteristic acquired during development in the uterus or during the birth process and not through heredity.

THE FAMILY   The child's first social environment, which is usually the family, has important influences on her intellectual functioning. Studies have found that across social classes several very specific aspects of family interaction are related to differences in measured intelligence. For example, a supportive, warm home environment that encourages a child to become self-reliant, to express her curiosity, and to explore has been linked to higher intellectual functioning (Gottfried & Gottfried, 1984; Petrill & Deater-Deckard, 2004). Parents who are emotionally and verbally responsive to their children, who provide appropriate play and reading materials, who encourage their children's interest in and efforts at learning, and who provide their children with a variety of learning experiences tend to have children with higher IQ scores (Bradley et al., 2001; Wachs, 2000). It's important to note, however, that such family environments do not uniformly produce high-achieving children. Recall from Chapter 2 that even though children in the same family have many shared environmental influences, they are also subject to nonshared environmental stimuli that may counteract other influences and affect their intellectual development (Rowe, 1994; Scarr, 1992). Moreover, because the home environment is not independent of inherited intelligence factors, the ways in which the family environment is related to children's intellectual functioning are complex.

SCHOOLS AND PEER GROUPS   Although people with higher intelligence levels complete more years of school, education may also influence intelligence. In other words, more years of school and higher-quality schooling are related to increases in intelligence scores. The contrary is also true. Deficits in education may cause IQ scores to decline (Ceci, 1996; Ceci & Williams, 1997). Lack of formal education, dropping out, and too much time off from school have been associated with declines in intellectual skills. Numerous studies have also shown that children who have attended a high-quality preschool have higher skill levels than children who have not, even when the two groups are similar in socioeconomic status, family environment, and prior skill levels (Wachs, 2000).

Poor and minority students in inner-city and rural neighborhoods in the United States often face substantial disadvantage in the school quality compared with those in wealthier areas. In addition, these students, due to a variety of environmental factors, are likely to enter school with no preschool experience and with lower levels of skills as compared with their middle-class peers. Furthermore, disadvantaged students tend to fall further behind as they progress into middle and high school (Molfese & Martin, 2001; Stipek & Ryan, 1997; Turkheimer, Haley, Waldron, D'Onofrio, & Gottesman, 2003). Cultural differences and negative teacher attitudes may also hinder adjustment and learning for these children (Comer, 1988, 1991).

Peer culture plays an enormously important role in children's attitudes toward, and success in, academic work. For example, one study found that peer groups of Asian American students supported each others' academic pursuits and participated in education-related activities such as studying together (Steinberg, Dornbush, & Brown, 1992). Another study found that dating and general socializing—activities that often interfere with studying—were less common among Asian American students than among European American peers (Chen & Stevenson, 1995).

Some researchers have reported a different pattern of behavior among African American students (Steinberg et al., 1992). Often, African American peer groups express antiacademic attitudes, ridiculing and isolating students who try to succeed in school (Ogbu, 1988). Because of the strong adolescent need to belong in a peer culture, many low-income black children face a tough choice, and the effect of negative feedback from their peers may often outweigh parental encouragement of academic achievement (Steinberg et al., 1992). Often, African American children who succeed in school choose strategies to hide or camouflage their true attitudes toward schoolwork and their actual efforts to achieve academic success (Fordham & Ogbu, 1986). For example, a student may excel in athletics or take on a role such as class comedian to disguise her intellectual pursuits.

THE COMMUNITY The community as a cultural unit may have significant effects on a child's cognitive and intellectual development. For example, studies have shown that children living in isolated circumstances, such as rural areas, score lower on IQ tests than children in suburban or metropolitan areas (Kennedy, 1969; Sherman & Key, 1932). Similarly, economically disadvantaged areas of modern cities are often associated with slowed intellectual development. The poor diets, unsafe housing, and high levels of violence and unemployment that characterize impoverished areas may all contribute to less adequate intellectual functioning (Bronfenbrenner, McClelland, Wethington, Moen, & Ceci, 1996; Evans, 2003; Garbarino, 1995; Pollitt, 1994).

It's important to note, however, that in some cases environments stimulate and help children to develop abilities that are highly adaptive in their specific circumstances. For instance, the Pulawat islanders of Micronesia, who have little formal education or technology, have developed an amazing navigational system that reveals a sophisticated understanding of the relations among direction, winds, tides, and currents that enables them to sail long distances out of the sight of land (Gladwin, 1970). Nevertheless, these skilled navigators would not perform well either on a standard test of intelligence or on Piagetian tasks of formal operations, despite the fact that their navigational skills evidence formal operational functioning, and even though they demonstrate highly advanced deductive reasoning on culturally relevant problems. Observations like these show us how important it is to analyze intellectual performance within the individual's cultural context (Ceci, 1996; Hutchins, 1996).

ACHIEVEMENT MOTIVATION AND INTELLECTUAL PERFORMANCE

Children's academic performance is affected not only by their experiences in the family, school, peer group, and community, but also by their own **achievement motivation**—that is, their tendency to strive for successful performance, to evaluate their performance against specific standards of excellence, and to experience pleasure as a result of having performed successfully (Wigfield et al., 2006). Variations in achievement motivation and

achievement motivation A person's tendency to strive for successful performance, to evaluate her performance against standards of excellence, and to feel pleasure at having performed successfully.

intellectual performance are often related to a child's emotions and opinions of himself as a person and a learner—in short, to self-esteem. Some children have negative feelings about specific learning tasks and may be convinced of their inability to learn in certain areas. Sometimes a child's feelings and beliefs about his ability to succeed are sufficiently negative that they distract the learner from the task itself and may prevent him from learning (Brown, Bransford, Ferrara, & Campione, 1983).

Researchers have identified two different response patterns among children working on a challenging task at which they could fail (Heckhausen & Dweck, 1998). In an early study, fifth- and sixth-grade children attempted to solve a series of difficult problems that resembled a game of Twenty Questions (Diener & Dweck, 1978). At first the children were able to solve the problems, but then the experimenter presented several very hard problems that they failed. Some children, whom the researchers called *mastery-oriented*, maintained or even improved their level of performance despite failure on some of the hard problems. In contrast, other children, whom the researchers labeled *helpless*, tended to give up easily or to show marked performance deterioration when working on challenging problems. Once these children failed a difficult task, they often began to use inefficient strategies.

When mastery-oriented children performed poorly, they expressed neutral or even positive emotions, attributed their failure to insufficient effort rather than to lack of ability, and maintained high expectations for future success. Helpless children, on the other hand, expressed negative emotions such as frustration, blamed their own lack of ability for their performance, and expressed low expectations for future performance.

What might cause different children to react so differently to the same task? Helpless and mastery-oriented children do not differ in their actual ability levels; rather, they *think* differently about ability and achievement (Dweck, 2001; Heckhausen & Dweck, 1998; Kamins & Dweck, 1999). Mastery-oriented children tend to have *learning goals*. In other words, they are more concerned with improving their skills and learning new things than they are with specific judgments of their ability. Children who show the helpless pattern, on the other hand, tend to have *performance goals*—that is, they are concerned with "looking smart," obtaining positive judgments, and avoiding negative judgments of their ability. Dweck and her colleagues have proposed that these different goals are associated with different beliefs or views about the nature of ability itself. That is, mastery-oriented children tend to hold an *incremental* view of intelligence, viewing intelligence as a body of skills and knowledge that can be increased with effort. In contrast, helpless children tend to hold an *entity* view of intelligence, believing, if implicitly, that intelligence is a fixed and unchangeable entity that people possess in varying degrees.

Dweck suggests that the two views of intelligence and the two goals orient children to react very differently to achievement tasks. As Table 10-4 illustrates, when children are successful at tasks, they do not appear to differ in their behavior; even children with an entity view and performance goals are likely to show the mastery-oriented pattern. It may be that in this situation children believe that their good performance indicates high ability. However, when children fail at a task, their different views of intelligence and types of goals find expression in either mastery-oriented or helpless behavior. Under these circumstances, mastery-oriented children may interpret their failure as an indication that they must work harder to learn more, whereas helpless children may see failure as evidence of their lack of ability and may give up. Of course, different situations can elicit different responses, and mastery-oriented children may occasionally show helpless responses when examiners or others put a lot of stress on performance goals (Dweck, 2001; Heckhausen & Dweck, 1998).

Some environmental conditions may even promote helplessness in children. In research on rural children in upstate New York, Gary Evans (2003) found that children living in poverty who experienced a number of physical stresses, such as crowding and poor-quality housing, and psychosocial stresses, such as family turmoil or violence, were more likely to behave in a helpless manner when presented with a challenging puzzle task than were poor children who had fewer stresses in their lives.

Table 10-4   Views of intelligence, goal orientations, and behavior patterns

View of Intelligence	Goal Orientation	Present Performance Level	Behavior Pattern
Entity (intelligence is fixed)	**Performance** (to gain positive, avoid negative judgments of competence)	High	**Mastery-oriented** (seeking challenge, persistence)
		Low	**Helpless** (avoiding challenge, low persistence)
Incremental (intelligence is malleable)	**Learning** (to increase competence)	High	**Mastery-oriented** (seeking challenge that fosters learning, persistence)
		Low	**Mastery-oriented** (seeking challenge that fosters learning, persistence)

Sources: Dweck, 2001; Dweck & Leggett, 1988.

Culture may also play a role. Chen and Stevenson (1995) found that European American students tended to endorse "having a good teacher" as the most important factor in their performance in mathematics, whereas Asian students reported that "studying hard" was the most important factor (Figure 10-2). Chen and Stevenson and their colleagues (Chen & Stevenson, 1995; Stevenson, 2001; Stevenson, Lee, & Mu, 2000) found that, compared with Asian students and their parents, European American students had lower standards for their academic work, and their parents more often attributed their children's performance to innate ability.

Finally, the timing of certain school-related experiences may affect children's achievement or their motivation to achieve. Traditionally, the first eight years of elementary school (or nine, including kindergarten) and the four years of high school were arranged in two separate segments, but other organizational schemes have emerged in recent years. In the alternative that's most often seen today, the first six years of elementary school are grouped together, followed by three years of junior high or "middle" school (grades 7–9), followed by three years of high school (grades 10–12).

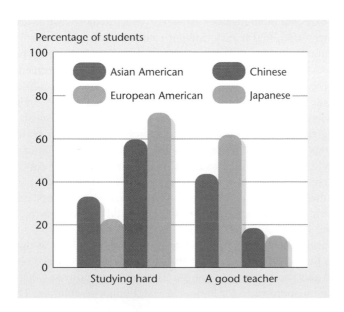

Figure 10-2

To study hard, or to be taught well—is there a question?
When researchers asked Chinese and Japanese high school students in their own countries, and Asian and European American students in the United States, to choose among several factors that may influence students' academic performance, the majority chose either "studying hard" or "having a good teacher." Within these choices, the Japanese and Chinese students were far more likely to choose the first of these factors, whereas U.S. high school students were much more likely to choose the second.

Source: Chen & Stevenson, 1995.

Family members have a great influence on intellectual development. Here a mother is using marbles and printed numbers to encourage her son in learning to match number symbols and names with quantities of actual objects.

Research suggests that such organizational variations make a difference in children's academic experience. Simmons, Blyth, and McKinney (1984) compared students moving from the sixth to the seventh grade in an eight-year elementary school and in a junior high school where this transition involved moving to a new school. In comparison to the seventh graders who stayed in elementary school, the junior high schoolers had lower self-concepts, were less involved in activities and clubs, and perceived themselves as less integrated into their school and peer groups (Roeser, Eccles, & Sameroff, 2000). For preadolescents and adolescents, the onset of puberty, the start of dating, or some disruption in family life may make the burden of shifting to a new school especially heavy. Simmons, Burgeson, Carlson-Ford, and Blyth (1987) found that children, especially girls, who were undergoing three or more transitions had lower self-esteem, participated less in extracurricular activities, and had lower grade-point averages.

ETHNICITY, SOCIAL CLASS, AND INTELLECTUAL PERFORMANCE

As we have already indicated, ethnicity and social class are related to intellectual performance. In this section we discuss these relations in greater depth. *Social class* is a broad term that includes such variables as education, occupation, income, lifestyle, housing, possessions, and use of leisure time. Three of these variables—education, occupation, and income—are generally reliable and valid measures of social class: they are easily quantified and data on all three are readily available from U.S. government sources. And the term *socioeconomic status* (or SES) is often used to refer to a combined assessment of these three variables (Benokraitis, 1998). Because these factors are also frequently associated with each other, researchers have generally explored them together. However, because these factors are closely associated, researchers often find it very difficult to disentangle one factor from another—for example, the effects of having a particular occupation from being poor.

The factor of ethnicity presents particular problems of measurement and analysis because researchers tend to lump subcultures together. Thus, a study of "Asians" or "Asian Americans" may turn out to have included Chinese, Filipinos, Indians, Japanese, Koreans, and Vietnamese as one group; as a result, the study will mask important differences among the groups included. Another problem related to both ethnicity and social class is that researchers' assumptions may influence the kinds of questions they ask and the way they ask them. For example, many studies of Asian Americans ask why these children are successful in school, whereas similar studies of African Americans may ask why these children perform poorly. Research that focuses on each group's strengths, as well as on the areas in which each could improve, is recommended by scholars working in this area (see, e.g., Fisher et al., 1998).

With these limitations on existing research in mind, let's look at three main types of explanations for the differences in IQ and intellectual performance observed among different ethnic and socioeconomic groups. The first type proposes that existing standardized tests are inappropriate for lower-class and minority children. The second type attempts to focus specifically on the roles socioeconomic factors play in intellectual performance. The third type explores how parent-child interactions may differ among social classes and ethnic groups.

Are Intelligence Tests Biased against Minority Groups?

Those who argue that existing tests of intelligence are biased against a sizable group of the American population point out that the most widely used tests were standardized on European American middle-class people. They maintain that for this reason test items do not accurately measure adaptive or problem-solving abilities appropriate to the circumstances in which low-income groups and some members of ethnic groups live. These tests, their detractors insist, draw on language, experience, and values of middle-class European American children. For example, the vocabulary used on traditional IQ tests often differs from the dialect or even language some children use every day. On this view, some researchers have argued that minority children's lower verbal scores may reflect cultural bias, not lack of intelligence.

Tests such as the Kaufman Battery, aimed at minimizing cultural bias, show less difference between the scores of African American and European American children than do standard IQ tests. However, on the Raven Progressive Matrices Test—another test often described as culture-fair, which tests the ability to detect, evaluate, and match graphic patterns—the more educated the test takers are, the better they do (Anastasi, 1988). This suggests that even a test of pattern discrimination may be tapping knowledge not available to people with fewer educational opportunities. Or perhaps the format of the testing situation itself may lead to differences. After all, one sure consequence of more years in school is increased opportunity and practice at taking tests (Rogoff, 2003).

In his concept of **stereotype threat,** Claude Steele (1997) has offered yet another explanation for poor performance on IQ tests among ethnic minority youth. According to Steele, people are aware of the stereotypes that society holds about their particular groups—for example, the stereotype that certain ethnic groups are intellectually inferior to other ethnic groups. In situations in which this stereotype can be tested, Steele believes that individuals from the group for which there is a negative stereotype have self-doubt and worry about confirming the stereotype in their test performance. This self-doubt has the effect of hurting the individual's performance, which, in turn, confirms the stereotype. Steele and Aronson (1995) demonstrated this process in a study in which the researchers gave a test of verbal intelligence to African American and European American college students. Half of the students were told the test was diagnostic of intelligence and the other half were told the test was not diagnostic of intelligence. The African American students who were told the test was diagnostic performed worse than the African American students who were told it was not diagnostic of intelligence. The European American students were unaffected by the instructions.

stereotype threat Being at risk of confirming a negative stereotype about the group to which one belongs.

ETHNIC GROUPS MAY EXCEL IN DIFFERENT AREAS   One criticism of IQ tests is that they fail to measure the ability to cope with everyday activities and problems of life with which people must contend. Following up on this criticism, Mercer (1971) studied a large group of children and young adults whose IQ scores classified them as mentally retarded. Mercer tested these individuals in their adaptive abilities—that is, their abilities to perform skills required for such things as self-care (e.g., dressing), household tasks (e.g., shopping, cooking), holding a job, and traveling alone to and from their jobs. The results were amazing: 90 percent of the African American children and 60 percent of the Latino children who had IQs below 70 (i.e., these children scored in the range of measured intelligence traditionally

This child is working on the block design subtest in the Wechsler Intelligence Scale for Children (WISC).

labeled "mentally defective") *passed* Mercer's test, but every European American child with an IQ below 70 *failed* it! The disturbing implications of these findings were that minority children are far more likely than European American children to be inappropriately classified as mentally retarded—a label that will have a pervasive effect on their life experiences and on others' expectations of them.

Jensen (1973) found that in poor areas of the rural South, African American children did less well than European Americans on both verbal and performance tests and that this difference increased as the children grew older (from 5 to 18 years of age). Interestingly, among children raised in better circumstances, African Americans and European Americans showed no appreciable difference on performance tests. On verbal tests, however, African American children did less well than European American children, and these differences tended to increase with age. These and other findings (e.g., Neisser et al., 1995) have led some investigators to reason that it may be more useful to look at achievement levels on different kinds of cognitive skills than at overall IQ levels.

On the theory that members of different groups may show different patterns of abilities on tests, one study compared the verbal skills, reasoning, and numerical abilities of middle- and lower-class African American, Chinese American, Jewish, and Puerto Rican children between about 6 and 7 years of age (Lesser, Fifer, & Clark, 1965). Lesser and his colleagues found that these four groups did indeed have different profiles of ability scores. For instance, Jewish American and Chinese American children scored higher on these tests than African American and Puerto Rican children; African American children showed greater verbal abilities than Chinese American children and scored better on reasoning than Puerto Rican children; and Puerto Rican children scored slightly above African Americans on numerical and spatial abilities. Social class influenced score levels for all groups; however, differences in score level due to socioeconomic factors were greatest for African Americans, suggesting that social class disadvantages had relatively greater impact on these children.

THE EFFECT OF CONTEXT ON INTELLECTUAL PERFORMANCE   Not only may traditional intelligence tests be biased in their content and approach, but the conditions under which they are administered to minority children of lower socioeconomic status may have interfered with these children's ability to perform. Recall that the newer, information-processing approaches to intelligence testing have pointed to the importance of context in children's intellectual performance. Researchers influenced by these ideas have tried to familiarize children with the test environment and test materials, to encourage them specifically on various tasks, and to use material rewards, such as candy, to motivate performance. These efforts have been successful with some low-income and minority-group children; in fact, they have been significantly more successful with economically deprived children than with middle-class children (Zigler, Abelson, Trickett, & Seitz, 1982). These findings support the view that intelligence tests do not measure the competencies of low-income and ethnic minority children as well as they measure the abilities of middle-class European American children.

Social-Class Influences on Intellectual Performance

Separating the closely interwoven influences on intelligence and achievement of class and ethnicity is enormously challenging. Yet, if nongenetic factors contribute about 50 percent of the variation in IQ scores and intellectual performance, it is important to separate these influences to gain better understanding of the process of intellectual development. In this section we look first at some research efforts to isolate social-class factors in intellectual performance. We then explore research that has compared intellectual performance among various ethnic groups within the United States and that has also compared U.S. students' performance with that of students in China and Japan.

SOCIAL-CLASS FACTORS AND CUMULATIVE RISK The influence of social class on intellectual performance has begun to receive more research attention. Several investigators have described differences in performance on standardized intelligence tests among children from various social-class and ethnic groups (Brody, 1992; Neisser et al., 1995). In general, children in the lower socioeconomic classes score 10 to 15 IQ points below middle-class children, and African American children on average score 20 IQ points below European American children (Brody, 1992). These differences are generally observed before children enter school and remain consistent throughout the school years (Kennedy, 1969; Moffitt, Caspi, Harkness, & Silva, 1993). However, when factors such as family conditions and home environment are taken into account, the differences in scores are reduced somewhat (Brooks-Gunn et al., 2003).

The concept of **cumulative risk** may help us understand the significance of the effects of socioeconomic factors on intelligence and intellectual performance. If in the life circumstances of a given child only one of the many risk factors that may compromise healthy development, such as poverty, is present, many other factors in that child's environment may outweigh the risk that one factor poses for her. However, as more and more negative factors are added to the child's life experience, her risk of poor cognitive outcomes will increase (Rutter, 1983). To test this notion, Sameroff and colleagues (Sameroff, Seifer, Baldwin, & Baldwin, 1993; Sameroff, Seifer, Barocas, Zax, & Greenspan, 1987) identified specific environmental factors likely to present risks to children's cognitive development (Table 10-5) and then, among 215 4-year-old African American, European American, and Puerto Rican children, examined the links between these risks and IQ scores. As you can see in Figure 10-3, the findings were striking. Children with only one risk factor had verbal IQ scores

cumulative risk The notion that risk factors in children's life circumstances have cumulative negative effects on their intellectual performance.

Poor maternal mental health
High maternal anxiety
Low maternal education
Head of household either unemployed or in unskilled occupation
Father absent from family
Minority-group membership
Family in which there were more than four children
High incidence of stressful events such as illness, job loss, or death in the family

Table 10-5

Major risk factors that endanger children's cognitive development

Source: Sameroff, Seifer, Baldwin, & Baldwin, 1993.

Figure 10-3

Risk and intellectual performance

This graph dramatically illustrates the relationship between risk factors and intellectual performance. The more risk factors (e.g., poverty, hunger, poor clothing, family stress) in the lives of these 4-year-olds, the lower their scores on the Wechsler Preschool and Primary Scale of Intelligence.

Source: Sameroff, Seifer, Baldwin, & Baldwin, 1993.

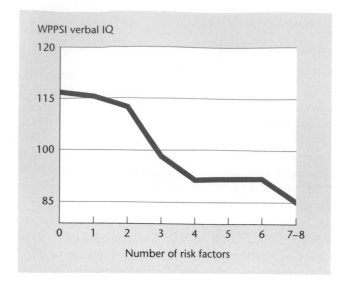

well above average; an IQ of 115 is considered "bright normal." As the number of environmental risk factors increased, however, IQ scores dropped, and children whose life circumstances included seven or eight of the risk factors had IQs 30 points lower, putting them in the "dull normal" range.

Social class did not appreciably affect these findings: The presence of several risk factors was associated with low IQs in families of both low and high socioeconomic status. However, any one of these factors was more likely to be present in low-income families than in families with more financial advantages. A follow-up study (Sameroff et al., 1993) of 152 of the same families when the children were 13 years old revealed a similar pattern: a 30- to 35-point IQ difference between the children whose risks were few and those who confronted many risk factors.

These findings argue for the notion that children who confront multiple risk factors face potential declines in their performance on intelligence tests. The findings also allow us to hypothesize that in the absence of such risk factors children should achieve higher test scores. Psychologists have tested this hypothesis by studying African American children who were adopted by economically well-off European American parents (Scarr & Weinberg, 1976). As you can see from Figure 10-4,

Figure 10-4

How do children adopted into middle-class European American homes fare?

Both African and European American children adopted into middle-class European American homes obtained IQ scores that were substantially above the national averages for their respective groups. And the earlier the child was adopted, the better the IQ score. It is not known why the European American adoptees fared somewhat better than the African Americans.

Source: Adapted from Scarr & Weinberg, 1976.

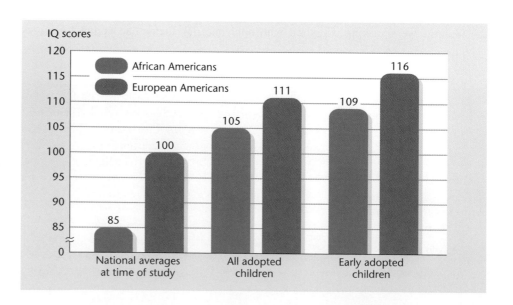

adopted African American children achieved scores some 20 points above the national average for black children, and the younger they were at adoption, the higher their scores were. Follow-up studies (Scarr, 1997, 1998b; Weinberg, Scarr, & Waldman, 1992) found that the adoptees experienced a gain in IQ similar to the gains of biological children of the adoptive parents. Although the adoptees' IQ scores more closely resembled those of their biological parents than their adoptive parents, their higher scores and continued gain showed the strong influence environment may have on IQ and on the long-term maintenance of gains. Other adoption studies have echoed these results (e.g., Capron & Duyme, 1989).

SOCIAL CLASS AND PARENT-CHILD INTERACTIONS Several investigators have suggested that maternal behavior differs across social classes and may differentially affect children's intellectual performance in the school setting. Studies have shown that middle- and lower-class mothers tend to differ most in their use of language. Middle-class mothers were more likely than lower-class mothers to speak in response to their babies' vocalizations (Hart & Risley, 1995; Lewis & Wilson, 1972), and their infants tended to stop vocalizing and listen when their mothers spoke. In contrast, lower-class children were more likely to continue vocalizing when their mothers were speaking (Lewis & Freedle, 1973). Some scholars have suggested that these early differences in the way infants attend to their mothers' speech may be related to later differences in the ease with which children learn from verbal information (Golden & Birns, 1983; Hoff, 2002).

Barnard, Bee, and Hammond (1984) found that mothers who had gone beyond a high school education were more highly involved with their infants than mothers who had not finished high school; these differences, measured at several intervals before the children reached age 2, were significantly related to the children's IQ scores at age 4. Specific behaviors that are important include reading to young children before they enter school. On average, 73 percent of young children whose mothers graduated from college were read to every day by a family member, compared with 60 percent of children whose mothers had some years of college, 49 percent of children whose mothers only finished high school, and 42 percent of children whose mothers had not finished high school (Federal Interagency Forum on Child and Family Statistics, 2001). These different rates are significant in that reading with an adult in the preschool years is associated with better reading achievement in elementary school (Bus, van IJzendoorn, & Pelligrini, 1995).

Many researchers have argued that stress, presumably more commonly experienced by lower-class parents than by middle-class parents, may directly influence parental styles of interaction—for example, leading parents to be more concerned with discipline than with positive emotional communication (Goldstein, 1990; McLloyd, Jayaratne, Ceballo, & Borguez, 1994). Studying the interactions among maternal control techniques, teaching styles, language, and children's cognitive development, Robert Hess and Virginia Shipman (1967) found a number of differences between middle-class and lower-class African American mothers. The former were more responsive to their children's feelings, provided them with more rational and complex reasons for rules and guidelines, and generally encouraged their children to become aware of the complexities of the social and physical environment and to attend to relevant cues in problem-solving situations. In contrast, lower-class mothers' communications with their children were more restricted and generic; they were less likely to respond to specific questions or statements offered by their children. Hess and Shipman concluded that the lower-class mothers' communicative style was less likely to help their children learn to make the kinds of discriminations necessary to develop effective problem-solving skills.

In China, where there are relatively small differences in income across groups who vary in education, Tardif (1993) found that less-educated parents used more imperatives with their toddlers than better-educated mothers. This style of interaction is likely to be associated with poorer cognitive development.

Culture, Family Practices, and Intellectual Performance

In recent years, both scholarly and lay publications have documented a trend in North American students' academic performance that is disturbing to many. These reports have warned that in mathematics and science, and even in the language arts, American students are falling behind students in other countries, particularly countries in Asia. The Perspectives on Diversity box in this section (Box 10.1) recounts a series of studies by Harold Stevenson and his colleagues that have followed groups of North American, Chinese (in Beijing, China, and Taipei, Taiwan), and Japanese (in Sendai, Japan) students from the first through the eleventh grades and that demonstrate the importance of differing family influences on cognitive development in these children. The findings of these longitudinal studies raise several provocative questions about American education practices and policies (Chen et al., 1995; Stevenson & Stigler, 1992).

One question is whether patterns of interaction in Asian American families can explain the high levels of performance frequently shown by Asian American children. Whereas African American, European American, and Latino American parents also value education highly, their children do not experience the same level of academic success seen in Asian American families. Asian American parents strongly support their children's academic achievement (Chao, 2001). They hold high expectations for their children's education and also tend to convey the idea that achievement is part of children's duty to parents. Asian American families often strictly monitor the time their children spend in homework and in free play. In addition, they frequently profess the belief that effort will be rewarded (Slaughter-Defoe, Nakagawa, Takanishi, & Johnson, 1990). This research suggests that the critical family factors that determine the different patterns of achievement across diverse ethnic groups merit further study.

COGNITIVE INTERVENTION STUDIES

As we have seen, a sizeable number of factors contribute to a child's intellectual functioning. When some of these factors are negative and impede children's intellectual development, as well as their ability and motivation to use their intellectual powers to grow and prosper, can we alter them to improve a child's intellectual functioning? Cognitive intervention studies are designed to address this question.

Head Start and Similar Programs

Beginning in the 1960s, researchers and policymakers have implemented a great many programs aimed at modifying the development of learning-disabled or economically deprived children. Some *preventive* programs were designed to prevent the decline in cognitive skills that was theorized to occur in preschool children who were relatively disadvantaged in society; other *interventionist*, or remedial, programs focused on school-age children who already had demonstrated learning difficulties. Some programs emphasized the teaching of specific skills such as counting or vocabulary, and others focused on teaching general problem-solving strategies, communication patterns, and principles of logical thought. Still others tried to alter such things as self-concept and achievement motivation. One of the most well-known cognitive intervention programs is **Head Start,** a federally funded program for severely economically deprived preschoolers begun in 1965. This program is intended to provide 3- and 4-year-old children with daily preschool, and it originally included social

Head Start A federally funded program that provides disadvantaged young children with preschool experience, social services, and medical and nutritional assistance.

Box 10.1
Perspectives on Diversity

MAKING THE GRADE IN JAPAN, TAIWAN, AND THE UNITED STATES

The declining school achievement of U.S. children decried by the media has often been attributed to failures of the North American school system. Teachers and educators who, particularly in inner-city schools, have struggled to help children from varying backgrounds and life circumstances learn to read, write, do mathematics, and, most important, enjoy learning, have felt deeply wronged by these reports. Longitudinal studies by Harold Stevenson and his associates (Chen, Stevenson, Hayward, & Burgess, 1995; Stevenson, Chen, & Lee, 1993; Stevenson, Chen, & Uttal, 1990) have now provided evidence that in the earliest months of first grade, children in the United States already lag behind other children in academic achievement. Thus, although differences in academic performance may well

reflect varying educational systems, that these differences appear when children have as yet had little exposure to formal education suggests more is involved than inadequate educational practices.

Over a 10-year period, Stevenson and colleagues administered tests of reading and mathematics ability to groups of first, fifth, and eleventh graders in classrooms in two U.S. metropolitan areas (Minneapolis, Minnesota, and Fairfax County, Virginia), in two East Asian cities (Beijing, China, and Taipei, Taiwan), and in Japan (Sendai). The U.S. students included four cultural groups—European, Chinese, African, and Latino Americans, although not all these groups were represented in every study. To the degree possible, the investigators retested the same students at different ages

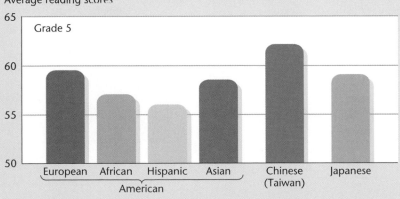

Figure 10-5

Reading scores in China, Japan, and the United States

Overall, across both first and fifth grades, Chinese and Japanese students tended to do better in reading than any of the U.S. cultural groups. In first grade, Asian American students ran second to Japanese students but, for some reason, dropped down by fifth grade. The relations among European, African, and Latino American students remained fairly stable from first to fifth grade; these groups scored from higher to lower, respectively.

Source: Adapted from Chen, Stevenson, Hayward, & Burgess, 1995.

(Continues)

Box 10.1 (*Concluded*)

Perspectives on Diversity

and in all studies; over the 10-year span, Stevenson and his associates tested several thousand children. In each study the researchers interviewed teachers, students, and students' mothers on a variety of topics, such as the value of education, beliefs about learning, attitudes toward school, and family involvement in children's schoolwork.

In one study, there were noticeable differences in reading test scores among seven groups of students even in the first grade (Figure 10-5). In first grade, Japanese students scored highest, followed fairly closely by Asian American, Taiwanese, and European American students; African American and Latino American students scored the lowest. By fifth grade, Taiwanese and European American students had

jumped ahead of Japanese and Asian Americans. American students scored considerably below others on a mathematics test, and between first and fifth grade these differences became more pronounced (Figure 10-6): At both times, Chinese (Beijing, Taiwan) and Japanese students had the highest scores, Asian Americans following close behind.

What could be contributing to these results? Stevenson and his colleagues found no evidence that the American children had lower intellectual levels, and parental education levels were highest among European American students. However, there were marked differences in parents' beliefs, their reported activities with their children, and the evaluations they made of their children and their educational systems. Chinese

Figure 10-6

Mathematics skills in China, Japan, and the United States

As in reading, Chinese and Japanese students outscored U.S. students in mathematics. Although the differences were small in grade 1, they were large in grade 5, and Asian American students clearly led their American peers.

Source: Adapted from Chen, Stevenson, Hayward, & Burgess, 1995.

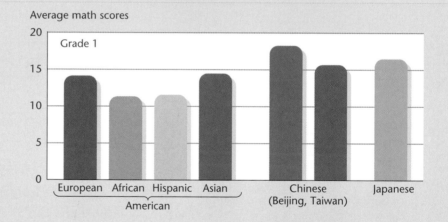

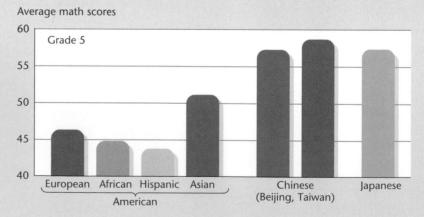

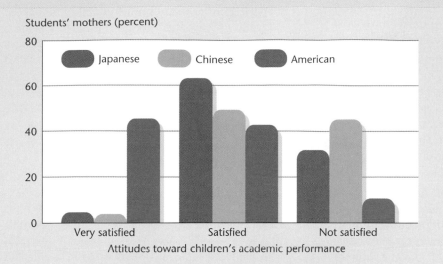

Students' mothers (percent)

Japanese   Chinese   American

Attitudes toward children's academic performance

Figure 10-7

Mothers' attitudes toward their children's academic performance

In 1990, more Japanese and Chinese mothers than U.S. mothers were "satisfied" with their children's academic performance. However, more than 40 percent of American mothers, but fewer than 5 percent of Chinese and Japanese mothers, were "very satisfied."

Source: Reprinted with permission from *Science, 259* (1993). Stevenson, H. W., Chen, C., and Lee, S. Y., "Mathematics achievement of Chinese, Japanese, and American children: Ten years later," pp. 53–58. Copyright © 1993 AAAS.

and Japanese mothers generally viewed academic achievement as the child's most important pursuit. Once children entered school, Chinese and Japanese families mobilized to help their children and to provide an environment conducive to achievement. Japanese mothers in particular were likely to see themselves as *kyoiku mamas,* that is, "education moms" responsible for assisting, directing, and supervising their children's learning.

American mothers were less likely to be actively involved in helping their children with homework than mothers in other groups. They tended to put more emphasis on the role of innate ability in school performance and less on the role of effort. Mothers in all three countries viewed their children's academic performance as above average but, as Figure 10-7 shows, American mothers voiced the most positive views about their children's scholastic achievement and experience, even though they were aware of the country's low rank in comparative studies of children's performance.

American children spend significantly less time on homework and reading for pleasure and more time playing and doing chores than Japanese or Taiwanese children do. Differences with Taiwanese families may be especially notable. In one study, only 17 percent of

first-grade and 28 percent of fifth-grade Taiwanese children did chores, in contrast to 90 and 95 percent of American first and fifth graders, respectively. When researchers asked one Taiwanese mother why she did not assign her children chores, she replied, "It would break my heart. Doing chores would consume time that the child should devote to studying."

American mothers appeared to be more interested in their children's general cognitive development than in their academic achievement per se, attempting to provide the children with experiences that fostered cognitive growth (Stevenson et al., 1990). These mothers reported reading more frequently to their young children, taking them on excursions, and accompanying them to more cultural events than did Chinese or Japanese parents (Stevenson et al., 1993).

What might Americans do to improve U.S. students' competitive status? Some school districts have moved toward lengthening the academic year, which has traditionally been much shorter than the school year in Asian countries. The shorter U.S. school day may also contribute to the fact that American students spend more time than Asian students in extracurricular pursuits, including sports activities, socializing, and dating. But if Stevenson and his colleagues are right, intervention needs to begin earlier and at home.

Box 10.2

Risk and Resilience

EARLY INTERVENTION WITH CHILDREN AT RISK

One of the most successful intervention efforts yet undertaken, the Carolina Abecedarian Project involves both day care and parent education (Campbell, Pungello, Miller-Johnson, Burchinal, & Ramey, 2001; Ramey, Campbell, & Blair, 1998). The Carolina program is a structured, cognitively and socially stimulating day-care program that focuses on developing children's communication skills as well as on intensive parent education. In one study within this program, a group of high-risk children began attending the preschool center, most by the age of 3 months, while a second, control group received no intervention. As Figure 10-8 shows, by the time the children in both groups were 12 months old, their cognitive performances had already begun to diverge. By the time the children were 4 years old, the IQ scores of those in the combined day-care plus parent-education (preschool intervention) group were some 13 points higher than the scores of those in the nontreated high-risk (control) group (Ramey et al., 1998).

When the children were between the ages of 2 and 4, the researchers classified some 40 percent of control-group children as mentally retarded (IQ 84 or below) but found that only 8 percent of the intervention-group children had IQs this low. The combined treatment program had prevented the deterioration in intellectual skills that ordinarily occurs by this age in such economically deprived, high-risk populations.

Figure 10-8   Early cognitive intervention works

The Carolina Abecedarian Project has produced significant gains in intellectual performance. At 12 months of age, the children in both the intervention and control groups received similar Mental Development Index scores on the Bayley scales, but their subsequent Stanford-Binet IQ scores were significantly different. When the two groups of children were 4 years old, the intervention group's average IQ score was some 13 points above the score for the control group, almost a full standard deviation. (The vertical dashed line marks the transition from Bayley scales to Stanford-Binet assessment measures.)

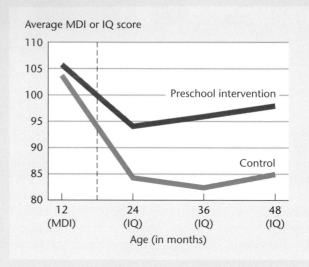

Source: Adapted from Ramey, Campbell, & Blair, 1998.

services, medical care, and health education for the parents. However, funding cuts starting in the 1970s eliminated many of the parent services, and many eligible children cannot be accommodated in the preschool component in most areas.

Studies have shown children have higher scores on IQ and other ability measures immediately after these programs end, whether the programs are preventive or interventionist. In the early grades, Head Start children show higher cognitive and social skills than similar children who have not participated in the program, but differences in IQ scores fade within a few years (Brooks-Gunn, 1995; Lee, Brooks-Gunn, & Schnur, 1988; Lee, Brooks-Gunn, Schnur, & Liaw, 1990).

Long-term studies have shown other effects that last well into adulthood, however. Compared with similar children who remained on the waiting list but did not participate in the program, Head Start children showed higher scores on achievement tests, they were more likely to graduate from high school and attend college, and they had higher earnings as adults (Barnett, Macmann, & Carey, 1992). Several other programs have shown similar results (Reynolds & Temple, 1998; Seitz, 1990; Seitz,

Figure 10-9   Early cognitive intervention has long-lasting effects

When the children in the original Carolina program reached 15 years of age, those who had been in the preschool intervention group were much less likely to have been retained in a grade than the children in the control group.

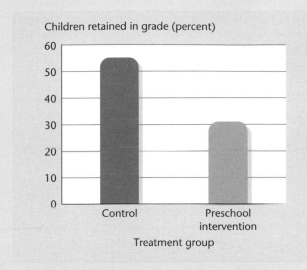

Children retained in grade (percent)

Source: Adapted from Ramey, Campbell, & Blair, 1998.

Lasting effects have been reported for this program. At age 15, children in the preschool intervention were less often assigned to special education than controls, and less often retained in grade, as Figure 10-9 shows. They had higher cognitive and academic achievement test scores in repeated testing from age 3 to age 21 (Campbell et al., 2001).

Ramey and his colleagues also randomly assigned some children to a later-starting intervention involving family services in early elementary school, assigning others to both preschool and later interventions. They found that the children assigned to both interventions performed at the highest levels. Children who received only the preschool support were close behind, however, showing that the early program was more effective by itself than was the later one. However, those who received only the later program still achieved at higher levels than the controls who received no intervention at all (Campbell et al., 2001).

This project has reported the strongest and most durable positive effects of any early intervention program. The results are particularly meaningful because the intervention was a true experiment, in which children were randomly assigned to treatment and control conditions.

Rosenbaum, & Apfel, 1985; Smith, 1995). One of the most successful has been the Carolina Abecedarian Project, featured in Box 10.2. It differs from Head Start in some important ways: It starts earlier, within the first year of life, and is more intensive, involving a full-day experience for the children which lasts from shortly after birth until the child starts school. Parent services are important components of the program and may be continued until the child is in grade 3.

Characteristics of Successful Intervention Programs

The earlier intervention programs start and the longer they continue, the more successful they are likely to be (Ramey & Ramey, 1992). Table 10-6 lists seven principles on which the most effective intervention programs have been based. Children from impoverished settings who are not given early intervention efforts suffer a

These children in a Head Start program seem very interested in what the teacher is saying and showing them.

significant loss in both cognitive and social-emotional development during the second and third years of life (Blair, Ramey, & Hardin, 1995). Moreover, it is not very likely that children can ever achieve a complete catch-up in these areas of development, although later intervention programs can effect some gains.

Intervention endeavors that focus on improving both the parent-child relationship and the family's natural support systems and that place the child in an educationally stimulating program are among the most successful (Slaughter, 1988; Smith, 1995). Almost as successful are programs that involve low-income parents actively in their children's education. In some cases, mothers are employed as teaching aides in preschool centers; in others, program staff visit mothers in their homes and instruct and support them in their educational activities with their children. Some successful programs offer support that stretches beyond the home and preschool environments. The goal of these **two-generation programs** is to support both parents and children as they try to improve their futures (Stipek & McCroskey, 1989). They enable parents to take advantage of community resources in furthering their own educations, getting job training and finding work, or strengthening family relationships and family functioning through supportive social relationships (Ramey et al., 2006; Smith, 1995).

Table 10-6 Seven principles of successful early intervention programs

Principle	Description
1. Timing	Interventions should begin during the first two years of life and continue at least until children enter kindergarten, and they should engage families earlier rather than later.
2. Intensity	The more intensive the intervention—that is, the greater the number of hours per day, days per week, and weeks per year during which intervention activities take place—the more positive the program's effects, particularly in families in which parents have the lowest education levels and during the first five years of the child's life.
3. Direct provision of learning experiences	Intervention programs that offer services directly to the child rather than through an intermediary, such as a parent or a home visitor, are more successful than others.
4. Breadth	The broader the spectrum of services provided and the more routes used to enhance children's development, the more successful the program.
5. Recognition of individual differences	Programs must recognize the varying needs of individuals. In the lives of poor families, myriad reasons may account for one individual's failure to do well; thus, individualization of treatment interventions is very important.
6. Environmental maintenance of development	Unless poor or at-risk children are supported in multiple domains of development beyond the preschool years, they will not develop the skills, motivation, health, and resources needed to succeed in school settings. Two-generation programs may, by helping parents, create the support system children need to make academic progress.
7. Cultural appropriateness and relevance of intervention strategies	To be valued, used, and incorporated into participants' everyday lives, interventions must be culturally relevant and welcome to family and child. Because individuals within cultures vary greatly, stereotyping cultures will lead to failure.

Sources: Based on Ramey & Ramey, 1998; Ramey, Ramey, Gaines, & Blair, 1995; Ramey, Ramey, & Lanzi, 2006.

BEYOND THE NORMS: GIFTEDNESS AND MENTAL RETARDATION

Children vary greatly in the rate and manner in which they learn. Some children are exceptionally talented, learning much faster than classmates, whereas others function at significantly lower intellectual levels than their peers. Traditionally, specialists in intelligence testing have held that an IQ score above 130 signals **intellectual giftedness;** a score below 70, coupled with difficulty in coping with age-appropriate activities of everyday life, indicates **mental retardation.** Finally, some children, many of whom have normal or even high intelligence levels, have specific difficulties that interfere with learning, such as speech or language impairments or reading disabilities like dyslexia. These children are identified as having **learning disabilities.** We look first at the evidence on giftedness and then at the contemporary view of retardation and the prospects for fulfilling lives for those who fall into this category. Then we examine children with learning disabilities.

The Intellectually Gifted

> Do children who are intellectually gifted burst upon society, speaking when they're only a year old, solving problems in calculus at the age of 2? Not usually. Often, however, gifted children show special interests and talents quite early, and they apply themselves to these interests with enthusiasm and perseverance. (Winner, 2000)

The question of how to educate and encourage exceptionally bright and talented children is controversial (Sternberg, 1988; Winner, 1997, 2000). Should these children be permitted to begin school early? Should they skip grades? Some argue that these sorts of steps are necessary to maintain an exceedingly bright child's interest and motivation. Critics retort, however, that if we adopt such an approach, we may meet the child's intellectual needs at the expense of her social and emotional development. Placing such a child with older peers, critics claim, may cause her to be socially isolated. Opposing this view is the fact that very bright children often seek out the company of older children and adults. According to Terman (1954), one of the earliest leaders in the study of the gifted child, bright children are usually far ahead of their age mates, not just intellectually, but socially and physically as well, and some research supports this view (Richardson & Benbow, 1990). Are gifted children unique? Veronica Dark and Camilla Benbow (1993) suggest that the processes that underlie the cognitive feats of gifted children are not unique—it's simply that such children use their cognitive skills more efficiently than the rest of us. For example, gifted children seem to be able to process information more rapidly than others.

Education alternatives for gifted children include enrichment programs, which attempt to provide these children with extra stimulation without advancing them to higher grades. In another type of program, the school sets up a special subject or activity meant to enrich the educational lives of a group of intellectually talented students, for example, a special class in science or social studies. A third type of enrichment program offers gifted students instruction in creative writing or foreign languages or opportunities for study in the arts, such as painting and dance. Critics argue that the "enrichment" offered by these types of program may be mostly busy work and are often unrelated to the area of a particular child's talent, thus failing to encourage the child's development of that talent. Nevertheless, under the influence of Gardner's argument that children display multiple intelligences, more schools have begun to offer programs to nurture the specific talents of children who are gifted in particular ways (Gardner, 1993).

Children with Intellectual Deficits

We first encountered the problem of mental retardation in Chapter 2, where we discussed three specific disorders that are accompanied by serious intellectual deficits:

two-generation program A program of early cognitive intervention that extends help to parents as well as to their children.

intellectual giftedness A characteristic defined by an IQ score of 130 or over; gifted children learn faster than others and may show early exceptional talents in certain areas.

mental retardation A characteristic defined by an IQ score below 70 together with difficulty in coping with age-appropriate activities of everyday life.

learning disabilities Deficits in one or more cognitive processes important for learning.

 LifeMap CD

What's it like to be a teenage genius? Find out by watching the video on "The Adolescent Brain" in Chapter 10 of your CD.

Down syndrome, phenylketonuria (PKU), and fragile X syndrome. Down and fragile X syndromes, you'll recall, are chromosomal disorders, whereas the cause of PKU is lack of a specific enzyme for processing phenylalanine. Mental retardation that results from genetic causes or other factors that are clearly biological is referred to as *organic* retardation (Hodapp, 2002). Intellectual deficits that derive from factors surrounding the birth process (e.g., lack of sufficient oxygen) and those that are the result of conditions of infancy or childhood (e.g., infections, traumas, or lack of nurturance) are considered *familial* retardation. In some 30 to 40 percent of cases, it is not possible to determine the cause or etiology of mental retardation; about 35 percent of cases appear to be organic, and 30 to 35 percent are considered familial (American Psychiatric Association, 1994). In general, organic retardation is more severe than familial retardation.

Mental retardation is diagnosed by two basic measures: assessments of the child's mental functioning and of his adaptive behavior (American Psychiatric Association, 1994). Traditionally, an IQ score below 70, together with adaptive behavior deficits, has indicated mental retardation. Each of four IQ score ranges reflects an increasingly serious degree of retardation: mild mental retardation, IQ 50–55 to 70; moderate retardation, IQ 35–40 to 50–55; severe retardation, IQ 20–25 to 35–40; and profound retardation, IQ below 20 or 25. In addition, according to the guidelines of the American Association on Mental Retardation (2002), to be classified as mentally retarded children must show deficits in their ability to function in the real world. Young children who can dress themselves, find their way around the neighborhood, and use the telephone, for example, are less likely to be identified as mentally retarded than children with the same IQs who do not exhibit these practical competencies.

By far the majority of mentally retarded people—some 95 percent—can learn and can hold jobs of more or less complexity and live in the community. Children with mild retardation (about 85% of all retarded children) usually acquire social and communicative skills during preschool years and may be indistinguishable from other children until they reach their teens, at which time they may begin having difficulty with more advanced academic work. Children who are moderately retarded (about 10%) generally acquire communication skills in early childhood, and although they can benefit from vocational training, they are limited in their grasp of academic subjects. Young people in both of these groups may join the workforce and live in supervised settings or, in some cases, independently.

The severely retarded (3% to 4% of all retarded children) may learn to speak and communicate but have rarely progressed beyond reading a few words. Finally, profoundly retarded children (1% to 2%) require close supervision in sheltered settings. Such children may learn communicative skills and some self-care. Both of the latter groups can learn to do some simple tasks with close supervision; young people in both these groups must live in supervised settings.

Whether the competencies of any or all of these groups of mentally retarded children can be improved is yet to be determined. As you will recall from Chapter 7, researchers at the Language Research Center in Georgia have succeeded in enabling nonspeaking severely and moderately retarded youngsters to communicate intelligibly with adults and peers for the first time using a computerized keyboard device and have begun to explore the use of this device with $1\frac{1}{2}$- to $3\frac{1}{2}$-year-old children at risk for failure to develop language. And, as we mentioned in Chapter 2, with caring parenting that includes extra stimulation and training, many children with Down syndrome can lead very productive lives (Hodapp, 2002).

Children with Learning Disabilities

Not all children learn at the same pace or in the same way. Some learn faster than their classmates, but others with various learning disabilities may learn more slowly. Of the more than 5 million U.S. children classified as disabled, a little more than 50 percent are considered learning disabled, about 20 percent have speech or language difficulties, about 9 percent are emotionally disturbed, about 12 percent are mentally retarded, and about 8 percent have various other kinds of handicaps (U.S. Department of Education, 1997). Children identified as learning disabled are a very heterogeneous group in terms of the types of cognitive and social abilities they possess (National Joint Committee on Learning Disabilities, 1994). The diversity among learning disabled children makes it particularly difficult to know exactly what types of interventions are most useful for this group of children.

A major question in recent years has been whether these "special needs" children should be placed in separate classes or integrated into regular classrooms. Currently, more than half of disabled students spend most of their school days in regular classrooms (U.S. Department of Education, 1997). Many schools have adopted the approach of **inclusion** (also called *integration* or *mainstreaming*), in which children of all ability levels are included in the same classroom. Other schools have placed children with learning disabilities and other special needs in separate, special education classes. The success of these different approaches is still being debated. Some argue that inclusion programs enhance the academic achievement of learning disabled children (Buysse & Bailey, 1993), whereas others argue that such programs put children at risk for peer rejection or inappropriate labeling (Weissberg & Greenberg, 1998).

inclusion A policy by which children of all ability levels, whether learning disabled, physically handicapped, or mentally retarded, are included in the same classroom.

CREATIVITY

The nature of creativity and its relationship to intelligence have long been of interest to psychologists. Some investigators, like Robert Sternberg, see intelligence and creativity as intertwined, but others, like Howard Gardner, see clear distinctions between the two. In this section, we look first at some of the definitions and theories of creativity and then at some evidence on the distinctions between creativity and intelligence. We then consider children's creative behaviors and conclude with some thoughts on how to encourage creativity in children.

Definitions and Theories

Defining creativity is just about as hard as defining intelligence; both are multifaceted qualities that vary as a function of personal characteristics (which are both inherited and learned), the context in which they are exercised, the risk factors that may inhibit them, and the environmental supports that may encourage and sustain them. The key to creativity is the notion of *uniqueness*. Most people—including most psychologists—would agree that the creative product is novel. In some way, it is unlike anything else in its class. But many authorities, such as Gardner (1998), also agree that a truly creative idea or product must be characterized by *usefulness*. It must be of benefit in some area of life, whether that be astrophysics, the visual arts (e.g., painting, sculpture), household products, literature, microbiology, music, or another field of human endeavor. And still others argue that knowledge is crucial. For instance, Keegan (1996) discusses how Charles Darwin amassed an enormous body of knowledge of natural history before he offered his ideas about evolution to the world.

Relationship between Creativity and Intelligence

Are IQ and creativity related to each other? **Creativity** is defined as the ability to solve problems, create products, or pose questions in a way that is different (novel, unique) from the approaches most other people use (Gardner, 1998). To explore the relation of creativity to IQ, Wallach and Kogan (1965) administered WISC subtests and other intelligence tests as well as a set of tasks designed to tap creative modes of thinking to a group of fifth graders. The researchers found only minimal correlations between "correct" answers on the intelligence tests and answers judged creative on the more

creativity The ability to solve problems, create products, or pose questions in a way that is novel or unique.

open-ended tasks. The results suggested that the intelligent person excels at *convergent thinking,* or thinking with the goal of recognizing or remembering specific information or solving traditional problems for the correct answers, and the creative person excels at *divergent thinking,* or thinking that is imaginative and seeks variety, novelty, and uniqueness. Thus, although highly creative people tend to be above average in intelligence, a higher IQ does not predict creativity (Gardner, 1998). Clearly, the true relationship between creativity and intelligence is yet to be determined. One thing people do agree on, however, is that both are desirable characteristics.

Are Children Creative?

When a kindergartner proudly shows you the painting he created that truly looks unique to you, is this evidence that he is creative? Some psychologists do not believe that very young children are capable of true creativity.

Although we know that children are capable of gathering significant bodies of knowledge, psychologists who specialize in creativity, such as Runco (1996), hold that because young children often cannot distinguish between reality and fantasy, children cannot be truly creative until they reach preadolescence and can make this distinction. However, others point out that even though young children are not creative in the full sense of the term, their play—especially fantasy, or pretend, play—gives children a chance to practice the kind of divergent thinking that can lead them someday to invent new things or ideas (Russ, 1996). Vygotsky thought that play facilitated creativity: "The child's play activity is not simply a recollection of past experience but a creative reworking that combines impressions and construct-forming new realities addressing the needs of the child" (1930 [1967], p. 7).

If children may eventually be capable of creativity, are there ways that this creativity can be fostered or encouraged? Formal school instruction tends to be focused on learning specific content, passing tests, and advancing in grade. According to Albert (1996), a number of researchers have identified a period in middle childhood through preadolescence when early signs of creativity seem to disappear as children concentrate on well-organized (and thus well-controlled) learning skills. Divergent thinking simply does not have much opportunity to flourish in the classroom. However, outside of school parents can contribute by encouraging their children's creative impulses (Russ, 1996).

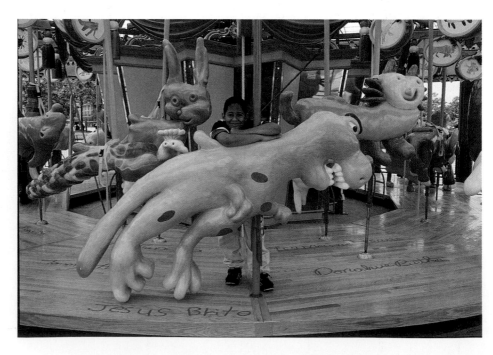

Jesus Brito smiles proudly above his lunging *Tyrannosaurus rex,* one of the Totally Kid Carousel's marvelous steeds that were all created by children. Mike Mottola, designer of the carousel, turned 36 of the 1,000 drawings submitted by first and second graders in New York City schools into mounts for this merry-go-round in the city's Riverbank State Park. Encouraging children's creative expression clearly can produce things that are unique and useful!

Making the Connections 10

There are many links between concepts and ideas in one area of development and concepts and ideas in other areas. Here are some of the connections between ideas in Chapter 10 and discussions in other chapters of this book.

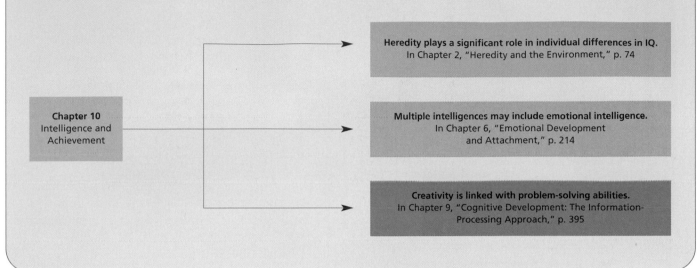

Chapter 10
Intelligence and
Achievement

Heredity plays a significant role in individual differences in IQ.
In Chapter 2, "Heredity and the Environment," p. 74

Multiple intelligences may include emotional intelligence.
In Chapter 6, "Emotional Development
and Attachment," p. 214

Creativity is linked with problem-solving abilities.
In Chapter 9, "Cognitive Development: The Information-
Processing Approach," p. 395

SUMMARY

Theories of Intelligence

- It is generally agreed that intelligence is composed of multiple abilities and is not a single, general construct. **Factor analysis** has been instrumental in research leading to this view. However, contemporary intelligence specialists have confirmed the existence of a general factor of cognitive ability, derived from Spearman's original **general factor (g).** This modern middle-ground position, which also recognizes Spearman's concept of **specific factors (s),** holds that children may vary both in overall intellectual power and in their proficiency in specific aspects of cognitive functioning.

- An information-processing approach to intelligence, Sternberg's **triarchic theory of intelligence** holds that intelligent behavior is built on information-processing skills, experience with particular kinds of tasks and problems, and the abilities to adapt to a particular context, or environment, and to shape others to one's needs.

- Gardner's **theory of multiple intelligences** suggests that each of eight kinds of intelligence has its own developmental path and is guided by different forms of perception, learning, and memory. Each type of intelligence is likely to characterize individuals with particular interests and endeavors, and a single individual may possess one or more types.

The Traditional Approach: Testing Intelligence

- Interest in intelligence has traditionally centered on the products of intelligence rather than on the processes of intellectual endeavor. Specialists in intelligence testing have generally described intelligence by means of an **intelligence quotient (IQ).** However, it is important to remember that what is measured on an IQ test is performance; capacity cannot be directly measured.

- Intelligence tests have three primary purposes: predicting academic performance, predicting performance on the job, and assessing general adjustment and health. Although traditional tests predict school performance fairly well, they have been criticized as unfair to minority groups, and efforts have been made to develop **culture-fair tests.**

- The widely used **Bayley Scales of Infant Development,** designed for infants and very young children, measure mostly sensorimotor abilities characteristic of certain developmental milestones and are generally used with children thought to be at risk of abnormal development. The newer **Fagan Test of**

451

Infant Intelligence is designed to measure processing skills.

- The intelligence test developed by French scientists Binet and Simon focused on verbal and problem-solving abilities. The **Stanford-Binet Test** is an American adaptation of Binet's test.

- Binet developed the concept of **mental age,** an index of a child's performance level as compared with her true age. Stern combined chronological age with mental age to create the intelligence quotient.

- The **Wechsler Intelligence Scales** (adult and child versions) are probably the most commonly used intelligence tests today, in part because they include a substantial performance section. Their scoring is based on a **deviation IQ,** or the relation between an individual's score and the distribution of scores for the group of which she is a member.

- Emphasizing the processes of intelligence, the **Kaufman Assessment Battery for Children (K-ABC)** also attempts to be culture-fair. Examiners teach a child who fails an item how to solve it before moving on to the next item.

- **Psychometricians** establish **test norms** by administering a test to groups having particular characteristics, such as age. The stimuli, instructions, and scoring of test items are also carefully **standardized** so that the test procedures will be the same when administered by different people.

- Intelligence tests must have both **validity**—that is, the test measures what it claims to measure, and **reliability**—that is, that the same score will be obtained for an individual across time or successive testings. IQ scores can and do fluctuate, because they measure current performance rather than underlying ability. Early studies indicated that scores on intelligence tests during infancy were not predictive of later performance, but recent research suggests that measures of infant attention may be related to IQ in early childhood. After about age 8, prediction of intelligence becomes more accurate. The rate of mental growth varies among children, however, and major stresses or changes in life circumstances may temporarily disrupt cognitive performance.

Why Do People Differ in Measured Intelligence?

- Most estimates of the heritability of intelligence have indicated that 40 to 50 percent of the variability in intelligence among middle-class white Americans is due to genetic factors.

- Many psychologists continue to debate the heritability of intelligence, some holding that it is less than 50 percent, others that it is more. Arthur Jensen, the most extreme representative of the latter group, proposes two types of learning, both inherited—**associative learning** and **cognitive learning.** According to Jensen, all people share the first type of learning, but the second type is more prevalent among certain ethnic groups.

- When we estimate heritability among people within a specific cultural or ethnic group, our estimates of heritability will be higher because such people by definition share some characteristics that are both inherited and environmental. It is inappropriate to apply heritability indexes based on one group to members of another. In addition, because heritability estimates are based on specific groups of people, they yield average numbers; thus, they do not necessarily apply to an individual member of a group.

- Significant environmental factors that affect the child's intellectual functioning include events during pregnancy and the child's birth that can result in **congenital** defects as well as the interpersonal relationships that the child develops with family members, teachers, peers, and members of the community at large.

Achievement Motivation and Intellectual Performance

- Children's intellectual performance is influenced by their own **achievement motivation,** the emotions they associate with learning tasks, the ways they view themselves and their abilities, and their responses to success and failure.

- In one approach to understanding achievement motivation, children who see themselves as helpless tend to give up easily or show deterioration when working on hard problems. In contrast, mastery-oriented children use failure feedback to maintain or improve their performance. Helpless children may hold an entity view of intelligence, whereas mastery-oriented children may hold an incremental view.

Ethnicity, Social Class, and Intellectual Performance

- According to those who hold that intelligence tests are biased against members of minority groups, the content of standard IQ tests is drawn from European American middle-class language, experience, and values and thus is inappropriate for other groups. Although more tests that attempt to be culture-fair are now available, on even some of these more educated and advantaged children do better.

- Context is an important factor in children's intellectual performance. Testing conditions, such as unfamiliar surroundings and European-American examiners, may negatively affect the performance of lower-class and minority children.

- The concept of **cumulative risk** suggests that the more negative aspects of experience that are present in a child's life, and put the child at risk for healthy development, the more likely he is to score poorly on tests of intellectual skills.

- Varying styles of parent-child interactions in different social classes may influence a child's development of verbal and cognitive skills. Studies indicate that early differences in mothers' use of language and infants' attention to their mothers' speech may account for later differences in the use of verbal information.

- Research indicates that cultural differences in parents' attitudes and enthusiasm for education may affect children's performance on academic tasks. Chinese and Japanese students have been found to perform at a higher intellectual level, particularly in mathematics, than Asian American students who, in turn, score higher than European American, African American, and Latino American students. **Stereotype threat** may also interfere with the performance of ethnic minority youth on achievement tests.

Cognitive Intervention Studies

- Since the 1960s educationists and government offices have launched many programs aimed at modifying the development of learning-disabled or economically deprived children. One of the most well-known and successful is **Head Start,** a federally funded program for severely economically deprived preschool children. In general, these programs have reported short-term gains in academic performance, though some others have reported a loss over time of the initial advances.

- Keys to long-term success may be involving children in these programs within the first two years of their lives, continuing intervention efforts at least until children enter kindergarten, and offering **two-generation programs,** in which educational, occupational, health, and counseling services are provided to the children's parents at the same time as intervention efforts proceed with the children themselves.

Beyond the Norms: Giftedness and Mental Retardation

- Whether or not to advance children who display **intellectual giftedness** to higher grades in school remains controversial, although some such programs have shown considerable success. Although some voice concerns that advancement to sometimes much older peer groups will isolate gifted young children socially, others hold that such children are generally advanced socially as well as intellectually.

- Some 95 percent of children with **mental retardation** can pursue academic studies to a greater or lesser degree, hold jobs, and as adults live either independently or in supervised settings. Only 4 to 6 percent of children afflicted with mental retardation must live under close supervision throughout their lives.

- More than half the children with special education needs are identified as having specific **learning disabilities** that interfere with cognitive processing in some way. Schools differ in terms of how these children are integrated into the classroom; some schools place children with learning disabilities in classes with normally functioning children and other schools separate these children into special education classes.

Creativity

- The defining features of **creativity** are uniqueness and usefulness. The relationship between creativity and intelligence continues to be debated, but current theory suggests that the sources of creativity lie in intelligence and motivation as well as a willingness to meet challenges, overcome obstacles, and take risks.

- Because children lack the knowledge base required to evaluate true creative efforts, some psychologists believe that creativity begins in preadolescence. Others, however, hold that young children have novel ideas, engage in creative acts, and use play to practice divergent thinking. These psychologists believe that encouraging imaginative play in children may promote future creativity.

EXPLORE AND DISCUSS

1. How important is IQ? What do IQ tests predict, and what do they not predict?
2. Why do you think the overall IQ score has improved over the last century, as described in the Flynn effect?
3. How can schools be organized in a multicultural society to provide equal opportunity for all children to attain their academic potential?
4. Should government funds be spent on early intervention programs for children at risk for educational failure? Why or why not?

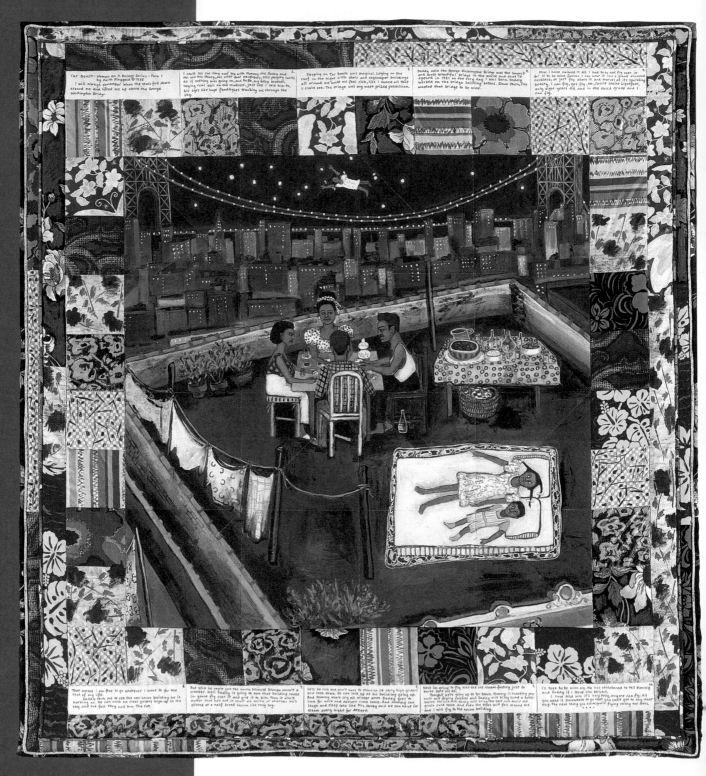

Faith Ringgold (b. 1930). *Tar Beach,* 1988. Solomon R. Guggenheim Musuem, New York.

11.

The Family

The family is both the earliest and the most sustained source of social contact for the child. What is a family? A family is a social unit in which the adult partners or spouses and the children share economic, social, and emotional rights and responsibilities as well a sense of commitment or identification with each other. Even though many contemporary families have new and different structures, family relationships remain the most intense and enduring of all interpersonal and social bonds. Family members share not only their memories of the past but also their expectations of sharing future events and experiences. It is largely this continuity over time that makes the family relationship qualitatively different from the shorter-lived relationships children have with playmates and friends, teachers, neighbors, and ultimately coworkers. Children carry their memories of past family interactions in their perceptions and feelings about family members and in the standards they hold not only for family behavior but for the behavior of people in general.

In the child's earliest years, his sole interpersonal relationships may be with his parents, and parents generally present cultural beliefs, values, and attitudes to their children in a highly personalized and selective fashion. Clearly parents' own personalities, family backgrounds, attitudes, values, education, religious beliefs, socioeconomic status, and gender influence the way they socialize their children. However, parents play a crucial role in this **socialization** process—ensuring that their child's standards of behavior, attitudes, skills, and motives conform as closely as possible to those regarded as desirable and appropriate to her role in society. We will see in the next several chapters that peers, school, churches, the media, and other forces also contribute importantly to a child's socialization. From the moment of birth, however, "whether the child is wrapped in a pink or blue blanket, swaddled and placed on a cradleboard . . . nestled in a mobile-festooned bassinet, indulged by a tender mother, or left to cry it out by a mother who fears spoiling the child, socialization has begun" (Hetherington & Morris, 1978, p. 3).

We begin this chapter by examining the family system from the ecological systems perspective that we described in Chapter 1. We explore the several subsystems of the family—including the relationships

socialization The process by which parents and others ensure that a child's standards of behavior, attitudes, skills, and motives conform closely to those deemed appropriate to her role in society.

between and among marital partners, parents and children, and siblings—and examine how the family as a whole contributes to the child's socialization. We look then at the effects of social class, socioeconomic status, and ethnicity on the family and its role as socializing agent. In addition, we explore some of the major changes in the structure and functioning of the American family that have occurred in recent decades. In a majority of families today, both parents work outside the home, a change that can have important effects on children's development. In addition, there is enormous diversity in the way modern families are structured—some families are headed by a single and/or divorced parent, some families are blended by divorce and remarriage, and still other families are headed by gay or lesbian parents. In some families, partners are becoming parents at later ages; in other families, parents cherish adopted children. We also consider the development of children born to teenage parents or unwed mothers. Our discussion of child abuse crosses all of the aforementioned family categories.

THE FAMILY SYSTEM

It's not uncommon for people to see socialization as a process by which parents modify children's behavior, but it would be more accurate to think of this phenomenon as a process of mutual shaping. That is, parents do indeed influence and direct their children, but their children also influence them and, in fact, play an active role in their own socialization (Bronfenbrenner & Morris, 2006; Kuczynski, 2003). In a complex system in which members are interdependent, changes in structure or in the behavior of a single family member can affect the functioning of the entire system. Moreover, families do not function in isolation; they are influenced by the larger physical, cultural, social, and historical settings and events around them. And families are not static; they change over time. Every family member, from the youngest infant to the oldest adult, is changing all the time, and these changes are reflected in family relationships.

The Ecological Systems Perspective

The view of the family as an interdependent system that functions as a whole has two principal origins: the realization by psychotherapists that to change the behavior of a troubled child one usually must change the family system as well (Kreppner, 2002; Minuchin, 2002), and the work of psychologists like Urie Bronfenbrenner. You will recall from Chapter 1 that Bronfenbrenner's ecological theory is concerned both with the relationships between the child and the many nested systems within which she develops as well as with the relationships among these systems themselves, from the familiar microsystem to the larger social and cultural setting of the macrosystem (Bronfenbrenner & Morris, 2006).

To refresh your memory, look back at Table 1-2 (Chapter 1), which used the family system to illustrate several important principles of systems theory. We learned there that a system is *complex* and *organized;* that it has an ongoing *identity* of its own; and that although it maintains a certain *stability* over time, it must also be capable of *morphogenesis,* adapting to changes both within the system and outside of it. In addition, a system demonstrates *equifinality* as time goes by, developing many similarities with other systems like it, even though such systems (e.g., families in different cultures) may express these similarities in different ways.

Before we discuss the family's major subsystems, we need to consider one or two other principles that govern system functioning. *Interdependency* explains why the functioning of the family system is not always smooth. Because each family member and family subsystem influences and is influenced by each other member and subsystem, both cooperative behavior and hostile or antisocial behavior may have widespread effects on the system as a whole. Parents who have a good relationship with each other are more likely than not to be caring and supportive with their children, and in turn the latter are likely to be cooperative and responsible. On the other hand, parents whose marriages are unhappy may become irritable with their children, and the latter may exhibit antisocial behavior that may in turn intensify problems in the parents' relationship.

Families tend to attain equilibrium, or *homeostasis,* in their functioning and to become resistant to forces that might alter this balance. This can be useful when routines and rituals help establish a sense of family history, identity, and tradition, making interactions easier and more comfortable. On the other hand, adaptability is the central criterion of a well-functioning family; when family members are unbending in the face of parental dissension or family distress over an aggressive child, routines can solidify and intensify negative patterns of interaction (Dishion & Bullock, 2002; Katz & Gottman, 1997). In these circumstances, members may make no effort to communicate rationally, defuse anger, protect others, or solve problems and may become locked into a pattern of interaction that promotes or sustains maladaptive behavior in one or more family members. Resistance to change can prevent parents or other family members from recognizing problems and can cause members to blame all family difficulties on one child, who becomes the target for everyone else.

Finally, families have *boundaries* that vary in how permeable or vulnerable they are to outside influences. A well-functioning family tends to have permeable boundaries that allow members to maintain satisfying relationships both within and outside of the family itself. If families are too rigidly bounded, members may have difficulty disengaging appropriately from the family as, for example, in adolescence, starting college, marrying, or, in time of need, making use of resources outside of the family. Such families may have few positive community contacts and social supports and may be more likely than others to perceive their children negatively and to be punitive and inconsistent with them (Wahler & Dumas, 1987). On the other hand, families whose boundaries are too permeable can be vulnerable to disruptions by external forces such as intrusive in-laws or peer groups whose behavior is at odds with the family's own standards.

This family is clearly pleased with their snowman. Such shared activities can reinforce family members' interdependency and increase positive feelings among them.

The Marital System

Both partners in a marriage, or other form of committed relationship, make up the marital system, the first and indeed the founding subsystem within the family system. Although the marital relationship still predominates in contemporary society, there are now other forms of committed arrangements between adult partners, such as civil unions and cohabitation by domestic partners. Many of the principles that we will describe probably apply equally to marital and other forms of stable couple arrangements. However, at this point in time we know considerably less about these newer relationships than about the more traditional marriage. Developmentalists sometimes tend to downplay the significance of the marital system, but the nature of the partners' interpersonal relationship unquestionably has an important impact on their children. Indeed, a relationship satisfactory to both adult partners is often regarded as the cornerstone of good family functioning. Directly or indirectly, it facilitates good parenting, good sibling relationships, and the healthy development of all the family's children.

HOW DOES THE MARITAL RELATIONSHIP AFFECT CHILDREN?

As we've suggested, when partners offer each other emotional and physical support and comfort, the likelihood that they will provide the same kind of support and caring to their children is greatly increased. Research has shown that when partners are mutually supportive, they are more involved with their children and their relationships with their children demonstrate affection, sensitivity, and competent childrearing practices (Cowan & Cowan, 2002; Katz & Gottman, 1997).

Couples who share child care and household chores have more time for playful and pleasurable interactions with their children and increase their chances of witnessing developmental milestones like a child's first words or staggering steps. Moreover, children's academic, social, and athletic successes are more fun if involved partners share them. Couples who cooperate in caring for their children also help each other shoulder some of the special burdens new parents experience, such as 2 A.M. feedings, changing dirty diapers, and soothing a crying or sick child.

Conflict between partners, however, can have seriously negative effects on both parents and children (Grych & Fincham, 2001; Kitzman, 2000). Even when a family's children are infants or preschool age, conflict between parents has been found to reflect insecure attachments of the children to both parents (Frosch, Mangelsdorf & McHale, 2000; also see Chapter 6). Studying school-age children, Katz and Gottman (1993, 1996) found that not only the level of conflict but the way adult partners manage their conflict can have deleterious effects on a couple's children. Within families whose marital partners typically confronted conflicts with hostility, belligerence, and contempt, children tended to display more aggressive and acting-out behavior than other children. In addition, fathers who had an angry and withdrawn style of dealing with marital disputes had children who were more likely to be depressed than others.

The effect of marital conflict on children takes two pathways: direct and indirect (Grych & Fincham, 2001; Parke & O'Neil, 2000). Children may be affected by such conflict *indirectly* when marital difficulties cause parents to change their childrearing practices in unfamiliar ways. In the Katz and Gottman (1997) work, parents in conflicted marriages had a poor parenting style that was characterized as cold, unresponsive, angry, and deficient in providing structure and setting limits; the children of these couples tended to display a lot of anger and noncompliance in interacting with their parents. Children may also be affected *directly* by marital conflict when they are actual witnesses to arguments and fights. In a series of studies, Mark Cummings and his colleagues have shown children real or videotaped interactions between adult actors behaving like two parents in a home setting. For example, the actors might disagree about which movie to see or argue about who will wash the dishes. The more frequent and violent the conflict, and the more often the arguments were about something a child had done or said, the more likely the children were to show distress, shame, and self-blame (Cummings, Goeke-Morey, & Graham, 2002; Frosch & Mangelsdorf, 2001). Moreover, when the actors failed to settle their dispute, the children expressed more anger and distress than when the actors resolved a conflict (Figure 11-1; Cummings, Simpson, & Wilson, 1993). Fighting in front of the kids has never been a good idea, but if partners handle their discussions constructively, showing respect for one another's opinions and expressing mutual warmth and support, they can lessen the harmful effects that their argument may have on their children. Moreover, they can model healthy conflict negotiation for their children.

Mothers and fathers may influence their children's outcomes in different ways. Kahen et al. (1994) found that when each parent was hostile toward the other, during

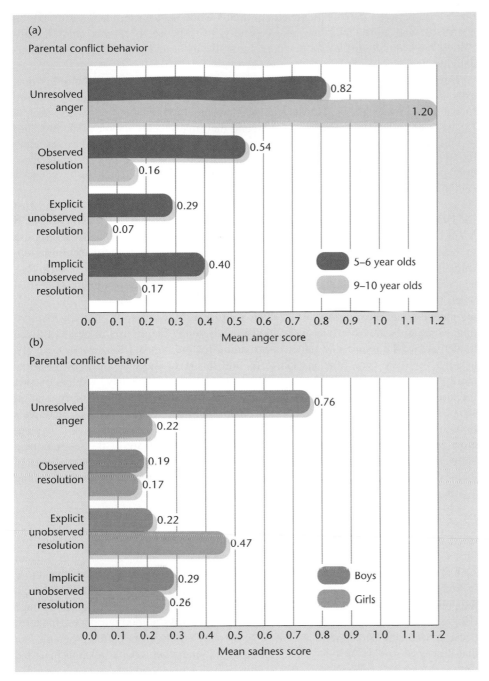

(a)
Parental conflict behavior

0.82

1.20

0.54

0.16

0.29

0.07

0.40

0.17

■ 5–6 year olds

■ 9–10 year olds

0.0 0.1 0.2 0.3 0.4 0.5 0.6 0.7 0.8 0.9 1.0 1.1 1.2
Mean anger score

(b)
Parental conflict behavior

0.76

0.22

0.19

0.17

0.22

0.47

0.29

0.26

■ Boys

■ Girls

0.0 0.1 0.2 0.3 0.4 0.5 0.6 0.7 0.8 0.9 1.0 1.1 1.2
Mean sadness score

Figure 11-1

How children respond to parental conflict

Parents' failure to resolve an angry conflict was the most likely behavior to arouse children's anger and caused the most displays of anger in older children (a). Such a failure was also more likely to trigger sadness in boys, but girls were more likely to be sad when parents resolved a conflict out of their presence and made only a brief reference to it later (b).

Source: Adapted from Cummings et al., 1993.

a parent-child interaction task fathers were more likely to be intrusive—that is, to physically interfere with children's actions—and children were more likely to express anger. Fathers' intrusiveness also predicted more negative peer play and more aggressive play with a best friend. Interestingly, these researchers also discovered that one parent's style of handling conflict may be related to the quality of his partner's relationships with the children. When fathers were angry and withdrawn in a conflict resolution task, mothers were more critical and intrusive in their interactions with their children, and, in turn, the children tended to be unresponsive or to "tune out" their mothers. In addition, the children's teachers rated them as tending to *internalize* problems—that is, to be shy and withdrawn—a finding that Cowan, Cowan, Schulz, and Heming (1994) replicated. Both these groups of researchers also found that hostile interaction between parents predicted children's tendency to *externalize,* or to exhibit aggressive and antisocial behaviors. Typically, in response to parents' marital difficulties, boys tend to display more externalizing behavior and girls to show more internalizing behavior.

Boys are much more susceptible to the negative effects of family disharmony than girls. Why should this be so? It seems that boys are more likely to be directly exposed to parental bickering and physical abuse than are girls (Hetherington & Stanley-Hagen, 2002). Parents quarrel more often and their quarrels are longer in the presence of their sons. If parents begin to disagree when daughters are present, they are more likely to raise their eyebrows, nod in the child's direction, and mutter "We'll talk about this later." Parents are simply more protective of daughters than of sons.

IMPACT OF A NEW BABY ON THE MARITAL/PARTNER SYSTEM   Just as the relationship between marital partners affects their response to their children, the presence and behavior of a child influences the marital relationship. The most immediate effect—especially after the birth of a couple's first child—is a shift toward a more traditional division of labor between husband and wife, even when the initial role arrangement was egalitarian (Cowan & Cowan, 2000). Despite the changes that have occurred in gender roles in recent years, an implicit assumption seems to be that the role of the mother with young children is in child care and homemaking, the role of the father in providing for the family (Parke, 2002). Rarely, a father will take time from his job to be with his wife and newborn, but that time hardly ever exceeds two weeks. In families where both partners have worked outside the home, the wife is most likely to give up her job. Thus, not surprisingly, marital satisfaction declines more markedly in women than men after the birth of a couple's first child (Cowan & Cowan, 2000). Fathers' marital satisfaction also takes a dive but more slowly; it may be only gradually that men become aware of the restrictions a baby imposes on their lives and realize that they are no longer the central focus of their wives' attention. In general, mothers get more of the responsibilities of raising a child, but they also often have more of the pleasures (Coltrane, 1996).

Children can influence the relationship between their parents in other ways. For example, children who are temperamentally difficult or handicapped in some way often are the cause of heightened family stress that may be translated into marital conflict. Couples who were satisfied with their relationship before the child's birth weather such pressures reasonably well, and their relationships show fewer disruptions than those of couples who were experiencing dissension before a child's arrival. Thus, although the presence of a difficult child may be enough to further undermine a fragile marriage (Hogan & Msall, 2002), the birth of a child rarely destroys a good marriage. However, because becoming parents does pose risks to a young family, intervention programs like that described in Box 11.1 have been designed to strengthen couple relationships and reduce the adverse consequences of the transition to parenthood.

The Parent-Child System

Most parents have some beliefs about the qualities they would like to see their children develop and the childrearing methods that ought to encourage them. There are many paths to the development of positive as well as negative social behaviors, however, and there is no magic childrearing formula. Parents have to try to adapt their methods to each child's temperament and needs and to the demands of the culture, but it's important to keep in mind that individual children may develop very differently within the same family situation. It is also important to remember that, as we saw in Chapter 3 (Box 3.3), even in adverse environments some children seem to be relatively resilient (Cicchetti & Toth, 2006; Luthar et al., 2000).

Child Psychology in Action

HELPING NEW PARENTS COPE WITH BECOMING A FAMILY

Although the Becoming a Family Project didn't succeed in immunizing young families forever from adversity and marital problems, this intervention effort did get 24 expectant couples and their new babies through at least five years of pretty healthy growth and development. Reviewing their results, the researchers who undertook this program concluded that to sustain the good family functioning that the project facilitated, it might be necessary to give "booster shoots" from time to time over the family life cycle (Cowan & Cowan, 2000).

From a group of 72 couples who were expecting their first babies, and 24 other couples who had not yet decided whether to become parents, the researchers selected a third of the expectant couples to participate in a six-month group intervention that concluded three months after the birth of the couples' babies. In weekly sessions, a clinically trained married couple encouraged the participants to raise any issues they were grappling with. Both wives and husbands described their dreams of creating an ideal family and talked about the families they grew up in and about the impending birth. Interestingly, everyone had trouble imagining what would happen after the baby was born.

As each couple's baby was born, the couples began bringing their infants to the group. It was only then that partners began to try to find their way through the common changes, problems, and conflicts people encounter in becoming a family. Who could give up what? Who would take responsibility for what? How could they keep the marital relationship fulfilling while dealing with the child's incessant demands? The researchers assessed family functioning, the quality of the marital relationship, parenting effectiveness, and parents' and children's adjustment in late pregnancy and when the baby was 6 months, 18 months, 3 years, and 5 years old.

At the 18-month follow-up, the effects of the intervention were encouraging. Compared with fathers in the nonintervention group, fathers in the intervention group were more involved and satisfied in parenting and reported less negative change in marital satisfaction, sexual relations, and social supports. In comparison to mothers in the nonintervention group, mothers in the intervention group saw their nonfamily roles—for example, as worker or student—as more important. Intervention mothers were more satisfied with the division of labor between themselves and their husbands and with their marriages overall; they were happier with their sexual relations, and they seemed better able to balance life stresses and social supports. In addition, at the 18-month and 3-year follow-ups, significantly fewer of the intervention couples were separated or divorced.

By the time the couples' children were in kindergarten, however, the positive effects of the early intervention had waned. Marital satisfaction was beginning to decline, and there were few differences between the intervention and nonintervention groups in either parenting style or children's adaptation. Early interventions clearly do not last forever. However, later findings from this research project indicated that another intervention (e.g., parent training to deal with problems unique to rearing toddlers) when the child was 2 could address some of the issues that led to later declines in marital satisfaction, to disruptions in family functioning, and to children's behavior problems. As new changes and challenges arise over the family life cycle, continued intermittent intervention focusing on new issues may be necessary to sustain good family functioning. Some family therapists have even suggested that, just as we go for regular medical checkups, we should go for regular checkups of family well-being to identify family problems and prevent them from escalating.

HOW PARENTS SOCIALIZE CHILDREN Attachment between parent and infant, as we discussed in Chapter 6, forms the foundation for later family relationships. Although socialization begins at birth, it seems to become more conscious and systematic as the child achieves greater mobility and begins to use formal language. Parents cuddle and pet the child and praise her for all sorts of achievements that parents and society regard as desirable, such as learning to use a spoon, naming objects, and repeating new words. On the other hand, whereas up to now parents have accepted and even indulged a number of "cute" behaviors, all of a sudden the air rings with "No!" "Don't!" and "Stop!" as children climb out of their cribs, totter to the head of the stairs, and discover the grand fun that can be had with the pots and pans so conveniently stored in cabinets at their own level. Practicing their newfound motor skills and exploring the world about them becomes a real trial when exploration is restrained by playpen bars and parents make serious attempts at toilet training.

In teaching their children social rules and roles, parents rely on several of the learning principles we discussed earlier. For example, they use *reinforcement* when they explain acceptable standards of behavior and then praise or discipline their children according to whether they conform to or violate these rules. Parents also teach their children by *modeling* behaviors they want the children to adopt. Recall Bandura's observational learning theory from Chapter 1. An important difference between these two approaches is that whereas parents knowingly use reinforcement techniques, observational learning may occur by chance. As a result, the modeled behavior may not always be what they want to produce. Suppose a child sees a churchgoing, platitude-spouting, moralizing parent lie about his golf score, cheat on his income tax, bully his children, and pay substandard wages to his help. Do you think the child will emulate his parent's hypocritical words or his actual behavior? The "do as I say, not as I do" approach to socialization doesn't work.

Parents also manage aspects of their children's environment that will influence their social development. They choose the neighborhoods and home in which the child lives, decorate the child's room in a masculine or feminine style, provide the child with toys and books, and expose the child to television viewing. They also promote the child's social life and activities by arranging social events and enrolling the child in activities such as sports, art, music, and other social and skill enhancement programs (Furstenberg, Brooks-Gunn, & Chase-Lansdale, 1999; Ladd & Pettit, 2002).

DIMENSIONS OF PARENTAL BEHAVIOR   Parenting patterns and styles tend to reflect two primary dimensions of behavior. The first revolves around emotionality: Parents may be warm, responsive, and child-centered in their approach to their children, or they may be rejecting, unresponsive, and essentially uninvolved with their children and more focused on their own needs and wishes. The second dimension concerns the issue of control: Parents may be very demanding of their children, restricting their behavior, or they may be permissive and undemanding, pretty much allowing the child to do as he wishes. We discuss some aspects of these two dimensions and then consider four parental patterns of behavior to which they contribute.

Emotionality   Parental *emotionality* is crucial in the socialization process. When a parent is warm and loving, the child is likely to want to maintain the parent's approval and to be distressed at any prospect of losing the parent's love (Baumrind, 1991; Maccoby & Martin, 1983). If a parent is cold and rejecting, however, the threat of withdrawal of love is unlikely to be an effective mechanism of socialization. From such a parent, what has the child to lose? Physical punishment too is more effective in the hands of warm parents, again probably because the child wants to conform to his parents' standards. But also, the child knows from experience that his parents are involved and concerned with his well-being and that they will give him information about socially acceptable alternative behaviors. The child with

Warm and loving parents tend to have children who are secure, feel good about themselves, and return their parents' affection.

rejecting parents has no such expectation. It is easier to learn the rules of the game if someone not only tells you what they are but also explains why you should play that way (Holden, 1997).

Warmth and nurturance are likely to be associated with parental responsiveness to the child's needs. Loving parents make children feel good about themselves, dispelling anxiety and building their sense of security and their self-esteem. Children with such parents are more likely to learn and to accept and internalize parental standards than children of rejecting parents (Crockenberg & Litman, 1990). The high levels of tension and anxiety likely to be associated with hostile parents and frequent physical punishment may make it very difficult for the child to learn the social rules the parent is attempting to teach.

Control   The goal of socialization is to enable the child eventually to *control* her own behavior and to choose socially responsible alternatives. Although the process of socialization does involve mutual influence between parents and children, the parent usually has more control than the child in interactions. Indeed, if parents are not in charge, the family is likely to be dysfunctional (Baumrind, 1991, 1993). When, rather than issue unexplained ultimatums, parents use suggestions and reasoning and present possible alternative courses of action, the child is more likely to comply with their wishes. Moreover, if parents are consistent in their discipline, use the minimum amount of pressure necessary to change the child's behavior, and encourage the child to view his compliance as self-initiated, children are more likely to cooperate and to adopt or internalize their parents' standards (Crockenberg & Litman, 1990; Holden, 1997).

As you might expect, warm, responsive parents are generally better at exercising control than hostile, rejecting parents. If parents use *power-assertive* methods of discipline that rely heavily on the superior power of the parent or are demeaning to the child, such as physical punishment, threats, or humiliation, children may come to view themselves as helpless or unworthy. Furthermore, although such techniques may enable a parent to gain immediate control of a child's behavior, in the long run they are likely to be deleterious. For example, suppose a hostile parent tries to control a child's aggressive behavior through physical punishment. By frustrating the child the parent may make her angry, and by offering an aggressive model to the child the parent may encourage the very behavior she is trying to eliminate. Moreover, the child may now try to avoid contact with the punishing parent, which gives the parent less opportunity to socialize the child, and may displace her aggressive urges to people outside the family of whose retaliation she is less certain. Again, the parent's method of discipline has simply intensified the behavior she was trying to get rid of (Gershoff, 2002).

Age plays an important role in children's responses to discipline. As children grow older, they resist being controlled and manipulated by others, and self-reinforcement for appropriate social behavior becomes increasingly important. Even older preschool children try to negotiate with their parents:

Child: I'll do it after I finish my painting. All right?

Parent: How about if you and I do it together?

As the child gains in social and cognitive competence and becomes more autonomous, parents rely increasingly on reasoning, and the child engages more and more in active bargaining (Kuczynski, 2003). This gradual shift from control by parents and others to self-control becomes critical for the child as he begins to spend time out of the home. Parents' opportunities to monitor and control the child's activities directly decline markedly in the elementary school years and even more in adolescence (Mounts, 2000).

Fortunately, over the school years, children become more able to substitute long-term rewards for immediate gratification and more oriented toward the welfare of others. Older children's more efficient information-processing skills improve their ability to interpret events, to consider their motives and those of others, and to weigh

Figure 11-2

Parenting styles

Although recent multicultural and cross-cultural studies suggest that these four parenting styles are not universally applicable, the essential characteristics and qualities on which they were based remain valid measures of behavior in many settings. New research may further refine these categories and add qualifying information based on cultural variations.

Source: From *Handbook of Child Psychology, 4* (E. M. Hetherington, Ed.), by Maccoby, E. E. and Martin, J. A., "Socialization in the context of the family: Parent-child interaction." Copyright © 1983 by John Wiley & Sons, Inc. Reprinted with permission of John Wiley & Sons, Inc.

	Emotionality	
	Warm, responsive	Rejecting, unresponsive
Restrictive, demanding	Authoritative	Authoritarian
Permissive, undemanding	Permissive	Uninvolved

alternative outcomes. For this reason, using immediate rewards or punishments to control behavior is much more effective with younger than with older children (Maccoby & Martin, 1983). Parents' effectiveness as agents of socialization is determined ultimately by a mix of factors: their emotional relationship with the child, the types of controls they try to use, and the appropriateness of these controls to the child's age and personality and the demands of the particular situation.

PARENTING STYLES   Family systems theorists would argue that what is important in a child's socialization is not any particular parental dimension of behavior but the overall combination of these behaviors. The four parenting styles shown in Figure 11-2—authoritative, authoritarian, permissive, and uninvolved—are composed of different combinations of the warm-responsive/rejecting-unresponsive and the restrictive-demanding/permissive-undemanding dimensions that we've discussed. They also reflect research that has explored the relationships between each parenting style and children's emotional, social, and cognitive development. In a now-classic study, Baumrind (1967) linked the first three of these styles with specific and quite distinctive patterns of children's interactions with their parents. Maccoby and Martin (1983) extended the Baumrind typology, adding the fourth, "uninvolved" parenting style. We discuss Baumrind's work first and then examine this fourth parenting style.

Observing nursery-school children in their daily activities for 14 weeks, Baumrind (1967) identified three groups of children who had widely varying patterns of behavior: energetic-friendly children, conflicted-irritable children, and impulsive-aggressive children. Baumrind then interviewed each of the children's parents and observed them interacting with their children both at home and in the laboratory, finding that three of the parenting styles depicted in Figure 11-2 were related to the three patterns of child behavior that she observed. Baumrind (1991) then followed her original authoritarian, authoritative, and permissive parents and their children through adolescence. **Authoritative parenting** was correlated with the behavior of the energetic-friendly children, who exhibited positive emotional, social, and cognitive development. Authoritative parents were not intrusive and permitted their children considerable freedom. At the same time, they imposed restrictions in areas in which they had greater knowledge or insight, and they were firm in resisting children's efforts to get them to acquiesce to their demands. In general, warmth and moderate restrictiveness, with the parents expecting appropriately mature behavior from their children, setting reasonable limits but also being responsive and attentive to their children's needs, were associated with the children's development of self-esteem, adaptability, competence, internalized control, popularity with peers, and low levels of antisocial behavior. Authoritative

authoritative parenting
Parenting that is warm, responsive, and involved yet unintrusive, and in which parents set reasonable limits and expect appropriately mature behavior from their children.

parenting continued to be associated with positive outcomes for adolescents, as it was with younger children; responsive, firm parent-child relationships were especially important in the development of competence in sons. In contrast, **authoritarian parenting** was linked with the behavior of conflicted-irritable children, who tended to be fearful, moody, and vulnerable to stressors. These parents were rigid, power-assertive, harsh, and unresponsive to their children's needs. In these families, children had little control over their environment and received little gratification. (See Chapter 14 for further discussion of punishment as a disciplinary tactic.) Baumrind proposed that these children often felt trapped and angry but also fearful of asserting themselves in a hostile environment. Authoritarian child rearing had more negative long-term outcomes for boys than for girls. Sons of authoritarian parents were low in cognitive and social competence. Their academic and intellectual performance was poor. They were unfriendly and lacked self-confidence, initiative, and leadership in their relations with peers.

Finally, **permissive parenting,** although it produced affectionate relationships between parents and children, was correlated with children's impulsive-aggressive behavior. Excessively lax and inconsistent discipline and encouragement of children's free expression of their impulses were associated with the development of uncontrolled, noncompliant, and aggressive behavior in children. Figure 11-3 summarizes Baumrind's findings on some major dimensions of parents' behaviors; parents of the energetic-friendly children scored highest on all these dimensions during both home and lab observations.

The fourth type, **uninvolved parenting,** identified by Maccoby and Martin (1983), characterized parents who were indifferent to or actively neglected their children and were "motivated to do whatever is necessary to minimize the costs in time and effort of interaction with the child." Uninvolved parents are parent centered, rather than child centered; they focus on their own needs. Particularly when a child is older, these parents fail to monitor the child's activity or to know where she is, what she's doing, or who her companions are. This parenting pattern is sometimes found in mothers who are depressed (Goodman & Gotlib, 2002) and in people under the stress of such things as marital discord or divorce (Hetherington & Kelly, 2002). Their own anxiety and emotional neediness may drive some parents to pursue self-gratification at the expense and neglect of their children's welfare (Patterson & Capaldi, 1991). Table 11-1 summarizes the characteristics of parents who display the four parenting styles as well as the kinds of behaviors the children of each group of parents manifest.

Parental involvement plays a crucial role in the development of both social and cognitive competence in children. In infants, lack of parental involvement is associated with disruptions in attachment (Thompson, 2006), and in older children it is associated with impulsivity, aggression, noncompliance, moodiness, and low self-esteem (Baumrind, 1991). In a kind of "double whammy," children of uninvolved parents tend not only to be socially incompetent, irresponsible, immature, and alienated from their families but to show disruptions in cognitive development, achievement, and school performance (Baumrind, 1991; Hetherington & Stanley-Hagen, 2002). Adolescents and young adults whose parents are uninvolved are likely to be truant, to spend time on the streets with friends whom the parents dislike, to be precociously sexually active, to have drinking problems, and to be delinquent (Dishion & Bullock, 2002). In a recent study, coercive discipline and poor monitoring of $4\frac{1}{2}$-year-old children predicted conduct problems in African American boys and girls at age 6 (Kilgore, Snyder, & Lentz, 2000).

What happens when parents use different disciplinary styles? Parenting is often less effective when the child is confronted by different styles because it is difficult and confusing for a child to respond appropriately to inconsistent feedback from her parents (Block, Block, & Morrison, 1981; Gershoff, 2002). As we discuss later, parents who co-parent, or cooperate and support each other, are more effective than others in socializing their children.

authoritarian parenting Parenting that is harsh, unresponsive, and rigid, and in which parents tend to use power-assertive methods of control.

permissive parenting Parenting that is lax and in which parents exercise inconsistent discipline and encourage children to express their impulses freely.

uninvolved parenting Parenting that is indifferent and neglectful and in which parents focus on their own needs rather than their children's needs.

Figure 11-3

Dimensions of parental behavior and children's characteristics
Not only did the parents of energetic-friendly children get higher scores on all four dimensions measured—control, demands for mature behavior, communication, and nurturance—but the scores of these parents were more consistent within each child group and across two observational settings, one at home and one in the laboratory.

Source: Adapted from Baumrind, 1967.

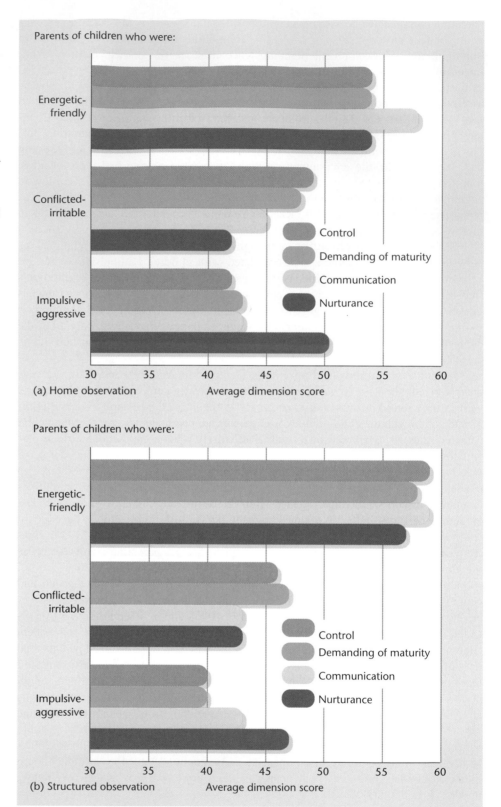

Table 11-1   Relation between parenting styles and children's characteristics

Parenting Style	Children's Characteristics
Authoritative Parent	*Energetic-Friendly Child*
Warm, involved, responsive; shows pleasure and support of child's constructive behavior; considers child's wishes and solicits her opinions; offers alternatives	Cheerful
	Self-controlled and self-reliant
	Purposive, achievement oriented
Sets standards, communicates them clearly, and enforces them firmly; does not yield to child's coercion; shows displeasure at bad behavior; confronts disobedient child	Shows interest and curiosity in novel situations
	Has high energy level
Expects mature, independent, age-appropriate behavior	Maintains friendly relations with peers
Plans cultural events and joint activities	Cooperates with adults; is tractable
	Copes well with stress
Authoritarian Parent	*Conflicted-Irritable Child*
Shows little warmth or positive involvement	Moody, unhappy, aimless
Does not solicit or consider child's desires or opinions	Fearful, apprehensive; easily annoyed
Enforces rules rigidly but doesn't explain them clearly	Passively hostile and deceitful
Shows anger and displeasure; confronts child regarding bad behavior and uses harsh, punitive discipline	Alternates between aggressive behavior and sulky withdrawal
Views child as dominated by antisocial impulses	Vulnerable to stress
Permissive Parent	*Impulsive-Aggressive Child*
Moderately warm	Aggressive, domineering, resistant, noncompliant
Glorifies free expression of impulses and desires	Quick to anger but fast to recover cheerful mood
Does not communicate rules clearly or enforce them; ignores or accepts bad behavior; disciplines inconsistently; yields to coercion and whining; hides impatience, anger	Lacks self-control and displays little self-reliance
	Impulsive
	Shows little achievement orientation
Makes few demands for mature, independent behavior	Aimless; has few goal-directed activities
Uninvolved Parent	*Neglected Child*
Self-centered, generally unresponsive, neglectful	Moody, insecurely attached, impulsive, aggressive, noncompliant, irresponsible
Pursues self-gratification at expense of child's welfare	
Tries to minimize costs (time, effort) of interaction with child	Low self-esteem, immature, alienated from family
Fails to monitor child's activity, whereabouts, companions	Lacks skills for social and academic pursuits
May be depressive, anxious, emotionally needy	Truancy, association with troubled peers, delinquency and arrests, precocious sexuality
Vulnerable to marital discord, divorce	

Sources: Baumrind, 1967, 1991; Hetherington & Clingempeel, 1992; Maccoby & Martin, 1983.

CHALLENGES TO THE PARENTING STYLES APPROACH

Other investigators have challenged the parenting style approach, asserting that more research is needed on several fronts. First, some have suggested that we need to identify more clearly the components of each style that contribute to its relative effectiveness or ineffectiveness in respect to the child's development. Second, some authorities propose giving greater attention to how much the child's temperament and behavior influences the parent's style (Kochanska, 1997). Finally, recent work has raised serious questions about the generalizability of these styles across either socio-economic or ethnic/cultural groups (Baldwin, Baldwin, & Cole, 1990; Chao, 1994,

2001). There are two primary issues: Do all groups use the parenting styles we've identified to the same degree, and are the advantages and disadvantages of each style for the child's development similar across groups? The answer to both of these questions seems to be no.

For one thing, neighborhoods make a difference in children's development, not only by confronting them with physical and social challenges that may or may not be beneficial but also by determining the kinds of socialization strategies parents adopt (Leventhal & Brooks-Gunn, 2000). For example, although an authoritative childrearing style may promote social and academic competence in children living in low-risk environments (Baumrind, 1991; Steinberg et al., 1992), it may not work in other situations. Several studies have found that poor minority parents who used more authoritarian childrearing practices, especially those who lived in dangerous neighborhoods, had better-adjusted children than those who relied on authoritative strategies (Baldwin et al., 1990; Furstenberg, 1993; Parke & O'Neil, 2000). Parental social integration into the neighborhood may also be an important predictor of more adequate parenting practices (Furstenberg 1993; Steinberg, Darling, & Fletcher, 1995). The more socially integrated the parents, the more vigilant they may be about their children's behavior, although this probably holds true only when families reside in neighborhoods where "good parenting" is the norm.

In Chinese families, a style of childrearing that may appear to be authoritarian is quite common, but some have argued that there are major differences between the U.S. and Chinese conceptions of *authoritarian* and that the application of such a style to Chinese parents may be ethnocentric and misleading (Box 11.2). According to Ruth Chao (1994, 2001), the childrearing styles described here reflect a U.S. perspective that emphasizes an individualistic view of childhood socialization and development; we revisit Chao's views in the section on cultural patterns in childrearing. In summary, it is important to consider contextual and cultural issues in developing new concepts of parenting styles.

The Co-parenting System

co-parenting Parenting in which spouses work together as a team, coordinating their childrearing practices with each other; co-parenting can be cooperative, hostile, or characterized by different levels of investment in the parenting task.

Although parents often act separately in dealing with a child, mothers and fathers sometimes *co-parent* as a team. **Co-parenting,** in which spouses coordinate their childrearing practices with one another, ideally working as a team, can take many forms. In families where parents' co-parenting patterns reflect warmth, cooperation, cohesion, and child centeredness, there may be a high degree of family harmony (McHale, Lauretti, Talbot, & Pouquette, 2002). On the other hand, parents who are hostile may actively compete against one another, and in some cases spouses may invest different amounts of time and energy in the parenting task, leading to an imbalance between the amount of involvement each parent displays with the child. These different co-parenting patterns have been observed across a range of studies with infants, preschoolers, and school-age children and in both European American and African American families (Brody, Flor, & Neubaum, 1998; Fivaz-Depeusinge & Corboz-Warnery, 1999).

Gatekeeping is one form of co-parenting in which one parent limits or controls the other parent's level of participation. For example, if a mother assumes that women are biologically more fit for parenting than men, she may set up subtle barriers that limit the father's involvement in the care of an infant (Beitel & Parke, 1998). There are clear links between early co-parenting dynamics and later indices of a child's social adaptation. McHale and Rasmussen (1998) found that hostile-competitive co-parenting during infancy was related to aggression in children. When there were large discrepancies between the input of each parent, parents rated children as displaying anxiety. Other investigators have found links between problematic family alliances in the first year and insecure mother-child attachments and, in the preschool years, behavior problems, such as acting out or withdrawal (McHale et al., 2002).

Box 11.2

Perspectives on Diversity

PARENTAL CHILDREARING STYLES CARRY DIFFERENT MEANINGS IN DIFFERENT CULTURES

There may be more than one explanation of why Asian American students outstrip European American and other cultural groups in academic performance. As we discuss elsewhere, Steinberg and his colleagues (1991, 1992) have proposed that the character of the peer groups with whom Asian and other students identify and socialize makes the difference; Asian students on average are more supportive of academic achievement. According to Ruth Chao (1994, 2001), however, other, much earlier factors in children's lives may also be at work. It seems likely that the supportive Asian peer group is reflecting a kind of childrearing that has no real U.S. equivalent.

In response to the finding that Chinese parents score high on U.S. psychologists' "authoritarian" scales, Chao points out that *authoritarian* does not mean in Chinese what it means in English. Thus, when Chinese parents get such high scores, they may be expressing behavior patterns that are quite different from the U.S. patterns that illustrate this concept. Moreover, this culturally based difference may hold also for parents from other Asian cultures who espouse such Confucian principles as family unity and respect for elders and may help explain why Asian American students typically do better in school than other U.S. students. (Confucius was a Chinese philosopher of the sixth to fifth centuries B.C. whose system of ethical precepts informs modern-day Confucianism.)

Whereas the American concept of authoritarianism subsumes many quite negative beliefs, attitudes, and behaviors (see Table 11-1), the Chinese style of parenting characterized by the concepts of *chiao shun* ("training") and *guan* ("to govern") requires a high degree of involvement with the child, physical closeness to the child, and devotion—mainly by the mother—of a great amount of time and effort. These concepts subsume teaching or educating children, focusing particularly on children's performance in school (for it is the Chinese belief that education is the key to success) and also connote "loving" and "caring for" the children. In this sense, these notions are antithetical to the concept of authoritarianism as it is defined in Western society. As Chao (1994) suggests, the seemingly restrictive behaviors that cause Asian parents to get high scores on Western scales may be equated with parental concern, caring, and involvement, and Asian parental control may reflect a more organizational effort designed to keep the family running smoothly and to foster family harmony.

It seems likely that the Chinese concepts of *chiao shun* and *guan* may actually resemble authoritativeness more than authoritarianism. The major difference between Chinese and Western concepts is the U.S. emphasis on soliciting the child's opinions, considering her wishes, and offering her alternatives (Table 11-1). As Chao (2001) points out, the Chinese notion of the self does not emphasize independence and autonomy, as the Western notion does. Instead, it derives from the Confucian notion of *jen* ("humanity" or "humankindness"), which holds that human beings are bound to one another and defined by their relationships with one another. For Chinese—and many other Asian—parents, adhering to social rules of conduct and interaction and developing a sensitive knowledge of others and their expectations are more crucial than focusing on the free expression of internal attitudes, feelings, and thoughts. Whereas the Western child is socialized to achieve according to some internalized standards of excellence, the Chinese child is encouraged to achieve according to family and social norms and expectations (Chao, 1995, 2001). These studies underscore the importance of recognizing how different cultures interpret various childrearing practices.

To return to the suggestion by Steinberg and his colleagues that peer group support explains why Asian students excel in school despite their "authoritarian" upbringing, it is just possible that the peer groups are reflecting the *chiao shun* and *guan* that these peers have received from their parents. In effect, then, they support a given child's motivation and endeavor to achieve because they have the same parent-taught motivation and belief in hard work.

Figure 11-4

Family systems and children's socialization
This model proposes that the family unit itself is a subsystem of the overall family system with as important an influence on children's socialization as the influence wielded by parent-child, marital, co-parenting, and sibling subsystems.

Source: From *Handbook of Personal Relationships,* 2nd ed. (S. Duck, Ed.) by Parke, R. D. and O'Neil, R., p. 56. © 2000 John Wiley & Sons Limited. Reproduced with permission.

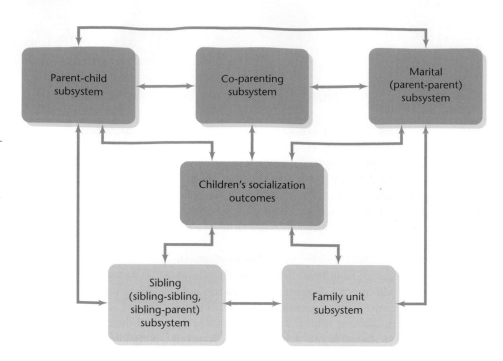

As Figure 11-4 illustrates, the impact of the co-parenting subsystem on children is independent of the effects of either the parent-child relationship or the marital relationship. This suggests that co-parenting makes a unique contribution to children's development.

The Sibling System

Over 80 percent of U.S. families have more than one child, and the number, gender, spacing, and relations among a family's children affect the functioning of the entire family unit. These factors affect not only parent-child interactions but also the relations among *siblings,* or sisters and brothers. In fact, most children probably spend more time in direct interaction with their siblings than with their parents or other people significant in their lives (Dunn, 1994; Larson & Verma, 1999). Interactions between siblings provide plenty of opportunities for learning about positive and negative behaviors, and the emotional intensity of these exchanges may be greater than that of exchanges with other family members and friends (Katz, Kramer, & Gottman, 1992).

HOW ARE SIBLINGS AFFECTED BY BIRTH ORDER?   A child's position in the family—that is, whether he is the firstborn or a later-born child—affects him, his siblings, his parents, and the interactions among all family members. Each child's experience is different, but the experience of the firstborn child is unique. He is the only child who reigns supreme in the love and attention of his parents until he is displaced by the birth of a new baby, with whom he now must share his parents' affection. The only child, of course, enjoys his parents' exclusive attention all his life. Firstborn children are generally more adult-oriented, helpful, and self-controlled than their siblings, and they also tend to be more studious, conscientious, and serious and to excel in academic and professional achievement (Herrera, Zajonc, Wieczorkowska, & Cichomski, 2003; Zajonc & Mullally, 1997; and see Figure 11-5). Indeed, firstborns are overrepresented in *Who's Who* and among Rhodes scholars and eminent Americans in the fields of letters and science!

Interestingly, however, research has found that second-born sons support innovative theories in major scientific controversies related to such issues as evolution,

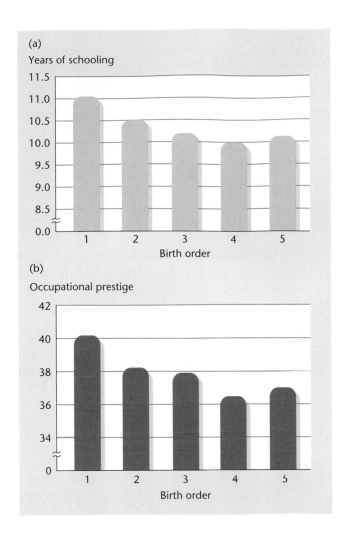

(a)
Years of schooling

Birth order

(b)
Occupational prestige

Birth order

Figure 11-5

Birth order and academic and occupational achievement
This research showed a clear positive relationship between a person's rank in the family and her degree of achievement in academic endeavors (a) and in working or professional life (b).

Source: Adapted from Herrera et al., 2003.

whereas firstborn sons support the status quo (Sulloway, 1995). It may be that the greater expectations and demands parents typically place on their firstborns are responsible for some other, less desirable characteristics of firstborns. For example, they tend to be more fearful and anxious than their siblings, to experience more guilt, to have more difficulty coping alone with stressful situations, to be admitted more often to child guidance clinics, and to have less self-confidence and social poise.

Although the only child has sometimes been called a "spoiled brat," research findings suggest that in many ways the only child has advantages over other children, especially children in families with three or more siblings. An only child is exposed to the same high level of parental demands as other firstborns, but does not have to adapt to displacement and competition with siblings. Like firstborns, the only child tends to be a high achiever, sustained by her close relationship with her parents, but she tends to be less anxious and to show more personal control, maturity, and leadership (Falbo & Polit, 1986). In social relations both outside and inside the home, only children seem to make more positive adjustments than children who are involved in sibling rivalry.

BIRTH ORDER AND PARENT-CHILD INTERACTIONS   The parents, to a great extent, determine whether the firstborn child will find seriously distressing the changes wrought by the arrival of a sibling (Teti, 2002). If a mother continues to be responsive to the needs of the older child and helps him to understand the feelings of the younger child, intense sibling rivalry is unlikely to occur

(Howe & Ross, 1990). And if a father becomes increasingly involved with his first-born child, this too can counter the child's feelings of displacement and jealousy. In fact, one positive effect of the birth of a second child may be that a father participates more in child care (Kramer & Ramsburg, 2002; Parke, 2002). Friends, too, can serve as buffers in this potentially stressful transition. Kramer and Gottman (1992) found that preschoolers who had good friendships showed less upset than children who did not get along well with friends. Moreover, these preschoolers were more accepting and behaved more positively toward their new sibling.

On the other hand, the birth of a new baby usually decreases the amount of interaction both between spouses and between mothers and older children, and firstborn boys are especially likely to show emotional and behavioral problems (Dunn, 1993). After the birth of a second child, mothers tend to become more coercive with their firstborns and to engage in fewer playful interactions with them (Dunn, 1993; Teti, 2002).

Do siblings themselves notice that parents treat them differently? Yes, they do. In addition, as we saw in Chapter 2, differential reactions by siblings to parental treatment form the nonshared environmental experiences that help us understand how siblings grow up to be quite different from each other. And such differential parental treatment can, for a disfavored sibling, have adverse effects such as heightened sibling rivalry and increased stress (Teti, 2002). At the same time, children's own interpretation of differential treatment by parents may defuse such effects. As Kowal and Kramer (1997) found in their study of 11- to 13-year-old siblings, only 25 percent of adolescents viewed parental treatment as unfair or capricious. The majority accepted it and understood that age, needs, and personal attributes of their siblings accounted for their parent's behavior. Only when siblings didn't understand or tolerate parental differential treatment did they view their relationships with their siblings negatively.

Older siblings in large families are often assigned the supervisory and disciplinary roles that parents play in smaller families. According to Edwards and Whiting (1993), girls are more likely to fulfill such roles; a firstborn 12-year-old girl in a large family may warm bottles, change diapers, and soothe a squalling infant with the alacrity and skill of a young mother. In African American and Latino American families, older siblings, especially females, often serve as caretakers (Harwood, Leyendecker, Carlson, Asencio, & Miller, 2002; Zukow-Goldring, 2002). In other cultures, such as Polynesia, sibling caretakers are common (Whiting & Edwards, 1988; Wiesner, 1993), and in still others—for example, Mexico—siblings rather than parents are the major play partners (Zukow-Goldring, 2002).

Parents can help prepare their children for the arrival of a new sibling. Bringing the older sibling to visit mother and new baby in the hospital and providing maternal support both help with this transition (Kramer & Ramsburg, 2002). However, as is often the case, the parent-advice books often exceed what we really know about how to best deal with this issue (Kramer & Ramsburg, 2002).

SIBLING INTERACTIONS AND BIRTH ORDER   Position in the family also affects a child's interactions with his siblings. The eldest child is often expected to assume some responsibility for the younger sibling who has displaced him. Older siblings may function as tutors, managers, or supervisors of their younger siblings' behavior during social interactions and may also act as gatekeepers who extend or limit siblings' opportunities to interact with other children outside of the family (Edwards & Whiting, 1993; Parke & O'Neil, 2000). Parents are likely to restrain or punish the eldest child for showing signs of jealousy or hostility toward a younger sibling, and they often protect and defend the younger child. On the other hand, the eldest child is dominant and more competent and can either bully or help and teach younger offspring. So it's not surprising that older children tend to show both more antagonistic behavior, such as hitting, kicking, and biting, and more nurturant, prosocial behavior toward their younger siblings than the younger ones show toward them (Dunn, 1993; Teti, 2002).

Eldest children focus on parents as their main sources of social learning, whereas younger children use both parents and older siblings as models and teachers (Dunn, 1993). Younger siblings, even infants as young as a year old, tend to watch, follow, and imitate their older siblings (Pepler, Corter, & Abramovitch, 1982). When children enter school, the older child's teaching role may become more formalized; 70 percent of children report getting help with homework from siblings, especially from older sisters (Zukow-Goldring, 2002). As we will explore in Chapter 15, older siblings can sometimes serve as deviant or negative influences, encouraging early sexual activity, drug use, or delinquency in their brothers or sisters (East, 1996; Garcia, Shaw, Winslow, & Yaggi, 2000). On the other hand, older siblings who are responsible and nondeviant can help younger siblings—for example, the practice of safe sex by older siblings may promote acceptance of such practices by the younger ones (Kowal & Blinn-Pike, 2004).

Siblings may also serve as resources in times of stress (Conger & Elder, 1994; Hetherington & Kelly, 2002; Teti, 2002). Children are most likely to turn to each other when a supportive adult is not available. For example, East and Rook (1993) found that children who had few peer relationships were buffered from adjustment problems when they had positive relationships with a favorite sibling. Boys are less likely to obtain support from siblings and tend to "go it alone" in times of family crises, whereas female siblings may become mutually protective.

Sibling relationships change with age. In adolescence, early overt sibling rivalry and ambivalence may diminish and intimacy may arise in which a sibling serves as the most trusted confidant and source of emotional support. In concerns about appearance, peer relations, social problems, and sexuality, siblings can often communicate more openly with each other than with peers or parents (Dunn, 1994). Female siblings often become closer over the life span.

When older children are secure in their parents' affection, they often make good teachers and guides for their younger siblings.

The Family Unit as an Agent of Children's Socialization: Family Stories and Rituals

Although we need to focus attention on marital, parent-child, co-parenting, and sibling influences on children's socialization, we mustn't fail to recognize the important role that the family unit itself plays as an agent of socialization (Parke, 1988). As systems theory emphasizes, the properties, functions, and effects of the family unit cannot necessarily be inferred by analyzing only the parent-child, marital, and sibling subsystems (Minuchin, 2002; Sameroff, 1994). Families as units change across development and develop distinct *climates, styles* of responding to events, and *boundaries,* all of which provide differing socialization contexts for the developing child (McHale et al., 2002; Sameroff, 1994). Families develop stories and rituals—activities in which all family members share—and these help transmit family values and roles, reinforcing the uniqueness of the family as a unit.

Generally, parents and other members of the family recount *family stories* in naturalistic contexts and in the presence of their children. Family members may transmit family-of-origin experiences across generations by telling stories and sharing memories, in this way shaping contemporary interaction between family members. Parents can teach children about the importance of their grandparents and other members of their extended family through stories. Listen to the story this mother told to her 4-year-old child:

> When I was a little girl I lived with my grandfather and grandmother. Grandpa had a big, comfy chair, and I would crawl up on his lap, and he would tell me stories. And one of my favorite things was to comb Grandpa's hair. One day I decided to comb his hair, but he didn't know that I had some little ponytail holders and some pins, and I put little curls all on the top of his head, and he fell asleep. And when he woke up he had the prettiest curls you ever saw all over his head, and he didn't even mind. Wasn't that nice? (Fiese & Bickham, 2004, p. 268)

The child learns through this story about the acceptance and playfulness of grandparents.

Fiese (1990) found that mothers who told stories of their own childhood that emphasized themes of closeness, nurturance, and play engaged in more turn taking and reciprocal interactions with their children. On the other hand, mothers who told stories of either achievement or rejection were less engaged and, when they interacted with their children, more intrusive and directive. Parents may also tell stories designed both to compensate for their own childhood difficulties and to ensure that their children do not suffer the same problems. Putallaz, Costanzo, and Smith (1991) found that mothers with predominantly anxious/lonely recollections of their own childhood experiences with peers took a particularly active role in their children's social development and had more socially competent children than mothers without such backgrounds.

People have known for decades of the importance of *family rituals* in family life, but it's only recently that researchers have recognized the socialization function of these rituals (Fiese, 2006). According to Sameroff (1994), family rituals range from formal and intricate religious observances, such as a first communion or a bat or bar mitzvah, to less-articulated daily interaction patterns like the kind of greeting family members give to someone returning home.

Rituals serve an important protective function (Cicchetti & Toth, 2006; Luthar et al., 2000). Researchers have found, for example, that children who came from families who were able to preserve family rituals such as dinner and holiday routines were less likely to become alcoholic as adults and that adolescents from families who attach more meaning to their rituals tend to have higher self-esteem than other children (Fiese, 2006; Pratt & Fiese, 2004). Rituals offer a powerful clue to the nature and quality of family functioning and have clear protective advantages for the child.

In sum, stories and rituals show us that families function not just as collections of individuals but also as true systems. Moreover, families differ from one another in special ways, much the way individuals differ from each other. In a sense, just as each individual develops a unique personality, so families develop ways of interacting that give them a unique signature or identity.

SOCIAL CLASS, ETHNICITY, AND SOCIALIZATION

No culture is entirely homogeneous. Subgroups within a culture may have different values, attitudes, and beliefs as well as different problems to cope with. Any or all of these differences may be reflected in unique goals of socialization and methods for achieving it.

Table 11-2

Some facts about U.S. children and their families: 2002

Source: Adapted from Children's Defense Fund, 2004.

1 in 2	Lives with a single parent at some point during childhood
1 in 3	Is born to unmarried parents
1 in 5	Is born poor
1 in 5	Is born to a mother who does not graduate from high school
1 in 5	Has a foreign-born mother
1 in 6	Is born to a mother who received no prenatal care during the first three months of her pregnancy
1 in 7	Has no health insurance
1 in 7	Lives in a family that is poor even though one adult works
1 in 8	Is born to a teenage mother
1 in 8	Lives in a family that receives food stamps
1 in 15	Is born into a family living at less than half the poverty level
1 in 24	Lives with neither parent
1 in 60	Sees his parents divorce in any year

Poverty and Powerlessness

Both scholarly and lay writers have focused much attention, in recent years, on the differences between the life situations of families of the lower and middle social classes in the American culture. Of particular importance is the prevalence of children living in poverty and under extremely unfavorable circumstances (see Table 11-2). Since the early 1970s, the percentage of U.S. children under 18 living in poverty has risen by more than 60 percent. In 2002, over 12 million children (nearly 17% of America's children) were living in poverty (see Figure 11-6; also, Brooks-Gunn, Britto, & Brady, 1999; Children's Defense Fund, 2004; Duncan & Brooks-Gunn, 2000). Moreover, an American child is more likely to be poor than a child in Canada or Europe. A child

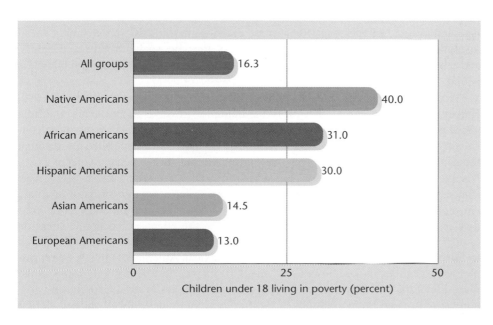

Children under 18 living in poverty (percent)

Figure 11-6

Children living below the poverty line, 2000

Whereas the percentages of European and Asian American children living below the poverty line are below the average figure for all U.S. children, the percentages of Native, African, and Latino American children far exceed the average.

Source: Based on Children's Defense Fund, 2002.

Figure 11-7   How economic stress can lead to children's adjustment problems

Adverse economic conditions may combine with personal financial stressors to create worry and insecurity in parents, which can lead to family conflict that may interfere with children's and adolescents' healthy adjustment.

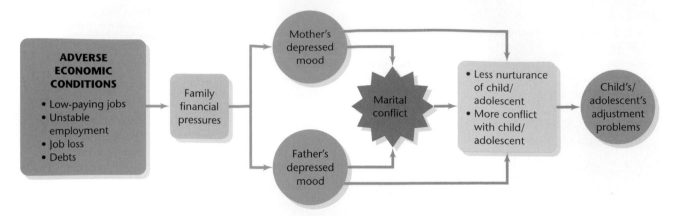

Source: Adapted from Conger, Conger, Elder, Lorenz, Simons, & Whitbeck, 1992.

in the United States is five to eight times more likely to be poor than a child in Sweden, Norway, or Finland (Children's Defense Fund, 2004). Although the most obvious differences between the lower and middle classes are seen in the indicators of socioeconomic status—income, education, and occupation—other related and pervasive features of the lives of the lower and middle classes may be more directly relevant to the socialization process (e.g., dangerous neighborhoods, chronic stress).

ECONOMIC HARDSHIP   Powerlessness is a basic problem of the poor. The poor have less influence over the society in which they live and are less likely than members of the middle class to be treated adequately by social organizations and with appropriate concern. The poor receive fewer health and public services, and their lack of power, information, and educational and economic resources restrict the options available to them. The poor have little choice of occupation or housing and little contact with other social groups; they are vulnerable to job loss, financial stress, and illness and subject to impersonal bureaucratic decisions in the legal system and in social institutions such as welfare agencies. Agents of the law, social workers, educators, and others are more likely to violate their individual rights than those of middle-class people.

According to McLoyd and her colleagues (McLoyd & Ceballo, 1998; McLoyd, Harper, & Copeland, 2001), in view of the multiple stresses, few resources, and little social power possessed by poor parents, it is not surprising that many experience considerable psychological distress, feel helpless, insecure, and controlled by external forces, and are unable to support and nurture their children adequately (Figure 11-7). Nor is it only poor families who suffer in this way. As Conger and Elder (1994) have shown, families at a variety of income levels who suffer economic stress of any kind are more likely than nonstressed families to experience depression and marital conflict and to be harsh with their children. Moreover, the effects of economic stress on family functions have been documented in families of many ethnic derivations, such as European American, African American, and Mexican American families. For example, white families in the midwestern United States who lost their family farms in the recession of the late 1980s, poor African American families in rural Georgia, and economically stressed Latino families in California in the mid-1990s all showed similar responses to economic hardship (Brody, Dorsey, Forehand, & Armistead, 2002; Conger & Elder, 1994; Parke et al., 2004). Clearly, economic hardship affects families regardless of race or ethnicity.

Only the phenomenon of mutual assistance and support among the poor themselves relieves this dismal picture. Perhaps the very stresses that highlight their powerlessness lead working-class families to form extensive support networks of kin, friends, and neighbors; such networks are particularly common among economically deprived black families (Brody, Stoneman, & Flor, 1996; Gadsden, 1999). These systems provide families not only with emotional support but also with unpaid services that could not otherwise be purchased. Families and friends render each other mutual assistance in meeting emergency needs in times of unemployment, childbirth, illness, and death, as well as the day-to-day needs of family life (Gadsden, 1999).

CYCLES OF DISADVANTAGE   The poor get involved in *cycles of disadvantage*. That is, the economic disadvantages they suffer lead them into successive failures that tend to spiral downward in such a way that not only can they not acquire more resources but they tend to lose the ones they have. Consider, for example, the situation of the teenage girl who becomes pregnant, often out of wedlock. She is likely not only to drop out of school but also to fail to catch up educationally after her baby is born; if she has already left school, she is unlikely to return. Without education, she is limited in the kinds of jobs she can secure, and her earning power is low. She can rarely afford child care and, unless relatives or others can care for her child, she may give up her job and go on welfare. Without money or education, or the opportunity to acquire either, she may find herself in a recurring cycle of low educational attainment, few skills, economic dependence, and poverty. Happily, as we will see later in the chapter, some teenage mothers can develop better lives for themselves and their children.

How does poverty affect children's development? First, poor children face more risks to physical health than do children of affluent families: Poor children are 1.9 times more likely to have low birthweight, 2.8 times more likely to have inadequate prenatal care, 3.5 times more likely to suffer lead poisoning, 1.7 times more likely to die during childhood, 2.0 times more likely to endure a short-term hospital stay, and 8 times as likely to have had too little food some time in the last four months. In short, being poor is bad for a child's health (Children's Defense Fund, 2004; Duncan & Brooks-Gunn, 2000). Nor is poverty helpful for children's achievement. Children in poverty are twice as likely to be retained in a grade and 3.5 times as likely to drop out of high school (Children's Defense Fund, 2004). Poor children are 1.3 times more likely to suffer emotional or behavior problems, 6.8 times more likely to suffer child abuse or neglect, and over 2.2 times more likely to encounter violent crime.

Timing of poverty matters. Being poor in early childhood is much more detrimental than being poor in middle childhood or adolescence (Duncan & Brooks-Gunn, 2000). A $10,000 increment to income over the first five years of life for children in low-income families is associated with nearly a threefold increase in the chances of finishing high school. Increasing income later in childhood has been seen as less effective in producing a change (Duncan, Young, Brooks-Gunn, & Smith, 1998). Poverty affects children through several pathways. First, the quality of the home environment differs in poor and nonpoor families (Bradley et al., 2001). Children in poor homes have fewer physical resources (books, toys, educational games, computers); they also receive fewer learning opportunities and less cognitive stimulation (parents less often read to children or engage in other developmentally appropriate activities) than children in nonpoor homes. In fact, the difference in home learning environments of higher- and lower-income children accounts for nearly half of the effect of income on the achievement scores of preschool children (Klebanov, Brooks-Gunn, McCardon, & McCormick, 1998). Second, the quality of care young children receive outside the home also matters, and poor children are often placed in poorer-quality child-care settings. Third, as we just noted, poverty and economic stress are linked with parent-child conflict; this leads to lower grades and impairs emotional and social development. A fourth effect of poverty is that poor families often live in high-risk neighborhoods characterized by social disorganization (crime, unemployment, low parental supervision) and limited resources (fewer playgrounds, after-school programs, child-care and health-care facilities); such poor neighborhoods can adversely affect children's development (Leventhal & Brooks-Gunn, 2000). Finally, poor parents often suffer more physical and emotional problems that impair their parenting abilities. Children suffer as a result of this reduced parental competence.

We have painted a bleak picture of the impact of poverty on children, but there is some good news: The effects of poverty are reversible. Recent evidence based on experimental studies in which families received supplemental income suggests that an increase in family income is linked with improvement in poor children's school engagement and social behavior (Morris & Gennetian, 2003). How do recent changes in welfare policies affect children's development? As a result of legislation in the 1990s, welfare reform efforts have been directed at reducing family dependence on welfare and at increasing families' participation in the workforce. Researchers have found that when reforms increased work opportunities and provided the kinds of financial support that led to a net gain in income for working families, children achieved higher levels of school performance and showed more positive social behavior. In contrast, welfare reforms that mandated work but did not result in an overall financial gain had few effects on children (Morris, Huston, Duncan, Crosby, & Bos, 2001).

Research also shows that when decreased dependence on welfare is linked with increased income, parents as well as children benefit (Gennetian & Miller, 2002). Children were found to exhibit fewer problem behaviors and to perform better in school, and mothers were less depressed and reported less domestic violence.

Cultural Patterns in Childrearing

In general, social-class differences in family relations are more marked than variations based on race or ethnicity (Parke & Buriel, 2006). However, because race and social class do tend to be related, separating these factors has often been difficult; minorities are overrepresented in poorer and less educated families. Keep in mind, though, that over 10 percent of white children in the United States also live in poverty (see Figure 11-6). Unfortunately, investigators have often treated ethnic groups as if they were homogeneous; rarely have they recognized the great variability within such groups. For example, in the United States there are many distinct Hispanic groups—Mexican, Puerto Rican, Cuban, Spanish, Colombian, Chilean, and Dominican, to name only a few. Spanish-speaking people of these and other groups have quite different socioeconomic, cultural, and linguistic characteristics—moreover, within each group there are subgroups within which there is great individual variation (Leyendecker & Lamb, 1999).

Parents' and children's behavior must always be understood in the context of the meanings and values of the individual's particular socioculture (Demo et al., 2000; McLoyd et al., 2001; Parke & Buriel, 2006). For example, in socializing their children, many ethnic minorities are more likely than the European American majority to place emphasis on continuity of ethnic values and worldviews and on social interdependence. In many groups we see reflections of such interdependence in the important role played by the **extended family**—the family inclusive of grandparents, aunts, uncles, nieces, and nephews (McLoyd & Ceballo, 1998). This emphasis on interdependence is also reflected in a concern with cooperation, obligation, sharing, and reciprocity, which contrasts with North American ideals of self-reliance and competition. On the other hand, Chinese American parents and parents in other Asian

extended family A family that includes relatives such as grandparents, aunts, uncles, nieces, and nephews within the basic family unit of parents and children.

Both the nuclear and the extended family are important in most Hispanic cultures, which emphasize sharing and cooperation in both good times and bad.

American subcultures, who also emphasize family cooperation and obligation, encourage self-sufficiency and achievement even more than do European American parents (Chao & Tseng, 2002). Once again, we must always know what group we're talking about when we make general statements.

Different parenting styles are found among many U.S. subcultural groups, but the effects of these styles seem to vary among some groups. Studying more than 20,000 high school students from varying ethnic and class backgrounds, Steinberg and colleagues (1992) found that in European American, African American, and Asian American families, authoritative parenting had similar benefits in promoting better psychosocial adjustment and in minimizing depression and delinquency in adolescents. However, these researchers found that the relations specifically between authoritative parenting and school performance were less consistent for African American and Asian American adolescents than for European American and Latino American adolescents (Steinberg et al., 1995; Steinberg et al., 1991). European and Latino American adolescents were more likely to benefit academically from authoritative parenting than were African American or Asian American adolescents. Within African American and Asian American groups, adolescents with authoritative parents did not show greater academic achievement than those with nonauthoritative parents. How can these findings be explained?

Research has often shown that African American and Latino American students earn lower grades, drop out more often, and attain less education than non-Hispanic white students, whereas the academic performance of Asian American students exceeds that of the other three groups (Chao & Tseng, 2002; Fuligni, 1997). Moreover, even when such factors as socioeconomic status and family structure are controlled for, these ethnic differences in achievement appear. In their study, Steinberg and his colleagues concluded that differences in achievement in students of different ethnic backgrounds may well reflect the nature of the peer groups with whom students associate. Mapping the social structure of these groups across the students' schools, these investigators found that students from one ethnic group rarely knew or associated with students from other ethnic groups. Even more interesting was their finding that across all ethnic groups, children performed best when both their parents and their peer groups supported achievement. They did less well, however, with support from only one of these sources, and least well when neither their parents nor their peers supported achievement.

European American and Asian American adolescents were more likely to belong to peer groups that encouraged engagement in school activities and academic achievement. In Steinberg's study, both Latino American and Asian American parents tended to be authoritarian, a parenting style that has been associated with low achievement. The researchers postulated that it was the Asian American students' access to supportive peer groups that enabled them to perform better. Recall our discussion of this issue in Box 11.2, however, which suggests that this parenting style, at least among Chinese parents, may encourage achievement (Chao, 1994, 2001) and, moreover, that same-culture peer groups are likely to reflect same-parental training.

Supportive, achievement-oriented peer groups were less available to African American adolescents—even to those with authoritative parents. According to Ogbu (1997), African American children often view achievement as giving in to the system, or as "white" behavior, and thus they often find themselves torn between the wish to be popular and the wish to perform well in school. As a result, high-achieving African American students often do cross ethnic lines, associating with students from other cultural groups (Liederman, Landsman, & Clark, 1990).

THE CHANGING AMERICAN FAMILY

The American family has been changing for some years now, and although some have predicted the demise of the family, it seems more accurate to say that family forms and family members' roles are becoming more varied. Most children still live in families with two parents who have been married only to each other. However, the proportion of **traditional nuclear families**—composed of two parents and children, with the father as the sole breadwinner—is declining. What are some of the main changes in family structure and functioning that are occurring?

traditional nuclear family
The traditional family form, composed of two parents and one or more children, in which the father is the breadwinner and the mother the homemaker.

The average household size has decreased to 2.6 people. The average number of children in a U.S. family is 1.8, and it is even lower in some other countries. In Japan and the Netherlands, for example, the rate is 1.5 and in Germany it is 1.3 children per family (Bellamy, 2000). There are a greater number of single-adult households. This is attributable, in part, to delays in marriage, declines in birth rates and in remarriages, and an increase in the number of elderly people living alone.

There are more single-parent households today, primarily because of the rising divorce rate but secondarily because more unmarried women are having children. The divorce rate doubled between 1960 and 1985; it is estimated that 40 to 50 percent of marriages today will end in divorce, and that 60 percent of these divorces will involve children. In 2000, nearly 28 percent of children under 18 lived with a single parent, but this figure was much higher for some ethnic groups (Figure 11-8). It was also much higher for U.S. families than for those in other industrialized countries (Figure 11-9). One-third of children will experience the remarriage of one or both of their parents, and 62 percent of remarriages end in divorce. Thus, more parents and children are undergoing multiple marital transitions and rearrangements in family relationships.

Over the past 40 years or so, out-of-wedlock births have doubled. Whereas in 1960 there were 22 births per 1,000 unmarried females, in 2002, 44 births per 1,000 unmarried females were recorded (Children's Defense Fund, 2004). Seventy percent of African American women have borne babies out of wedlock; among Native Americans the percentage was 57, among Latino Americans 43, among European Americans 25, and among Asians and Pacific Islanders 16 (Children's Defense Fund, 1997). Contrary to popular wisdom, more than twice as many unmarried mothers are women over 20 years old, not under 20. We examine teenage pregnancies later in the chapter.

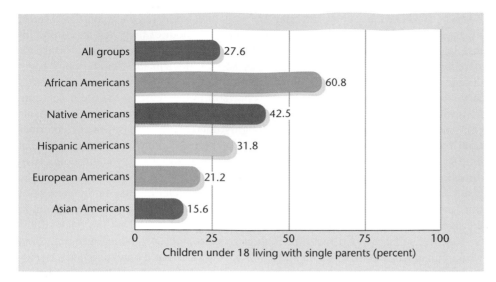

Figure 11-8

Children living with single parents, 1996

Like children living in poverty (see Figure 11-6), children living with a single parent are much more likely to be African, Native, or Latino American than European or Asian American.

Source: Based on Children's Defense Fund, 1997.

The number of working mothers has increased. In 2002, 68 percent of mothers with children under the age of 18 were in the labor force (Children's Defense Fund, 2003). Young mothers, poor mothers, and mothers from single-parent families are most likely to enter the labor force because of economic need. Two-thirds of mothers in single-parent families work outside the home, and another 20 percent are seeking employment. Eighty-six percent of black mother-headed households and 38 percent of white mother-headed households fall below the poverty line, in contrast to 46 percent and 16 percent, respectively, of two-parent households.

We look first, in this section, at changes in the family that are associated with maternal employment, and then at the kinds of changes that unwed single parenting, divorce, and remarriage bring about. As we will see, although many children of divorce continue to live with their mothers, joint custody arrangements have become somewhat more common.

Parental Employment and Child Development

Since the 1970s increasing numbers of mothers, particularly of preschool children, have been entering the labor market. As mothers spend more time on the job and less in the home, family roles and patterns of functioning are changing. What are some of the changes that have already occurred, and how do they influence children's behavior? How does work-related stress influence children?

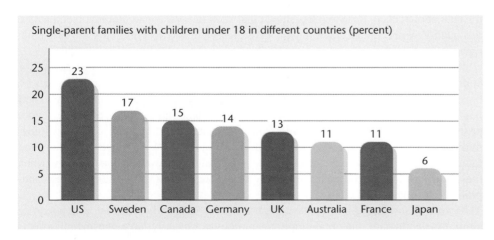

Figure 11-9

Single-parent families in some industrialized countries

The United States has by far the greatest percent of single-parent families with underage children of all the countries represented; the U.S. rate is almost four times the percent of such families in Japan.

Source: Santrock, 2005.

ROLE MODELS   One shift may be a growing similarity between the roles of the mother and father. When children more often see both of their parents as providing for the family and as participating actively in family and childrearing tasks, the stereotypical roles of the breadwinner father and the homemaking mother may begin to fade away (Pleck, 2004). Note, however, that although father participation increases in dual-career families, currently mothers are still doing most of the child care and housework (Coltrane, 2000). According to one recent estimate, since about 1970 men's contributions to inside housework have roughly doubled, whereas women's contributions have decreased by about a third (Coltrane, 1996). Of course, because up to that time women were shouldering almost all the homemaking, they were still doing two-thirds of this work. In the late 1980s, men were doing about 20 to 25 percent of the inside chores (Coltrane, 1996), but, rather than an absolute increase in the amount of time men devote to household tasks, this apparent change may reflect a reduction in the amount of time wives devote to housework and child care.

Working mothers report that time is their scarcest and most valued resource. Both working mothers and their school-age children complain that the mothers have too little time to spend with their children (Booth, Clarke-Stewart, Vandell, McCartney, & Owen, 2002; Perry-Jenkins, Repetti, & Crouter, 2000). However, greater father involvement may compensate for some of these problems. In both dual-earner and single-earner families, high father involvement is associated with higher IQ and achievement test scores, as well as with greater social maturity in children (Gottfried, Gottfried, & Bathurst, 2002).

The role model working mothers provide has pronounced effects on both daughters' and sons' perceptions of men and women. Children of working mothers have more egalitarian views of gender roles (Hoffman, 2000; Hoffman & Youngblade, 1999), and children in middle-class families whose mothers are employed have higher educational and occupational goals. These differences in goals are due to the fact that, compared with homemaker mothers, working mothers encourage children to be self-sufficient and independent at earlier ages (Hoffman, 2000). Daughters are less likely to display traditional feminine interests and characteristics and more often perceive the woman's role as involving freedom of choice, satisfaction, and competence—daughters themselves are career- and achievement-oriented, independent and assertive, and high in self-esteem (Hoffman, 2000). The sons of working mothers, in contrast to sons of full-time homemaker mothers, not only perceive women as more competent but view men as warmer and more expressive.

What are the long-term effects of maternal employment? Gottfried and colleagues (2002) found no relationship between maternal employment and children's development from infancy to the age of 12 and concluded that no sleeper effects were associated with mothers working outside the home. The children of both mothers who were full-time homemakers and mothers who worked outside the home were similar in cognitive, socioemotional, academic, motivational, and behavioral domains from infancy through adolescence. Research has shown that such factors as parental involvement and the quality of the home environment were clearly linked to children's development, regardless of mothers' occupations (Bradley et al., 2001; Parke & Buriel, 2006).

It appears that individual differences among mothers are more significant for children's development than a mother's status as employee outside the home or as a homemaker. Mothers who derive a sense of satisfaction and self-efficacy from their homemaking role, and working mothers who enjoy their employment, both show more positive relations with their husbands and with their children than unhappy homemakers who would like to be employed (Hoffman, 2000). However, mothers and fathers both display more negative feelings and behavior toward their children when their attitudes toward maternal employment and the wife's work status are not congruent (Hoffman, 2000).

Despite many predictions to the contrary, studies have indicated that with adequate alternative child care, maternal employment does not usually have detrimental effects on children. It is important, however, that in evaluating the effects of maternal employment we consider all relevant factors, such as the mother's reasons for working, her level of job satisfaction, the demands her employment may place on other family members, the attitudes of these family members toward her employment, and the quality of the substitute care and supervision provided for the children.

WORK STRESS AND CHILDREN'S ADJUSTMENT What determines how parental employment affects a child's development? It is not just whether one parent or the other works, the nature of the work situation determines the effects of parental employment on a child's development. As we have seen, maternal employment per se does not put children at risk. However, a parent's experience of stress on the job may take its toll on children, parents, and marriages (Crouter & Bumpus, 2001). Fathers who worked in a high-stress occupation, air traffic control, withdrew from their wives and were more irritable with their children after a stressful day (Repetti, 1989, 1996). Similarly, mothers were more likely to withdraw from their children after particularly stressful work days (Repetti & Wood, 1997). Finally, children of mothers who work nonstandard schedules (evening, night, or rotating shifts) have poor early cognitive and language development (Han, 2005). In sum, it is not merely working or not working that matters, but the conditions under which adults work that make a difference in children's lives.

SELF-CARE: THE CASE OF LATCHKEY CHILDREN The need for child care that we discussed earlier (Chapter 6) does not stop when children enter school, and it is a cause of concern for working parents. Over 2 million children care for themselves without the benefit of parental supervision: Approximately 20 percent of 6- to 12-year-olds are **latchkey children,** who must let themselves into their homes because one or both parents are at work elsewhere (Zigler & Finn-Stevenson, 1993; Urban Institute, 2000). Not surprisingly, self-care increases with age, and by adolescence many children are in self-care at least some of the time. What are the effects of unsupervised care? On the positive side, self-care places greater demands on children for responsibility and maturity (Belle, 1999). And some children appreciate the positive aspects of being left on their own.

latchkey children Children who must let themselves into their homes after school because a parent or both parents are working outside the home.

One reason some schoolchildren come home to empty houses—estimates of the numbers of latchkey children have run as high as 10 million—is the lack of sufficient child-care and after-school programs.

As one child noted, the best things about her unsupervised arrangement are "being able to come home. Being able to have unstructured time. Being able to relax after school. Having flexibility. Being able to decide last minute to play with another friend . . ." (Belle, 1999, p. 87). But there is a downside for children to being left on their own. Children who are left unsupervised are at higher risk for a variety of problems such as increased delinquency and antisocial behavior, poorer grades, heightened stress, and greater substance abuse (Belle, 1999). And the risks of leaving children unsupervised are not lost on parents. As one mother fretted: "It puts more pressure on me worrying about what she's doing in the afternoon. From 3 P.M. on I can't be totally relaxed. I'm thinking about whether she's home doing homework" (Belle, 1999, p. 87).

What helps reduce the risks associated with self-care? *Distal monitoring* in which parents check in by phone can be useful, as can devising clear rules and expectations about permitted activities, friends, and places (Belle, 1999). Perhaps the most helpful alternative is after-school care programs. Children who are enrolled in high-quality after-school programs during the elementary school years benefit in many ways. They have better grades, avoid drugs and delinquency, and have better relationships with their peers (Vandell & Shumow, 1999; NICHD Early Child Care Research Network, 2004a). And parents feel better too: "Justin's after-school program relieves me of the fear of him being caught on the streets unattended. He's playing with a selected group of kids. He's not . . . [strapped] to the T.V. I feel so comfortable with the program and teachers" (Belle, 1999, p. 88).

Just as we saw in the case of child care for younger children, quality is the key. Poorly supervised and disorganized after-school programs can be detrimental to children's development. In short, parents need to be careful to choose quality after-school care.

Marital Transitions

LifeMap CD

What do experts say about how parents can help their children cope with divorce? Find out by watching the "Children and Divorce" video in Chapter 11 of your CD.

We need to view divorce and remarriage not as discrete events but as steps in a transition that will modify the lives and development of parents and children. Children's experiences in earlier family situations will modify their response to this transition. The response of family members to divorce and to life in a single-parent family is generally a function of the quality of family life that preceded the separation and divorce. In like fashion, the response to remarriage will be shaped by experiences in the earlier marriage and the subsequent single-parent household. Both divorce and remarriage force a restructuring of the household and changes in family roles and relationships (Clarke-Stewart & Bretano, 2005; Hetherington & Kelly, 2002).

Although divorce is sometimes a positive solution to destructive family functioning, for many family members the transition period following separation and divorce is highly stressful. During the first year after a divorce, parents' feelings of distress and unhappiness, troubled parent-child relationships, and children's social and emotional adjustment actually get worse (Hetherington & Stanley-Hagen, 2002). In the second year, however, when families are adapting to their new single-head-of-household status, many parents experience a dramatic improvement in their sense of personal well-being, interpersonal functioning, and family relations. In the long run, children in stable, well-functioning single-parent households are better adjusted than children in conflict-ridden nuclear families.

Some researchers have suggested that when parents delay divorcing—sometimes in the hope of protecting their children—those children show behavior problems long before the divorce finally takes place. Moreover, these problems may be greater than those of children whose parents have some difficulties but remain in their marriage (Cherlin et al., 1991; Clarke-Stewart, Vandell, McCartney, Owen, & Booth, 2000). It is possible that children respond adversely to the acrimony and conflict in

a stressed marriage, particularly when it is suppressed; or behavior problems in children may exacerbate difficulties in a troubled marriage and help to precipitate a divorce.

DIVORCE AND THE SINGLE-PARENT HOUSEHOLD   What are the most important effects of divorce on children? When divorce leads, as it usually does, to children living in a single-parent household, how does the family's lifestyle and functioning differ? What kinds of stresses are single-parent households more likely than nuclear families to encounter? Can a single parent cope with all that two parents have handled up to now? Does the single parent have time to be a parent?

When divorced parents and their children do not experience additional stresses following divorce, most are coping reasonably well by the second or third year after a divorce. However, one-parent mother-headed households are at increased risk of encountering multiple stresses that make it difficult to raise children successfully, and, in fact, a period of diminished parenting often follows divorce (Hetherington & Stanley-Hagan, 2002). Custodial mothers may become self-involved, erratic, uncommunicative, nonsupportive, and inconsistently punitive in dealing with their children. They may also fail to control and monitor their children's behavior adequately. Not uncommonly, children reciprocate in the immediate aftermath of divorce by being demanding, noncompliant, and aggressive or by whining and being overly dependent. Not a very winning combination! Divorced mothers and sons are particularly likely to engage in escalating, mutually coercive exchanges. Some desperate divorced mothers have described their relationships with their children right after a divorce as "declared war," a "struggle for survival," "the old Chinese water torture," or "like getting bitten to death by ducks." Although inept parenting is most marked in the first year following divorce—parenting improves markedly in the second year—problematic parenting is more likely to be sustained with sons—especially temperamentally difficult sons—than with daughters. Divorced mothers and their daughters are likely eventually to form exceptionally close relationships, although mothers may have to weather their daughters' acting-out behavior in adolescence (Hetherington & Clingempeel, 1992; Hetherington & Kelly, 2002). Despite the foregoing, Wolchick and colleagues (2000) found that when divorced mothers are high in warmth and consistent in their discipline, 8- to 15-year-olds had fewer adjustment problems than their peers in less warm and consistent families.

Although we have emphasized the increasing salience of the custodial parent in the child's development, noncustodial parents can continue to play a significant role in their children's development. When divorced parents agree on childrearing methods and maintain a reasonably friendly attitude toward each other, frequent visits between the children and the noncustodial parent may be associated with positive adjustment and self-control in the children. When the mother has custody, such visits are particularly helpful for sons. When there is continued conflict between parents, however, especially conflict where the child feels caught in the middle or when the parent is a nonauthoritative parent or is poorly adjusted, frequent contact between the noncustodial parent and the child may be associated with disruptions in the child's behavior (Buchanan, Maccoby, & Dornbusch, 1992a; Buchanan & Heiges, 2001). Clearly, what counts is the quality of the contact with a noncustodial parent and the exposure of the child to conflict and stress.

FAMILY INTERACTION IN REMARRIED FAMILIES Family members' experience in their original family setting greatly affects their response to remarriage. For divorced women, remarriage is the most common route out of poverty, and a new partner may give a custodial mother not only economic but emotional support as well as help in childrearing.

Children sometimes resist the arrival of a stepparent, creating stress in the new marital relationship. Sons, who have often been involved in coercive relationships with their custodial mothers, may have little to lose and much to gain from a relationship with a caring stepfather. Daughters, on the other hand, may feel the intrusion of stepfathers into their close relationships with their mothers as more threatening and disruptive. Among preadolescent children, divorce seems to have more adverse consequences for boys, and remarriage seems to be more difficult for girls; in adolescence, however, such gender differences are rarely found (Cherlin et al., 1991; Hetherington & Clingempeel, 1992; Hetherington & Stanley-Hagen, 2002).

In general, neither stepmothers nor stepfathers take as active a role in parenting as biological parents (Clarke-Stewart & Bretano, 2005). Even after they've been in the family for two years, stepfathers are likely to exhibit an uninvolved parenting style. Indeed, many stepfathers are rather like polite strangers with their stepchildren, hesitating to become involved in controlling or disciplining them. Biological fathers are more likely to praise children for good behavior, to be affectionate and interested in their children's activities, to set limits, and to criticize children for undesirable behavior—for not cleaning up their rooms, not getting their homework done, or fighting with a younger sibling. Stepmothers, who walk into the maternal role, are forced to take a more active role in discipline than are stepfathers (Cherlin & Furstenberg, 1994). This may in part explain the finding that children are more resistant and have poorer adjustment in stepmother families (Cherlin & Furstenberg, 1994; Hetherington, Bridges, & Insabella, 1998). In addition, a child's age at the time of a parent's remarriage will affect both the child's attitude toward the new marriage and the likelihood that she will develop any kind of problem behavior. Adolescents have a particularly difficult time accepting a parent's remarriage (Hetherington, 1991a; Hetherington & Stanley-Hagen, 2002).

Although we have been focusing on the effects of divorce and remarriage on parent-child relations, sibling relations also are often disrupted. More antagonistic, nonsupportive relations are found among siblings in divorced and remarried families than among those in nondivorced families (Conger & Conger, 1996; Dunn & Davies, 2000; Hetherington et al., 1998). These adverse effects are most marked for male siblings, whereas some pairs of female siblings serve as mutual supports in coping with their parents' marital transitions.

CHILDREN IN DIVORCED AND REMARRIED FAMILIES Over time, most boys and girls adjust reasonably well to their parents' marital transitions. Exhibiting remarkable resiliency, some children actually become stronger through coping with divorce and remarriage. In fact, only about 25 percent have long-term problems (Hetherington & Kelly, 2002). Authoritative parenting is associated with more positive adjustment in children in divorced and remarried families, just as it is in nondivorced families. If divorce reduces stress and conflict and leads to better functioning on the part of the custodial parent, or if the child's loss of an uninvolved or incompetent father eventually results in the acquisition of a more accessible, responsive father figure, the child often benefits in the long run from divorce and remarriage. Preadolescent boys in particular may benefit from a close, caring relationship with a stepfather.

The most commonly reported sustained problem behaviors found in children of divorced and remarried families are aggressive, noncompliant, antisocial behavior; a decline in prosocial behaviors; and disruptions in peer relations (Clarke-Stewart & Bretano, 2005; Hetherington et al., 1998). Adolescence seems to trigger behavior problems in both boys and girls in divorced and remarried families, even in some who have previously been functioning well. Depression is common, and substance abuse and precocious sexual activity are found in both boys and girls in mother-headed one-parent families (Hetherington & Clingempeel, 1992). Problems in academic achievement, school adjustment, and school dropout are greater for boys than for girls in divorced families.

As children mature, girls continue to do somewhat better than boys. Following up on an initial study, Hetherington (1989) found that six years after divorce and in families in which the mother was still single, girls who were relatively well adjusted after two years remained so. These girls had more responsibility and more power within the family and had close relationships with their mothers. Among girls, adjustment problems are more evident at the onset of adolescence. During the teen years, girls of divorce may show increased conflict with their mothers, increased noncompliance, antisocial behavior, emotional disturbance, loss in self-esteem, and problems in heterosexual relations and sexual behavior (Chase-Lansdale & Hetherington, 1990; Hetherington, 1998). The risk of being a teenage mother increases three times as a result of divorce, going from 11 percent in intact families to 33 percent in divorced families. Hetherington also found that these young women were more likely to have married at a young age, to have been pregnant before marriage, and to have selected husbands who were more psychologically unstable and less educated and economically secure than women in intact or widowed families (Hetherington, 1998). Survey studies of nationally representative samples confirm the increased difficulties experienced in heterosexual relationships by young women whose parents divorce (Cherlin, 1996). Adult women from divorced families were more likely than those from nondivorced families to have higher rates of divorce themselves (Hetherington, 1987).

Boys continue to experience problems after a divorce. Hetherington (1993) found that divorced mothers spent less time with their sons than mothers in nondivorced families. Mothers continued to be ineffective in their control efforts and to engage in coercive interactions with their sons. Monitoring of boys' activities was lower in divorced nonremarried households, and the boys engaged in more antisocial behavior and spent more time away from home with peers.

Figure 11-10

Education and one-parent families

As measured in four separate studies, the risk of dropping out of high school was nearly twice as high for children living in one-parent families (including stepfamilies) as for those living with two parents.

Source: From *Growing Up with a Single Parent* by Sara McLanahan and Gary Sandefur. Cambridge, MA: Harvard University Press, 1994, p. 41.

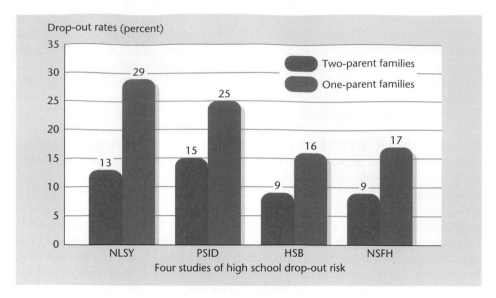

Note: NLSY = National Longitudinal Survey of Youth; PSID = Panel Study of Income Dynamics; HSB = High School and Beyond Study; NSFH = National Survey of Families and Households.

What are the long-term effects of divorce and remarriage on a family's children? National survey studies suggest that divorce is related to several negative outcomes (Amato, 2000, 2001; McLanahan & Sandefur, 1994). The risk of dropping out of high school was nearly twice as high for children of divorced families as it was for children in intact families (Figure 11-10), and failing to finish school may reduce future employment and educational opportunities.

Perhaps the most dramatic evidence of the long-term effects of divorce comes from a study of the predictors of longevity (Freidman et al., 1995). In a follow-up investigation of a group of gifted children originally studied by Lewis Terman in the 1920s, individuals who experienced parental divorce during childhood were likely to die sooner than those whose parents stayed married. Although these individuals were more likely themselves to divorce as adults, even after taking this into account, parental divorce was still a predictor of premature death. Clearly divorce has long-term consequences, although the mechanisms by which divorce alters longevity are still not well understood.

JOINT CUSTODY   In view of the changes that increasing maternal employment has brought about, especially the realization that fathers not only can be highly competent caregivers but also can derive pleasure from being with their children, it is not surprising that the traditional doctrine of sole custody has been reexamined. Perhaps children and ex-spouses would all benefit if joint custody was always an option in divorce cases involving children: "At its best, joint custody presents the possibility that each family member can 'win' in post-divorce life" (Thompson, 1994, p. 17). Neither mother nor father is identified as a better or worse parent, and mothers and fathers each win a significant future role in the lives of their children. Perhaps even more important, the children win.

Joint custody takes two main forms. In **joint legal custody,** both mother and father retain and share responsibility for decisions concerning their children's lives, but the children usually reside with one parent. Under a **joint physical custody** arrangement, the children live with each parent for certain periods throughout the year. Although the length and timing of these periods vary, it is expected that children will have physical access to both parents on a regular basis. To examine the impact of joint custody on children, Maccoby and Mnookin (1992) followed 1,100 families for three and a half years, beginning with each married couple's separation, and found that nearly

joint legal custody A form of child custody in which both parents retain and share responsibility for decisions regarding the child's life, although the child usually resides with one parent.

joint physical custody As in *joint legal custody,* parents make decisions together regarding their child's life, but they also share physical custody, so that the child lives with each parent for a portion of the year.

80 percent of the families had joint legal custody. Mothers received sole physical custody in more than 67 percent of the cases, whereas fathers received sole physical custody less than 10 percent of the time. Even when joint physical custody was the legal decision, only about half of the children actually lived in dual residence arrangements, and a third lived with their mothers. Overall, more than two-thirds of the families opted for a mother residence arrangement and continued with this residence plan for the period of the study. However, boys were more likely to live with their fathers or in dual residence than girls, who more often lived with their mothers. Moreover, older children were more likely to live with their fathers and 3- to 8-year-old children to live in dual residence arrangements. Finally, arrangements were not static; many children changed their residential arrangements over the course of the study. More than one-quarter (28%) of the children changed houses during the three and a half years of the study.

Joint custody works best when conflict between parents decreases and when children don't "feel caught" in the middle (e.g., as a messenger) between warring parents (Buchanan, Maccoby, & Dornbusch, 1996). Older adolescents and girls were more likely to feel caught in the between-parent squeeze. Adolescents with stronger feelings of "being caught" were more likely to experience depression and anxiety and to engage in more deviant behavior (e.g., smoking, drug use, fighting, cheating, stealing) than adolescents who experienced more interparental cooperation (Buchanan & Heiges, 2001).

The degree of parental conflict, rather than the custody arrangement itself, seems to be the best predictor of children's adjustment (Buchanan & Heiges, 2001; Goodman, Emery, & Haugaard, 1998). Joint custody is clearly not a panacea for divorced families or for divorced fathers in particular. Fathers' influence and contact with their children seems less governed by custody arrangements than by other factors, such as geographic distance and relationship with the ex-spouse. In the long run, the advantage of joint custody may be its "symbolic value to parents and children" (Emery, 1988): It may offer a sign to fathers that they retain some rights and obligations as a parent and a message to their children that their fathers are still significant figures in their lives. At the same time, it is evident that joint custody is not a problem-free solution, especially if interparental conflict continues after divorce (Buchanan & Heiges, 2001). Evaluations are needed of the long-term impact of differing types of custody arrangements on children as well as on their parents.

PARENTING AFTER THIRTY   People are not only marrying later today than in earlier times (three or four years later than they did in the 1950s) but they are also becoming first-time parents at later ages. Although there may be many reasons for later parenthood, important factors are doubtless widespread maternal employment, more flexibility in gender roles for both men and women, and greater availability of support services such as child care. In addition, by the time a couple are in their thirties, they have usually completed their educations and are fairly well established in their careers.

Delaying the decision to become parents sometimes means that a couple will have difficulty in conceiving (Henig, 2004; Paulson & Sachs, 1999), and in fact, older prospective parents are major consumers of the new reproductive technologies (see Box 2.2, Chapter 2). As Hahn and DePietro (2001) note, "Research on the effects of reproductive technologies has been fueled by the speculation that the emotional distress associated with previous infertility and the unusual form of transition to parenthood may influence a [formerly] infertile couple's relationship, their quality of parenting and, ultimately, the parent-child relationship" (p. 37). Are these concerns warranted?

Research to date suggests that children born via the technique of donor insemination, for example, function as well as children born in the usual manner (Golombok, 2002; Patterson, 2002). And recent study of the technique of surrogacy suggests not only that the offspring of surrogate mothers develop well but also that these children may benefit from parent-child relationships that are even more positive than many that obtain in naturally conceived families. In part, this may be due to the eagerness of couples who must make extraordinary efforts to become parents (Golombok, Murray, Jadva, MacCallum, & Lycett, 2004).

Both mothers and fathers who delay parenting seem to interact differently with their infants. Mothers may not only feel more responsibility in caretaking but also enjoy it more and express more positive affect with their infants (Ragozin, Bashman, Crnic, Greenberg, & Robinson, 1982). In addition, older mothers tend to spend more social time with their babies and to be more successful in eliciting vocal and imitative responses from them, perhaps because these mothers have gained more social and cognitive teaching skills.

The older father, with more flexibility and freedom in balancing the demands of work and family, is three times as likely as a younger father to have regular responsibility for some part of a preschool child's daily care (Daniels & Weingarten, 1988). Moreover, the older father may be generally more involved in the parental role and may experience more positive affect associated with childrearing (Cooney, Pedersen, Indelicato, & Palkovitz, 1993; NICHD Early Child Care Research Network, 2000b). The fact that younger fathers tend to engage in more strenuous physical play with their children and older fathers to use more cognitive mechanisms in their play may reflect a lessening of physical energy rather than a less stereotypical view of men's and women's roles in parenting (Neville & Parke, 1997; Parke & Neville, 1995).

As family systems theory would predict, greater participation by fathers in caring for and playing with their children may help facilitate the more enjoyable and productive relations that older mothers enjoy with their children. Clearly, the timing of first parenthood is a powerful organizer of both maternal and paternal roles. Future investigations of marital and parenting interaction patterns need to consider timing as well as other factors.

Adoption: Another Route to Parenthood

Couples choose adoption for many reasons: Some are unable to conceive a child; some are older and thus at risk for some of the problems we discussed in Chapter 2; others may wish to avoid a family-related genetic disorder. In the United States, 2 to 4 percent of children are adopted (Stolley, 1993). Twenty or thirty years ago, people commonly adopted infants born in the United States. Today, however, because contraceptive methods are more effective, abortion is more available, and young unwed mothers often keep their babies, couples are more likely to find their little adoptees in other countries and/or among the numbers of developmentally at-risk infants and children in the United States. Currently, babies are most often adopted from China, Russia, Guatemala, and South Korea. In 1999, over 16,000 foreign-born children were adopted into the United States (National Adoption Information Clearinghouse, 2000).

How do adopted children fare in terms of their development? There are two perspectives on this issue. According to one view, adoption is a protective measure if it removes an infant or child from adverse social conditions such as long-term foster care or institutional environments such as orphanages. Children who are able to escape these poor rearing environments through adoption have better developmental outcomes than children who remain in deprived and nonstimulating environments (Rutter, 2002a, 2002b). The success of adoption as an intervention, however, depends on a variety of factors, perhaps most importantly, on the age of the adopted child. Children who are adopted at any early age out of adverse circumstances fare better than those who remain for longer periods in such circumstances. For example, Rutter and colleagues (2001a) found that infants adopted from the infamous Romanian orphanages before they were 6 months old were similar to British adoptees who had not suffered early deprivation. This suggests that a normal family environment can help adopted children catch up and develop normally. On the other hand, many adopted children have not necessarily suffered the extreme adversity that characterized institutionalized Romanian infants. And in general, adopted children are at greater risk for psychological problems, including hyperactivity, externalizing behavior, academic problems, and learning disabilities (Brodzinsky & Pinderhughes, 2002).

Several factors affect an adopted child's relative risk for developmental problems: being a boy; being older at the time of placement; and having had more adverse prior experiences, such as multiple placements in foster care or being abused or neglected, are all linked with poorer adjustment. At the same time, the vast majority of adoptees fall within the range of normal development, and the differences between the progress of adopted and biological children are often small. For most adopted children and for most couples who adopt, the benefits clearly outweigh the risks.

Gay and Lesbian Parents

Another recent change in the American family is the greater number of lesbian and gay parents. Although we have only estimates at the moment, most authorities suggest that there are somewhere between 1 and 5 million lesbian mothers and between 1 and 3 million gay fathers and that gay or lesbian parents are rearing between 6 and 14 million children (Patterson, 2002).

Homosexual families are diverse. The largest group of children with gay or lesbian parents are children who were born to one of the homosexual partners before they established their relationship, in the context of a heterosexual relationship or marriage. Within this group there are two primary variations: When one of a child's biological parents declares a same-gender sexual preference and the couple divorce, the gay or lesbian parent may then form a new, homosexual relationship in which these partners together care for the child. In another arrangement, a gay or a lesbian couple who do not have children from previous relationships may choose to become parents. One partner in a lesbian relationship may choose to bear a child through donor insemination. Or either gay or lesbian couples may adopt children.

Research suggests that heterosexual mothers and lesbian mothers who have divorced their heterosexual partners differ little in terms of self-concept, general happiness, overall adjustment, and presence of psychiatric problems (Patterson, 2002). We know less about divorced gay fathers because only a small minority of these men are granted custody of their children or live with them (Patterson, 2004). Most of our knowledge of gay and lesbian parenting comes from studies of couples who, after establishing their relationship, chose to become parents (Patterson, 2002). Research that compared these couples' households with heterosexual households found that both gay and lesbian couples tended to share household duties more equally (McPherson, 1993; Solomon, Rothbaum, & Balsam, 2004). Among lesbian partners, biological mothers appeared to be more involved in child care and nonbiological mothers to spend longer hours in paid employment (Figure 11-11; Patterson, 1995a). At the same time, children in lesbian families, like those in heterosexual families, were likely to be better adjusted when both partners shared child care more or less equally, and lesbian parents were also likely to be more satisfied (Patterson, 1995a).

What about the children? According to Patterson (2002), the evidence suggests that children of lesbian mothers are developing in a normal fashion. We have no evidence that these children have any greater emotional or social problems—including peer relationships and relationships with adults—than other children, nor is there any appreciable evidence of altered gender roles among lesbian parents' children (see also Chapter 13). In similar fashion, the great majority of gay fathers' children grow up to

Figure 11-11

Lesbian mothers and paid employment

Among lesbian parents, biological mothers spent less time in paid employment (only 40% worked a full week) and more time in child care (a), whereas nearly three-quarters of nonbiological mothers were engaged in full-time employment (b).

Source: Adapted from Patterson, 1995a.

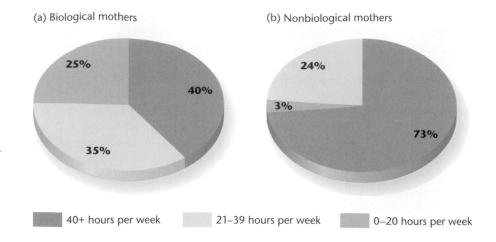

(a) Biological mothers

25%
40%
35%

(b) Nonbiological mothers

24%
3%
73%

■ 40+ hours per week   ■ 21–39 hours per week   ■ 0–20 hours per week

be heterosexual adults. There is no evidence that these children are victims of sexual abuse nor that they are at any significant disadvantage in comparison with children of heterosexual fathers. Moreover, although gay fathers undoubtedly face prejudice and discrimination, children have described their relationships with gay fathers as warm and supportive (Patterson 2004).

Finally, we need to monitor the impact on same-sex couples of the ongoing legal and political discussion about same-sex marriage and the opportunities for these couples to adopt children. The available evidence suggests that greater acceptance of gay and lesbian parents will be beneficial for the children reared in these households.

Teen Pregnancy: Children Having Children

Why do teenagers have babies out of wedlock? The immediate causes include the facts that young people among all major cultural groups in the United States are

Lesbian partners who choose to become parents tend to share childrearing and home-making tasks more equally than heterosexual couples.

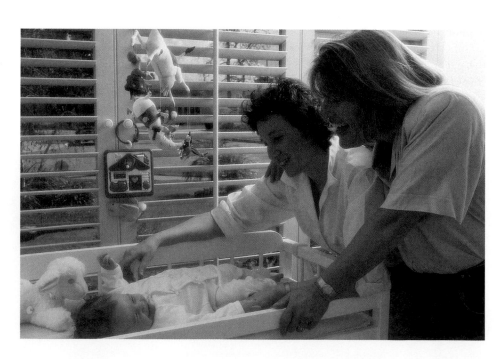

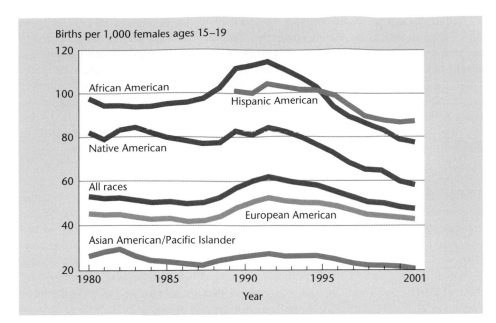

Figure 11-12

Teen birth rates, 1980–2001
Among U.S. black teens, birth rates peaked in the early 1990s but have been declining fairly steadily since that time. And birth rates for other teen groups have also been declining over the last decade or so. However, the United States continues to have the highest rates of teen pregnancy and births in the industrialized countries of the Western world.

Source: Children's Defense Fund, 2004.

initiating sexual behavior earlier and that people generally are marrying later. The underlying causes are complicated and difficult to combat. Poverty, being socially and economically disadvantaged, having models (parents and other adults) who also have children out of wedlock, and growing up too soon all play particularly important roles in early teen pregnancy (Moore & Brooks-Gunn, 2002). Early sexual activity leads not just to unplanned pregnancies but also to declining school achievement and interest and to sexually transmitted diseases (STDs). Teenagers have the highest STD rates of any age group and one-fifth of all AIDS cases start in adolescence (Brody, 1998; Tinsley et al., 2004).

How many teen pregnancies are there in a year? As Figure 11-12 shows, birth rates for teenagers are high, especially for some non-white groups. However, birth rates for teens have declined in recent years; since 1991, rates for white teens have dropped 14 percent and for Latino teens 12 percent and, most dramatically, by 26 percent for African American teens (Children's Defense Fund, 2004). Minority U.S. teens are one and a half to two times as likely as European teens to bear children, and all together, American teenagers have almost twice as many babies as United Kingdom adolescents, more than four times as many babies as teens in France, and more than eight times as many babies as are born to teenagers in Japan (Singh & Darroch, 2000). Although almost a quarter of teenage mothers are married, and another third have fairly stable relationships with the fathers of their babies, more than half face personal, economic, and social problems that make it very difficult for them to support and care for their children (Wakchlag et al., 2001). Thus, these half million babies have poor prospects, largely because of the economic constraints most teen mothers confront, and the younger the mother the greater the risk:

> During the preschool years, signs of delays in cognitive development begin to emerge and tend to grow more evident as the children age. Preschool children of teen mothers also tend to display higher levels of aggression and less ability to control impulsive behavior. By adolescence, children of teen mothers have, on the whole, higher rates of grade failure and more delinquency. They also become sexually active earlier [and have] a greater likelihood of pregnancy before age 20. (Children's Defense Fund, 1998, p. 98)

According to one recent estimate, the sons of teen mothers are 13 percent more likely than others to be incarcerated, and daughters are 22 percent more likely to become teen mothers themselves (Children's Defense Fund, 2004). Even the younger sisters of teenage mothers can be affected by the early arrival of a nephew or niece. Often they must take time away from schoolwork to help care for the child, and they are at increased risk for drug and alcohol use and for becoming pregnant themselves (East & Jacobsen, 2001). Teen parents and their children pay huge prices, and society pays in lost productivity and in the need to provide public care and services for disadvantaged children.

TEEN PARENTING AND THE FATHER'S ROLE   Largely because of personal problems and a lack of resources, teenage parents are thought to be less competent caregivers (Moore & Brooks-Gunn, 2002). Teenage mothers may be less warm and nurturing than older mothers and less likely to stimulate their babies verbally and cognitively, reading to them less and being less involved in their school activities. Young unwed mothers may also have lower educational aspirations for their children, and there is some suggestion that these mothers may more often engage in aggressive behavior with their children and abuse or neglect them (Moore & Brooks-Gunn, 2002).

Adolescent males are more likely to become teenage fathers if they are poor, substance abusers, delinquent, and prone to behavior problems (Moore & Florsheim, 2001). Although society tends to fault teenage fathers for their failure to support their babies and the babies' mothers, some but not all young men see their children regularly and provide help with caregiving (Coley & Chase-Lansdale, 1998). Moreover, two-thirds of European American fathers and nearly as many Latino fathers were found to marry the mothers of their babies (Sullivan, 1993). Among the African American fathers, only 23 percent married, but job opportunities were least favorable for these young men. According to Cherlin (1996), male partners in unwed teenage pregnancy and parenting contribute little support for several reasons. First, most teenage boys lack the earning power to help much; second, the mothers' parents may try to keep the young father out, assuming that his support is unlikely anyway; third, some teen fathers simply don't want the responsibility. Some teenage fathers do support their children, but the determinants of father involvement are still unclear.

PREVENTION AND INTERVENTION   Teenagers whose parents are not only educated and reasonably comfortable financially but also warm and responsive to their children have a better chance at avoiding teen pregnancy (Moore & Brooks-Gunn, 2002). A family's active involvement with religious beliefs and practices also is a protective factor that can help avoid early sexual activity and childbearing among the children. The use of contraceptives by teenagers who have initiated sexual activity can of course prevent pregnancy as well as serious and life-threatening sexual diseases. According to Cherlin (1996), although the rate at which teenagers use contraceptives has been increasing, so far this rate of increased protection has just managed to keep up with the increase in numbers of young people who are sexually active.

Once an unwed teen has become a parent, what are her options for avoiding some of the negative effects of early parenthood? Marriage is one of the most important routes out of poverty, largely because of the husband's income, but marriage is also a difficult route. The majority of marriages entered into by the teenage mothers that Cherlin (1996) studied had ended by the time he interviewed the women again 22 years later. One factor in the failure of such marriages may be immaturity of the young people and their inability to judge what makes for a good life partner.

According to Hetherington (1998), getting a good education and limiting future births are other important ways for a teenage mother to improve her lot. In addition, when the children of unwed mothers have good-quality relationships with their fathers, they tend to achieve higher educational levels and to be less subject to depression and less likely to be imprisoned for misbehaviors or crimes (Hetherington, 1998). Particularly for African American children, having a stepfather join the family seems to have positive effects, increasing the likelihood that the children will be successful in life.

The negative impact of the conditions under which teenage mothers and their children live is greater for the children than for the mothers. This may be because the children have always lived under these conditions, whereas some of the mothers at least may have known better. In any event, evidence indicates that if the mother's situation changes for the better, and particularly if she moves off welfare, becomes economically independent, acquires more education, or enters a stable marriage before her child becomes an adolescent, the child's adjustment and academic performance may be enhanced (Moore & Brooks-Gunn, 2002).

CHILD ABUSE WITHIN THE FAMILY

Although it is difficult to obtain precise figures on how many children in the United States suffer from maltreatment, it is estimated that every year between 1 and 3 million children are physically or psychologically abused and that the majority of these children are abused by family members (Children's Defense Fund, 2004; National Committee to Prevent Child Abuse, 1997). In 2002, Child Protective Services received reports of approximately 3 million cases of child abuse, about 31 percent of which were substantiated (Children's Defense Fund, 2004; Golden, 2000; Goodman et al., 1998). Of these children, nearly 20 percent were infants or toddlers (Children's Defense Fund, 1997). About 60 percent of the children who were maltreated suffered neglect, 20 percent suffered physical abuse, 10 percent suffered sexual abuse, and the rest multiple kinds of abusive behavior (Children's Defense Fund, 2004). Because many instances of child abuse are not even reported or are discovered only after abuse has continued for a long time or the child is dead, these figures are conservative. Children are subjected to verbal abuse; they are starved, beaten, burned, cut, chained, isolated, left to lie filthy and in their own excrement, or sexually molested, and not a small number are murdered. In 2002 in the United States, more than 1,400 children died as a result of child abuse—almost four children every day (Children's Defense Fund, 2004).

What can possibly lead to this inhuman treatment of children? Some of the contributing risk factors are characteristics of parents and their abused children, some are ecological factors such as the quality of the neighborhood and available support systems, and still others are life experiences and stresses that family members encounter. Abuse is unlikely to occur when only one risk factor is present. It is the presence of multiple risk factors and of interaction among them that often leads to abuse, especially when the family and the child have few protective factors such as a warm and caring marital relationship, a supportive social network, accessible community resources, high intelligence, education, good health, and adaptability (Azar, 2002; Cicchetti & Toth, 2006). Many African Americans and Native Americans still live under such stressful conditions—poverty, substandard housing, lack of educational opportunities, and poor health—that it is in these groups that we find the most cases of child maltreatment. (See Figure 11-13.) Asians and European Americans—who tend not to live in circumstances of this sort—have many fewer cases of child abuse. As we will see, ethnic differences of these kinds and other stress-related factors, such as single parenthood, probably account for these variations among U.S. subcultures.

Figure 11-13

Child abuse in different U.S. ethnic and racial groups
Child abuse is more common in some ethnic groups than others. At present, the families in whom children are most commonly mistreated tend to be African and Native American; people in these groups often find it difficult to obtain good jobs, typically receive low wages, and often live in areas where delinquency and crime are more common.

Source: Adapted from U.S. Department of Health and Human Services, 2001.

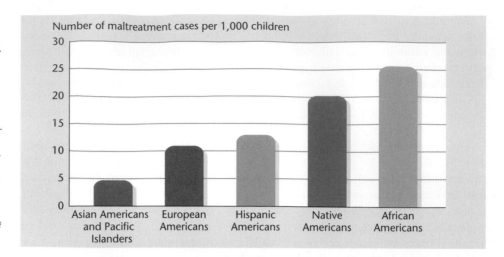

Abused Children and Their Parents

Most students reading this book probably think that no one they know would ever abuse a child or that only someone who is really mentally ill would inflict grievous physical harm on defenseless children. However, although chronic maltreatment is most likely to occur in economically deprived, poorly educated families, child abusers are found in all social classes and all religious, racial, and ethnic groups. In addition, there is little evidence that severe mental illness or specific personality traits consistently distinguish abusive from nonabusive parents. Shocking as it may seem, mothers are frequently the persons who abuse children. Why might this be? For one thing, some mothers feel locked into a stressful family situation, and mothers generally spend a good deal more time with a child than do other family members (Azar, 2002; Cicchetti & Toth, 2006).

Certain characteristics of the child and family also are associated with maltreatment of children. Child physical abuse is more likely to occur in large families and to children under the age of 3. A higher-than-normal incidence of birth anomalies, physical and intellectual deviations, irritability, negativism, and other behaviors that parents often find exasperating are seen in many of these children. **Sexual abuse** occurs from infancy through adolescence; for females, the peak onset occurs between 7 and 8 years of age, and for boys, the peak onset is before puberty. Female children are four times more likely to be victims of sexual abuse than male children (Azar, 2002; Trickett & Putnam, 1998).

Two factors most commonly associated with abusive behavior by parents are a distressed, often sexually unsatisfying marriage and the abuse of one or both marital partners by his or her own parents. Both competent, loving parenting and incompetent, abusive parenting may to some extent be transmitted across generations (Azar, 2002). This does not mean that young parents are locked into their own parents' style of parenting. Only about a third of parents who were abused when they were young abuse their own children (Cicchetti & Toth, 2006). Mothers who break this intergenerational cycle are more likely to have had a warm, caring adult in their background, to have established a close marital relationship, and at some time to have received therapy (Egeland, Jacobvitz, & Sroufe, 1988).

Parents in these families often have conflicts with each other and are socially isolated (Belsky, 1993). They seem to have fewer friends, relatives, or neighbors to whom they can turn in times of stress. The isolation may contribute, in part, to the fact that these parents frequently do not seem to recognize the seriousness of their behavior and blame the child rather than themselves for what is occurring.

sexual abuse Inappropriate sexual activity between an adult and a child for the perpetrator's pleasure or benefit; the abuse may be direct (sexual contact of any type) or indirect (exposing a child to pornography or to the live exhibition of body parts or sexual acts).

Table 11-3

Words can hurt, too
Source: Based on Schaefer, 1997.

Category of Verbal Abuse	Example
1. Rejection or withdrawal of love	"Nobody could love you."
2. Verbal put-downs	"You dummy."
3. Demands for perfection	"How come you came in second?"
4. Negative predictions	"You're never going to amount to anything."
5. Negative comparison	"Why can't you be like your sister?"
6. Scapegoating	"You're the reason your mother and I are getting a divorce."
7. Shaming	"Look, everybody, at what a baby Tom is."
8. Cursing or swearing	"Go to hell."
9. Threats	"I'm going to kill you."
10. Inducing guilt	"How could you do that after all I've done for you?"

In addition, abusive parents are likely to have unrealistic beliefs about parent-child relationships and to respond less appropriately to their children's behavior than do nonabusive parents. They often expect their children to perform in a manner far beyond what is normal for their stage of development or to exhibit levels of independence and self-control that are unlikely in children of their ages (Azar, 2002).

Physical violence does not suddenly emerge in usually well-controlled parents. Child abuse is preceded by an escalating cycle of other forms of verbal and physical aggression (Straus & Donnelly, 1994). As compared with nonabusive mothers, abusive mothers show fewer positive behaviors toward their children and more severe negative behaviors, such as threatening commands, strong criticism, and physical punishment (Cicchetti & Toth, 2006). In addition, the behavior of abusive parents is unpredictable and less contingent on the type of behavior the child actually exhibits (Mash, Johnston, & Kovitz, 1983). A mother's response may not distinguish between a tantrum and a task well done. This failure of maltreating mothers to discriminate between desirable and undesirable children's behavior is also reflected in physiological measures. Abusive mothers, in contrast to nonabusive ones, show a similar pattern of autonomic arousal in response to either a smiling or a crying baby (Frodi & Lamb, 1980). They seem to be experiencing both the crying baby and the pleasant, happy baby as emotionally aversive. We have spoken earlier of the importance of parents' accurately reading and responding to children's cues. This distorted perception of the child's behavior must greatly increase the stress and confusion in already disturbed parent-child relationships. Although abusive parents usually use verbal abuse along with physical forms of maltreatment, even verbal abuse alone can be devastating to a child. In an effort to define what constitutes such abuse, Schaefer (1997) asked mental health professionals and parents to rate categories of verbal abuse that abusing parents had heaped on their children. Table 11-3 shows the 10 categories of abuse that the participants rated "never acceptable."

The Ecology of Child Abuse

Recognizing that individuals and families do not operate in a social vacuum but are embedded in a variety of important social contexts outside the family can improve our understanding of child abuse (Azar, 2002; Cicchetti & Toth, 2006). This level of analysis—Bronfenbrenner's exosystem—includes neighborhoods and communities as well as schools, workplaces, peer groups, and religious institutions. Research has shown that the social support and guidance that these contexts provide can alter parental attitudes, knowledge, and childrearing practices, which in turn can modify the likelihood of abuse.

First, poverty makes a difference. Although violence against children occurs in all social classes, it is greater in poor families (Duncan & Brooks-Gunn, 2000). Several reasons have been suggested: Among them are the stressors associated with being poor, the greater number of single-parent families who live in poverty, the violence that often pervades poor neighborhoods, and limited access to social services. Although physical abuse and neglect both have been linked with poverty, sexual abuse has not. In fact, according to some experts, sexual abuse appears to be more common in middle-class families.

Unemployment is related to rates of child abuse as well as to poverty. Steinberg, Catalano, and Dooley (1981) found that occurrences of child abuse followed a period of high job loss. Fathers are especially likely to be affected by losing their jobs. Stress, frustration, and increased contact between parents and children may all contribute to the link between job loss and child abuse.

Neighborhoods matter, and neighborhoods differ considerably in abuse rates, even after holding poverty level constant. Some neighborhoods serve a protective or buffering function against abuse, whereas others seem to exacerbate or increase the family's risk for abuse. Protective or low-risk neighborhoods have more social resources, and the families tend to use these resources—friends, neighbors, and relatives, as well as community centers—for advice, guidance, and physical and financial assistance in a balanced and reciprocal fashion. High-risk neighborhoods, on the other hand, are less friendly places; people rely on each other for guidance and support less often and tend to exploit each other more when they do exchange goods and services. Such neighborhoods are physically run down, they experience a high degree of transient behavior, people moving in and out frequently, and they are dangerous (Leventhal & Brooks-Gunn, 2000; Steinberg et al., 1995). And child abuse rates—even after controlling for race and poverty levels—are higher in the high-risk neighborhoods (Garbarino & Sherman, 1980).

Families are embedded not just in communities, but also in a set of cultural and societal contexts that shape their values, attitudes, and practices. Broad cultural changes in American society may play a role in the emergence of abusive patterns. For example, increased divorce rates, increased mobility, limited availability of day care, lack of medical coverage, and lack of paid leave at the birth of a child may increase stress that may, in turn, contribute to abuse. In addition, societal attitudes with regard to both the privacy of the family and the issue of children's versus parents' rights may also play a role (Petersen, 1993). Finally, a widespread indifference to violence or even acceptance of violence as a solution to social problems may contribute to the rise in child abuse in American society (Straus & Donnelly, 1994). As we saw in Chapter 1, children's exposure to violence in television and films may help set the stage for later violence in their own lives.

Some social scientists have suggested that the high incidence of child abuse in the United States may owe something to the American culture's general acceptance of the physical punishment of children (Gershoff, 2002; Straus & Donnelly, 1994). Child abuse is relatively uncommon in cultures like that of the Chinese, who rarely punish children physically. Thus, the cultural approval of violence, such as spanking in childrearing, may sometimes combine with caretakers' lack of social, economic, and emotional resources to produce child abuse.

In summary, no single factor leads to child abuse. It involves complex interactions among dysfunctional family relationships, multiple stressful experiences, a disorganized or nonsupportive environment, and cultural values that tolerate or justify aggression and physical punishment.

Consequences of Abuse

The consequences of abuse are devastating. More than 1,000 children die each year; 65 percent of these children die as a direct result of physical abuse, and another 36 percent die from the consequences of neglect. And it is the youngest children who are most likely to die from abusive treatment: 77 percent of all the children who died from abuse or neglect in 2001 were younger than 4 years of age (Coser & Cohen, 2003). If abused or neglected children do not die, they may suffer brain dysfunction, neuromotor handicaps, physical defects, stunted growth, mental retardation, or serious psychological disturbance. Abuse can also slow intellectual development and cause psychosocial problems.

Even as infants, physically abused children show less secure attachment and more noncompliant, resistant, and avoidant behavior toward their mothers (Cicchetti & Toth, 2006; Lyons-Ruth & Jacobvitz, 1999). Moreover, abused children are more likely to have problems in regulating their emotions, tend to show less prosocial behavior and empathy, and are more aggressive with their peers and more likely than nonabused children to be rejected by their classmates (Bolger & Patterson, 2001; Howe, Aquan-Assee, Bukowski, Lehowx, & Rinaldi, 2001; Shields, Ryan, & Cicchetti, 2001). In infancy and early childhood, sexually abused children, particularly girls, often display bed-wetting problems (called *enuresis*). Abused boys are more likely to have somatic complaints, such as stomachache. Both boys and girls display inappropriate sexual behavior and have higher anxiety and social withdrawal. Among sexually abused children, delays in cognitive and academic development are common as well (Trickett & Putnam, 1998).

As abused children advance through the school years, they tend not only to show problems in relations with peers, teachers, and caregivers but also to have academic problems and low self-esteem, to exhibit behavior problems, and, not surprisingly, to be depressed and withdrawn (Cicchetti & Toth, 2006). Problems are greater if abuse begins early (prior to age 5) rather than later (Keiley, Howe, Dodge, Bates, & Pettit, 2001). Most abused children do not become delinquents or violent offenders. Long-term effects of abuse are most likely to appear if children remain in low-income socioeconomic environments with multiple stresses and few supports available (Cicchetti & Lynch, 1995). In sexually abused children, it is common to find inappropriate sexual behavior directed toward themselves or other children and adults as well as play and fantasy with sexual content (Trickett & Putnam, 1998). Higher rates of fears, nightmares, aggressive behavior, behavior problems, and self-injurious behavior have also been found (Cicchetti & Toth, 2006). Finally, more learning problems and poorer academic performance, as well as a greater number of attention deficit/hyperactivity problems have been found in sexually abused children (Trickett & Putnam, 1998).

Prevention of Child Abuse

A variety of strategies help reduce rates of abuse (Golden, 2000; Thompson, 1995). First, increasing parents' understanding of children's developmental timetables reduces unrealistic expectations about children's progress. Second, teaching parents nonpunitive disciplinary tactics, such as time-out and reasoning can help decrease abuse rates. Third, providing support networks, both formal and informal, to reduce the isolation of abusing families is helpful. And fourth, as some argue, another way to lessen the incidence of child abuse in our society may be to change our tendency to tolerate and even justify the use of violence in dealing with interpersonal and social problems (Thompson, 1995).

Making the Connections 11

There are many links between concepts and ideas in one area of development and concepts and ideas in other areas. Here are some of the connections between ideas in Chapter 11 and discussions in other chapters of this book.

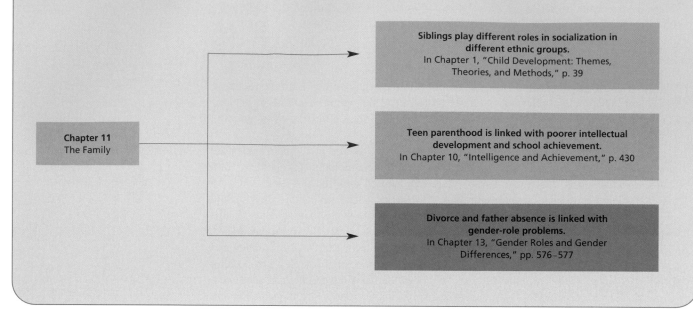

Chapter 11
The Family

Siblings play different roles in socialization in different ethnic groups.
In Chapter 1, "Child Development: Themes, Theories, and Methods," p. 39

Teen parenthood is linked with poorer intellectual development and school achievement.
In Chapter 10, "Intelligence and Achievement," p. 430

Divorce and father absence is linked with gender-role problems.
In Chapter 13, "Gender Roles and Gender Differences," pp. 576–577

SUMMARY

- The family is both the earliest and most sustained source of social contact for the child. The beliefs and values of the culture are filtered through the parents, whose interpretation is influenced by their own personalities, religion, social class, education, and gender. Although rearrangements in family ties are increasingly common, family relationships remain the most intense and enduring bonds.

- Parents, siblings, peers, and teachers are major agents of **socialization.** They may influence the child by directly teaching standards, rules, and values; by providing role models; by making attributions about the child; and by creating the environment in which the child lives.

The Family System

- The family is a complex system involving interdependent members whose functioning may be altered by changes in the behavior of one member, or relationships among family members, and by changes over time. In addition, family functioning is influenced by the larger physical, cultural, and social setting in which the family lives.

- Family processes involve mutual influences among family members and adaptation to changes in family members and their relationships as well as to circumstances external to the family. In addition to the systems theory principles discussed in Chapter 1, the family system is governed by the principles of interdependency and homeostasis and by the types of boundaries it establishes.

- The functioning of the marital system, parent-child system, and sibling system are interrelated and influence children's adjustment. A satisfying marital relationship is often regarded as the basis of good family functioning, which directly or indirectly affects the interactions with the children. Increased parent-child involvement and positive parent-child relationships have been found when spouses are mutually supportive.

- Marital conflict, which can affect children either directly or indirectly, is associated with negative feelings and behaviors directed toward the children and with disruptions in children's social and cognitive competence. Particularly when conflicts are unresolved, children are likely to react with anger, sadness, or other negative emotions. Boys are more susceptible to the negative effects of family disharmony than girls because they are more likely to be directly exposed to family conflict, whereas girls are more likely to be protected from it.

- Children have an impact on the marital relationship. Pregnancy and the birth of a first child are associated with a shift toward more traditional masculine and feminine roles, so that the mother does more of the child care. Both mothers and fathers report declines in marital satisfaction following the birth of their first child, but fathers are slower to express such declines than mothers. In addition, temperamentally difficult, deviant, or handicapped children place additional strain on the marriage and may be enough to destroy an already fragile marriage.

- Parents typically begin to consciously and systematically socialize their child during the second year by saying "no" to some behaviors and by praising other behaviors. They also teach social rules directly, serve as models with whom the child may identify or imitate, and choose the environment and social life that their child will experience.

- Parents' relationships with their children have frequently been categorized along the dimensions of emotionality and control. Parental warmth and responsiveness are regarded as important to socialization, and some degree of parental control is necessary for positive social development. The goal should be the child's learning of self-regulation rather than continuing external control by the parents. Thus, discipline strategies that present alternatives and rely on reasoning and attributions about the child's positive intentions are the most effective.

- The interaction of the dimensions of warmth and responsiveness with those of permissiveness and control creates a four-way typology: **authoritative, authoritarian, permissive,** and **uninvolved parenting.** In a classic study Baumrind found that distinctive types of parental behavior were related to specific patterns of child behavior. She found that authoritative parenting involving high-warmth responsiveness and communication, but also consistent and firm control and high-maturity demands, led to the most positive emotional, social, and cognitive development in children and adolescents.

- Critics of this typology have cited the need to identify more clearly the components of each style that contribute to its effects on the child's development, the need to pay more attention to the role played by the child's temperament and behavior, and the question of the generalizability across cultures of the original findings. As one example, the most effective Chinese style of parenting may fall somewhere between authoritative and authoritarian. In addition, in China and many

other Asian countries, the relative emphasis on the relation of the self to the group is quite different from the emphasis on the individual self that is common in the United States and other Western nations.

- **Co-parenting,** in which ideally spouses or partners take a team approach in their childrearing practices, can contribute to cooperation, cohesiveness, and harmony in the family. However, if parents compete with one another or fail to match each other's investment of time and energy in the work of parenting, the children may react with aggression, anxiety, or other kinds of problem behavior.

- Most families in the United States have more than one child. The functioning of the family is affected by the number, gender, and spacing of the children. These factors influence both parent-child interaction and sibling interaction. As family size increases, parents and children have less opportunity for extensive contact, but siblings experience more contact. This may result in greater independence but lower self-esteem and academic achievement in children from large families.

- Although parents often act separately in dealing with a child, mothers and fathers sometimes co-parent as a team. Some parents are cooperative, but others are hostile. Hostile-aggressive parenting can have negative outcomes for the child.

- Variations in interactions with parents and siblings have been associated with birth order. Firstborn children often show emotional and behavioral problems after the birth of a sibling, but the outcome is mediated by the mother's reaction, by efforts to include the firstborn, and by the father's involvement. In general, parents tend to stay highly involved with firstborn children throughout their lives, often having higher expectations, exerting greater pressure for achievement, and requiring the acceptance of more responsibility.

- Different characteristics have been ascribed to firstborn and later-born children. Firstborns are more adult-oriented, helpful, self-controlled, conforming, and anxious than their siblings, and they tend to excel in academic and professional achievement. Although only children experience many of the same parental demands of firstborns, they do not have to compete with siblings. Thus, they tend to be high in achievement, but lower in anxiety, and make more positive adjustments in social relations both within and outside of the home.

- Birth order is associated with variations in sibling relations. Eldest children are typically expected to assume some responsibility for younger children, and this may lead to either antagonistic behavior or to more nurturant behavior toward younger siblings. Eldest children tend to focus on parents as sources of social learning, whereas younger children use both parents and older siblings as models and teachers.

- The family as a unit is as much a family subsystem as are the marital, parent-child, and sibling subsystems. The family unit is particularly responsible for the development and perpetuation of family stories and rituals, which transmit values, teach family roles, and reinforce the family's uniqueness.

Social Class, Ethnicity, and Socialization

- Subgroups within our culture have both divergent values and different problems with which to cope. These may have an impact on the goals and methods of socialization parents choose.

- In addition to obvious differences in income, education, and occupation, lower-class and middle-class families may differ in other ways. Poor families generally experience little power within all of the systems (e.g., education, health) that they encounter, leading them to feel helpless, insecure, and controlled by external forces. In addition, they may be involved in cycles of disadvantage, associated with accumulating risk factors that make childrearing difficult and lead to adverse outcomes in the next generation. However, the stresses experienced by poor families often result in the formation of extensive support networks, which involve both emotional support and services that cannot be purchased.

- Social class, ethnicity, race, and culture have been related to differences in childrearing. Among these four, race is probably the least significant factor. Among other things, childrearing may differ according to whether a given cultural group emphasizes the **traditional nuclear family** or the **extended family;** the former is likely to be found among people who stress individualism, the latter among those who stress the importance of the relationships between the individual and the group. Specific differences in styles of childrearing and their effect on children are also influenced by other systems—for example, the workplace, the neighborhood, peers, and the school—that in turn are influenced by culture and society.

The Changing American Family

- In recent years, family roles and forms have become more varied. As the number of working mothers has increased, the average size of households has decreased. Single-parent households have increased greatly in number due largely to rising divorce rates and increases in out-of-wedlock births.

- Effects on maternal employment have been attributed to the mother's reason for working, the mother's satisfaction with her role, the demands placed on other family members, the attitudes of the other family members, and the quality of substitute care provided for the children. If each of these is positive, maternal employment not only has no detrimental effects on children but instead may have specific positive effects, especially for girls.

- Children's self-care is growing in response to increases in maternal employment. Although self-care has positive features, such as encouraging children to take responsibility for themselves, there are risks for **latchkey children,** such as increased delinquency and substance abuse. After-school care programs, however, are beneficial, promoting better grades and lessening the occurrence of problem behaviors.

- Divorce, life in a one-parent family, and remarriage should be viewed as part of a series of transitions that modify family roles and relationships and the lives of parents and children. In the first year following divorce, the children in single-parent households tend to be more disturbed, but in the long run most are able to adapt to their parents' divorce. However, single, custodial mothers suffer from task overload, a marked decline in income, and a lack of social support.

- Family interactions immediately following divorce are characterized by inept parenting on the part of custodial parents—usually mothers—and distressed, demanding, noncompliant behavior on the part of children. These effects seem to last longer and to be more negative for preadolescent sons than for daughters.

- Children's responses to remarriage vary depending on the previous family experience—but the age at which the remarriage occurs is associated with the child's acceptance of the new parent. It is particularly difficult for adolescents to cope with a parent's—or both parents'—remarriage. Antisocial behavior, depression and anxiety, school problems, and disruptions in peer relations have been associated with divorce and remarriage. In preadolescence, boys show the most negative responses to divorce and girls the most lasting resistance to remarriage; however, gender differences are rarely found in adolescence.

- Although in nearly 75 percent of divorce and custody cases the children reside with the mother, a divorced couple may select either **joint legal custody** or **joint physical custody** arrangements. Even when parents choose the latter, however, close to half of children live full-time with their mothers.

- The timing of first parenthood is a powerful organizer of parental roles. People are marrying and becoming parents later today than in earlier years. There are some positive aspects to later parenthood—for example, parents may be better established in careers, feel more responsibility, and be more flexible about family roles.

- Between 2 and 4 percent of children in the United States are adopted, often from other countries. Adoption can protect infants and children by removing them from adverse rearing environments, such as orphanages. Adopted children are at high risk for psychological and academic problems, but age, gender, and prior living conditions determine the adopted child's risk for these sorts of problems. Most adoptees fall in the normal range of development.

- Gay and lesbian families are becoming increasingly common, whether composed of children from former heterosexual marriages or of children adopted or conceived by various assisted reproductive techniques. The evidence suggests that the children of gay and lesbian couples develop as children of heterosexual marriages do, that they generally adopt heterosexual lifestyles, and that their concepts of gender roles do not differ from those of children of heterosexual parents.

- Although births to teenage parents have declined somewhat, births to unwed adolescent mothers more than tripled between the 1960s and the 1990s. Largely because of economic constraints on unmarried mothers, the children of teen mothers are at particular risk. The younger the mother, the more likely the child is to experience cognitive and eventual academic deficits. Children of teen mothers are more likely to have behavior problems, to have less self-control, and to show more antisocial behavior, such as the misuse of drugs and delinquency.

- Education, a comfortable economic situation, and religious faith can help to prevent teenage pregnancy, as of course can the proper use of contraceptives. Once an unmarried teenager has had a child, getting an education, limiting future births, and forming a stable marriage may help her pull herself out of poverty and give her child a chance for good adjustment and academic performance.

Child Abuse within the Family

- In 1996 nearly a million cases of child abuse or neglect were substantiated, another 2 million cases were reported, and the number of unreported incidents was unknown. The severe abuse of children is most likely to occur in the presence of multiple risk factors and the absence of protective factors such as community resources, good health, high intelligence, education, and a supportive social network.

- Child abuse is more likely to occur in large families, to children under age 3, and to children with physical and intellectual deficits or excessive fussiness and crying. Parents in abusive families often are socially isolated and have unrealistic beliefs about young children's abilities and about the parent-child relationship. Child abuse is preceded by escalating verbal and physical aggression that is often unpredictable and not contingent on the child's actual behaviors.

- Family members may engage in the **sexual abuse** of children when they are just infants. Girls are four times as likely as boys to be abused sexually; the peak years of such maltreatment are from 7 to 8. Among boys, the peak period of sexual abuse occurs in the years just before puberty. Child sexual abuse may lead to various somatic complaints, inappropriate sexual behavior, anxiety, social withdrawal, and delays in cognitive development and in academic achievement.

- Parents who abuse their children are frequently involved in a distressed marriage, have been abused by their own parents, and are unemployed, poorly educated, and economically deprived. No single factor leads to abuse. It is a product of the interactions among family characteristics, nonsupportive environments, and cultural values that tolerate aggression and physical punishment as well as poverty, unemployment, and high-risk, dangerous neighborhoods. The latter sort of neighborhood may promote insecurity, feelings of helplessness, and vulnerability.

- The devastating consequences of child abuse include less secure attachment in infants; problems with emotional regulation and aggressive behavior in toddlers; poor relations with peers and adults, academic problems, and low self-esteem as children get older; brain dysfunction; mental retardation, neuromotor deficits, physical handicaps—and death.

EXPLORE AND DISCUSS

1. Consider our discussion of how families have continued to change across time. For example, more mothers work outside the home than ever before. What other changes have occurred in the past several decades that have modified our definition of a family?

2. Parenting is sometimes viewed as encompassing practices that are universal, but recent evidence suggests that culture shapes parenting practices. Based on your own experience and observations, do you think that parenting is influenced by culture? Explain your answer.

3. Divorce has many negative effects on children's adjustment. It has been proposed that we should make it harder to obtain a divorce. What might be the problems with this proposal? Should the government be involved in decisions about divorce? Why or why not?

Pavel Kuznetsov (1878–1968). *Pushball*. Tretyakov Gallery, Moscow.

12.

Expanding the Social World: Peers and Friends

We have become increasingly aware, in recent years, of how important people outside the family are in socializing children. The roles that peers, friends, and teachers play in this process have gained significance as more and more mothers have begun to work outside the home and as preschool care and education have become more prevalent. This chapter focuses on how children's friends and peers contribute to their socialization.

Children's relationships with their peers differ from relations with their parents in several ways. In general, relations with peers are less enduring than those with family and especially parents. And interactions among age-mates are freer and more egalitarian. This greater fluidity offers children the opportunity for a new kind of interpersonal exploration. In particular, it facilitates the growth of social competence, it encourages a sense of social justice, and it opens the way for children to form relationships with people outside the family.

We start out by looking at the child's first encounters with peers, in early infancy. Then we examine the special roles peers play in children's socialization, such as modeling behaviors for each other. Next, we consider the many factors that affect children's acceptance by peers, including the ability to interact with others smoothly. We explore the kinds of problems that children can face in peer relationships, and consider some ways of resolving them. Next we explore the roles of parents, teachers, and others in promoting children's acceptance by peers, and look at the ways in which children make friends and eventually enter into romantic relationships. We then reflect on the continuing debate as to whether it is parents or peers who exert the most influence on children's behavior. Then we turn to children's behaviors in groups, examining the way children form "pecking orders" and cliques, or groups of friends that are often exclusive. Finally, we look at some cultural differences in peer relationships. Throughout these discussions we will see changes over time in children's relations with their peers, changes that are reflected in our Turning Points chart on page 509.

HOW PEER INTERACTIONS BEGIN: DEVELOPMENTAL PATTERNS

Interactions with peers begin to shape children's behavior at an early age. Even in their earliest months, babies begin to react to each other, and when children begin to utter their first words and phrases, social interaction really gets under way. Gradually, children spend increasing amounts of time with peers, and by the time they're 3 toddlers generally prefer interaction with peers to that with adults.

Infancy: First Social Encounters

Babies are really curious about each other! In the first six months of life, they touch and look at each other and are surprisingly responsive to each other's behaviors. If one child cries, another may cry too. But these early responses can't be considered truly social in the sense of an infant's seeking and expecting a response from another child. It is not until the second half of their first year that infants begin to recognize a peer as a social partner (Brownell, 1990; Howes, 1987). Between 6 and 12 months, an infant will start trying to influence another child by vocalizing, by looking at or waving at the child, or by touching him. Although babies do hit and push sometimes, a considerable amount of social behavior among the baby crowd is friendly (Bronson, 1981; Eckerman & Didow, 1988; Rubin et al., 2006). Here's a classic example:

> Larry sits on the floor and Bernie turns and looks toward him. Bernie waves his hand and says "da," still looking at Larry. He repeats the vocalization three more times before Larry laughs. Bernie vocalizes again and Larry laughs again. Then, the same sequence of one child saying "da" and the other laughing is repeated twelve more times before Bernie turns away from Larry and walks off. Bernie and Larry become distracted at times during the interchange. Yet, when this happens, the partner reattracts attention either by repeating his socially directed action or by modifying it, as when Bernie both waves and says "da," reengaging Larry. (Mueller & Lucas, 1975, p. 241)

As children develop competence in interacting with peers, they shift toward increased social play and exhibit a clear preference for playing with peers rather than adults. In a classic study of social play in children between 10 months and 2 years of age, Eckerman, Whatley, and Kutz (1975) found that solitary play changed very little from the youngest to the oldest group of children. However, they also found that older children engaged in significantly more social play than younger ones did. In addition, the older children were less interested than the younger children in playing with their mothers and more interested in playing with peers (Figure 12-1).

Social exchanges with mothers differ from those with peers (Rubin et al., 2006; Vandell & Wilson, 1987). Babies find mothers more reliable and more responsive than infants. Exchanges with mothers are longer and more sustained, but often a bit one-sided. Mothers tend to bear the larger responsibility for maintaining the interaction, whereas in exchanges between infant peers, the two partners contribute more equally. Mothers make it easy; peers make you work for your social life!

Social Exchange among Toddlers

Between the ages of 1 and 2, children make gains in locomotion and language that increase the complexity of their social exchange (Dunn, 2005; Rubin et al., 2006). During this period, they develop the capacity to engage in complementary social interaction (Howes, 1987). That is, partners take turns and exchange roles in their play, so that, for example, Jason may play "hider" and Samantha "seeker," and then Samantha may hide while Jason seeks. Peers also begin to imitate each other's activity and to

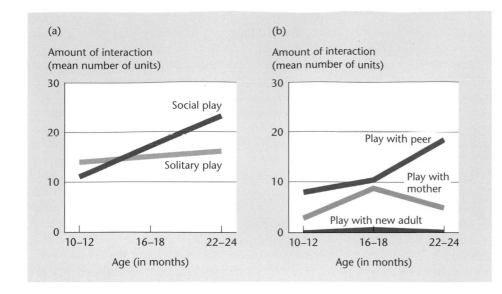

Figure 12-1

The development of social play

In this study of 1- to 2-year-olds, the oldest children were twice as likely to engage in social play as the youngest ones (a) and almost twice as likely to play with peers (b).

Source: Eckerman, Whatley, & Kutz, 1975.

show awareness that they're being imitated (Eckerman, 1993). Now, too, when children engage in positive social interactions, they're more likely to smile or laugh or display other kinds of positive affect (Mueller & Brenner, 1977). And interactions last longer (Ross & Conant, 1992).

In the late toddler period (25 to 36 months), the child's main social achievement is the ability to share meaning with a social partner (Mueller, 1989). "When children communicate meanings, they know how to suggest playing a particular game (eye gaze, plus run to wagon), the signal to switch roles ('my turn' plus a tug) and how to communicate that they share this knowledge . . . children's communication of meaning makes possible a wider range of games and variations on the themes of games, as well as early forms of pretend play" (Howes, 1987, p. 260).

Table 12-1 summarizes Parten's (1932) classic description of the types of play that characterize the social exchanges of $2\frac{1}{2}$- to 4-year-olds. The complexity of toddlers' play increases over age: Solitary play and parallel play diminish as the child grows

Table 12-1

Types of play in preschool-age children

Solitary Play

Children play by themselves and generally ignore other children who are near. About half of 2-year-olds engage in this type of play.

Parallel Play

Two children play in similar activities, often side by side, but do not engage one another. This type of play is common in 2-year-olds but diminishes by the time a child is 3 or 4 years old.

Associative Play

Children play with other children but do not necessarily share the same goals or agendas. They share toys and materials, and they may even react to or comment on another child's ongoing activities (e.g., sharing paints or remarking on another child's artwork). However, they are still not fully engaged with each other in a joint project. This type of play is commonly seen in 3- and 4-year-olds, less often in 2-year-olds.

Cooperative Play

At age 3 to 4, children begin to engage in this sophisticated type of play in which they cooperate, reciprocate, and share common goals. Some examples of cooperative play are building a sand castle, drawing a picture together, and playing a fantasy game in which characters interact with each other.

older, and associative and cooperative play both increase in frequency. There is of course overlap: Some 4-year-olds are still engaging in solitary play, whereas some precocious $2\frac{1}{2}$-year-olds are busily engaged in cooperative play bouts.

As children develop, negative exchanges and conflict also increase (Hay & Ross, 1982; Rubin et al., 2006). In fact, socializing and getting into conflicts seem to go together. As Brown and Brownell (1990) found, toddlers who frequently initiated conflicts with peers were also the most sociable and the most likely to initiate interactions. It takes a little time to learn how to manage your social interchanges effectively.

As children become familiar with each other, their early peer interactions tend to develop into relationships. In a **relationship** two acquaintances share an ongoing succession of interactions that continue over time and that affect each other (Dunn, 2005; Rubin et al., 2006). That is, in every encounter between the partners both their history of past interactions and their expectations of future interactions influence the nature and course of events. Hildy Ross and her colleagues (Ross, Conant, Cheyne, & Alevizos, 1992) have found that toddlers develop relationships based on both positive and negative exchanges. In their simple give-and-take exchanges, these young peers display an elementary form of friendship. Interestingly, children between 1 and 2 develop preferences for particular playmates: It is a clear sign of early friendship formation that not just any other child will do. And these early social choices of special friends are not temporary—50 to 70 percent of early friendships last over a year, and in some cases over several years (Dunn, 2005; Howes, 1996). Although Rubin and colleagues argue that "it is doubtful that [these relationships] carry the same strength of psychological meaning as the friendships of older children" (1998, p. 634), clearly the beginnings of friendship are formed far earlier than we have heretofore believed. We explore the topic of friendship later in some detail.

Preschool and Elementary School Society

As children move into preschool and elementary school, they continue to seek and engage in more and more peer interactions. With whom do children of various ages spend time? In their study of social interaction, Ellis, Rogoff, and Cromer (1981) found that the 400 children they observed were alone 26 percent of the time, with other children 46 percent, and with adults and peers 15 percent of the time. As Figure 12-2 shows, over time children spend more hours with child companions and fewer with adults. These trends continue into adolescence, when children spend more time either alone or with friends (Larson, 1997).

relationship A continuing succession of interactions between two people that are affected by their shared, past interactions and that also affect their future interactions.

Figure 12-2

Peers preferred
At about the age of $2\frac{1}{2}$, children begin to prefer other children as companions, and their choice of adults for companionship dwindles rapidly over time.

Source: Ellis, Rogoff, & Cromer, 1981.

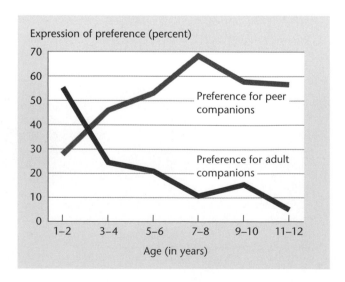

Turning Points

PEER RELATIONSHIPS AND SOCIAL INTERACTION

0–6 MONTHS	• Touches and looks at another infant and cries in response to the other's crying
6–12 MONTHS	• Tries to influence another baby looking, touching, vocalizing, or waving • Interacts with other infants in a generally friendly way, but may sometimes hit or push another
13–24 MONTHS	• Begins to adopt complementary behavior (e.g., taking turns, exchanging roles) • Engages in more social play throughout the period • Begins to engage in imaginative play
25–36 MONTHS	• In play and other social interaction, begins to communicate meaning (e.g., invites another to play or signals that it's time to switch roles) • Begins to prefer peers over adults as companions
3 YEARS	• Begins to engage in complex cooperative and dramatic play • Starts to prefer same-gender playmates
4 YEARS	• Shares more with peers than 3-year-olds do
$4\frac{1}{2}$ YEARS	• Begins to sustain longer play sequences • Is more willing to accept roles other than protagonist
6 YEARS	• Reaches a peak in imaginative play
3–7 YEARS	• Main friendship goal: coordinated and successful play
7 YEARS	• Shows stable preference for same-gender playmates
7–9 YEARS	• Expects friends to share activities, offer help, be physically available
8–12 YEARS	• Main friendship goal: to be accepted by same-gender peers
9–11 YEARS	• Expects friends to accept and admire him and to be loyal and committed to the relationship • Is likely to build friendships on the basis of earlier interactions
11–13 YEARS	• Expects genuineness, intimacy, self-disclosure, common interests, and similar attitudes and values in friends
13–17 YEARS	• Important friendship goal: understanding of the self
16–17 YEARS	• Expects friends to provide emotional support

Note: Developmental events described in this and other Turning Points charts represent overall trends identified in research studies. Individual children vary greatly in the ages at which they achieve these developmental changes.

Sources: Rubin, Bukowski, & Parker, 2006; Schneider, 2000.

Figure 12-3

Girls/boys aren't so bad after all

This study showed that both girls and boys in elementary and middle school generally chose same-gender others for companions (a and b in left column), but that beginning in the ninth grade, the amount of time children spent with opposite-gender friends increased significantly, especially for girls, who mature earlier than boys (a and b in right column).

Source: Richards, Crowe, Larson, & Swarr, 1998.

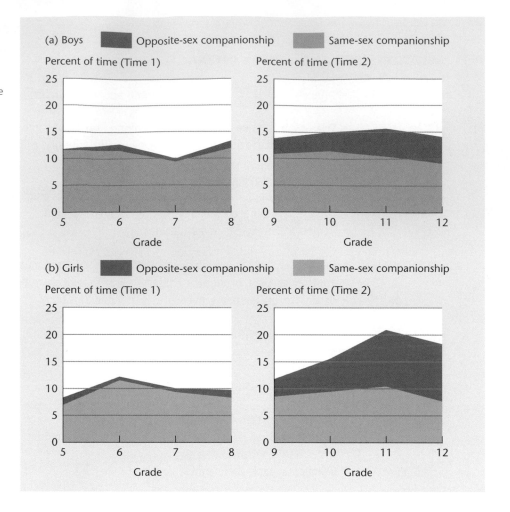

Larson (1997) found that among both European American and African American preadolescents and adolescents talking with peers increased dramatically between ages 10 and 15. Interestingly, when Larson (Larson & Verma, 1999) compared U.S., Korean, and Japanese twelfth graders, they found that the U.S. teens spent more than twice as much time each day talking with each other (2.5 hours per day) as did the Korean and Japanese teens (1.0 hours per day).

The kinds of peers children choose to spend time with change also. Age becomes a more important factor—for example, companionship with peers of the same age grows over time. Gender, too, begins to matter. Up to age 3 or 4, children choose same- and opposite-gender companions, but after this, both boys and girls prefer same- to opposite-gender play partners. Adolescence, of course, heralds a reversal, as cross-gender friendships begin to blossom once again (Richards, Crowe, Larson, & Swoff, 1998; Rubin et al., 2006; and see Figure 12-3).

PEERS AS SOCIALIZERS

Peers play a role in socializing children, just as families do. Peers offer a perspective quite different from that of the family—the perspective of equals who share common abilities, goals, and problems. How does the peer group influence the child's development? In many of the same ways parents do—through modeling, reinforcement, and social comparison and by providing opportunities for learning and socializing.

Modeling Behaviors

Peers influence each other by serving as social models. Children acquire knowledge behaviors simply by observing the behavior and actions of their peers. For example, Colin is spending his first day at a new school. Through observing the other students, he rapidly learns that children are expected to stand when the teacher enters the room, that it is risky to shoot spitballs, and that he should avoid the big redheaded kid because he's the class bully. Colin may learn new social skills by modeling, or imitating, Melissa and Tom, who appear to be the class leaders and more socially skilled than some other members of the class (Grusec & Abramovitch, 1982).

Children also imitate older, more powerful, and more prestigious peer models (Bandura, 1989; Rubin et al., 2006). As children develop and internalize the rules of their society, they need to rely on and imitate others less often (Grusec & Abramovitch, 1982). But imitation serves other purposes besides rule learning. It can often be an important way of maintaining social interaction. As Eckerman (1989, 1993) has shown, even in 2-year-olds, imitation sustains joint play between partners and leads to more sophisticated forms of play in social games such as tossing a ball back and forth.

As we will see, in many cultures siblings are primary caregivers for infants and toddlers. This allows the young child to learn from peers of different age groups. Some writers have suggested that the rigid age grading common to many Western institutions, such as schools and sports organizations, may alter or at least limit children's opportunities to learn. What do you think?

Teaching and Reinforcing

As children develop, they begin to reinforce their peers' behaviors. To "reinforce" is to pay attention to another's behavior, to praise or criticize it, or to share in it. No one knows this better than parents—especially parents of adolescents—who often bemoan the fact that their children ignore wise parental advice and instead listen to, and emulate, their peers. As the concept of "peer pressure" implies, peers can convince children and adolescents to take risks and engage in deviant behavior. Clearly, peers' influence can be harmful as well as beneficial. Throughout the preschool years, peers are increasingly likely to reinforce each other: One study found that 4-year-olds praised, attended to, or shared with their peers significantly more than 3-year-olds did (Charlesworth & Hartup, 1967). And reciprocity begins to grow, as nursery schoolers reinforce the same peers who reinforce them.

The notion that peer reinforcement in the form of attention and approval affects a child's behavior patterns has considerable research support. For example, in one study, experimenters had adults instruct a child's peers to attend to only certain behaviors and to ignore others. For example, they were to attend to the child's helpful and cooperative behaviors but to ignore any mean or aggressive behaviors. The peers' differential reinforcement produced significant changes in the target child's behavior (Furman & Gavin, 1989).

Children respond to negative reinforcement too. Just think of the looks and comments an adolescent who wears the wrong clothes is likely to elicit or of the reactions preschoolers are likely to get if they play with toys regarded as meant only for the opposite sex. Peers can quickly whip an errant child into shape by looks or biting comments or by ostracizing the child from the group (Lamb & Roopnarine, 1979).

Interaction with peers also provides an opportunity for specific instruction and learning (Zarbatany, Hartmann, & Rankin, 1990). In Western cultures, one can see this in school games and sports and in tutorial arrangements, in which children teach each other and acquire new skills together. In some other cultures, such as those of India, Kenya, and Mexico, both older peers and siblings teach and are caretakers for young children (Maynard, 2002; Rogoff, 2002; Whiting & Edwards, 1988).

These kinds of interactions with peers provide children not only with the venue for acquiring social skills but also with the opportunity to develop personal and group relationships and a sense of belonging (Zarbatany et al., 1990). And as children begin to spend increasing amounts of time with their peers, these functions grow in importance (Larson & Richards, 1994).

Social Comparison and the Developing Self

social comparison The process by which we evaluate our own abilities, values, and other qualities by comparing ourselves with others, usually our peers.

Peers may help a child develop her self-image and self-esteem by providing standards against which to measure herself. There are few objective ways to rate one's own characteristics, abilities, and values, and children turn to other people, particularly to peers, for help. Through **social comparison,** children watch and talk with their peers and then use what they've learned to evaluate themselves.

Research has shown that in the early elementary school years children display a marked increase in their use of social comparison, with the peer group as a common means of self-evaluation (Harter, 1990, 2006; Zarbatany et al., 1990). And the child's self-image and self-acceptance are closely associated with how he is received by peers. This social comparison process helps the child define his own self-image and self-esteem (Harter, 2006). How well children think they "stack up" against their peers plays a major role in the development of their self-esteem. If you think that you are as good as your peers your self-esteem is high, but if you see yourself as falling short, your self-esteem suffers.

How do we choose the particular person with whom we want to compare ourselves? It's likely that if a child wants to know how good a fighter he is, he thinks about how he's done in neighborhood scuffles and how tough his peers seem to think he is; he doesn't compare himself with Mike Tyson. If a child wants to evaluate her reading ability, she probably compares herself with her classmates; she's pretty unlikely to judge herself by how many words her mother can read or by how rapidly her teacher reads. As a basis for self-definition, the peer group is unequaled.

LifeMap CD

To learn more about the formation of identity and how this process varies from one culture to another, watch the video on "The Self and Culture" in Chapter 12 of your CD.

Tugs-of-war and other play activities help children compare their abilities with those of others.

PEER ACCEPTANCE

Children place enormous significance on being accepted by peers, and peer acceptance is of great importance to children's social development. Interacting with peers is the child's first experience of social behavior beyond the family, and when this experience is positive it can help lay the foundation for healthy adult social behavior. In this section, we look first at the ways psychologists study peer acceptance and assess children's status among their peers and at their discoveries about the factors that affect children's judgments of others. Then we examine the way that children are affected by their peers' view of them and interactions with them. Based on our findings here, we go on to consider how we can promote healthy social interaction in children.

How Do We Study Peer Acceptance?

A common way of studying peer acceptance is to measure and compare the status of each child in a specific peer group. To do this, developmental psychologists generally use **sociometric techniques** in which they ask children to rate peers on scales of aggressiveness or helpfulness, or to compare peers as to likeability or to identify those whom they like best.

Why do psychologists ask children, rather than teachers or other adults, to provide them with data on children's peer status? First, as insiders in the group, peers see a wider range of relevant behaviors than do adults. Second, peers have extended and varied experience with each other. And third, by gathering data from many individuals who've interacted with the child who is the subject of study, we prevent any single individual's view from dominating our results.

Let's look at a method of study called the *nominations technique,* in which an investigator begins by asking each child in a group to name a specific number (usually three) of peers whom he likes "especially" and the same number of peers whom he doesn't like "very much." Next, the investigator sums the scores of all the "like most" and "like least" choices and assigns children to one of several groups. **Popular children** are those who have received the greatest number of positive nominations and the fewest negative ones. Children whom their peers judge popular are friendly and assertive but not disruptive or aggressive. When they join a play group, they do it so smoothly that the ongoing action can continue without interruption (Black & Hazen, 1990; Newcomb, Bukowski, & Pattee, 1993). Children like this are good at communication; they help set the rules and norms for their groups, and they engage in more prosocial behavior than less popular children.

Not all popular children fit this profile. Some children who are perceived as popular are characterized not only as athletic and cool, but as domineering, arrogant, and both physically and relationally aggressive. These children and adolescents may wield high levels of social influence, even though their actions are often manipulative in nature (Cillessen & Mayeux, 2004; Rodkin, Farmer, Pearl, & Van Acker, 2000). In short, there is more than one pathway to popularity.

Average children receive some of both types of nominations but are neither as well liked as popular peers nor as disliked as peers in other categories. **Neglected children** are isolated, often friendless, children but aren't necessarily disliked by classmates; they receive few like or dislike votes. And children termed neglected are less aggressive, less talkative, and more withdrawn. **Controversial children** receive many positive nominations but also a lot of negative ones. **Rejected children** receive many negative nominations. **Aggressive rejected children** are characterized by aggressiveness, poor self-control, and behavior problems, whereas **nonaggressive rejected children** tend to be anxious, withdrawn, and socially unskilled (Bierman, Smoot, & Aumiller, 1993; Crick & Ladd, 1993; Parkhurst & Asher, 1992). However, as we saw in our discussion of types of popular children, aggressive children who are

sociometric technique A procedure for determining children's status within their peer group; each child in the group either nominates others whom she likes best and least or rates each child in the group for desirability as a companion.

popular children Children who are liked by many peers and disliked by very few.

average children Children who have some friends but who are not as well liked as popular children.

neglected children Children who are often socially isolated and, although they are not necessarily disliked by others, have few friends.

controversial children Children who are liked by many peers but also disliked by many.

rejected children Children who are disliked by many peers and liked by very few.

aggressive rejected children *Rejected* children who have low self-control, are highly aggressive, and exhibit behavior problems.

nonaggressive rejected children *Rejected* children who tend to be anxious, withdrawn, and socially unskilled.

competent and developing social networks are unlikely to be rejected and may even be popular (Cairns & Cairns, 1994).

Factors That Affect Peer Status

Once we've placed every child in a group somewhere in this mixed bag of categories, we need to find out what reasons underlie the judgments made by each child's peers. What factors influence children's appraisals of one another? Research suggests that probably the single most significant factor is a child's demonstrated cognitive and social skills—his ability to initiate interactions with others, to communicate effectively and interact comfortably with them, to be responsive to others' interests and behaviors, and to cooperate with others in play and school activities (Coie, Dodge, & Kupersmidt, 1990; Schneider, 2000). In this section, we focus first on exploring these kinds of skills and the ways in which children develop them.

We will also have to look, however, at some less crucial factors in peer acceptance that are as influential with children as they are with adults. When people meet others, especially for the first time, they are likely to base their initial appraisals of the person on such superficial characteristics as name or physical appearance or even enduring characteristics such as race, gender, or age. Unfortunately, children often do this too.

ACQUIRING SOCIAL-COGNITIVE SKILLS Think about how you react when new people join a group of which you're a member. What do you think of a person who smiles in a friendly way and asks you about yourself and the group? What do you think of someone who stands on the edge of the group and makes no effort to approach anyone? Which person would you be most likely to chat with or invite to join you in a particular activity? Probably the first, although of course there are always extenuating circumstances.

In the same way, the child who asks new acquaintances for information (e.g., "Where do you live?"), offers information (e.g., "My favorite sport is basketball"), or invites another child to join in an activity (e.g., "Wanna help me build this fort?") is well on the way to being accepted by the group (Putallaz & Gottman, 1981). On the other hand, the child who tries to initiate social interaction by hovering about a group silently or by making inappropriate or aggressive remarks is behind before she gets started. To feel comfortable approaching a new social situation, a child needs to want to interact with others, to feel confident that she has something useful to contribute to the group, and to be interested in learning what others in the group are like—what their interests are and what they think about many things.

PROCESSING AND ACTING ON SOCIAL INFORMATION Approaching a new social situation is similar to solving a cognitive problem or puzzle. A child approaching that new group of peers needs to understand others' communications clearly, to interpret their behavior accurately, to formulate her own goals and strategies based on these interpretations, to make useful decisions, to communicate clearly to others, and to try out and then evaluate her strategies. This is quite a large order, especially for a young child, and some are better at it than others. To examine the interplay of these complicated functions in a social situation, Crick and Dodge (1994) devised the model of social information-processing illustrated in Figure 12-4. Although the model stresses the cognitive steps in evaluating problems that a child confronts when interacting with others, it is important to remember that individual biological predispositions, such as a tendency to be impulsive, also play a role in accounting for variations in the decision-making process (Dodge & Pettit, 2003). As we study a child's progress through this scheme of processing, we'll see that at every one of the six steps outlined the child must make a decision or take an action that may be accurate or inaccurate, helpful or unhelpful.

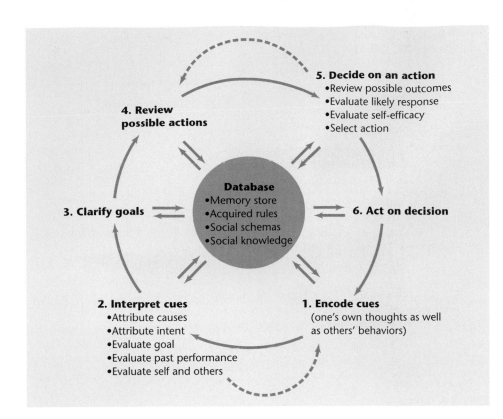

Figure 12-4

An information-processing model of children's social behavior

The model outlines the way children perceive and interpret a social situation, decide what they want to achieve in that situation, choose a behavior they think likely to accomplish their goal, and act on their decisions (steps 1–6). Note that the child's "database" consists of memories of other situations and acts, learned rules of social behavior, and her general social knowledge. As the double arrows indicate, the child's thinking and action both draw on the database and contribute to it. The dashed-line arrows point out that the child may refer back to the preceding step and perhaps change her plan for the one she's about to take.

Source: Adapted from Crick & Dodge, 1994.

Rochelle, 7 years old and quite socially competent, approaches two children playing a board game. She notices that one of the girls smiles at her in a friendly way (step 1, encode cues). She concludes that the girl would like her to play too (step 2, interpret cues), and decides that she wants to make friends (step 3, clarify goals). Next, she reviews possible actions to further her goal—smile back, ask to join in—and considers how the girls might react to each possible choice (step 4, review actions/responses). Rochelle decides to make a friendly comment about the girls' game (step 5, decision). Just then the smiling girl looks up again, and Rochelle smiles back and says, "Looks like fun" (step 6, act). The girls invite her to play the next game.

Now replace Rochelle with Jamie, 6 years old and less competent socially. Jamie sees two boys playing, but, because he's looking at their sneakers he misses the friendly look one boy gives him (step 1, encodes the wrong cues). Jamie decides that the boys are unfriendly (step 2, incorrectly interprets cues) and wonders what he might do. He thinks of some hostile things—ask the boys why they don't ask him to play, call them mean—and fails to consider how they might react (steps 3 and 4, fails to both clarify goal and review possible acts and responses). Jamie decides on the latter approach (step 5, decides) and blurts out, "You two are really selfish not to let me play!" (step 6, acts). It's no great surprise that the boys ignore him and move off.

Using these models, Dodge (1986) and his colleagues compared 5- to 7-year-old children who were rated either socially competent or socially incompetent by their teachers and peers. They presented children with a videotape of situations similar to the ones just described, where a child is trying to join the play of two other children, and asked their participants about what they would do in each of five steps (the researchers omitted step 3 in this study). Predicting that children of different levels of competence would respond differently, the researchers found just that. The incompetent children were less likely to notice and interpret the cues correctly, generated fewer competent responses, chose less appropriate responses, and in the next phase of the experiment, were less skilled at actually enacting or carrying out the behavior. The researchers then asked the children to participate in an actual peer-group entry task

Figure 12-5

Social competence, aggression, and social processing skills

Children who were more socially competent (a) and who were nonaggressive and better adjusted (b) displayed fewer deficits in their ability to process cues and other information in social situations than children who were socially incompetent and aggressive.

Source: Adapted from Dodge, Pettit, McClaskey, & Brown, 1987.

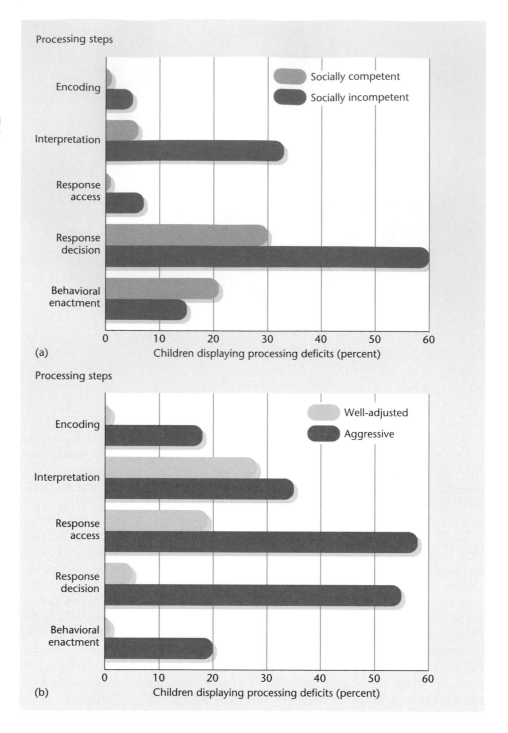

with two peers from their classroom. Measures of each of the five steps in the model predicted children's competence and success at this task; children who understood what to do were better at the real task of gaining entry into the peer group (see Figure 12-5a). In a related study, well-adjusted children, as well as aggressive 8- to 10-year-olds, were presented with a situation involving their response to a peer's provocation (e.g., a peer knocks over a child's block tower in an ambiguous way so the child can't tell if it was accidental or not). Figure 12-5b shows that aggressive children showed more deficits at each of the processing steps. In addition, children's processing ability successfully predicted how children responded when another child actually provoked them. These studies provide strong support for the role of cognitive factors in understanding children's social relationships with peers. Deficits in social understanding can lead to poor social relationships. In this case, thought and action are clearly linked.

Let's look at some of these steps in more detail, for others have found support for many of the components of the Crick and Dodge model. First, rejected children, especially aggressive ones, tend to view others in hostile terms and to make hostile attributions about other peers' intentions (Burks, Laird, Dodge, Pettit, & Bates, 1999). Second, not all children have the same goals and strategies in social situations. Chung and Asher (1996) suggest that one needs to be aware of one's goals in a social situation and to have the ability to devise a few strategies to achieve those goals. Not surprisingly, certain kinds of social goals tend to be accompanied by certain kinds of strategies. For example, children who want to have relationships with others are more likely to use prosocial strategies in interacting with their peers. On the other hand, children who want to control others may choose hostile and coercive strategies.

Some researchers have found that the social goals and behavioral strategies of children whom their peers judge either high or low status may differ quite a bit (Crick & Dodge, 1994). Renshaw & Asher (1983), for example, asked third to sixth graders to choose a goal for each of the following social situations:

- Your family has moved to a new town, and this is your first day at a new school. Recess starts, and the children go out to play. What would you like to do?
- You invite a child who's just moved into your neighborhood to come over and watch TV one Saturday morning. After about 10 minutes, the child you've invited suddenly changes the channel you chose. What would you do?

High-status children had clear goals and strategies. For example, some said they would "want to start making friends" with the children in the schoolyard and that they would ask other children to play with them. These children described outgoing, sociable, and sympathetic behaviors designed to achieve this general goal. In contrast, some low-status children tried to avoid the situation—for instance, "I'd probably just go play outside by myself." Others described hostile goals and strategies—for example, "I'd want to get back at" the child who changed the TV channel without asking.

Why do some children develop positive goals and strategies and others negative goals and behaviors? One important explanation is that children differ in the way they perceive themselves and in the way they explain why they are sometimes successful at a task and sometimes unsuccessful. When Goetz and Dweck (1980) asked elementary school children how they explained "what happened" when their efforts to begin a new relationship with a peer were rebuffed, some children said either that there was a misunderstanding or that they simply hadn't tried hard enough and expressed confidence that they could succeed the next time. In contrast, some other children said that it was just hard for them to make friends. The first group saw the problem as temporary and fixable; the latter saw it as a reflection of some presumably permanent lack of ability within themselves.

As we said earlier, an important quality in peer interaction is the ability to try alternative strategies when initial efforts are unsuccessful. Clearly, a child who thinks that he didn't succeed at something because he just didn't try hard enough may well try again, but the child who believes that there's something lacking within himself may give up. Dweck, whose research on children's differing beliefs about their abilities to master new learning that we explored in Chapter 10, suggests that one way to circumvent the latter kind of thinking is to prevent the child from seeing a task or problem as a measure of her ability to perform and instead to focus the child's attention on just trying out something new and possibly useful.

In a study testing this notion, Erdley, Loomis, Cain, Dumas-Hines, and Dweck (1997) told children that they were trying out for membership in a pen-pal club, and they divided the children into a learning-goal group and a performance-goal group.

The researchers told the children in the first group that the important thing was that the task would help them "practice and improve" their ways of making friends. "So think of it as a chance to work on your skills," they continued, "and maybe learn some new ones" (Erdley et al., 1997). Then they told the children in the second group that what they were interested in was "how good" they were at striking up new friendships: "Think of it as a chance for you to see how good you are at making friends." As the researchers predicted, the children given the learning goal were more persistent and ultimately more successful than the children given the performance goal. The latter were much more likely to give up.

It is important to recognize that the relations between the information-processing steps in the model and actual behavior with peers are reciprocal. Although we assume that biased processing of social information leads to maladaptive social behavior and poor peer acceptance, the model recognizes that maladaptive behavior over time can lead to the development of social-information-processing deficits as well (Gifford-Smith & Rabiner, 2004). For example, Dodge and his colleagues (2003) found that children who were rejected by peers in kindergarten became, as the researchers predicted, less competent social processers in grades 2 and 3. The experience of early peer rejection, either by confirming biased processing patterns or by limiting a child's ability to acquire necessary social experience, leads to greater cognitive deficits—which, in turn, contribute to maladaptive behavior and less acceptance by peers.

BEAUTY MAY BE ONLY SKIN DEEP, BUT IT'S COOL When they encounter someone new, children are just as likely as adults to base their impressions on the person's physical appearance. As you'll recall from Chapter 4, when newborns view pictures of unfamiliar faces that have been judged "attractive" and "unattractive," they look more at the attractive ones (Langlois et al., 2000; Slater et al., 2000). And 3-year-olds show the same preference, choosing attractive over unattractive faces (Langlois, 1985).

People in general tend to attribute positive qualities to those who are physically attractive, and children and adolescents go right along with this tendency (Langlois & Stephan, 1981; Langlois et al., 2000). Children expect to find characteristics such as friendliness, willingness to share, fearlessness, and self-sufficiency in good-looking peers and often think unattractive children are likely to be aggressive, antisocial, and mean. Teenagers almost uniformly prefer good-looking partners, viewing unattractive ones as unacceptable.

Have our expectations that attractive people will demonstrate positive characteristics and behavior any basis in reality? In a recent review, Langlois and her colleagues (2000) confirmed many of these expectations and underscored that beauty and attractiveness may be more important than we thought. Attractive children are judged more positively than unattractive children—even by those who know them. The attractive children were rated higher on social appeal, adjustment, and interpersonal competence. You get treated better if you're attractive too. The more attractive children were treated more positively and less negatively by others, even by people who were familiar with these children. Finally, attractive children were more popular, better adjusted, and even displayed greater intelligence. Perhaps it's time to reevaluate our cultural myths: Beauty is more than just skin deep after all (Langlois et al., 2000).

Ordinarily, very young children don't pay much attention to their peers' physical characteristics, although even they can react negatively to serious overweight or obesity. When peers taunt or criticize others because of their physical appearance, however, the children who are targeted in this way may incorporate the criticism into their self-images, where it can affect their social development over time (Lerner, Petersen, & Brooks-Gunn, 1987). Rosenblum and Lewis (1999) have found that adolescent girls' own body images tended to worsen from 13 to 18 years, which may reflect feedback from others. Among the girls these authors studied, obesity was a major factor in negative self-appraisals. In an interesting contrast, these researchers also found that boys tended to express greater satisfaction with their bodies over the same age range.

"WE LIKE TO HAVE BOYS (GIRLS)"   Preschoolers Jake and Danny are playing on the big swing, and Laura runs up, calling excitedly, "Can I get on?" "No!" says Jake emphatically, "We don't want you on here. We only want boys on here." When researcher Zick Rubin (1980) asks why the boys won't play with Laura, Jake replies simply, "Because we like boys—we like to have boys." Up to the age of 7, children are usually willing to play with peers of either gender, but, as you see, even in the preschool years gender discrimination can occur!

The tendency to gender-exclusivity increases throughout elementary school (Maccoby, 1998), and it's not until early adolescence that children once again choose opposite-gender companions—this time, as dates. There are exceptions to this rule, but they often operate underground. For example, a girl and boy may spend time together in church work or in neighborhood activities but keep their friendship a secret from classmates (Gottman, 1986; Thorne, 1986). Too bad, say some researchers, for cross-gender play can introduce both boys and girls to a broader range of behavioral styles and activities (Rubin, 1980). It can expand their pool of potential friends and promote a better understanding of qualities often shared by both sexes.

Some support for these notions comes from research by Kovacs, Parker, and Hoffman (1996), whose study of a group of third and fourth graders revealed that children who had cross-gender friendships as well as same-gender friendships were among the most well-accepted, socially skilled children in the group. In contrast, children whose primary friendships, or only friendships, were with peers of the opposite gender were less well accepted, judged less skilled academically and socially, and tended to report lower self-esteem. Similarly, others have found that boys who had girls in their friendship networks reported greater intimacy with their same-gender best friends (Zarbatany, McDougall, & Hymel, 2000).

Why do girls and boys segregate themselves from each other? Researchers have described a number of factors. According to Thorne (1986), girls tend to play (1) low-energy games (2) in small groups (3) near school buildings and (4) close to adult supervision. They tend to prefer play involving artistic endeavors, books, or dolls. In addition, girls appear to prefer unstructured, unorganized activities, such as talking and walking (Savin-Williams, 1987). In general, girls were more intimate, exchanged more information, and were less aggressive in their interactions than boys (Lansford & Parker, 1999; Zarbatany et al., 2000).

Boys, on the other hand, tend to play high-energy, run-and-chase games that take up nearly ten times as much as space as girls' play. Rough-and-tumble, boisterous play, often with blocks, cars, or trucks generally characterizes boys' play, and boys, as they become older, tend to prefer organized games that are controlled by rules (Eisenberg, Murray, & Hite, 1982; Maccoby, 1998). Even the nature of **pretend play** differs: Boys are more

pretend play A form of play, most often social, in which children use symbolic meanings to act out fantasies, in this way learning social roles and how to interact with others. Also called *imaginative* and *fantasy play*.

Boys in the elementary school years still tend to choose same-gender playmates for team sports. However, as interest in girls' team sports continues to grow, we may see changes in playmate choices over time.

likely to enact superhero roles, whereas girls often portray family characters (Haight & Miller, 1993). Play may not go well when Batman and Robin meet Mom and her little baby! Perhaps, as traditional gender roles continue to change, more shared interests may emerge and boys and girls will accept and interact with one another more. We return to the issue of gender segregation in Chapter 13.

It is important not to exaggerate the differences in peer relationship styles of boys and girls (Underwood, 2004). Boys and girls participate in both cooperative and competitive activities—team sports, for example, foster both types of goals. And, as we will see in Chapter 14, girls can be as aggressive as boys but generally express aggression differently. In addition, recent work has questioned the claim that boys' and girls' social networks are different in size or structure; for example, girls and boys are equally likely to be central members of their respective cliques (Bagwell, Coie, Terry, & Lochman, 2000; Cairns & Cairns, 1994). There are many similarities in the behaviors of boys and girls in their respective peer relationships.

WHAT'S IN A NAME? OR AN AGE?   Children learn very quickly what given names are popular among their peers and thus "acceptable," and often they may think another child's name "funny" or worry that their own name is odd. As a result, they're more likely to be friendly to a peer with a name that's familiar to them, such as Michelle or Jason, than to a child with a name that's currently out of favor, such as Horace or Myrtle (Rubin et al., 2006). Few children realize that fashions in names change constantly.

In Western societies play groups, especially those of young children, tend to be age-graded. U.S. children spend most of their time with same-age peers, playing less than a third of the time with children who are more than 2 years older or younger than themselves (Ellis et al., 1981). In contrast, as we've already noted, in many other cultures older children often play with younger ones as well as care for and teach them (Edwards, 1992; Whiting & Edwards, 1988; Zukow-Goldring, 2002).

Across the continents of Africa, Asia, and North America, even young children seem to understand that older and younger peers serve different functions. Typically, children expect to play with age-mates and younger peers and to get help from older peers (Edwards & Lewis, 1979; Rubin et al., 2006). However, children with emotional or social problems may find it easier to gain acceptance among children who are younger than they are. Children whose social skills are not yet fully developed may be less threatening to a socially immature child (Hetherington, Cox, & Cox, 1979). Recall our discussion in Chapter 6 of Harlow's classic studies of socialization in rhesus monkeys: Harlow and colleagues also discovered that if young monkeys were isolated from others early on, the negative effects of this could be reversed by giving them sustained contact with younger monkeys at a later time (Suomi & Harlow, 1972). This finding led Furman, Rahe, and Hartup (1979) to examine the effect on withdrawn 4- and 5-year-old children of contact with younger peers. As the researchers predicted, the target children became more sociable.

The bottom line, however, is that children's typical preference for play with same-age peers does serve a special role in social development. After all, children share interests most closely with those who are at similar points in their cognitive, emotional, social, and physical development (Maccoby, 1998). And it is largely their peers with whom they will be interacting on a continuing basis in their schooling, their work, and their communities.

Consequences of Being Unpopular

In order to understand the consequences of being rejected by peers, we need to take a closer look at how children actually express their rejection of others as well as at the factors that modify children's reaction to rejection. Then we'll consider the short-term and long-term consequences of being rejected, including the stability of peer status over time.

Table 12-2 How kids reject other kids

Major Methods	Some Examples of Subtypes
Excluding, shunning, or otherwise terminating interaction with a child; psychologically or physically ejecting him from one's presence or from a group	• Purposely ignoring a child's comments or efforts to join in an activity • Refusing a child's offer to join in play: "We're not going to play with you ever." • Telling a child, "I don't like you." • Telling a child to leave: "Get away!"
Dominating or controlling a child	• In a hostile manner, ordering a child to do something • In a hostile way, telling a child that something she said was wrong (e.g., "That's stupid" or "You don't know anything")
Involving a third party in a statement that expresses rejection of another child	• Telling a child that someone said something unpleasant about him: "Mrs. Jones [a teacher] said you're dumb and always get bad grades." • Saying to a third party something nasty about another child when the latter is within hearing • Telling a third party that a child did something the speaker describes as wrong or stupid
Denying a child access either to other people or to desirable things	• Taking another child's toy away from her or taking her place at a particular resource: "Get off, Jackee, get off." • Refusing to let a child speak to or play with the speaker or with another child: "You aren't in the club—we don't need you." • Assigning a child to a less desirable resource or position: "You mess up too bad."
Specifically attacking a child, either psychologically or physically	• Calling a child names or maligning his characteristics or behavior: "You know what you got in your brain? A load of bricks." • Purposely damaging or breaking a child's possessions: Sam grabs Conrad's pizza and then wipes his hands on Conrad's clothes • Attacking a child physically, biting, scratching, pulling hair, hitting, punching, knocking down

Source: Adapted from Asher, Rose, & Gabriel, 2001.

HOW CHILDREN EXPRESS REJECTION According to Asher, Rose, and Gabriel (2001), children have a lot of very unpleasant ways of expressing their dislike of peers or their rejection of them. Observing a group of children in grades 3 through 6 at a Midwestern public elementary school, these researchers compiled a taxonomy that included five major methods of rejection and many subtypes. In Table 12-2, we reproduce the five primary classifications and offer some examples of the subtypes.

Children are creative and cruel in the ways they reject the children whom they dislike. Sometimes children exclude others from their group or activities; sometimes children bully or dominate others in the classroom. Or children can be sneaky, telling another child that they dislike a third child. In more direct action, children can deny others access to other people or objects—for example, children may not let a preschooler play on a swing or slide. Finally, children can directly attack a disliked peer, either verbally or physically.

Box 12.1
Risk and Resilience

VICTIMIZATION BY PEERS: IT HELPS TO HAVE FRIENDS

Peer victimization occurs when a child is bullied by other peers. This kind of persecution can take several forms. Some children physically attack or threaten others, especially boys, with physical harm if they don't obey their peers (Perry, Hodges, & Egan, 2001). Girls, on the other hand, are more likely to be targets of **relational victimization,** in which peers try to damage or control their relationships with others. For example, a girl may be excluded from an important event such as a birthday party when she fails to comply with a peer request, or she may be the target of a hostile rumor within her peer group (Crick & Bigbee, 1998; Crick,

Casas, & Ku, 1999a). Both of these forms of victimization have harmful consequences for children's adjustment. Victimized children are more anxious, depressed, and lonely. They are more likely to be rejected by peers, to hold more negative perceptions of their own competence, and to experience greater school adjustment problems (Boulton & Smith, 1994; Olweus, 1993).

Some children are the regular targets of victimization, and it's unfortunate that, although we can often identify these victims of aggression early, they frequently remain victims throughout the school years (Khatri, Kupersmidt, & Patterson, 1994; Kochenderfer-Ladd &

Ignoring another child or purposely excluding her from a conversation or activity can be a form of relational victimization.

peer victimization Ill treatment of one child by another (or by others) that can range from teasing to bullying to serious physical harm; typically, victimizing is a continuing behavior that persists over time.

relational victimization The attempt by a peer to damage or control another child's relationships with others.

Many rejected children, especially those who are not aggressive, tend to be victimized by their classmates. For an exploration of this problem see Box 12.1.

WHAT DETERMINES HOW CHILDREN REACT TO REJECTION?
Kids respond in many different ways to being rejected by their peers, and according to Asher, Rose & Gabriel (2001), a number of factors determine rejected children's behavior. You may find it helpful to look at Table 12-3 as you read on. To begin with, the situation in which an exchange between peers occurs is often ambiguous and subject to interpretation. For example, if Tamara refuses Brittany's offer of part of a sandwich, she may simply be indicating that she's not hungry, not that she doesn't want food from *Brittany*. The next factor is the tendency of children to joke with one another by pretending to insult each other. Children, like some adults, are

Wardrop, 2001). Recent cross-national surveys suggest that from 6 to 22 percent of children report moderate to severe levels of peer abuse while in school or traveling to or from school (Nansel et al., 2001).

Who are these children that peers pick on, tease, or attack? Some are children who, unwittingly, send implicit signals that they are unlikely to defend themselves or to retaliate. These children may cry easily, they may exhibit anxiety, or they may appear weak (Hodges & Perry, 1999). They tend to lack self-esteem and self-confidence, and they're often missing a sense of humor. And again, without realizing it, they may encourage their attackers by being submissive, by not being very good at persuading others, or by giving in to a bully's demands and surrendering possessions (Crick et al., 1999a; Perry, Williard, & Perry, 1990; Juvonen, Graham, & Schuster, 2003).

Other victimized children are more outgoing in their responses. They argue, disrupt bullies' actions, and attempt to return the attack—but even so they aren't very effective. Instead, they somehow provoke and irritate other children without actually threatening them or giving them the idea that they'll follow through on their hostile displays. Olweus (1999) has termed these children "provocative victims." Not surprisingly, such a child is also physically weak. If he were the school fullback, even bullies would leave him alone (Olweus, 1999). Some children are both bullies and victims: They are victimized by others, and they themselves act as bullies, often against weaker children.

Victimization takes its toll on children. Those who are victimized are likely to have lower social status and lower self-esteem, to experience more social anxiety, to be lonely, to avoid school, and to show increasing depression over time (Hodges, Malone, & Perry, 1997;

Juvonen et al., 2003; Rigby, 2002). Further, in early adulthood, people who as young adolescents have been abused by peers report elevated depression and low self-esteem (Olweus, 1993, 1999).

What factors protect or buffer children from being victimized? Hodges, Malone, and Perry (1997) tested the notion that children at risk of being attacked or bullied will be more likely to become victims if they lack friends or are rejected by their peers. Indeed, in these researchers' study, children who were at risk were increasingly less likely to be victimized as their numbers of friends grew. But not just any friend will do; it was children whose friends had characteristics that served a protective function (e.g., physical strength, aggressiveness) who were less likely to be victimized. Moreover, Hodges, Boivin, Vitaro, and Bukowski (1999) found that friendship may not only protect children from victimization but may increase the likelihood that a target child will maintain self-esteem and will not "invite" attack or submit to it, at least over the one year of these researchers' study. Although being victimized by peers can cause a child's social behavior to become less effective, this is less likely to occur when she has a best friend.

Rejection by a peer group is another social risk factor related to increased victimization for children at risk. In other words, the link between each behavioral risk factor (e.g., physical weakness, showing anxiety, low self-confidence) and victimization was greater for peer-rejected children than for better-accepted children.

These findings support the notion that the expression of an individual's vulnerabilities often depends on social context factors (Hodges et al., 1997). Having friends—the right kind of friends—can serve to buffer the at-risk child from victimization.

often unaware of the fine line between joking and insult. And making distinctions between behaviors that closely walk this line seems to be trickier for some children than for others. The rejection-sensitive child is likely to expect rejection and thus perceive it. The child who is relatively insensitive to social cues probably won't interpret ambiguous behaviors as rejecting but over the long term may have as many problems in social interaction as the child who expects rejection (Asher et al., 2001).

A third factor is the frequency with which children experience negative feedback from peers. As you might expect, the more often that such feedback characterizes a child's social interactions, the more likely he is to expect it again and again. According to Asher and coworkers, children who are repeatedly rejected over several years report more loneliness than those who get such feedback in just one grade. These researchers also point out that a child's reaction to disregard or mistreatment may be

Table 12-3   What determines how rejected kids react to peers?

Ambiguity of communication	Other's intent to reject may be unclear (e.g., in a noisy cafeteria, it may be difficult to tell whether one child is ignoring the other or simply didn't hear her).
Identity of rejector	Being rejected by a close friend or a family member is likely to be more distressing than being rejected by a peer whom one knows only casually.
Target child's personality	More likely to be distressed by perceived rejection are children who brood over slights; children who attribute negative events to their own inadequacies rather than to external causes (a rejecting child may simply be a hateful person); children who believe they can't change their own abilities or characteristics; children who approach social situations as tests of their "okayness" rather than as opportunities to meet new people and learn new things.
Child's own behavior	A child's response to rejection may strongly influence the intensity and duration of the rejecting behavior and thus its effect on the target child (e.g., responding vengefully or failing to stand up for oneself can make a situation worse). Children who can respond with a sense of humor may succeed in turning a rejection situation into something funny and thus gain others' acceptance.
Child's social support	Children can cope with rejection much more easily when they have friends and other sources of support.
Consistency of rejection	The more consistently a child experiences rejection, the more likely he is to expect and even anticipate it.

Source: Adapted from Asher, Rose, & Gabriel, 2001.

strongly affected by who is doing the rejecting. A sibling's rejection may hurt one more than a classmate's; alternatively, rejection by an admired peer may cause a child more distress than similar behavior on the part of a family member to whom she's not close.

A child's relative self-confidence is a fourth factor in dealing with rejection. Children who are fairly certain of their own abilities and skills may be less troubled by criticism or rejection than children who feel they're inadequate in some way or, especially, who believe that they cannot change their abilities and skills. Children who approach social situations in a positive and friendly manner, rather than dreading that they won't measure up in some way, are more likely to suffer distress at rejection.

The fifth factor is a child's ability to respond to rejection in such a way as to counteract or negate it. For example, the child who can maintain a sense of humor and respond in a joking or playful way can often turn a situation around and gain the acceptance he seems at first to be denied. But children who react aggressively or who shrink back and fail to defend themselves may be rejected again and again.

SHORT-TERM AND LONG-TERM CONSEQUENCES OF REJECTION   Being unpopular can lead to both short-term and long-term problems. Loneliness among children is one of the primary results of being rejected or ignored, and it has many faces (see Table 12-4). Unpopular children have often reported feeling lonely and socially dissatisfied (Asher & Hopmeyer, 2001; Asher, Hymel, & Renshaw, 1984; Cassidy & Asher, 1992). Research suggests that although neglected children may be no lonelier than average children, rejected children are much more likely than average or neglected children to feel lonely (Asher et al., 1984; see also Figure 12-6). Being actively disliked by many of one's peers can lead to strong feelings of social isolation and alienation. Even among kindergarten children, being verbally and physically victimized by peers is associated with greater degrees

Table 12-4

Loneliness is not having
anyone around

Source: Hayden, Turulli, & Hymel, 1988.

Girl, Grade 6

"Today everybody's going to Mary Ann's party in the group. I'm sort of the one that gets left behind. I'm not invited to the party, so I won't do anything on the weekend. Anywhere the whole group goes, I don't."

(Why did that make you feel lonely?) "I'm just the person that gets left back. Maybe they don't realize that I get left, that I'm there, but it happens all the time."

Boy, Grade 5

"I was living in Greenvalley. It was a Sunday. All the stores were closed, I had no money. Jason, a friend, had to go to his aunt's. I decided to call on Jamie, but no one was home. I went to turn on the TV and only church stuff was on. I went upstairs to play with my toys, but it was so boring. The dog was behind the couch so I didn't want to bother him. Mom was sleeping. My sister was babysitting. It wasn't my day."

(Why did that make you feel lonely?) "There was no one to talk to or play with, nothing to listen to."

of loneliness (Kochenderfer & Ladd, 1996b). And nonaggressive rejected children are likely to feel lonelier than aggressive rejected children (Parkhurst & Asher, 1992).

As social relationships change, feelings of loneliness can change too. Renshaw and Brown (1993) tracked a group of Australian children in grades 3 through 6 for a year and found that those who showed considerable increases in loneliness over time were those who lost friends, became less accepted by peers, and made more remarks about how hard it was for them to make friends. It helps, though, to have at least one friend. Rejected children who have a stable friendship with just one other child may feel less lonely than rejected and totally friendless children (Parker & Asher, 1993; Sanderson & Siegal, 1991).

What are the long-term consequences for a child of being accepted by only a few of his peers? According to Parker and Asher (1987), poor achievement, school avoidance, and loneliness. These researchers found that children who were poorly accepted by their peers were less cooperative in the classroom than well-accepted children and were also more likely to drop out of school entirely and to develop patterns of criminal activity. As Box 12.2 shows, even children who are shy and withdrawn follow a different life-course pattern than less shy children.

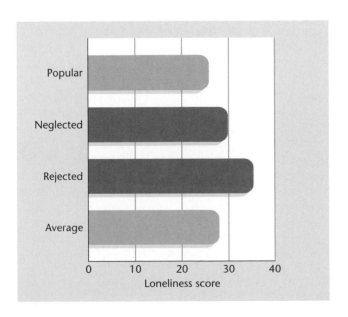

Figure 12-6

Loneliness and peer
status

In this study, being rejected triggered considerably more loneliness than being either popular or average—or even than being neglected.

Source: Asher et al., 1984.

Box 12.2

Child Psychology in Action

WHAT HAPPENS TO SHY CHILDREN—THIRTY YEARS LATER?

What happens to shy children as they grow up? To find out, Caspi, Elder, and Bem (1988) had teachers rate children between 8 and 10 years old on shyness and then traced the developmental patterns of these children for 20 to 30 years. At the outset of this study, the researchers defined shyness as both social anxiety and inhibited social behavior. Teachers rated children on a scale that ranged from highly shy (from acutely uncomfortable to feeling panic in social situations) to low shyness (enjoying meeting new people). On a scale of social reserve, children who scored high were so emotionally inhibited that other people reported feelings of strain and awkwardness when in their company; children who scored low were "spontaneous and uninhibited in their expression of feelings." Their teachers rated the shy boys and girls less friendly, less sociable, more reserved, and more withdrawn than others, seeing them as followers rather than leaders.

Some 20 to 30 years later, the researchers reinterviewed their former participants as adults. Boys rated shy in childhood had delayed in marrying, in having children, and in establishing stable careers (see Figure 12-7). Moreover, as adults these men held jobs of less stature than the jobs their more assertive peers held. In contrast, shy girls were more likely than others to follow a conventional pattern of marriage, childbearing, and homemaking. Of women with a childhood history of shyness, 56 percent were likely either to have no history of employment outside the home or to have left the labor force at marriage or childbirth. Only 36 percent of their more outgoing peers followed this pattern. In addition, women with a history of childhood shyness typically were married to men who had higher occupational status at midlife than other women's husbands.

Clearly, the life course of these men and women was partly shaped by cultural gender-role prescriptions. Although shyness in men has never been thought desirable, at the time this group were growing up, shyness in women was widely considered a positive attribute, suited to the wife-mother-homemaker role then deemed by many to be appropriate for women.

Probably no shy child has ever thought that shyness was a good thing. Fortunately, interventions designed to help such children gain poise and self-confidence can begin very early. One kindergarten teacher had her class

Figure 12-7 Life transitions for shy boys

Boys who were shy late in childhood were likely to establish careers later, marry later, and have children later than other boys.

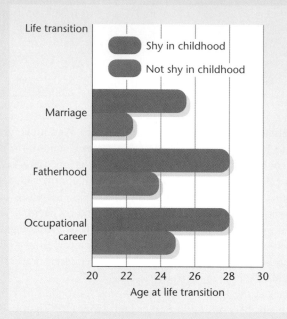

Source: Caspi et al., 1988.

draw pictures about events in their lives and then, one by one, display their drawings to the class, briefly describing what they had portrayed. In the first presentation session, many children looked at the ground and spoke in whispers or not at all, but after a few such sessions and with coaching and encouragement from the teacher, even the shyest child was looking coolly around at his audience, making sure of everyone's attention, and then calmly presenting his work.

In this vein, psychologists have developed a variety of formal programs to help shy and withdrawn children become more socially outgoing (Rubin et al., 1998). Shyness does seem to have a genetic component, but temperament is not destiny (Goleman,1995; Kagan, 1994). Children can often overcome their shyness through coaching, modeling, and instruction (see the text section on "Teachers Can Facilitate Healthy Social Interaction").

CAN PEER STATUS CHANGE?   In a study by Coie and Dodge (1983), both popular and neglected children were fairly stable in their social standing over a five-year span. Interestingly, though, popular children sometimes lost their high status and neglected children occasionally gained some social acceptance. In general, however, once a child was rejected she was more likely than others to maintain this status over a considerable time span. It seems that poor peer relationships in childhood do have implications for later adjustment.

The stability of peer rejection appears to be greater even among kindergartners than the stability of any other category of peer acceptance (Parke et al., 1997). In part, this is the result of **reputational bias,** or the tendency of children to interpret peers' behavior on the basis of past encounters and feelings about these children (Hymel, Wagner, & Butler, 1990). When we ask children to judge a negative behavior by a peer whom they earlier liked or disliked, they are likely to excuse the behavior of a peer they earlier liked, giving her the benefit of the doubt, but not to excuse a peer they didn't like. Reputation colors children's interpretations of peers' actions and helps account for the stability of behavior across time (Hymel, 1986).

Reputation, however, is not the only component in peer status stability. The behavior and characteristics of the children who have experienced rejection are important too. For example, Coie and colleagues (1990) found that when boys were brought together into new and different social groups (whose members had no knowledge of the boys' earlier reputations), they tended to be assigned the same peer status they'd had before. This was as true of boys who'd been considered popular as of those who'd been rejected (Coie & Kupersmidt, 1983). As we said earlier, although peers' judgments of other children are often bound by relatively superficial and unimportant factors, such as physical appearance, it is largely children's social skills that determine their social status. Clearly, we need to find ways to help children with lower status improve these skills and gain greater acceptance among their peers.

reputational bias Children's tendency to interpret peers' behavior on the basis of past encounters with, and feelings about, them.

PROMOTERS OF PEER ACCEPTANCE: PARENTS AND TEACHERS

The task of increasing peer acceptance among children is huge. We need to help socially isolated or rejected children to gain peer acceptance. We need to lessen the loneliness that results from being less popular than others. We need to encourage children who are "popular" or "average" in social status to be more generous toward their less socially adept peers—to make a greater effort to understand these peers and to find ways of including them in social groups. We may as well ask how we can get people to be more understanding, more accepting, more inclusive of other people, for these issues are hardly limited to the childhood years.

Indeed, the struggles between insiders and outsiders and between people of different cultural backgrounds, varying talents and skills, and many different skin colors and ethnic traditions continue to fuel the globe's most barbaric and most destructive human conflicts. Some believe that early training in social skills may eventually help developing children to find ways to celebrate strengths in one another and offer support for each others' weaknesses. Who is to provide this training? It must rest with parents and teachers, the prime members of Clinton's (1996) "village," a village that ultimately must encompass all of society.

Parents can draw on a variety of resources in helping their children develop healthy peer relationships (Parke & O'Neil, 2000). As Figure 12-8 shows, they start as trusted partners with whom their children can begin to acquire skills of social interaction. Recall from Chapter 6 that secure attachments to parental figures can form the basis for later social competence (Elicker, Egeland, & Sroufe, 1992; Schneider et al., 2001). In addition, researchers have found clear relationships between parents' specific ways

Figure 12-8

How parents help their children develop peer relationships

Children learn social interaction by practicing with their parents, through their parents' coaching and other educational methods, and through their parents' facilitation of opportunities for interaction with peers. The upper two-way arrow symbolizes the reciprocal relationship between parent-child interactive experience and parents' decisions about opportunities for social interaction; that experience and those decisions affect each other. The lower two-way arrows signal that children's experience in peer interaction provides feedback to parents and children on useful adjustments in social interaction patterns.

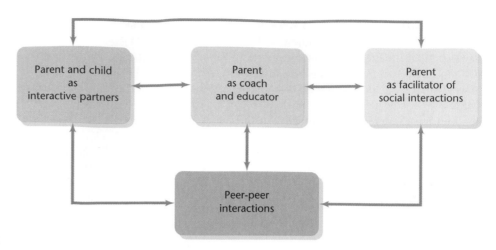

of interacting with their children and the children's social behavior with their peers. For example, Martha Putallaz and her colleagues (Putallaz, 1987; Putallaz & Heflin, 1990) found that higher-sociometric-status first graders had mothers who interacted in a positive and agreeable manner with their children and were concerned with the child's feelings as well as their own. In contrast, these researchers found that the mothers of lower-status children exhibited more negative and controlling behaviors with their children. Studying the interactions between fathers of higher- and lower-sociometric-status children, Parke and O'Neil (2000) documented similar findings.

Recently Clark and Ladd (2000) found that in parent-child relationships characterized by connectedness (e.g., mutual warmth and intimacy) and autonomy (responsiveness and validation, or acceptance of the child's views), children were better accepted by their peers. Why? These types of parent-child relationships promote in children a prosocial orientation (the tendency to treat other children in an empathic manner) that, in turn, invites greater acceptance by peers.

No one is more eager than a young child to learn, to know, and to try. Parents are also significant reinforcers of children's behavior, praising and rewarding useful attempts and suggesting alternative approaches when efforts fail. Equally important is the parent's role as model. Children observe everything their parents do and say, but it's easy for a parent to forget this as she interacts with other adults or children. One of the most important tasks for parents is to be "on" at all times: at once, they must be ever conscious of how their behavior may look to their infants and toddlers, and they must consciously attempt to model healthy, confident behavior for their young children. For some parents this may come naturally, but for others it may be exhausting!

Parents Are Coaches

Parents can also prepare their children for successful and satisfying social relationships through specific coaching, or teaching (Bhavnagri & Parke, 1991; Ladd & Pettit, 2002; Pettit & Mize, 1993). In coaching, parents teach a child a general concept or strategy, give examples of successful behaviors, and then guide the child through multiple rehearsals of a particular action. Following that, they review both concept and rehearsal in order to show the child how to evaluate his own behavior and its result. In this way, parents can advise a child on helpful approaches in interacting with peers, direct him to the most useful strategies, and support him as he tries new ideas.

Of course, this kind of coaching is most helpful when parents themselves are socially adept. In an Australian study (Finnie & Russell, 1988; Russell & Finnie, 1990), researchers found clear differences between the coaching methods mothers of children of high social status and those of children of lower status used when their children were confronted with a peer problem. The former generally used positive approaches (e.g., suggesting that a child propose a third, positive alternative action when he and another child cannot agree) and more rule-oriented strategies (e.g., suggesting that a child propose turn taking instead of fighting over a particular toy). In contrast, the mothers of low-status children tended to suggest avoidance strategies (e.g., that a child ignore unfriendly behavior) or nonspecific tactics (e.g., "just get to know the children"). When they actually joined in the children's activities, the two groups of mothers showed different degrees of skillfulness. For example, the first group encouraged communication among the children generally and actively helped their own children to join in conversation. The second group, however, often took control of a game, disrupted the children's play patterns, or simply avoided supervising the group.

Parents Are Social Arrangers

Another way parents can influence their children's relations with peers is by providing opportunities for interaction with other children (Ladd, 2005; Ladd, Muth, & Hart, 1992; Ladd & Pettit, 2002). The first step in this effort is often finding housing in a neighborhood where children are likely to find suitable playmates and where there are good facilities for children's play. Like many other things that help children grow and develop, a good neighborhood is generally more accessible to families at the higher socioeconomic levels. But even affluent neighborhoods differ: One parent told researchers, "Just look at this street—kids, swing sets, swimming pools. . . . It's a kid's paradise. . . . We had a beautiful house (before we moved here from another section of town), but there weren't many kids to play with" (Rubin & Sloman, 1984).

Socioeconomic factors can affect friendship patterns in surprising ways. In another study, Elliot Medrich and his colleagues (Medrich, 1981) discovered that friendships were more abundant and easy in a low-income neighborhood than in a more affluent one. In the well-to-do California community they studied, friends often lived so far apart that typically parents chauffeured their children to preplanned social events. In contrast, in the low-income inner-city neighborhood the researchers studied, where predominantly black families lived, friends were abundant and nearby, and children's play tended to be more spontaneous and frequent. In the first neighborhood, children were selective in their friendships; many had only one or two friends whom they chose because "we have something in common." In the second neighborhood, children typically had four or five close friends and spent considerable time in large groups.

Thus, the physical environment can sometimes counteract other factors in the endeavor to help children get to know one another. And even in dangerous and unsafe neighborhoods, parents can protect their children by monitoring their activities and their children's choices of peers (Brody et al., 2001; O'Neil, Parke, & McDowell, 2001). In a later chapter (Chapter 14), we will talk about the finding of Patterson, who showed that parents who monitor their children are less likely to have children who associate with deviant peers and more likely to avoid antisocial activities.

Because 2-year-olds aren't too good at finding playmates without their parents' help, being good social arrangers is particularly important for the parents of these very young children. Parents can schedule visits between young friends and enroll their children in organized activities and then, of course, chauffeur their children to and from such visits and gatherings (Ladd & Pettit, 2002). And this effort pays off. Comparing the social activities of children whose parents were good arrangers with those of children whose parents didn't facilitate peer contacts, Gary Ladd and colleagues (Ladd & Golter, 1988; Ladd et al., 1992; Ladd & Pettit, 2002) found that the boys in the first group of children had a clear advantage. They had a larger range of play-mates and more frequent play companions outside of school than boys in the second group. Girls in both groups were equally well accepted by their peers, but peer acceptance for boys was greater for those whose parents initiated peer contacts.

When Parents Fail: Abused Children and Peer Rejection

Although parents usually promote their children's friendships with other kids, parents who abuse a child often thereby prevent the child from developing healthy peer relationships. Recently, Bolger and Patterson (2001) found that preadolescents who were chronically abused were more likely to be rejected by their peers. As Figure 12-9 shows, the more extensive the abuse, the more likely a child was to be rejected by her peers. Moreover, maltreated children, especially if the abuse occurred in the preschool years, had difficulty forming and maintaining friendships. Neglected children were more likely to be social isolates who had infrequent contact with peers (Bolger, Patterson, & Kupersmidt, 1998; Garbarino & Kostelny, 2002). As we saw in Chapter 11, being abused can cause a child to exhibit aggressive behavior with others, and elevated levels of aggression accounted for the links between chronic maltreatment and peer rejection. Other work (Shields et al., 2001) suggests that the inability of many maltreated children to regulate their emotions often leads peers to reject them. Finally, abuse in the family also makes it more likely that children, especially boys, wll be victimized by their peers (Schwartz, Dodge, Pettit, & Bates, 1997; also see Box 12.1).

Teachers Can Facilitate Healthy Social Interaction

Teachers can help children who are lonely or socially awkward improve their people skills and increase their acceptance among their peers. We should note, though, that

Figure 12-9

Abused children are often rejected
In this study, not only were children who had been abused found to be often rejected by their peers, but the longer the abuse continued, the more likely these children were to be rejected by others.

Source: Bolger & Patterson, 2001.

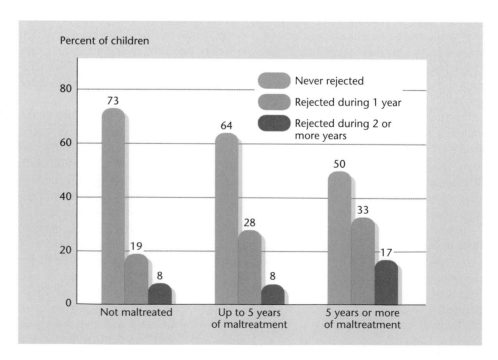

not every child who appears to be unpopular needs intervention. According to Coie and Dodge (1983) many neglected children become more socially competent and accepted over time. And there is nothing intrinsically wrong about solitary play, a common form of play among 2-year-olds, as we saw earlier in this chapter. Often a child who plays alone simply has a passion for certain kinds of experiences and activities. The time a child spends with Lego sets or paints or the computer may or may not produce the next Frank Lloyd Wright or Picasso or Bill Gates, but in any case, the child may become quite socially competent.

Studying a group of preschoolers, however, Rubin (Rubin, 1982; Rubin & LeMare, 1990) found that the children who often engaged in simple repetitive activities such as banging on the table, whether alone or close to other children, tended to be less socially competent. Similarly, children who engaged in solitary dramatic play (e.g., pretending to be Spider-Man all by oneself) were not very socially skilled either. And at greatest risk for later social adjustment problems were rejected children.

Using coaching techniques, Ladd and colleagues (Ladd, 1981; Mize & Ladd, 1990) were able to improve the social relationships of unpopular third-grade children as well as of neglected and rejected preschoolers. These researchers taught the third-graders to use three particular methods of communication: asking positively toned questions, offering useful suggestions, and making supportive statements. (For a sample protocol of a coaching session, see Table 12-5). Over a three-week period, children participated in eight sessions, each about an hour long, in which the adult coach offered instruction and guidance through rehearsals, let the children practice on their own, and then reviewed the practice sessions with them. Both immediately after these

Table 12-5

Coaching a child in group participation

Source: Oden & Asher, 1977.

Coach: Okay, I have some ideas about what makes a game fun to play with another person. There are a couple of things that are important to do. You should cooperate with the other person. Do you know what cooperation is? Can you tell me in your own words?

Child: Ahh . . . sharing.

Coach: Yes, sharing. Okay, let's say you and I are playing the game you played last time. What was it again?

Child: Drawing a picture.

Coach: Okay, tell me then, what would be an example of sharing when playing the picture-drawing game?

Child: I'd let you use some pens, too.

Coach: Right. You would share the pens with me. That's an example of cooperation. Now let's say you and I are doing the picture-drawing game. Can you also give me an example of what would not be cooperating?

Child: Taking all the pens.

Coach: Would taking all the pens make the game fun to play?

Child: No.

Coach: So you wouldn't take all the pens. Instead, you'd cooperate by sharing them with me. Can you think of some more examples of cooperation? [The coach waited for a response.] Okay, how about taking turns. . . . Let's say you and I [the coach gives examples]. Okay, I'd like you to try out some of these ideas when you play [a particular new game] with [another child]. Let's go and get [the other child], and after you play, I'll talk to you again for a minute or so and you can tell me if these things seem to be good ideas for having fun at a game with someone.

Teachers and parents often act as coaches, encouraging children to include others in their play and helping them to settle disputes.

sessions and four weeks later, the researchers' assessments indicated that the children's classroom behavior improved and their popularity increased. A control group, who received no coaching, showed no improvement. A similar intervention with a preschool group achieved comparable results (Mize & Ladd, 1990).

Interventions of the sort we've described are not undertaken only with young children. Programs have targeted preadolescents who were not well accepted by peers and who were either aggressive or isolated (Bienert & Schneider, 1995). When interventions were tailored to children's specific deficits (i.e., training was designed to reduce either isolation or aggression), both groups of children gained in peer-group acceptance. More recently, prevention programs aimed at both parents and peers have been found to be helpful as well (Conduct Problems Prevention Research Group, 2004). We review these programs in Chapter 14.

Recently, Asher and Hopmeyer (2001) found that some 10 percent of elementary school children report "extremely high levels of loneliness." According to these researchers, this distressing emotional state reflects the degree to which children are accepted by their peers and whether or not they have best friends. Among these investigators' suggestions for useful interventions with lonely children are the following:

- Teaching such skills as how to cooperate with others, how to be a responsive communicator, and how to support or validate others' ideas and actions
- Teaching specific games and sports activities
- Changing classroom and school organizational patterns

The notion of teaching specific skills is based on Asher and Hopmeyer's (2001) finding that lonely people are likely not to try hard to interact with others. They are generally less prosocial, or helpful, in their peer relations and tend to be negative, withdrawn, and nonresponsive. Anxiety and fear of rejection may prevent such individuals from risking friendly overtures. Asher and Hopmeyer also suggest that games and sports activities can offer useful contexts for teaching the skills they've identified as well as offer children a chance to display and develop the competence that can gain them social acceptance.

In addition to improving the lonely child's skills and behaviors, Asher and Hopmeyer (2001) suggest changing elements in the child's environment so as to reduce or eliminate conditions that may be hindering her development of good social skills. For example, in a Norwegian study (Olweus, 1991b, 1993) researchers persuaded a school to lower its tolerance for bullying and succeeded in altering classroom interactions, such as encouraging teachers to offer public praise to lonely children. These investigators also propose altering class organization patterns: One possibility is to use the homeroom pattern of elementary grades in secondary schools in order to avoid the constant changing from room to room. Another is "looping," in which one teacher stays with a given class for several years as the classmates move up in grade level.

WHEN PEERS BECOME FRIENDS

In our discussions so far, we have focused on how well children may be accepted by their classmates or peer group. Although this group perspective is an important one, children also develop the close, dyadic relationships with a few peers that we call friendships. The essentials of a **friendship,** according to Hartup (1989), are reciprocity and commitment between people who see themselves more or less as equals. As the following exchange indicates, young children don't always find it easy to explain friendship. Here's one child's attempt:

Interviewer: Why is Caleb your friend?

Tony: Because I like him.

Interviewer: And why do you like him?

Tony: Because he's my friend.

Interviewer: And why is he your friend?

Tony (with mild disgust): Because—I—choosed—him—for—my—friend. (Rubin, 1980)

friendship A reciprocal commitment between two people who see themselves more or less as equals.

Expectations and Obligations of Friendship

Children do have certain expectations about relationships with friends (Schneider, 2000). And these expectations about friends seem to evolve over time in three stages. Note, in the following list, that the expectations that emerge at each stage do not disappear with the next; in fact, those shown in italics tend to increase with age (Bigelow, 1977; Bigelow & LaGaipa, 1975).

1. **Reward-cost stage (Grades 2–3):** Children expect friends to *offer help, share common activities,* provide stimulating ideas, be able to join in organized play, *offer judgments, be physically nearby,* and be demographically similar to them.
2. **Normative stage (Grades 4–5):** Children now expect friends to *accept* and *admire* them, to bring *loyalty and commitment* to a friendship, and to express similar values and attitudes toward rules and sanctions.
3. **Empathic stage (Grades 6–7):** Children begin to expect *genuineness* and the *potential for intimacy* in their friends; they expect friends to understand them and to be willing to engage in **self-disclosure;** they want friends to accept their help, to share *common interests,* and to hold similar attitudes and values across a range of topics (not just rules). At this stage, kids may enter into "chumship," the unique kind of intimacy described by Sullivan (1953).

self-disclosure The honest sharing of information of a very personal nature, often with a focus on problem solving; a central means by which adolescents develop friendships.

The obligations of friendship change as well. Studying 10- to 17-year-olds, Youniss and his colleagues (Smollar & Youniss, 1982; Youniss, 1980) found that friendship obligations undergo marked shifts over adolescence. Although 80 percent of the 10- to 11-year-olds thought friends should "be nice to one another and help each other," only 11 percent of the 16- to 17-year-olds indicated that this was a central obligation. In contrast, 62 percent of the 16- to 17-year-olds thought that providing emotional support was important, but only 5 percent of the 10- to 11-year-olds agreed. Reasons change too. Young children view obligations as important "so he'll be nice to you too" or "to keep the relation going good." Obligations are important to older children because they would benefit the other person ("because she'll be happier if you do") or because they define the relationship ("That's what friends are supposed to do"). Gender is also a factor: Females at all ages are more likely than males to be concerned with emotional assistance and to stress reasons based on benefiting the other person (Ladd, 2005; Schneider, 2000).

Unfortunately, there is no clear evidence that these expectations always translate into action! What children—and many adults—say they expect and what they do are not highly related. Nor are friendships always smooth and everlasting. Fights often occur, friends can and do hurt each other, and friendships do end. Box 12.3 discusses

Box 12.3

Child Psychology in Action

WHEN "LOVE THY NEIGHBOR" FAILS: PEERS AS MUTUAL ENEMIES

Peer interaction can have a dark side, as studies of peer rejection and bullying reveal. A relationship that clearly partakes of this dark aspect of social behavior is that of **mutual antipathy**—a situation in which two or more children dislike or even hate each other. Some mutual antipathies involve children of the same gender; others occur between opposite-gender children. What effect do such relationships have on children's social adjustment?

In a recent study of American third graders, 65 percent of the children reported at least one same-sex mutual antipathy, and some children had as many as three (Hembree & Vandell, 2000). Such relationships of mutual dislike are found in older children as well. In a recent study of Dutch children, Abecassis and colleagues (2002) found that both fifth and eighth graders reported mutual antipathies. In this case, boys were more likely to have these kinds of relationships than girls were. And, not surprisingly, among children at many ages (third, fifth, and eighth grades), rejected and controversial children were more likely to be involved in these kinds of relationships than were popular and average children. Sadly, mutual antipathies can have very negative effects on both children's and adolescents' developmental outcomes. The more numerous the same-sex antipathies a child is involved in, the poorer his or her socioemotional adjustment and academic performance (Hembree & Vandell, 2000).

During preadolescence, all children with same-sex antipathies are more likely than those without such relationships to be antisocial and to fight and bully or be victimized. In contrast, the effects of mixed-sex antipathies (boy/girl dislikes and is disliked by girl/boy) differ between boys and girls. Boys with these problems tend to be antisocial, but in girls, antisocial behavior does not seem to be linked with mixed-sex antipathies. Instead, girls in mixed-sex antipathies were less socially skilled and less prosocial; they had fewer friends, they were more likely to be victimized, and they reported more somatic and depressive symptoms.

Moreover, having enemies in preadolescence foreshadows later problems during adolescence. Boys who had same-sex mutual antipathies at age 10 were more likely, three years later in adolescence, to exhibit addiction and delinquency, and to have more somatic complaints and less support from friends (Abecassis et al., 2002). For girls, same-sex antipathies in preadolescence predicted lower achievement scores in adolescence. Cross-gender antipathies in preadolescence were not related to adolescent outcomes for either boys or girls.

Having friends is clearly a protective factor in children's development. Having enemies, on the other hand, puts children at risk for later problems. Just as it isn't good for countries to have enemies, it's not good for children, either. "Love thy neighbor" is clearly a better policy for countries and children alike!

mutual antipathy A relationship of mutual dislike between two people.

a particularly unhappy kind of relationship in which two people develop mutual antipathy rather than friendship. In the next section, we explore how children make friends and how they behave with their friends.

Making Friends

Although psychologists and others have studied children's peer relations for many decades, we still find it difficult to answer a simple question, "How do children become friends?" Gottman and his colleagues (Gottman, 1983; Gottman & Parker, 1986; Parker & Gottman, 1989) tried to provide an answer in a series of studies of children ranging in age from 3 to 7 years old. These researchers set up tape recorders in children's homes and listened while some children played with their best friends and other children played with strangers. While groups of "best friends" and groups of

Table 12-6   The social processes of friendship formation

Process	Definition	Example
Communication clarity and connectedness	Request for message clarification followed by appropriate clarification of the message.	Child A: Give it to me. Child B: Which one? Child A: The purple one with yellow ears.
Information exchange	Asking questions and eliciting revelant information.	Where do you live? What color is your crayon?
Establishing common ground	Finding something to do together and/or exploring partners' similarities and differences.	Let's play trucks. I like tea parties, do you?
Self-disclosure of feelings	Questions about feelings by one child are followed by expression of feelings by the partner.	I'm really scared of the dark and snakes, too.
Positive reciprocity	One partner responds to the other's positive behavior or extends or lengthens a positive exchange: usually involves joking, gossip, or fantasy.	Child A: Did you hear what happened to Mary's sister? Child B: No, tell me and then I'll tell you another thing about Mary.
Conflict resolution	The extent to which play partners resolve disputes and disagreements successfully.	Child A: I want the blue truck. Child B: No, I'm playing with it. Child A: I want it. Child B: OK let's play with it together.

Source: Adapted from Gottman, 1983.

unacquainted peers played in their homes for three sessions, the researchers tracked the behavior of each. The study found that friends communicated more clearly, disclosed themselves more, had more positive exchanges, established common ground more easily, exchanged more information, and were able to resolve conflict more effectively than strangers. Interestingly, unacquainted children who got along well and were rated as likely to become friends scored higher on these dimensions than others in the stranger group. One of this study's achievements was the description of a set of social processes that successfully distinguished between the play patterns of friends and strangers (see Table 12-6).

Studies with children at varying ages confirm many of these findings. Not surprisingly, children spend more time with friends and express more positive affect in these interactions than they do with nonfriends (Hartup, 1996; Ladd, 2005; Schneider, 2000). They share more with their friends (Jones, 1985), although when friends are tough competitors, sharing with each other may decrease somewhat (Berndt, 1986). Being friends does not mean never disagreeing (Hartup, 1996; Laursen, Hartup, & Koplas, 1996). In fact, friends disagree more than nonfriends, but their conflicts are less heated and they're more likely to stay in contact after an argument than nonfriends (Hartup, Laursen, Stewart, & Eastenson, 1988). Friends are more likely to resolve conflicts in an equitable way and to ensure that the resolution preserves the friendship (Hartup, 1996; Laursen et al., 1996). And friends, of course, are more intimate and self-disclosing with each other than with simple acquaintances

(Berndt & Perry, 1990; Simpkins & Parke, 2001). Friends are more knowledgeable about each other than nonfriends—they know each other's strengths and secrets as well as their wishes and weaknesses (Ladd & Emerson, 1984; Schneider, 2000). As someone once said, "A friend is one who knows our faults but doesn't give a damn!"

Friendships Evolve over Time

How do friendship patterns change across development? Parker and Gottman (1989) suggest that the goals and central processes involved in successful friendship formation shift across age. For young children (ages 3 to 7 years), the goal of peer interaction is coordinated play, with all the social processes organized to promote successful play. In the second developmental phase—the 8- to 12-year period—the goal changes from playful interaction to a concern with being accepted by one's same-gender peers. Children are concerned with the norms of the group, figuring out which actions will lead to acceptance and inclusion, and which to exclusion and rejection. The most salient social process in middle childhood is **negative gossip,** which involves sharing some negative information about another child. When this works well, the partner responds with interest, more negative gossip, and often feelings of solidarity.

negative gossip Sharing some negative information about another child with a peer.

Both boys and girls engage in gossip, ritual insults, and teasing during this period, and at times this behavior reaches organized levels. One study found, for example, that in some schools, girls kept "slam books" in which each girl wrote nasty things about other girls (Giese-Davis, cited by Gottman, 1986). Here is an example of two girls, Erica and Mikaila, gossiping about another girl, Katie.

> **Erica:** Katie does lots of weird things. Like, every time she makes a mistake, she says, "Well, *sorry*." (Sarcastic tone)
>
> **Mikaila:** I know.
>
> **Erica:** And stuff like that.
>
> **Mikaila:** She's mean. She beat me up once. (Laughs) I could hardly breathe she hit me in the stomach so hard.
>
> **Erica:** She acts like . . .
>
> **Mikaila:** She's the boss. (Gottman, 1986)

Often gossip is used as a way of establishing the norms for the group, and as this example shows, it is important not to be too aggressive or bossy. As we will see in Chapter 14, gossip sometimes expresses hostility. Girls tend to use this kind of relational aggression rather than the forms of physical aggression that boys more commonly use. In the third developmental period (13 to 17 years), the focus shifts to understanding the self. Self-exploration and self-disclosure are the principal social processes this time, and they're accompanied by intense honesty and a lot of problem solving. Table 12-7 summarizes these developmental periods.

Losing Friends

Friendships, like most everything else in life, change over time. Children form new friendships and lose, renew, and replace friendships, sometimes as quickly as within days or weeks, sometimes over a span of years. To trace changes in friendship patterns, Parker and Seal (1996) studied 216 children ages 8 to 15, at a summer camp. Within this larger group, these researchers identified five subgroups based on common patterns in friendships. In the *rotation* group were children who readily formed new relationships but whose social ties showed little stability. These children were

Table 12-7   How friendship patterns develop

	Early Childhood (3–7 years old)	Middle Childhood (8–12 years old)	Adolescence (13–17 years old)
Primary concerns	To maximize excitement, entertainment, and enjoyment through play	To be included by peers; to avoid rejection; to present oneself to others in a positive way	To explore oneself—to come to know oneself, define oneself
Main processes and purposes of communication	To coordinate play; to escalate and de-escalate play activity; talking about activities; resolving conflict	To share negative gossip with others	To disclose oneself to another or others; to solve problems
Emotional development	Learning to manage arousal during interaction	Acquiring rules for showing feelings; rejecting sentiment	Getting logic and emotion together; understanding the implications of emotions for relationships

Source: Adapted from Gottman & Mettetal, 1986.

considered playful teasers and were always up on the latest interesting gossip, but they were also aggressive, bossy, and untrustworthy. The *growth* group comprised children who added new relationships and kept existing ones. These children were neither bossy nor easily pushed around. In the *decline* group were children whose friendships often broke up and who failed to replace these relationships. These children were caring, shared with others, and, like those in the rotation group, engaged in playful teasing; they were often judged to be "show-offs." Children in the *static* group maintained a stable pool of friendships but added no new ones. The girls in this group were known for honesty, and the group members were less apt to tease others; at the same time, they were less caring than others. Finally, the *friendless* group made no friends at all throughout the summer. These children were perceived by others as timid, shy, and as preferring to play alone. They couldn't deal with teasing and were easily angered. In addition, they were rated lower than other children on caring, honesty, and sharing. And as we might expect, these children were more lonely than others.

Another examination of the evolution of friendships revealed gender as a factor in the stability of children's peer relationships. Benenson and Christakos (2003) found that girls' closest same-sex friendships appeared more fragile and less lasting than those of boys. Based on a study of 10- to 15-year-olds, they suggest that the tendency of girls to form close relationships with each other in isolation from a larger group may jeopardize these relationships in a way not seen in boys' friendships. Boys' same-sex friendships are more often embedded in a larger group of relationships, which provides a kind of safety net. The easy recourse to third party mediators, allies, and alternative partners helps keep boys' friendship ties intact.

Although the greater intimacy expressed in girls' friendships may be rewarding, it may also place the friendships at greater risk. Girls may be more likely to worry that a relationship might end or to feel that they've done something to damage a friendship. When things go wrong, girls may intensify the problem by divulging intimate secrets about their partners to others, and this betrayal may hasten the demise of a friendship. Boys, on the other hand, seem to be less intimate with one another, less likely to divulge personal information about their partners, and, when problems arise, more likely to confront their partners directly.

The Pros and Cons of Friendship

For most children, having friends is a positive accomplishment. As we saw earlier in the chapter, peers and friends provide support, intimacy, and guidance. Children with friends are less lonely and depressed (Hartup, 1996), and even their long-term outcomes are better. Bagwell and colleagues (1998) found that fifth graders who had a reciprocated best friendship were better adjusted at the age of 23. Compared with friendless children, these individuals experienced less depression, exhibited less delinquent behavior, did better in college, and had better relationships with family and peers. Having a childhood friendship forecasts more successful adult development.

Not all friendships are beneficial, for they may pose risks as well as offer protective factors (Bagwell, 2004). Even rejected children form friendships, but often they choose as friends other rejected (and often aggressive) classmates. Moreover, compared with the friendships of nonrejected/nonaggressive children, the friendships of rejected children are often of poorer quality—that is, they tend to be less satisfying, less intimate, and more likely to be conflict-ridden (Poulin, Dishion, & Haas, 1999). Rejected children who are friends often encourage each other's deviant behavior, such as cheating, aggression, and substance use or abuse (Bagwell, 2004). Thus it is important to consider the common activities that form the basis of a friendship in addition to the quality of the relationship. We return to this issue in Chapter 15 when we explore the role of peers and friends in the development of psychological difficulties.

Romantic ties form earlier than some people believe, as these preteens illustrate.

The Romantic Relationship: A Developmental Milestone

Andrew Collins, a student of adolescence, recently observed that "Popular culture is suffused with images of the dreaminess, preoccupation, shyness, self-consciousness and sexual awakening of adolescents in love" (Collins, 2003). Many dismiss romantic relationships as no more than flings or even a fiction of popular culture. If they've no developmental significance, why then should we discuss adolescent romantic relationships? Let's examine some of the myths that surround these kinds of relationships and try to separate fact from fancy.

TEENAGE LOVE AFFAIRS REALLY DO MATTER Here are four of the most commonly held mistaken ideas about adolescent romantic relationships:

Myth 1: Adolescent romantic relationships are transitory. According to this belief, these relationships are fleeting and superficial.

Reality: Adolescent romantic relationships are neither uncommon nor transitory. In one study, 25 percent of 12-year-olds, nearly 50 percent of 15-year-olds, and 70 percent of 18-year-olds reported having a romantic relationship within the preceding 18 months (Carver, Joyner, & Udry, 2003).

And a surprising percentage of adolescents in dating relationships reported that their relationships had lasted 11 months or more. Among adolescents 14 and under, 20 percent reported a similar length of relationship history, and 60 percent of 17- and 18-year-olds indicated that their romantic ties lasted nearly a year or longer (Carver et al., 2003).

Myth 2: Adolescent romantic relationships are trivial. Even if romantic ties last a fair amount of time, they are of little significance to adolescent development.

Reality: According to recent evidence, adolescent romantic alliances are quite significant in adolescent functioning and possibly in longer-term outcomes. As we all know, romance has its costs as well as its rewards. Adolescents in romantic relationships report more conflict, have more mood swings, and experience more symptoms of depression (Joyner & Udry, 2000; Larson & Richards, 1994; Laursen, 1995). Note that it is often the breakup that triggers depression, not the relationship itself. But there are positive outcomes associated with romantic relationships too. Being in such a relationship is linked with a feeling of self-worth, a sense of competence, and a feeling that one is part of the peer group (Connolly, Craig, Goldberg, & Pepler, 2004; Harter, 2006). **Peer-group networks** and romantic relationships, in fact, probably support each other: Peer networks support early romantic pairings, and these ties facilitate connections with other peers (Connolly, Furman, & Konarski, 2000; Furman, 2002). Furthermore, early romantic relationships help us to understand interpersonal relationships in adolescence. In a longitudinal German study, Seiffge-Krenke, Shulman, and Klessinger (2001) found that the quality of romantic relationships in midadolescence was significantly and positively related to commitment in other relationships in young adulthood.

On the other hand, early dating with a large number of different partners may forecast relationships of poorer quality in young adulthood (Collins, 2003). Although these studies suggest that quality, timing, and duration of relationships are all possible determinants of the long term consequences of adolescent romantic ties, one recent report found no link between adolescent romantic involvement and adult adjustment (Roisman et al., 2004). Although the short-term significance of adolescent romance is clear, the verdict on its long-term significance for adult functioning is not yet in.

Myth 3: Romantic relationships don't differ from other relationships. According to this myth, these relationships simply mirror relationships with family members, friends, and other peers.

Reality: It is true that the quality of family relationships and same-sex friendships are often predictive of the quality of romantic ties. Conger, Bryant, and Elder (2000) found that nurturant parenting during adolescence predicted the quality of romantic relationships five years later: a close parent-adolescent relationship was linked with a better-quality romantic relationship. Neither sibling nor marital relationship quality predicted romantic ties. On the other hand, inadequate parenting (insufficient monitoring of child behavior, inconsistent discipline) is related not only to increased antisocial, aggressive behavior in general but to increased risk for aggression and violence toward a romantic partner (Capaldi & Clark, 1998; Simons, Lin, & Gordon, 1998). Clearly, quality of the parent-child relationship is an important predictor of the quality of children's later romantic alliances.

Similarly, children with high-quality same-sex friendships in middle childhood have healthier romantic ties (more intimacy and disclosure) during adolescence (Collins & Sroufe, 1999). However, family, peer, and friendship relationships are clearly different from romantic ones. In fact, even 9-year-olds expect different things from friends and romantic partners (Connolly & Goldberg, 1999). Children

peer-group network The cluster of peer acquaintances who are familiar with and interact with one another at different times for common play or task-oriented purposes.

expect more intimacy, for example, from romantic partners than friends. Furman and his colleagues (2002) found very low correlations among high school seniors' representations of their relationships with parents, friends, and romantic partners.

Myth 4: Romantic relationships are important mainly as harbingers of problem behavior. Early dating, and especially early sexual activity, are linked with a variety of behavior problems, such as drug use and classroom difficulties (Davies & Windle, 2000).

Reality: There is some truth to this statement, and dating at an early age can be problematic. Delaying dating until it is more normative and until the adolescent is more mature—at 15 or 16—is associated with reduced risk for later problems. Dating many different partners can also increase risk for behavior problems, such as acting out and aggression. Male and female adolescents who dated many partners between the ages of 12 and 16 showed an increase in behavior problems compared with those who dated fewer people (Zimmer-Gembeck, Siebenbruner, & Collins, 2001).

CHANGES IN ROMANTIC ALLIANCES OVER TIME   Adolescents at all ages develop romantic ties, but the romantic experience changes between early and late adolescence (Collins, 2003). Just as the frequency of romantic involvement increases across development, the length of time in a specific relationship also increases. A recent study showed that among 14- to 15-year-olds, 35 percent were in relationships that lasted 11 months or more, whereas 55 percent of those 16 or older were in long-term relationships (Carver et al., 2003).

The peer group plays a major role in partner choice among young adolescents. You date partners that your peer network approves of or views as "cool." Appearance, clothes, status, and other superficial features guide young adolescents' choices, but older adolescents focus more on characteristics that underlie intimacy and compatibility, such as personality, values, and particular interests (Zani, 1993). Among older adolescents, there is more interdependence between partners in romantic relationships (Laursen & Jensen-Campbell, 1999). Older adolescents are more likely than younger ones to compromise with their partners as a way of solving problems.

In sum, romantic relationships do represent an important developmental milestone in adolescence. Romance is a harbinger of later adaptations; we need to accept and understand its importance to healthy adolescent development.

PARENTS, PEERS, OR BOTH?

Many writers have seen preadolescence and adolescence as highly stressful periods during which children are buffeted by the often conflicting behavioral standards of parents and contemporaries. Others, on the other hand, have argued that these standards conflict far less frequently than is suggested and that in fact there is often remarkable agreement between parental and peer values (Brown & Huang, 1995; Collins, Maccoby, Steinberg, Hetherington, & Bornstein, 2000; Vandell, 2000). A better question than whether peers or adults are more influential is, "Under what conditions and with what behaviors are peers or adults influential?"

Peers and parents each have their own areas of expertise. Although peers are not generally the best advisers on occupational choices, parents are not the best source for the latest and best music recordings and videos. Peers exert more influence on teens' styles of interpersonal behavior, their selections of friends, and their choices of fashions and entertainment. Parents have more impact on their teenagers' academic choices, their job preferences, and their future aspirations (Hartup, 1996). Moreover, when adolescents are with parents and peers they generally engage in very different types of activities—work and task activities with parents, recreation and conversation with peers (Larson & Richards, 1994; Larson & Verma, 1999).

Much of a child's behavior reflects a mix of peer and parental influence (Elder & Conger, 2000; Ladd, 2005). Studying the use of marijuana, Kandel (1973) found that among teenagers whose best friends were nonusers, but whose parents were users, only 17 percent smoked marijuana. If friends used drugs, however, and parents did not, 56 percent of adolescents reported using marijuana. When both parents and peers were users, 67 percent of the adolescents used marijuana. Studies on the use of alcohol, tobacco, and illegal drugs, and of early and risky sexual behavior, have reported similar numbers (Dishion, Poulin, & Medici Skaggs, 2000; Mounts & Steinberg, 1995). Thus, drug usage by parents and peers had a combined impact on adolescents' use of marijuana.

In Chapter 11, we discussed several approaches to parenting, noting that the authoritative style is generally more effective than the authoritarian approach to childrearing. Children's susceptibility to peer pressure, it turns out, can be greatly reduced by warm, supportive, authoritative parenting. Examining the after-school activity of 865 adolescents, Steinberg (1986) found that spending time at home was far more likely to buffer these young people from undesirable peer influence than unsupervised "hanging out." In the study illustrated in Figure 12-10, children whose parents were more authoritative were considerably less susceptible to peer pressure than were children whose parents were less authoritative.

It also helps if a child's *friends* have authoritative parents. Steinberg and colleagues (Fletcher, Darling, Steinberg, & Dornbusch, 1995) discovered that adolescents with friends who described their own parents as authoritative were less likely to use drugs and run afoul of the law than teenagers whose friends described their parents as authoritarian. Note that, even after considering the target adolescent's own family influence, the effect of the friend's family's childrearing style was evident. Perhaps well-adjusted adolescents seek out similar peers as friends, or maybe parents encourage their children to associate with such peers. In any event, it's clear that parenting style carries over to peer settings and can either contribute to children's vulnerability to peer pressure or protect them from it.

According to Brown and Huang (1995), adolescents' behavior reflects an interaction between parental influence and peer experience. Exploring this notion, these

Authoritative parents who maintain close relationships with their children help them to resist peer pressure more effectively.

Figure 12-10

Hanging out and peer pressure

In this study, the adolescent sons of parents rated low on authoritativeness were more susceptible to peer pressure, even when at home, than the sons of parents rated high on authoritativeness. Daughters of such parents were considerably more likely than sons to conform to parental guidelines when they were at home, but when hanging out they didn't differ too much from sons in susceptibility to peer pressure. Among children of highly authoritative parents, boys showed little difference in vulnerability to peer pressure whether at home or with peers, but these girls showed a little more responsiveness to peers when hanging out.

Source: Steinberg, 1986.

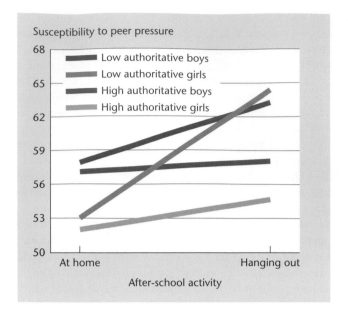

researchers designed a study to measure the effects on groups of teenagers of two types of parenting style and two types of peer groups. Parenting style was considered *facilitative* if parents measured high on one of four dimensions: *warmth, demandingness, psychological autonomy granting,* and *encouragement of education.* If parents measured low on one of these dimensions, their style was considered *inhibitive.* A peer group was considered *adaptive* if it was composed largely of brainy kids; if a group included drug users or other outsiders it was considered *maladaptive.* Brown and Huang then proposed that facilitative parents would affect their children's behavior positively and more so in an adaptive crowd than in a maladaptive one. Conversely, they hypothesized, inhibitive parents would affect their children's behavior negatively, and more so in a maladaptive crowd than in an adaptive one.

And this is exactly what they found. Teenagers whose parents were facilitative spent more time on homework than those with inhibitive parents, and the more adaptive their peer group was the harder they studied (Figure 12-11a). Further, across the board, these teens were less likely to use drugs—and the more facilitative their parents were, the more the teenagers resisted drug use (Figure 12-11b). By contrast, the findings for adolescents with inhibitive parents were almost exactly opposite: No matter which type of crowd they joined, these teens did less homework and used more drugs. Moreover, these effects were stronger in the maladaptive peer group than in the adaptive one. In sum, the beliefs that parental influence is soon replaced by peer influence and that parenting really doesn't matter are wrong. Although parental influence wanes as peer influence increases, both parents and peers play a significant role in determining the child/adolescent's social development.

FROM DYADS TO GROUPS

As recent American TV reality shows clearly illustrate, people form alliances and pacts and make other kinds of social connections in order to overcome obstacles and to reach common goals. In similar fashion, children form alliances and develop group

Figure 12-11   Parenting style, crowd type, academic effort, and drug use

The more facilitative the parents of adolescents were, and the more adaptive the crowd with which teenagers associated, the more likely the teens were to do their homework (a) and the less likely they were to engage in drug use (b).

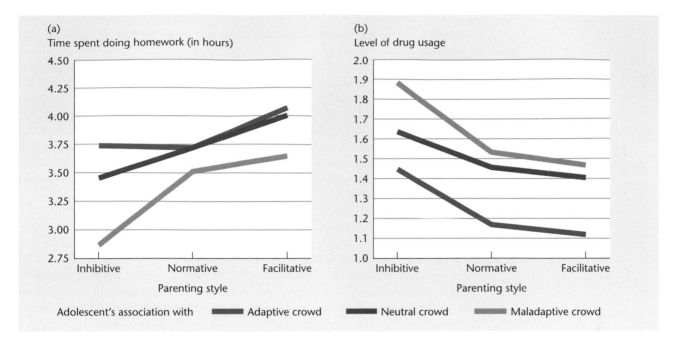

Source: Brown & Huang, 1995.

structures with common goals and rules of behavior. Group structures are different from dyadic friendships but are another way that children can achieve their social goals. Groups usually develop a hierarchical structure that identifies and characterizes the relationship of each member of the group to each other member and facilitates member interaction. Inevitably, some group members are identified as dominant, and their leadership roles clearly differ from the roles of the other children in the group.

Dominance Hierarchies

Children in a group will form a **dominance hierarchy,** or "pecking order," even in preschool. In fact, Hawley and Little (1999) found clear evidence of a social dominance hierarchy in children between the ages of one year four months and three years two months. Although preschool children tend to perceive their own positions as a bit higher in the pecking order than they really are, they become increasingly accurate at judging their own status (Hawley, 1999). Moreover, although preschool children's dominance hierarchies are simpler and more loosely differentiated than those of older children, as these children age they tend to agree in identifying group status structures (Hawley, 1999). Other evidence suggests that dominance hierarchies emerge very quickly. In a study by Dodge, Coie, Pettit, & Price (1990), within the first 45 minutes of contact, unacquainted first- and third-grade boys began to develop a coherently organized social structure.

What predicts a child's ability to be dominant over her peers? A variety of attributes, such as attractiveness, physical strength, and cognitive maturity, all lead to dominance (Hawley, 1999). Even familiarity and experience in the preschool setting can

dominance hierarchy An ordering of individuals in a group from most to least dominant; a "pecking order."

give a young child some advantage (Hawley & Little, 1999). Persistence helps too—the more persistent children become the more dominant (Hawley & Little, 1999). Among toddlers, especially the one-to-three-year-old set, girls may be dominant over boys (Hawley & Little, 1999), but after age 3, boys more often take dominant roles. Girls' early leadership underscores the fact that the road to dominance may as easily be gained by prosocial strategies, such as "seizing the day" and being persuasive, as by aggression and conquest.

The qualities by which a leader is measured change over time. Young children seem to appraise a peer's potential for dominance on the basis of the ability to direct others' behavior, leadership in play, physical coercion, and physical toughness. In contrast, status structures among older children are more likely to be based on leadership skills, appearance, academic performance, athletic prowess, and pubertal development (Hawley, 1999). Dominance and status affect social interaction as well. Peers watch and imitate dominant children more than nondominant children (Hawley & Little, 1999). In addition, children are more likely to conform to the opinions and behavior of high-status peers (Rubin et al., 2006).

What functions do hierarchies serve? First, they reduce aggression among the group members, and enable the establishment of nonaggressive means of resolving conflict. For example, a high-ranking member may use a threat gesture to keep a lower-ranking group member in line. In fact, aggression is rarely seen in a group with a well-established hierarchy (Hawley & Little, 1999). A second purpose is to help divide the tasks and labor of the group, with worker roles being assumed by the lower-status members and leadership roles going to the more dominant members. Third, dominance hierarchies determine the allocation of resources—especially limited resources (Charlesworth, 1988; Hawley, 1999). Rank has as many privileges in the nursery school set as among adolescents (Charlesworth & Dzur, 1987; Savin-Williams, 1987). In a study of adolescent summer campers, Savin-Williams (1987) found that the dominant teens "frequently ate the bigger piece of cake at mealtimes, sat where they wanted to during discussions and slept in the preferred sleeping sites during camp-outs (near the fire)—all scarce resources at summer camp" (p. 934). Clearly, dominance hierarchies play important roles in regulating interaction, but as is often the case, the ones at the top of the hierarchy seem to benefit most.

Cliques and Crowds

clique A voluntary group formed on the basis of friendship.

In middle childhood, children begin to form cliques, voluntary groups based on friendship (Schneider, 2000). A **clique** may range in size from three to nine children, and members usually are of the same gender and same race (Kindermann, McCollam, & Gibson, 1995). By the time children are 11, most of their interaction with peers is in the context of the clique. Membership in cliques enhances children's psychological well-being and their ability to cope with stress (Rubin et al., 2006), just as social acceptance and friendship are buffers against loneliness.

crowd A collection of people whom others have stereotyped on the basis of their perceived shared attitudes or activities; for example, *populars* or *nerds*.

Cliques are evident in adolescence as well but decline across the high school years (Shrum & Cheek, 1987), when they are superseded by crowds. A **crowd** is a collection of people who share attitudes or activities that define a particular stereotype—for example, jocks, brains, eggheads, loners, burnouts, druggies, populars, and nerds—and who may or may not spend much time together (Brown, 1990; Brown & Huang, 1995). Crowd affiliation is assigned by consensus of the peer group; adolescents don't select it themselves (Rubin et al., 2006). The salience of crowds probably peaks in ninth or tenth grade and decreases throughout high school (Brown, 1990; Brown & Huang, 1995). Like friendships, peer groups are not always beneficial to participants—for example, as we will see in Chapter 15, gang membership is often linked with delinquency and other negative outcomes.

Some cliques, like this high-school Latino group, include members of both sexes.

PEER GROUPS IN DIFFERENT CULTURES

Are peers equally important in all cultures or in all parts of one culture? Is America a uniquely peer-oriented culture? Even within cultures, patterns of peer interaction may differ—for example, comparison of urban and rural peers indicates that Israeli children reared in rural kibbutzim are more cooperative and supportive than city-reared children (Schneider, 2000). In the United States, African American children tend to have more friendships as well as more opposite-sex friendships than European American children (Kovacs et al., 1996). Perhaps African American children are socialized to develop larger peer networks or may live in extended family systems that encourage and make feasible broader social ties (Ladd, 2005).

In some countries, peers play an even more influential role, whereas in others the family and adult agents are more important. Compared with American youths, adolescents in Japan spend less time with peers and more time at home (Rothbaum et al., 2000a). In Japan, parental values play a more prominent role than peer values in the formation and structure of adolescent peer groups than in the United States (Rothbaum et al., 2000a). Similarly, in Latino cultures, children are more family-oriented and less influenced by peers (DeRosier & Kupersmidt, 1991). In Mexico and Central America, parents often maintain this family orientation by directly discouraging peer interaction (Ladd, 2005; Schneider, 2000).

Finally, even styles of relating to peers vary cross culturally. (See Box 12.4.) Research has suggested that Italian children are more likely than Canadian children to embrace debates and disputes with their friends (Casiglia, Lo Coco, & Zapplulla, 1998; Schneider et al., 1997). In these studies, Italian children's friendships were seen as more stable than those of Canadian children, and the investigators suggest that cultural differences in tolerance for conflict may account for this finding. There are even cultural differences in the factors that contribute to the formation of cliques. For example, an adolescent's academic achievement or standing is a stronger determinant of clique membership in China than it is in North America (Chen, Chang, & He, 2003). In North America, as we saw earlier, a wider range of factors, from academic achievement to athletic prowess to deviant orientation, influence clique membership.

Box 12.4

Perspectives on Diversity

CROSS-CULTURAL VARIATIONS IN CHILDREN'S PEER RELATIONSHIPS

Cultures often differ in the way they view the relative importance of the individual or the group. In individual-oriented societies, such as Canada, the United States, and Western Europe, identity is determined largely by personal accomplishments. In contrast, in group-oriented societies, such as China and Japan and in Native American tribes, a greater proportion of a person's identity is related to his membership in the larger group (Schneider, 2000). Just as adult relationships are shaped by these cultural orientations, so are children's peer relationships.

In China and Canada, Orlick, Zhou, and Partington (1990) found differences in the tendencies to be cooperative, to share, to engage in prosocial behavior; to get involved in conflict, and to be aggressive. Among 5-year-olds, 85 percent of Chinese children were cooperative and more likely to share than Canadian children. And 78 percent of the "individualistic" Canadian children were involved in conflicts.

Across these two cultures, the behavioral correlates of peer acceptance showed both similarities and differences. In both China and Canada, middle-school-age children who were sociable and engaged in prosocial behaviors were accepted by peers, whereas those who were aggressive were often rejected (Chen & Rubin, 1994). Canadian children 7 to 9 years old tended to reject other children who were shy and sensitive, whereas in China the same characteristics were met with peer acceptance (Chen, Rubin, & Sun, 1992). These perceptions appear to change across development: among 12-year-old Chinese children, shyness-sensitivity *was* related to peer rejection (Chen & Rubin, 1994). This shift is due in part to changing pressures from Chinese parents for achievement and academic excellence in this age group, as well as to the expectation that as children grow older, they must become more assertive.

Moreover, historical changes in China are modifying the links between shyness and peer acceptance. Chen et al. (2005) found that shyness was related to peer acceptance for 10-year-old Chinese children in a 1990 sample; in a 2002 sample of 10-year-olds, shyness was related to peer rejection. Perhaps the shift toward a market-oriented economy in China with a focus on assertiveness and self-direction is responsible for this shift.

Among Chinese Canadian children, those who were competitive in academic tasks were well liked, whereas those who were competitive in physical or athletic activities were disliked (Udvari, Schneider, Labovitz, & Tassi, 1995). In contrast, non–Asian Canadian children who were competitive in athletics were well liked, and among these children academic competition was unrelated to peer acceptance. These findings highlight the value that Chinese people place on educational attainment (recall the Chapter 10 discussion of cross-national achievement). Clearly, in our efforts to understand peer relationships we need to recognize the broader cultural contexts in which these relationships develop.

Children in all cultures spend time with peers, but the ways they interact often differ. Chinese children, for example, are more cooperative than U.S. children and less aggressive.

Making the Connections 12

There are many links between concepts and ideas in one area of development and concepts and ideas in other areas. Here are some of the connections between ideas in Chapter 12 and discussions in other chapters of this book.

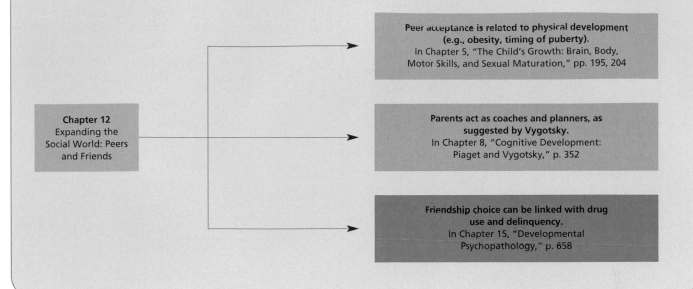

Chapter 12
Expanding the Social World: Peers and Friends

Peer acceptance is related to physical development (e.g., obesity, timing of puberty).
In Chapter 5, "The Child's Growth: Brain, Body, Motor Skills, and Sexual Maturation," pp. 195, 204

Parents act as coaches and planners, as suggested by Vygotsky.
In Chapter 8, "Cognitive Development: Piaget and Vygotsky," p. 352

Friendship choice can be linked with drug use and delinquency.
In Chapter 15, "Developmental Psychopathology," p. 658

SUMMARY

- Children's interactions with peers are freer and more egalitarian than their interactions with their parents. This greater fluidity facilitates interpersonal exploration and encourages growth in social competence and the development of a sense of social justice.

How Peer Interactions Begin: Developmental Patterns

- During the second half of the first year, infants begin to recognize peers as social partners and attempt to influence one another by such means as vocalizing and touching. In the early toddler period, peers begin to exchange both turns and roles during social interactions; in the late toddler period, a major achievement is the ability to share meaning with a social partner. As children's competence with peers develops, they begin to form true **relationships.** They shift toward increased social play and a preference for playing with peers rather than adults, a trend that continues throughout the preschool and elementary years.

- After about age 7, children are more likely to choose same-gender rather than opposite-gender play partners; this remains the case until adolescence, when interest in the opposite gender begins.

Peers as Socializers

- The peer group influences the development of the child using many of the same techniques that parents do, such as modeling and reinforcement. Children acquire a wide range of knowledge and a variety of responses by observing and imitating the behaviors of their peers. Imitation may serve as a way to both learn social rules and maintain social interaction.

- Peers reinforce one another with increasing frequency throughout the preschool years, and reinforcement commonly is reciprocated.

- Peers also serve as standards against which children evaluate themselves. Research indicates that the use of **social comparison** with the peer group as a means of self-evaluation increases dramatically in the early elementary school years. Comparing oneself with others forms one building block for one's self-image and self-esteem.

- Peers provide opportunities for socializing and forming relationships as well as for developing a sense of belonging.

Peer Acceptance

- Researchers assess peer status with **sociometric techniques,** in which children identify peers whom they like and those whom they don't like. On the basis of these nominations, children have been classified as **popular, rejected, neglected,** and **average. Controversial** children are liked by some peers and disliked by others.

- Popular children engage in more prosocial behavior and help set the norms for a group, whereas rejected children are often aggressive, aversive, and socially unskilled. Neglected children are less talkative and more withdrawn.

- For a child to interact effectively with others, she needs self-confidence, persistence, and the ability to try a new approach when another has been unsuccessful. A model of the cognitive decision-making process describes six steps that children must negotiate in social interaction: Children must evaluate a social situation, assess other children's behavior, decide what their own goals in a situation are and how they may best achieve them, decide on certain actions, and act on their decisions. Children who show social competence use this process most successfully.

- Achieving such competence may be difficult for children who approach social interactions with a focus on their inadequacies and the belief that they cannot change their own abilities and behaviors. In addition, when children attribute the causation of events to factors outside of themselves, they may believe they can have no effect on a situation and not try their best.

- In general, children prefer spending time with peers of the same age and the same gender. Although age preferences may be due to the age-grading of many institutions, some research suggests that children would choose same-age playmates on their own. Segregation by gender is clearly self-imposed, and it seems to be related to differences in the interests and play patterns of girls and boys. Until the onset of adolescence, opposite-gender friendships are somewhat rare. One reason is that boys and girls have traditionally sought different types of play, girls preferring play involving such things as books, art, and conversation, boys preferring rough-and-tumble activities and organized games. As girls become more involved in team sports, these preferences may change.

- Children often form first impressions of others on the basis on appearance. By age 3, children distinguish attractive from unattractive children in the same way that adults do, and they attribute more negative characteristics to children judged to be unattractive.

- Being unpopular among peers can lead to both short-term and long-term problems. Unpopular children (especially rejected ones) feel lonely and socially dissatisfied, and are more likely to drop out of school and develop criminal behavior patterns. **Peer victimization** can take a heavy toll on children; having at least one friend can lessen the loneliness this may cause.

- Social standing tends to remain stable across time and situations, showing the most stability for rejected children. Some programs designed to help these children by shaping socially desirable behavior through reinforcement and coaching in social skills have proved beneficial. Although not all unpopular children need help in peer interactions, rejected children clearly can benefit from intervention. Loneliness, a common result of being rejected or ignored, can be lessened if a rejected child has one stable friendship.

Promoters of Peer Acceptance: Parents and Teachers

- Parents play an important role in promoting a child's peer relations. They serve as partners with whom the child acquires social skills that help him interact with other children. They also act as coaches or educators by giving advice and support, reinforcing useful behaviors, and modeling strategies for conduct with peers. They provide opportunities for peer interaction through their choice of neighborhood and their willingness to schedule visits with friends (especially for preschoolers). But a child who is abused by parents may develop aggressive behaviors with peers and thus incur their rejection.

- Teachers can play a role in helping children improve their social skills. Good results have been gained through coaching children in more effective ways of communicating, and in changing children's environments, such as penalizing bullies and using the homeroom pattern at the secondary level.

When Peers Become Friends

- Children develop **friendships** with only a few peers. Expectations of a friend change during the elementary school years from someone who simply shares activities to someone who can also keep secrets and be understanding.

- Friends interact with each other in a way that differs from their interactions with unacquainted peers and the goals of friendship change with development. For young children (ages 3 to 7), the goal is coordinated play, whereas for older children (ages 8 to 12) the goal is establishing group norms and being accepted by peers. During this period, **self-disclosure** becomes important. By adolescence (ages 13 to 17), the focus shifts to understanding the self, making self-disclosure a critical component of friendship.

- Although children who are friends often disagree and fight, they tend to communicate more clearly, disclose more, exchange more information, establish more common ground, and become able to resolve conflicts more effectively than strangers. They also share more and express more positive affect toward each other.

- As children become concerned with acceptance into peer groups and figuring out which actions will promote this, they may engage in **negative gossip** about other children. This may result in more bonding between those who share the gossip.

- Over time, children form new friendships and lose or replace old friendships. A child's personal characteristics may influence her ability to form and keep friendships. A particularly unhappy situation among peers is the formation of **mutual antipathies**, in which two people seriously dislike each other. These relationships can interfere with both his socioemotional adjustment and his academic performance.

- Romantic involvements differ from family and other relationships, and can have positive effects on the adolescent's development. Although the teenager may experience more conflict and more mood swings, she may also gain a sense of competence, self-worth, and a feeling of belonging to the group.

Parents, Peers, or Both?

- Parents and peers each have their own areas of expertise and influence in children's lives. Peers have more influence in the preadolescent and adolescent years, when they have lot of impact on such things as selection of friends, styles of dress, and choices of entertainment. Parents have greater impact on academic choices and work, job preferences, and on a child's aspirations for the future.

- Activities such as using drugs and engaging in other risky behaviors are less attractive to teenagers with authoritative parents who are warm and supportive, who encourage their kids in education and grant them psychological autonomy but who also demand that they conform to rules of behavior. And teens whose friends have parents with these characteristics are further protected from undesirable peer pressure. Adolescents whose parents do not possess these qualities may be particularly susceptible to negative peer influence

From Dyads to Groups

- In addition to friendships, children form groups that possess common goals and rules of conduct. Such groups are usually hierarchically organized to identify members' relationships with one another and to facilitate interaction. **Dominance hierarchies** within groups are apparent even among preschoolers, and a "pecking order" appears to develop within a short time after the first contact. The criteria for establishing dominance changes with age from physical toughness to leadership and academic abilities.

- Within groups of children, hierarchies serve the purposes of resolving conflict, dividing tasks, and allocating resources. A child's position in a hierarchy will affect the degree to which other children associate with her and imitate her.

- In middle childhood, children may form **cliques,** which enhance their well-being and ability to cope with stress. Later children may be assigned by their peers to **crowds,** whose salience decreases by the end of high school.

Peer Groups in Different Cultures

- Within and between cultures, patterns of peer interaction differ. Varying socialization concepts and practices give peers more or less influence on children. In Mexico and Central America, for example, family influences remain strong throughout adolescence. Latino parents often directly discourage peer interaction.

EXPLORE AND DISCUSS

1. Are the same characteristics likely to make a child popular or rejected in all cultures? Support your answer with examples.
2. Girls' and boys' friendships differ in a number of ways, but they also share some common characteristics. Discuss and differentiate the genders' friendship patterns and try to explain the reasons for their differences.
3. Romantic relationships are often a mixed blessing. What do you think are the positive and negative effects of romantic relationships on adolescent development?

Berthe Morisot (1841–1895). *The Children of M. Gabriel Thomas*, 1894. Musee d'Orsay, Paris.

13.

Gender Roles and Gender Differences

In most societies, men and women behave differently, are viewed and treated differently by others, and play distinctive roles. At the same time, there are many situations in which the two genders behave alike or nearly so, receive equal treatment from others, and play very similar roles. The challenge to psychologists is to determine how these differences and similarities originate and find expression in the developing child and to articulate the processes that contribute to gender-specific patterns of behavior.

Five primary theories have sought to explain these patterns. First, Freud's psychoanalytic theory proposed that the child, through a process of **identification**, acquired either feminine or masculine traits and behaviors by identifying with a same-sex parent. As we saw in Chapter 1, Freud noted that children's developing curiosity about their own bodies, around the ages of 5 or 6, alerts them to the differences in sexual anatomy between males and females. This observation formed the basis for his proposal that this period was critical to the formation of gender identity. Second, cognitive social learning theory, which we introduced in Chapter 1, holds that children acquire gender identification both through parents' direct guidance and encouragement and by imitating parents and others about them. According to this view, children understand gender quite early, and the fact that parents behave differently toward their male and female babies from the moment of birth may be influential in this understanding. Third, gender-schema theory, an information-processing approach, proposes that children as young as $2\frac{1}{2}$ begin to develop their own naive theories about gender differences and gender-appropriate behaviors. Fourth, Lawrence Kohlberg's cognitive developmental theory asserts that children categorize themselves as female or male on the basis of physical and behavioral clues and then proceed to behave in what they understand to be gender-appropriate ways. According to Kohlberg, it's not until children are about 6 or 7 that they make stable gender-typed choices.

Finally, as we saw in Chapter 1, evolutionary approaches to psychology stress the principles of natural selection and adaptation.

identification The Freudian notion that children acquire gender identity by identifying with and imitating their same-sex parents.

gender typing The process by which children acquire the values, motives, and behaviors considered appropriate for their gender in their particular culture.

gender-based beliefs Ideas and expectations about what is appropriate behavior for males and females.

gender stereotypes Beliefs that members of a culture hold about how females and males ought to behave; that is, what behaviors are acceptable and appropriate for each sex.

gender roles Composites of the behaviors actually exhibited by a typical male or female in a given culture; the reflection of a *gender stereotype* in everyday life.

gender identity The perception of oneself as either masculine or feminine.

These concepts can be applied to gender-related behaviors, especially behaviors that increase the likelihood that a person's genes will be passed across generations (Buss, 1994; Geary, 1998). To be able to pass genes from one generation to the next, individuals need to have mating strategies that enhance their reproductive success. According to Buss and Schmidt (1993), males and females use different strategies to achieve reproductive success. Males have developed aggressive and competitive skills in order to compete successfully with other males in attracting mates. Females have developed strategies for attracting and keeping males who are able to provide resources, including protection, for their joint offspring. These two sets of strategies complement each other and have led to the evolution of gender differences in both animals and humans. Other biological factors also contribute to differences in female and male attitudes and behaviors, such as specific hormones and levels of those hormones, as well as male-female differences in brain lateralization. As we've stressed throughout this book, most human characteristics are products of the interplay between genetic and environmental forces, and gender behavior is no different.

We begin this chapter by examining some standards of male and female behavior common to the American culture and take a brief look at some quite different cross-cultural behaviors. We then consider some actual patterns of gender differences and ask how stable these patterns are over the life course. With at least a rudimentary understanding of what we're talking about in this chapter, we turn to the issue of biological influences in gender behavior. Next we explore cognitive factors, focusing on Kohlberg's approach and gender-schema theory. The balance of the chapter is devoted to considering the influences on gender behavior of parental teaching, reinforcement, and modeling and of the social forces represented by peer groups, schools, and the media. Essentially, these sections on family and extrafamilial influences illuminate the cognitive social learning approach, but they also incorporate concepts from the other cognitive theories we discuss in this chapter. We conclude with a brief look at androgyny, the quality of possessing within oneself both masculine and feminine psychological characteristics.

DEFINING SEX AND GENDER

Before we move into the world of the child as male or female, we need to define some of the terms that guide research and thinking in the area of gender differences. To begin with, we use the terms *gender* and *sex* more or less interchangeably, for both refer to identity as either female or male. Traditionally, gender has been used to refer to cognitive and social matters and sex to biological and physiological ones, but it is often very difficult to separate these issues. Of course, we use the term sex solely when discussing either primary or secondary sex characteristics or specifically sexual behavior.

The process by which children acquire the values, motives, and behaviors viewed as appropriate to their gender in a specific culture, referred to as **gender typing,** is a multidimensional concept (Ruble, Martin, & Berenbaum, 2006). Children begin by developing **gender-based beliefs,** or ideas and expectations about what behaviors are appropriate for males and females. These beliefs are derived largely from **gender stereotypes,** which are the beliefs that members of an entire culture hold about the attitudes and behaviors acceptable and appropriate for each sex. These stereotypes prescribe the way males and females *should* be and *should* act. For example, in America, boys have traditionally been expected to be sports-oriented and aggressive, girls to be nonaggressive and to like caring for others. **Gender roles** are composites of the distinctive behaviors that males and females in a culture actually exhibit and thus are essentially the reflections of a culture's gender stereotypes. Early in life, children develop a **gender identity,** or a perception of themselves as either masculine or feminine and as having the characteristics and interests that are appropriate to their gender. And finally, children develop **gender-role preferences,** or desires to possess certain gender-typed characteristics. Children's choices of toys and of play partners reflect these preferences. Later in the chapter we will encounter and define two other important terms: *gender stability* and *gender constancy*.

gender-role preferences
Desires to possess certain gender-typed characteristics.

GENDER-ROLE STANDARDS AND STEREOTYPES

When children are still young infants, parents and other agents of socialization attempt systematically to teach them standards for behavior that are gender based and to shape different behaviors in boys and in girls (Maccoby, 1998). In fact, this process starts immediately after a baby's birth, when parents give the baby a name and bring the infant home to a nursery often decorated in gender-typed ways—flowered bumper pads and pale, beribboned lampshades, or bright-colored curtains with sports or space themes. Parents dress male and female children in distinctive clothes, style their hair in different ways, select toys and activities for them that they deem gender appropriate, promote children's association with same-gender playmates, and often react negatively when children behave in ways they consider gender inappropriate.

One investigator who was studying gender differences in infancy and did not want participants in the study to know whether they were watching boys or girls complained that, even in the first few days of life, some parents brought their infant girls to the laboratory with pink bows tied to their wisps of hair or taped to their little bald heads. Later, when she tried again to conceal the children's gender by asking mothers to dress their infants in overalls, girls appeared in pink overalls and boys in blue ones! The frustrated experimenter commented to a colleague, "And would you believe, overalls with *ruffles*?"

In Western cultures particularly, the women's movement and the rise of feminism have led us to revise our ways of thinking about gender differences and gender roles. However, these topics remain highly controversial. In this chapter's discussions, you will find two major threads. One is the continuing challenge offered by social scientists to the traditional view that apparent differences between males and females—such as women's superior abilities at verbal tasks and men's superior performance on mathematical problems—are fixed for all time. The other thread is modern scientists' consistent focus, in their theorizing about gender behavior and roles, on the multiple influences that shape our gender roles, including biological, cognitive, and social factors.

Cultures are internally quite consistent with regard to their standards of "appropriate" gender-role behavior. In this chapter, unless we are specifically referring to people in another country, when we talk about culturally defined behavior as either masculine or feminine, we will be talking about U.S. culture. Keep in mind, however, that within U.S. culture, gender roles and stereotypes vary as a function of a person's ethnic and social-class background. It is also important to note that we do not use the term *appropriate* to mean "desirable"; we mean, instead, what people in general *think* is appropriate—what is typical and generally accepted. Finally, although some of the gender-role standards we discuss may seem outdated to you, just remember that according to a considerable body of research, few gender stereotypes have changed since the 1970s!

In American society, the male role is seen, stereotypically, as charged with controlling and manipulating the environment. Men are expected to be independent, assertive, dominant, and competitive in social and sexual relations. The female role is seen, again stereotypically, as supporting husband and family. Women are expected to be relatively passive, loving, sensitive, and supportive in family and social relationships. In general, people regard the expression of warmth in personal

Despite the changes that have occurred in recent years in men's and women's roles in society, gender-stereotypical roles are still widespread. In Japan, some women continue to teach their daughters to perform the formal and highly ritualized tea ceremony, and in the Philippines, some men train their sons in traditional male skills—here, a young boy learns the blacksmith trade.

relationships, the display of anxiety under pressure, and the suppression of overt aggression and sexuality as more appropriate for women than for men (Broverman, Vogel, Broverman, Clarkson, & Rosenkrantz, 1972). Despite the concern with gender equality that has grown over nearly 30 years, a recent comparison of the way college students expressed gender stereotypes in 1972 and again in 1988 found no evidence of shifts over the intervening 16 years (Bergen & Williams, 1991; Twenge, 1997). But things may actually be changing and in some domains more than in others. For example Spence and Buckner (2000) recently found that self-endorsement by males of personality traits such as toughness and aggression has declined since the 1970s.

Nevertheless, as we saw in Chapter 5, the paucity of change in stereotypes includes attitudes about people's preferences for sexual partners of either the same or the opposite gender. And, according to Liben and Bigler (2002), the world of work remains stereotypically gendered. Both children and adults still tend to think of mechanics and doctors as male and of librarians and nurses as female. Interestingly, cross-cultural studies have found these stereotypical roles widespread not only in North American culture but in a wide range of societies. Researchers have found a similar pattern of gender stereotypes in some 25 countries from Middle and South America, Europe, Africa, Asia, and Oceania (Whiting & Edwards, 1988; Williams & Best, 1990).

There is, however, some variation in culturally accepted gender-role standards both within the United States and across cultures. Within the United States, these standards vary with ethnicity, age, education, and occupation. For example, African American families are more likely to socialize children without strict boy-girl gender-role distinctions. These families value early independence for both boys and girls, and they make fewer gender distinctions in deciding who is to carry out which family roles and tasks (Gibbs, 1989). Moreover, African American families encourage girls to be aggressive and assertive and boys to express emotion and nurturance (Allen & Majidi-Abi, 1989; Basow, 1992). Among Mexican Americans, however, gender-role socialization standards for boys and girls are much more clearly differentiated (Coltrane, 1998). In this subculture, boys are expected to show independence earlier than females.

Age and education alter gender-role expectations as well. Young children are especially rigid in their gender stereotyping; indeed, children between 3 and 6 years old do more of this than adults (Golombok & Fivush, 1994; Signorella, Bigler, & Liben, 1993). This sense of absolutism about rules is common among young children. As they develop, children become more differentiated and flexible in their attitudes about a variety of concepts, including gender issues.

In the United States, female students and other, college-educated women between the ages of 18 and 35 are more likely than older or less educated females to perceive the feminine role as involving independence and desire for achievement. Children whose mothers who are employed in skilled occupations and professions are more likely than children whose mothers are full-time homemakers to think that acquiring an education and having a profession is appropriate for women and that it's also all right for men to assume housekeeping and child-care tasks. At the same time, researchers have found that even young, educated men maintained more stereotyped gender-role standards than did women (Basow, 1992; Ruble et al., 2006). Moreover, single-earner fathers were found to be more traditional in their gender-typed attitudes than fathers from dual-earner families, but mothers, whether they worked within or outside the home, did not differ in these attitudes (Coltrane, 1998; McHale, Bartko, Crouter, & Perry-Jenkins, 1990).

Adult men and women differ in the way they view gender typing in children. For example, one study found that men were more likely than women to rate the behaviors of 18-month-old female and male toddlers as typical of each gender—even when the behaviors were in fact similar (Fagot, 1973). Perhaps these men saw what they expected to see. It is common to find fathers more concerned than mothers that their children maintain behaviors appropriate to their gender, and fathers have been seen to play a more important role in children's gender typing than mothers (Ruble et al., 2006). However, researchers have recently challenged this view, suggesting that in the light of recent shifts in male and female roles, mothers and fathers may play more similar roles in gender typing than previously thought (Lytton & Romney, 1991). It is interesting that in spite of some variations in gender-role standards among groups in the United States, almost all groups, regardless of gender, social class, and education, still view aggression as more characteristic of men and view interpersonal sensitivity as more common in women (Dodge et al., 2006). Note, however, that even within groups there are important individual differences in the *strength* with which people endorse these and other gender stereotypes (Beal, 1994; Maccoby, 1998).

One of the most frequently cited reports of divergence among cultures in gender role standards and behavior is Margaret Mead's study of social roles in three primitive tribes: the Arapesh, the Mundugumor, and the Tchambuli (Mead, 1935). The Mundugumor and the Arapesh actually prescribed little if any gender-role differentiation. However, the Arapesh men and women both exhibited behaviors that in many societies would be regarded as feminine, whereas the Mundugumor displayed behaviors traditionally thought of as masculine. The Arapesh were passive, cooperative, and unassertive, whereas both men and women in the Mundugumor tribe were hostile, aggressive, cruel, and restrictive. Both Arapesh mothers and fathers were actively involved in raising infants. In fact, Mead remarks, "If one comments upon a middle-aged Arapesh man as good-looking, the people answer: 'Good looking? Ye-e-e-s? But you should have seen him before he bore all those children!'" (Mead, 1935, p. 56).

Among the Tchambuli, Mead found a reversal of traditional gender roles. The men were dependent, socially sensitive, and concerned with the feelings of others, and interested in arts and crafts. The women were independent and aggressive and played the controlling role in decision making. Although around the world the gender roles Western society labels traditional seem to be the most common, there is enough variability within and across cultures to suggest considerable plasticity in the development of masculine and feminine behaviors. If there are actually genetically based social and cognitive differences between males and females, apparently these differences can be considerably modified by cultural forces.

GENDER DIFFERENCES IN DEVELOPMENT

How accurately do gender stereotypes reflect differences in the actual gender-role behaviors of males and females? As Table 13-1 shows, although clear gender differences have been found in some characteristics, many others that have been

Table 13-1   Gender differences: Real, occasional, or mythical?

Some Gender Differences Are Real . . .

Physical, Motor, and Sensory Development

At birth, girls are physically and neurologically more advanced. They walk earlier, and they attain puberty earlier. Boys have more mature muscular development and larger lungs and heart, and at birth they are less sensitive to pain. With increasing age, boys become superior at activities involving strength and gross motor skills. On the other hand, male fetuses are more likely to be miscarried, boys have a higher rate of infant mortality, and boys are more vulnerable to malnutrition, disease, and many hereditary anomalies. In terms of physiological vulnerability, females are clearly not the weaker sex.

Cognitive Development

From infancy through the early school years, girls display superior verbal abilities, including vocabulary acquisition, reading comprehension, and verbal creativity. During middle childhood and adolescence, gender differences are either nonexistent or very small. From about age 10, boys display greater visual-spatial ability, which is involved in such tasks as reading maps, aiming at a target, and manipulating objects in two- or three-dimensional space, Beginning at about age 12, boys excel in some kinds of mathematics, especially geometry.

Social and Emotional Development

Even in early social play, boys are more often the aggressors and the victims of aggression, particularly physical aggression. Girls tend to use more indirect forms of aggression, such as excluding another child from social interaction. As early as age 2, girls are more likely to comply with the demands of parents and other adults. Boys are more variable in their responses to adult direction. Gender differences in compliance with peers are not consistent, but preschool boys are less likely to comply with girls' demands than with those of other boys, and they are also less likely than girls to comply with partners of either gender. Girls are more nurturant toward younger children.

Atypical Development

Boys are more likely to have genetic defects, physical disabilities, mental retardation, reading disabilities, speech defects, and school and emotional problems.

Others May Be Found Only Sometimes . . .

Activity Level

Many studies find no gender differences in activity level. When they do find differences, it is usually boys who are more active than girls.

Dependency

Younger children do not display gender differences in dependency. Older girls and women tend to rate themselves as more dependent, but this is probably changing.

Fear, Timidity, and Anxiety

Again, young children do not exhibit consistent gender differences in timidity. Older girls and women report themselves as being more fearful, and males are more likely to involve themselves in physically risky recreations and occupations. On the other hand, many women today are in dangerous occupations (e.g., firefighting, high-steel construction) and enjoy risky sports (e.g., mountain climbing, hang gliding).

Exploratory Activity

Studies do not find consistent gender differences in exploratory activity. A number of studies of early exploratory activity have found boys to be more venturesome and curious and more likely to attack barriers intervening between themselves and a desirable object.

Vulnerability to Stress

Findings over the last decade suggest that males may be more vulnerable to family disharmony and interpersonal stress, as evidenced by an overrepresentation of boys in child guidance clinics. However, we need further research to draw firm conclusions.

Orientation to Social Stimuli

Some evidence indicates that infant girls may orient to faces more than boys and may recognize their mother's faces at an earlier age.

(Continued)

Table 13-1 *Concluded*

And Still Others Are Wholly Mythical . . .
Sociability
Boys and girls are equally social; they spend as much time with others and are equally responsive to others. There's no gender difference in the need for love and attachment. Males and females are equally capable of nurturance, although girls and women do more actual caring for children, relatives, and friends.
Suggestibility and Conformity
Girls and boys do not differ in suggestibility or in the tendency to conform to the standards of a peer group or to imitate the responses of others.
Learning Style
Boys and girls are equally good at rote learning and simple repetitive tasks. They also display similar skills in tasks involving the inhibition of previously learned responses and in complex cognitive tasks. Girls and boys are equally responsive to visual and auditory stimuli.
Achievement
Girls and boys generally display equal levels of achievement motivation. Under neutral conditions, girls are often more achievement-oriented than boys, but in a competitive situation, boys are more likely than girls to exhibit enhanced achievement motivation.
Self-Esteem
Boys and girls do not differ in self-esteem. However, girls rate themselves as more competent in social skills, and boys view themselves as stronger and more powerful.
Verbal Aggressiveness and Hostility
Girls and boys engage equally in verbal aggression but use different approaches: Girls tend to gossip and exclude others; boys are more directly verbally assaultive.

Sources: Dodge et al., 2006; Halpern, 2000, 2004; Hyde & Linn, 1988; Hyde & Plant, 1995; Linn & Hyde, 1989; Maccoby, 1998; Maccoby & Jacklin, 1974; Ruble et al., 2006; Tavris, 1992; Underwood, 2003, 2004; Wigfield et al., 2006.

considered gender linked seem only questionably so, and still others are wholly mythical. Because gender differences that we don't observe at all times are, by definition, suggestive only, we need more research in order to draw definite conclusions. Moreover, as children develop into adulthood, men and women develop many differences that are influenced not only by biological factors but by the environmental factors that shape and regulate our lives: terms of employment and work opportunities; power and status in the workplace; homemaking, child-care, and family obligations; sexual experiences and concerns; and, of course, reproductive experiences (Beal, 1994; Ruble et al., 2006).

As you examine Table 13-1 and study our discussions of gender differences, keep in mind that the characteristics of males and females overlap considerably. Some males are more compliant, verbal, and interested in the arts than some females. Similarly, although males are physically designed for greater strength and thus are generally better adapted for successful aggressive interactions, many women display considerable physical strength as well: Not only do women have greater health and longevity, but they are increasingly successful in team sports such as basketball, soccer, and hockey. In addition, in the area of intellectual and occupational achievement there are outstanding women architects, mathematicians, engineers, and scientists. Changing societal expectations and opportunities clearly play a role in the maintenance and/or modification of gender differences, although biological constraints suggest that some of these differences are unlikely to disappear!

Figure 13-1

Preschool choices among gender-typed toys

Preschool boys clearly preferred toys considered appropriate for boys, but the girls were more eclectic in their choices.

Source: O'Brien, Huston, & Risley, 1983.

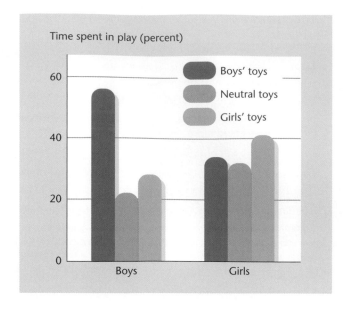

Developmental Patterns of Gender Typing

Children develop gender-typed behavior patterns at an early age (Beal, 1994; Ruble et al., 2006). Even before they can tell us about their gender-based preferences, infants and toddlers clearly express their choices through their looking behavior. Using techniques that we described in Chapter 4 with respect to visual perception in babies, Lisa Serbin and her colleagues (2001) found that boys and girls differ in their preferences for dolls and cars from a very early age. As Figure 13-1 shows, by the time they were a year old, girls had begun to show a greater preference for dolls than boys did, and this gender difference was even stronger by the time the children were $1\frac{1}{2}$ to 2 years old. In contrast, boys showed much stronger preferences for vehicles such as cars and trucks than girls did by the ages of $1\frac{1}{2}$ and 2. And these contrasting preferences continue to be observed: In a study of 15- to 36-month-old toddlers in a day-care center, boys and girls had already developed clear preferences for toys that were gender appropriate (O'Brien, Huston, & Risley, 1983). Note, however, that girls more often than boys chose gender-inappropriate toys. Why do you suppose girls are more likely to play with a truck than boys are to cuddle a doll? Let's look at some reasons.

Western culture is basically male-oriented, according greater esteem, privileges, and status to the masculine role. The male role is more clearly defined, and there is greater pressure for boys than for girls to conform to narrow, gender-appropriate standards. Although the situation is gradually changing, boys shy away from things that are "for girls," fearing derision from other boys, whereas girls may want to do things that are regarded as higher status. In short, although we tolerate tomboys, we reject sissies. Parents and peers condemn boys for crying, retreating in the face of aggression, wearing feminine apparel, or playing with dolls. In contrast, we tend to accept a girl's occasional temper tantrums, rough-and-tumble play, wearing of jeans, or playing with trucks. In fact, one survey found that more than 50 percent of women and girls described themselves as being or having been tomboys, participating in sports and playing with boys' toys at some point during childhood (Morgan, 1998).

Although as we have said, many girls engage in masculine activities, boys and girls do develop distinctive patterns of interest that are consistent with gender stereotypes. In a national survey of more than 2,000 children between the ages of 7 and 11, Zill (1986) found that boys liked guns, boxing, wrestling, karate, team sports, and fixing and making things more than girls did. In contrast, girls enjoyed dolls, sewing, cooking, dancing, and looking after younger children more than boys did. More recent studies of girls in middle childhood and adolescence have found that girls spent more time in feminine leisure activities (e.g., dance, handicrafts, art, writing stories and letters) than in masculine activities (e.g., competitive sports, hunting/fishing, building) (McHale, Shanahan, Updorgraff, Crouter, & Booth, 2004). Parents and others encourage these patterns of interest in a variety of ways, including assigning household tasks. Even in the twenty-first century, girls are more likely to make beds, clean, prepare meals, wash dishes, and do laundry. Boys are more likely to fix things, take out the garbage, and mow lawns (Parke, 2002; Goodnow, 1988, 1996). As we will see below, a variety of theoretical perspectives, which include cognitive and social learning as well as evolutionary approaches, can help account for these findings. Unfortunately, as Box 13.1 suggests, parents and others in society also differentially encourage and discourage certain academic interests in boys and girls, which may be detrimental to both in the long run.

Remember that families differ, and some boys wash dishes and some girls fix cars! Nevertheless, a great many "old" stereotypes still persist in contemporary roles for boys and girls.

Stability of Gender Typing

Although children develop masculine and feminine interests and behaviors early, as we have noted, many girls participate in both female and male pursuits during childhood. By adolescence, however, there is a movement back toward increased sex typing. To explain this, the *gender intensification hypothesis* argues that with adolescence—and especially with the onset of puberty—there is a shift toward more common sex-typed patterns of behavior (Larson & Richards, 1994; McHale et al., 2004). For example, in one study of self-identified tomboys, girls indicated that at about age 12 they began to adopt more traditionally feminine interests and behaviors owing to pressures from both parents and peers and to their own increasing interest in romantic relationships (Burn, O'Neil, & Nederend, 1996; see also Chapter 12).

In spite of normative developmental fluctuations in sex typing during childhood and adolescence, individual children who are strongly masculine or feminine during childhood tend to be similarly sex typed during adulthood. For example, the longitudinal Fels Institute Study, which examined the development of a group of middle-class children from birth to adulthood, found that adult behavior could be predicted from gender-typed interests in elementary school (Kagan & Moss, 1962). Boys who were interested in competitive games, activities that required gross motor skills, and such things as mechanics, and girls who were interested in cooking, sewing, reading, and noncompetitive games were involved in similar gender-typed activities in adulthood.

The stability of many of the personality characteristics investigated in the Fels Study was related to cultural acceptance. That is, when a characteristic conflicted with gender-role standards, it led in adulthood to some more socially acceptable behavior (e.g., dependence in a boy might lead to entrepreneurial endeavors in an adult). But when a characteristic was congruent with cultural standards, it tended to remain stable from childhood to maturity (e.g., dependence in a girl might lead to a less aggressive role in business in an adult). In some cases, stability appeared to be related to gender: In males, but not in females, childhood sexuality and aggression were predictive of adult sexuality and anger. In females, but not in males, childhood passivity was predictive of similar adult behaviors. However, this study was conducted several decades ago, and less stability may be evident in the new millennium. Recall from Chapter 1 that people born in a specific era form a cohort, and when we study rapidly changing areas such as gender roles, we may see that different cohorts of individuals experience very different circumstances and influences.

Children are likely to repress behaviors that society regards as gender inappropriate. In both genders, however, such behaviors often emerge in adulthood but in altered forms. For example, girlhood anger and tantrums may evolve into intellectual

Box 13.1

Child Psychology in Action

WILL WE LET COMPUTERS WIDEN THE GENDER GAP?

Computers are commonplace in classrooms, but are boys and girls benefiting equally from the technological revolution? Studying many types of computer activities available to children, including home use of a computer and courses in school, after-school clubs, and summer camps, Mark Lepper (1985; Lepper & Gurtner, 1989) found large gender differences in girls' and boys' use of these opportunities. In formal computer programs, there were as many as 5 to 10 boys for every girl, and this difference in participation rates increased as activities became more costly and more effortful. In California schools, boys outnumbered girls in introductory programming classes by a 2 to 1 ratio, but in advanced programming classes, the ratio was as high as 10 to 15 boys for each girl.

What might be the reasons for this gender gap? The computer field—like the fields of math and science—has long been dominated by males, in large part because of the myth that males are more capable than females in technical subjects. Thus the computer science field has few female role models. Computer labs in schools are often competitive, noisy, and high-activity environments in which boys may feel more comfortable than girls.

The kinds of software often used to introduce students to computers seem also to have been written for boys (Subrahmanyam, Greenfield, Kraut, & Gross, 2001). Among computer games, the most common themes are war and violence and male-gender-typed sports such as football. Even the titles of specifically educational games may turn girls off: Alien Addition, Demolition Division, Spelling Baseball. It's not surprising, therefore, to find that boys play electronic games more often than girls and that they tend to make more gender distinctions about the acceptability of these games for either boys or girls. According to Funk and Buchman (1996), although most fourth and fifth graders of both genders thought both girls and boys could play video games, boys were considerably more likely than

girls to say that playing video games was not an acceptable activity for girls. Boys clearly spent more time at such games, and they were a good deal more likely than girls to describe video game playing as their favorite activity. A number of boys also said that girls who spent a lot of time playing video games were not popular, and that if girls wanted to be popular they ought not play such games, especially "the fighting games." Few girls agreed with these statements; as many as a third held that fighting games were okay for girls. This result is consistent with research that suggests females are more flexible than males in their attitudes toward gender roles.

Despite the fact that computers have many varied uses, including word processing and graphic design, schools typically present computers as mathematical tools. Computer labs are usually found in the math department, and math teachers supervise their use. In addition, credits for computer courses often count toward math requirements. Inasmuch as girls have long been brainwashed into believing that they can't do math as well as boys, this arrangement both keeps girls away from computers and reinforces the myth. The ultimate result is to turn girls ever further away from careers in math and science (Shea, Lubinski, & Benbow 2001). However, according to recent trends, the gender gap in computer use may be closing, partly because of the expanding range of applications that are available, including e-mails, chat rooms, and educational pursuits—not just games.

Recent data suggests that girls and boys are reporting equal levels of computer usage and are equally confident in their computer skills. But they still differ in the type of usage they favor—for example, girls often use computers for social contact, whereas boys use them to play games. "Girls and boys both appear to embrace computers—they merely require functions that fit their interests" (Subrahmanyam et al., 2001, p. 130).

competitiveness, masculine interests, and conflict over dependency needs in an adult woman. Passivity in boys, for instance, might be related in adult men to social apprehension, noncompetitiveness, and sexual anxiety. Even in adulthood there is evidence of stability: In one longitudinal study that spanned a 10-year period, researchers found that 54 percent of adults continued to be rated similarly by observers in terms of masculinity or femininity (Hyde, Krajnik, & Skuldt-Neiderberger, 1991).

However, not all adults maintain the same gender roles over their life course. Gender roles fluctuate as adults change to meet the demands of new situations and circumstances. One of the most important transitions—parenthood—is associated with a sharp divergence of gender roles. Even among egalitarian couples who are committed to equal sharing of household tasks, the onset of parenthood generally heralds a return to traditional gender roles (Cowan & Cowan, 2000; Parke, 2002). In these roles, women are seen as having more **expressive characteristics**—they are more nurturant, concerned with feelings, and child-oriented. Men, on the other hand, are thought to have more **instrumental characteristics**—they are more task and occupation-oriented. Self-perceptions of gender roles shift with age as well. As they grow older, men tend to become more expressive and nurturant, especially in old age. Women tend to become more autonomous as they develop, but return to a more feminine gender-role orientation in old age, perhaps in part because as one becomes less self-sufficient, one has a greater need for help (Hyde et al., 1991; Maccoby, 1998). Thus, gender typing is best viewed as an ongoing and changing process; development in this area clearly continues across adulthood.

BIOLOGICAL FACTORS IN GENDER DIFFERENCES

Most research on the influence of biological factors on gender-role typing has focused on two principal areas: hormonal function and brain lateralization, or the association of particular processes and behaviors with one or the other half of the brain (look back at Chapter 5 if you need to refresh your understanding of these concepts). In this section, we begin by exploring the ways that hormones influence gender typing, both in social behavior and in the development of cognitive skills. We then examine how the lateralization of brain function affects gender differences in development and discover that females are more bilateral than males. Finally, we consider the ways in which biology and cultural notions of gender-appropriate behaviors interact to influence gender typing.

Hormones and Social Behavior

Hormones, as you'll recall from Chapter 5, are powerful and highly specialized chemical substances produced by the cells of certain body organs and have a regulatory effect on the activities of certain other organs. Those hormones associated with sexual characteristics and with reproductive functions are present in differing concentrations in males and females from infancy through adulthood. Among male hormones, called *androgens, testosterone* is the principal and most potent one. Women's principal hormones are various forms of *estrogen* and *progesterone*. However, each sex also has small amounts of the other's hormones: Women have a little testosterone and men have some estrogen and progesterone. The differences in the concentrations of these hormones are not great in prepubertal boys and girls, of preschool and elementary-school age, but they become quite pronounced in adolescents and adults.

Both the prenatal and pubertal periods may be critical in terms of the effect of hormonal action on human development (Collaer & Hines, 1995). In the prenatal period, hormones organize the fetus's biological and psychological predispositions to be masculine or feminine, and the surge in hormonal function during puberty (Chapter 5) activates these early predispositions.

Hormonal differences experienced prenatally or during the subsequent course of development may contribute to differences in the social behavior of males and females. When Young, Goy, and Phoenix (1967) injected pregnant monkeys with testosterone during the second quarter of pregnancy, the monkeys' offspring were

expressive characteristics Presumably typical of females, these characteristics include nurturance and concern with feelings.

instrumental characteristics Presumably typical of males, these characteristics include task and occupation orientation.

pseudohermaphroditic females who exhibited not only physical changes in their genitalia but also social behavior patterns that are characteristic of male monkeys. These infant female monkeys manifested masculine behaviors such as threatening gestures, a lesser tendency to withdraw from approach or threat by other animals, more mounting behavior, and more rough-and-tumble play.

Subsequent studies have found that if male hormones are injected into normal female monkeys after birth but preceding puberty, these females also become more assertive, sometimes even attaining prime dominance status in their monkey troop. They may restrict males' sexual behavior and rough-and-tumble play and demand more restrained and docile behavior from their followers (Wallen, 1996).

A dramatic example of the way social experience can modify the effects of hormonal factors can be seen in the classic studies of John Money and his colleagues (Money, 1987; Money & Ehrhardt, 1972). These investigators studied prenatal hormonal anomalies, such as high levels of androgen in a female fetus, which masculinized the female child and caused mistaken sexual identity. Many of the participants in these studies were female infants who had normal internal female reproductive organs but an enlarged clitoris that resembled a penis and labial folds that were often fused, resembling a scrotum. Money found that even if such a child were reassigned to her correct feminine gender role after the first few years of life, her gender typing was inadequate, and she made a poor psychological adjustment. Money found that 25 fetally androgenized girls who were raised as girls—and given corrective surgery if necessary—were characterized by behaviors and interests that have traditionally been associated more with boys than with girls. These girls enjoyed vigorous athletic activities, such as ball games. They showed little interest in such things as playing with dolls, babysitting, or caring for younger children. They also preferred simple utilitarian clothing, such as slacks and shorts, and showed little concern with cosmetics, jewelry, or hairstyles. Not only were these girls' play and grooming interests more like those of boys, but their assertiveness and attitudes toward sexuality and achievement resembled male behavior.

Later studies of these fetally androgenized girls (Berenbaum & Snyder, 1995; Hines & Kaufman, 1994; Reiner & Gearhart, 2004; Zucker, 2001) confirmed some of Money's findings—for example, the girls preferred boys as playmates, chose toys usually preferred by boys, and exhibited behaviors more common to males, such as rough-and-tumble play. In addition, researchers found evidence that the greater the girl's exposure to androgen when a fetus, the stronger were her preferences for masculine play and activities (Berenbaum, Duck, & Bryk, 2000). However, even though these children behaved in some ways more like boys, they continued to identify themselves as girls (Berenbaum & Bailey, 2003). Clearly, biology plays a role in determining gender roles, even in the face of social pressures to overcome biological influences. However, it would be premature to conclude that "biology is destiny." In a later section we will learn more about the role that social influences play in gender typing.

Hormones and Cognitive Skills

Researchers have suggested that at a critical period in prenatal development sex hormones may determine a fetus's potentials for brain organization and hemispheric lateralization and that these events may, in turn, lead to gender differences in males' and females' verbal and spatial skills. Studies suggest, for example, that prenatal hormones may sensitize female brains to process verbal information more effectively and male brains to process spatial information more accurately. To date, however, research relating early hormonal levels to later abilities has yielded mixed findings.

In one study, girls whose blood at birth showed high-normal levels of androgens (testosterone and androstanedione) had lower scores on tests of spatial ability when they entered school than girls whose blood at birth showed low-normal androgen

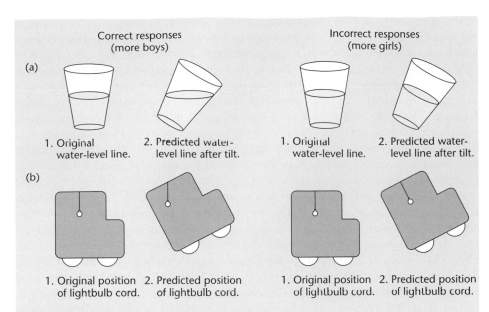

Figure 13-2

Boys' and girls' understanding of horizontal and vertical relations

Between the ages of about 8 or 9 to about 16 or 17, boys tend to make correct predictions of changes in horizontals and verticals following tilt, whereas girls are more likely to predict the results incorrectly. In general, boys seem to be more skilled at visual-spatial tasks.

Source: Liben & Golbeck, 1980.

levels (Jacklin, Wilcox, & Maccoby, 1988). Similarly, a later study (Finegan, Niccols, & Sitarenios, 1992) found that female fetuses with higher levels of androgens later showed lesser spatial and numerical abilities than other girls. However, in nonnormal samples, when prenatal androgen levels in female fetuses are exceptionally high, these effects may be reversed. In adolescence, such girls had better visual-spatial skills than other girls did (Collaer & Hines, 1995). Perhaps the "masculine" behavior of these girls led parents and others to encourage them in activities such as team sports, which then facilitated their spatial abilities.

Some evidence of gender differences in spatial abilities comes from studies of children's understanding of horizontals and verticals. Consider the following situations. A glass of water is tipped from an upright position to an angle of 50 degrees. What would the water level in the glass look like? Or, how would a lightbulb suspended by a cord hanging from the ceiling of a van look if the van drove up a hill inclined at 50 degrees? As Figure 13-2 shows, boys and girls in grades 3 to 11 answer differently. Boys are more likely to make correct judgments about both the water level and the position of the lightbulb (Liben, 1991). Although males and females continue to differ in these kinds of judgments at all ages, both girls and boys improve as they become older. Studies have shown, for example, that experience with blocks, models, or video games can enhance the spatial skills of both boys and girls (Subrahmanyam et al., 2001a, 2001b). These findings suggest that genetically based sex differences that result in different levels of prenatal androgens can be modified by environmental experiences, as we saw in Chapters 2 and 5.

Studies of male superiority at spatial processing have helped to explode the myth that males are superior to females in math (DeLisi & McGillicuddy-DeLisi, 2002; Halpern, 2000). Why? Because, according to Hyde, Fennema, and Lamon (1990), male superiority in math is generally restricted to performance in geometry, a form of mathematics that requires spatial visualization skills! In fact, girls do better in computational skills than boys, and there are no gender differences in girls' and boys' performance on tests either of basic math knowledge or on algebra—which is less reliant on spatial ability than geometry (Halpern, 2000; Hyde et al., 1990). In sum, males' performance is generally superior to that of females when math problems require a spatially based strategy, but there are no sex differences when a verbal strategy is available—that is, when a computational problem is stated in words (Gallagher, Levin,

& Cahalan, 2002). Spatial reasoning ability may depend, in part, on participation in physical activities in which one must understand one's body position vis-à-vis one's teammates and have the ability to judge size and distance (e.g., hit a home run or drop a ball in the basket). According to Beal (1994), girls' greater participation in sports in recent years may have something to do with the fact that their performance in spatial reasoning has also improved (DeLisi & McGillicuddy-DeLisi, 2002; Halpern, 2000). We still have a long way to go on this issue, for even in today's schools, girls rarely have the opportunity to participate in a full range of sports.

It is very important to note not only that the demonstrated difference between males and females in spatial ability is relatively small but also that even if researchers established a clearly biological basis for this gender difference, it would not mean that spatial abilities are not culturally influenced and environmentally modifiable (Caplan & Caplan, 1999; Ruble et al., 2006). For example, it has been suggested that boys are encouraged more often than girls to play with toys that involve spatial abilities, such as building sets, and to undertake mathematical and scientific endeavors (Beal, 1994). Moreover, U.S. researchers have found that mothers of first-grade children *believe* that boys are better at mathematics and girls at reading. Investigators in other countries—for example, Japan and Taiwan—have found the same thing (Lummis & Stevenson, 1990). Perhaps it is in part because of the faulty assumptions people make about girls' math abilities that girls enroll in increasingly fewer mathematics and science courses over the high school and college years. Indeed, it becomes more difficult to interest even those girls who have displayed superior mathematical abilities in remaining involved in the subject (Eccles, 1985; Shea et al., 2001). For example, in a study of California schools between 1983 and 1987, girls made up only about 38 percent of physics classes, 34 percent of advanced physics classes, and 42 percent of chemistry classes (Linn & Hyde, 1991). Fortunately, recent evidence suggests that this particular gender gap is narrowing (DeLisi & McGillicuddy-De Lisi, 2002; Halpern, 2000, 2004). Perhaps changing gender-role standards are beginning to have some effects.

To summarize, hormonal differences between males and females do play a role in their respective spatial abilities. As in the case of many skills, however, environmental factors can modify these biologically influenced patterns of differences between males and females.

Brain Lateralization and Gender Differences

Behavior is determined to some extent by the organization of the two cerebral hemispheres, and brain functioning becomes increasingly specialized and lateralized with age. As we discussed in Chapter 5, in most people the right hemisphere is more involved in processing spatial information and the left hemisphere in processing verbal information.

There is some evidence that men's brains are more lateralized than women's (Halpern, 2000). For example, women whose left hemispheres suffer damage are less likely than men with similar damage to experience verbal deficits, and right-hemisphere-damaged women show fewer spatial deficits than do men (Halpern, 2000). Also supporting the notion that women are more bilateral than men are the results of a study in which boys and girls between the ages of 6 and 13 had to recognize shapes merely by handling them. Boys were more accurate in recognizing shapes with their left hands, but girls were just as accurate in perceiving shapes with their right as with their left hands (Witelson, 1978). Other studies of spatial tasks have yielded similar evidence of lesser lateralization in females (Halpern, 2000; Reite et al., 1993).

Recent studies using brain-imaging techniques that detect blood flow in the brain as people perform different cognitive tasks have confirmed this greater bilateralism among females. In a task in which men and women participants were asked to decide if nonsense words rhymed, both left and right sides of women's brains were activated; in men, however, only the left hemisphere was activated (Shaywitz, Shaywitz, Pugh, & Constable, 1995). Recall from Chapter 5 that even infants show this gender difference in patterns of brain activation in a word comprehension task.

Biology and Cultural Expectations

Researchers have asked what role people's physical bodies play in shaping both gender-role standards and gender typing. For example, are the female's abilities to carry a fetus to term and to breast-feed her child related to some kind of biological programming that causes her to be more responsive than a male to the sights and signals of infants and children? Investigators have found that by the age of 4 or 5, girls interact more with babies and in a more active way than boys do. When asked to care for a baby, boys are inclined to watch the baby passively, whereas girls are more likely to engage actively in taking care of the baby (Berman, 1987; Blakemore, 1990). These observations are consistent with the evolutionary theoretical perspective that argues that females are more committed to parental activities than males.

These behavioral tendencies, however, could as easily be due to cultural expectations and training as to biological differences (Parke, 2002). Interestingly, in adolescents and adults, such gender-based differential behavior is less apparent under conditions of privacy than in situations where people know that someone is observing them (Berman, 1987). And when experimenters have used subtle measures of responsiveness to an infant's crying, such as changes in blood pressure, electrical skin conductance, or other responses of the autonomic nervous system, they have not detected any differences in mothers' and fathers' responses to the child (Frodi, Lamb, Leavitt, & Donovan, 1978; Lamb, 1997). Indeed, factors other than gender may determine responsiveness to a child. For example, research has shown that young mothers are more responsive to babies than are childless women (Maccoby, 1998). It seems very likely that men's and women's responses to babies are to a considerable extent conditioned by culturally sanctioned gender roles. Biological and evolutionary programming notwithstanding, culture may have considerable impact on behavior.

LifeMap CD

To learn more about how girls and boys differ in their cognitive development, and theories about why, watch the "Sex Differences and School" video in Chapter 13 of your CD.

COGNITIVE FACTORS IN GENDER TYPING

Biology and social influences are not the only determinants of gender typing. Children's own understanding of gender roles and rules may contribute to the developmental process of gender-role acquisition. Two related questions are central to understanding the role of cognition in the development of gender differences. First, when do children acquire different types of gender information? (As you study this section and the rest of the chapter you may find it useful to refer to our Turning Points chart on page 566, which offers some chronological information about children's development of gender concepts.) Second, does knowledge modify children's gender-role activities and behavior? In this section we explore two cognitive approaches to gender typing: Kohlberg's cognitive developmental theory and an information-processing-based approach called gender-schema theory. Both theories share the assumption that human beings take an active role in perceiving and interpreting information from the environment—that we are not passively shaped by environmental forces. Cognitively oriented scientists assume that people use implicit theories to interpret environmental information and that in so doing they create environments that will support their theories (Ruble et al., 2006). For example, our views of appropriate gender roles may lead us to select activities and social partners consistent with these views.

Turning Points

Note: Developmental events described in this and other Turning Points charts represent overall trends identified in research studies. Individual children vary greatly in the ages at which they achieve these developmental changes.

Sources: Beal, 1994; Golombok & Fivush, 1994; Maccoby, 1998; Ruble et al., 2006.

Kohlberg's Cognitive Developmental Theory

cognitive developmental theory of gender typing Kohlberg's theory that children use physical and behavioral clues to differentiate gender roles and to gender-type themselves very early in life.

Lawrence Kohlberg's (1966) provocative **cognitive developmental theory of gender typing** proposes that children's differentiation of gender roles and their perception of themselves as more like same-gender than opposite-gender models begins very early. These processes, Kohlberg says, begin not only before the Freudian process of identification but without the reinforcement or modeling hypothesized by cognitive social learning theory. According to Kohlberg, children, using physical and behavioral clues such as hairstyle or occupation, categorize themselves as male or female; they then find it rewarding to behave in a gender-appropriate manner and to imitate same-gender models. For example, the girl's thinking goes something like this: "I am a girl because I am more like my mother and other girls than like boys; therefore I want to dress like a girl, play girl games, and feel and think like a girl." Consonance between children's actual gender—the way they see themselves—and their behaviors and values is critical in sustaining their self-esteem.

Kohlberg thinks all children go through three phases in gaining an understanding of gender. First, as we have just seen, the child acquires basic gender identity,

4–5 YEARS	• Children begin to understand the concept of gender stability but do not grasp it fully until about the age of 7
	• Children 4 and younger tend to rely more on gender schemas than do children 5 and older
	• By $4\frac{1}{2}$, children spend three times as much time with same-gender playmates as with other-gender peers
	• Girls interact more with babies and in a more active way than boys do
5 YEARS	• Few children this age show knowledge of personality traits
4–6 YEARS	• Boys are more likely than girls to congregate in same-gender groups
$6\frac{1}{2}$ YEARS	• Children spend 11 times as much time with same-gender playmates as with other-gender children
6–7 YEARS	• Children now understand gender stability and also grasp gender constancy
7–11 YEARS	• Children develop distinct patterns of interest in activities that are consistent with cultural gender stereotypes
8 YEARS	• Most children display knowledge of gender-typed traits
6–13 YEARS	• Studies of children in this age range suggest that female brains may be more bilaterally organized than male brains

recognizing that she is a girl or he is a boy, which in turn serves to organize incoming information and attitudes (Ruble et al., 2006). Children acquire gender identity, according to Kohlberg, between the ages of 2 and 3. Second, the child acquires the concept of **gender stability** by the age of 4 or 5, accepting that males remain male and females remain female. The little boy no longer thinks he might grow up to be a mommy, and the little girl gives up her heady hopes of becoming Spiderman. And, third, by about 6 or 7 the child acquires the notion of **gender constancy,** recognizing that superficial changes in appearance or activities do not alter gender. Even when a girl wears jeans or plays football, or when a boy wears long hair or has a burning interest in needlepoint, the child recognizes—and peers recognize, too—that gender remains constant. This achievement is important because Kohlberg argues that gender constancy should influence sex-typed choices.

What is the evidence for Kohlberg's developmental progression? Researchers who have tested his theory have confirmed that both boys and girls acquire gender identity first, an understanding of stability next, and finally an appreciation of constancy (Martin & Little, 1990; Slaby & Frey, 1975). Moreover, children in other cultures (Belize, Kenya, Nepal, and American Samoa) show a similar progression in their understanding of gender (Munroe, Shimmin, & Munroe, 1984). Working-class children and children in nonindustrialized cultures generally reach

gender stability The notion that gender does not change; males remain male and females remain female.

gender constancy The awareness that superficial alterations in appearance or activity do not alter gender.

These children do not seem worried that either rock climbing, stereotypically a male activity, or baking, often considered a female task, will affect their gender identities. Clearly, they have grasped the notion of gender constancy.

these milestones about a year later than middle-class U.S. children (Frey & Ruble, 1992).

Some researchers have suggested that the process by which children come to recognize males and females as distinct categories probably has its origins in early infancy—well before babies can understand labels and language. In one study, 75 percent of 12-month-old infants were able to recognize male and female faces as belonging to distinctive categories (Leinbach & Fagot, 1992). This is not the same thing as recognizing that you yourself belong to one of these categories, but it does suggest that the process of understanding gender begins earlier than Kohlberg originally thought.

The ability to understand gender labels such as *boy* and *girl* is not far behind. By the time they're 2 years old, children can correctly label their own gender, but they still have a very limited understanding of gender identity (Fagot & Leinbach, 1992). Young children have some understanding of gender words such as *man* and *woman* and recognize that some activities and objects are associated with each gender. For example, they recognize that men wear neckties and women don't and that women sometimes wear skirts but men never do. It's not until they're about 3 years old, however, that they grasp the concept that they themselves, along with other children, belong to a *gender class* or *group*.

We think now that children begin to grasp the notions of gender stability and constancy around the age of 5, but that they do not fully appreciate the meaning of these concepts until they are about 7. Consider the following exchange between two 4-year-old boys. Jeremy, who wore a barrette to nursery school, was accused by Leo of being a girl because "only girls wear barrettes." Jeremy pulled down his pants to show that he really was a boy. His young classmate replied, "Everyone has a penis; only girls wear barrettes" (Bem, 1983, p. 607). Clearly he did not yet understand gender constancy.

Genital knowledge is an important determinant of gender constancy (Ruble et al., 2006). Bem (1989, 1993) showed nursery schoolers anatomically correct photos of a nude boy and girl and then showed the youngsters pictures of the same children dressed in either clothing appropriate to their gender or clothing appropriate to the opposite gender. Even when boys wore dresses or girls wore pants, nearly 40 percent of the children correctly identified the gender of the child. When Bem then tested the preschoolers' understanding of genital differences between the sexes, she found that nearly 60 percent of the children who possessed genital knowledge, but only 10 percent of those who lacked it, had displayed gender constancy.

Children appear to apply gender constancy to themselves earlier than they apply it to others (Martin, Ruble, & Szkrybalo, 2002; Ruble et al., 2006; Wehren & DeLisi, 1983). Preschoolers (ages $2\frac{1}{2}$ to 6) could label their own gender before the gender of other children (95% versus 90%), showed better understanding of their own gender stability than the gender stability of others (87% versus 82%), and showed a similar pattern for gender constancy (30% versus 20%). Children achieved gender constancy by $4\frac{1}{2}$ years of age when considering themselves but did not understand that this concept applied to other children until they were $5\frac{1}{2}$ years old. Young children are certain that no matter how much they might want to be transformed into a member of the opposite gender, this could not happen, but they are not so sure about that kid down the street! In addition, as you might expect, gender constancy is related to a child's level of cognitive functioning and to performance on Piagetian tasks of physical conservation (Chapter 8). The ability to conserve requires that a child recognize the constancy of physical objects in spite of the appearance of superficial transformations (Halpern, 2000; Szkrybalo & Ruble, 1999).

Gender-Schema Theory: An Information-Processing Approach

Another cognitive approach to sex typing, **gender-schema theory,** derives from modern information-processing perspectives (Bem, 1993, 1998; Martin & Halverson, 1983; Martin & Ruble, 2004; Martin et al., 2002). According to this viewpoint, children develop *schemas,* or naive theories, that help them organize and structure experience related to gender differences and gender roles. These schemas tell the child what kinds of information to look for in the environment and how to interpret such information. In Chapter 10 we discussed how children's theories about intelligence may cause them to perceive and respond to achievement situations and to success and failure in different ways. In a similar manner, according to Martin and Halverson (1981), children's beliefs about gender stereotypes are important because they are relevant to their emerging self-concepts and because they are salient in their everyday worlds.

Do gender-role schemas affect the way children see things? To find out, Martin and Halverson (1983) showed 5- and 6-year-olds pictures of males and females involved in activities that were either gender consistent (e.g., a boy playing with a train) or gender inconsistent (e.g., a girl sawing wood). A week later the researchers asked the children to recall the pictures. Recalling the gender-inconsistent pictures, children tended to distort information by changing the gender of the actor; when they recalled gender-consistent pictures, they were more confident of their memory. A variety of studies report similar findings—for example, girls and boys remember feminine and masculine toys and objects, respectively, more easily, and both also remember more about same-gender peers and activities (Signorella, Bilger, & Liben, 1998). Research has also found that children's memory for schema-consistent information grows stronger as they grow older (Martin & Ruble, 2004).

Gender identity matters too. Boys who view themselves as more feminine in sixth grade were more likely to develop increasingly egalitarian gender attitudes by the end of seventh grade (Liben & Bigler, 2002). The degree to which children rely on gender schemas in interpreting their social world varies among individual children and across age (Martin, & Ruble, 2004). Young children (4 years or younger) appear to rely relatively more on gender schemas than older children (5 years or older). This is partly because older children have more complete and elaborate knowledge of gender roles, attach less importance to these roles, and are less rigid in applying their knowledge (Levy, 1994). Similarly, children vary in

gender-schema theory The notion that children develop schemas, or naive theories, that help them organize and structure their experience related to gender differences and gender roles.

Figure 13-3

Gender constancy and attention to TV characters
Grasping the concept of gender constancy led both boys and girls to pay more attention to same-gender characters on TV. Because both girls and boys who haven't yet grasped this concept tend to pay more attention to female characters, constancy did not alter girls' viewing patterns very much, although it reversed the boys' patterns.

Source: Based on Luecke-Aleska, Anderson, Collins, & Schmitt, 1995.

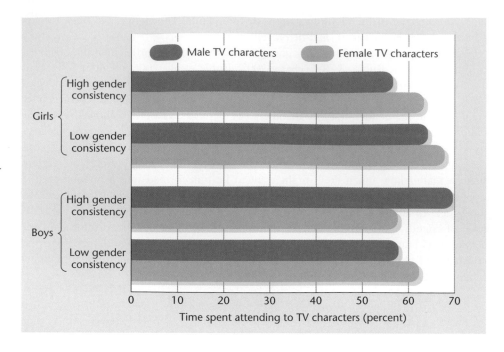

the extent to which they have well-formed gender schemas (Signorella et al., 1998). Some children are "gender schematic" and highly sensitive to gender notions, whereas other children are "gender aschematic" and focus more on nongender aspects of information in their environment. Not surprisingly, gender-schematic children display better memories for gender-consistent information and are more likely to distort gender-inconsistent information than less gender-schematic children (Levy, 1994). Part of their ability to remember may be due to differential attention to same-gender information. In a naturalistic study of TV viewing, Luecke-Aleksa, Anderson, Collins, and Schmitt (1995) found that boys who had a better grasp of gender constancy watched male characters more and programs that featured a greater number of males than did boys who had not yet fully achieved gender constancy (Figure 13-3). High gender-constant girls also watched same-gender characters more than they watched male TV characters. In contrast girls whose constancy was not yet secure watched male and female TV characters about the same amount. Interestingly, gender-constant girls also watched more action programs; the researchers hypothesized that this may be the result of women's having more glamorous and key roles in such programs, even though these roles are still subordinate to those of the men. These studies remind us that it is important to consider individual as well as developmental differences in understanding cognitive approaches to gender typing. In short, gender-role schemas clearly alter the ways in which children process social information and either recall it accurately or distort it to suit their prior concepts.

A Comparison of the Cognitive Developmental and Gender-Schema Theories

Does increasingly sophisticated gender-typed knowledge influence children's gender-role activities and behavior? Kohlberg's cognitive developmental theory and gender-schema theory provide different answers (Martin & Ruble, 2004). Kohlberg's theory predicts that the achievement of gender constancy should influence children's gender-typed choices. Therefore, prior to the 5- to 7-year age period, there should be little preference for gender-appropriate activities. Gender-schema theory, on the

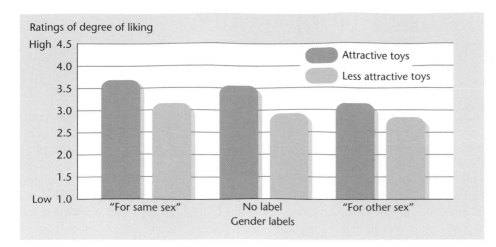

Figure 13-4

Toys for the other gender are "hot potatoes"

For preschoolers, the attractiveness of a toy increased its likeability, particularly if experimenters described it as a toy either that children of the same gender or all children really liked. Children liked a toy a lot less if it was described as something that other-gender children really liked, treating these toys like "hot potatoes."

Source: Martin, Eisenbud, & Rose, 1995.

other hand, suggests that children may need only basic information about gender, such as identification of the sexes (Martin & Ruble, 2004). According to this theory, merely labeling the genders is sufficient for children to begin to form rules concerning gender.

Apparently the gender-schema theorists are correct. Contrary to Kohlberg's proposals, gender labeling is sufficient to affect gender-typed activity preferences—an achievement that occurs well before the child develops gender constancy (Martin & Ruble, 2004; Martin & Little, 1990). As Fagot and Leinbach (1989) found, children who developed gender identity early (before 27 months) engaged in more gender-typed play than children who gained gender identity later in development. In short, the early boys were more likely to be playing with trucks and trains, while the early girls were more likely to be found in the doll corner! Moreover, at age 4, the early gender-role identifiers also possessed greater knowledge of gender-role stereotypes. Children even respond to novel toys based on gender labels. As Martin, Eisenbud, and Rose (1995) found, even when novel toys were very attractive, children showed a "hot potato" effect: They quickly lost interest in toys after being told that they were for the opposite gender (Figure 13-4).

Another kind of basic gender category information that is important in organizing gender-typed preferences is children's recognition of their membership in a gender class or group (Maccoby, 1998). Recognition of their gender membership as male or female is related to children's gender-typed preferences and to their gender-role knowledge (Martin & Little, 1990; Martin & Ruble, 2004; Ruble et al., 2006).

Gender-typed play such as choosing trucks or dolls as appropriate for one's gender does not seem to depend on the achievement of gender stability or gender constancy. Instead, the first stage—the acquisition of basic gender identity—seems sufficient for the emergence of gender-typed play. However, according to Smetana and Letourneau (1984), choice of playmate may depend on the level of gender understanding. In this study, girls who had acquired gender stability chose to play with other girls more than did girls who had acquired only gender identity. "Lacking the certainty that gender is invariant across contexts and situations, females may actively seek the presence of same-sex peers to affirm their conceptions of themselves as females" (1984, p. 695). Once girls acquire gender constancy and their gender concepts are firmly established, they are less rigid in their choice of playmates. Girls at the highest level of gender understanding are confident that play with boys will not alter their gender. Cognitive understanding, in this case, brings increased freedom of social choice (McHale et al., 2001b). Together, these studies suggest that the link between acquiring gender concepts and behavior varies across both the stage of gender understanding and the kind of behavior.

INFLUENCE OF THE FAMILY ON GENDER TYPING

Parents have an enormous impact on children's gender-role behaviors and gender typing (McHale, Crouter, & Whiteman, 2003). As we noted in our discussion of family influences on children's peer relationships (Chapter 12), parents influence their children's sex-typed behaviors in several ways as well: as interaction partners, as direct instructors, and as providers of opportunities to learn sex-role attitudes and behaviors (McHale et al., 2003; Parke & Buriel, 2006). Parents speak differently to male and female babies, they hold and move them differently, and, as we've said, they tend to choose clothing, room decor, and toys that are considered appropriate for either girls or boys. As children grow, parents encourage them in gender-appropriate activities, and they disapprove or reinforce their children's behaviors according to whether they are gender appropriate or inappropriate. And by their own behaviors and lifestyles parents provide models that children can follow in developing their gender-role choices and behaviors. And parents provide different opportunities for boys and girls to learn sex-typed behaviors by enrolling them in different kinds of gender-typed activities, clubs, and sports.

Cognitive social learning theory predicts that parents should play an important role as encouraging and reinforcing agents and as models in shaping children's gender-role behaviors and attitudes, and it seems likely that they do. Parents are the first people children observe, and they're also the first people who try to teach children or shape their behavior. As we will see, there is considerable evidence of the influence of social factors in children's gender typing.

Parents' Influence on Children's Gender-Typed Choices

Well before children are making lists of toys they'd like to receive for their birthdays or holidays, parents are actively shaping their children's tastes and preferences. Have you ever compared the bedrooms of girls and boys? This is exactly what several researchers did. Carefully and systematically, they recorded the kinds of toys, decorations, furniture, and even the curtains and bedspreads that adorned the bedrooms of boys and girls between 1 month and 6 years old (Pomerleau, Bolduc, Malcuit, & Cossette, 1990; Rheingold & Cook, 1975). Boys' rooms contained more vehicles, machines, army equipment, soldiers, and sports equipment. In contrast, girls' rooms

cathy®   **by Cathy Guisewite**

were more likely to house dolls and floral-patterned and ruffled furnishings (e.g., floral curtains with lace). The toys of boys were more action-oriented; girls' toys were less action-oriented and more family focused. Of particular interest was the finding that there was little difference between the results of studies conducted in 1975 and 1990; the times, they may be a-changin', but not children's rooms!

Parents often announce the gender of their offspring to the world by the way they dress their children, subtly shaping their children toward "appropriate" gender roles (Parke & Brott, 1999). When a group of researchers watched 1- to 13-month-olds in a shopping center, they found baby girls in pink, puffed sleeves, ruffles, and lace. Boys wore blue or red, but few bows, barrettes, or ribbons (Shakin, Shakin, & Sternglanz, 1985). According to Fagot and Leinbach (1987), gender-typed clothing serves not only to announce a child's gender but to ensure that even strangers will respond to the child in gender-appropriate ways.

Parents' Behavior toward Girls and Boys

Both mothers and fathers tend to behave differently with their male and female babies, but mothers are more likely than fathers to treat girls and boys in an egalitarian manner. Fathers show a preference for sons, perhaps partly because they feel free to talk and play with them in a more rough-and-tumble way (Parke, 2002). As children grow older, however, both parents tend to encourage their children in play and other activities that the culture sees as gender appropriate.

INFANTS AND TODDLERS   From earliest infancy, parents are likely to view their sons and daughters differently. Parents are more likely to describe their newborn daughters as smaller, softer, less attentive, cuter, more delicate, and more finely featured than their sons. And fathers, even if they have only seen and not yet handled their infants, are more extreme than mothers in emphasizing the size, strength, coordination, and alertness of sons versus the fragility and beauty of daughters (Rubin, Provenzano, & Luria, 1974; Stern & Karraker, 1989). These expectations are, of course, consistent with predictions from an evolutionary theoretical approach to gender differences, which emphasizes strength and competitiveness in boys and nurturance in girls (Geary, 1998). In view of such differences in parents' perceptions of their male and female infants, it is not surprising that, from the earliest days of life, boys and girls are treated differently and

When we first meet an infant we often use clothing as a clue to the child's gender. If the beruffled infant in pink and the baby decked out in blue exchanged clothes, would you be able to make an accurate judgment of the first as a girl and the second as a boy?

that this differential treatment is most marked among fathers (Stern & Karraker, 1989). Researchers have also found that adults will play in more masculine ways with a baby they have been led to believe is a boy and in a gentler fashion with an infant they think is a girl, regardless of the infant's actual gender! Gender-role stereotypes clearly serve to shape our treatment of children—even in infancy.

From the time women learn they are pregnant, fathers-to-be generally show a strong preference for sons (Hoffman, 1977). And after children are born, fathers are more likely to play and talk with sons than with daughters, especially when the new babies are firstborns (Parke, 2002). As children grow older, fathers spend more time in play with male toddlers, and they watch and touch their infants more. They indulge in rough-and-tumble antics with male infants and may talk with them in a kind of macho way, saying things like "Hey, Tiger!" (Parke, 2002). Fathers are more likely to cuddle their infant daughters gently than to engage in active play with them. In contrast, mothers tend to treat female and male babies pretty much the same way (Lytton & Romney, 1991; Siegel, 1987). Both parents, however, are more verbally responsive to girls; they talk to them more, and they use more supportive and directive speech with daughters than they do with sons (Leaper, Anderson, & Sanders, 1998).

This pattern of differences in mothers' and fathers' interactions with sons and daughters suggests that the social forces involved in gender-role typing may begin almost at birth and that fathers, through their more markedly different treatment of boys and girls, may play a more important role in the gender-typing process than do mothers. As Ruble and colleagues (2006) point out, however, today some parents may be making conscious efforts to encourage egalitarian behaviors in both boys and girls, although they may tend to do this more often with older than with younger children. Perhaps the twenty-first century may see more equal roles for moms and dads in the gender-typing process.

OLDER CHILDREN   As children grow older, do parents actively encourage and reinforce them for behaving in a gender-stereotypic manner? If the environment has anything to do with gender behavior, social learning theory would predict that both reinforcement and modeling should play important roles, and it seems likely that they do. Langlois and Downs (1980) observed how mothers and fathers reacted to their 3- and 5-year-old girls' and boys' play, purposely manipulating the children's choices of toys. Both "masculine" toys, such as soldiers and a gas station, and "feminine" toys, such as a dollhouse and kitchen utensils, were available to the children, but the researchers specifically told the children to play with what were either gender-appropriate or cross-gender toys. They then recorded parents' reactions to their children's choices of toys, mothers in one session, and fathers in another.

Fathers consistently exerted pressure on their children—both boys and girls—to play with gender-typed toys. They were also quite consistent in rewarding both sons and daughters for play with gender-appropriate toys and in punishing them for play with cross-gender toys. With daughters, mothers took the same approach, but their responses to their sons were inconsistent: They sometimes punished and sometimes rewarded them for playing with cross-gender toys. Other studies found that when children are engaged in other-gender behaviors, fathers disapprove more than mothers (Leve & Fagot, 1997).

These findings are consistent with other evidence that men are more likely to gender-type toys and to purchase such toys than women are, especially playthings for boys (Fisher-Thompson, 1990). The findings are also consistent with the view that the father is the principal agent of gender-role socialization and that the mother plays a less influential role in this process (Parke, 2002).

In general, parents seem to be more protective of daughters' than of sons' physical well-being. Parents tend to encourage dependency and close family ties in girls and to put more emphasis on independence, early exploration, achievement, and competition in boys. Whereas parents typically display similar expectations for boys' and girls' independence and maturity in relation to such safe activities as tidying up rooms, putting away toys or clothes, or getting dressed, they treat boys and girls differently in areas where there are greater risks. Parents generally think boys should be able to play away from home without telling parents where they are, run errands in the neighborhood, cross the street alone, use sharp scissors, and indulge in other venturesome activities at an earlier age than girls. Parents are also less likely to pick up or supervise boys after school (Hoffman, 1977; Ruble et al., 2006). Moreover, parents often communicate these messages quite directly: Pomerantz and Ruble (1998) found that parents were more likely to tell sons specifically that they were free to do certain activities than they were to grant such freedom to daughters.

Not all cultural groups make these kinds of gender-based distinctions. As we saw earlier, African American parents treat boys and girls more similarly than do European American parents. Many psychologists are concerned, however, that among those groups that do tend to gender-type their children along traditional lines, girls may suffer. Restricting girls' freedom more than boys' may lead girls to lack feelings of self-efficacy and to discourage them from exploring their worlds and taking intellectual and creative risks. Under these conditions, girls may continue to be much more likely than boys to conform to cultural norms and values; clearly, this may sometimes be useful, but it may also be detrimental (Ruble et al., 2006).

Parents' gender-differentiated behaviors often seem to be associated with their interest in their children's achievement. Fathers, who are particularly prone to differentiate among boys and girls in this regard, are more likely to stress the importance of a career or occupational success for sons than for daughters (Block, 1983; Hoffman, 1977). Differential treatment of boys and girls is particularly marked in the area of mathematical achievement (DeLisi & McGillicuddy-DeLisi, 2002). For example, parents are likely to encourage boys more often than girls to work on math or science-related activities at home (Eccles, Freedman-Doan, Frome, Jacobs, & Yoon, 2000). In one study, even when families visited a science museum parents were more likely to explain interactive exhibits to their sons than to their daughters (Crowley, Callahan, Tennenbaum, & Allen, 2001). In a variety of cultures, including Japan, Taiwan, and the United States, parents still believe boys do better in math than girls and that girls are superior readers (Lummis & Stevenson, 1990).

In both teaching and problem-solving situations, fathers of boys are more attuned to achievement and to the cognitive aspects of the situation. Fathers of girls seem to be less concerned with performance and more concerned with interpersonal interactions with their daughters (Block, 1983). And even mothers, when reading bedtime stories, teach their boys more than their girls. They supply unfamiliar names for sons ("Look, here's a giraffe. Can you say *giraffe?*"), but with daughters they emphasize enjoying the time spent with them (Weitzman, Birns, & Friend, 1985) or they focus on feelings and emotions rather than the cognitive aspects of the exchange (Cervantes & Callanan, 1998). And these parental behaviors are not lost on children. Eccles and colleagues (Eccles et al., 1993; Wigfield et al., 2006) found that parents who held stronger stereotyped beliefs about boys' and girls' skills in English, math, and sports had matching expectations about their own children's abilities in these areas. Moreover, even when the researchers controlled for children's actual levels of skill in these areas, the children's performance and their perceptions of their own competence matched their parents' expectations.

Modeling Parents' Characteristics

To what degree do children's imitations of a parent's characteristics explain the development of gender typing? Although warm and nurturant parents may by example encourage children of their own gender to learn the roles they have adopted, for boys especially parental power has an even greater impact on gender typing. In boys' masculine identification, the combination of a dominant mother and a passive father is particularly destructive, whereas this combination has no particular effect on girls' femininity. A boy with a weak father and a powerful mother is likely to exhibit feminine characteristics.

Modeling a parent's behavior is one of the most important ways a child learns social roles and the skills judged appropriate to those roles.

Fathers who are dominant and decisive in setting limits and dispensing rewards and punishments, however, are likely to have very masculine sons (Hetherington, 1967).

Turner and Gervai (1995) have confirmed the role of parent characteristics in children's gender typing. Parents who are highly traditional in their gender roles have children who are also highly gender typed, especially in terms of their knowledge of gender stereotypes, but who don't necessarily give expression to this knowledge in their actual behavior. This was particularly true with regard to children's choice of same- or other-gender play partners. Both sons and daughters of very "masculine" fathers were more assertive and less emotionally expressive than children of men judged less masculine (Hetherington, 1967).

The roles parents play within the family—whether traditional or nontraditional—have a strong impact on children's gender-typed preferences and behavior (Ruble et al., 2006). In less traditional families where mothers are employed outside the home, both boys and girls may have less stereotyped concepts of gender-appropriate behavior, and girls may display fewer gender-typed behaviors (Ruble et al., 2006). However, maternal employment is now so prevalent that children's gender concepts may be affected just by the presence of women in the workplace; it doesn't seem to matter whether their own mothers work outside the home (Ruble et al., 2006; Serbin, Polwishta, & Gulko, 1993). As we discussed in Chapter 1, secular trends affect children's development—as the social contexts of children's lives change, the sources of critical socializing influence change as well.

The ways in which parents divide household tasks also influence gender typing. An egalitarian division of labor is linked to less traditional occupational choices, and fathers who modeled nontraditional behaviors had children with less advanced knowledge of gender distinctions (Serbin et al., 1993; Turner & Gervai, 1995). In a unique longitudinal study of families in which fathers were the primary caregivers during children's preschool years, the children, when they became adolescents, endorsed nontraditional employment and childrearing roles (Radin, 1999).

Parental Absence or Unavailability

Particularly because the father plays such an important role in gender typing, we might expect that children from homes in which the father is either permanently absent or away for long periods would show disruptions in gender typing. When there is no father in the home, the mother must, of necessity, assume a more decisive role in rearing her children. The absence of a male model and the lack of opportunity for children to interact with a father may contribute to children's difficulties in developing both gender identity and gender typing (Hetherington, 1989).

When fathers are permanently gone owing to divorce or death, when they are temporarily absent or unavailable because of occupational demands or wartime service, and when they simply show little interest in their children, young boys especially may have problems with gender identity and gender role (Ruble et al., 2006). Disruptions in gender roles are most apparent in preadolescent boys and are most severe when the separation has occurred before the child was 5 (Hetherington, 1966). As the child grows older and has wider social contacts, other models such as peers, siblings, surrogate fathers, teachers, and people in the mass media can partially mitigate the effects of father absence on gender-role adoption (Ruble et al., 2006).

The effects of parental absence on gender typing in preadolescent girls appear to be minimal. However, studies of adolescents suggest that parental absence may have a delayed effect on girls' gender typing. Father absence may cause adolescent daughters to have difficulties relating to other males; these difficulties may take different forms for daughters of widows and of divorcées. In some studies, adolescent girls from divorced homes appeared to be more sexually precocious and assertive with males, whereas those whose mothers were widowed were characterized as excessively anxious about sexuality and as shy and uncomfortable around males (Hetherington, 1991a; Newcomer & Udry, 1987).

Recently these findings were confirmed in both the United States and New Zealand. Following girls from age 5 to 18, Ellis and colleagues (2003) found that father absence was associated with elevated risk for both early sexual activity and adolescent pregnancy. Moreover, there was a *dose-response* relationship between the timing of the onset of father absence and early sexual outcomes. That is, as the "dose," the length of father absence, increased, the "response," sexual outcomes for adolescents, increased. In this case, girls who suffered father absence early in their lives (i.e., before age 5) had the highest rates of both early sexual activity and adolescent pregnancy, followed by girls who experienced father absence later on (i.e., after age 6). The father-present girls were lowest on these sex-related outcomes. The rates of teenage pregnancy, in fact, were seven to eight times higher among early father-absent girls but only two to three times higher among late father-absent girls as compared with rates for father-present girls. (See Figure 13-5.)

Perhaps the ill effects of father absence are the result of adverse family and economic conditions, such as poverty, exposure to violence, inadequate parental guidance, and lack of supervision. However, Ellis and his colleagues found that even after controlling for these factors, the links between father absence and sexual behavior were still evident.

What explains these relations between father absence and female sexual risk taking? According to social learning models, daughters learn to feel competent and to

Figure 13-5 The effects of father absence or presence on girls' early sexual activity and teen pregnancy

Teenage girls in both the United States and New Zealand were far more likely to engage in early sexual activity when, at an early age, they were bereft of their fathers, and even girls who lost their fathers later in their development were more likely to engage in such activity than girls whose fathers were consistently present. A similar pattern was found for rates of teenage pregnancy.

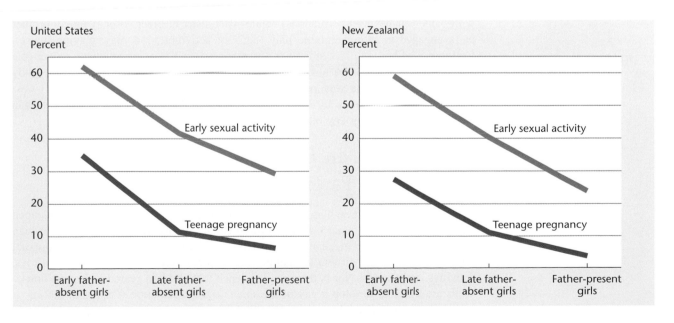

Source: Ellis et al., 2003.

value and acquire the social skills necessary for effective heterosexual relationships by interacting with warm, responsive, masculine fathers who reward and enjoy their daughters' femininity. The father-absent girls not only lacked positive male models, but may have been exposed to irresponsible or unpalatable dating and repartnering behaviors on the part of their mothers. These exposures may have encouraged earlier onset of sexual behavior, with its risk of pregnancy.

According to the evolutionary perspective, girls in homes without a father view male parental investment in families as unreliable and unimportant (Bjorklund & Schackelford, 1999; Geary, 1998). As a result, these girls as adolescents are more likely to form sexual liaisons, to be more casual in their sexual encounters, and thus to be likely to risk pregnancy. As in many domains, many different theories can help us understand children's social development. Studies of paternal absence again indicate the important role of the father in girls' social development. Mothers can moderate the effects of father absence on their daughters, however. Women who cast their former husbands and their relationships with them in a positive light, and who themselves demonstrate emotional stability, can lessen the deleterious effects of father absence.

Siblings as Gender Socialization Agents

Siblings as well as parents can influence children's gender choices, attitudes, and behaviors. For example, a variety of both classic and contemporary studies have found that the gender typing of children varies with the sex of their siblings (Brim, 1958; Rust et al., 2000). Children with sisters tend to develop more feminine qualities, whereas those with brothers generally develop more masculine qualities (Rust et al., 2000).

Now consider a recent longitudinal study by McHale, Updegraff, Helms-Erikson, and Crouter (2001). The goal of these researchers was to assess whether the gender-role attitudes, leisure activities, and gendered personality qualities (e.g., expressivity versus instrumentality) of firstborn children predicted these same outcomes in their second-born siblings, two years later. The researchers found that older siblings did indeed influence younger siblings' gender typing. Moreover the links between siblings' attributes were stronger than the links between a child's attributes and those of his mother or father. Moreover, second-borns were more likely to model their older, firstborn siblings than the other way round.

Moreover, the sex of the older sibling matters too (Stoneman, Brody, & MacKinnon, 1986). Brother-brother pairs engaged in more stereotypically masculine play (e.g., play with balls, vehicles, or toy weapons), while sister-sister or older sister–younger brother pairs engaged in more feminine play (e.g., art activities, doll play, playing house). Children who had an older sibling of the other sex had less stereotypical gender-role concepts. Even parents are susceptible to the impact of the sex of siblings. In the study we cited earlier of the way parents decorate children's rooms (Rheingold & Cook, 1975), the bedroom décor of the boys with older brothers was more stereotyped than the décor found among any other group of infants and children.

Gender Roles in Children of Gay and Lesbian Parents

Recent studies of children who grow up in a lesbian or gay household have challenged the importance of the father's contribution to gender typing. Children reared in lesbian families do not differ in gender-role behavior from children reared in heterosexual households. Boys and girls in lesbian homes choose traditionally gender-oriented toys, activities, and friends. Nor is there any evidence that children reared in lesbian households are likely to develop a gay or a lesbian sexual orientation (Patterson, 2002).

Similarly, recent evidence suggests that boys raised by gay fathers are largely heterosexual in their sexual orientations and that this is so regardless of how long sons lived with their gay fathers (Bailey et al., 1995; Patterson, 2002). As we discussed in Chapter 11, the socioemotional adjustment of children in lesbian households seems very similar to that of children reared in traditional families. Research in this area has raised important questions about the role of environmental and biological influences on the development of gender-related orientations and behaviors. Although fathers do appear to have the greater role in children's gender-role typing, these studies suggest that children can learn gender roles in a variety of family arrangements.

EXTRAFAMILIAL INFLUENCES ON GENDER ROLES

Families are the first among the many social forces that play a role in shaping our gender-linked behaviors, but they are not the only influences. As children grow older, influences outside the family, present from early on, become increasingly important in shaping gender typing. Among the earliest of these forces are the books that parents read to children and the television programming that children watch. Peers and peer groups have considerable impact on a child's assumption of a gender identity and of gender roles, as does the child's own understanding of what is appropriate and inappropriate behavior for her gender. And, as we will see, the schools and teachers with whom children spend so much of their time have great influence on gender typing, both for good and for ill. Once again, we review research results that support cognitive social learning theory.

In this section, we explore some of the forces that may contribute to children's amazingly clear distinctions about what's gender appropriate and inappropriate. Sixth and ninth graders, asked to rate various activities (e.g., reading or doing math, art, or mechanical tasks) as to how "boyish" or "girlish" they were, how important accomplishment in each was, how well they thought they would perform in each activity, and with what minimum standard of performance they would be satisfied, drew very clear gender-based distinctions (Ruble et al., 2006). These young people attached more importance to achievement in activities they viewed as appropriate to their own gender, set higher minimum standards for these tasks, and expected to do better on them than on activities they considered inappropriate for their gender.

Books and Television

Male and female roles are portrayed in similarly gender-stereotyped ways in children's stories and on television. Although there has been pressure within educational circles for more egalitarian treatment of boys and girls, as well as of different cultural groups, children's literature and schoolbooks still contain many gender stereotypes. A comparative study of elementary school children's readers over a period of some 15 years offered some hopeful signs: Girls appeared as often as boys did in the books surveyed in 1989 and in a wider range of activities than they enjoyed in 1975 books (Purcell & Stewart, 1990). Nevertheless, books still often show females as more passive, dependent, and engaged in a narrower range of occupations than men and show males as more assertive and action-oriented (Turner-Bowker, 1996).

Males on television are more likely than females to be depicted as aggressive, decisive, professionally competent, rational, stable, powerful, and tolerant. In contrast, females tend to be portrayed as warmer, more sociable, more emotional, and happier. When women on television are aggressive, they are usually inept or unsuccessful aggressors, and they are more likely to be shown as victims than as initiators of violence. There are exceptions, of course, such as "Xena: Warrior Princess" and cartoon characters like Catwoman. Females are less likely to be leading characters and are more likely to be in comedy roles, to be married or about to be married, and to be younger than males (Huston & Wright, 1998), although there is a trend, as in books, toward depicting women in a wider range of occupational roles (Allan & Coltrane, 1996; Coltrane, 1998; Douglas, 2003). In fact, according to a recent survey, only 4 percent of female TV characters were portrayed as homemakers (Heintz-Knowles, 2001). Even in television commercials, males more often portray authorities and make more voice-over comments about a product's merits. Women are more likely to play the role of the consumer, displaying interest in product demonstrations (Coltrane, 1998). When women are shown as experts, they are likely to be discussing food products, laundry, soap, or beauty aids. These trends have been identified in the United States as well as in other countries (Best & Williams, 1993; Singer & Singer, 2001).

The likelihood that these stereotypical presentations of male and female roles have a real impact on children is underscored by findings that children who are heavy TV viewers are more likely to have stereotypical notions of gender and race and to show conformity to culturally accepted gender-role typing (Berry, 2000). When television was first introduced in a small town in Canada (see the section on natural experiments in Chapter 1), analysts recorded marked increases in traditional gender attitudes two years later (Kimball, 1986; MacBeth, 1996).

Television can also be used to change children's gender-role stereotypes. In one study, 5- and 6-year-olds who were shown a cartoon in which the characters played nontraditional roles (girls helped boys build a clubhouse) developed less conventional gender-role attitudes (Davidson, Yasuna, & Tower, 1979). Similarly, "Freestyle," a television series that tries to counteract children's gender and ethnic stereotypes, has been moderately successful in increasing acceptance of boys and girls who exhibit nontraditional gender-typed behaviors. For example, 9- to 12-year-old viewers were more accepting of girls who participated in athletics and mechanical activities and of boys who engaged in nurturant activities (Johnston & Ettema, 1982). However, the effects of most TV-based interventions have been relatively modest and short-lived and are more effective with younger than with older children (Bigler & Liben, 1992; Maccoby, 1998). It will probably take much more change in books, television, and many other spheres of life to alter gender-role stereotypes and attitudes.

Peers, Gender Roles, and Gender Segregation

Peers often serve as enforcers of society's gender-role standards, and they may also help to define them. In these roles, peers may also help the individual child to define herself and to solidify a gender identity. The importance of forging a clear gender identity stems from its link with self-esteem. Researchers have found that children who were masculine or androgynous (combining both masculine and feminine characteristics) had higher self-esteem than those who had a feminine gender identity (Boldizar, 1991; Ruble et al., 2006). As the feminine role becomes more equal to the male role, this link with self-esteem is likely to change, but girls and women still suffer more discrimination than men in many spheres of society.

Observing 200 preschoolers at play over several months' time, Fagot (1985a) found that peers displayed marked reactions when children violated appropriate gender-role behavior patterns. Boys who play with dolls rather than trucks have a tough time; their classmates criticize them five to six times more often than they heckle children who conform. On the other hand, peers aren't as harsh in their treatment of girls who would rather play firefighter than nurse; they tend to ignore rather than criticize such girls.

When peers rewarded children for appropriate gender-role behavior, the children tended to persist longer in the rewarded type of activity. However, the source of the reinforcement makes a difference, too. Boys respond to feedback from boys, but not from girls, whereas girls are more receptive to feedback from other girls. This pattern of responsiveness can lead to gender segregation which, in turn, may provide additional opportunities to learn accepted gender roles (Fagot, 1985a; Maccoby, 1998).

On any school playground, you can see that children have a very strong tendency to associate and play with children of the same gender. When children are $4\frac{1}{2}$ years old, they spend nearly three times as much time with same-gender play partners as with children of the other gender. By age $6\frac{1}{2}$, the effect is even stronger: Children spend 11 times as much time with same-gender as with opposite-gender partners (Maccoby, 1998). Between ages 4 and 6, boys tend even more than girls to congregate in same-gender groups (Benenson, Apostoleris, & Parnass, 1997). And grade-school children like same-gender peers better and are less likely to behave negatively toward same-gender classmates (Underwood, Schockner, & Hurley, 2001).

To further illustrate the segregation effect, Martin and Fabes (2001) followed preschoolers throughout the school year. They found not only an increase in gender segregation but clear differences in activities between boys and girls when each were in same-gender groups. During the year, the more time that a boy spent with other boys the greater his activity level. He engaged in more and more rough-and-tumble play and overt aggression, spent less time with or near adults, and expressed more positive emotion (i.e., had fun). In contrast, girls in groups with other girls showed a drop in activity level, their aggressive behavior lessened, and they spent more time in proximity to adults. In short, as this study found and as we noted in Chapter 12, same-gender groups provide markedly distinctive socializing experiences for boys and girls (Maccoby, 1998).

These stylistic differences in boys' and girls' groups have led Maccoby (1998) to suggest several reasons for gender segregation. First, girls view boys' rough-and-tumble play style and their competition-dominance orientation as aversive; as a result, girls avoid interactions with boys. Second, girls find it difficult to influence boys. They influence one another successfully, using their preferred method of making polite suggestions. These tactics are not very effective with boys, who prefer to make more direct demands. "Girls find it aversive to try to interact with someone who is unresponsive, and they begin to avoid such partners" (Maccoby, 1990, p. 515).

This phenomenon is evident across many cultures, ranging from the United States to India to some African countries, and it occurs without adult encouragement, guidance, or pressure. Although earlier parental influence may play a role in setting the process in motion, children spontaneously choose same-gender play partners. Although individual children may differ in their masculinity or femininity, or in their grasp of gender stability and gender constancy, they all show the same preference for same-gender playmates (Maccoby, 1998). Thus, from preschool onward, children choose to live in segregated play worlds that, in turn, encourage separate styles of interaction that are distinctly male and female. This **self-socialization,** or children's spontaneous adoption of gender-appropriate behavior, may be another powerful way of learning and maintaining gender roles. Thus children themselves and their peer groups play an important role in gender-role socialization. Of course, gender segregation is not permanent; by adolescence, interest in opposite-sex partners is in full swing (Larson et al., 2002).

self-socialization The child's spontaneous adoption of gender-appropriate behavior.

Schools and Teachers

Teachers and schools deliver a number of gender-related messages to children (Ruble et al., 2006). To begin with, the structure of the school system is predominantly male—men hold many more of the positions of power, such as principal and superintendent—whereas the teaching staff is predominantly female. This mirrors the power structure in the traditional family and in society at large. In addition, teachers sometimes structure classroom activities by gender and provide differential rewards and punishments to boys and girls. In this section, we consider the differential impact of the school culture and environment on girls and boys, and we explore some specific effects of teachers' attitudes and practices.

THE SCHOOL CULTURE   Although teachers in individual classrooms often seem to pay more attention to boys than to girls, the general culture of the school may in some ways favor girls. The school system often frowns upon the independent, assertive, competitive, and boisterous qualities that the culture has encouraged in boys from infancy. In contrast, the more verbally oriented girls, who are generally better

Teachers often segregate a child from the rest of the class for a period of time as a way of controlling unruly behavior. Many more boys than girls get the "time out" treatment.

behaved and who follow rules more readily than boys, may find more acceptance from teachers who—at least in the early grades—are likely to be female. Is it surprising, then, that from the start girls tend to like school more than boys and to perform better in their academic work? For many boys, school may not be a happy place. Boys may feel that their teachers like them less than girls and they may have more difficulty adjusting to school routines—they may create more problems for teachers and elicit more criticism from them; and, most important, they may perform not only at a lower level than their female classmates but well below their own abilities (McCall, Beach, & Lan, 2000; Ruble et al., 2006).

What might be the implications of young boys' perception of school as a gender-inappropriate institution? Clearly, one potential effect is that boys may be unlikely to be as motivated and interested in school-related activities as girls, who are likely to view school as consistent with their own gender-role identity. Girls outperform their male peers in the early grades, especially in reading skills; some surveys have found that boys are between three and six times as likely as girls to experience problems in learning to read (Halpern, 2000; Lummis & Stevenson, 1990). On the other hand, the school environment and culture as we've described them do not explain the often greater eventual achievement of boys and men in the late high school and college years.

It seems that although girls may have an advantage in the early grades, this jump start, as it were, has a short-lived effect. Girls' achievement levels decline as they grow older, and by college, the proportion of female underachievers exceeds the proportion of male underachievers (Eccles et al., 1993; Wigfield et al., 2006). The kinds of conforming and dependent behaviors that schools encourage in girls may, in the long run, be detrimental. Dependency is negatively related to intellectual achievement. Independence, assertiveness, and nonconformity are much more likely to lead to creative thinking and problem solving and to high levels of achievement in both girls and boys (Dweck, 2001; Dweck & Leggett, 1988). The many conflicting messages that girls receive in the school years can put them at risk, if not for failure, for lives that are less than satisfying.

Over the years, psychologists have found that public achievement, particularly in competitive activities, is often threatening to girls and women. Some girls cope with their conflict about achievement by concealing their abilities, particularly from boys (Ruble et al., 2006). For example, a girl may tell a male peer that she received lower grades than she actually did in a course they both attend. Or she may lower her effort, intentionally performing below her capabilities. And even women who are highly successful professionals sometimes seek to disguise their achievement striving by appearing superfeminine—they may try not only to be super career women but super wives, super mothers, and super volunteers. What boy or man would try to hide his ambition and his accomplishments from others?

IMPACT OF TEACHER ATTITUDES AND BEHAVIORS Even in the preschool years, teachers respond differently to boys and girls, often reacting to boys and girls in gender-stereotypic ways (Fagot, 1985a). Researchers have found that teachers interrupt girls more frequently than boys during conversations and pay more attention to boys' assertive behavior than to girls' pushing and shoving (Hendrick & Stange, 1991). On the other hand, teachers respond to girls' social initiatives, such as talking and gesturing, more than to these same behaviors in boys. Moreover, although teachers may encourage boys to engage in quiet activities rather than aggressive and rough-and-tumble play, both teachers and peers criticize boys for cross-gender behaviors (e.g., dressing up or playing with dolls) but are much less likely to criticize girls for cross-gender play (Fagot, 1985a).

Not surprisingly, differential teacher attention has an impact. Fagot (1985a) found that nine months after she first observed a group of preschoolers, clear gender differences had emerged. Girls talked to the teacher more, and boys exhibited a higher level of assertiveness. Although educators once believed that increasing the number of male teachers would counteract female teachers' apparently differential treatment of boys and girls, Fagot (1985b) discovered that both male and female teachers reacted more positively to children involved in stereotypical female gender-role behaviors, such as art activities and helping others, no matter what the individual child's gender! At the same time, some evidence indicates that male teachers may have more nontraditional gender beliefs and preferences as well as nontraditional views of the teacher's role (e.g., they may hold less stereotyped beliefs about boys' verbal abilities and girls' math skills than have been common among teachers) (Mancus, 1992).

As we have seen, boys and girls have traditionally differed in their performance on verbal and quantitative tasks, girls doing better in English and boys in mathematics (Shea et al., 2001; Wigfield et al., 2006). We have also discussed the finding, however, that girls' lower math achievement is apparently caused by their often lesser ability to deal with geometry and that this, in turn, is related to boys' superior abilities in spatial relations. In fact, we said, girls are better at computational skills and do not differ from boys in respect either to basic mathematical knowledge or knowledge of algebra. Why, then, do enrollments in school courses, selections of college majors and college degrees, and adult career choices continue to reflect the old idea that boys and men are better at math?

For one thing, teachers and others who continue to encourage boys more than girls in mathematical pursuits may be unaware of these findings (Shepardson & Pizzini, 1992; Wigfield et al., 2006). And if people in general are unaware of researchers' data, males may continue to perceive themselves as more competent in mathematics, and females may continue to view mathematics as a male-achievement domain, which would then make the study of math inconsistent with their gender-role identity. Eccles (1985) found that 668 children in the fifth through the twelfth grades thought boys were better at math and could make more use of it than girls, despite the fact that these children displayed no gender differences in their actual mathematics performance!

Interestingly, as they grew older, girls expressed a decreasing liking for mathematics and more enjoyment of English, but boys' attitudes toward both subjects remained fairly stable. Lacking any positive reinforcement for studying math, more girls than boys dropped math during their high school years (Shea et al., 2001). In contrast, boys' course enrollment decisions reflected their past performance; if they had done well in math, they continued to take math courses. It seems that educators may need further education about children's educational skills and potential capabilities!

ANDROGYNY

Many psychologists believe that traditional ideas of masculinity and femininity have been socially and psychologically destructive. To speak and act as if each individual person is either "masculine" or "feminine" in interests, attitudes, and behaviors makes little sense when we know that in reality most people possess a combination of characteristics traditionally viewed as masculine or feminine. Any person, male or female, can be tender and nurturant with children, professionally successful, fiercely competitive on the tennis court, and an excellent cook. Many people are **androgynous**—that is, they possess both masculine and feminine psychological characteristics (Bem, 1981, 1998; Spence, 1993).

androgynous Possessing both feminine and masculine psychological characteristics.

Children, as well as adults, can be androgynous and such children are less likely to make stereotyped choices of play, activities, and occupations (Hebert, 2000; Harter, Waters, & Whitesell, 1998); they are better adjusted and more creative too (Norlander et al., 2000). And gender-oriented interests and concerns tend to change with age. Women may become more feminine and men more androgynous; thus, each gender may become more feminine with age. Of course, the increase in femininity in later life may also reflect the increased dependency both genders may experience as they continue to age (Hyde et al., 1991).

It is important to recognize that not only do gender-related traits such as expressiveness, nurturance, instrumentality, or assertiveness vary across individual males and females, but individual people will display one or another of these characteristics in different situations, settings, and tasks (Spence, 1993; Spence & Hall, 1996). Facilitating the development of desirable characteristics such as social sensitivity, nurturance, open expression of positive feelings, appropriate assertiveness, and independence in both males and females would seem to be constructive.

Can children's gender-role stereotypes be modified? Can children be taught to be more androgynous? Can children learn that fashion models and firefighters can be either males or females? The study we discuss in Box 13.2 suggests that they can; but, as the following exchange illustrates, the task may not be easy.

A psychologist overheard her 4-year-old son trying to explain her occupation to a young friend:

Son: My mother helps people. She's a doctor.

Friend: You mean a nurse.

Son: No. She's not that kind of doctor. She's a psychologist. She's a doctor of psychology.

Friend: I see. She's a nurse of psychology.

multischematic Possessing both multiple cultural schemas for responding to the environment and the necessary criteria for deciding what schema to use in a particular situation.

Work by Bigler and Liben (1990, 1992) does suggest that children can learn to use fewer stereotypes. Using 10 occupations that children view as typically masculine (e.g., dentist, farmer, construction worker) or feminine (e.g., beautician, flight attendant, librarian), these researchers tried to lessen children's stereotyping of these work roles. They taught the children, first, that gender is irrelevant. Then they focused the childrens' attention on two other ways of looking at job appropriateness: liking a job, and having the skills needed for the job. For example, construction workers must like to build things, and they must acquire the skill to drive big machines. The investigators gave one group of children practice problems for which they had to specify why the job (e.g., construction worker) was a good match for the person. If the children based their answers on gender rather than on interest or skills they received corrective feedback. In a control group, children participated in a group discussion about the roles of specific occupations within the community, with no emphasis on gender stereotyping. Children in the experimental group later gave more nonstereotyped answers not only for the occupations involved in the "lessons" but for a range of other occupations as well. For instance, when they were asked who could do various specific activities, such as police work and nursing, they gave more "Both men and women" responses. Children in the control group, however, still argued that "girls can't be firefighters!"

Consistent with the theory of gender schemas, they found that children in the experimental intervention showed better recall of counterstereotypic information in a later memory test. Although children in both the experimental and control groups remembered stories about Frank the firefighter and Betty the beautician, children who were in the experimental group remembered stories about Larry the librarian and Ann the astronaut far better than did children in the control group. These findings suggest that even children's ways of thinking about gender roles can be modified.

Some parents and schools are working toward the goal of reducing gender typing (Bigler, 1995). In open preschools, where the staff consciously attempts to minimize gender stereotyping, children spend more time in mixed-gender groups and less time in conventional gender-typed activities than children in traditional schools. In nontraditional preschools, children of both genders are likely to be playing house and gassing up their toy trucks (Bianchi & Bakeman, 1983). Clearly, gender roles and attitudes are modifiable. Attitudes toward gender roles are slowly changing, but there is no single formula for what may be appropriate behaviors for males and females. Individuals, families, and cultures vary widely, and no single script for gender roles will suit these many variations.

Box 13.2

Perspectives on Diversity

CHILDREARING IN COUNTERCULTURAL FAMILIES

One of the most powerful demonstrations of the plasticity, or modifiability, of gender roles can be seen in the lifestyles of families who deliberately choose to emphasize gender-role equality in their overall lifestyle. These countercultural families often show a high commitment to questioning conventional cultural dictates and institutions. Often products of the 1960s cultural rebellion, these parents frequently endorse more egalitarian attitudes toward gender roles.

Beginning in the mid-1970s, the Family Lifestyles Project followed a group of more than 200 of these nontraditional families, studying the relationship between family lifestyle and child development and focusing particularly on the variables that affected the socialization of children (Eiduson, Kornfein, Zimmerman, & Weisner, 1988). All families were European American. Some were composed of single parents, some of common-law (living together but not legally married) couples, and some of traditionally married couples. Other families lived in communes or in similar group living arrangements.

Interested in the way parents put their gender egalitarian values into practice in raising their children, Thomas Weisner and Jane Wilson-Mitchell (1990) brought the children and their parents to a southern California university center for a daylong visit when the children were about 6 years old—in kindergarten, first, and second grade. These researchers interviewed the parents on several issues and assessed the children's gender typing in several specific areas: appearance, activities and interests, personal-social attributes (e.g., "adventurous," "considerate," "outgoing," "calm"), and gender-based social relationships.

In comparison with children reared by conventional married couples, these countercultural children were less gender typed in a variety of ways. They were more androgynous in their chosen activities and interests and more likely to assume that girls could be engineers or firefighters and boys could be librarians or nursery school teachers. Indeed, more than 70 percent of these children gave non-gender-typed answers to questions about appropriate occupations for boys and girls, whereas only 40 percent of the children in the comparison group gave such answers.

It is important to note that these countercultural children were also very like other children in a variety of ways. In their play preferences, and in their basic knowledge of the way familiar play objects (e.g., dishes, trucks, dolls, racing cars) are culturally gender typed, they were similar to conventionally reared children. All children acquired the normative cultural schemas for gender typing, regardless of their family lifestyle; they were not counter-stereotyped. Instead, these children tended to be **multischematic:** They displayed either conventional or more egalitarian gender-typing schemas depending on the situation or the domain. "These children have more than one cultural schema available for responding to their world and have developed selective criteria for when to recognize and use either [a] conventional or [an] egalitarian schema" (Weisner & Wilson-Mitchell, 1990, p. 19).

This capacity to be flexible and multischematic is part of a more general pattern that characterizes the kinds of families multischematic children come from. These families regularly "engage in negotiations and conversation regarding all kinds of cultural standards, reflexively debate and question these standards, and include children in these negotiations. When focused on [gender] typing schemas and [gender] roles, this process encourages children to think about and question beliefs rather than to always adopt either conventional or alternative beliefs. . . . Overall [these children] have acquired the ability to think about situations, and to [purposefully] select the type of schema best suited for [a particular] situation" (Weisner & Wilson-Mitchell, 1990, p. 20).

Some family styles, however, can make children even more rigidly gender typed. Investigators found that children reared in devotional communes that strongly emphasized culturally conventional gender typing were even less likely to be androgynous than children in conventional married families (Weisner & Wilson-Mitchell, 1990). Socializing institutions such as families and schools can modify children's gender roles, but the form that these shifts assume clearly depends on the value system of the social agent.

Making the Connections 13

There are many links between concepts and ideas in one area of development and concepts and ideas in other areas. Here are some of the connections between ideas in Chapter 13 and discussions in other chapters of this book.

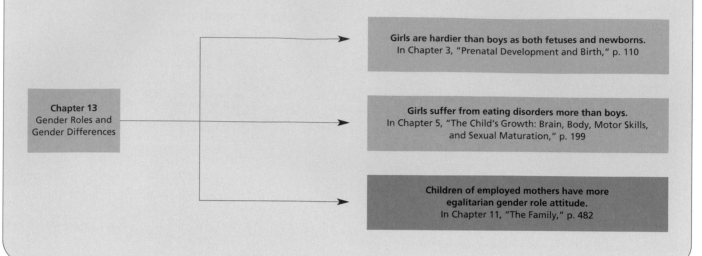

Chapter 13
Gender Roles and Gender Differences

Girls are hardier than boys as both fetuses and newborns.
In Chapter 3, "Prenatal Development and Birth," p. 110

Girls suffer from eating disorders more than boys.
In Chapter 5, "The Child's Growth: Brain, Body, Motor Skills, and Sexual Maturation," p. 199

Children of employed mothers have more egalitarian gender role attitude.
In Chapter 11, "The Family," p. 482

SUMMARY

- Both biological and psychological factors influence gender-based behaviors. There are four principal psychological explanations of gender-linked behavior patterns: Freudian theory's process of **identification, cognitive social learning theory, gender-schema theory,** and Kohlberg's **cognitive developmental theory of gender typing.**

- The process by which children acquire the motives, values, and behaviors viewed as appropriate for males and females within a culture is called **gender typing.** Children develop **gender-based beliefs,** largely on the basis of **gender stereotypes;** the latter are reflected in **gender roles.** Children adopt a **gender identity** early in life and develop **gender-role preferences** as well.

Gender-Role Standards and Stereotypes

- Both within and across cultures we find great consistency in standards of desirable gender-role behavior. Males are expected to be independent, assertive, and competitive; females are expected to be more passive, sensitive, and supportive. These beliefs have changed little over the past 20 years within the United States, and apparently around the world as well.

- There is, however, some variation in cultural gender-role standards both within the United States and in other cultures. Within the United States, standards vary depending on ethnicity, age, education, and occupation. For example, African American families are less likely to adhere to strict gender-role distinctions when socializing their children, whereas Mexican-American families are more likely to highlight gender differences.

- Divergence between cultures is also clearly seen in Margaret Mead's classic study of three primitive tribes. In each of two tribes, both men and women displayed what the Western world considers to be either feminine or masculine characteristics. In a third tribe the genders reversed the traditional Western roles. However, even within groups, individual differences in the strength of stereotypes often outweigh group characteristics.

Gender Differences in Development

- Of the many traditionally held differences between the behaviors of males and females, some are real, some are found only inconsistently, and some are wholly mythical.

- Girls are more physically and neurologically advanced at birth. Boys have more mature muscular development but are more vulnerable to disease and hereditary anomalies. Girls excel early in verbal skills, but boys excel in visual-spatial and math skills. Boys' superior mathematic abilities reflect only a better grasp of geometry, however, which depends on visual-spatial abilities. Boys are more aggressive, and girls more nurturant. Boys have more reading, speech, and emotional problems than girls.

- More equivocal are gender differences in activity level, dependency, timidity, exploratory activity, and vulnerability to stress. There are no gender differences in sociability, conformity, achievement, self-esteem, or verbal hostility.

- Although differences exist, it is important to remember that the overlap between the distributions is always greater than the differences between them. In addition, noting the existence of the differences does not tell us why they exist. Clearly, girls and boys have many different experiences and opportunities as they develop, and that these may either lead to divergent outcomes or highlight existing differences.

- Children develop gender-typed patterns of behavior and preferences as early as age 15 to 36 months. Girls tend to conform less strictly to gender-role stereotypes than do boys, possibly because parents and teachers exert greater pressure on boys to adhere to the masculine role. Girls may also imitate the male role because it has greater status and privilege in our culture. Although some boys and girls receive support for cross-gender behavior, most are encouraged to behave according to traditional stereotypes.

- A longitudinal study found that adult behavior could be predicted from gender-typed interests in elementary school. Greater stability was found when a characteristic was related to culturally accepted standards; culturally nontraditional childhood behaviors tended to emerge in divergent forms in adulthood. Thus gender-typed interests tended to remain stable from childhood to maturity.

- Research indicates that gender roles fluctuate across the life course as adults change to meet the demands of new situations and circumstances, such as childrearing. Whatever their roles up to this point, in parenthood women tend to show more **expressive characteristics** and men more **instrumental characteristics.**

- In studying stability over time of any characteristic or behavior it is important to take into consideration the fact that cohorts of different eras may experience different influences.

Biological Factors in Gender Differences

- Biological factors that are thought to shape gender differences include hormones and lateralization of brain function. Hormones may organize a biological predisposition to be masculine or feminine during the prenatal period, and the increase in hormones during puberty may activate that predisposition. In addition, social experiences may alter the levels of such hormones as testosterone.

- Gender differences in the brain's organization may be reflected in the greater lateralization of brain functioning in males, which may help explain male success at spatial and some math tasks. It may also explain female tendencies to be more flexible than males and to better withstand injury to the brain.

- Androgenized female fetuses may become girls whose behavior and interests are more traditionally male. Exceptionally high prenatal androgen levels in females may be correlated with greater visuo-spatial skills later on, but the evidence is mixed. Environmental factors also influence both sexes' development of traditional and nontraditional gender-based abilities and interests.

Cognitive Factors in Gender Typing

- Cognitive factors in children's understanding of gender and gender stereotypes may contribute to their acquisition of gender roles. Two cognitive approaches to gender typing have looked at the time at which children acquire different types of gender information and at the way such information modifies their gender-role activities and behaviors. Kohlberg's three-stage **cognitive developmental theory of gender typing** suggests that children begin by categorizing themselves as male or female, then feel rewarded by behaving in gender-consistent ways. To do this, they must develop gender identity, **gender stability,** and **gender constancy.**

- According to **cognitive developmental theory,** we should not see gender-typed behavior until a child has achieved gender constancy (around age 6). However, children express gender-typed toy and activity preferences much earlier, and show a preference for same-sex playmates later. These findings suggest that the link between the acquisition of gender concepts and behavior varies depending on gender understanding and the kind of behavior.

- **Gender-schema theory** suggests that children may need only basic information about gender in order to develop naive mental schemas that help them organize their experiences and form rules concerning gender. Research findings to date give the nod to gender-schema theory, which has shown that gender labeling is enough to affect gender-typed preferences well before a child has achieved gender constancy. However, as research has also shown, some children are more "gender-schematic" than others. We may thus expect individual differences in this area.

Influence of the Family on Gender Typing

- Families play an active role in gender-role socialization in the way they organize their children's environment. They dress boys and girls differently, give them different toys to play with, and furnish their bedrooms differently. In addition, parents—especially fathers—treat girls and boys differently. Parents tend to see boys as stronger, even at birth, and to treat them more roughly and play with them more actively than with girls. As children grow older, parents protect girls more and allow them less autonomy than boys. Parents also expect boys to achieve more than girls in the areas of mathematics and careers.

- As predicted by cognitive social learning theory, parents influence children's gender typing through role modeling. Parental power has a great impact on gender typing in boys, but not in girls. Femininity in girls, however, is related to the father's masculinity, his approval of the mother as a model, and his reinforcement of his daughter's participation in feminine activities.

- Because the father plays such a critical role in the development of children's gender roles, his absence has been related to disruptions in gender typing in preadolescent boys and to problems in relationships with peers of the opposite sex for adolescent females. Recent cross-cultural research has shown that a father's absence may be associated both with his teenage daughter's early sexual activity and with her likelihood of becoming pregnant. The earlier in her life that a girl's father becomes absent, the higher her risks for both of these eventualities. Studies have also shown that the effects of a father's absence on his daughter's interactions with men are long lasting, extending to marital choices.

- Siblings can have an important impact on one another's gender socialization. If a child has siblings of the opposite gender, he may be likely to model his sisters' behavior. Younger siblings tend to model their older siblings' behaviors no matter what their gender; a young girl may model her older brother. In addition, the sex of the older sibling may determine the character of his or her play with a younger sibling. This situation can also result in the younger sibling's development of less stereotypical gender-role concepts.

- There is no evidence of differences in the gender roles of boys and girls raised in gay or lesbian families. Most children of such families grow up to have heterosexual orientations.

Extrafamilial Influences on Gender Roles

- Many extrafamilial influences affect gender-role typing. Male and female roles are portrayed in gender-stereotypic ways in many children's books and on television. Males are more likely than females to be portrayed as aggressive, competent, rational, and powerful in the workforce. Females are more often portrayed as involved primarily in housework or caring for children.

- Females are less likely to be leading characters on TV, and male characters are overrepresented in children's books—although some change toward greater equality has occurred in recent years. Children who are heavy TV viewers hold more gender-stereotyped views; however, this may be due to their interpretations of what they see based on previously held stereotypes. A few attempts to use television to change gender stereotypes have been successful, but the effects typically have been modest and short-lived.

- Peers also serve as an important source of gender-role standards. Children who have masculine or androgynous characteristics are likely to have higher self-esteem than those who have traditionally feminine characteristics.

- Children are likely to react when other children violate gender-typical behaviors, and boys' cross-gender behaviors are more likely to meet with negative reactions from peers. Reactions from peers typically result in changes in behavior, particularly if the feedback is from a child of the same sex. This pattern of responsiveness may lead to gender segregation, which, in turn, provides opportunities to learn gender-typical roles. In **self-socialization,** children often spontaneously adopt gender-appropriate behavior.

- Teachers also treat girls and boys differently. Schools emphasize quiet and conformity to rules. Girls tend to like school better and perform better than boys in the early grades. Even in preschool, teachers, who often react to children in gender-stereotypic ways, tend to criticize boys more than girls. If young boys perceive school as gender inappropriate, they may be less motivated to participate in school activities. This may in part explain the higher rate of learning problems found in boys in the early grades.

- The kinds of conforming and dependent behaviors encouraged in girls may be detrimental to their later academic success. The fact that many people are unaware of research findings—for example, that in most areas of math girls do as well as boy—may prevent parents and others from encouraging girls to excel in these areas.

Androgyny

- Most people are not strictly feminine or masculine but possess both masculine and feminine characteristics. Children who are more **androgynous** make less stereotyped play and activity choices.

- Children of nonconventional parents who place a high value on gender egalitarianism are less gender typed in their beliefs about possible occupations for males and females, although they are no different from other children on play preferences and knowledge of cultural sex typing. Such children are **multischematic,** holding more than one gender schema for responding to the world. Research interventions and the experience of nontraditional preschools clearly indicate that children's gender stereotypes can be modified or eliminated.

EXPLORE AND DISCUSS

1. Girls and boys exhibit different levels of achievement in mathematics and computer-related activities. Do you believe that these differences are biologically based or the result of various cultural influences? How would you propose to equalize male and female skills and achievement in this area?

2. Do you think that girls and boys should go to same-sex schools, or do you think that co-ed schools are better for children's learning? Explain your answer.

3. Parents, peers, schools, and the media all influence gender roles. Do you think one or more of these factors is more important than the others for children's learning of these roles? Or do you think that each influence source affects a particular aspect of gender-role learning? If so, which aspect does each impact?

Illustration in the border of a page of Latin text from the Luttrell Psalter: *A boy stealing cherries from a tree*, c1300–c1340. British Library, London.

14.

Morality, Altruism, and Aggression

Anyone who spends time observing children in the classroom or on the playground must be impressed by the great diversity of children's behaviors. Some children play together cooperatively, some help or share with others, and some try to soothe classmates who have broken toys or scraped knees. Other children are involved in one altercation after another—successive bouts of name calling, quarreling, shoving, and pushing, with occasional bursts of more violent physical fighting. And watch children during an exam—some are whispering or peeking surreptitiously at a neighbor's exam paper or stealthily slipping out crib notes concealed in their desks. Others sit with their brows furrowed in focused attention, trying to solve the problems on the exam.

What contributes to such marked variations in children's behavior toward one another and in their apparent attitudes toward ethical issues? How do moral values and behaviors develop in the young child? How does the child become capable of self-control, resistance to temptation, and personal sacrifices for the welfare of others? This chapter traces the course of moral development, the evolution of prosocial and altruistic behaviors, and the development and control of aggressive behaviors. We begin by discussing two of the most important theories of moral development, those of Jean Piaget and Lawrence Kohlberg. We examine the relationship between moral judgment and moral actions and the consistency of these behaviors across situations and over time. We then explore the development of prosocial and altruistic behaviors, asking how early these behaviors begin, how they change, and how parents influence their emergence in the child. Finally, we consider the topic of aggression, raising a number of issues: How does aggression develop? How does it change in form and frequency? How do biological and environmental factors—the family encompasses both—influence the development of aggressive behaviors? And how can we control aggression most effectively?

AN OVERVIEW OF
MORAL DEVELOPMENT

In every culture, one of socialization's most basic tasks is communicating ethical standards to the developing child and shaping and enforcing her practice of "good" behaviors. Although the specific values and behaviors regarded as desirable vary among cultures, every society has a system of rules about the rightness and wrongness of certain behaviors. Adults expect children to learn these rules and to experience satisfaction when conforming to them, emotional discomfort or guilt when violating them.

Initially, parents control the young child's behavior largely through immediate external factors, such as their displeasure or the child's fear of punishment. As children mature, however, they begin to regulate their own behavior by means of internalized standards of conduct. They become able, in the absence of external restraints, to exert self-control. As we've discussed earlier in the book, it is through *internalization* that children incorporate others' ideas and beliefs into their own concepts of themselves, thus developing personal standards of conduct. Many psychologists argue that internalization is the fundamental and essential process in the development of morality.

Psychological research has focused on the development of three basic components of morality—cognitive, behavioral, and emotional—and the relationships among these three factors and their roles in the process of internalization. The cognitive component involves knowledge of ethical rules and judgments of the "goodness" or "badness" of various acts. The behavioral component has to do with people's actual behavior in situations that invoke ethical considerations, and the emotional component focuses on people's feelings about situations and behaviors that involve moral and ethical decisions. As we will see, these same three components can help us understand the development of altruism and of aggression.

In general, studies of moral behavior in children have investigated activities that most adults consider wrong, such as lying or cheating and failing to delay gratification, to resist temptation, or to control aggressive behavior. Recently, however, researchers have begun to study positive behaviors, such as sharing, helping, cooperating, and performing prosocial or altruistic acts. Studies of the emotional dimension of morality have also traditionally focused on negative aspects, such as feelings of guilt after a transgression, but recent work has focused on positive emotions such as empathy for other people's misfortunes or distress (Eisenberg, Fabes, & Spinrad, 2005). The particular theory a researcher embraces generally determines the specific aspect of moral development that she explores. Cognitive theories drive investigations of moral judgments, learning theories provide the underpinning for studies of ethical behaviors, and psychoanalytic theories underlie examinations of the affective components of morality.

COGNITIVE THEORIES
OF MORAL DEVELOPMENT

Jean Piaget and Lawrence Kohlberg have offered alternative explanations for the acceptance and development of moral standards. As you will see, Piaget's theory of moral development involves many of his principles and processes of cognitive growth that we discussed in Chapter 8. Indeed, both Piaget and Kohlberg consider moral development essentially an aspect of cognitive development as this development bears on the specific topic of ethics and morality.

Jean Piaget's Cognitive Theory of Moral Development

Piaget proposes a cognitive developmental theory of moral development in which the child's moral concepts evolve in an unvarying sequence through three stages. The first, *premoral stage* runs from birth to the age of 5; the *stage of moral realism* runs from 6 to 10 years of age; and the third stage of *morality of reciprocity,* or *autonomous morality,* runs from 11 onward. One cannot reach the stage of moral reciprocity without first passing through the stage of moral realism. According to Piaget, mature morality includes both an understanding and acceptance of social rules and a concern for equality and reciprocity in human relationships; these qualities form the basis of justice. Piaget investigated children's developing moral judgment in two main ways: by studying how children change their attitudes toward rules in common games and by examining the way they change their judgments of the seriousness of transgressions over time.

LEARNING THE RULES OF MORAL BEHAVIOR   The preschool child is in the **premoral stage;** she shows little concern for, or awareness of, rules. In games like marbles, children of this age don't try to play systematically with the intention of winning but seem rather to gain satisfaction from manipulating the marbles and finding out how they can be used in different ways. By the time children are 5, however, they move into the stage of **moral realism,** in which they develop great concern and respect for rules that come from authority, usually their parents, and see rules as immutable—unchanging and not to be questioned. In this stage, what Piaget calls *moral absolutism* prevails. If we ask children of this age if children in other countries could play marbles with different rules, they will assure us that they could not. We see a similar rigidity in the way children approach social interactions, frequently falling back on a "my mommy says" ploy to solve disputes.

In addition, young children subscribe to the notion of **immanent justice:** They see any deviation from the rules as inevitably resulting in punishment. Someone or something is going to get you, one way or another! Such retribution might take the form of accidents or mishaps controlled by inanimate objects or by God. A child who has

premoral stage Piaget's first stage of moral development, in which the child shows little concern for rules.

moral realism Piaget's second stage of moral development, in which the child shows great respect for rules but applies them quite inflexibly.

immanent justice The notion that any deviation from rules will inevitably result in punishment or retribution.

Children, like these Moroccan boys, often learn the meaning of rules by playing formal games. The games they learn and the ways in which they establish and change rules may vary across different cultures.

lied to her mother may later fall off her bike, skin her knees, and think, "That's what I get for lying to Mom." In this stage, children also evaluate the seriousness of an act solely in terms of its consequences; they don't take the perpetrator's intentions into account. The two factors that contribute to young children's moral realism are their *egocentrism*—their inability to subordinate their own experiences and to perceive situations as others may—and their *immature way of thinking,* which leads them to confuse external reality with their own thought processes and subjective experiences.

Piaget argues that a **morality of reciprocity** begins to emerge in older children at about the age of 11. The child's moral judgments are now characterized by his recognition that social rules are arbitrary agreements that can be questioned and changed. He realizes that obedience to authority is neither necessary nor always desirable and that violations of rules are not always wrong, nor inevitably punished. In judging another's behavior, the child considers the other's feelings and viewpoint. In this stage, children believe that if behavior is to be punished, the punishment should be related to both the wrongdoer's intentions and the nature of the transgression. The punishment, the child thinks, should also be of such a nature that it somehow makes up for the harm done or helps teach the wrongdoer to behave better in the future. Children in this stage also believe in "equalitarianism"—that is, they believe that there should be equal justice for all.

Some of the shifts in attitude from the stage of moral realism to the stage of moral reciprocity are vividly illustrated in Piaget's account of his investigations, *The Moral Judgment of the Child* (1932). Piaget would read paired stories to a child and then ask the child if the children in each story were equally guilty, which child was the naughtier, and why.

> *Story I.*
>
> A little boy who is called John is in his room. He is called to dinner. He goes into the dining room. But behind the door there [is] a chair, and on the chair there [is] a tray with 15 cups on it. John couldn't have known that there was all this behind the door. He goes in, the door knocks against the tray, "bang" to the 15 cups and they all get broken!

> *Story II.*
>
> Once there was a little boy whose name was Henry. One day when his mother was out he tried to get some jam out of the cupboard. He climbed up on a chair and stretched out his arm. But the jam was too high up and he couldn't reach it and have any. But while he was trying to get it, he knocked over a cup. The cup fell down and broke. (Piaget, 1932, p. 122)

Clearly, Henry tried to deceive his mother. But the child in the stage of moral realism regards John as less ethical because he broke more cups, even though John's act was an accident and unintentional. In contrast to Piaget's young subject, René, who is 10, shows signs that he's reached the stage of moral reciprocity when he responds that the child who wanted to take the jam was the naughtier. When asked if it makes any difference that the other child broke more cups, René replies: "No, because the one who broke 15 cups didn't do it on purpose" (Piaget, 1932, p. 130).

EVALUATION OF PIAGET'S THEORY How well has Piaget's theory fared over half a century? Most cognitive theories of moral development hold that people progress from one level of moral judgment to another in a fixed and invariant sequence, and Piaget's developmental progression from moral realism to moral reciprocity has been supported (Lapsley, 1996). In industrialized Western countries such as the United States, Great Britain, France, and Switzerland, across a wide range of populations and social classes, and among both genders, investigators find regular age trends in the development of moral judgment. However, the findings in other cross-cultural studies are less consistent. For example, Havinghurst and Neugarten (1955) found that among the people of 10 Native American tribes, the belief in immanent justice increased

---

morality of reciprocity
Piaget's third stage of moral development, in which the child recognizes that rules may be questioned and altered, considers the feelings and views of others, and believes in equal justice for all.

rather than decreased over time. Also, only 2 of the 10 groups showed the predicted shift toward greater flexibility in the conception of rules with age.

Although research on moral development lends support to the general developmental sequence, it also suggests that Piaget underestimated the cognitive capacities of young children. In judging the behavior of others, even 6-year-old children are able to consider an actor's intentions when the situation is described in a way they can comprehend. For example, when Chandler, Greenspan, and Barenboim (1973) presented stories to 6-year olds by videotape, rather than orally, the younger children responded to the intentions of the actors as well as older children did. Videotape probably helps younger children by providing them with more information, such as facial expressions that signal emotional states; these additional clues can help younger ones better infer the actor's intentions.

Another methodological shortcoming in Piaget's early studies may help account for his underestimation of young children's ability to make moral judgments. Piaget always mixed action outcome with actor intention. Thus he invariably required children to judge whether a child who causes a small amount of damage in the service of bad intentions is "worse" than a child who causes a large amount of damage but has good intentions. When researchers present stories in which good and bad intentions can be evaluated separately from good and bad outcomes, even elementary-school-age children can use intentions as a basis for judgment (Bussey, 1992; Helwig, Zelazo, & Wilson, 2001). For example, if the case of the broken cups is presented with a focus on intention (i.e., the child breaks cups *in trying to help his mother* or *in trying to sneak a cookie*), but the outcome is the same for all stories (i.e., the child breaks 6 cups), children have no trouble understanding the role of intention. By cleverly creating variations on these basic stories, researchers have been able to isolate factors that affect moral judgment. Just as in real life, many issues influence our judgments about rightness and wrongness and about whether or not the consequences of actions are positive or negative and whether the consequences are intended or accidental.

The "simple" tasks that Piaget devised more than half a century ago have become much more complicated today! Clearly, there are many more factors to consider in understanding moral reasoning than simply intentions and consequences. In the next section, we will see that Kohlberg has offered a more complex approach to the study of moral judgment.

Lawrence Kohlberg's Cognitive Theory of Moral Development

Lawrence Kohlberg (1969, 1985) has based his theory of moral development on Piaget's theory, but he has refined and expanded the stages and extended the age periods covered. Like Piaget, Kohlberg holds that the child's cognitive capabilities determine the evolution of her moral reasoning. Moreover, moral development builds on concepts grasped in preceding stages; the attainments of each stage build on the achievements of earlier stages.

To test his theory, Kohlberg began by interviewing boys between the ages of 10 and 16, presenting them with a series of moral dilemmas in which they had to choose either to obey rules and authority or to ignore such regulatory forces and respond to the needs and welfare of other people. Here is a representative story presented to Kohlberg's young participants:

> Heinz needs a particular expensive drug to help his dying wife. The pharmacist who discovered and controls the supply of the drug has refused Heinz's offer to give him all the money he now has, which would be about half the necessary sum, and to pay the rest later. Heinz must now decide whether or not to steal the drug to save his wife; that is, whether to obey the rules and laws of society or to violate them to respond to the needs of his wife. What should Heinz do, and why?

Table 14-1   Kohlberg's theory of moral development

Level I Preconventional Morality	
Stage 1	
Obedience and punishment orientation	To avoid punishment, the child defers to prestigious or powerful people, usually the parents. The morality of an act is defined by its physical consequences.
Stage 2	
Naive hedonistic and instrumental orientation	The child conforms to gain rewards. The child understands reciprocity and sharing, but this reciprocity is manipulative and self-serving rather than based on a true sense of justice, generosity, sympathy, or compassion. It is a kind of bartering: "I'll lend you my bike if I can play with your wagon." "I'll do my homework now if I can watch the late night movie."
Level II Conventional Morality: Conventional Rules and Conformity	
Stage 3	
Good boy morality	The child's good behavior is designed to maintain approval and good relations with others. Although the child is still basing judgments of right and wrong on others' responses, he is concerned with their approval and disapproval rather than their physical power. It is to maintain goodwill that he conforms to families' and friends' standards. However, the child is starting to accept others' social regulations and to judge the goodness or badness of behavior in terms of a person's intent to violate these rules.
Stage 4	
Authority and morality that maintain the social order	The person blindly accepts social conventions and rules and believes that if society accepts these rules, they should be maintained to avoid censure. He now conforms not just to other individuals' standards but to the social order. This is the epitome of "law and order" morality, involving unquestioning acceptance of social regulations. The person judges behavior as good according to whether it conforms to a rigid set of rules. According to Kohlberg, many people never go beyond this conventional level of morality.
Level III Postconventional Morality: Self-Accepted Moral Principles	
Stage 5	
Morality of contract, individual rights, and democratically accepted law	People now have a flexibility of moral beliefs they lacked in earlier stages. Morality is based on an agreement among individuals to conform to norms that appear necessary to maintain the social order and the rights of others. However, because this is a social contract, it can be modified when people within a society rationally discuss alternatives that might be more advantageous to more members of the society.
Stage 6	
Morality of individual principles and conscience	People conform both to social standards and to internalized ideals. Their intent is to avoid self-condemnation rather than criticism by others. People base their decisions on abstract principles involving justice, compassion, and equality. This is a morality based on a respect for others. People who have attained this level of development will have highly individualistic moral beliefs that may at times conflict with rules accepted by the majority of a society. According to Kohlberg, among the nonviolent, activist students who demonstrated in the mid to late 1960s against the Vietnam War, more had attained the postconventional level of morality than had nonactivist students.

Source: Kohlberg, 1969.

On the basis of his findings, Kohlberg formulated a series of three broad levels of moral development and subdivided these into six stages. Each stage was based not only on participants' choices of either an obedient or a need-serving act but on the reasons participants gave and on the ways they justified their choices. Table 14-1 presents these levels and stages of moral development. Kohlberg argues that although the sequence of all six stages is fixed—that is, all people pass through the stages in the same order—they may occur in different people at different ages. Moreover, many

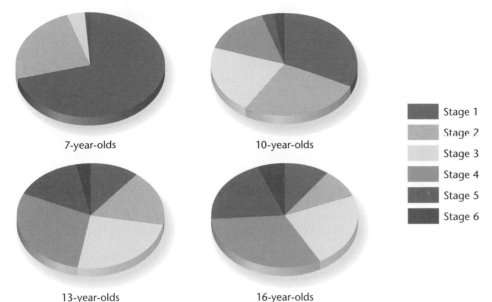

7-year-olds   10-year-olds

13-year-olds   16-year-olds

- Stage 1
- Stage 2
- Stage 3
- Stage 4
- Stage 5
- Stage 6

Figure 14-1

Use of Kohlberg's six stages of moral reasoning and judgment

Most 7-year-olds responded at Level I (Stages 1 and 2), although a very few offered some Level III (Stage 5) responses. The 10-year-olds showed the most regular pattern: In descending order of frequency, they gave Stages 1, 2, 3, 4, 5, and 6 responses! Among 16-year-olds, the most common responses were at Level II (Stages 3 and 4). Quite a few participants in this age group responded at Level III (Stages 5 and 6), but there were also some Level I responses.

Source: Adapted from Kohlberg, 1969.

people may never attain the highest level of moral judgment, and even some adults continue to think in immature terms.

Kohlberg sees behavior at the **preconventional level** as based on the desire to avoid punishment and gain rewards (see Table 14-1, Level I). At Level II, the **conventional level,** although the child identifies with his parents and conforms to what they regard as right and wrong, what he has internalized is the motive to conform, not the notion of ethical standards. It is only at Level III, the **postconventional level,** that moral judgment is rational and internalized and that conduct is controlled by an internalized ethical code that is relatively independent of others' approval or castigation. At this level, moral conflict is resolved in terms of broad ethical principles, and violating these principles results in guilt and self-condemnation.

In Kohlberg's original and later studies (Colby & Kohlberg, 1987; Kohlberg, 1985), young children gave more preconventional (Level I) responses and older children gave more postconventional responses (Figure 14-1). Although as we've said, Kohlberg predicts no specific level of response at any particular age, the general sequence of stages is followed in these participants' responding. The sequence should be invariant across cultures, Kohlberg asserts, although the ultimate level attained may vary among cultures and for individuals within the same society. Once a person has attained a high level of moral cognition, especially Stage 6, he will not regress and go back to earlier stages.

MORAL DEVELOPMENT IN GIRLS AND WOMEN Have you perhaps missed something so far in our account of Kohlberg's theory of moral development? Did you notice that the participants in his studies were boys and male adolescents? A lot of women have! Feminists contend that Kohlberg's theory is biased against females. Carol Gilligan, the foremost spokesperson for this view, argued eloquently in her book *In a Different Voice* (1982) that Kohlberg failed to take account of possible differences in the moral orientations of females and males. Citing the fact that women usually score lower than men on Kohlberg's tests, Gilligan (1982) points out that "the very traits that traditionally have defined the 'goodness' of women are those that mark them as deficient in moral development" (p. 18). Researchers have rated most women's moral judgments on these tests at Stage 3, the stage in which morality is conceived in terms of goodness and badness. In this stage the person is motivated primarily to maintain the goodwill and approval of others, although she is

preconventional level
Kohlberg's first level of moral development, in which he sees the child's behavior as based on the desire to avoid punishment and gain rewards.

conventional level
Kohlberg's second level of moral development, in which the child's behavior is designed to solicit others' approval and maintain good relations with them. The child accepts societal regulations unquestioningly and judges behavior as good if it conforms to these rules.

postconventional level
Kohlberg's third level of moral development, in which the child's judgments are rational and his conduct is controlled by an internalized ethical code that is relatively independent of the approval or disapproval of others.

beginning to accept the notion of social regulations and to judge behaviors in terms of whether people conform to or violate these rules.

According to Gilligan, Kohlberg's theory, based as it is on the study of boys and men only, fails to take account of gender-based differences. For example, women tend to take a more caring and interpersonal approach to moral dilemmas, whereas men tend to emphasize less clearly personal values such as individual rights and principles of justice. Consider how two children—a boy and a girl—responded to the question, Should Heinz steal the drug to save his wife's life?

Jake, age 11:

For one thing, a human life is worth more than money, and if the druggist only makes $1,000, he is still going to live, but if Heinz doesn't steal the drug, his wife is going to die. [Why is life worth more than money?] Because the druggist can get a thousand dollars from rich people with cancer, but Heinz can't get his wife again. [Why not?] Because people are all different and so you couldn't get Heinz's wife again. (Gilligan, 1982, p. 26)

Jake's response emphasizes logic and the balance between life and property rights, according to Gilligan, a masculine orientation.

Amy, age 11:

Well, I don't think so. I think there might be other ways besides stealing it, like if he could borrow the money or make a loan or something, but he really shouldn't steal the drug—but his wife shouldn't die either. If he stole the drug, he might save his wife then, but if he did, he might have to go to jail, and then his wife might get sicker again, and he couldn't get more of the drug, and it might not be good. So, they should really just talk it out and find some other way to make the money. (Gilligan, 1982, p. 28)

Instead of focusing on the issues of property or law, Amy focuses on the impact the theft might have on Heinz, his wife, his wife's condition, and their relationship—an interpersonal orientation to morality.

Others have found support for Gilligan's claim of separate moral orientations for males and females. Walker, deVries, and Trevethan (1987) found that when they asked adults to recall real-life dilemmas (e.g., birth control, abortion, the preservation of life, the inequitable character of a will), women were more likely to express a caring orientation, whereas men more often adopted a "rights" orientation. Women were also more likely to recall dilemmas that concerned personal relationships, whereas men recalled more impersonal kinds of dilemmas. Interestingly, when men and women were asked to respond to similar real-life dilemmas, both men and women focused more on caring than justice (Walker, 1995). Other studies using both hypothetical and real-life situations have yielded no clear pattern of gender differences (Jaffe & Hyde, 2000; Turiel, 2006).

Although there is some basis for Gilligan's contention that there may be different orientations to morality, we have little evidence of a gender bias in moral reasoning (Turiel, 2006). Reviewing data from more than 10,000 research participants, Walker (1988) found little support for the notion that females and males differ in the levels of their moral judgments. At the same time, Gilligan (1993) argues that the caring and interpersonal perspective should be added to the understanding of moral reasoning in all people. Interestingly, this view has received some support from cross-cultural studies. Consider, for example, the research described in Box 14.1 (pp. 600–601). The case is not closed, and the debate continues.

EFFECTS OF SOCIAL INTERACTIONS ON MORAL DEVELOPMENT Kohlberg has emphasized the importance for the child's moral development of social interactions that involve role taking. Children who participate in more social activities are more often elected group leaders, are rated by peers and teachers as more popular, and are rated more mature in moral judgments (Enright & Sutterfield, 1980). In contrast, researchers have found that children in restricted social environments (e.g., isolated communities or schools that offered little opportunity for role-taking experience) tended to give relatively simplistic descriptions of social roles, a finding that might well be accompanied by limitations in these children's role-taking abilities, which are basic to moral judgment (Rest, Narvaez, Bbeau, & Thoma, 2000).

Researchers have devised educational programs to foster the development of moral judgment based on Kohlberg's theory. Designed for classroom use, these programs usually focus on peer discussion of controversial moral issues. Key ingredients in these programs, which explore the relationship between social interaction and moral development, are practice in exploring solutions to moral dilemmas and experience in negotiating with others. The programs also provide a way of evaluating Kohlberg's theory. Although we have some evidence that these educational interventions foster moral judgment and promote closer links between judgments and behavior (Youniss & Yates, 1997), they are still controversial. Some programs fail to meet their goals, and it is still unclear what specific teaching tactics or curriculum materials are most effective in helping children develop their moral reasoning (Damon, 1988).

Kohlberg argues that parents do not play a crucial role in moral development; others, however, have found that both parents and peers facilitate the development of moral judgments (Walker, Hennig, & Krettenauer, 2000). When parents use consistent disciplinary techniques that involve reasoning and explanation, when they initiate discussion of the feelings of others, and when they promote a democratic family-discussion style, children evidence more mature moral judgments and more self-controlled behavior (Hoffman, 1984, 2000; Parke, 1977; Walker et al., 2000).

In fact, children's understanding of moral rules may begin at a very early age. Observing the natural interactions among young children and members of their families, Judy Dunn (1987, 1989) and her colleagues found that the children showed not only the beginnings of moral understanding but rapid increases in such understanding between the ages of 2 and 3. They showed clear awareness of rules, for example, looking at their mothers and laughing when carrying out a forbidden act or pointing out the consequences of the rule violation, such as a broken object. As early as 16 months, mothers and children engaged in "moral dialogues" about rules, with children often nodding, shaking their heads, or providing verbal answers to their mothers' inquiries about rules. Interestingly, even children at a young age commented on their own responsibility for transgressions:

Ella (21 months): [At table, throws toy to floor, a previously forbidden act. Looks at mother.]

Mother: No! What's Ella?

Child: Bad bad baba.

Mother: A bad bad baba.

Children also joined in conversations between mother and siblings to comment on the transgressions of others:

Older sibling: [shows mother that she has drawn on a piece of jigsaw puzzle.] Look.

Mother [to older sibling]: You're not supposed to draw on them, Caroline. You should know better. You only draw on pieces of paper. You don't draw on puzzles.

Younger sibling: (24 months): [to mother] Why?

Mother [to younger sibling]: Because they aren't pieces of paper.

Younger sibling: Naughty.

Mother: Yes, that is a naughty thing to do.

As children develop, they learn to justify their actions. By 36 months, in nearly a third of their disputes with mothers and siblings, children produced justifications,

Box 14.1

Perspectives on Diversity

JUSTICE VERSUS INTERPERSONAL OBLIGATIONS: INDIA AND THE UNITED STATES

The debate about the significance of a caring and interpersonal perspective for a model of moral reasoning may have broader implications than Gilligan foresaw when she first challenged Kohlberg's model of moral development. Cross-cultural research that has pitted interpersonal obligations against justice obligations has revealed significant differences between the choices American and Hindu Indian children and adults make in the face of moral dilemmas. Miller and Bersoff (1992) found that whereas more than 80 percent of Indian schoolchildren and adults endorsed interpersonal considerations in judging these issues, little more than a third of U.S. schoolchildren and adults endorsed such considerations.

According to Miller (Baron & Miller, 2000; Miller & Bersoff, 1992), Kohlberg's model is based on a philosophical tradition (Kantian) that sees "beneficence" obligations (obligations to care for others) as subordinate to justice obligations. The latter are based on "fairness, rights [and] the Golden Rule" (Kohlberg, 1973, quoted in Miller & Bersoff, 1992, p. 431). In contrast, concerns for the welfare of others that subsume such things as caring, prosocial behavior, loyalty, and charity are matters of either beneficence or interpersonal responsibility. According to Miller and Bersoff, Americans attribute a personal moral status to such interpersonal responsibilities and assume that rather than rules of justice, personal choice applies. These researchers find that "American children believe that only justice obligations, and not helping behavior, should be rule governed" (1992, p. 542). On the other hand, Hindu Indian children and adults apparently see helping others as fully moral—that is, as involving "a sense of objective obligation and as being within the scope of legitimate regulation" (p. 542).

Comparing groups of third- and seventh-grade children and college-age adults in New Haven, Connecticut, and in Mysore, a city in southern India, Miller and Bersoff asked their participants first to rate the undesirability of single incidents in which people were described as breaching either justice or interpersonal obligations. In this phase of the study, the researchers

endeavored to adjust their examples so as to ensure that participants considered all incidents of the same or nearly the same degree of importance. In the second phase of the study, the researchers presented participants with fully described conflict situations in which the respondents could fulfill one kind of behavioral obligation (justice or interpersonal) only by violating the other (interpersonal or justice). Here is one of the conflict situations presented to participants (personal names, names of cities, and other details were altered in the versions presented to Indian participants):

> Ben was in Los Angeles on business. When his meetings were over . . . Ben planned to travel to San Francisco . . . to attend [his best friend's wedding]. He needed to catch the very next train if he was to be on time for the ceremony, as he had to deliver the wedding rings.
>
> However, Ben's wallet was stolen in the train station. He lost all of his money as well as his ticket to San Francisco. . . . He approached several officials as well as passengers . . . and asked them to loan him money to buy a new ticket. But . . . no one was willing to lend him the money he needed.
>
> While Ben was sitting on a bench trying to decide what to do next, a well-dressed man sitting next to him walked away for a minute. . . . Ben noticed that the man had left his coat unattended. Sticking out of the man's coat pocket was a train ticket to San Francisco. Ben knew that he could take the ticket and use it to travel to San Francisco on the next train. He also saw that the man had more than enough money in his coat pocket to buy another train ticket.

In this example, participants were asked to decide which of the following two alternative actions Ben should choose. Note that both the purpose that would be fulfilled and the obligation that would be violated by each choice was clearly stated:

1. *Ben should not take the ticket from the man's coat pocket*—even though it means not getting to San Francisco in time to deliver the wedding rings to his best friend.

2. *Ben should go to San Francisco to deliver the wedding rings to his best friend*—even though it means taking the train ticket from the other man's coat pocket.

As Figure 14-2 shows, in this series of studies, Indian participants at all age levels were more than twice as likely to decide in favor of interpersonal alternatives than were American participants. The more serious the breach of an obligation, the more likely Hindu Indians were to switch to a justice choice, but even in these circumstances Indians clearly preferred the interpersonal alternatives. Indians also tended to categorize their recommendations as moral imperatives whether they opted for justice or interpersonal alternatives. Americans, however, tended to describe an interpersonal alternative as a personal-moral or personal-choice decision. Interestingly, when Americans and Indians considered life-threatening situations, they both viewed helping others as moral issues; they disagreed, however, when the dilemmas were less extreme. It seems that Indians tend to view helping others in fully moral terms no matter how minor the issue, a view more compatible with the view of morality Gilligan originally proposed as more "feminine."

Kohlberg's model specifies that at Stage 6, "individuals conform both to social standards and to internalized ideals [and] . . . make decisions that are based on abstract principles that include compassion . . . [evidencing] a morality that is based upon a respect for others" (see Table 14-1). This formulation certainly does not seem to rule out so-called interpersonal concerns. Moreover, as we have noted in the text, many researchers who have used Kohlberg's model have failed to find the gender differences that early research detected. The Hindu religion holds that all life is sacred, and Hindu Indian culture emphasizes "social duties as the starting point of society" (Miller & Bersoff, 1992, p. 552). These views are not greatly different from those many in Western society have attributed to a "feminine" perspective. It seems likely that caring and interpersonal moral reasoning is not "feminine," but rather a view of morality that differs from a moral perspective based on the concept of justice and individual rights.

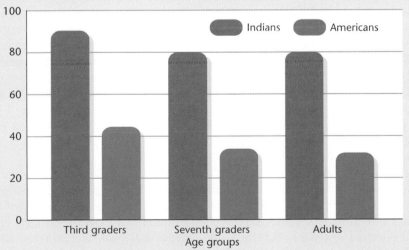

Solutions based on interpersonal considerations (percent)

Figure 14-2

Moral dilemmas and interpersonal-versus-justice considerations

In every age group, Indians were far more likely than Americans to cite interpersonal considerations in choosing solutions to moral dilemmas.

Source: Based on Miller & Bersoff, 1992.

Figure 14-3

How does moral reasoning evolve into adulthood?
Although Level I reasoning was significant in preadolescence, Stage 1 disappeared in the teens and Stage 2 had virtually disappeared by 30. At age 36, Level II, Stage 4 reasoning was the most common, and Level III was barely represented, with a small percentage of Stage 5 responses.

Source: Adapted from Colby, Kohlberg, Gibbs, & Lieberman, 1983.

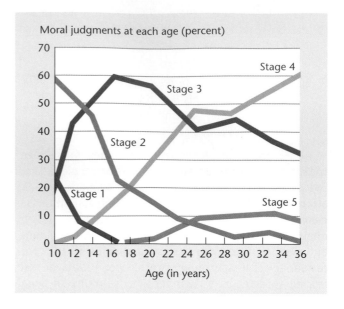

which were often in terms of their own wants, needs, or feelings. (For example, one child said, "But, I need that" as a sibling tried to take the child's spoon); "That doesn't belong to you," in reference to social rules; "Rachel will be cross if you do that," referring to the feelings of another; and "You'll break it if you do that," indicating the material consequences of actions. Children emerge at an early age as budding moral philosophers.

EVALUATION OF KOHLBERG'S THEORY   Kohlberg's theory of moral judgment maintains more current support than Piaget's, but there are critics as well as defenders (Snarey, 1995; Turiel, 2006). The notion that children proceed through the stages of moral judgment in an invariant fashion has received general support (Rest et al., 2000; Turiel 2006; Walker, Gustafson, & Hennig, 2001). The most impressive evidence comes from a longitudinal study of 58 males who were 10, 13, and 16 years old at the start of the study (Colby, Kohlberg, Gibbs, & Lieberman, 1983). Over a 20-year period and at three- and four-year intervals, the participants were asked to make judgments about moral dilemmas. All but two participants moved from lower to higher stages over the course of the study, and no one skipped stages. Although the vast majority stopped at Stage 4, a few (10%) continued to develop their moral reasoning in their twenties, reaching Stage 5 in young adulthood (Figure 14-3). None, however, reached Stage 6. The dominant pattern of moral reasoning in most adults appears to be conventional (Level II, Stages 3 or 4). Perhaps Mother Teresa is a model for fewer of us than Kohlberg originally imagined.

Role-playing and modeling studies that have attempted to learn whether people can be induced to shift their moral reasoning to another level have generally found that it is easier to advance a person's moral judgment to a higher stage than to a lower one (Turiel, 2006). Moreover, participants who are exposed to a model's reasoning about a moral dilemma at a stage above or a stage below their own stage of moral development prefer the more advanced to the less advanced stage (Rest et al., 2000; Turiel, 2002, 2006). These findings are generally consistent with both Piaget's and Kohlberg's views that progress should be toward higher rather than lower stages.

How does the theory fare in cross-cultural studies? Studies in Turkey (Nisan & Kohlberg, 1982), Taiwan (Lei & Cheng, 1989), and Israel (Snarey, Reimer, & Kohlberg, 1985) have supported the proposal that individuals, regardless of their cultural background, would develop through the stage sequence in the same manner. In addition, in this study few participants skipped or regressed to lower stages. On the other hand, some research suggests the possibility of cultural bias. For example, in New Guinea, people place community obligations over individual rights, whereas in India, people emphasize the sacredness of all forms of life. As Box 14.1 suggests, Kohlberg's focus on individual rights and obligations may lead to underestimates of moral development in other cultures or may exclude some culturally unique domains of morality (Kahn, 1997; Shweder, Much, Mahapatra, & Park, 1997; Snarey 1995).

Note, too, that people's moral judgments differ depending on the way in which questions are presented to them. When an issue is couched in abstract form, rather than embedded in a realistic description of a particular situation of conflict, respondents are more likely to support the default position (Helwig, 1995, 2003). Consider the following example, in which children were asked to evaluate freedom of speech and religion. When respondents were simply asked whether they endorsed freedom of speech and religion in the United States and in other countries, nearly all seventh-grade, eleventh-grade, and college age students said yes, they did. However, when respondents were asked the same question but in a context in which these freedoms were described as conflicting with other liberties, such as freedom from physical and psychological harm and equality of opportunity, the pattern of results was quite different. For example, when researchers presented respondents with a scenario in which an individual gave a speech in which he advocated physical violence against members of a rival political party and then asked the students whether they endorsed freedom of speech, 19 percent of seventh graders, 56 percent of eleventh graders, and 50 percent of college students said they would. In short, moral judgments often involve the need to balance competing moral issues, and the original Kohlbergian approach may have oversimplified the nature of the dilemmas that people face in everyday moral decision making.

History often shapes people's views of morality as they develop, just as the life span perspective (Chapter 1) would predict. Events—such as the Watergate political crisis, the Vietnam War, the struggles of African Americans and women for equality, and the tragic deaths of thousands of people in the terrorist destruction of New York City's World Trade Center towers and attack on Washington D.C.'s Pentagon—have in recent years sensitized people to issues of fairness and justice. People who grew up in other eras (e.g., the Great Depression of the 1930s) may have different understandings of moral issues. For example, those who suffered severe economic loss may be more sensitive to the plight of the poor and less affluent and thus may endorse more liberal attitudes. Changes in moral judgment, in short, may be affected by the sociopolitical context of the times in which people live (Rest et al., 2000; Turiel, 2002, 2006).

In spite of criticisms and limitations, Kohlberg's pioneering work revolutionized the way we think about moral development. Due to his influence, cognitive judgment and understanding are central concerns of a contemporary approach to the issue of morality.

Distinguishing Moral Judgments from Other Social Rules

Children must learn many rules for behavior. At the same time that they learn moral strictures against cheating, lying, and stealing they learn many other nonmoral, **social-convention rules** about everyday conduct: table manners, kinds of dress, modes of greeting, forms of address, and other rules of social etiquette. According to Elliot Turiel (1983, 2002), children make clear distinctions between reasoning about moral issues and reasoning about social conventions. In one study of nursery-school-age children (Nucci & Turiel, 1978), researchers asked children how wrong it would be to hit someone, lie, or steal (violate moral rules), and how wrong to address teachers by their first names, for a boy to enter a girl's bathroom, or to eat lunch with one's fingers (violate rules of social convention). In support of Turiel's argument that

social-convention rules
Socially based rules about everyday conduct.

Source: MISS PEACH. By permission of Mell Lazarus and Creators Syndicate, Inc.

morality and social conventions represent independent domains, children and adolescents from second grade to college consistently viewed the moral violations as more wrong than the violations of social convention.

Even children as young as 3 can distinguish moral from social-convention issues (Smetana & Braeges, 1990). However, young children can generally make this distinction only with respect to familiar situations. When children reach the ages of 9 or 10, they can apply the distinction to both familiar and unfamiliar issues (Smetana, 1995; Turiel, 2006). Children view moral violations as more wrong because they result in harm to another and violate norms of justice and others' rights, whereas they see deviations from social conventions as being impolite or disruptive and as violations of social rules and traditions (Turiel, 2006).

Children also learn to distinguish issues that involve morality and social convention from those that touch on the **personal domain** (Nucci, 1996). The latter include such issues as friendship choices, personal conversations, personal diaries, and choices of such things as hairstyle and clothing. Even in cultures with a more collectivist than individualistic orientation, children and adolescents distinguish moral and social-convention issues from personal ones. In Brazil and Hong Kong, for example, children made this distinction increasingly over time (Nucci, Camino, & Milnitsky-Sapiro, 1996; Yau & Smetana, 1996). This domain appears to be essential for children's development of individuality and for their construction of a self-concept and personal identity (Erikson, 1970; Nucci, 1996).

Children agree with the notion that although moral issues are fixed, absolute, and invariant across cultures, social conventions are arbitrary and relative and vary across communities, cultures, and domains (Helwig & Jasiobedzka, 2001; Turiel, 2002, 2006; Wainryb, Shaw, Laupa, & Smith, 2001). When asked if it would be acceptable to steal in a country that had no laws against stealing, children as young as 6 thought it was wrong to steal. On the other hand, children thought that people in different countries could play games by different rules (Turiel, Killen, & Helwig, 1988). In many countries, including Brazil, India, Indonesia, Korea, Nigeria, and Zambia, children and adolescents judge moral issues (e.g., welfare and justice) differently from social-convention issues (e.g., eating and bathing) (Bersoff & Miller, 1993; Turiel, 2002, 2006).

This work has implications for understanding another aspect of moral development—the development of tolerance or the willingness to recognize the legitimacy of beliefs with which you disagree. In the light of children's abilities to distinguish moral issues from other types of beliefs (e.g., social conventions), it is not surprising that children's tolerance does not increase in a simple linear way across development. Instead, children are selective of the beliefs they tolerate. Although they are intolerant of moral violations, they often accept not only divergent social conventions but also different psychological and metaphysical beliefs (Wainryb et al., 2001). For example, when researchers asked third graders, seventh graders, and college students about such psychological beliefs as "a person who believes that the way to be really good friends with people is never to tell them how you feel about anything" or that "doing nice things for other people makes these people spoiled and selfish," all respondents were

personal domain An area of rules and conventions distinct from moral rules; involves issues such as choice of friends and styles of dress.

equally accepting of divergent beliefs in these areas. Children at different ages are similarly tolerant of divergent metaphysical beliefs about such things as the transcendent and supernatural—for example, "a person who believes there are 38 gods" or "only people who die on Tuesday become angels." Tolerance is not a unitary attitude or disposition; instead, even children are sensitive to variations across different belief domains and make their judgments according to the domain involved. In short, children are much more discerning, and perhaps more tolerant of other people's beliefs, than we had thought.

How do children learn to distinguish between moral and social-convention transgressions? Probably parents and other family members help children learn these distinctions (Nucci & Weber, 1995). Children learn from their parents at a very early age that eating your spaghetti with your hands or spilling your milk has different consequences than taking your brother's toy or pulling your kid sister's pigtail. Mothers of 24- to 26-month-olds responded to social-convention violations with rules about social order and social regulation that focused on the disorder that the act created ("Look at the mess you made!"). In contrast, mothers' responses to moral transgressions focused on the consequences of the acts for other's rights and welfare or by perspective-taking requests ("Think how you would feel if somebody hit you!") (Smetana, 1989, 1995). Moreover, mothers tend to allow children much more choice and freedom around personal issues (Nucci & Weber, 1995).

Parents influence adolescents as well as young children. Even teenagers understand and accept that parents may legitimately regulate moral behavior (Smetana, 1995). Adolescents even agree with parents on parental regulation of social-convention matters; however, adolescents view parental regulation of moral issues as more legitimate (Smetana & Asquith, 1994; Smetana & Gaines, 1999). Neither European American nor African American adolescents agree that parents have a right to regulate personal matters (e.g., appearance, friendship choices, spending decisions). Conflicts most often arise in this area, and they arise with increasing frequency as the adolescent grows older (Smetana, 2000). Conflicts that mix social-convention and personal issues—for example, cleaning one's own room, which affects the entire home—are more intense.

Other socializing agents, including teachers and peers, play a part, too. In day-care centers, adults respond differently to the moral and social-convention transgressions of 12-month-old toddlers than to those of 36-month-old toddlers (Smetana, 1984, 1995, 1997). Even other children react differently to these different kinds of violations: Smetana found that 2- and 3-year-olds reacted more emotionally and retaliated more often in the face of moral transgressions than when confronting social-convention transgressions. Not surprisingly, children become more sophisticated in their responses as they develop. For example, the 3-year-olds displayed more adult responses than the 2-year-olds. The older children were more likely to make statements about rights (e.g., "That's not fair," or "The rules say that you can't do that"), a major accomplishment for a 3-year-old! In sum, children can distinguish different kinds of violations and can do so at a surprisingly early point in development. As in other areas of development—perception, cognition, language, emotion—we're learning that children are more competent at earlier ages than previous generations of developmental psychologists assumed.

Do Moral Judgments Always Lead to Moral Behavior?

Knowledge of the maturity of a child's moral judgments does not necessarily predict how a child will actually behave in a situation where she must choose between ethically desirable and undesirable behavior. Moral judgments and moral behavior are often unrelated, especially in young children (Blasi, 1983; Straughan, 1986). Much behavior is impulsive and not guided by rational and deliberate thought (Burton, 1984). A child may have reached Kohlberg's Stage 3, the level of "good girl morality," where she is concerned with maintaining parental approval. However, when her younger brother breaks her favorite toys, she may kick him even if the parent is present to disapprove of her action. Later, the child may even be able to offer mature reasoning that it is wrong to hit young children because they do not really know what they're doing (Batson & Thompson, 2001). Thought does not always guide action!

We do have some evidence, however, that in older children, moral judgments and moral behavior may be linked. People who have reached Kohlberg's Level III (Stages 5 and 6) are less likely to cheat than those at earlier levels, less likely to inflict pain on others, and more likely to endorse free speech and due process and to oppose capital punishment (Gibbs, Potter, & Goldstein, 1995; Kohlberg & Candee, 1984). Nevertheless, as we noted earlier, relatively few people may reach Stage 6 in Kohlberg's moral scheme. Thus although moral judgments may relate to behavior among older children, the link between moral cognition and action among young children is very weak.

Although it's convenient to divide the world of morality into separate parts—cognitive, emotional, and behavioral—in real life these different aspects often operate together in determining how a child will act when faced with a moral decision. Rest et al. (2000) propose a four-step process in executing a moral action (this process is reminiscent of Dodge's information-processing approach to social interaction that we considered in Chapter 12). When faced with a situation that requires such action, in Step 1 the child first interprets the situation in terms of how other people's welfare could be affected by his possible actions. Then, in Step 2, the child must figure out what the ideally moral course of action would be, given the possibilities presented in Step 1. In Step 3 the child must decide what he actually intends to do, and finally, in Step 4, the child actually performs the action chosen. So far we have considered Steps 1 and 2; in the next section we'll be exploring Steps 3 and 4.

THE BEHAVIORAL SIDE OF MORAL DEVELOPMENT

People don't just think about actions, they act, and to differing degrees in moral ways. In this section, we focus on the action, or behavioral, component of moral judgment—deciding what to do and doing it.

Self-Regulation and the Delay of Gratification

self-regulation The child's ability to control behavior on her own without reminders from others.

One goal in socializing the child is to help her achieve **self-regulation,** or the ability to control her behavior on her own, without reminders from others. In the context of moral development, the child must also learn to inhibit or direct her actions to conform to social or moral rules. Life is full of temptations, traps, and tugs that try to pull the young child away from socially acceptable courses of action. A child's ability to resist these forces is a consequence of both her own emerging cognitive and representational capacities and the guidance that parents, siblings, and other socializing agents provide.

control phase According to Kopp, the first phase in learning self-regulation, when children are highly dependent on caregivers to remind them about acceptable behaviors.

How does this capacity to monitor and regulate one's own behavior develop? According to Kopp (1982, 2002), the child proceeds through several phases. In the **control phase** (12 to 18 months), "children show awareness of social and task demands that have been defined by caregivers and initiate, maintain, modulate or cease acts accordingly upon demand . . . In [this] phase, children are highly dependent upon the caregiver for reminder signals about acceptable behaviors" (Kopp, 1987, p. 38). And, in fact, children do begin to show compliance to caregiver demands during this period. Next, in the **self-control phase,** the child gains the ability to comply with caregiver expectations in the absence of external monitors. Kopp suggests that development of representational thinking and recall memory permits the child to remember family rules and routines involved in common activities such as eating, dressing, and playing. At last, in the **self-regulation phase,** children become able to use strategies and plans to direct their behavior and to help them resist temptation and to **delay gratification.** For example, Vaughn, Kopp, and Krakow (1984) displayed attractive objects such as a toy telephone, an attractively wrapped gift, or a raisin under a cup to 18-, 24-, and 30-month-olds and then told the children not to touch the objects right away. Whereas the 18-month-olds were able to wait only 20 seconds, the 24-month-olds waited 70 seconds, and the 30-month-olds waited nearly 100 seconds before touching the attractive but forbidden objects! Other research confirms the progression in self-control over the preschool period (Kochanska, Coy, & Murray, 2001; Kopp, 2002).

Although we've described a normative progression in the child from control by others through self-control to self-regulation, some children progress more rapidly and achieve higher levels of control than others. Some children reach the self-regulation phase and internalize the rules and values of the society by 4 or 5 years of age, whereas others continue to rely on sustained parental control in order to comply with rules. Recently, Kochanska (2002) studied the backgrounds of children who were self-regulators and of others who were more situationally compliant. Children who are self-regulators have a stronger sense of "moral self"; they endorse parental values and rules, and it is this sense of moral self that helps these children obey rules even in the absence of parental authority.

The development of self-control is influenced not only by the child's own efforts but by the actions of parents and other caregivers as well. Various kinds of parental disciplinary practices, such as consistent and carefully timed punishment, as well as the provision of a rationale for compliance, help increase resistance to temptation (Kuczynski, Marshall, & Shell, 1997; Parke, 1977). Moreover, as children age, mothers shift their control strategies from physical to verbal modalities; explanations, bargaining, and reprimands increase as the child grows older, and distraction techniques decrease (Kuczynski, Kochanska, Radke Yarrow, & Girnius-Brown, 1987). This suggests that parents shift their strategies to match the increasingly sophisticated quality of the child's cognitive and language capacities. In turn, this adjusted parental input heightens the child's own abilities to use verbally based control strategies (Kopp, 1987, 2002). In addition, a mutually responsive orientation involving cooperation and shared positive affect between mother and child aids in conscience development. Children who, as toddlers, enjoyed this kind of mother-child relationship developed a higher level of conscience at 5 years of age than children in a less mutually responsive mother-child relationship (Kochanska & Murray, 2000).

Self-control may also be affected by temperament. According to Kochanska (1995), the process of internalization through which children develop self-regulatory capabilities involves two particular aspects of temperament: the passive and active inhibition systems. The *passive inhibition system* is driven primarily by fear and anxiety and often operates outside of awareness. The *active inhibition system,* on the other hand, is expressed in conscious, effortful control, by which the person regulates her behavior, particularly when desirable behavior requires giving up or postponing pleasurable outcomes (Kochanska et al., 2001; Rothbart, Ahadi, & Evans, 2000). Researchers assess these aspects of temperament by measuring how a child slows down motor activity, makes a clear effort to attend, and suppresses or initiates activity in response to a specific signal. For example, Kochanska (1995) found that fearful toddlers who responded with distress and withdrawal in laboratory situations when researchers presented them with novel or mildly risky events were more likely to inhibit prohibited behavior than less fearful children.

This boy may be trying to guess what's in the packages or just itching to start tearing off the paper—or both! Learning to delay gratification is a significant part of self-regulation.

self-control phase According to Kopp, the second phase in learning self-regulation, when the child becomes able to comply with caregiver expectations in the absence of the caregiver.

self-regulation phase According to Kopp, the third phase in learning self-regulation, when children become able to use strategies and plans to direct their own behavior and to delay gratification.

delay gratification To put off until another time possessing or doing something that gives one pleasure.

Children who are high in effortful control show more internalization of rules of conduct than children who display little control of this sort. Moreover, these links between effortful control and measures of internalization are evident both cross-sectionally and longitudinally. Kochanska has also found that effortful control increases with age and is a stable individual difference among children (Kochanska et al., 2001).

Because children differ in temperament, it is not surprising that varying parental disciplinary strategies are effective with different children. And indeed, Kochanska's findings suggest that there are different routes to the emergence of **conscience**— internalized values and standards of behavior—and children's control of their actions. Kochanska (1995, 1997) has found that for children who were relatively fearful as 2-year-olds, mothers' gentle discipline that deemphasized power was correlated with strong evidence of conscience at toddler and preschool ages. In contrast, with relatively fearless children, low-key maternal discipline did not work; instead, parental strategies that focused on positive motivation promoted higher levels of self-control. Overall, a mother-child relationship that was positive, responsive, and cooperative was linked with strong conscience development in young children. This work illustrates the important interplay between children's temperamental characteristics and parents' childrearing practices. As they say, "Different strokes for different folks."

conscience The child's internalized values and standards of behavior.

The Affective Side of Morality

The development of moral standards and behavior is not all cognition. Human beings feel as well as think, and there is clearly an affective, or emotional, aspect to moral development. We have all experienced "feeling bad" when we break a rule. We may feel remorse, or shame, or guilt. What are the origins of these emotional reactions, and how do they relate to the way children act when faced with temptations or with moral dilemmas or after they have violated moral standards?

In order to track the development of guilt in young children, Kochanska and her colleagues (2002) tested young children at 22 months, 45 months, and finally at 56 months. To induce feelings of guilt in the children, the experimenter presented each child with an object that belonged to her (to the experimenter; e.g., a favorite stuffed animal from her childhood or a toy she had assembled herself) and asked the child to be very careful with it. However, each object had been "rigged" and fell apart as soon as a child began to handle it. Then, by noting the child's reaction to the mishap, the experimenter was able to record the ways in which the child expressed guilt at different ages.

You'll remember from Chapter 6 that although children display shame as early as 18 months or so, expressions of guilt are somewhat slower to appear because the child needs to internalize standards of behavior and to develop a sense of personal responsibility for her own behavior. At younger ages (22 months), children "looked" guilty— they showed negative affect. At older ages (45 months), children were better at masking their guilty reactions—they maintained visual contact with the adult and expressed fewer overt negative emotions. Instead, among older toddlers, guilt leaked out or spilled over in the form of subtle signs such as changes in posture, squirming, hanging the head, and other indications of arousal and upset. As we saw in Chapter 6, children's emotional regulation capacities improve with age, and it is this improved skill that may be evident in the way guilt is expressed as children get older.

Do boys and girls differ in their level of guilt? Studying boys and girls as young as 33 months old, Kochanska and her colleagues (1995, 2002) found that girls were more prone to guilt than boys. Other researchers have reported similar gender differences in middle childhood (Zahn-Waxler, 2000). This heightened level of guilt may reflect the fact that girls are expected to obey more and to adhere more closely to rules than boys and thus may experience more upset, such as guilt, when they break rules.

What are the determinants of guilt? Both temperament and parental socialization predict levels of guilt in children. Fearful children are more likely to respond with discomfort, worry, and concern to stressful events in general (Kagan, 1998) and to experience more guilt after rule violations as well (Kochanska et al., 2002). Similarly, fearful infants are rated by their parents, when they are 6 to 7 years old, as more prone to guilt and shame (Rothbart, Ahadi, & Hershey, 1994).

Guilt may be the mechanism by which fearful individuals achieve better self-control. Fearful children react to their own transgressions with greater guilt and, in turn, their guilt helps prevent later transgressions. In short, the anticipation of guilt, especially in fearful, guilt-prone children, serves as a deterrent to misbehavior and rule violation. In contrast, fearless individuals, such as people with antisocial personalities, do not experience remorse, guilt, or shame if they violate rules, and the lack of guilt does not deter them from rule violations.

Parents influence the development of guilt too. Parents who use power-assertive disciplinary techniques such as physical punishment (see Chapter 11) have children who show less guilt at later ages. And the development of a sense of self is a further determinant of guilt. As we discussed earlier, guilt and shame are self-conscious emotions (Lewis, 1992), and children who show a stronger sense of self develop more pronounced guilt. Children who showed more awareness of themselves separate from others at 18 months exhibited more guilt at 30 months. Moreover, children who showed early signs of guilt developed stronger moral selves at later ages. The guilty children described themselves as more concerned about rules, more committed to rule-compatible behavior, and generally more morally concerned at 56 months (Kochanska, 2002). And children who exhibit guilt early in life were less likely to violate rules in a "resistance to temptation" situation later.

Clearly, guilt may make us uncomfortable but clearly serves a positive role in children's social development. Whether too much guilt is detrimental to children's lives remains less well understood.

Consistency across Situations and Time

Are children consistent in their moral behavior across situations? To answer this question, let's look at the most extensive investigation of moral behavior in children ever attempted. In this classic study, Hartshorne and May (1928) gave 11,000 school-age children the opportunity to cheat, steal, and lie in a wide variety of situations—athletics, social events, the school, the home, alone, or with peers—and then examined their behaviors. Some years after the close of this study, Burton (1963, 1984) analyzed the measures that were proved reliable from Hartshorne's and May's studies in deceit and found strong evidence for a general factor of moral behavior, just as we saw in the case of intelligence (Chapter 10). Burton concluded that every child does have a different general predisposition to behave morally or immorally in a variety of situations. The more similar the situations, the greater the consistency in self-control; the less the situations resemble each other, the less likely the child's response will be the same on each occasion. For example, measures of cheating on achievement tests in the classroom correlated more highly with each other than they did with measures of cheating on games in the home. Such findings underscore the importance of situational variables, such as fear of detection, peer support for deviant behavior, and the instigation of other powerful motivational factors, such as the temptation to cheat on an exam to get a better grade. Because these measures also showed considerable variability among individual children, however, they also suggest that some children are more likely than others to yield to situational demands.

Are children consistent in their moral behavior over time? There is evidence to suggest that children who are able to delay gratification in early life are able to cope better socially and academically as adolescents (Mischel, Shoda, & Peake, 1988; Shoda, Mischel, & Peake, 1990). Researchers gave 4-year-olds a simple test of self-control in order to evaluate their ability to wait for an attractive reward (a toy or candy).

They gave the children the option of obtaining a small reward immediately or a much larger and more attractive one later. Some children were very poor at waiting; others were able to delay taking their prize for a considerable period. Ten years later, when these children were adolescents, Mischel asked the parents to rate their children on a variety of traits. Parents rated the children who had been able to delay gratification in nursery school as more socially and cognitively competent. They were playful, resourceful, skillful, attentive, and able to deal with frustration and stress—a cluster of traits that are important ingredients in successfully coping with the academic and social demands of adolescence. More recently, investigators found that this same pattern of self-regulatory connections carries over into early adulthood (Peake, Hebl, Ahrens, Lepper, & Mischel, 2001). In sum, the early ability to inhibit impulses and delay gratification may have been an important antecedent of these children's later competence.

THE EVOLUTION OF PROSOCIAL AND ALTRUISTIC BEHAVIORS

Consider two different children. One preschool child, Amanda, is ready to share her toys, and whenever another child gets upset, she steps in and tries to comfort the distressed classmate. Another toddler, Jerome, is stingy with his toys, seldom shares, and is often indifferent to other children's upset and discomfort. He generally goes right on with his activities when another child is distressed; others' problems don't seem to trouble him. These two children clearly differ in their prosocial behavior and, as we will see, these styles of reacting to others' needs are related to later behaviors as well. In this section, we explore the origins and determinants of prosocial behavior.

prosocial behavior Behavior designed to help or benefit other people.

altruism An unselfish concern for the welfare of others.

altruistic behavior Intrinsically motivated behavior that is intended to help others without expectation of acknowledgment or concrete reward.

Prosocial behavior is voluntary behavior intended to benefit another. It may be performed for a variety of motives, including egoistic, other-oriented, and practical concerns (Eisenberg et al., 2006). **Altruism** is an unselfish concern for the welfare of other people. Altruistic behavior, like prosocial behavior, is voluntary behavior designed to help someone else. However, what distinguishes **altruistic behavior** from prosocial behavior is the willingness to help another without any thought of recompense. Altruistic acts are motivated by "internalized values, goals, and self-rewards rather than by the expectation of concrete or social rewards" (Eisenberg et al., 2006, p. 3). People may act prosocially, sharing and cooperating with others, helping or caring for them, sympathizing and comforting others in times of distress and need, and performing acts of kindness toward others. Prosocial behavior can also encompass actions designed to help groups of people, societies, nations, even the world. When people act altruistically, however, they do so without thought for their own immediate welfare, without expectation of reciprocity or acknowledgment (they often act anonymously), and sometimes even at the sacrifice of their own longer-term needs and wishes. According to Eisenberg and colleagues (2006), we see the beginnings of prosocial behavior in quite young children, whereas truly altruistic behavior, seen as a refinement of prosocial behavior, arises later on.

In this section, we explore how prosocial behavior evolves and changes. We consider both biological and environmental determinants of prosocial behavior and then examine the influence of the child's evolving cognitive capabilities on prosocial reasoning and activity. Our concluding discussion examines the child's ability to understand and empathize with others' feelings and circumstances.

How Prosocial Behavior Evolves

As the Turning Points chart on page 611 shows, prosocial behavior may begin even before an infant is 6 months old. For example, when children point out or show things to others or share their toys, they are engaging in prosocial behavior (Hay, 1994). As

PROSOCIAL AND ALTRUISTIC BEHAVIOR

BIRTH–6 MONTHS
- Responds positively to others (smiles, laughs with others)
- Participates in social games (e.g., peek-a-boo)
- Reacts emotionally to others' distress (crying or general upset)

6–12 MONTHS
- Takes an active role in social games
- Exhibits sharing behaviors
- Displays affection to familiar persons

12–24 MONTHS
- Refines ability to point with index finger
- Complies with simple requests
- Indicates knowledge of rules of cooperative games
- Shows knowledge of caregiving skills
- Comforts people in distress
- Participates in adults' work, household tasks
- Shows and gives toys to adults

24–36 MONTHS
- Draws person's attention to objects with words as well as gestures
- Exhibits increasingly planned caregiving and helping behaviors
- Verbally expresses own intentions to help and knowledge of tasks
- Gives helpful verbal advice
- Tries to protect others

3–ABOUT 7 YEARS
- Is hedonistically motivated to perform prosocial acts

3–11 YEARS
- Recognizes others' needs even when they conflict with own

6–17 YEARS
- Justifies prosocial or nonprosocial behavior by reference to stereotypical notions of good and bad and considerations of approval and acceptance from others

10–17 YEARS
- Empathizes with others and feels pride or guilt about consequences of own actions

14–17 YEARS
- May justify helping or not helping by internalized values and by concern with rights and dignity of others
- May believe in individual and social obligations, the equality of all individuals, and may base self-respect on living up to own values and accepted norms

Note: Developmental events described in this and other Turning Points charts represent overall trends identified in research studies. Individual children vary greatly in the ages at which they achieve these developmental changes.

Sources: Based on Eisenberg, Fabes, & Spinrad, 2006; Hay & Rheingold, 1983.

we noted in Chapter 7, even before the end of the first year, children learn to use such gestures as pointing to communicate with others; this gesturing can be seen as a way of sharing interesting sights and objects with others. Rheingold and her colleagues have found that among 12- to 18-month-old children, showing and giving toys to a variety of adults (mothers, fathers, and strangers) is very common (Hay, 1994; Rheingold, Hay, & West, 1976). Moreover, children engage in these early sharing activities without prompting or direction and without being reinforced by praise. According to these authors, such behaviors as holding an object up for others to see and offering an object to another person represent developmental milestones. "That children so young share contradicts the egocentricity so often ascribed to them and reveals them instead as already contributors to social life" (Rheingold et al., 1976, p. 1157).

CHANGES IN PROSOCIAL BEHAVIORS   Sharing and showing are not the only ways in which young children reveal their capacity for prosocial action. From an early age, children engage in a variety of other behaviors such as caring for siblings, helping adults with housework, or comforting others in distress; this is striking evidence that prosocial behavior begins very early in life (Garner, Jones, & Palmer, 1994). Children between 10 and 12 months old typically become agitated or cry in response to another child's distress, but they make little effort to help the other child. By the time they're 13 or 14 months old, however, they will often approach and comfort another child in distress. This comforting, though, is often general and not specific to the source of distress. When children are a year and a half old, they will not only approach a distressed person but offer specific kinds of help. For example, they may offer a toy to a child with a broken toy or a Band-Aid to a mother with a cut finger. And by the age of 2, children engage in a wide range of prosocial actions, including verbal advice ("Be careful"), indirect helping (getting their mother to retrieve the baby's rattle), sharing (giving food to a sister), distraction (closing a picture book that has made their mother sad), and protection/defense (trying to prevent another from being injured, distressed, or attacked). Others have found a clear developmental increase in prosocial responding of toddlers not only to their mothers' distress (van der Mark, van IJzendoorn, & Bakermans-Kranenburg, 2002) but also to peer distress as well (Lamb & Zakhireh, 1997). As Box 14.2 discusses, when young children begin to react to the distress of another, parents can encourage their emerging sense of altruism.

Children's altruistic behavior changes in form and expression as children develop. Children do not always show prosocial reactions to others' distress and, indeed, they sometimes laugh or behave aggressively or even become distressed themselves (Lamb & Zakhireh, 1997; Radke-Yarrow & Zahn-Waxler, 1983; Zahn-Waxler, Radke-Yarrow, Wagner, & Chapman, 1992b). However, based on a recent *meta-analysis* (a large-scale review of relevant studies), Eisenberg et al. (2005) found clear evidence that as children grow older they are generally more likely to engage in prosocial behaviors. Specifically prosocial behavior increases from infancy and the preschool years through middle childhood to adolescence. As Hoffman (2000) has proposed, prosocial behavior increases with cognitive maturation. Toddlers who display self-recognition thus (indicating that they understand the self-other distinction) are more empathic and prosocial (Zahn-Waxler, Schiro, Robinson, Emde, & Schmitz, 2001). Children's perspective taking in the second year and at ages 4 and 5 was positively linked to their prosocial behavior (Zahn-Waxler, Cole, Welsh, & Fox, 1995). An increase in emotional knowledge, such as beginning to understand emotional cues, is another development linked to increase in prosocial behavior (Denham, 1998; Garner, Jones, & Palmer, 1994). This may be in part because, over time, children become increasingly able to detect subtle cues that someone needs help (Eisenberg et al., 2006). Presenting 4- and 8-year-old children with a series of vignettes in which the explicitness of distress cues varied (from a slight frown to a full-blown cry), Pearl (1985) found that the children were equally likely to note distress when the cues were explicit. However,

Box 14.2

Child Psychology in Action

HOW PARENTS CAN TEACH CHILDREN PROSOCIAL BEHAVIOR

To find out how children learn to react in helpful ways when they have caused distress in another person, or when they see another person suffering, Carolyn Zahn-Waxler and her colleagues (Zahn-Waxler, Radke-Yarrow, & King, 1979) devised a clever scheme. They trained mothers of 18-month-olds to tape record their children's reactions to others' distress that the children themselves either caused or witnessed. The mothers recorded both the child's and their own behavior over a nine-month period, during which observers occasionally visited the home to check on the accuracy of the mothers' records. The researchers also asked the mothers to simulate distress from time to time: For example, mothers might pretend to be sad (sobbing for five to ten seconds), to be in pain (bumping their feet or heads, saying "Ouch," and rubbing the injured parts), or to suffer respiratory distress (coughing/choking).

How did the children respond to others' distress? Overall, whether they had hurt someone else or merely witnessed another person's distress, they reacted in a helpful fashion about a third of the time. However, some children responded in most distress situations (between 60% and 70%), whereas some failed to respond at all.

Zahn-Waxler's research also revealed that mothers' reactions to their own children's harmful behavior toward others, as well as to the sight of another person's distress, can influence their children's development of helpful behavior in distress situations. Some mothers linked a child's behavior with its consequences for the child's victim; the children of these mothers were more likely to respond in a helpful way when they caused harm to someone. These mothers might say, for

example, in a clear but objective manner, "Tom's crying because you pushed him." Other mothers' discussions of distress situations had strong emotional overtones, and these explanations appeared to be even more effective. The children of these mothers were more likely to intervene in bystander situations where they did not cause any harm but saw that someone else was upset. These mothers might say something like "You must never poke anyone's eyes," or "When you hurt me, I don't want to be near you. I am going away from you."

Other studies have confirmed these findings. For example, Denham, Renwick-DeBardi, and Hewes (1994) found that the children of mothers who pointed out a peer's personal distress in an affectively charged manner reacted in a sad fashion. On the other hand, some maternal tactics were ineffective in encouraging prosocial behavior. For example, physical restraint (simply moving away from the child or moving her away from a victim), physical punishment (a mother might have reported, "I swatted him a good one"), or unexplained prohibitions ("Stop that!") may even interfere with the development of prosocial behavior. These researchers also found that when mothers showed anger as they delivered their disciplinary reasoning and tried to induce guilt in children, preschoolers were unlikely to engage in parent-directed prosocial actions.

Prosocial and altruistic behavior can begin early, and parents play an important role. They can facilitate and encourage the child's emerging altruistic behaviors by helping children make connections between their own actions and other people's emotional states. Altruism truly does begin at home!

when cues were subtle, 4-year-olds were less likely to see a problem or to suggest help. Naturalistic studies have shown similar results. Radke-Yarrow, Zahn-Waxler, and Chapman (1983) found that after 2- and 7-year-old children viewed a TV report of a family killed in a fire, the 7-year-olds were better able to deal with subtle cues and more abstract kinds of distress and to consider feelings other than those expressed in the immediate situation. For example, one child said, "I hope that those children weren't so young, so they had a chance to have some life before having to die."

STABILITY IN STYLES OF PROSOCIAL BEHAVIOR Does knowledge of children's early prosocial tendencies help predict their helpful behavior at later ages? In a classic study, Baumrind (1971) measured nursery school children's

Donating to a school food drive to help people less fortunate than themselves is an important lesson in prosocial behavior for young children.

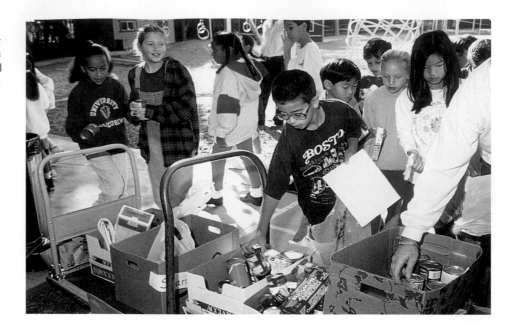

nurturant and sympathetic behaviors toward their peers, their thoughtfulness, and their understanding of other children's viewpoints and then assessed these characteristics in the same children five or six years later. Between the two points in time, this investigator found that the characteristics showed moderate stability. More recent longitudinal studies tell a similar story. Studying children's tendencies to donate to needy children and to assist an adult (e.g., by helping pick up paper clips), researchers found that both donating and helping behaviors were consistent between 10 and 12 years of age. Children who were highly prosocial at one age were likely to remain so at later ages (Eisenberg et al., 2006). The continuity of helpfulness in elementary school children between 6 and 12 years old is considerable. Children who were rated as helpful in kindergarten finished elementary school at similar levels of helpfulness (Coté et al., 2002). It seems likely that there is a fair amount of consistency or stability in children's prosocial behavior across time.

We can look at the issue of stability from other angles. Radke-Yarrow and Zahn-Waxler (1983) found that children showed their prosocial tendencies in different ways: Their prosocial responses varied in both frequency and quality. Consider the reactions of Althea, Jenny, Talia, and Kim—all 2-year-olds—when their mothers cry after reading a sad story in the newspaper. Althea begins to tense up and fights back her tears. Jenny shows little emotion but asks, "What's wrong, Mommy?" Talia tears up the newspaper that makes her mother cry, whereas Kim covers her ears and turns the other way. As these very different reactions illustrate, infants and children develop their own styles of dealing with others' distress. Some children are very emotional, like Althea, and show a great deal of upset. Other youngsters, like Jenny, are cool and reflective and appear to approach the situation more cognitively, by inspecting, exploring, and asking questions. Still others, like Talia, show an aggressive, defensive prosocial approach—for example, "hit the person who made the baby cry." Finally, some children, like Kim, try to "shut out" signals of distress and turn or run away.

These researchers, who observed their young participants first when they were 2 years old and again when they were 7, found stability in style of reaction in about two-thirds of the children. The same style of reacting to others' upset and discomfort was evident both in infancy and five years later. Similarly, the pattern of intense, empathic, affective prosocial attempts made by certain toddlers was still evident at age 7, and the combative responders, the problem-solvers, and the anxious-guilty types were still exhibiting their characteristic styles five years later. Of course, not all children responded similarly across time and for some, "development meant change" (Radke-Yarrow & Zahn-Waxler, 1983, p. 16).

Are Girls More Prosocial than Boys?

Based on our discussions in Chapter 13, we might expect to find that girls are more responsive, empathic, and prosocial than boys. Although girls tend to be more generally oriented toward helping others than do boys, the reality is more complex. Gender differences vary depending on what type of prosocial behavior we're looking at (Eisenberg et al., 2006; Fabes & Eisenberg, 1996). Differences are greatest for kindness and consideration. Girls are apparently also higher in instrumental helping, comforting, sharing, and donating, but gender differences on these behaviors were less dramatic.

Interestingly, gender differences are more pronounced in data derived from self-reports and reports of others (family members, peers) than in data gathered by observational techniques. This may suggest that some gender differences "reflect people's conceptions of what boys and girls are *supposed* to be like rather than how they actually behave" (Eisenberg et al., 2006, p. 123). Parents stress the importance of politeness and prosocial behavior more for daughters than for sons (Maccoby, 1998). When girls behave prosocially, parents attribute such behaviors to inborn tendencies, whereas they attribute boys' prosocial behaviors to the influences of the environment and socialization. These findings do not mean that gender differences are *only* in the eye of the self or the beholder, but that these cultural stereotypes and beliefs may contribute to the gender differences researchers have found.

Closely related are gender differences in **empathy,** the capacity to experience the emotions that others feel. Girls are clearly more empathic than boys (Zahn-Waxler et al., 2001), and the gender difference becomes greater as children develop (Eisenberg et al., 2006). Again, self-report measures have shown the greatest gender differences. According to Eisenberg et al. (2006), gender differences in empathy may increase as children become more aware of gender stereotypes and expectations and are then perhaps more likely to internalize these in their self-images.

empathy The capacity to experience the same emotion that someone else is experiencing.

Determinants of Prosocial Development

Like most behaviors, prosocial behavior and **prosocial reasoning**—thinking about and judging prosocial issues—may have both genetic and environmental determinants. So far, however, the evidence for a biological contribution is modest, so our discussions in this section emphasize environmental influences such as parental behavior—both teaching and modeling—cultural customs and practices, and the media, particularly television programming.

prosocial reasoning Thinking and making judgments about prosocial issues.

BIOLOGICAL INFLUENCES   Some argue that human beings have a biological predisposition to respond with empathy and that we are biologically prepared to engage in prosocial behavior, a view that is consistent with evolutionary theory (see Chapter 1). In his book *Sociobiology* (1975), the evolutionary biologist E. O. Wilson cites evidence of helping and sharing among infrahuman animals and argues that evolution has prepared us for such behavior. For example, helping and sharing is seen among many animals; Preston and deWaal (2002) report both empathy and consoling behavior in chimpanzees. Krebs (2000), a psychologist, also suggests that human prosocial behavior has evolutionary roots and points out that it is adaptive for children and adults to cooperate and share with each other. Research supports this view as well. Some theorists have claimed that the fact that newborn infants cry in response to the cries of other infants is evidence of such a biological predisposition to behave in an empathic fashion (Hoffman, 1981, 2000).

There is some evidence that individual differences in prosocial behavior may have a genetic basis. Identical twins have been found more alike in respect to prosocial behavior than fraternal twins (Davis, Luce, & Kraus, 1994). However, other research has provided only limited support to the notion that prosocial behavior may be inherited (Zahn-Waxler et al., 1992b, 2001). In a study of 2-year-olds, identical and nonidentical twins did not differ in their observed prosocial behaviors, but the researchers found modest evidence for the heritability of empathic concern for a victim in (simulated) distress (Zahn-Waxler, Klimes-Dougan, & Kendizora, 1998). Other studies of identical twins underscore the combined role of genetic and environmental factors in the development of children's prosocial behavior. For example, in a study of identical preschool-age twins, Deater-Deckard et al. (2001) found that both genetic and environmental factors (e.g., maternal supportive and punitive behaviors) contributed to children's prosocial behavior. Further support for the genetic basis of prosocial behavior comes from our understanding of children with certain genetic abnormalities. Children who have Williams syndrome (marked by loss of the long arm of chromosome 7) are more sociable, empathic, sympathetic, and prosocial than children who do not have Williams or than children with other types of genetic disorders (Mervis & Klein-Tasman, 2000; Semal & Rosner, 2003).

Finally, recent work is beginning to isolate the neurological roots of prosocial behavior. For example, studies using the PET scan, a form of neuroimaging that we introduced in Chapter 5, revealed that neural structures associated with emotions (in particular, the *amygdala*) were more activated in response to sad than to neutral stories (Decety & Chaminade, 2003).

Temperament may play a role in sympathetic responding and prosocial behaviors, just as it appears to influence children's ability to inhibit undesirable responses. Highly inhibited 2-year-olds become more upset by another's distress than their less inhibited peers (Young, Fox, & Zahn-Waxler, 1999).

Prosocial children are generally better at regulating their emotions and impulses than other children (Denham, 1998; Wilson, 2003). For example, comforting behavior has been associated with physiological self-regulation, as indexed by measures of heart rate (Eisenberg, Fabes, Guthrie, & Murphy, 1996b).

In sum, a variety of biological factors—genetic, neurological, and temperamental—may predispose children to behave in a prosocial manner. As we have emphasized throughout, these biological influences interact with environmental factors in achieving their effects. We turn to environmental influences in the next section.

ENVIRONMENTAL INFLUENCES Whatever the biological contribution to prosocial behavior may be, environmental factors including the family, mass media, and culture clearly make a difference. Laboratory studies in which children see people donate to or share with others as well as real-life situations in which parents, peers, and others model prosocial behaviors support this social-learning notion of the acquisition of prosocial behavior (Eisenberg et al., 2006; Hart & Fegley, 1995). And adolescents who have opportunities to engage in prosocial actions, such as volunteering at homeless shelters, develop more prosocial attitudes and behavior; they also exhibit fewer school problems and antisocial behavior (Johnson, Beebe, Mortimer, & Snyder, 1998; Metz, McLellan, & Youniss, 2003). Interestingly, Rosenhan (1972) showed, in a now-classic study, that the civil rights activists he interviewed came from families in which parents were committed to altruistic and humanitarian causes.

Parents may act as models, or they may directly encourage, elicit, and shape prosocial behaviors in their children (Eisenberg et al., 2006). As the study in Box 14.2 shows, mothers' childrearing practices do contribute to children's reactions to others' distress. Parents who use power-assertive techniques (e.g., physical punishment) and little reasoning and who show little warmth are unlikely to have altruistic children. In a study in the Netherlands, Dekovic and Janssens (1992) found that democratic parenting (parenting that is warm, supportive, and demanding, and that provides guidance and positive feedback) was linked to more prosocial behavior in children as rated by both teachers and peers. Studies in the United States and Great Britain found that mothers who were negative and controlling had children who showed increasingly less empathic tendencies and prosocial behavior (Asbury, Dunn, Pike, & Plomin, 2003; Biringen, Robinson, & Emde, 1994). Similarly, Canadian children's prosocial behavior was found to be more frequent when parents responded in a tolerant and nonpunitive manner to emotional distress (Strayer & Roberts, 2004).

Most of the time, however, children probably acquire prosocial concepts and behavior through modeling and imitation rather than direct teaching (Bandura, 1989). For example, parents may show things to their infants, thus encouraging the infants to imitate these actions, and at other times parents may request things of their infants—things that belong to the babies. "Such experiences inform infants about situations in which certain actions are socially appropriate and offer them opportunities for practicing and refining the actions" (Hay & Rheingold, 1983, pp. 28–29).

Parents who explicitly model prosocial behavior and at the same time provide opportunities for children to perform these actions may be particularly successful in promoting altruism (Eisenberg et al., 2006). A common way parents provide opportunities for learning prosocial behavior is by assigning children responsibility for household tasks. Even children as young as 2 will spontaneously help adults in a variety of tasks such as sweeping, cleaning, and setting tables (Rheingold, 1982). And allowing children to help in these ways may be important for their prosocial development. As Rheingold wryly notes, parents' "efficient execution of chores makes for inefficient teaching of the young" (1982, p. 124). Nor are the effects limited to infants and toddlers. McLellan and Youniss (2003) found that adolescent volunteering was related to the extent to which the adolescents' parents engaged in volunteer activities. Adolescents even modeled the types of voluntary services in which their parents engaged, such as working in a homeless shelter or working for an environmental cause.

Finally, peers act as models and shapers of children's prosocial behavior. In one study, preschoolers who were exposed to prosocial peers at the beginning of the school year engaged in more positive and prosocial peer interactions later in the year (Fabes, Martin, & Hanish, 2002). Although peers clearly have the potential to encourage and model prosocial behavior for each other, children who were low in prosocial behavior generally played with other low prosocial children, and high prosocial children played together (Fabes et al., 2002). As a result of this kind of "prosocial segregation," children who are low in prosocial behavior may have few chances to learn more prosocial practices from their prosocial peers.

TV and Prosocial Behavior   Models of prosocial behavior are not confined to the family; television may be an important additional learning medium for such behavior. A variety of studies have assessed the impact on young children's prosocial behavior of watching "Mister Rogers' Neighborhood," a program focusing on understanding the feelings of others, expressing sympathy, and helping. The children who watched "Mister Rogers' Neighborhood" not only learned the specific prosocial content of the program but were able to apply that learning to other situations involving peers. In comparison to children who watched shows with neutral content, the children who saw the prosocial programs learned generalized rules about prosocial behavior (Friedrich & Stein, 1973; Huston & Wright, 1998; Singer & Singer, 2001). Similarly, shows such as "Sesame Street" and "Barney," which encourage prosocial behaviors like helping, sharing, and cooperating, increase prosocial actions in their young viewers. This is especially so among young children from middle-to-upper-class families whose parents watch the programs with them and who encourage altruistic behavior in their youngsters (Mares & Woodward, 2001).

Cross-Cultural Perspectives   As we noted in Chapter 11, children in some cultures often are given the responsibility to take care of siblings and other children as well as to perform household tasks (Eisenberg et al., 2005). What effect does this have? Cross-cultural studies of children from a wide range of societies—Mexico, the Philippines, Okinawa, India, and Kenya—suggest that "children who perform more domestic chores, help more with economic tasks and spend more time caring for their infant brothers, sisters, and cousins, score high on the altruistic dimension" (Whiting & Edwards, 1988; Whiting & Whiting, 1975). Researchers have made similar findings in some cultures that stress prosocial and communal values, such as the Aitutaki of Polynesia, the Papago Indian tribe in Arizona, and many Asian cultures (Chen, 2000; Eisenberg et al., 2006). On the other hand, prosocial behaviors are rare, and hostility and cruelty are the norms in cultures such as the Ik of Uganda (Eisenberg, 1992; Eisenberg et al., 2006; Goody, 1991). Further evidence of both the role of culture and the modifiability of prosocial behavior comes from studies of children raised in Israeli kibbutzim, which stress prosocial and cooperative values, as you will recall from our discussion in Chapter 6. Researchers found children reared in these communal settings more prosocial than their city-reared peers (Aviezer, Van IJzendoorn, Sagi, & Schuengel, 1994). Similarly, Mexican and Mexican American children are more prosocial than European American children (Knight, Nelson, Kagan, & Gumbiner, 1982). However, as these children become teenagers and more acculturated to U.S. norms and behavior, they tend to report less prosocial behavior (de Guzman & Carlo, 2004).

The Influence of Cognitive Development

We've said that prosocial behavior shifts in form and expression across development. These changes reflect alterations in prosocial reasoning, and these alterations, in turn, reflect changes in children's cognitive development. As you can see in Table 14-2, Nancy Eisenberg and her colleagues (Eisenberg, Guthrie, Murphy, Cumberland, & Carlo, 1999; Eisenberg et al., 2001b, 2006) have proposed a model of the development of prosocial reasoning that is in some ways similar to the Kohlberg model of the development of moral reasoning. To test the model's depiction of how children's thinking about prosocial acts changes across development, Eisenberg devised a number of accounts of hypothetical interpersonal or social dilemmas. Here is a sample:

> One day a girl (boy) named Mary (Eric) was going to a friend's birthday party. On her (his) way she (he) saw a girl (boy) who had fallen down and hurt her (his) leg. The girl (boy) asked Mary (Eric) to go to her (his) house and tell her (his) parents so the parents could come and take her (him) to the doctor. But if Mary (Eric) did run and get the child's parents, she (he) would be late to the birthday party and miss the ice cream, cake, and all the games. What should Mary (Eric) do? Why?

Eisenberg and her colleagues tested groups of children across 19 years, when they were $4\frac{1}{2}$ and $11\frac{1}{2}$ years old, and again in early adulthood. As the children matured they became less egocentric, and more other-oriented, and they became more capable of abstract reasoning about prosocial dilemmas. The first type of reasoning shown in Table 14-2, **hedonistic reasoning,** in which the child bases his decision to perform a prosocial act on the promise of material reward, decreased with age. The second type, **needs-oriented reasoning**—still a relatively simple type of reasoning—in which children express concern for the needs of others, even though these needs may conflict with their own, peaked in midchildhood and then leveled off. However, the third, fourth, and fifth types of reasoning described in the table—all of which fall under the rubric of prosocial reasoning—all increased with age. The gender differences we've discussed emerged as well; in early adolescence, girls made more use of empathic reasoning than boys. Predictably, sharing and empathy were both negatively related to hedonistic reasoning, and needs-oriented reasoning was positively related to prosocial behavior (Carlo et al., 1996, 2003). Prosocial moral reasoning was more likely to be linked with prosocial behaviors that required some cognitive reflection

hedonistic reasoning
Making a decision to perform a prosocial act on the basis of expected material reward.

needs-oriented reasoning
Reasoning in which children express concern for others' needs even though their own needs may conflict with those needs.

Table 14-2   Evolution of prosocial reasoning

Level	Age Group	Orientation	Mode of Prosocial Reasoning
1	Preschoolers and younger elementary school children	Hedonistic, self-focused	Child is concerned with self-oriented consequences rather than moral considerations. Decision to help or not help another is based on consideration of direct gain to self, future reciprocity, and concern for people to whom the child is bound by affectional ties.
2	Preschoolers and elementary school children	Recognition of needs of others	Child expresses concern for the physical, material, and psychological needs of others even if these needs conflict with her own. Concern is expressed in the simplest terms, without verbal expressions of sympathy, evidence of self-reflective role taking, or reference to internalized affect such as guilt.
3	Elementary and high school students	Seeking others' approval and acceptance	Child uses stereotyped images of good and bad persons and behaviors and considerations of others' approval and acceptance in justifying prosocial or nonhelping behaviors.
4	Older elementary school and high school students	(a) Empathic	Child's judgments include evidence of sympathetic responding, self-reflective role taking, concern with the other's humanness, and guilt or positive affect related to the consequences of her actions.
	Minority of high school students	(b) Transitional (empathic and internalized)	Child's justifications for helping or not helping involve internalized values, norms, duties, or responsibilities, and may refer to the necessity of protecting the rights and dignity of other persons. These ideas, however, are not clearly stated.
5	Only a small minority of high school students and virtually no elementary school children	Strongly internalized	Child's justifications for helping or not helping are based on internalized values, norms, or responsibilities, the desire to maintain individual and societal contractual obligations, and the belief in the dignity, rights, and equality of all individuals. Child also construes her self-respect as based on living up to her own values and accepted norms.

Source: Adapted from Eisenberg, Lennon, & Roth, 1983.

than with a simple, low-cost prosocial action, such as helping someone pick up books he dropped (Carlo, Hausmann, Christiansen, & Randall, 2003).

Finally, prosocial behavior may be related to other aspects of cognitive development such as children's theory of mind (see Chapter 9). Moore and colleagues (Moore, Barresi, & Thompson, 1998) found that preschoolers whose theory of mind was more advanced were able to delay gratification longer to secure a reward to share with a partner. In short, both self-control and sharing may be linked with increasing sophistication in a child's theory of mind.

Assessing the possible relationships between children's levels of prosocial and moral reasoning, Eisenberg and her colleagues found only modest correlations. It may be that children's development within these two domains follows parallel but more or less independent paths. On the other hand, if helping behavior involves an important value or principle—for example, helping support or defeat legislative action to "save the refugees"—a person's level of prosocial reasoning is likely to be relevant. As Eisenberg et al. (2006) note, "Moral reasoning is more likely to be associated with children's prosocial behavior in situations involving a cost because consideration of the cost is likely to evoke cognitive conflict and morally relevant decision making" (p. 96).

Making cross-cultural comparisons of children's (and adults') moral and prosocial thinking and behavior is difficult, for cultural norms relevant to the issue of social responsibility vary widely, and cultures differ in the ways they value specific kinds of prosocial actions (Eisenberg et al., 2006). In general, there are relatively few differences in prosocial moral reasoning among children of industrialized Western cultures but quite a considerable difference between the way these children reason and the children of non-Western developing nations think. In cultures such as that of Hindu India, for example, people tend to have a more stringent, duty-based view of social responsibility than do most people in the United States, where interpersonal responsiveness and caring is more of a personal choice (Miller, Bersoff, & Harwood, 1990; see also Box 14.1).

Beliefs about morality and appropriate behavior toward others are grounded in bodies of religious and philosophical thought that have deep roots in the histories of many cultures. For example, as we've discussed earlier, many people in Asian countries take a more collective approach to social and interpersonal behavior than do people in Western nations, placing their emphasis on the welfare of the group or nation rather than of the individual. And indeed, some researchers argue that the norms that characterize the American culture are more linked with an emphasis on individual rights (Miller & Bersoff, 1992). When people live in communal fashion, as in traditional societies or developing nations, where people are more interdependent in their daily existence, or in the modern Israeli kibbutzim, ties of responsibility and reciprocity may be more binding.

Investigators have found that in Germany and Israel, school-age children were more likely than American children to emphasize direct reciprocity, whereby children expect to receive similar payback for their prosocial actions (Eisenberg, Boehnke, Schuler, & Sibereisen, 1985), and Brazilian urban adolescents were less likely to use higher-level prosocial reasoning than U.S. teens (Eisenberg, Zhou, & Keller, 2001). Clearly, as we saw earlier, cultural experiences and values not only shape prosocial behaviors but organize the ways in which people think about their prosocial obligations to others.

Empathy, Sympathy, Perspective Taking, and Altruism

Two important determinants of altruism are empathy and perspective-taking ability, or the capacity to understand another's point of view (Eisenberg et al., 2005; Hoffman, 2000). According to Hoffman, children have the capacity to feel or empathize with another person's emotional states. Another child's distress can elicit a similar emotion in a child observing the first, just as a child can experience another person's joy or happiness. This empathic ability often motivates children to engage in prosocial actions that relieve not only another person's distress but also their own emotional upset. In turn, prosocial acts that result in positive feelings can vicariously produce similar positive emotions in the helping child. Children who are more empathic behave in a more prosocial manner (Eisenberg et al., 2006; Eisenberg et al., 1990). These relations are found in a variety of cultures, including Italy, Japan, and Turkey (Asakawa, Iwawaki, Mondori, & Minami, 1987; Bandura, Caprara, Barbaranelli, Gerbino, & Pastorelli, 2003; Kumru & Edwards, 2003) as well as North America (Vitaglione & Barnett, 2003). Moreover, the daughters of mothers who are sensitive

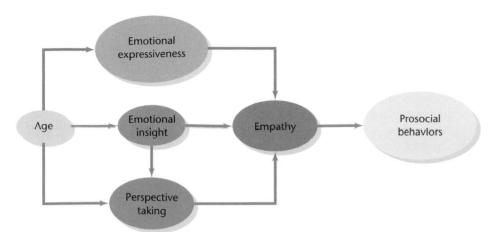

Figure 14-4

How empathy and other qualities combine to produce prosocial behavior
According to this model, empathy is the principal determinant underlying prosocial behavior. Underlying empathy are emotional expressiveness, emotional insight, and perspective-taking abilities, and all of these qualities are driven by age.

Source: Adapted from Roberts & Strayer, 1996.

to their children's emotions (i.e., try to find out why children feel bad and listen to them when they are anxious and upset) display more prosocial behavior—for example, they will comfort an infant in distress (Eisenberg et al., 1993). The way that mothers talk about emotions matters, too. Preschoolers whose mothers explain their own feelings when they are sad display more prosocial behavior (Denham, 1998).

Researchers have found clear links between the capacity for perspective taking and altruism (Eisenberg et al., 2006; Strayer & Roberts, 2004). However, perspective-taking ability alone may not be enough to produce prosocial behavior if a child doesn't have the motivation or the social assertiveness necessary to act prosocially. Several researchers have found that children who demonstrated ability in perspective taking and who also either were socially assertive or who expressed **sympathy**—the feeling of sorrow or concern for a distressed or needy person—were more prosocial than children good at perspective taking alone (Denham, 1998). In one study, the children who donated money to help a child who was burned in a fire were those who were sympathetic, had perspective-taking ability, and understood units and value of money (Knight, Nelson, Kagan, Carlo, & Eisenberg, 1994).

sympathy The feeling of sorrow or concern for a distressed or needy person.

Considering the question of how these various factors might interrelate with empathy to produce prosocial behavior, Roberts and Strayer (1996) proposed the model shown in Figure 14-4. They then tested this model with groups of 5-, 9-, and 13-year-olds, and found that all the measures—emotional expressiveness, emotional insight, and perspective taking—did indeed work together to determine empathy and, in turn, prosocial behavior. Interestingly, empathy predicted boys' general level of prosocial behavior, but in girls it predicted prosocial behavior only toward friends. Because girls' friendships are generally closer and more intimate than boys' friendships, empathy may be a more important predictor of prosocial behavior toward friends for girls than for boys (see Chapter 12). Again, it is important to consider gender as we strive to achieve a better understanding of prosocial behavior.

Altruism is expressed in a complex and multiply determined set of behaviors. Although we are gradually learning more about prosocial action, we are not yet in a position to write a prescription for raising a helpful and caring child. Perhaps that ultimate prescription will include the prevention of the very troublesome aspect of social development to which we now turn—aggression.

THE DEVELOPMENT OF AGGRESSION

Altruism is a behavior that parents, peers, and teachers view positively; aggression, on the other hand, is seen as an unwelcome but common occurrence. For decades, psychologists have puzzled over the knotty problem of aggression. Why do some children attack others? Why do some adults cheat, rob, attack, murder others? Do patterns of aggression change over time, and if so, how? What roles do families, peers, and the mass media play in the development of aggression? Most important, how can we control aggression in our children?

Before we go any farther, we need to clarify what we mean by **aggression.** The term is usually defined as behavior that is intended to and does harm other people by inflicting pain or injury on them. The notion of intention is crucial here, for we need to separate acts of aggression from the actions taken by parents, for example, in disciplining their children, or from the actions of doctors, dentists, surgeons, and other medical personnel who must at times cause pain to others in order to preserve and protect their physical health. What distinguishes painful actions of these kinds from acts of aggression is that the intent of the former is not to cause pain or harm but to help and better the condition of others.

How Aggressive Behavior Develops in Children

A visit to a nursery school and a stopover at an elementary school playground reveal some striking age differences in the form and frequency of aggressive behavior. (Our Turning Points chart on page 623 offers a brief outline of how aggression changes over time.) Nursery school children display **instrumental aggression,** since they are more likely to quarrel and fight over toys and possessions. In contrast, in the older children (6- and 7-year-olds) we see **hostile aggression,** or more personally oriented aggressive acts in which a child criticizes, ridicules, tattles on, and calls names (Dodge, Coie, & Tremblay, 2006). This shift from fighting over things to fighting over human characteristics and behaviors may occur as older children acquire a greater ability to infer the intentions and motives of others (Ferguson & Rule, 1980). Thus, when older children recognize that another person wants to hurt them, they are more likely to retaliate by a direct assault on the tormentor than by an indirect attack on the aggressor's possessions.

Despite children's gradually improved ability to infer intent, individual children differ in how accurately they can "read" another person's intentions. Some children, especially those who are highly aggressive, have more difficulty judging the intentions of their peers. Again, recall our discussion in Chapter 12 of the information-processing model of social behavior. We can apply this model to understanding aggressive behavior as well (Crick & Dodge, 1994). According to Dodge, applying this model is especially helpful in ambiguous situations, where children's intentions are not clearly either aggressive or prosocial. In such situations, boys who are rated by their classmates as aggressive are likely to react in a hostile way—as if the other person intended to be aggressive. Aggressive boys see the world as a threatening and hostile place. They perceive the actions of others differently and see more anger and aggression in others than do less aggressive boys. Dodge and Frame (1982) found that aggressive boys not only committed more unprovoked aggressive acts but were the targets of more aggressive attacks than nonaggressive boys. They thus concluded that "the biased attributions of aggressive boys may have a basis in their experience. Their collective expectancy that peers will be biased in aggressing toward them is consistent with their experience" (Dodge & Frame, 1982, p. 28). Researchers have found this bias toward hostile attribution in a variety of samples, including European American, African American, and Latino American children (Graham & Hudley, 1994; Guerra & Huesmann, 2003).

The kind of aggression a child displays can be characterized in yet another way. Some children act aggressively only in response to being attacked, threatened, or frustrated, displaying **reactive aggression.** In contrast, other children show **proactive aggression,** using force to dominate another person or to bully or threaten others to gain a prized object or possession. Boys who display reactive aggression are

aggression Behavior that intentionally harms other people by inflicting pain or injury on them.

instrumental aggression Quarreling and fighting with others over toys and possessions.

hostile aggression Directing aggressive behavior at a particular person or group, criticizing, ridiculing, tattling on, or calling names.

reactive aggression Aggressive behavior as a response to attack, threat, or frustration.

proactive aggression The use of force to dominate another person or to bully or threaten others.

Turning Points

THE DEVELOPMENT OF AGGRESSIVE BEHAVIOR

INFANCY:
0–2 YEARS
- The child expresses anger and frustration
- Shows some early signs of aggression (pushing, shoving)
- Temperamental differences in irritability predict later aggression

PRESCHOOL YEARS:
2–5 OR 6 YEARS
- If encouraged by family members in antisocial behavior, the child may later begin to display seriously aggressive behavior
- The child tends to display instrumental aggression, fighting over toys and possessions, and to rely on the physical expression of aggression
- Girls exhibit more verbal and relational aggression, excluding and gossiping about others, whereas boys are more physical

6–7 YEARS
- Children display hostile aggression, using criticism, ridicule, name calling, and tattling, as they begin to infer and to judge the intentions of others
- Instrumental aggression decreases

ELEMENTARY SCHOOL AGE:
7–10 YEARS
- Differences between boys' reliance on physical aggression and girls' reliance on relational aggression become more marked
- In both boys and girls physical aggression gradually declines, and verbal aggression becomes more common
- Children may begin to do poorly in school and to be rejected by peers if aggressive
- In the fourth or fifth grade, parental monitoring becomes particularly important to deter delinquency and vandalism

ADOLESCENCE
- Aggressive children select aggressive and deviant peer groups
- Among some youths, vandalism, use of guns, and delinquency increase
- Gender differences are marked: Rates of delinquency and violent behavior are much higher among boys than girls
- Hormonal changes, such as rising levels of testosterone, are associated with increases in reactive aggression in boys; individual differences in hormonal levels are important determinants of the levels of aggression

Note: Developmental events described in this and other Turning Points charts represent overall trends identified in research studies. Patterns of aggressive behavior vary greatly among individual children (see especially "The Family as a Training Center for Aggression").

Sources: Coie & Dodge, 1998; Crick et al., 1998; Dodge, Coie, & Tremblay, 2006; Underwood, 2004.

more likely to misinterpret others' intentions, whereas those who are proactively aggressive—like the playground bully—are less likely to misread another's intent (Poulin & Boivin, 2000). Like instrumental aggression, proactive aggression generally decreases across development. For example, in a recent report (NICHD Early Child Care Research Network, 2004b), "hits others" occurred in 70 percent of the sample at ages 2 and 3 but declined to 20 percent by ages 4 and 5 and to 12 percent by third grade.

The way children express aggression also changes over development. Whereas toddlers rely more on physical attacks, older children, with their improved communication skills, are likely to aggress verbally rather than physically (Dodge et al., 2006). These developmental shifts in the style of expressing aggression are due not only to increased verbal skills but to changes in adult expectations and rules. Most adults become less tolerant of physical aggression as children mature, whereas they are more likely to ignore a "battle of words" even among older children. On the other hand, different measures of aggression may reflect the same underlying pattern at different ages. For example, fighting at age 8, vandalism at age 12, and homicide at age 18 may all be indices of aggression, a reminder that the same trait is expressed differently at different ages (Farrington, 1993).

Although the level of aggression gradually declines across development as children learn to solve problems and conflicts through more socially acceptable means, one can still ask whether individual levels of aggression compared with others remain stable over time. How stable, then, is aggression over time? For both males and females, aggression appears to be moderately stable (Cairns & Cairns, 1994; Dodge et al., 2006; Olweus, 1982). If you were rated as more aggressive than your classmates at one point, it is likely that you will retain that relative rank. In fact, aggression is as stable as intelligence. For both genders, as the time between assessment points stretches out, the degree of stability decreases. Earlier research such as the Fels Longitudinal Study, which we've mentioned before, found greater stability of aggression for boys (Kagan & Moss, 1962). More recent studies have confirmed that physical aggression by boys in early elementary school predicts physical violence as well as other forms of delinquency in adolescence (Broidy et al., 2003). In contrast, these same studies have also found that childhood physical aggression is not predictive of later delinquency in girls. However, perhaps owing to changing societal values, girls are beginning to show greater stability in assertive and aggressive behaviors. Even more important, if we distinguish between the kinds of aggression typically displayed by males (physical) and by females (verbal) we find that aggression is stable for both (Cairns & Cairns, 1994). Even across a 22-year span, aggression shows a moderate degree of consistency. In a follow-up study of more than 600 individuals who were originally seen at 8 years of age, researchers (Bushman & Huesmann, 2001; Huesmann, Eron, Lefkowitz, & Walder, 1984) found that the more aggressive 8-year-olds were, at age 30, still more aggressive than their peers. The boys who were rated in childhood as aggressive were more likely as adults to have more moving traffic violations, to have been arrested for drunk driving, and to have abused their wives. Moreover, both males and females who were rated aggressive as children were more likely to have criminal convictions by age 30 (Figure 14-5).

Early aggression may have similar long-term consequences for males and females. Men who were rated ill-tempered as 8- to 10-year-old boys had, by the age of 40, experienced more erratic work lives, held poorer jobs than their parents, and were more likely to have divorced than their even-tempered peers. Ill-tempered girls married men with lower occupational mobility; were less adequate and more ill-tempered mothers; and were also more likely to divorce (Caspi et al., 1987; Kokko & Pulkkinen, 2000). Clearly, an early pattern of aggressive behavior leaves its mark.

A word of caution: Not all aggressive children remain aggressive. In fact, as noted earlier, most children decrease markedly in their level of aggression across age, and few children increase in their aggression levels over time. However, a small percentage remain at a high level. For example, in one study, about 18 percent of children remained consistently high in their level of aggression between 24 months and third grade (NICHD Early Child Care Research Network, 2004b). In another study (Nagin & Trembay, 1999), about one-eighth (12.5%) of aggressive 5-year-olds were

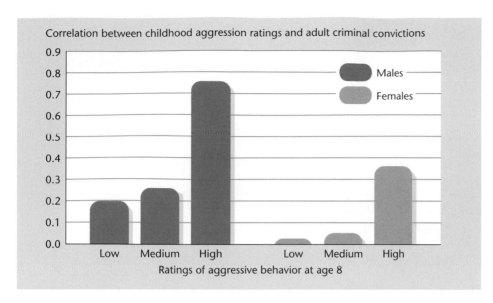

Figure 14-5

The relation between childhood aggression and adult criminal behavior
Among males, the correlation between highly aggressive behavior in childhood and the number of criminal convictions in later life was .75, which is extremely high. The same correlations for boys who showed little or only moderate aggressiveness in childhood were much lower, as were all the same correlations for females. Note, however, that among females we see the same tendency of rising correlations as the degree of early aggression escalates.

Source: Adapted from Huesmann, Eron, Lefkowitz, & Walder, 1984.

highly aggressive at adolescence. As we will see later in the chapter, interventions and experience can shift the development trajectory toward a more peaceful pathway.

Gender Differences in Aggression

One of the most striking aspects of these developmental trends is the markedly divergent courses that boys and girls follow. Although there are few gender differences in aggression in infancy, by the time of toddlerhood, and in the preschool years, boys are more likely than girls to instigate and be involved in aggressive incidents (Loeber & Hay, 1993; Maccoby, 1998). This gender difference is evident not only across U.S. socioeconomic groups but across cultures including Britain, Canada, Switzerland, Ethiopia, Kenya, India, the Philippines, Mexico, New Zealand, and Okinawa (Broidy et al., 2003; Dodge et al., 2006; Whiting & Whiting, 1975). Boys' and girls' aggressive patterns differ in other important ways. Boys are more likely than girls to retaliate after being attacked (Darvill & Cheyne, 1981), and they are more likely to attack a male than a female (Barrett, 1979). Boys are more physically confrontational, and their expressions of aggression are more frequent than those of girls. Boys are less likely than girls to engage in negative self-evaluation, they are less likely to anticipate parental disapproval for acting aggressively, and they are also more likely to approve of aggression (Huesmann & Guerra, 1997; Perry, Perry, & Weiss, 1989).

In attempting to resolve conflicts, girls tend to use such strategies as verbal objection and negotiation, methods that may make the escalation of a quarrel into overt aggression less likely (Eisenberg, Fabes, Nyman, Bernzweig, & Pinuelas, 1994). This does not mean that girls are not aggressive, but rather that they use different tactics in achieving their goals. Especially in the elementary school years, girls often use what is called **relational aggression,** or the damaging or destruction of interpersonal relationships (Crick et al., 1999; Crick, Ostrov, Appleyard, Jansen, & Casas, 2004; Underwood, 2003). In this mode, according to Dodge et al. (2006), girls may attempt "to exclude peers from group participation, besmirch another's reputation, and gossip about another's negative attributes" (p. 791). For example, some researchers have found that seventh-grade girls may choose to harm others by means of social ostracism rather than by direct confrontation. Other investigators have found that as girls enter adolescence, they tend to make increasing use of the aggressive strategy of excluding others from social cliques (Crick et al., 1999, 2004; Underwood, 2003; Xie, Cairns, & Cairns, 2005).

relational aggression
Damaging or destroying interpersonal relationships by such means as excluding another or gossiping about or soiling another's reputation.

Overt Aggressors	Relational Aggressors
Hit, kick, punch other children	Try to make other children dislike a certain child by spreading rumors about that person
Say mean things to insult others or put them down	When angry, get over it by excluding another person from group of friends
Tell other children that they will beat them up unless the children do what they say	Tell friends that they will stop liking them unless the friends do what they say
Push and shove others	When angry at a person, ignore the person or stop talking to them
Call other children mean names	Try to keep certain people out of their own group during activity or play time

Although relational aggression becomes more common in the elementary school grades, even preschool girls show significantly more relational aggression and are less overtly aggressive than preschool boys (Crick, Casas, & Mosher, 1997). Moreover, relational aggression is significantly related to social and psychological maladjustment; boys or girls who engage in this type of aggression are more likely to be rejected by their peers, both in the United States and in Italy (Crick, 1997; Crick et al., 2004). Although this kind of aggression may be less overt, other children don't fail to notice it, and they ostracize those who engage in it. More girls than boys view this type of aggression as hurtful, even though they tend to use it themselves, and indeed view both relational and physical aggression as equally hurtful (Galen & Underwood, 1997; Underwood, 2003). Boys, on the other hand, tend to view physical aggression as more hurtful than relational aggression. Table 14-3 and Figure 14-6 illustrate some of the differences between these two types of aggression and between girls' and boys' use of these behaviors.

The preschool gender differences are not only perpetuated but become more salient as children develop. Marked male-female differences in aggressive behavior are evident in adolescence and adulthood (Moffit, Caspi, Rutter, & Silva, 2001).

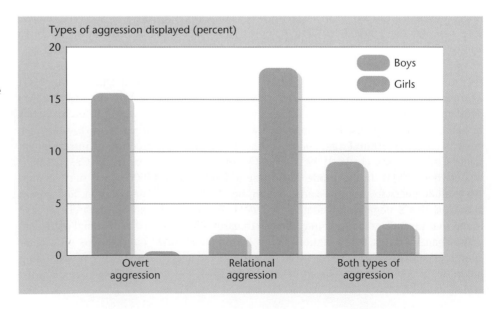

Figure 14-7 Serious violent crime among adolescents and young adults: Self-reports

Serious violent offenses (SVOs), which include aggravated assault (assault with intent to commit a crime), robbery, and rape, rise sharply between the ages of 12 and 17. Although more males than females commit violent offenses, girls are likely to get involved in criminal behavior when they are about two years younger than boys (14 versus 16).

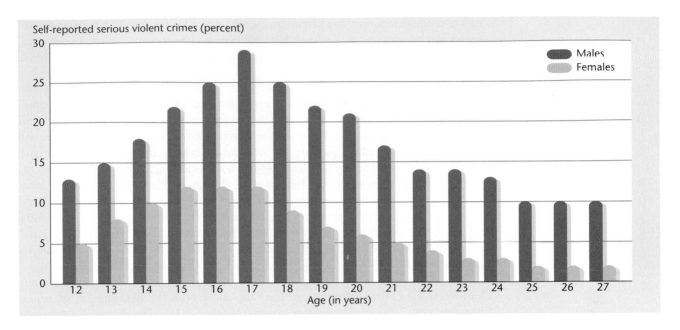

Source: Coie & Dodge, 1998.

Approximately five times as many adolescent boys as girls are arrested for violent crimes (e.g., robbery, aggravated assault, criminal homicide), although in recent years the number of females found guilty of such crimes has increased (Cairns & Cairns, 1994; Moffitt et al., 2001). Figure 14-7 displays data on violent criminal behavior among young people in the mid-1990s.

Origins of Aggressive Behavior

The theme of the interplay between biological and environmental influences reappears once again, as we explore the possible causes of aggressive behavior. As we will see, there is some evidence for the influence of biological factors, at least as they act in concert with environmental influences. Equally impressive, however, is the evidence for the effects of the child's early learning within the family and, later in development, the influence of the peer group on the emergence of aggression. As we have argued throughout, both biological and environmental factors act together in accounting for developmental outcomes.

THE ROLE OF BIOLOGY Does aggression have a biological basis? Let's look at the physiological evidence first. Biology's impact on aggression may be seen rather clearly in adolescence, when, as we saw in Chapter 5, hormone levels are rising (Moeller, 2001). Brooks and Reddon (1996) found that in the United States, adolescent violent offenders had higher levels of testosterone than nonviolent or even sexual offenders. A study of 15- to 17-year-old boys in Sweden (Olweus, Mattson, Schalling, & Low, 1988) found an indirect link between testosterone and aggression. Boys whose blood showed higher levels of testosterone rated themselves as more likely to respond aggressively to provocations and threats from others. In this case, the hormone would seem to have a direct effect on the aggressive behavior. Moreover, boys with high blood levels of testosterone were more impatient or irritable, which in turn increased their readiness to engage in unprovoked and destructive kinds of aggressive behavior (e.g., to start fights or say hostile things without provocation). The effect was construed as indirect, inasmuch as the hormone affected the level of irritation, which in turn altered the tendency to aggression. Tremblay and his Canadian colleagues (1998) found another form of indirect link between testosterone and aggression. In this case, testosterone was related to body mass which, in turn, was linked with increased physical aggression.

Although temperament and childrearing practices are important contributing factors in aggression, even when researchers controlled for these factors, the hormonal effects held. Interestingly, other work has suggested that there may be reciprocal effects—that is, dominance or success in conflict may lead to a rise in testosterone levels (Schaal, Tremblay, Soussignan, & Susman, 1996). Boys rated as tough and social leaders had the highest testosterone levels, although they were not necessarily higher in aggression on a routine basis. Tough, dominant boys, however, may be more likely to respond aggressively to provocation by lower-status peers. Hormones may affect aggression in girls as well. Levels of hormones, especially estradiol, that increase during puberty were positively linked with adolescent girls' expressions of anger and aggression during interactions with their parents (Inoff-Germain et al., 1988).

Recently, research has examined the links between aggression and neurotransmitters, chemical compounds that can facilitate and inhibit the transmission of neural impulses within the central nervous system (Moeller, 2001). For example, a two-year study found a negative relationship between levels of the neurotransmitter *serotonin* and the severity of children's physically aggressive behavior—the lower a child's level of serotonin, the higher his level of aggression (Kruesi, Hibbs, Zahn, & Keysor, 1992). Serotonin, which is involved in regulating the activity of the endocrine glands (see Chapter 5), can affect attention and emotional states and may also be involved in depression.

Twin studies have given some support to a role for genetic factors in aggressive behavior (Dionne, Tremblay, Boivin, Laplante, & Perusse, 2003; Rhee & Waldman, 2002). Based on parental ratings of their children's physical aggression, Dionne and her colleagues (2003) found that 18-month-old Canadian identical twins were more similar than nonidentical twins. Studies of adolescents have produced similar findings. Responding to a questionnaire about aggression that contained such items as "Some people think that I have a violent temper," identical twins rated themselves as more similar than did nonidentical twins (Gottesman & Goldsmith, 1994). Researchers in the Netherlands, Sweden, and Britain have obtained similar results (Eley, Lichtenstein, & Stevenson, 1999; Van Den Oord et al., 1994).

Temperament also may be linked with tendencies toward aggressive behavior. As you'll recall from Chapters 2 and 4, infants differ in temperament, some being difficult and others easygoing. Recent evidence suggests that difficult babies—those who are irritable, whiny, unpredictable, hard to soothe, and prone to negative affect—may be more likely to develop aggressive behavior patterns at later ages. At 3 years of age, infants who had been rated difficult at 6, 13, and 24 months were rated higher in anxiety, hyperactivity, and hostility (Rothbart & Bates, 1998). Similarly, S. B. Campbell (2000) found that two-thirds of noncompliant, overactive and ill-tempered 3-year-olds had externalizing problems such as aggression six years later.

Temperamental predisposition and biological factors such as levels of hormones and neurotransmitters don't act independently of the social environment, of course; rather, they interact with it (Leve, Winebarger, Fagot, Reid, & Goldsmith, 1998; Moeller, 2001). It may be that hormones are more influential at certain points in development, such as adolescence, and under certain conditions, such as provoking and threatening situations (Dodge et al., 2006). Although some individuals may be more likely than others to be aggressive because of their biological makeup, they may be even more likely to engage in aggressive acts if they live in a high-risk and conflict-ridden environment. In a Swedish study of adopted males, if both the biological and adoptive parents were criminals, 40 percent of adopted males were likely to engage in criminal acts. If only the biological parent was a criminal, the percentage declined to 12; if only the adoptive parent was a criminal, it declined to 7 percent. If neither parent was a criminal, the proportion of adopted males who engaged in criminal acts dropped to 3 percent (Cloninger, Sigvardsson, Bohman, & van Knoring, 1982). A similar gene-environment interaction has been reported for females (Cloninger, Christiansen, Reich, & Gottesman, 1978).

THE FAMILY AS A TRAINING CENTER FOR AGGRESSION

The family, as we have said, is the child's first social environment. Do parents play a role in children's tendencies to be aggressive or nonaggressive? They do indeed; a child's early relationships with his parents matter, especially when the family faces external stressors. Although some evidence indicates that insecure forms of attachment (especially disorganized attachment) are linked to aggressive behavior at 5 and 7 years of age (Lyons-Ruth, 1996; Lyons-Ruth & Jacobvitz, 1999), other research suggests that it is when insecure attachment combines with other risk factors that the child is in danger of developing aggression-related problems. For example, in a study of more than 4,000 males in Denmark, a combination of birth complications and early rejection by the mother (unwanted pregnancy, abortion attempts) predicted that adolescents would be involved in violent crime by the time they were between 17 and 19 years old. Among the young offenders who had experienced both risk factors, 40 percent became violent, whereas only 20 percent of those who experienced only one risk factor committed violent crimes (Lyons-Ruth, 1996).

Whether her parents have spanked her or spanked a sibling in her presence, this little girl has clearly gotten the message that misbehavior is to be punished severely.

Although some parents may deliberately teach their children, especially boys, to "defend" themselves or to "be a man," most parents do not view themselves as giving aggression tutorials (Anderson, 1998). As we saw in our earlier discussion of gender roles (Chapter 13), cultural groups differ: African American families, for example, are more likely than are European American families to encourage daughters to be more assertive and to defend themselves. However, as we saw in Chapter 11, when parents argue or fight with one another and, especially, fail to resolve their conflicts in positive ways, they may well be giving implicit instruction to their children. In addition, parents' typical control tactics may contribute to their children's aggression. Parents who use physical punishment, especially on an inconsistent basis, are likely to have aggressive, hostile children, and this is true whether their children are playground bullies or juvenile delinquents (Cohen & Brook, 1995; Patterson, 2002). Physical punishment is especially likely to lead to aggressive behavior in a child when the parent-child relationship is lacking in warmth and otherwise unsatisfying (Deater-Deckard & Dodge, 1997). However, ethnicity of the child matters: The link between physical punishment and aggression is clear in European American families and children, but this link is not evident in African American families (Deater-Deckard, Dodge, Bates, & Pettit, 1996). Just as we saw in Chapter 11, children from different ethnic backgrounds may view parental practices differently and in turn, these practices have different consequences for children.

In considering the effect of the family environment on the development of aggressive tendencies in children, the work of Gerald R. Patterson (1982, 2002) is of particular importance. Since the 1970s Patterson's Social Learning Center in Eugene, Oregon, has been one of the world's leading research institutions devoted to understanding the origins of aggressive behavior, the developmental pathways that children follow toward delinquent behavior, and ways of treating and changing children who have problems with aggression. Patterson has based his conclusions on actual observations of families of aggressive and nonaggressive children, especially boys, in their home environments. Schools and clinical agencies refer aggressive children to the center for treatment of their excessive antisocial, aggressive behavior.

Patterson (1982, 2002) has found that the family environments of aggressive and nonaggressive children are strikingly different. Aggressive children's families tended to be erratic and inconsistent in their use of punishment for deviant behaviors and ineffective in rewarding their children for prosocial behaviors. Moreover, these families not only punished their boys more often but punished them even when the children were behaving appropriately! Such inept parenting practices often lead to cycles of mutually coercive behavior. (Recall our Chapter 11 discussion of coercive interactions between child and parent, especially in the single-parent family following a divorce.) Children are not passive victims in this sort of process; they often develop behavior patterns in which they quite purposely use aversive behaviors—such as whining and being difficult or committing directly aggressive acts—to coerce parents into giving them what they want. Children learn that such coercive behaviors can help them control other family members' behavior including that of siblings. When brother or sister pairs engage in coercive exchanges, especially if the older sibling is already delinquent, the younger sibling is more likely to become delinquent, too (Slomkowski, Rende, Conger, Sinous, & Conger, 2001). A combination of sibling conflict and rejecting parenting is an especially potent recipe for later conduct problems (Garcia et al., 2000). The most appropriate model of discipline is thus a bidirectional one, which recognizes that parent, sibling and child influence one another, and that all contribute to the development of aggression.

Parents don't only influence their own children; parental influence often continues across generations as well. We saw in the case of attachment that patterns of infant-parent attachment in one generation continued in the next. To evaluate whether hostile parenting increases the risk of aggressive behavior in the next generation was the goal of a recent study by Scaramella and Conger (2003). These researchers examined patterns of parent-adolescent interaction and then reexamined these same adolescents when they became parents themselves. The investigators found that adolescents who received hostile parenting were more likely to repeat this style of angry and coercive parenting with their 2-year-olds. In turn, these toddlers exhibited more problem behaviors, including aggressive and disruptive behaviors.

Cross-generational continuity is not inevitable; in many instances there are differences or discontinuities between generations. One factor that may control cross-generation consistency or inconsistency is the child's level of emotional reactivity (i.e., how much the child reacts to parental control by angry emotional reactions). In families in which a young child was high in negative emotional reactivity, there was continuity in hostile parenting from generation to generation, but when the child was less emotionally reactive there was no link across generations. This illustrates again the interplay between temperament and parenting and suggests that the type of child plays a role in shaping parenting not only in one generation but across generations as well.

Families not only contribute directly to their children's aggressive tendencies through the control tactics they use but also shape the development of aggression indirectly. For example, their monitoring or lack of monitoring of their children's

Lack of parental monitoring of a child's activities is associated with aggression and delinquency.

whereabouts, activities, and social contacts can be an important determinant of whether children will develop aggressive behavior. Some parents are fully aware of their children's activities, problems, and successes and can report accurately what their children are doing, whom they're with, and where they are. Other parents are largely oblivious to their children's lives. They don't know if their children are hanging around on street corners or are at a school dance, whether they are habitual truants or involved students, or even whether their child is the friendly neighborhood drug dealer. Lack of parental monitoring is associated, among seventh and tenth graders, with high rates of delinquency, attacks against property, and poorer relations with peers and teachers (Patterson, 2004; Pettit, Laird, Dodge, Bates, & Criss, 2001).

Monitoring children's friends and activities is not just a parental job but a shared responsibility between children and parents (Kerr & Stattin, 2000; Laird, Pettit, Dodge, & Bates, 2003). The ability to monitor relies on the extent to which children share information about their activities and choices of companions with their parents. As Laird et al. (2003) found, monitoring is higher and antisocial behavior is lower when parents and adolescents spend more time together and have more enjoyable relationships, and when adolescents view monitoring as an appropriate parenting activity. In short, "it takes two" to monitor successfully.

To understand the development of aggression in the home, we must view the family unit not only as a social system in which all the interrelations among family members are important but also as a gatekeeper in respect to external influences. Children's development of aggressive behaviors may depend as much on parents' awareness of activities in the surrounding community, and their efforts to control negative aspects of these activities, as on their direct childrearing practices. Training parents to use more effective disciplinary techniques and to increase their monitoring of their children's activities may help reduce aggressive behavior (Reid, Patterson, & Snyder, 2002).

Patterson, DeBarshyshe, & Ramsey, (1989) have shown how children may progress from conduct problems in early childhood to full-fledged delinquency in adolescence as a consequence of the early experience of poor parental disciplinary practices and lack of monitoring. As you can see from Figure 14-8, when such children enter school, two things typically happen: Their peer group rejects them, and they experience academic failure (Ladd, Birch, & Buhs, 1999; Buhs & Ladd, 2001). In late childhood and early adolescence, these now antisocial children may seek out deviant peers who, in turn, provide further training in antisocial behavior and opportunities for delinquent activities (Dishion, Poulin, & Burraston, 2001). Antisocial youth are more likely to be school dropouts, to be employed only sporadically, to experience marital problems, and to end up in jail (Patterson & Bank, 1989). Interestingly, it matters a great deal whether the child starts along a deviant path early or later in development. If the family environment is already encouraging antisocial behavior before age 5 or 6, the child is more likely to develop serious and persistent delinquent behavior than if the child starts on the deviancy road at a later age—in middle to late adolescence

Figure 14-8   Evolution and progression of antisocial behavior

Note that parents, peers, and school all play a role in the evolution of antisocial behavior but at different stages in the child's development.

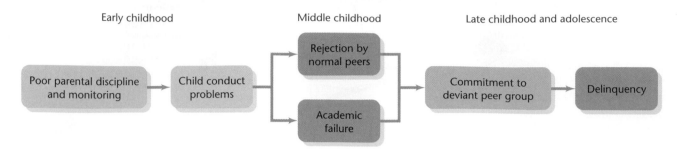

Source: Adapted from Patterson, DeBarshyshe, & Ramsey, 1989.

(Dishion et al., 2001; Moffitt, 1993). The late starter may have avoided the social rejection and school failure common among early starters. Interestingly, the early starters are more often boys than girls by a ratio of 10 to 1 (Moffit et al., 2001).

As we noted earlier, biological as well as social factors are important determinants of later aggression. In fact, early starters who persist in their aggression are at greater risk owing not only to social circumstances but also to biological factors as well (Brennan, Hall, Bar, Najman, & Williams, 2003). Children in whom biological risks—such as perinatal and birth complications, maternal illness during pregnancy, poor infant temperament, low receptive vocabulary (age 5), and deficits in executive functioning—were combined with social risks such as poverty were the most likely to be aggressive adolescents at age 15. Clearly, the developmental timing of earlier experience makes an important difference in determining whether childhood aggression leads to serious delinquent behaviors.

TELEVISION VIEWING, VIDEO GAMES, AND AGGRESSION

As we saw in Chapter 1, exposure to aggressive models on TV can increase children's subsequent aggressive behavior (Bushman & Huesmann, 2001; Comstock & Scharrer, 2006; Huston & Wright, 1998), and aggressive and violent behaviors are endemic in the medium. Heavy doses of TV violence can affect both attitudes and behavior, leading children to view violence as an acceptable and effective way to solve interpersonal conflict (Bushman & Huesmann, 2001). Children learn a lesson from TV that "violence works, for both the good guys and the bad guys; it gets things done" (Dominick & Greenberg, 1972, p. 331). Moreover, the effect of TV violence on aggression in children is not a strictly American phenomenon. Cross-cultural studies indicate that children in Australia, Finland, Great Britain, Israel, the Netherlands, and Poland show similar reactions to violent TV fare (Bushman & Huesmann, 2001; Huesmann & Miller, 1994).

There are other outcomes. For example, frequent viewers may become immune to violence; they show less emotional reaction when viewing televised aggression (Cantor, 2000). Children who watch televised violence may also become indifferent to real-life violence (Drabman & Thomas, 1976). However, exposure to TV violence affects children differently at different ages, due to shifts in children's cognitive abilities. Children who can distinguish between fantasy and reality and between what is acceptable and unacceptable may react differently from those who cannot make these distinctions. Children who were told that a violent film clip was real (i.e., a newsreel of an actual riot) later reacted more aggressively than children who believed that the film was a Hollywood production (Atkin, 1983). As children develop and are able to make this fiction-reality distinction, many TV programs may have less impact (Bushman & Huesmann, 2001).

Nor is it just television that is the culprit. Children in the new millennium have other forms of media such as video and computer games that may influence aggressive behaviors as well (Comstock & Scharrer, 2006). The most notorious case of this possible effect is the 1999 Columbine High School incident in which two students shot several classmates. The shooters were described as being "obsessed with the violent video game Doom—in which the players try to rack up the most kills—and played it every afternoon" (Glick et al., 1999). Such an incident does not prove the case, but the evidence clearly suggests that violent games—like violent television—can increase aggression (Comstock & Scharrer, 2006). As in the case of other media, careful use can be beneficial but watching or playing too many violent games can lead to elevated aggression.

PEERS, GANGS, AND NEIGHBORHOODS   As we saw in Chapter 12, peers, especially deviant peers, can encourage other children's aggressive tendencies. One study found that if a child's friends engaged in disruptive behavior (e.g., disobedience or truancy), the child was more likely to engage in either overt (e.g., fighting) or covert (e.g., stealing) delinquent behavior both concurrently and a year later (Keenan, Loeber, Zhang, Stouthamer-Loeber, & Van Kammen, 1995; Thornberry, Krohn, Lizotte, Smith, & Tobin, 2003). Similarly, association with gangs is likely to increase violent activity (Thornberry et al., 2003). Individuals in a gang are three times more likely to engage in violent offenses than those not in a gang (Spergel, Ross, Curry, & Chance, 1989). Joining a gang increases a child's illegal and violent activity, and leaving one decreases these activities (Thornberry et al., 2003; Zimring, 1998).

Other environmental conditions such as living in a poor, high-crime neighborhood will increase aggression, but these effects are generally due to changes in family functioning associated with poverty, unemployment, or childrearing practices. Several researchers (Guerra, Huesmann, Tolan, Van Acker, & Eron, 1995; McLoyd, 1998) have found that poor African American mothers who experienced stress and lack of social support were more likely to display ineffective and coercive parenting; this in turn led to aggressive behavior in their children and greater gang involvement (Tolan, Gorman-Smith, & Henry, 2003). On the other hand, parents can help: For African American

Members of this California gang flash signs of solidarity and display their weapons.

adolescents, high levels of parental control (clear rules and consistent discipline) predicted decreased gang involvement over time—even after controlling for peer behavior (Walker-Barnes & Mason, 2001).

Control of Aggression

How can we control aggression in our children? One of the most commonly offered solutions, and yet one whose beneficial effects have been seriously questioned, is the notion of *catharsis,* popularly known as letting off steam. We look at the myth of catharsis first and then turn to cognitive modification strategies, in which parents and others may attempt to explain the consequences of aggression and to teach alternative problem-solving behaviors.

catharsis Presumably, discharging aggressive impulses by engaging in actual or symbolic aggressive acts that do not impinge on another person.

THE CATHARSIS MYTH   One of the most persistent beliefs about aggression is that if people have ample opportunity to engage in aggressive acts, whether in actuality or symbolically, a process known as **catharsis,** they will be less likely to act on hostile aggressive urges. The catharsis doctrine asserts that aggressive urges build up in an individual, and that unless this accumulating reservoir of aggressive energies is drained, a violent outburst will occur. The implications are clear: Provide people with a safe opportunity to behave aggressively, and the likelihood of antisocial aggression will be lessened. In clinical circles there is widespread belief in catharsis. People are often encouraged to express aggression in group-therapy sessions. There are punching bags on many wards in mental hospitals, and Bobo dolls, pounding boards, and toy guns and knives in many play-therapy rooms.

Advice columnists in the media have sometimes propagated a similar view. For example, Ann Landers once advised a reader that "Hostile feelings must be released" and went on to recommend that children be taught to vent their anger against furniture rather than against other people. Another reader replied: "I was shocked at your advice to the mother whose 3-year-old had temper tantrums. . . . My younger brother used to kick the furniture when he got mad. . . . He's 32 years old now and still kicking the furniture. . . . He is also kicking his wife, the cat, the kids, and anything else that gets in his way. . . . Why don't you tell mothers that children must be taught to control their anger? This is what separates civilized human beings from savages."

The research evidence on the value of catharsis tends to support the position of the Landers' reader. Most studies suggest that aggressive experiences may promote rather than "drain off" aggressive urges. In a classic test of the issue, Mallick and McCandless (1966) allowed third-grade children to shoot a toy gun after being frustrated by a peer who interfered with a task they were working on. Another group of children were allowed to work on arithmetic problems after the peer upset them. Then all the children were given a chance to express their aggression toward the peer who had upset them. The researchers used a rigged procedure in which children thought they were delivering a shock to the other child; in reality, of course, they were not delivering shocks to anyone. Whether the children, after being frustrated by the peer, had shot the toy gun or worked on math problems made little difference in their delivery of "shocks." Thus catharsis appeared to be insufficient to reduce aggression. As you'll recall from our discussion of research ethics (Chapter 1), such a study would be unlikely to be permitted today.

socially unskilled Being unskilled at solving interpersonal problems.

COGNITIVE MODIFICATION STRATEGIES   According to the social information-processing approach to aggression, aggressive children may behave in a hostile and inappropriate fashion because they are **socially unskilled**—that is, they're not very skilled at solving interpersonal problems (Dodge et al., 2006). In several studies (Crick & Dodge, 1994; Slaby & Guerra, 1988), researchers who asked children and adolescents to come up with solutions to conflict problems in social situations found that aggressive participants in the studies offered fewer solutions than their nonaggressive peers. Moreover, the proposals that aggressive children and adolescents made for resolving social disputes were generally less effective than the solutions less aggressive individuals offered.

Making aggressive children and adolescents aware of the negative consequences of aggression for themselves and others through modeling and explanations can reduce aggression, and teaching and encouraging children to use alternative problem-solving behaviors such as cooperation or turn taking have also been found to reduce aggression (Chittenden, 1942; Guerra, Eron, Huesmann, Tolan, & Van Acker, 1997). One study found that teaching children how to read another person's behavior more accurately—especially helping them to reduce if not wholly give up their biases toward making hostile attributions about other people and their behavior—led to a decrease in aggression among African American boys (Hudley & Graham, 1993). This approach is especially effective with reactively aggressive children, who are poor at reading other people's intentions. Empathy and sympathy also play important roles in the control of aggression. There is a clear link between sympathy, empathy, and lower levels of aggression in children, as well as less delinquency in adolescents (Laible, Carlo, & Raffaelli, 2000; Strayer & Roberts, 2004). Training children and adolescents to be more empathic and sensitive to the views, perspectives, and feelings of other individuals can be an effective way of controlling aggression (Guerra et al., 1997).

Some psychologists are putting these findings into practical use. Curricula have been developed to improve the social problem-solving skills of aggressive children, and some success has been reported in studies in both the United States and Sweden (Stevahn, Johnson, Johnson, Oberle, & Wahl, 2000; Weissberg & Greenberg, 1998). Recently, Aber, Brown, & Jones (2003) found that when teachers taught lessons in conflict resolution to their first and sixth graders, these children were less aggressive over time. The children made fewer hostile attributions, showed fewer conduct problems, and exhibited less aggressive behavior and more prosocial behavior. Box 14.3 describes a Swedish example of a successful school-based intervention program.

AGGRESSION PREVENTION: A MULTIPRONGED EFFORT

As we have stressed, many factors influence aggression and as a result, we need to consider many variables in changing levels of aggression. We conclude the chapter with a brief description of one national experiment in controlling aggression, known as Fast Track (Conduct Problem Prevention Research Group, 2004).

In four U.S. cities, over 200 first graders from poor families, over half of whom were from minority families, were treated to a variety of interventions to help prevent aggressive and antisocial behavior. Another 200 children served as the control group. Children in the intervention group participated in a program to help them with social problem solving, emotional understanding, and communication and to teach them how to self-regulate in the face of frustrating events. For the children with the most serious problems (10% of the group) there was a more intensive program involving academic tutoring, extra social skills training, and a parent intervention designed to improve parenting skills. It worked! Children in the intervention group were less aggressive, improved academically, and developed better social-emotional skills. Moreover, peer relationships improved; children got along better and were better liked by their peers. And parents benefited too: Their parenting skills improved and they were more involved in school-related activities. By the end of the third grade, 37 percent of the children in the program had no conduct problems—and 27 percent of the control group also had no such problems! Clearly, by mounting a broad-based assault on aggression, children's antisocial behavior can be reduced.

LifeMap CD

Bullying is a form of aggression that is receiving increased attention. Learn more about it by watching the video on "Characteristics of Children Who Bully" in Chapter 14 of your CD.

Box 14.3

Child Psychology in Action

REDUCING BULLYING IN SCHOOLS

Bullying is a worldwide problem. Parents and professionals in Europe, Australia, Japan, New Zealand, Canada, and the United States have all expressed concern about this school-centered problem (Smith et al., 1999b). What is bullying? "Bullying is aggression directed repeatedly and specifically toward a specific victim who is, in most cases, weaker than the bully" (Schneider, 2000, p. 106). Between 5 and 40 percent of children report being victims of bullying (Fonzi et al., 1999; Smith et al., 1999a). In fact, according to a Canadian observational study (Craig & Pepler, 1997), an incident of bullying occurs every seven minutes.

What can be done about this problem? One of the most ambitious efforts comes from Dan Olweus (1993), who launched a nationwide campaign to reduce bullying in schools in Norway and Sweden. The program enunciated four primary goals:

1. Increase awareness of the problem of aggression among the general public and provide schools with information to increase their knowledge about aggressive behavior

2. Get teachers and parents actively involved in the program

3. Develop clear classroom rules to combat aggressive behavior, such as the following:

   We will not bully others.

   We will help students who suffer bullying by others.

   We will include students who have been excluded.

4. Provide support and protection for the victims of aggression

Because it is well known that parents, teachers, and children themselves may all contribute to the levels and kinds of aggressive behavior children display, the program was designed to target all three groups. The program's main components were as follows:

A booklet was prepared for school personnel that described the nature and scope of aggression in the schools and that offered practical suggestions about what teachers and other school personnel could do to control or prevent aggressive behavior. For example, the booklet stressed the importance of increasing not only teachers' awareness of their responsibility to control interpersonal aggression in school but the awareness of other adult personnel as well and the importance of providing more adequate supervision of students during recess times. The booklet encouraged teachers to intervene in bullying situations, and to give students the clear message that "aggression is not acceptable in our school." In addition, the booklet's guidelines advised teachers to initiate serious talks with victims, their aggressors, and the children's parents if aggressive attacks persisted.

A four-page folder was designed to address all parents, giving them basic information and in particular offering assistance to parents of both victims and aggressors.

A videocassette was prepared, showing episodes from the everyday lives of two children who were victims of aggressive attacks.

Students were asked to fill out a short questionnaire anonymously, providing information about the frequency of aggressor/victim problems in the school and describing the ways teachers and parents had responded, including how aware they were of the problem and how ready to take action to deal with it.

Although the program was made available to all schools in Norway and Sweden, the researchers based their detailed evaluation of its effectiveness on data from about 2,500 students in 112 fourth- to seventh-grade classes in 42 primary and junior high schools in Bergen, Norway. Did this multilevel cross-national campaign aimed at reducing aggression work? The answer was clearly yes.

Both 8 and 20 months after the intervention program was initiated, the levels of aggressive behavior the researchers reported were markedly reduced. Fewer children reported being attacked by others, and fewer children reported that they themselves had acted aggressively. Peer ratings told a similar story: Classmates reported that both the "number of students being bullied in the class" and "the number of students bullying others" showed a marked drop. In addition, general antisocial behavior such as vandalism, theft, and truancy declined significantly, and student satisfaction with school life rose appreciably. Similar programs have been launched in many countries with at least some success (Smith et al., 1999b). Although we can't be sure just which aspect of this program (class rules, teacher awareness, parental intervention) was most important in achieving these effects, intervention clearly can make a difference!

Making the Connections 14

There are many links between concepts and ideas in one area of development and concepts and ideas in other areas. Here are some of the connections between ideas in Chapter 14 and discussions in other chapters of this book.

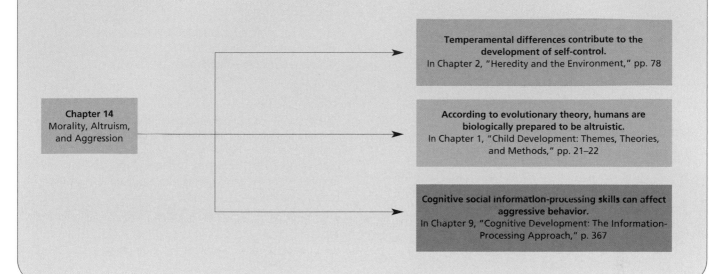

Chapter 14
Morality, Altruism, and Aggression

Temperamental differences contribute to the development of self-control.
In Chapter 2, "Heredity and the Environment," pp. 78

According to evolutionary theory, humans are biologically prepared to be altruistic.
In Chapter 1, "Child Development: Themes, Theories, and Methods," pp. 21–22

Cognitive social information-processing skills can affect aggressive behavior.
In Chapter 9, "Cognitive Development: The Information-Processing Approach," p. 367

SUMMARY

An Overview of Moral Development

- The socialization of moral beliefs and behavior is one of the main tasks in all cultures. Psychological research has focused on the three basic components of morality—the cognitive, the behavioral, and the emotional components.

- Research, which has in the past focused mostly on nonmoral, nonethical behaviors, is beginning to give more attention to other aspects of moral behavior such as sharing, helping, and cooperating with others.

Cognitive Theories of Moral Development

- Jean Piaget and Lawrence Kohlberg have both proposed theories involving invariant sequences of stages of moral development through which children progress as their cognitive capacities become increasingly sophisticated.

- Piaget proposed a three-stage approach: the **premoral stage,** the stage of **moral realism,** and the stage ruled by a **morality of reciprocity,** also called *autonomous*

morality. Moral absolutism and a belief in **immanent justice** and objective responsibility characterize moral realism. In contrast, children in the stage of reciprocity recognize intentionality and the arbitrariness of social rules in their moral judgments.

- Later research has shown that young children can distinguish between intentions and consequences if material is presented to them in a less complex manner. Many other factors affect children's judgments.

- Kohlberg proposed a theory of the development of moral judgment in which each of three levels contains two stages. The order of development is fixed and invariant, and movement is generally from lower levels—the **preconventional** and **conventional levels**—toward higher ones. Moral judgments continue to develop into adulthood, but few individuals reach the most advanced **postconventional level** (Stages 5 and 6).

- Gilligan has proposed that Kohlberg's model emphasizes a masculine orientation, focusing on rights and logic, whereas an interpersonal and caring orientation

637

may more accurately describe women's moral reasoning and judgments.

- Piaget emphasized the role of peers, and Kohlberg emphasizes the importance of varied opportunities for role taking in the development of moral judgments. Both views tend to minimize the influence of parents in the development of moral judgments. Data suggest that a combination of consistent discipline, involving reasoning and explanation, and concern with the feelings of others tends to produce more mature moral judgments in children. There is also evidence that maturity of moral reasoning is related to cognitive maturity.

- Educational programs in which students explore possible solutions to moral dilemmas may be useful in developing moral reasoning.

- Kohlberg's theory may be flawed in some ways. The theory's third level is controversial; relatively few people reach this level, and in particular, the sixth stage of moral reasoning. In addition, cross-cultural research suggests that Kohlberg's theory is culture-bound.

- Rules of **social convention,** such as table manners and forms of address, are distinct from moral rules and follow a different developmental course; in fact, children learn quite early to distinguish these kinds of rules from each other. Children also distinguish issues of morality and of social convention from those that belong to the **personal domain.** Moral judgments do not always lead to moral behavior, particularly among very young children.

The Behavioral Side of Moral Development

- **Self-regulation,** the ability to inhibit one's impulses and to behave in accord with social or moral rules, proceeds through three stages—the **control phase,** the **self-control phase,** and the **self-regulation phase.** In the latter phase, children become capable of **delaying gratification.**

- Children can learn to use strategies and plans to help them postpone rewards and attend to a task at hand. Specific verbal plans are more useful to children than general directions.

- Self-control or moral behavior is strongly influenced by situational factors. As the elements of situations and types of behavior assessed become more similar, moral conduct becomes more consistent. The development of **conscience** is linked with children's achievement of self-regulatory capacities. Both self-regulation and the development of conscience are linked with mother-child relationships that are positive, responsive, and cooperative.

- Some evidence indicates that children's early ability to regulate their behavior is related to later social and cognitive competence.

The Evolution of Prosocial and Altruistic Behaviors

- **Prosocial behavior** begins very early; helping, sharing, and exhibiting emotional reactions to the distress of others appear in the first and second years of life. **Altruism** may also appear quite early.

- Parents influence the emergence of **altruistic behavior** by their direct teaching in "distress" situations, by providing models, and by arranging for opportunities to behave in prosocial ways. Opportunities for children to take responsibility appear to lead to increased altruistic behavior. Similarly, role playing and **empathy** both contribute to the development of altruism and helping behavior.

- Girls tend to be more prosocial than boys, but gender differences depend on the type of prosocial behavior being expressed. Such differences are largest for expressions of kindness and consideration.

- Evidence of helping and sharing behavior in infrahuman animals leads some scientists to argue that evolution has prepared both humans and animals for prosocial behavior.

- Environmental factors, including the family, the mass media, and general cultural influences help shape prosocial and altruistic behaviors, but children probably learn such behaviors most often from modeling parental behaviors.

- Children's **prosocial reasoning** evolves over time through a number of stages including **hedonistic reasoning** and **needs-oriented reasoning,** as values and norms become increasingly internalized.

- Both empathy and perspective taking contribute to the child's capacity for altruistic behavior.

The Development of Aggression

- **Aggression** undergoes important developmental shifts: Younger children show more **instrumental aggression,** whereas older children display more person-oriented or **hostile aggression.** Children's ability to correctly infer intent in others—which varies among individual children—may account, in part, for these shifts. **Proactive aggression,** which is used to dominate another person, decreases across development more than **reactive aggression,** which occurs in response to being attacked.

- The expression of aggression changes over time, becoming more verbal as children mature, but the amount and quality of aggression remain fairly stable. Clear gender differences in aggression are evident, with boys instigating and retaliating more than girls. Girls are more likely to use **relational aggression** than boys, who are more likely to use physical aggression. Aggression is moderately stable over age for both sexes.

- Certain parental disciplinary practices, especially ineffectual and erratic physical punishment, contribute to high levels of aggression in children. Lack of parental monitoring of children is another contributor to later aggressive behavior or even serious delinquency.

- Biological influences on aggression include genetic, temperamental, and hormonal factors. All of these factors find expression in interaction with the environment.

- Association with deviant peers can increase the possibility that a child will engage in aggressive or

delinquent activities. Poverty and high-crime neighborhoods can also promote aggressive behavior.

- **Catharsis** theory, the belief that behaving aggressively against a safe target can reduce aggression, has been seriously challenged by research evidence. Strategies that involve cognitive modification may be more successful. Some aggressive children who are **socially unskilled** may be helped to learn more prosocial behaviors through teaching them how to read others' behavior more accurately and encouraging them to be more sensitive to the views and feelings of others.

- Increasing children's awareness of the harmful effects of aggression is an effective control technique, as are eliciting cooperation and improving problem-solving skills of aggressive children.

EXPLORE AND DISCUSS

1. Morality has behavioral, emotional, and cognitive components. When a child is confronted with a moral problem, how do you think that each of these components comes into play?

2. Altruistic behavior involves helping or assisting others. Do you think acting in this manner has a positive effect on the actor? On the person receiving the help? Explain your answers.

3. Violence in schools has received a great deal of attention in the mass media. How can we explain events such as the shootings, killings, and suicides perpetrated in 1999 by two students at Columbine High School in Littleton, Colorado? And what do you think we, as a society, can do to prevent future such tragedies?

Donald Martin (20th century). *Stripes.*

15.

Developmental Psychopathology

Throughout the first fourteen chapters of this book we have spoken mostly about the development of the normal child. In this introduction to developmental psychopathology, we turn to an intriguing but often painful and poorly understood area of development—the psychological disorders of childhood. Shifting our focus from the normal to what is considered abnormal, we now pursue an understanding of why some children develop problems or difficulties that require special treatment and intervention. We address such questions as, what is "abnormal"? How have psychologists defined abnormality? What is unique about a developmental approach to psychopathology? How do risk factors, vulnerabilities, and protective processes interact to promote or protect against the development of abnormal behavior? How ought we classify the psychological disorders of childhood?

In this exploration, we consider a few specific psychological disorders that may occur in children. Some of these disorders are not uncommon, but others are relatively rare. Children with problems such as attention deficit/hyperactivity disorder appear unable to control their own behavior and are excitable, in constant motion, and generally disruptive. In contrast, children with problems such as depression seem to control their behavior too tightly, internalizing things that trouble them and having difficulty expressing their distress. Finally, children with problems such as autistic disorder evidence extreme disturbances that invade many spheres of functioning. Fortunately, disorders such as autism are relatively rare.

In discussing these and other disorders, we ask what may cause these problems and how we can treat different kinds of disorders effectively. We also consider the efforts now being made to prevent children from developing serious psychological disturbances. To introduce you to the topics of this discussion and to illustrate the range of problems that children can exhibit, we offer the following brief case studies:

> Victor had always been a "handful" in his parents' eyes. As an infant, he cried frequently, woke up at all hours, and soon gave up his afternoon nap in favor of exploring tabletops and other forbidden territories. As a toddler, he raced

around from dawn until dark, always seeming to run when others walked. When he was 4, one of his favorite games was scrambling onto the roof of the family car and fearlessly diving off into his father's tired arms.

During times like these, Victor's parents would try to discipline him by reasoning with him, but that tactic rarely worked. Instead, they would tolerate—and often secretly enjoy—his antics until they reached their limit, at which point they found it necessary to simply force Victor to comply. Although Victor exhausted them, his parents never considered him to have a real problem—until he started school. At the end of first grade, Victor's principal called his parents in for a conference. The principal told them that Victor wasn't paying attention in class, was consequently falling behind in his work, and required more supervision than his teacher said she could give. In addition, his antics in the classroom were distracting other children and disrupting the entire class. The principal suggested that Victor's parents talk to their pediatrician about how to do something to change Victor's behavior before he started the second grade. If not, the school was going to consider placing Victor in their "resource room" next year—a special class for "emotionally disturbed" children.

Emi was beginning to worry her mother. She was a very well-behaved and helpful 12-year-old, but to her mother Emi seemed unhappy. She really didn't have any close friends, and her mother wondered why the phone wasn't constantly ringing for Emi as it had for her when she was Emi's age. To her mother, Emi seemed to be spending too much of her time alone in her room and not enough time socializing. More than that, her mother was concerned about Emi's schoolwork. Her straight As in sixth grade had slipped down to mostly Bs and even one C for the first term in her new junior high school, and Emi had dropped out of the one thing that her mother thought she really seemed to enjoy—orchestra. Her mother tried to talk with Emi about how she was feeling, but both times she tried to approach her, Emi first got angry at her mother's "bugging her" and then ended up running to her room in tears. Her mother blamed Emi's unhappiness on Emi's father and their divorce six years earlier. But what could she do about that now?

Pauli was becoming a source of grave concern to his parents. At age 3, he had not yet spoken his first, and they could not ignore his unusual behavior. He spent hours every day sitting and spinning a top that he had played with since he was 2, and he became violently upset if the toy was taken away from him. Pauli showed no interest in other children and would jerk away from his mother or father if they tried to give him a hug. Even as an infant Pauli had resisted being held and stiffened at physical contact, and his mother could not remember a time when they had really cuddled. She commented that holding Pauli was more like holding a log than a baby since he did not mold or cling to her shoulder the way most babies do. His rejection of his parents didn't seem to be one of anger; rather it almost seemed as if it were physically painful for Pauli to be touched by someone.

Although Pauli had been an exceptionally good baby, his failure to speak and endless repetitive play gradually became more distressing to his parents. The pediatrician's calm reassurances when Pauli was younger had now ceased, and he suggested that Pauli be taken for an evaluation at a special hospital for exceptional children in a city 200 miles away. Pauli's parents were frightened by this possibility. Would they be asked to leave him at the hospital, and, if so, for how long?

All the children described in these brief case histories are exhibiting some behavior that concerns their parents. Victor's loving parents could tolerate and even appreciate his boundless energy, but his uncontrolled activity is causing trouble for him, his teacher, and his classmates in school. Does Victor have a special problem that differentiates him from his peers and may require special attention? Should he be placed in a special classroom? His teacher seems to think so. As for Emi, her apparent unhappiness may be a problem, but we don't really know how she feels about herself and her life. Is she feeling depressed, helpless, and angry at her mother and father for getting divorced? Or is she going through a "stage," feeling confused and lonely as she enters puberty? Perhaps Emi is simply experiencing the normal feelings of a quiet girl who is going through a transition to a new school. Of the three children, Pauli is exhibiting the most disturbing behavior. But why is he behaving in this unusual manner? Is Pauli suffering from some sort of an emotional problem, or is he perhaps mentally retarded? We will meet Victor, Emi, and Pauli again as we explore the complexities of developmental psychopathology.

THE DEVELOPMENTAL APPROACH TO PSYCHOPATHOLOGY

When a child—a person still developing cognitively, emotionally, and behaviorally— appears to be experiencing unusual psychological distress, to understand and help this young person we need to invoke principles of what is called developmental psychopathology. *Psychopathology* is the study of disorders of the *psyche*—that is, of the mind. **Developmental psychopathology,** which combines the study of psychopathology with the study of development, involves the investigation of the origins, course, changes, and continuities in disordered or maladaptive behavior over the individual's life span. The principles of developmental psychopathology are applicable to people of all ages, for people change and go on changing as long as they live. Life transitions—such as graduation, a new job, marriage, childbirth, divorce, and retirement—all have their effects on people's functioning and have the potential to create shifts in developmental trajectories. Here, of course, we are concerned with the usefulness of these principles for understanding the special influences that biological, emotional, social, and environmental factors have on the young developing person.

The unique approach of *developmental* psychopathology is embodied in four basic principles (Cicchetti & Toth, 2006; Cummings et al., 2000). First, because, as we've pointed out, child disorders occur in a developing organism, *we must take into account the role of development in interpreting the symptoms, searching for the origins, and understanding the course of any given disorder.* The frequency and patterns of symptoms in behavior disorders vary across the course of development. For example, children may suffer depression as they move from preadolescence to adolescence. Although there are no gender differences in the incidence of depression among preadolescents, depression increases notably in adolescent girls. Depression in young children is typically characterized by social withdrawal and a *dysphoric* (unhappy, dejected, anxious, and/or self-doubting) mood. However, childhood depression is often masked by other, more strictly behavioral symptoms such as hyperactivity, bed wetting, learning problems, and antisocial behavior. Young children—especially those between the ages of about 8 and 11—do not manifest the general slowing of mental and physical activity or the motivational deficits that depressed adults typically evidence (Gelfand & Drew, 2003). In depressed adolescents, suicidal thoughts, which are quite uncharacteristic of younger children, begin to appear, and the depressed adult's symptoms of low self-worth, guilt, depressed mood, negative self-attributions, and inactivity also emerge (Lewinsohn, Rohde, & Seeley, 1993). The increase in depression and suicidal behavior at adolescence is probably associated with the onset of pubertal changes, advances in cognitive development, and the many stresses and adaptive challenges young people encounter in this developmental period (Hammen, 1997, 2002).

developmental psychopathology The investigation of the origins, course, changes, and continuities in disordered or maladaptive behavior over a person's life span.

Depressive episodes are not uncommon in teenage girls and may well be linked to the changes of puberty and the stresses and challenges of adolescence. When depression lingers and is associated with expressions of guilt, low self-worth, or suicidal ideation, however, knowledgeable adults need to intervene to prevent the adolescent from sinking into self-destructive behaviors such as the abuse of drugs.

Second, *psychopathology in a child must be viewed in relation both to children's normal development and to the major developmental tasks and changes that occur as children mature.* By definition, psychopathology is concerned with deviations from normal behavior, and developmental psychopathology is concerned with deviations from normal attainments of people of the same age as the person under consideration. A critical issue is how to distinguish between developmental disruptions within the normal range and those reflecting more serious disordered behavior (Rutter, 1996). As we will see, all children have some problems at some times in their lives, and at some points in development certain problems occur with such frequency as to be regarded as normal. For example, although temper tantrums are common in 2-year-olds, they would be viewed as somewhat deviant in adolescents.

Third, *developmental psychopathology studies the earliest precursors of disordered behavior.* Although psychopathology is less clearly defined and less stable in younger children than in adults, early behaviors are often associated with later disturbances. Two such warning signs are noncompliant behaviors and rejection by peers, as we discuss in Chapters 11 and 12. These two precursors of later antisocial behavior may also be related. Young children who are resistant, coercive, nonconforming, and confrontational with parents are also likely to be insensitive, unskilled, aggressive, and hence unaccepted in peer relations. Peer rejection eventually may drive children to associate with a deviant peer group and to become involved in antisocial behavior. Thus, although neither early noncompliance and coercive behavior nor rejection by peers are necessarily pathological, these events can be associated with more serious later conduct disorders such as stealing, setting fires, drug abuse, and physical violence (Dishion et al., 2000; Gelfand & Drew, 2003).

The fourth and last principle points out that *there are multiple pathways to both normal and abnormal adjustment over the course of development* (Cicchetti & Toth, 2006). Many factors—genetic, environmental, and experiential—interact to deflect a child either into a deviant trajectory or back into a normal developmental pathway. To the degree that we can identify risk factors of all sorts in the young child, we may be able to prevent many children from following an abnormal path. We return to this notion at the close of this exploration, when we discuss the efforts at preventive intervention undertaken in the field of community psychology.

WHAT IS ABNORMAL?

Defining abnormal psychological behavior is no easy task. Many cultural, societal, ethnic, and personal values affect what we consider normal and abnormal, and all of these values vary among regions, nations, and subcultures within nations. However, because some behavior is so unusual that it causes great distress either to the actor or to those with whom she interacts, or places one or more people in danger, we need at least a working model. We begin with the medical approach to defining and classifying psychological disorders. Then we look at two common views: abnormality as different from most common behaviors and abnormality as different from what we hold as ideal behavior. We then consider a factor of great importance in child psychopathology—the fact that disorder in children is often judged by the adults who are closest to them. And finally we consider how likely it is that childhood disorder will continue into adulthood.

The Medical Model

Many who have studied abnormal behavior have attempted to further our knowledge of the psychological problems that children experience by borrowing from medical science—or the field of psychiatry—ideas about the causes and treatments of emotional problems. Unfortunately, however, using the term *psychopathology* to describe the unusual or abnormal behaviors of childhood leads many people to believe that such behaviors reflect some form of *disease* of the mind analogous to a physical illness. Indeed, the medical model generally assumes that the psychological disorder—like a physical disease—resides within the individual and results from abnormal physiological or *intrapsychic* (mental) processes.

Most child psychologists—both researchers and clinicians—feel that the medical model offers an inappropriate, or at least insufficient, means of explaining much of what is called abnormal child behavior. Critics of the medical model argue that what we call developmental psychopathology is better thought of as a collection of problems in living that are caused by environmental circumstances. At the same time, however, it is important to recognize that research is gradually delineating genetic roots of problems such as *autism* and *attention deficit/hyperactivity disorder* (discussed later in the chapter) even though the expression of these and other disorders may be dependent on environmental conditions (Ding et al., 2002). Such problems are said to be abnormal on the basis of social judgments rather than objective medical tests. In general, people's view of abnormality depends on their individual and cultural values. What is abnormal are those behaviors, thoughts, and feelings that a group of individuals agree are deviant. At the same time, although this view may be preferable to the physical-illness analogy, you can easily see that there are problems in this definition. For example, different groups of people use different criteria to define abnormality, and these criteria may often conflict. To understand developmental psychopathology, we must first gain an awareness and an understanding of such diverse views of how to define abnormal child behavior.

Abnormality as Deviation from the Average

The term *abnormal* literally means "departing from the normal"; therefore, one way of defining abnormality is to view as abnormal any behaviors or feelings that differ in some degree from the average. This method of defining abnormality is referred to as the *statistical model*. Although there are problems with the statistical definition of abnormality, this model is often used as a guide to what constitutes deviance. For example, as we discuss in Chapter 10, part of the definition of mental retardation offered by the American Association of Mental Retardation (AAMR) stipulates that children may be considered retarded if their IQ test scores are two standard deviations below the mean. On the Wechsler Intelligence Scale for Children–Revised, a score of 100 is average, and one standard deviation is equal to 15 points; by this rule, an IQ score of less than 70 indicates mental retardation.

The statistical model may seem appealing because it is so clear-cut, but things are not so simple as the model may suggest. Although it may work for something like intelligence, which is measured on a numerical scale and can be either lower than normal or higher, it doesn't work for a concept like normality-abnormality. There is no statistically measurable mean, and if there were, what would be "above" and what would be "below"? Deviation from a mean can go in either direction. By this rule, if we were to consider an IQ of 100 "normal," we would have to consider scores of both 70 and 130 "abnormal." Most people would be understandably reluctant to call superior cognitive functioning a sign of abnormality! Another problem with the statistical model is that it gives us no guidance as to how much of a difference is abnormal and under what circumstances differences matter. Why choose two standard deviations below the mean to determine mental retardation—why not one? or three? Indeed, as we explain in Chapter 10, the AAMR includes three factors in considering a diagnosis of mental retardation—IQ score, whether or not disability emerges before the age of 18, and the child's relative ability to function adaptively in the real world.

Abnormality as Deviation from the Ideal

An alternative to the statistical model is to define abnormality as a deviation from the ideal. Rather than define a normal or healthy average, this model identifies an ideal healthy personality and claims that deviations from this ideal state are abnormal. The main problem with this approach is the question of how to define the ideal healthy personality. Personality theorists such as Freud and Maslow have suggested guidelines for what they propose to be the ideal personality, but who is to say they are right? What do you consider to be ideal adjustment? And are you willing to say that anyone who falls short of this ideal is abnormal? Are you prepared to accept someone else's judgment of what ideal functioning is? Your parents' definition perhaps? The answers to these questions are clearly in doubt. To define such an ideal seems too big a task for anyone, no matter how brilliant or how highly regarded, to assume.

Elements of this concept of abnormality, however, are seen in Western definitions of psychopathology. In Western cultures, people are expected to work hard, to love forever, and, further, to be happy in achieving these two goals. When someone falls short of these cultural criteria (e.g., a high school dropout), Western societies become concerned. However, in Eastern and other cultures, other ideals may prevail. Box 15.1 discusses some differences in how adults in the United States and Thailand perceive the significance of childhood behavior problems. This cross-cultural study demonstrates clearly that implicit ideals affect cultural definitions of abnormality.

The Social Judgment of Child Psychopathology

Consider the information provided by a brief excerpt from a case history. Tom lives with his aunt and cousin and is enrolled in elementary school. He often skips school, however, because he hates it, and he frequently sneaks out of the house at night to meet friends. Just before he ran away from home, Tom's thinking was along these lines:

> Tom's mind was made up now. He was gloomy and desperate. He was a forsaken, friendless boy, he said; nobody loved him; when they found out what they had driven him to do, perhaps they would be sorry; he had tried to do right and get along, but they would not let him; since nothing would do them but to be rid of him, let it be so; and let them blame him for the consequences—why shouldn't they? What right had the friendless to complain? Yes, they had forced him to it at last; he would lead a life of crime. There was no choice.

What can you conclude from this very brief account about the normality or abnormality of Tom's behavior? Does Tom differ sufficiently from the average to be considered abnormal according to the statistical model? Certainly he deviates from many people's ideals, including, we might presume, the ideals of some of the people with whom Tom interacts. Put yourself in the position of a psychologist who has been asked to evaluate Tom's general adjustment. Are you suspicious that he is exhibiting some form of developmental psychopathology, or are you more inclined to dismiss his behavior as nothing to worry about?

Let us provide you with some help in weighing your decision. The "case" of Tom is actually an excerpt from Mark Twain's *The Adventures of Tom Sawyer* (Twain, 1976, p. 493). Is Tom Sawyer abnormal? Why, no indeed, he's just the opposite: Tom represents the prototype of the ideal all-American boy. He is hardly a candidate for psychotherapy! But taken out of context, Tom seems quite deeply troubled, and he is proposing to leave his home, quit school, and take up what most would consider a clearly deviant lifestyle. Had someone with some degree of authority heard his thoughts, he might well have been judged abnormal and remanded for formal treatment or rehabilitation. Clearly, something other than a child's behavior in any given situation affects people's social judgments as to what constitutes abnormal behavior.

Because children rarely refer themselves for formal help but rather are identified by an adult as disturbed and in need of the attention of mental health professionals,

Box 15.1

Perspectives on Diversity

THAI AND AMERICAN VIEWS ON CHILD BEHAVIOR PROBLEMS

Cultural values may determine whether adults consider a child's psychological problems to be serious enough to require professional help. John Weisz and colleagues (Lambert, Weisz, & Knight, 1989; Weisz et al., 1988, 1995) investigated adults' concern about overcontrolled and undercontrolled child behavior problems in Thailand and the United States. The teachings of Thai Buddhism propose that some unhappiness in life is inevitable, that all things change for the better, and that an individual's behavior on any given occasion is not reflective of an unchanging personality.

In contrast, Americans may be sensitized to view children's problems as more serious than members of other cultures consider them to be. In schools, colleges, and universities and every day in the media Americans are exposed to theories and ideas about child psychology, childrearing, and deviant behavior. In the study by Weisz and his colleagues (1988, 1995) parents, teachers, and psychologists in the United States and Thailand read vignettes describing two children, one with symptoms of overcontrolled behavior, such as shyness, fearfulness, depression, worrying, and dependency; the other with problems in undercontrol, such as aggression, cruelty, disobedience, and lying. The adults were asked to rate each child on the seriousness of the problems, their level of concern about the problems, whether the children's behavior would improve over time, and which child had a greater need for professional help.

As Figure 15-1 shows, consistent with their beliefs, Thais rated both children's behaviors as less serious and worrisome and more likely to improve than the U.S. adults judged them. Cross-national differences were less extreme in psychologists' responses than in the responses of parents and teachers, perhaps because their professional training exposed them to these childhood problems more often. Childhood psychopathology is to some extent in the eye of the beholder, and the beholder's perspective is modified by his cultural context.

Figure 15-1   Are Thai children's problem behaviors less of a problem?

Rating the seriousness of children's problems (several behaviors combined) on a scale of 1 to 7 (from "not serious at all" to "very serious"), in general Thai adults thought such behaviors less problematic than did American adults (a). Asked "How serious is this child's problem?" Thai parents and teachers differed from U.S. ones, but in both countries psychologists' ratings were similar (b).

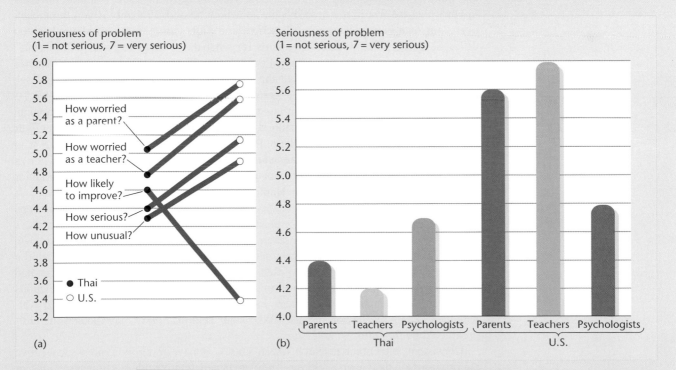

Source: Weisz, et al., 1988.

psychologists must constantly be alert to factors other than the child's behavior itself. Thus, therapists must always ask themselves, Has this child really a problem or has the adult who has referred him to me a distorted view of the child for some reason? Three sets of factors that may subtly influence a referring adult's perception are the characteristics of the child, the characteristics of the adult, and contextual influences.

CHARACTERISTICS OF THE CHILD   Parents and other adults are more likely to perceive and respond to a behavior as deviant if it occurs in boys, in children who have been temperamentally difficult infants, in unattractive children, or in children with a history of other forms of deviance (Cummings et al., 2000; Putnam, Sanson, & Rothbart, 2002). In addition, people are less likely to judge a behavior displayed by a socially skilled child as abnormal than they are to make the same judgment about similar behavior in a socially unskilled child (Gelfand & Drew, 2003). Social judgments of abnormality are influenced by behaviors other than the ones that are being judged directly.

One reason that you, the psychologist, are probably not inclined to view Tom Sawyer as having a psychological problem, even when he misbehaves, is that you know other, positive things about Tom. He's smart—he gets other boys to finish painting the fence he's supposed to paint. He's attractive, and he's head over heels in love with Becky Thatcher. Moreover, although his Aunt Polly often tweaks him by the ear, not even she can get really angry at him.

CHARACTERISTICS OF THE REFERRING ADULT   Certain characteristics of the adult who has identified a child as disturbed can distort one's judgment as to whether a child's behavior is normal or abnormal. Anyone, including teachers and health professionals, may express a view about a child that, although it may reveal something real about the child's behavior, may also say something about the adult. Huck Finn, Tom's best friend, could tell you that different adults have different views of the same children. The Widow Douglas apparently saw potential for good in Huck that the rest of the townspeople somehow missed. Probably if you think back over your own experiences in grade school and high school, you can remember that different teachers had different standards for what they considered acceptable behavior. And suppose you, the psychologist considering Tom's case, had a sibling who ran away from home, disappearing into the streets of a large city; even you might see danger in Tom's ruminations that apparently wasn't there.

Although it might seem that parents would know their children better than anyone, not uncommonly parents have a distorted view of their children's behavior and of their children's need for psychological help. Parents who are depressed or abusive or who refer their children to a clinic for help are likely to report their children's behavior as much more negative and deviant than observations of the child's actual behavior support (Cicchetti & Toth, 2006; Hammen, 2002). Consider a study by Bauer & Twentyman (1985), in which the researchers examined abusive parents' attributions about the causes of their children's positive and negative behaviors. The researchers showed abusive and nonabusive mothers a series of photographs of either their own child or an unfamiliar child acting in a variety of social situations in which children were either (a) transgressing against each other, (b) engaged in a play situation that had a destructive outcome, or (c) involved in a competitive situation that had an ambiguous outcome. They then asked the mothers a series of questions that required them to evaluate the children's behavior and also asked them to explain why they thought the children acted as they did.

Consistent with other research (Azar, 2002), abusive mothers expressed negative expectations of their own children. They attributed their children's transgressions or failures to internal, stable causes—that is, they saw them as reflecting continuing traits and thus as likely to be repeated. On the other hand, when their own children were successful and when other children were the transgressors or failed at a task, these mothers attributed other children's behaviors to external, unstable causal factors. They implied that these behaviors were specific to the particular situation and thus unlikely to be repeated. Nonabusive mothers offered almost the exact opposite pattern of causal explanations: They emphasized their children's positive attributes as leading to success, and they suggested that either special circumstances or unusual behaviors were the causes of their children's transgressions.

These findings indicate that adults' judgments of children's behavior involve complex processes. It is not enough for a therapist to help a parent see a child as behaving in a more positive way; the parent also must attribute the child's behavior to internal, stable causes. For example, if a parent who has referred a child to a psychologist concludes that the child is doing better "only because he is in therapy," the parent is unlikely to maintain a positive view of the child. Ultimately, the goal must be for the parent to see the child as doing better as a result of internal, stable factors: It's "because he's basically a good kid."

Finally, it has been found that two different adults, whether they are mother and father or parent and teacher, frequently disagree about whether a given child has a problem. Trained professionals often cannot even agree with each other as to what constitutes developmental psychopathology; thus it is not surprising that laypeople frequently disagree.

THE CHILD'S ENVIRONMENT   The context in which adults observe a child's behavior also influences their judgments of developmental psychopathology. That is, they may judge the same behavior differently according to the demands of different situations. Let's go back to Victor, whom we described at the beginning of this introduction to child psychopathology. Victor's parents judged his inattentive and overactive behavior tiresome, but they accepted it in their home. But when Victor began school, the demands and stricter standards of the classroom context led teachers to judge his behavior abnormal. Victor's behavior did not change, but the setting in which it occurred did.

Contextual influences on the evaluation of children's psychological adjustment include still other factors. For example, a child's social background, race, and prior behavior can create contexts that influence the way adults judge a current behavior. Such factors often lead people to tag children with value-laden labels: "retarded," "a child from a broken home," "delinquent," "high-risk." Unfortunately, such labels can create a context in which others perceive and respond to a child's behavior in a way that has adverse consequences for the child's development. Consider Tom Sawyer and Huck Finn. Tom was well regarded by the community, whereas Huck was considered an outcast, someone no self-respecting family would allow their children to associate with. Huck's father was the town drunk, but Tom's Aunt Polly was a devout churchgoer. Do people view the act of a child from a lower-status family as more problematic than that same act committed by a child from a mainstream family? Some police officers apparently do: When arrested for similar offenses, more lower-class minorities than middle-class whites are sent on to court (Moeller, 2001). Such treatment may lead to detrimental self-labeling and expose children to additional risks that push them toward more deviant behavior.

Although it is important to recognize that adults' views of what constitutes developmental psychopathology may reflect distorted judgments, we must not overstate the potential for distortion. Adults' judgments *are* influenced by a child's actual behavior! And there are children with psychological problems whose behavior is abnormal according to all standards—statistical, ideal, and social. The remainder of this exploration is devoted to some of the more important behavior disorders of childhood.

Table 15-1 Common problem behaviors of children and adolescents

Problem Behavior	1½–2 years	3–5 years	6–10 years	11–14 years	15–18 years
Inattentiveness	x				
Demanding attention constantly	x	x			
Refusal to do things when asked	x	x			
Overactivity	x	x	x		
Specific fears	x	x	x		
Temper tantrums	x	x	x	x	
Negativism		x			
Oversensitivity		x	x		
Lying		x	x		
Jealousy			x	x	
Excessive reserve			x	x	
Moodiness				x	
School achievement problems			x	x	x
Skipping school					x
Cheating on exams					x
Depression					x
Drinking					x
Smoking					x
Drug misuse					x
Early sexual activity					x
Trespassing					x
Shoplifting					x
Other minor law violations					x

Source: Adapted from Gelfand, Jensen, & Drew, 1997.

Continuity over Time

Whether or not a particular behavior problem is viewed as abnormal depends greatly on the child's age and the probability that the behavior will continue over time and be manifested in some form of adult disorder (Rutter, 1996). Some problems, such as bed-wetting, thumb-sucking, temper tantrums, and tics, decline with age; others, such as nail-biting, increase from early childhood to adolescence; still others, such as disturbing dreams and nightmares, peak in preadolescence at about age 10 and then decline (Gelfand & Drew, 2003). Table 15-1 displays some problem behaviors that, when they occur at the ages indicated, are fairly common among normal children and thus not necessarily indicative of serious trouble. On the other hand, some problem behaviors are cause for concern. As we will see, childhood disorders such as hyperactivity, autism, and overly aggressive and antisocial behaviors are more likely to be associated with later adult dysfunction (Dodge et al., 2006; Gelfand & Drew, 2003).

Many investigators are interested in the changes over time in behavioral manifestations of particular disorders as well as in processes and factors that maintain problem behaviors. Caspi and colleagues (1987) studied the stability of behavior in children who at age 8 had been identified as having an irritable social interactional style, manifested in temper tantrums, explosiveness, and verbal abuse (see Chapter 14). Boys who were irritable school-age children were, 30 years later, undercontrolled, moody, and unsociable. As adults they were also less dependable, less ambitious, and less productive, as reflected in erratic work patterns and downward occupational mobility. For both males and females, early explosive, ill-tempered behavior was associated with marital problems and divorce, and for women, with marriage to a man of low socioeconomic status and with an irritable, inept parenting style.

Caspi and colleagues propose that the stability of maladaptive behaviors is sustained by two related processes: cumulative continuity and interactional continuity. **Cumulative continuity** is similar to niche picking (Chapter 2). Specifically in this case, however, the child promotes experiences or selects environments that support or reinforce maladaptive predispositions. Cumulative continuity also involves the notion of *transactional stressors* — for example, being irritable increases the chance that stressful life experiences such as school dropout and job loss will occur, leading to increased frustration and irascibility. **Interactional continuity** involves interaction with others and another cyclical process: People who are irritable are likely both to evoke and to be the targets of hostile responses from those with whom they interact. It seems likely that both genetic and experiential factors contribute to continuities and discontinuities in problem behavior.

CLASSIFYING CHILD PSYCHOPATHOLOGY

Given our many problems in defining abnormal child behavior, it is not surprising that psychiatrists (physicians who specialize in psychological disorders), psychologists, and others disagree over how to classify the different forms of developmental psychopathology. Until quite recently, childhood psychological problems were viewed as variations of recognized adult disorders, and the diagnostic categories developed for adults were applied to children as well (Achenbach, 1995). The irony of viewing disturbed children as munchkins with adult problems is striking, for most theories of mental and emotional disturbance view psychological functioning during adult life as a product of child development!

Although many authorities argue that the seeds of abnormal development are sown in childhood, researchers and others have spent far less time studying abnormal behavior in children than adult psychological disorders. As you know by now, children are not simply little adults either physically or psychologically, and recent years have seen an increasing interest in the psychological problems unique to childhood. We look next at two important means of assessing and classifying childhood psychopathology: the diagnostic approach and the empirical method.

The Diagnostic Approach

The diagnostic approach to assessing and classifying psychopathology is rooted in the medical tradition. In medicine, a **diagnosis** is useful or valid if it conveys information about the **etiology,** or cause, of a disorder, about its likely course, or about the kind of treatment likely to be effective in curing or alleviating the disorder. The classification of illnesses is based on information gleaned from a number of sources, including diagnoses and courses of treatment. Because the classification of childhood

cumulative continuity The tendency to seek out experiences and environments that support or reinforce maladaptive predispositions. *Transactional stressors*, such as chronic irritability, fuel a cycle of experiences like job loss which, in turn, heightens irritability.

interactional continuity The tendency for negative temperamental or personality characteristics to evoke negative responses from others, which then reinforce the negative characteristics.

diagnosis The identification of a physical or mental disorder on the basis of symptoms and of knowledge of the cause or causes of the disorder and its common course. A diagnosis may also include information about effective forms of treatment.

etiology In medicine and psychiatry, the cause or causes of a specific disorder.

Table 15-2   Some examples of *DSM-IV*'s "Disorders Usually First Diagnosed in Infancy, Childhood, or Adolescence"

Mental Retardation	*Attention-Deficit and Disruptive Behavior Disorders*
Mild mental retardation	Attention deficit/hyperactivity disorder
Moderate mental retardation	Conduct disorder
Severe mental retardation	Oppositional defiant disorder
Profound mental retardation	*Feeding and Eating Disorders of Infancy or Early Childhood*
Learning Disorders	Rumination disorder (regurgitation and rechewing of food)
Reading disorder	*Tic Disorders (stereotyped motor movements or vocalizations)*
Mathematics disorder	Tourette's disorder (multiple tics)
Disorder of written expression	Chronic motor or vocal tic disorder
Motor Skills Disorder	*Elimination Disorders*
Developmental coordination disorder	Encopresis (incontinence of feces)
Communication Disorders	Enuresis (bed-wetting)
Expressive language disorder	*Other Disorders of Infancy, Childhood, or Adolescence*
Phonological disorder (difficulties in articulating speech)	Separation anxiety disorder
Stuttering	Selective mutism
	Reactive attachment disorder of infancy or early childhood
Pervasive Developmental Disorders	Stereotypic movement disorder
Autistic disorder	
Rett's disorder (usually associated with severe or profound mental retardation)	
Childhood disintegrative disorder (usually associated with severe mental retardation)	

Source: Based on American Psychiatric Association, 2000.

psychopathology is still in its infancy, many diagnostic categories devised to characterize specific disorders are based largely on description—including such things as patterns of behavior and specific kinds of thoughts and feelings—and few can make firm statements about either etiology or treatment.

The diagnostic classification system most widely used in the field of psychiatry has been compiled by the American Psychiatric Association (APA). The current *Diagnostic and Statistical Manual* (American Psychiatric Association, 2000) is the fourth classification scheme that APA has developed (it is commonly referred to as *DSM-IV*). Table 15-2 displays some examples of *DSM* categories that relate specifically to childhood disorders. This section has grown considerably over the more than 50 years since *DSM-I* was published in 1952, a sign of the increased interest in psychological disorders of childhood. Today *DSM-IV* contains 43 diagnostic categories applicable to children, 41 more than were included in *DSM-I*. Inasmuch as this change reflects a trend away from viewing children as little adults, it is to be applauded.

DSM-IV is not without its critics, however (Campbell, 1998, 2002). Perhaps its biggest problem is that many of its diagnostic categories are neither valid nor reliable (Beutler & Malik, 2002). **Diagnostic reliability** is a measure of how often two or more clinicians arrive independently at the same diagnosis of a particular disorder. Without reliability no system of classification can be valid. If two psychologists cannot

diagnostic reliability A measure of how often two or more clinicians arrive independently at the same diagnosis of a particular disorder.

agree, for example, on whether a child is clinically depressed, we cannot learn much about depression in childhood. If psychologist Smith decides that Emi, one of the children we discussed at the beginning of the chapter, suffers from depression, but psychologist Jones determines that Emi is merely experiencing the normal ups and downs of preadolescence, we learn nothing. In one study, researchers found that diagnosticians within a large hospital and medical center agreed on a diagnosis of depression quite well, but when diagnostic results in sites across the United States were compared, agreement on this diagnosis was poor (Keller et al., 1995). Even when a physician or other professional diagnoses the same person on two occasions, six months apart, the two diagnoses may differ (Carson, 1991). One study found that clinicians diagnosing depression in a child agreed only about 40 percent of the time, far below an acceptable level of diagnostic reliability (Cantwell, Russell, Mattison, & Will, 1979). On the other hand, the diagnostic reliability of some of *DSM-IV*'s categories—such as the diagnosis of attention deficit/hyperactivity disorder, which we will discuss shortly—is acceptably high. The psychiatric profession is endeavoring to improve the reliability of the *DSM*'s diagnostic categories and has developed training guides for diagnosticians (Ottoson, Ekselius, Grann, & Kullgren, 2002).

The Empirical Method

An alternative to the diagnostic approach we have discussed is the empirical or rating-scale method (Achenbach, 1995, 1997). Using this method, an adult who is familiar with a child who displays signs of emotional disturbance—usually a parent or a teacher—rates a large number of problem behaviors according to whether and to what degree the child displays the behaviors. Investigators then use statistical techniques to determine which problem behaviors are associated with one another. There is considerable overlap among the classifications arrived at by the diagnostic and the empirical methods, but there are also many disparities (Achenbach, 1995). Researchers may also have peers rate the likelihood that other children will engage in risky behaviors (Tinsley, Holtgrave, Erdley, & Reise, 1997) in an approach similar to the sociometric techniques we discuss in Chapter 12. Because peers influence children's risky behavior, this approach is a particularly useful way of identifying children and adolescents at risk for harmful behaviors such as smoking and using alcohol and other drugs.

Both classification methods generally agree on the broader, major categories, such as "mental retardation," but often disagree—both with each other and within their own systems—on narrower subcategories, such as "mild mental retardation" and "moderate mental retardation" (see Table 15-2). The finer the distinction one tries to draw between collections of symptoms and behaviors, the more difficult the task. If symptoms and behaviors were always exactly the same, with enough study it should be possible to draw these distinctions once and for all. But human beings are infinitely variable—so the work goes on!

SOME PSYCHOLOGICAL DISORDERS THAT AFFECT CHILDREN

Because the *DSM*'s approach to the psychological disorders of childhood is not entirely in line with the way child psychologists view these disorders, developmentalists have modified the *DSM* classification system for their use. Many times throughout the book, we talk about the developing child's need to internalize parental and societal values and standards and to learn how to control not only her behaviors but her inner thoughts, feelings, and attitudes. This aspect of the developmental process can be especially challenging for some children, for either biological (inherited) or

Table 15-3

How children's fears wax and wane

Ages	Fears
0–12 months	Loss of support; loud noises; unexpected, looming objects; strangers
12–24 months	Separation from parent; injury; strangers
24–36 months	Separation from parent; animals, especially large dogs; darkness
36 months–6 years	Separation from parent; animals; darkness; strangers; bodily harm
6–10 years	Imaginary beings; snakes; injury; darkness; being alone
10–12 years	Social evaluations; school failure; thunderstorms; ridicule; injury; death
Adolescence	Peer rejection; school failure; war and other disasters; family issues; future plans (especially in boys)

undercontrolled disorders A group of psychological disturbances in which a child appears to lack self-control and to act out in a variety of ways, through such behaviors as noncompliance, disobedience, and aggression.

overcontrolled disorders A group of psychological disturbances in which a child appears overly controlled, withdrawing from others, lacking spontaneity, and generally appearing to be not a happy child.

environmental reasons. (In some cases, this challenge continues to be a difficult one throughout a person's life span.) And whereas some children respond to the challenge with inadequate attempts to control their behavior, others seek to control their behavior too rigidly.

We find it useful, therefore, to discuss some representative child disorders in terms of the degree to which they reflect the nature of the control children exert over their behavior. In **undercontrolled disorders,** the child fails to control his behavior in such a way as to suit the demands of a given environment. Examples of undercontrolled behaviors include noncompliance, disobedience, rule violation, and aggression. These kinds of behaviors are particularly characterized by their impact on those people in the child's environment. Although ultimately these behaviors hurt the child himself, they are initially most disturbing to those about him. Because undercontrolled behaviors are defined largely by this negative impact on others, and because most childhood psychological disorders are defined by adults' social judgments, it is not surprising that undercontrolled behavior disorders are the most frequently reported of all the psychological problems of childhood. In this section, we discuss two of these types of disorders: conduct disorders, and attention deficit/hyperactivity disorder.

In contrast to undercontrolled disorders, **overcontrolled disorders** tend to have a more adverse effect on the child himself, who seems to withdraw from others, lack spontaneity, and, in general, to be not the "happy child" every parent wants. Various negative emotions such as fear, anxiety, and sadness characterize such children, who seem restrained and overly controlled in the way they relate to others. *Phobias* (excessive fears) may cause considerable discomfort for some children and their families; happily, research indicates that 80 percent of children's phobias disappear within two years, even without treatment (Gelfand & Drew, 2003). (Table 15-3 lists some fears that are common at different stages of normal development.) However, some fears and phobias are more long lasting, persisting across the life span. These include *acrophobia* (fear of heights) or fear of physical illness. Anxiety disorders characterized by a general apprehensiveness and low self-confidence can also last into the adult years (Ollendick & King, 1998).

As a representative of overcontrol we will discuss childhood depression. This disorder is not listed in Table 15-2, because *DSM-IV* covers depression in childhood in its discussion of *Mood Disorders* in adults, as it also covers the expression in children of anxiety and phobias under the adult category of *Anxiety Disorders.* For several reasons, it is often difficult to identify overcontrolled problems in children. Because the definition of childhood psychopathology depends on an adult's social judgment, and because it is much more difficult for adults to evaluate children's inner feelings (like sadness) than it is to judge their overt behavior (like aggression), the diagnostic labels for overcontrolled disorders are often vague and controversial. Finally, it is important to remember that undercontrolling and overcontrolling behaviors often occur together. For example, the child who acts out and displays aggression may also experience depression and use drugs. So even though we discuss them separately, keep in mind that "bad things" as well as good ones often occur together (Kim, Conger, Elder, & Lorenz, 2003). **Comorbidity** is the term often used to describe this co-occurrence of two or more problem behaviors (Pennington, 2002).

Although the problems of delinquency, hyperactivity, and depression are serious, some children exhibit even more marked forms of psychological distress that do not really fit under either the overcontrolled or undercontrolled designations. The term **pervasive developmental disorders** describes a collection of disorders characterized by gross deficits in many areas of cognitive, emotional, and social development that are linked with severe and pervasive impairment of social interaction and communication skills (American Psychiatric Association, 2000). Children with these kinds of disorders are extremely disturbed. Although these disorders have sometimes been referred to as *psychoses* (broadly, disturbances in which the person's functioning is so maladaptive that he or she is said to be out of touch with reality), the unusual behaviors seen in these children are even more general and incapacitating than those in most psychoses.

Pervasive developmental disorders have often been confused with schizophrenia, a common and seriously incapacitating disorder that, like some of these disorders, is characterized by loss of contact with reality. However, schizophrenia is also characterized by hallucinations, delusions, and other kinds of thought disorders not found in the pervasive developmental disorders. In addition, these two kinds of disorder have very different ages of onset: The pervasive developmental disorders are evident in the first few years of life, whereas schizophrenia most commonly emerges in late adolescence or early adulthood. Schizophrenia is not found with any great frequency in children.

In this introduction to psychopathology, we discuss one of the most widely known pervasive developmental disorders, that of autistic disorder (also known as *early infantile autism* and *childhood autism*). Autism has been one of the most baffling of childhood disturbances, but, as we will see, some progress has been made in treating the children who suffer from it.

comorbidity The co-occurrence of two or more problem behaviors.

pervasive developmental disorders Childhood disorders characterized by gross deficits in many areas of cognitive, emotional, and social development that are linked with severe and pervasive impairment of social interaction and communication skills.

Conduct Disorders

A **conduct disorder** is characterized by a repetitive and persistent pattern of behavior in which a child or adolescent violates the basic rights of others or major age-appropriate societal norms or rules (American Psychiatric Association, 2000). (See Table 15-4 for the *DSM-IV* description of conduct disorders.) Thus it is considered a disorder of *undercontrol*. When a young person exhibits this kind of behavior primarily in the company of peers, the problem is termed a *socialized* conduct disorder, whereas when the behavior occurs primarily when the child is alone, the disorder is said to be *unsocialized*. More than three times as many boys as girls are reported to exhibit conduct disorders (American Psychiatric Association, 2000; Moffit et al., 2001; Reid et al., 2002). In our discussion of aggression in Chapter 14, we touch on some of the problems that can contribute to the evolution of conduct disorders.

RULE VIOLATIONS When rule breaking involves a violation not just of norms or others' rights but of the law, the youth is said to be *delinquent*. **Delinquency** is not a psychological term but is the legal designation for juvenile behavior that violates the law. Juveniles can be judged delinquent for two types of offenses. A youth may be charged with a **status offense,** such as possession of alcohol, if she is under

conduct disorder A disorder characterized by a repetitive and persistent pattern of behavior in which a young person violates the basic rights of others or major age-appropriate societal norms or rules.

delinquency Juvenile behavior in violation of the law.

status offense Illegal behavior in an underage offender.

Table 15-4

DSM-IV-TR diagnostic criteria for conduct disorder

Source: Reprinted with permission from the *Diagnostic and Statistical Manual of Mental Disorders*, Copyright 2000. American Psychiatric Association.

Repetitive and persistent pattern of behavior in which the basic rights of others or major age-appropriate societal norms or rules are violated, as manifested by the presence of three (or more) of the following criteria in the past 12 months, with at least one criterion present in the past 6 months:

Aggression to People and Animals

1. Often bullies, threatens, or intimidates others

2. Often initiates physical fights

3. Has used a weapon that can cause serious physical harm to others (e.g., a bat, brick, broken bottle, knife, gun)

4. Has been physically cruel to people

5. Has been physically cruel to animals

6. Has stolen while confronting a victim (e.g., mugging, purse snatching, extortion, armed robbery)

7. Has forced someone into sexual activity

Destruction of Property

8. Has deliberately engaged in fire setting with the intention of causing serious damage

9. Has deliberately destroyed others' property (other than by fire setting)

criminal offense Behavior that is illegal.

the age at which drinking is legal. **Criminal offenses** are illegal regardless of the age of the individual. Criminal offenses committed by juveniles are no small matter. The bad news is that they accounted for 17 percent of all criminal arrests and 16 percent of arrests for serious violent crime in 1999 (Children's Defense Fund, 2001). The good news, however, is that the arrest rate for juveniles has dropped 23 percent since 1995 (see Figure 15-2). The juvenile murder arrest rate has declined even more rapidly, dropping over 55 percent since the late 1980s (Children's Defense Fund, 2001). In

Figure 15-2   Young people and violent crime

Beginning in the mid to late 1980s, arrests of youths aged 10 to 17 for violent crimes (robbery, aggravated assault, rape, or murder) began to climb from about 300 per 100,000 youth each year to nearly 500 per 100,000 youth annually. About 1995, however, the rate of these arrests began to drop, and by 1999 it had almost returned to the earlier level.

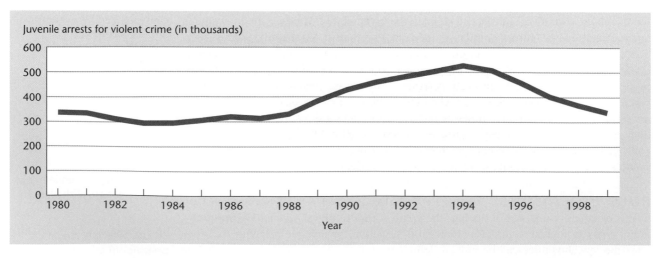

Source: Children's Defense Fund, 2001.

Table 15-5

DSM-IV-TR criteria for substance abuse

Source: Reprinted with permission from the *Diagnostic and Statistical Manual of Mental Disorders,* Copyright 2000. American Psychiatric Association.

A. A maladaptive pattern of substance use leading to clinically significant impairment or distress, as manifested by one (or more) of the following, occurring within a 12-month period:

   (1) Recurrent substance use resulting in a failure to fulfill major role obligations at work, school, or home (e.g., repeated absences or poor work performance related to substance use; substance-related absences, suspensions, or expulsions from school; neglect of children or household)

   (2) Recurrent substance use in situations in which it is physically hazardous (e.g., driving an automobile or operating a machine when impaired by substance use)

   (3) Recurrent substance-related legal problems (e.g., arrests for substance-related disorderly conduct)

   (4) Continued substance use despite having persistent or recurrent social or interpersonal problems caused or exacerbated by the effects of the substance (e.g., arguments with spouse about consequences of intoxication, physical fights)

B. The symptoms have never met the criteria for Substance Dependence for this class of substance.

addition to harming others, youthful offenders are themselves victims of violent crimes. Although the number of child victims of violent crime has declined in recent years, recent data show that 22 percent of violent crime victims in the United States are juveniles (Children's Defense Fund, 2001). Boys, except in the case of sexual assault, are more likely to be victims of violent crime than girls (Moeller, 2001)—for males the increase was about 33 percent, for females about 77 percent. African American youth are more likely than European Americans to be the victims of violent crime; in 1994 about 13 percent more black youth were victimized than white youth.

DRUG ABUSE *DSM-IV* considers *substance-related disorders* a category separate from the disorders diagnosed in childhood—largely because drug abuse is a serious and pervasive problem among adults. However, we discuss substance abuse here because among children and adolescents this problem—again, one of undercontrol—has been and continues to be the cause of much concern. **Substance abuse** is the excessive use of legal or illegal drugs in such a way as to interfere with one or more important areas of functioning in life: work, intimacy with another, and general interpersonal and social relationships. Table 15-5 lists the *DSM-IV* criteria for a diagnosis of substance abuse. Drug use among youths rose dramatically in the late 1960s and early 1970s, and then began a decline. However, 10- to 15-year trends in eighth, tenth, and twelfth graders' use of both legal and illegal drugs show both that decline and a resurgence, primarily in the use of alcohol and illicit drugs such as marijuana, cocaine, heroin, and hallucinogens, beginning in the 1990s (Federal Interagency Forum on Child and Family Statistics, 1997). We do not yet know what has caused this rise in drug use. We have evidence that those who use drugs may be starting at younger ages (Johnston, O'Malley, & Bachman, 1997). As Figure 15-3 shows, Leshner (2001) found that even 12-year-olds were likely to use drugs such as inhalants, and that 13- and 14-year-olds were using marijuana. Among the twelfth graders sampled in the National Youth Survey, boys were considerably more likely to drink regularly and to use illicit drugs than girls, but girls were just as likely as boys to smoke cigarettes. Whites were more likely than Latinos to smoke cigarettes and to use illicit drugs, and of the three groups, blacks were least likely to use these substances. Nearly twice as many white as African American adolescents are smokers (39% versus 20%), and about 33 percent of Hispanic teenagers were smokers (Children's Defense Fund, 2001).

substance abuse The excessive use of legal or illegal drugs in such a way as to interfere seriously with one or more important areas of functioning in life: work, intimacy with another, general interpersonal and social relationships.

Figure 15-3

Young people's use of illegal drugs in the late 1990s

According to one study, the percentages of adolescents who used drugs rose fairly steadily over the three-year period of the study, although the proportion of teenagers who were users was still relatively low. Note that at 12, young people preferred inhalants, but by 13, their use of marijuana began to rise, becoming their favorite by the age of 14. Inhalants gradually declined in use between ages 13 and 14.

Source: Leshner, 2001.

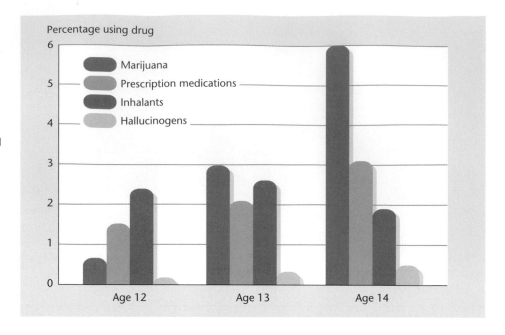

A number of surveys, notably school-based surveys of high school seniors, support these racial-ethnic findings. These surveys have indicated that Native Americans, particularly those living on reservations, show the highest drug-use rates. Mexican American and white American youths are the next highest, and Asians and blacks have the lowest rates of use (Oetting & Beauvais, 1990).

Table 15-6 lists some factors that, in general, influence children's use or nonuse of drugs. The relative importance of these factors in a specific case depends on the drug of choice. Regardless of whether an adolescent is Latino, African American, or European American, one of the best predictors of his smoking is whether his best friend smokes (Gritz, 2004). In addition, a number of factors contribute to the likelihood that a particular child will become a frequent drug user. Children who are undercontrolled, impulsive, risk taking, moody, and who overreact to minor frustrations are more likely to become frequent drug users (Epstein, Griffin, & Botvin, 2001). Heavy drug use by parents and peers is related to children's use of both alcohol and marijuana; peers and situational factors are somewhat more influential in children's marijuana use (Smith, 2001; Willis & Yeager, 2003). Also related to marijuana use are poor academic records, truancy, minor delinquency, and the desire to experiment. Finally, the rates of drug use in a particular school will affect the chance that an individual student there will use drugs. The more peers in the school who use tobacco and alcohol, the more opportunities there are for others to begin to use these substances. Thus individual students are more likely to use these substances in high-drug-use schools than in low-use ones (Cleveland & Wiebe, 2003).

The use of illicit drugs seems to depend both on situational factors and on a young person's response to psychological problems such as depression, anxiety, low self-esteem, or rejection (Gelfand & Drew, 2003). If a youth uses marijuana to resolve such personal or psychological problems rather than as a response to social situations, she is likely to go on to use hard drugs. Serious delinquent offenses, resistance to adult authority, drug dealing, social alienation, and the need to increase self-insight are also associated with the use of illicit drugs. The more adolescents experience such risk factors, the more likely they are to be involved in drug abuse (Willis & Yeager, 2003). Across all types of legal and illegal drugs, a close relationship with a responsible, stable family helps to buffer adolescents against drug abuse (Gelfand & Drew, 2003).

Table 15-6 Some characteristics of young users and nonusers of drugs

	Users	Nonusers
Cultural Influences		
Attitudes toward drug use	Acceptance	Low acceptance
Drug use in society	High exposure	Low exposure
Contextual and Neighborhood Influences		
Crime	High crime	Low crime
Employment	Unemployment	Low unemployment
Schools	Inadequate schools	Adequate schools
Availability of drugs	Readily available drugs	Drugs are not readily available
Educational and career opportunities	Lack of legitimate opportunities	Legitimate opportunities available
Family Influences		
Drug use	Parents are users (especially mothers)	Parents do not use drugs
Religion	Not religious	Religious faith
Values	Nontraditional values	Traditional values
Family conflict	More family conflict	Less family conflict
Siblings	Siblings are users	Siblings do not use drugs
Peer Influences		
Drug use	Best friend is user	Best friend does not use drugs
Peer power	Peers are more influential	Peers are less influential
Individual Factors		
Opportunity	Opportunity to take drugs	No opportunity to take drugs
History	Good experiences with drugs	Unpleasant drug experiences
Adjustment	Possible adjustment problems	Possible superior adjustment
Attitude toward authority	More rebellious and questioning	More conforming
Attitude toward deviance	More tolerant of deviance	Less tolerant of deviance
Deviance	More deviant behavior	More conforming behavior
Attitude toward school achievement	Less concerned about school achievement	More concerned about school achievement
Self-esteem	Low self-esteem and low self-efficacy	High self-esteem and self-efficacy
Mood	Depressed mood	Not depressed
Coping skills	Poor coping skills	Adequate coping skills
Biological susceptibility to drug addiction	Higher biological susceptibility to drug addiction	Low biological susceptibility to drug addiction

Sources: Based on Gelfand & Drew, 2003; Gelfand et al., 1997; Petraitis, Flay, & Miller, 1995.

What is the common pathway to serious drug use? Few adolescents start with hard drugs, such as cocaine; they begin with drugs such as alcohol and tobacco, which are easy to obtain. In the next step they go from these legal drugs to marijuana, which is illegal, and from there some move on to more serious illegal drugs such as LSD, cocaine, or, in a few cases, narcotics such as heroin. "Only a small minority of teenagers eventually obtain the most dangerous drugs, but their route from experimentation to heavy drug use is highly predictable. Most begin with familiar substances of abuse and stop there while a few are drawn to increasingly dangerous and expensive drug habits" (Gelfand et al., 1997, p. 153). As in the case of aggression and violent behavior, those who start their drug careers early (before age 15) are at the highest risk for developing a serious drug problem and for continuing to use drugs into adulthood (Hawkins et al., 1997). As is true of many other disorders, drug abuse in adolescence is related to a series of associated adverse events such as school dropout, instability in early marriage and childrearing, and high rates of divorce (Gelfand & Drew, 2003).

Finally, it is important to underscore that problem behaviors such as drug use and delinquency often co-occur; an adolescent who smokes marijuana may also be the one who has trouble in school, steals cars, and gets into fights with peers. In short, although we have discussed disorders in separate categories, in real life different forms of psychopathology often occur together.

TREATING CONDUCT DISORDERS The most successful approaches to treatment for conduct disorders have employed social learning and behavioral techniques (Reid, Patterson, & Snyder, 2002). Parents can be trained to teach and reinforce appropriate behavior and to use nonreinforcement and what is called **time out**—removing children from a situation or context in which they are acting inappropriately until they are able and ready to act in an appropriate manner—to suppress undesirable behaviors. These approaches have been found to reduce rates of conduct disorders among aggressive, delinquent boys (Patterson, 2002) as well as to reduce disruptive behavior in classrooms (Walker, 1995). A variety of prevention programs involving parent training, home visits, social skill training, academic tutoring, and classroom intervention have been mounted, and early returns are promising (Conduct Problems Prevention Research Group, 2004; Weissberg & Greenberg, 1998; see also "Aggression Prevention: A Multipronged Effort," in Chapter 14).

Despite the great concern over youth substance abuse, our social policies and intervention programs have not dealt effectively with this problem. The best-run programs—which typically involve detoxification, total abstinence from a drug, and intensive educational and counseling efforts over a period of weeks or months—have much higher recidivism rates than they would like. These rates, according to Newcomb and Bentler (1989), can range as high as 70 percent. Moreover, drug-abuse rates remain unacceptably high, and treatment programs are not available for the majority of adolescents (Roche, 1998). In the case of tobacco use, for example, Shiffman (1993) estimated that one treatment program produced abstinence from smoking for one year in about 38 percent of the young people in the program; thus 60 to 70 percent of those in treatment had relapsed by the end of that year. As we will see later in the chapter, prevention efforts to reduce substance use in preadolescence can be successful in stemming the onset and level of substance use (Spoth, Redmond, & Shin, 2003). Box 15.2 discusses gender and ethnic differences in drug abuse and offers some suggestions for useful interventions.

Using or abusing drugs, having unprotected sexual intercourse, and engaging in delinquent behavior occur so often in the same individuals that some investigators have argued that these behaviors involve a single syndrome of problem behavior (Jessor, 1992). Continuing research in this area may give us some answers.

Attention Deficit/Hyperactivity Disorder

Some authorities question whether conduct disorders differ from the disorder called attention deficit/hyperactivity disorder. The essential feature of **attention deficit/ hyperactivity disorder (ADHD)** is a persistent pattern of inattention and hyperactivity or impulsivity that is far in excess of such behaviors observed in children at

time out Removing children from a situation or context in which they are acting inappropriately until they are able and ready to act appropriately.

attention deficit/hyperactivity disorder (ADHD) A childhood disorder characterized by a persistent pattern of inattention and hyperactivity or impulsivity that far exceeds such behaviors observed in children at comparable levels of development.

Box 15.2

Perspectives on Diversity

ETHNIC AND GENDER DIFFERENCES IN DRUG USE

Recent studies of the use of legal and illicit drugs among elementary and junior high school students suggest that European American students may be more likely to use alcohol and tobacco than African American students and to initiate drug use earlier. Across ethnic groups, although boys are more likely to drink than girls, girls are just as likely to smoke cigarettes as boys. Among students in elementary grades, no ethnic or gender differences were found with respect to the students' use of marijuana.

Catalano, Hawkins, Krenz, and Gillmore (1993) followed about 1,700 students from the first to the fifth grade, asking questions about drug use and measuring family bonding and aggressive and delinquent behavior over time. These researchers found that European American children were more likely than African American children to use both alcohol and tobacco. Among European Americans, boys used more tobacco and alcohol than girls, but among African Americans there were no significant differences in drug use between girls and boys. European Americans also initiated drinking and smoking earlier than African Americans. There were neither ethnic nor gender differences in the use of marijuana by these youngsters.

At the same time, African American children were more likely to report having siblings whose behavior was deviant. Teachers tended to rate African American students as more aggressive than European Americans, and African American students were more likely to rate themselves as evidencing delinquent behaviors. Interestingly, they also rated their parents as stricter and as strongly discouraging them from using drugs. This strong family management by parents may account for the children's slower awakening to drug use. Parental discipline may also to some degree reflect the necessity to control siblings' behavior and to ensure that their other children—those in the present study—were more restrained. These children's tendency to rate themselves as delinquent might also reflect their realization of their teachers' perceptions of them, which, in turn, could be related to the teachers' knowledge of sibling behavior.

In this study a number of risk factors appeared to affect children's behavior in regard to drug use. For example, the less available drugs were, the less antisocial behavior the children demonstrated. In addition, the more adequate parents' management of the family was, and the more after-school activities the children were able to participate in, the less likely they were to use either alcohol or tobacco.

Similar findings emerged from a study of cigarette smoking by Robinson and Klesges (1997). Among seventh graders, European Americans were more likely to smoke than African Americans. Indeed, 13 percent of European American students smoked regularly, whereas among African Americans, only 2 percent said they were regular smokers. These researchers found gender differences as well: In both groups, boys were more likely to smoke than girls.

European Americans were more than twice as likely to report smoking among family members than were African Americans. African Americans reported stronger feelings of social support and success and less risk-taking behavior, although this was more true of girls than of boys. African American children were more likely to disapprove of smoking and, as in the Catalano study, to report that their parents specifically discouraged them from smoking.

Taking a slightly different approach, Farrell and Danish (1993) studied the relationship between emotional restraint, peer models, and peer pressure in seventh and eighth graders, 92 percent of whom were African American. These researchers found emotional restraint—which they defined as the ability to suppress aggression, control impulses, accept responsibility, and be considerate of others—to be closely and negatively related to drug use. Their findings of gender differences—girls showed more emotional restraint than boys, whereas boys were more likely to engage in drug use and reported more peer pressure to do so—supported the significance of the emotional restraint factor.

According to Catalano and colleagues (1993), it may be useful to direct prevention programs focused on alcohol and tobacco use at European American elementary school children particularly. At the same time, these researchers point out that because drug-related problems may simply arise later in African American children, intervention efforts need to target these children as well, perhaps capitalizing on the factors that inhibit their early drug use. Farrell and Danish (1993) recommend interventions designed to help boys and male adolescents to deal more effectively with anger and frustration as a way of helping them to resist seeking an outlet in drug use.

Table 15-7

DSM-IV-TR definition of ADHD

Source: Reprinted with permission from the *Diagnostic and Statistical Manual of Mental Disorders,* Copyright 2000. American Psychiatric Association.

Criterion	Description
Criterion A	The essential feature of attention-deficit/hyperactivity disorder is a persistent pattern of inattention and/or hyperactivity-impulsivity that is more frequent and severe than is typically observed in individuals at a comparable level of development.
Criterion B	Some hyperactive-impulsive or inattentive symptoms that cause impairment must have been present before age 7 years, although many individuals are diagnosed after the symptoms have been present for a number of years.
Criterion C	Some impairment from the symptoms must be present in at least two settings (e.g., at home and at school or work).
Criterion D	There must be clear evidence of interference with developmentally appropriate social, academic, or occupational functioning.
Criterion E	The disturbance does not occur exclusively during the course of a pervasive developmental disorder, schizophrenia, or other psychotic disorder and is not better accounted for by another mental disorder (e.g., mood disorder, anxiety disorder, dissociative disorder, or personality disorder).

comparable levels of development (American Psychiatric Association, 2000; see also Table 15-7 for the DSM criteria for the diagnosis of ADHD). ADHD—another problem of undercontrol—leads to difficulties in the home, the classroom, and the peer group (American Psychiatric Association, 2000; Barkley, 1998). A variety of studies have demonstrated that hyperactive children not only run into conflict with adults in their environment but perform more poorly than other children in school, present serious classroom-management problems to the teacher, have difficult peer relations, and often think of themselves as being "no good" (S. B. Campbell, 2000). Perhaps even more important, in at least 60 percent of these children, some of these problems persist into adolescence and early adulthood (Weiss, Hechtman, & Weiss, 1999). Adults who have been hyperactive children often describe themselves as inattentive, restless, impulsive, depressed, and lacking in self-esteem. In many cases, however, adults complain less about attentional problems because, in part, they select jobs and activities that require minimal amounts of sustained attention (Weiss et al., 1999). Attention deficit disorders occur more frequently and are more sustained in boys than in girls. Minimally, these disorders are seen in twice as many boys as girls, and depending on the particular cluster of symptoms, they may trouble nine times as many boys as girls (American Psychiatric Association, 2000).

How does a hyperactive child differ from other children? The case of Victor presented earlier illustrates many of the problems hyperactive children encounter. Like Victor, most hyperactive children go undiagnosed until they enter school or some highly structured environment, although many have a history of being born prematurely (Anderson et al., 2003), being overactive infants whose biological functions such as sleeping and eating were irregular and who progressed to become tireless and fearless preschoolers (S. B. Campbell, 2000). ADHD is usually first identified in elementary school because of the combination of the stricter demands of the

A prime characteristic of hyperactive children is their inability to attend for long or to stay with a specific activity or task, particularly one that requires them to sit quietly and concentrate.

school environment and the particular cluster of problem behaviors hyperactive children exhibit.

CHARACTERISTICS OF THE DISORDER   Children with this disorder display overactivity, poorly sustained attention, impulsivity, and problems with adherence to instructions and rules (Barkley, 1998; Reiff & Tippins, 2004). The *DSM* distinguishes three subtypes of ADHD, namely *inattentive, hyperactive,* and *impulsive* or *combined.* Probably the most marked symptom that parents and teachers notice about hyperactive children is their inappropriately high activity level. Note, however, that hyperactive and nonhyperactive children differ more in the *quality* of their activity level than in the *quantity* of their activity (S. B. Campbell, 2000). For example, research indicates that in free-play situations, hyperactive children cannot be discriminated from their peers in terms of activity level (Barkley, 1998). It is in structured situations like the classroom, which demand controlled, task-oriented behavior, that activity level discriminates the two groups (Barkley, 1998). The hyperactive child's behavior is likely to disturb peers and further disrupt the classroom (Barkley, 1998; S. B. Campbell, 2000). The behaviors of the typical ADHD child help account for the fact that 50 to 60 percent of these children are rejected by their peers (Henker & Whalen, 1999). As Gelfand and Drew (2003) note, "A child who fidgets, taps his foot, is unable to keep his hands to himself, and who talks out of turn may constantly come to the attention of the teacher and be perceived as overly active. A child who is engaged in the same amount of motor activity but who is diligently working is judged to be normally active" (p. 204).

The hyperactive child's inappropriate activity appears to diminish during adolescence; unfortunately, other clinically important problems persist through these years (Weiss et al., 1999). One of the most persistent problems that hyperactive children exhibit is *inattention,* which becomes especially problematic in school, where teachers may have to expend considerable effort to keep them interested in learning tasks (S. B. Campbell, 2000; Zilleson, Scheverpfug, Fallgatter, Strik, & Warnke, 2001). Note that this inattention reflects an inability to sustain attention and stay focused on a task, not an inability to screen out irrelevant distractions (Barkley, 1998).

The third major problem some hyperactive children experience is *impulsivity.* Hyperactive children often seem to act before they think. Impulsivity, like inattention, appears to be a relatively stable aspect of hyperactivity; it can be seen in the frequent accidents of the preschooler and the poorly thought-out test answers of the school-age child. It may continue into adult life, where more frequent changes in residence and a higher incidence of automobile accidents are found among formerly hyperactive children (American Psychiatric Association, 2000; S. B. Campbell, 2000).

Children with attention deficit/hyperactivity disorder also have deficiencies in *rule-governed behavior,* finding it difficult to follow rules that parents, teachers, or others have constructed to describe behavioral contingencies—that is, what will happen if certain things occur. Such a rule might be, "When your little brother takes one of your toys, don't hit him, or you will be sent to your room." In responding to such rules, hyperactive children have problems in *tracking.* That is, although these children may be able to inhibit undesirable behavior in response to a rule when it's first given them, they are unable to use these rules to track or maintain their behavior over time (Barkley, 1998).

Hyperactive children tend to do poorly in school. It is likely that their relatively poor academic performance is, in large part, the result of the problems they typically have with impulsivity, overactivity, and inattention and the difficulties they experience in following rules. As measured by both classroom assessments and standardized achievement tests, hyperactive children typically function one to two years below grade level despite normal IQs (Barkley, 1998; Pisecco, Baker, Silva, & Brooke, 2001). It's fairly common for a hyperactive child to be retained in the same grade or placed in special classes as a consequence of academic and behavioral problems.

LifeMap CD

The "Attention Deficit Disorder" video in Chapter 15 of your CD provides additional insights into what it's like to have this condition and how it can affect the entire family.

Although many hyperactive children continue to have academic problems throughout their school years, ordinarily they achieve occupational status and satisfaction equal to that of their peers (S. B. Campbell, 2000). Perhaps this is because they find jobs that reward their strengths and make fewer demands in their areas of weakness.

CAUSAL FACTORS IN ADHD

What is the cause of this frustrating collection of problems, and how can we help hyperactive children? Among the potential answers to these questions, no single and unquestionable solution has been discovered. Research on this topic has been complicated because so many explanations for the etiology and treatment of hyperactivity have been offered, and some speculations test the limits of believability. Of the more credible explanations of hyperactivity, one suggests that the problem has a biological origin while the other implicates the environment.

Biological Factors   For years, the leading biological explanation of hyperactivity suggested that this particular cluster of problems was caused by some form of *minimal brain dysfunction,* a controversial term that bases the notion of brain dysfunction on what are called "soft" neurological signs such as abnormal reflexes. Many children with ADHD do not show clear signs of brain damage (Barkley, 1998; Dinn, Robbins, & Harris, 2001). However, modern computer imaging techniques such as computed tomography (CT) and magnetic resonance imaging (MRI) scans have revealed brain abnormalities in three areas: the frontal lobes, the basal ganglia, and the cerebellum (Casey, 2001; Voellor, 2001). Recall our discussion of these brain imaging techniques in Chapter 5. This recent tentative evidence supports the position that some children with attention deficit/hyperactivity disorder may have some brain dysfunction. Different individuals respond in diverse ways to the same level of stimulation and require different levels of stimulation for optimal functioning. Some people are overreactive and may require less stimulation, others are underreactive and may seek out higher levels of stimulation. Barkley (1998) has suggested that children with ADHD are underreactive and that their excessive activity and impulsive behavior are attempts to obtain more stimulation. It is hypothesized that neurotransmitter abnormalities in the brain underlie hyperactivity, but this proposal is still speculative.

psychostimulant medications Drugs, such as amphetamines and caffeine, that increase alertness and attention as well as psychomotor activity.

The strongest piece of evidence for some type of brain dysfunction was thought to be the paradoxical effect on hyperactive children of **psychostimulant medications**—drugs such as caffeine, amphetamine, or methylphenidate (one brand name is Ritalin) that, in adults, increase alertness and are sometimes used, legally or illegally, to heighten arousal, increase energy, and combat fatigue (Whalen, 2001). When these drugs were first used with hyperactive children, in the 1960s, their effect in *slowing down* such children was seen as paradoxical. However, a classic study by Rapoport and her colleagues (Rapoport et al., 1978) showed that psychostimulants had the same effect on normal children—and on adults given *small* dosages—that they had on hyperactive children. The medication appears to increase attention and, as a result, reduce extraneous activity, enabling the child to focus on a task and complete it. Today, psychostimulants are a common treatment for ADHD children, some of whom refer to these medications as their "arithmetic pills" (Gelfand & Drew, 2003). However, use of these drugs is still controversial and in 2005 Canada banned Adarol, an ADHD psychostimulant medication.

Largely because of the discovery that psychostimulant effects on children were not, after all, paradoxical, many researchers in the field have now abandoned the minimal brain dysfunction hypothesis (S. B. Campbell, 2000). At present, perhaps the most popular biological hypothesis is that ADHD is a genetic disorder. For example, evidence suggests that activity level is more similar between normal monozygotic twins than between dizygotic twins (Plomin, 1990b). More recent evidence suggests that genetic links may be stronger for some characteristics of ADHD, such as hyperactivity-impulsivity and reading disabilities, than other characteristics, such as inattentiveness (Nadder, Silberg, Rutter, Maes, & Eaves, 2001). As Gelfand and colleagues (1997) suggest, "The exact role of genetics is still difficult to determine. . . . Probably there is an interplay of multiple causes such as genetics, biological factors, the environment, and family stresses that increases the vulnerability of a child to the ADHD condition" (p. 119).

Psychological Factors As an alternative to biological explanations of ADHD, some researchers have suggested that hyperactivity is environmentally caused. Diverse social and familial stressors such as poverty, low levels of education, marital discord and disruption, household disorganization, and inept parenting have been associated with ADHD (S. B. Campbell, 2000). Much research has focused on parent-child relations and has found that the mothers of hyperactive children generally are more controlling and intrusive and less affectionate and reinforcing than the mothers of normal children. However, most investigators think that, rather than the cause of a child's behavior, excessive parental control and lessened affectional response are likely reactions to that behavior.

A number of researchers have developed a clever method for testing this question (Barkley, 1998). They have compared the interactions between hyperactive children and their mothers when the children are on psychostimulant medication with their interactions at times when the children are merely taking *placebos,* that is, sugar pills with no active ingredients. The researchers hypothesized that because the psychostimulant drug directly affects the child's behavior, any differences in mother-child interaction between the two conditions would indicate that mothers were reacting to the hyperactive child's difficult behavior, not causing it. This, in fact, is exactly what they found. When their children were on medication, mothers interacted with them much differently from the way they interacted with the children when they were off medication (Barkley, 1998). During the medication condition, the hyperactive child-mother pairs were similar to normal child-mother pairs. Although this research once again underlines the importance of children's influences on adults, reciprocal influence in interactions between hyperactive children and their mothers should not be ignored. Whereas a mother's intrusive, nonreinforcing behavior may initially be a reaction to a hyperactive child, in time her reaction may exacerbate the child's problems. It thus seems worthwhile to direct at least some efforts toward altering mother-child interactions.

Given the inconclusiveness of the evidence for either the biological or the environmental explanations of hyperactivity, what can we say about the cause of this disorder? The best answer is that there is no one cause; rather, hyperactivity appears to be a heterogeneous disorder with multiple causes. Brain damage may cause hyperactivity in some instances, and inheritance, environmental lead poisoning, or dietary agents eventually may explain other cases. It also seems likely that some children's hyperactivity is exacerbated by the specific environments in which they are reared. We cannot at present determine the cause of hyperactivity for any one individual child, nor can we predict what treatment will work best for that child. Again, part of the difficulty in isolating the causes is the fact that hyperactivity—just as we saw in the case of drug use and externalizing behaviors—often co-occurs with other forms of psychopathology such as anxiety or depression (Pennington, 2002). Let's look now at the treatments that have shown the most promise to date.

TREATING HYPERACTIVITY At this point, there is little doubt that psychostimulant medication (e.g., Ritalin) improves the behavior of about 80 percent of all hyperactive children, at least in the short term (Cunningham, 1999; Mehta, Sahakian, & Robbins, 2001). Improvement is quite rapid and noticeable to parents and teachers, who quickly become advocates of the medication approach. Hyperactive children become less impulsive, oppositional, and disruptive and more attentive and manageable when on medication; to say this is a relief to some tired and worried parents is an understatement (Whalen, 2001). The impact of psychostimulants is so dramatic that it is estimated that between 1 and 2 percent of American schoolchildren are currently taking the drugs. On the other hand, many observers object to the use of these medications, citing concerns that range from the philosophical stance that altering children's behavior with drugs is inappropriate to questions about the side effects of psychostimulants, which include suppression in the rate of physical growth, irritability, insomnia, weight loss, and abdominal pain (Barkley, 1998; Gelfand & Drew, 2003).

behavior therapy A psychological form of treatment, often used in treating conduct disorders, that is based on such learning principles as reinforcement and social learning.

The major alternative treatment available for hyperactivity is **behavior therapy,** a psychological intervention based on social learning principles, primarily reinforcement. In traditional behavior therapy programs, parents and teachers are taught to identify and monitor various specific, troublesome aspects of the hyperactive child's behavior (e.g., not completing class assignments on time) and to systematically reward the child for making improvements in the targeted problem area (Hardman, Drew, & Egan, 2002). In related behavior therapy programs, teachers and parents also work directly with the child in an attempt to teach cognitive self-control strategies, Barkley (1998) has developed an 8- to 10-week program for parents that trains them to focus on appropriate behaviors and discourage inappropriate behaviors. Although continuous monitoring is necessary, results suggest that the program works to improve children's behavior and academic success (Barkley, 1998).

To address the ongoing controversy of whether drugs, psychosocial intervention, or both are the best way to treat children with ADHD, the National Institute of Mental Health launched a large clinical trial (Jensen et al., 2001; Wells, 2001). Nearly 600 children ages 7 to 9 with a primary diagnosis of ADHD were randomly assigned to one of four treatment conditions. One group received only medication; a second group received only psychosocial treatment consisting of parent training, teacher consultation, and cognitive-behavioral and behavioral treatments aimed at fostering academic, social, and sports skills. Children in the third group received a combination of both medication and psychosocial treatment, while those in the fourth group receive only routine treatment from their community pediatrician or the school. Results indicated that children in all four treatment groups improved after the 14 months of treatment and 10 months of follow-up relative to their initial levels of function. Not only did ADHD symptoms decrease, but symptoms of oppositional defiant disorder and internalizing symptoms decreased as well. Moreover, social skills, academic achievement, and parent-child relationships improved. But not all treatments were equally effective. Children receiving medication or the combined treatment (medication and psychosocial intervention) showed greater improvement than those receiving psychosocial treatment alone or community treatment, especially in ADHD symptoms. Moreover, children in the combined group showed the most impressive improvement on other measures, such as oppositional symptoms, internalizing symptoms, social skills, and reading achievement.

An especially interesting finding was that these gains were achieved in spite of the fact that children in the combined group were managed on somewhat lower doses of medication. Especially in view of the concerns about medication that parents and professionals express, this is welcome news! Medication clearly is effective, but its effectiveness is enhanced and its dosage may be reduced if drugs are combined with psychosocial interventions. Although we still are unclear about the long-term effects, these findings suggest that we can help children with ADHD. Children, parents, and teachers will all benefit from the improvements in children's behavior these interventions facilitate.

Depression in Childhood

You've often heard people use the word *depression* to refer to feelings of sadness, loneliness, or "the blues." However, in its clinical use, the term has a much more specific meaning. Because there is so much controversy over what depression actually is, let's

	Behaviors
Infants	Sadness, crying, apathy, motor retardation, failure to thrive, vomiting, irritability, developmental delays, feeding or sleeping difficulties
Toddlers and preschoolers	Irritability, social withdrawal, negative self-image, peer problems, anxiety, phobias, weeping, loss of interest or pleasure in usual activities, loss of appetite, sleep disturbances, changed activity rates, failure to thrive, aggression, self-endangering behaviors, somatic disorders including urinary and fecal incontinence, asthma, eczema, desire to die
Schoolchildren	Irritability, loss of interest or pleasure in usual activities, fatigue, somatic complaints, sleeping and eating disturbances, changed activity rates, guilt, low self-esteem, sudden schoolwork problems, aggression, decreased ability to concentrate, phobias, anxiety, separation anxiety problems, depressed facial expression, suicidal thoughts
Adolescents	Disturbed sleep, appetite or weight changes, changed activity rates, fatigue, loss of interest or pleasure in usual activities, self-devaluation, difficulty in concentrating, indecisiveness, anxiety, phobias, somatic disorders, excessive emotional dependency, withdrawal, reckless behavior, suicidal thoughts or attempts

Table 15-8

Depressive behaviors in children and adolescents

Source: From *Understanding Child Behavior Disorders,* 4th edition by Gelfand/Drew. © 2003. Reprinted with permission of Wadsworth, a division of Thomson Learning: www.thomsonrights.com. Fax 800-730-2215. Sources: American Psychiatric Association (2000); Herzog & Rathbun (1982); Nottelmann & Jensen (1995); Poznanski, Mokros, Grossman, & Freeman (1985).

start with a working definition of **depression in childhood,** based largely on *DSM-IV.* Depression—considered an overcontrolled disorder—is diagnosed when a person has seemed depressed or has lost interest or pleasure in nearly all activities for at least two weeks. Note, however, that in children and adolescents the dominant mood may be one of irritability and crankiness rather than sadness and dejection. Family members often notice social withdrawal or neglect of activities formerly enjoyed—for example, a child who used to enjoy playing soccer may begin to make excuses not to practice. Recall our discussion of Emi, who was suffering from many of these same symptoms. Depression often interferes with appetite and eating, and parents may note a failure to make normal or expected weight gains. Another common effect of depression is an impaired ability to think, to concentrate, or to focus on a task; a precipitous drop in grades may signal depressive problems in a child or adolescent. Because depression is often linked with fear and anxiety, we may see signs of separation anxiety in young children. In addition, somatic complaints (e.g., headache, stomachache) are not uncommon in depressed children. Table 15-8 lists some behaviors that are common in depressed children and adolescents.

Because distractibility can occur in both attention deficit/hyperactivity disorder and depression, one must be cautious in diagnosing depression in a child whose mood disturbance is more one of irritability than of sadness or loss of interest. On the other hand, it is also possible that manic-depressive symptoms may mask ADHD in older children or adolescents, who sometimes evidence truancy, antisocial behavior, school failure, or substance abuse. (Depression in adults in some cases alternates with periods of excitability and manic activity, as in *manic-depressive disorder.*) In general, however, ADHD has an earlier onset than depressive disorder.

To be judged clinically depressed, an adult or a child must not only experience extreme sadness or affective disturbance but must display changes in cognitive

depression in childhood
Like adult depression, a mood disorder often manifested in a depressed mood and loss of interest in familiar activities, but also likely to be expressed as irritability and crankiness. Difficulty concentrating or focusing on tasks and concomitant drops in school grades are not uncommon, and depressed children often complain of physical problems such as headache.

Figure 15-4

Clinical depression among children and adolescents

Clinical, or serious, depression is not seen often among children, but beginning at about the age of 15 it is diagnosed in a considerable number of young people. About twice as many females as males are found to be seriously depressed, and depression continues to rise slowly as young women enter adulthood.

Source: Hankin et al., 1998.

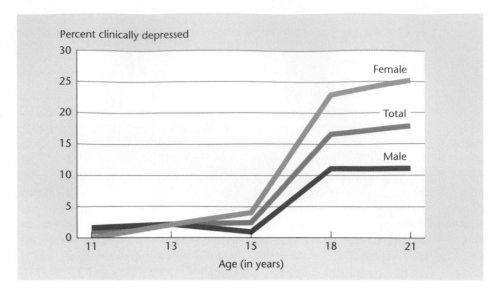

functioning and behavior. Possible changes in cognitive functioning include guilt and feelings of worthlessness, complaints about inability to concentrate, slowed thinking, and recurrent thoughts of death and suicide. Although some authorities have argued that because children's cognitive and personality development is immature or incomplete children can't be clinically depressed, most clinicians and researchers agree that childhood depression does exist; they just don't agree on precisely what it is (Hammen & Rudolph, 1996). A basic question is whether it is possible to determine accurately when children are experiencing the affective, cognitive, and behavioral disturbances that define clinical depression (Goodman & Gotlib, 2002). Many of the symptoms of depression, such as appetite and sleep disturbances, occur with such a high frequency among children that they are considered developmentally normal events; other phenomena, such as crying, do not carry the same significance in children that they do in adults (Goodman & Gotlib, 2002; Hammen, 1997).

In addition, we do not really know how aware children of different ages are of their inner lives. And if children are aware of unpleasant feelings and thoughts, can they label these states and describe their feelings accurately to an adult? Can a preschool child honestly tell you that she is depressed? Some research indicates that 5-year-old children rarely admit to being sad, although 6- and 7-year-old children more commonly recognize this emotion in themselves (Glasberg & Aboud, 1982). Recalling the Piagetian model of development, this would suggest that the transition from preoperational thought to concrete operations is related to children's awareness and ability to report on their inner feelings. Still, depression in childhood is low (1.7%), due in part to the difficulty of reliably diagnosing depression in childhood (Gelfand & Drew, 2003).

The fact that treating professionals diagnose depression in children more frequently as children grow older probably reflects both that difficulty and the fact that depressive disorder is experienced at its fullest only when the child's cognitive capacities reach the stage of formal operations. As Figure 15-4 shows, depression is rarely diagnosed among children under the age of 10, but the diagnosis rises in frequency quite dramatically among adolescent females from the age of 15 and continues to rise into adulthood. The diagnosis rises for males as well at about 15 but levels off at about 18. Nearly twice as many girls as boys experience depression (Goodman & Gotlib, 2002). "Both the hormonal and other physical changes of puberty and the social roles of females and males have been suggested as possible causes of the large preponderance of depressed women" (Gelfand et al., 1997, p. 184). However, depression rates among young males are rising, in part owing to the fact that the current generation of young men are more accepting of emotional sensitivity and vulnerability in themselves (Gelfand & Drew, 2003). Indeed, in contrast to its rarity during childhood, depressive disorder is so frequent among adults as to be referred to as "the common cold of psychopathology" (Seligman, 1973).

One unfortunate consequence of the increased rate of depression during adolescence is a concomitant increase in the rate of suicide. Although suicide is very rare among children younger than 12, it is estimated to be the third leading killer of adolescents, following only accidents and homicide, and among 15- to 24-year-olds the rate has tripled since 1950 (Centers for Disease Control and Prevention, 2002a, 2002b). Among college students it is the second leading cause of death; about 10,000 individuals attempt suicide and of those, 1,000 succeed each year. About 3 percent of older adolescent girls and 1 percent of boys make at least one serious suicide attempt (Centers for Disease Control and Prevention, 2002a, 2002b). About 16 percent of high school students make specific suicide plans (Centers for Disease Control and Prevention, 1998a), but 75 percent of these students received no intervention in the year following their suicide plans or attempts. The most notable increases in successful suicides have been in males, particularly white males. Females are much more likely to attempt but to fail at suicide than are males. One reason is that females more often use such methods as overdosing with drugs or poisons, whereas males tend to use methods that have faster and surer results, such as hanging, shooting, or explosives.

Culture plays a role in suicide as well as age and gender. Suicide rates are high in some countries such as Japan, where there is a long history of viewing suicide as an honorable tradition. In Muslim and Catholic countries, where suicide is viewed as a violation of religious teachings, rates are low. In North America, Native American youth have high rates of suicide; one recent study found the rate to be five times higher than that for youth in the general population (Chandler, Lalonde, Sokol, & Hallett, 2003). Many factors including poverty, loss of their traditional culture, limited educational and job opportunities, and alcohol and drug use contribute to these elevated rates. Among inner-city African American and Latino American gangs, suicide rates are rising as well (Rotherman Borus, Piacentini, Cantwell, Belin, & Song, 2000). Although depression and suicide are often linked, this is not always the case (Jellinek & Snyder, 1998). In one large study of adolescents, 42 percent of those who attempted suicide did *not* have a history of depression (Andrews & Lewinsohn, 1992). Basically, suicide is related to a general sense of overwhelming hopelessness, although it also may result from the accumulation of adverse life events such as family conflicts; loss of a family member due to illness, death, or divorce; breakups or problems in romantic relationships or friendships; school failure; being apprehended in a delinquent, forbidden, or embarrassing act or situation; or real or imagined mental or physical illness (Jellinek & Snyder, 1998). Adolescents who attempt suicide often feel they have no source of emotional support. They frequently are alienated from their families and may have had disruptions or losses in intimate relations and relations with peers that give them an increasing sense of isolation and helplessness. Although not all teenagers who commit suicide alert others to their intentions, many do. Parents and others should listen to and take very seriously any threat by a child or adolescent of suicide and, if necessary, take concrete action to prevent it.

CAUSES OF CHILDHOOD DEPRESSION   Theories of the etiology of depression are abundant. Like many human disorders, depression is very likely caused by multiple factors. Thus, in discussing biological, social and psychological, and cognitive theories, we will be looking not for one answer but for many, and we will be seeking to learn how such contributing factors interact.

Biological Theories   Biological theories of the cause of depression have focused more on adults than on children. Although a causal role has not been demonstrated, evidence has linked depression among adults with low levels of chemicals that

A mother's depression and listlessness may lead the child to become depressed later on. Disruption in early attachment, as well as modeling, may contribute to the link between parent and child depression.

facilitate the transmission of neural impulses (Jacobs, 2004); however, similar biochemical evidence has not been consistently obtained in depressed children (Wicks-Nelson & Israel, 2000). At the same time, by age 3 children of chronically depressed parents showed lower activation in a variety of brain regions than children of nondepressed mothers (Embry & Dawson, 2002). Infants of mothers who were depressed, but whose depression improved, showed normal brain activity at 3 years of age. This suggests that environmental factors play a role in early depression and in early brain development as well (Embry & Dawson, 2002). It seems likely that environmental factors play a considerable role in childhood depression (Cummings et al., 2000; Hammen, 1997). The relative contributions of family interaction and genetic influences remain an open question (Hops, 2001; Silberg, Rutter, & Eaves, 2001).

Social and Psychological Theories   One of the earliest theories of the causes of childhood depression linked it to the loss of maternal affection or the failure of attachment (Bowlby, 1960). Although some research has supported this position, other factors, such as parental conflict, maternal depression, negative life events, lack of effective social supports, and, especially for girls, problems with peers and unpopularity, have been linked with depression in children (Cummings et al., 2000; Hammen, 1997).

The link between depression in parents and children has received considerable attention in the recent research literature. Depression is more likely to occur in children of clinically depressed parents (Cicchetti & Toth, 2006; Goodman & Gotlib, 2002). Indeed, children of depressed parents are at risk for higher rates not only of depression but of a wide range of other disorders such as separation anxiety, academic failure, attention deficit disorders, and conduct disorders, especially if the depression is chronic or sustained (Embry & Dawson, 2002; Hammen, 1997; Weissman, Warner, Wickramaratne, Morean, & Olfson, 1997). Although twin and adoption studies indicate that this association between depression in children and parents may be in part genetic, other studies show that the experiences of children with a depressed mother may differ from those with a nondepressed mother. Depressed mothers are more tense, disorganized, resentful, and ambivalent, and less sensitive, communicative, and affectionate with their children (Cummings et al., 2000; NICHD Early Child Care Research Network, 1999). Furthermore they are more likely to perceive their children's behavior negatively (Hammen, 1997, 2002). It is not surprising, then, that children of depressed mothers are more likely to be insecurely attached, fearful, and lower in self-esteem and to have problems in subsequent social relations (Cicchetti & Toth, 2006; Lyons-Ruth, Lyubchik, Wolfe, & Bronfman, 2002).

It is not just mothers who contribute to children's depression. Recently, Jacob and Johnson (1997) found that both paternal and maternal depression were associated with child adjustment problems, such as depression, as well as with undercontrolled behaviors. As family systems theory would predict, when one parent is depressed, the marital relationship suffers, and this may, in turn, lead to inadequate parenting (Jacob & Johnson, 1997; Phares, Dubig, & Watkins, 2002). As we saw in Chapter 12, peers can play a role in children's mental health too. Elementary school children who were socially anxious (shy, inhibited) and who were excluded by their peers were at higher risk for depression than nonanxious and better accepted classmates (Gazelle and Ladd, 2003). Life stressors as well can contribute to internalizing problems such as depression (Hammen, 2002). Recently, Kim et al. (2003) found a reciprocal link between stressful life events (e.g., financial crises, physical stressors, breaking up with a boy or girlfriend, changing schools) and both internalizing and externalizing behavior in seventh- and twelfth-grade adolescents. For these youths, stressful events increased their internalizing problems, and across time the problems predicted other stressful life events. In other words, negative life events experienced during early adolescence can intensify symptoms of sadness and fear which, in turn, can increase adolescents' risk for incurring future adversities and life crises.

Finally, our cultural expectations that emphasize achievement, success, and wealth may contribute to the emergence of depression and other forms of childhood psychopathology as well. Failure to meet their own expectations or those of their parents and peers may contribute to children's mental health problems. Box 15.3 discusses this and other problems facing even affluent youth in American society.

Cognitive Theories   An alternative theoretical explanation of depression invokes the concept of **learned helplessness,** a kind of behavior that results from the belief that one is helpless to control the events in one's world and their outcomes (Seligman, 1974). In *Child Psychology* we stress that one of the developmental cornerstones of both cognitive and social competence is the development of a sense of self-efficacy. The learned helplessness theory of depression proposes that depressed people not only experience feelings of helplessness but attribute their failures in controlling the world to enduring personal shortcomings. Essentially, this cognitive theory asserts that people become depressed when they perceive themselves as having failed to achieve desired outcomes in their lives (Garber & Martin, 2002).

Here is one of the places where those who argue against the reality of childhood depression hang their hats. Children's cognitive capabilities, they assert, have not yet matured sufficiently for them to have developed a true sense of self-efficacy, to say nothing of lamenting their failure to have developed such a sense.

learned helplessness A kind of behavior that results from the belief that one is helpless to control the events in one's world.

TREATING CHILDHOOD DEPRESSION   Children and adolescents with depressive disorders benefit from a wide range of interventions. In general, they respond more favorably to psychosocial and psychotherapeutic interventions than do children with conduct disorders. Although the newer antidepressant drugs such as fluoxetine (Prozac) and sertraline (Zoloft) are widely prescribed for teenagers, they are generally less effective in treating depression in children and adolescents than they are in helping adults (Stark, Napolitano, Swearer, & Schmidt, 1996). However, some recent evidence (Emslie et al., 1997) is encouraging; 56 percent of children with major depression improved with Prozac compared with only 33 percent of a placebo control group. Unfortunately, antidepressant drugs are dangerous, and an overdose can be lethal (Gelfand & Drew, 2003). In fact, in 2004 the U.S. federal government began to require that warning labels accompany these antidepressant drugs in light of the increased risk of suicide associated with their use in a small percentage of adolescents. This cautionary step is important in view of the dramatic increase in antidepressant use among children and adolescents in the United States: Between 1998 and 2002, there was a 49 percent increase in the use of antidepressants among children younger than 18 years of age (Delate, Gelenberg, Simmons, & Motheral, 2004).

Cognitive behavior therapy is one of the most effective approaches for treating depression in adolescents. This type of therapy is typically conducted in small groups of three to eight adolescents twice a week over an eight-week period. The goals are to reduce the teenagers' self-consciousness and feelings of being different and to provide them with strategies such as relaxation techniques and self-control tactics to help them control their dark moods. The therapy also emphasizes positive strategies such as improving peer relations, setting realistic goals, and learning how to get more fun out of activities. Results have been impressive. In one series of studies, between 54 and 67 percent of treated adolescents no longer met the *DSM* criteria for depression (Clarke, Hops, Lewinsohn, & Andrews, 1992; Lewinsohn & Rhode, 1993). By contrast, among teenagers with similar depressive problems who were on a waiting list for therapy and served as controls, only 5 to 48 percent no longer met the criteria. Unfortunately, the long-term effectiveness of cognitive behavior therapy is not established: Nearly one-third of adolescents

cognitive behavior therapy A group therapy technique particularly useful in treating depression in adolescents. Therapeutic goals include reducing self-consciousness and feelings of being different and teaching strategies for dealing with depressive moods and for acquiring a more positive outlook and improving social interactions.

Box 15.3

Risk and Resilience

DOES A CULTURE OF AFFLUENCE PROTECT CHILDREN AND YOUTH FROM THE RISK OF PSYCHOPATHOLOGY?

In many Western cultures, such as that of the United States, affluence and the acquisition of material goods are revered. But does wealth buy happiness and protect children from the development of psychological problems? According to recent surveys, in spite of historical trends that show that "Americans have far more luxuries than they had in the 1950s with twice as many cars per person and microwave ovens, VCRs, air conditioners, and color TVs . . . they are no more satisfied with their lives" (Diener, 2000) (Cited by Luthar, 2003, p. 1584). Or as Myers (2000) has observed, "Americans are twice as rich and no happier. Meanwhile the divorce rate doubled. Teen suicide tripled. Depression rates have soared, especially among teens and young adults . . . I call this conjunction of material prosperity and social recession *the American Paradox*. The more people strive for extrinsic goals such as money, the more numerous their problems and the less robust their well-being" (cited by Luthar, 2003, p. 1584).

But what about children and adolescents? Are they not better off growing up in the relative affluence of suburban life, as compared with children and adolescents who grow up in poverty in the inner cities? Are suburban youth not happier and less likely to suffer from mental health problems such as depression, delinquency, and substance abuse? A recent study of nearly 1,000 American teenagers revealed a negative relation between parent's socioeconomic status and their adolescent's happiness (Csikszentmihalyi & Schneider, 2000). Rich youth of America are not only less happy, but may be at risk for a variety of mental health problems. It is not just the poor, the disadvantaged, and

members of minority cultures who are at risk for psychopathology. Recent evidence suggests that privileged children from wealthy homes are also at risk for alcohol and illegal drug abuse.

Suniya Luthar (Luthar, 2003; Luthar & Becker, 2002; Luthar & D'Avanzo, 1999) has directed her attention to the high cost of affluence for American youth. In a sample of tenth-grade students in an affluent suburban community, she found that suburban youth reported significantly higher levels of anxiety symptoms, and of cigarette, alcohol, marijuana, and hard drug use (Luthar & D'Avanzo, 1999) than did their economically disadvantaged, inner-city peers. Compared with national samples, more than one in five suburban girls (22%) reported clinically significant depressive symptoms—rates three times as high as those in normative samples (7%). Rates of clinically significant anxiety among boys (22%) and girls (26%) were higher than national average rates for boys (17%) and girls (21%). Similarly, when compared with national samples, affluent young people displayed a higher frequency of substance abuse, particularly of alcohol and among girls (72% during the past year versus 61% in normative samples) and of illicit drug use among affluent boys (rates of 59% versus 38%).

Moreover, the reasons for substance use may differ across rich and poor adolescents. In the case of affluent teens, substance use and maladjustment (anxiety, depression) were related, whereas there were no links between adjustment and drug use among poor adolescents. Affluent adolescents appear to use drugs as a way of "self-medicating" in order to relieve their

treated with cognitive behavior therapy experienced recurrence within two years (Birmaher et al., 2000).

Prevention programs have been effective in reducing depression, too (Gladstone & Beardsley, 2002; Hammen, 1997). In one study (Gillham, Reivich, Jaycox, & Seligman, 1995), children at risk for depression were given training in cognitive and problem-solving skills. Two years later, when researchers evaluated these children they found fewer depressive symptoms among them than among a control group. These findings helped underscore the value of prevention.

In general, study of the causes and treatment of childhood depression is still in its early stages. As is the case with many of the overcontrolled disorders, sound research on etiology and treatment must await the development of better definitions of the

anxiety and depression. This is particularly troubling, because adolescents who use drugs as mood regulators are more likely to continue to be regular users in later adolescence and adulthood (Zucker, Fitzgerald, & Moses, 1995). Moreover, peer groups in affluent, suburban settings were more likely than inner-city peer groups to endorse substance use among boys. Peer popularity was linked with high substance use among boys of higher socioeconomic status, but among inner-city boys it was not so linked. There are several reasons for these patterns. First, affluent youth are under high pressure to achieve, and that pressure takes its toll on their adjustment. Adolescents who were rated high in perfectionistic strivings (e.g., "The fewer mistakes I make, the more people will like me; my parents expect excellence from me") had elevated distress and delinquency scores that, in turn, were linked with substance use. Second, adolescents' reports of lack of closeness to their mothers were linked with distress, delinquency, and substance abuse for both boys and girls. Third, minimal after-school supervision was related to girls' distress, delinquency, and substance abuse (recall the links between low parental monitoring and aggression that we discussed in Chapter 14). In sum, the combination of excessively high expectations and isolation from adults in wealthy families puts affluent youth at risk for drug and alcohol problems. Clearly being rich is not a protective factor, and it may be a risk factor for these forms of developmental ills.

Are there factors that protect and buffer individuals from the effects of stress and that promote coping and good adjustment in the face of the parental and peer pressure that affluent children may encounter? As you'll recall from our earlier discussion of the Kauai Longitudinal Study (Chapter 3) and other work (Luthar et al., 2000), there are three types of protective factors: positive individual attributes, a supportive family environment, and extrafamilial individuals or social agencies (such as schools, peer groups, or churches) that support the child's coping efforts. As we saw in our earlier discussion of the Kauai study, these factors may be relevant for children across the range of economic circumstances. Children who are intelligent and independent and have easy temperaments, high self-esteem, and an internal locus of control are more adaptable in the face of stressful life experiences (Garmezy & Masten, 1994; Luthar et al., 2000; Werner, 1995). As the work on affluent children and youth illustrates, the lack of parental availability puts children at risk for maladjustment. At the same time, the presence of one warm supportive parent can help buffer the adverse effects of social and academic pressures experienced by affluent children, just as a supportive parent can protect children from the ill effects of divorce, family discord, and child abuse (Luthar et al., 2000).

The effects of all these protective factors are not automatic, however. Protection does not lie in the availability of potentially supportive resources but in the child's use of them. Thus, children's own strengths make an extremely important contribution to the resilience they show in the face of risk. Sadly, even the most resilient child can develop problems when stressful life events are so intense and so massed that they overwhelm the available protective factors (Luthar et al., 2000; Werner 1995). For children—rich or poor—achieving a balance between risk and protective factors is a major challenge that will play an important role in whether or not they develop as healthy children or as children plagued by behavioral and emotional problems.

---

disorders themselves (Cicchetti & Toth, 2006; Hammen, 1997). In the area of childhood depression, such definitions must consider children's differing behavioral, emotional, and cognitive capacities at various stages of development. In spite of these uncertainties Emi's mother could help her daughter reduce her depression symptoms by either medication and/or cognitive therapy.

Autistic Disorder

The mostly widely recognized of the pervasive developmental disorders is **autistic disorder,** also known as *early infantile autism* or *childhood autism.* Children with this

autistic disorder A disorder in which children's ability to communicate and interact socially is seriously impaired; autistic children have specific language deficiencies, demonstrate a need for sameness in their environment, and often engage in repetitive and stereotyped kinds of behaviors.

disorder were first identified by psychiatrist Leo Kanner (another name for the disorder is *Kanner's autism*), who noted many of the disorder's most puzzling and disturbing characteristics (Kanner, 1943). These features include:

Extreme autistic aloneness, expressed as a lack of interest in other people that sometimes appears to be an actual aversion to contact with other human beings

Language abnormalities, ranging from nonspeech to repeating others' exact words rather than reply or engage in conversation

Attempts to preserve sameness in the environment that may lead to repetitive behaviors or total and extended concentration on something like a spinning top

These are the behaviors exhibited by Pauli to whom you were introduced at the beginning of this chapter.

How prevalent is this disorder? Estimates range from 6 to over 20 per 10,000 individuals (American Psychiatric Association, 2000; Patterson & Rafferty, 2001). Autism is more commonly found in boys than in girls; the ratio is three to five boys to one girl (American Psychiatric Association, 2000). Recently, rates of autism have increased, owing not only to better detection but also to the use of broader diagnostic criteria that increase the number of children being labeled autistic. Because of books and films such as *Rainman* there is also more public awareness of the condition.

Asperger's disorder, a related syndrome first recognized in the 1980s, is sometimes confused with autism and may thus help to account for the apparent increased prevalence of the latter. Although Asperger's disorder shares some of the social and affective deficits associated with autism, children with Asperger symptomatology do not show significant language delays and are often able to progress in school at a satisfactory rate (Gelfand & Drew, 2003; Pennington, 2002).

It is difficult to imagine just how disturbed an autistic child is, but once you have observed one of these unfortunate children, the memory will last forever. If two autistic children are placed side by side in a room full of toys, chances are that they will ignore each other and most of the toys. These children seem to be living in a world much different from our own, a world in which they seem to prefer inanimate objects to human interaction. Autistic children often avoid eye contact with others and fail to modulate social interaction in any way. Often they appear to be unaware not only of

Autistic children often fail to develop a useful means of communication with others, whether verbal or nonverbal. Such children may be highly resistant to change and to new patterns of behavior. At the same time, because these children often seem to prefer inanimate objects to human interaction, psychologists are exploring the approach of teaching children with autism to communicate by means of a computer.

other people but even of themselves. Some autistic children frequently seem not to recognize themselves as independent social beings (Dawson, Meltzoff, Osterling, & Rinaldi, 1998). As we discuss in Chapter 8, children normally develop the ability to recognize their mirror images as themselves around the age of 2. Do autistic children show deficits in self-recognition ability? Spiker and Ricks (1984) tested the self-recognition capacity of 52 autistic children who were 12 years old and younger. Using a procedure that will be familiar to you, these investigators, under the pretext of wiping a child's nose clean, unobtrusively smeared green makeup on each child's face. When Spiker and Ricks showed these autistic children a mirror, fully 31 percent failed to demonstrate recognition of their mirror images. The children's ability to recognize themselves was strongly related to their levels of communicative speech: Those children who had at least some speech ability were much more likely to wipe their noses upon seeing the mirror image than were those children who had no communicative speech. However, even the children who showed evidence of self-recognition demonstrated little emotional response.

As we saw earlier, normal children typically respond with giggling when they see their green noses in the mirror, saying something like "You tricked me!" In this study, children had no such reactions, suggesting that their social impairment may include disturbances in their concepts of themselves as social beings. Other studies, however, have used subtle measures of attention, such as heart rate, to show that autistic children are aware of the presence of other people, even though they may not reflect this knowledge in their overt behavior (Baron-Cohen, 1995). Many autistic children seem to manifest a lack of attachment and empathy in social relations, although a small subgroup demonstrate attachment behavior that seems normal (Sigman & Mundy, 1989). The consequences for children's social relations with peers are severe: Most fail to develop normal friendships, and peers view them as social isolates (American Psychiatric Association, 2000; Baron-Cohen, 2003).

Communication deficits constitute one of the most incapacitating problems autistic children face. Autistic children display these deficits in both nonverbal and verbal communication. They have difficulty in understanding facial expressions of emotion and in integrating or using instrumental gestures such as those meaning "be quiet" or "come here" or pointing gestures indicating "look" or "over there" (Baron-Cohen, 2003; Baron-Cohen, Baldwin, & Crowson, 1997). For example, Dawson and her colleagues (2004) recently found that 3-year-old autistic children were less likely than typically developing children or developmentally delayed nonautistic children to orient to a social signal (e.g., responding when called by name or to a person snapping his fingers) or to show *joint attention* (responding to an examiner's point and gaze). In comparison with other groups of children, autistic preschoolers displayed less attention to the distress of another person, such as an adult examiner's hurt finger (see Chapter 14). In addition, some 50 percent of autistic children never develop meaningful, useful speech, and most others have limited and sometimes bizarre means of verbal expression. The development of useful speech by age 5 is the best predictor of adult outcome (Kanner, 1973). **Echolalia** is one frequent language problem found among autistic children who are not mute (Broderick & Kasa-Hendrickson, 2001). Echolalic children will repeat what is said to them, sometimes over and over again. If you were to ask an echolalic child, "What is your name?" the child would reply, "What is your name?" Pronoun reversals are another common language problem found in autism. Autistic children often refer to themselves as "you" and to others as "I." Even when autistic children acquire speech, they often do not use it effectively for social communication. Autistic children rarely "chat" or respond to the verbal comments of other people (Baron-Cohen, 1995, 2003).

Many autistic children learn to master only a few of the tasks necessary to function in the world and need constant help with feeding, dressing, toileting, and cleaning. Although their senses function adequately when tested, autistic children behave

echolalia Repeating word for word what is said by another rather than responding to a question or making a statement of one's own; a common problem in autistic children.

obsessive self-stimulatory behavior Behavior common in autistic children in which they engage in repetitive actions that seemingly have no purpose.

as if they have sensory deficits. For example, autistic children spend much of their time engaging in **obsessive self-stimulatory behavior** such as repetitively spinning objects, switching lights on and off, or flapping their hands in front of their eyes (Baker, 2000). It is thought that the primary purpose of this bizarre-appearing behavior may be to provide sensory stimulation.

Whether autistic children are of normal, below-average, or superior intelligence has been the topic of much discussion. Kanner and others have suggested that autistic children have normal or even superior intelligence but that it is hidden beneath a blanket of psychopathology and, perhaps, a deficit in information processing (Smith & Bryson, 1994). Several pieces of circumstantial evidence support this speculation. The parents of autistic children are somewhat more likely to have higher than average IQs (Cantwell, Baker, & Rutter, 1978), and an autistic child's normal physical appearance and motor development does distinguish autism from many forms of mental retardation. Furthermore, some autistic children show a type of intelligence traditionally associated with the *idiot savant*. This is a person who typically has some unusual talents—particularly in the area of mathematical abilities—such as being able to quickly and accurately predict the day of the week on which some date far in the future will fall. Some autistic children show remarkable memory in being able to repeat television commercials verbatim or to sing operatic arias or even complete musical scores. Despite such seeming indications of superior intelligence, about 70 percent of all autistic children score in the retarded range on commonly used measures of intelligence, and this below-average performance is quite stable over time (Kauffman, 2001).

Recent research indicates that some of the cognitive deficits children with autistic disorders display relate to metacognition, or the theory of mind, which we discuss in Chapter 9 (Leslie & Roth, 1993; Siegler & Alibali, 2005). This is not surprising, when we consider the difficulties autistic children experience in social relations. They seem unable to understand that mental states such as knowledge, beliefs, and expectations exist and are connected to people's behavior (Baron-Cohen, 1995, 2003). This lack of a theory of mind or deficiency in metacognition makes it difficult for autistic children to anticipate and predict others' responses and thus makes it hard for them to engage in effective social interactions.

CAUSES OF AUTISM   At present the cause of autism is unknown. Some investigators, including Kanner himself, once suggested that the cause might be of psychological origin and attributed the disorder to parents who were cold and aloof. Scientists who held this view described parents of autistic children as "refrigerator parents" who thawed out just long enough to conceive a child. Such assertions were unfounded and have created unnecessary guilt and anxiety among the parents of autistic children. If these parents seem somewhat distant from their children, it is much more likely to be a reaction to their child's social aversion than a cause of the child's disorder. Furthermore, the onset of the disorder comes so early in life, and other children have been found to be so resilient even in the face of catastrophic environmental events, that it hardly seems likely that a disorder as severe as autism could be caused by parents' "unconscious rejection" of their child.

Currently, it is almost universally accepted that autism has a biological cause yet to be specified. Twin studies have partially implicated genetics, suggesting a higher incidence of the disorder in monozygotic than in dizygotic twins (Nigg & Goldsmith, 1994; Rutter, 2003). In fact, in one study, the concordance rate for autism in monozygotic twins was 60 percent, whereas for dizyotic twins it was only 5 percent (Bailey et al., 1995). Inasmuch as the heritability rate for mental illnesses such as depression and bipolar disorder is considerably lower, it would seem that autism is one of the most heritable of psychiatric disorders. In addition, a larger percentage of families than would be expected by chance (2%) have two or more autistic children. Furthermore, parents and siblings of autistic children show more problems in cognition and language than are found in the general population (Rutter, 2003). Biological dysfunction is also suggested by the fact that the chromosomal abnormalities responsible for fragile X syndrome, brain damage, metabolic disturbance, and abnormally high levels of the neurotransmitter serotonin have been found in some autistic children (Drew, Hardman, & Logan, 1996). Although genetic inheritance is clearly a factor in the development of autism, other, environmental factors play a role as well. There are wide differences in both IQ and clinical symptomatology within monozygotic twin pairs, which suggests that environmental influences play a major role in shaping the form that autism will assume (Pennington, 2002; Rutter, 2000).

Recently, it has been suggested that the use of mercury in some immunization compounds and flu shots might trigger autism, but as of this writing no clear evidence has emerged to support this theory. The exact nature of the cause or causes of autism is unclear.

TREATING AUTISTIC DISORDER   To date, autism has proven to be a discouraging disorder to treat. Professionals treating autistic children have increasingly used medications—especially medication designed to reduce serotonin levels—but although such medications have shown moderate success in reducing some problem behaviors, such as hyperactivity, they have not succeeded in dealing with the core symptoms, primarily self-injurious behavior. Moreover these medications are often accompanied by adverse side effects (Drew & Hardman, 2000). Of the host of treatments tried, **operant behavior therapy** appears to be most effective (Clarke, 2001; Lovaas & Smith, 1988). Unfortunately, although the changes this time-consuming treatment produces may help the children in day-to-day functioning, it usually leaves them still performing well below the normal range (Clarke, 2001). By carefully monitoring the autistic child's behavior, and by systematically rewarding appropriate behavior with such things as food, operant behavior therapy programs have been quite successful in teaching autistic children basic self-care skills. Such techniques have not been as successful in the teaching of generalizable language skills, however. Although autistic children show improvement in their functional language as a result of these treatment programs, the process is often painfully slow. Furthermore, some of the autistic children who do learn words never seem to acquire the meaning of language (Cantwell et al., 1978). That is, they don't generate new word combinations, and their new vocabulary and other therapeutic gains can quickly deteriorate if the children move from their highly structured teaching environment (Lovaas & Smith, 1988). More recently, teaching sign language rather than oral speech, intervening at earlier ages, involving parents in training programs, and working with children in their natural environment are alternatives that are being more widely used (Clarke, 2001).

One study has offered evidence that an intensive program of one-to-one behavior modification, directed at both parents and their autistic children, could help some autistic children (Lovaas & Smith, 1988). In this program, one group (Group I) of autistic children, who were younger than 4 when the study began, received 40 hours a week of treatment for two or more years. A second group (Group II) of autistic children received only 10 hours a week of treatment over this period, and a third group (Group III) received no treatment at all. Although before the treatment children in all three groups had similar IQ scores, fewer than 10 percent scored in the normal range. As Table 15-9 shows, after the intervention, the intensive treatment group had made considerable gain in intellectual functioning in comparison to the other two groups. A follow-up study showed that some of these gains were maintained into adolescence and early adulthood (McIntosh, 1999).

Although behavior therapy may not be the solution to all of the problems of the autistic child, it does offer these children the opportunity to develop many more skills than they would otherwise acquire, and the prognosis of autism without treatment is

operant behavior therapy
A form of behavior therapy in which behavior is carefully monitored and consistently rewarded with such things as food.

Table 15-9 Effects of behavioral intervention with autistic children

	Group I (intensive treatment)		Group II (10 hours of treatment)		Group III (no treatment)	
	Percentage of Children	IQ	Percentage of Children	IQ	Percentage of Children	IQ
Children who completed regular first grade	47	107	0		5	99
Children in language-handicapped and learning-disabled class	42	70	42	74	48	67
Children in first-grade class for autistic-retarded children	11	30	58	36	48	44

Source: Adapted from Lovaas, 1987.

gloomy indeed. Kanner himself noted that of 96 children he diagnosed as autistic before 1953, only 10 percent had what was considered to be a good outcome—that is, they were able to live independently (Kanner, 1973). The remainder required special care in institutions or other protected settings. Similar results have been reported by other researchers (Remschmidt, Schulz, Martin, & Warnke, 1994). In a 28-year follow-up study, Kanner (1992) found that institutional placement was ineffective for autistic children: They deteriorated in social skills and general adjustment. In contrast, children who were placed on farms did better: They took on regular chores and were generally accepted by the farm communities in which they lived. Unfortunately, even what is called a "good" outcome for an autistic child—although a dramatic change—is far from the sort of life that most of us would consider ideal.

TREATING AND PREVENTING CHILD PSYCHOLOGICAL DISORDERS

A parent seeking help for a child with a psychological problem may receive very different advice on appropriate treatment from different mental health professionals. The treatment suggestions that such professionals make depend, in part, on their diagnosis of the problem. As we have said, however, the diagnosis of developmental disorders is imprecise because of conflicting theories about etiology and possible outcomes. Thus clinicians' varying theoretical views influence their treatment recommendations. In this section, we describe the goals of five commonly used general approaches: psychoactive medication, play therapy, behavior therapy, family therapy, and community psychology, which combines treatment with serious efforts at prevention.

Psychoactive Medication

psychoactive medications
Medications designed to alter mood and/or thinking processes.

Of the various **psychoactive medications**—chemical substances designed to alter mood and/or thinking processes—that have been used to treat abnormal behavior in children, by far the most commonly used drugs are the psychostimulants we discussed in connection with attention deficit/hyperactivity disorder. As we noted, one of the most serious concerns associated with psychostimulants is the suppression of growth that long-term use of these drugs can cause. It appears, however, that when use of a psychoactive drug is discontinued there may be a "growth rebound"—that is, a period of rapid growth during which the child catches up with peers (Barkley, 1998).

Concerns about effectiveness and side effects notwithstanding, perhaps the two most controversial issues about the use of medications are philosophical and political. First, should drugs be used to alter children's behavior when no firm evidence indicates that a disturbance is the result of a disease process? This issue subtly pervades the research on hyperactivity and, in many respects, underlies the debate as to whether hyperactivity and conduct disorders are different problems (S. B. Campbell, 2000). When hyperactivity is viewed as a distinct disorder, there is often a hidden implication that it *is* a "disease," and therefore appropriate for treatment with drugs. If we view a hyperactive child as just another "brat," on the other hand, drug treatment may be considered inappropriate.

A second issue is that a disproportionate number of minority and economically deprived children undertake drug treatment. Some authorities are concerned that children from less advantaged families may be seen as deviant for reasons other than their apparently disturbed behavior and may be offered drug treatment rather than more costly and time-consuming psychological therapies. Ultimately, it is parents who must decide whether psychostimulants or other drugs should be used to alter their children's behavior. However, mental health professionals have a responsibility to inform parents and families of all social classes, and all ethnic and racial backgrounds, of the state of the art and of the alternative treatments available (Gelfand & Drew, 2003). The issue of how quality medical treatment and care can be made available to all members of society continues to be debated.

Play Therapy

Play therapy, one of the most common forms of psychotherapy used with young children, was devised in response to children's limited ability to express themselves verbally (Leblanc & Ritchie, 2001). In **play therapy,** children are encouraged to participate in free play with toys the therapist provides. Often toys thought to be symbolically important—mommy and daddy dolls, for example—are available. In psychoanalytic play therapy, children's play is viewed as an expression of their unconscious impulses and conflicts that gives the therapist a window into children's minds. The therapist's goal in play therapy is to help the child gain insight into her unconscious psychodynamics by interpreting the play. More recently, some psychoanalytically oriented therapists have been broadening their treatment to include mother-child dyads (Stern, 2004), and some analysts have begun to include home visits, education about development, and supportive services for at-risk parents and children (Lieberman & Zeanah, 1999; McDonough, 2004).

Although there is very little evidence that psychoanalytic play therapy is an effective treatment by itself, many clinicians agree that play, especially in combination with other interventions, can be an effective therapeutic tool. For most nonanalytically oriented clinicians, however, the goal of play therapy is not to help the child gain emotional insight but to build a trusting relationship with the child. Few would argue that play cannot be helpful in achieving that important goal.

play therapy A form of psychotherapy in which therapists encourage children in free play with dolls and toys on the premise that such play will reveal a child's unconscious conflicts and concerns.

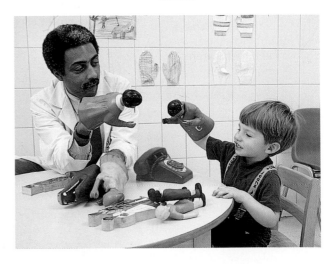

For many child therapists, play is a pleasurable activity that children enjoy and a helpful means of building rapport with their young clients.

Behavior Therapy

Behavior therapy, which we have discussed in connection with several disorders, is not a single approach. The term actually refers to a collection of different treatment techniques all derived from the principles of social learning and from the operant learning laboratory (Gelfand & Drew, 2003). The basic goal of behavior therapy with children is to teach them new ways of behaving through changing cognitive and emotional processes, changing the environment, and teaching new skills. Behavior therapists not only rely on operant conditioning but also use techniques based on classical conditioning, modeling, and theories of cognitive processing. In general, behavior therapists can be applauded for the care with which they have studied and reported on the effectiveness of their therapeutic interventions. The evidence suggests that behavior therapy procedures have proven useful in treating a variety of psychological disorders in children (Clarke, 2001; Gelfand & Drew, 2003).

As we noted in discussing depression, cognitive behavior therapies combine behavioral approaches with a focus on the child's thoughts and feelings (Cummings et al., 2000). In addition to treating depressive disorders, this approach has been used with considerable success in treating fears, phobias, and anxiety (March, Franklin, Nelson, & Foa, 2001; Ollendick & King, 1998).

Family Therapy

family therapy A form of psychotherapy in which all family members join in to find solutions to a child's problem behaviors.

Family therapy is being used with increasing frequency as an intervention with children and their families. In **family therapy,** all relevant family members, not just the child, meet together with a therapist in an attempt to resolve the child's problem. Family therapists argue that a child's psychological problems do not occur in isolation but within the family system and as an expression of some disruption within that system (Minuchin, 2002). On this view, the child's behavior is an indication that something is wrong with the entire system, not just the child. Thus family therapists tend to view specific childhood disorders as "symptoms" of underlying disturbances within the entire family system. Family systems theory, which we introduce in Chapter 1 and discuss at greater length in Chapter 11, forms the basis for this type of therapy. The importance of this family-based approach stems in part from the fact that there is considerable evidence of intergenerational continuity of risk for development of psychopathology over time

Family therapy in which all family members participate is often an effective intervention for both troubled children and their parents.

(Serbin & Karp, 2003). By treating the family, including the parents as well as the child, the chance of breaking this intergenerational cycle of risk increases.

According to the family therapy approach, a child's symptoms serve to maintain the family's equilibrium. When the "symptom" is removed, it may precipitate a distressing crisis and a need to reorganize and restabilize the family system. For example, a passive father may gain vicarious gratification out of a child's aggressive assaults and verbal abuse toward his domineering wife. If the child becomes less aggressive, the father may become anxious and angry, and conflict between the husband and wife may escalate. In such cases it is not uncommon for the parents to withdraw the family from therapy just when the behavior of the child on whose behalf they sought the therapy is improving.

Family therapy is a relatively new approach to treating childhood disorders. Initial research suggests that it holds promise although there has been little well controlled work on its effectiveness (Cummings et al., 2000).

Community Psychology and Prevention

In each of the four forms of treatment that we've discussed in this section, the focus has been on treating children who have already been identified as suffering from emotional difficulties. Furthermore, the interventions discussed represent a progressively broadening ecological focus, moving from treating the child in isolation (medication) to treating not only the child but her social context (family therapy). **Community psychology** takes an even broader ecological perspective, attempting to change general social conditions that play a role in children's and adults' psychological distress. Community psychologists also focus much more on the prevention of disorder than on its treatment (Wandersman & Florin, 2003).

Community psychologists generally recognize three levels of preventive intervention (Weissberg & Greenberg, 1998; Weissberg, Kumpfer, & Seligman, 2003). In **primary prevention,** mental health professionals attempt to alter social conditions that are thought to give rise to psychological difficulties. Improving school curriculums, teaching childrearing skills to new parents, and reducing the amount of lead in the environment are all primary prevention efforts. In **secondary prevention,** such professionals attempt to identify problems at their onset or as early as possible and to provide treatment to groups of children already at risk for developing cognitive or social disorders. Project Head Start, a preschool program largely focused on economically deprived children, is one example of an effort at secondary prevention. Finally, **tertiary prevention** involves providing treatment to children and families who have been identified as suffering from a variety of problems. The various medical and psychological treatments that we have discussed in this introduction to developmental psychopathology are examples of tertiary prevention.

The recent evaluation of a family-based primary prevention program aimed at reducing substance use (use of alcohol and tobacco among sixth to tenth graders) suggests that the incidence of this sort of problem can be reduced (Guyll, Spoth, Chao, Wickrama, & Russell, 2004; Spoth et al., 2003). The investigators taught families in the experimental condition a variety of skills including the following:

1. Increasing prosocial involvement within the family
2. Improving parenting and child management practices
3. Teaching children how to resist peer pressure
4. Reducing family conflict
5. Facilitating the expression of positive emotion among family members

Compared with children of families in the control group, who were not offered treatment, children in the treatment group were slower to develop use of alcohol and tobacco and, at the end of a four-year period, exhibited less overall substance use.

community psychology A form of social and psychological intervention in which psychologists try both to change general social conditions that play a role in children's—and adults'— psychological problems and to treat such problems.

primary prevention A form of *community psychology* in which mental health professionals attempt to alter social conditions, such as changing school curricula and teaching childrearing skills to new parents.

secondary prevention A form of *community psychology* in which mental health professionals try to identify people's problems at the outset and to undertake interventions to prevent disorders in those at risk.

tertiary prevention A form of *community psychology* in which mental health professionals provide treatment to children and families who are suffering various psychological problems.

Box 15.4

Child Psychology in Action

TREATING SERIOUS MULTIPROBLEM JUVENILE OFFENDERS

Adolescents, especially males, have higher crime rates in most categories than any other age group (Dodge et al., 2006), and they are one of the most difficult groups to treat successfully. Recidivism rates among serious juvenile offenders, even those who receive treatment of some sort, are often more than 70 percent. This is true in part because these delinquent adolescents have multiple problems and in part because most treatment methods tend to be either too narrow, focusing on only one or two characteristics of youths' ecology, or too broad, placing juveniles in institutions or foster homes.

Serious antisocial behavior is related to personal problems and difficulties in functioning in the family, peer group, school, and community. Henggeler, Melton, and Smith (1992b) used Bronfenbrenner's ecological model of development (Chapter 1) in developing a multisystemic therapy (MST) to treat serious juvenile offenders and their multiproblem families (Borduin & Henggeler, 1990). MST attempts to change systems and processes—such as parental discipline, familial emotional reactions, peer associations, and school performance—that research has identified as related to adolescent antisocial behavior. Thus, in addition to the focus on altering family relations characteristic of traditional family therapy, MST attempts to modify dysfunctional interactions in various settings. MST uses principles of family therapy and behavior therapy to alter not only relationships but patterns of social response, and therapy is carried out in familiar settings such as the home or school. MST also tries to be sensitive to individual and sociocultural differences in juvenile offenders.

Henggeler and his associates (1992b) randomly assigned 96 juvenile offenders to either an MST treatment group or a typical treatment situation involving social agencies, curfew, enforced school attendance, and monitoring by a probation officer. Although these adolescents were on average only 15 years of age, they were serious offenders, not just a group of rambunctious youths. They had averaged more than three previous arrests and eight weeks of prior incarceration, and 59 percent had had at least one arrest for a violent crime. They were well down the road toward a life of criminal activity. The average duration of treatment was just over 13 weeks, and MST treatment involved 33 hours of direct contact with a therapist.

The researchers used a multimethod battery of measures to assess pre- and posttreatment levels of criminal activity and duration of incarceration; improvements in family relations, peer relations, and social competence; and decreases in psychopathology in both youths and their parents. At the time of the posttreatment assessment, 59 weeks after the participants' first referral, the recidivism rate for the MST group was 42 percent, compared with 62 percent for the group who received typical treatment. In addition, 68 percent of the typical treatment group had been incarcerated after the study ended, whereas only 20 percent of the MST youth spent time in jail between the study and the posttreatment evaluation. On average, the MST youth were incarcerated for 73 fewer days than the typical treatment group. Important factors associated with the MST group's marked decrease in criminal activity and jail time included increased family cohesiveness as well as less aggressive and more positive relationships with peers.

Prevention efforts are not restricted to substance use. The success of recent prevention programs such as the Fast Track Program (Conduct Problems Prevention Research Group, 2004) is clear testimony that prevention efforts on behalf of children with problems of aggressive behavior can work (see Chapter 14). First-grade children at risk for later aggressive and conduct problems received school, family, and individual cognitive and social interventions. Early returns—at the end of third grade— suggest that the prevention efforts are helping children both academically and socially. The work by Henggeler and his colleagues presented in Box 15.4 demonstrates how effective a research-based, ecological, multisystem intervention method can be in treating a most resistant group—serious juvenile offenders.

Making the Connections 15

There are many links between concepts and ideas in one area of development and concepts and ideas in other areas. Here are some of the connections between ideas in Chapter 15 and discussions in other chapters of this book.

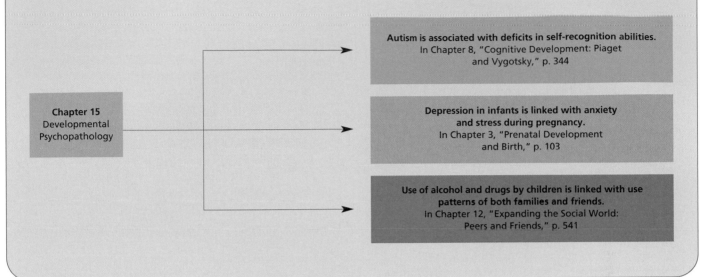

Chapter 15
Developmental
Psychopathology

Autism is associated with deficits in self-recognition abilities.
In Chapter 8, "Cognitive Development: Piaget and Vygotsky," p. 344

Depression in infants is linked with anxiety and stress during pregnancy.
In Chapter 3, "Prenatal Development and Birth," p. 103

Use of alcohol and drugs by children is linked with use patterns of both families and friends.
In Chapter 12, "Expanding the Social World: Peers and Friends," p. 541

SUMMARY

- Children exhibit a wide array of problem behaviors, some of which are relatively common and others quite rare. Many of these behaviors are marked by either a lack of control or excessive internalizing of troublesome issues.

The Developmental Approach to Psychopathology

- **Developmental psychopathology** involves the study of the origins, changes, and continuities in maladaptive behavior over the life span. The four basic principles of developmental psychopathology are (1) the role of development must be considered in interpreting the symptoms of a disorder and in seeking to understand its origins and course; (2) psychopathology must be viewed in relation both to the child's normal development and to the developmental tasks of children of her age; (3) the earliest precursors of disordered behavior must be studied; and (4) there are multiple pathways to both normal and abnormal behavior.

- There is great variability in response to biological and environmental risk factors, including permanent developmental delays, sleeper effects, and even enhanced coping ability. The child's resilience is greatest in the presence of three main protective factors: positive individual attributes, a supportive family environment, and supportive extrafamilial people or groups.

What Is Abnormal?

- Most researchers and clinicians think that developmental psychopathology is best thought of as problems in living. The medical model's view of problems as pathological may obscure the role of social judgments that depend on cultural and individual values. The statistical model views as abnormal any behaviors or feelings that differ from the average. Abnormality may also be defined as deviation from the ideal.

- Children are usually referred to mental health professionals by their parents or other adults, and factors other than the child's behavior may influence the referring adult's judgment about the child. Three kinds of factors that may influence the adult's perceptions are the child's characteristics, characteristics of the referring adult, and characteristics of the child's environment.

- Whether or not a particular behavior is viewed as normal depends on the child's age and the likelihood that it will continue over time. Some problems, such as bed-wetting, decline with age; others, such as nightmares, increase until adolescence and then decline. However, some childhood disorders are associated with later adult dysfunction.

- Continuity in some problem behaviors can be maintained by **cumulative continuity,** the selection of environments that support maladaptive behavior, or by **interactional continuity,** the evoking of negative responses from others that create and maintain dysfunctional interactions.

Classifying Child Psychopathology

- Two major ways of assessing and classifying developmental psychopathology are the diagnostic approach and the empirical method. Diagnoses are based on descriptions of clusters of behaviors and disturbing thoughts or feelings classified into various diagnostic categories. A **diagnosis** must convey information about the **etiology** and course of a disorder to be useful. The most widely used diagnostic classification system is the American Psychiatric Association's *DSM-IV.* Although this system has been revised several times, it still presents problems of reliability and validity.

- **Diagnostic reliability** is crucial in a classification system. The empirical approach involves having adults familiar with the child rate a large number of problem behaviors and then use statistical techniques to determine which disorders are related.

- **Undercontrolled disorders,** such as conduct and attention deficit/hyperactivity disorders, are the most frequently reported of all psychological problems of childhood and have considerable impact on the child's social environment. **Overcontrolled disorders,** such as childhood depression, have a greater effect on children themselves, who bottle up their feelings and concerns. Children with **pervasive developmental disorders** such as autism are characterized by gross deficits and extreme disturbances.

Some Psychological Disorders That Affect Children

- Children with either socialized or unsocialized **conduct disorders** repeatedly violate the rights of others or age-appropriate societal norms. Children who violate the law are termed **delinquent** and run the risk of being charged with either **status** or **criminal offenses.** Young offenders commit a sizable percentage of major offenses, and they are also often the victims of violent crime. Juvenile crime rose signifi-

cantly in the 1980s but declined somewhat in the early 1990s.

- Although among young people **substance abuse,** one kind of conduct disorder, also began a decline in the 1980s, it began an upswing in the 1990s. The evidence suggests that European American youths are more likely than Latino or African American adolescents to use legal and illegal drugs, although the data may not include youths who are dropouts or absent from school. Personal factors, such as anxiety and depression, are significant causes of drug abuse, and the common pathway to abuse starts with legal drugs such as alcohol and tobacco.

- Behavioral techniques, including reinforcement of appropriate behavior and the **time out** method, are among the most successful treatments for conduct disorders. Prevention programs that involve both family and school show early promise.

- **Attention deficit/hyperactivity disorder,** often not diagnosed until children enter the structured environment of school, is characterized by overactivity, impulsivity, poor attention, and difficulties with rule-governed behavior. Although the inappropriate activity of hyperactive children tends to diminish with age, some problems may persist, resulting in poor academic performance.

- Although biological explanations for this disorder, such as minimal brain damage, have received little empirical support, some genetic component may be involved. Environmental explanations, such as dysfunctional parent-child interaction patterns, have received some research support. At present, it appears that hyperactivity may have multiple causes. It is often treated by **psychostimulant medications, behavior therapy,** or a combination of the two.

- **Depression in childhood** may be characterized by depressed mood, changes in cognitive functioning such as inability to concentrate, behavioral signs such as irritability and crankiness, and such physical problems as loss of appetite and weight loss. Depression in children is hard to diagnose because children may not be able or willing to talk about feelings of overwhelming sadness until they have reached a certain level of cognitive maturity.

- Diagnoses of depression increase dramatically in adolescence, as does the rate of suicidal thinking and actual suicide attempts. A number of causes of depression have been hypothesized. Biological theories emphasize genetic and biochemical causes. Social and psychological theories suggest such causes as maternal depression and parental conflict. Cognitive theories suggest that feelings of personal inadequacy, or **learned helplessness,** may lead to depression.

- Antidepressant drugs are generally more successful at treating adults than children. **Cognitive behavior therapy** is one of the most effective treatments for childhood depression. Training in cognitive and problem-solving skills is a promising method for preventing depression.

- The most widely recognized pervasive developmental disorder is **autistic disorder,** which is characterized by a lack of interest in other people, various language abnormalities, such as **echolalia,** and an intense desire to preserve sameness in the environment. **Obsessive self-stimulation** may be seen as an effort to control sensory stimulation.

- Psychologists and others continue to debate the intelligence of autistic children. Such children sometimes exhibit specific talents in mathematics or the ability to repeat television commercials verbatim, but they score in the retarded range on IQ tests.

- The cause of autism is thought to have a biological basis. Treatment, which has included medication and **operant behavior therapy,** has met with limited success. Although treatment allows the children to develop many skills they would not otherwise acquire, their range of abilities remains quite limited.

Treating and Preventing Child Psychological Disorders

- Five approaches to the treatment of developmental disorders are commonly used. **Psychoactive medications** result in short-term benefits but have some side effects. Controversy about this form of treatment centers on the use of a drug when no firm evidence indicates the existence of an underlying biological disorder.

- **Play therapy** is often used with children because of their limited ability to express themselves verbally. The therapist attempts to gain insight into the child's concerns by interpreting the child's play.

- **Behavior therapy** is a collection of different treatment techniques derived from the principles of social learning and operant conditioning. The goal is to teach the child new ways of behaving by changing environmental contingencies.

- **Family therapy** views the child as part of a system and assumes that the child's behavior is an indication that something is wrong in that system. The therapist meets with all members of the family and works on modifying family relationships and interactions.

- **Community psychology** works to prevent disorders at the community level through **primary prevention**—providing interventions aimed at changing social conditions, **secondary prevention**—identifying and providing services for at-risk groups, and **tertiary prevention**—treating families who have already been identified as having problems.

EXPLORE AND DISCUSS

1. Are developmental problems of childhood culturally specific or do children in all cultures show all of the same kinds of problems? If you believe that these problems are culturally specific, support your answer with examples.

2. Some forms of psychopathology, such as autism, seem to be more prevalent than they were a decade ago. What do you think may be some of the reasons for the increased incidence of this kind of developmental disorder?

3. Why do you think that boys are more prone to externalize problems, for example, to engage in aggressive behavior that is often physical, whereas girls are more likely to internalize their concerns and then to express them in anxiety and depression?

Epilogue

Michael Escoffery (contemporary). *Circle of Love.*
1996. Private Collection.

Throughout this book we have reviewed the results of many studies of children's development. Beginning in our first chapter, we have described and critiqued theories that attempt to explain and interpret the detailed and complex information amassed by theorists and researchers in their efforts to understand child development. We have also identified and discussed the themes and methods of development that we first introduced in Chapter 1. Although psychology's understanding of children's development is vast, much remains that we do not yet understand. And as society and culture change, the process of development also changes. As is true in any field of science, our information is constantly expanding and changing. Child development is a vibrant and exciting area of study, and we are sure you will agree that advancing our knowledge and understanding of the field can contribute substantially to the betterment of society and to the healthy development of children everywhere.

We realize that much of the information discussed in this book will be reexamined and modified in the near future. With this in mind, we have identified some broad principles that characterize, first, our views on the current state of psychology's knowledge about child development and, second, our ideas about knowledge that is on the horizon. In this connection we make some suggestions about what the field needs to do in respect to both building theory and selecting the kinds of research methods that will make it possible to secure this developing knowledge.

OUR KNOWLEDGE OF CHILD DEVELOPMENT AT PRESENT

1. **The child is competent.** Recent years have seen a dramatic change in our view of the capacities of children. Scientists once considered infants and young children to be helpless, passive creatures who, with limited sensory, perceptual, and social abilities, were simply awaiting the imprint of the adult world. In contrast, today's child psychologists view children as competent and active beings who from an early age possess a wide range of perceptual, motoric, cognitive, emotional, and social capabilities.
2. **The child's behavior is organized.** From the very beginning of children's lives, organization is evident in their behavior. Actions such as sucking and looking are not disorganized reflexes or reactions but highly structured response patterns that enable even newborns to interact with and to learn from the social and physical world.
3. **The different aspects of psychological development are interdependent.** Although developmentalists often focus on distinct areas of growth such as social, emotional, physical, linguistic, or cognitive development, all these areas overlap and exert mutual influence on each other.

4. **The child's behavior has multiple causes.** Current understanding of development suggests that most behaviors have multiple causes, and that causation often involves interaction among biological, environmental, and experiential factors.

5. **There is no single pathway to normal or abnormal development.** Children may take alternative routes to normal development; no single pathway is necessarily the "best" one to follow. It is a well-established observation that individual adults who are intellectually and socially competent often have reached their goals by very different routes. Children's development is profoundly influenced both by varying kinds of experiences and by the timing of these experiences. At one time or another a child may confront a risk with greater or lesser resilience. Moreover, these same principles hold true with respect to development that is less than ideal: children whose lives become dysfunctional to one degree or another may reach this state by a variety of pathways.

6. **The child's development is generally continuous but is marked by periods of more rapid, more dramatic change.** These periods of change are often accompanied by the onset of biological and social changes, such as puberty and school transitions, or by unexpected or nonnormative events, such as the loss of a parent or of a friendship. In addition, the characterization of development as continuous or discontinuous depends, in part, on how closely we look. A detailed examination will reveal that even though developmental progress is, in the main, quite gradual, periods of rapid developmental advance sometimes occur.

7. **Development is a lifelong process.** Although this book focuses on the development of the child, it is important to recognize that the adults who are influential in a child's development continue to develop throughout their own lives—physically, socially, emotionally, and cognitively. As human beings in every stage of the life cycle, we respond to, learn from, and change through experiences of many kinds. So to understand children we need to recognize that their development occurs in the context of the continuing development experienced by their parents and by other socializing agents.

8. **The child influences other people.** As children grow, they influence the behavior of the adults and children with whom they interact. Even infants play an active role in modifying the behaviors of their parents and others. Now widely accepted, this *bidirectional* view of development underscores the fact that children play an influential part in their own development.

9. **The child's behavior varies across situations and settings.** One important feature of human behavior is the ability to adapt to the demands of different situations. The same child may behave differently with different people or in different situations—in the home, the laboratory, the school, or the peer play group. Thus we need to study children in multiple settings and to exercise caution in generalizing our interpretations of children's behaviors from one situation to another.

10. **The child's behavior is influenced by social systems.** The child is embedded in a variety of systems, and the members of these systems influence one another's behavior. Social systems range from the smaller and more immediate, such as the family or the peer group, to the larger and more remote, such as the school, the community, or the greater society. The child may have considerable influence in smaller systems but often has less control in larger ones.

11. **Child development occurs in a cultural context.** Cultural contributions to development are important and complex. In multicultural societies like the United States, because cultural systems range from the ethnic neighborhood to the broader culture of the society at large, children experience a number

of cultural influences. In other societies in which most members share a similar cultural background, this cultural context greatly influences the developing child. In all types of cultural settings, tensions among the generations may evolve as elders expect younger people to carry on valued cultural traditions and the young resist these expectations. To achieve a full understanding of child development, we need to pay attention to both intercultural and intracultural variations in children's experience.

12. **Children develop in an historical context.** As social conditions shift, children and families undergo changes that alter their behavior. The experiences of children who grew up in the Great Depression of the 1930s differed dramatically from those of children growing up in the 1990s. The changes in gender roles that have occurred in the mid- and later twentieth century have altered family lifestyles. When both parents work outside the home and divide household labor differently, children's lives are altered, too. One of the aims of child psychology is to examine these and other changes so as to determine how they affect children's behavior.

KNOWLEDGE ON THE HORIZON

1. **Child psychologists need to employ multiple research methods.** In examining the complex and multifaceted aspects of children's development we cannot rely on any single research method. A wide variety of methods, including naturalistic observations, laboratory and field experiments, self-reports, clinical studies, and standardized tests can provide us with different types of information about children. In addition, we need to gather information from the many different people who interact with children, including parents, peers, and teachers. With the information that each of these people can provide and the unique perspectives that each offers, we will gain a broader and deeper understanding of the developing child.

2. **Child psychologists need multiple samples.** To fully understand how children grow and develop, we need to select multiple samples in our research. Doing so will enable us to capture the cultural and ethnic richness—the diversity—of children's development, both within the United States and throughout the world.

3. **Child psychologists need multiple theories of development.** Theories like those of Piaget, Freud, and Vygotsky—theories that attempt to provide a full and comprehensive account of development—have inspired a great deal of very useful research. Contemporary psychologists believe, however, that the complex and multidetermined nature of development requires us to explain smaller pieces of the developmental puzzle before we attempt to assemble an all-encompassing theory. Thus, today's developmental psychologists are more likely to advance theories of more specific phenomena—such as gender typing, memory function, aggression, or language development—than to formulate the kinds of grand theories that were put forward during much of the twentieth century.

4. **A full understanding of child development will require a multidisciplinary effort.** Many scientific disciplines besides child psychology contribute in important ways to our understanding of children. For example, anthropology provides a cross-cultural perspective on child socialization, and sociology offers a societal viewpoint on the systems and institutions which children experience. Pediatrics illuminates the role of physical health in the child's development, while clinical psychology and psychiatry offer an understanding of deviant and abnormal development in children. Finally, history views children's development through the lens of time. Multidisciplinary approaches

are increasingly common in studies of children's development, as they are in other areas of scientific study.

5. **Child development research influences, and is influenced by, social policy.** As we have stressed throughout this book, research in child development and the application of its findings are closely linked. For example, basic research on the importance for development of children's early environment stimulated government efforts like Head Start and the growth of day-care programs. Child psychologists are actively involved in issues of concern to society, such as poverty, problems of family breakdown, schooling that accommodates different cultural styles of learning, and the influence on the growing child of violent content in television and other media. Contributing to the formation and evaluation of social policy that affects children is both an opportunity and a responsibility of the field of child development.

Glossary

accommodation Modifying an existing schema to fit a new experience.

achievement motivation A person's tendency to strive for successful performance, to evaluate her performance against standards of excellence, and to feel pleasure at having performed successfully.

acquired immune deficiency syndrome (AIDS) A viral disease that attacks the body's immune system; transmitted to a fetus or newborn in the form of the *human immunodeficiency virus (HIV)*, this disorder weakens the immune system and may ultimately cause the child's death.

active genetic-environmental interaction A kind of interaction in which people's genes encourage them to seek out experiences compatible with their inherited tendencies.

adaptation Adjusting one's thinking to fit with environmental demands.

age cohort People born within the same generation.

age of viability Twenty-two to 26 weeks from conception, at which point the fetus's physical systems are advanced enough that it may survive premature birth.

aggression Behavior that intentionally harms other people by inflicting pain or injury on them.

aggressive rejected children *Rejected* children who have low self-control, are highly aggressive, and exhibit behavior problems.

allele An alternate form of a gene; typically, a gene has two alleles, one inherited from the individual's mother and one from the father.

alphafetoprotein (AFP) assay A blood test performed on a pregnant woman to detect such problems in the fetus as Down syndrome, the presence of multiple embryos, and defects of the central nervous system.

altruism An unselfish concern for the welfare of others.

altruistic behavior Intrinsically motivated behavior that is intended to help others without expectation of acknowledgment or concrete reward.

amniocentesis A technique for sampling and assessing fetal cells for indications of abnormalities in the developing fetus; performed by inserting a needle through the abdominal wall and into the amniotic sac and withdrawing a small amount of the amniotic fluid.

amniotic sac A membrane that contains the developing organism and the amniotic fluid around it; sac and fluid protect the organism from physical shocks and temperature changes.

androgynous Possessing both feminine and masculine psychological characteristics.

animistic thinking The attribution of life to inanimate objects.

anorexia nervosa An eating disorder in which the person, usually a young woman, is preoccupied with avoiding obesity and often diets to the point of starvation.

anoxia A lack of oxygen in brain cells.

approach/avoidance behavior A pattern of interaction in which the infant or child shows an inconsistent pattern of approaching and retreating from a person or an object.

assimilation Applying an existing schema to a new experience.

associative learning According to Jensen, lower-level learning tapped in tests of such things as short-term memorization and recall, attention, rote learning, and simple associative skills. Also called *level I learning*.

attachment A strong emotional bond that forms between infant and caregiver in the second half of the child's first year.

Attachment Q Sort (AQS) An assessment method in which a caregiver or observer judges the quality of a child's attachment based on the child's behavior in naturalistic situations that often include brief separations from parents.

attention The identification and selection of particular sensory input for closer inspection and more detailed processing.

attention deficit/hyperactivity disorder (ADHD) A childhood disorder characterized by a persistent pattern of inattention and hyperactivity or impulsivity that far exceeds such behaviors observed in children at comparable levels of development.

authoritarian parenting Parenting that is harsh, unresponsive, and rigid, and in which parents tend to use power-assertive methods of control.

authoritative parenting Parenting that is warm, responsive, and involved yet unintrusive, and in which parents set reasonable limits and expect appropriately mature behavior from their children.

autistic disorder A disorder in which children's ability to communicate and interact socially is seriously impaired; autistic children have specific language deficiencies, demonstrate a need for sameness in their environment, and often engage in repetitive and stereotyped kinds of behaviors.

autobiographical memory A collection of memories of things that have happened to a person at a specific time or place.

automatization The process of transforming conscious, controlled behaviors into unconscious and automatic ones.

autosomes The 22 paired non-sex chromosomes.

autostimulation theory The theory that during REM sleep the infant's brain stimulates itself and that this in turn stimulates early development of the central nervous system.

average children Children who have some friends but are not as well liked as popular children.

babbling An infant's production of strings of consonant-vowel combinations.

basic reflex activity An infant's exercise of, and growing proficiency in, the use of innate reflexes.

Bayley Scales of Infant Development A set of nonverbal tests that measure specific developmental milestones and are generally used with children who are thought to be at risk for abnormal development.

behavior therapy A form of psychological treatment, often used in treating conduct disorders as well as other disorders (autistic spectrum disorders), that is based on such learning principles as reinforcement and social learning.

behaviorism A learning perspective which holds that theories of psychology must be based on observations of actual behavior rather than on speculation about motives or unobservable factors.

bilingualism The acquisition of two languages at the same time.

brain hemispheres The two halves of the brain's cerebrum, left and right.

Brazelton Neonatal Assessment Scale A scale containing a battery of tests used to measure an infant's sensory and perceptual capabilities, motor development, range of states, and ability to regulate these states, as well as whether the brain and central nervous system are properly regulating involuntary responses.

bulimia nervosa An eating disorder in which people, usually young women, alternate periods of binge eating with vomiting and other means of compensating for the weight gained.

canalization The genetic restriction of a phenotype to a small number of developmental outcomes, permitting environmental influences to play only a small role in these outcomes.

case study method A form of research in which investigators study an individual person or group very intensely.

catch-up growth The tendency for human beings to regain a normal course of physical growth after injury or deprivation.

categorical speech perception The tendency to perceive as the same a range of sounds belonging to the same phonemic group.

catharsis Presumably, discharging aggressive impulses by engaging in actual or symbolic aggressive acts that do not impinge on another person.

center care A child-care context in which children are cared for in a "school-like" environment by professional caregivers.

centration Focusing one's attention on only one dimension or characteristic of an object or situation.

cephalocaudal development The pattern of human physical growth in which development begins in the area of the brain and proceeds downward, to the trunk and legs.

cerebral cortex The covering layer of the cerebrum that contains the cells that control specific functions such as seeing, hearing, moving, and thinking.

cerebrum The two connected hemispheres of the brain.

cesarean delivery The surgical delivery of a baby; the baby is removed from the mother's uterus through an incision made in her abdomen and uterus in a procedure also known as *cesarean section*.

child development A field of study that seeks to account for the gradual evolution of the child's cognitive, social, and other capacities first by describing changes in the child's observed behaviors and then by uncovering the processes and strategies that underlie these changes.

chlamydia Probably the most widespread bacterial sexually transmitted disease; can cause pneumonia or a form of conjunctivitis in a pregnant woman's baby.

chorionic villi sampling A technique for sampling and assessing cells withdrawn from the chorionic villi, projections from the *chorion* that surrounds the amniotic sac; cells are withdrawn either through a tube inserted into the uterus through the vagina or through a needle inserted through the abdominal wall.

chromosomes Threadlike structures located in the nucleus of a cell, that carry genetic information to help direct development.

chronosystem The time-based dimension that can alter the operation of all other systems in Bronfenbrenner's model, from *microsystem* through *macrosystem*.

classical conditioning A type of learning in which two stimuli are repeatedly presented together until individuals learn to respond to the unfamiliar stimulus in the same way they respond to the familiar stimulus.

clique A voluntary group formed on the basis of friendship.

codominance A genetic pattern in which heterozygous alleles express the variants of the trait for which they code simultaneously and with equal force.

cognition The mental activity through which humans acquire and process knowledge.

cognitive behavior therapy A group therapy technique particularly useful in treating depression in adolescents. Therapeutic goals include reducing self-consciousness and feelings of being different and teaching strategies for dealing with depressive moods and for acquiring a more positive outlook and improving social interactions.

cognitive developmental theory of gender typing Kohlberg's theory that children use physical and behavioral clues to differentiate gender roles and to gender-type themselves very early in life.

cognitive developmental view of attachment The view that to form attachments infants must both differentiate between mother and stranger and understand that people exist independent of the infant's interaction with them.

cognitive learning According to Jensen, higher-level learning tapped in tests of such things as abstract thinking, symbolic processing, and the use of language in problem solving. Also called *level II* learning.

cognitive map A mental representation of the spatial layout of a physical or geographic place.

cognitive processes Ways that the human mental system operates on information.

cognitive social learning theory A learning theory that stresses the importance of observation and imitation in the acquisition of new behaviors, with learning mediated by cognitive processes.

colic A prolonged period of unexplained crying in an infant.

communicative competence The ability to convey thoughts, feelings, and intentions in a meaningful and culturally patterned way.

community of learners An approach to classroom learning in which adults and children work together in shared activities, peers learn from each other, and the teacher serves as a guide.

community psychology A form of social and psychological intervention in which psychologists try both to change general social conditions that play a role in children's—and adults'—psychological problems and to treat such problems.

comorbidity The co-occurrence of two or more problem behaviors.

computer-assisted instruction A form of instruction embodied in computer software programs that typically pose questions or problems, give the student a chance to respond, and then tell her if she is correct.

concrete operations stage Stage in which the child is able to reason logically about materials that are physically present.

conduct disorder A disorder characterized by a repetitive and persistent pattern of behavior in which a young person violates the basic rights of others or major age-appropriate societal norms or rules.

congenital Describes characteristic acquired during development in the uterus or during the birth process and not through heredity.

connectionist models Information-processing approaches that are based on the biological idea of neural networks and that often uses computer simulations; these models emphasize human cognition's different layers and networks of cognitive processing.

conscience The child's internalized values and standards of behavior.

conservation The understanding that altering an object's or a substance's appearance does not change its basic attributes or properties.

constructivist view The idea that children actively create their understanding of the world as they encounter new information and have new experiences.

control group In an experiment, the group that is not exposed to the treatment, or the *independent variable*.

control phase According to Kopp, the first phase in learning self-regulation, when children are highly dependent on caregivers to remind them about acceptable behaviors.

controversial children Children who are liked by many peers but also disliked by many.

conventional level Kohlberg's second level of moral development, in which the child's behavior is designed to solicit others' approval and maintain good relations with them. The child accepts societal regulations unquestioningly and judges behavior as good if it conforms to these rules.

cooing A very young infant's production of vowel-like sounds.

cooperative learning A teaching technique in which small groups of students work together to master material to be learned.

coordination of secondary circular reactions An infant's combination of different schemata to achieve a specific goal.

co-parenting Parenting in which spouses work together as a team, coordinating their childrearing practices with each other; co-parenting can be cooperative, hostile, or characterized by different levels of investment in the parenting task.

core knowledge systems Ways of reasoning about ecologically important objects and events, such as the solidity and continuity of objects.

corpus callosum The band of nerve fibers that connects the two hemispheres of the brain.

correlational method A research design that permits investigators to establish relations among variables as well as assess the strength of those relations.

creativity The ability to solve problems, create products, or pose questions in a way that is novel or unique.

creole language A language spoken by children of pidgin-language speakers that, in contrast with pidgin, is highly developed and rule governed.

criminal offense Behavior that is illegal.

critical period A specific period in children's development when they are sensitive to a particular environmental stimulus that does not have the same effect on them when encountered before or after this period.

crossing over The process by which equivalent sections of homologous chromosomes switch places randomly, shuffling the genetic information each carries.

cross-sectional method A research method in which researchers compare groups of individuals of different age levels at approximately the same point in time.

crowd A collection of people whom others have stereotyped on the basis of their perceived shared attitudes or activities; for example, *populars* or *nerds*.

culture-fair test A test that attempts to minimize cultural biases in content that might influence the test taker's responses.

cumulative continuity The tendency to seek out experiences and environments that support or reinforce maladaptive predispositions. *Transactional stressors*, such as irritability, fuel a cycle in which irritability leads to job loss, which heightens irritability.

cumulative risk The notion that risk factors in children's life circumstances have cumulative negative effects on their intellectual performance.

deductive reasoning Logical thinking that involves reaching a necessary and valid conclusion based on a set of premises.

deferred imitation Mimicry of an action some time after having observed it; requires that the child have some sort of mental representation of the action.

delay of gratification Putting off until another time possessing or doing something that gives one pleasure.

delinquency Juvenile behavior in violation of the law.

deoxyribonucleic acid (DNA) A ladderlike molecule that stores genetic information in cells and transmits it during reproduction.

dependent variable The variable, or factor, that researchers expect to change as a function of change in the independent variable.

depression in childhood Like adult depression, a disorder often manifested in a depressed mood and loss of interest in familiar activities, but also likely to be expressed as irritability and crankiness. Difficulty concentrating or focusing on tasks and concomitant drops in school grades are not uncommon, and depressed children often complain of physical problems such as headache.

developmental psychopathology The investigation of the origins, course, changes, and continuities in disordered or maladaptive behavior over a person's life span.

deviation IQ An IQ score that indicates the extent to which a person's performance on a test deviates from age-mates' average performance.

diagnosis The identification of a physical or mental disorder on the basis of symptoms and of knowledge of the cause or causes of the disorder and its common course. A diagnosis may also include information about effective forms of treatment.

diagnostic reliability A measure of how often two or more clinicians arrive independently at the same diagnosis of a particular disorder.

diethylstilbestrol (DES) A synthetic hormone once prescribed for pregnant women to prevent miscarriage but discontinued when cancer and precancerous conditions were detected in their children.

differentiation view The notion that the child learns to identify and discriminate among the important features of objects and relationships from the rich source of information sensory input provides.

direct observation A method of observation in which researchers go into settings in the natural world or bring participants into the laboratory to observe behaviors of interest.

discourse Socially based conversation.

dizygotic Characterizing *fraternal* twins, who have developed from two separate fertilized eggs.

dominance hierarchy An ordering of individuals in a group from most to least dominant; a "pecking order."

dominant The more powerful of two *alleles* in a heterozygous combination.

Down syndrome A form of chromosome abnormality in which the person suffers disabling physical and mental development and is highly susceptible to such illnesses as leukemia, heart disorders, and respiratory infections.

dynamic systems theory A theory that proposes that individuals develop and function within systems and that studies the relationships among individuals and systems and the processes by which these relationships operate.

dyslexia A term for the difficulties some people experience in reading or learning to read.

echolalia Repeating word for word what is said by another rather than responding to a question or making a statement of one's own; a common problem in autistic children.

ecological theory A theory of development that stresses the importance of understanding not only the relationships between organisms and various environmental systems but the relations among such systems themselves.

ecological validity The degree to which a research study accurately represents events and processes that occur in the natural world.

ego In Freudian theory, the rational, controlling component of the personality, which tries to satisfy needs through appropriate, socially acceptable behaviors.

egocentric speech According to Vygotsky, a form of self-directed dialogue by which the child instructs herself in solving problems and formulating plans; as the child matures, this becomes internalized as *inner speech*.

egocentrism The tendency to view the world from one's own perspective and to have difficulty seeing things from another's viewpoint.

elaboration A memory strategy in which one adds to information to make it more meaningful and thus easier to remember.

elementary mental functions Psychological functions with which the child is endowed by nature, including attention, perception, and involuntary memory, that emerge spontaneously during children's interaction with the world.

embryo The developing organism between the second and eighth week of gestation; the embryonic period comprises the differentiation of the major physiological structures and systems.

emotional display rules Rules that dictate which emotions one may appropriately display in particular situations.

emotional script A complex scheme that enables a child to identify the emotional reaction likely to accompany a particular sort of event.

emotions Subjective reactions to the environment that are usually experienced cognitively as either pleasant or unpleasant, generally accompanied by physiological arousal, and often expressed in some visible form of behavior.

empathy The capacity to experience the same emotion that someone else is experiencing.

encoding The transformation of information from the environment into a mental representation.

ends over means focus Consideration of only the end state of a problem in evaluating an event; failure to consider the means by which that end state was obtained.

enrichment view The notion that the child acquires additional information about an object from each repeated experience with it, further modifying and enriching these data with information from existing schemata.

episodic memory Memory for specific events, often autobiographical in nature.

estrogens Hormones that, in the female, are responsible for sexual maturation.

ethological theory A theory that holds that behavior must be viewed and understood as occurring in a particular context and as having adaptive or survival value.

ethological theory of attachment Bowlby's theory that attachment derives from the biological preparation of both infant and parents to respond to each other's behaviors in such a way that parents provide the infant with care and protection.

etiology In medicine and psychiatry, the cause or causes of a specific disorder.

event sampling A technique by which investigators record participants' behavior only when an event of particular interest occurs.

evocative genetic-environmental interaction The expression of the genes' influence on the environment through an individual's inherited tendencies to evoke certain environmental responses; for example, a child's smiling may elicit smiles from others.

evolutionary psychology An approach that holds that critical components of psychological functioning reflect evolutionary changes and are critical to the survival of the species.

executive control process A cognitive process that serves to control, guide, and monitor the success of a problem-solving approach that a child uses.

executive control structure According to Case, a mental blueprint or plan for solving a class of problems.

exosystem The collection of settings, such as a parent's daily work, that impinge on a child's development but in which the child does not play a direct role.

expansion A technique adults use in speaking to young children in which they imitate and expand or add to a child's statement.

experience-dependent processes Brain processes that are unique to the individual and responsive to particular cultural, community, and family experiences.

experience-expectant processes Brain processes that are universal, experienced by all human beings across evolution.

experimental group In an experiment, the group that is exposed to the treatment, or the *independent variable*.

expressive characteristics Qualities such as nurturance, concern for feelings, and child orientation; thought to be more common in women.

extended family A family that includes relatives such as grandparents, aunts, uncles, nieces, and nephews, as well as the basic family unit of parents and children.

factor analysis A statistical procedure used to determine which of a number of factors, or scores, are both closely related to each other and relatively independent of other groups of factors, or scores.

Fagan Test of Infant Intelligence A test of how infants process information, including encoding attributes of objects and seeing similarities and differences across objects; designed to be culture-fair.

family child care A child-care arrangement in which an individual cares for three or four children in her home.

family therapy A form of psychotherapy in which all family members join to find solutions to a child's problem behaviors.

fast-mapping A technique in which a child learns to link a new word with a concept that he or she already understands.

fetal alcohol syndrome A disorder exhibited by infants of alcoholic mothers and characterized by stunted growth, a number of physical and physiological abnormalities, and, often, mental retardation.

fetus The developing organism from the third month of gestation through delivery; during the fetal period bodily structures and systems develop to completion.

field experiment An experiment in which researchers deliberately create a change in a real-world setting and then measure the outcome of their manipulation.

Flynn effect Increase in the average IQ score in the populations of the United States and other developed countries since the early 1900s, a phenomenon identified by J. R. Flynn.

formal operations stage Stage in which the child becomes capable of abstract thinking, complex reasoning, and hypothesis testing.

fragile X syndrome A form of chromosomal abnormality, more common in males than in females, in which an area near the tip of the X chromosome is narrowed and made fragile due to a failure to condense during cell division. Symptoms include physical, cognitive, and social problems.

friendship A reciprocal commitment between two people who see themselves more or less as equals.

gender-based beliefs Ideas and expectations about what is appropriate behavior for males and females.

gender constancy The awareness that superficial alterations in appearance or activity do not alter gender.

gender identity The perception of oneself as either masculine or feminine.

gender-role preferences Desires to possess certain gender-typed characteristics.

gender roles Composites of the behaviors actually exhibited by a typical male or female in a given culture; the reflection of a *gender stereotype* in everyday life.

gender-schema theory The notion that children develop schemas, or naive theories, that help them organize and structure their experience related to gender differences and gender roles.

gender stability The notion that gender does not change; males remain male and females remain female.

gender stereotypes Beliefs that members of a culture hold about how females and males ought to behave; that is, what behaviors are acceptable and appropriate for each sex.

gender typing The process by which children acquire the values, motives, and behaviors considered appropriate for their gender in their particular culture.

gene A portion of DNA located at a particular site on a chromosome; codes for the production of certain kinds of proteins.

general factor (*g*) General mental energy, or ability, involved in all cognitive tasks.

generalization The application of a strategy learned while solving a problem in one situation to a similar problem in a new situation.

genital herpes A common viral infection spread primarily through sexual contact; if contracted by an infant during birth can cause blindness, motor abnormalities, mental retardation, and a wide range of neurological disorders.

genotype The particular set of genes that a person inherits from his or her parents.

glial cell A nerve cell that supports and protects neurons and serves to encase them in *myelin sheaths*.

gonorrhea A sexually transmitted bacterial infection that, in a pregnant woman, can cause blindness in her infant; normally treatable with antibiotics.

goodness of fit A measure of the degree to which a child's temperament is matched by her environment; the more effectively parents and other agents of socialization accept and adapt to the child's unique temperament, the better this "fit."

grammar The structure of a language; consists of *morphology* and *syntax*.

guided participation Learning that occurs as children participate in activities of their community and are guided in their participation by the actions of more experienced partners in the setting.

habituation A process of learning by which an individual reacts with less and less intensity to a repeatedly presented stimulus, eventually responding only faintly or not at all.

Head Start A federally funded program that provides disadvantaged young children with preschool experience, social services, and medical and nutritional assistance.

hedonistic reasoning Making a decision to perform a prosocial act on the basis of expected material reward.

hemispheric specialization Differential functioning of the two cerebral hemispheres; the left controlling the right side of the body, the right controlling the body's left side.

hemophilia A disorder caused by an X-linked recessive gene, in which the blood fails to clot; found more often in males than in females.

heritability factor A statistical estimate of the contribution heredity makes to a particular trait or ability.

heterozygous Characterizing an individual who has inherited different *alleles* for a particular trait from each parent.

hierarchical categorization The organization of concepts into levels of abstraction that range from the specific to the general.

higher mental functions Psychological functions, such as voluntary attention, complex memory processes, and problem solving, that entail the coordination of several cognitive processes and the use of *mediators*.

holophrase A single word that appears to represent a complete thought.

homozygous Characterizing an individual who has inherited identical *alleles* for a particular trait from each parent.

horizontal décalage The term Piaget used to describe unevenness in children's thinking within a particular stage; for example, in developing an understanding of conservation children conserve different objects or substances, at different ages.

hormones Powerful and highly specialized chemical substances that are produced by the cells of certain body organs and that have a regulatory effect on the activity of certain other organs.

hostile aggression Directing aggressive behavior at a particular person or group, criticizing, ridiculing, tattling on, or calling names.

human behavior genetics The study of the relative influences of heredity and environment on the evolution of individual differences in traits and abilities.

Huntington disease A genetically caused, fatal disorder of the nervous system that begins in midadulthood and is manifested chiefly in uncontrollable spasmodic movements of the body and limbs and eventual mental deterioration.

id In Freudian theory, the person's instinctual drives; the first component of the personality to evolve, the id operates on the basis of the *pleasure principle*.

identification The Freudian notion that children acquire gender identity by identifying with and imitating their same-sex parents.

immanent justice The notion that any deviation from rules will inevitably result in punishment or retribution.

imprinting The process by which birds and other infrahuman animals develop a preference for the person or object to which they are first exposed during a brief, critical period after birth.

inclusion A policy by which children of all ability levels, whether learning disabled, physically handicapped, or mentally retarded, are included in the same classroom.

independent variable The variable, or factor, that researchers deliberately manipulate in an experiment.

infant state A recurring pattern of arousal in the newborn, ranging from alert, vigorous, wakeful activity to quiet, regular sleep.

infant-directed, or child-directed, speech A simplified style of speech parents use with young children, in which sentences are short, simple, and often repetitive and the speaker enunciates especially clearly, slowly, and in a higher-pitched voice, often ending with a rising intonation. Also called *motherese*.

information-processing approaches Theories of development that focus on the flow of information through the child's cognitive system and particularly on the specific operations the child performs between input and output phases.

informed consent Agreement, based on a clear and full understanding of the purposes and procedures of a research study, to participate in that study.

inner speech Internalized *egocentric speech* that guides intellectual functioning.

insecure-avoidant attachment A type of attachment shown by babies who seem not to be bothered by their mothers' brief absences but specifically avoid them on their return, sometimes becoming visibly upset.

insecure-disorganized attachment A type of attachment shown by babies who seem disorganized and disoriented when reunited with their mothers after a brief separation.

insecure-resistant attachment A kind of attachment shown by babies who tend to become very upset at the departure of their mothers and who exhibit inconsistent behavior on their return, sometimes seeking contact, sometimes pushing their mothers away.

instrumental aggression Quarreling and fighting with others over toys and possessions.

instrumental characteristics Qualities such as task and occupation orientation; thought to be more typical of males than of females.

intellectual giftedness A characteristic defined by an IQ score of 130 or over; gifted children learn faster than others and may show early exceptional talents in certain areas.

intelligence quotient (IQ) An index of the way a person performs on a standardized intelligence test relative to the way others her age perform.

interactional continuity The tendency for negative temperamental or personality characteristics to evoke negative responses from others, which reinforce the negative characteristics.

interactive synchrony A term that characterizes mother-infant interactions in which the mother constantly adjusts her behavior to that of her baby, responding to and respecting the baby's signals as to when she is ready for and wants engagement and interaction.

intermodal perception The use of sensory information from more than one modality to identify a stimulus and make sense of it; also, the identification of a stimulus already identified by means of one modality by the use of another modality.

internal working model According to Bowlby, a child's mental representation of himself as a child, his parents, and the style of his interaction with his parents, as he reconstructs and interprets that interaction; also referred to as an *attachment representation*.

intuitive substage The second substage of the preoperational stage, during which the child begins to solve problems by using mental operations but cannot explain how she arrives at the solutions.

inventing new means by mental combination Children begin to combine schemata mentally and rely less on physical trial and error.

iron-deficiency anemia A disorder in which inadequate amounts of iron in the diet cause listlessness and may retard a child's physical and intellectual development.

joint legal custody A form of child custody in which both parents retain and share responsibility for decisions regarding the child's life, although the child usually resides with one parent.

joint physical custody As in *joint legal custody*, parents make decisions together regarding their child's life, but they also share physical custody, so that the child lives with each parent for a portion of the year.

Kaufman Assessment Battery for Children (K-ABC) An intelligence test designed to measure several types of information-processing skills as well as achievement in some academic subjects.

Klinefelter's syndrome A form of chromosome abnormality in which a male inherits an extra X sex chromosome, resulting in the XXY pattern, many feminine physical characteristics, language deficits, and, sometimes, mental retardation.

laboratory experiment A research design that allows investigators to determine cause and effect by controlling variables and treatments and assigning participants randomly to treatments.

language A communication system in which words and their written symbols combine in rule-governed ways and enable speakers to produce an infinite number of messages.

Language Acquisition Device (LAD) Chomsky's proposed mental structure in the human nervous system that incorporates an innate concept of language.

Language Acquisition Support System (LASS) According to Bruner, a collection of strategies and tactics that environmental influences—initially, a child's parents or primary caretakers—provide the language-learning child.

lanugo A fine, soft hair that covers the fetus's body from about the fifth month of gestation on; may be shed before birth or after.

latchkey children Children who must let themselves into their homes after school because a parent or both parents are working outside the home.

lateralization The process by which each half of the brain becomes specialized for the performance of certain functions.

learned helplessness A kind of behavior that results from the belief that one is helpless to control the events in one's world.

learning disabilities Deficits in one or more cognitive processes important for learning.

learning theory of attachment The theory that infants become attached to their mothers because a mother provides food, or primary reinforcement, and thus becomes a *secondary reinforcer*.

life-span perspective A view of development as a process that continues throughout the life cycle, from infancy through adulthood and old age.

longitudinal method A method of research in which investigators study the same people repeatedly at various times in the participants' lives.

long-term memory The mental processing unit in which information may be stored permanently and from which it may later be retrieved.

macrosystem The system that surrounds the *microsystem*, *mesosystem*, and *exosystem*; represents the values, ideologies, and laws of the society or culture.

magic window thinking The tendency of very young children to believe that TV images are as real as the people and things around them.

maturation A genetic or biologically determined process of growth that unfolds over a period of time.

mediational deficiency Inability to use strategies to store information in long-term memory.

mediators Psychological tools and signs—such as language, counting, mnemonic devices, algebraic symbols, art, and writing—that facilitate and direct thinking processes.

meiosis The process by which a germ cell divides to produce new germ cells with only half the normal complement of chromosomes; male and female germ cells (sperm and ovum) each contain only 23 chromosomes but when they unite, the new organism they form has 46 chromosomes, half from each parent.

memory span The amount of information one can hold in short-term memory.

menarche In females, the beginning of the menstrual cycle.

mental age An index of a child's actual performance on an intelligence test as compared with his true age.

mental representation Information stored in some form (e.g., verbal, pictorial, procedural) in the cognitive system after the person has encountered it in the environment.

mental retardation A characteristic defined by an IQ score below 70 and difficulty in coping with age-appropriate activities of everyday life.

mesosystem The interrelations among the components of the *microsystem*.

metacognition The individual's knowledge about knowing and his control of cognitive activities.

metalinguistic awareness The understanding that language is a rule-bound system of communicating with others.

microgenetic analysis A very detailed examination of how a child solves a problem over a single learning episode or over several episodes that occur close in time.

microgenetic change Change associated with learning that occurs over the period of a specific learning experience or episode.

microsystem In Bronfenbrenner's ecological theory, the context in which children live and interact with the people and institutions closest to them, such as parents, peers, and school.

mitosis The process in which a body cell divides in two, first duplicating its chromosomes so that the new daughter cells each contain the usual 46 chromosomes.

modifier genes Genes that exert their influence indirectly, by affecting the expression of still other genes.

monozygotic Characterizing *identical* twins, who have developed from a single fertilized egg.

moral realism Piaget's second stage of moral development, in which the child shows great respect for rules but applies them quite inflexibly.

morality of reciprocity Piaget's third stage of moral development, in which the child recognizes that rules may be questioned and altered, considers the feelings and views of others, and believes in equal justice for all.

morpheme A language's smallest unit of meaning, such as a prefix, a suffix, or a root word.

morphology The study of morphemes, language's smallest units of meaning.

multischematic Possessing both multiple cultural schemas for responding to the environment and the necessary criteria for deciding what schema to use in a particular situation.

multistore model A model of information processing that depicts information as moving through a series of organized processing units—*sensory register, short-term memory,* and *long-term memory.*

mutual antipathy A relationship of mutual dislike between two people.

myelination The process by which glial cells encase neurons in sheaths of the fatty substance *myelin.*

naming explosion The rapid increase in vocabulary that the child typically shows at about the age of $1\frac{1}{2}$.

narrative form A temporally sequenced account that conveys meaning about an event.

national survey A method of sampling in which a very large, nationally representative group of people are selected for a particular study.

natural experiment An experiment in which researchers measure the results of things that occur naturally in the real world.

needs-oriented reasoning Reasoning in which children express concern for others' needs even though their own needs may conflict with those needs.

negative evidence According to Pinker, corrective feedback that parents may give to young language-learning children.

negative gossip Sharing with a peer some negative information about another child.

neglected children Children who are often socially isolated and, although they are not necessarily disliked by others, have few friends.

neonate A newborn baby.

neo-Piagetian theories Theories of cognitive development that reinterpret Piaget's concepts from an information-processing perspective.

neural migration The movement of neurons within the brain that ensures that all brain areas have a sufficient number of neural connections.

neuron A cell in the body's nervous system, consisting of a cell body, a long projection called an *axon,* and several shorter projections called *dendrites;* neurons send and receive neural impulses, or messages, throughout the brain and nervous system.

neuron proliferation The rapid proliferation of neurons in the developing organism's brain.

neuronal death The death of some neurons that surround newly formed synaptic connections among other neurons; also called *programmed cell death.*

niche picking Seeking out or creating environments compatible with one's own genetically based predispositions.

nonaggressive rejected children *Rejected* children who tend to be anxious, withdrawn, and socially unskilled.

nonshared environment A set of conditions or activities experienced by one child in a family but not shared with another child in the same family.

nucleotide A compound containing a nitrogen base, a simple sugar, and a phosphate group.

obesity A condition in which a person's weight is 30 percent or more in excess of the average weight for his or her height and frame.

object permanence The notion that entities external to the child, such as objects and people, continue to exist independent of the child's seeing or interacting with them.

observer bias The tendency of observers to be influenced in their judgments by their knowledge of the hypotheses guiding the research.

obsessive self-stimulatory behavior Behavior common in autistic children in which they engage in repetitive actions that seemingly have no purpose.

operant behavior therapy A form of behavior therapy in which behavior is carefully monitored and consistently rewarded with such things as food.

operant conditioning A type of learning that depends on the consequences of behavior; rewards increase the likelihood that a behavior will recur, whereas punishment decreases that likelihood.

operations Schemata based on internal mental activities; a Piagetian term.

organization A memory strategy that involves putting together in some organized form the information to be remembered; usually entails categorization and hierarchical relations. In Piagetian terms, combining simple mental structures into more complex systems.

overcontrolled disorders A group of psychological disturbances in which a child appears overly controlled, withdrawing from others, lacking spontaneity, and generally appearing to be not a happy child.

overextension The use, by a young child, of a single word to cover many different things.

overregularization The application of a principle of regular change to a word that changes irregularly.

ovum The female germ cell, or egg.

passive genetic-environmental interaction The interactive environment created by parents with particular genetic predispositions who encourage the expression of these tendencies in their children.

patterned speech A form of pseudospeech in which the child utters strings of phonemes that sound very much like real speech but are not.

peer-group network The cluster of peer acquaintances who are familiar with and interact with one another at different times for common play or task-oriented purposes.

peer victimization Ill treatment of one child by another (or by others) that can range from teasing to bullying to serious physical harm; typically, victimizing is a continuing behavior that persists over time.

perception The interpretation of sensations to make them meaningful.

permissive parenting Parenting that is lax and in which parents exercise inconsistent discipline and encourage children to express their impulses freely.

personal domain An area of rules and conventions distinct from moral rules; involves issues such as choice of friends and styles of dress.

pervasive developmental disorders Childhood disorders characterized by gross deficits in many areas of cognitive, emotional, and social development that are linked with severe and pervasive impairment of social interaction and communication skills.

phenotype The visible expression of the person's particular physical and behavioral characteristics; created by the interaction of a person's genotype, or genetic makeup, with the environment.

phenylketonuria (PKU) A disease caused by a recessive allele that fails to produce an enzyme necessary to metabolize the protein phenylalanine; if untreated immediately at birth, damages the nervous system and causes mental retardation.

phoneme The basic unit of a language's phonetic system; phonemes are the smallest sound units that affect meaning.

phonological awareness The understanding of the sounds of a language and of the properties, such as the number of sounds in a word, related to these sounds.

phonology The system of sounds that a language uses.

Piagetian theory A theory of cognitive development that sees the child as actively seeking new information and uses two basic principles of biology and biological change: organization and adaptation.

pituitary gland A so-called master gland, located at the base of the brain, that triggers the secretion of hormones by all other hormone-secreting, or endocrine, glands.

placenta A fleshy, disclike structure formed by cells from the lining of the uterus and from the *zygote,* and that, together with the *umbilical cord,* serves to protect and sustain the life of the growing organism.

planning The deliberate organization of a sequence of actions oriented toward achieving a goal.

plasticity The capacity of the brain, particularly in its developmental stages, to respond and adapt to input from the external environment.

play therapy A form of psychotherapy in which therapists encourage children in free play with dolls and toys on the premise that such play will reveal a child's unconscious conflicts and concerns.

popular children Children who are liked by many peers and disliked by very few.

postconventional level Kohlberg's third level of moral development, in which the child's judgments are rational and his conduct is controlled by an internalized ethical code that is relatively independent of the approval or disapproval of others.

pragmatics A set of rules that specify appropriate language for particular social contexts.

preconceptual substage The first substage of Piaget's preoperational stage, during which the child's thought is characterized by the emergence of *symbolic function*, the rapid development of language, animistic thinking, and egocentricity.

preconventional level Kohlberg's first level of moral development, in which he sees the child's behavior as based on the desire to avoid punishment and gain rewards.

premoral stage Piaget's first stage of moral development, in which the child shows little concern for rules.

preoperational stage In this stage, the ability to use symbols facilitates the learning of language; this stage is also marked by semilogical reasoning, egocentricity—in which the child sees the world from her own point of view—and intuitive behavior, in which the child can solve problems using mental operations but cannot explain how she did so.

pretend play A form of play, most often social, in which children use symbolic meanings to act out fantasies, in this way learning social roles and how to interact with others. Also called *imaginative* and *fantasy play.*

preterm A term describing a premature baby who is born before its due date and whose weight, although less than that of a full-term infant, may be appropriate to its gestational age.

primary circular reactions Behaviors focused on the infant's own body that the infant repeats and modifies because they are pleasurable and satisfying.

primary prevention A form of *community psychology* in which mental health professionals attempt to alter social conditions, such as changing school curricula and teaching child-rearing skills to new parents.

proactive aggression The use of force to dominate another person or to bully or threaten others.

problem solving The identification of a goal and of steps to reach that goal.

production deficiency Inability to generate and use known memory strategies spontaneously.

productive language The production of speech.

progesterone A hormone that, in females, helps regulate the menstrual cycle and prepares the uterus to receive and nurture a fertilized egg.

propositional reasoning Logical thinking that involves evaluating a statement based on the information in the statement alone.

prosocial behavior Behavior that is designed to help or benefit other people.

prosocial reasoning Thinking and making judgments about prosocial issues.

protodeclarative A gesture that an infant uses to make some sort of statement about an object.

protoimperative A gesture that an infant or a young child may use to get someone to do something she or he wants.

proximal-distal pattern The pattern of human physical growth wherein development starts in central areas, such as the internal organs, and proceeds to more distant areas, such as arms and legs.

psychoactive medications Medications designed to alter mood and/or thinking processes.

psychoanalytic theory of attachment Freud's theory that babies become attached first to the mother's breast and then to the mother herself as a source of oral gratification.

psychodynamic theory On this view of development, which is derived from Freudian theory, development occurs in discrete stages and is determined largely by biologically based drives shaped by encounters with the environment and through the interaction of the personality's three components—the *id, ego,* and *superego.*

psychometrician A psychologist who specializes in the construction and use of tests designed to measure psychological constructs such as intelligence and various personality characteristics.

psychosocial theory Erikson's theory of development that sees children developing through a series of stages largely through accomplishing tasks that involve them in interaction with their social environment.

psychostimulant medications Drugs, such as amphetamines and caffeine, that increase alertness and attention as well as psychomotor activity.

puberty The onset of sexual maturity.

random assignment The technique by which researchers assign individuals randomly to either an *experimental* or *control group.*

range of reaction The notion that the human being's genetic makeup establishes a range of possible developmental outcomes, within which environmental forces largely determine how the person actually develops.

reactive aggression Aggressive behavior as a response to attack, threat, or frustration.

recast A technique adults use in speaking to young children in which they render a child's incomplete sentence in a more complex grammatical form.

receptive language Understanding the speech of others.

recessive The weaker of two *alleles* in a heterozygous combination.

reciprocal instruction A tutoring approach based on the ideas of the *zone of proximal development* and *scaffolding.*

recovery The ability to recognize a new stimulus as novel and to direct attention to it in preference to a familiar stimulus.

reflex A human being's involuntary response to external stimulation.

reflex smile A smile seen in the newborn that is usually spontaneous and appears to depend on some internal stimulus rather than on something external such as another person's behavior.

rehearsal A memory strategy in which one repeats a number of times either mentally or orally the information one wants to remember.

rejected children Children who are disliked by many peers and liked by very few.

relational aggression Damaging or destroying interpersonal relationships by such means as excluding another or gossiping about or soiling another's reputation.

relational victimization The attempt by a peer to damage or control another child's relationships with others.

relationship A succession of interactions between two people that are altered by their shared, past interactions and that also affect their future interactions.

reliability The degree to which a test yields consistent results over time or successive administrations.

REM sleep REM, or rapid eye movement sleep, is characterized by rapid, jerky movements of the eyes and, in adults, is often associated with dreaming.

representativeness The degree to which a sample actually possesses the characteristics of the larger population it represents.

reputational bias Children's tendency to interpret peers' behavior on the basis of past encounters with, and feelings about, them.

respiratory distress syndrome A condition of the newborn marked by labored breathing and a bluish discoloration of the skin or mucous membranes; can result in infant death.

reversibility The understanding that the steps of a procedure or operation can be reversed and that the original state of the object or event can be obtained.

Rh factor incompatibility A condition in which an infant's Rh-negative blood opposes its mother's Rh-positive blood and which threatens fetuses in later births, when the mother's body has had time to produce antibodies that will attack fetal blood cells.

sample A group of individuals who are representative of a larger population.

scaffolding An instructional process in which the more knowledgeable partner adjusts the amount and type of support he or she offers to the child to fit with the child's learning needs over the course of the interaction.

schema (plural, *schemata*) An organized unit of knowledge that the child uses to try to understand a situation; a schema forms the basis for organizing actions to respond to the environment.

scientific method The use of measurable and replicable techniques in framing hypotheses and collecting and analyzing data to test a theory's usefulness.

script A mental representation of an event or situation of daily life, including the order in which things are expected to happen and how one should behave in that event or situation.

secondary circular reactions Behaviors focused on objects outside the infant's own body that the infant repeatedly engages in because they are pleasurable and satisfying.

secondary prevention A form of *community psychology* in which mental health professionals try to identify people's problems at the outset and to undertake interventions to prevent disorders in those who are at risk.

secondary reinforcer A person or other stimulus that acquires reinforcing properties by virtue of repeated association with a primary reinforcer.

secular trend A shift in the normative pattern of a characteristic, such as height, that occurs over a historical period, such as a decade or century.

secure attachment A kind of attachment displayed by babies who are secure enough to explore novel environments, who are minimally disturbed by brief separations from their mothers, and who are quickly comforted by their mothers when they return.

secure base According to Ainsworth, a caregiver to whom an infant has formed an attachment and whom the child uses as a base from which to explore new things and as a safe haven in times of stress.

selective attention A strategy in which one focuses on some features of the environment and ignores others.

self-acceptance A general sense of one's personal worth combined with a positive view of one's sexual orientation.

self-control phase According to Kopp, the second phase in learning *self-regulation,* when the child becomes able to comply with caregiver expectations in the absence of the caregiver.

self-disclosure The honest sharing of information of a very personal nature, often with a focus on problem solving; a central means by which adolescents develop friendships.

self-regulation The child's ability to control behavior on her own, without reminders from others.

self-regulation phase According to Kopp, the third phase in learning *self-regulation,* when children become able to use strategies and plans in directing their own behavior and to delay gratification.

self-report Information that people provide about themselves, either in a direct interview or in some written form, such as a questionnaire.

self-socialization The child's spontaneous adoption of gender-appropriate behavior.

semantic memory All the world knowledge and facts a person possesses.

semantic organization Organizing information to be remembered by means of categorization and hierarchical relationships.

semantics The study of word meanings and word combinations, as in phrases, clauses, and sentences.

sensation The detection of stimuli by the sensory receptors.

sensitive care Consistent and responsive caregiving that begins by allowing an infant to play a role in determining when feeding will begin and end and at what pace it will proceed.

sensorimotor stage Piaget's first stage of cognitive development, during which children change from basic reflexive behavior to the beginnings of symbolic thought and goal-directed behaviors.

sensory register The mental processing unit that takes information from the environment and stores it in original form for brief periods of time.

separation protest An infant's distress reaction to being separated from his or her mother, which typically peaks at about 15 months of age.

sequential method A research method that combines features of both the *cross-sectional* and the *longitudinal* methods.

sex chromosomes In both males and females, the 23rd pair of chromosomes, which determine the individual's sex and are responsible for sex-related characteristics; in females, this pair normally comprises two X chromosomes, in males an X and a Y chromosome.

sexual abuse Inappropriate sexual activity between an adult and a child for the perpetrator's pleasure or benefit; the abuse may be direct (sexual contact of any type) or indirect (exposing a child to pornography or to the live exhibition of body parts or sexual acts).

shape constancy The ability to perceive an object's shape as constant despite changes in its orientation and the angle from which one views it.

shared environment A set of conditions or experiences shared by children raised in the same family; a parameter commonly examined in studies of individual differences.

short-term, or working, memory The mental processing unit in which information may be stored temporarily; the "work space" of the mind, where a decision must be made to discard information, work on it at present, or transfer it to permanent storage in *long-term memory.*

sickle-cell anemia A disorder, caused by a recessive gene, in which the red blood cells become distorted when low in oxygen, causing fatigue, shortness of breath, and severe pain and posing a threat to life from blockage of crucial blood vessels.

size constancy The tendency to perceive an object as constant in size regardless of changes in its distance from the viewer and in the image it casts on the retinas of the eyes.

small for date A term describing a premature baby who may be born close to its due date but who weighs significantly less than would be appropriate to its gestational age.

social comparison The process by which we evaluate our own abilities, values, and other qualities by comparing ourselves with others, usually our peers.

social referencing The process of "reading" emotional cues in others to help determine how to act in an uncertain situation.

social-convention rules Socially based rules about everyday conduct.

socialization The process by which parents and others ensure that a child's standards of behavior, attitudes, skills, and motives conform closely to those deemed appropriate to her role in society.

socially unskilled Being unskilled at solving interpersonal problems.

sociocultural theory A theory of development, proposed by Lev Vygotsky, that sees development as emerging from children's interactions with more skilled people and the institutions and tools provided by their culture.

sociometric technique A procedure for determining children's status within their peer group; each child in the group either nominates others whom she likes best and least or rates each child in the group for desirability as a companion.

specific factors (s) Factors unique to particular cognitive tasks.

specimen record A technique in which researchers record everything a person does within a given period of time.

speech acts One- or two-word utterances that clearly refer to situations or to sequences of events.

sperm The male germ cell.

spermarche In males, the first ejaculation of semen-containing ejaculate.

stages of development Comprehensive, qualitative changes over time in the way a child thinks.

standardization The process by which test constructors ensure that testing procedures, instructions, and scoring are identical, or as nearly so as possible, on every testing occasion.

Stanford-Binet Test The modern version of the first major intelligence test; emphasizes verbal and mathematical skills.

status offense Illegal behavior in an underage offender.

stereoscopic vision The sense of a third spatial dimension, that of depth, produced by the brain's fusion of the separate images contributed by each eye, each of which reflects the stimulus from a slightly different angle.

stereotype threat Being at risk of confirming a negative stereotype about the group to which one belongs.

Strange Situation A testing scenario in which mother and child are separated and reunited several times; enables investigators to assess the nature and quality of a mother-infant attachment relationship.

stranger distress A fear of strangers that typically emerges in infants around the age of 8 to 9 months.

strategies Conscious cognitive or behavioral activities used to enhance mental performance.

structural-organismic perspectives Theoretical approaches that describe psychological structures and processes that undergo qualitative or stagelike changes over the entire course of development.

structured observation A form of observation in which researchers structure a situation so that behaviors they wish to study are more likely to occur.

substance abuse The excessive use of legal or illegal drugs in such a way as to interfere seriously with one or more important areas of functioning in life: work, intimacy with another, general interpersonal and social relationships.

successful intelligence Ability to fit into, mold, and choose environments that best fulfill one's own needs and desires as well as the demands of society and culture. Includes analytical, creative, and practical abilities.

sudden infant death syndrome (SIDS) The sudden, unexplained death of an infant while sleeping, also called *crib death*.

superego In Freudian theory, the personality component that is the repository of the child's internalization of parental or societal values, morals, and roles.

symbolic function The ability to use symbols, such as images, words, and gestures, to represent objects and events in the world.

symbolic thought The use of mental images and concepts to represent people, objects, and events.

sympathy The feeling of sorrow or concern for a distressed or needy person.

synapse A specialized site of intercellular communication where information is exchanged between nerve cells, usually by means of a chemical *neurotransmitter*.

synaptic pruning The brain's disposal of the axon and dendrites of a neuron that is not often stimulated.

synaptogenesis The forming of synapses between neurons.

syntax The part of grammar that prescribes how words may combine into phrases, clauses, and sentences.

syphilis A sexually transmitted bacterial disease that can usually be treated with antibiotics, but if untreated in the pregnant woman can cause miscarriage or blindness, mental retardation, or other physical abnormalities in her baby.

tacit knowledge Implicit knowledge that is shared by many people and that guides behavior.

telegraphic speech Two-word utterances that include only the words essential to convey the speaker's intent.

temperament The individual's typical mode of response to the environment, including such things as activity level, emotional intensity, and attention span; used particularly to describe infants' and children's behavior.

teratogen An environmental agent, such as a drug, medication, dietary imbalance, or polluting substance, that may cause developmental deviations in a growing human organism; most threatening in the embryonic stage but capable of causing abnormalities in the fetal stage as well.

tertiary circular reactions Behaviors in which infants experiment with the properties of external objects and try to learn how objects respond to various actions.

tertiary prevention A form of *community psychology* in which mental health professionals provide treatment to children and families who are suffering various psychological problems.

test norms Values, or sets of values, that describe the typical test performance of a specific group of people.

testosterone A hormone that, in the male, is responsible for the development of primary and secondary sex characteristics and is essential for the production of sperm.

thalidomide A drug once prescribed to relieve morning sickness in pregnant women but discontinued when found to cause serious fetal malformations. Current controversy surrounds possible use in treating symptoms of such diseases as AIDS, cancer, and leprosy.

theory of mind Understanding of the mind and how it works.

theory of multiple intelligences Gardner's multifactorial theory that proposes eight distinct types of intelligence.

time out Removing children from a situation or context in which they are acting inappropriately until they are able and ready to act appropriately.

time sampling A technique in which researchers record any of a set of predetermined behaviors that occur within a specified period of time.

toxoplasmosis A parasitic disease acquired by eating undercooked meat or by contact with feces as in handling cat litter.

traditional nuclear family The traditional family form, composed of two parents and one or more children, in which the father is the breadwinner and the mother the homemaker.

transitive inference The mental arrangement of things along a quantitative dimension.

triarchic theory of intelligence A theory that proposes three major components of intelligent behavior: information-processing skills, experience with a particular situation, and ability to adapt to the demands of a context.

Turner syndrome A form of chromosome abnormality found in females, in which secondary sex characteristics develop only if female hormones are administered, and abnormal formation of internal reproductive organs leads to permanent sterility.

two-generation program A program of early cognitive intervention that extends help to parents as well as to their children.

ultrasound A technique that uses sound waves to visualize deep body structures; commonly used to reveal the size and structure of a developing fetus. Also called *ultrasonography*.

umbilical cord A tube that contains blood vessels connecting the growing organism and its mother by way of the *placenta*; it carries oxygen and nutrients to the growing infant and removes carbon dioxide and waste products.

undercontrolled disorders A group of psychological disturbances in which a child appears to lack self-control and to act out in a variety of ways, through such behaviors as noncompliance, disobedience, and aggression.

underextension The use, by a young child, of a single word in a restricted and individualistic way.

uninvolved parenting Parenting that is indifferent and neglectful and in which parents focus on their own needs rather than their children's needs.

utilization deficiency Inability to use a known memory strategy or to benefit from the use of such a memory strategy.

validity The extent to which a test actually measures what it claims to measure.

visual acuity Sharpness of vision; the clarity with which fine details can be detected.

visual cliff An apparatus that tests an infant's depth perception by using patterned materials and an elevated, clear glass platform to make it appear that one side of the platform is several feet lower than the other.

visual preference method A method of studying infants' abilities to distinguish one stimulus from another in which researchers measure and compare the amounts of time babies spend attending to different stimuli.

Wechsler Intelligence Scales Three intelligence tests for preschool children, school-age children, and adults that yield separate scores for verbal and performance IQ as well as a combined IQ score.

world knowledge What a child has learned from experience and knows about the world in general.

X-linked genes Genes that are carried on the X chromosome and that, in males, may have no analogous genes on the Y chromosome.

zone of proximal development (ZPD) The region of sensitivity for learning characterized by the difference between the developmental level of which a child is capable when working alone and the level she is capable of reaching with the aid of a more skilled partner.

zygote The developing organism from the time sperm and egg unite to about the second week of gestation; the period of the zygote comprises the implantation of the fertilized egg in the wall of the uterus.

References

Abbecassis, M., Hartup, W. W., Haselager, G., Scholte, R., & van Lieshout, C. F. M. (2002). Mutual antipathies in middle childhood and adolescence. *Child Development, 73,* 1543–1556.

Abbott, S. (1992). Holding on and pushing away: Comparative perspectives on an Eastern Kentucky child-rearing practice. *Ethos, 1,* 33–65.

Abel, E. L. (1998). *Fetal alcohol abuse syndrome.* New York: Plenum.

Aber, J. L., Brown, J. L., & Jones, S. M. (2003). Developmental trajectories toward violence in middle childhood: Course, demographic differences and response to school-based interventions. *Developmental Psychology, 39,* 324–348.

Achenbach, T. M. (1995). Developmental issues in assessment, taxonomy and diagnosis of child and adolescent psychopathology. In D. Cicchetti & D. J. Cohen (Eds.), *Developmental psychopathology, Vol. 1: Theory and methods* (pp. 57–82). New York: Wiley.

Achenbach, T. M. (1997). What is normal? What is abnormal? Developmental perspectives on behavioral and emotional problems. In S. S. Luthar, J. A. Burack, D. Cicchetti, & J. R.Weisz (Eds.), *Developmental psychopathology perspectives on adjustment, risk and disorder* (pp. 93–114). New York: Cambridge University Press.

Ackerman, B. P. (1996). Induction of a memory retrieval strategy by young children. *Journal of Experimental Child Psychology, 62,* 243–271.

Acredolo, L. P., & Goodyn, S. W. (1998). *Baby signs: How to talk with your baby before your baby can talk.* Chicago: NTB/Contemporary Publishers.

Adamson, L. B. (1995). *Communication development during infancy.* Madison, WI: Brown & Benchmark.

Adamson, L. B., & Bakeman, R. (1991). The development of shared attention during infancy. In R. Vasta (Ed.), *Annals of child development* (Vol. 8, pp. 1–41). London: Kingsley.

Adelson, E., & Fraiberg, S. (1974). Gross motor development in infants blind from birth. *Child Development, 45,* 114–126.

Adolph, K. & Berger, S. E. (2006). Motor development. In W. Damon & R. M. Lerner (Eds.) and D. Kuhn & R. Siegler (Vol. Eds.), *Handbook of child psychology: Vol. 2. Perceptual and cognitive development* (6th ed.). New York: Wiley.

Adolph, K. E., Verijken, B., & Denny, M. A. (1998). Learning to crawl. *Child Development, 69,* 636–653.

Adolph, K. E., Vereijken, B., & Shrout, P. E. (2003). What changes in infant walking and why. *Child Development, 74,* 475–497.

Affleck, G., Tennen, H., & Rowe, J. (1990). Mothers, fathers and the crisis of newborn intensive care. *Infant Medical Health Journal, 11,* 12–25.

Agras, W. S. (1988). Does early eating behavior influence later adiposity? In N. A. Krasnegor, G. D. Grave, & N. Kretchmer (Eds.), *Childhood obesity: A biobehavioral perspective* (pp. 49–66). Caldwell, NJ: Telford Press.

Ahmed, N. U., Zeitlin, M. F., Beiser, A. S., Super, C. M., & Gershoff, S. N. (1993). A longitudinal study of the impact of behavioural change intervention on cleanliness, diarrhoeal morbidity and growth of children in rural Bangladesh. *Social Science and Medicine, 37,* 159–171.

Ainsworth, M. D. (1963). The development of infant-mother interaction among the Ganda. In D. M. Foss (Ed.), *Determinants of infant behavior* (Vol. 2, pp. 67–104). New York: Wiley.

Ainsworth, M. D. (1973). The development of infant-mother attachment. In B. Caldwell & H. Ricciuti (Eds.), *Review of child development research* (Vol. 3). Chicago: University of Chicago Press.

Ainsworth, M. D., Blehar, M., Waters, E., & Wall, S. (1978). *Patterns of attachment.* Hillsdale, NJ: Erlbaum.

Albert, R. S. (1996, Summer). Some reasons why childhood creativity often fails to make it past puberty into the real world. In M. A. Runco (Ed.), *Creativity from childhood through adulthood: The developmental issues* [Special issue]. *New Directions for Child Development,* No. 72, 43–56.

Alessandri, S. M., & Lewis, M. (1996). Differences in pride and shame in maltreated and nonmaltreated preschoolers. *Child Development, 67,* 1857–1869.

Allan, K., & Coltrane, S. (1996). Gender-displaying television commercials: A comparative study of television commercials in the 1950s and 1980s. *Sex Roles, 35,* 185–203.

Allen, J. P., McElhaney, K. B., Land, D. J., Kuperminic, G. P., Moore, C. W., O'Beirne-Kelly, H., & Kilmer, S. L. (2003). A secure base in adolescence: Markers of attachment security in the mother-adolescent relationship. *Child Development, 74,* 292–307.

Allen, L., & Majidi-Abi, S. (1989). Black American children. In J. T. Gibbs & L. N. Huang (Eds.), *Children of color.* San Francisco: Jossey-Bass.

Als, H., Gilkerson, L., Duffy, F. H., McAnulty, G. B., Buehler, D. M., Vandenberg, K., Sweet, N., Sell, E., Parad, R. B., Ringer, S. A., Butler, S. C., Blickman, J. G., & Jones, K. J. (2003). A three-center, randomized, controlled trial of individualized developmental care for very low-birthweight preterm infants: Medical, neurodevelopmental, parenting, and caregiving effects. *Journal of Developmental & Behavioral Pediatrics, 24,* 399–408.

Amato, P. (2000). The consequences of divorce for adults and children. *Journal of Marriage and the Family, 62,* 1269–1287.

Amato, P. R. (2001). Children of divorce in the 1990's: An update of Amato & Keith (1991) meta-analysis. *Journal of Family Psychology, 13,* 355–370.

American Association of Mental Retardation. (2002). *Mental retardation: Definition, classification, and systems of supports* (10th ed.). Annapolis, MD: Author.

American Psychiatric Association (1994). *Diagnostic and statistical manual of mental disorders* (4th ed.). Washington, DC: Author.

American Psychiatric Association (2000). *Diagnostic and statistical manual for mental disorders* (4th ed., Text Revision). Washington, DC: American Psychiatric Association.

American Psychological Association (1992). Ethical principles of psychologists: Code of conduct. *American Psychologist, 44,* 1597–1611.

American Society for Reproductive Medicine (2002). Assisted reproductive technology in the United States: 1998 results generated from the American Society for Reproductive Medicine/Society for Assisted Reproduction Registry. *Fertility & Sterility, 77,* 18–31.

Anastasi, A. (1988). *Psychological testing* (6th ed.). New York: Macmillan.

Anderson, D. R., Lorch, E. P., Field, D. E., & Sanders, J. (1981). The effects of TV program comprehensibility on preschool children's visual attention to television. *Child Development, 52,* 151–157.

Anderson, E. (1998). The social ecology of youth violence. In M. Tenry & M. H. Moore (Eds.), *Youth violence: Crime and justice* (pp. 65–104). Chicago: University of Chicago Press.

Anderson, P., Doyle, L. W., Callahan, C., Carse, E., Casalaz, D., Charlton, M. P. et al. (2003). Neurobehavioral outcomes of school-age children born extremely low birth weight or very preterm in the 1990s. *Journal of American Medical Association, 289,* 3264–3272.

Anderson, W. F. (1995). Gene therapy. *Scientific American, 273,* 124–128.

Andrews, J. A., & Lewinsohn, P. M. (1992). Suicidal attempts among older adolescents: Prevalence and co-occurrence with psychiatric disorders. *Journal of American Academy of Child and Adolescent Psychiatry, 31,* 655–662.

Angier, N. (1997). Evolutionary necessity or glorious accident? Biologists ponder the self. *The New York Times,* April 22, p. C1.

Anisfeld, E., Casper, V., Nosyce, M., & Cunningham, N. (1990). Does infant-carrying promote attachment? An experimental study of the effects of increased physical contact on the development of attachment. *Child Development, 61,* 1617–1627.

Anisfeld, M. (1991). Neonatal imitation. *Developmental Review, 11,* 60–97.

Annual Editions. (2003). *Child growth and development 03/04* (10th ed.). New York: McGraw-Hill.

Anooshian, L. J., & Siegel, A. W. (1985). From cognitive to procedural mapping. In C. J. Brainard & M. Pressley (Eds.), *Basic process in memory development.* New York: Springer-Verlag.

Antonarakis, S. E., & Down Syndrome Collaborative Group. (1991). Parental origin of the extra chromosome in trisomy 21 as indicated by analysis of DNA polymorphisms. *New England Journal of Medicine, 324,* 872–876.

Apgar, V. (1953). A proposal for a new method of evaluation of the newborn infant. *Current Research in Anesthesia and Analgesia, 32,* 260–267.

Aries, P. (1962). *Centuries of childhood.* New York: Knopf.

Arterberry, M. E., & Bornstein, M. H. (2001). Three-month-old infants' categorization of animals and vehicles based on static and dynamic attributes. *Journal of Experimental Child Psychology, 80,* 333–346.

Asakawa, K., Iwawaki, S., Mondori, Y., & Minami, H. (1987, July). *Altruism in school and empathy: A developmental study of Japanese pupils.* Paper presented at the International Society for the Study of Behavioral Development, Tokyo.

Asbury, K., Dunn, J. F., Pike, A., & Plomin, R. (2003). Nonshared environmental influences on individual differences in early behavioral development: A monozygotic twin differences study. *Child Development, 74,* 933–943.

Asher, S., & Hopmeyer, A. (2001) Loneliness in childhood. In G. G. Baer, K. M. Minke, & A. Thomas (Eds.) *Children's needs: Development, problems and alternatives* (pp. 279–292). Silver Spring, MD: National Association of School Psychologists.

Asher, S. R., Hymel, S., & Renshaw, P. D. (1984). Loneliness in children. *Child Development, 55,* 1456–1464.

Asher, S. R., Rose, A. J., & Gabriel, S. W. (2001). Peer rejection in everyday life. In M. R. Leary (Ed.), *Interpersonal rejection* (pp. 105–142). New York: Oxford.

Aslin, R. (1987). Visual and auditory development in infancy. In J. Osofsky (Ed.), *Handbook of infant development* (2nd ed.). New York: Wiley.

Aslin, R. N., Jusczyk, P. W., & Pisoni, D. B. (1998). Speech and auditory processing during infancy: Constraints on and precursors to language. In W. Damon (Gen. Ed.), D. Kuhn, & R. Siegler (Vol. Eds.), *Handbook of child psychology: Vol. 2. Cognition, perception and language.* New York: Wiley.

Aslin, R. N., Woodward, J. Z., LaMendola, N. P., & Bever, T. G. (1996). Models of work segmentation in fluent maternal speech to infants. In J. L. Morgan & K. Dermuth (Eds.), *Signal to syntax.* Hillsdale, NJ: Erlbaum.

Atkin, C. (1983). Effects of realistic TV violence vs. fictional violence on aggression. *Journalism Quarterly, 60,* 615–621.

Atkinson, R. C., & Shiffrin, R. M. (1968). Human memory: A proposed system and its control processes. In K. W. Spence & J. Spence (Eds.), *Advances in the psychology of learning and motivation: Research and theory* (Vol. 2). New York: Academic.

Attie, I., & Brooks-Gunn, J. (1989). Development of eating problems in adolescent girls: A longitudinal study. *Developmental Psychology, 25,* 70–79.

Atweh, G. F., et al. (1999). Sustained induction of fetal hemoglobin by pulse butyrate therapy in sickle cell disease. *Blood, 93,* 1790–1797.

Au, K., & Jordan, C. (1981). Teaching reading to Hawaiian children: Finding a culturally appropriate solution. In H. Tureba, G. Guthrie, & K. Au (Eds.), *Culture and the bilingual classroom: Studies in classroom ethnography* (pp. 139–152). Rowley, MA: Newbury House.

Au, T. K., Sidle, A. L., & Rollins, K. B. (1993). Developing intuitive understanding of conservation and contamination: Invisible particles of a plausible mechanism. *Developmental Psychology, 29,* 286–289.

Aviezer, D., Sagi, A., Joels, T., & Ziv, Y. (1999). Emotional availability and attachment representations in kibbutz infants and their mothers. *Developmental Psychology, 35,* 811–821.

Aviezer, O., Van IJzendoorn, M. H., Sagi, A., & Schuengel, C. F. (1994). "Children of the dream" revisited: 70 years of collective early child care in Israeli kibbutzim. *Psychological Bulletin, 116,* 99–116.

Avis, J., and Harris, P. L. (1991). Belief-desire reasoning among Baka children: Evidence for a universal conception of mind. *Child Development, 62,* 460–467.

Axia, G., Bonichini, S., & Benini, F. (1999). Attention and reaction to distress in infancy, a longitudinal study. *Developmental Psychology, 35,* 500–504.

Azar, S. T. (2002). Parenting and child maltreatment. In M. Bornstein (Ed.), *Handbook of parenting* (Vol. 4, pp. 361–388). Mahwah, NJ: Erlbaum.

Baca Zinn, M., & Wells, B. (2000). Diversity within Latino families: New lessons for family social sciences. In D. H. Demo, K. R. Allen, & M. Fine (Eds.), *Handbook of family diversity* (pp. 252–273). New York: Oxford University Press.

Bagwell, C. L. (2004). Friendships, peer networks and antisocial behavior. In J. B. Kupersmidt & K. A. Dodge (Eds.), *Children's peer relations* (pp. 37–57). Washington, DC: American Psychological Association.

Bagwell, C. L., Coie, J. D., Terry, R. A., & Lochman, J. E. (2000). Peer clique participation and social status in preadolescence. *Merrill-Palmer Quarterly, 46,* 280–305.

Bagwell, C. L., Newcomb, A., & Bukowski, W. M. (1998). Preadolescent friendships and peer rejection as predictors of adult adjustment. *Child Development, 69,* 140–153.

Bailey, A., LeCouteur, A., Gottesman, I., Bolton, P., Simonoff, E., Yuzda, F. Y., & Rutter, M. (1995). Autism as a strongly genetic disorder: Evidence from a British twin study. *Psychological Medicine, 25,* 63–77.

Bailey, J., Bobrow, D., Wolfe, M., & Mikach, S. (1995). Sexual orientation of adult sons of gay fathers. Special Issue: Sexual orientation and human development. *Developmental Psychology, 31,* 124–129.

Bailey, J. M., Pillard, R. C., Neale, M. C., & Agyei, Y. (1993). Heritable factors influence sexual orientation in women. *Archives of General Psychiatry, 50,* 217–223.

Bailey, J. M., & Zucker, K. J. (1995). Childhood sex-typed behavior and sexual orientation: A conceptual analysis. *Developmental Psychology, 31,* 43–55.

Baillargeon, R. (1986). Representing the existence and the location of hidden objects: Object permanence in 6- and 8-month-old infants. *Cognition, 23,* 21–41.

Baillargeon, R. (1993). The object concept revisited: New directions in the investigation of infants' physical knowledge. In C. E. Granrud (Ed.), *Visual perception and cognition in infancy.* Hillsdale, NJ: Erlbaum.

Baillargeon, R. (1994). How do infants learn about the physical world? *Current Directions in Psychological Science, 3,* 133–140.

Baillargeon, R. (2002). The acquisition of physical knowledge in infancy: A summary in eight lessons. In U. Goswami (Ed.), *Blackwell Handbook of Childhood Cognitive Development* (pp. 47–83). Oxford: Blackwell Publishing.

Baillaregeon, R., & Wang. S. (2002). Event categorization in infancy. *Trends in Cognitive Science, 6,* 85–93.

Bainum, C. K., Lounsbury, K. R., & Pollio, H. R. (1984). The development of laughing and smiling in nursery school children. *Child Development, 55,* 1946–1957.

Bakeman, R., & Gottman, J. (1997). *Observing behavior* (2nd ed.). New York: Cambridge University Press.

Bakermans-Kranenburg, M. J., van IJzendoorn, M. H., & Juffer, F. (2003). Less is more: Meta-analyses of sensitivity and attachment interventions in early childhood. *Psychological Bulletin, 129,* 195–215.

Baldwin, A., Baldwin, C., & Cole, R. E. (1990). Stress-resistant families and stress-resistant children. In J. E. Rolf, A. S. Masten, D. Cicchetti, K. N. Wechterlein, & S. Weintraub (Eds.), *Risk and protective factors in the development of psychopathology* (pp. 257–280). New York: Cambridge University Press.

Bandura, A. (1989). Social cognitive theory. In R. Vasta (Ed.), *Annals of child development: Six theories of child development* (Vol. 6). Greenwich, CT: JAI Press.

Bandura, A. (1997). *Self-efficacy.* New York: W. H. Freeman & Co.

Bandura, A., Caprara, G.V., Barbaranelli, C., Gerbino, M., & Pastorelli, C. (2003). Role of affective self-regulatory efficacy in diverse spheres of psychosocial functioning. *Child Development, 74,* 769–782.

Banish, J. T. (1998). Integration of information between the cerebral hemispheres. *Current Directions in Psychological Science, 7,* 32–37.

Banks, M. S., Aslin, R. N., & Letson, R. D. (1975). Sensitive period for the development of human binocular vision. *Science, 190,* 675–677.

Banks, M. S., & Salapatek, P. (1983). Infant visual perception. In M. H. & J. Campos (Eds.), *Handbook of child psychology; Biology and infancy.* New York: Wiley.

Banks, M. S., & Shannon, E. (1993). Spatial and chromatic visual efficiency in human neonates. In C. Granrud (Ed.), *Visual perception and cognition in infancy* (pp. 1–46). Hillsdale, NJ: Erlbaum.

Barglow, P., Vaughn, B. E., & Molitor, N. (1987). Effects of maternal absence due to employment on the quality of infant-mother attachment in a low-risk sample. *Child Development, 58,* 945–954.

Baringa, M. (1996). Learning defect identified in the brain. *Science, 273,* 867–868.

Barkley, R. A. (1998). *Attention deficit/hyperactivity disorder: A handbook for diagnosis and treatment* (2nd ed.). New York: Guilford Press.

Barnard, K. E., & Bee, H. L. (1983). The impact of temporally patterned stimulation on the development of preterm infants. *Child Development, 54,* 1156–1167.

Barnard, K. E., Bee, H. L., & Hammond, M. A. (1984). Home environment and cognitive development in a healthy, low-risk sample: The Seattle study. In A. W. Gottfried (Ed.), *Home environment and early cognitive development* (pp. 117–149). Orlando, FL: Academic.

Barnas, M. V., & Cummings, E. M. (1994). Caregiver stability and toddlers' attachment-related behavior towards caregivers in day care. *Infant Behavior and Development, 17,* 141–147.

Baron, J., & Miller, J. G. (2000). Limiting the scope of moral obligations to help: A cross-cultural investigation. *Journal of Cross-Cultural Psychology, 31,* 703–725.

Baron-Cohen, S. (1995). *Mindblindness: An essay on autism and theory of mind.* Cambridge, MA: MIT Press.

Baron-Cohen, S. (2003). *The essential difference: Male and female brains and the truth about autism.* New York: Basic Books.

Baron-Cohen, S., Baldwin, D. A., & Crowson, M. (1997). Do children with autism use the speaker's-direction-of-gaze strategy to crack the code of language? *Child Development, 68,* 48–57.

Barr, H. M., Steissguth, A. P., Darby, B. L., & Sampson, P. D. (1990). Prenatal exposure to alcohol, caffeine, tobacco, and aspirin: Effects on fine and gross motor performance in 4-year-old children. *Developmental Psychology, 26,* 339–348.

Barrett, D. E. (1979). A naturalistic study of sex differences in children's aggression. *Merrill-Palmer Quarterly, 25,* 193–203.

Basow, S. A. (1992). *Gender stereotypes and roles.* Pacific Grove, CA: Brooks/Cole.

Bates, D., Thal, D., Whitsell, K., Fenson, L., & Oakes, L. (1989). Integrating language and gesture in infancy. *Developmental Psychology, 25,* 1004–1019.

Bates, E. (1976). *Language and context: The acquisition of pragmatics.* New York: Academic.

Bates, E. (1999). On the nature of language. In R. Levi-Montalcini, D. Baltimore, R. Dulbecco, & F. Jacob (Series Eds.), and O. E. Bizzi, P. Calissano, & V. Vorterra (Vol. Eds.), *The brain of homo sapiens.* Rome: Giovanni Trecami.

Bates, E., & Goodman, J. (1999). On the emergence of grammar from the lexicon. In B. MacWhinney (Ed.), *The emergence of language* (pp. 29–80). Mahwah, NJ: Erlbaum.

Bates, E., & Roe, K. (2002). Language development in children with unilateral brain injury. In C. A.

Nelson & M. Luciana (Eds.), *Handbook of developmental cognitive neuroscience.* Cambridge, MA: MIT Press.

Batson, C. D., & Thompson, E. R. (2001). Why don't moral people act morally? Motivational considerations. *Current Directions in Psychological Science, 10,* 54–57.

Bauer, P. J. (1996). What do infants recall of their lives? *American Psychologist, 51,* 29–41.

Bauer, P. J. (2002). Long-term recall memory: Behavioral and neuro-developmental changes in the first 2 years of life. *Current Directions in Psychological Science, 11,* 137–141.

Bauer, P. J. (2006). Event memory. In W. Damon & R. M. Lerner (Series Eds.) and D. Kuhn & R. Siegler (Vol. Eds.), *Handbook of child psychology,* Vol. 2, 6th ed. New York: Wiley.

Bauer, P. J., & Dow, G. A. (1994). Episodic memory in 16- and 20-month-old children: Specifics are generalized but not forgotten. *Developmental Psychology, 30,* 403–417.

Bauer, P. J., & Mandler, J. M. (1992). Putting the horse before the cart: The use of temporal order in recall of events by one-year-old children. *Developmental Psychology, 28,* 441–452.

Bauer, P. J., & Thal, D. J. (1990). Scripts or scraps: Reconsidering the development of sequential understanding. *Journal of Experimental Child Psychology, 50,* 287–304.

Bauer, P. J., Wenner, J. A., Dropik, P. L., & Wewerka, S. S. (2000). Parameters of remembering and forgetting in the transition from infancy to early childhood. *Monographs of the Society for Research in Child Development, Vol. 65 (4),* No. 263.

Bauer, W. D., & Twentyman, C. T. (1985). Abusing, neglectful, and comparison mothers' responses to child-related and non-child-related stressors. *Journal of Consulting and Clinical Psychology, 53,* 335–343.

Baumeister, A. A. (1967). The effects of dietary control on intelligence in phenylketonuria. *American Journal of Mental Deficiency, 71,* 840–847.

Baumrind, D. (1967). Child care practices anteceding three patterns of preschool behavior. *Genetic Psychology Monographs, 75,* 43–88.

Baumrind, D. (1971). Current patterns of parental authority. *Developmental Psychology Monographs, 1,* 1–103.

Baumrind, D. (1991). Effective parenting during the early adolescent transition. In P. A. Cowan & E. M. Hetherington

(Eds.), *Family transitions* (pp. 111–164). Hillsdale, NJ: Erlbaum.

Baumrind, D. (1993). The average expectable environment is not good enough: A response to Scarr. *Child Development, 64,* 1299–1317.

Bayley, N. (1969). *Bayley scales of infant development.* New York: Psychological Corporation.

Bayley, N. (1993). *Bayley scales of infant development* (revised ed.). New York: Psychological Corporation.

Beal, C. R. (1994). *Boys and girls: The development of gender roles.* New York: McGraw-Hill.

Bedard, J., & Chi, M. T. H. (1992). Expertise. *Current Directions in Psychological Science, 1,* 135–139.

Begley, S. (1997). How to build a baby's brain. *Newsweek Special Issue.* Spring/Summer, 28–32.

Beilin, H. (1992). Piaget's enduring contribution to developmental psychology. *Developmental Psychology, 28,* 191–204.

Beitel, A. H., & Parke, R. D. (1998). Parental involvement in infancy: The role of maternal and paternal attitudes. *Journal of Family Psychology, 12,* 268–288.

Bell, R. Q. (1968). A reinterpretation of the direction of effects in studies of socialization. *Psychological Review, 75,* 81–95.

Bell, S., & Ainsworth, M. D. (1972). Infant crying and maternal responsiveness. *Child Development, 43,* 1171–1190.

Bellamy, C. (2000). *The state of the world's children.* New York: Oxford University Press.

Belle, D. (1999). *The after-school lives of children.* Mahwah, NJ: Erlbaum.

Bellugi, U., Van Hoek, K., Lillo-Martin D., & O'Grady, L. (1993). The acquisition of syntax and space in young deaf signers. In D. Bishop & K. Mogford (Eds.), *Language development in exceptional children* (pp. 132–149). Hove, England: Erlbaum.

Belsky, J. (1993). Etiology of child maltreatment: A developmental-ecological analysis. *Psychological Bulletin, 114,* 413–434.

Belsky, J. (1999). Interactional and contextual determinants of attachment security. In J. Cassidy & P. Shaver (Eds.), *Handbook of attachment* (pp. 249–264). New York: Guilford Press.

Belsky, J., & Cassidy, J. (1994). Attachment: Theory and evidence. In M. Rutter, D. Hay, & S. Baron-Cohen (Eds.), *Developmental principles and clinical issues in psychology and psychiatry.* Oxford: Blackwell.

Belsky, J., & Rovine, M. (1988). Nonmaternal care in the first year of life and infant-parent attachment

security. *Child Development, 57,* 1224–1231.

Belsky, J., Spritz, B., & Crnic, K. (1996). Infant attachment security and affective cognitive information processing at age 3. *Psychological Science, 7,* 111–114.

Belsky, J., Steinberg, L. D., & Walker, A. (1983). The ecology of day care. In M. E. Lamb (Ed.), *Nontraditional families.* Hillsdale, NJ: Erlbaum.

Bem, S. L. (1981). Gender schema theory: A cognitive account of sex typing. *Psychological Review, 88,* 354–364.

Bem, S. L. (1983). Gender schema theory and its implications for child development: Raising gender-aschematic children in a gender-schematic society. *Signs: Journal of Women in Culture and Society, 8,* 598–616.

Bem, S. L. (1989). Genital knowledge and gender constancy in preschool children. *Child Development, 60,* 649–662.

Bem, S. L. (1993). *The lenses of gender: Transforming the debate on sexual inequality.* New Haven, CT: Yale University Press.

Bem, S. L. (1998). *An unconventional family.* New Haven, CT: Yale University Press.

Benbow, C. P., & Lubinski, D. J. (Eds.). (1996). Intellectual talent: Psychometric and social issues. Baltimore, MD: Johns Hopkins University Press.

Benenson, J. F., Apostoleris, N. H., & Parnass, J. (1997). Age and sex differences in dyadic and group interaction. *Developmental Psychology, 33,* 538–543.

Benenson, J. F., & Christakos, A. (2003). The greater fragility of females' versus males' closest same-sex friendships. *Child Development, 74,* 1123–1129.

Benloucif, S., Bennett, E. L., & Rosenzweig, M. R. (1995). Norepinephrine and neural plasticity: The effects of Xylamine on experience-induced changes in brain weight, memory and behavior. *Neurobiology of Learning and Memory, 63,* 33–42.

Benokraitis, N. V. (1996). *Marriages and families: Changes, choices, and constraints* (2nd ed.). Upper Saddle River, NJ: Prentice Hall.

Benokraitis, N. V. (1998). Personal communication.

Benson, E. S. (2004). Behavior genetics: Meet molecular biology. *Monitor on Psychology, 35,* 42–45.

Bentley, D. B. (1996). Genomic sequence information should be released immediately and freely in the public domain. *Science, 274,* 533–534.

Bentzen, B. L., & Mitchell, P. A. (1995). Audible signage as a way-finding aid: Verbal landmark versus talking signs. *Journal of Visual Impairment & Blindness, 88,* 494–505.

Berenbaum, S. A., & Bailey, J. M. (2003). Effects on gender identity of prenatal androgens and genital appearance: Evidence from girls with congenital adrenal hyperplasia. *Journal of Clinical Endocrinology and Metabolism, 88,* 1102–1106.

Berenbaum, S. A., & Snyder, E. (1995). Early hormonal influences on childhood sex-typed activity and playmate preferences: Implications for the development of sexual orientation. *Developmental Psychology, 31,* 31–42.

Berg, W. K., & Berg, K. M. (1987). Psychophysiologic development in infancy: State, startle and attention. In J. Osofsky (Ed.), *Handbook of infancy* (2nd ed.). New York: Wiley.

Bergen, D. J., & Williams, J. E. (1991). Sex stereotypes in the United States revisited: 1972–1988. *Sex Roles, 24,* 413–423.

Berger, S. E., & Adolph, K. E. (2003). Infants use handrails as tools in a locomotor task. *Developmental Psychology, 39,* 594–605.

Berk, L. E. (1992). Children's private speech: An overview of theory and the status of research. In R. M. Diaz & L. E. Berk (Eds.), Private speech: From social interaction to self-regulation (pp. 17–53). Hillsdale, NJ: Erlbaum.

Berlin, L. J., & Cassidy, J. (1999). Relations among relationships: Contributions from attachment theory and research. In J. Cassidy & P. Shaver (Eds.), *Handbook of attachment* (pp. 688–712). New York: Guilford Press.

Berman, P. W. (1987). Children caring for babies: Age and sex differences in response to infant signals and to the social context. In N. Eisenberg (Ed.), *Contemporary topics in developmental psychology.* New York: Wiley.

Berndt, T. J. (1986). Sharing between friends: Contexts and consequences. In E. C. Mueller & C. R. Cooper (Eds.), *Process and outcome in peer relationships.* New York: Academic.

Berndt, T. J., & Perry, T. B. (1990). Distinctive features and effects of adolescent friendships. In R. Montemeyer, G. R. Adams, & T. P. Gullotta (Eds.), *From childhood to adolescence: A transition period?* London: Sage.

Bernstein, D., & Nash, P. (2005). *Essentials of psychology.* Boston: Houghton-Mifflin.

Berry, G. (2000). Multicultural media portrayals and the changing demographic landscape: The psychosocial impact of television

representations on the adolescent of color. *Journal of Adolescent Health, 275,* 57–60.

Bersoff, D. M., & Miller, J. (1993). Culture, context, and the development of moral accountability judgments. *Developmental Psychology, 29,* 664–676.

Bertenthal, B. I. (1996). Origins and early development of perception, action and representation. *Annual Review of Psychology, 47,* 431–459.

Bertenthal, B., & Bai, D. L. (1989). Infants' sensitivity to optical flow for controlling posture. *Developmental Psychology, 25,* 936–945.

Bertenthal, B. I., Campos, J. J., & Kermoian, R. (1994). An epigenetic perspective on the development of self-produced locomotion and its consequences. *Current Directions in Psychological Science, 3,* 140–145.

Bertenthal, B. I., & Clifton, R. K. (1998). Perception and action. In W. Damon (Gen. Ed.), D. Kuhn, & R. Siegler (Vol. Eds.), *Handbook of child psychology: Vol. 2. Cognition, perception and language* (pp. 51–102). New York: Wiley.

Bertenthal, B. I., Proffitt, D. R., & Cutting, J. E. (1984). Infant sensitivity to figural coherence in biomechanical motions. *Journal of Experimental Child Psychology, 37,* 213–230.

Bertenthal, B. I., Proffitt, D. R., & Kramer, S. J. (1987). The perception of biomechanical motions. Implementation of various processing constraints. *Journal of Experimental Psychology. Human Perception and Performance, 13,* 577–585.

Berthier, N. E., DeBlois, S., Poirier, C. R., Novak, J. A., & Clifton, R. K. (2000). Where's the ball? Two- and three-year-olds reason about unseen events. *Developmental Psychology, 36,* 394–401.

Berthoud-Papandropoulou, I. (1978). An experimental study of children's ideas about language. In A. Sinclair, R. J. Jarvella, & W. J. M. Levelt (Eds.), *The child's conception of language* (Vol. 2). Heidelberg: Springer.

Best, D. L. (1993). Inducing children to generate mnemonic organizational strategies: An examination of long-term retention and materials. *Developmental Psychology, 29,* 324–336.

Best, D. L., & Ornstein, P. A. (1986). Children's generation and communication of mnemonic organizational strategies. *Developmental Psychology, 22,* 845–853.

Best, D. L., & Williams, J. E. (1993). A cross-cultural viewpoint. In A. E. Beall & R. J. Sternberg (Eds.), *The psychology of gender.*

(pp. 215–248). New York: Guilford Press.

Beutler, L. E., & Malik, M. L. (2002). *Rethinking the DSM: A psychological perspective.* Washington, DC: American Psychological Association.

Bhavnagri N., & Parke, R. D. (1991). Parents as direct facilitators of children's peer relationships: Effects of age of child and sex of parent. *Journal of Social and Personal Relationships, 8,* 423–440.

Bialystok, E. (1997). Effects of bilingualism and biliteracy on children's emerging concepts of print. *Developmental Psychology, 33,* 429–440.

Bialystok, E. (1999). Cognitive complexity and attentional control in the bilingual mind. *Child Development, 70,* 636–644.

Bianchi, B. D., & Bakeman, R. (1983). Patterns of sex typing in an open school. In M. B. Liss (Ed.), *Social and cognitive skills: Sex roles and children's play.* New York: Academic.

Bickerton, D. (1983). Creole languages. *Scientific American, 249,* 116–122.

Bickerton, D. (1990). *Language and species.* Chicago: University of Chicago Press.

Bierman, K. (2004). *Peer rejection: Causes and consequences.* New York: Guilford.

Bigelow, B. J. (1977). Children's friendship expectations: A cognitive-developmental study. *Child Development, 48,* 246–253.

Bigelow, B. J., & LaGaipa, J. J. (1975). Children's written descriptions of friendship: A multidimensional analysis. *Developmental Psychology, 11,* 857–858.

Bigler, R. S. (1995). The role of classification skill in moderating environmental influences on children's gender stereotyping: A study of the functional use of gender in the classroom. *Child Development, 68,* 530–548.

Bigler, R. S., & Liben, L. S. (1990). The role of attitudes and interventions in gender-schematic processing. *Child Development, 61,* 1440–1452.

Bigler, R. S., & Liben, L. S. (1992). Cognitive mechanisms in children's gender stereotyping: Theoretical and educational implications of a cognitive-based intervention. *Child Development, 63,* 1351–1363.

Bilger, B. (2004, April 5). The height gap. *New Yorker,* 38–45.

Binet, A. (1909/1973). *Les idées modernes sur les enfants.* Paris: Flammarion.

Birch, E. E. (1993). Stereopsis in infants and its developmental relation to visual acuity. In K.

Simons (Ed.), *Early visual development: Normal and abnormal* (pp. 224–236). New York: Oxford University Press.

Birch, L. L., & Fisher, J. A. (1995). Appetite & eating behavior in children. *Pediatric Clinics of North America, 42,* 931–953.

Birch, L. L., McPhee, L., Shoba, B. C., Steinberg, L., & Krehbeil, R. (1987). "Clean up your plate." Effects of child feeding practices on the conditioning of meal size. *Learning & Motivation, 18,* 301–317.

Biringen, Z., Emde, R. N., Campos, J. J., & Appelbaum, M. I. (1995). Affective reorganization in the infant, the mother, and the dad: The role of upright locomotion and its timing. *Child Development, 66,* 499–514.

Biringen, Z., Robinson, J. L., & Emde, R. N. (1994). Maternal sensitivity in the second year: Gender-based relations in the dyadic balance of control. *American Journal of Orthopsychiatry, 64,* 78–90.

Birmaher, B., Brent, B. A., Kolko, D., Baugher, M., Bridge, J., Holder, D., Iyengar, S., & Ulloa, R. E. (2000). Clinical outcome after short-term psychotherapy for adolescents with major depressive disorder. *Archives of General Psychiatry, 57,* 29–36.

Bivens, J. A., & Berk, L. E. (1990). A longitudinal study of the development of elementary school children's private speech. *Merrill-Palmer Quarterly, 36,* 443–463.

Bjorklund, D. F. (2005). *Children's thinking: Developmental function and individual differences* (4th ed.). Belmont, CA: Wadsworth.

Bjorklund, D. F., Miller, P. H., Coyle, T. R., & Slawinski, J. L. (1997). Instructing children to use memory strategies: Evidence of utilization deficiencies in memory training studies. In D. F. Bjorklund & P. H. Miller (Eds.), *New themes in strategy development.*

Bjorklund, D. F., & Pelligrini, A. D. (2002). *The origins of human nature: Evolutionary developmental psychology.* Washington, DC: American Psychological Association.

Bjorklund, D. F., Schneider, W., Cassel, W. S., & Ashley, E. (1994). Training and extension of a memory strategy: Evidence for utilization deficiencies in the acquisition of an organizational strategy in high- and low-IQ children. *Child Development, 65,* 951–965.

Bjorkland, D. F., & Shackelford, T. K. (1999). Differences in parental investment contribute to important differences in men and women. *Current Directions in Psychological Science, 8,* 86–89.

Black, B., & Hazen, N. (1990). Social status and patterns of communication in acquainted and unacquainted preschool children. *Developmental Psychology, 26,* 379–387.

Black, J. E., & Greenough, W. T. (1998). Developmental approaches to the memory process. In J. Martinez & R. Kesner (Eds.), *Neurobiology of learning and memory.* New York: Academic Press.

Black, J. E., Jones, T. A., Nelson, C. A., & Greenough, W. T. (1998). Neuronal plasticity and the developing brain. In N. E. Alessi, J. T. Coyle, S. I. Harrison, & E. Eth (Eds.), *Handbook of child and adolescent psychiatry* (Vol. 6, pp. 31–53). New York: Wiley.

Black, M., Schuler, M., & Nair, P. (1993). Prenatal drug exposure: Neurodevelopmental outcome and parenting environment. *Journal of Pediatric Psychology, 18,* 605–620.

Blair, C., Ramey, C. T., & Hardin, M. (1995). Early intervention for low birthweight premature infants: Participation and intellectual development. *American Journal of Mental Retardation, 99,* 542–554.

Blakemore, J. (1990). Children's nurturant interactions with their infant siblings: An exploration of gender differences and maternal socialization. *Sex Roles, 22,* 43–57.

Blanchard, R., Zucker, K J., Bradley, S. J., & Hume, C. S. (1995). Birth order and sibling sex ratio in homosexual male adolescents and probably prehomosexual feminine boys. *Developmental Psychology, 31,* 22–30.

Blasch, B. B., Long, R. G., & Griffin-Shirley, N. (1989). Results of a national survey of electronic travel aid use. *Journal of Visual Impairment & Blindness, 82,* 449–453.

Blasi, A. (1983). Moral cognition and moral action: A theoretical perspective. *Developmental Review, 3,* 178–210.

Blass, E., Ganchrow, J. R., & Steiner, J. E. (1984). Classical conditioning in newborn humans 2–48 hours of age. *Infant Behavior and Development, 7,* 223–234.

Block, J. H. (1983). Differential premises arising from differential socialization of the sexes: Some conjectures. *Child Development, 54,* 1335–1354.

Block, J. H., Block, J., & Morrison, A. (1981). Parental agreement-disagreement on childrearing

orientations and gender-related personality correlates in children. *Child Development, 52,* 965–974.

Blomeke, S. C. (1999). A surrogacy agreement that could have and should have been enforced. RR. V. M. H., 689 N. E. 2nd 790 (Mass. 1998). *University of Dayton Law Review, 24,* 513–542.

Bloom, L. (1970). *Language development: Form and function in emerging grammars.* Cambridge, MA: MIT Press.

Bloom, L. (1976). *An interactive perspective on language development.* Keynote address, Child Language Research Forum, Stanford University, Stanford, CA.

Bloom, L. (1991). *Language development from two to three.* New York: Cambridge University Press.

Bloom, L. (1993). *The transition from infancy to language.* New York: Cambridge University Press.

Bloom, L. (1998). Language acquisition in its developmental context. In W. Damon (Gen. Ed.), R. Siegler, & D. Kuhn (Vol. Eds.), *Handbook of child psychology: Vol. 2. Cognition, perception, and language* (5th ed., pp. 309–370). New York: Wiley.

Bloom, L., Lifter, K., & Broughton, J. (1985). The convergence of early cognition and language in the second year of life: Problems in conceptualization and measurement. In M. Barrett (Ed.), *Single word speech.* London: Wiley.

Bloom, L., & Tinker, E. (2001). The intentionality model and language acquisition. *Monographs of the Society for Research in Child Development, 66* (4), Serial No. 267.

Bloom, P. (2000). *How children learn the meanings of words.* Cambridge, MA: The MIT Press.

Blum, L. M. (2000). *At the breast: Ideologies of breastfeeding and motherhood in the contemporary United States.* Boston: Beacon Press.

Boccia, M., & Campos, J. (1989). Maternal emotional signals, social referencing, and infants' reactions to strangers. In N. Eisenberg (Ed.), *Empathy and related emotional responses: New directions for child development* (pp. 25–49). San Francisco: Jossey-Bass.

Bogartz, R. S., Shinskey, J. L., & Schilling, T. H. (2000). Object permanence in five-and-a-half-month-old infants? *Infancy, 1,* 403–428.

Bohannon, J. N., III, & Stanowicz, L. (1988). The issue of negative evidence: Adult responses to children's language errors. *Developmental Psychology, 24,* 684–689.

Bohannon, J. N., III, & Warren-Leubecker, A. (1988). Recent developments in child-directed speech: We've come a long way, baby talk. *Language Sciences, 10,* 89–110.

Bohlin, G., & Hagekull, B. (1993). Stranger wariness and sociability in the early years. *Infant Behavior and Development, 16,* 53–67.

Boismier, J. D. (1977). Visual stimulation and wake-sleep behavior in human neonates. *Developmental Psychobiology, 10,* 219–227.

Bolger, K. E., & Patterson, C. J. (2001). Developmental pathways from child maltreatment to peer rejection. *Child Development, 72,* 549–568.

Bolger, K. E., Patterson, C., & Kupersmidt, J. B. (1998). Peer relationships and self-esteem among children who have been maltreated. *Child Development, 69,* 1171–1197.

Bonvillian, J. D., Orlansky, M. D., & Folven, R. J. (1990). Early acquisition: Implications for theories of language acquisition. In V. Volterra & C. J. Erting (Eds.), *From gesture to language in hearing and deaf children.* Heidelberg: Springer-Verlag.

Bonvillian, J. D., Orlansky, M. D., Novack, L. I., & Folven, R. J. (1983). Early sign language acquisition and cognitive development. In D. R. Rogers & J. A. Sloboda (Eds.), *The acquisition of symbolic skills.* New York: Plenum.

Booth, A. E., Pinto, J., & Bertenthal, B. I. (2002). Perception of the symmetrical patterning of human gait by infants. *Developmental Psychology, 38,* 554–563.

Booth, C. A., Clarke-Stewart, K. A., Vandell, D. L., McCartney, K., & Owen, M. T. (2002). Child care usage and mother-infant "quality time." *Journal of Marriage and Family, 64,* 16–26.

Borduin, C. M., & Henggeler, S. W. (1990). A multisystemic approach to the treatment of serious delinquent behavior. In R. J. McMahon & R. D. Peters (Eds.), *Behavior disorders of adolescence: Research, intervention, and policy in clinical and school settings* (pp. 63–80). New York: Plenum Press.

Borke, H. (1971). Interpersonal perception of young children: Egocentrism or empathy. *Developmental Psychology, 5,* 263–269.

Borke, H. (1975). Piaget's mountains revisited: Changes in the egocentric landscape. *Developmental Psychology, 11,* 240–243.

Bornstein, M. H., & Sigman, M. D. (1986). Continuity in mental

development from infancy. *Child Development, 57,* 251–274.

Bornstein, M. H., & Tamis, C. (1986). *Origins of cognitive skills in infants.* Paper presented at the International Conference on Infant Studies, Los Angeles.

Bouchard, C. (1994). *The genetics of obesity.* Boca Raton, FL: CRC Press.

Bouchard, T. J., & McGue, M. (1981). Familial studies of intelligence: A review. *Science, 212,* 1055–1059.

Boulton, M. J., & Smith, P. K. (1994). Bully/victim problems in middle-school children: Stability, self-perceived competence, peer perceptions and peer acceptance. *British Journal of Developmental Psychology, 12,* 315–329.

Bower, T. G. R. (1979). Visual development in the blind child. In V. Smith & J. Keen (Eds.), *Visual handicap in children.* Clinics in Development Medicine, No. 73. London: Lippincott.

Bower, T. G. R. (1989). *The rational infant: Learning in infancy.* San Francisco: W. H. Freeman.

Bowlby, J. (1958). The nature of the child's tie to his mother. *International Journal of Psychoanalysis, 39,* 350–373.

Bowlby, J. (1960). Grief and mourning in infancy and early childhood. *The Psychoanalytic Study of the Child, 15.*

Bowlby, J. (1969). *Attachment and loss: Vol. 1. Attachment.* New York: Basic Books.

Bowlby, J. (1973). *Separation and loss.* New York: Basic Books.

Boyum, L., & Parke, R. D. (1995). Family emotional expressiveness and children's social competence. *Journal of Marriage and Family, 57,* 593–608.

Brackbill, Y., McManus, K., & Woodward, L. (1985). *Medication in maternity: Infant exposure and maternal information.* Ann Arbor, MI: University of Michigan Press.

Bradley, R. H., Corwyn, R. F., Burchinal, M., McAdoo, H. P., & Garcia-Coll, C. (2001). The home environments of children in the United States Part II: Relations with behavioral development through age thirteen. *Child Development, 72,* 1868–1886.

Bradley, R. H., Whiteside, L., Mundfrom, D. J., Casey, P. H., Kelleher, K. J., & Pope, S. K. (1994). Early indications of resilience and their relation to experiences in the home environments of low birthweight, premature infants living in poverty. *Child Development, 65,* 346–360.

Brainerd, C. J., & Reyna, V. F. (1990). Inclusion illusions: Fuzzy trace theory and perceptual salience effects in cognitive development. *Developmental Review, 10,* 365–403.

Bransford, J. D., Brown, A. L., & Cocking, R. R. (1999). *How people learn: Brain, mind, experience, and school.* Washington, DC: National Academy Press.

Braungart-Rieker, J. M., Garwood, M. M., Powers, B. P., & Wang, X. (2001). Parental sensitivity, infant affect and affect regulation: Predictors of later attachment. *Child Development, 72,* 252–270.

Brazelton, T. B. (1972). Implications of infant development among the Mayan Indians of Mexico. *Human Development, 15,* 90–111.

Brazelton, T. B. (1984). *Neonatal behavioral assessment scale.* Philadelphia: Lippincott.

Brazelton, T. B., & Nugent, J. K. (1995). *Neonatal behavioral assessment scale* (3rd ed.). London, England: MacKeith Press.

Brazelton, T. B., Nugent, J. K., & Lester, B. M. (1987). Neonatal behavioral assessment scale. In J. Osofsky (Ed.), *Handbook of infancy* (2nd ed.). New York: Wiley.

Brener, R. (1940). An experimental investigation of memory span. *Journal of Experimental Psychology, 33,* 1–19.

Brennan, P. A., Hall, J., Bor, W., Najman, J. M., & Williams, G. (2003). Integrating biological and social processes in relation to early-onset persistent aggression in boys and girls. *Developmental Psychology, 32,* 309–323.

Bretherton, I., & Munholland, K. A. (1999). Internal models in attachment relationships: A construct revisited. In J. Cassidy & P. Shaver (Eds.), *Handbook of attachment* (pp. 89–114). New York: Guilford Press.

Bridges, L. J., & Grolnick, W. S. (1995). The development of emotional self-regulation in infancy and early childhood. In N. Eisenberg (Ed.), *Social development. Review of personality and social psychology* (pp. 185–211). Thousand Oaks, CA: Sage.

Brim, O. G. (1958). Family structure and sex role learning by children: A further analysis of Helen Koch's data. *Sociometry, 21,* 1–16.

Britt, G. C., & Myers, B. J. (1994). The effects of Brazelton intervention: A review. *Infant Mental Health Journal, 15,* 278–292.

Brockington, I. (1996). *Motherhood and mental health.* Oxford, England: Oxford University Press.

Broderick, A. A., & Kasa-Hendrickson, C. (2001). "Say just one word first.": The emergence of reliable speech in a student labeled

with autism. *Journal of the Association for Persons with Severe Handicaps, 26,* 13–24.

Brody, G. H., Dorsey, S., Forehand, R., & Armistead, L. (2002). Unique and protective contributions of parenting and classroom processes to the adjustment of African-American children living in single-parent families. *Child Development, 73,* 274–286.

Brody, G., Flor, D., & Neubaum, E. (1998). Coparenting process and child competence among rural African-American families. In M. Lewis & C. Feiring (Eds.), *Families, risk, and competence* (pp. 227–343). Mahwah, NJ: Erlbaum.

Brody, G. H., Ge, X., Conger, R., Gibbons, F. X., Murry, V. M., Gerrard, M., & Simons, R. L. (2001). The influence of neighborhood disadvantage, collective socialization and parenting on African American children's affiliation with deviant peers. *Child Development, 72,* 1231–1246.

Brody, G. H., Stoneman, Z., & Flor, D. (1996). Parental religiosity, family processes, and youth competence in rural, two-parent African American families. *Developmental Psychology, 32,* 696–706.

Brody, J. E. (1998). Personal health: Teenagers and sex—Younger and more at risk. *The New York Times,* Sept. 15.

Brody, L. (2000). The socialization of gender differences in emotional expression: Display rules, infant termperament, and differentiation. In A. H. Fischer (Ed.), *Gender and emotion: Social psychological perspectives. Studies in emotion and social interaction* (2nd Series, pp. 24–47). New York: Cambridge University Press.

Brody, L. (2002). Emotions, defenses, and gender. In R. F. Bornstein & J. M. Masling (Eds.), The psychodynamics of gender and gender role. *Empirical studies in psychoanalytic theories* (Vol. 10, pp. 203–249). Washington, DC: American Psychological Association.

Brody, L. R. (1996). Gender, emotional expression and parent-child boundaries. In R. D. Kavanaugh, B. Zimmerberg, & S. Fein (Eds.), *Emotion: Interdisciplinary perspectives.* Hillsdale, NJ: Erlbaum.

Brody, N. (1992). *Intelligence* (2nd ed.). San Diego: Academic Press.

Brodzinsky, D. M., & Pinderhughes, E. (2002). Parenting and child development in adoptive families. In M. Bornstein (Ed.), *Handbook of*

parenting (rev. ed., Vol. 1, pp. 279–311). Mahwah, NJ: Erlbaum.

Broidy, L. M., Nagin, D. S., Tremblay, R. E., Bates, J. E., Brame, B., Dodge, K. A. et al. (2003). Developmental trajectories of childhood discipline behaviors and adolescent delinquency: A six-site, cross-national study. *Developmental Psychology, 39,* 222–245.

Bronfenbrenner, U. (1979). *The ecology of human development.* Cambridge, MA: Harvard University Press.

Bronfenbrenner, U., McClelland, P., Wethington, E., Moen, P., & Ceci, S. J. (1996). *The state of Americans: This generation and the next.* New York: Free Press.

Bronfenbrenner, U., & Morris, P. (2006). The ecology of developmental processes. In W. Damon & R. M. Lerner (Series Eds.) and R. M. Lerner (Vol. Ed.) *Handbook of child psychology* (6th ed.), vol., New York: Wiley.

Bronson, W. (1981). Toddlers' behaviors with age mates: Issues of interaction, cognition and affect. *Monographs on Infancy, 1,* 127.

Brooks, J., & Lewis, M. (1976). Infants' responses to strangers: Midget, adult, and child. *Child Development, 47,* 323–332.

Brooks, J. H., & Reddon, J. R. (1996). Serum testosterone in violent and non-violent young offenders. *Journal of Clinical Psychology, 52,* 475–483.

Brooks-Gunn, J. (1988). Antecedents and consequences of variations in girls' maturational timing. *Journal of Adolescent Health Care, 9,* 1–9.

Brooks-Gunn, J. (1995). Children in families in communities: Risk and intervention in the Bronfenbrenner tradition. In P. Moen, G. H. Elder, & K. Lescher (Eds.), *Examining lives in context* (pp. 467–519). Washington, D.C.: American Psychological Association.

Brooks-Gunn, J., Berlin, L. J., Leventhal, T., & Fuligni, A. S. (2000). Depending on the kindness of strangers: Current national data initiatives and developmental research. *Child Development, 71,* 257–268.

Brooks-Gunn, J., Britto, P. J. R., & Brady, C. (1999). Struggling to make ends meet: Poverty and child development. In M. E. Lamb (Ed.), *Parenting and child development in "nontraditional" families* (pp. 279–304). Mahwah, NJ: Erlbaum.

Brooks-Gunn, J., Klebanov, P. K., Smith, J., Duncan, G. J., & Lee, K. (2003). The black-white test score gap in young children:

Contributions of test and family characteristics. *Applied Developmental Science, 7,* 239–252.

Brooks-Gunn, J., & Lewis, M. (1984). The development of early visual self-recognition. *Developmental Review, 4,* 215–239.

Brooks-Gunn, J., & Moore, K. (2002). Adolescent parents. In M. Bornstein (Ed.), *Handbook of parenting* (2nd ed.). Mahwah, NJ: Erlbaum.

Brooks-Gunn, J., & Ruble, D. N. (1984). The experience of menarche from a developmental perspective. In J. Brooks-Gunn & A. C. Petersen (Eds.), *Girls at puberty: Biological, psychological and social perspectives.* New York: Plenum.

Brooks-Gunn, J., Smith, J., Berlin, L. J., & Lee, K. (2001). Familywork: Welfare changes, parenting and young children. In G. K. Brookins (Ed.), *Exits from poverty.* New York: Cambridge University Press.

Brooks-Gunn, J., & Warren, W. P. (1985). The effects of delayed menarche in different contexts: Dance and nondance students. *Journal of Youth and Adolescence, 14,* 285–300.

Broverman, I. K., Vogel, S. R., Broverman, D. M., Clarkson, F. E., & Rosenkrantz, P. S. (1972). Sex-role stereotypes: A current appraisal. *Journal of Social Issues, 28,* 59–78.

Brown, A. L. (1975). The development of memory: Knowing, knowing about knowing, and knowing how to know. In H. W. Reese (Ed.), *Advances in child development and behavior* (Vol. 10). New York: Academic Press.

Brown, A. L. (1989). Analogical learning and transfer: What develops? In S. Vosniagou & A. Ortony (Eds.), *Similarity and analogical reasoning.* Cambridge, UK: Cambridge University Press.

Brown, A. L. (1994). The advancement of learning. *Educational Researcher, 23,* 4–12.

Brown, A. L., Bransford, T. D., Ferrara, R. A., & Campione, J. C. (1983). Learning, remembering and understanding. In J. H. Flavell & E. M. Markman (Eds.), *Handbook of child psychology: Vol. 3. Cognitive development.* New York: Wiley.

Brown, A. L., & Campione, J. C. (1997). Designing a community of young learners: Theoretical and practical lessons. In N. M. Lambert & B. L. McCombs (Eds.), *How students learn: Reforming schools through learner-centered education* (pp. 153–186). Washington, DC:

American Psychological Association.

Brown, A. L., Kane, M. J., & Echols, C. H. (1986). Young children's mental models determine analogical transfer across problems with a common goal structure. *Cognitive Development, 1,* 103–121.

Brown, B. B. (1990). Peer groups and peer cultures. In S. S. Feldman & G. R. Elliott (Eds.), *At the threshold* (pp. 171–196). Cambridge, MA: Harvard University Press.

Brown, B. B., & Huang, B. (1995). Examining parenting practices in different peer contexts: Implications for adolescent trajectories. In L. J. Crockett & A. C. Crouter (Eds.), *Pathways through adolescence: Individual development in relation to social contexts.* Mahwah, NJ: Erlbaum.

Brown, E., & Brownell, C. A. (1990). *Individual differences in toddlers' interaction styles.* Paper presented at International Conference on Infant Studies, Montreal.

Brown, R. (1973). *A first language: The early stages.* Cambridge, MA: Harvard University Press.

Brown, R., & Bellugi, U. (1964). Three processes in the child's acquisition of syntax. In E. G. Lenneberg (Ed.), *New directions in the study of language.* Cambridge, MA: MIT Press.

Brown, R., & Hanlon, C. (1970). Derivational complexity and order of acquisition in child speech. In J. Hayes (Ed.), *Cognition and the development of language* (pp. 11–54). New York: Wiley.

Brownell, C. A. (1990). Peer social skills in toddlers: Competencies and constraints illustrated by same age and mixed-age interaction. *Child Development, 61,* 838–848.

Bruck, M., & Ceci, S. J. (1999). The suggestibility of children's memory. *Annual Review of Psychology, 50,* 419–439.

Bruner, J. (1983). *Children's talk.* New York: Norton.

Bruner, J. (1990). *Acts of meaning.* Cambridge, MA: Harvard University Press.

Bruner, J. S. (1966). On cognitive growth. In J. S. Bruner, R. R. Olver, & P. M. Greenfield (Eds.), *Studies in cognitive growth.* New York: Wiley.

Bryant, P. E., & Trabasso, J. (1971). Transitive inferences and memory in young children. *Nature, 232,* 456–458.

Bryden, M. P. (1988). Does laterality make any difference? Thoughts on the relation between asymmetry and reading. In D. L. Molfese & S. J. Segalowitz (Eds.), *Brain lateralization in children* (pp. 509–525). New York: Guilford Press.

Bryden, M. P., & Saxby, L. (1986). Developmental aspects of cerebral lateralization. In J. E. Obrzat & G. W. Hynd (Eds.), *Child neuropsychology: Vol. 1. Theory and research.* Orlando, FL: Academic.

Buchanan, C. M., & Heiges, K. L. (2001). When conflict continues after the marriage ends: Effects of postdivorce conflict on children. In J. Grych & F. D. Fincham (Eds.), *Interparental conflict and child development* (pp. 337–362). New York: Cambridge University Press.

Buchanan, C. M., Maccoby, E. E., & Dornbusch, S. M. (1991). Caught between parents: Adolescents experience in divorced homes. *Child Development, 62,* 1008–1029.

Buchanan, C. M., Maccoby, E. E., & Dornbusch, S. M. (1996). *Adolescents after divorce.* Cambridge, MA: Harvard University Press.

Buckroyd, J. (1996). Eating disorders as psychosomatic illness: The implications for treatment. *Psychodynamic Counseling, 1,* 106–118.

Budwig, N. (2002). A developmental-functionalist approach to mental state talk. In E. Amsel and J. P. Byrnes (Eds.), *Language, literacy, and cognitive development* (pp. 59–86). Mahwah, NJ: Erlbaum.

Bugental, D., & Grusec, J. (2006). Socialization processes. In W. Damon & R. M. Lerner (Series Eds.) & N. Eisenberg (Vol. Ed.), *Handbook of child psychology* (6th ed., Vol. 3). New York: Wiley.

Bugental, D. B., & Happaney, K. (2004). Predicting infant maltreatment in low-income families: The interactive effects of maternal attributions and child status at birth. *Developmental Psychology, 40,* 234–243.

Buhs, E. S., & Ladd, G. W. (2001). Peer rejection as an antecedent of young children's school adjustment: An examination of mediating processes. *Developmental Psychology, 37,* 550–560.

Bullinger, A., & Chatillon, J. (1983). Recent theory and research of the Genevan school. In P. H. Mussen (Ed.), *Handbook of child psychology* (Vol. 3). New York: Wiley.

Bullock, D. (1983). Seeking relations between cognitive and social-interactive transitions. In K. W. Fischer (Ed.), *Levels and transitions in children's development: New directions in child development.* San Francisco: Jossey-Bass.

Bullock, D., & Merrill, L. (1980). The impact of personal preference on consistency through time: The case of childhood aggression. *Child Development, 51,* 808–814.

Bullock, M. (1985). Animism in childhood thinking: A new look at an old question. *Developmental Psychology, 21,* 217–225.

Burks, V., Laird, R., Dodge, K., Pettit, G., & Bates, J. (1999). Knowledge structures, social information processing, and children's aggressive behavior. *Social Development, 8,* 220–236.

Burn, S. M., O'Neil, A. K., & Nederend, S. (1996). Childhood tomboyism and adult androgyny. *Sex Roles, 34,* 419–428.

Burns, G. W., & Bottino, P. J. (1989). *The science of genetics* (6th ed.). New York: Macmillan.

Burns, K. A., Deddish, R. B., Burns, K., & Hatcher, R. P. (1983). Use of oscillating waterbeds and rhythmic sounds for premature infant stimulation. *Developmental Psychology, 19,* 746–751.

Burton, R. V. (1963). The generality of honesty reconsidered. *Psychological Review, 70,* 481–499.

Burton, R. V. (1984). A paradox in theories and research in moral development. In W. M. Kurtines & J. L. Gewirtz (Eds.), *Morality, moral behavior, and moral development.* New York: Wiley.

Bus, A. G., van IJzendoorn, M. H., & Pelligrini, A. D. (1995). Joint book reading makes for success in learning to read: A meta-analysis on intergenerational transmission of literacy. *Review of Educational Research, 65,* 1–21.

Bushman, D., & Huesmann, L. R. (2001). Effects of televised violence on aggression. In D. Singer & J. Singer (Eds.), *Handbook of children and the media.* Thousand Oaks, CA: Sage.

Buss, D. M. (1994). *The evolution of desire.* New York: Basic Books.

Buss, D. M., & Schmitt, D. P. (1993). Sexual strategies theory: An evolutionary perspective on human mating. *Psychological Review, 100,* 204–232.

Bussey, K. (1992). Lying and truthfulness: Children's definitions, standards and evaluative reactions. *Child Development, 63,* 129–137.

Butler, S. C., Berthier, N. E., & Clifton, R. K. (2002). Two-year-olds' search strategies and visual tracking in a hidden displacement task. *Developmental Psychology, 38,* 581–590.

Butterfield, E. C., & Siperstein, G. N. (1972). Influence of contingent auditory stimulation upon non-nutritional suckle. In J. F. Bosoma (Ed.), *Third symposium on oral sensation and perception: The mouth of the infant.* Springfield, IL: Charles C Thomas.

Butterworth, G., & Grover, L. (1990). Joint visual attention, manual pointing, and preverbal communication in human infancy. In M. Jeannerod (Ed.), *Attention and performance XIII.* Hillsdale, NJ: Erlbaum.

Buysse, V., & Bailey, D. B. (1993). Behavioral and developmental outcomes in young children with disabilities in integrated and segregated settings: A review of comparative studies. *Journal of Special Education, 26,* 434–461.

Byrne, J. M., & Horowitz, F. D. (1981). Rocking as a soothing intervention: The influence of direction and type of movement. *Infant Behavior and Development, 4,* 207–218.

Cairns, R. B. (1998). The making of developmental psychology. In W. Damon (Series Ed.), & R. M. Lerner (Vol. Ed.), *Handbook of child psychology, Vol. 1* (pp. 25–105). New York: Wiley.

Cairns, R. B., & Cairns, B. D. (1994). *Lifelines and risks: Pathways of youth in our time.* Cambridge, England: Cambridge University Press.

Callanan, M. A., & Oakes, L. M. (1992). Preschoolers' questions and parents' explanations: Causal thinking in everyday activity. *Cognitive Development, 7,* 213–233.

Campbell, A. L., & Namy, L. L. (2003). The role of social-referential context in verbal and nonverbal symbol learning. *Child Development, 74,* 549–563.

Campbell, D. (2000). *The Mozart effect for children.* New York: William Morrow.

Campbell, F. A., Pungello, E. P., Miller-Johnson, S., Burchinal, M., & Ramey, C. T. (2001). The development of cognitive and academic abilities: Growth curves from an early childhood educational experiment. *Developmental Psychology, 37,* 231–242.

Campbell, S. B. (1998). Developmental considerations in child psychopathology. In T. Ollendick & M. Hersen (Eds.), *Handbook of child psychopathology* (3rd ed., pp. 1–35). New York: Plenum.

Campbell, S. B. (2000). Developmental perspectives on attention deficit disorder. In A. Sameroff, M. Lewis, & S. Miller (Eds.), *Handbook of child psychopathology* (2nd ed., pp. 383–401). New York: Plenum.

Campbell, S. B. (2002). *Behavior problems in preschool children: Clinical and developmental issues* (2nd ed.). New York: Guilford Press.

Campos, J. J., Anderson, D. I., Barbu-Roth, M. A., Hubbard, E. M., Hertenstein, M. J., & Witherington, D. (2000). Travel broadens the mind. *Infancy, 1,* 149–220.

Campos, J. J., & Bertenthal, B. I. (1989). Locomotion and psychological development in infancy. In F. Morrison, C. Lord, & D. Keating (Eds.), *Applied developmental psychology* (Vol. 3). New York: Academic.

Campos, J. J., Bertenthal, B., & Kermonian, R. (1992). Early experience and emotional development: The emergence of wariness of heights. *Psychological Science, 3,* 61–64.

Campos, J., Hiatt, S., Ramsey, D., Henderson, C., & Svejda, M. (1978). The emergence of fear on the visual cliff. In M. Lewis & L. Rosenblum (Eds.), *The origins of affect.* New York: Plenum.

Campos, J. J., Langer, A., & Krowitz, A. (1970). Cardiac responses on the visual cliff in prelocomotor human infants. *Science, 170,* 196–197.

Campos, J. J., Svejda, M., Bertenthal, B., Benson, N., & Schmid, D. (1981, April). *Self-produced locomotion and wariness of heights: New evidence from training studies.* Paper presented at the meeting of the Society for Research in Child Development, Boston.

Campos, R. P. (1989). Soothing pain-elicited distress in infants with swaddling and pacifiers. *Child Development, 60,* 781–792.

Camras, L. A., Malatesta, C., & Izard, C. (1991). The development of facial expressions in infancy. In R. Feldman & B. Rime (Eds.), *Fundamentals of nonverbal behavior.* New York: Cambridge University Press.

Canfield, R. L., & Haith, M. M. (1991). Young infants' visual expectations for symmetrical and asymmetrical sequences. *Developmental Psychology, 27,* 198–208.

Cantor, N. (2000). Life task problem solving: Situational affordances and personal needs. In E. T. Higgins, A. W. Kruglanski, & W. Arie (Eds.), *Motivational science: Social and personality perspectives. Key reading in social psychology* (pp. 100–110). New York: Psychology Press.

Cantwell, D. P., Baker, L., & Rutter, M. (1978). Family factors. In M. Rutter & E. Schopier (Eds.), *Autism: A reappraisal of concepts and treatment.* New York: Plenum.

Cantwell, D. P., Russell, A. T., Mattison, R., & Will, L. A. (1979). A comparison of DSM-II and DSM-III in the diagnosis of childhood psychiatric disorders. *Archives of General Psychiatry, 36,* 1208–1228.

Capaldi, D., & Clark, S. (1998). Prospective family predictors of aggression toward female partners for at-risk young men. *Developmental Psychology, 34,* 1175–1188.

Caplan, P. J., & Caplan, J. B. (1999). *Thinking critically about research on sex and gender* (2nd ed.). New York: Longman.

Capron, C., & Duyme, M. (1989). Assessment of effects of socioeconomic status on IQ in a cross-fostering study. *Nature, 340,* 552–554.

Cardon, L. R. (1994). Height, weight, and obesity. In J. C. DeFries, R. Plomin, & D. W. Fulker (Eds.), *Nature and nurture during middle childhood.* Oxford: Blackwell.

Carey, S. (1994). Does learning a language require the child to reconceptualize the world? In L. Gleitman & B. Landau (Eds.), *The acquisition of the lexicon* (pp. 143–168). Cambridge, MA: Elsevier/MIT Press.

Carlo, G., Hausmann, A., Christiansen, S., & Randall, B. A. (2003). Sociocognitive and behavioral correlates of a measure of prosocial tendencies for adolescents. *Journal of Early Adolescence, 23,* 107–134.

Carlo, G., Koller, S. H., Eisenberg, N., Pacheco, P., & Loquercio, A. (1996). Prosocial cognitions, emotions and behavior: A cross-cultural study of adolescents from Brazil and the United States. *Developmental Psychology, 32,* 231–240.

Carlson, E. A., Sroufe, L. A., & Egeland, B. (2004). The construction of experience: A longitudinal study of representation and behavior. *Child Development, 75,* 66–83.

Carlson, V., Cicchetti, D., Barnett, D., & Braunwald, K. (1989). Disorganized/ disoriented attachment relationships in maltreated infants. *Developmental Psychology, 25,* 525–531.

Carmichael, M. (2004). Have it your way: Redesigning birth. *Newsweek,* May 10, 70–71.

Carr, M., & Jessup, D. L. (1995). Cognitive and metacognitive predictors of mathematics strategy use. *Learning and Individual Differences, 7,* 235–247.

Carraher, T. N., Schliemann, A. D., & Carraher, D. W. (1988). Mathematical concepts in everyday life. *New Directions for Child Development, 41,* 71–87.

Carroll, J. B. (1993). *Human cognitive abilities: A survey of factor analytic studies.* New York: Cambridge University Press.

Carroll, J. B. (1997). Psychometrics, intelligence, and public perception. *Intelligence, 24,* 25–52.

Carroll, J. M., Snowling, M. J., Hulme, C., & Stevenson, J. (2003). The development of phonological awareness in preschool children. *Developmental Psychology, 39,* 913–923.

Carson, R. C. (1991). Dilemmas in the pathway of the DSM-IV. *Journal of Abnormal Psychology, 100,* 302–307.

Carson, R. C., & Butcher, J. N. (1992). *Abnormal psychology and modern life* (9th ed.). New York: HarperCollins.

Carter, C. S., Freeman, J. H., & Stanton, M. E. (1995). Neonatal medial prefrontal lesions and recovery of spatial delayed alternation in the rat: Effects of delay interval. *Developmental Psychobiology, 28,* 269–279.

Carver, K., Joyner, K., & Udry, J. R. (2003). National estimates of adolescent romantic relationships. In P. Florsheim (Ed), *Adolescent romantic relations and sexual behavior: Theory, research, and practical implications* (pp. 23–56). Mahwah, NJ: Erlbaum.

Carver, P. R., Egan, S. K., & Perry, D. G. (2004). Children who question their heterosexuality. *Developmental Psychology, 40,* 43–53.

Case, R. (1984). The process of stage transition: A neo-Piagetian view. In R. Sternberg (Ed.), *Mechanisms of cognitive development.* New York: Freeman.

Case, R. (1985). *Intellectual development: Birth to adulthood.* New York: Academic.

Case, R. (1992). Neo-Piagetian theories of child development. In R. J. Sternberg & C. A. Berg (Eds.), *Intellectual development,* (pp. 161–196). New York: Cambridge University Press.

Case, R. (1996). Modeling the dynamic interplay between general and specific change in children's conceptual understanding. *Monographs of the Society for Research in Child Development, 61,* Serial No. 246 Nos. 1 & 2, 156–188.

Case, R. (1998). The development of conceptual structures. In W. Damon (Series Ed.) & D. Kuhn & R. S. Siegler (Vol. Eds.), *Handbook of child psychology: Vol. 2, Cognition, perception, and language* (5th ed.). New York: Wiley.

Case, R., Hayward, S., Lewis, M., & Hurst, P. (1988). Toward a neo-Piagetian theory of cognitive and emotional development. *Developmental Review, 8,* 1–51.

Casey, B. J. (2001). Disruption of inhibitory control in developmental disorders: A mechanistic model of implicated frontostriatal circuitry. In J. McClelland & R. Siegler (Eds.), *Mechanisms of cognitive development* (pp. 327–349). Mahwah, NJ: Erlbaum.

Cashon, C. H., & Cohen, L. B. (2000). Eight-month-old infants' perception of possible and impossible events. *Infancy 1,* 429–446.

Casiglia, A. C., Lo Coco, A., & Zapplulla, C. (1998). Aspects of social reputation and peer relationships in Italian children: A cross-cultural perspective. *Developmental Psychology, 34,* 723–730.

Casper, L. M., & Hogan, D. P. (1990). Family networks in prenatal and postnatal health. *Social Biology, 37*(1–2), 84–101.

Caspi, A., Elder, G. H., & Bem, D. J. (1987). Moving against the world: Life course patterns of explosive children. *Developmental Psychology, 23,* 308–313.

Caspi, A., Elder, G. H., & Bem, D. J. (1988). Moving away from the world: Life-course patterns of shy children. *Developmental Psychology, 24,* 824–831.

Caspi, A., Lyman, D., Moffitt, T. E., & Silva, P. A. (1993). Unraveling girls' delinquency: Biological, dispositional and contextual contributors to adolescent misbehavior. *Developmental Psychology, 29,* 19–30.

Caspi, A., Sugden, K., Moffitt, T. E., Taylor, A., Craig, I. W., Harrington, H., et al. (2003). Influence of life stress on depression: Moderation by a polymorphism in the 5-HTT gene. *Science, 301,* 386–389.

Cassidy, J. (1988). Child-mother attachment and the self in six-year-olds. *Child Development, 59,* 121–135.

Cassidy, J. (1999). The nature of the child's ties. In J. Cassidy & P. R. Shaver (Eds.), *Handbook of attachment: Theory, research, and clinical applications.* New York: Guilford Press.

Cassidy, J., & Asher, S. R. (1992). Loneliness and sociometric status among young children. *Child Development, 63,* 350–365.

Cassidy, J., & Berlin, L. J. (1994). The insecure/ambivalent pattern of attachment: Theory and research. *Child Development, 65,* 971–991.

Cassidy, J., Kirsh, S. J., Scolton, K. L., & Parke, R. D. (1996). Attachment and representations of peer relationships. *Developmental Psychology, 32,* 892–904.

Cassidy, K. W., Fineberg, D. S., Brown, K., & Perkins, A. (2005). Theory of mind may be contagious, but you don't catch it from your twin. *Child Development, 76,* 97–106.

Catalano, R. F., Hawkins, J. D., Krenz, C., & Gilmore, M. (1993). Using research to guide culturally appropriate drug abuse prevention. *Journal of Consulting and Clinical Psychology, 61,* 804–811.

Ceci, S. J. (1996). *On intelligence: A bioecological treatise on intellectual development* (Exp. ed.). Cambridge, MA: Harvard University Press.

Ceci, S. J., & Bruck, M. (1998). Children's testimony: Applied and basic issues. In W. Damon (Gen. Ed.), I. Sigel, & K. A. Renninger (Vol. Eds.), *Handbook of child psychology: Vol. 4* (pp 713–774). New York: Wiley.

Ceci, S. J., Bruck, M., & Battin, D. (2000). The suggestibility of children's testimony. In D. F. Bjorklund (Ed.), *False-memory creation in children and adults: Theory, research, and implications.* Mahwah, NJ: Erlbaum.

Ceci, S. J., Leichtman, M. D., & White, T. (1998). Interviewing preschoolers' remembrance of things planted. In D. P. Peters (Ed.), *The child witness in context cognitive, social and legal perspectives.* Holland: Kluwer.

Ceci, S. J., Ross, D. F., & Toglia, M. P. (1987). Suggestibility of children's memory: Psycholegal implications. *Journal of Experimental Psychology: General, 116,* 38–49.

Ceci, S., & Williams, W. (1997). Schooling, intelligence, and income. *American Psychologist, 52,* 1051–1058.

Centers for Disease Control and Prevention. (1993). Rates of cesarean delivery—United States, 1991. *Morbidity and Mortality Weekly Report, 42,* 285–289.

Centers for Disease Control and Prevention. (1996). Summary of notifiable diseases, United States, 1996. *Morbidity and Mortality Weekly Report, 46.*

Centers for Disease Control and Prevention. (2000). Trends in the attendant, place, and timing of births and in the use of obstetric interventions in the United States, 1989–1997. *Mortality and Morbidity Weekly Report, 49,* 1–4.

Centers for Disease Control and Prevention. (2003). *HIV/AIDS Report, 15,* 1–29.

Cervantes, C. A., & Callanan, M. (1998). Labels and explanations in mother-child emotion talk: Age and gender differentiation. *Developmental Psychology, 34,* 88–98.

Chandler, M. J., Greenspan, S., & Barenboim, C. (1973). Judgments of intentionality in response to videotaped and verbally presented moral dilemmas: The medium is the message. *Child Development, 44,* 315–320.

Chandler, M. J., Lalonde, C. E., Sokol, B. W., & Hallett, D. (2003). Personal persistence, identity development, and suicide. *Monographs of the Society for Research on Child Development, 68* (1, Serial No. 273).

Chandler, S., & Field, P. A. (1997). Becoming a father: First-time fathers' experience of labor and delivery. *Journal of Nurse-Midwifery, 42,* 17–24.

Chang, H. W., & Trehub, S. E. (1977). Infants' perception of grouping in auditory patterns. *Child Development, 48,* 1666–1670.

Chao, R. K. (1994). Beyond parental control and authoritarian parenting style: Understanding Chinese parenting through the cultural notion of training. *Child Development, 65,* 1111–1119.

Chao, R. K. (1995). Chinese and European American cultural models of the self reflected in mothers' childrearing beliefs. *Ethos, 23,* 328–354.

Chao, R. K. (2001). Extending research on the consequences of parenting style for Chinese Americans and European Americans. *Child Development, 72,* 1832–1843.

Chao, R. K., & Tseng, V. (2002). Asian-American parents. In M. Bornstein (Ed.), *Handbook of parenting: Vol. 4: Social conditions and applied parenting* (2nd ed.) (pp. 59–93). Mahwah, NJ: Erlbaum.

Charlesworth, R., & Hartup, W. W. (1967). Positive social reinforcement in the nursery school peer group. *Child Development, 38,* 993–1002.

Charlesworth, W. (1988). Resources and resource acquisition during ontogeny. In K. MacDonald (Ed.), *Sociobiological perspectives on human development.* New York: Springer-Verlag.

Charlesworth, W., & Dzur, C. (1987). Gender comparison of preschoolers' behavior and resource utilization. *Child Development, 58,* 191–200.

Charlton, A. (1994). Children and passive smoking: A review. *Journal of Family Practice, 38,* 267–277.

Chase, W. G., & Simon, H. A. (1973). The mind's eye in chess. In W. G. Chase (Ed.), *Visual information processing.* New York: Academic.

Chase-Lansdale, P. L., & Hetherington, E. M. (1990). The impact of divorce on life-span development: Short and long-term effects. In D. Featherman & R. M. Lerner (Eds.), *Life span development and behavior* (Vol. 10, pp. 105–150). Orlando, FL: Academic Press.

Chavkin, W. (1995). Substance abuse in pregnancy. In B. P. Sachs, R. Beard, E. Papiernik, & C. Russel (Eds.), *Reproductive health care for women and babies* (pp. 305–321). New York: Oxford University Press.

Chen, C., & Stevenson, H. W. (1995). Motivation and mathematics achievement: A comparative study of Asian-American, Caucasian-American and East Asian high school students. *Child Development, 66,* 1215–1234.

Chen, C., Stevenson, H. W., Hayward, C., & Burgess, S. (1995). Culture and academic achievement: Ethnic and cross-national differences. In P. Pintrich & M. Maehr (Eds.), *Advances in motivation and achievement: Vol. 9. Culture, race, ethnicity, and motivation.* New York: Plenum.

Chen, X. (2000). Growing up in a collectivist culture: Socialization and socioemotional development in Chinese children. In A. L. Comunian & U. P. Gielen (Eds.), *Human development in cross-culture perspective.* Padua, Italy: Cedam.

Chen, X., Cen, G., Li, D., & He, Y. (2005). Social functioning and adjustment in Chinese children: The imprint of historical time. *Child Development, 76,* 182–195.

Chen, X., Chang, L., & He, Y. (2003). The peer group as context: Mediating and moderating effects on relations between academic achievement and social functioning in Chinese children. *Child Development, 74,* 710–727.

Chen, X., & Rubin, K. H. (1994). Family conditions, parental acceptance, and social competence and aggression in Chinese children. *Social Development, 3,* 269–290.

Chen, X., Rubin, K. H., & Sun, Y. (1992). Social reputation and peer relationships in Chinese and Canadian children: A cross-cultural study. *Child Development, 63,* 1336–1343.

Chen, Z., & Daehler, M. W. (1989). Positive and negative transfer in analogical problem solving by 6-year-old children. *Cognitive Development, 4,* 327–344.

Chen, Z., Sanchez, R. P., & Campbell, T. (1997). From beyond to within their grasp: The rudiments of analogical problem solving in 10- and 13-month-olds. *Developmental Psychology, 33,* 790–801.

Cherlin, A. (1996). *Sociology of the family.* Englewood Cliffs, NJ: Prentice Hall.

Cherlin, A. J., Furstenberg, F. F. Jr., Chase-Lansdale, P. L., Kiernan, K. E., Robins, P. K., Morrison, D. R., & Teitler, J. O. (1991). *Longitudinal studies of the effects of divorce on children in Great Britain and the United States. Science, 252,* 1386–1389.

Cherlin, A. J., & Furstenberg, F. F. (1994). Stepfamilies in the United States: A reconsideration. *Annual Review of Sociology, 20,* 359–381.

Chi, M. T. H. (1976). Short term memory limitations in children: Capacity or processing deficits? *Memory and Cognition, 4,* 559–572.

Chi, M. T. H. (1978). Knowledge structures and memory development. In R. S. Siegler (Ed.), *Children's thinking: What develops?* Hillsdale, NJ: Erlbaum.

Chi, M. T. H., & Koeske, R. D. (1983). Network representation of a child's dinosaur knowledge. *Developmental Psychology, 19,* 29–39.

Childers, J. B., & Tomasello, M. (2002). Two-year-olds learn novel nouns, verbs, and conventional actions from massed or distributed exposure. *Developmental Psychology, 38,* 967–978.

Children's Defense Fund. (1997). *The state of America's children: 1997.* Washington, DC: Author.

Children's Defense Fund. (1998). *The state of American's children: 1998.* Washington, DC: Author.

Children's Defense Fund. (2001). *The state of America's children: 2001.* Washington, DC: Author.

Children's Defense Fund. (2002). *The state of America's children: 2002.* Washington, DC: Author.

Children's Defense Fund. (2004). *The state of America's children: 2004.* Washington, DC: Author.

Chisholm, J. S. (1963). *Navajo infancy: An ethological study of child development.* New York: Aldine.

Chittenden, G. E. (1942). An experimental study in measuring and modifying assertive behavior in young children. *Monographs of the Society for Research in Child Development, 7* (Serial No. 31).

Chomitz, V. R., Cheung, L. W. Y., & Lieberman, E. (2000). The role of lifestyle in preventing low birthweight. In K. L. Freiberg (Ed.), *Human Development 00/01* (28th ed., pp. 18–28). Guilford, CT: Duskin/McGraw-Hill.

Chomsky, N. (1968). *Language and mind.* New York: Harcourt, Brace & World.

Chung, T., & Asher, J. R. (1996). Children's goals and strategies in peer conflict situations. *Merrill Palmer Quarterly, 42,* 125–147.

Cicchetti, D., & Toth, S. L. (2006). Developmental psychopathology and preventive intervention. In W. Damon & R. M. Lerner (Gen. Eds.) and K. A. Renninger & I. E. Sigel (Vol. Eds.), *Handbook of child psychology: Vol. 4. Child psychology and practice* (6th ed.). New York: Wiley.

Cicero, T. J. (1994). Effects of paternal exposure to alcohol on offspring development. *Alcohol Health and Research World, 18,* 37–41.

Cillessen, A. H. N., & Mayeux, L. (2004). Sociometric status and peer group behavior: Previous findings and current directions. In J. B. Kupersmidt & K. A. Dodge (Eds.), *Children's peer relations* (pp. 3–20). Washington, DC: American Psychological Association.

Clancy, P. (1985). Acquisition of Japanese. In D. I. Slobin (Ed.), *The cross-linguistic study of language acquisition: Vol. 1. The data* (pp. 323–524). Hillsdale, NJ: Erlbaum.

Clapp, J. (1996). Morphometric and neurodevelopmental outcome at age 5 years of the offspring of women who continued to exercise regularly throughout pregnancy. *Journal of Pediatrics, 129,* 856–863.

Clark, E. V. (1983). Meanings and concepts. In P. H. Mussen (Eds.), *Handbook of child psychology* (Vol. 3). New York: Wiley.

Clark, J. E., & Phillips, S. J. (1993). A longitudinal study of intralimb coordination in the first year of independent walking: A dynamical systems analysis. *Child Development, 64,* 1143–1157.

Clark, K. E., & Ladd, G. W. (2000). Connectedness and autonomy support in parent-child relationships: Links to children's socioemotional orientation and peer relationships. *Developmental Psychology, 36,* 485–498.

Clarke, D. J. (2001). Treatment of schizophrenia. In A. Dosen & K. Day (Eds.)., *Treating mental illness and behavior disorders in children and adults with mental retardation* (pp. 183–200). Washington, DC: American Psychiatric Press.

Clarke, G., Hops, H., Lewinsohn, P. M., & Andrews, J. (1992). Cognitive-behavioral group treatment of adolescent depression: Prediction of outcome. *Behavior Therapy, 23,* 341–354.

Clarke-Stewart, K. A. (1978). And daddy makes three: The father's impact on mother and young child. *Child Development, 49,* 466–478.

Clarke-Stewart, K. A. (1987). Predicting child development from day care forms and features: The Chicago study. In D. A. Phillips (Ed.), *Quality in child care: What does research tell us? Research Monographs of the National Association for the Education of*

Young Children (Vol. 1, pp. 21–42). Washington, DC: National Association for the Education of Young Children.

Clarke-Stewart, K. A. (1989). Infant day care: Maligned or malignant? *American Psychologist, 44,* 266–273.

Clarke-Stewart, K. A. (1993). *Daycare* (rev. ed.). Cambridge, MA: Harvard University Press.

Clarke-Stewart, K. A., & Allhusen, V. D. (2002). Nonparental caregiving. In M. Bornstein (Ed.), *Handbook of parenting* (2nd ed., pp. 215–252). Mahwah, NJ: Erlbaum.

Clarke-Stewart, K. A., & Allhusen, V. D. (2005). *What we know about childcare.* Cambridge, MA: Harvard University Press.

Clarke-Stewart, K. A., & Bretano, C. (2005). *Till divorce do us part.* New Haven: Yale University Press.

Clarke-Stewart, K. A., Goodens, F., & Allhusen, V. (2001). Measuring infant-mother attachment: Is the strange situation enough? *Social Development, 10,* 143–169.

Clarke-Stewart, K. A., Vandell, D. L., McCartney, K., Owen, M. T., & Booth, C. (2000). Effects of parental separation and divorce on very young children. *Journal of Family Psychology, 14,* 304–326.

Cleveland, H. H., & Wiebe, R. P. (2003). The moderation of adolescent to peer similarity in tobacco and alcohol use by school levels of substance abuse. *Child Development, 74,* 279–291.

Clifton, R. K. (1992). The development of spatial hearing in human infants. In L. A. Werner & E. W. Rubel (Eds.), *Develop mental psychoacoustics* (pp. 135–157). Washington, DC: American Psychological Association.

Clinton, H. R. (1996). *It takes a village.* New York: Simon & Schuster.

Cloninger, C. R., Christiansen, K. O., Reich, T., & Gottesman, I. I. (1978). Implications of sex differences in the prevalences of antisocial personality, alcoholism, and criminality for familial transmission. *Archives of General Psychiatry, 35,* 941–951.

Cloninger, C. R., Sigvardsson, S., Bohman, M., & van Knoring, A. L. (1982). Predisposition to petty criminality in Swedish adoptees: II. Cross-fostering analyses of gene-environmental interactions. *Archives of General Psychiatry, 39,* 1242–1247.

Cochi, S. L., Edmonds, L. E., Dyer, K., Grooves, W. L., Marks, J. S., Rovira, E. Z., Preblud, S. R., & Orenstein, W. A. (1989). Congenital rubella syndrome in the United States, 1970–1985: On the verge of

elimination. *American Journal of Epidemiology, 129,* 349–361.

Cohen, P., & Brook, J. S. (1995). The reciprocal influence of punishment and child behavior disorder. In J. McCord (Ed.), *Coercion and punishment in long-term perspectives* (pp. 154–164). New York: Cambridge University Press.

Coie, J. D., & Dodge, K. A. (1983). Continuities and changes in children's social status: A five-year longitudinal study. *Merrill-Palmer Quarterly, 29,* 261–282.

Coie, J. D., & Dodge, K. A. (1998). Aggression and antisocial behavior. In W. Damon (Gen. Ed.) & N. Eisenberg (Vol. Ed.), *Handbook of child psychology: Social, emotional, and personal development* (Vol. 3, pp. 779–862). New York: Wiley.

Coie, J. D., Dodge, K. A., & Kupersmidt, J. (1990). Peer group behavior and social status. In S. R. Asher & J. D. Coie (Eds.), *Peer rejection in childhood.* New York: Cambridge University Press.

Coie, J. D., & Kupersmidt, J. B. (1983). A behavioral analysis of emerging social status in boys' groups. *Child Development, 54,* 1400–1416.

Colby, A., & Kohlberg, L. (1987). *The measurement of moral judgment* (Vols. 1–2). New York: Cambridge University Press.

Colby, A., Kohlberg, L., Gibbs, J., & Lieberman, M. (1983). A longitudinal study of moral judgment. *Monographs of the Society for Research in Child Development, 48* (Serial No. 200).

Cole, M. (1985). The zone of proximal development: Where culture and cognition create each other. In J. V. Wertsch (Ed.), *Culture, communication and cognitive: Vygotskian perspectives.* Cambridge: Cambridge University Press.

Cole, M. (1996). *Cultural psychology: A once and future discipline.* Cambridge, MA: Harvard University Press.

Cole, M. (2006). Culture and cognitive development in phylogenetic, historical and ontogenetic perspective. In W. Damon & R. M. Lerner (Series Eds.) and D. Kuhn & R. Siegler (Vol. Eds.), *Handbook of child psychology,* Vol 2, 6th ed. New York: Wiley.

Cole, P. M., Bruschi, C. J., Tamang, B. L. (2002). Cultural differences in children's emotional reactions to difficult situations. *Child Development, 73,* 983–996.

Coley, R. L., & Chase-Lansdale, L. (1998). Adolescent pregnancy and parenthood: Recent evidence and

future directions. *American Psychologist, 53,* 152–166.

Colin, V. L. (1996). *Human attachment.* New York: McGraw-Hill.

Collaer, M. L., & Hines, M. (1995). Human behavioral sex differences: A role for gonadal hormones during early development. *Psychological Bulletin, 118,* 55–107.

Collins, W. A. (2003). More than myth: The developmental significance of romantic relationships during adolescence. *Journal of Research on Adolescence, 13,* 1–24.

Collins, W. A., Maccoby, E. E., Steinberg, L., Hetherington, E. M., & Bornstein, M. H. (2000). Contemporary research on parenting: The case for nature and nurture. *American Psychologist, 55,* 218–232.

Collins, W. A., & Repinski, D. J. (2001). Parents and adolescents as transformers of relationships: Dyadic adaptation to developmental change. In J. R. M. Gerris (Ed.), *Dynamics of parenting* (pp. 429–444). Leuven, Belgium: Garant.

Collins W. A., & Sroufe, L. A. (1999). Capacity for intimate relationships: A developmental construction. In W. Furman et al. (Eds.), *The development of romantic relationships in adolescence. Cambridge studies in social and emotional development* (pp. 125–147). New York: Cambridge University Press.

Coltrane, S. (1996). *Family man: Fatherhood, housework, and gender equity.* New York: Oxford University Press.

Coltrane, S. (1998). *Gender and families.* Thousand Oaks, CA: Pine Forge Press.

Coltrane, S. (2000). Research on household labor: Modeling and measuring the social embeddedness of routine family work. *Journal of Marriage & the Family, 62,* 1208–1233.

Comer, J. (1988). The education of low-income black children. *Scientific American, 259,* 42–48.

Comer, J. (1991). The Black child in school. In M. Lewis (Ed.), *Child and adolescent psychology: A comprehensive textbook.* Baltimore: Williams & Wilkins.

Comstock, G., & Scharrer, E. (2006). Media and pop culture. In W. Damon & R. M. Lerner (Senes Eds.) and K. A. Renninger & I. Sigel (Vol. Eds.), *Handbook of child psychology* (Vol. 4, 6th ed.). New York: Wiley.

Conduct Problems Prevention Research Group. (2004). The Fast Track experiment: Translating the developmental model into a prevention design. In J. B. Kupersmidt & K. A. Dodge (Eds.) *Children's peer relations: From development to intervention* (pp. 181–208). Washington, DC: American Psychological Association.

Conel, J. L. (1939/1967). *The postnatal development of the human cerebral cortex* (Vols. 1 & 8). Cambridge, MA: Harvard University Press.

Conger, J. J., & Petersen, A. C. (1984). *Adolescence & youth* (3rd ed.). New York: Harper & Row.

Conger, R. D., & Conger, K. J. (1996). Sibling relationships. In R. L. Simons et al. (Eds.), *Understanding differences between divorced and intact families* (pp. 104–124). Thousand Oaks, CA: Sage.

Conger, R. D., Conger, K. J., Elder, G. J., Jr., Lorenz, F. O., Simons, R. L., & Whitbeck, L. B. (1992). A family process model of economic hardship and adjustment of early adolescent boys. *Child Development, 63,* 526–541.

Conger, R. D., Cui, M., Bryant, C. M., & Elder, G. H. (2000). Competence in early adult romantic relationships: A developmental perspective on family influences. *Journal of Personality and Social Psychology, 79,* 224–237.

Conger, R. D., & Elder, G. H. (Eds.). (1994). *Families in troubled times: Adapting to change in rural America.* New York: Aldine.

Connolly, J. A., Craig, W., Goldberg, A., & Pepler, D. (2004). Mixed-gender groups, dating, and romantic relationships in early adolescence. *Journal of Research on Adolescence, 14,* 185–207.

Connolly, J. A., Furman, W., & Konarski, R. (2000). The role of peers in the emergence of heterosexual romantic relationships in adolescence. *Child Development, 71,* 1395–1408.

Connolly, K. J., & Dalgleish, M. (1989). The emergence of tool-using skill in infancy. *Developmental Psychology, 25,* 894–912.

Connor, E. M., Sperling, R. S., Gelber, R., Kiselev, P., Scott, G., O'Sullivan, M. J., Van Dyke, R., Bey, M., Shearer, W., & Jacobsen, R. L. (1994). Reduction of maternal-infant transmission of human immunodeficiency virus type 1 with treatment. Pediatric AIDS Clinical Trial Group Protocol 076 Study Group. *New England Journal of Medicine, 331,* 1173–1180.

Connor, P. D., Sampson, P. D., Bookstein, F. L., Barr, H. M., & Streissguth, A. P. (2001). Direct and indirect effects of prenatal alcohol damage on executive function. *Developmental Neuropsychology, 18,* 331–354.

Conoley, J. C. (1990). Review of the K-ABC: Reflecting the unobservable. *Journal of Psychoeducational Assessment, 8,* 369–375.

Contreras, J. M., Kerns, K., Weimer, B. L., Gentzler, A. L., & Tomich, P. L. (2000). Emotional regulation as a mediator of association between mother-child attachment and peer relationships in middle childhood. *Journal of Family Psychology, 14,* 111–124.

Cooney, R. S., Pedersen, F. A., Indelicato, S., & Palkowitz, R. (1993). Timing of fatherhood: Is "on time" optimal? *Journal of Marriage and the Family, 44,* 621–631.

Cooper, R. P., & Aslin, R. N. (1990). Preference for infant-directed speech in the first month after birth. *Child Development, 61,* 1584–1595.

Coren, S. (1992). *The left-hander syndrome: The causes and consequences of left-handedness.* New York: Free Press.

Cornell, E. H., Hadley, D. C., Sterling, T. M., Chan, M. A., & Boechler, P. (2001). Adventure as a stimulus for cognitive development. *Journal of Environmental Psychology, 21,* 219–231.

Corner, G. W. (1961). Congenital malformations: The problem and the task (pp. 7–17). Papers and discussions presented at the First International Conference on Congenital Malformations. Philadelphia: Lippincott.

Corter, C. M., & Minde, K. K. (1987). Impact of infant prematurity on family systems. In M. Wolbraich (Ed.), *Advances in developmental and behavioral pediatrics* (Vol. 8). Greenwich, CT: JAI Press.

Coser, C., & Cohen, J. (2003). *America's babies.* Washington, DC: Zero to Three Press.

Cosgrove, J. M., & Patterson, C. J. (1977). Plans and the development of listener skills. *Developmental Psychology, 13,* 557–564.

Cosmides, L., & Tooby, J. (1987). From evolution to behavior: Evolutionary psychology as the missing link. In J. Dupre (Ed.), *The latest and best essays on evolution and optimality.* Cambridge, MA: MIT Press.

Costello, E. (1983). *Signing: How to speak with your hands.* New York: Bantam.

Coté, S., Tremblay, P., Nagin, D., Zocolillo, M. & Vitaro, F. (2002). The development of impulsivity, fearfulness and helpfulness during childhood: Patterns of consistency and change in trajectories of boys and girls. *Journal of Child Psychology and Psychiatry, 43,* 609–618.

Courage, M. L., & Adams, R. J. (1990). Visual acuity assessment from birth to three years using the acuity card procedures: Cross-longitudinal samples. *Optometry and vision science, 67,* 713–718.

Cowan, C. P., & Cowan, P. A. (2000). *When partners become parents: The big life change for couples.* Mahwah, NJ: Erlbaum.

Cowan, P. A., & Cowan, C. P. (2002). What an intervention design reveals about how parents affect their children's academic achievement and behavior problems. In J. Borkowski, S. L. Ramey, & M. Bristol-Power (Eds.), *Parenting and the child's world* (pp. 75–98). Mahwah, NJ: Erlbaum.

Cowan, P. A., Cowan, C. P., Schulz, M. C., & Heming, G. (1994). Prebirth to preschool family factors in children's adaptation to kindergarten. In R. D. Parke & S. Kellam (Eds.), *Exploring family relationships with other social contexts* (pp. 75–114). Hillsdale, NJ: Erlbaum.

Cowley, G. (2001). Generation XXL. In K. L. Frieberg (Ed.), *Human development 01/02* (29th ed., pp. 120–121). Guilford, CT: Duskin/McGraw-Hill.

Cox, B. C., Ornstein, P. A., Naus, M. J., Maxfield, D., & Zimler, J. (1989). Children's concurrent use of rehearsal and organizational strategies. *Developmental Psychology, 25,* 619–627.

Coyle, T. R., & Bjorklund, D. F. (1997). Age differences in, and consequences of, multiple and variable-strategy use on a multitrial sort-recall task. *Developmental Psychology, 33,* 372–380.

Craig, W., & Pepler, D. J. (1997). Observations of bullying and victimization in the schoolyard. *Canadian Journal of School Psychology, 13,* 41–57.

Crain-Thoreson, C., & Dale, P. S. (1992). Do early talkers become early readers? Linguistic precocity, preschool language and emergent literacy. *Developmental Psychology, 28,* 421–429.

Cratty, B. J. (1999). *Movement behavior and motor learning.* Ann Arbor, MI: Books on Demand.

Crick, N. R. (1997). Engagement in gender normative versus nonnormative forms of aggression: Links to social-psychological adjustment. *Developmental Psychology, 33,* 610–617.

Crick, N. R., & Bigbee, M. A. (1998). Relational and overt forms of peer victimization: A multi-informant approach. *Journal of Consulting and Clinical Psychology, 66,* 337–347.

Crick, N. R., Casas, J. F., & Ku, H. (1999). Relational and physical forms of peer victimization in preschool. *Developmental Psychology, 35,* 376–385.

Crick, N. R., Casas, J. F., & Mosher, M. (1997). Relational and overt aggression in preschool. *Developmental Psychology, 33,* 579–588.

Crick, N. R., & Dodge, K. A. (1994). A review and reformulation of social information processing mechanisms in children's social adjustment. *Psychological Bulletin, 115,* 74–101.

Crick, N. R., & Grotpeter, J. K. (1995). Relational aggression, gender, and social-psychological adjustment. *Child Development, 66,* 710–722.

Crick, N. R., & Ladd, G. W. (1993). Children's perceptions of their peer experiences: Attributions, loneliness, social anxiety, and social avoidance. *Developmental Psychology, 29,* 244–254.

Crick, N. R., Ostrov, J. M., Appleyard, K., Jansen, E. A., & Casas, J. F. (2004). Relational aggression in early childhood: "You can't come to my birthday party unless." In M. Puttalaz & K. L. Bierman (Eds.), *Aggression, antisocial behavior, and violence among girls* (pp. 71–89). New York: Guilford.

Crisafi, M., & Brown, A. L. (1986). Analogical transfer in very young children: Combining two separately learned solutions to reach a goal. *Child Development, 57,* 953–968.

Crockenberg, S. B. (1981). Infant irritability, mother responsiveness and social support influences on the security of infant-mother attachment. *Child Development, 52,* 857–865.

Crockenberg, S., & Litman, D. (1990). Autonomy as competence in 2-year-olds: Maternal correlates of child defiance, compliance and self assertion. *Developmental Psychology, 26,* 916–971.

Crouter, A. C., & Bumpus, M. F. (2001). Linking parents' work stress to children's and adolescents' psychological adjustment. *Current Directions in Psychological Science, 10,* 156–159.

Crowell, J., & Treboux, D. (1995). A review of adult attachment measures: Implications for theory and research. *Social Development, 4,* 294–327.

Crowell, J. A., Treboux, D., & Waters, E. (2002). Stability of attachment representations: The transition to marriage. *Developmental Psychology, 38,* 467–479.

Crowley, K., Callahan, M. A., Tennenbaum, H. R., & Allen, E. (2001). Parents explain more often to boys than to girls during shared scientific thinking. *Psychological Science, 12,* 258–261.

Crowley, K., & Siegler, R. S. (1993). Flexible strategy use in young children's tic-tac-toe. *Cognitivie Science, 17,* 531–561.

Csikszentmihalyi, M., & Schneider, B. (2000). *Becoming adult: How teenagers prepare for the world of work.* New York: Basic Books.

Cummings, E. M., Davies, P., & Campbell, S. (2000). *Developmental psychopathology and family process.* New York: Guilford.

Cummings, E. M., Goeke-Morey, M. C., & Graham, M. A. (2002). Interparental relations as a dimension of parenting. In J. Borkowski, S. L. Ramey, & M. Bristol-Power (Eds.), *Parenting and the child's world* (pp. 251–264). Mahwah, NJ: Erlbaum.

Cummings, E. M., Simpson, K. S., & Wilson, A. (1993). Children's responses to interadult anger as a function of information about resolution. *Developmental Psychology, 29,* 978–985.

Cunningham, C. E. (1999). In the wake of the MTA: Charting a new course for the study and treatment of children with attention-deficit hyperactivity disorder. *Canadian Journal of Psychiatry, 44,* 999–1006.

Cunningham, F. G., MacDonald, P. C., & Grant, N. F. (1993). *Williams obstetrics.* Norwalk, CT: Appleton & Lange.

Curtiss, S. (1989). The independence and task-specificity of language. In M. H. Bornstein & J. S. Bruner (Eds.), *Interaction in human development* (pp. 105–138). Hillsdale, NJ: Erlbaum.

D'Augelli, A. R. (1998). Developmental implications of victimization of lesbian, gay, & bisexual youth. In G. M. Herek (Ed.), *Stigma and sexual orientation: Understanding prejudice against lesbians, gay men, and bisexuals* (pp. 187–210). Thousand Oaks, CA: Sage.

D'Augelli, A. R. (2004). Developmental and contextual factors and mental health among lesbians, gay, and bisexual youths. In A. Omoto & H. Kurtzman (Eds.), *Recent research on sexual orientation.* Washington, DC: American Psychological Association.

D'Augelli, A. R., Hershberger, S. L., & Pilkington, N. W. (1998). Lesbian, gay, and bisexual youth and their families: Disclosure of sexual orientation and its consequences. *American Journal of Orthopsychiatry, 68,* 361–371.

D'Augelli, A. R., & Patterson, C. (Eds.). (2001). *Lesbian, gay and bisexual identities among youth: Psychological perspectives.* New York: Oxford University Press.

Dale, P. S. (1976). *Language development: Structure and function* (2nd ed.). New York: Holt.

Damon, W. (1988). Socialization and individuation. In G. Handel (Ed.), *Childhood socialization* (pp. 3–10). New York: Hawthorne.

Daniels, P., & Weingarten, K. (1988). The fatherhood click: The timing of parenthood in men's lives. In P. Bronstein & C. P. Cowan (Eds.), *Fatherhood today: Men's changing role in the family* (pp. 36–52). New York: Wiley.

Dannemiller, J. L., & Stephens, B. R. (1988). A critical test of infant pattern perception models. *Child Development, 59,* 210–216.

Dark, V. J., & Benbow, S. P. (1993). Cognitive differences among the gifted: A review and new data. In D. K. Detterman (Ed.), *Current topics in human intelligence* (Vol. 3). Norwood, NJ: Ablex.

Darvill, D., & Cheyne, J. A. (1981). *Sequential analysis of response to aggression: Age and sex effects.* Paper presented at the biennial meeting of the Society for Research in Child Development, Boston.

Darwin, C. (1872). *The expression of emotions in animals and man.* London: John Murray.

Dasen, P. R. (1975). Concrete operational development in three cultures. *Journal of Cross-Cultural Psychology, 6,* 156–172.

Dasen, P. R. (1984). The cross-cultural study of intelligence: Piaget and the Baoulé. *International Journal of Psychology, 19,* 407–434.

Dasen, P. R., Inhelder, B., Lavallée, M., & Retschitzki, J. (1978). *Naissance de l'intelligence chez l'enfant Baoulé de Côte d'Ivoire.* Berne, Hans Huber.

Davidson, D. (1996). The effects of decision characteristics on children's selective search of predecisional information. *Acta Psychologica, 92,* 263–281.

Davidson, E. S., Yasuna, A., & Tower, A. (1979). The effects of television cartoons on sex role stereotyping in young girls. *Child Development, 50,* 597–600.

Davidson, R. J. (1994). Temperament, affective style, and frontal lobe asymmetry. In G. Dawson & K. W. Fischer (Eds.), *Human behavior and the developing brain.* New York: Guilford Press.

Davies, P. T., & Windle, M. (2000). Middle adolescents' dating pathways and psychosocial adjustment. *Merrill-Palmer Quarterly, 46,* 90–118.

Davis, M. H., Luce, C., & Kraus, S. J. (1994). The heritability of characteristics associated with dispositional empathy. *Journal of Personality, 62,* 369–391.

Dawson, G. (1994). Development of emotional expression and regulation in infancy. In G. Dawson & K. W. Fischer (Eds.), *Human behavior and the developing brain.* New York: Guilford Press.

Dawson, G., Meltzoff, A. N., Osterling, J., & Rinaldi, J. (1998). Neuropsychological correlates of early symptoms of autism. *Child Development, 19,* 1276–1285.

Dawson, G., Toth, K., Abbott, R., Osterling, J., Munson, J., Estes, A., & Liaw, J. (2004). Early social attention impairments in autism: Social orienting, joint attention, and attention to distress. *Developmental Psychology, 40,* 271–283.

Day, N. L., & Richardson, G. A. (1994). Comparative teratogenicity of alcohol and other drugs. *Alcohol Health and Research World, 18,* 42–48.

De Boysson-Bardies, B., Vihman, M., Roug-Hellichius, L., Durand, C., Landberg, I., & Arao, F. (1992). Material evidence of infant selection from target language: A cross-linguistic study. In C. A. Ferguson, L. Menn, & C. Stoel-Gammon (Eds.), *Phonological development* (pp. 369–391). Timonium, MD: York Press.

de Guzman, M. R. T., & Carlo, G. (2004). Family, peer, and acculturative correlates of prosocial development among Latino youth in Nebraska. *Great Plains Research, 14,* 185–202.

de Houwer, A. (1995). Bilingual language acquisition. In P. Fletcher & B. MacWhinney (Eds.), *The handbook of child language* (pp. 219–250). Oxford: Basil Blackwell.

Dean, R. S., & Anderson, J. L. (1997). Lateralization of cerebral function. In A. M. Horton, D. Wedding, & J. Webster (Eds.), *The neuropsychology handbook* (Vol. 1, pp. 138–139). New York: Springer.

Deater-Deckard, K., & Dodge, K. A. (1997). Externalizing behavior problems and discipline revisited: Nonlinear effects and variation by culture, context, and gender. *Psychological Inquiry, 8,* 161–175.

Deater-Deckard, K., Dodge, K. A., Bates, J. E., & Pettit, G. S. (1996). Physical punishment among African American and European American mothers: Links to children's externalizing behaviors. *Developmental Psychology, 32,* 1065–1072.

Deater-Deckard, K., Pike, A., Petrill, S. A., Cutting, A. L., Hughes, C., & O'Connor, T. G. (2001). Nonshared environmental processes in social-emotional development: An observational study of identical twin differences in the preschool period. *Developmental Science, 4,* F1–F6.

DeCarie, T. C. (1961). A study of the mental and emotional development of the thalidomide child. In B. Foss (Ed.), *Determinants of infant behavior* (Vol. 4). London: Methuen.

DeCasper, A., & Fifer, W. (1980). Of human bonding: Newborns prefer their mothers' voices. *Science, 12,* 305–317.

DeCasper, A., & Spence, M. (1991). Auditory mediated behavior during the perinatal period. A cognitive view. In M. Weiss & P. Zelazo (Eds.), *Newborn attention.* Norwood, NJ: Ablex.

DeCasper, A. J., & Spence, M. (1986). Newborns prefer a familiar story over an unfamiliar one. *Infant Behavior and Development, 9,* 133–150.

Decety, J., & Chaminade, T. (2003). Neural correlates of feeling sympathy. *Neuropscyhologia, 41,* 127–138.

Dekovic, M., & Janssens, J. M. (1992). Parents' child-rearing style and child's sociometric status. *Developmental Psychology, 28,* 925–932.

Delate, T., Gelenberg, A. J., Simmons, V. A., & Motheral, B. R. (2004). Changes in use of antidepressants among children and adolescents. *Psychiatric Services, 55,* 387–391.

DeLisi, R., & McGillicuddy-DeLisi, A. V. (2002). Sex differences in mathematical abilities and achievement. In A. V. McGillicuddy & R. DeLisi (Eds.), *Biology, society and behavior: The development of sex differences in cognition.* Westport, CT: Ablex.

DeLoache, J. S. (1987). Rapid change in symbolic functioning of very young children. *Science, 238,* 1556–1557.

DeLoache, J. S. (1995). Early understanding and use of symbols: The model model. *Current Directions in Psychological Science, 4,* 109–113.

DeLoache, J. S. (2000). Dual representation and young children's use of scale models. *Child Development, 71,* 329–338.

DeLoache, J. S., & Brown, A. L. (1983). Very young children's memory for the location of objects in a large-scale environment. *Child Development, 54,* 888–897.

DeLoache, J. S., Miller, K. F., & Pierroutsakos, S. L. (1998). Reasoning and problem solving. In W. Damon (Gen. Ed.), D. Kuhn, & R. S. Siegler (Vol. Eds.), *Handbook of child psychology, Vol. 2. Cognition, perception, and language* (pp. 801–850). New York: Wiley.

DeLoache, J. S., Miller, K., & Rosengren, K. (1997). The credible shrinking room: Very young children's performance in symbolic and non-symbolic tasks. *Psychological Science, 8,* 308–314.

DeLoache, J. S., & Smith, C. M. (1999). Early symbolic representation. In I. E. Sigel (Ed.), *Development of mental representation: Theories and applications.* Mahwah, NJ: Erlbaum.

Deloukas, P., et al. (1998). A physical map of 30,000 human genes. *Science, 282,* 744–746.

Demetriou, A., Christou, C., Spanoudis, G., & Platsidou, M. (2002). The development of mental processing: Efficiency, working memory, and thinking. *Monographs of the Society for Research in Child Development, Vol. 67 (1),* No. 268.

Demo, D. H., Allen, K. R., & Fine, M. A. (Eds.) (2000). *Handbook of family diversity.* New York: Oxford University Press.

Dempster, F. N. (1985). Proactive interference in sentence recall: Topic similarity effects and individual differences. *Memory and Cognition, 13,* 81–89.

Denham, S. (1998). *Emotional development in young children.* New York: Guilford.

Denham, S. A., Renwick-DeBardi, S., & Hewes, S. (1994). Emotional communication between mothers and preschoolers: Relations with emotional competence. *Merrill-Palmer Quarterly, 40,* 488–508.

Dennis, W. (1940). Does culture appreciably affect patterns of infant behavior? *Journal of Social Psychology, 12,* 305–317.

DeRosier, M., & Kupersmidt, J. B. (1991). Costa Rican children's perceptions of their social networks. *Developmental Psychology, 27,* 656–662.

deVilliers, P. A., & deVilliers, J. G. (1979). *Early language.* Cambridge, MA: Harvard University Press.

deVilliers, P. A., & deVilliers, J. G. (1992). Language development. In M. E. Lamb & M. H. Bornstein (Eds.), *Developmental psychology: An advanced textbook* (3rd ed.). Hillsdale, NJ: Erlbaum.

DeVries, M. (1984). Temperament and infant mortality among the Masai of East Africa. *American Journal of Psychiatry, 141,* 1189–1194.

DeVries, M., & Sameroff, A. J. (1984). Culture and temperament: Influences on temperament in three East African societies. *American Journal of Orthopsychiatry, 54,* 83–96.

Dewey, K. (2001). Nutrition, growth and complementary feeding of the breastfed infant. *Pediatric Clinics of North America, 48,* 87–104.

Diaz, R. M. (1983). Thought and two languages: The impact of

bilingualism on cognitive development. *Review of Research in Education, 10,* 23–54.

Diaz, R. M. (1985). Bilingual cognitive development: Addressing three gaps in current research. *Child Development, 56,* 1376–1388.

Dick, D. M., Rose, R. J., Viken, R. J., & Kaprio, F. (2000). Pubertal timing and substance use between and within families across late adolescence. *Developmental Psychology, 36,* 180–189.

Diedrich, F. T., & Warren, W. H., Jr. (1995). Why change gaits? Dynamics of the walk-run transition. *Journal of Experimental Psychology: Human Perception & Performance, 21,* 183–202.

Diener, C. I., & Dweck, C. S. (1978). An analysis of learned helplessness: Continuous changes in performance, strategy and achievement cognitions following failure. *Journal of Personality and Social Psychology, 36,* 451–462.

Diener, E. (2000). Subjective well-being: The science of happiness and a proposal for a national index. *American Psychologist, 55,* 34–43.

Diesendruck G., & Markson, L. (2001). Children's avoidance of lexical overlap: A pragmatic account. *Developmental Psychology, 37,* 630–641.

Dieter, J. N., Field, T., Hernandez-Reif, M., Emory, E. K., & Redzepi, M. (2003). Stable preterm infants gain more weight and sleep less after five days of massage therapy. *Journal of Pediatric Psychology, 28,* 403–411.

Dietrich, K. N., Berger, O. G., Succop, P. A., Hammond, P. B., & Bornschein, R. L. (1993). The developmental consequences of low to moderate prenatal and postnatal lead exposure: Intellectual attainment in the Cincinnati Lead Study cohort following school entry. *Neurotoxicology and Teratology, 13,* 37–44.

DiLalla, L. F., Thompson, L. A., Plomin, R., Phillips, K., Faga, J. F., Haith, M. M., Cyphers, L. H., & Fulker, D. W. (1990). Infant predictors of preschool and adult IQ: A study of infant twins and their parents. *Developmental Psychology, 26,* 759–769.

DiMatteo, R., & Kahn, K. L. (1997). Psychosocial aspects of childbirth. In S. J. Gallant, G. P. Keita, & R. Royak-Schaler (Eds.), *Health care for women: Psychological, social, and behavioral influences* (pp. 175–186). Washington, DC: American Psychological Association.

Ding, Y. C., Chi, H. C., Grady, D. L., Morishima, A., Kidd, J. R., & Kidd, K. K. et al. (2002). Evidence of positive selection acting at the

human dopamine receptor D4 gene locus. *Proceedings of the National Academy of Science, 99,* 309–314.

Dinn, W. M., Robbins, N. C., & Harris, C. L. (2001). Adult attention-deficit/hyperactivity disorder: Neuropsychological correlates and clinical preservation. *Brain and Cognition, 46,* 114–121.

Dionne, G., Tremblay, R., Boivin, M., Laplante, D., & Perusse, D. (2003). Physical aggression and expressive vocabulary in 19-month-old twins. *Developmental Psychology, 39,* 261–273.

DiPietro, J. A. (2004). The role of prenatal maternal stress in child development. *Current Directions in Psychological Science, 13,* 71–74.

Dishion, T., & Bullock, B. M. (2002). Parenting and adolescent problem behavior: An ecological analysis of the nurturance hypothesis. In J. Borkowski, S. L. Ramey, & M. Bristol-Power (Eds.), *Parenting and the child's world* (pp. 231–249). Mahwah, NJ: Erlbaum.

Dishion, T. J., Poulin, F., & Burraston, B. (2001). Peer group dynamics associated with iatrogenic effects in group interventions with high-risk young adolescents. In D. W. Nangle & C. A. Erdley (Eds.), *The role of friendship in psychological adjustment. New directions for child and adolescent development, No. 91* (pp. 79–92). San Francisco: Jossey-Bass.

Dishion, T. J., Poulin, F., & Medici Skaggs, N. (2000). The ecology of premature autonomy in adolescence: Biological and social influences. In K. A. Kerns & A. M. Neal-Barnett (Eds.), *Family and peers: Linking two social worlds.* Westport, CT: Praeger.

Dittrichova, J. (1969). The development of premature infants. In R. J. Robinson (Ed.), *Brain and early development.* London: Academic.

Dobson, V., & Teller, D. Y. (1978). Visual acuity in human infants: A review and comparison of behavioral and electrophysiological studies. *Vision Research, 18,* 1469–1483.

Dodge, K., Coie, J., Pettit, G., & Price, J. M. (1990). Peer status and aggression in boys' groups: Developmental and contextual analyses. *Child Development, 55,* 163–173.

Dodge, K., Coie, J., & Tremblay, R. F. (2006). Aggression. In W. Damon & R. L. Lerner (Series Eds.) & N. Eisenberg (Vol. Ed.), *Handbook of child psychology: Vol. 3* (6th ed.). New York: Wiley.

Dodge, K., Landsford, J., Burks, V., Bates, J., Pettit, G., Fontaine, R., & Price, J. (2003). Peer rejection

and social information processing factors in the development of aggressive behavior problems in children. *Child Development, 74,* 374–393.

Dodge, K. A. (1986). A social information processing model of social competence in children. In M. Perlmutter (Ed.), *The Minnesota Symposium on Child Psychology: Vol. 18* (pp. 77–125). Hillsdale, NJ: Erlbaum.

Dodge, K. A., & Frame, C. L. (1982). Social cognitive biases and deficits in aggressive boys. *Child Development, 53,* 620–635.

Dodge, K. A., & Pettit, G. S. (2003). A biopsychological model of the development of chronic conduct problems in adolescence. *Developmental Psychology, 39,* 189–190.

Dodge, K. A., Pettit, G. S., McClaskey, C. L., & Brown, M. M. (1987). Social competence in children. *Monographs of the Society for Research in Child Development, 51* (2, Serial No. 213).

Dominick, J. R., & Greenberg, B. S. (1972). Attitudes toward violence: The interaction of television exposure, family attitudes, and social class. In G. A. Comstock & E. A. Rubenstein (Eds.), *Television and social behavior: Television and adolescent aggressiveness* (Vol. 3, pp. 314–335). Washington, DC: Government Printing Office.

Donaldson, M. (1978). *Children's minds.* New York: Norton.

Doris, J. (Ed.). (1991). *The suggestibility of children's recollections.* Washington, DC: American Psychological Association.

Douglas, W. (2003). *Television families.* Mahwah, NJ: Erlbaum.

Downs, R. M., & Liben, L. S. (1986). Children's understanding of maps. In P. Ellen & C. Thinus-Blanc (Eds.), *Cognitive processes and spatial orientation in animal and man: Vol. 1. Neurophysiology of spatial knowledge and developmental aspects.* Dordrecht, Holland: Martinus Nijhoff.

Drabman, R. S., & Thomas, M. H. (1976). Does watching violence on television cause apathy? *Pediatrics, 52,* 329–331.

Drew, C. J., & Hardman, M. L. (2000). *Mental retardation: A life cycle approach* (7th ed.). Columbus, OH: Merrill.

Dryfoos, J. (1994). *Full service schools: A revolution in health and social services for children, youth and families.* San Francisco: Jossey-Bass.

Dube, E. M., Savin-Williams, R. C., & Diamond, L. M. (2001). Intimacy development, gender, and ethnicity among sexual minority youth. In A. R. D'Augelli & C. Patterson (Eds.), *Lesbian, gay, and bisexual identities among youth: Psychological perspectives* (pp. 129–182). New York: Oxford University Press.

Dubowitz, L., & Dubowtiz, V. (1981). *The neurological assessment of the preterm and full-term newborn infant.* Philadelphia: Lippincott.

Duke, P. M., Carlsmith, J. M., Jennings, D., Martin, J. A., Dornbusch, S. M., Siegel-Gorelick, B., & Gross, R. T. (1982). Educational correlates of early and late sexual maturation in adolescence. *Journal of Pediatrics, 100,* 633.

Duncan, G., Young, W. J., Brooks-Gunn, J., & Smith, J. R. (1998). How much does childhood poverty affect life choices of children? *American Sociological Reviews, 63,* 406–423.

Duncan, G. O., & Brooks-Gunn, J. (2000). Family parenting, welfare reform and child development. *Child Development, 71,* 188–195.

Dunham, P. J., Dunham, R., & Curwin, A. (1993). Joint-attentional states and lexical acquisition at 18 months. *Developmental Psychology, 29,* 827–831.

Dunn, J. (1987). The beginning of moral understanding. In J. Kagan and S. Lamb (Eds.), *The emergence of morality in young children.* Chicago: University of Chicago Press.

Dunn, J. (1988). *The beginnings of social understanding.* Cambridge, MA: Harvard University Press.

Dunn, J. (1993). *Young children's close relationships.* Newbury Park, CA: Sage.

Dunn, J. (1994). Changing minds and changing relationships. In C. Lewis & P. Mitchell (Eds.), *Children's early understanding of mind: Origins and development* (pp. 297–310). Hove, England: Erlbaum.

Dunn, J. (2005). *Children's friendships: The beginnings of intimacy.* Oxford, UK: Blackwell.

Dunn, J., & Davies, L. (2000). Sibling relationships and interpersonal conflict. In J. Grych & F. F. Fincham (Eds.), *Interparental conflict and child development* (pp. 273–290). New York: Cambridge University Press.

Dunn, J., & Hughes, C. (2001). Young children's understanding of emotions within close relationships. *Cognition and Emotion, 12,* 171–190.

Dunn, J., & Kendrick, C. (1982). The speech of two- and three-year-olds to infant siblings: "Baby talk" and the context of communication. *Journal of Child Language, 9,* 579–595.

Dunn, J., & Plomin, R. (1991). Why are siblings so different? The significance of differences in sibling experiences within the family. *Family Process, 30,* 271–283.

Duyme, M. (1988). School success and social class: An adoption study. *Developmental Psychology, 24,* 203–209.

Dweck, C. (2001). Caution—Praise can be dangerous. In K. L. Frieberg (Ed.), *Human development 01/02* (29th ed., pp. 105–109). Guilford, CT: Dushkin/McGraw-Hill.

Dweck, C. S., & Leggett, E. L. (1988). A social-cognitive approach to motivation and personality. *Psychological Review, 95,* 256–273.

East, P. L. (1996). The younger sisters of childrearing adolescents: Their attitudes, expectations, and behaviors. *Child Development, 67,* 953–963.

East, P. L., & Jacobson, J. L. (2001). The younger siblings of teenage mothers: A follow-up of their pregnancy risk. *Developmental Psychology, 37,* 254–264.

East, P. L., & Rook, K. S. (1993). Compensatory patterns of support among children's peer relationships: A test using school friends, nonschool friends, and siblings. *Developmental Psychology, 28,* 163–172.

Eberhart-Phillips, J. E., Frederick, P. D., & Baron, R. C. (1993). Measles in pregnancy: A descriptive study of 58 cases. *Obstetrics & Gynecology, 82,* 797–801.

Eccles, J. S. (1985). Sex differences in achievement patterns. In T. Sonderegger (Ed.), *Nebraska symposium on motivation.* Lincoln: University of Nebraska Press.

Eccles, J. S., Freedman-Doan, C., Frome, P., Jacobs, J., & Yoon, K. S. (2000). Gender socialization in the family: A longitudinal approach. In T. Ecker & H. Trautner (Eds.), *The developmental social psychology of gender* (pp. 333–365). Mahwah, NJ: Erlbaum.

Eccles, J. S., Jacobs, J., Harold, R., Yoon, K. S., Abreton, A., & Freedman-Doan, C. (1993). Parents' and gender-role socialization during the middle childhood and adolescent years. In S. Oskamp & M. Costanzo (Eds.), *Gender issues in contemporary society* (pp. 59–83). Newbury Park, CA: Sage.

Eckerman, C. O. (1989). *Imitation and the achievement of coordinated action.* Paper presented at the biennial meeting of the Society for Research in Child Development, Kansas City, KS.

Eckerman, C. O. (1993). Imitation and toddlers' achievement of coordinated action with others. In J.

Nadel & L. Camaioni (Eds.), *New perspectives in early communicative development* (pp. 116–156). New York: Routledge.

Eckerman, C. O., & Didow, S. M. (1988). Lessons drawn from observing young peers together. *Acta Paeditrica Scandinavica, 77* (Suppl. 344), 55–70.

Eckerman, C. O., Whatley, J. L., & Kutz, S. L. (1975). Growth of social play with peers during the second year of life. *Developmental Psychology, 11,* 42–49.

Edmonson, M. B., Stoddard, J. J., & Owens, L. M. (1997). Hospital readmission with feeding-related problems after early postpartum discharge of normal newborns. *The Journal of the American Medical Association, 278,* 299–303.

Edwards, C. P. (1992). Cross-cultural perspectives on family-peer relations. In R. D. Parke & G. W. Ladd (Eds.), *Family-peer relationships: Modes of linkage* (pp. 285–316). Hillsdale, NJ: Erlbaum.

Edwards, C. P., & Lewis, M. (1979). Young children's concepts of social relations: Social functions and social objects. In M. Lewis & L. A. Rosenblum (Eds.), *The child and its family: Genesis of behavior* (Vol. 1). New York: Plenum.

Edwards, C. P., & Whiting, B. B. (1993). "Mother, older sibling, and me": The overlapping roles of caregivers and companions in the social world of two- and three-year-olds in Ngeca, Kenya. In K. MacDonald (Ed.), *Parent-child play: Descriptions and implications* (pp. 305–329). Albany, NY: State University of New York Press.

Egan, S. K., & Perry, D. G. (2002). Gender identity: A multidimensional analysis with implications for psychological adjustment. *Developmental Psychology, 37,* 451–463.

Egeland, B., Jacobvitz, D., & Sroufe, L. A. (1988). Breaking the cycle of abuse. *Child Development, 59,* 1080–1088.

Eiduson, B. T., Kornfein, M., Zimmerman, I. L., & Weisner, T. S. (1988). Comparative socialization practices in traditional and alternative families. In G. Handel (Ed.), *Childhood socialization* (pp. 73–101). Hawthorne, NY: Aldine de Gruyter.

Eilers, R. E., Oller, D. K., Levine, S., Basinger, D., Lynch, M. P., & Urbano, C. (1993). The role of prematurity and socioeconomic status in the onset of canonical babbling in infants. *Infant Behavior & Development, 16,* 297–315.

Eimas, P. D. (1994). Categorization in early infancy and the continuity of development. *Cognition, 50,* 83–93.

Eimas, P. D., Quinn, P. C., & Cowan, P. (1994). Development of exclusivity in perceptually based categories of young infants. *Journal of Experimental Child Psychology, 58,* 418–431.

Eisen, M., Goodman, G., & Quas, J. (2002). *Memory and suggestibility in the forensic interview.* Hillsdale, NJ: Erlbaum.

Eisenberg, N. (1992). *The caring child.* Cambridge, MA: Harvard University Press.

Eisenberg, N., Boehnke, K., Schuhler, P., & Silbereisen, R. K. (1985). The development of prosocial behavior and cognitions in German children. *Journal of Cross-Cultural Psychology, 16,* 69–82.

Eisenberg, N., Cumberland, A., Spinard, T. L., Fabes, R. A., Shepard, S. A., Reiser, M., Murphy, B., Losoya, S. H., & Guthrie, I. K. (2001a). The relation of regulation and emotionality to children's externalizing and internalizing problem behavior. *Child Development, 72,* 1112–1134.

Eisenberg, N., Fabes, R. A., Carlo, G., Speer, A. L., Switzer, G., Karbon, M., & Troyer, D. (1993). The relations of empathy-related emotions and maternal practices to children's comforting behavior. *Journal of Experimental Child Psychology, 55,* 131–150.

Eisenberg, N., Fabes, R. A., Guthrie, I. K., & Murphy, B. C. (1996b). The relations of regulation and emotionality to problem behavior in elementary school children. *Development & Psychopathology, 8,* 141–162.

Eisenberg, N., Fabes, R. A., Miller, P. A., Shell, C., Shea, R., & May-Plumlee, T. (1990). Preschoolers' vicarious emotional responding and their situational and dispositional prosocial behavior. *Merrill-Palmer Quarterly, 36,* 507–529.

Eisenberg, N., Fabes, R. A., & Murphy, B. C. (1996a). Parents' reactions to children's negative emotions: Relations to children's social competence and comforting behavior. *Child Development, 67,* 2227–2247.

Eisenberg, N., Fabes, R. A., Nyman, M., Bernzweig, J., & Pinuelas, A. (1994). The relations of emotionality and regulation to children's anger-related reactions. *Child Development, 65,* 109–128.

Eisenberg, N., Fabes, R. A., & Spinrad, T. (2006). Prosocial development. In W. Damon & R. M. Lerner (Series Eds.) & N. Eisenberg (Vol. Ed.), *Handbook of child psychology: Vol. 3* (6th ed.). New York: Wiley.

Eisenberg, N., Gershoff, E. T., Fabes, R. A., Shepard, S. A., Cumberland, A. J., Lososyna,

et al. (2001b). Mothers' emotional expressivity and children's behavior problems and social competence: Mediation through children's regulation. *Developmental Psychology, 37*, 475–490.

Eisenberg, N., Guthrie, I. K., Murphy, B. C., Cumberland, A., & Carlo, G. (1999). Consistency and development of prosocial dispositions. *Child Development, 70*, 1370–1372.

Eisenberg, N., Lennon, R., & Roth, K. (1983). Prosocial development: A longitudinal study. *Developmental Psychology, 19*, 846–855.

Eisenberg, N., Murray, E., & Hite, T. (1982). Children's reasoning regarding sex-typed toy choices. *Child Development, 49*, 500–504.

Eisenberg, N., Zhou, Q., & Koller, S. (2001a). Brazilian adolescents' prosocial moral judgments and behavior: Relations to sympathy perspective taking, gender-role orientation, and demographic characteristics. *Child Development, 72*, 518–534.

Ekman, P., Davidson, R., & Friesen, W. V. (1990). The Duchenne smile: Emotional expression and brain physiology. *Journal of Personality and Social Behavior, 58*, 342–353.

Ekman, P., Friesen, W. V., O'Sullivan, M., Chan, A., Diacoyanni-Tarlatzis, I., Heider, K., Krauss, R., LeCompte, W. A., Pitcairn, T., Ricci Bilti, P. E., Scherer, K., Tomita, M., & Tzavaras, A. (1987). Universals and cultural differences in the judgments of facial expressions of emotion. *Journal of Personality and Social Psychology, 52*, 712–717.

Elbers, L., & Ton, J. (1985). Playpen monologues: The interplay of words & babbles in the first words period. *Journal of Child Language, 12*, 551–565.

Elder, G. H., & Shanahan, M. J. (2006). The life course and human development. In W. Damon & R. M. Lerner (Series Eds.), & R. M. Lerner (Vol. Ed.), *Handbook of child psychology: Vol. 1. Theoretical models of human development* (6th ed.). New York: Wiley.

Elder, G. H. (1974). *Children of the Great Depression.* Chicago: University of Chicago Press.

Elder, G. H., & Conger, R. D. (2000). *Children of the land.* Chicago: University of Chicago Press.

Eldredge, L., & Salamy, A. (1988). Neurobehavioral and neurophysiological assessment of healthy and "at risk" full-term infants. *Child Development, 59*, 186–192.

Eley, T. C., Lichtenstein, P., & Stevenson, J. (1999). Sex differences in the etiology of aggressive and nonaggressive antisocial behavior: Results from two twin studies. *Child Development, 70*, 155–168.

Elicker, J., Egeland, B., & Sroufe, L. A. (1992). Predicting peer competence and peer relationships from early parent-child relationships. In R. D. Parke & G. W. Ladd (Eds.), *Family-peer relationships: Modes of linkage.* Hillsdale, NJ: Erlbaum.

Ellis, B. J., Bates, J. E., Dodge, K. A., Fergusson, D. M., Horwood, L. J., Pettit, G. S., & Woodward, L. (2003). Does father absence place daughters at special risk for early sexual activity and teenage pregnancy? *Child Development, 74*, 801–821.

Ellis, B. J., McFadyen-Ketchum, S., Dodge, K. A, Pettit, G. S., & Bates, J. E. (1999). Quality of early family relationships and individual differences in the timing of pubertal maturation in girls: A longitudinal test of an evolutionary model. *Journal of Personality and Social Psychology, 77*, 387–401.

Ellis, S., Rogoff, B., & Cromer, C. (1981). Age segregation in children's social interactions. *Developmental Psychology, 17*, 399–407.

Ellsworth, C. P., Muir, D. W., & Hains, S. M. J. (1993). Social competence and person-object differentiation: An analysis of the still-face effect. *Developmental Psychology, 29*, 63–73.

Elman, J. L., Bates, E. A., Johnson, M. H., Karmiloff-Smith, A., Parisi, D., & Plunkett, K. (1998). *Rethinking innateness: A connectionist perspective on development.* Cambridge, MA: MIT Press.

Embry, L., & Dawson, G. (2002). Disruptions in parenting related to maternal depression: Influences on children's behavioral and psychobiological development. In J. G. Borkowski, S. Ramey, & M. Bristol-Power (Eds.), *Parenting and the child's world* (pp. 203–213). Mahwah, NJ: Erlbaum.

Emde, R. N., Gaensbauer, T. J., & Harmon, R. J. (1976). Emotional expression in infancy: A biobehavioral study. *Psychological Issues* (Vol. 10, No. 37). New York: International Universities Press.

Emde, R. N., Harmon, R. J., Metcalf, D., Koenig, K. L., & Wagonfeld, S. (1971). Stress and neonatal sleep. *Psychosomatic Medicine, 33*, 491–497.

Emery, R. E. (Ed.). (1988). *Marriage, divorce and children's adjustment.* Newbury Park, CA: Sage.

Emory, E. K., Schlackman, L. J., & Fiano, K. (1996). Drug-hormone interactions on neurobehavioral responses in human neonates. *Infant Behavior & Development, 19*, 213–220.

Emslie, G. J., Rush, A. J., Weinberg, W. A., Kowatch, R. A., Hughes, C. W., Carmody, T., & Rintelmann, J. (1997). A double-blind, randomized, placebo-controlled trial of fluoxetine in children and adolescents with depression. *Archives of General Psychiatry, 54*, 1031–1037.

Engel, S. (1995). *The stories children tell: Making sense of the narratives of childhood.* New York: Freeman.

Engel, S., & Li, A. (2004). Narratives, gossip, and shared experience: How and what young children know about the lives of others. In J. M. Lucariello, J. A. Hudson, R. Fivush, & P. J. Bauer (Eds.), *The development of the mediated mind: Sociocultural context and cognitive development* (pp. 151–174). Mahwah, NJ: Erlbaum.

Enright, R. D., & Sutterfield, S. J. (1980). An ecological validation of social cognitive development. *Child Development, 51*, 156–161.

Entwisle, D. R., & Alexander, K. L. (1987). Long-term effects of cesarean delivery on parents' beliefs and children's schooling. *Developmental Psychology, 23*, 676–682.

Entwisle, D. R., & Frasure, N. E. (1974). A contradiction resolved: Children's processing of syntactic cues. *Developmental Psychology, 10*, 852–857.

Epstein, J. A., Griffin, K. W., & Botvin, G. J. (2001). Risk taking and refusal assertiveness in a longitudinal model of alcohol use among inner-city adolescents. *Prevention Science, 2*, 193–200.

Epstein, L. H., Saelens, B. E., Myers, M. D., & Vito, D. (1997). Effects of decreasing sedentary behaviors on activity choice in obese children. *Health Psychology, 16*, 107–113.

Epstein, L. H., Valoski, A. M., Vara, S., McCurley, J., Wisniewski, L., Kalarchian, M. A., Klein, K. R., & Shrager, L. R. (1995). Effects of decreasing sedentary behavior and increasing activity on weight change in obese children. *Health Psychology, 14*, 109–115.

Epstein, L. R., Valoski, A., Wing, R. R., & McCurley, J. (1994). Ten-year outcomes of behaviorally family-based treatment for childhood obesity. *Health Psychology, 13*, 373–383.

Erdley, C. A., Cain, K. M., Loomis, C. C., Dumas-Hines, F., & Dweck, C. S. (1997). Relations among children's social goals, implicit personality theories, and responses to social failure. *Developmental Psychology, 33*, 263–272.

Erikson, E. H. (1970). Reflections on the dissent of contemporary youth. *International Journal of Psycho-Analysis, 51*, 11–22.

Ervin-Tripp, S. (1979). Children's verbal turn taking. In E. Ochs & B. Schieffelin (Eds.), *Developmental pragmatics.* New York: Academic.

Evans, D. W., & Gray, F. L. (2000). Compulsive-like behavior in individuals with Down syndrome: Its relation to mental age level, adaptive and maladaptive behavior. *Child Development, 71*, 288–300.

Evans, G. W. (2003). A multimethodological analysis of cumulative risk and allostatic load among rural children. *Developmental Psychology, 39*, 924–933.

Fabes, R., Eisenberg, N., Nyman, N., & Michealieu, Q. (1991). Young children's appraisals of others' spontaneous emotional reactions. *Developmental Psychology, 27*, 858–866.

Fabes, R. A., & Eisenberg, N. (1996). *An examination of age and sex differences in prosocial behavior and empathy.* Unpublished data, Arizona State University.

Fabes, R. A., Eisenberg, N., Smith, M. C., & Murphy, B. (1996). Getting angry at peers: Associations with liking of the provocateur. *Child Development, 67*, 942–956.

Fabes, R. A., Martin, C. L., & Hanish, L. D. (2002, October). *The role of sex segregation in young children's prosocial behavior and disposition.* Paper presented at the Groningen Conference on Prosocial Dispositions and Solidarity, Groningen, Netherlands.

Fagan, J., & Hawkins, A. J. (Eds.). (2001). *Clinical and educational interventions with fathers.* New York: Haworth Press.

Fagan, J. F., III. (1992). Intelligence: A theoretical viewpoint. *Current Directions in Psychological Science, 1*, 82–86.

Fagan, J. F., III, Drotar, D., Berkoff, K., Peterson, N., Kiziri-Mayengo, R., Guay, L., Ndugwa, C., & Zaidan, S. (1991). The Fagan Test of Infant Intelligence: Cross-cultural and racial comparisons. *Journal of Developmental and Behavioral Pediatrics, 12*, 168.

Fagot, B. I. (1973). Sex-related stereotyping of toddlers' behaviors. *Developmental Psychology, 9*, 429.

Fagot, B. I. (1985a). Beyond the reinforcement principle: Another step toward understanding sex role development. *Developmental Psychology, 21,* 1097–1104.

Fagot, B. I. (1985b). Changes in thinking about early sex role development. *Developmental Review, 5,* 83–98.

Fagot, B. I., & Leinbach, M. D. (1987). Socialization of sex roles within the family. In D. B. Carter (Ed.), *Current conceptions of sex roles and sex typing: Theory and research* (pp. 89–100). New York: Praeger.

Fagot, B. I., & Leinbach, M. D. (1989). The young child's gender schema: Environmental input, internal organization. *Child Development, 60,* 663–672.

Fagot, B. I., & Leinbach, M. D. (1992). Gender-role development in young children: From discrimination to labeling. *Developmental Review, 13,* 205–224.

Fairburn, C. G., Cooper, A., Doll, H. A., & Welch, S. L. (1999). Risk factors for anorexia nervosa: Three integrated case-control comparisons. *Archives of General Psychiatry, 56,* 468–476.

Falbo, T., & Polit, D. F. (1986). Quantitative review of the only child literature: Research evidence and theory development, *Psychological Bulletin, 100,* 176–189.

Fantz, R. (1963). Pattern vision in newborn infants. *Science, 140,* 296–297.

Farrar, M. J. (1992). Negative evidence and grammatical morpheme acquisition. *Developmental Psychology, 28,* 90–98.

Farrell, A. D., & Danish, S. T. (1993). Peer drug associations and emotional restraint: Causes or consequences of adolescents' drug use? *Journal of Consulting & Clinical Psychology, 61,* 327–334.

Farrington, D. P. (1993). The challenge of teenage antisocial behavior. In M. Rutter (Ed.), *Psychosocial disturbances in young people.* Cambridge: Cambridge University Press.

Farver, J. M., & Howes, C. (1993). Cultural differences in American and Mexican mother-child pretend play. *Merrill-Palmer Quarterly, 39,* 344–358.

Federal Interagency Forum on Child and Family Statistics. (1997). Washington, DC: U.S. Government Printing Office.

Feinberg, M., & Hetherington, M. E. (2001). Differential parenting as within-family variable. *Journal of Family Psychology, 15,* 22–37.

Feinman, S., & Lewis, M. (1983). Social referencing at ten months: A second-order effect on infants' responses to strangers. *Child Development, 54,* 878–887.

Feiring, C., & Lewis, M. (1987). The ecology of some middle class families at dinner. *International Journal of Behavioral Development, 10,* 377–390.

Feldman, R., & Eidelman, A. I. (2003). Skin-to-skin contact (kangaroo care) accelerates autonomic and neurobehavioral maturation in preterm infants. *Developmental Medicine and Child Neurology, 45,* 274–281.

Fenson, L., Dale, P. S., Reznick, J. S., Bates, E., Thal, D. J., & Pethick, S. J. (1994). Variability in early communicative development. *Monographs of the Society for Research in Child Development, 59* (Serial No. 242).

Ferguson, T. J., & Rule, B. G. (1980). Effects of inferential set, outcome severity and basis of responsibility on children's evaluations of aggressive acts. *Developmental Psychology, 16,* 141–146.

Fernald, A. (1992). Meaningful melodies in mothers' speech to infants. In H. Papousek, U. Jurgens, & M. Papousek (Eds.), *Nonverbal vocal communication* (pp. 262–282). Cambridge, England: Cambridge University Press.

Fernald, A., & Kuhl, P. K. (1987). Acoustical determinants of infant preference for motherese speech. *Infant Behavior and Development, 10,* 279–293.

Fernald, A., & Mazzie, C. (1991). Prosody and focus in speech to infants and adults. *Developmental Psychology, 27,* 209–221.

Fernald, A., & Morikawa, H. (1993). Common themes and cultural variations in Japanese and American mothers' speech to infants. *Child Development, 64,* 636–637.

Fernandes, O., Sabharwal, M., Srailey, T., Pastuszak, A., Koren, G., & Einarson, T. (1998). Moderate to heavy caffeine consumption during pregnancy and relationship to spontaneous abortion and abnormal fetal growth: A meta-analysis. *Reproductive Toxicology, 12,* 435–444.

Ferreira, F., & Morrison, F. J. (1994). Children's metalinguistic knowledge of syntactical constituents: Effects of age and schooling. *Developmental Psychology, 30,* 663–678.

Field, D. (1987). A review of preschool conservation training: An analysis of analyses. *Developmental Review, 7,* 210–251.

Field, T., & Goldson, E. (1984). Pacifying effects of nonnutritive sucking on term and preterm neonates during heelstick procedures. *Pediatrics, 74,* 1012–1015.

Field, T., Hernandez-Reif, M., & Freedman, J. (2004). Stimulation programs for preterm infants. *Social Policy Report, 18,* 1–19.

Field, T., Sandberg, D., Quetal, T. A., Garcia, R., & Rosario, M. (1985). Effects of ultrasound feedback on pregnancy, anxiety, fetal activity and neonate outcome. *Obstetrics and Gynecology, 66,* 525–528.

Field, T. M. (1978). Interaction behaviors of primary versus secondary caretaker fathers. *Developmental Psychology, 14,* 183–184.

Field, T. M. (1986). Affective responses to separation. In T. B. Brazelton & M. W. Yogman (Eds.), *Affective development in infancy.* Norwood, NJ: Ablex.

Field, T. M. (1990). *Infancy.* Cambridge, MA: Harvard University Press.

Field, T. M. (2001a). Massage therapy facilitates weight gain in preterm infants. *Current Directions in Psychological Science, 10,* 51–54.

Field, T. M. (2001b). *Touch.* Cambridge, MA: MIT Press.

Fiese, B. H. (1990). Playful relationships: A contextual analysis of mother-toddler interaction and symbolic play. *Child Development, 61,* 1648–1656.

Fiese, B. (2006). *Family routines and rituals.* New Haven, CT: Yale University Press.

Fiese, B. H., & Bickham, N. L. (2004). Pin-curling grandpa's hair in the comfy chair: Parents' stories of growing up and potential links to socialization in the preschool years. In M. W. Pratt & B. H. Fiese (Eds.), *Families, stories, and the life course* (pp. 259–278). Mahwah, NJ: Erlbaum.

Fiese, B. H., Tomcho, T., Douglas, M., Josephs, K., Poltrock, S., & Baker, T. (2002). Fifty years of research on naturally occurring rituals: Cause for celebration? *Journal of Family Psychology, 16,* 381–390.

Fifer, W. P., & Moon, C. (1989). Auditory experience in the fetus. In W. P. Smotherman & S. R. Robinson (Eds.), *Behavior of the fetus* (pp. 175–187). Caldwell, NJ: Telford Press.

Finegan, J. K., Niccols, G. A., & Sitarenios, G. (1992). Relations between prenatal testosterone levels and cognitive abilities at 4 years. *Developmental Psychology, 28*(6), 1075–1089.

Finnie, V., & Russell, A. (1988). Preschool children's social status and their mothers' behavior and knowledge in the supervisory role. *Developmental Psychology, 24,* 789–801.

Fischer, A., et al. (2000). Gene therapy of severe combined immunodeficiencies. *Immunological Review, 178,* 13–20.

Fischer, K. W., & Lazerson, A. (1984). A summary of parental development. In K. W. Fischer & A. Lazerson, *Human development* (p. 117). New York: Freeman.

Fischer, K. W., & Roberts, R. J. (1986). A developmental sequence of classification skills and errors in preschool children. Unpublished manuscript, Harvard University.

Fisher, C. B., & Brone, R. J. (1991). Eating disorders in adolescence. In R. M. Lerner, A. C. Petersen, & J. Brooks-Gunn (Eds.), *Encyclopedia of Adolescence* (Vol. 1). New York: Garland.

Fisher, C., Hall, D. G., Rakowitz, S., & Gleitman, L. (1994). When it is better to receive than to give: Syntactic and conceptual contraints on vocabulary growth. In L. Gleitman & B. Landau (Eds.), *The acquisition of lexicon* (pp. 333–376). Cambridge, MA: MIT Press/Elsevier.

Fisher, C. B., Jackson, J. F., & Villaruel, F. A. (1998). The study of ethnic minority children and youth in the United States. In W. Damon (Gen. Ed.) & R. M. Lerner (Vol. Ed.), *Handbook of child psychology: Vol. 1. Theoretical models of human development.* New York: Wiley.

Fisher-Thompson, D. (1990). Adult gender typing of children's toys. *Sex Roles, 23,* 291–303.

Fivaz-Depeursinger, E., & Corboz-Warner, A. (1999). *The primary triangle: A developmental systems view of fathers, mothers, and infants.* New York: Basic Books.

Fivush, R. (1988). The functions of event memory: Some comments on Nelson and Brasalou. In U. Neisser & E. Winograd (Eds.), *Remembering reconsidered: Ecological and traditional approaches to the study of memory* (pp. 277–282). New York: Cambridge University Press.

Fivush, R., Haden, C., & Reese, E. (1996). Remembering, recounting, and reminiscing: The development of autobiographical memory in social context. In D. C. Rubin (Ed.), *Remembering our past: Studies in autobiographical memory* (pp. 341–359). Cambridge, England: Cambridge University Press.

Fivush, R., & Hamond, N. R. (1989). Time and again: Effects of repetition and retention interval on two year olds' event recall. *Journal of Experimental Child Psychology, 47,* 259–273.

Fivush, R., Hudson, J., & Nelson, K. (1984). Children's long-term memory for a novel event: An exploratory study. *Merrill-Palmer Quarterly, 30,* 303–316.

Fivush, R., Kuebli, J., & Clubb, P. A. (1992). The structure of events and event representations: A developmental analysis. *Child Development, 63,* 188–201.

Flavell, J. H. (1963). *The developmental psychology of Jean Piaget.* Princeton, NJ: Van Nostrand.

Flavell, J. H. (1985). *Cognitive development.* Englewood Cliffs, NJ: Prentice Hall.

Flavell, J. H., Beach, D. R., & Chinsky, J. M. (1966). Spontaneous verbal rehearsal in a memory task as a function of age. *Child Development, 37,* 283–299.

Flavell, J. H., Friedricks, A. G., & Hoyt, J. D. (1970). Developmental changes in memorization processes. *Cognitive Psychology, 1,* 324–340.

Flavell, J. H., Green, F. L., & Flavell, E. R. (1995) Young children's knowledge about thinking. *Monographs of the Society for Research in Child Development, 60,* 243–256.

Flavell, J. H., & Miller, P. H. (1998). Social cognition. In W. Damon (Gen. Ed.), D. Kuhn, & R. S. Siegler (Vol. Eds.), *Handbook of child psychology: Vol. 2. Cognition, perception, and language.* New York: Wiley.

Flavell, J. H., Miller, P. H., & Miller, S. A. (1993). *Cognitive development* (3rd ed.). Englewood Cliffs, NJ: Prentice-Hall.

Fletcher, A. C., Darling, N. E., Steinberg, L., & Dornbusch, S. (1995). The company they keep: Relation of adolescents' adjustment and behavior to their friends' perceptions of authoritative parenting in the social network. *Developmental Psychology, 31,* 300–310.

Flynn, J. R. (1984). The mean IQ of Americans: Massive gains from 1932–1978. *Psychological Bulletin, 95,* 29–51.

Flynn, J. R. (1998). IQ trends over time: Intelligence, race, and meritocracy. In S. Durlauf, K. Arrow, & S. Bowles (Eds.), *Meritocracy and equality.* Princeton, NJ: Princeton University Press.

Fogel, A. (1993). *Developing through relationships: Origins of communication, self, and culture.* Chicago: University of Chicago Press.

Fonagy, P., Steele, H., & Steele, M. (1991). Maternal representations of attachment during pregnancy predict organization of infant-mother attachment at one year of age. *Child Development, 62,* 891–905.

Fonzi, A. F., Genta, M. L., Menesini, E., Bacchini, D., Bonino, S., & Constabile, A. (1999). In P. K. Smith, Y. Morita, J. Junger-Tas, D. Olweus, R. Catalano, & P. Slee (Eds.), *The nature of school bullying: A cross-national perspective* (pp. 140–156). New York: Routledge.

Fordham, S., & Ogbu, J. V. (1986). Black students' school success: Coping with the burden of acting white. *Urban Review, 18,* 176–206.

Forrester, L. W., Phillips, S. J., & Clark, J. E. (1993). Locomotor co-ordination in infancy: The transition from walking to running. In G. J. P. Savelsbergh (Ed.), *The development of coordination in infancy* (pp. 359–393). Amsterdam: Elsevier.

Forssberg, H. (1985). Ontogeny of human locomotor control: I. Infant stepping, supported locomotion and the transition to independent locomotion. *Experimental Brain Research, 57,* 480–493.

Fox, H. E., Steinbrecher, M., Pessel, D., Inglis, J., Medvid, L., & Angel, E. (1978). Maternal ethanol ingestion and the occurrence of human fetal breathing movements. *American Journal of Obstetrics and Gynecology, 132,* 1327–1328.

Fox, N. A. (1991). If it's not left, it's right: Electroencephalograph asymmetry and the development of emotion. *American Psychologist, 46,* 863–872.

Fox, N. A., Calkins, S. D., & Bell, M. A. (1994). Neural plasticity and development in the first two years of life: Evidence from cognitive and socioemotional domains. *Development and Psychopathology, 6,* 677–696.

Fox, N. A., & Davidson, R. J. (1988). Patterns of brain electrical activity during facial signs of emotion in 10-month-old infants. *Developmental Psychology, 24,* 230–236.

Fraiberg, S. (1977). *Insights from the blind.* New York: Basic Books.

Francis, P. L., Self, P. A., & Horowitz, F. D. (1987). The behavioral assessment of the neonate: An overview. In J. Osofsky (Ed.), *Handbook of infancy* (2nd ed.). New York: Wiley.

Franco, F., & Butterworth, G. (1996). Pointing and social awareness: Declaring and requesting in the second year. *Journal of Child Language, 23,* 307–336.

Fredrickson, D. D. (1993). Breastfeeding research priorities, opportunities, and study criteria: What have we learned from the smoking trail. *Journal of Human Lactation, 9,* 147–150.

Freedman, D. G. (1974). *Human infancy: An evolutionary perspective.* Hillsdale, NJ: Erlbaum.

Freidman, H. S., Tucker, J. S., Schwartz, J. E., Tomlinson-Keasey, C., Martin, L. R., Wingard, D. L., & Criqui, M. H. (1995). Psychosocial and behavioral predictors of longevity. *American Psychologist, 50,* 69–78.

Freud, A., & Dann, S. (1951). An experiment in group upbringing. In *The psychoanalytic study of the child* (Vol. 6). New York: International Universities Press.

Frey, K. S., & Ruble, D. N. (1992). Gender constancy and the "cost" of sex-typed behavior: A test of the conflict hypothesis. *Developmental Psychology, 28,* 714–721.

Frick, W. B. (1999). Flight into health: A new interpretation. *Journal of Humanistic Psychology, 3,* 58–81.

Fried, P. A., Watkinson, B., & Gray, R. (1998). Differential effects on cognitive functioning in 9- to 12-year-olds prenatally exposed to cigarettes and marijuana. *Neurotoxicology and Teratology, 20,* 203–306.

Friedman, J. M., & Polifka, J. E. (1996). The effects of drugs on the fetus and the nursing infant. Baltimore, MD: Johns Hopkins University Press.

Friedrich, L. K., & Stein, A. H. (1973). Aggressive and prosocial television programs and the natural behavior of preschool children. *Monographs of the Society for Research in Child Development, 38* (Serial No. 151).

Frodi, A. M., & Lamb, M. E. (1980). Child abusers' responses to infant smiles and cries. *Child Development, 51,* 238–241.

Frodi, A. M., Lamb, M. E., Leavitt, L. A., & Donovan, W. K. (1978). Father's and mother's responses to infant smiles and cries. *Infant Behavior and Development, 1,* 187–198.

Frosch, C. A., & Mangelsdorf, S. C. (2001). Marital behavior, parenting behavior and multiple reports of preschoolers' behavior problems: Mediation or moderation. *Developmental Psychology, 37,* 502–519.

Frosch, C. A., Mangelsdorf, S., & McHale, J. L. (2000). Marital behavior and the security of preschool-parent attachment relationships. *Journal of Family Psychology, 14,* 1438–1449.

Fuligni, A. J. (1997). The academic achievement of adolescents from immigrant families: The roles of family background, attitudes, and behavior. *Child Development, 68,* 351–363.

Funk, J. B., & Buchman, D. D. (1996). Children's perceptions of gender differences in social approval for playing electronic games. *Sex Roles, 35,* 219–232.

Furman, W. (2002). The emerging field of adolescent romantic relationships. *Current Directions in Psychological Science, 11,* 177–180.

Furman, W., & Gavin, L. A. (1989). Peers influence on adjustment and development. In T. J. Berndt & G. W. Ladd (Eds.), *Peer relationships in child development.* New York: Wiley.

Furman, W., Rahe, D., & Hartup, W. W. (1979). Social rehabilitation of low-interactive preschool children by peer intervention. *Child Development, 50,* 915–922.

Furman, W., Simon, V. A., Shaffer, L., & Bouchey, H. A. (2002). Adolescents' working models and styles of relationships with parents, friends and romantic partners. *Child Development, 73,* 241–255.

Furstenberg, F. F. (1993). How families manage risk and opportunity in dangerous neighborhoods. In W. J. Wilson (Ed.), *Sociology and the public agenda* (pp. 231–258). Newbury Park, CA: Sage.

Furstenberg, F. F., & Cherlin, A. J. (1991). *Divided families: What happens to children when parents part.* Cambridge, MA: Harvard University Press.

Furstenberg, F. F., Cook, T., Eccles, J., Elder G., & Sameroff, A. (1999). *Managing to make it.* Chicago: University of Chicago Press.

Furstenberg, F. F., Jr., Brooks-Gunn, J., & Chase-Lansdale, L. (1989). Teenage pregnancy and child bearing. *American Psychologist, 44,* 313–320.

Gadsden, V. L. (1999). Black families in international and cultural perspective. In M. E. Lamb (Ed.), *Parenting and child development in "nontraditional" families* (pp. 221–246). Mahwah, NJ: Erlbaum.

Galen, B. R., & Underwood, M. K. (1997). A developmental investigation of social aggression among children. *Developmental Psychology, 33,* 589–600.

Galinsky, E., Howes, C., & Kontos, S. (1995). *The family child care training study.* New York: Families and Work Institute.

Gallagher, A., Levin, J., & Cahalan, C. (2002). GRE research: Cognitive patterns of gender differences in mathematics admissions tests (ETS Report No. 12-19). Princeton, NJ: Educational Testing Service.

Gallaway, C., & Richards, B. J. (1994). *Input and interaction in language acquisition.* Cambridge: Cambridge University Press.

Ganger, J., & Brent, M. R. (2004). Reexamining the vocabulary spurt. *Developmental Psychology, 40,* 621–632.

Garbarino, J. (1982). Sociocultural risk: Dangers to competence. In C. Kopp & J. Krakow (Eds.), *Child development in a social context* (pp. 630–685). Reading, MA: Addison-Wesley.

Garbarino, J. (1995). *Raising children in a socially toxic environment.* San Francisco: Jossey-Bass.

Garbarino, J., & Kostelny, K. (2002). Parenting and public policy. In M. Borenstein (Ed.), *Handbook of parenting: Vol 3.* (rev. ed., pp. 419–436). Mahwah, NJ: Erlbaum.

Garbarino, J., & Sherman, D. (1980). High-risk neighborhoods and high-risk families: The human ecology of child maltreatment. *Child Development, 51,* 188–198.

Garber, J., & Mardin, N. C. (2002). Negative cognitions in offspring of depressed parents: Mechanisms of risk. In S. H. Goodman & I. N. Gotlib (Eds.), *Children of depressed parents.* Washington, DC: American Psychological Association.

Garcia Coll, C. T. (1990). Developmental outcome of minority infants: A process-oriented look into our beginnings. *Child Development, 61,* 270–289.

Garcia Coll, C. T., & Magnuson, K. (2000). Cultural differences as sources of developmental vulnerabilities and resources. In J. P. Shonkoff & S. J. Meisels (Eds.), *Handbook of early childhood intervention* (2nd ed., pp. 94–114). New York: Cambridge University Press.

Garcia, M. M., Shaw, D. S., Winslow, E. B., & Yaggi, K. E. (2000). Destructive sibling conflict and the development of conduct problems in young boys. *Developmental Psychology, 36,* 44–53.

Gardiner, H. W., & Kosmitzki, C. (2005). *Lives across cultures; Cross-cultural human development* (3rd ed.). Boston: Allyn & Bacon.

Gardner, H. (1983). *Frames of mind: The theory of multiple intelligences.* New York: Basic Books.

Gardner, H. (1993). *Multiple intelligences: The theory in practice.* New York: Basic Books.

Gardner, H. (1998). Extraordinary cognitive achievements (ECA): A symbol systems approach. In W. Damon (Gen. Ed.), and R. M. Lerner (Vol. Ed.), *Handbook of child psychology: Vol. 1. Theoretical models of human development* (5th ed., pp. 415–466). New York: Wiley.

Gardner, H. (1999). *Intelligence reframed.* New York: Basic Books.

Gardner, R. J. M., & Sutherland, G. R. (1996). *Chromosome abnormalities and genetic counseling* (2nd ed.). Oxford, England: Oxford University Press.

Garlick, D. (2003). Integrating brain science research with intelligence research. *Current Directions in Psychological Science, 12,* 185–189.

Garmezy, N., & Masten, A. S. (1994). Chronic adversities. In M. Rutter, E. Taylor, & L. Hersov (Eds.), *Child and adolescent psychiatry: Modern approaches* (3rd ed., pp. 191–208). London: Blackwell.

Garner, P. W. (1996). The relations of emotional role taking, affective/moral attributions, and emotional display rule knowledge to low-income school-age children's social competence. *Journal of Applied Developmental Psychology, 17,* 19–36.

Garner, P. W., Jones, D. C., & Palmer, D. (1994). Social cognitive correlates of preschool children's sibling caregiving behavior. *Developmental Psychology, 30,* 905–911.

Garner, P. W., & Power, T. G. (1996). Preschoolers' emotional control in the disappointment paradigm and its relation to temperament, emotional knowledge and family expressiveness. *Child Development, 67,* 1406–1429.

Garvey, C. (1990). *Play.* Cambridge, MA: Harvard University Press.

Gauvain, M. (1992). Social influences on the development of planning in advance and during action. *International Journal of Behavioral Development, 15,* 377–398.

Gauvain, M. (1993). The development of spatial thinking in everyday activity. *Developmental Review, 13,* 92–121.

Gauvain, M. (2001a). *The sociocultural context of cognitive development.* New York: Guilford.

Gauvain, M. (2001b). Cultural tools, social interaction, and the development of thinking. *Human Development, 44,* 126–143.

Gauvain, M. (2005). Sociocultural contexts of learning. In A. Maynard & M. Martini (Eds.), *The psychology of learning in context: Cultural artifacts, families, peers, and schools* (pp. 11–40). New York: Kluwer/Plenum.

Gauvain, M., & Rogoff, B. (1989). Collaborative problem solving and children's planning skills. *Developmental Psychology, 25,* 139–151.

Gazelle, H., & Ladd, G. W. (2003). Anxious solitude and peer exclusion: A diathesis-stress model

of internalizing trajectories in childhood. *Child Development, 74,* 257–278.

Ge, X., Brody, G., Conger, R., Simons, R., & Murry, V. M. (2002). Contextual amplification of pubertal transition effects on deviant peer affiliation and externalizing behavior among African-American children. *Developmental Psychology, 38,* 42–54.

Ge, X., Conger, R., & Elder, G. (1996). Coming of age too early: Pubertal influences on girls' vulnerability to psychological distress. *Child Development, 62,* 3386–3400.

Ge, X., Conger, R., & Elder, G. H. (2001). The relation between puberty and psychological distress in adolescent boys. *Journal of Research on Adolescence, 11,* 49–70.

Geary, D. C. (1998). *Male, female: The evolution of human sex differences.* Washington, DC: American Psychological Association.

Geary, D. C., Fan, L., & Bow-Thomas, C. C. (1992). Numerical cognition: Loci of ability differences comparing children from China and the United States. *Psychological Science, 3,* 180–185.

Gelfand, D. M., & Drew, C. J. (2003). *Understanding child behavior disorders.* Belmont, CA: Wadsworth.

Gelfand, D. M., Jensen, W. R., & Drew, C. J. (1997). *Understanding child behavior disorders* (3rd ed.). Fort Worth, TX: Harcourt Brace.

Gelman, R. (1972). Logical capacity of very young children: Number invariance rules. *Child Development, 43,* 75–90.

Gelman, R. (1978). Cognitive development. *Annual Review of Psychology, 29,* 297–332.

Gelman, R. (1979). Preschool thought. *American Psychologist, 34,* 900–905.

Gelman, R. (1980). What young children know about numbers. *Educational Psychologist, 15,* 54–68.

Gelman, R. (1990). First principles organize attention to and learning about relevant data: Number and the animate-inanimate distinction as examples. *Cognitive Science, 14,* 79–106.

Gelman, R., & Baillargeon, R. (1983). A review of some Piagetian concepts. In J. H. Flavell & E. M. Markman (Eds.), *Handbook of child psychology: Cognitive development* (Vol. 3). New York: Wiley.

Gelman, R., & Gallistel, C. R. (1978). *The child's understanding of number.* Cambridge, MA: Harvard University Press.

Gelman, R., & Shatz, M. (1977). Appropriate speech adjustments: The operation of conversational

restraints on talk to two-year-olds. In M. Lewis & L. Rosenblum (Eds.), *Interaction, conversation and the development of language.* New York: Wiley.

Gelman, R., & Williams, E. (1998). Enabling constraints for cognitive development and learning: Domain specificity and epigenesis. In D. Kuhn & R. Siegler (Eds.), W. Damon (Series Ed.), *Handbook of child psychology: Vol. 2. Cognition, perception and language* (5th ed., pp. 575–630). New York: Wiley.

Gelman, S. A., & Markman, E. M. (1987). Young children's inductions from natural kinds: The role of categories and appearances. *Child Development, 58,* 1532–1541.

Gelman, S. A., & O'Reilly, A. W. (1988). Children's inductive inferences within superordinate categories: The role of language and category structure. *Child Development, 59,* 876–886.

Gennetian, L. A., & Miller, C. (2002). Children and welfare reform: A view from an experimental welfare program in Minnesota. *Child Development, 73,* 601–620.

Gentner, D. (1982). Why nouns are learned before verbs: Linguistic relativity versus natural partitioning. In S. A. Kuczaj II (Ed.), *Language development: Vol. 2. Language, thought, and culture* (pp. 301–332). Hillsdale, NJ: Erlbaum.

Gentner, D., & Holyoak, K. J. (1997). Reasoning and learning by analogy: Introduction. *American Psychologist, 52,* 32–34.

Gentner, D., & Stuart, P. (1983, April). *Metaphor as structure mapping: What develops?* Paper presented at the biennial meeting of the Society for Research in Child Development, Detroit.

Gentner, D., & Toupin, C. (1986). Systematicity and surface similarity in the development of analogy. *Cognitive Science, 10,* 277–300.

Gershoff, E. T. (2002). Corporal punishment by parents and associated child behaviors and experiences: A meta-analytic and theoretical review. *Psychological Bulletin, 128,* 339–579.

Gesell, A. L. (1928). *Infancy and human growth.* New York: Macmillan.

Gewirtz, J. L. (1967). The course of infant smiling in four child-rearing environments in Israel. In B. M. Foss (Ed.), *Determinants of infant behavior* (Vol. 3, pp. 105–248). London: Methuen.

Gewirtz, J. L. (1969). Mechanisms of social learning: Some roles of stimulation and behavior in early human development. In D. A.

Goslin (Ed.), *Handbook of socialization theory and research.* Chicago: Rand McNally.

Gewirtz, J. L., & Peláez-Nogueras, B. F. (1992). Skinner's legacy to human infant behavior and development. *American Psychologist, 47,* 1411–1422.

Gibbs, J. C., Potter, G. B., & Goldstein, A. P. (1995). *The EQUIP program: Teaching youth to think and act responsibly through a peer helping approach.* Champaign, IL: Research Press.

Gibbs, J. T. (1989). Black American adolescents. In J. T. Gibbs & L. N. Huang (Eds.), *Children of color.* San Francisco: Jossey-Bass.

Gibson, D., & Harris, A. (1988). Aggregated early intervention effects for Down syndrome persons. *Journal of Mental Deficiency Research, 32,* 1–7.

Gibson, E. J. (1969). *Principles of perceptual learning and development.* New York: Appleton-Century-Crofts.

Gibson, E. J. (2000). Perceptual learning in development: Some basic concepts. *Ecological Psychology, 12,* 295–302.

Gibson, E. J., & Pick, A. D. (2000). *An ecological approach to perceptual learning and development.* London: Oxford University Press.

Gibson, E. J., & Walk, R. D. (1960). The "visual cliff." *Scientific American, 202,* 64.

Gick, M. L., & Holyoak, K. J. (1980). Analogical problem solving. *Cognitive Psychology, 12,* 306–355.

Gifford-Smith, M. E., & Rabiner, D. L. (2004). Social information processing and children's social adjustment. In J. Kupersmidt & K. A. Dodge (Eds.), *Children's peer relations* (pp. 61–79). Washington, DC: American Psychological Association.

Gillham, J. E., Reivich, K. J., Jaycox, L. H., & Seligman, M. E. (1995). Prevention of depressive symptoms in schoolchildren: Two-year follow-up. *Psychological Science, 6,* 343–351.

Gilligan, C. (1982). *In a different voice.* Cambridge, MA: Harvard University Press.

Gilligan, C. (1993). Woman's place in man's life cycle. In A. Dobrin (Ed.), *Being good and doing right: Readings in moral development* (pp. 37–54). Lanham, MD: University Press of America.

Gilliland, F. D., Li, Y-F, & Peters, J. M. (2001). Effects of maternal smoking during pregnancy and environmental tobacco smoke in asthma and wheezing in children. *American Journal of Respiratory and Critical Care Medicine, 163,* 429–436.

Gilliom, M., Shaw, D., Beck, J. E., Shonberg, M., & Lukon, J. L. (2002). Anger regulation in disadvantaged preschool boys: Strategies, antecedents, and the development of self-control. *Developmental Psychology, 38,* 222–235.

Ginsberg, H. P., Klein, A., & Starkey, P. (1998). The development of children's mathematical thinking: Connecting research with practice. In W. Damon (Series Ed.) & I. E. Sigel & K. A. Renninger (Vol. Eds.), *Handbook of child psychology, Vol. 4: Child psychology in practice* (pp. 401–476). New York: Wiley.

Giusti, R. M., Iwamoto, K., & Hatch, E. E. (1995). Diethylstilbestrol revisited: A review of the long-term health effects. *Annals of Internal Medicine, 122,* 778–788.

Gladstone, T. R. G., & Beardslee, W. R. (2002). Treatment, intervention, and prevention with children of depressed parents: A developmental perspective. In S. H. Goodman & I. Gotlib (Eds.), *Children of depressed parents: Mechanisms of risk and implications for treatment* (pp. 277–305). Washington, DC: American Psychological Association.

Gladwell, M. (1998). The Pima paradox. *The New Yorker,* Feb. 2, pp. 44–57.

Gladwin, T. (1970). *East is a big bird.* Cambridge, MA: Harvard University Press.

Glasberg, R., & Aboud, F. (1982). Keeping one's distance from sadness: Children's self-reports of emotional experience. *Developmental Psychology, 18,* 287–293.

Gleitman, L. (1990). The structural sources of verb meanings. *Language acquisition, 1,* 3–55.

Glucksberg, S., Krauss, R., & Higgins, E. T. (1975). The development of referential communication skills. In F. D. Horowitz (Ed.), *Review of child development research* (Vol. 4). Chicago: University of Chicago Press.

Goetz, T. E., & Dweck, C. S. (1980). Learned helplessness in social situations. *Journal of Personality and Social Psychology, 39,* 246–255.

Goldberg, S. (1966). Infant care and growth in urban Zambia. *Human Development, 15,* 77–89.

Goldberg, S., & DeVitto, B. (2002). Parenting children born premature. In M. Bornstein (Ed.), *Handbook of parenting* (vol. 1, 2nd ed.). Mahwah, NJ: Erlbaum.

Golden, M., & Birns, B. (1983). Social class and infant intelligence.

In M. Lewis (Ed.), *Origins of intelligence: Infancy and early childhood* (2nd ed., pp. 347–398). New York: Plenum.

Golden, O. (2000). The federal response to child abuse and neglect. *American Psychologist, 55,* 1050–1053.

Goldin-Meadows, S. (2006). Nonverbal communication: The hand's role in talking and thinking. In W. Damon & R. M. Lerner (Series Eds.) and D. Kuhn & R. Siegler (Vol. Eds.), *Handbook of child psychology,* Vol. 2, 6th ed. New York: Wiley.

Goldsmith, H. H. (1983). Genetic influences on personality from infancy to adulthood. *Child Development, 54,* 331–355.

Goldsmith, H. H., Aksan, N., Essex, M., Smider, N. A., & Vandell, D. L. (2001). Temperament and socioemotional adjustment to kindergarten: A multi-informant perspective. In T. D. Wachs & G. A. Kohnstamm (Eds.), *Temperament in context* (pp. 103–138). Mahwah, NJ: Erlbaum.

Goleman, D. (1995). *Emotional intelligence.* New York: Bantam Books.

Golinkoff, R. M. (1983). The preverbal negotiation of failed messages: Insights into the transition period. In R. M. Golinkoff (Ed.), *The transition from prelinguistic to linguistic communication* (pp. 57–78). Hillsdale, NJ: Erlbaum.

Golinkoff, R. M., & Hirsh-Pasek, K. (1999). *How babies talk.* New York: The Penguin Group.

Golinkoff, R. M., Hirsh-Pasek, K., Bailey, L. M., & Wenger, N. R. (1992). Young children and adults use lexical principles to learn new words. *Developmental Psychology, 28,* 99–108.

Golinkoff, R. M., Hirsh-Pasek, K., & Schweisguth, M. A. (2001). A reappraisal of young children's knowledge of grammatical morphemes. In J. Weissenborn & B. Hoehle (Eds.), *Approaches to bootstrapping: Phonological, syntactic, and neurophysical aspects of early language acquisition.* Amsterdam & Philadelphia: John Benjamins.

Golombok, S. (2002). Parenting and contemporary reproductive technologies. In M. Bornstein (Ed.), *Handbook of Parenting* (2nd ed., Vol. 3, pp. 339–362). Mahwah, NJ: Erlbaum.

Golombok, S., & Fivush, R. (1994). *Gender development.* New York: Cambridge University Press.

Golombok, S., Murray, C., Jadva, V., MacCallum, F., & Lycett, E. (2004). Families created through surrogacy arrangements:

Parent-child relationships in the first year of life. *Developmental Psychology, 40,* 400–411.

Goncz, L., & Kodzopeljic, J. (1991). Exposure to two languages in the preschool period: Metalinguistic development and the acquisition of reading. *Journal of Multilingual and Multicultural Development, 12,* 137–142.

Goodglass, H. (1993). *Understanding aphasia.* New York: Academic Press.

Goodman, G. S., Bottoms, B. L., Schwartz-Kenney, B. M., & Rudy, L. (1991). Children's testimony for a stressful event: Improving children's reports. *Journal of Narrative and Life History, 1,* 69–99.

Goodman, G. S., Emery, R. E., & Haugaard, J. J. (1998). Developmental psychology and law: Divorce, child maltreatment, foster care, and adoption. In W. Damon (Gen. Ed.), I. E. Sigel, & K. A. Renninger (Vol. Ed.), *Handbook of child psychology: Vol. 4. Child psychology in practice* (pp. 775–874). New York: Wiley.

Goodman, J. C. (1989). *The development of context effects of spoken word recognition.* Doctoral dissertation. The University of Chicago.

Goodman, S. H., & Gotlib, I. N. (Eds.). (2002). *Children of depressed parents.* Washington, DC: American Psychological Association.

Goodnow, J. (1988). Children's household work: Its nature and functions. *Psychological Bulletin, 103,* 5–26.

Goodnow, J. J. (1996). From household practices to parents' ideas about work and interpersonal relationships. In S. Harkness & C. Super (Eds.), *Parents' cultural belief systems* (pp. 313–344). New York: Guilford Press.

Goodnow, J. J., Miller, P. J., & Kessel, F. (1995). *Cultural practices as contexts for development.* San Francisco: Jossey-Bass.

Goody, E. (1991). The learning of prosocial behavior in small-scale egalitarian societies: An anthropological view. In R. A. Hinde & J. Groebel (Eds.), *Cooperation and prosocial behavior* (pp. 106–128). Cambridge, England: Cambridge University Press.

Goody, J. (1977). *The domestication of the savage mind.* Cambridge, UK: Cambridge University Press.

Goswami, U. (1995). Transitive relational mappings in 3- and 4-year-olds: The analogy of Goldilocks and the Three Bears. *Child Development, 66,* 877–892.

Goswami, U., & Brown, A. L. (1990). Higher-order structure and relational reasoning: Contrasting analogical and thematic relations. *Cognition, 36,* 207–226.

Goswami, U., & Bryant, P. (1990). *Phonological skills and learning to read.* Hillsdale, NJ: Erlbaum.

Gottesman, I. I. (1963). Genetic aspects of intelligent behavior. In N. Ellis (Ed.), *Handbook of mental deficiency: Psychological theory and research.* New York: McGraw-Hill.

Gottesman, I. I., & Goldsmith, H. H. (1994). Developmental psychopathology of antisocial behavior: Inserting genes into its ontogenesis and epigenesis. In C. A. Nelson (Ed.), *Threats to optimal development: Integrating biological, psychological, and social risk factors* (pp. 69–104). Hillsdale, NJ: Erlbaum.

Gottfredson, L. S. (Ed.). (1997). Intelligence and social policy [Special issue]. *Intelligence, 24,* 1–320.

Gottfredson, L. S. (2004). Schools and the *g* factor. *The Wilson Quarterly, Summer,* 35–45.

Gottfried, A. E., Gottfried, A. W., & Bathurst, K. (2002). Maternal and dual-earner employment status and parenting. In M. Bornstein (Ed.) *Handbook of parenting* (Rev. ed., pp. 207–230). Mahwah, NJ: Erlbaum.

Gottfried, A. W., & Gottfried, A. E. (1984). Home environment and cognitive development in young children of middle-socioeconomic-status families. In A. W. Gottfried (Ed.), *Home environment and early cognitive development* (pp. 57–115). Orlando, FL: Academic.

Gottlieb, G. (1991). Experiential canalization of behavioral development theory. *Developmental Psychology, 27,* 4–13.

Gottlieb, G. (1992). *Individual development and evolution: The genesis of novel behavior.* New York: Oxford University Press.

Gottlieb, G., Wahlsten, D., & Lickliter, R. (1998). The significance of biology for human development: A developmental psychobiological systems view. In W. Damon (Gen. Ed.) & R. M. Lerner (Vol. Ed.), *Handbook of child psychology: Vol. 1. Theoretical models of human development* (pp. 233–273). New York: Wiley.

Gottman, J. M. (1983). How children become friends. *Monographs of the Society for Research in Child Development, 48* (Serial No. 201).

Gottman, J. M. (1986). The world of coordinated play: Same and cross-sex friendship in young children. In J. M. Gottman & J. G. Parker (Eds.), *The conversations of friends.* New York: Cambridge University Press.

Gottman, J., Katz, L., & Hooven, C. (1996). *Meta-emotion.* Mahwah, NJ: Erlbaum.

Gottman, J. M., & Mettetal, G. (1986). Speculations on social and affective development: Friendship and acquaintanceship through adolescence. In J. M. Gottman & J. G. Parker (Eds.), *The conversations of friends.* New York: Cambridge University Press.

Gottman, J. M., & Parker, J. G. (Eds.). (1986). *The conversations of friends.* New York: Cambridge University Press.

Gould, E., Reeves, A. J., Graziano, M. S., & Gross, C. G. (1999). Neurogenesis in the neocortex of adult primates. *Science, 286,* 548–555.

Graber, J. A., Petersen, A. C., & Brooks-Gunn, J. (1996). Pubertal processes: Methods, measures and models. In J. A. Graber, J. Brooks-Gunn, & A. C. Petersen (Eds.), *Transitions through adolescence.* Mahwah, NJ: Erlbaum.

Graham, G. G. (1966). Growth during recovery from infantile malnutrition. *Journal of the American Medical Women's Association, 21,* 737–742.

Graham, S. (1992). Most of the subjects were white and middle class: Trends in published research on African-Americans in selected APA journals, 1970–1989. *American Psychologist, 47,* 629–639.

Graham, S., Doubleday, C., & Guarino, P. A. (1984). The development of relations between perceived controllability and the emotions of pity, anger and guilt. *Child Development, 55,* 561–565.

Graham, S., & Hudley, C. (1994). Attributions of aggressive and nonaggressive African-American male early adolescents: A study of construct accessibility. *Developmental Psychology, 30,* 365–373.

Grantham-McGregor, S., Powell, C., Walker, S., & Chang, S. (1994). The long-term follow up of severely malnourished children who participated in an intervention program. *Child Development, 65,* 428–439.

Grantham-McGregor, S. M., Powell, C. A., Walker, S. P., & Hines, J. H. (1991). Nutritional supplementation, psychological stimulation and mental development of stunted children: The Jamaican study. *Lancet, 338,* 1–5.

Green, J. A., Gustafson, G. E., & West, M. J. (1980). Effects of infant development on mother-infant interactions. *Child Development, 51,* 199–207.

Greenberg, M. (1999). Atttachment and psychopathology in childhood. In J. Cassidy & P. Shaver (Eds.), *Handbook of attachment* (pp. 449–456). New York: Guilford.

Greenberg, M., & Morris, N. (1974). Engrossment: The newborn's impact upon the father. *American Journal of Orthopsychiatry, 44,* 520–531.

Greenfield, P., & Cocking, R. (Eds.). (1995). *Cross-cultural perspectives on child development.* Hillsdale, NJ: Erlbaum.

Greenfield, P. M., & Childs, C. P. (1991). Developmental continuity in biocultural context. In R. Cohen & A. W. Siegel (Eds.), *Context and development.* Hillsdale, NJ: Erlbaum.

Greenfield, P. M., & Suzuki, L. K. (1998). Culture and human development: Implications for parenting, education, pediatrics and mental health. In W. Damon (Gen. Ed.), I. Sigel & A. Renninger (Vol. Eds.), *Handbook of child psychology* (Vol. 4). New York: Wiley.

Greenough, W., & Black, J. E. (1999). Experience, neural plasticity, and psychological development. In N. A. Fox, L. A. Leavitt, & J. G. Warhol (Eds.), *The role of early experience in infant development* (pp. 29–40). Johnson & Johnson Pediatric Institute.

Grief, E. B., & Gleason, J. B. (1980). Hi, thanks, and goodbye: More routine information. *Language in Society, 9,* 159–166.

Griffin, P. B., & Griffin, M. B. (1992). Fathers and childcare among the Cagayan Agta. In B. Hewlett (Ed.), *Father-child relations: Cultural and biosocial contexts* (pp. 297–320). New York: Aldine de Gruyther.

Grigorenko, E. L. (2002). In search of the genetic engram of personality. In D. Cervone & W. Mischel (Eds.), *Advances in personality science* (pp. 29–82). New York: Guilford.

Grilo, C. M. (2001). Pharmacological and psychological treatments of obesity and binge eating disorders. In M. T. Simmons & N. B. Schmidt (Eds.), *Combined treatment for medical disorders: A guide to psychological and pharmacological interventions* (pp. 239–269). Washington, DC: American Psychological Association.

Gritz, E. R. (2004). Smoking and friendship influence in three ethnic groups. *Nicotine and Tobacco Research, 11,* 109–115.

Groen, G. J., & Parkman, J. M. (1972). A chronometric analysis of simple addition. *Psychological Review, 79,* 329–302.

Gross, R. T., Spiker, D., & Haynes, C. W. (Eds.). (1997). Helping low-birthweight, premature infants. *The Infant Health and Development Program.* Stanford, CA: Stanford University Press.

Grossman, K., & Fremmer-Bombik, E. (June, 1994). Father's attachment representations and the quality of their interactions with their children in infancy and early childhood. Poster presented at the meeting of the International Society for the Study of Behavioral Development, Amsterdam.

Grossman, K. E., & Grossman, K. (1991). Attachment quality as an organizer of emotional and behavioral responses in a longitudinal perspective. In C. M. Parkes, J. Stevenson-Hinde, & P. Marris (Eds.), *Attachment across the life cycle* (pp. 93–114). London: Tavistock/ Routledge.

Grusec, J. E., & Abramovitch, R. (1982). Imitation of peers and adults in a natural setting: A functional analysis. *Child Development, 53,* 636–642.

Grych, J., & Fincham, F. F. (Eds.). (2001). *Interparental conflict and child development: Theory, research, and applications.* New York: Cambridge University Press.

Guerra, N., & Huesmann, R. (2003). A cognitive-ecological model of aggression. *Revue Internationale de Psychologie Sociale, 17,* 177–203.

Guerra, N. G., Eron, L. D., Huesmann, L. R., Tolan, P. H., & Van Acker, R. (1997). A cognitive-ecological approach to the prevention and mitigation of violence and aggression in innercity youth. In D. P. Fry & K. Bjorkqvist (Eds.), *Cultural variation in conflict resolution: Alternatives to violence* (pp. 199–213). Mahwah, NJ: Erlbaum.

Guerra, N. G., Huesmann, L. R., Tolan, P. H., Van Acker, R., & Eron, L. D. (1995). *Correlates of environmental risk for aggression among inner-city children: Implications for preventive interventions.* Unpublished manuscript. University of Illinois at Chicago.

Gunnar, M. (1980). Control, warning signals and distress in infancy. *Developmental Psychology, 16,* 281–289.

Gunnar, M. (1994). Psychoendocrine studies of temperament and stress in early childhood: Expanding current models. In J. Bates & T. Wachs (Eds.), *Temperament: Individual differences at the interface of biology and behavior.* New York: APA Press.

Gunnar, M. (1998). Quality of early care and buffering of neuroendocrine stress reactions: Potential effects on the developing human brain. *Preventive Medicine, 27,* 208–211.

Gunnar, M., Leighton, K., & Peleaux, R. (1984). *The effects of temporal predictability on year-old infants' reactions to potentially frightening toys.* Unpublished manuscript, University of Minnesota, Minneapolis.

Gunnar, M. R. (2000). Early adversity and the development of stress reactivity and regulation. In. C. A. Nelson (Ed.), *The Minnesota symposia on child psychology: Vol. 31. The effects of early adversity on neurobehavioral development* (pp. 163–200). Mahwah, NJ: Lawrence Erlbaum Associates.

Gunnar, M. R., Malone, S. M., Vance, G., & Fisch, R. O. (1985). Coping with aversive stimulation in the neonatal period: Quiet sleep and plasma cortisol levels during recovery from circumcision. *Child Development, 56,* 824–834.

Gustafson, G. E., & Harris, K. L. (1990). Women's responses to young infants' cries. *Developmental Psychology, 26,* 144–152.

Gutin, B., & Manos, T. M. (1993). Physical activity in the prevention of childhood obesity. In C. L. Williams & S. Y. S. Kimm (Eds.), *Prevention and treatment of childhood obesity* (pp. 115–126). Annals of the New York Academy of Sciences, Vol. 699. New York: The New York Academy of Sciences.

Guttentag, R. E. (1995). Mental effort and motivation: Influences on children's memory strategy use. In F. E. Weinert & W. Schneider (Eds.), *Memory performance and competencies: Issues in growth and development* (pp. 207–224). Mahwah, NJ: Erlbaum.

Guyll, M., Spoth, R. L., Chao, W., Wickrama, K. A. S., & Russell, D. (2004). Family-focused risk moderations of substance use trajectories. *Journal of Family Psychology, 18,* 293–201.

Haden, C. A., Ornstein, P. A., Eckerman, C. O., & Didow, S. M. (2001). Mother-child conversational interactions as events unfold: Linkages to subsequent remembering. *Child Development, 72,* 1016–1031.

Hagerman, J. J., & Cronister, A. (1996). *Fragile X syndrome: Diagnosis, treatment and research* (2nd ed.). Baltimore: Johns Hopkins University Press.

Hahn, C., & DiPietro, J. A. (2001). In vitro fertilization and the family: Quality of parenting, family functioning, and child psychosocial adjustment. *Developmental Psychology, 37,* 37–48.

Haight, W., & Miller, P. (1993). *The ecology and development of pretend play.* Albany: State University of New York Press.

Haith, M. M., & Benson, J. (1998). Infant cognition. In W. Damon (Gen. Ed.), D. Kuhn, & R. Siegler (Vol. Eds.), *Handbook of child psychology: Vol. 2. Cognition, perception and language.* New York: Wiley.

Hakuta, K. (1986). *Mirror of language: The debate on bilingualism.* New York: Basic Books.

Halberstadt, A. G., Crisp, V. W., & Eaton, K. L. (1999). Family expressiveness: A retrospective and new directions for research. In P. Philipott, R. S. Feldman, & E. Coats (Eds.), *The social context of nonverbal behavior.* New York: Cambridge University Press.

Halford, G. S. (1990). Is children's reasoning logical or analogical? Further comments on Piagetian cognitive developmental psychology. *Human Development, 33,* 356–361.

Halliday, M. A. K. (1975). *Learning how to mean: Exploration in the development of language.* London: Arnold.

Halpern, D. (2000). *Sex differences in cognitive abilities* (3rd ed.). Mahwah, NJ: Erlbaum.

Halpern, D. F. (2004). A cognitive-process taxonomy for sex differences in cognitive abilities. *Current Directions in Psychological Science, 13,* 135–139.

Halverson, C. F., & Deal, J. E. (2001). Temperamental changes, parenting and the family context. In T. D. Wachs & G. A. Kohnstamm (Eds.), *Temperament in context* (pp. 61–80). Mahwah, NJ: Erlbaum.

Halverson, H. M. (1931). An experimental study of prehension in infants by means of systematic cinema records. *Genetic Psychology Monographs, 10*(2–3), 107–286.

Halverson, L. E., & Williams, K. (1985). Developmental sequences for hopping over distance: A prelongitudinal screening. *Research Quarterly for Exercise and Sport, 56,* 37–44.

Hamer, D. H., Hu, S., Magnuson, V. L., Hu, N., & Pattatucci, A. M. L. (1993). A linkage between DNA markers on the X chromosome and male sexual orientation. *Science, 261,* 311–327.

Hamill, P., Drizd, T. A., Johnson, C. L., Reed, R. B., & Roche, A. F. (1976). HCHS growth charts. *Monthly Vital Statistics Report, 25* (Suppl. HRA), 76–112.

Hammen, C. (1997). *Depression.* Washington, DC: Brunner/Mazel.

Hammen, C. (2002). Context of stress in families with depressed parents. In S. H. Goodman & I. Gotlib (Eds.), *Children of depressed parents* (pp. 175–202). Washington, DC.: American Psychological Association.

Hammen, C., & Rudolph, K. D. (1996). Childhood depression. In E. J. Mash & R. A. Barkley (Eds.), *Child Psychopathology* (pp. 153–195). New York: Guilford Press.

Hamond, N. R., & Fivush, R. (1991). Memories of Mickey Mouse: Young children recount their trip to Disneyworld. *Cognitive Development, 6,* 433–448.

Han, W. (2005). Maternal nonstandard work schedules and child cognitive outcomes. *Child Development, 76,* 137–154.

Hankin, B. L., Abramson, L. Y., Moffit, T. E., Silva, P. A., McGee, R., & Angell, K. E. (1998). Development of depression from preadolescence to adulthood: Emerging gender differences in a 10 year longitudinal study. *Journal of Abnormal Psychology, 107,* 128–140.

Hanna, E., & Meltzoff, A. N. (1993). Peer imitation by toddlers in laboratory, home, and day-care contexts: Implications for social learning and memory. *Developmental Psychology, 29,* 701–710.

Hardman, M. L., Drew, C. J., & Egan, M. W. (2002). *Human exceptionality: Society, school and family* (7th ed.). Newton, MA: Allyn & Bacon.

Harkness, S., & Super, C. (1995). Culture and parenting. In M. Bornstein (Ed.), *Handbook of parenting* (Vol. 2, pp. 211–234). Hillsdale, NJ: Erlbaum.

Harlow, H. F., & Zimmerman, R. R. (1959). Affectional responses in the infant monkey. *Science, 130,* 421–432.

Harris, J. (1995). Where is the child's environment? A group socialization theory of development. *Psychological Review, 102,* 458–489.

Harris, P. L. (1989). *Children and emotion.* New York: Basil Blackwell.

Harris, P. L. (2006). Social cognition. In W. Damon & R. M. Lerner (Series Eds.) and D. Kuhn & R. Siegler (Vol. Eds.), *Handbook of child psychology,* Vol. 2, 6th ed. New York: Wiley.

Harris, P. L., Olthof, T., Meerum Terwogt, M., & Hardman, C. E. (1987). Children's knowledge of the situations that provide emotions. *International Journal of Behavioral Development, 10,* 319–343.

Harrison, L. J., & Ungerer, J. A. (2002). Maternal employment and infant-mother attachment security at 12 months postpartum. *Developmental Psychology, 38,* 758–773.

Hart, B., & Risley, T. R. (1995). *Meaningful differences in the everyday experience of young American children.* Baltimore, MD: Brookes.

Hart, B., & Risley, T. R. (1999). *The social world of children learning to talk.* Baltimore: Paul Brookes.

Hart, D., & Fegley, S. (1995). Prosocial behavior and caring in adolescence: Relations to self-understanding and social judgment. *Child Development, 66,* 1346–1359.

Hart, S., Field, T., DelValle, C., & Letourneau, M. (1998). Infants protest their mothers attending to an infant-size doll, *Social Development, 7,* 54–61.

Harter, S. (1990). Issues in the assessment of the self-concept of children and adolescents. In A. M. LaGrecca (Ed.), *Through the eyes of the child.* Boston: Allyn and Bacon.

Harter, S. (2006). The self. In W. Damon & R. M. Lerner (Series Eds.) & N. Eisenberg (Vol. Ed.), *Handbook of Child Psychology* (6th ed., Vol. 3). New York: Wiley.

Harter, S., & Buddin, B. J. (1987). Children's understanding of the simultaneity of two emotions: A five-stage developmental acquisition sequence. *Developmental Psychology, 23,* 388–399.

Harter, S., Waters, P., & Whitesell, N. R. (1998). Relational self-worth: Differences in perceived worth as a person across interpersonal contexts among adolescents. *Child Development, 69,* 756–766.

Hartshorne, H., & May, M. S. (1928). *Moral studies in the nature of character: Vol. 1. Studies in deceit; Vol. 2. Studies in self-control; Vol. 3. Studies in the organization of character.* New York: Macmillan.

Hartup, W. W. (1989). Social relationships and their developmental significance. *American Psychologist, 44,* 120–126.

Hartup, W. W. (1996). The company they keep: Friendships and their developmental significance. *Child Development, 67,* 1–13.

Hartup, W. W., Laursen, B., Stewart, M. I., & Eastenson, A. (1988). Conflict and the friendship relations of young children. *Child Development, 59,* 1590–1600.

Harwood, L., & Fergusson, D. (1998). Breastfeeding and later cognitive and academic outcomes. *Pediatrics, 101,* 1–7.

Harwood, R., Leyendecker, B., Carlson, V., Asencio, M., & Miller, A. (2002). Parenting among Latino families in the United States. In M. Bornstein (Ed.), *Handbook of parenting* (rev. ed., Vol. 4, pp. 21–46). Mahwah, NJ: Erlbuam.

Harwood, R. L., Miller, J. G., & Irizarry, N. L. (1995). *Culture and attachment: Perceptions of the child in context.* New York: Guilford.

Haslett, B. B. (1997). Basic concepts: Communication, cognition, and language. In B. B. Haslett & W. Samter (Eds.), *Children communicating: The first five years.* Mahwah, NJ: Erlbaum.

Hasselhorn, M. (1992). Task dependency and the role of category typicality and metamemory in the development of an organizational strategy. *Child Development, 63,* 202–214.

Havinghurst, R. F., & Neugarten, B. L. (1955). *American Indian and white children.* Chicago: University of Chicago Press.

Hawkins, J. (1999). Trends in anesthesiology during childbirth. *Anesthesiology, 91,* A1060.

Hawkins, J., Pea, R. D., Glick, J., & Scribner, S. (1984). "Merds that laugh don't like mushrooms": Evidence for deductive reasoning by preschoolers. *Developmental Psychology, 20,* 584–594.

Hawkins, J. D., Graham, J. W., Maguin, E., Abbott, R., Hill, K. G., & Catalane, R. F. (1997). Exploring the effects of age of alcohol use initiation and psychosocial risk factors on subsequent alcohol misuse. *Journal of Studies on Alcohol, 58,* 280–290.

Hawley, P. H. (1999). The ontogenesis of social dominance: A strategy-based evolutionary perspective. *Developmental Review, 19,* 97–132.

Hawley, P. H., & Little, T. D. (1999). On winning some and losing some: A social relations approach to social dominance in toddlers. *Merrill-Palmer Quarterly, 45,* 188–214.

Hay, D. F. (1994). Prosocial development. *Journal of Child Psychology & Psychiatry & Allied Disciplines, 35,* 29–71.

Hay, D. F., & Rheingold, H. L. (1983). *The early appearance of some valued social behaviors.* Unpublished manuscript, State University of New York at Stony Brook.

Hay, D. F., & Ross, H. S. (1982). The social nature of early conflict. *Child Development, 53,* 105–113.

Hayden, L., Turulli, D., & Hymel, S. (1988, May). Children talk about loneliness. Paper presented at the biennial meeting of the University of Waterloo Conference on Child Development, Waterloo, Ontario, Canada.

Hayes, A., & Batshaw, M. L. (1993). Down Syndrome. *Pediatric Clinics of North America, 40,* 523–535.

Hayes, D. S., Chemelski, B. E., & Birnbaum, D. W. (1981). Young children's incidental and intentional retention of televised events. *Developmental Psychology, 17,* 230–232.

Hayne, H., McDonald, S., & Barr, R. (1997). Developmental changes in the specificity of memory over the second year of life. *Infant Behavior and Development, 20,* 233–245.

Healy, B. (1995). *A new perspective for women's health.* New York: Viking.

Heath, S. B. (1998). Working through language. In S. M. Hoyle & C. Temple Adger (Eds.), *Kids' talk: Strategic language use in later childhood* (pp. 217–240). Oxford: Oxford University Press.

Hebert, T. P. (2000). Gifted males pursuing careers in elementary education: Factors that influence a belief in self. *Journal for the Education of the Gifted, 24,* 7–45.

Heckhausen, J., & Dweck, C. S. (Eds.). (1998). Motivation and self-regulation across the life span. New York: Cambridge University Press.

Hecox, K., & Deegan, D. M. (1985). Methodological issues in the study of auditory development. In G. Gottlieb & N. A. Krasnegor (Eds.), *Measurement of audition and vision in the first year of postnatal life: A methodological overview.* Norwood, NJ: Ablex.

Heintz-Knowles, K. E. (2001). Balancing acts: Work-family issues on prime-time T.V. In J. Bryant & J. A. Bryant (Eds.), *Television and the American Family* (2nd ed., pp. 177–206). Mahwah, NJ: Erlbaum.

Helm, P., & Grolund, J. (1998). A halt in the secular trend toward earlier menarche in Denmark. *Acta Obstetrics and Gynecology Scandinavia, 77,* 198–200.

Helwig, C. C. (1995). Adolescents' and young adults' conceptions of civil liberties: Freedom of speech and religion. *Child Development, 66,* 152–166.

Helwig, C. C. (2003). Culture and the construction of concepts of personal autonomy and democratic decision making. In J. E. Jacobs & P. A. Klaczynski (Eds.) *The development of judgment and decision making in children and adolescents.* Mahwah, NJ: Erlbaum.

Helwig, C. C., & Jasiobedzka, U. (2001). The relation between law and morality: Children's reasoning about socially beneficial and unjust laws. *Child Development, 72,* 1382–1393.

Helwig, C. C., Zelazo, P. D., & Wilson, M. (2001). Children's judgments of psychological harm in normal and noncanonical situations. *Child Development, 72,* 66–81.

Hembree, S. E., & Vandell, D. (2000). *Reciprocity in rejection: The mutual role of antipathy and children's adjustment.* Unpublished manuscript, University of Wisconsin, Madison.

Hendrick, J., & Stange, T. (1991). Do actions speak louder than words? An effect of the functional use of language on dominant sex role behavior in boys and girls. *Early Childhood Research Quarterly, 6,* 565–576.

Henggeler, S. W., Melton, G. B., & Smith, L. A. (1992). Multisystemic treatment of serious juvenile offenders: An effective alternative to incarceration. *Journal of Consulting and Clinical Psychology, 60,* 229–241.

Henig, R. M. (2004). *Pandora's baby: How the first test tube baby sparked the reproductive revolution.* New York: Ecco.

Henker, B., & Whalen, C. K. (1999). The child with attention deficit/hyperactivity disorder in school and peer settings. In H. C. Quay & A. E. Hogan (Eds.). *Handbook of disruptive behavior disorders* (157–178). New York: Plenum.

Hepper, P. (1992). Fetal psychology: An embryonic science. In J. Niijhuis (Ed.), *Fetal behavior: Developmental and perinatal aspects* (pp. 129–156). New York: Oxford University Press.

Herbert, J., & Hayne, H. (2000). Memory retrieval by 18- to 30-month olds: Age-related changes in representational flexibility. *Developmental Psychology, 36,* 473–484.

Herman, L. M., & Uyeyama, R. K. (1999). The dolphin's grammatical competency: Comments on Kako. *Animal Learning & Behavior, 27,* 18–23.

Herman-Giddens, M. E., Slora, E. J., Wasserman, A. C., Bourdony, C. J., Bhapkar, M. V., Koch, G. G., & Hasemeie, C. M. (1997). Secondary sexual characteristics and menses in young girls seen in office practice: A study from the pediatric research in office settings network. *Pediatrics, 99,* 505–512.

Herrera, N. C., Zajonc, R. B., Wieczorkowska, G., & Cichomski, B. (2003). Beliefs about birth rank and their reflection in reality. *Journal of Personality and Social Psychology, 85,* 142–150.

Herrnstein, R. (1971). I. Q. *Atlantic, 228,* 44–64.

Herrnstein, R., & Murray, C. (1994). *The bell curve: Intelligence and class structure in American life.* New York: Basic Books.

Hershberger, S. L., & D'Augelli, A. R. (1995). The impact of victimization on the mental health and suicidality of lesbian, gay, and bisexual youths. *Developmental Psychology, 31,* 65–74.

Hespos, S. J., & Baillargeon, R. (2001). Infants' knowledge about occlusion and containment events: A surprising discrepancy. *Psychological Science, 12,* 140–147.

Hess, R. D., & Shipman, V. (1967). Cognitive elements in maternal behavior. In J. Hill (Ed.), *Minnesota symposia on child psychology* (pp. 57–81). Minneapolis: University of Minnesota Press.

Hesse, E. (1999). The adult attachment interview: Historical and current perspectives. In J. Cassidy & P. Shaver (Eds.), *Handbook of attachment* (pp. 395–433). New York: Guilford.

Heth, C. D., & Cornell, E. H. (1980). Three experiences affecting spatial discrimination learning by ambulatory children. *Journal of Experimental Child Psychology, 30,* 246–264.

Hetherington, E. M. (1966). Effects of paternal absence on sex-typed behaviors in Negro and white preadolescent males. *Journal of Personality and Social Psychology, 4,* 87–91.

Hetherington, E. M. (1967). The effects of familial variables on sex typing, on parent-child similarity and on imitation in children. In J. P. Hill (Ed.), *Minnesota symposia on child psychology* (Vol. 1, pp. 82–107). Minneapolis: University of Minnesota Press.

Hetherington, E. M. (1987). *Long-term impact of divorce on children's marital stability.* Unpublished manuscript, University of Virginia, Charlottesville.

Hetherington, E. M. (1989). Coping with family transitions: Winners, losers and survivors. *Child Development, 60,* 1–14.

Hetherington, E. M. (1991a). Families, lies and videotapes. *Journal of Adolescent Research, 1*(4), 323–348.

Hetherington, E. M. (1991b). The role of individual differences and family relationships in children's coping with divorce and remarriage. In P. A. Cowan & E. M. Hetherington (Eds.), *Family transitions* (pp. 165–194). Hillsdale, NJ: Erlbaum.

Hetherington, E. M. (1993). An overview of the Virginia longitudinal study of divorce and remarriage with a focus on early adolescence. *Journal of Family Psychology, 7,* 39–56.

Hetherington, E. M. (1998). Social capital and the development of youth from nondivorced, divorced, and remarried families. In A. Collins (Ed.), *Relationships as developmental contexts: The 29th Minnesota symposium on child psychology.* Hillsdale, NJ: Erlbaum.

Hetherington, E. M., Bridges, M., & Insabella, G. M. (1998). Five perspectives on the association between divorce and remarriage and children's adjustment. *American Psychologist, 53,* 167–184.

Hetherington, E. M., & Clingempeel, W. G. (1992). Coping with marital transitions: A family systems perspective. *Monographs of the Society for Research in Child Development, 57* (2, 3, Serial No. 227).

Hetherington, E. M., Cox, M., & Cox, R. (1979). Play and social interaction in children following divorce. *Journal of Social Issues, 35,* 26–49.

Hetherington, E. M., & Kelly, J. (2002). *For better or for worse.* New York: Norton.

Hetherington, E. M., & Morris, W. N. (1978). The family and primary groups. In W. H. Holtzman (Ed.), *Introductory psychology in depth: Developmental topics.* New York: Harper & Row.

Hetherington, E. M., & Stanley-Hagan, M. (2002). Parenting in divorced, single-parent, and stepfamilies. In M. H. Bornstein (Ed.), *Handbook of parenting* (2nd ed.). Mahwah, NJ: Erlbaum.

Hewlett, B. S., Lamb, M. E., Slanner, D., Leyendecker, B., & Scholmerich, A. (1998). Culture and early infancy among central African foragers and farmers. *Developmental Psychology, 34,* 653–661.

Higgins, A. T., & Turnure, J. E. (1984). Distractibility and concentration of attention in children's development. *Child Development, 55,* 1799–1810.

Hinde, R. A. (1994). Developmental psychology in the context of the other behavioral sciences. In R. D. Parke, P. Ornstein, J. Reisen, & C. Zahn-Waxler (Eds.), *A century of developmental psychology.* Washington, DC: American Psychological Association.

Hindley, C. B., Filliozat, A. M., Klackenberg, G., Nicolet-Neister, D., & Sand, E. A. (1966). Differences in age of walking for five European longitudinal samples. *Human Biology, 38,* 264–379.

Hines, M., & Kaufman, F. R. (1994). Androgen and the development of human sex-typical behavior: Rough-and-tumble play and sex of preferred playmates in children with congenital adrenal hyperplasia (CAH). *Child Development, 65,* 1042–1053.

Hirsch, J., & Kim, K. (1997). New views of early language. *Nature, 103,* 1141–1143.

Hirsch-Pasek, K., & Golinkoff, R. (2003). *Einstein never used flash cards: How our children really learn and why they need to play more and memorize less.* Rodale Publishers.

Hitch, G. J., & Towse, J. N. (1995). Working memory: What develops? In F. E. Weinert & W. Schneider (Eds.), *Memory performance and competencies: Issues in growth and development* (pp. 3–21). Mahwah, NJ: Erlbaum.

Hodapp, R. (2002). Parenting children with Down syndrome and other types of mental retardation. In M. Bornstein (Ed.), *Handbook of parenting* (2nd ed.). Mahwah, NJ: Erlbaum.

Hodges, E. V. E., Boivin, M., Vitaro, F., & Bukowski, W. M. (1999). The power of friendship: Protection against an escalating cycle of peer victimization. *Developmental Psychology, 35,* 94–101.

Hodges, E. V. E., Malone, M. J., & Perry, D. G. (1997). Individual risk and social risk as interacting determinants of victimization in the peer group. *Developmental Psychology, 33,* 1032–1039.

Hodges, E. V. E., & Perry D. G. (1999). Personal and interpersonal antecedents and consequences of victimization by peers. *Journal of Personality and Social Policy, 76,* 677–685.

Hoff, E. (2001). *Language development* (2nd ed.). Belmont, CA: Wadsworth/Thomson.

Hoff, E., Laursen, B., & Tardif, T. (2002). Socioeconomic status and parenting. In M. Bornstein (Ed.), *Handbook of parenting* (2nd ed., pp. 231–252). Mahwah, NJ: Erlbaum.

Hoff-Ginsberg, E., & Shatz, M. (1982). Linguistic input and the child's acquisition of language. *Psychological Bulletin, 92,* 3–26.

Hoffman, L. W. (1977). Changes in family roles, socialization and sex differences. *American Psychologist, 32,* 644–657.

Hoffman, L. W. (1991). The influence of the family environment on personality: Accounting for sibling differences. *Psychological Bulletin, 110,* 187–203.

Hoffman, L. W. (2000). Maternal employment: Effects of social context. In R. D. Taylor & M. C. Wang (Eds.), *Resilience across contexts: Family, work, culture and community* (pp. 147–176). Mahwah, NJ: Erlbaum.

Hoffman, L. W., & Youngblade, L. M. (1999). *Mothers at work: Effects on children's well-being.* New York: Cambridge University Press.

Hoffman, M. L. (1981). Is altruism part of human nature? *Journal of Personality and Social Psychology, 40,* 121–137.

Hoffman, M. L. (1984). Empathy, its limitations, and its role in a comprehensive moral theory. In W. M. Kurtines & J. L. Gewirtz (Eds.), *Morality, moral behavior and moral development.* New York: Wiley.

Hoffman, M. L. (2000). *Empathy and moral development. Implications for caring and justice.* Cambridge, UK: Cambridge University Press.

Hofsten, C. von, & Rönnqvist, L. (1993). The structuring of neonatal arm movement. *Child Development, 64,* 1046–1057.

Hogan, D., & Msall, M. E. (2002). Family structure and resources and the parenting of children with disabilities and functional limitations. In J. G. Borkowski, S. L. Ramey, & M. Bristol-Power (Eds.), *Parenting and the child's world* (pp. 311–328). Mahwah, NJ: Erlbaum.

Hohne, E. A., & Jusczyk, P. W. (1994). Two-month old infants sensitivity to allophonic differences. *Perception and Psychophysics, 56,* 613–623.

Holden, G. W. (1988). Adults' thinking about a child-rearing problem: Effects of experience, parental status and gender. *Child Development, 59,* 1623–1632.

Holden, G. W. (1997). *Parents and the dynamics of child rearing.* Boulder, CO: Westview Press.

Holditch-Davis, D. (1990). The development of sleeping and waking states in high-risk preterm infants. *Infant Behavior and Development, 13,* 513–531.

Hollich, G. J., Hirsh-Pasek, K., & Golinkoff, R. M. (2000). Breaking the language barrier: An emergentist coalition model for the origins of word learning. *Monographs of the Society for Research in Child Development, Vol. 65* (3), Serial No. 262.

Holt, S. A., Fogel, A., & Wood, R. W. (1998). Innovation in social games. In M. D. P. deLyra & J. Valsiner (Eds.), *Construction of psychological processes in interpersonal communication* (vol. 4, pp. 787–823). Norwood, NJ: Ablex.

Holyoak, K. J., Junn, E. N., & Billman, D. O. (1984). Development of analogical problem-solving skills. *Child Development, 55,* 2042–2055.

Honzik, M. (1983). Measuring mental abilities in infancy: The value and limitations. In M. Lewis (Ed.), *Origins of intelligence: Infancy and early childhood* (2nd ed.) (pp. 67–105). New York: Plenum.

Honzik, M. P. (1976). Value and limitations of infant tests: An overview. In M. Lewis (Ed.), *Origins of intelligence.* New York: Plenum.

Honzik, M. P., Macfarlane, J. W., & Allen, L. (1948). The stability of mental test performance between two and eighteen years. *Journal of Experimental Education, 17,* 309–324.

Hopkins, B. (1991). Facilitating early motor development: An intracultural study of West Indian mothers and their infants living in Britain. In J. K. Nugent, B. M. Lester, & T. B. Brazelton (Eds.), *The cultural context of infancy: Vol. 2. Multicultural and interdisciplinary approaches to parent-infant relations* (pp. 93–143). Norwood, NJ: Ablex.

Hopkins, B., & Westra, T. (1988). Maternal handling and motor development: An intracultural study. *Genetic Psychology Monographs, 14,* 377–420.

Hopkins, B., & Westra, T. (1990). Motor development, maternal expectations, and the role of handling. *Infant Behavior and Development, 13,* 117–122.

Hoppu, U., Kalliomaki, M., Laiho, K., & Isolauri, E. (2001). Breast milk—immunomodulatory signals against allergenic disease. *Allergy, 56,* 23–26.

Hops, H. (2001). Intergenerational transmission of depressive symptoms: Gender and developmental considerations. In C. Mundt, M. Goldstein, K. Hahlweg & P. Fiedler (Eds.), *Proceedings of the symposium of interpersonal factors in the origin and course of affective disorders.* London: Royal College of Psychiatrists.

Hossain, Z., Field, T., Gonzalez, J., Malphurs, J., De Valle, C., & Pickens, J. (1994). Infants of depressed mothers interact better with their non-depressed fathers. *Infant Mental Health Journal, 15,* 348–357.

Howe, N., & Ross, H. S. (1990). Socialization perspective taking and the sibling relationship. *Developmental Psychology, 26,* 160–165.

Howe, P. E., & Schiller, M. (1952). Growth responses of the school child to changes in diet and environment factors. *Journal of Applied Physiology, 5,* 51–61.

Howes, C. (1987). Social competence with peers in young children. Developmental sequences. *Developmental Review, 7,* 252–272.

Howes, C. (1996). The earliest friendships. In W. M. Bukowski, A. F. Newcomb, & W. W. Hartup (Eds.), *The company they keep: Friendship in childhood and adolescence* (pp. 66–86). New York: Cambridge University Press.

Howes, C. (1999). Attachment relationships in the context of multiple caregivers. In J. Cassidy & P. R. Shaver (Eds.), *Handbook of attachment: Theory, research, and clinical applications* (pp. 671–687). New York: Guilford.

Hsu, L. Y. F. (1998). Prenatal diagnosis of chromosomal abnormalities through amniocentesis. In A. Milunsky (Ed.), *Genetic disorders and the fetus* (4th ed.). Baltimore: Johns Hopkins University Press.

Hubbard, F. O. A., & van IJzendoorn, M. H. (1991). Maternal unresponsiveness and infant crying across the first 9 months: A naturalistic longitudinal study. *Infant Behavior and Development, 14,* 299–312.

Hudley, C., & Graham, S. (1993). An attributional intervention to reduce peer-directed aggression among African-American boys. *Child Development, 64,* 124–138.

Hudson, J. A. (1990). The emergence of autobiographical memory in mother-child conversation. In R. Fivush & J. A. Hudson (Eds.), *Knowing and remembering in young children* (pp. 166–196). Cambridge, UK: Cambridge University Press.

Huesmann, L. R., Eron, L. D., Lefkowitz, M. M., & Walder, L. O. (1984). The stability of aggression over time and generations. *Developmental Psychology, 20,* 1120–1134.

Huesmann, L. R., & Guerra, N. G. (1997). Children's normative beliefs about aggression and aggressive behavior. *Journal of Personality and Social Psychology, 72,* 408–419.

Huesmann, L. R., & Miller, L. S. (1994). Long-term effects of repeated exposure to media violence in childhood. In L. R. Huesmann (Ed.), *Aggressive behavior: Current perspectives* (pp. 153–186). New York: Plenum Press.

Hughes, C., & Dunn, J. (1998). Understanding mind and emotional understanding: Longitudinal associations with mental-state talk between friends. *Developmental Psychology, 34,* 1026–1037.

Hughes, M. (1975). Egocentrism in pre-school children. The University of Edinburgh: Unpublished doctoral dissertation. Edinburgh, Scotland.

Humphrey, M. M. (1982). Children's avoidance of environmental, simple task internal, and complex task internal distractors. *Child Development, 53,* 736–745.

Hunt, C. E. (2001). Sudden infant death syndrome and other causes of infant mortality: Diagnosis, mechanisms and risk of recurrence

for siblings. *American Journal of Respiratory and Critical Care Medicine, 164,* 346–357.

Huston, A. C., McLloyd, V., & Garcia-Coll, C. (1994). Children and poverty: Issues in contemporary research. *Child Development, 65,* 275–282.

Huston, A. C., & Wright, J. C. (1998). Mass media and children's development. In W. Damon (Gen. Ed.), I. E. Sigel, & K. A. Renninger (Vol. Eds.), *Handbook of child psychology: Vol. 4. Child psychology in practice* (pp. 999–1058). New York: Wiley.

Hutchins, E. (1980). *Culture and inference: A Trobriand case study.* Cambridge, MA: Harvard University Press.

Hutchins, E. (1996). *Cognition in the wild.* Cambridge, MA: MIT Press.

Huttenlocher, J. (1974). The origins of language comprehension. In R. L. Solso (Ed.), *Theories in cognitive psychology.* Hillsdale, NJ: Erlbaum.

Huttenlocher, J., Haight, W., Bryk, A., Seltzer, M., & Lyons, T. (1991). Early vocabulary growth: Relation to language impact and gender. *Developmental Psychology, 27,* 236–248.

Huttenlocher, J., & Lui, F. (1979). The semantic organization of some simple nouns and verbs. *Journal of Verbal Learning and Verbal Behavior, 18,* 141–162.

Huttenlocher, J., & Smiley, P. (1987). Early word meanings: The case of object names. *Cognitive Psychology, 19,* 63–89.

Huttenlocher, J., Smiley, P., & Charney, R. (1987). Emergence of action categories in the child: Evidence from verb meanings. *Psychological Review, 90,* 72–93.

Huttenlocher, P. R. (1994). Synaptogenesis, synapse elimination, and neural plasticity in human cerebral cortex. In C. A. Nelson (Ed.), *Threats to optimal development. The Minnesota symposia on child psychology* (Vol. 27, pp. 35–54). Hillsdale, NJ: Erlbaum.

Huttenlocher, P. R., & Dabholkar, A. J. (1997). Regional differences in synaptogenesis in the human cerebral cortex. *Journal of Comparative Neurology, 387,* 167–178.

Hutton, N. (1996). Health prospects for children born to HIV-infected women. In R. R. Faden & N. E. Kass (Eds.), *HIV, AIDS, and childbearing* (pp. 63–77). New York: Oxford University Press.

Hwang, C. P. (1986). Behavior of Swedish primary and secondary

caretaking fathers in relation to mothers' presence. *Developmental Psychology, 22,* 749–751.

Hyde, J. S., Fennema, E., & Lamon, S. J. (1990). Gender differences in mathematics performance: A meta-analysis. *Psychological Bulletin, 107,* 139–155.

Hyde, J. S., Krajnik, M., & Skuldt-Neiderberger, K. (1991). Androgyny across the life span: A replication and longitudinal follow-up. *Developmental Psychology, 27,* 516–519.

Hyde, J. S., & Linn, M. C. (1988). Gender differences in verbal ability: A meta-analysis. *Psychological Bulletin, 104,* 53–69.

Hyde, J. S., & Plant, E. A. (1995). Magnitude of psychological gender differences. *American Psychologist, 50,* 159–161.

Hymel, S. (1986). Interpretations of peer behavior: Affective bias in childhood and adolescence. *Child Development, 57,* 431–445.

Hymel, S., Wagner, E., & Butler, L. (1990). Reputational bias: View from the peer group. In S. R. Asher & J. D. Coie (Eds.), *Peer rejection in childhood.* New York: Cambridge University Press.

Hymes, D. H. (1972). Models of the interaction of language and social life. In J. Gumprez & D. Hymes (Eds.), *Directions in sociolinguistics: The ethnography of communication* (pp. 35–71). New York: Holt, Rinehart & Winston.

Ikonomov, O. G., Stoynev, A. G., & Shisheva, A. C. (1998). Integrative coordination of circadian mammalian diversity: Neuronal networks and peripheral clocks. *Progress in Neurobiology, 54,* 87–97.

Ingersoll, E. W., & Thoman, E. B. (1999). Sleep/wake states of preterm infants: Stability, developmental change, diurnal variation, and relation with caregiving activity. *Child Development, 70,* 1–10.

Ingram, D. (1989). *First language acquisition.* New York: Cambridge University Press.

Inhelder, B., & Piaget, J. (1958). *The growth of logical thinking from childhood to adolescence.* New York: Basic Books.

Inoff-Germain, G., Arnold, G. S., Nottleman, E. D., Susman, E. J., Cutler, G. B., & Chrousos, G. P. (1988). Relations between hormone levels and observational measures of aggressive behavior of young adolescents in family interactions. *Developmental Psychology, 24,* 129–139.

Institute of Medicine. (1999). *Reducing the odds.* Washington,

DC: National Academy of Sciences Press.

Institute of Medicine. (2004). *Ethical conduct of clinical research involving children.* Washington, DC: The National Academic Press.

International Human Genome Sequencing Consortium (2004). Finishing the euchromatic sequencing of the human genome. *Nature, 431,* 931–945.

Isabella, R. (1993). Origins of attachment: Maternal interactive behavior across the first year. *Child Development, 64,* 605–621.

Israel, A. C. (1988). Parental and family influences in the etiology and treatment of childhood obesity. In N. A. Krasnegor, G. D. Grave, & N. Kretchmer (Eds.), *Childhood obesity: A behavioral perspective.* Caldwell, NJ: Telford Press.

Izard, C. E. (1994). Innate and universal facial expressions: Evidence from developmental and cross-cultural research. *Psychological Bulletin, 115,* 288–299.

Izard, C. E., Fantauzzo, C. A., Castle, J. M., Haynes, O. M., & Slomine, B. S. (1995). *The morphological stability and social validity of infants' facial expressions.* Unpublished manuscript, University of Delaware.

Izard, C. E., Hembree, E., & Huebner, R. (1987). Infants' emotional expressions to acute pain: Developmental changes and stability of individual differences. *Developmental Psychology, 23,* 105–113.

Jacklin, C. N., Wilcox, K. T., & Maccoby, E. E. (1988). Neonatal sex steroid hormones and intellectual abilities of six-year-old boys and girls. *Developmental Psychobiology, 21,* 567–574.

Jacob, T., & Johnson, S. L. (1997). Parent-child interaction among depressed fathers and mothers: Impact on child functioning. *Journal of Family Psychology, 11,* 391–409.

Jacobs, B. L. (2004). Depression: The brain finally gets into the act. *Current Directions in Psychological Science, 13,* 103–106.

Jacobs, P. A. (1991). The fragile X syndrome. *Journal of Human Genetics, 28,* 809–810.

Jacobsen, T., & Hofmann, V. (1997). Children's attachment representations: Longitudinal relations to school behavior and academic competency in middle childhood and adolescence. *Developmental Psychology, 33,* 703–710.

Jacobson, J. L., & Jacobson, S. W. (1996). Prospective longitudinal assessment of developmental neurotoxicity. *Environmental Health Perspectives, 104,* 275–283.

Jacobson, J. L., Jacobson, S. W., Padgett, R. J., Brumitt, G. A., & Billings, R. L. (1992). Effects of prenatal PCB exposure on cognitive processing efficiency and sustained attention. *Developmental Psychology, 28,* 297–306.

Jaffe, S., & Hyde, J. (2000). Gender differences in moral orientation: A meta-analysis. *Psychological Bulletin, 126,* 703–726.

Jahoda, G. (1980). Theoretical and systematic approaches in cross-cultural psychology. In H. C. Triandis & W. W. Lambert (Eds.), *Handbook of cross-cultural psychology, Vol. 1, Perspectives* (pp. 69–142). Boston: Allyn & Bacon.

Jakobson, R. (1968). *Child language, aphasic, and phonological universals.* The Hague: Mouton.

Jeffrey, R. W. (2001). Public health strategies for obesity treatment and prevention. *American Journal of Health Behavior, 25,* 252–259.

Jellinek, M. B., & Snyder, J. B. (1998). Depression and suicide in children and adolescents. *Pediatric Review, 19,* 255–264.

Jensen, A. R. (1969). How much can we boost IQ and scholastic achievement? *Harvard Educational Review, 39,* 1–123.

Jensen, A. R. (1973). *Genetics, educability, and subpopulation differences.* London: Methuen.

Jensen, A. R. (1993). Test validity: "g" versus "tacit knowledge." *Current Directions in Psychological Science, 2,* 9–109.

Jensen, P. S., Hinshaw, S. P., Swanson, J. M., Greenhill, L. L., Conners, C. K., & Arnold, L. E. et al. (2001). Findings from the NIMH multi-modal treatment study of ADHD (MTA): Implications and applications for primary care providers. *Journal of Developmental and Behavioral Pediatrics, 22,* 60–73.

Jessor, R. (1992). Risk behavior in adolescence: A psychosocial framework for understanding and action. *Developmental Review, 12,* 374–390.

Johnson, J. S., & Newport, E. L. (1989). Critical period effects in second language learning: The influence of maturational state on the acquisition of English as a second language. *Cognitive Psychology, 21,* 60–99.

Johnson, M., Beebe, L., Mortimer, J., & Snyder, M. (1998). Volunteerism in adolescence: A process perspective. *Journal of Research on Adolescence, 8,* 309–330.

Johnson, M. H. (1997). *Developmental cognitive neuroscience.* Oxford, England: Blackwell.

Johnson, M. H. (1998). The neural basis of cognitive development. In W. Damon (Series Ed.) and D. Kuhn & R. S. Siegler (Vol. Eds.), *Handbook of child psychology* (Vol. 2, pp. 1–49). New York: Wiley.

Johnson, M. H. (2000). Functional brain development in infants: Effects of an interactive specialization network. *Child Development, 71,* 75–81.

Johnson, S. P., Bremner, J. G., Slater, A., Mason, U., Foster, K., & Cheshire, A. (2003). Infants' perception of object trajectories. *Child Development, 74,* 94–108.

Johnson, W., Bouchard, T. J., Krueger, R. F., McGue, M., & Gottesman, I. I. (2004). Just one g: Consistent results from three test batteries. *Intelligence, 32,* 95–107.

Johnson, W., Emde, R. N., Pannabecker, B., Stenberg, C., & Davis, M. (1982). Maternal perception of infant emotion from birth through 18 months. *Infant Behavior and Development, 5,* 313–322.

Johnston, J., & Ettema, J. S. (1982). *Positive images: Breaking stereotypes with children's television.* Beverly Hills, CA: Sage.

Johnston, L. D., O'Malley, P. M., & Bachman, J. G. (1997). National Survey Results on drug use from the Monitoring the Future study, 1975–1995. Rockville, MD: National Institutes of Health.

Jones, D. C. (1985). Persuasive appeals and responses to appeals among friends and acquaintances. *Child Development, 56,* 757–763.

Jones, G., Riley, M., & Dwyer, T. (2000). Breastfeeding early in life and bone mass in prepubertal children: A longitudinal study. *Osteoporosis International, 11,* 146–152.

Jones, M. C., & Bayley, N. (1950). Physical maturing among boys as related to behavior. *Journal of Educational Psychology, 41,* 129–148.

Jones, T. A., & Greenough, W. T. (1996). Ultrastructural evidence for increased contact between astrocytes and synapses in rats reared in a complex environment. *Neurobiology of Learning and Memory, 65,* 48–56.

Jourdan, C. (1991). Pidgins and creoles: The blurring of categories. *Annual Review of Anthropology, 20,* 187–209.

Joyner, K., & Udry, J. R. (2000). You don't bring me anything but down: Adolescent romance and depression. *Journal of Health and Social Behavior, 41,* 369–391.

Jusczyk, P., Houston, D. M., & Newsome, M. (1999). The beginnings of word segmentation in English-learning infants. *Cognitive Psychology, 39* (3–4), 159–207.

Jusczyk, P. W., Friederici, A. D., Wessels, J., Svenkerud, V. Y., and Jusczyk, A. M. (1993). Infants' sensitivity to the sound patterns of native language words. *Journal of Memory & Language, 32,* 402–420.

Jusczyk, P. W., Rosner, B. S., Cutting, J. E., Foard, F., & Smith, L. B. (1977). Categorical perception of non-speech sounds by two-month-old infants. *Perception and Psychophysics, 21,* 50–54.

Juvonen, J., Graham, S., & Schuster, M. A. (2003). Bullying among young adolescents: The strong, the weak, and the troubled. *Pediatrics, 112,* 1231–1237.

Kagan, J. (1969). Inadequate evidence and illogical conclusions. *Harvard Educational Review, 39,* 274–277.

Kagan, J. (1994). *Galen's prophecy.* New York: Basic Books.

Kagan, J. (1998). Biology and the child. In W. Damon (Series Ed.) & N. Eisenberg (Vol. Ed.), *Handbook of child psychology: Vol. 3* (pp. 177–235). New York: Wiley.

Kagan, J., Kearsley, R. B., & Zelazo, P. R. (1978). *Infancy: Its place in human development.* Cambridge, MA: Harvard University Press.

Kagan, J., & Moss, H. A. (1962). *Birth to maturity: A study in psychological development.* New York: Wiley.

Kagan, J., & Zentner, M. (1996). Early childhood predictors of adult psychopathology. *Harvard Review of Psychiatry, 3,* 341–350.

Kahen, V., Katz, L. F., & Gottman, J. M. (1994). Linkages between parent-child interaction and conversations of friends. From family to peer group: Relations between relationships. *Social Development, 3,* 238–254.

Kahn, P. H. (1997). Bayous and jungle rivers: Cross-cultural perspectives on children's environmental moral reasoning. In H. D. Saltzstein (Ed.), *Culture as a context for moral development* (pp. 23–37). San Francisco: Jossey-Bass.

Kail, R. (1991). Development of processing speed in childhood and adolescence. In H. W. Reese (Ed.), *Advances in child development and behavior* (Vol. 23). San Diego: Academic.

Kail, R. (1995). Processing speed, memory, and cognition. In F. E. Weinert & W. Schneider (Eds.), *Memory performance and competencies: Issues in growth and development* (pp. 71–88). Mahwah, NJ: Erlbaum.

Kail, R. (2000). Speed of information processing: Developmental change and links to intelligence. *Journal of School Psychology, 38,* 51–61.

Kail, R., & Park, Y. (1994). Processing time, articulation time, and memory span. *Journal of Experimental Child Psychology, 57,* 281–291.

Kako, E. (1999). Elements of syntax in the systems of three language-trained animals. *Animal Learning and Behavior, 27,* 1–15.

Kamins, M. L., & Dweck, C. (1999). Person-versus-process praise and criticism: Implications for contingent self-worth and coping. *Developmental Psychology, 35,* 835–847.

Kandel, D. (1973). Adolescent marijuana use: Role of parents and peers. *Science, 181,* 1067–1070.

Kandel, E. R., Schwartz, J. H., & Jessell, T. M. (2000). *Principles of neuroscience* (4th ed.). New York: McGraw-Hill.

Kanner, L. (1943). Autistic disturbances of affective contact. *Nervous Child, 2,* 217–250.

Kanner, L. (1973). How far can autistic children go in matters of social adaptation? In L. Kanner (Ed.), *Childhood psychosis: Initial studies and new insights.* Washington, DC: Winston.

Kanner, L. (1992). Follow-up study of 11 autistic children originally reported from 1943. *Focus on Autistic Behavior, 7*(5), 1–11.

Karass, J., & Braungart-Rieker, J. M. (2004). Infant negative emotionality and attachment: Implications for preschool intelligence. *International Journal of Behavioral Development, 28,* 221–229.

Katchadourian, H. (1977). *The biology of adolescence.* San Francisco: Freeman.

Katz, L. F., & Gottman, J. M. (1993). Patterns of marital conflict predict children's internalizing and externalizing behaviors. *Developmental Psychology, 29,* 940–950.

Katz, L. F., & Gottman, J. M. (1996). Spillover effects of marital conflict: In search of parenting and co-parenting mechanisms. In J. P. McHale & P. A. Cowan (Eds.), *Understanding how family-level dynamics affect children's development: Studies of two-parent families* (pp. 57–76). San Francisco: Jossey-Bass.

Katz, L. F., & Gottman, J. M. (1997). Buffering children from marital conflict and dissolution. *Journal of Clinical Child Psychology, 26,* 157–171.

Katz, L. F., Kramer, L., & Gottman, J. M. (1992). Conflict and emotions in marital, sibling, and peer relationships. In C. U. Shantz & W. W. Hartup (Eds.), *Conflict in child and adolescent development* (pp. 122–149). Cambridge, England: Cambridge University Press.

Kauffman, J. (2001). *Characteristics of emotional and behavioral disorders of children and youth* (7th ed.). Columbus, OH: Merrill/Prentice Hall.

Kaufman, A. S., & Kaufman, N. L. (1983). *Kaufman assessment battery for children: Interpretive manual*. Circle Pines, MN: American Guidance Service.

Kaye, K. L., & Bower, T. G. R. (1994). Learning and intermodal transfer of information in newborns. *Psychological Science, 5*, 286–288.

Keating, D. P. (1990). Adolescent thinking. In J. Adelson (Ed.), *Handbook of adolescent psychology*. New York: Wiley.

Kee, D. W. (1994). Developmental differences in associative memory: Strategy use, mental effort, and knowledge-access interaction. In H. W. Reese (Ed.), *Advances in child development and behavior* (Vol. 25, pp. 7–32). New York: Academic Press.

Keefer, C. H., Dixon, S., Tronick, E. Z., & Brazelton, T. B. (1991). Cultural mediation between newborn behavior and later development: Implications for methodology in cross-cultural research. In J. K. Nugent, B. M. Lester, & T. B. Brazelton (Eds.), *The cultural context of infancy: Vol. 2. Multicultural and interdisciplinary approaches to parent-infant relations* (pp. 39–61). Norwood, NJ: Ablex.

Keegan, R. T. (1996, Summer). Creativity from childhood to adulthood: A difference of degree and not of kind. In M. A. Runco (Ed.), *Creativity from childhood through adulthood: The developmental issues* [Special issue]. *New Directions for Child Development*, No. 72, 57–66.

Keen, R. (2003). Representation of objects and events: Why do infants look so smart and toddlers look so dumb? *Current Directions in Psychological Science, 12*, 79–83.

Keenan, K., Loeber, R., Zhang, Q., Stouthamer-Loeber, M., & Van Kammen, W. B. (1995). The influence of deviant peers on the development of boys' disruptive and delinquent behavior: A temporal analysis. *Development and Psychopathology, 7*, 715–726.

Keeney, T. J., Cannizzo, S. R., & Flavell, J. H. (1967). Spontaneous and induced rehearsal in a recall task. *Child Development, 38*, 953–966.

Keil, F. (2006). Cognitive science and cognitive development. In W. Damon & R. M. Lerner (Series Eds.) and D. Kuhn & R. Siegler (Vol. Eds.), *Handbook of child psychology*, Vol. 2, 6th ed. New York: Wiley.

Keiley, M. K., Howe, T. R., Dodge, K. A., Bates, J. E., & Pettit, G. S. (2002). The timing of child physical maltreatment: A cross-domain growth analysis of impact on adolescents' externalizing and internalizing problems. *Development and Psychopathology, 13*, 891–912.

Keller, M. B., Klein, D. N., Hirshfield, R. M., Kocsis, J. H., McCullough, M., et al. (1995). Results of the DSM-IV mood disorders field trial. *American Journal of Psychiatry, 152*, 843–849.

Kellman, P. J., & Arterberry, M. E. (2006). Infant visual perception. In W. Damon & R. M. Lerner (Series Eds.) and D. Kuhn, & R. Siegler (Vol. Eds.), *Handbook of child psychology, Vol. 2*, 6th ed. New York: Wiley.

Kennedy, W. A. (1969). A follow-up normative study of Negro intelligence and achievement. *Monographs of the Society for Research in Child Development, 34* (2, Serial No. 126).

Kennell, J., Klaus, M., McGrath, S., Robertson, S., & Hinckley, C. (1991). Continuous emotional support during labor in a U.S. hospital. *Journal of the American Medical Association, 265*, 2197–2201.

Kennell, J. H., & McGrath, S. K. (1993, September). *Labor support by a doula plus father vs father alone for middle class couples: The effect on perinatal outcomes.* Paper presented at the meeting of the Society for Behavioral Pediatrics, Providence, RI.

Kerr, M. (2001). Culture as a context for temperament: Suggestions from the life courses of shy Swedes and Americans. In T. D. Wachs & G. A. Kohnstamm (Eds.), *Temperament in context* (pp. 139–152). Mahwah, NJ: Erlbaum.

Kerr, M., & Stattin, H. (2000). What parents know, how they know it and several forms of adolescent adjustment: Further support for a reinterpretation of monitoring. *Child Development, 36*, 366–380.

Kessen, W., Leutzendoff, A. M., & Stoutsenberger, K. (1967). Age, food deprivation, non-nutritive sucking and movement in the human newborn. *Journal of Comparative and Physiological Psychology, 63*, 82–86.

Khatri, P., Kupersmidt, J., & Patterson, C. (1994, April). Aggression and peer victimization as predictors of self-report of behavioral and emotional adjustment. Poster

presented at the biennial meeting of the Conference in Human Development, Pittsburgh, PA.

Kilgore, K., Snyder, J., & Lentz, C. (2000). The contribution of parental discipline, parental monitoring and school risk to early-onset conduct problems in African American boys and girls. *Developmental Psychology, 36*, 835–845.

Kim, J. K., Conger, R. D., Elder, G. H., & Lorenz, F. O. (2003). Reciprocal influences between stressful life events and adolescent internalizing and externalizing problems. *Child Development, 74*, 127–143.

Kimball, M. M. (1986). Television and sex role attitudes. In T. M. Williams (Ed.), *The impact of television: A natural experiment in three communities* (pp. 265–301). Orlando, FL: Academic Press.

Kimm, S. Y., Glynn, N. W., Kriska, A. M., Barton, B. A., Kronsberg, S. S., Daniels, S. R., Crawford, P. B., Sabry, Z. I., & Liu, K. (2002). Decline in physical activity in black girls and white girls during adolescence. *New England Journal of Medicine, 347*, 709–715.

Kindermann, T. A., McCollam, T. L., & Gibson, E., Jr. (1995). Peer networks and students' classroom engagement during childhood and adolescence. In K. Wentzel & J. Juvonen (Eds.), *Social motivation: Understanding children's school adjustment.* New York: Cambridge University Press.

Kisilevsky, B. S., & Muir, D. W. (1991). Human fetal and subsequent newborn responses to sound and vibration. *Infant Behavior and Development, 14*, 1–26.

Kitzmann, K. M. (2000). Effects of marital conflict on subsequent triadic family interactions and parenting. *Developmental Psychology, 36*, 3–13.

Klahr, D., & MacWhinney, B. (1998). Information processing. In W. Damon (Ed.), D. Kuhn, & R. Siegler (Vol. Eds.), *Handbook of child psychology, Vol. 2. Cognition, perception and language.* (5th ed.). New York: Wiley.

Klaus, M. H., & Kennell, J. H. (1982). *Parent-infant bonding.* St. Louis: Mosby.

Klaus, M. H., Kennell, J. H., & Klaus, P. H. (1995). *Bonding: Building the foundations of secure attachment and independence.* Reading, MA: Addison-Wesley.

Klebanov, P. K., Brooks-Gunn, J., McCardon, C., & McCormick, M. C. (1998). The contribution of neighborhood and family income to developmental test scores over the first three years of life. *Child Development, 65*, 1420–1436.

Klebanov, P. K., Brooks-Gunn, J., & McCormick, M. C. (2001). Maternal coping strategies and emotional distress: Results of an early intervention program for low-birthweight young children. *Developmental Psychology, 37*, 654–667.

Klebonoff, M. A., Levine, R. J., Der Simonian, R., Clemens, J. D., & Wilkins, D. G. (1999). Maternal serum paraxanthine, a caffeine metabolite and the risk of spontaneous abortion. *New England Journal of Medicine, 341*, 1639–1644.

Knight, G. P., Johnson, L. G., Carlo, G., & Eisenberg, N. (1994). A multiplicative model of the dispositional antecedents of a prosocial behavior. Predicting more of the people more of the time. *Journal of Personality and Social Psychology, 66*, 178–183.

Knight, G. P., Nelson, W., Kagan, S., & Gumbiner, J. (1982). Cooperative-competitive social orientation and school achievement among Anglo-American and Mexican-American children. *Contemporary Educational Psychology, 7*, 97–106.

Kochanska, G. (1995). Children's temperament, mother's discipline, and security of attachment: Multiple pathways to emerging internalization. *Child Development, 66*, 597–615.

Kochanska, G. (1997). Multiple pathways to conscience for children with different temperaments: From toddlerhood to age 5. *Developmental Psychology, 33*, 228–240.

Kochanska, G. (2002). Committed compliance, moral self and internalization: A mediational model. *Developmental Psychology, 38*, 339–351.

Kochanska, G., Coy, K. C., & Murray, K. T. (2001). The development of self-regulation in the first four years of life. *Child Development, 72*, 1091–1111.

Kochanska, G., Gross, J. N., Mei-Hua, L., & Nichols, K. E. (2002). Guilt in young children: Development, determinants, and relations with a broader system of standards. *Developmental Psychology, 73*, 461–482.

Kochanska, G., & Murray, K. T. (2000). Mother-child mutually responsive orientation and conscience development: From toddler to early school age. *Child Development, 71*, 417–431.

Kochanska, G., Murray, K., & Harlan, E. T. (2000). Effortful control in early childhood: Continuity and change, antecedents, and implications for social development. *Developmental Psychology, 36,* 220–232.

Kochenderfer, B. J., & Ladd, G. W. (1996). Peer victimization: Manifestations and relations to school adjustment. *Journal of School Psychology, 34,* 267–283.

Kochenderfer-Ladd, B., & Wardrop, J. (2001). Chronicity and instability in children's peer victimization experiences as predictors of loneliness and social satisfaction trajectories. *Child Development, 72,* 134–151.

Kohlberg, L. (1969). *Stages in the development of moral thought and action.* New York: Holt.

Kohlberg, L. (1985). *The psychology of moral development.* San Francisco: Harper & Row.

Kohlberg, L. A. (1966). A cognitive-developmental analysis of children's sex-role concepts and attitudes. In E. E. Maccoby (Ed.), *The development of sex differences* (pp. 82–173). Stanford, CA: Stanford University Press.

Kohlberg, L., & Candee, D. (1984). The relationship of moral judgment to moral action. In W. M. Kurtines & J. L. Gewirtz (Eds.), *Morality, moral behavior and moral development.* New York: Wiley.

Kokko, K., & Pulkkinen, L. (2000). Aggression in childhood and long-term unemployment in adulthood: A cycle of maladaptation and some protective factors. *Developmental Psychology, 36,* 463–472.

Kolb, B., Gorny, G., Li, Y., Samaha, A., & Robinson, T. E. (2003). Amphetamine or cocaine limits the ability of later experience to promote structural plasticity in the neocortex and nucleus accumbens. *Proceedings of the National Academy of Sciences, 100,* 10523–10528.

Kopp, C. B. (1982). The antecedents of self-regulation. *Developmental Psychology, 18,* 199–214.

Kopp, C. B. (1987). The growth of self-regulation: Caregivers and children. In N. Eisenberg (Ed.), *Contemporary topics in developmental psychology.* New York: Wiley.

Kopp, C. B. (1994). *Baby steps: The "whys" of your child's behavior in the first two years.* New York: W. H. Freeman.

Kopp, C. B. (2002). Self-regulation in childhood. In N. J. Smelson & P. B. Baltes (Eds.), *International encyclopedia of the social and behavioral sciences* (vol. 3). New York: Pergamon.

Koren-Karie, N., Oppenheim, D., Dolev, S., Sher, E., & Etzion-Carasso, A. (2002). Mothers' insightfulness regarding their infants' internal experience: Relations with maternal sensitivity and infant attachment. *Developmental Psychology, 38,* 534–542.

Korner, A. (1974). The effect of the infant's state, level of arousal, sex and ontogenic stage on the caregiver. In M. Lewis & L. Rosenblum (Eds.), *The effect of the infant on its caregiver.* New York: Wiley.

Korner, A. F. (1989). Infant stimulation: The pros and cons in historical perspective. *Bulletin of National Center for Clinical Infant Programs, 10,* 11–17.

Korner, A. F., & Thoman, E. (1970). Visual alertness in neonates as evoked by maternal care. *Journal of Experimental Child Psychology, 10,* 67–78.

Kotchick, B. A., Shaffer, A., Miller, K. S., & Forehand, R. (2001). Adolescent sexual risk behavior: A multi-system perspective. *Clinical Psychology Review, 21,* 493–519.

Kotelchuck, M. (1995). Reducing infant mortality and improving birth outcomes for families of poverty. In H. E. Fitzgerald, B. M. Lester & B. S. Zuckerman (Eds.), *Children of poverty: Research, health, and policy issues, Reference books on family issues* (Vol. 23, pp. 151–166). New York: Garland Publishing.

Kovacs, D.M., Parker, J.G., & Hoffman, L.W. (1996). Behavioral, affective and social correlates of involvement in cross-sex friendship in elementary school. *Child Development, 67,* 2269–2286.

Kowal, A., & Kramer, L. (1997). Children's understanding of differential parental treatment. *Child Development, 68,* 113–126.

Kowal, A. K., & Blinn-Pike, L. (2004). Sibling influences on adolescents' attitudes toward safe sex practices. *Family Relations, 53,* 377–384.

Kozulin, A. (1990). *Vygotsky's psychology: A biography of ideas.* Cambridge, MA: Harvard University Press.

Kramer, L., & Gottman, J. M. (1992). Becoming a sibling—with a little help from my friends. *Developmental Psychology, 28,* 685–699.

Kramer, L, & Ramsburg, D. (2002). Advice given to parents on welcoming a second child: A critical review. *Family Relations, 51,* 2–14.

Kraus, N., McGee, T. J., Carrell, T. D., Zecler, S. G., Nicol, T. G., & Koch, D. B. (1996). Auditory neurophysiologic responses and discrimination deficits in children with learning problems. *Science, 273,* 971–973.

Krebs, D. L. (2000). The evolution of moral dispositions in the human species. In D. Le Croy & P. Moller (Eds.), Evolutionary perspectives in human reproductive behavior. *Annals of the New York Academy of Science, 907,* 132–148.

Kreppner, K. (2002). Retrospect and prospect in the psychological study of families as systems. In J. McHale & W. Grolnick (Eds.), *Retrospect and prospect in the psychological study of families* (pp. 225–257). Mahwah, NJ: Erlbaum.

Kreutzer, M. A., Leonard, C., & Flavell, J. H. (1975). An interview study of children's knowledge about memory. *Monographs of the Society for Research in Child Development, 40,* 1–60.

Krogman, W. M. (1972). *Child growth.* Ann Arbor: University of Michigan Press.

Kruesi, M. J., Hibbs, E. D., Zahn, T. P., & Keysor, C. S. (1992). A 2-year prospective follow-up study of children and adolescents with disruptive behavior disorders: Prediction by cerebrospinal fluid 5-hydroxyindoleacetic acid, homovanillic acid and autonomic measures? *Archives of General Psychiatry, 49,* 429–435.

Kuchner, J. F. R. (1980). *Chinese-American and European-American: A cross-cultural study of infant and mother.* Unpublished doctoral dissertation. University of Chicago.

Kuczaj, S. A. (1982). *Language development: Syntax and semantics* (Vol. 1). Hillsdale, NJ: Erlbaum.

Kuczynski, L. (Ed.) (2003). *Handbook of dynamics in parent-child relations.* Thousand Oaks, CA: Sage.

Kuczynski, L., Kochanska, G., Radke-Yarrow, M., & Girnius-Brown, O. (1987). A developmental interpretation of young children's noncompliance. *Developmental Psychology, 23,* 799–806.

Kuczynski, L., Marshall, S., & Schell, K. (1997). Value socialization in a bidirectional context. In J. E. Grusec & L. Kuczynski (Eds.), *Parenting and children's internalization of values: A handbook of contemporary theory* (pp. 23–50). New York: Wiley.

Kuhl, P. K., Andruski, J. E., Christovich, I. A., Christovich, L. A., Kozhovnikova, E. A., Ryskina, V. L., Stolyarouva, E. I., Sandberg, U., & Lacerda, F. (1997). Cross-language analysis of phonetic units in language addressed to infants. *Science, 277,* 685–686.

Kuhl, P. K., & Miller, J. D. (1975). Speech perception by the chinchilla: voice-voiceless distinction in alveolar plosive consonants. *Science, 190,* 69–72.

Kuhl, P. K., Williams, K. A., Lacerda, F., Stevens, K. N., & Lindblom, B. (1992). Linguistic experience alters phonetic perception in infants by 6 months of age. *Science, 255,* 606–608.

Kuhn, D., & Franklin, S. (2006). The second decade: What develops (and how?). In W. Damon & R. M. Lerner (Series Eds.) and D. Kuhn & R. Siegler (Vol. Eds.), *Handbook of child psychology,* Vol, 2, 6th ed. New York: Wiley.

Kumanyika, S. (1993). Ethnicity and obesity development in children. In C. L. Williams & S. Y. S. Kimm (Eds.), *Prevention and treatment of childhood obesity* (pp. 81–92). Annals of the New York Academy of Sciences, Vol. 699. New York: The New York Academy of Sciences.

Kumru, A., & Edwards, C. P. (2003, April). Gender and adolescent prosocial behavior within the Turkish family. Poster presented at the biennial meeting of the Society for Research in Child Development, Tampa, Florida.

Kunkel, D., & Canepa, J. (1994). Broadcasters' license renewal claims regarding children's educational programming. *Journal of Broadcasting and Electronic Media, 38,* 397–416.

Kupersmidt, J. & Dodge, K. A. (Eds.) (2004), *Children's peer relations: From development to intervention.* Washington, DC: American Psychological Association.

Kurtz, B. E., & Borkowski, J. G. (1987). Development of strategic skills in impulsive and reflective children: A longitudinal study of metacognition. *Journal of Experimental Child Psychology, 43,* 129–148.

Kirtler, A. F., La Greca, A. M., & Prinstein, M. J. (1999). Friendship qualities and social-emotional functioning of adolescents with close, cross-sex friendships. *Journal of Research on Adolescence, 93,* 339–366.

La Barbera, J. D., Izard, C. E., Vietze, P., & Parisi, S. A. (1976). Four- and six-month-old infants' visual responses to joy, anger, and neutral expressions. *Child Development, 47,* 535–538.

Labarthe, J. C. (1997). Are boys better than girls at building a tower or a bridge at 2 years of age? *Archives of Disease in Childhood, 77,* 140–144.

Lacković-Grgin, K., Dekovic, M., & Opačić, G. (1994). Pubertal status, interaction with significant others, and self-esteem of adolescent girls. *Adolescence, 29,* 681–700.

Ladd, G. W. (1981). Effectiveness of a social learning method for enhancing children's social interaction and peer acceptance. *Child Development, 52,* 171–178.

Ladd, G. W. (2005). *Peer relationships and social competence of children and youth.* New Haven, CT: Yale University Press.

Ladd, G. W., Birch, S. H., & Buhs, E. S. (1999). Children's social and scholastic lives in kindergarten: Related spheres of influence? *Child Development, 70,* 1373–1400.

Ladd, G. W., & Emerson, E. S. (1984). Shared knowledge in children's friendships. *Developmental Psychology, 20,* 932–940.

Ladd, G. W., & Golter, B. S. (1988). Parents' management of preschoolers' peer relations: Is it related to children's social competence? *Developmental Psychology, 24,* 109–117.

Ladd, G. W., Muth, S., & Hart, C. H. (1992). Parents' management of children's peer relations: Is it related to children's social competence? *Developmental Psychology, 24,* 109–117.

Ladd, G. W., & Pettit, G. S. (2002). Parents and children's peer relationships. In M. Bornstein (Ed.), *Handbook of parenting: Vol. 4* (2nd ed., pp. 377–409). Hillsdale, NJ: Lawrence Erlbaum & Associates.

LaFrance, M., Hecht, M. A., & Levy Paluck, E. (2003). The contingent smile: A meta-analysis of sex differences in smiling. *Psychological Bulletin, 129,* 305–334.

La Freniere, P. J. (2000). *Emotional development: A biosocial perspective.* New York: Wadsworth.

Laible, D. J., Carlo, G., & Raffaelli, M. (2000). The differential relations of parent and peer attachment to adolescent adjustment. *Journal of Youth and Adolescence, 29,* 45–59.

Laible, D. J., & Thompson, R. A. (1998). Attachment and emotional understanding in preschool children. *Developmental Psychology, 34,* 1038–1045.

Laird, R. D., Pettit, G. S., Dodge, K. A., & Bates, J. E. (2003). Change in parents' monitoring knowledge: Links with parenting, relationships quality, adolescent beliefs and antisocial behavior. *Social Development, 12,* 401–419.

Lamb, M. E. (Ed.). (1987). *The father's role: Cross-cultural perspectives.* New York: Wiley.

Lamb, M. E. (Ed.). (2004). *The role of the father in child development* (4th ed.). New York: Wiley.

Lamb, M. E., & Ahnert, L. (2006). Childcare and youth programs. In W. Damon & R. L. Lerner (Gen. Eds.) and K. A. Renninger &

I. E. Sigel (Vol. Eds.). *Handbook of child psychology: Vol. 4. Child psychology and practice* (6th ed.). New York: Wiley.

Lamb, M. E., & Campos, J. (1982). *Development in infancy.* New York: Random House.

Lamb, M. E., & Roopnarine, J. L. (1979). Peer influences on sex role development in preschoolers. *Child Development, 50,* 1219–1222.

Lamb, M. E., Suomi, S. J., & Stephenson, G. R. (1979). *Social interaction analysis: Methodological issues.* Madison, WI: University of Wisconsin Press.

Lamb, S., & Zakhireh, B. (1997). Toddlers' attention to the distress of peers in a day care setting. *Early Education and Development, 8,* 105–118.

Lambert, M. C., Weisz, J. R., & Knight, F. (1989). Over- and undercontrolled clinic referral problems of Jamaican and American children and adolescents: The culture general and the culture specific. *Journal of Consulting & Clinical Psychology, 57,* 467–472.

Lambert, S. R., & Drack, A. V. (1996). Infantile cataracts. *Survey of Ophthalmology, 40,* 427–458.

Lambert, W. E. (1987). The effects of bilingual and bicultural experiences on children's attitudes and social perspectives. In P. Homel, M. Palij, & D. Aranson (Eds.), *Childhood Bilingualism.* Hillsdale, NJ: Erlbaum.

Lander, E. S. (1996). The new genomics: Global views of biology. *Science, 274,* 536–538.

Landers, C. (1989). A psychobiological study of infant development in South India. In J. K. Nugent, B. M. Lester, & T. B. Brazelton (Eds.), *The cultural context of infancy: Vol. 1. Biology, culture, and infant development* (pp. 169–207). Norwood, NJ: Ablex.

Lane, H. (1976). *The wild boy of Aveyron.* Cambridge, MA: Harvard University Press.

Langlois, J. H. (1985). From the eye of the beholder to behavior reality: The development of social behaviors and social relations as a function of physical attractiveness. In C. P. Herman (Ed.), *Physical appearance, stigma, and social behavior.* Hillsdale, NJ: Erlbaum.

Langlois, J. H., & Downs, C. A. (1980). Mothers, fathers and peers as socialization agents of sex-typed play behaviors in young children. *Child Development, 51,* 1237–1247.

Langlois, J. H., Kahakanis, L., Rubenstein, A. J., Larson, A., Hallam, N., & Smoot, M. (2000). Maxims or myths of beauty: A meta-analytic and theoretical

review. *Psychological Bulletin, 126,* 390–423.

Langlois, J. H., Roggman, L. A., Casey, R. J., Ritter, J. M., Rieser-Danner, L. A., & Jenkins, V. Y. (1987). Infant preferences for attractive faces: Rudiments of a stereotype? *Developmental Psychology, 23,* 363–369.

Langlois, J. H., Roggman, L. A., & Rieser-Danner, L. A. (1990). Infants' differential social responses to attractive and unattractive faces. *Developmental Psychology, 26,* 153–159.

Langlois, J. H., & Stephan, C. (1981). Beauty and the beast: The role of physical attractiveness in the development of peer relations and social behavior. In S. S. Brehm, S. H. Kassin, & F. X. Gibbons (Eds.), *Developmental social psychology.* New York: Oxford University Press.

Lansford, J. E., & Parker, J. G. (1999). Children's interactions in triads: Behavioral profiles and effects of gender and patterns of friendships among members. *Developmental Psychology, 35,* 80–93.

Lapsley, D. K. (1996). *Moral psychology.* Boulder, CO: Westview.

Larson, R. (1997). The emergence of solitude as a constrictive domain of experience in early adolescence. *Child Development, 68,* 80–93.

Larson, R., & Richards, M. H. (1994). *Divergent realities: The emotional lives of mothers, fathers and adolescents.* New York: Basic Books.

Larson, R., & Verma, S. (1999). How children and adolescents around the world spend time: Work, play, and developmental opportunities. *Psychological Bulletin, 125,* 701–736.

Larson, R. W., Monetia, G., Richards, M. H., & Wilson, S. (2002). Continuity, stability, and change in daily emotional experience across adolescence. *Child Development, 73,* 1151–1165.

Laursen, B. (1995). Conflict and social interaction in adolescent relationships. *Journal of Research on Adolescence, 5,* 55–70.

Laursen, B., Hartup, W. W., & Koplas, A. L. (1996). Towards understanding peer conflict. *Merrill-Palmer Quarterly, 42,* 76–102.

Laursen, B., & Jensen-Campbell, L. A. (1999). The nature and functions of social exchange in adolescent romantic relationships. In W. Furman, B. Brown, B. Bradford et al. (Eds.), *The development of romantic relationships in adolescence. Cambridge studies in social and emotional development*

(pp. 50–74). New York: Cambridge University Press.

Leaper, C., Anderson, K. J., & Sanders, P. (1998). Moderators of gender effects on parents' talk to their children: A meta-analysis. *Developmental Psychology.*

Leblanc, M., & Ritchie, M. (2001). A meta-analysis of play therapy outcomes. *Counseling Psychology Quarterly, 14,* 149–163.

Lecanuet, J.-P., Fifer, W., Krasnegor, N., & Smotherman, W. (1995). *Fetal development: A psychobiological perspective.* Hillsdale, NJ: Erlbaum.

Lederberg, A. R., Prezbindowski, A. K., & Spencer, P. E. (2000). Word-learning skills of deaf preschoolers: The development of novel mapping and rapid word-learning strategies. *Child Development, 71,* 1571–1585.

Lee, V. E., Brooks-Gunn, J., & Schnur, E. (1988). Does Head Start work? A 1–year follow-up comparison of disadvantaged children attending Head Start, no preschool, and other preschool programs. *Developmental Psychology, 24,* 210–222.

Lee, V. E., Brooks-Gunn, J., Schnur, E., & Liaw, F. (1990). Are Head Start effects sustained? A longitudinal follow-up comparison of disadvantaged children attending Head Start, no preschool, and other preschool programs. *Child Development, 61,* 495–507.

Lefrancois, G. R. (1973). *Of children.* Belmont, CA: Wadsworth.

Lei, T., & Cheng, S. (1989). A little but special light on the universality of moral judgment development. In L. Kohlberg, D. Candee, & A. Colby (Eds.), *Rethinking moral development.* Cambridge, MA: Harvard University Press.

Leichtman, M. D., & Ceci, S. J. (1995). The effects of stereotypes and suggestions on preschoolers' reports. *Developmental Psychology, 31,* 758.

Leiderman, P. H. (1983). Social ecology and childbirth: The newborn nursery as environmental stressor. In N. Garmezy & M. Rutter (Eds.), *Stress, coping and development in children.* New York: McGraw-Hill.

Leinbach, M. D., & Fagot, B. I. (1992). *Gender-schematic processing in infancy: Categorical habituation to male and female faces.* Unpublished manuscript. University of Oregon, Eugene.

Leippe, M. R., & Romanczyk, A. (1989). Reactions to child (versus adult) eyewitnesses: The influence of jurors' preconceptions and witness behavior. *Law & Human Behavior, 13,* 103–132.

Lemerise, E. A., & Arsenio, W. F. (2000). An integrated model of emotion process and cognition in social information processing. *Child Development, 71,* 107–118.

Lengua, L. J. (2002). The contribution of emotionality and self-regulation to the understanding of children's response to multiple risk. *Child Development, 73,* 144–161.

Lenneberg, E. H. (1967). *Biological foundations of language.* New York: Wiley.

Lenneberg, E. H., Rebelsky, F. G., & Nichols, I. A. (1965). The vocalizations of infants born to deaf and hearing parents. *Human Development, 8,* 23–37.

Lepper, M. R. (1985). Microcomputers in education: Motivation and social issues. *American Psychologist, 40,* 1–18.

Lepper, M. R., & Gurtner, J. (1989). Children and computers: Approaching the twenty-first century. *American Psychologist, 44,* 170–178.

Lerner, R. M., Fischer, C. B., & Weinberg, R. A. (2000). Towards a science for and of the people: Promoting civil society through the application of developmental science. *Child Development, 71,* 11–20.

Lerner, R. M., Petersen, A., & Brooks-Gunn, J. (1987) (Eds.). *Encyclopedia of Adolescence.* New York: Garland.

Leshner, A. (2001, August). Understanding the risks of prescription drugs. NIDA notes. Directors Column. http://www.aida.nih.gov/NIDA_Notes/NNVol16N3/DirRepVol16N3.html.

Leslie, A. M., & Roth, D. (1993). What autism teaches us about metarepresentation. In S. Baron-Cohen, H. Tager-Flusberg, & D. J. Cohen (Eds.), *Understanding other minds: Perspectives on autism.* Oxford, England: Oxford University Press.

Lesser, G. S., Fifer, G., & Clark, D. H. (1965). Mental abilities of children from different social class and cultural groups. *Monographs of the Society for Research in Child Development, 30* (4, Serial No. 102), 1–115.

Lester, B. M. (1988). Neurobehavioral assessment of the infant at risk. *Early identification of infants with developmental disabilities.* New York: Grune & Stratton.

Lester, B. M. (2005). *Why is my baby crying? The parent's survival guide for coping with crying problems and colic.* New York: HarperCollins.

Lester, B. M., Als, H., & Brazelton, T. B. (1982). Regional obstetric anesthesia and newborn behavior: A reanalysis toward synergistic effects. *Child Development, 53,* 687–692.

Lester, B. M., Boukydis, C. F. Z., Garcia-Coll, C. T., Hole, W., & Peuker, M. (1992). Infantile colic: acoustic cry characteristics, maternal perception of cry, and temperament. *Infant Behavior and Development, 15,* 15–26.

Lester, B. M., Boukydis, C. F. Z., & Twomey, J. E. (2000). Maternal substance abuse and child outcome. In C. H. Zeanah (Ed.), *Handbook of infant mental health* (pp. 161–175). New York: Guilford.

Lester, B. M., Corwin, M., & Golub, H. (1988). Early detection of the infant at risk through cry analysis. In J. N. Newman (Ed.), *The psychological control of mammalian vocalization.* Hillsdale, NJ: Erlbaum.

Leve, L. D., & Fagot, B. I. (1997). Gender-role socialization and discipline processes in one- and two-parent families. *Sex Roles, 36,* 1–12.

Leve, L. D., Winebarger, A. A., Fagot, B. I., Reid, J. B., & Goldsmith, J. H. (1998). Environmental and genetic variance in children's observed and reported maladaptive behavior. *Child Development, 69,* 1286–1298.

Levenkron, S. (2000). *Anatomy of anorexia.* New York: W. W. Norton.

Leventhal, T., & Brooks-Gunn, J. (2000). The neighborhoods they live in: The effects of neighborhood residence on child and adolescent outcomes. *Psychological Bulletin, 126,* 309–337.

Levine, L., Tuber, S. B., Slade, A., & Ward, M. J. (1991). Mothers' mental representations and their relationship to mother-infant attachment. *Bulletin of the Menninger Clinic, 55,* 454–469.

Levine, L. J. (1995). Young children's understanding of the causes of anger and sadness. *Child Development, 66,* 697–709.

Levinson, S. C. (1997). Language and cognition: The cognitive consequences on spatial description in the Guugu Yimithirr. *Journal of Linguistic Anthropology, 7,* 98–131.

Levitt, M. J., Weber, R. A., & Clark, M. C. (1986). Social network relationships as sources of maternal support and well-being. *Developmental Psychology, 22,* 310–316.

Levy, G. D. (1994). High and low gender schematic children's release from proactive interference. *Sex roles, 30,* 93–108.

Lewinsohn, P. M., & Rohde, P. (1993). The cognitive-behavioral treatment of depression in adolescents: Research and suggestions. *The Clinical Psychologist, 46,* 177–183.

Lewinsohn, P. M., Rohde, P., & Seeley, J. R. (1993). Psychosocial characteristics of adolescents with a history of suicide attempts. *Journal of the American Academy of Child and Adolescent Psychiatry, 32,* 600–668.

Lewis, M. (1983). On the nature of intelligence: Science or bias? In M. Lewis (Ed.), *Origins of intelligence: Infancy and early childhood* (2nd ed., pp. 1–24). New York: Plenum.

Lewis, M. (1992). *Shame: The exposed self.* New York: The Free Press.

Lewis, M. (1995). Embarrassment: The emotion of self-exposure and evaluation. In J. P. Tangney & K. Fischer (Eds.), *Self-conscious emotions* (pp. 198–218). New York: Guilford.

Lewis, M. (1998). Emotional competence and development. In D. Pushkar, W. M. Bukowski, A. E. Schwartzman, D. M. Stack, & D. R. White (Eds.), *Improving competence across the lifespan* (pp. 27–36). New York: Plenum Press.

Lewis, M., Alessandri, S., & Sullivan, M. W. (1992). Differences in shame and pride as a function of children's gender and task difficulty. *Child Development, 63,* 630–638.

Lewis, M., & Brooks, J. (1974). Self, other, and fear: Infants' reactions to people. In M. Lewis & L. Rosenblum (Eds.), *The origins of fear.* New York: Wiley.

Lewis, M., & Brooks-Gunn, J. (1979). *Social cognition and the acquisition of self.* New York: Plenum.

Lewis, M., & Freedle, R. (1973). The mother-infant dyad. In P. Pilner, L. Kranes, & T. Holoway (Eds.), *Communication and affect: Language and thought.* New York: Academic.

Lewis, M., & Michaelson, L. (1985). *Children's emotions and moods.* New York: Plenum.

Lewis, M., Ramsey, D. S., & Kawakami, K. (1993). Differences between Japanese infants and Caucasian American infants in behavioral and cortisol response to inoculation. *Child Development, 64,* 1722–1731.

Lewis, M., & Wilson, C. D. (1972). Infant development in lower-class American families. *Human Development, 15,* 112–127.

Lewis, M. D. (2000). The promise of dynamic systems approaches for an integrated account of human development. *Child Development, 71,* 36–43.

Leyendecker, B., & Lamb, M. E. (1999). Latino families. In M. E. Lamb (Ed.), *Parenting and child development in "nontraditional" families* (pp. 247–262). Mahwah, NJ: Erlbaum.

Liben, L. S. (1991). Adults' performance on horizontality tasks: Conflicting frames of reference. *Developmental Psychology, 27,* 285–294.

Liben, L. S. (1999). Developing an understanding of external spatial representations. In I. E. Sigel (Ed.), *Development of mental representation: Theories and applications* (pp. 297–321). Mahwah, NJ: Erlbaum.

Liben, L. S., & Bigler, R. S. (2002). The developmental course of gender differentiation. *Monographs of the Society for Research in Child Development, 67* (269, Pt. 2).

Liben, L. S., & Golbeck, S. L. (1980). Sex differences in performance on Piagetian spatial tasks: Differences in competence or performance. *Child Development, 51,* 594–597.

Liberman, I. Y., Shankweiler, D., Liberman, A. M., Fowler, C., & Fischer, F. W. (1976). Phonetic segmentation and recoding in the beginning reader. In A. S. Reber & D. Scarborough (Eds.), *Reading: Theory and practice.* Hillsdale, NJ: Erlbaum.

Lieberman, A. F., & Zeanah, C. H. (1999). Contributions of attachment theory to infant-parent psychotherapy and other interventions with infants and young children. In J. Cassidy & P. Shaver (Eds.), *Handbook of attachment* (pp. 555–574). New York: Guilford.

Liebert, R. M., & Baron, R. A. (1972). Some immediate effects of televised violence on children's behavior. *Developmental Psychology, 6,* 469–475.

Liederman, P. H., Landsman, M., & Clark, C. (1990, March). *Making it or blowing it: Coping strategies and academic performance in a multiethnic high school population.* Paper presented at the biennial meeting of the Society for Research on Adolescence, Atlanta.

Lifshitz, F., Finch, N., & Lifshitz, J. (1991). *Children's nutrition.* Boston: Jones & Bartlett.

Lillard, A. S. (1993). Pretend play skills and the child's theory of mind. *Child Development, 64,* 348–371.

Lillard, A. S. (1998). Ethnopsychologies: Cultural variations in theory of mind. *Psychological Bulletin, 123,* 3–33.

Lillard, A. S. (2005). *Montessori: The science behind the genius.* Oxford: Oxford University Press.

Lindberg, M. (1980). Is knowledge base development a necessary and sufficient condition for memory development? *Journal of Experimental Child Psychology, 30*, 401–410.

Lindberg, M. A., Jones, S., McComas-Collard, L., & Thomas, S. W. (2001). Similarities and differences in eyewitness testimonies of children who directly versus vicariously experience stress. *Journal of Genetic Psychology, 162*, 314–333.

Lindell, S. G. (1988). Education for childbirth: A time for change. *Journal of Obstetrics, Gynecology and Neonatal Nursing, 17*, 108–112.

Linn, M. C., & Hyde, J. S. (1989). Gender, mathematics, and science. *Educational Researcher, 18*, 17–27.

Linn, M. C., & Hyde, J. S. (1991). Trends in cognitive and psychosocial gender differences. In R. M. Lerner, A. C. Petersen, & J. Brooks-Gunn (Eds.), *The encyclopedia of adolescence.* New York: Garland.

Linn, S., Lieberman, E., Schoenbaum, S. C., Monson, R. R., Stubblefield, P. G., & Ryand, K. J. (1988). Adverse outcomes of pregnancy in women exposed to diethylstilbestrol in utero. *Journal of Reproductive Medicine, 33*, 3–7.

Lipsitt, L. P. (1990). Learning and memory in infants. *Merrill-Palmer Quarterly, 36*, 53–66.

Lipsitt, L. P., & Werner, J. S. (1981). The infancy of human learning processes. In E. Gollin (Ed.), *Developmental plasticity.* New York: Academic Press.

Little, G. A. (1992). The fetus at risk. In F. A. Hoekelman, S. B. Friedman, N. M. Nelson, & H. M. Seidel (Eds.), *Primary pediatric care* (2nd ed.). St. Louis: Mosby Yearbook.

Little, R. (1975). *Maternal alcohol use and resultant birth weight.* Unpublished doctoral dissertation. Johns Hopkins University, Baltimore, MD.

Liu, L. L., Clemens, C. J., Shay, D. K., Davis, R. L., & Novack, A. H. (1997). The safety of newborn early discharge. *The Journal of the American Medical Association, 278*, 293–298.

Localio, A. R., Lawthers, A. G., Bengston, J. M., Herbert, L. E., Weaver, S. L., Brennan, T. A., & Landis, J. R. (1993). Relationship between malpractice claims and caesarean delivery. *Journal of the American Medical Association, 269*, 366–373.

Loeber, R., & Hay, D. F. (1993). Developmental approaches to aggression and conduct problems. In M. Rutter & D. F. Hay (Eds.), *Development through life: A handbook for clinicians*

(pp. 488–516). Oxford: Blackwell Scientific Publications.

Loehlin, J. C., Willerman, L., & Horn, J. M. (1988). Human behavior genetics. *Annual Review of Psychology, 39*, 101–133.

Lorch, E. P., Bellack, D. R., & Augsbach, L. H. (1987). Young children's memory for televised stories: Effects of importance. *Child Development, 58*, 453–463.

Lorenz, K. (1952). *King Solomon's ring.* New York: Crowell.

Lovaas, O. I. (1987). Behavioral treatment and normal educational and intellectual functioning in young autistic children. *Journal of Consulting and Clinical Psychology, 55*, 3–9.

Lovaas, O. I., & Smith, P. (1988). Intensive behavioral treatment for young autistic children. In B. Lahey & A. Kazdin (Eds.), *Advances in clinical child psychology* (Vol. 2). New York: Plenum.

Lovett, S. B., & Pillow, B. H. (1995). Development of the ability to distinguish between comprehension and memory: Evidence from strategy-selection tasks. *Journal of Educational Psychology, 87*, 523–536.

Lowes, J. & Triggerman, M. (2003). Weight concerns of young children. *British Journal of Health Psychology, 8*, 135–147.

Lozoff, B., Jimenez, J. M., Hagen, J., Mollen, E., & Wolf, A. W. (2000). Poorer behavioral and developmental outcomes more than ten years after treatment for iron deficiency in infancy. *Pediatrics, 105*, E51.

Luecke-Aleksa, D., Anderson, D. R., Collins, P. A., & Schmitt, K. L. (1995). Gender constancy and television viewing. *Developmental Psychology, 31*, 773–780.

Lummis, M., & Stevenson, H. W. (1990). Gender differences in beliefs and achievement: A cross-cultural study. *Developmental Psychology, 26*, 254–263.

Luria, A. R. (1971). Towards the problem of the historical nature of psychological processes. *International Journal of Psychology, 6*, 259–272.

Luria, A. R. (1976). *Cognitive development: Its cultural and social foundation.* Cambridge, MA: Harvard University Press.

Luthar, S. S. (2003). The culture of affluence: Psychological costs of material wealth. *Child Development, 74*, 1581–1593.

Luthar, S. S., & Becker, B. E. (2002). Privileged but pressured? A study of affluent youth. *Child Development, 73*, 1593–1610.

Luthar, S., Burack, J., Ciccetti, D., & Weisz, J. (1997). *Developmental psychopathology: Perspectives in*

adjustment risk and disorder. New York: Cambridge University Press.

Luthar, S. S., Cicchetti, D., & Becker, B. (2000). The construct of resilience: A critical evaluation and guidelines for future work. *Child Development, 71*, 543–562.

Luthar, S. S., & D'Avanzo, K. (1999). Contextual factors in substance use: A study of suburban and inner-city adolescents. *Development and Psychopathology, 11*, 845–867.

Lykken, D. T., McGue, M., Tellegen, A., & Bouchard, T. J., Jr. (1992). Genetic traits that may not run in families. *American Psychologist, 47*(12), 1565–1577.

Lynch, M. P., Eilers, R. E., Oller, D. K., & Urbano, R. C. (1990). Innateness, experience, and music perception. *Psychological Science, 1*, 272–276.

Lyons, T. D. (2002). Applying suggestibility research to the real world: The case of repeated questions. *Law and Contemporary Problems, 65*, 97–126.

Lyons-Ruth, K. (1996). Attachment relationships among children with aggressive behavior problems: The role of disorganized early attachment patterns. *Journal of Consulting and Clinical Psychology, 64*, 572–585.

Lyons-Ruth, K., & Jacobvitz, D. (1999). Attachment disorganization. In J. Cassidy & P. Shaver (Eds.), *Handbook of attachment* (pp. 520–554). New York: Guilford.

Lyons-Ruth, K., Lyubchik, A., Wolfe, R., & Bronfman, E. (2002). Parental depression and child attachment: Hostile and helpless profiles of parent and child behavior among families and risk. In S. H. Goodman & I. Gotlib (Eds.), *Children of depressed parents* (pp. 89–120). Washington, DC: American Psychological Association.

Lytton, H., & Romney, D. M. (1991). Parents' differential socialization of boys and girls: A meta-analysis. *Psychological Bulletin, 109*, 267–296.

MacBeth, T. M. (1996). Indirect effects of television: Creativity, persistence, school achievement, and participation in other activities. In T. M. Mac Beth (Ed.), *Tuning in to young viewers.* Thousand Oaks, CA: Sage.

Maccoby, E. E. (1988). Gender as a social category. *Developmental Psychology, 24*, 755–765.

Maccoby, E. E. (1990). Gender and relationships: A developmental account. *American Psychologist, 45*, 513–521.

Maccoby, E. E. (1998). *The two sexes.* Cambridge, MA: Harvard University Press.

Maccoby, E. E., & Jacklin, C. N. (1974). *The psychology of sex differences.* Stanford, CA: Stanford University Press.

Maccoby, E. E., & Martin, J. A. (1983). Socialization in the context of the family: Parent-child interaction. In E. M. Hetherington (Ed.), *Socialization, personality, and social development: Vol. 4. Handbook of child psychology.* New York: Wiley.

Maccoby, E. E., & Mnookin, R. (Eds.). (1992). *Dividing the child.* Cambridge, MA: Harvard University Press.

MacDonald, K., & Parke, R. D. (1986). Parent-child physical play: The effects of sex and age of children and parents. *Sex Roles, 15*, 367–378.

MacFarlane, J. A. (1975). Olfaction in the development of social preferences in the human neonate. In M. A. Hofer (Ed.), *Parent-infant interaction.* Amsterdam: Elsevier.

Mackey, M. C. (1995). Women's evaluation of their childbirth performance. *Maternal-Child Nursing Journal, 23*, 57–72.

MacWhinney, B. (1996). Lexical connectionism. In P. Broeder & J. M. J. Murre (Eds.), *Models of language acquisition: Inductive and deductive approaches.* Cambridge, MA: MIT Press.

Magai, C., & McFadden, S. H. (1995). *The role of emotions in social and personality development.* New York: Plenum.

Magnusson, D. (1988). Individual development from an interactional perspective: A longitudinal study. In D. Magnusson (Ed.), *Paths through life* (Vol. 1). Hillsdale, NJ: Erlbaum.

Magnusson, D. (1996). Towards a developmental science. In D. Magnusson (Ed.), *The lifespan development of individuals.* Cambridge, England: Cambridge University Press.

Magnusson, D., & Stattin, H. (1998). Person-context interaction theories. In W. Damon (Ed.), *Handbook of child psychology* (Vol. 1). New York: Wiley.

Main, M. (1973). *Exploration, play and level of cognitive functioning as related to child-mother attachment.* Unpublished doctoral dissertation. Johns Hopkins University, Baltimore, MD.

Main, M., & Cassidy, J. (1988). Categories of response to reunion with the parent at age 6: Predictable from infant attachment classification and stable over a 1-month period. *Developmental Psychology, 24*, 415–426.

Main, M., & Hesse, E. (1990). Parents' unresolved traumatic experiences are related to infant disorganized attachment status: Is frightened and/or frightening parental behavior the linking mechanism? In M. T. Greenberg, D. Cicchetti, & E. M. Cummings (Eds.), *Attachment in the preschool years: Theory, research, and intervention* (pp. 161–182). Chicago, IL: University of Chicago Press.

Main, M., Kaplan, N., & Cassidy, J. (1985). Security in infancy, childhood, and adulthood: A move to the level of representation. *Monographs of the Society for Research in Child Development, 50,* 66–104.

Main, M., & Weston, D. (1981). The quality of the toddler's relationship to mother and father: Related to conflict behavior and readiness to establish new relationships. *Child Development, 52,* 932–940.

Malatesta, C. Z. (1982). The expression and regulation of emotion: A lifespan perspective. In T. Field & A. Fogel (Eds.), *Emotion and early interaction* (pp. 1–24). Hillsdale, NJ: Erlbaum.

Malatesta, C. Z., Culver, C., Tesman, J., & Shepard, B. (1989). The development of emotional expression during the first two years of life: Normative trends and patterns of individual differences. *Monographs of the Society for Research in Child Development, 54,* 1–2.

Malcolm, L. A. (1970). Growth of the Asai child of the Madang district of New Guinea. *Journal of Biosocial Science, 2,* 213–226.

Mallick, S. K., & McCandless, B. R. (1966). A study of catharsis of aggression. *Journal of Personality and Social Psychology, 4,* 591–596.

Mancus, D. S. (1992). Influence of male teachers on elementary school children's stereotyping of teacher competence. *Sex Roles, 26,* 109–128.

Mandler, J. M. (1998). Representation. In W. Damon (Gen. Ed.), D. Kuhn, & R. S. Siegler (Vol. Eds.), *Handbook of child psychology: Vol. 2. Cognition, perception, and language* (pp. 255–308). New York: Wiley.

Mandler, J. M., & Bauer, P. J. (1988). The cradle of categorization: Is the basic level basic? *Cognitive Development, 3,* 247–264.

Mangelsdorf, S., Watkins, S., & Lehn, L. (1991, April). *The role of control in the infant's appraisal of strangers.* Paper presented at the biennial meeting of the Society for Research in Child Development, Seattle, Washington.

Mangelsdorf, S. C., Plunkett, J. W., Dedrick, C. F., Berlin, M., Meisels, S. J., McHale, J. L., &

Dichtellmiller, M. (1996). Attachment security in very-low-birthweight infants. *Developmental Psychology, 32,* 914–920.

Mangelsdorf, S. C., Shapiro, J. R., & Marzolf, D. (1995). Developmental and temperamental differences in emotion regulation in infancy. *Child Development, 66,* 1817–1828.

Maratsos, M. (1983). Some current issues in the study of the acquisition of grammar. In P. H. Mussen (Ed.), *Handbook of child psychology* (Vol. 3). New York: Wiley.

Maratsos, M. (1989). Innateness and plasticity in language acquisition. In M. Rice & R. L. Shiefelbusch (Eds.), *The teachability of language.* Baltimore, MD: Brooks/Cole.

Maratsos, M. (1993). Discussion in the symposium "Issues in the acquisition of inflectional processes," presented at the meetings of the Society for Research in Child Development, New Orleans.

Maratsos, M. (1998). The acquisition of grammar. In W. Damon (Gen. Ed.), D. Kuhn, & R. S. Siegler (Vol. Eds.), *Handbook of child psychology: Vol. 2. Cognition, perception, and language* (5th ed., pp. 421–466). New York: Wiley.

March, J. S., Franklin, M., Nelson, A., & Foa, E. (2001). Cognitive-behavioral psychotherapy for pediatric obsessive-compulsive disorder. *Journal of Clinical Child Psychology, 30,* 8–18.

Marcus, G. F. (1995). Children's overregularization of English plurals: A quantitative analysis. *Journal of Child Language, 22,* 447–460.

Marean, G. C., Werner, L. A., & Kuhl, P. K. (1992). Vowel categorization by very young infants. *Developmental Psychology, 28,* 396–405.

Mares, M., & Woodward, E. H. (2001). Prosocial effects on children's interactions. In D. G. Singer & J. Singer (Eds.), *Handbook of children and the media* (pp. 183–203). Thousand Oaks, CA: Sage.

Markman, E. M. (1973). Facilitation of part-whole comparisons by use of the collective noun "family." *Child Development, 44,* 837–840.

Markman, E. M. (1977). Realizing that you don't understand: A preliminary investigation. *Child Development, 48,* 986–992.

Markman, E. M. (1979). Realizing that you don't understand: Elementary school children's awareness of inconsistencies. *Child Development, 50,* 643–655.

Markman, E. M. (1989). *Categorization and naming in children.* Cambridge, MA: MIT Press.

Markman, E. M., & Hutchinson, J. E. (1994). Children's sensitivity to constraints on word meaning: Taxonomic versus thematic relations. *Cognitive Psychology, 16,* 1–27.

Markson, L., & Bloom, P. (1997). Evidence against a dedicated system for word learning in children. *Nature, 385,* 813–815.

Marlier, L., Schaal, B., & Soussignan, R. (1998). Neonatal responsiveness to the odor of amniotic and lacteal fluids: A test of perinatal chemosensory continuity. *Child Development, 69,* 611–623.

Martin, C., & Fabes, R. (2001). The stability and consequences of young children's same-sex peer interactions. *Developmental Psychology, 37,* 431–446.

Martin, C. L., Eisenbud, L., & Rose, H. (1995). Children's gender-based reasoning about toys. *Child Development, 52,* 1119–1134.

Martin, C. L., & Halverson, C. F. (1981). A schematic-processing model of sex typing and stereotyping in children. *Child Development, 52,* 1119–1134.

Martin, C. L., & Halverson, C. F. (1983). The effects of sex-typing schemas on young children's memory. *Child Development, 54,* 563–574.

Martin, C. L., & Little, J. K. (1990). The relation of gender understanding to children's sex-typed preferences and gender stereotypes. *Child Development, 61,* 1427–1439.

Martin, C. L., & Ruble, D. N. (2004). Children's search for gender cues. *Current Directions in Psychological Science, 13,* 67–70.

Martin, C. L., Ruble, D. N., & Szkybalo, J. (2002). Cognitive theories of early gender development. *Psychological Bulletin, 128,* 903–933.

Martinez, F. D., Wright, A. L., & Taussig, L. M. (1994). The effect of paternal smoking on the birthweight of newborns whose mothers do not smoke. *American Journal of Public Health, 84,* 1489–1491.

Martini, F. H. (1995). *Anatomy and physiology* (3rd ed.). Upper Saddle River, NJ: Prentice Hall.

Martini, J. (1993). *Fundamentals of anatomy and physiology.* Upper Saddle River, NJ: Prentice Hall.

Martini, M., & Kirkpatrick, J. (1981). Early interactions in the Marquesas Island. In T. M. Field, A. M. Sostek, P. Vietze, & P. H. Leiderman (Eds.), *Culture and early interactions.* Hillsdale, NJ: Erlbaum.

Martorell, R. (1984). Genetics, environment and growth: Issues in the assessment of nutritional status. In A. Velasquez & H. Bourges (Eds.), *Genetic factors in nutrition.* Orlando, FL: Academic Press.

Martorell, R., Mendoza, F. S., Baisden, K., & Pawson, R. G. (1994). Physical growth, sexual maturation, and obesity in Puerto Rican children. In G. Lamberty & C. G. Coll (Eds.), *Puerto Rican women and children: Issues in health, growth, and development.* New York: Plenum.

Mash, E. J., Johnston, C., & Kovitz, K. A. (1983). A comparison of the mother-child interactions of physically abused and nonabused children during play and task situations. *Journal of Clinical Child Psychology, 12,* 337–346.

Massey, C. M., & Gelman, R. (1988). Preschooler's ability to decide whether a photographed unfamiliar object can move itself. *Developmental Psychology, 24,* 307–317.

Masten, A. S., & Coatsworth, J. D. (1998). The development of competence in favorable and unfavorable environments: Lessons from research on successful children. *American Psychologist, 53,* 205–220.

Matas, L., Arend, R., & Sroufe, L. A. (1978). Continuity of adaptation in the second year. The relationship between quality of attachment and later competence. *Child Development, 49,* 547–556.

Mattson, S. N., Riley, E. P., Delis, D. C., & Jones, K. L. (1998). Neuropsychological comparison of alcohol-exposed children with or without physical features of fetal alcohol syndrome. *Neuropsychology, 12,* 146–153.

Maurer, D., & Maurer, C. (1988). *The world of the newborn.* New York: Basic Books.

Maurer, D., & Salapatek, P. (1976). Developmental changes in the scanning of faces by young infants. *Child Development, 47,* 523–527.

Maurer, D., Stagner, C. L., & Mondlach, C. J. (1999). Cross-modal transfer of shape is difficult to demonstrate in one-month-olds. *Child Development, 70,* 1047–1057.

Maynard, A. E. (2002). Cultural teaching: The development of teaching skills in Maya sibling interactions. *Child Development, 73,* 969–982.

McCabe, A., & Peterson, C. (1991). *Developing narrative structure.* Hillsdale, NJ: Erlbaum.

McCall, R., Beach, S. R., & Lan, S. (2000). The nature and correlates of underachievement among elementary school children in

Hong Kong. *Child Development, 71,* 785–801.

McCall, R. B., Applebaum, M. I., & Hogarty, P. S. (1973). Developmental changes in mental performance. *Monographs of the Society for Research in Child Development, 38* (3, Serial No. 150), 1–84.

McCall, R. B., Hogarty, P. S., & Hurlburt, N. (1972). Transitions in infant sensorimotor development and the prediction of childhood IQ. *American Psychologist, 27,* 728–748.

McCartney, K., Harris, M. J., & Berniere, F. (1990). Growing up and growing apart: A developmental meta-analysis of twin studies. *Psychological Bulletin, 107,* 226–237.

McCarty, M. E., & Ashmead, D. H. (1999). Visual control for reaching and grasping in infants. *Developmental Psychology, 35,* 620–631.

McCauley, E., Ito, J., & Kay, T. (1986). Psychosocial funtioning in girls with Turner syndrome and short stature. *Journal of the American Academy of Child Psychiatry, 25,* 105–112.

McCauley, E., Kay, T., Ito, J., & Treeler, R. (1987). The Turner syndrome: Cognitive defects, affective discrimination and behavior problems. *Child Development, 58,* 464–473.

McClintock, M. K., & Herdt, G. (1996). Rethinking puberty: The development of sexual attraction. *Current Directions in Psychological Science, 5,* 178–183.

McConaghy, N., & Silove, D. (1992). Do sex linked behaviors in children influence relationships with their parents? *Archives of Sexual Behavior, 21,* 409–479.

McDonald, M. A., Sigman, M., Espinosa, M. P., & Neumann, C. G. (1994). Impact of a temporary food shortage on children and their mothers. *Child Development, 65,* 404–416.

McDonough, S. C. (2004). Interaction guidance: Promoting and nurturing the caregiving relationship. In A. J. Sameroff, S. C. McDonough, & K. L. Rosenblum (Eds.), *Treating parent-infant relational problems* (pp. 79–96). New York: Guilford.

McDowell, D. J., O'Neil, R., & Parke, R. D. (2000). Display rule application in a disappointing situation and children's emotional reactivity: Relations with social competence. *Merrill-Palmer Quarterly, 46,* 306–324.

McDowell, D. J., & Parke, R. D. (2000). Differential knowledge of display rules for positive and negative emotions: Influences from

parents influences on peers. *Social Development, 9,* 415–432.

McGraw, M. (1940). Neuromuscular development of the human infant as exemplified in the achievement of erect locomotion. *Journal of Pediatrics, 17,* 747–771.

McGue, M., & Bouchard, T. J. (1987). Genetic and environmental determinants of information processing and special mental abilities: A twin analysis. In R. J. Sternberg (Ed.), *Advances in the psychology of human intelligence* (Vol. 5). Hillsdale, NJ: Erlbaum.

McGuire, S. (2001). Nonshared environment research: What is it and where is it going? *Marriage and Family Review, 33,* 31–56.

McHale, J., & Rasmussen, J. (1998). Coparental and family group-level dynamics during infancy: Early family predictors of child and family functioning during preschool. *Developmental and Psychopathology, 10,* 39–58.

McHale, J. P., Laurette, A., Talbot, J., & Pouquette, C. (2002). Retrospect and prospect in the psychological study of coparenting and family group process. In J. P. McHale & W. Grolnick (Eds.), *Retrospect and prospect in the psychological study of families* (pp. 127–165). Mahwah, NJ: Erlbaum.

McHale, S. M., Bartko, W. T., Crouter, A. C., & Perry-Jenkins, M. (1990). Children's housework and psychosocial functioning: The mediating effects of parents' sex-role behaviors and attitudes. *Child Development, 61,* 1413–1426.

McHale, S. M., Crouter, A. C., & Whiteman, S. D. (2003). Family contexts of gender development in childhood and adolescence. *Social Development, 12,* 125–148.

McHale, S. M., Shanahan, L., Updergraff, K. A., Crouter, A. C., & Booth, A. (2004). Developmental and individual differences in girls' sex-typed activities in middle childhood and adolescence. *Child Development, 75,* 1575–1593.

McHale, S. M., Updegraff, K. A., Helms-Erikson, H., & Crouter, A. C. (2001). Sibling influences on gender development in middle childhood and early adolescence: A longitudinal study. *Developmental Psychology, 37,* 115–125.

McIntire, D. D., Bloom, S. L., Casey, B. M., & Leveno, K. J. (1999). Birthweight in relation to morbidity and mortality among newborn infants. *New England Journal of Medicine, 340,* 1234–1238.

McIntosh, H. (1999). Two autism studies fuel hope and skepticism. *Monitor in Psychology, 30,* 28.

McKenna, J. J., & Mosko, S. (1990). Evolution and the sudden infant death syndrome (SIDS). *Human Nature, 1,* 291–330.

McKenna, J. J., & Mosko, S. (1993). Evolution and infant sleep: An experimental study of infant-parent co-sleeping and its implications for SIDS. *Acta Paediatrica, 389* (Suppl.), 31–36.

McLanahan, S., & Sandefur, G. (1994). *Growing up with a single parent.* Cambridge, MA: Harvard University Press.

McLellan, J. A., & Youniss, J. (2003). Two systems of youth service: Determinants of voluntary and required youth community service. *Journal of Youth and Adolescence, 32,* 47–58.

McLoyd, V. C. (1998). Socioeconomic disadvantage and child development. *American Psychologist, 53,* 185–204.

McLoyd, V. C., & Ceballo, R. (1998). Conceptualizing and assessing economic context: Issues as the study of race and child development. In V. C. McLoyd & L. Steinberg (Eds.), *Studying minority adolescents: Conceptual, methodological and theoretical issues* (pp. 251–278). Mahwah, NJ: Erlbaum.

McLoyd, V. C., Harper, C. I., & Copeland, N. L. (2001). Ethnic minority status, interparental conflict and child adjustment. In J. Grych & F. D. Fincham (Eds.), *Interparental conflict and child development* (pp. 98–125). New York: Cambridge University Press.

McLoyd, V. C., Jayaratne, R. E., Ceballo, R., & Borguez, J. (1994). Unemployment and work interruption among African-American single mothers: Effects on parenting in adolescent socioemotional functioning. *Child Development, 65,* 562–589.

McNeill, D. (1970). *The acquisition of language: The study of developmental psycholinguistics.* New York: Harper & Row.

McPherson, D. (1993). *Gay parenting couples: Parenting arrangements, arrangement satisfaction, and relationship satisfaction.* Unpublished doctoral dissertation, Pacific Graduate School of Psychology, Palo Alto, CA.

Mead, M. (1935). *Sex and temperament in three primitive societies.* New York: Morrow.

Medrich, E. A. (1981). *The serious business of growing up: A study of children's lives outside the school.* Berkeley: University of California Press.

Mehler, J., Dupoux, E., Nazzi, T., & Dehaene-Lambertz, G. (1996). Coping with linguistic diversity: The infant's viewpoint. In J. L.

Morgan & K. Demuth (Eds.), *Signal to syntax: Bootstrapping from speech to grammar in early acquisition* (pp. 101–116). Mahwah, NJ: Erlbaum.

Mehler, J., Jusczyk, P., Lambertz, G., Halsted, N., Bertoncini, J., & Amieltison, C. (1988). A precursor of language acquisition in young infants. *Cognition, 29,* 143–178.

Mehler, P. S., & Crews, C. K. (2001). Refeeding the patient with anorexia nervosa. *Eating Disorders: The Journal of Treatment and Prevention, 9,* 167–171.

Mehta, M. A., Sahakian, B. J., & Robbins, T. (2001). Comparative psychopharmacology of methylphenidate and related drugs in human volunteers, patients with ADHD, and experimental animals. In M. V. Solanto, A. F. T. Arnsten, & F. X. Castellanos (Eds.)., *Stimulant drugs and ADHD: Basic and clinical neuroscience* (pp. 303–331). New York: Oxford University Press.

Meier, R. P., & Newport, E. L. (1990). Out of the hands of babes: On a possible sign advantage in language acquisition. *Language, 66*(1), 1–23.

Meisel, J. M. (1995). Parameters in acquisition. In P. Fletcher & B. MacWhinney (Eds.), *The handbook of child language.* Oxford: Blackwell.

Meltzoff, A. N. (1981). Imitation, intermodal coordination and representation in early infancy. In G. Butterworth (Ed.), *Infancy and epistemology.* Brighton: Harvester Press.

Meltzoff, A. N. (1988a). Infant imitation and memory: Nine-month-old infants in immediate and deferred tests. *Child Development, 59,* 217–225.

Meltzoff, A. N. (1988b). Infant imitation after a 1-week delay: Long-term memory for novel acts and multiple stimuli. *Developmental Psychology, 24,* 470–476.

Meltzoff, A. N. (1990). Towards a developmental cognitive science. *Annals of the New York Academy of Sciences, 608,* 1–37.

Meltzoff, A. N., & Borton, R. W. (1979). Intermodal matching by human neonates. *Nature, 282,* 403–404.

Meltzoff, A. N., & Moore, M. K. (1983). Newborn infants imitate adult facial gestures. *Child Development, 54,* 702–709.

Meltzoff, A. N., & Moore, M. K. (1994). Imitation, memory and the representation of persons. *Infant Behavior and Development, 17,* 83–99.

Mennella, J. A., & Beauchamp, G. K. (1993). The effects of repeated exposure to garlic-flavored milk on the nursling's behavior. *Pediatric Research, 34,* 805–808.

Mennella, J. A., & Beauchamp, G. K. (1996). The human infants' response to vanilla flavors in mother's milk and formula. *Infant Behavior & Development, 19,* 13–19.

Mercer, J. R. (1971). Sociocultural factors in labeling mental retardates. *Peabody Journal of Education, 48,* 188–203.

Meredith, H. V. (1975). Somatic changes during prenatal life. *Child Development, 46,* 603–610.

Merewood, A. (2000). Sperm under siege. In K. L. Freiberg (Ed.), *Human development 00/01* (28th ed., pp. 41–45). Guilford, CT: Dushkin/McGraw-Hill.

Merriman, W., & Bowman, L. (1989). The mutual exclusivity bias in children's word learning. *Monographs of the Society for Research in Child Development, 54* (serial no. 220).

Merriman, W. E., Evey-Burkey, J. A., Marazita, J. M., & Jarvis, L. H. (1996). Young two-year-olds' tendency to map novel verbs onto novel actions. *Journal of Experimental Child Psychology, 63,* 466–498.

Mervis, C. B., & Klein-Tasman, B. P. (2000). Williams syndrome: Cognition, personality, and adaptive behavior. *Mental Retardation and Developmental Disabilities Research Review, 6,* 148–158.

Mervis, C. B., & Mervis, C. A. (1982). Leopards are kitty cats: Object labeling by mothers for their thirteen-month-olds. *Child Development, 53,* 267–273.

Messinger, D. S., Fogel, A., & Dickson, K. L. (2001). All smiles but some smiles are more positive than others. *Developmental Psychology, 37,* 642–653.

Metz, E., McLellan, J., & Youniss, J. (2003). Types of voluntary service and adolescents' civic development. *Journal of Adolescent Research, 18,* 188–203.

Meyer-Bahlburg, H. F. L., Ehrhardt, A. A., Rosen, L. R., Gruen, R. S., Veridiano, N. P., Vann, F. H., & Neuwalder, H. A. (1995). Prenatal estrogens and the development of homosexual orientation. *Developmental Psychology, 31,* 12–21.

Miller, G. A. (1956). The magical number seven, plus or minus two: Some limits on our capacity for processing information. *Psychological Review, 63,* 81–97.

Miller, J. G., & Bersoff, D. M. (1992). Culture and moral judgment: How are conflicts between justice and interpersonal responsibilities resolved? *Journal of Personality and Social Psychology, 62,* 541–554.

Miller, J. G., Bersoff, D. M., & Harwood, R. L. (1990). Perceptions of social responsibilities in India and in the United States: Moral imperatives or personal decisions? *Journal of Personality & Social Psychology, 58,* 33–47.

Miller, J. L., & Eimas, P. D. (1994). Observations on speech perception, its development, and the search for a mechanism. In J. C. Goodman & H. C. Nusbaum (Eds.), *The development of speech perception: The transition from speech sounds to spoken words* (pp. 37–56). Cambridge, MA: MIT Press.

Miller, K. F., Smith, C. M., Zhu, J., & Zhang, H. (1995). Preschool origins of cross-national differences in mathematical competence: The role of number-naming systems. *Psychological Science, 6,* 56–60.

Miller, L. T., & Vernon, P. A. (1997). Developmental changes in speed of information processing in young children. *Developmental Psychology, 33,* 549–554.

Miller, M. N., & Pumariega, A. J. (2001). Eating disorders: Bulimia and anorexia nervosa. In V. H. Booney & A. Pumariega (Eds.), *Clinical assessment of child and adolescent behavior* (pp. 234–268). New York: Wiley.

Miller, P., & Sperry, L. L. (1987). The socialization of anger and aggression. *Merrill-Palmer Quarterly, 33,* 1–31.

Miller, P. H. (1990). The development of strategies of selective attention. In D. F. Bjorklund (Ed.), *Children's strategies: Contemporary views of cognitive development* (pp. 157–184). Hillsdale, NJ: Erlbaum.

Miller, P. H. (2002). *Theories of developmental psychology* (4th ed.). New York: Worth.

Miller, P. H., & Aloise-Young, P. A. (1995). Preschoolers' strategic behavior and performance on a same-different task. *Journal of Experimental Child Psychology, 60,* 284–303.

Miller, P. H., & Seier, W. L. (1994). Strategy utilization deficiencies in children: When, where, and why. In H. W. Reese (Ed.), *Advances in child development and behavior* (Vol. 25, pp. 107–156). New York: Academic Press.

Miller, P. H., Seier, W. L., Probert, J. S., & Aloise, P. A. (1991). Age differences in the capacity demands of a strategy among spontaneously strategic children. *Journal of Experimental Child Psychology, 52,* 149–165.

Miller, P. H., & Weiss, M. G. (1981). Children's attention allocation, understanding of attention, and performance on the incidental learning task. *Child Development, 52,* 1183–1190.

Miller, P. J., & Moore, B. B. (1989). Narrative conjunctions of caregiver and child: A comparative perspective on socialization through stories. *Ethos, 17,* 428–449.

Mills, J. L. (1999). Cocaine, smoking, and spontaneous abortion. *New England Journal of Medicine, 340,* 380–381.

Milstein, R. M. (1980). Responsiveness in newborn infants of overweight and normal parents. *Appetite, 1,* 65–74.

Minami, M., & McCabe, A. (1995). Rice balls and bear hunts: Japanese and North American family narrative patterns. *Journal of Child Language, 22,* 423–446.

Minuchin, P. (2002). Looking toward the horizon: Present and future in the study of family systems. In J. McHale & W. Grolnick (Eds.), *Retrospect and prospect in the psychological study of families* (pp. 259–278). Mahwah, NJ: Erlbaum.

Mischel, W., Shoda, Y., & Peake, P. K. (1988). The nature of adolescent competencies predicted by preschool delay of gratification. *Journal of Personality and Social Psychology, 54,* 687–696.

Mishra, R. (1997). Cognition and cognitive development. In J. W. Berry, P. R. Dasen, & T. S. Saraswathi (Eds.), *Handbook of cross-cultural psychology: Vol. 2, Basic process and human development* (2nd ed., pp. 143–175). Boston: Allyn & Bacon.

Mistry, J., Rogoff, B., & Herman, H. (2001). What is the meaning of meaningful purpose in children's remembering? Istomina revisited. *Mind, Culture, & Activity, 8,* 28–41.

Mitchell, E. A., Ford, R. P. K., Stewart, A. W., Taylor, B. J., Becroft, D. M., Thompson, J. M. P., Scragg, R., Hassall, I. B., Barry, D. M. J., Allen, E. M., & Roberts, A. P. (1993). Smoking and the sudden infant death syndrome. *Pediatrics, 91,* 893–896.

Mitchell, J. E., Fletcher, L., Hanson, K., Mussell, M. P., Siem, H., Crosby, R., & Albanna, M. (2001). The relative efficacy of fluoxetine and manual-based self-help in the treatment of outpatients with bulimia nervosa. *Journal of Clinical Psychopharmacology, 21,* 298–304.

Mitchell, P. (1997). *Introduction to theory of mind.* London: Arnold.

Mize, J., & Ladd, G. W. (1990). Toward the development of successful social skills for preschool children. In S. R. Asher & J. D. Coie (Eds.), *Peer rejection in childhood.* New York: Cambridge University Press.

Moeller, T. G. (2001). *Youth aggression and violence.* Mahwah, NJ: Erlbaum.

Moffitt, A. R. (1971). Consonant cue perception by twenty- to twenty-four week old infants. *Child Development, 42,* 717–732.

Moffitt, T. E. (1993). Adolescence-limited and life-course-persistent antisocial behavior: A developmental taxonomy. *Psychological Review, 100,* 674–701.

Moffitt, T. E., Caspi, A., Belsky, J., & Silva, P. A. (1992). Childhood experience and the onset of menarche: A test of a sociobiological model. *Child Development, 63,* 47–58.

Moffitt, T. E., Caspi, A., Harkness, A. R., & Silva, P. A. (1993). The natural history of change in intellectual performance: Who changes? How much? Is it meaningful? *Journal of Child Psychology & Psychiatry & Allied Disciplines, 34,* 455–506.

Moffitt, T. E., Caspi, A., Rutter, M., & Silva, P. A. (2001). *Sex differences in antisocial behavior.* Cambridge, UK: Cambridge University Press.

Mohn, G., & van Hof-van Duin (1986). Development of binocular and monocular visual fields of human infants during the first year of life. *Clinical Visual Science, 1,* 51–64.

Molfese, D. L. (1973). Cerebral asymmetry in infants, children, and adults: Auditory evoked responses to speech and musical stimuli. *Journal of the Acoustical Society of America, 53,* 363.

Molfese, D. L., & Betz, J. C. (1988). Electrophysiological indices of the early development of lateralization for language and cognition, and their implications for predicting later development. In D. L. Molfese & S. J. Segalowitz (Eds.), *Brain lateralization in children: Developmental implications* (pp. 171–190). New York: Guilford Press.

Molfese, D. L., & Molfese, V. J. (1980). Cortical response of preterm infants to phonetic and nonphonetic speech stimuli. *Developmental Psychology, 16,* 574–581.

Molfese, D. L., & Molfese, V. J. (1985). Electrophysiological indices of auditory discrimination in newborn infants: The bases for predicting later language development? *Infant Behavior and Development, 8,* 197–211.

Molfese, D. L., Morse, P. A., & Peters, C. J. (1990). Auditory evoked responses to names for different objects: Cross-modal processing as a basis for infant language acquisition. *Developmental Psychology, 26,* 780–795.

Molfese, V. J., & Martin, T. B. (2001). Intelligence and achievement: Measurement and prediction of developmental variations. In D. L. Molfese & V. J. Molfese (Eds.), *Developmental variations in learning* (pp. 1–22).

Molina, J., Chotro, M., & Dominguez, H. (1995). Fetal alcohol learning resulting from contamination of the prenatal environment. In J.-P. le Canuet, W. Fifer, N. Krasnegor, & W. Smotherman (Eds.), *Fetal development: A psychobiological perspective* (pp. 419–438). Hillsdale, NJ: Erlbaum.

Money, J. (1987). Propaedeutics of dioecious G-I/R: Theoretical foundations for understanding dimorphic gender-identity/role. In J. M. Reinisch, L. A. Rosenblum, & S. A. Sanders (Eds.), *Masculinity/femininity: Basic perspectives.* New York: Oxford University Press.

Money, J. (1993). Specific neurocognitional impairments associated with Turner (45, X) and Klinefelter (47, XXY) syndromes: A review. *Social Biology, 40,* 147–151.

Money, J., & Ehrhardt, A. A. (1972). *Man and woman, boy and girl.* Baltimore, MD: Johns Hopkins University Press.

Monk, C., Fifer, W. P., Myers, M. M., Sloan, R. P., Trien, L., & Hurtado, A. (2000). Maternal stress responses and anxiety during pregnancy: Effects on fetal heart rate. *Developmental Psychology, 36,* 67–77.

Montague, D. P. F., & Walker-Andrews, A. S. (2002). Mothers, fathers, and infants: The role of person familiarity and parental involvement in infants' perception of emotion expressions. *Child Development, 75,* 1339–1352.

Moore, C., Barresi, J., & Thompson, C. (1998). The cognitive basis of future-oriented prosocial behavior. *Social Development, 1,* 198–218.

Moore, D. R., & Florsheim, P. (2001). Interpersonal processes and psychopathology among expectant and non-expectant adolescent couples. *Journal of Consulting and Clinical Psychology, 69,* 101–111.

Moore, D. S. (2001). *The dependent gene: The fallacy of "nature vs. nurture."* New York: Freeman.

Moore, K. L., & Persaud, T. V. N. (1998). *Before we are born* (5th ed.). Philadelphia: Saunders.

Moore, M. R., & Brooks-Gunn, J. (2002). Adolescent parenthood. In

M. H. Bornstein (Ed.), *Handbook of parenting* (2nd ed.) (pp. 173–214). Mahwah, NJ: Erlbaum.

Morelli, G., Rogoff, B., & Angellio, C. (2003). Cultural variation in young children's access to work or involvement in specialised child-focused activities. *International Journal of Behavioral Development, 27,* 264–274.

Morelli, G. A., Rogoff, B., Oppenheim, D., & Goldsmith, D. (1992). Cultural variation in infants' sleeping arrangements: Questions of independence. *Developmental Psychology, 28,* 604–613.

Morelli, G. A., & Tronick, E. Z. (1992). Male care among Efe foragers and Lese farmers. In B. Hewlett (Ed.), *Father-child relations: Cultural and biosocial contexts* (pp. 231–262). New York: Aldine de Gruyther.

Morgan, B. L. (1998). A three-generational study of tomboy behavior. *Sex Roles, 39,* 787–858.

Morgan, G. A., & Ricciuti, H. (1969). Infants' responses to strangers during the first year. In B. M. Foss (Ed.), *Determinants of infant behavior* (Vol. 4, pp. 253–272). London: Methuen.

Morgan, J. L. (1990). Input, innateness and induction in language acquisition. *Developmental Psychology, 23,* 661–678.

Morgan, J. L. (1994). Converging measures of speech segmentation in preverbal infants. *Infant Behavior and Development, 17,* 387–403.

Morgan, J. L., Bonamo, K. M., & Travis, L. L. (1995). Negative evidence on negative evidence. *Developmental Psychology, 31,* 180–197.

Morgan, J. L., & Demuth, K. (1996). *Signal to syntax: Bootstrapping from speech to grammar in early acquisition.* Mahwah, NJ: Erlbaum.

Morgan, J. L., & Saffran, J. R. (1995). Emerging integration of sequential and suprasegmental information in preverbal speech segmentation. *Child Development, 16,* 911–936.

Morris, P., Huston, A. C., Duncan, G. J., Crosby, D. A., & Bos, J. M. (2001). *How welfare and work policies affect children: A synthesis of research.* New York: Manpower Demonstration Research Corporation.

Morris, P. A., & Gennetian, L. A. (2003). Identifying the effects of income on children's development using experimental data. *Journal of Marriage and Family, 65,* 716–729.

Morrison, F. J., Holmes, D. L., & Haith, M. M. (1974). A developmental study of the effect

of familiarity on short-term visual memory. *Journal of Experimental Child Psychology, 18,* 412–425.

Morrongiello, B. A., Hewitt, K. L., & Gotowiec, A. (1991). Infant discrimination of relative distance in the auditory modality: Approaching versus receding sound sources. *Infant Behavior Development, 14,* 187–208.

Mosedale, L. (1991). Fathers in the delivery room. *Self,* April, 104–108.

Moshman, D. (1998). Cognitive development beyond childhood. In W. Damon (Gen. Ed.), D. Kuhn & R. S. Siegler (Vol. Eds.), *Handbook of child psychology: Vol. 2. Cognition, perception, and language* (pp. 947–978). New York: Wiley.

Moss, H. (1967). Sex, age and state as determinants of mother-infant interaction. *Merrill-Palmer Quarterly, 13,* 19–36.

Moss, M., Colombo, J., Mitchell, D. W., & Horowitz, F. D. (1988). Neonatal behavioral organization and visual discrimination at 3 months of age. *Child Development, 59,* 1211–1220.

Mounts, N. S. (2000). Parental management of adolescent peer relationships: What are its effects on friend selection? In K. Kerns, J. Contreras, & A. M. Neal-Barnett (Eds.), *Family and peers: Linking two social worlds* (pp. 169–194). Westport, CT: Praeger.

Mounts, N. S., & Steinberg, L. (1995). An ecological analysis of peer influences on adolescent grade point average and drug use. *Developmental Psychology, 31,* 915–922.

Mueller, E. (1989). Toddlers' peer relations: Shared meaning and semantics. In W. Damon (Ed.), *Child development today and tomorrow.* San Francisco: Jossey-Bass.

Mueller, E., & Brenner, J. (1977). The origins of social skills and interaction among playgroup toddlers. *Child Development, 48,* 854–861.

Mueller, E., & Lucas, T. A. (1975). A developmental analysis of peer interaction among toddlers. In M. Lewis & L. A. Rosenblum (Eds.), *Friendship and peer relations.* New York: Wiley.

Muir, D., & Clifton, R. (1985). Infants' orientation to location of sound sources. In G. Gottlieb & N. Krasnegor (Eds.), *Measurement of audition and vision in the first year of postnatal life. A methodological overview.* Norwood, NJ: Ablex.

Muir, D., & Field, T. M. (1979). Newborn infants orient to sounds. *Child Development, 50,* 431–436.

Mullen, M. K., & Yi, S. (1995). The cultural context of talk about the past: Implications for the development of autobiographical

memeory. *Cognitive Development, 10,* 407–419.

Mumme, D. L., Fernald, A., & Herrera, C. (1996). Infants' responses to facial and vocal emotional signals in a social referencing paradigm. *Child Development, 67,* 3219–3237.

Munakata, U., McClelland, J. L., Johnson, M. J., & Siegler, R. S. (1997). Rethinking infant knowledge: Toward an adaptive process account of successes and failures in object permanence tasks. *Psychological Review, 104,* 686–713.

Munroe, R. H., Munroe, R. L., & Brasher, A. (1985). Precursors of spatial ability: A longitudinal study among the Logoli of Kenya. *The Journal of Social Psychology, 125,* 23–33.

Munroe, R. H., Shimmin, H. S., & Munroe, R. L. (1984). Gender understanding and sex role preference in four cultures. *Developmental Psychology, 20,* 673–682.

Munte, T. F., Altenmuller, E., & Jancke, L. (2002). The musician's brain as a model of neuroplasticity. *National Review of Neuroscience, 3,* 473–478.

Murray, T. A. (1996). *The worth of a child.* Berkeley, CA: University of California Press.

Myers, D. G. (2000). *The American paradox: Spiritual hunger in an age of plenty.* New Haven, CT: Yale University Press.

Myers, N. A., Clifton, R. K., & Clarkson, M. G. (1987). When they were young: Almost-threes remember two years ago. *Infant Behavior and Development, 10,* 123–132.

Myles-Worsley, M., Cromer, C. C., & Dodd, D. H. (1986). Children's preschool script reconstruction: Reliance on general knowledge as memory fades. *Developmental Psychology, 22,* 22–30.

Nachmias, M., Gunnar, M., Mangelsdorf, S., Parritz, R. H., & Buss, K. (1996). Behavioral inhibition and stress reactivity: The moderating role of attachment security. *Child Development, 67,* 508–522.

Nadder, T. S., Silberg, J. L., Rutter, M., Maes, H., & Eaves, J. (2001). Comparison of multiple measures of ADHD symptomatology: A multivariate of genetic analysis. *Journal of Child Psychology and Psychiatry and Allied Disciplines, 42,* 475–486.

Nader, P. R. (1993). The role of the family in obesity: Prevention and treatment. In C. L. Williams & S. Y. S. Kimm (Eds.), *Prevention and treatment of childhood obesity* (pp. 147–153). Annals of the New York Academy of Sciences,

Vol. 699. New York: The New York Academy of Sciences.

Nagin, D., & Tremblay, R. E. (1999). Trajectories of boys' physical aggression, opposition, and hyperactivity on the path to physically violent and nonviolent juvenile delinquency. *Child Development, 70,* 1181–1196.

Nansel, T. R., Overpeck, M., Pilla, R. S., Ruan, W. J., Simons-Morton, B., & Scheidt, P. (2001). Bullying behaviors among US youth. *Journal of the American Medical Association, 285,* 2094–2100.

Nash, J. M. (1997). Fertile minds. *Time,* Feb. 3, pp. 49–62.

National Adoption Information Clearinghouse (2000). Transsocial adoption. www.calib/naic/pubs/s-trans.html.

National Center for Health Statistics (1976). *NCHS growth charts.* Washington, DC.

National Center for Health Statistics (2002). Overweight prevalence. www.cdc.gov/nchs/ fastats/overwt.htm

National Committee to Prevent Child Abuse (1997). *Current trends in child abuse reporting and fatalities: Results of the 1996 annual 50-state survey.* Chicago: Author.

National Institutes of Health (2002). *The National Human Genome Research Institute Website.* www.nhgri.nih.gov/

National Joint Committee on Learning Disabilities (1994). Learning disabilities: Issues on definition, a position paper of the National Joint Committee on Learning Disabilities. In *Collective perspectives on issues affecting learning disabilities: Position papers and statements.* Austin, TX: Pro-Ed.

National March of Dimes Foundation (2001). Report on pregnancy-related diseases. White Plains, NY: March of Dimes Foundation.

Naus, M. J. (1982). Memory development in the young reader: The combined effects of knowledge base and memory processing. In W. Otto & S. White (Eds.), *Reading expository text.* New York: Academic.

Nazzi, T., & Gopnik, A. (2001). Linguistic and cognitive abilities in infancy: When does language become a tool for categorization? *Cognition, 80,* 30–37.

Neal, M. V. (1968). Vestibular stimulation and developmental behavior of the small premature infant. *Nursing Research Report, 3,* 2–5.

Needleman, H. L., Leviton, A., & Bellinger, D. (1982). Lead-associated intellectual deficits. *New England Journal of Medicine, 306,* 367.

Neisser, U., Boodoo, G., Bouchard, T. J., Boykin, A. W., Brody, N., Ceci, S. J., Halpern, D. F., Loehlin, J. C., Perloff, R., Sternberg, R. J., & Urbina, S. (1995). *Intelligence: Knowns and unknowns.* Washington, DC: American Psychological Association.

Nelson, C. A. (1987). The recognition of facial expressions in the first two years of life. *Child Development, 58,* 889–909.

Nelson, C. A. (1999a). Change and continuity in neurobehavioral development: Lessons from the study of neurobiology and neural plasticity. *Infant Behavior and Development, 22,* 415–429.

Nelson, C. A. (1999b). Neural plasticity and human development. *Current Directions in Psychological Science, 8,* 42–45.

Nelson, C. A., & Bosquet, M. (2000). Neurobiology of fetal and infant development: Implications for infant mental health. In C. Zeanah (Ed.), *Handbook of Infant Mental Health* (pp. 37–59). New York: Guilford.

Nelson, C. A., Thomas, K., & de Haan, M. (2006). Neural basis of cognition. In W. Damon & R. M. Lerner (Gen. Eds.) and D. Kuhn & R. Siegler (Vol. Eds.). *Handbook of child psychology, Vol. 2: Perceptual and cognitive development* (6th ed.). New York: Wiley.

Nelson, K. (1973). Structure and strategy in learning to talk. *Monographs of the Society for Research in Child Development, 38* (1, 2).

Nelson, K. (1977). Aspects of language acquisition and form use from age 2 to age 20. *Journal of the American Academy of Child Psychiatry, 16,* 121–132.

Nelson, K. (1989). Strategies for first language teaching. In M. L. Rice & R. L. Schiefelbusch (Eds.), *The teachability of language.* Baltimore, MD: Brooks/Cole.

Nelson, K. (1993). Events, narratives, memory: What develops? In C. A. Nelson (Ed.), *Memory and affect in development. The Minnesota symposia on child psychology* (Vol. 26, pp. 1–24). Hillsdale, NJ: Erlbaum.

Nelson, K. (1996). *Language in cognitive development: The emergence of the mediated mind.* New York: Cambridge University Press.

Nelson, K., Carskadden, G., & Bonvillian, J. D. (1973). Syntax acquisition: Impact of experimental variation in adult verbal interaction with the child. *Child Development, 44,* 497–504.

Nelson, K. E., Welsh, J., Camarata, S. M., Butkovsky, L., &

Camarata, M. (1995). Available input for language-impaired children and younger children of matched language levels. *First Language, 15,* 1–17.

Netley, C. T. (1986). Summary overview of behavioral development in individuals with neonatally identified X and Y aneuploidy. *Birth Defects, 22,* 293–306.

Neumarker, K. (1997). Mortality and sudden death in anorexia nervosa. *International Journal of Eating Disorders, 21,* 205–212.

Neville, B., & Parke, R. D. (1997). Waiting for paternity: Interpersonal and contextual implications of the timing of fatherhood. *Sex Roles, 37,* 45–59.

Neville, H. J. (1991). Neurobiology of cognitive and language processing: Effects of early experience. In K. R. Gibson & A. C. Petersen (Eds.), *Brain maturation and cognitive development: Comparative and cross-cultural perspectives* (pp. 355–380). New York: Aldine de Bruyter.

Neville, H. J., Bevelier, D., Corina, J., Rauschecker, A., Karni, A., Lalwani, A., Braun, V., Clark, P., & Turner, R. (1998). Cerebral organization for language in deaf and hearing subjects: Biological constraints and effects of experience. *Proceedings of the National Academy of Sciences, 95,* 922–929.

Neville, H. J., & Bruer, J. T. (2001). Language processing: How experience affects brain organization. In D. B. Bailey, J. T. Bruer, F. J. Simons, & J. W. Lichtman (Eds.), *Critical thinking about critical periods* (pp. 151–172). Baltimore: Paul H. Broker.

Nevin, M. M. (1988). Dormant dangers of DES. *The Canadian Nurse, 84,* 17–19.

Newcomb, A. F., Bukowski, W. M., & Pattee, L. (1993). Children's peer relations: A meta-analytic review of popular, rejected, neglected, controversial, and average sociometric status. *Psychological Bulletin, 113,* 99–128.

Newcomb, M. D., & Bentler, P. M. (1989). Substance use and abuse among children and teenagers. *American Psychologist, 44,* 242–248.

Newcombe, N., & Huttenlocher, J. (1992). Children's early ability to solve perspective-taking problems. *Developmental Psychology, 28,* 635–643.

Newcombe, N. S., & Huttenlocher, J. (2003). *Making space: The development of spatial representation and reasoning.* Cambridge, MA: MIT Press.

Newcombe, N. S., Huttenlocher, J., Drummey, A. B., & Wiley, J. (1998). The development of spatial

location coding: Place learning and dead reckoning in the second and third years of life. *Cognitive Development, 13,* 185–200.

Newcomer, S., & Udry, J. R. (1987). Parental marital status effects on adolescent sexual behavior. *Journal of Marriage and the Family, 48,* 235–240.

Newell, K., Scully, D. M., McDonald, P. V., & Baillargeon, R. (1989). Task constraints and infant grip configurations. *Developmental Psychobiology, 22,* 817–832.

Newman, D., Riel, M., & Martin, L. (1983). Cultural practices and Piagetian theory: The impact of a cross-cultural program. In D. Kuhn & J. Meacham (Eds.), *On the development of developmental psychology.* Basel, Switzerland: Karger.

Newman, J. (1995). How breast milk protects newborns. *Scientific American, 273,* 76–79. www.unicef.org/fgf/04/Breast feeding. Facts of life.

Newport, E. L. (1990). Maturational constraints on language learning. *Cognitive Science, 14,* 11–28.

NHLBI Growth and Health Study Research Group. (1992). *American Journal of Public Health, 82,* 1613–1620.

NICHD Early Child Care Research Network (1999). Chronicity of maternal depressive symptoms, maternal sensitivity, and child functioning at 36 months. *Developmental Psychology, 35,* 1297–1310.

NICHD Early Child Care Research Network (2000a). The relation of child care to cognitive and language development. *Child Development, 71,* 960–980.

NICHD Early Child Care Research Network (2000b). Factors associated with fathers' caregiving activities and sensitivity with young children. *Journal of Family Psychology, 14,* 200–219.

NICHD Early Child Care Research Network (2001). Before Head Start: Income and ethnicity, family characteristics, child care experiences and child development. *Early Education and Development, 12,* 545–576.

NICHD Early Child Care Research Network (2003). Does amount of time spent in child care predict socioemotional adjustment during the transition to kindergarten? *Child Development, 74,* 976–1005.

NICHD Early Child Care Research Network (2003). Frequency and intensity of activity of third grade children in physical education. *Archives of Pediatrics and Adolescent medicine, 157,* 185–190.

NICHD Early Child Care Research Network (2004a). Are child developmental outcomes related to before/after school care arrangements. *Child Development, 75*, 280–295.

NICHD Early Child Care Research Network (2004b). Trajectories of physical aggression from toddlerhood to middle childhood: Predictors, correlates, and outcomes. *Monographs of the Society for Research in Child Development.*

Nickolls, K. B., Cassel, J., & Kaplan, B. H. (1972). Psychosocial assets, life crisis and the prognosis of pregnancy. *American Journal of Epidemiology, 95,* 431–441.

Nigg, J. T., & Goldsmith, H. H. (1994). Genetics of personality disorders: Perspectives from personality and psychopathology research. *Psychological Bulletin, 115,* 346–380.

Nightingale, E. O., & Meister, S. B. (1987). *Prenatal screening, policies, and values: Three examples of neural tube defects.* Cambridge, MA: Harvard University Press.

Ninio, A., & Snow, C. (1996). *Pragmatic development.* Boulder, CO: Westview Press.

Nisan, M., & Kohlberg, L. (1982). Universality and variation in moral judgment: A longitudinal and cross-sectional study in Turkey. *Child Development, 53,* 865–876.

Nisbett, R. E. (1998). Race, genetics, and IQ. In C. Jencks & M. Phillips (Eds.), *The black-white test score gap* (pp. 86–102). Washington, DC: Brookings Institution.

Norlander, T., Erixon, A., & Archer, T. (2000). Psychological androgyny and creativity: Dynamics of gender roles and personality traits. *Social Behavior and Personality, 28,* 423–435.

Norman, D. A. (1993). *Things that make us smart: Defending human attributes in the age of machines.* Reading, MA: Addison-Wesley.

Novak, G. (1996). *Developmental psychology: Dynamic systems and behavioral analysis.* Reno, NV: Context Press.

Novosad, C., & Thoman, E. B. (2003). The Breathing Bear: An intervention for crying babies and their mothers. *Journal of Developmental and Behavioral Pediatrics, 24,* 89–95.

Nsamenang, A. B., & Lamb, M. E. (1994). Socialization of Nso children in the Bamenda Grassfields of Northwest Cameroon. In P. M. Greenfield & R. R. Cocking (Eds.), *Cross cultural roots of minority child development.* Hillsdale, NJ: Erlbaum.

Nucci, L. P. (1996). Morality and the personal sphere of action. In E.

Reed, E. Turiel, & T. Brown (Eds.), *Values and knowledge* (pp. 41–60). Hillsdale, NJ: Erlbaum.

Nucci, L. P., Camino, C., & Milnitsky-Sapiro, C. (1996). Social class effects on northeastern Brazilian children's conceptions of areas of personal choice and social regulation. *Child Development, 67,* 1223–1242.

Nucci, L. P., & Turiel, E. (1978). Social interactions and the development of social concepts in preschool children. *Child Development, 49,* 400–407.

Nucci, L. P., & Weber, E. (1995). Social interactions in the home and the development of young children's conceptions of the personal. *Child Development, 66,* 1438–1452.

Nugent, J. K., Lester, B. M., & Brazelton, T. B. (Eds.). (1989). *Biology, culture, and development.* Norwood, NJ: Ablex.

Nugent, J. K., Lester, B. M., & Brazelton, T. B. (1991). *The cultural context of infancy, Vol. 2: Multicultural and interdisciplinary approaches to parent-infant relations.* Westport, DT: Ablex.

Nunes, T., & Bryant, P. (1996). *Children doing mathematics.* Oxford, UK: Blackwell.

Nwokah, E. E., Hsu, H., Dobrowolska, O., & Fogel, A. (1994). The development of laughter in mother-infant communication: Timing parameters and temporal sequences. *Infant Behavior & Development, 17,* 23–35.

O'Brien, M., Huston, A. C., & Risley, T. (1983). Sex-typed play of toddlers in a day care center. *Journal of Applied Developmental Psychology, 4,* 1–9.

O'Connor, T., Heron, J., Glover, V., & the ALSPAC Study Team. (2002). Antenatal anxiety predicts child behavior/emotional problems independently of postnatal depression. *Journal of the American Academy of Child and Adolescent Psychiatry, 41,* 1470–1477.

O'Neil, R., Parke, R. D., & McDowell, D. J. (2001). Objective and subjective features of children's neighborhoods: Relations to parental regulatory strategies and children's social competence. *Journal of Applied Developmental Psychology, 21,* 135–155.

O'Sullivan, J. T. (1996). Children's metamemory about the influence of conceptual relations on recall. *Journal of Experimental Child Psychology, 62,* 1–29.

O'Sullivan, J. T., & Pressley, M. (1984). Completeness of instruction and strategy transfer. *Journal of Experimental Child Psychology, 38,* 275–288.

Ochs, E. (1988). *Culture and language development.* Cambridge: Cambridge University Press.

Oden, S., & Asher, S. R. (1977). Coaching children in social skills for friendship making. *Child Development, 48,* 495–506.

Oehler, J. M., Eckerman, C. D., & Wilson, W. H. (1988). Social stimulation and the regulation of premature infant's state prior to term age. *Infant Behavior and Development, 12,* 341–356.

Oetting, E. R., & Beauvais, F. (1990). Adolescent drug use: Findings of national and local surveys. *Journal of Consulting and Clinical Psychology, 58,* 385–394.

Ogbu, J. (1988). Black education: A cultural-ecological perspective. In H. P. McAdoo (Ed.), *Black families* (pp. 169–186). Beverly Hills, CA: Sage.

Ogbu, J. U. (1997). Understanding the school performance of urban blacks: Some essential background knowledge. In H. J. Walberg, O. Reyes, & R. P. Weissberg (Eds.), *Children and youth: Interdisciplinary perspective* (pp. 190–222). Thousand Oaks, CA: Sage.

Ollendick, T. H., & King, N. J. (1998). Empirically supported treatments for children with phobic and anxiety disorders: Current status. *Journal of Clinical Child Psychology, 22,* 156–167.

Oller, D. K., & Eilers, R. E. (1988). The rate of audition in infant babbling. *Child Development, 59,* 441–449.

Oller, D. K., Wieman, L. A., Doyle, W. J., & Ross, C. (1976). Infant babbling and speech. *Journal of Child Language, 3,* 1–11.

Olsen, O. (1997). Meta-analysis of the safety of home birth. *Birth, 24,* 4–13.

Olson, D. R. (1994). *The world on paper: The conceptual and cognitive implications of writing and reading.* Cambridge, UK: Cambridge University Press.

Olweus, D. (1982). Development of stable aggressive reaction patterns in males. In R. Blanchard & C. Blanchard (Eds.), *Advances in the study of aggression* (Vol. 1). New York: Academic.

Olweus, D. (1991). Bully/victim problems among schoolchildren: Basic facts and effects of a school based intervention program. In D. J. Pepler, & K. H. Rubin (Eds.), *The development and treatment of childhood aggression* (pp. 411–448). Hillsdale, NJ: Lawrence Erlbaum Associates, Inc.

Olweus, D. (1993). *Bullying and school: What we know and what we can do.* Oxford: Blackwell.

Olweus, D. (1999). Bullying in Norway. In P. K. Smith, Y. Morita, J. Junger-Tas, D. Olweus, R.

Catalano, & P. Slee (Eds.), *The nature of school bullying: A cross-national perspective* (pp. 28–48). New York: Routledge.

Olweus, D., Mattson, A., Schalling, D., & Low, H. (1988). Circulating testosterone levels and aggression in adolescent males: A causal analysis. *Psychosomatic Medicine, 50,* 261–272.

Opie, I., & Opie, P. (1959). *The lore and language of schoolchildren.* Oxford: Clarendon Press.

Orlick, T., Zhou, Q., & Partington, J. (1990). Co-operation and conflict within Chinese and Canadian kindergarten settings. *Canadian Journal and Behavioural Science, 22,* 20–25.

Ornstein, P. A., Larus, D. M., & Clubb, P. A. (1992). Understanding children's testimony: Implications of research on the development of memory. In R. Vasta (Ed.), *Annals of Child Development* (Vol. 8). London: Jessica Kingsley Publishers.

Ornstein, P. A., Naus, M. J., & Liberty, C. (1975). Rehearsal and organizational processes in children's memory. *Child Development, 46,* 818–830.

Ottosson, H., Ekselius, Grann, M., & Kullgren, G. (2002). Cross-system concordance of personality disorder diagnosis of DSM-IV and Diagnostic Criteria for Research of ICD-10. *Journal of Personality Disorders, 16,* 283–292.

Overton, W. F., & Byrnes, J. P. (1991). Cognitive development. In R. M. Lerner, A. C. Petersen, & J. Brooks-Gunn (Eds.), *Encyclopedia of adolescence* (Vol. 1). New York: Garland.

Öztürk C., Durmazlar, N., Ural, B., Karaagooglu, E., Yalaz, K., & Anlar, B. (1999). Hand and eye preference in normal preschool children. *Clinical Pediatrics, 38,* 677–680.

Paarlberg, K. M., Vingerhoets, A. J. J. M., Passchier, J., Dekker, G. A., & van Giegn, H. P. (1995). Psychosocial factors and pregnancy outcomes: A review with emphasis on methodological issues. *Journal of Psychosomatic Research, 39,* 563–595.

Paley, B., Cox, M. J., Burchinal, M. R., & Payne, C. C. (1999). Attachment and family functioning: Comparison of spouses with continuous-secure, earned-secure, dismissing and preoccupied attachment stances. *Journal of Family Psychology, 13,* 580–597.

Palincsar, A. S., & Brown, A. L. (1984). Reciprocal teaching of comprehension fostering and comprehension monitoring activities. *Cognitive and Instruction, 1,* 117–175.

Parke, R. D. (1977). Punishment in children: Effects, side effects and alternative strategies. In H. Hom & P. Robinson (Eds.), *Psychological processes in early education* (pp. 71–97). New York: Academic.

Parke, R. D. (1988). Families in life-span perspective: a multilevel developmental approach. In E. M. Hetherington, R. M. Lerner, & M. Perlmutter (Eds.), *Child development in life span perspective* (pp. 159–190). Hillsdale, NJ: Erlbaum.

Parke, R. D. (1996). *Fatherhood.* Cambridge, MA: Harvard University Press.

Parke, R. D. (2002). Fatherhood. In M. Bornstein (Ed.), *Handbook of parenting* (2nd ed.). Mahwah, NJ: Erlbaum.

Parke, R. D., & Brott, A. (1999). *Throwaway dads.* Boston: Houghton-Mifflin.

Parke, R. D., & Buriel, R. (2006). Socialization in the family: Ethnic and ecological perspectives. In W. Damon & R. M. Lerner (Gen. Eds.) & N. Eisenberg (Vol. Ed.), *Handbook of child psychology: Vol. 3. Social, emotional and personality development* (6th ed.). New York: Wiley.

Parke, R. D., Coltrane, S., Duffy, S., Buriel, R., Dennis, J., Powers, J., French, S., & Widaman, K. F. (2004). Economic stress, parenting and child adjustment in Mexican-American and European-American families. *Child Development, 75,* 1632–1656.

Parke, R. D., McDowell, D. J., Kim, M., & Leidy, M. S. (2005). Family-peer relationships: The role of emotional regulatory processes. In D. K. Snyder, J. A. Simpson, & J. N. Hughes (Eds.), *Emotional regulation in families: Pathways to dysfunction and health.* Washington, DC: American Psychological Association.

Parke, R. D., & Neville, B. (1995). Late-timed fatherhood: Determinants and consequences for children and families. In J. L. Shapiro, M. J. Diamond, & M. Greenberg (Eds.), *Becoming a father: Contemporary, social, developmental, and clinical perspectives* (Vol. 8, pp. 104–116). New York: Springer.

Parke, R. D., & O'Leary, S. E. (1976). Father-mother-infant interaction in the newborn period: Some findings, some observations and some unresolved issues. In K. Riegel & J. Meacham (Eds.), *The developing individual in a changing world: Social and environmental issues* (Vol. 2). The Hague: Mouton.

Parke, R. D., & O'Neil, R. (2000). The influence of significant others on learning about relationships: From family to friends. In R. S. L. Mills & S. Duck (Eds.), *The developmental psychology of personal relationships* (pp. 15–47). New York: Wiley.

Parke, R. D., O'Neil, R., Spitzer, S., Isley, S., Welsh, M., Wang, S., Lee, J., Strand, C., & Cupp, R. (1997). A longitudinal assessment of sociometric stability and the behavioral correlates of children's social acceptance. *Merrill-Palmer Quarterly, 43,* 635–662.

Parker, J. G., & Asher, S. R. (1987). Peer acceptance and later personal adjustment: Are low-accepted children at risk? *Psychological Bulletin, 102,* 357–389.

Parker, J. G., & Asher, S. R. (1993). Friendship and friendship quality in middle childhood. *Developmental Psychology, 29,* 611–621.

Parker, J. G., & Gottman, J. M. (1989). Social and emotional development in a relational context: Friendship interaction from early childhood to adolescence. In T. J. Berndt & G. W. Ladd (Eds.), *Peer relationships in child development.* New York: Wiley.

Parker, J. G., & Seal, J. (1996). Forming, losing, renewing and replacing friendships: Applying temporal parameters to the assessment of children's friendship experiences. *Child Development, 67,* 2248–2268.

Parkhurst, J. T., & Asher, S. R. (1992). Peer rejection in middle school: Subgroup differences in behavior, loneliness and interpersonal concerns. *Developmental Psychology, 28,* 231–241.

Parten, M. (1932). Social play among preschool. *Journal of Abnormal and Social Psychology, 28,* 231–241.

Pasamanick, B., & Knoblock, H. (1966). Retrospective studies on the epidemiology of reproductive casualty: Old and new. *Merrill-Palmer Quarterly, 12,* 7–26.

Pascalis, O., de Haan, M., & Nelson, C. A. (2002). Is face processing species-specific during the first year of life? *Science, 5,* 427–434.

Pascalis, O., De Schonen, S., Morton, J., Deruelle, C., & Fabre-Grenet, M. (1995). Mother's face recognition by neonates: A replication and extension. *Infant Behavior and Development, 18,* 79–85.

Pascual-Leone, J. (1980). Constructive problems for constructive theories. In R. H. Kluwe & H. Spada (Eds.), *Developmental models of thinking.* New York: Academic.

Pascual-Leone, J. A. (1989). Constructive problems for constructive theories: The current relevance of Piaget's work and a critique of information processing simulation psychology. In H. Spada & R. Kluwe (Eds.), *Developmental models of thinking.* New York: Academic.

Patterson A., & Rafferty, A. (2001). Making it work: Towards employment for the young adult with autism. *International Journal of Language and Communication Disorders, 36* (Suppl.), 475–480.

Patterson, C. (2004). Gay fathers. In M. E. Lamb (Ed.), *The role of the father in child development* (pp. 397–416). New York: Wiley.

Patterson, C. J. (1995). Families of the lesbian baby boom: Parents' division of labor and children's adjustment. *Developmental Psychology, 31,* 115–123.

Patterson, C. J. (2002). Lesbian and gay parenthood. In M. H. Bornstein (Ed.), *Handbook of parenting* (2nd ed.). Mahwah, NJ: Erlbaum.

Patterson, C. J., & Kister, M. C. (1981). Development of listener skills for referential communication. In W. P. Dickerson (Eds.), *Children's oral communication skills.* New York: Academic.

Patterson, G. R. (1982). *Coercive family process.* Eugene, OR: Castalia Press.

Patterson, G. R. (1996). Some characteristics of a developmental theory for early-onset delinquency. In M. F. Lenzenweger & J. J. Haugaard (Eds.), *Frontiers of developmental psychopathology* (pp. 81–124). New York: Oxford University Press.

Patterson, G. R. (2002). The early development of coercive family processes. In J. B. Reid, G. R. Patterson, & J. Snyder (Eds.), *Antisocial behavior in children and adolescents* (pp. 25–44). Washington, DC: American Psychological Association.

Patterson, G. R., & Bank, L. (1989). Some amplifying mechanisms for pathologic processes in families. In M. Gunnar & E. Thelen (Eds.), *Systems and development: The Minnesota symposium on child psychology* (Vol. 22, pp. 167–209). Hillsdale, NJ: Erlbaum.

Patterson, G. R., & Capaldi, D. M. (1991). Antisocial parents: Unskilled and vulnerable. In P. A. Cowan & E. M. Hetherington (Eds.), *Family transitions.* Hillsdale, NJ: Erlbaum.

Patterson, G. R., DeBarshyshe, B., & Ramsey, R. (1989). A developmental perspective on antisocial behavior. *American Psychologist, 44,* 329–335.

Paulson, R. J., & Sachs, J. (1999). *Rewinding your biological clock.* New York: Freeman.

Peake, P. K., Hebl, M., Ahrens, C., Lepper, M., & Mischel, W. (2001). Early adult correlates of preschool delay of gratification and obedience to authority. Unpublished manuscript, Columbia University, New York.

Pearl, R. (1985). Children's understanding of others' need for help: Effects of problem explicitness and type. *Child Development, 56,* 735–745.

Pearson, B. Z., Fernandez, S. C., Lewedeg, V., & Oller, D. K. (1997). The relation of input factors of lexical learning by bilingual infants (ages 8 to 30 months). *Applied Psycholinguistics, 18,* 41–58.

Pearson, B. Z., Fernandez, S. C., & Oller, D. K. (1993). Lexical development in bilingual infants and toddlers: Comparison to monolingual norms. *Language Learning, 43,* 93–120.

Peck, M. N., & Lundberg, O. (1995). Short stature as an effect of economic and social conditions in childhood. *Social Science and Medicine, 41,* 733–738.

Pedersen, F. A., Zaslow, M., Cain, R., & Anderson, B. (1980). *Cesarean birth: The importance of a family perspective.* Paper presented at the International Conference on Infant Studies, New Haven, CT.

Pegg, J. E., Werker, J. F., & McLeod, P. J. (1992). Preference for infant-directed over adult-directed speech: Evidence from 7-week-old infants. *Infant Behavior and Development, 15,* 325–345.

Pennington, B. (2002). *The development of psychopathology.* New York: Guilford Press.

Pepler, D., Corter, C., & Abramovitch, R. (1982). Social relations among children. Comparisons of siblings and peer interaction. In K. Rubin & H. S. Ross (Eds.), *Peer relationships and social skills in childhood* (pp. 209–227). New York: Springer-Verlag.

Pepperberg, I. M. (2000). *The Alex studies: Cognitive and communicative abilities of grey parrots.* Cambridge, MA: Harvard University Press.

Perner, J., Ruffman, T., & Leekam, S. R. (1994). Theory of mind is contagious: You can catch it from your sibs. *Child Development, 65,* 1228–1238.

Perry, B. D. (1997). Incubated in terror: Neurodevelopmental factors in the "cycle of violence." In J. D.

Osofsky (Ed.), *Children in a violent society* (pp. 124–149). New York: The Guilford Press.

Perry, D. G., Hodges, E. V., & Egan, S. (2001). Determinants of chronic victimization by peers: A review and new model of family influence. In J. Juvonen & S. Graham (Eds.), *Peer harassment in school: The plight of the vulnerable and victimized* (pp. 73–104). New York: Guilford Press.

Perry, D. G., Perry, L. C., & Weiss, R. J. (1989). Sex differences in the consequences children anticipate for aggression. *Developmental Psychology, 25,* 312–320.

Perry, D. G., Williard, J. C., & Perry, L. C. (1990). Peers' perceptions of the consequences that victimized children provide aggressors. *Child Development, 61,* 1310–1325.

Perry-Jenkins, M., Repetti, R., & Crouter, A. C. (2000). Work and family in the 1990s. *Journal of Marriage and the Family, 62,* 981–998.

Peters, A. M. (1983). *The units of language.* New York: Cambridge University Press.

Petersen, A. C. (Ed.). (1993). *Understanding child abuse and neglect.* Washington: National Academy Press.

Petersen, A. C., & Taylor, B. (1980). The biological approach to adolescence. In J. Adelson (Ed.), *Handbook of adolescent psychology.* New York: Wiley.

Petitto, L. (1993). On the ontogenetic requirements for early language acquisition. In B. de Boysson-Bardies, S. de Schonen, P. W. Jusczyk, P. McNeilage, & J. Morton (Eds.), *Developmental neurocognition: Speech and face processing in the first year of life* (pp. 365–383). Dordrecht, Netherlands: Kluwer Academic Press.

Petitto, L., & Marenette, P. (1991). Babbling in the manual mode: Evidence for the ontogeny of language. *Science, 251,* 1493–1496.

Petitto, L. A., Holowka, S., Sergio, L. E., & Ostry, D. (2001). Language rhythms in baby hand movements. *Nature, 413,* 35–36.

Petrill, S. A., & Deater-Deckard, K. (2004). Task orientation, parental warmth and SES account for a significant proportion of the shared environmental variance in general cognitive ability in early childhood: Evidence from a twin study. *Developmental Science, 7,* 25–32.

Pettit, G. S., Laird, R. D., Dodge, K. A., Bates, J. E., & Criss, M. N. (2001). Antecedents and behavior problem outcomes of parental monitoring and psychological control in early adolescence. *Child Development, 72,* 283–598.

Pettit, G. S., & Mize, J. (1993). Substance and style: Understanding the ways in which parents teach children about social relationships. In S. Duck (Ed.), *Understanding relationship processes: Vol. II. Learning about relationships* (pp. 118–151). Newbury Park, CA: Sage.

Phares, V., Dubig, A. M., & Watkins, M. M. (2002). Family contexts: Fathers and other supports. In S. H. Goodman & I. Gotlib (Eds.)., *Children of depressed parents* (pp. 203–226). Washington, DC: American Psychological Association.

Phillips, J. (1969). *The origin of intellect: Piaget's theory.* San Francisco: Freeman.

Phillips, R. B., Sharma, R., Premachandra, B. R., Vaughn, A. J., & Reyes-Lee, M. (1996). Intrauterine exposure to cocaine: Effect on neurobehavior of neonates. *Infant Behavior & Development, 19,* 71–81.

Piaget, J. (1926). *Language and thought of the child.* London: Kegan Paul, Trench, & Trubner.

Piaget, J. (1929). *The child's conception of the world.* London: Kegan Paul, Trench, & Trubner.

Piaget, J. (1932). *The moral judgment of the child.* New York: Harcourt, Brace.

Piaget, J. (1950). *The psychology of intelligence.* London: Kegan Paul, Trench, & Trubner.

Piaget, J. (1960). *The child's conception of the world.* London: Routledge.

Piaget, J. (1965). *The child's conception of number.* New York: Norton.

Piaget, J. (1985). *The equilibration of cognitive structures.* Chicago: University of Chicago Press.

Pickens, J. N. (1994). Perception of auditory-visual distance relations by 5-month-old infants. *Developmental Psychology, 30,* 537–544.

Pinhas, H. O., & Zeitler, P. (2000). "Who is the wise man?—the one who forsees consequences": Childhood, obesity, new associated co-morbidity, and prevention. *Preventive Medicine, 31,* 702–705.

Pinker, S. (1989). *Learnability and cognition: The acquisition of argument structure.* Cambridge, MA: MIT Press.

Pinker, S. (1994). *The language instinct: How the mind creates language.* New York: Morrow.

Pisecco, S., Baker, D. B., Silva, P. A., & Brooke, M. (2001). Boys with reading disabilities and/or ADHD: Distinctions in early childhood. *Journal of Learning Disabilities, 43,* 98–106.

Pleck, E. (2004). Two dimensions of fatherhood: A history of the good dad-bad dad complex. In M. Lamb (Ed.), *The role of the father in child development* (4th ed., pp. 32–57). New York: Erlbaum.

Plomin, R. (1990). *Nature & nurture: An introduction to human behavioral genetics.* Pacific Grove, CA: Brooks/Cole.

Plomin, R. (1995). Genetics and children's experiences in the family. *Journal of Child Psychology and Psychiatry, 36,* 33–68.

Plomin, R., & Daniels, D. (1987). Why are children in the same family so different from one another? *The Behavioral and Brain Sciences, 10,* 1–16.

Plomin, R., DeFries, J. C., Craig, I. W., & McGuffin, P. (2002). *Behavior genetics in the postgenomic era.* Washington, DC: American Psychological Association.

Plomin, R., DeFries, J. C., McClearn, G. E., & McGuffin, P. (2001). *Behavioral genetics* (4th ed.). New York: Worth.

Plomin, R., DeFries, J. C., McClearn, G. E., & Rutter, M. (1997). *Behavior genetics* (3rd ed.). New York: W. H. Freeman.

Plomin, R., McClearn, G. E., Pedersen, N. L., Nesselroade, J. R., & Bergeman, C. S. (1988). Genetic influence on childhood family environment perceived retrospectively from the last half of the life span. *Developmental Psychology, 24,* 738–745.

Plomin, R., & Petrill, S. A. (1997). Genetics and intelligence: What's new? *Intelligence, 24,* Special issue, 53–78.

Plomin, R., & Rutter, M. (1998). Child development, molecular genetics and what to do with genes once they are found. *Child Development, 69,* 1223–1242.

Plunkett, K., Karmiloff-Smith, A., Bates, E., Elman, J. L., & Johnson, M. H. (1997). Connectionism and developmental psychology. *Journal of Child Psychology and Psychiatry, 38,* 53–80.

Pollak, S. D., & Sinha, P. (2002). Effects of early experience on children's recognition of facial displays of emotion. *Developmental Psychology, 38,* 784–791.

Pollitt, E. (1994). Poverty and child development: Relevance of research in developing countries to the United States. *Child Development, 65,* 283–295.

Pollitt, E., Gorman, K., & Metallinos-Katsaras, E. (1992). Long-term developmental consequences of intrauterine and postnatal growth retardation in rural Guatemala. In G. J. Suci & S. R. Robertson (Eds.), *Future directions in infant development research* (pp. 43–70). New York: Springer-Verlag.

Pomerantz, E. M., & Ruble, D. N. (1998). A multidimensional perspective of control: Implications for the development of sex differences in self-evaluation and depression. In J. Heckhausen & C. Dweck (Eds.), *Motivation and self-regulation across the life span.* New York: Cambridge University Press.

Pomerleau, A., Bolduc, D., Malcuit, G., & Cossette, L. (1990). Pink or blue: Environmental gender stereotypes in the first two years of life. *Sex Roles, 22,* 359–367.

Porges, S. W. (1995). Orienting in a defensive world: Mammalian modifications of our evolutionary heritage. A Polyvagal theory. *Psychophysiology, 32,* 301–318.

Porter, R. H., Makin, J. W., Davis, L. B., & Christensen, K. M. (1992). Breast-fed infants respond to olfactory cues from their own mother and unfamiliar lactating females. *Infant Behavior and Development, 15,* 85–93.

Posada, G., Gao, Y., Wu, F., Posada, R., Tascon, M., Schelmerich, A., Sagi, A., Kondo-Ikemura, K., Haaland, W., & Synnevaag, B. (1995). The secure-base phenomenon across cultures: Children's behavior, mothers' preferences, and experts' concepts. In E. Waters, B. E. Vaughn, G. Posada, & K. Kondo-Ikemura (Eds.), *Caregiving, cultural, and cognitive perspectives on secure-base behavior and working models: New growing points of attachment theory and research. Monographs of the Society for Research in Child Development, 60*(2–3, Serial No. 244).

Posada, G., Jacobs, A., Richmond, M. K., Carbonell, O. A., Alzate, G., Bustamante, M. R., & Zuiceno, J. (2002). Maternal caregiving and infant security in two cultures. *Developmental Psychology, 38,* 67–78.

Postlethwait, J. H., & Hopson, J. L. (1995). *The nature of life* (3rd ed.). New York: McGraw-Hill.

Poulin, F., & Boivin, M. (2000). The role of proactive and reactive aggression on the formation of boys' friendships. *Developmental Psychology, 36,* 233–240.

Poulin, F., Dishion, T., & Haas, E. (1999). The peer influences paradox: Friendship quality and deviancy training within male adolescents. *Merrill-Palmer Quarterly, 45,* 42–61.

Povinelli, D. J., Bering, J., & Giambrone, S. (2000). Toward a science of other minds: Escaping the argument by analogy. *Cognitive Science, 24,* 509–541.

Povinelli, D. J., & Giambrone, S. (2001). Reasoning about beliefs: A human specialization? *Child Development, 72,* 691–695.

Pratt, M. W., & Fiese, B. H. (Eds.). (2004). *Family stories and the life course*. Mahwah, NJ: Erlbaum.

Pressley, M., Cariglia-Bull, T., Deane, S., & Schneider, W. (1987). Short-term memory, verbal competence, and age as predictors of imagery instructional effectiveness. *Journal of Experimental Child Psychology, 43*, 194–211.

Preston, S. D., & de Waal, F. B. M. (2002). Empathy: Its ultimate and proximate bases. *Behavioral and Brain Sciences, 25*, 1–72.

Price-Williams, D. R., Gordon, W., & Ramirez, M., III. (1969). Skill and conservation: A study of pottery-making children. *Developmental Psychology, 1*, 769.

Purcell, P., & Stewart, L. (1990). Dick and Jane in 1989. *Sex Roles, 22*, 177–185.

Putallaz, M. (1987). Maternal behavior and socioenomic status. *Child Development, 58*, 324–340.

Putallaz, M., Costanzo, P. R., & Smith, R. B. (1991). Maternal recollections of childhood peer relationships: Implications for their children's social competence. *Journal of Social and Personal Relationships, 8*, 403–422.

Putallaz, M., & Gottman, J. M. (1981). Social skills and peer acceptance. In S. R. Asher & J. M. Gottman (Eds.), *The development of children's friendships*. New York: Cambridge University Press.

Putallaz, M., & Heflin, A. H. (1990). Parent-child interaction. In S. R. Asher & J. D. Coie (Eds.), *Peer rejection in childhood*. New York: Cambridge University Press.

Putnam, S. P., Sanson, A. V., & Rothbart, M. K. (2002). Child temperament and parenting. In M. Bornstein (Ed.), *Handbook of parenting* (2nd ed., pp. 255–278). Mahwah, NJ: Erlbaum.

Quinn, P. C., Cummins, M., Kuse, J., Martin, E., & Weissman, T. K. (1996). Development of categorical representations for above and below spatial relations in 3- to 7-month-old infants. *Developmental Psychology, 32*, 942–950.

Quinn, P. C., & Eimas, P. D. (1998). Perceptual cues that permit categorical differentiation of animal species by infants. *Journal of Experimental Child Psychology, 63*, 189–211.

Rabinowitz, F. M., Grant, M. J., Howe, M. L., & Walsh, C. (1994). Reasoning in middle childhood: A dynamic model of performance on transitivity tasks. *Journal of Experimental Child Psychology, 58*, 252–288.

Radin, N. (1999). Fathers in non-traditional families. In M. Lamb (Ed.), *Parenting and child development in non-traditional families*. Mahwah, NJ: Erlbaum.

Radke-Yarrow, M., & Zahn-Waxler, C. (1983). Roots, motives and patterns in children's prosocial behavior. In J. Reykowski, T. Karylowski, D. Bar-Tal, & E. Staub (Eds.), *Origins and maintenance of prosocial behaviors*. New York: Plenum.

Radke-Yarrow, M., Zahn-Waxler, C., & Chapman, M. (1983). Children's prosocial dispositions and behavior. In E. M. Hetherington (Ed.), *Handbook of child psychology: Vol. 4. Socialization, personality and social development*. New York: Wiley.

Radziszewska, B., & Rogoff, B. (1988). Influence of adult and peer collaborators on the development of children's planning skills. *Developmental Psychology, 24*, 840–848.

Ragozin, A. S., Bashman, R. B., Crnic, K. A., Greenberg, M. T., & Robinson, N. M. (1982). Effects of maternal age on the parenting role. *Developmental Psychology, 18*, 627–634.

Rakic, P. (1995). Corticogenesis in human and nonhuman primates. In M. S. Gazzaniga (Ed.), *The cognitive neurosciences* (pp. 127–145). Cambridge, MA: MIT Press.

Ramey, C. T., Campbell, F. A., & Blair, C. (1998). Enhancing the life course for high-risk children: Results from the Abecedarian Project. In J. Crane (Ed.), *Social programs that work*. New York: Sage.

Ramey, C. T., & Ramey, S. L. (1992). Early educational intervention with disadvantaged children—to what effect? *Applied and Preventive Psychology, 1*, 130–140.

Ramey, C. T., & Ramey, S. L. (1998). Early intervention and early experience. *American Psychologist, 53*, 109–130.

Ramey, C. T., Ramey, S. L., Gaines, K. R., & Blair, C. (1995). Two-generation early intervention programs: A child development perspective. In S. Smith (Ed.), *Two-generation programs for families in poverty: A new intervention strategy* (pp. 202–215). Norwood, NJ: Ablex.

Rank, O. (1929). *The trauma of birth*. New York: Harcourt Brace.

Rapoport, J. L., Buchsbaum, M. S., Zahn, T. P., Weingartner, H., Ludlow, C., & Mikkelson, E. J. (1978). Dextroamphetamine: Cognitive and behavioral effects in normal prepubertal boys. *Science, 199*, 560–563.

Ray, J. W., & Klesges, R. C. (1993). Influences on the eating behavior of children. In C. L. Williams & S. Y. S. Kimm (Eds.), *Prevention and treatment of childhood obesity* (pp. 57–69). Annals of the New York Academy of Sciences, Vol. 699. New York: The New York Academy of Sciences.

Raynor, H. A., & Epstein, L. H. (2001). Dietary variety, energy regulation, and obesity. *Psychological Bulletin, 127*, 325–341.

Reid, J. B., Patterson, G. R., & Snyder, J. J. (Eds.). (2002). *Antisocial behavior in children and adolescents*. Washington, DC: American Psychological Association.

Reiff, M. I., & Tippins, S. (Eds.). (2004) *ADHD: A complete authoritative guide*. Elk Grove Village, IL: American Academy of Pediatrics.

Reilly, T. W., Entwisle, D. R., & Doering, S. G. (1987). Socialization into parenthood: A longitudinal study of the development of self evaluations. *Journal of Marriage and the Family, 49*, 295–308.

Reiner, W. G., & Gearhart, J. P. (2004). Discordant sexual identity in some genetic males with cloacal exstrophy assigned to female sex at birth. *The New England Journal of Medicine, 350*, 333–341.

Reiss, D., Neiderhiser, J. M., Hetherington, E. M., & Plomin, R. (2000). *The relationship code: Deciphering genetic and social influences on adolescent development*. Cambridge, MA: Harvard University Press.

Reite, M., Cullum, C. M., Stocker, J., Teale, P., et al. (1993). Neuropsychological test performance and MEG-based brain lateralization: Sex differences. *Brain Research Bulletin, 32*, 325–328.

Remschmidt, H. E., Schulz, E., Martin, M., & Warnke, A. (1994). Childhood-onset schizophrenia: History of the concept and recent studies. *Schizophrenia Bulletin, 20*, 727–745.

Renshaw, P. D., & Asher, S. R. (1983). Children's goals and strategies for social interaction. *Merrill-Palmer Quarterly, 29*, 353–374.

Renshaw, P. D., & Brown, P. J. (1993). Loneliness in middle childhood: Concurrent and longitudinal predictors. *Child Development, 64*, 1271–1284.

Repetti, R. (1989). Effects of daily workload on subsequent behavior during marital interaction: The roles of withdrawal and spouse support. *Journal of Personality and Social Psychology, 57*, 651–659.

Repetti, R. (1996). Short-term and long-term linking job stressors to father child interaction. *Social Development, 1*, 1–15.

Repetti, R., & Wood, J. (1997). The effects of stress and work on mothers' interactions with preschoolers. *Journal of Family Psychology, 1*, 90–108.

Rescorla, L. A. (1980). Overextension in early language. *Journal of Child Language, 7*, 321–335.

Rest, J. R., Narvaez, D., Bbeau, M., & Thoma, S. J. (2000). *Postconventional moral thinking: A neoKohlbergian approach*. Mahwah, NJ: Erlbaum.

Restak, R. M. (1994). *The Brain*. New York: Bantam.

Revelle, G. L., Wellman, H. M., & Karabenick, J. D. (1985). Comprehension monitoring in preschool children. *Child Development, 56*, 654–663.

Reynolds, A. J., & Temple, J. A. (1998). Extended early childhood intervention and school achievement: Age thirteen findings from the Chicago Longitudinal Study. *Child Development, 69*, 231–246.

Rhee, S. H., & Waldman, I. D. (2002). Genetic and environmental influences on antisocial behavior: A meta-analysis of twin and adoption studies. *Psychological Bulletin, 128*, 490–529.

Rheingold, H. L. (1982). Little children's participation in the work of adults, a nascent prosocial behavior. *Child Development, 53*, 114–125.

Rheingold, H. L., & Cook, K. V. (1975). The content of boys' and girls' rooms as an index of parent behavior. *Child Development, 46*, 459–463.

Rheingold, H. L., & Eckerman, C. (1970). The infant separates himself from his mother. *Science, 168*, 78–83.

Rheingold, H. L., & Eckerman, C. O. (1973). The fear of strangers hypothesis: A critical review. In H. Reese (Ed.), *Advances in child development and behavior* (Vol. 8, pp. 185–222). New York: Academic.

Rheingold, H. L., Hay, D. F., & West, M. J. (1976). Sharing in the second year of life. *Child Development, 47*, 1148–1158.

Ricci, C. M., & Beal, C. R. (1998). Effect of questioning techniques and interview setting on young children's eyewitness memory. *Expert Evidence, 6*, 127–128.

Richards, M. H., Crowe, P. A., Larson, R., & Swarr, A. (1998). Developmental patterns and gender differences in the experience of peer companionship during adolescence. *Child Development, 69*, 154–163.

Richardson, T. M., & Benbow, C. P. (1990). Long-term effects of acceleration on the social-emotional adjustment of mathematically precocious youths. *Journal of Educational Psychology, 82*, 464–470.

Riese, M. L. (1990). Neonatal temperament in monozygotic and dizygotic twin pairs. *Child Development, 61,* 1230–1237.

Riesen, A. H. (1947). The development of visual perception in man and chimpanzee. *Science, 106,* 107–108.

Rigby, K. (2002). Bullying in childhood. In P. K. Smith & C. H. Hart (Eds.). *Handbook of Childhood Social Development* (pp. 549–568). Oxford, UK: Blackwell.

Rivera, S. M., Wakeley, A., & Langer, J. (1999). The drawbridge phenomenon: Representational reasoning or perceptual preference? *Developmental Psychology, 35,* 427–435.

Roberton, M. A., & Halverson, L. E. (1988). The development of locomotor coordination: Longitudinal change and invariance. *Journal of Motor Behavior, 20,* 197–241.

Roberts, W., & Strayer, J. (1996). Empathy, emotional expressiveness and prosocial behavior. *Child Development, 67,* 449–470.

Robin, D. J., Berthier, N. E., & Clifton, R. K. (1996). Infants' predictive reaching for moving objects in the dark. *Developmental Psychology, 32,* 824–835.

Robinson, A., Bender, B. G., & Linden, M. G. (1992). Prenatal diagnosis of sex chromosome abnormalities. In A. Milunsky (Ed.), *Genetic disorders and the fetus: Diagnosis, prevention and treatment.* Baltimore: Johns Hopkins University Press.

Robinson, J. L., Kagan, J., Reznick, J. S., & Corley, R. (1992). The heritability of inhibited and uninhibited behavior. A twin study. *Developmental Psychology, 28,* 1030–1037.

Robinson, L. A., & Klesges, R. C. (1997). Ethnic and gender differences in risk factors for smoking onset. *Health Psychology, 16,* 499–505.

Roche, A. F. (Ed.). (1979). Secular trends: Human growth, maturation, and development. *Monographs of the Society for Research in Child Development, 44* (Serial No. 179).

Roche, A. M. (1998). Alcohol and drug education: A review of key issues. *Drugs: Education, Prevention and Policy, 5,* 85–99.

Rock, A. M. L., Trainor, L. J., & Addison, T. L. (1999). Distinctive messages in infant-directed lullabies and songs. *Developmental Psychology, 35,* 527–534.

Rodin, J. (1981). Current status of the internal-external hypothesis for obesity: What went wrong? *American Psychologist, 36,* 361–372.

Rodkin, P. C., Farmer, T. W., Pearl, R., & Van Acker, R. (2000). Heterogeneity of popular boys: Antisocial and prosocial

configurations. *Developmental Psychology, 30,* 14–24.

Roeser, R. W., Eccles, J. S., & Sameroff, A. J. (2000). School as a context of early adolescents' academic and social-emotional development: A summary of research findings. *Elementary School Journal, 100,* 443–471.

Roffwarg, H. P., Muzio, J. N., & Dement, W. C. (1966). Ontogenetic development of the human sleep-dream cycle. *Science, 152,* 604–619.

Rogoff, B. (1990). *Apprenticeship in thinking: Cognitive development in social context.* New York: Oxford University Press.

Rogoff, B. (1998). Cognition as a collaborative process. In D. Kuhn & R. Siegler (Eds.), W. Damon (Series Ed.), *Handbook of child psychology: Vol. 2. Cognition, perception and language* (5th ed., pp. 679–744). New York: Wiley.

Rogoff, B. (2002). How can we study cultural aspects of human development? *Human Development, 45,* 387–389.

Rogoff, B. (2003). *The cultural nature of human development.* New York: Oxford University Press.

Rogoff, B., Goodman Turkanis, C., & Bartlett, L. (2001). *Learning together: Children and adults in a school community.* New York: Oxford University Press.

Rogoff, B., & Mistry, J. (1990). The social and functional context of children's remembering. In R. Fivush & J. A. Hudson (Eds.), *Knowing and remembering in young children* (pp. 197–222). New York: Cambridge University Press.

Rogoff, B., & Waddell, K. J. (1982). Memory for information organized in a scene by children from two cultures. *Child Development, 53,* 1224–1228.

Roisman, G. I., Masten, A. S., Coatsworth, J. D., & Tellegen, A. (2004). Salient and emerging development tasks in the transition to adulthood. *Child Development, 75,* 123–133.

Roisman, G. I., Padron, E., Sroufe, L. A., & Egeland, B. (2002). Earned-secure attachment states in retrospect and prospect. *Child Development, 73,* 1204–1219.

Rolls, B. J., Engell, D., & Birch, L. L. (2000). Serving portion size influences 5-year-old but not 3-year-old children's food intake. *Journal of American Dietetic Association, 100,* 232–234.

Romski, M. A., & Sevcik, R. A. (1996). *Breaking the speech barrier: Language development through augmented means.* Baltimore: Brookes.

Roopnarine, J. (1992). Father-child play in India. In K. MacDonald

(Ed.), *Parent-child play.* Albany: State University of New York Press.

Rose, S. A., & Feldman, J. F. (1995). Prediction of IQ and specific cognitive abilities at 11 years from infancy measures. *Developmental Psychology, 31,* 685–696.

Rose, S. A., & Feldman, J. F. (1996). Memory and processing speed in preterm children at eleven years: A comparison with full-terms. *Child Development, 67* (5), 2005–2021.

Rose, S. A., Feldman, J. F., Wallach, I. F., & McCarton, C. (1989). Infant visual attention: Relation to birth status and developmental outcome during the first 5 years. *Developmental Psychology, 25,* 560–576.

Rose, S. A., Jankowski, J. J., & Feldman, J. F. (2002). Speed of processing and face recognition at 7 and 12 months. *Infancy, 3,* 435–455.

Rosenblum, G. D., & Lewis, M. (1999). The relations among body image, physical attractiveness, and body mass in adolescence. *Child Development, 70,* 50–64.

Rosenblum, T., & Pinker, S. (1983). Word magic revisited: Monolingual and bilingual children's understanding of the word-object relationships. *Child Development, 54,* 773–780.

Rosenhan, D. (1972). Prosocial behavior of children. In W. W. Hartup (Ed.), *The young child* (Vol. 2, pp. 340–359). Washington, DC: National Association for the Education of Young Children.

Rosenstein, D., & Oster, H. (1988). Differential facial response to four basic tastes in newborns. *Child Development, 59,* 1555–1568.

Rosenzweig, M. R. (2003). Effects of differential experience on brain and behavior. *Developmental Neuropsychology, 24,* 523–540.

Rosenzweig, M. R., Leiman, A. S., & Breedlove, S. M. (1996). *Biological psychology.* Sunderland, MA: Sinauer Associates.

Ross, H. S., & Conant, C. L. (1992). The social structure of early conflict: Interactions, relationships, and alliances. In C. U. Shantz & W. W. Hartup (Eds.), *Conflict in child and adolescent development.* Cambridge: Cambridge University Press.

Ross, H. S., Conant, C., Cheyne, J. A., & Alevizos, E. (1992). Relationships and alliances in the social interactions of kibbutz toddlers. *Social Development, 1,* 1–17.

Ross, H. S., & Goldman, B. D. (1977). Infants' sociability toward strangers. *Child Development, 48,* 638–642.

Rothbart, M., & Bates, J. (1998). Temperament. In W. Damon (Gen. Ed.) & N. Eisenberg

(Vol. Ed.), *Handbook of child psychology: Vol. 3. Social and emotional development* (5th ed.). New York: Wiley.

Rothbart, M. K. (1981). Measurement of temperament in infancy. *Child Development, 52,* 569–578.

Rothbart, M. K., Ahadi, S. A., & Evans, D. E. (2000). Temperament and personality: Origins and outcomes. *Journal of Social Psychology, 78,* 122–135.

Rothbart, M. K., Ahadi, S. A., & Hershey, K. L. (1994). Temperament and social behavior in childhood. *Merrill-Palmer Quarterly, 40,* 21–39.

Rothbaum, F., Pott, M., Azuma, H., Miyake, K., & Weisz, J. (2000a). The development of close relationships in Japan and the United States: Paths of symbiotic harmony and generative tension. *Child Development, 71,* 1121–1142.

Rothbaum, F., Weisz, J., Pott, M., Miyake, K., & Morelli, G. (2000b). Attachment and culture: Security in the United States and Japan. *American Psychologist, 35,* 1093–1104.

Rotherman-Borus, M. J., & Langabeer, K. A. (2001). Developmental trajectories of gay, lesbian, & bisexual youths. In A. R. D'Augelli & C. Patterson (Eds.), *Lesbian, gay, and bisexual identities among youth: Psychological perspectives* (pp. 97–128). New York: Oxford University Press.

Rotherman-Borus, M. J., Piacentini, J., Cantwell, C., Belin, T. R., & Song, J. (2000). The 18-month impact of an emergency room intervention for adolescent female suicide attemptees. *Journal of Consulting and Clinical Psychology, 68,* 1081–1093.

Rovee-Collier, C. K. (1986). *Infants and elephants: Do they ever forget?* Paper presented at a Science and Public Policy Seminar, Washington, DC.

Rovee-Collier, C. K. (1987). Learning and memory in infants. In J. D. Osofsky (Ed.), *Handbook of infant development* (pp. 98–148). New York: Wiley.

Rovee-Collier, C. K. (1999). The development of infant memory. *Current Directions in Psychological Science, 8,* 80–85.

Rovee-Collier, C. K., & Gerhardstein, P. (1997). The development of infant memory. In C. Nelson & C. Hulme (Eds.), *The development of memory in childhood: Studies in developmental psychology.* East Sussex, England: Psychology Press.

Rovee-Collier, C. K., & Lipsitt, L. P. (1982). Learning, adaptation and memory in the newborn. In P. Stratton (Ed.), *Psychobiology of the human newborn*. New York: Wiley.

Rovee-Collier, C. K., & Shyi, G. (1992). A functional and cognitive analysis of infant long-term retention. In C. J. Brainard, M. L. Howe, & V. Reyna (Eds.), *Development of long-term retention* (pp. 3–55). New York: Springer-Verlag.

Rovet, J., Netley, C., Keenan, M., Bailey, J., & Stewart, D. (1996). The psychoeducational profile of boys with Klinefelter syndrome. *Journal of Learning Disabilities, 29*, 180–196.

Rowe, D. (1994). *The limits of family influence: Genes, experience, and behavior*. New York: Guilford Press.

Rozin, P. (1996). Towards a psychology of food and eating: From motivation to module to model to marker, morality, meaning, and metaphor. *Current Directions in Psychological Science, 5*, 18–24.

Rubenstein, A. J., Kalakanis, L., & Langlois, J. H. (1999). Infant preferences for attractive faces: A cognitive explanation. *Developmental Psychology, 35*, 848–855.

Rubin, J. Z., Provenzano, F. J., & Luria, A. (1974). The eye of the beholder: Parents' views on sex of newborns. *American Journal of Orthopsychiatry, 43*, 720–731.

Rubin, K., Bukowski, W., & Parker, J. (2006). Peer interaction and social competence. In W. Damon & R. M. Lerner (Series Eds.) & N. Eisenberg (Vol. Ed.), *Handbook of child psychology. Vol. 3* (6th ed.). New York: Wiley.

Rubin, K. H. (1982). Non-social play in preschoolers: Necessarily evil? *Child Development, 53*, 651–657.

Rubin, K. H., & LeMare, L. (1990). Social withdrawal in childhood: Assessment issues and social commitments. In S. R. Asher & J. D. Coie (Eds.), *Children's status in the peer group*. New York: Cambridge University Press.

Rubin, Z. (1980). *Children's friendships*. Cambridge, MA: Harvard University Press.

Rubin, Z., & Sloman, J. (1984). How parents influence their children's friendship. In M. Lewis (Ed.), *Beyond the dyad*. New York: Plenum.

Ruble, D., Martin, C., & Berenbaum, S. (2006). Gender development. In W. Damon & R.M. Lerner (Series Eds.) & N. Eisenberg (Vol. Ed.), *Handbook of child psychology: Vol. 3* (6th ed.). New York: Wiley.

Rudolph, K. D., Lambert, S. F., Clark, A. G., & Kurlakowsky, K. D. (2001). Negotiating the transition to middle school: The role of self-regulatory processes. *Child Development, 72*, 929–946.

Rudy, G. S., & Goodman, G. S. (1991). The effects of participation on children's reports: Implications for children's testimony. *Developmental Psychology, 27*, 527–538.

Ruff, H. A., & Capozzoli, M. C. (2003). Development of attention and distractibility in the first 4 years of life. *Developmental Psychology, 39*, 877–890.

Ruff, H. A., & Rothbart, M. K. (1996). *Attention in early development: Themes and variations*. New York: Oxford University Press.

Runco, M. A. (1996, Summer). Personal creativity: Definition and developmental issues. In M. A. Runco (Ed.), *Creativity from childhood through adulthood: The developmental issues* [Special issue]. *New Directions for Child Development*, No. 72, 3–30.

Russ, S. W. (1996, Summer). Development of creative processes in children. In M. A. Runco (Ed.). *Creativity from childhood through adulthood: The developmental issues* [Special issue]. *New Directions for Child Development*, No. 72, 31–42.

Russell, A., & Finnie, V. (1990). Preschool children's social status and maternal instructions to assist group entry. *Developmental Psychology, 26*, 603–611.

Russell, A., Russell, G., & Midwinter, D. (1991). Observer effects on mothers and fathers: Self-reported influence during a home observation. *Merrill-Palmer Quarterly, 38*, 263–283.

Rust, J., Golombok, S., Hines, M., Johnston, K., Golding, J., & The ALSPAC Study Team. (2000). The role of brothers and sisters in the gender development of preschool children. *Journal of Experimental Child Psychology, 77*, 292–303.

Rutter, M. (1983). Statistical and personal interactions: Facets and perspectives. In D. Magnusson & V. Allen (Eds.), *Human development: An interactional perspective* (pp. 295–319). New York: Academic Press.

Rutter, M. (1992). Nature, nurture and psychopathology. In B. Tizard & V. Varma (Eds.), *Vulnerability and resilience in human development*. London: Jessica Kingsley.

Rutter, M. (1996). Transitions and turning points in developmental psychopathology: As applied to the age span between childhood and mid-adulthood. *International Journal of Behavioral Development, 19*, 603–626.

Rutter, M. (2000). Genetic studies of autism: From the 1970s into the millennium. *Journal of Abnormal Child Psychology, 28*, 3–14.

Rutter, M. (2002). Nature, nurture, and development: From evangelism through science toward policy and practice. *Child Development, 73*, 1–21.

Rutter, M. (Ed.). (2003). *Autism: Neural basis and treatment possibilities*. London: Novartis.

Rutter, M., Kreppner, J., O'Conner, T., & the English & Romanian Adoptees (ERA) Study Team. (2001a). Risk and resilience following profound early global privation. *British Journal of Psychiatry, 179*, 97–103.

Rutter, M., Pickles, A., Murray, R., & Eaves, L. (2001c). Testing hypotheses on specific environmental causal effects on behavior. *Psychological Bulletin, 127*, 291–324.

Rymer, R. (1993). *Genie: A scientific tragedy*. New York: HarperCollins.

Saarni, C. (1999). *The development of emotional competence*. New York: Guilford.

Saarni, C., Campos, J. J., & Camras, L. (2006). Emotional development. In W. Damon & R. M. Lerner (Gen. Eds.) & N. Eisenberg (Vol. Ed.). *Handbook of child psychology: Vol 3. Social, emotional, and personality development* (6th ed.). New York: Wiley.

Sachs, J. (1985). Prelinguistic development. In J. Berko-Gleason (Ed.), *The development of language*. Columbus, OH: Merrill.

Sadeh, A. (1996). Stress, trauma, and sleep in children. *Child & Adolescent Psychiatric Clinics of North America, 5*, 685–700.

Saffran, J. R., Aslin, R. N., & Newport, E. L. (1996). Statistical learning by 8-month-old infants. *Science, 274*, 1926–1928.

Saffran, J. R., & Griepentrog, G. J. (2001). Absolute pitch on infant auditory learning: Evidence for developmental reorganization. *Developmental Psychology, 37*, 74–85.

Saffran, J. R., Werker, J., & Werner, L. A. (2006). The infant's auditory world. In W. Damon & R. M. Lerner (Series Eds.) and D. Kuhn & R. Siegler (Vol. Eds.), Vol. 2, 6th ed. New York: Wiley.

Sagi, A., Koren-Karie, N., Gini, M., Ziv, Y., & Joels, T. (2002). Shedding further light on the effects of various types and quality of early child care on infant-mother attachment relationship: The Haifa study of early child care. *Child Development, 73*, 1166–1186.

Sagi, A., van IJzendoorn, M. H., Aviezer, O., Donnell, Koren-Karie, N., Joels, T., & Harel, Y. (1995). Attachments in a multiple-caregiver and multiple infant environment: The case of the Israeli kibbutzim. In E. Waters, B. E. Vaughn, G. Posada, & K. Kondo-Ikemura (Eds.), *Caregiving, cultural, and cognitive perspectives on secure-base behavior and working models: New growing points of attachment theory and research. Monographs of the Society for Research in Child Development, 60* (2–3, Serial No. 244).

Sagi, A., van IJzendoorn, M. H., Aviezer, O., Donnell, F., & Mayseless, O. (1994). Sleeping out of home in a kibbutz community arrangement: It makes a difference for infant-mother attachment. *Child Development, 65*, 992–1004.

Salapatek, P. (1969, December). *The visual investigation of geometric pattern by the one- and two-month-old infant*. Paper presented at the meeting of the American Association for the Advancement of Science, Boston.

Salapatek, P., & Kessen, W. (1966). Visual scanning of triangles by the human newborn. *Journal of Experimental Child Psychology, 3*, 155–167.

Sallis, J. F., McKenzie, T. L., Alcaraz, J. E., Kolody, B., Hovell, M. F., & Nader, P. R. (1993). Project SPARK: Effects of physical education on adiposity in children. In C. L. Williams & S. Y. S. Kimm (Eds.), *Prevention and treatment of childhood obesity* (pp. 127–136). Annals of the New York Academy of Sciences, Vol. 699. New York: The New York Academy of Sciences.

Sameroff, A. J. (1989). General systems and the regulation of development. In M. R. Gunnar & E. Thelen (Eds.), *Systems and development* (Vol. 22, pp. 219–235). Hillsdale, NJ: Erlbaum.

Sameroff, A. J. (1994). Developmental systems and family functioning. In R. D. Parke & S. G. Kellam (Eds.), *Exploring family relationships with other social systems* (pp. 199–214). Hillsdale, NJ: Erlbaum.

Sameroff, A. J., & Chandler, M. J. (1975). Reproductive risk and the continuum of caretaking casualty. In F. Horowitz (Ed.), *Review of child development research* (Vol. 4). Chicago: University of Chicago Press.

Sameroff, A. J., & Seifer, R. (1983). Familial risk and child competence. *Child Development, 54*, 1254–1268.

Sameroff, A., Seifer, R., Baldwin, A., & Baldwin, C. (1993). *Continuity of risk from childhood to adolescence*. Unpublished paper. University of Rochester.

Sameroff, A. J., Seifer, R., Barocas, R., Zax, M., & Greenspan, S.

(1987). Intelligence quotient scores of 4-year-old children: Social-environmental risk factors. *Pediatrics, 79,* 343–350.

Sampaio, R., & Truwit, C. (2001). Myelination in the developing human brain. In C. Nelson & M. Luciana (Eds.), *Handbook of developmental cognitive neuroscience* (pp. 35–44). Cambridge, MA: MIT Press.

Samuels, C. A., Butterworth, G., Roberts, T., & Graupner, L. (1994). Babies prefer attractiveness to symmetry. *Perception, 23,* 823–831.

Samuelson, L. K., & Smith, L. B. (2000). Grounding development in cognitive processes. *Child Development, 71,* 1555–1570.

Sanderson, J. A., & Siegal, M. (1991). *Loneliness in young children.* Unpublished manuscript. University of Queensland, Brisbane, Australia.

Santrock, J. (2005). *Life span development* (9th ed.). New York: McGraw-Hill.

Sarnthein, J., vonStein, A., Rappelsberger, P., Petsche, H., Rauscher, F. H., & Shaw, G. (1997). Persistent patterns of brain activity: An EEG coherence study of the positive effect of music on spatial-temporal reasoning. *Neurological Research, 19,* 107–116.

Savage-Rumbaugh, S., & Shanker, S. (1998). *Apes, language, and the human mind.* New York: Oxford University Press.

Savin-Williams, R. (1987). *Adolescence: An ethological perspective.* New York: Springer-Verlag.

Savin-Williams, R. (1998). *". . . and then I became gay". Young men's stories.* New York: Routledge.

Savin-Williams, R. (2001). *"Mom, Dad, I'm Gay." How families negotiate coming out.* Washington, DC: American Psychological Association.

Savin-Williams, R., & Diamond, L. M. (2000). Sexual identity trajectories among sexual minority youths: Gender comparisons. *Archives of Sexual Behavior, 29,* 607–627.

Savin-Williams, R., & Ream, G. (2003). Sex variations in the disclosure to parents of same-sex attractions. *Journal of Family Psychology, 17,* 429–438.

Saxe, G. B. (1979). Developmental relations between notational counting and number conservation. *Child Development, 50,* 180–187.

Saxe, G. B. (1982). Developing forms of arithmetic thought among the Oksapmin of Papua New Guinea. *Developmental Psychology, 18,* 583–594.

Saxe, G. B. (1988). The mathematics of child street vendors. *Child Development, 59,* 1415–1425.

Saxe, G. B. (1991). *Culture and cognitive development: Studies in mathematical understanding.* Hillsdale, NJ: Erlbaum.

Saxe, G. B., Guberman, S. R., & Gearhart, M. (1987). Social processes in early number development. *Monographs of the Society for Research in Child Development, 52,* 162.

Saywitz, K. J., & Lyons, T. D. (2002). Coming to grips with children's suggestibility. In M. Eisen, G. Goodman, & J. Quas (Eds.), *Memory and suggestibility in the forensic interview* (pp. 85–113). Hillsdale, NJ: Erlbaum.

Scaramella, L. V, & Conger, R. D. (2003). Intergenerational continuity of hostile parenting and its consequences: The moderating influence of children's negative emotional reactivity. *Social Development, 12,* 420–439.

Scarr, S. (1992). Developmental theories for the 1990s: Development and individual differences. *Child Development, 63,* 1–19.

Scarr, S. (1996). How people make their own environments: Implications for parents and policy makers. *Psychology, Public Policy & Law, 2,* 204–228.

Scarr, S. (1997). Behavior-genetic and socialization theories of intelligence: Truce and reconciliation. In R. J. Sternberg & E. Grigorenko (Eds.), *Intelligence, heredity, and environment* (pp. 3–41). New York: Cambridge University Press.

Scarr, S. (1998). How do families affect intelligence? Social-environmental and behavior-genetic predictions. In J. J. McArdle & R. W. Woodcock (Eds.), *Human cognitive abilities in theory and practice* (pp. 113–136). Mahwah, NJ: Erlbaum.

Scarr, S., & McCartney, K. (1983). How people make their own environments: A theory of genotype environment effects. *Child Development, 54,* 424–435.

Scarr, S., & Weinberg, R. A. (1976). IQ test performance of black children adopted by white families. *American Psychologist, 31,* 726–739.

Scarr, S., & Weinberg, R. A. (1983). The Minnesota adoption studies: Genetic differences and malleability. *Child Development, 54,* 260–267.

Schaal, B., Tremblay, R. E., Soussignan, R., & Susman, E. J. (1996). Male testosterone linked to high social dominance but low physical aggression in early adolescence. *Journal of the American Academy of Child & Adolescent Psychiatry, 19,* 1322–1330.

Schaefer, C. (1997). Defining verbal abuse of children: A survey. *Psychological Reports, 80,* 626.

Schaffer, H. R. (1971). *The growth of sociability.* London: Penguin.

Schaffer, H. R. (1974). *The development of sociability.* New York: Penguin.

Schaffer, H. R. (1977). *Mothering.* Cambridge, MA: Harvard University Press.

Schaffer, H. R. (1996). *Social development.* Cambridge, MA: Blackwell.

Schaffer, H. R., & Emerson, P. E. (1964). The development of social attachments in infancy. *Monographs of the Society for Research in Child Development, 29*(3, Serial No. 94).

Schank, R. C., & Abelson, R. P. (1977). *Scripts, plans, goals and understanding.* Hillsdale, NJ: Erlbaum.

Schellenberg, E. G., & Trehub, S. E. (1996). Natural musical intervals: Evidence from infant listeners. *Psychological Science, 7,* 272–277.

Schellenberg, E. G., & Trehub, S. E. (1999). Culture-general and culture-specific factors in the discrimination of melodies. *Journal of Experimental Child Psychology, 74,* 107–127.

Schieffelin, B. B., & Ochs, E. (1987). *Language socialization across cultures.* New York: Cambridge University Press.

Schmuckler, M. A., & Tsang-Tong, H. Y. (2000). The role of visual and body movement information in infant search. *Developmental Psychology, 36,* 499–510.

Schneider, B. H. (2000). *Friends and enemies: Peer relations in childhood.* London: Arnold.

Schneider, B. H., Atkinson, L., & Tardif, C. (2001). Child-parent attachment and children's peer relations: A quantitative review. *Developmental Psychology, 37,* 86–100.

Schneider, B. H., Smith, A., Poisson, S. E., & Kwan, A. B. (1997). Cultural dimensions of children's peer relations. In S. Duck (Ed.), *Handbook of personal relationships* (2nd ed., pp. 121–146). New York: Wiley.

Schneider, W., & Bjorklund, D. F. (1998). Memory. In W. Damon (Gen. Ed.), and D. Kuhn, & R. S. Siegler (Vol. Eds.), *Handbook of child psychology: Vol. 2. Cognition, perception, and language* (pp. 467–521). New York: Wiley.

Scholl, T. O., Heidiger, M. L., & Belsky, D. (1996). Prenatal care and maternal health during adolescent pregnancy: A review and meta-analysis. *Journal of Adolescent Health, 15,* 444–456.

Schwartz, D., Dodge, K., Pettit, G., & Bates, J. (1997). The early socialization of aggressive victims of bullying. *Child Development, 68,* 665–675.

Schwartz, L. L. (2003). A nightmare for King Solomon: The new reproductive technologies. *Journal of Family Psychology, 17,* 229–237.

Schwartz, R. G., & Leonard, L. B. (1984). Words, objects and actions in early lexical acquisition. *Journal of Speech and Hearing Research, 27,* 119–127.

Scribner, S. (1985). Vygotsky's use of history. In J. V. Wertsch (Ed.), *Culture, communication and cognition: Vygotskian perspectives.* New York: Cambridge University Press.

Seiffge-Krenke, I., Shulman, S., & Klessinger, N. (2001). Adolescent precursors of romantic relationships in young adulthood. *Journal of Social and Personal Relationships, 18,* 327–346.

Seitz, V. (1990). Intervention programs for impoverished children: A comparison of educational and family support models. *Annals of Child Development, 7,* 73–103.

Seitz, V., Rosenbaum, L. K., & Apfel, N. H. (1985). Effects of family support intervention: A ten-year follow-up. *Child Development, 56,* 376–391.

Seligman, M. E. P. (1973, June). Fall into helplessness. *Psychology Today,* pp. 43–48.

Seligman, M. E. P. (1974). Depression and learned helplessness. In R. J. Friedman & M. M. Katz (Eds.), *The psychology of depression: Contemporary theory and research.* Washington, DC: Winston-Wiley.

Selman, R. L. (1980). *The growth of interpersonal understanding.* New York: Academic.

Selman, R. L., & Byrne, D. F. (1974). A structural-developmental analysis of levels of role taking in middle childhood. *Child Development, 45,* 803–806.

Selman, R. L. & Dray, A. (2006). Risk and prevention: Building bridges between research and practice. In W. Damon & R. L. Lerner (Gen. Eds.) and K. A. Renninger & I. E. Sigel (Vol. Eds.), *Handbook of child psychology: Vol 4, Child Psychology and Practice* (6th ed.). New York: Wiley.

Selman, R. L., & Jacquette, D. (1978). Stability and oscillation in interpersonal awareness: A clinical-developmental analysis. In C. B. Keasey (Ed.), *The XXV Nebraska symposium on motivation.* Lincoln: Univ. of Nebraska Press.

Semel, E., & Rosner, S. R. (2003). *Understanding Williams syndrome: Behavioral patterns and interventions.* Mahwah, NJ: Erlbaum.

Senghas, A., & Coppola, M. (2001). Children creating language: How

Nicaraguan sign language acquired a spatial grammar. *Psychological Science, 12*(4), 323–328.

Serbin, L., & Karp, J. (2003). Intergenerational studies of parenting and the transfer of risk from parent to child. *Current Directions in Psychological Science, 12,* 138–142.

Serbin, L. A., Polwishta, K. K., & Gulko, J. (1993). The development of sex-typing in middle childhood. *Monographs of the Society for Research in Child Development, 58* (Serial No. 232).

Serbin, L. A., Poulin-Dubois, K. A., Colburne, K. A., Sen, M. G., & Eichstedt, J. A. (2001). Gender stereotyping in infancy: Visual preferences for and knowledge of gender-stereotyped toys in the second year. *International Journal of Behavioral Development, 25,* 7–15.

Serpell, R., & Hatano, G. (1997). Education, schooling, and literacy. In J. W. Berry, P. R. Dasen, & T. S. Saraswathi (Eds.), *Handbook of cross-cultural psychology: Vol. 2, Basic process and human development* (2nd ed., pp. 339–376). Boston, MA: Allyn & Bacon.

Shakin, M., Shakin, D., & Sternglanz, S. H. (1985). Infant clothing: Sex labeling for strangers. *Sex Roles, 12,* 955–963.

Shanley, M. L. (2001). *Making babies, making families.* Boston: Beacon Press.

Shantz, C. V. (1983). Social cognition. In J. H. Flavell & E. M. Markman (Eds.), *Handbook of child psychology: Cognitive development* (Vol. 3). New York: Wiley.

Shatz, M. (1983). Communication. In P. H. Mussen (Eds.), *Handbook of child psychology* (Vol. 3). New York: Wiley.

Shatz, M. (1994). Theory of mind and the development of socio-linguistic intelligence in early childhood. In C. Lewis & P. Mitchell (Eds.), *Children's early understanding of mind: Origins and development* (pp. 311–329). Hillsdale, NJ: Erlbaum.

Shatz, M., & Gelman, R. (1973). The development of communication skills: Modifications in the speech of young children as a function of listener. *Monographs of the Society for Research in Child Development, 38* (5, Serial No. 152), 1–37.

Shaywitz, B. A., Shaywitz, S. E., Pugh, K. R., & Constable, R. T. (1995). Sex differences in the functional organization of the brain for language. *Nature, 373,* 607–609.

Shea, D. L., Lubinski, D., & Benbow, C. P. (2001). Importance of assessing spatial ability in intellectually talented young adolescents: A 20-year longitudinal study. *Journal of Educational Psychology, 93,* 604–614.

Shepardson, D. P., & Pizzini, E. L. (1992). Gender bias in female elementary teachers' perceptions of the scientific ability of students. *Science Education, 76*(2), 147–153.

Sherman, M., & Key, C. B. (1932). The intelligence of isolated mountain children. *Child Development, 3,* 279–290.

Sherwood, N. E., Neumark-Sztainer, D., Story, M., Beuhring, T., & Resnick, M. D. (2002). Weight-related sports involvement in girls: Who is at risk for disordered eating? *American Journal of Health Promotion, 16,* 341–344.

Shields, A., Ryan, R. M., & Cicchetti, D. (2001). Narrative representations of caregivers and emotional dysregulation as predictors of maltreated children's rejection by peers. *Developmental Psychology, 37,* 321–337.

Shiffman, S. (1993). Smoking cessation treatment: Any progress? *Journal of Consulting and Clinical Psychology, 61,* 718–722.

Shirley, M. M. (1931). *The first two years, a study of twenty-five babies: I Postural & locomotor development.* Minneapolis, MN: University of Minnesota Press.

Shoda, Y., Mischel, W., & Peake, P. K. (1990). Predicting adolescent cognitive and self-regulatory competencies from preschool delay of gratification: Identifying diagnostic conditions. *Developmental Psychology, 26,* 978–986.

Shonkoff, J., & Phillips, D. (Eds.). (2000). *From neurons to neighborhoods.* Washington, DC: National Academy Press.

Shrum, W., & Cheek, N. H. (1987). Social structure during the school years: Onset of the degrouping process. *American Sociological Review, 52,* 218–223.

Shweder, R. A., Goodnow, J., Hatano, G., LeVine, R. A., Markus, H., & Miller, P. (1998). The cultural psychology of development: One mind, many mentalities. In W. Damon (Gen. Ed.) & R. M. Lerner (Vol. Ed.), *Handbook of child psychology* (Vol. 1, pp. 865–938). New York: Wiley.

Shweder, R. A., Much, N. C., Mahapatra, M., & Park, L. (1997). The "big three" of morality (autonomy, community, divinity) and the "big three" explanations of suffering. In A. M. Brandt, P. Rozin (Ed.), *Morality and health* (pp. 119–169). Florence, KY: Taylor & Frances/Routledge.

Siddiqui, A. (1995). Object size as a determinant of grasping in infancy. *Journal of Genetic Psychology, 156,* 345–358.

Siegel, A. W., & White, S. H. (1975). The development of spatial representatives of large scale environments. In H. W. Reese (Eds.), *Advances in child development and behavior* (Vol. 10). New York: Academic.

Siegel, M. (1987). Are sons and daughters treated more differently by fathers than mothers? *Developmental Review, 7,* 183–209.

Siegler, R. S. (1978). The origins of scientific reasoning. In R. S. Siegler (Ed.). *Children's thinking: What develops?* Hillsdale, NJ: Erlbaum.

Siegler, R. S. (1992). The other Alfred Binet. *Developmental Psychology, 28,* 179–190.

Siegler, R. S. (1994). Cognitive variability: A key to understanding cognitive development. *Current Directions in Psychological Science, 3,* 1–5.

Siegler, R. S. (1996). *Emerging minds: The process of change in children's thinking.* New York: Oxford University Press.

Siegler, R. S. (2000). The rebirth of children's learning. *Child Development, 71,* 26–36.

Siegler, R. S., & Alibali, M. W. (2005). *Children's thinking* (4th ed.). Upper Saddle River, NJ: Prentice Hall.

Siegler, R. S., & Chen, Z. (2002). Development of rules and strategies: Balancing the old and new. *Journal of Experimental Child Psychology, 81,* 446–457.

Siegler, R. S., & Stern, E. (1998). Conscious and unconscious strategy discoveries: A microgenetic analysis. *Journal of Experimental Psychology: General, 127,* 377–397.

Sigman, M. (1995). Nutrition and child development: More food for thought. *Current Directions in Psychological Science, 4,* 52–55.

Sigman, M., & Capps, L. (1997). *Children with autism: A developmental perspective.* Cambridge, MA: Harvard University Press.

Sigman, M., & Mundy, P. (1989). Social attachments in autistic children. *Journal of the American Academy of Child and Adolescent Psychiatry, 28,* 74–81.

Signorella, M. L., Bigler, R. S., & Liben, L. S. (1993). Developmental differences in children's gender schemata about others: A meta-analytic review. *Developmental Review, 13,* 147–183.

Signorella, M. L., Bilger, R. S., & Liben, L. S. (1998). A meta-analysis of children's memories for own-sex and other-sex information. *Journal of Applied Developmental Psychology, 18,* 425–445.

Silberg, J. L., Rutter, M., & Eaves, L. J. (2001). Genetic and environmental influences on the temporal association between early anxiety and later depression in girls. *Biological Psychology, 49,* 1040–1049.

Silverstein, B., Petersen, B., & Perdue, L. (1986). Some correlates of the thin standard of bodily attractiveness for women. *International Journal of Eating Disorders, 5,* 895–906.

Simmons, R. G., & Blyth, D. A. (1987). *Moving into adolescence: The impact of pubertal change and school context.* Hawthorne, NY: Aldine.

Simmons, R. G., Blyth, D. A., & McKinney, K. L. (1984). The social and psychological effects of puberty on white females. In J. Brooks-Gunn & A. C. Peterson (Eds.), *Girls at puberty: Biological, psychological and social perspectives.* New York: Plenum.

Simmons, R. G., Burgeson, R., Carlson-Ford, S., & Blyth, D. A. (1987). The impact of cumulative change in early adolescence, *Child Development, 58,* 1220–1234.

Simons, R. L., Lin, K., & Gordon, L. C. (1998). Socialization in the family of origin and male dating violence: A prospective study. *Journal of Marriage and the Family, 60,* 467–478.

Simpkins, D., & Parke, R. D. (2001). The relations between parental friendships and children's friendships: Self-report and observational analysis. *Child Development, 72,* 569–582.

Singer, D., & Singer, J. (Eds.). (2001). *Handbook of children and the media.* Thousand Oaks, CA: Sage.

Singh, S., & Darroch, J. E. (2000). Adolescent pregnancy and childbearing: Levels and trends in developed countries. *Family Planning Perspectives, 32,* 14–23.

Skinner, B. F. (1957). *Verbal behavior.* New York: Appleton-Century-Crofts.

Slaby, R. G., & Frey, K. S. (1975). Development of gender constancy and selective attention to same-sex models. *Child Development, 46,* 849–856.

Slaby, R. G., & Guerra, N. G. (1988). Cognitive mediators of aggression in adolescent offenders: I. Assessment. *Developmental Psychology, 24,* 580–588.

Slater, A. (2000). Visual perception in the young infant: Early organization and rapid learning. In D. Muir & A. Slater (Eds.), *Infant development: The essential readings* (pp. 95–116). Oxford, UK: Blackwell.

Slater, A. M., Bremner, G., Johnson, S. P., Sherwood, P., Hayes, R., & Brown, E. (2000). Newborn preferences for attractive faces: The role of internal and external facial features. *Infancy, 1,* 265–274.

Slaughter-Defoe, D. T., Nakagawa, K., Takanishi, R., & Johnson, D. J. (1990). Toward cultural/ecological perspectives on schooling and achievement in African- and Asian-American children. *Child Development, 61,* 363–383.

Slobin, D. I. (1968). Imitation and grammatical development in children. In N. S. Endler, L. R. Boulter, & H. Osser (Eds.), *Contemporary issues in development in psychology.* New York: Holt.

Slobin, D. I. (1979). *Psycholinguistics.* Glenview, IL: Scott, Foresman.

Slobin, D. I. (1982). Universal and particular in the acquisition of language. In L. R. Gleitman & H. E. Wanner (Eds.), *Language acquisition: The state of the art.* New York: Cambridge University Press.

Slobin, D. I. (1985). *The cross-linguistic study of language acquisition* (Vols. 1 & 2). Hillsdale, NJ: Erlbaum.

Slobin, D. I. (Ed.). (1992). *The cross-linguistic study of language acquisition: Vol. 3.* Hillsdale, NJ: Erlbaum.

Slomkowski, C., Rende, R., Conger, K. J., Simons, R. L., & Conger, R. D. (2001). Sisters, brothers, and delinquency: Evaluating social influence during early and middle adolescence. *Child Development, 72,* 271–283.

Smetana, J. G. (1984). Toddler's social interaction regarding moral and conventional transgressions. *Child Development, 55,* 1767–1776.

Smetana, J. G. (1989). Toddlers' social interactions in the context of moral and conventional transgressions in the home. *Developmental Psychology, 25,* 499–508.

Smetana, J. G. (1995). Morality in context: Abstractions, ambiguities, and applications. In R. Vasta (Ed.), *Annals of child development* (Vol. 10, pp. 83–130). London: Jessica Kingsley.

Smetana, J. G. (1997). Parenting and the development of social knowledge reconceptualized: A social domain analysis. In J. E. Grusec & L. Kuczynski (Eds.), *Parenting and children's internalization of values* (pp. 162–192). New York: Wiley.

Smetana, J. G. (2000). Middle-class African American adolescents' and parents' conceptions of parental authority and parenting practices: A longitudinal investigation. *Child Development, 71,* 1672–1686.

Smetana, J. G., & Asquith, P. (1994). Adolescents' and parents' conceptions of parental authority and adolescent autonomy. *Child Development, 65,* 1147–1162.

Smetana, J. G., & Braeges, J. L. (1990). The development of toddler's moral and conventional judgments. *Merrill-Palmer Quarterly, 36,* 329–346.

Smetana, J. G., & Gaines, C. (1999). Adolescent-parent conflict in middle-class African American families. *Child Development, 70,* 1447–1463.

Smetana, J. G., & Letourneau, K. J. (1984). Development of gender constancy and children's sex-typed free play behavior. *Developmental Psychology, 20,* 691–696.

Smith, B. A., & Blass, E. M. (1996). Taste-mediated calming in premature, preterm and full term human infants. *Developmental Psychology, 32,* 1084–1089.

Smith, B. A., Fillion, T. J., & Blass, E. M. (1990). Orally mediated sources of calming in 1- to 3-day-old human infants. *Developmental Psychology, 26,* 731–737.

Smith, C. L. (1979). Children's understanding of natural language hierarchies. *Journal of Experimental Child Psychology, 27,* 437–458.

Smith, D. (2001). Prevention: Still a young field. *Monitor on Psychology, 3,* 70–72.

Smith, D. J., Stevens, M. E., Sudanagunta, S. P., Bronson, R. T., Makhinson, M., Watabe, A. M., O'Dell, T. J., Fung, J., Weier, H. U., Chang, J. F., & Rubin, E. M. (1997). Functional screening of 2Mb of human chromosome 21q22.2 in transgenic mice implicates minibrain in learning defects associated with Down syndrome. *Nature Genetics, 16,* 28–36.

Smith, H. (1992). The detrimental health effects of ionizing radiation. *Nuclear Medicine Communications, 13,* 4–10.

Smith, I. M., & Bryson, S. E. (1994). Imitation and action in autism: A critical review. *Psychological Bulletin, 116,* 259–273.

Smith, L. (2000). Learning how to learn words: An associative crane. In R. M. Golinkoff, K. Hirsh-Pasek, N. Akhtar, L. Bloom, G. Hollich, K. Plunkett, L. Smith, M. Tomasello, & A. Woodward (Eds.), *Breaking the word learning barrier: What does it take?* New York: Oxford Press.

Smith, P. K., & Drew, L. M. (2002). Grandparenthood. In M. H. Bornstein (Ed.), *Handbook of parenting* (2nd ed.). Mahwah, NJ: Erlbaum.

Smith, P. K., Madsen, K. C., & Moody, J. C. (1999a). What causes the age decline in reports of being bullied at school? Towards a developmental analysis of risks of being bullied. *Educational Research, 41,* 267–285.

Smith, P. K., Morita, Y. M., Junger-Tas, J., Olweus, D., Catalano, R. F., & Slee, P. (Eds.). (1999b). *The nature of school bullying: A cross-national perspective.* New York: Routledge.

Smith, P. K., & Sloboda, J. (1986). Individual consistency in infant-stranger encounters. *British Journal of Developmental Psychology, 4,* 83–92.

Smith, S. (Ed.) (1995). *Two-generation programs for families in poverty: A new intervention strategy.* Norwood, NJ: Ablex.

Smith, T. M. (1994). Adolescent pregnancy. In R. Simeonsson (Ed.). *Risk, resilience, and prevention: Promoting the well-being of all children.* Baltimore: Brooks Publishing.

Smollar, J., & Youniss, J. (1982). Social development through friendship. In K. H. Rubin & H. S. Ross (Eds.), *Peer relationships and social skills in childhood.* New York: Springer-Verlag.

Snarey, J. (1993). *How fathers care for the next generation: A four decade study.* Cambridge, MA: Harvard University Press.

Snarey, J. R. (1995). In a communitarian voice: The sociological expansion of Kohlbergian theory, research, and practice. In W. Kurtines & J. Gewirtz (Eds.), *Moral development: An introduction* (pp. 109–134). Boston: Allyn & Bacon.

Snarey, J. R., Reimer, J., & Kohlberg, L. (1985). Development of social-moral reasoning among kibbutz adolescents: A longitudinal cross-cultural study. *Developmental Psychology, 21,* 3–17.

Snow, C. E. (1989). Understanding social interaction and language acquisition: Sentences are not enough. In M. H. Bornstein & J. S. Bruner (Eds.), *Interaction in human development* (pp. 83–104). Hillsdale, NJ: Erlbaum.

Society for Research in Child Development. (1993). Ethical standards of research with children. In *Directory of Members* (pp. 337–339). Ann Arbor, MI: SRCD.

Sokolov, J. L. (1993). A local contingency analysis of the fine-tuning hypothesis. *Developmental Psychology, 29,* 1008–1023.

Solomon, J., & George, C. (1999). The measurement of attachment security in infancy and childhood. In J. Cassidy & P. Shaver (Eds.), *Handbook of attachment* (pp. 287–318). New York: Guilford.

Solomon, S. E., Rothbaum, E. D., & Balsam, K. F. (2004). Pioneers in partnership: Lesbian and gay male couples in civil unions and married heterosexual siblings. *Journal of Family Psychology, 18,* 275–286.

Sommer, K. S., Keogh, D., & Whitman, T. L. (1995, March). *Prenatal predictors of cognitive and emotional development in children of adolescent mothers.* Poster session presented at 61st biennial meeting of the Society for Research in Child Development, Indianapolis.

Sontag, L. W. (1944). Differences in modifiability of fetal behavior and physiology. *Psychosomatic Medicine, 6,* 151–154.

Sorahan, T., Lancashire, R. J., Hulten, M. A., Peck, I., & Stewart, A. M. (1997). Childhood cancer and parental use of tobacco: Deaths from 1953 to 1955. *British Journal of Cancer, 75,* 134–138.

Sosa, R., Kennell, J., Klaus, M., Robertson, S., & Urrutia, J. (1980). The effect of a supportive companion on perinatal problems, length of labor and mother-infant interaction. *New England Journal of Medicine, 303,* 597–600.

Sostek, A. M., & Anders, T. F. (1981). The biosocial importance and environmental sensitivity of infant sleep-wake behaviors. In K. Bloom (Ed.), *Prospective issues in infancy research.* Hillsdale, NJ: Erlbaum.

Sowell, E. R., Peterson, B. S., Thompson, P. M., Welcome, S. E., Henkenius, A. L., & Toga, A. W. (2003). Mapping cortical change across the human life span. *Nature Neuroscience, 6,* 309–315.

Spangler, G., & Grossman, K. E. (1993). Biobehavioral organization in securely & insecurely attached infants. *Child Development, 64,* 1439–1450.

Spearman, C. (1927). *The abilities of man.* New York: Macmillan.

Speer, J. R., & Flavell, J. H. (1979). Young children's knowledge of the relative difficulty of recognition and recall memory tasks. *Developmental Psychology, 15,* 214–217.

Spelke, E. (2000). Core knowledge. *American Psychologist, 55,* 1233–1243.

Spelke, E. S. (1987). The development of intermodal perception. In P. Salapatek & L. Cohen (Eds.), *Handbook of infant perception: Vol. 2. From perception to cognition* (pp. 233–274). New York: Academic.

Spelke, E. S., & Cortelyou, A. (1981). Perceptual aspects of social knowing: Looking and listening in infancy. In M. E. Lamb & L. R. Sherrod (Eds.), *Infant social cognition* (pp. 6–84). Hillsdale, NJ: Erlbaum.

Spence, J. (1993). Gender-related traits and gender ideology: Evidence for a multifactorial theory. *Journal of Personality and Social Psychology, 64,* 624–635.

Spence, J., & Buckner, C. (2000). Instrumental and expressive traits, trait stereotypes, and sexist attitudes. *Psychology of Women Quarterly, 24*, 44–62.

Spence, J. T., & Hall, S. K. (1996). Children's gender-related self-perceptions, activity preference and occupational stereotypes: A test of three models of gender constructs. *Sex Roles, 35*, 659–691.

Spencer, J. P., & Thelen, E. (2000). Spatially specific changes in infants' muscle coactivity as they learn to reach. *Infancy, 1*, 275–302.

Spergel, I. A., Ross, R. E., Curry, G. D., & Chance, R. (1989). *Youth gangs: Problem and response.* Washington, DC: Office of Juvenile Justice and Delinquency Prevention.

Sperling, G. (1960). The information available in brief visual presentations. *Psychological Monographs, 74*.

Spiker, D., & Ricks, M. (1984). Visual self-recognition in autistic children: Developmental variations. *Child Development, 55*, 214–225.

Spoth, R., Redmond, C., & Shin, C. (2003). Randomized trial of brief family interventions for general populations: Adolescent substance use outcomes four years following baseline. *Journal of Consulting and Clinical Psychology, 69*, 627–642.

Springer, S. P., & Deutsch, G. (1993). *Left brain, right brain.* New York: W. H. Freeman.

Sroufe, L. A. (1996). *Emotional development: The organization of emotional life in the early years.* New York: Cambridge University Press.

Sroufe, L. A. (2002). From infant attachment to promotion of adolescent autonomy. In J. G. Borkowski, S. L. Ramey, & M. Bristol-Power (Eds.), *Parenting and the child's world* (pp. 187–202). Mahwah, NJ: Erlbaum.

Sroufe, L. A., Waters, E., & Matas, L. (1974). Contextual determinants of infant affectional response. In M. Lewis & L. Rosenblum (Eds.), *Origins of fear.* New York: Wiley.

Sroufe, L. A., & Wunsch, J. P. (1972). The development of laughter in the first year of life. *Child Development, 43*, 1326–1344.

St. Clair, P. A., Smeriglio, V. L., Alexander, C. S., & Celentano, D. D. (1989). Social network structure and prenatal care utilization. *Medical Care, 27*(8), 823–831.

St. Peters, M. (1993). *The ecology of mother-child interaction.* Unpublished doctoral dissertation, University of Kansas, Lawrence.

Stams, G. J. M., Juffer, F., & van IJzendoorn, M. H. (2002). Maternal sensitivity, infant attachment and temperament in early childhood predict adjustment in middle childhood: The case of adopted children and their biologically unrelated parents. *Developmental Psychology, 38*, 806–821.

Stark, K. D., Napolitano, S., Sweaver, S., & Schmidt, K. (1996). Issues in the treatment of depressed children. *Applied & Preventive Psychology, 5*, 59–83.

Starr, A. S. (1923). The diagnostic value of the audio-vocal digit memory span. *Psychological Clinic, 15*, 61–84.

Stattin, H., & Magnusson, D. (1990). *Pubertal maturation in female development* (Vol. 2). Hillsdale, NJ: Erlbaum.

Steckel, Richard. (1997). Ohio State University. As reproduced in "2000: The Millennium Notebook," *Newsweek,* June 2, p. 10.

Steele, C. M. (1997). A threat in the air: How stereotypes shape intellectual identity and performance. *American Psychologist, 52*, 613–629.

Steele, C. M., & Aronson, J. (1995). Stereotype threat and the intellectual test performance of African Americans. *Journal of Personality and Social Psychology, 69*, 797–811.

Stein, Z. A., & Susser, M. W. (1976). Prenatal nutrition and mental competence. In J. D. Lloyd-Still (Ed.), *Malnutrition and intellectual development* (pp. 39–80). Littleton, MA: Publishing Sciences Group.

Steinberg, L. (1986). Latchkey children and susceptibility to peer pressure. An ecological analysis. *Developmental Psychology, 22*, 433–439.

Steinberg, L. (1987). Impact of puberty on family relations: Effects of pubertal status and pubertal timing. *Developmental Psychology, 23*, 451–460.

Steinberg, L., Catalano, R., & Dooley, D. (1981). Economic antecedents of child abuse and neglect. *Child Development, 52*, 975–985.

Steinberg, L., Darling, N. E., & Fletcher, A. C. (1995). Authoritative parenting and adolescent adjustment: An ecological journey. In P. Moen, G. H. Elder, Jr., & K. Luscher (Eds.), *Examining lives in context: Perspectives on the ecology of human development* (pp. 423–466). Washington: American Psychological Assocation.

Steinberg, L., Dornbusch, S. M., & Brown, B. B. (1992). Ethnic differences in adolescent achievement: An ecological perspective. *American Psychologist, 47*, 723–729.

Steinberg, L., Mounts, N. S., Lamborn, S. D., & Dornbusch, S. M. (1991). Authoritative parenting and adolescent adjustment across varied ecological niches. *Journal of Research on Adolescence, 1*, 19–36.

Steiner, J. E. (1979). Human facial expression in response to taste and smell stimulation. In H. W. Reese & L. P. Lipsitt (Eds.), *Advances in child development and behavior* (Vol. 13). New York: Academic.

Steinschneider, A. (1975). Implications of the sudden infant death syndrome for the study of sleep in infancy. In A. D. Pick (Ed.), *Minnesota symposia on child psychology* (Vol. 9). Minneapolis, MN: University of Minnesota Press.

Stenberg, C., & Campos, J. (1989). *The development of anger expressions during infancy.* Unpublished manuscript. University of Denver, Denver, Colorado.

Stenberg, C., Campos, J., & Emde, R. N. (1983). The facial expression of anger in seven-month-old infants. *Child Development, 54*, 178–184.

Stephan, K. E., Marshall, J. C., Friston, K. J., Rowe, J. B., Ritzl, A., Zilles, K., & Fink, G. R. (2003). Lateralized cognitive processes and lateralized task control in the human brain. *Science, 301*, 384–386.

Stern, D. N. (1974). Mother and infant at play: The dyadic interaction involving facial, vocal, and gaze behaviors. In M. Lewis & L. A. Rosenblum (Eds.), *The effect of the infant on its caregiver.* New York: Wiley.

Stern, D. N. (2004). The motherhood constellation: Therapeutic approaches to early relationship problems. In A. J. Sameroff, S. C. McDonough, & K. L. Rosenblum (Eds.), *Treating parent-infant relational problems* (pp. 29–42). New York: Guilford.

Stern, M., & Karraker, K. H. (1989). Sex stereotyping of infants: A review of gender labeling studies. *Sex Roles, 20*, 501–522.

Sternberg, R. J. (1985). *Beyond IQ: A triarchic theory of human intelligence.* Cambridge, England: Cambridge University Press.

Sternberg, R. J. (1988). *The triarchic mind.* New York: Viking.

Sternberg, R. J. (2001). Successful intelligence: Understanding what Spearman had rather than what he studied. In J. M. Collis & S. Messick (Eds.), *Intelligence and personality* (pp. 347–373). Mahwah, NJ: Erlbaum.

Sternberg, R. J., Grigorenko, E. L., & Bundy, D. A. (2001). The predictive value of IQ. *Merrill-Palmer Quarterly, 47*, 1–41.

Sternberg, R. J., Torff, B., & Grigorenko, E. L. (1999). Teaching triarchically improves school achievement. *Journal of Educational Psychology, 90*, 374–384.

Sternberg, R. J., & Wagner, R. K. (1993). The geocentric view of intelligence and job performance is wrong. *Current Directions in Psychological Science, 2*, 1–6.

Sternberg, R. J., & Wagner, R. K. (1994). *Mind in context.* New York: Cambridge University Press.

Sternberg, R. J., Wagner, R. K., & Okagaki, L. (1993). Practical intelligence: The nature and role of tacit knowledge in work and at school. In H. W. Reese & W. Puckett (Eds.), *Advances in lifespan development* (pp. 205–227). Hillsdale, NJ: Erlbaum.

Stevahn, L., Johnson, D. W., Johnson, R. T., Oberle, K., & Wahl, L. (2000). Effects of conflict resolution training integrated into a kindergarten curriculum. *Child Development, 71*, 772–784.

Stevenson, H. W. (2001). Schools, teachers, and parents. In A. Thornton (Ed.), *The well-being of children and families: Research and data needs* (pp. 341–355). Ann Arbor: The University of Michigan Press.

Stevenson, H. W., Chen, C., & Lee, S. Y. (1993). Mathematics achievement of Chinese, Japanese, and American children: Ten years later. *Science, 259*, 53–58.

Stevenson, H. W., Chen, C., & Uttal, D. H. (1990). Beliefs and achievement: A study of black, white, and Hispanic children. *Child Development, 61*, 508–523.

Stevenson, H. W., & Lee, S. Y. (1990). Context of achievement. *Monographs of the Society for Research in Child Development, 55*, Serial No. 221.

Stevenson, H. W., Lee, S., & Mu, X. (2000). Successful achievement in mathematics: China and the United States. In C. F. M. Van Lieshout & P. G. Heymans (Eds.), *Developing talent across the life span* (pp. 167–183). Philadelphia: Psychology Press.

Stevenson, H. W., & Stigler, J. W. (1992). *The learning gap.* New York: Summit Books.

Stice, L., Presnell, K., & Bearman, S. K. (2000). Relation of early menarche to depression, eating disorder, substance abuse and comorbid psychopathology among adolescent girls. *Developmental Psychology, 37*, 608–619.

Stiles, J. (2000). Spatial cognitive development following prenatal or perinatal focal brain injury. In H. S. Levin & J. Grafman (Eds.), *Cerebral reorganization of function after brain damage* (pp. 207–217). New York: Oxford University Press.

Stipek, D., & McCroskey, J. (1989). Investing in children: Government and workplace policies for parents. *American Psychologist, 44*, 416–423.

Stipek, D. J., & Ryan, R. H. (1997). Economically disadvantaged preschoolers: Ready to learn but further to go. *Developmental Psychology, 33,* 711–723.

Stolley, K. S. (1993). Statistic on adoption in the United States. *The Future of Children, 3,* 26–42.

Stone, R. (1990, August 20). An artificial eye may be within sight. *The Washington Post,* p. A3.

Stoneman, Z., Brody, G., & MacKinnon, C. E. (1986). Same sex and cross-sex siblings: Activity choices, roles, behavior, and gender stereotypes. *Sex Roles, 15,* 495–511.

Straughtan, R. (1986). Why act on Kohlberg's moral judgments? In S. Modgil & C. Modgil (Eds.), *Lawrence Kohlberg: Consensus and controversy.* Philadelphia: Falmer Press.

Straus, M., & Donnelly, D. (1994). *Beating the devil out of them: Corporal punishment in American families.* New York: Lexington Books.

Strayer, J., & Roberts, W. (2004). Children's anger, emotional expressiveness, and empathy: Relations with parents' empathy, emotional expressiveness, and parenting practices. *Social Development, 13,* 229–254.

Streissgath, A. P. (1997). *Fetal alcohol syndrome.* New York: Oxford University Press.

Streissgath, A. P., Bookstein, F. L., Sampson, P. D., & Barr, H. M. (1995). Attention: Prenatal alcohol and continuities of vigilance and attentional problems from 4 through 14 years. *Development & Psychopathology, 1,* 419–446.

Streri, A., Lhote, M., & Dutilleul, S. (2000). Haptic perception in newborns. *Developmental Science, 3,* 319–327.

Streri, A., & Pecheux, M. (1986). Tactual habituation and discrimination of form in infancy: A comparison with vision. *Child Development, 57,* 100–104.

Stunkard, A. J. (1958). The management of obesity. *New York Journal of Medicine, 58,* 79–87.

Stunkard, A. J., Foch, T. T., & Hrubeck, Z. (1986a). A twin study of human obesity. *Journal of the American Medical Association, 256,* 51–54.

Stunkard, A. J., Sorenson, T. I., Hanis, C., Teasdale, T. W., Chakraborty, R., Schull, W. J., & Schulsinger, F. (1986b). An adoption study of human obesity. *New England Journal of Medicine, 314,* 193–198.

Subrahmanyam, K., Greenfield, P., Kraut, R., & Gross, E. (2001a). The impact of computer use on children's and adolescents' development. *Journal of Applied Developmental Psychology, 22,* 7–30.

Subrahmanyam, K., Kraut, R. E., Greenfield, P. M., & Gross, E. F. (2001b). New forms of electronic media: The impact of interactive games and Internet on cognition, socialization, and behavior. In D. Singer & J. Singer (Eds.), *Handbook of children and the media.* Thousand Oaks, CA: Sage.

Sugarman, S. (1987). *Piaget's construction of the child's reality.* Cambridge, England: Cambridge University Press.

Sugita, Y. (2004). Experience in early infancy is indispensable for color perception. *Current Biology, 14,* 1267–1271.

Sullivan, H. S. (1953). *The interpersonal theory of psychiatry.* New York: Norton.

Sullivan, M. L. (1993). Culture and class as determinants of out-of-wedlock childbearing and poverty during late adolescence. *Journal of Research on Adolescence, 3,* 295–316.

Sulloway, F. J. (1995). Birth order and evolutionary psychology: A meta-analytic overview. *Psychological Inquiry, 6,* 75–80.

Suomi, S. J., & Harlow, H. F. (1972). Social rehabilitation of isolate-reared monkeys. *Developmental Psychology, 6,* 487–496.

Super, C. M., & Harkness, S. (1981). The infant's niche in rural Kenya and metropolitan America. In L. L. Adler (Ed.), *Cross-cultural research at issue* (pp. 47–55). New York: American Press.

Super, C. M., Herrera, M. G., & Mora, J. O. (1990). Long-term effects of food supplementation and psychosocial intervention on the physical growth of Columbian infants at risk of malnutrition. *Child Development, 61,* 29–49.

Susman-Stillman, A., Kalkoske, M., Egeland, B., & Waldman, I. (1996). Infant temperament and maternal sensitivity as predictors of attachment security. *Infant Behavior & Development, 19,* 33–47.

Swain, I. U., Zelazo, P. R., & Clifton, R. K. (1993). Newborn infants' memory for speech sounds retained over 24 hours. *Developmental Psychology, 29,* 312–323.

Szkrybale, J., & Ruble, D. (1999). "God made me a girl": Sex category constancy judgments and explanations revisited. *Developmental Psychology, 35,* 392–402.

Tager-Flusberg, H. (1985). Putting words together: Morphology and syntax in the preschool years. In J. Berko-Gleason (Ed.), *The development of language.* Columbia: Bell D. Howell.

Tamis-LeMonda, C. S., Bornstein, M. H., & Baumwell, L. (2001). Maternal responsiveness and children's achievement of language milestones. *Child Development, 72,* 748–767.

Tamis-LeMonda, C. S., & McLure, J. (1995). Infant visual expectation in relation to feature learning. *Infant Behavior and Development, 18,* 427–434.

Tangney, J. P. (1998). How does guilt differ from shame? In J. Bybee (Ed.), *Guilt and children* (pp. 1–17). San Diego: Academic Press.

Tanner, J. M. (1970). Physical growth. In P. H. Mussen (Ed.), *Carmichael's manuscript of child psychology* (Vol. 1, pp. 77–155). New York: Wiley.

Tanner, J. M. (1978). *Fetus into man: Physical growth from conception to maturity.* Cambridge, MA: Harvard University Press.

Tanner, J. M. (1990). *Fetus into man: Physical growth from conception to maturity.* Cambridge, MA: Harvard University Press.

Tardif, T. (1993). *Audit-to-child speech and language acquisition in Mandarin Chinese.* Unpublished doctoral dissertation. New Haven, CT.

Tardif, T. (1996). Nouns are not always learned before verbs: Evidence from Mandarin speakers' early vocabularies. *Developmental Psychology, 32,* 492–504.

Tasbihsazan, R., Nettelbeck, T., & Kirby, N. (2003). Predictive validity of the Fagan Test of Infant Intelligence. *British Journal of Developmental Psychology, 21,* 585–597.

Tavris, C. (1992). *The mismeasure of woman.* New York: Simon & Schuster.

Teller, D. Y. (1997). First glances. The vision of infants. The Friedenwald Lecture. *Investigative Ophthalmology & Visual Science, 38,* 2183–2203.

Teller, D. Y., & Bornstein, M. H. (1987). Infant color vision. In P. Salapatek & L. B. Cohen (Eds.), *Handbook of infant perception.* New York: Academic.

Terman, L. M. (1954). The discovery and encouragement of exceptional talent. *American Psychologist, 9,* 221–230.

Tessier, R., Cristo, M. B., Velez, S., Giron, M., Line, N., Figueroa de Calume, Z., Ruiz- Palaez, J. G., & Charpak, N. (2003). Kangaroo mother care: A method for protecting high-risk low-birth weight and premature infants against developmental delay. *Infant Behavior Development, 26,* 384–397.

Teti, D. M. (2002). Retrospect and prospect in the study of sibling relationships. In J. McHale & W. Grolnick (Eds.), *Retrospect and prospect in the psychological study of families* (pp. 193–224). Mahwah, NJ: Erlbaum.

Tharp, R. G. (1994). Intergroup differences among Native Americans in socialization and child cognition: An ethnogenetic analysis. In P. M. Greenfield & R. R. Cocking (Eds.), *Cross-cultural roots of minority child development.* Hillsdale, NJ: Erlbaum.

Tharp, R. G., & Gallimore, R. (1988). *Rousing minds to life: Teaching, learning, and schooling in social context.* New York: Cambridge University Press.

Thelen, E. (1995). Motor development: A new synthesis. *American Psychologist, 50,* 79–95.

Thelen, E., Corbetta, D., Kamm, K., Spencer, J. P., Schneider, K., & Zernicke, R. F. (1993). The transition to reaching: Mapping intention and intrinsic dynamics. *Child Development, 64,* 1058–1098.

Thelen, E., & Smith, L. (2006). Dynamic systems theory. In W. Damon & R. L. Lerner (Gen. Eds.) and R. L. Lerner (Vol. Ed.). *Handbook of child psychology: Vol 1, Theoretical models of human development* (6th ed.). New York: Wiley.

Thelen, E., & Smith, L. B. (1994). *A dynamic systems approach to the development of cognition and action.* Cambridge, MA: MIT Press.

Thelen, E., Ulrich, B. D., & Niles, D. (1987). Bilateral coordination in human infants: Stepping on a split-belt treadmill. *Journal of Experimental Psychology, 13,* 1405–1410.

Thevenin, D. M., Eilers, R. E., Oller, D. K., & LaVoie, L. (1985). Where's the drift in babbling drift? A cross-linguistic study. *Applied Psycholinguistics, 6,* 3–15.

Thiessen, E. D., & Saffran, J. D. (2003). When cues collide: Use of stress and statistical cues to word boundaries by 7- to 9-month-old infants. *Developmental Psychology, 39,* 706–716.

Thoman, E. (1987). Self-regulation of stimulation by prematures with a breathing blue bear. In J. Gallagher & C. Ramey (Eds.), *The malleability of children.* Baltimore/London: Paul H. Brookes.

Thoman, E. B., Hammond, K., Affleck, G., & DeSilva, H. N. (1995). The breathing bear with preterm infants: Effects on sleep, respiration, and affect. *Infant Mental Health Journal, 16,* 160–168.

Thomas, A., & Chess, S. (1986). The New York Longitudinal Study: From infancy to early adult life. In R. Plomin & J. Dunn (Eds.), *Changes, continuities and challenges.* Hillsdale, NJ: Erlbaum.

Thompson, I. (2000). Human gene therapy: Harsh lessons, high hopes. *FDA Consumer, 34,* 19–24.

Thompson, R. A. (1989). Causal attributions and children's

emotional understanding. In C. Saarni & P. L. Harris (Eds.), *Children's understanding of emotions*. New York: Cambridge University Press.

Thompson, R. A. (1994). *Fatherhood and divorce: The future of children.* Los Altos, CA: Center for the Future of Children.

Thompson, R. A. (1995). *Preventing child maltreatment through social support: A critical analysis.* Thousand Oaks, CA: Sage.

Thompson, R. A. (2006). The development of the person: Social understanding, relationships, self, conscience. In W. Damon & R. M. Lerner (Gen. Eds.) & N. Eisenberg (Vol. Ed.), *Handbook of Child Psychology* (6th ed, Vol 3.). New York: Wiley.

Thompson, R. A., Lamb, M. E., & Estes, D. (1982). Stability of infant-mother attachment and its relationship to changing life circumstances in an unselected middle-class sample. *Child Development, 53,* 144–148.

Thornberry, T. P., Krohn, M. D., Lizotte, A. J., Smith, C. A., & Tobin, K. (2003). *Gangs and delinquency in developmental perspective.* New York: Cambridge University Press.

Thorne, B. (1986). Girls and boys together . . . but mostly apart: Gender arrangements in elementary schools. In W. W. Hartup & Z. Rubin (Eds.), *Relations and relationships.* Hillsdale, NJ: Erlbaum.

Thurber, C. A., & Weisz, J. R. (1997). "You can try or you can just give up": The impact of perceived control and coping style on childhood homesickness. *Developmental Psychology, 33,* 508–517.

Thurstone, L. L. (1938). *Primary mental abilities.* Chicago: University of Chicago Press.

Tinsley, B. J. (2003). *How children learn to be healthy.* New York: Cambridge University Press.

Tinsley, B. J., Holtgrave, D. R., Erdley, C. A., & Reise, S. P. (1997). A multi-method analysis of risk perceptions and health behaviors in children. *Educational and Psychological Measurement, 57,* 197–209.

Tinsley, B. J., Lees, N. B., & Sumartojo, E. (2004). Children & adolescent HIV risk: Familial and cultural perspectives. *Journal of Family Psychology, 18,* 208–224.

Tobin-Richards, M., Boxer, A. O., & Petersen, A. C. (1984). The psychological impact of pubertal change: Sex differences in perceptions of self during early adolescence. In J. Brooks-Gunn & A. C. Petersen (Eds.), *Girls at puberty: Biological, psychological, and social perspectives.* New York: Plenum.

Tolan, P. H., Gorman-Smith, D., & Henry, D. B. (2003). The developmental ecology of urban males' youth violence. *Developmental Psychology, 39,* 274–291.

Tolman, E. C. (1948). Cognitive maps in rats and men. *Psychological Review, 55,* 189–209.

Tomasello, M. (1995). Language is not an instinct. *Cognitive Development, 10,* 131–156.

Tomasello, M. (Ed.). (1998). *The new psychology of language: Cognitive and functional approaches to language structure.* Mahwah, NJ: Erlbaum.

Tomasello, M. (1999). *The cultural origins of human cognition.* Cambridge, MA: Harvard University Press.

Tomasello, M. (2006). Acquiring metalinguistic constructions. In W. Damon & R. M. Lerner (Series Eds.) and D. Kuhn & R. Siegler (Vol. Eds.), *Handbook of child psychology,* Vol. 2, 6th ed. New York: Wiley.

Tomasello, M., & Farrar, J. (1986). Joint attention and early language. *Child Development, 57,* 1454–1463.

Torff, B., & Gardner, H. (1999). The vertical mind—The case for multiple intelligences. In M. Anderson (Ed.), *The development of intelligence.* East Sussex, England: Psychology Press.

Towers, H., Spotts, E., & Reiss, D. (2003). Unraveling the complexity of genetic and environmental influences on family. In F. Walsh (Ed.), *Normal family processes* (3rd ed., pp. 608–631). New York: Guilford.

Trabasso, T., Issen, A. M., Dolecki, P., McLanahan, A., Riley, C., & Tucker, T. (1978). How do children solve class-inclusion problems? In R. S. Siegler (Ed.), *Children's thinking: What develops?* Hillsdale, NJ: Erlbaum.

Tracey, A. E., & Maroney, D. (1999). *Your premature baby and child.* New York: Berkeley Books.

Trainor, L. J. (1996). Infant preferences for infant-directed versus non-infant directed playsongs and lullabies. *Infant Behavior and Development, 19,* 83–92.

Treffers, P. E., Eskes, M., Kleiverda, G., Van Alten, D. (1990). Home births and minimal medical interventions. *Journal of the American Medical Association, 264,* 2207–2208.

Trehub, S. E., & Trainor, L. J. (1993). Listening strategies in infancy: The roots of music and language development. In S. McAdams & E. Bigand (Eds.), *Thinking in sound: The cognitive psychology of human audition* (pp. 278–327). New York: Oxford University Press.

Tremblay, R. E., Schall, B., Boulerice, B., Arsonault, L., Soussignan, R. G., & Paquette, D. (1998). Testosterone, physical aggression, and dominance and physical development in adolescence. *International Journal of Behavioral Development, 22,* 753–777.

Trickett, P. K., & Putnam, F. W. (1998). The developmental impact of sexual abuse. In P. Trickett & C. Schellenbach (Eds.), *Violence against children in the family and the community.* Washington: APA Books.

Tronick, E. Z. (1989). Emotions and emotional communication in infants. *American Psychologist, 44,* 112–119.

Tronick, E. Z., Morelli, G. A., & Ivey, P. K. (1992). The Efe forager infant and toddler's pattern of social relationships: Multiple and simultaneous. *Developmental Psychology, 28,* 568–577.

Tronick, E. Z., Thomas, R. B., & Daltabuit, M. (1994). The Quechua manta pouch: A caretaking practice for buffering the Peruvian infant against the multiple stressors of high altitude. *Child Development, 65,* 1005–1013.

True, M. M., Pisani, L., & Oumar, F. (2001). Infant-mother attachment among the Dogan of Mali. *Child Development, 72,* 1451–1466.

Turati, C. (2004). Why faces are not special to newborns: An alternative account of the face preference. *Current Directions in Psychological Science, 13,* 5–8.

Turati, C., Simion, F., Milani, I., & Umilta, C. (2002). Newborns' preference for faces: What is crucial? *Developmental Psychology, 38,* 875–882.

Turiel, E. (1983). *The development of social knowledge: Morality and convention.* New York: Cambridge University Press.

Turiel, E. (2001). The discontents and contents in cultural practices: It depends on where you sit. In W. Edelstein & G. Nunner-Winkler (Eds.), *Morality in context.* Frankfurt: Shurkamp.

Turiel, E. (2002). *The culture of morality.* New York: Cambridge University Press.

Turiel, E. (2006). The development of morality. In W. Damon & R. M. Lerner (Series Eds.) & N. Eisenberg (Vol. Ed.), *Handbook of child psychology: Vol. 3* (6th ed.). New York: Wiley.

Turiel, E., Killen, V., & Helwig, F. (1988). Morality: Its structure, functions and vagaries. In J. Kagan and S. Lamb (Eds.), *The emergence of morality in young children.* Chicago: University of Chicago Press.

Turkewitz, G. (1991). Perinatal influences on the development of

hemispheric specialization and complex information processing. In M. J. S. Weiss, & P. R. Zelazo (Eds.), *Newborn attention: Biological constraints and the influence of experience.* Norwood, NJ: Ablex.

Turkheimer, E. (1991). Individual and group differences in adoption studies of IQ. *Psychological Bulletin, 110,* 392–405.

Turkheimer, E. (2000). Three laws of behavior genetics and what they mean. *Current Directives in Psychological Science, 9,* 160–164.

Turkheimer, E., Haley, A., Waldron, M., D'Onofrio, B., & Gottesman, I. I. (2003). Socioeconomic status modifies heritability of IQ in young children. *Psychological Science, 14,* 623–628.

Turner, J. S., & Rubinson, L. (1993). *Contemporary human sexuality.* Englewood Cliffs, NJ: Prentice Hall.

Turner, P. J., & Gervai, J. (1995). A multidimensional study of gender typing in preschool children and their parents: Personality, attitudes, preferences, behavior & cultural differences. *Developmental Psychology, 31,* 759–772.

Turner-Bowker, D. M. (1996). Gender stereotyped description in children's picture books: Does "Curious Jane" exist in literature? *Sex Roles, 35,* 461–488.

Turnure, J. E. (1970). Children's reactions to distractors in a learning situation. *Developmental Psychology, 2,* 115–122.

Twain, M. (1976). The adventures of Tom Sawyer. In L. Teacher (Ed.), *The unabridged Mark Twain.* Philadelphia: Running Press.

Twenge, J. M. (1997). Changes in masculine and feminine traits over time. A meta-analysis. *Sex Roles, 36,* 305–325.

Udvari, S., Schneider, B. H., Labovitz, G., & Tassi, F. (1995, August). *A multidimensional view of competition in relation to children's peer relations.* Paper presented to the American Psychological Association. New York, NY.

Underwood, M. K. (2003). *Social aggression among girls.* New York: Guilford.

Underwood, M. K. (2004). Gender and peer relations. In J. Kupersmidt & K. A. Dodge (Eds.), *Children's peer relations* (pp. 21–36). Washington, DC: American Psychological Association.

Underwood, M. K., Schockner, A. E., & Hurley, J. C. (2001). Children's responses to same- and other-gender peers: An experimental investigation with 8-, 10-, and 12-year-olds. *Developmental Psychology, 37,* 362–372.

Ungerer, J. A., Brody, L. R., & Zelazo, P. R. (1978). Long-term memory for speech in 2- to 4-week-old infants. *Infant Behavior and Development, 7,* 177–186.

UNICEF. Facts for life: Breastfeeding. http://unicef.org/ffl/04/ (retrieved Oct. 21, 2004).

U.S. Bureau of the Census (1999). *Statistical abstract of the United States* (119th ed.). Washington, DC: U. S. Government Printing Office.

U.S. Department of Commerce (1996, October). *Statistical Abstract of the United States, 1996. The National Data Book* (116th ed.). Washington, DC: U.S. Department of Commerce.

U.S. Department of Education, National Center for Educational Statistics (1997). *Children with special educational needs.* Washington, DC: US Government Printing Office.

U.S. Department of Health and Human Services (2001). Washington, DC: Government Printing Office.

Urban Institute (2000). *Child care patterns of school-age children with employed mothers.* Washington, DC: The Urban Institute Press.

Uttal, D. (2000). Seeing the big picture: Map use and the development of spatial cognition. *Developmental Science, 3,* 247–286.

Uzgiris, I. C. (1989). Infants in relation: Performers, pupils and partners. In W. Damon (Ed.), *Child development: Today and tomorrow.* San Francisco: Jossey-Bass.

Valenzuela, M. (1997). Maternal sensitivity in a developing society: The context of urban poverty and infant chronic malnutrition. *Developmental Psychology, 33,* 845–855.

Valian, V. (1986). Syntactic categories in the speech of young children. *Developmental Psychology, 22,* 562–579.

Valsiner, J. (Ed.). (1989). *Child development in cultural context.* Toronto, Canada: Hogrefe and Huber.

Van Den Bergh, B. R. H. (1992). Maternal emotions during pregnancy and fetal and neonatal behavior. In J. G. Nijhuis (Ed.), *Fetal behavior: Development and perinatal aspects.* New York: Oxford University Press.

Van den Boom, D. C. (1994). The influence of temperament and mothering on attachment and exploration: An experimental manipulation of sensitive responsiveness among lower-class mothers with irritable infants. *Child Development, 65,* 1457–1477.

Van Den Oord, E. J., Boomsma, I., & Verhulst, F. C. (1994). A study of problem behaviors in 10-to-15 year old biologically related and unrelated international adoptees. *Behavior Genetics, 24,* 193–205.

van der Mark, I. L., van IJzendoorn, M. H., & Bakermans-Kranenburg, M. J. (2002). Development of empathy in girls during the second year of life: Associations with parenting, attachment, and temperament. *Social Development, 11,* 451–468.

Van Egeren, L. A., Barratt, M. S., & Roach, M. A. (2001). Mother-infant responsiveness: Timing, mutual regulation, and interactional context. *Developmental Psychology, 37,* 684–697.

van IJzendoorn, M. H. (1995). Associations between adult attachment representations and parent-child attachment, parental responsiveness and clinical status: A meta-analysis on the productive validity of the Adult Attachment Interview. *Psychological Bulletin, 117,* 387–403.

van IJzendoorn, M. H., & Sagi, A. (1999). Cross-cultural patterns of attachment: Universal and contextual dimensions. In J. Cassidy & P. Shaver (Eds.), *Handbook of attachment* (pp. 713–734). New York: Guilford.

van IJzendoorn, M. H., Sagi, A., & Lamberman, M. W. E. (1992). The multiple caretaker paradox: Data from Holland & Israel. In R. C. Planta (Ed.) *Beyond the parent: The role of other adults in children's lives* (pp. 5–24). San Francisco: Jossey-Bass.

Van Os, J., & Selton, J. (1998). Prenatal exposure to maternal stress and subsequent schizophrenia. *British Journal of Psychiatry, 172,* 324–326.

Vandell, D. L. (2000). Parents, peer groups, and other socializing influences. *Developmental Psychology, 36,* 699–710.

Vandell, D. L., Henderson, V. K., & Wilson, K. S. (1988). A longitudinal study of children with varying quality day care experiences. *Child Development, 59,* 1286–1292.

Vandell, D. L., & Shumow, L. (1999). After school programs. *The Future of Children: When School Is Out, 9,* 64–80.

Vandell, D. L., & Wilson, K. (1987). Infants' interactions with mother, siblings and peer contacts and relations between interaction systems. *Child Development, 58,* 176–186.

Vander, A. J., Sherman, J. H., & Luciano D. S. (1994). *Human physiology.* 6th ed. New York: McGraw-Hill.

Vaughn, B. E., & Bost, K. K. (1999). Attachment and temperament. In J. Cassidy & P. Shaver (Eds.), *Handbook of attachment* (pp. 198–225). New York: Guilford.

Vaughn, B. E., Kopp, C. B., & Krakow, J. B. (1984). The emergence and consolidation of self-control from eighteen to thirty months of age: Normative trends and individual differences. *Child Development, 55,* 990–1004.

Venter, J. C., et al. (2001). The sequence of the human genome. *Science, 291,* 1304–1351.

Verp, M. S. (1993). Environmental causes of pregnancy loss and malformation. In C. Lin, M. S. Verp, & R. E. Sabbagha (Eds.). *The high-risk fetus: Pathophysiology, diagnosis, and management.* New York: Springer-Verlag.

Vinden, P. G. (1996). Junin Quechua children's understanding of mind. *Child Development, 67,* 1707–1716.

Vitaglione, G. D., & Barnett, M. A. (2003). Assessing a new dimension of empathy: Empathic anger as a predictor of helping and punishing desires. *Motivation and Emotion, 27,* 301–324.

Volling, B. L., McElwain, N. L., & Miller, A. L. (2002). Emotion regulation in context: The jealousy complex between young siblings and its relations with child and family characteristics. *Child Development, 73,* 581–600.

Voorhees, C. V., & Mollnow, E. (1987). Behavioral teratogenesis: Long-term influences on behavior from early exposure to environmental agents. In J. D. Osofsky (Ed.), *Handbook of infant development* (2nd ed., pp. 913–971). New York: Wiley.

Vosniadou, S. (1987). Children and metaphors. *Child Development, 58,* 870–885.

Vurpillot, E. (1968). The development of scanning strategies and their relation to visual differentiation. *Journal of Experimental Child Psychology, 6,* 632–650.

Vygotsky, L. S. (1934). *Thought and language.* Cambridge, MA: MIT Press.

Vygotksy, L. S. (1967). *Vaobraszeniye i tvorchestvo v deskom voraste* [Imagination and creativity in childhood]. Moscow: [Originally published 1930].

Vygotsky, L. S. (1978). *Mind in society: The development of higher psychological functions.* Cambridge, MA: Harvard Univerity Press.

Wachs, T. D. (2000). *Necessary but not sufficient: The respective roles of individual and multiple influences on individual development.* Washington, DC: American Psychological Association.

Wachs, T. D., & Kohnstamm, G. A. (Eds.). (2001). *Temperament in context.* Mahwah, NJ: Erlbaum.

Waddington, C. H. (1962). *New patterns in genetics and development.* New York: Columbia University Press.

Waddington, C. H. (1966). *Principles of development and differentiation.* New York: Macmillan.

Wadman, M. (1996, December 16). The DNA hard sell. *New York Times.*

Wahler, R. G. (1967). Infant social attachments: A reinforcement theory interpretation and investigation. *Child Development, 38,* 1079–1088.

Wahler, R. G., & Dumas, J. E. (1987). Family factors in childhood psychology: Toward a coercion-neglect model. In T. Jacob (Ed.), *Family interaction and psychopathology: Theories, methods, and findings* (pp. 581–625). New York: Plenum.

Wainryb, C., Shaw, L. A., Laupa, M., & Smith, K. R. (2001). Children's, adolescents', and young adults' thinking about different types of disagreements. *Developmental Psychology, 37,* 373–386.

Wakschlag, L. S., Gordon, R. A., Lahey, B. B., Loeber, R., Green, S. M., & Leventhal, B. L. (2001). Maternal age at first birth and boys' risk for conduct disorders. *Journal of Research on Adolescence, 10,* 417–441.

Walden, T. (1991). Infant social referencing. In J. Garber & K. Dodge (Eds.), *The development of emotional regulation and dysregulation.* New York: Cambridge University Press.

Walker, H. M. (1995). *The acting out child: Coping with classroom disruption.* Longmont, CO: Sopris West.

Walker, L. J. (1988). The development of moral reasoning. *Annals of Child Development, 5,* 33–78.

Walker, L. J., deVries, B., & Trevethan, J. D. (1987). Moral stages and moral orientations in real-life and hypothetical dilemmas. *Child Development, 58,* 842–858.

Walker, L. J., Gustafson, P., & Hennig, K. H. (2001). The consolidation/transition model in moral reasoning development. *Developmental Psychology, 37,* 187–197.

Walker, L. J., Hennig, K. H., & Krettenauer, T. (2000). Parent and peer contexts for children's moral reasoning development. *Child Development, 71,* 1033–1048.

Walker-Barnes, C. J., & Mason, C. A. (2001). Ethnic differences in the effect of parenting on gang involvement and gang delinquency: A longitudinal, hierarchical linear modeling perspective. *Child Development, 72,* 1814–1831.

Wallach, M. A., & Kogan, N. (1965). *Modes of thinking in young children: A study of the creativity-intelligence distinction.* New York: Holt, Rinehart and Winston.

Wallen, K. (1996). Nature needs nurture: The interaction of hormonal and social influences on the development of behavioral sex differences in rhesus monkeys. *Hormones & Behavior, 30,* 364–378.

Walton, G. E., Bower, N. J. A., & Bower, T. G. R. (1992). Recognition of familiar faces by newborns. *Infant Behavior and Development, 15,* 265–269.

Wandersman, A., & Florin, P. (2003). Community interventions and effective prevention. *American Psychologist, 58,* 441–448.

Wang, Q. (2004). The emergence of cultural self-constructs: Autobiographical memory and self-description in European American and Chinese children. *Developmental Psychology, 40,* 3–15.

Wartella, E. (1995). The commercialization of youth: Channel One in context. *Phi Delta Kappan,* 448–451.

Wartner, A. G., Grossman, K., Fremmer-Bombik, E., & Suess, G. (1994). Attachment patterns at age six in South Germany: Predictability from infancy and implications for preschool behavior. *Child Development, 49,* 483–494.

Watamura, S. E., Donzella, B., Alwin, J., & Gunnar, M. R. (2003). Morning to afternoon increases in cortisol concentration for infants and toddlers at child care: Age differences and behavioral correlates. *Child Development, 74,* 1006–1020.

Waters, E. (1995). The attachment Q Set, Version 3.0. In E. Waters, B. Vaughn, G. Posada, & K. Kondo Ikemura (Eds.), Caregiving, cultural, and cognitive perspectives on secure-base phenomena and working models: New growing points of attachment theory and research. *Monographs of the Society for Research in Child Development, 60* (2–3, Serial No. 244), 133–145.

Waters, E., Merrick, S., Treboux, D., Crowell, J., & Albersheim, L. (2000). Attachment security in infancy and early childhood: A twenty-year longitudinal study. *Child Development, 71,* 684–689.

Waters, E., Vaughn, B. E., Posada, G., & Kondo-Ikemura, K. (1995). Caregiving, cultural, and cognitive perspectives on secure-base behavior and working models: New growing points of attachment theory and research. *Monographs of the Society for Research in Child Development, 60* (2–3, Serial No. 244).

Waters, H. S. (2000). Memory strategy development: Do we really

need another deficiency? *Child Development, 71,* 1001–1012.

Watkins, B. A., Calvert, S. L., Huston-Stein, A., & Wright, J. C. (1980). Children's recall of television material: Effects of presentation mode and adult labeling. *Developmental Psychology, 16,* 672–674.

Watkins, W. E., & Pollitt, E. (1997). "Stupidity or worms": Do intestinal worms impair mental performance? *Psychological Bulletin, 121* (2), 171–191.

Watson, J. B. (1926). What the nursery has to say about instincts. In C. Murcheson (Ed.), *Psychologies of 1925* (pp. 1–35). Worcester, MA: Clark University Press.

Watson, J. B. (1928). *Psychological care of infant and child.* New York: Norton.

Watson-Gegeo, K. A., & Gegeo, D. W. (1986). Calling-out and repeating routines in Kwara'ae children's language socialization. In B. B. Schieffelin & E. Ochs (Eds.), *Language socialization across cultures* (pp. 17–50). Mahwah, NJ: Erlbaum.

Waxman, S., & Gelman, R. (1986). Preschoolers' use of superordinate relations in classification and language. *Cognitive Development, 1,* 139–156.

Waxman, S. R., & Lidz, J. L. (2006). Early word learning. In W. Damon & R. M. Lerner (Series Eds.) and D. Kuhn & R. Siegler (Vol. Eds.), *Handbook of child psychology,* Vol. 2, 6th ed. New York: Wiley.

Waxman, S. R., Shipley, E. F., & Shepperson, B. (1991). Establishing new subcategories: The role of category labels and existing knowledge. *Child Development, 62,* 127–138.

Wechsler, D. (1952). *Wechsler Intelligence Scale for Children.* New York: Psychological Corporation.

Wechsler, D. (1958). *The measurement and appraisal of adult intelligence* (4th ed.). Baltimore: Williams & Wilkins.

Wechsler, D. (2003). *Wechsler Intelligence Scale for Children* (4th ed.) New York: Psychological Corporation.

Wegman, M. E. (1994). Annual summary of vital statistics—1993. *Pediatrics, 93,* 771–782.

Wegman, M. E. (1995). Annual summary of vital statistics—1994. *Pediatrics, 94,* 792–803.

Wehren, A., & DeLisi, R. (1983). The development of gender understanding: Judgments and explanations. *Child Development, 54,* 1568–1578.

Weinberg, R. A. (1989). Intelligence and IQ: Landmark issues and great

debates. *American Psychologist, 44,* 98–104.

Weinberg, R. A., Scarr, S., & Waldman, I. D. (1992). The Minnesota Transracial Adoption Study: A follow-up of IQ test performance at adolescence. *Intelligence, 16,* 117–135.

Weinraub, M., & Lewis, M. (1977). The determinants of children's responses to separation. *Monographs of the Society for Research in Child Development, 42* (Serial No. 172).

Weisner, T. S. (1993). Overview: Sibling similarity and difference in different cultures. In C. W. Nuckolls (Ed.), *Siblings in South Asia: Brothers and sisters in cultural context* (pp. 1–17). New York: Guilford Press.

Weisner, T. S., & Wilson-Mitchell, J. E. (1990). Nonconventional family lifestyles and multischematic sex typing in six year olds. *Child Development, 61,* 1915–1933.

Weiss, M., Hechtman, L. T., & Weiss, G. (1999). *ADHD in adulthood: A guide to current theory, diagnosis and treatment.* Baltimore, MD: Johns Hopkins University Press.

Weissberg, R., & Greenberg, M. (1998). School and community competence-enhancement and prevention programs. In W. Damon (Gen. Ed.), I. Sigel, & K. A. Renninger (Vol. Eds.), *Handbook of child psychology: Vol. 4. Child psychology in practice.* New York: Wiley.

Weissberg, R. P., Kumpfer, & Seligman, M. (2003). Prevention that works for children and youth: An introduction. *American Psychologist, 58,* 425–432.

Weissman, M., Warner, V., Wickramaratne, P., Moreau, D., & Olfson, M. (1997). Offspring of depressed parents: Ten years later. *Archives of General Psychiatry, 54,* 932–940.

Weisz, J. R., Chaiyasit, W., Weiss, B., & Eastman, K. L., et al. (1995). A multimethod study of problem behavior among Thai and American children in school: Teacher reports versus direct observations. *Child Development, 66,* 402–415.

Weisz, J. R., Suwanlert, S., Chaiyasit, W., Weiss, B., Walter, B. R., & Anderson, W. W. (1988). Thai and American perspectives on over- and under-controlled child behavior problems: Exploring the threshold model among parents, teachers, and psychologists. *Journal of Consulting and Clinical Psychology, 56,* 601–609.

Weitzman, N., Birns, B., & Friend, R. (1985). Traditional and

nontraditional mothers' communication with their daughters and sons. *Child Development, 56,* 894–898.

Weizman, Z. O., & Snow, C. E. (2001). Lexical output as it relates to children's vocabulary acquisition: Effects of sophisticated exposure as a support for meaning. *Developmental Psychology, 37,* 265–279.

Wellman, H. M. (1977). Preschoolers' understanding of memory relevant variables. *Child Development, 48,* 1720–1723.

Wellman, H. M. (1978). Knowledge of the interaction of memory variables: A developmental study of metamemory. *Developmental Psychology, 14,* 24–29.

Wellman, H. M., Collins, J., & Glieberman, J. (1981). Understanding the combinations of memory variables: Developing conceptions of memory limitations. *Child Development, 52,* 1313–1317.

Wellman, H. M., Cross, D., & Watson, J. (2001). Meta-analysis of theory-of-mind development: The truth about false belief. *Child Development, 72,* 655–684.

Wellman, H. M., & Gelman, S. A. (1992). Cognitive development: Foundational theories of core domains. *Annual Review of Psychology, 43,* 337–375.

Wellman, H. M., & Gelman, S. A. (1998). Knowledge acquisition in foundational domains. In W. Damon (Gen. Ed.), D. Kuhn, & R. S. Siegler (Vol. Eds.), *Handbook of child psychology: Vol. 2. Cognition, perception, and language* (pp. 523–573). New York: Wiley.

Wellman, H. M., & Lempers, J. D. (1977). The naturalistic communicative abilities of two-year-olds. *Child Development, 48,* 1052–1057.

Wells, K. C. (2001). Comprehensive versus matched psychosocial treatment in the MTA study: Conceptual and empirical issues. *Journal of Clinical Child Psychology, 30,* 131–135.

Wendland-Carro, J., Piccinini, C. A., & Miller, W. S. (1999). The role of an early intervention on enhancing the quality of mother-infant interaction. *Child Development, 70,* 713–721.

Werker, J. F. (1989). Becoming a native listener. *American Scientist, 77,* 54–59.

Werker, J. F., & McLeod, P. J. (1989). Infant preference for both male and female infant-directed talk: A developmental study of attentional and affective responsiveness. *Canadian Journal of Psychology, 43,* 230–246.

Werker, J. F., Pegg, J. E., & McLeod, P. J. (1994). A cross-language investigation of infant preference for infant-directed communication. *Infant Behavior & Development, 17,* 323–333.

Werker, J. F., & Polka, L. (1993). Developmental changes in speech perception: New challenges and new directions. *Journal of Phonetics, 21,* 83–101.

Werker, J. F., & Vouloumanos, A. (2001). Speech and language processing in infancy: A neurocognitive approach. In C. A. Nelson & M. Luciana (Eds.), *Handbook of developmental cognitive neuroscience* (pp. 269–280). Cambridge, MA: MIT Press.

Werner, E. (1995). Resilience in development. *Current Directions in Psychological Science, 4,* 81–85.

Werner, E. E. (1984). Resilient children. *Young Children, 40,* 68–72.

Werner, E. E. (1993). Risk, resilience, and recovery: Perspectives from the Kauai Longitudinal Study. *Development and Psychopathology, 5,* 503–515.

Werner, E. E., Bierman, J. M., & French, F. F. (1971). *The children of Kauai.* Honolulu: University of Hawaii.

Werner, E. E., & Smith, R. S. (1977). *Kauai's children come of age.* Honolulu: University of Hawaii.

Werner, E. E., & Smith, R. S. (1982). *Vulnerable but invincible: A longitudinal study of resilient children and youth.* New York: McGraw-Hill.

Werner, E. E., & Smith, R. W. (1992). *Overcoming the odds: High risk children from birth to adulthood.* Ithaca, NY: Cornell University Press.

Werner, J. S., & Siqueland, E. R. (1978). Visual recognition memory in the preterm infant. *Infant Behavior and Development, 1,* 79–84.

Wertsch, J. V. (1985). *Vygotsky and the social formation of mind.* Cambridge: Harvard University Press.

Wertsch, J. V., & Kanner, B. G. (1992). A sociocultural approach to intellectual development. In *Intellectual development.* R. J. Sternberg, C. A. Berg, (Eds.) Cambridge University Press, New York, NY. pp. 328–349.

Wertsch, J. V., & Tulviste, P. (1992). L. S. Vygotsky and contemporary developmental psychology. *Developmental Psychology, 28,* 543–553.

Whalen, C. K. (2001). ADHD treatment in the 21st century: Pushing the envelope. *Journal of Clinical Child Psychology, 30,* 136–140.

Whitall, J., & Clark, J. E. (1994). The development of bipedal interlimb co-ordination. In S. P. Swinnen, J. Massion, & H. Heuer

(Eds.), *Interlimb co-ordination: Neural, dynamical and cognitive constraints.* San Diego, CA: Academic Press.

White, B. L. (1967). An experimental approach to the effects of the environment on early human behavior. In J. P. Hill (Ed.), *Minnesota Symposia on Child Psychology* (Vol. 1). Minneapolis: University of Minnesota Press.

Whitehurst, G. J., & Lonigan, C. J. (1998). Child development and emergent literacy. *Child Development, 69,* 848–872.

Whiting, B., & Edwards, C. (1988). *Children of different worlds. The formation of social behavior.* Cambridge, MA: Harvard University Press.

Whiting, B. B., & Whiting, J. W. M. (1975). *Children of six cultures: A psychocultural analysis.* Cambridge, MA: Harvard University Press.

Whitman, T. L., Borkowski, J., Keogh, D. A., & Weld, K. (2001). *Interwoven lives: Adolescent mothers and their children.* Mahwah, NJ: Erlbaum.

Wichstrom, L. (1999). The emergence of gender difference in depressed mood during adolescence: The role of intensified gender socialization. *Developmental Psychology, 35,* 232–245.

Wicks-Nelson, R., & Israel, A. C. (2000). *Behavior disorders in childhood.* Upper Saddle River, NJ: Prentice Hall.

Wiesenfeld, A., Malatesta, C., & DeLoache, L. (1981). Differential parental response to familiar and unfamiliar infant distress signals. *Infant Behavior and Development, 4,* 281–295.

Wigfield, A., Eccles, J. & Schiefele, U. (2006). Motivation. In W. Damon & R. M. Lerner (Series Eds.) and N. Eisenberg (Vol. ed.). *Handbook of child psychology, Vol. 3* (6th ed.). New York: Wiley.

Wilcox, A. J., Baird, D. D., & Weinberg, C. R., et al. (1995). Fertility in men exposed prenatally to diethylstilbestrol. *New England Journal of Medicine, 332,* 1411–1416.

Wilcox, A., Kobayashi, L., & Murray, I. (1997). Twenty-five years of obstetric patient satisfaction in North America: A review of the literature. *Journal of Perinatal and Neonatal Nursing, 10,* 36–47.

Wilkinson, A. C. (1984). Children's partial knowledge of the cognitive skill of counting. *Cognitive Psychology, 16,* 28–64.

Willatts, P. (1990). Development of problem solving strategies in infants. In D. F. Bjorklund (Ed.), *Children's strategies* (pp. 23–66). Hillsdale, NJ: Erlbaum.

Williams, J. E., & Best, D. L. (1990). *Measuring sex stereotypes: A multinational study* (rev. ed.). Newbury, CA: Sage.

Williams, P. E., Weiss, L. G. & Rolfhus, E. (2003). *WISC-IV— Wechsler Intelligence Scale for Children, 4th ed, Theoretical Model and Test Blueprint,* Technical Report #1, The Psychological Corporation, Houston TX.

Williams, W. M., & Ceci, S. J. (1997a). A person-process-context-time approach to understanding intellectual development. *Review of General Psychology, 1,* 288–310.

Williams, W. M., & Ceci, S. J. (1997b). Are Americans becoming more or less alike? Trends in race, class, and ability differences in intelligence. *American Psychologist, 52,* 1226–1235.

Willinger, M., Hoffman, H. T., & Hartford, R. B. (1994). Infant sleep position and risk for sudden infant death syndrome. *Pediatrics, 93,* 814–819.

Willis, T. A., & Yaeger, A. M. (2003). Family factors and adolescent substance use: Models and mechanisms. *Current Directions in Psychological Science, 12,* 222–226.

Wilson, B. J. (2003). The role of attentional processes in children's prosocial behavior with peers: Attention shifting and emotion. *Development and Psychopathology, 15,* 313–329.

Wilson, B. J., & Weiss, A. J. (1993). The effects of sibling coviewing on preschooler's reactions to a suspenseful movie scene. *Communication Research, 20,* 214–248.

Wilson, E. O. (1975). *Sociobiology: The new synthesis.* Cambridge, MA: Belknap Press of Harvard University Press.

Wilson, R. S. (1983). The Louisville twin study: Developmental synchronies in behavior. *Child Development, 54,* 298–316.

Wilson, R. S., & Harpring, E. B. (1972). Mental and motor development in infant twins. *Developmental Psychology, 7,* 277–287.

Wimmer, H. (1980). Children's understanding of stories: Assimilation by a general schema for actions or coordination of temporal relations. In F. Wilkening, J. Becker, & T. Trabasso (Eds.), *Information integration by children.* Hillsdale, NJ: Erlbaum.

Wimmer, H., & Perner, J. (1983). Beliefs about beliefs: Representation and constraining function of wrong beliefs in young children's understanding of deception. *Cognition, 13,* 103–128.

Winner, E. (1988). *The point of words: Children's understanding of metaphor and irony.* Cambridge, MA: Harvard University Press.

Winner, E. (1997). Special intelligence and lifelong learning. *American Psychologist, 52,* 1070–1081.

Winner, E. (2000). Giftedness: Current theory and research. *Current Directions in Psychological Science, 9,* 153–156.

Winner, E., McCarthy, M., Kleinman, S., & Gardner, H. (1979). First metaphors. In D. Wolf (Eds.), *Early symbolization: New directions for child development.* San Francisco CA: Jossey-Bass.

Wintre, M. G., & Vallance, D. D. (1994). A developmental sequence in the comprehension of emotions: Intensity, multiple emotions and valence. *Developmental Psychology, 30,* 509–514.

Witelson, S. F. (1978). Sex differences in the neurology of cognition: Psychological, social, educational and clinical implications. In S. Sullerto (Ed.), *La fait feminin.* Paris: Fayard.

Witelson, S. F. (1983). Bumps on the brain: Neuroanatomical asymmetries as a basis for functional symmetries. In S. Segalowitz (Ed.), *Language functions and brain organization* (pp. 117–144). New York: Academic.

Wolchik, S. A., Wilcox, K. L., Tein, J-Y., & Sandler, I. N. (2000). Maternal acceptance and consistency of discipline as buffers of divorce stressors on children's psychological adjustment problems. *Journal of Abnormal Child Psychology, 28,* 87–102.

Wolf, A. M., Gortmaker, S. L., Cheung, L., Gray, H. M., Herzog, D. B., & Colditz, G. A. (1993). Weight-related sports involvement in girls: Who is at risk for disordered eating? *American Journal of Public Health, 83,* 1635–1627.

Wolff, P. H. (1966). The causes, controls and organizations of behavior in the neonate. *Psychological Issues, 5* (1, Whole No. 17).

Wolff, P. H. (1987). *The development of behavioral states and the expression of emotions in early infancy: New proposals for investigation.* Chicago: University of Chicago Press.

Wood, D., Bruner, J., & Ross, G. (1976). The role of tutoring in problem solving. *Journal of Child Psychology and Psychiatry, 17,* 89–100.

Woodward, J. Z., & Aslin, R. N. (1990, April). *Segmentation cues in maternal speech to infants.* Paper presented at the 7th biennial meeting of the International Conference on Infant Studies, Montreal, Quebec, Canada.

Worchel, F. F., & Allen, M. (1997). Mothers' ability to discriminate cry types in low-birthweight premature and full-term infants. *Children's Health Care, 26,* 183–195.

Wright, J. C., & Huston, A. C. (1995). *Effects of educational TV viewing of lower income preschoolers on academic skills, school readiness, and school adjustment one to three years later.* Report to Children's Television Workshop, Center for Research on the Influences of Television on Children, University of Kansas, Lawrence.

Wyshak, G., & Frisch, R. E. (1982). Evidence for a secular trend in age of menarche. *New England Journal of Medicine, 306,* 1033–1035.

Xie, H., Cairns, B. D., & Cairns, R. B. (2005). The development of aggressive behavior among girls: Measurement issues, social functions, and differential trajectories. In D. J. Pepler, K. C. Madsen, C. Webster, and K. S. Levene (Eds.), *The development and treatment of girlhood aggression* (pp. 105–136). Mahwah, NJ: Erlbaum.

Xu, F., & Spelke, E. S. (2000). Large number discrimination in 6-month-old infants. *Cognition, 74,* B1–B11.

Yale, M. E., Messinger, D. S., Cobo-Lewis, A. B., & Delgado, C. F. (2003). The temporal coordination of early infant communication. *Developmental Psychology, 39,* 815–824.

Yarmey, A. D., & Jones, H. P. (1983). Accuracy of memory of male and female eyewitnesses to a criminal assault and rape. *Bulletin of the Psychonomic Society, 21,* 89–92.

Yau, J., & Smetana, J. G. (1996). Adolescent-parent conflict among Chinese adolescents in Hong Kong. *Child Development, 67,* 1262–1275.

Yonas, A., Arterberry, M. E., & Granrud, C. E. (1987). Space perception in infancy. *Annals of Child Development* (Vol. 4, pp. 1–34). Greenwich, CT: JAI Press.

Young, C., McMahon, J., Bowman, V., & Thompson, D. (1989).

Maternal reasons for delayed prenatal care. *Nursing Research, 38*(4).

Young, S. K., Fox, N. A., & Zahn-Waxler, C. (1999). The relations between temperament and empathy in two-year-olds. *Developmental Psychology, 35,* 1189–1197.

Young, W. C., Goy, R. W., & Phoenix, C. H (1967). Hormones and sexual behavior. *Science, 143,* 212–218.

Youniss, J. (1980). *Parents and peers in social development.* Chicago: University of Chicago Press.

Youniss, J., & Yates, M. (1997). *Community service and social responsibility in youth.* Chicago: The University of Chicago Press.

Yuill, N., & Pearson, A. (1998). The development of bases for trait attribution: Children's understanding of traits as casual mechanisms based on desire. *Developmental Psychology, 34,* 574–586.

Yussen, S. R., & Berman, L. (1981). Memory predictions for recall and recognition in first, third, and fifth grade children. *Developmental Psychology, 17,* 224–229.

Zahn-Waxler, C. (2000). The development of empathy, quiet and internalization of distress: Implications for gender differences in internalizing and externalizing problems. In R. Davidson (Ed.), *Anxiety, depression, and emotion: Wisconsin Symposium on Emotion: Vol. 1* (pp. 222–235). New York: Oxford University Press.

Zahn-Waxler, C., Cole, P. M., Welsh, J. D., & Fox N. A. (1995). Psychophysiological correlates of empathy and prosocial behaviors in preschool children with problem behaviors. *Development and Psychopathology, 7,* 27–48.

Zahn-Waxler, C., Klimes-Dougan, B., & Kendziora, K. T. (1998). The study of emotion socialization: Conceptual, methodological, and developmental considerations. *Psychological Inquiry, 9,* 313–316.

Zahn-Waxler, C., Radke-Yarrow, M., & King, R. A. (1979). Child rearing and children's prosocial initiations toward victims of distress. *Child Development, 50,* 319–330.

Zahn-Waxler, C., Radke-Yarrow, M., Wagner, E., & Chapman, M.

(1992b). Development of concern for others. *Developmental Psychology, 28,* 126–136.

Zahn-Waxler, C., Schiro, K., Robinson, J. L., Emde, R. N., & Schmitz, S. (2001). Empathy and prosocial patterns in young MZ and DZ twins: Development and genetic and environmental influences. In R. N. Emde & J. K. Hewitt (Eds.), *Infancy to early childhood* (pp. 141–162). New York: Oxford University Press.

Zajonc, R. B., & Mullally, P. R. (1997). Birth order: Reconciling conflicting effects. *American Psychologist, 52,* 685–699.

Zani, B. (1993). Dating and interpersonal relationships in adolescence. In S. Jackson & H. Rodriguez-Tome (Eds.), *Adolescence and its social worlds* (pp. 95–119). Hillsdale, NJ: Lawrence Erlbaum Associates, Inc.

Zarbatany, L., Hartmann, D. P., & Rankin, D. B. (1990). The psychological functions of preadolescent peer activities. *Child Development, 61,* 1067–1080.

Zarbatany, L., McDougall, P., & Hymel, S. (2000). Gender-differentiated experience in the peer culture: Links to intimacy in preadolescence. *Social Development, 9,* 62–69.

Zeifman, D., Delaney, S., & Blass, E. M. (1996). Sweet taste, looking and calm in 2- and 4-week old infants: The eyes have it. *Developmental Psychology, 32,* 1090–1099.

Zelazo, N. A., Zelazo, P. R., Cohen, K. M., & Zelazo, P. D. (1988, April). *Specificity of practice effects on elementary neuromotor patterns.* Paper presented at the International Conference on Infant Studies, Washington, D.C.

Zelazo, P. R. (1972). Smiling and vocalizing: A cognitive emphasis. *Merrill-Palmer Quarterly, 18,* 349–365.

Zelazo, P. R. (1983). The development of walking: New findings and old assumptions. *Journal of Motor Behavior, 15,* 99–137.

Zelazo, P. R., Zelazo, N. A., & Kolb, S. (1972). "Walking" in the newborn. *Science, 176,* 314–315.

Zerbe, K. J. (1993). *The body betrayed: Women, eating disorders, and treatment.* Washington, D.C.: American Psychiatric Press.

Zhang, J., et al. (1999). Epidural analgesia in association with duration of labor and mode of delivery: A quantitative review. *American Journal of Obstetrics & Gynecology, 180,* 970–977.

Zigler, E., Abelson, W. D., Trickett, P. K., & Seitz, V. (1982). Is an intervention program necessary in order to improve economically disadvantaged children's IQ scores? *Child Development, 53,* 340–348.

Zigler, E., & Finn-Stevenson, M. (1993). *Children in a changing world: Developmental and social issues.* Pacific Grove, CA: Brooks/Cole.

Zill, N. (1986). *Happy, healthy and insecure.* New York: Cambridge University Press.

Zimmer-Gembeck, M. J., Siebenbruner, J., & Collins, W. A. (2001). Diverse aspects of dating: Associations with psychosocial functioning from early to middle adolescence. *Journal of Adolescence. Special adolescent romance: From experiences to relationships, 24,* 313–336.

Zimring, F. E. (1998). *American youth violence* New York: Oxford University Press.

Zucker, K. J. (2001). Biological influences on psychosexual differentiation. In R. K. Unger (Ed.), *Handbook of the psychology of women and gender* (pp. 101–118). New York: Wiley.

Zucker, R. A., Fitzgerald, H. E., & Moses, H. D. (1995). Emergence of alcohol problems and the several alcoholisms: A developmental perspective on etiologic theory and life course trajectory. In D. Cicchetti & D. Cohen (Eds.), *Developmental psychopathology: Vol. 2. Risk, disorder and adaptation* (pp. 677–711). New York: Wiley.

Zukow-Goldring, P. (2002). Sibling caregiving. In M. H. Bornstein (Ed.), *Handbook of parenting* (vol. 3, pp. 177–208). Mahwah, NJ: Erlbaum.

Credits

TEXT AND LINE ART

Table 2-5: Adapted with permission from *Science, 212* (1981). Bouchard, T. J. and McGue, M., "Familial studies of intelligence: A review," pp. 1055–1059. Copyright 1981 AAAS.

Figure 2-7: From *Handbook of Mental Deficiency: Psychological Theory and Research* (N. Ellis, Ed.). Gottesman, I.I., "Genetic aspects of intelligent behavior." New York: McGraw-Hill, 1963. Reprinted by permission of Irving I. Gottesman.

Figure 2-8: From *Individual Development and Evolution: The Genesis of Novel Behavior* by Gilbert Gottlieb, Figure 14.3, p. 186. Copyright © 1991 by Oxford University Press, Inc. Used by permission of Oxford University Press, Inc.

Figure 2-10: From *Developmental Psychology, 7* (1972). Wilson, R. S. and Harpring, E. B., "Mental and motor development in infant twins," pp. 277–287. Copyright © 1972 by the American Psychological Association. Adapted with permission.

Figure 3-1: Adapted from *The Nature of Life*, 3rd ed., by Postlethwait, J. H. and Hopson, J. L. New York: McGraw-Hill, 1995, pp. 348–349. By permission of Janet L. Hopson.

Figure 3-5: From *Human Physiology*, 6th ed., by Vander, A. J., Sherman, J. H., and Luciano, D. S., p. 683. Copyright © 1994 by The McGraw-Hill Companies, Inc. Adapted by permission of the publisher.

Table 3-3: Adapted from *Current Researches in Anesthesia and Analgesia, 32* (1953). Apgar, V. A., "A proposal for a new method of evaluation of the newborn infant," pp. 260–267. Reprinted by permission of Lippincott Williams & Wilkins.

Figure 4-1: From *Prospective Issues in Infancy Research* (K. Bloom, Ed.). Sostek, A. M. and Anders, T. F., "The biosocial importance and environmental sensitivity of infant sleep-wake behaviors," p. 108. Copyright © 1981 Lawrence Erlbaum Associates, Inc. Reprinted by permission of the publisher.

Figure 4-2: Reprinted from *Journal of Experimental Child Psychology, 10,* Korner, A. F. and Thoman, E., "Visual alertness in neonates as evoked by maternal care," pp. 67–78. Copyright 1970, with permission from Elsevier.

Table 4-3: Adapted from *Handbook of Infant Development*, 2nd ed. (J. Osofsky, Ed.). Brazelton, T. B., Nugent, J. K., and Lester, B. M., "Neonatal behavioral assessment scale," pp. 780–817. Copyright © 1987 by John Wiley & Sons, Inc. Reprinted with permission of John Wiley & Sons, Inc.

Figure 4-3: From Daphne Maurer and Charles Maurer, *The World of the Newborn.* New York: Basic Books, 1988. Reprinted with permission of Goodman Associates.

Figure 4-5: Reprinted from *Journal of Experimental Child Psychology, 37,* Bertenthal, B. I., Proffitt, D. R., and Cutting, J. E., "Infant sensitivity to figural coherence in biomechanical motions," pp. 213–230. Copyright 1984, with permission form Elsevier.

Figure 4-6: From *Child Development, 47* (1976). Maurer, D. and Salapatek, P., "Developmental changes in the scanning of faces by young infants," pp. 523–527. Reprinted with permission of the Society for Research in Child Development.

Figure 4-7: From *Child Development, 59* (1988). Dannemiller, J. L. and Stephens, B. R., "A critical test of infant pattern preference models," pp. 210–216. Reprinted with permission of the Society for Research in Child Development.

Figure 4-14: From *American Psychologist, 51* (1996). Bauer, P. J., "What do infants recall of their lives?" pp. 29–41. Copyright © 1996 by the American Psychological Association. Reproduced with permission.

Figure 5-1: From *A Child's World*, 7th edition, by Papalia, D. E. and Olds, S. W., p. 172. Copyright © 1996 by The McGraw-Hill Companies, Inc. Reprinted with permission of the publisher.

Figure 5-2: From *Biological Psychology* by Rosenzweig, M. R., Leiman, A. L., and Breedlove, S. M., Fig. 4.1, p. 100. Copyright © 1996 by Sinauer Associates, Inc., Publishers. Reprinted with permission.

Figure 5-3: From *The Nature of Life*, 3rd ed., by Postlethwait, J. H. and Hopson, J. L. New York: McGraw-Hill, 1995, Figure 32.8A, p. 718. Reprinted by permission of Janet L. Hopson.

Figure 5-7: From *American Psychologist, 46* (1991). Fox, N. A., "If it's not left, it's right: Electroencephalograph asymmetry and the development of emotion," pp. 863–872. Copyright © 1991 by the American Psychological Association. Adapted with permission.

Table 5-1: From Bernstein, Douglas A. and Peggy W. Nash, *Essentials of Psychology*, Third Edition. Copyright © 2005 by Houghton Mifflin Company. Adapted with permission.

Figure 5-9: From *Child Development, 45* (1974). Adelson, E. and Fraiberg, S., "Gross motor development in infants blind from birth," pp. 114–126. Reprinted with permission of the Society for Research in Child Development.

Figure 5-10: Reprinted with permission from *Science, 176* (1972). Zelazo, P. R., Zelazo, N. A., and Kolb, S., "'Walking' in the Newborn," pp. 314–315. Copyright 1972 AAAS.

Figure 5-12: From "2CCC: The Millennium Notebook." From *Newsweek*, June 2, 1997, p. 10. © 1997 Newsweek, Inc. All rights reserved. Reprinted by permission.

Figure 5-14: Reprinted from *Journal of the American Dietetic Association, 100,* Rolls, B. J., Engell, D., and Birch, L. L., "Serving portion size influences 5-year-old but not 3-year-old children's food intake," pp. 232–234. Copyright 2000, with permission from American Dietetic Association.

Figure 5-15: From *Health Psychology, 14* (1995). Epstein, L. H., Valoski, A. M., Vara, L. S., McCurley, J., Wisniewski, L., Kalarchian, M. A., Klein, K. R., and Shrager, L. R., "Effects of decreasing sedentary behavior and increasing activity on weight change in obese children," pp. 109–115. Copyright © 1995 by the American Psychological Association. Reproduced with permission.

Figure 5-16: Adapted from *The Nature of Life*, 3rd ed., by Postlethwait, J. H. and Hopson, J. L. New York: McGraw-Hill, 1995, p. 716. By permission of Janet L. Hopson.

Figure 5-17: From *Monographs of the Society for Research in Child Development, 44* (Serial No. 179, 1979). Roche, A. F., "Secular trends in human growth, maturation, and development." Reprinted with permission of the Society for Research in Child Development.

Figure 5-18: From *Girls at Puberty: Biological, Psychological, and Social Perspectives* (J. Brooks-Gunn and A. C. Petersen, Eds.). Tobin-Richards, M., Boxer, A. O., and Petersen, A. C., "The psychological impact of pubertal change: Sex differences in perceptions of self during early adolescence," pp. 127–154. Copyright © 1983 by Plenum Press. With kind permission of Springer Science and Business Media.

Figure 6-1: From *Determinants of Infant Behaviour*, Vol. 3 (B. M. Foss, Ed.). Gewirtz, J. L., "The course of infant smiling in four child-rearing environments in Israel." London: Methuen, 1965, pp. 105–248. Reprinted by permission of Routledge, a division of Taylor & Francis, UK.

Figure 6-2: From *Child Development, 43* (1972). Sroufe, L. A. and Wunsch, J. P., "The development of laughter in the first year of life," pp. 1326–1344. Reprinted with permission of the Society for Research in Child Development.

Figure 6-3: Reprinted from *Psychological Issues*, Vol. 10. Emde, R. N., Gaensbauer, T. J., and Harmon, R. J., "Emotional expression in infancy: A biobehavioral study." By permission of International Universities Press, Inc. Copyright 1976 by IUP.

Figure 6-4: From *The Origins of Fear* (M. Lewis and L. Rosenblum, Eds.). Lewis, M. and Brooks, J., "Self, other, and fear: Infants' reactions to people," pp. 195–227. New York: Wiley, 1974. Reprinted by permission of Michael Lewis.

Figure 6-6: From *Developmental Psychology, 33* (1997). Thurber, C. A. and Weisz, J. R., "'You can try or you can just give up': The impact of perceived control and coping style on childhood homesickness," pp. 508–517. Copyright © 1997 by the American Psychological Association. Reproduced with permission.

Figure 6-7: From *Child Development, 63* (1992). Lewis, M., Alessandri, S., and Sullivan, M. W., "Differences in shame and pride as a function of children's gender and task difficulty," pp. 630–638. Reprinted with permission of the Society for Research in Child Development.

Figure 6-8: From *Emotional Development in Young Children* by Denham, S. A. New York: Guilford, 1998, Figure 1.2, p. 15. Reprinted by permission of the publisher.

Table 6-2: From *Social Development* by Schaffer, H. R., Table 15, p. 129. Copyright © H. Rudolph Schaffer 1996. Reprinted by permission of Blackwell Publishing Ltd., Oxford, UK.

Table 6-3: From *Social Development* by Schaffer, H. R., Table 16, p. 136. Copyright © H. Rudolph Schaffer 1996. Reprinted by permission of Blackwell Publishing Ltd., Oxford, UK.

Table 6-4: From *Review of Child Development Research*, Vol. 3, 1973 (B. Caldwell and H. Ricciuti, Eds.). Table 1 from Ainsworth, M. D., "The development of infant-mother attachment."

Reprinted with permission of the Society for Research in Child Development.

Figure 6-9: From *Child Development, 75* (2004). Carlson, E. A., Sroufe, L. A., and Egeland, B., "The construction of experience: A longitudinal study of representation and behavior," pp. 66–83. Reprinted with permission of the Society for Research in Child Development.

Figure 6-10: From *Social Cognition and the Acquisition of Self* by Lewis, M. and Brooks-Gunn, J. New York: Plenum Press. Copyright © 1979 by Michael Lewis and Jeanne Brooks-Gunn. With kind permission of Springer Science and Business Media.

Table 6-8: From *Social Development* by Schaffer, H. R., Table 22, p. 158. Copyright © H. Rudolph Schaffer 1996. Reprinted by permission of Blackwell Publishing Ltd., Oxford, UK.

Figure 7-1: Reprinted from *Cognitive Psychology, 21,* Johnson, J. S. and Newport, E. L., "Critical period effects in second language learning: The influence of maturational state on the acquisition of English as a second language," pp. 60–99. Copyright 1989, with permission from Elsevier.

Figure 7-2: From *Theories in Cognitive Psychology* (R. L. Solso, Ed.). Huttenlocher, J., "The origins of language comprehension." Copyright © 1974 Lawrence Erlbaum Associates, Inc. Reprinted by permission of the publisher.

Figure 7-3: From *Breaking the Speech Barrier: Language Development through Augmented Means* by Romski, M. and Sevcik, R. A. Baltimore: Paul H. Brookes Publishing Co., 1996, pp. 28, 56. Reprinted by permission.

Figure 7-4: From *Meaningful Differences in the Everyday Experience of Young American Children* by Hart, B. and Risley, T. R. Baltimore: Paul H. Brookes Publishing Co., 1995, pp. 234, 235. Reprinted by permission.

Figure 7-6: From *Signing: How to Speak with Your Hands* by Elaine Costello, copyright © 1983 by Elaine Costello. Used by permission of Bantam Books, a division of Random House, Inc.

Figure 7-7: From *Developmental Psychology, 10* (1974). Entwisle, D. R. and Frasure, N. E., "A contradiction resolved: Children's processing of syntactic cues," pp. 852–857. Copyright © 1974 by the American Psychological Association. Adapted with permission

Figure 8-1: Reprinted from *Cognition, 23,* Baillargeon, R., "Representing the existence and the location of hidden objects: Object permanence in 6- and 8-month-old infants," pp. 21–41. Copyright 1986, with permission from Elsevier.

Figure 8-2: From *Psychological Science, 12* (2001). Hespos, S. J. and Baillargeon, R., "Infants' knowledge about occlusion and containment events: A surprising discrepancy," pp. 140–147. Reprinted by permission of Blackwell Publishing Ltd., Oxford, UK.

Figure 8-5: From *Children's Minds* by Margaret Donaldson. Copyright © 1978 by Margaret Donaldson. Used by permission of W. W. Norton & Company, Inc. and A. P. Watt Ltd.

Figure 8-6: From *Of Children: An Introduction to Child Development* by Lefrançois, G. R. (Belmont, CA: Wadsworth, 1973), p. 305. Reprinted by permission of the author.

Table 8-3: Reprinted from the *1977 Nebraska Symposium on Motivation* (C. B. Keasy, Ed.). Selman, R. and Jacquette, D., "Stability and oscillation in interpersonal awareness: A clinical-developmental analysis," Table 1, p. 266. By

permission of the University of Nebraska Press. Copyright © 1978 by the University of Nebraska Press.

Figure 8-8: Adapted from *Child Development, 45* (1974). Selman, R. L. and Byrne, D. F., "A structural-developmental analysis of levels of role taking in middle childhood," pp. 803–806. Reprinted with permission of the Society for Research in Child Development.

Figure 8-9: From *Developmental Psychology, 24* (1988). Radziszewska, B. and Rogoff, B., "Influence of adult and peer collaborators on the development of children's planning skills," pp. 840–848. Copyright © 1988 by the American Psychological Association. Adapted with permission.

Figure 9-1: Reprinted from *The Psychology of Learning and Motivation, Vol. 2: Advances in Research and Theory* (K. W. Spence and J. Spence, Eds.). Atkinson, R. C. and Shiffrin, R. M., "Human memory: A proposed system and its control processes," pp. 89–195. New York: Academic Press. Copyright © 1968, with permission from Elsevier.

Figure 9-3: From *Children's Thinking: What Develops?* (R. S. Siegler, Ed.). Chi, M. T. H., "Knowledge structures and memory development." Copyright © 1978 Lawrence Erlbaum Associates, Inc. Reprinted by permission of the publisher.

Figure 9-4: From *Developmental Psychology, 39* (2003). Berger, S. E. and Adolph, K. E., "Infants use handrails as tools in a locomotor task," pp. 594–605. Copyright © 2003 by the American Psychological Association. Reproduced with permission.

Figure 9-5: From *Attention in Early Development: Themes and Variations* by Holly Alliger Ruff and Mary Klevjord Rothbart, Figure 7.6, p. 130, copyright © 1996 by Oxford University Press, Inc. Used by permission of Oxford University Press, Inc.

Table 9-2: Reprinted from *Acta Psychologica, 92,* Davidson, D., "The effects of decision characteristics on children's selective search of predecisional information," pp. 263–281. Copyright © 1996, with permission from Elsevier.

Figure 9-8: Reprinted from *Journal of Experimental Child Psychology, 6,* Vurpillot, E., "The development of scanning strategies and their relation to visual differentiation," pp. 632–650. Copyright 1968, with permission form Elsevier.

Figure 9-9: Reprinted from *Intellectual Development: Birth to Adulthood* by Case, R. New York: Academic Press. Copyright 1985, with permission form Elsevier.

Figure 9-10: From *Developmental Psychology, 33* (1997). Coyle, T. R. and Bjorklund, D. F., "Age differences in, and consequences of, multiple- and variable-strategy use on a multitrial sort-recall task," pp. 372–380. Copyright © 1997 by the American Psychological Association. Reproduced with permission.

Figure 9-13: Reprinted from *Journal of Environmental Psychology, 21,* Cornell, E. H., Hadley, D. C., Sterling, T. M., Chan, M. A., and Boechler, P., "Adventure as a stimulus for cognitive development," pp. 219–231. Copyright 2001, with permission from Elsevier.

Figure 9-15: From *Psychological Science, 6* (1995). Miller, K. F., Smith, C. M., Zhu, J., and Zhang, H., "Preschool origins of cross-national differences in mathematical competence: The role of number-naming systems," pp. 56–60. Reprinted

by permission of Blackwell Publishing Ltd., Oxford, UK.

Table 10-1: From *Current Directions in Psychological Science, 2* (1993). Sternberg, R. J. and Wagner, R. K., "The geocentric view of intelligence and job performance is wrong," pp. 1–6. Reprinted by permission of Blackwell Publishing Ltd., Oxford, UK.

Table 10-2: From *Frames of Mind: The Theory of Multiple Intelligences* by Howard Gardner. Copyright © 1983 by Howard Gardner. Published by Basic Books and William Heinemann. Reprinted by permission of Basic Books, a member of Perseus Books, L.L.C., and The Random House Group Ltd.

Figure 10-1: From *Origins of Intelligence* (M. Lewis, Ed.). Honzik, M. P., "Value and limitations of infant tests: An overview," p. 67. © 1976 Plenum Press. With kind permission of Springer Science and Business Media.

Figure 10-2: From *Child Development, 66* (1995). Chen, C. and Stevenson, H. W., "Motivation and mathematics achievement: A comparative study of Asian-American, Caucasian-American, and east Asian high school students," pp. 1215–1234. Reprinted with permission of the Society for Research in Child Development.

Figure 10-4: From *American Psychologist, 31* (1976). Scarr, S. and Weinberg, R. A., "IQ test performance of black children adopted by white families," pp. 726–739. Copyright © 1976 by the American Psychological Association. Adapted with permission.

Figure 10-5: Reprinted from *Advances in Motivation and Achievement: Vol. 9. Culture, Race, Ethnicity, and Motivation* (P. Pintrich and M. Maehr, Eds.). Chen, C., Stevenson, H. W., Hayward, C., and Burgess, S., "Culture and academic achievement: Ethnic and cross-national differences," pp. 119–151. Copyright 1995, with permission from Elsevier.

Figure 10-6: Reprinted from *Advances in Motivation and Achievement: Vol. 9. Culture, Race, Ethnicity, and Motivation* (P. Pintrich and M. Maehr, Eds.). Chen, C., Stevenson, H. W., Hayward, C., and Burgess, S., "Culture and academic achievement: Ethnic and cross-national differences," pp. 119–151. Copyright 1995, with permission from Elsevier.

Figure 10-8: From Ramey, Craig T. Jr., et al. Figure 6.3, "Bayley Mental Development Index and Stanford Binet IQ at Twelve, Twenty-Four, Thirty-Six, and Forty-Eight Months for Abecedarian Children." In *Social Programs that Work*, edited by Jonathan Crane. © 1998 Russell Sage Foundation, 112 East 64th Street, New York, NY 10021. Reprinted with permission.

Figure 10-9: From Ramey, Craig T. Jr., et al. Figure 6.7, "Children Retained in Grade by Age Fifteen, Abecedarian Project." In *Social Programs that Work*, edited by Jonathan Crane. © 1998 Russell Sage Foundation, 112 East 64th Street, New York, NY 10021. Reprinted with permission.

Figure 11-3: From *Genetic Psychology Monographs, 75* (1967), pp. 43–88. Baumrind, D., "Child care practices anteceding three patterns of preschool behavior." Reprinted with permission of the Helen Dwight Reid Educational Foundation. Published by Heldref Publications, 1319 Eighteenth St., NW, Washington, DC 20036-1802. Copyright © 1967.

Table 11-1: From *Genetic Psychology Monographs, 75* (1967), pp. 43–88. Baumrind, D., "Child care practices anteceding three patterns of preschool behavior." Reprinted with permission of the Helen Dwight Reid Educational Foundation. Published by Heldref Publications, 1319 Eighteenth St., NW, Washington, DC 20036-1802. Copyright © 1967.

Figure 11-5: From *Journal of Personality and Social Psychology, 85* (2003). Herrera, N. C., Zajonc, R. B., Wieczorkowska, G., and Cichomski, B., "Beliefs about birth rank and their reflection in reality," pp. 142–150. Copyright © 2003 by the American Psychological Association. Reproduced with permission.

Table 11-2: Reprinted by permission. Children's Defense Fund, *The State of America's Children: 2001.* Washington, DC: Children's Defense Fund, 2001.

Figure 11-7: From *Child Development, 63* (1992). Conger, R. D., Conger, K. J., Elder, G. J., Jr., Lorenz, F. O., Simons, R. L., and Whitbeck, L. B., "A family process model of economic hardship and adjustment of early adolescent boys," pp. 526–541. Reprinted with permission of the Society for Research in Child Development.

Figure 11-9: From *Life Span Development*, 8th ed., by Santrock, J. W. Copyright © 2002 by The McGraw-Hill Companies, Inc. Reprinted with permission of the publisher.

Figure 11-11: From *Developmental Psychology, 31* (1995). Patterson, C. J., "Families of the lesbian baby boom: Parents' division of labor and children's adjustment," pp. 115–123. Copyright © 1995 by the American Psychological Association. Adapted with permission.

Figure 11-12: Reprinted by permission. Children's Defense Fund, *The State of America's Children: 2004.* Washington, DC: Children's Defense Fund, 2004, p. 156.

Figure 12-1: From *Developmental Psychology, 11* (1975). Eckerman, C. O., Whatley, J. L., and Kutz, S. L., "Growth of social play with peers during the second year of life," pp. 42–49. Copyright © 1975 by the American Psychological Association. Reproduced with permission.

Figure 12-2: From *Developmental Psychology, 17* (1981). Ellis, S., Rogoff, B., and Cromer, C., "Age segregation in children's social interactions," pp. 399–407. Copyright © 1981 by the American Psychological Association. Reproduced with permission.

Figure 12-3: From *Child Development, 69* (1998). Richards, M. H., Crowe, P. A., Larson, R., and Swarr, A., "Developmental patterns and gender differences in the experience of peer companionship during adolescence," pp. 154–163. Reprinted with permission of the Society for Research in Child Development.

Figure 12-4: From *Psychological Bulletin, 115* (1994). Crick, N. R. and Dodge, K. A., "A review and reformulation of social information processing mechanisms in children's social adjustment," pp. 74–101. Copyright © 1994 by the American Psychological Association. Adapted with permission.

Figure 12-5: From *Monographs of the Society for Research in Child Development, 51* (2, Serial No. 213, 1986). Dodge, K. A., Pettit, G. S., McLaskey, C. L., and Brown, M. M., "Social competence in children," p. 40. Reprinted with permission of the Society for Research in Child Development.

Figure 12-6: From *Child Development, 55* (1984). Asher, S. R., Hymel, S., and Renshaw, P. D., "Loneliness in children," pp. 1456–1464. Reprinted with permission of the Society for Research in Child Development.

Figure 12-7: From *Developmental Psychology, 24* (1988). Caspi, A., Elder, G. H., and Bem, D. J., "Moving away from the world: Life-course patterns of shy children," pp. 824–831. Copyright © 1988 by the American Psychological Association. Reproduced with permission.

Figure 12-9: From *Child Development, 72* (2001). Bolger, K. E. and Patterson, C. J., "Developmental pathways from child maltreatment to peer rejection," pp. 549–568. Reprinted with permission of the Society for Research in Child Development.

Table 12-5: From *Child Development, 48* (1977). Oden, S. and Asher, S. R., "Coaching children in social skills for friendship making," pp. 495–506. Reprinted with permission of the Society for Research in Child Development.

Table 12-6: From *Monographs of the Society for Research in Child Development, 48* (Serial No. 201, 1983). Gottman, J. M., "How children become friends." Reprinted with permission of the Society for Research in Child Development.

Table 12-7: From *Conversations of Friends: Speculations on Affective Development* (J. M. Gottman and J. G. Parker, Eds.). Gottman, J. M. and Mettetal, G., "Speculations on social and affective development: Friendship and acquaintanceship through adolescence." New York: Cambridge University Press, 1986, p. 237. Reprinted with the permission of Cambridge University Press.

Figure 12-10: From *Developmental Psychology, 22* (1986). Steinberg, L., "Latchkey children and susceptibility to peer pressure: An ecological analysis," pp. 433–439. Copyright © 1986 by the American Psychological Association. Reproduced with permission.

Figure 12-11: From *Pathways through Adolescence: Individual Development in Relation to Social Contexts* (L. J. Crockett and A. C. Crouter, Eds.). Brown, B. B. and Huang, B., "Examining parenting practices in different peer contexts: Implications for adolescent trajectories." Copyright © 1995 Lawrence Erlbaum Associates, Inc. Reprinted by permission of the publisher.

Figure 13-1: Reprinted from *Journal of Applied Developmental Psychology, 4,* O'Brien, M., Huston, A. C., and Risley, T., "Sex-typed play of toddlers in a day care center," pp. 1–9. Copyright 1983, with permission from Elsevier.

Figure 13-2: From *Child Development, 51* (1980). Liben, L. S. and Golbeck, S. L., "Sex differences in performance on Piagetian spatial tasks: Differences in competence or performance," pp. 594–597. Reprinted with permission of the Society for Research in Child Development.

Figure 13-3: From *Developmental Psychology, 31* (1995). Luecke-Aleksa, D., Anderson, D. R., Collins, P. A., and Schmitt, K. L., "Gender constancy and television viewing," pp. 773–780. Copyright © 1995 by the American Psychological Association. Adapted with permission.

Figure 13-4: From *Child Development, 66* (1995). Martin, C. L., Eisenbud, L., and Rose, H., "Children's gender-based reasoning about toys," pp. 1453–1471. Reprinted with permission of the Society for Research in Child Development.

Figure 13-5: From *Child Development, 74* (2003). Ellis, B. J., Bates, J. E., Dodge, K. A., Fergusson, D. M., Horwood, L. J., Pettit, G. S., and Woodward, L., "Does father absence place daughters at special risk for early sexual activity and teenage pregnancy?" pp. 801–821. Reprinted

with permission of the Society for Research in Child Development.

Table 14-2: From *Developmental Psychology, 19* (1983). Eisenberg, N., Lennon, R., and Roth, K., "Prosocial development: A longitudinal study," pp. 846–855. Copyright © 1983 by the American Psychological Association. Adapted with permission.

Figure 14-4: From *Child Development, 67* (1996). Roberts, W. and Strayer, J., "Empathy, emotional expressiveness, and prosocial behavior," pp. 449–470. Reprinted with permission of the Society for Research in Child Development.

Figure 14-5: From *Developmental Psychology, 20* (1984). Huesmann, L. R., Eron, L. D., Lefkowitz, M. M., and Walder, L. O., "The stability of aggression over time and generations," pp. 1120–1134. Copyright © 1984 by the American Psychological Association. Adapted with permission.

Figure 14-7: From *Handbook of Child Psychology: Vol. 3: Social, Emotional, and Personality Development* (W. Damon and N. Eisenberg, Eds.). Coie, J. D. and Dodge, K. A., "Aggression and antisocial behavior," pp. 779–862. Copyright © 1998 by John Wiley & Sons, Inc. Reprinted with permission of John Wiley & Sons, Inc.

Figure 14-8: From *American Psychologist, 44* (1989). Patterson, G. R., DeBaryshe, B. D., and Ramsey, E., "A developmental perspective on antisocial behavior," pp. 329–335. Copyright © 1989 by the American Psychological Association. Adapted with permission.

Figure 15-1: from *Journal of Consulting and Clinical Psychology, 56* (1988). Weisz, J. R., Suwanlert, S., Chaiyasit, W., Weiss, B., Walter, B. R., and Anderson, W. W., "Thai and American perspectives on over- and under-controlled child behavior problems: Exploring the threshold model among parents, teachers, and psychologists," pp. 601–609. Copyright © 1988 by the American Psychological Association. Reproduced with permission.

Figure 15-2: Reprinted by permission. Children's Defense Fund, *Annual Report.* Washington, DC: Children's Defense Fund, 2001, p. 101.

Figure 15-4: From *Journal of Abnormal Psychology, 107* (1998). Hankin, B. L., Abramson, L. Y., Moffitt, T. E., Silva, P. A., McGee, R., and Angell, K. E., "Development of depression from preadolescence to young adulthood: Emerging gender differences in a 10 year longitudinal study," pp. 128–140. Copyright © 1998 by the American Psychological Association. Reproduced with permission.

PHOTOS

CHAPTER 1

p. 2, Photo © Superstock; © Estate of Pablo Picasso/Artists Rights Society (ARS), New York; **p. 4,** Courtesy Department of Library Services, American Museum of Natural History. Neg. #326799; **p. 11,** William Toby/Courtesy of Harvard University, Office of News & Public Affairs; **p. 12,** © Corbis; **p. 16 (left),** © Mike Yamashita/Woodfin Camp and Associates; **p. 16 (right),** © Lawrence Migdale/Stock Boston; **p. 20,** John Vachon/Library of Congress; **p. 28,** © Richard T. Nowitz/Photo Researchers, Inc.

CHAPTER 2

p. 46, Digital Image © The Museum of Modern Art/Licensed by SCALA / Art Resource, NY. © 2005 Banco de México, Diego Rivera & Frida Kahlo Museums Trust. Av. Cinco de Mayo No. 2, Centro, Del. Cuauhtémoc 06059, Mexico, D.F.; **p. 50,** © Alfred Pasieka/Photo Researchers, Inc.; **p. 53,** © CNRI/Science Photo Library/Photo Researchers, Inc.; **p. 59 (left),** © Ken Eward/Photo Researchers, Inc.; **p. 59 (right),** © Bill Longcore/Science Source/Photo Researchers, Inc.; **p. 60,** © Rob Lewine/Time Life Pictures/Getty Images; **p. 63,** © Alix/Photo Researchers, Inc.; **p. 67,** © SSPL/The Image Works; **p. 71,** © Jerry Berndt/Stock Boston

CHAPTER 3

p. 82, © Werner Forman/Art Resource, NY; **p. 86 (top),** © Dr. Yorgos Nikas/Photo Researchers, Inc.; **p. 86 (bottom),** © Anatomical Travelogue/Photo Researchers, Inc.; **p. 87 (top),** © Scott Camazine/Photo Researchers, Inc.; **p. 87 (bottom),** © Nestle/Petit Format/Photo Researchers, Inc.; **p. 90 (top),** © Lennart Nilsson/A Child is Born/Albert Bonniers Förlag; **p. 90 (middle left),** © Claude Edelmann/Photo Researchers, Inc.; **p. 90 (middle right),** © Dr. G. Moscoso/Photo Researchers, Inc.; **p. 90 (bottom),** © Nestle/Petit Format/Photo Researchers, Inc.; **p. 91 (top),** © Lennart Nilsson/A Child is Born/Albert Bonniers Förlag; **p. 91 (middle),** PhotoLink/Getty Images; **p. 91 (bottom),** TRBfoto/Getty Images; **p. 98,** © John Maier, Jr./The Image Works; **p. 104,** © Rubberball/PictureQuest; **p. 115,** Courtesy Evelyn Thoman; **p. 119,** © Mike Teruya/Free Spirt Photography

CHAPTER 4

p. 124, © Scala/Art Resource, NY; **p. 126,** © Mimi Forsyth; **p. 132,** Digital Stock; **p. 135,** © Terry E. Eiler/Stock Boston; **p. 138, 139,** PhotoDisc/Getty Images; **p. 141,** © Michael Siluk/Index Stock Imagery; **p. 143,** © Robert Ullmann; **p. 144 (top),** Maurer & Mauer, 1988; **p. 144 (bottom),** Images by Davida Teller and Tony Young. From Davida Teller, First Glances: The Vision of Infants. *Investigative Ophthalmology and Visual Science*, Vol. 13, No. 11, Oct. 97, pp. 2183–2203. Photos © Anthony Young, All rights reserved ; **p. 150,** © Jack Deutsch/Innervisions; **p. 154,** Courtesy Dr. Jeff N. Pickens; **p. 157,** © Michael Newman/PhotoEdit; **p. 159,** © Breck P. Kent

CHAPTER 5

p. 162, Photograph Courtesy of Gwendolyn Knight Lawrence/Art Resource, NY. © The Estate of Gwendolyn Knight Lawrence/Artists Rights Society (ARS), New York; **p. 172,** © Bill Bachmann/Stock Boston; **p. 177,** Courtesy of Children's Hospital of Michigan; **p. 178,** © Laura Dwight/Peter Arnold, Inc.; **p. 179,** © Laura Dwight/PhotoEdit; **p. 188,** © Mark Richards/PhotoEdit; **p. 193,** © Bob Daemmrich/Stock Boston; **p. 199,** © William Thomson/Index Stock Imagery

CHAPTER 6

p. 212, © David David Gallery/Superstock; **p. 219,** PhotoDisc/Getty Images; **p. 225,** © Tom McCarthy/PhotoEdit; **p. 228,** © Kathy McLaughlin/The Image Works; **p. 229,** © Jose Carillo/PhotoEdit; **p. 242,** © Big Cheese Photo/PictureQuest; **p. 254 (left),** © Bill Aron/PhotoEdit; **p. 254 (right),** © Erika Stone/Peter Arnold, Inc.; **p. 263,** © Lawrence Migdale/Photo Researchers, Inc.

CHAPTER 7

p. 268, Photograph Courtesy of Gwendolyn Knight Lawrence/Art Resource, NY. © The Estate of Gwendolyn Knight Lawrence/Artists Rights Society (ARS), New York; **p. 272,** PhotoDisc/Getty Images; **p. 278,** © Lon C. Diehl/PhotoEdit; **p. 282,** © Myrleen Ferguson-Cate/PhotoEdit; **p. 296, 297,** PhotoDisc/Getty Images; **p. 301,** © The McGraw-Hill Companies, Chris Kerrigan; **p. 302,** © Lilyan Aloma/PhotoEdit; **p. 307,** © Cassy Cohen/PhotoEdit; **p. 311,** © Billy E. Barnes/PhotoEdit

CHAPTER 8

p. 316, © Lee & Lee Communications/Art Resource, NY; **p. 318,** © Bettmann/Corbis; **p. 325, 327,** © Laura Dwight; **p. 329,** © Laura Dwight/Peter Arnold, Inc.; **p. 331,** Courtesy Neil Berthier and Carol Beale; **p. 335,** © Laura Dwight/PhotoEdit

CHAPTER 9

p. 364, © Christian Pierre/Superstock; **p. 372,** © David Young-Wolff/PhotoEdit; **p. 377,** © Ellen Senisi/The Image Works; **p. 379,** PhotoDisc/Getty Images; **p. 380,** Courtesy Patricia Miller, University of Florida; **p. 384,** © Spencer Grant/PhotoEdit; **p. 387,** © Syracuse Newspapers/Jennifer Grimes/The Image Works; **p. 397,** © Syracuse Newspapers/The Image Works; **p. 399,** © Bob Daemmrich/The Image Works; **p. 402,** Courtesy Judy S. DeLoache

CHAPTER 10

p. 414, © Scala/Art Resource, NY; **p. 419 (left),** © Larry Mulvehill/The Image Works; **p. 419 (right),** © Tony Savino/The Image Works; **p. 434,** © Sybil Shackman; **p. 436,** © Bob Daemmrich/The Image Works; **p. 446,** © Michael J. Doolittle/The Image Works; **p. 450,** © Christopher Hornsby, Courtesy Milo Mottola, Totally Kid Carousel

CHAPTER 11

p. 454, Solomon R. Guggenheim Museum, New York. Gift, Mr. and Mrs. Gus and Judith Lieber, 1988. 88.3620. Photograph by David Heald, © The Solomon R. Guggenheim Foundation, New York.; **p. 457,** © Rudi Von Briel/PhotoEdit; **p. 462,** © George Goodwin; **p. 473,** PhotoDisc/Getty Images; **p. 479,** © Tony Freeman/PhotoEdit; **p. 483,** © David Young-Wolff/PhotoEdit; **p. 492,** © Deborah Davis/PhotoEdit

CHAPTER 12

p. 504, © Scala/Art Resource, NY; **p. 512,** PhotoDisc/Getty Images; **p. 519, 522,** © Jeff Greenberg/The Image Works; **p. 532,** © Richard Hutchings/PhotoEdit; **p. 538,** © Robert W. Ginn/PhotoEdit; **p. 541,** © Tony Freeman/PhotoEdit; **p. 545,** © Michael Newman/PhotoEdit; **p. 546,** © Jeff Greenberg/PhotoEdit

CHAPTER 13

p. 550, © Scala/Art Resource, NY; **p. 554 (left),** © Michael Heron/Woodfin Camp and Associates; **p. 554 (right),** © Martha Cooper/Peter Arnold, Inc.; **p. 568 (left),** © Miro Vintoniv/Stock Boston; **p. 568 (right),** © Michelle D. Bridwell/PhotoEdit; **p. 573 (left),** © Charles Gupton/Stock Boston; **p. 573 (right),** © Myrleen Ferguson Cate/PhotoEdit; **p. 576,** © Syd M. Johnson/The Image Works

CHAPTER 14

p. 590, © HIP/Art Resource, NY; **p. 593,** © Phillip Jon Bailey/Index Stock Imagery; **p. 607,** © Tony Freeman/PhotoEdit; **p. 611,** PhotoDisc/Getty Images; **p. 614,** © David Young-Wolff/PhotoEdit; **p. 623,** PhotoDisc/Getty Images; **p. 629,** © Myrleen Ferguson Cate/PhotoEdit; **p. 633,** © A. Ramey/PhotoEdit

CHAPTER 15

p. 640, © Donald C. Martin/Superstock; **p. 643,** © David M. Grossman/The Image Works; **p. 662,** © Nancy Acevedo; **p. 670,** © Laura Dwight; **p. 674,** © Paul Conklin/PhotoEdit; **p. 679,** © Michal Heron; **p. 680,** © David Young-Wolff/PhotoEdit

EPILOGUE

p. 686, Photo © Michael Escoffery/Art Resource, NY. © Michael Escoffery/Artists Rights Society (ARS), New York

Name Index

Subject Index

Abnormality, 644–651
  continuity over time, 650–651
  cultural variations, 647
  deviation from average, 645
  deviation from ideal, 646
  issues in determining, 646–649
  medical model, 644–645, 651–653
Abortion, 61, 64–65
Absolutism, moral, 593
Abuse; see Child abuse
Academic achievement
  ADHD and, 663–664
  birth order and, 470–471
  cultural variations, 441–443
  gender and parental attitudes toward, 575
  motivation for, 431–434, 480
Accommodation
  definition of, 322
  in development, 12
Achievement motivation, 431–434, 480, 582
Acquired immune deficiency syndrome (AIDS), 106–107
Active genetic-environmental interaction, 70–71
Adaptation
  cognitive, 322–323
  definition of, 322
  in development, 12
Adarol, 664
ADHD; see Attention deficit/hyperactivity disorder
Adolescence
  aggression, 627–628
  antisocial youth, risks for, 631, 682
  attachment and, 251
  cognitive development, 340–341
  crime, 655–657, 682
  divorce and remarriage effects, 487
  eating disorders, 198–200
  Eriksonian theory of, 11–12
  gender typing, 559
  romantic relationships, 538–540
  sexual orientation, 206–208
  suicide and, 669
Adoption, 490–491
Adoption studies
  individual differences, 72–73
  intelligence, 75–76, 438–439
Adrenal cortex, 201
Affordances, 376
African Americans
  gender roles, 554
  infant mortality, 101
  intelligence, 427–429
  low birthweight babies, 111–112
  peer influence on intelligence, 431
  prenatal health care, 101
  sickle-cell anemia, 58–59
After-school programs, 483–484
Age
  companion choice and, 520
  maternal, and reproductive risk, 100, 102
  mental, 422
  ontogenetic change, 360
Age cohorts, 19, 36–37
Age of viability, 88
Aggression, 621–636
  behaviorism, 13
  biological factors, 627–629

boys, 625–628
catharsis and, 634
child care and, 264
cognitive modification strategies, 634–635
cognitive social learning theory, 13
control of, 634–635
definition of, 622
development of, 622–624
environmental factors, 629–634
family and, 629–632
gender and, 625–627
girls, 625–627
hostile, 622
information-processing approach, 622
instrumental, 622
parents and, 629–632
peers and, 633–634
physical versus verbal, 624
physiological basis for, 627–628
proactive, 622–623
punishment and, 629–630
reactive, 622–623
relational, 625–626
stability of, 624–625
television and video games, 31–33, 632–633
verbal versus physical, 624
XYY chromosome pattern and, 60
Aggressive rejected children, 513
AIDS (acquired immune deficiency syndrome), 106–107
Alcohol, prenatal risks from, 93, 95
Allele, 51
Alphafetoprotein (AFP) assay, 64
Altruism, 610, 620–621
Altruistic behavior, 610
Amenorrhea, 203
American Psychiatric Association (APA), 652
American Psychological Association, 39
American Sign Language (ASL), 297, 300–301
Amniocentesis, 62
Amniotic sac, 85
Anal stage of development, 10
Analogy, solving problems by, 397–398
Androgyny, 583–584
Anemia, 191
Anesthetics, 98–99
Animals
  and language, 276, 283
  prosocial behavior among, 615
Animistic thinking, 332–333
Anorexia nervosa, 199–200
Anoxia, 110
Antidepressant drugs, 671
Antipathy, mutual, 534
Antisocial behavior, 631–632
Apgar evaluation, 110
Apnea, 113, 130
Approach/avoidance behavior, 250
Asian Americans
  academic performance, 440
  achievement motivation, 433
  peer influence on intelligence, 431
Asperger's disorder, 674
Aspirin, 93, 98
Assimilation
  definition of, 322
  in development, 12

Assisted reproductive techniques, 61–63
Associative learning, 428
At-risk children; see Risk and Resilience
Attachment, 238–265
  aggression and, 629
  assessment of, 243, 245–247
  child care and, 260–264
  cognitive development, 256
  consequences of, 255–260
  cultural variations, 242, 248–249, 251–252
  definition of, 238
  development of, 240–241
  fathers, 241–242, 254, 257–258
  infant temperament and, 254–255
  intergenerational factors, 252–254
  mothers, 239–240, 250–254, 257–258
  multiple caregivers, 260–264
  parents' role, 247–256, 257–258
  security of, 243, 245–252
  sense of self, 259–260
  social development, 256–258
  stability of, 255
  targets of, 243
  theories of, 238–240
Attachment Q Sort, 247, 249
Attention
  control of, 377–378
  definition of, 375
  information-processing approach, 377–378, 380–383
  planning and, 382–383
  selective, 378, 380–382
Attention deficit/hyperactivity disorder (ADHD), 660, 662–666
  biological factors, 664–665
  characteristics, 663–664
  conduct disorder versus, 660
  definition of, 660, 662
  depression and, 667
  medications, 664, 665–666
  psychological factors, 665
  subtypes, 663
  treatment, 665–666
Auditory localization, 142
Authoritarian parenting, 465, 467, 468, 469, 480
Authoritative parenting, 464, 467, 479, 541
Autistic disorder, 673–678
  causes, 676–677
  characteristics, 674–676
  communication deficits, 675, 677
  definition of, 673
  intelligence, 676
  treatment, 677–678
Autobiographic memory, 392–395
Automatization, cognitive process of, 373
Autosomes, 49
Autostimulation theory, 131
Average children, 513

Babbling, 285–286
Babies; see Birth; Infants and infancy; Newborns
Bacterial infections, prenatal risks from, 105
Balance-scale problems, 395–396
Bandura's model of observational learning, 14
Basic reflex activity, 325
Bayley Scales of Infant Development (BSID), 421